BRADFORD'S
CROSSWORD
SOLVER'S
DICTIONARY

Collins

HarperCollins Publishers
Westerhill Road
Bishopbriggs
Glasgow
G64 2QT
Great Britain

Sixth Edition 2005

Reprint 10 9 8 7 6 5 4

© Anne R. Bradford 1986, 1993, 1997, 2000, 2003
This edition © Anne R. Bradford, 2005

First edition published by Longman; second, third and fourth editions published by Peter Collin Publishing Ltd

ISBN-13 978-0-00-720894-4
ISBN-10 0-00-720894-4

www.collins.co.uk

A catalogue record for this book is available from the British Library

Computing support and typesetting by Thomas Callan

Printed and bound in Germany by Bercker

Author's Preface

Every word has a definition – an identity. If it has only one definition we can look at it and know it for what it is, but some words are like cut stones with many facets; they can mean different things according to the way in which we use them. These are the words which add spice to the cryptic crossword puzzle – the setter plays with them and tries to deceive his solvers into believing he means what he does not. They are the basis of puns and word-play. Introduced to crossword puzzles at an early age, it soon became clear to me that some words are beloved of setters – rivers Po and Dee; the town of Diss in Norfolk; the diocesan 'see' of Ely. These and many more quickly became familiar, but now and again the odd one would elude the memory. It seemed logical then to write these down, and by a natural progression to start to turn the normal dictionary inside out – if 'flummery' is defined as a blancmange, then why not list it under 'blancmange' alongside other words which can be defined as such? Not a new idea, of course, but why stop at synonyms? There are words which have recognised associations with other words – descriptive words or words with literary connections, foreign words, archaic words, technical words and even folkloric words – all highly collectable. And so this crossword dictionary began to evolve. Every puzzle I have laid hands on for over forty-five years has been scrutinised, the clues broken down into definitions and cryptic parts; words indicating anagrams, reversals, puns, etc. all carefully recorded and stored.

It is now eighty years since the crossword puzzle arrived in this country and caught the attention of the populace so thoroughly. Today, the attraction is as strong as ever and, increasingly, crosswords are to be found on the universal web. Some today are set by artificial means using computers and word-banks, but nothing equals the challenge of pitting one's wits against the wiles of the human brain, and some of today's compilers show an amazing ingenuity.

This book is my personal word-bank. Once you are in the crossword mode, you should find the answer you seek somewhere within its covers. Truly, the solution is to hand!

A.R.B. 2005

Solving Crossword Clues

Crossword puzzles tend to be basically 'quick' or 'cryptic'. A 'quick' crossword usually relies on a one- or two-word clue which is a simple definition of the answer required. As has been stated, many words have different meanings, so that the clue 'ball' could equally well lead to the answer 'sphere', 'orb', or 'dance'. The way to solve 'quick' crosswords is to press on until probable answers begin to interlink, which is a good sign that you are on the right track.

'Cryptic' crosswords are another matter. Here the clue usually consists of a basic definition, given at either the beginning or end of the clue, together with one or more definitions of parts of the answer. Here are some examples taken from all-time favourites recorded over the years:

    1. '*Tradesman who bursts into tears*' (**Stationer**)

Tradesman is a definition of stationer. *Bursts* is cleverly used as an indication of an anagram, which *into tears* is of stationer.

    2. '*Sunday school tune*' (**Strain**)

Here *Sunday* is used to define its abbreviation S, *school* is a synonym for train, and put together they give strain, which is a synonym of *tune*.

    3. '*Result for everyone when head gets at bottom*' (**Ache**)
(used as a 'down' clue)

This is what is known as an '& lit' clue, meaning that the setter has hit on a happy composition which could literally be true. *Everyone* here is a synonym for each, move the *head* (first letter) of the word to the *bottom*, and the answer is revealed, the whole clue being the definition of the answer in this case.

    4. '*Tin out East*' (**Sen**)

In this example, *tin*, implying 'money', requires its chemical symbol Sn to go *out*(side) *East*, or its abbreviation, E, the whole clue being a definition of a currency (sen) used in the East.

5. '*Information given to communist in return for sex*' (**Gender**)

Information can be defined as gen; *communist* is almost always red, *in return* indicates 'reversed', leading to gen-der, a synonym for *sex*.

6. '*Row about no enclosure of this with sardines*' (**Tin-opener**)

Row is a synonym for tier, *about* indicates 'surrounding', *no enclosure* can be no pen, leading to ti-no pen-er, and another '& lit' clue.

7. '*Cake-sandwiches-meat, at Uncle Sam's party*' (**Clambake**)

Meat here is lamb, *sandwiches* is used as a verb, so we have C-lamb-ake, which is a kind of party in America. Uncle Sam or US is often used to indicate America.

8. '*Initially passionate meeting of boy and girl could result in it*' (**Pregnancy**)

Initially is usually a sign of a first letter, in this case 'p' for *passionate* + Reg (a boy) and Nancy (a girl), and another clever '& lit'.

With 'cryptic' clues the solver needs to try to analyse the parts to see what he or she is looking for – which word or words can be the straight definition, and which refer to the parts or hint at anagrams or other subterfuges. Whilst it would be unrealistic to claim total infallibility, practice has shown that in most crosswords some 90% of the answers are to be found in this work.

Anne R Bradford

How to use the Dictionary

This dictionary is the result of over forty-five years' analysis of some 300,000 crossword clues, ranging from plain 'quick' crosswords requiring only synonyms to the different level of cryptic puzzles. Therefore the words listed at each entry may be connected to the keyword in various ways, such as:

– a straightforward synonym

– a commonly-associated adjective

– an associated or proper noun

– a pun or other devious play on words

Keywords are listed alphabetically; in cases where the heading consists of more than one word, the first of these words is taken to be the keyword, and in cases where the end of a word is bracketed, the material up to the opening bracket is taken to be the keyword. Keywords marked with the symbol ▶ refer the user to other entries where additional information may be found. Keywords marked with the symbol ▷ give leads to anagrams and other ploys used by crossword setters. If the keywords found in the clue do not lead directly to the required answer, the solver should look under words given as cross-references to other entries. These are indicated by the symbol >, with the cross-referenced word shown in capitals.

As a completely innovative feature for this new edition, some entries have been divided into two parts – a general entry similar to the standard entries which appear elsewhere, and a panel entry which contains a list of more specific or encyclopedic material. So, for example, the entry 'Artist(ic)' includes not only a list of general words connected with 'Artist' or 'Artistic' in some way, such as 'Bohemian', 'Cubist', 'Fine' and 'Virtuoso', but also a panel with the heading 'Artists' containing a list of the names of specific artists, such as 'Bellini', 'Constable', and 'Rembrandt'. For added help, the words in these panels are arranged by length, with all three-letter words grouped together in alphabetical order, then all four-letter words, then all five-letter words, and so on.

About the Author

Anne Bradford's love of words began to make itself evident even in her schooldays, when, as Head Girl of her school, she instituted a novel punishment – instead of making rulebreakers write lines, she had them write out pages from a dictionary, on the grounds that this was a more useful exercise. Little did she know this was soon to be her own daily routine!

In time, crosswords became a magnificent obsession for Anne. All lovers of crosswords can understand the irresistible lure of solving them, but Anne's interest went much deeper than most people's, and when she stopped work in 1957 to have her first child, she found herself starting to note down answers to particularly tricky clues as an aid to memory, in case she should come across them again in another puzzle. It was from this simple beginning that this crossword dictionary evolved.

Over the space of 25 years, Anne continued to build on her collection of solutions, analysing every crossword clue as she solved it and adding it to her steadily growing bank of entries. This unique body of material eventually reached such proportions that she had the idea of offering it to her fellow crossword-solvers as a reference book, and since then, the book has gone from strength to strength, providing valuable help to countless cruciverbalists over a number of editions.

Anne Bradford continues to devote time each day to solving crosswords, averaging some 20 a week – both quick and cryptic – and still avidly collects new solutions for her *Crossword Solver's Dictionary* at a rate of around 150 a week, compiling each solution by hand (without the use of a computer!) This latest edition therefore includes much new material, gleaned by a true crossword lover who not only solves crosswords but, as an active member of the Crossword Club, can offer the user an insight into the mind of a cunning crossword compiler.

The Crossword Club

If you are interested in crosswords, you might like to consider joining the Crossword Club. Membership is open to all who enjoy tackling challenging crosswords and who appreciate the finer points of clue-writing and grid-construction. The Club's magazine, Crossword, contains two prize puzzles each month. A sample issue and full details are available on request.

The Crossword Club
Coombe Farm
Awbridge
Romsey, Hants.
SO51 0HN
UK

email: bh@thecrosswordclub.co.uk
website address: www.thecrosswordclub.co.uk

Aa

A, An Ack, Adult, Ae, Alpha, Angstrom, Are, Argon, D, Ein, Her, If, L, One, Per, They

A1 Tiptop

AA Milne

Aardvark Ant-bear, Ant-eater, Earth-hog, Ground-hog

Aaron's Rod Hagtaper

Aba, Abba Patriarch

Abacus Counter, Soroban

Abaft Astern, Sternson

Abalone Ormer, Paua, Perlemoen

Abandon(ed), Abandonment Abdicate, Abnegate, Abort, Adrift, Amoral, Apostasy, Back down, Cade, Cancel, Castaway, Corrupt, Decommission, Defect, Derelict, > **DESERT**, Desuetude, Discard, Disown, Dissolute, Ditch, Drop, Dump, Elan, Evacuate, Expose, Flagrant, Forhoo(ie), Forhow, Forlend, Forsake, Gomorra, Immoral, Jack(-in), Jettison, Jilt, Leave, Loose, Louche, Maroon, Old, Orgiastic, Profligate, Quit, Rat, Relinquish, Renounce, Reprobate, Scrap, Shed, Sink, Strand, Vacate, Waive, Wanton, Yield

Abase Degrade, Demean, Disgrace, Grovel, > **HUMBLE**, Kowtow, Lessen

Abash Daunt, Discountenance, Mortify

Abate(ment) Allay, Appal, Decrescent, Defervescence, Diminish, Let up, Lyse, Lysis, Moderate, Reduce, Remit, > **SUBSIDE**

▷ **Abate** *may indicate* a contention

Abattoir Knackery, Slaughterhouse

Abbey Abbacy, Bath, Buckfast, Cloister, Downside, Fonthill, Fountains, Glastonbury, Je(r)vaulx, Medmenham, Melrose, Minster, Nightmare, Northanger, Priory, Rievaulx, Tintern, Westminster, Whitby, Woburn

Abbot Aelfric, Archimandrite, Brother, Friar

Abbreviate, Abbreviation Abridge, Ampersand, Compendium, Condense, Curtail, > **SHORTEN**, Sigla

ABC Absey

Abdicate, Abdication Cede, Demission, Disclaim, Disown, Resign

Abdomen Belly, C(o)eliac, Epigastrium, Gaster, Hypochondrium, Paunch, Pleon, > **STOMACH**, Tummy, Venter

Abduct(ed), Abduction Enlèvement, Kidnap, Rapt, Ravish, Shanghai, Steal

Aberdeen Granite City

Aberrant, Aberration Abnormal, Aye-aye, Deviant, Idolon, Perverse

Abet(tor) Aid, Back, Candle-holder, Second

Abeyance, Abeyant Dormant, Shelved, Sleeping, Store

Abhor(rent) > **DETEST**, Execrable, > **HATE**, Loathe, Odious, Shun

Abide Dwell, Inhere, > **LAST**, Lie, Live, Observe, Remain, Stand, Tarry

Abigail Maid, Masham

Ability Aptitude, Calibre, Capacity, Cocum, > **COMPETENCE**, Efficacy, ESP, Facility, Faculty, Ingine, Instinct, Lights, Potential, Prowess, Savey,

Savoir-faire, Savv(e)y, Skill, Talent

Abject Base, Craven, Grovel, Humble, Servile, Slave

Abjure Eschew, Forswear, Recant, Renege, Reny

Ablaze Afire, Ardent

Able Ablins, Accomplished, > **ADEPT**, Aiblins, Apt, Capable, > **COMPETENT**, Fere, Proficient, Seaman, Yibbles

Abnormal(ity) Anomalous, Atypical, > **DEVIANT**, Dysfunction, Ectopic, Erratic, Etypical, Freakish, Odd, Preternatural, > **QUEER**, Sport, Unnatural, Varus

Aboard On

Abode Domicile, Dwelling, Habitat, > **HOME**, Lain, Libken, Midgard, Remain

Abolish, Abolition(ist) Annihilate, Annul, Axe, > **BAN**, D, Delete, Destroy, Eradicate, Erase, Extirpate, John Brown, Nullify, Repeal, Rescind

Abomasum Read

Abominable, Abominate, Abomination Bane, Cursed, > **HATE**, Nefandous, Nefast, Revolting, Snowman, Vile, Yeti

Aboriginal, Aborigine Adivasi, Ainu, Aranda, Autochthon, Binghi, Boong, Buck, Bushmen, Carib, Evolué, Fringe-dweller, Gin, Gurindji, Indigenous, Jacky(-Jacky), Kamilaroi, Koori, Lubra, Maori, Mary, Motu, Myall, Piljantjatjara, Pintubi, Pre-Dravidian, Sakai, San, Sican, Siwash, Truganini, Vedda(h)

Abort(ion), Abortive Apiol, Cancel, Ecbolic, Miscarry, Moon-calf, Slip, Sooterkin, Teras, Termination

Abound(ing) Bristle, Copious, Enorm, Rife, Teem

About A, Almost, Anent, Around, C, Ca, Circa, Circiter, Concerning, Encompass, Environs, Going, Near, Of, On, Over, Re, Regarding, Soon at

▷ **About** *may indicate* one word around another

Above Abune, Aforementioned, Aloft, Over, Overhead, Overtop, Owre, Sopra, Superior, Supra-, Suspicion, Upon

Abracadabra Cantrip, Heypass

Abrade, Abrasive Carbanado, Carborundum®, Chafe, Emery, Erode, File, Garnet paper, > **GRATE**, Rub, Sand, Scrape, Scrat, Scuff

Abraham Lincoln, Patriarch, Urite

Abreast Alongside, Au courant, Au fait, Beside, Level, Up

Abridge(ment) Audley, Compress, Condense, Cut, Digest, Dock, Epitome, Pot, Shorten, Trim

Abroad Afield, Away, Distant, Forth, Offshore, Out, Overseas

▷ **Abroad** *may indicate* an anagram

Abrogate Abolish, Repeal, Replace

▷ **Abrupt** *may indicate* a shortened word

Abrupt(ly) Bold, Brusque, Curt, Gruff, Offhand, Premorse, Prerupt, Short, Staccato, Terse

Abscess Gumboil, Impost(h)ume, Ulcer, Warble

Abscond Absquatulate, Decamp, Desert, Elope, Flee, Leg-bail, Levant, Welch

Abseil(ing) Dulfer, Rappel

Absence, Absent(ee), Absent-minded(ness) Abs, Abstracted, Away, Distant, Distracted, Distrait, Exile, Hookey, Mitch, Scatty, Skip, Truant, Vacuity, Void, Wanting, Wool-gathering

Absinthe Wormwood

Absolute(ly) Bang, Complete, Dead, Deep-dyed, Downright, Fairly, Implicit, Ipso facto, Just, Mere, Mondo, Nominative, Plenary, Plumb, Quite, Real, Sheer, Total, Truly, Unmitigated, Unqualified, Utter, Veritable, Very

Absolve, Absolution Acquit, Assoilzie, Clear, Exculpate, Excuse, Pardon, Shrive

Absorb(ed), Absorbent, Absorbing, Absorption Assimilate, Autism, Blot, Consume, Desiccant, Devour, Digest, Dope, Drink, > **ENGROSS**, Imbibe, Ingest, Intent, Merge(r), Occlude, Occupy, Osmosis, Porous, Preoccupation, Rapt, Sorbefacient, Spongy, Unputdownable

Absquatulate Skedaddle

Abstain(er), Abstemious, Abstinence, Abstinent Band of Hope, Celibacy, Chastity, Continent, Desist, Eschew, Forbear, Forgo, Maigre, Nazarite, Nephalism, Pioneer, Rechab(ite), Refrain, Resist, Sober, Temperate, TT

Abstract(ed), Abstraction Abrege, Abridge, Academic, Appropriate, Brief, Deduct, Digest, Discrete, Distrait, Epitome, Essence, Metaphysical, Musing, Notional, Précis, Prepossessed, Prescind, Remove, Resumé, Reverie, Stable, Steal, Summary, Syllabus, Tachism

Abstruse Deep, Esoteric, Obscure, Recondite

Absurd(ity) Alician, Apagoge, Fantastic, Farcical, Folly, Inept, Irrational, Laputan, Ludicrous, Madness, Nonsense, Paradox, Preposterous, Ridiculous, Silly, Solecism, Stupid, Toshy, Whim-wham

Abundance, Abundant A-gogo, Ample, Bounty, Copious, Excess, Flood, Flush, Fouth, Fowth, Fruitful, Galore, Lashings, Mickle, Mine, Mint, Oodles, Opulent, Over, Plenitude, Plenteous, > **PLENTIFUL**, Plenty, Pleroma, Plethora, Plurisie, Prolific, Relative, Replete, Rich, Rife, Routh, Rowth, Sonce, Sonse, Store, Tallents, Teeming, Tons, Uberous

Abuse, Abusive Assail, Billingsgate, Blackguard, Flak, Fustilarian, Fustil(l)irian, Hail, Insult, Invective, Limehouse, Maltreat, Miscall, > **MISTREAT**, Misuse, Obloquy, Opprobrium, Philippic, Rail, Rampallian, Rate, Rayle, Revile, Ritual, Satanic, Satire, Scarab(ee), Scurrilous, Serve, Sexual, Slang, Slate, Sledging, Snash, Solvent, Substance, Thersitical, Tirade, Vilify, Violate, Vituperation

Abut Adjoin, Border, Touch

Abysm(al), Abyss Avernus, Barathrum, Barranca, Chasm, Deep, Gulf, Swallet, Tartarean, Tartarus

AC Current, Erk

Acacia Bablah, Boree, Brigalow, Eumong, Eumung, Gidgee, Gidjee, Koa, Mimosa, Mulga, Myall, Sallee, Shittim, Wattle

Academic(ian) A, Acca, Acker, Della-Cruscan, Don, Erudite, Fellow, Hypothetic(al), Immortals, Literati, Master, Pedantic, PRA, Prof(essor), RA, Reader, Rector

Academy Athenaeum, Dollar, French, Loretto, Lyceum, Military, Naval, Royal, St Cyr, Sandhurst, School, Seminary, West Point

Acanthus Blankursine, Ruellia

Accelerate, Acceleration, Accelerator Antedate, Betatron, Bevatron, Collider, Cosmotron, Cyclotron, Festinate, G, Gal, Gun, Hasten, Increase, Linac, Linear, Rev, Signatron, Speed, Stringendo, Synchrotron

Accent(ed), Accentuate Acute, Beat, Breve, Brogue, Bur(r), Circumflex, Cut-glass, Doric, Drawl, Enclitic, Enhance, Grave, Hacek, Intonation, Kelvinside, Long, Macron, Martelé, Morningside, Mummerset, Nasal, Orthotone, Oxford, Oxytone, Paroxytone, Perispomenon, Pitch, Primary, Proparoxytone, Rhythm, Secondary, Stress, Tittle, Tone, Tonic, Twang

Accentor Dunnock

Accept(able), Acceptance, Accepted A, Accede, Admit, Adopt, Agree, Allow, Approbate, Bar, Believe, Buy, Can-do, Common, Consent, Cool, Cosher, Decent, Done, Grant, Kosher, Meet, Obey, On, Pocket, Putative, Settle, Stand, Swallow, Take, Tolerate, U, Wear, Widespread

Access(ible) Avenue, Card, Come-at-able, Credit, Direct, Door, Entrée, > **ENTRY**, Fit, Hack, Ingo, Key, Log in, Log on, Passe-partout, Password, Phreaking, Random, Recourse, Remote, Sequential, Spasm, Wayleave

Accessory, Accessories Abettor, Addition, Aide, Ally, Ancillary, Appendage, Appurtenance, Attribute, Bandanna, Bells and whistles, Cribellum, Findings, Fitment, Staffage, Trappings, Trimming

Accident(al) Adventitious, Bechance, Blowdown, Blunder, Calamity, > **CHANCE**, Circumstance, Contingency, Contretemps, Crash, Dent, Disaster, Fall, Fluke, Fortuitous, Hap, Hit and run, Mischance, Mishap, Promiscuous, Rear-ender, Shunt, Smash, Smash-up, Spill, Stramash, Wreck

Accidie Acedia, Sloth, Torpor

Acclaim Accolade, Applaud, Brava, Bravo, Cheer, Eclat, Fame, Fanfare, Hail, Kudos, Ovation, Praise, Salute

Accolade Award, Honour, Palm, Token, Tribute

Accommodate, Accommodation Adapt, B and B, Bedsit, Berth, Billet, Board, Botel, Bunkhouse, Camp, Chalet, Compromise, Crashpad, Digs, Flotel, Gaff, Gite, Grace and favour, Homestay, Hostel, Hotel, House, Lend, Loan, Lodge, Lodgement, Motel, > **OBLIGE**, Parador, Pension, Quarters, Rapprochement, Recurve, Room, Sheltered, Sorehon, Stabling, Stateroom, Steerage, Storage, Wharepuni, Xenodochium

▷ **Accommodating** *may indicate* one word inside another

Accompany(ing), Accompanied (by), Accompaniment, Accompanist Accessory, Alberti, And, Attend, Backing, Chaperone, Chum, Concomitant, Consort, Continuo, Descant, > **ESCORT**, Harmonise, Herewith, Obbligato, Obligate, Obligato, Repetiteur, Soundtrack, Trimmings, Vamp

Accomplice Abettor, Aide, > **ALLY**, Collaborator, Confederate, Federarie, Partner, Shill, Stale

Accomplish(ed), Accomplishment Able, > **ACHIEVE**, Arch, Attain, Clever, Complete, Consummate, Done, Effect, Master, Over, Perform, Polished, Realise, Ripe, Savant, Success, Tour de force

Accord(ingly), According to After, Agree, Ala, Allow, As per, Attune, Chime, Consensus, Give, Grant, Harmony, Jibe, Meech Lake, Meet, Sort, Thus

According to nature SN

Accordion Button, Concertina, Flutina, Piano, Squeeze-box

Accost Abord, Approach, Greet, Hail, Importune, Molest, Solicit, Tackle

Account(s) AC, Anecdote, Audit, Battels, Behalf, Bill, Cause, Charge, Checking, Chronicle, Current, Deposit, Discretionary, Drawing, Enarration, Expense, Explain, Exposition, Joint, Lawin, Ledger, Long, Memoir, Narration, Nostro, Numbered, Procès-verbal, Real, Reason, Recital, Regest, Register, > **REPORT**, Repute, Resumé, Sake, Short, Suspense, Swindlesheet, Tab, Tale, Thesis, Trust, Version, Vostro

Accountant Auditor, CA, Cost, Forensic, Hyde, Liquidator, Reckoner, Vestry-clerk

Accredit Attribute

Accumulate, Accumulation Accrue, Adsorb, Aggregate, > **AMASS**, Augment, Backlog, Build, Collect, Gather, Hoard, Lodg(e)ment, Pile, Rack up, Stockpile, Uplay

Accuracy, Accurate(ly) Bang-on, Cocker, > **CORRECT**, Dead-on, Fair, Fidelity, Minute, Precise, Right, Spot-on, True, Word-perfect

Accursed Argued, Blest, Blist, Sacred

Accusation, Accuse(d) Allege, Arraign, Attaint, Bill, Blame, Censure, Challenge, Charge, Criminate, Denounce, Dite, Gravamen, Impeach,

Incriminate, Panel, Suspect, Tax, Threap, Threep, Traduce, Wight, Wite, Wyte

Accustom(ed) Acquaint, Attune, Enure, General, Habituate, Inure, Teach, Wont, Woon

Ace(s) Basto, Crabs, Dinger, > EXPERT, Jot, Master, Mournival, One, Quatorze, Spadille, Spadill(i)o, Spot, Tib, Virtuoso, Wonderful

Acerbate Intensify

Ache, Aching Aitch, Die, Long, Mulligrubs, Nag, Otalgia, Pain, Stitch, Yearn, Yen

Achieve(ment) Accomplish, Acquisition, Attain, Come, Compass, > EFFECT, Exploit, Feat, Fulfil, Gain, Hatchment, Realise, Satisfice, Satisfy, Stroke, Succeed, Triumph, Trock, Troke, Truck

Acid(ity) Acrimony, Corrosive, Drop, EPA, Etchant, Hydroxy, Reaction, Ribosomal, Ribozyme, Solvent, Sour, Tart, Trans-fatty, Vinegar, Vitriol

ACIDS

2 letters:
PH

3 letters:
DNA
HCL
LSD
Oxo
RNA

4 letters:
Acyl
Dopa
Pyro
Uric
Wood

5 letters:
Amide
Amino
Auric
Boric
Caro's
Fatty
Folic
Iodic
L-dopa
Lewis
Malic
Mucic
Oleic
Orcin
Osmic
Trona

6 letters:
Adipic
Bromic
Capric
Cholic
Citric
Cyanic
Erucic
Formic
Gallic
Lactic
Lauric
Leucin
Lipoic
Lysine
Maleic
Marine
Niacin
Nitric
Oxalic
Oxygen
Pectic
Phenol
Picric
Quinic
Serine
Sialic
Sorbic
Tannic
Tiglic
Toluic
Valine

7 letters:
Abietic
Acrylic
Alanine
Alginic
Benzoic
Butyric
Caproic
Cerotic
Chloric
Chromic
Creatin
Cystine
Ellagic
Eugenic
Ferulic
Folacin
Fumaric
Fusidic
Glycine
Guanine
Leucine
Malonic
Meconic
Melanic
Muramic
Nitrous
Nucleic
Orcinol
Peracid
Proline
Prussic
Pteroic
Pyruvic
Racemic
Sebacic
Selenic
Silicic
Stannic

Stearic
Suberic
Terebic
Titanic
Valeric
Vanadic
Xanthic
Xylonic

8 letters:
Abscisic
Adenylic
Arginine
Ascorbic
Aspartic
Butanoic
Caprylic
Carbamic
Carbolic
Carbonic
Chlorous
Cinnamic
Creatine
Cresylic
Crotonic
Cyclamic
Cysteine
Decanoic
Ethanoic
Fulminic
Glutamic
Glyceric
Glycolic
Guanylic
Hippuric
Iopanoic

- Itaconic
- Linoleic
- Lysergic
- Manganic
- Margaric
- Muriatic
- Myristic
- Nonanoic
- Palmitic
- Periodic
- Phthalic
- Rhodanic
- Succinic
- Sulfonic
- Tantalic
- Tartaric
- Telluric
- Tungstic
- Tyrosine
- Uridylic
- Valproic

9 letters:
- Aqua-regia
- Citydylic
- Dichromic
- Histidine
- Hydrazoic
- Hydriodic
- Isocyanic
- Linolenic
- Methanoic
- Nalidixic

Nicotinic
Ornithine
Panthenic
Pentanoic
Polybasic
Propanoic
Propenoic
Saccharic
Salicylic
Sassolite
Selenious
Sulphonic
Sulphuric
Tellurous
Threonine

10 letters:
Aquafortis
Asparagine
Barbituric
Carboxylic
Citrulline
Dithionous
Dodecanoic
Glucoronic
Glutamatic
Glutaminic
Hyaluronic
Isoleucine
Margaritic
Methionine
Orthoboric
Pelargonic

Perchloric
Phosphoric
Proprionic
Pyrogallic
Ricinoleic
Thiocyanic
Thymidylic
Tryptophan

11 letters:
Arachidonic
Decanedioic
Ethanedioic
Ferricyanic
Ferrocyanic
Gibberellic
Hydnocarpic
Hydrobromic
Hydrocyanic
Hyponitrous
Methacrylic
Octanedioic
Pantothenic
Permanganic
Phosphorous
Ribonucleic
Sarcolactic
Taurocholic

12 letters:
Dicraboxylic
Hydrochloric
Hydrofluoric

Hypochlorous
Indoleacetic
Orthosilicic
Persulphuric
Phenylalanin
Polyadenalic
Propanedioic
Prostacyclin
Pyroligneous
Terephthalic

13 letters:
Galactosamine
Heptadecanoic
Indolebutyric
Phenylalanine
Prostaglandin
Pyrosulphuric
Thiosulphuric

14 letters:
Metaphosphoric
Pyrophosphoric

15 letters:
Orthophosphoric

16 letters:
Deoxyribonucleic

Acknowledge(ment) Accept, Admit, Allow, Answer, Avow, Confess, Credit, Grant, Mea culpa, Nod, Own, Receipt, Recognise, Resipiscence, Respect, Righto, Roger, Salute, Ta, Touché, Wilco, Yo
Acme Apex, Apogee, Climax, Comble, Crest, Peak, Summit, Top, Zenith
Acolyte Nethinim, Novice, Server, Thurifer
Acorn(s), Acorn-shell Balanus, Glans, Mast, Rac(c)ahout, Valonia
Acoustic(s) Harmonics, Phonics, Sonics
Acquaint(ance), Acquainted Advise, Cognisant, Enlighten, Familiar, > INFORM, Knowledge, Nodding, Notify, Tell, Versed
Acquiesce(nce), Acquiescent Accept, Bow, Conform, Resigned, Righto, Roger, Wilco, Yield
Acquire, Acquisition Acquest, Earn, Ern, Gain, > GET, Land, Obtain, Procure, Purchase, Steal, Take-over, Usucap(t)ion
Acquit(tal) Assoil, Cleanse, Clear, Exonerate, Free, Loose, Loste, Pardon
Acre(s) A, Area, Bigha, Hide, Rival, Rood
Acrid, Acrimony Bitter(ness), Empyreuma, Pungent, Rough, Sour, Surly
Acrobat(s), Acrobatics Equilibrist, Gymnast, Jerry-come-tumble, Ropedancer, Speeler, Splits, Trampoline, Tumbler, Wing-walker

Acropolis Citadel, Parthenon

Across A, Ac, Athwart, Opposite, Over, Through

Act(ing), Action, Acts A, Affirmative, Antic, Assist, Assumpsit, Auto,
Barnstorm, Behave, Bit, Business, Camp, Campaign, Case, Cause, Charade,
Come, Conduct, Coup, Daff, Deal, > DEED, Delaying, Deputise, Detinue,
Direct, Do, DORA, Double, Enabling, Enclosure, Epistasis, Excitement, Exert,
Exploit, Factory, Feat, Feign, Forth-putting, Function, Furthcoming, Habeas
corpus, Histrionic, Homestead, Identic, Impersonate, Improbation, Incident,
Industrial, Juristic, Lance-jack, Litigate, Locutionary, Measure, Method,
Movement, Mum, Mutiny, Navigation, Partypiece, Pas, Perform(ance),
Personate, Play, Positive, Pp, Practice, Pretence, Private, Procedure, Process,
Qua, Qui tam, Reflex, Replevin, Represent, Riot, Rising, Routine, Sasine,
Scenery, Secondary, Serve, Showdown, Shtick, Simulate, Stamp, Stanislavski,
Statute, Steps, Suit, Synergy, Terminer, Test, Theatricise, Thellusson, Thing,
Transitory, Treat, Trover, Truck, Turn, Twig, Uniformity, Union, Vicegerent,
War, Windlass

Actinium Ac

Actinon An

Activate Arm, Engage, Goad, Spark, Spur, Stur, Styre, Trigger

Active, Activist, Activity A, Agile, Alert, At, Athletic, Brisk, Busy, Cadre,
Deedy, DIY, Do(ing), Dynamited, Dynamo, Ecowarrior, Effectual, Energetic,
Energic, Exercise, Extra-curricular, Floruit, Fluster, Game, Go-go, Goings-on,
Hum, Hyper, Leish, Licht, Live, Mobile, Motile, Nimble, Ongo, On the go, Op,
Operant, Play, Rambunctious, Residual, Sprightly, Springe, Spry, Sthenic,
Surge, Third house, Vacuum, Voice, Wick, Wimble

Actor(s), Actor-like Agent, Alleyn, Artist, Ashe, Barnstormer, Benson,
Betterton, Burbage, Cast, Character, Company, Diseur, Donat, Equity, Gable,
Garrick, Gielgud, Guiser, Ham, Hamfatter, Heavy, Histrio(n), Jay, Juve(nile),
Kean, Luvvie, MacReady, Mime, Mummer, Olivier, Performer, Player, Playfair,
Roscian, Roscius, Savoyard, Sim, Stager, Strolling, Super, Thespian, Tragedian,
Tree, Tritagonist, Trouper, Understudy, Wolfit

Actress Bankhead, Duse, Ingenue, Pierrette, Siddons, Soubrette, Terry, West

Actual(ity), Actually De facto, Entelechy, Literal, Live, Material, Real, Real-life,
Tangible, True, Very

Acumen Insight

Acupressure Jin shin do, Shiatsu

Acupuncture Stylostixis

Acute Astute, Dire, Fitché, > INTENSE, Keen, Quick-witted, Sharp

Adage Aphorism, Gnome, Maxim, Motto, Paroemia, Proverb, Saw, Saying,
Truism

Adam Bede, Delved

Adamant Inexorable, Insistent, Obdurate, Rigid, Unbending

Adapt(er), Adaptable, Adaptor Bushing, Ecad, Flexible, Pliant, Reorient,
Resilient, Tailor, Timeserver, Transform, Versatile

Add(ed), Addendum, Adder Accrue, Adscititious, > APPENDIX, Attach, Cast,
Coopt, Dub, Ech(e), Eik, Eke, Elaborate, Embroider, Enhance, Fortify, Insert,
Lace, Puff, Reckon, Score, Spike, Sum, Summate, Tack on, Tot(e), Total, Viper

Addict(ion), Addicted Abuser, Acidhead, Base head, Buff, Couch potato,
Dependency, Devotee, Dope-fiend, Etheromaniac, Fan, Fiend, Freak, Hophead,
Hype, Jones, Joypopper, Junkie, Lover, Mainliner, Mania, Need, Pillhead,
Pillpopper, Pothead, Shithead, Slave, Space-cadet, Speedfreak, User, Vinolent,
Wino

Addison Spectator

Addition(al) Accession, Addend, Additive, Adscititious, Adulterant, Also, And, Annexure, (As an) in, Bolt-on, Braata, Codicil, Corollary, Eik, Eke, Encore, Epithesis, Etc, Extender, > **EXTRA**, Extramural, > **IN ADDITION**, Increment, Makeweight, Monkey, New, Odd, On, On top, Other, Padding, Paragog(u)e, Parergon, Plus, PS, Rider, Ripieno, Spare, Suffect, Suffix, Supplementary, Surcharge, Thereto, Top-up, Verandah

Address, Address system Accommodation, Accost, Adroit, Allocution, Apostrophe, Apostrophise, Appellation, Art, > **ATLAS**, Ave, Bub, Buster, Call, Compellation, Dedication, Delivery, Den, Diatribe, Direction, Discourse, Election, Epilogue, Epirrhema, Esquire, Gettysburg, Gospodin, Hail, Home, Homily, Lecture, Mester, Mister, Mush, Mynheer, Nkosi, Ode, Orate, Parabasis, Poste-restante, Prelection, Rig, Salute, Sermon, Sir(ree), Speech, Stance, Tact, Tannoy®, > **TITLE**, Towkay, Tuan, Valedictory, Wambenger, Wus, Y'all

Adduce Cite

Adelphic Adam

Adept Able, Adroit, Dab, Deacon, Don, > **EXPERT**, Fit, Handy, Mahatma

Adequate Condign, Does, Due, Egal, Equal, Ere-now, Passable, Proper, > **SUFFICIENT**, Tolerable, Valid

Adhere(nt), Adherence, Adhesive Allegiance, Ally, Araldite®, Bond, Burr, Child, Cling, Conform, Cow Gum®, Dextrin, Disciple, Epoxy, Fidelity, Follower, Glue, Goldsize, Guebre, Gum, Hot-melt, Impact, Jain(a), Mucilage, Partisan, Resin, Sectator, Servitor, Sticker, Supporter, Synechia, Waterglass

Adjacent, Adjoining Bordering, Conterminous, Contiguous, Handy, Nigh

Adjective Adnoun, Epithet, Gerundive

Adjourn(ment) Abeyance, Defer, Delay, > **POSTPONE**, Prorogate, Recess, Rise, Suspend

Adjudicate, Adjudicator Judge, Jury, Referee, Try, Umpire

Adjunct Addition, Aid, Ancillary, Rider

Adjust(able), Adjustment, Adjuster Accommodate, Adapt, Attune, Coapt, Dress, Ease, Fine-tune, Fit, Focus, Gang, Gauge, Gerrymander, J'adoube, Modify, Modulate, Orientate, Prepare, Reduce, Regulate, Reorientate, Reset, Scantle, Sliding, Suit, Tamper, Tram, Trim, True, Tune, Tweak, Vernier

▷ **Adjust** *may indicate* an anagram

Adjutant Aide, Argala, Officer, Stork

Adler Irene

Administer, Administration, Administrator Adhibit, Anele, Apply, Arrondissement, Bairiki, Bureaucrat, Control, Corridors of power, > **DIRECT**, Dispence, Dispense, Executive, Intendant, Intinction, > **MANAGE**, Raj, Regime, Registrar, Run, Secretariat, Soke, Steward

Admirable, Admiration, Admire(d), Admirer Clinker, Clipper, Conquest, Crichton, Esteem, Estimable, > **EXCELLENT**, Flame, Fureur, Ho, Iconise, Idolater, Laudable, Partisan, Regard, Ripping, Splendid, Toast, Tribute, Venerate, Wonder, Wow

Admiral Adm, Anson, Beatty, Beaufort, Benbow, Blake, Bligh, Boscawen, Butterfly, Byng, Byrd, Drake, Effingham, Fisher, Hood, Hornblower, Howard, Jellicoe, Keyes, Marrowfat, Navarch, Nelson, Raeder, Red, Rodney, Spee, Sturdee , Togo, Vanessa, Van Nieman, Van Tromp, White

Admission, Admit(ting), Admittance Accept, Access, Agree, Allow, Avow, Concede, > **CONFESS**, Enter, Entrée, Entry, Estoppel, Grant, Induct, Ingress, Initiate, Intromit, Ordain, Owe, Own, Recognise, Tho(ugh), Yield

Admonish, Admonition Chide, Lecture, Moralise, Pi-jaw, Rebuke, Reprimand,

> **SCOLD**, Tip, Warn

Ado Bother, Bustle, Fuss

Adolescent Developer, Grower, Halflin, Juvenile, Neanic, Teenager, Veal, Youth

Adonais Keats

Adonis Pheasant's Eye

Adopt(ed) Accept, Affect, Affiliate, Assume, Dalt, Embrace, Espouse, Father, Foster, Mother

Adoration, Adore Homage, Idolise, Latria, Love, Pooja(h), Puja, Revere, Venerate, Worship

Adorn(ed), Adornment Attrap, Banderol, Bedeck, Bedight, Bejewel, Caparison, Clinquant, Deck, Dight, Drape, Embellish, Emblaze, Emblazon, Embroider, Enchase, Equip, Festoon, Flourish, Furnish, Garnish, Grace, Graste, Ornament, Riband, Tattoo, Tatu, Tinsel, Trappings

Adrenaline Epinephrin(e)

Adroit Adept, Clever, Dextrous, Expert, Skilful

Adulate, Adulation Flatter(y), Praise, > **WORSHIP**

Adullam Cave

Adult Amadoda, Consenting, Grown-up, Man, Mature, Upgrown, X

Adulterant, Adulterate Cut, Debase, Impurify, Lime, Mix, Multum, > **POLLUTE**, Sophisticate, Weaken

Adulterer, Adultery Avoutery, Cuckold, Fornication, Francesca, Lenocinium

Advance(d) A, Abord, Accelerate, Anabasis, Ante, Approach, Assert, Charge, Develop, Extreme, Fore, Forge, Forward, Gain, Get on, Grubstake, Haut(e), Impress, Imprest, Incede, Late, Lend, > **LOAN**, March, Mortgage, On(ward), Overture, Pass, Piaffe, Posit, Postulate, Precocious, Prefer, Prest, Process, Progress, > **PROMOTE**, Propose, Propound, Ripe, Rise, Scoop, Sub, Submit, Tiptoe, Voorskot

Advantage(ous) Accrual, Aid, > **ASSET**, Avail, Batten, Benefit, Bisque, Boot, Edge, Emolument, Expedient, Exploit, Favour, Fruit, Gain, Grouter, Handicap, Handle, Head-start, Help, Interess, Interest, Lever(age), Odds, One-up, Pecuniary, Percentage, Plus, Privilege, Prize, Pro, Purchase, Salutary, Strength, Toe-hold, Upper-hand, Upside, Use, Van, Whiphand, Whipsaw

Advent(ist) Coming, Shaker

Adventure(r), Adventuress Argonaut, Assay, Aunter, Buccaneer, Casanova, Conquistador, Emprise, Enterprise, Escapade, > **EXPLOIT**, Filibuster, Gest, Lark, Mata Hari, Mercenary, Merchant, Picaresque, Picaro, Picaroon, Risk, Routier, Rutter, Swashbuckler, Vamp, Voyage

Adversary Antagonist, Cope(s)mate, Enemy, Foe

Adverse, Adversity Calamity, Cross, Down, Harrow, Misery, Reversal, Setback, Untoward, Woe

Advert(ise), Advertisement, Advertising Ad, Air, Allude, Bark, Bill, Blipvert, Circular, Classified, Coign(e), Coin, Commercial, Copy, Display, Dodger, Flier, Flyer, Flyposting, Flysheet, Hype, Infomercial, Jingle, Madison Avenue, Mailshot, Niche, Noise, > **NOTICE**, Packshot, Parade, Placard, Plug, > **POSTER**, Promo, Promote, Promulgate, Prospectus, Puff, Quoin, Refer, Semisolus, Sky-write, Splash, Spot, Stunt, Subliminal, Teaser, Tele-, Throwaway, Tout, Trailer, Trawl, Want(s) (ad)

Advice Conseil, Counsel, > **GUIDANCE**, Guideline, Information, Invoice, Opinion, Read, Recommendation, Re(e)de

Advise(d), Adviser, Advisable Acquaint, CAB, Cabal, Camarilla, Counsel, Egeria, Enlighten, Expedient, Genro, Induna, Inform, Instruct, Mentor, Oracle, Peritus, Politic, Prudent, > **RECOMMEND**, Tutor, Urge, Wise

Advocate(d) Agent, Argue, Attorney, Back, Counsel, Devil's, Exponent, Gospel, Lawyer, Move, Paraclete, Peat, Peddle, Pleader, Pragmatist, Preach, Proponent, Syndic, Urge

Aerial Aeolian, Aery, Antenna, Beam, Clover, Dipole, Dish, Ethereal, Ferriterod, Folded dipole, Frame, Ground plane, Long-wire, Loop, Parabolic, Rhombic, Satellite dish, Slot, Yagi

Aerobatics Stunt

Aerobics Pilates

▸ **Aeroplane** *see* AIRCRAFT

Aerosol Atomiser, Mace®

Aesir Loki

Aesthetic Arty, Tasteful

Affable Amiable, Avuncular, Benign, Suave, Urbane

Affair(s) Amour, Business, Concern, Current, Effeir, Effere, Event, External, Fight, Foreign, Go, Indaba, Internal, Intrigue, Matter, Pash, Pi(d)geon, Pidgin, Ploy, Relationship, Res, Romance, Shebang, Subject, Thing

Affect(ed), Affectation, Affection(ate) Air, Airtsy-mairtsy, Alter, Breast, Camp, Chi-chi, Concern, Crazy, Endearment, Euphuism, Foppery, Hit, Impress, Ladida, Lovey-dovey, Mimmick, Minauderie, Mincing, Minnick, Minnock, Mouth-made, Phoney, > POSE, Poseur, Precieuse, Preciosity, Pretence, Prick-me-dainty, Smitten, Spoilt, Stag(e)y, Storge, Susceptible, Sway, Sympathetic, Tender, Twee, Unction, Unnatural, Upend

Affiliate, Affiliation Adopt, Associate, Merge, Unite

Affinity Bro, Kin(ship), Penchant, Rapport, Tie

Affirm(ative), Affirmation Assert, Attest, Maintain, Predicate, Protestation, Uh-huh, > VERIFY, Yebo

Affix(ed) Append, Ascribe, > ATTACH, Connect, Fasten, On

Afflict(ed), Affliction Ail, Asthma, Cross, Cup, Curse, Disease, Furnace, Harass, Hurt, Lumbago, Molest, Nosology, Palsy, Persecute, Pester, Plague, Scourge, Smit, Sore, > SORROW, Stricken, Teen, Tene, Tic, Tribulation, > TROUBLE, Unweal, Visitation, Woe

Affluence, Affluent Abundance, Dinky, Fortune, Opulence, Wealth

Afford Allow, Bear, Give, Manage, Offer, Provide, Spare, Yield

Affray Brawl, Fight, Mêlée, Scuffle, Skirmish

Affront Assault, Defy, Facer, > INSULT, > OFFEND, Outrage, Scandal, Slight, Slur

Afghan(istan) Bactria, Dard, Hound, Kaf(f)ir, Pakhto, Pakhtu, Pashto, Pashtu, Pathan, Pushto(o), Pushtu

Afloat Aboard, Abroach, Adrift, Natant

Afoot Astir, Up

Aforesaid Above, Same

Afraid Adrad, Alarmed, Chicken, Fearful, Funk, Rad, Regretful, Scared, Timorous, Windy, Yellow

Africa(n) Abyssinian, Akan, Angolan, Ashanti, Baganda, Bambara, Bantu, Barbary, Barotse, Basotho, Basuto, Beento, Bemba, Beninese, Berber, Biafran, Bintu, Black, Boer, Botswana, Cairene, Carthaginian, Chewa, Chichewa, Congo(l)ese, Cushitic, Damara, Dinka, Duala, Dyula, Efik, Eritrean, Ethiopian, Eve, Fang, Fanti, Fingo, Flytaal, Fula(h), Gabonese, Galla, Gambian, Ganda, Gazankulu, Grikwa, Griqua, Gullah, Hamite, Hausa, Herero, Hottentot, Hutu, Ibibi, Ibo, Igbo, Impi, Kabyle, Kaffer, Kaf(f)ir, Kenyan, Khoikhoi, Kikuyu, Kongo, Lango, Lesotho, Liberian, Libyan, Lowveld, Lozi, Luba, Luo, Maghreb, Maghrib, Malawi, Malian, Malinke, Mande, Mandingo, Masai, Mashona, Matabele, Mende, Moor, Moroccan, Mossi, Mozambican, Mswahili,

Munt(u), Mzee, Nama, Nama(qua), Namibian, Negrillo, > **NEGRO**, Nguni, Nilot(e), Nubian, Nuer, Nyanja, Oromo, Ovambo, Pedi, Pied noir, Pondo, Rastafarian, Rhodesian, San, Shilluk, Shluh, Shona, Shono, Somali, Songhai, Sotho, Soweto, Sudanese, Susu, Swahili, Swazi, Temne, Tiv, Tonga, Transkei, Transvaal, Tshi, Tsonga, Tswana, Tuareg, Tutsi, Twi, Ugandan, Venda, Voltaic, Waswahili, Wolof, X(h)osa, Yoruban, Zairean, Zulu

Afrikaan(s), Afrikaner Crunchie, Hairyback, Mynheer, Taal, Volk, Voortrekker

After(wards) About, A la, At, Behind, Beyond, Eft, Epi-, > **LATER**, On, Once, Past, Rear, Since, Sine, Subsequent

Afterbirth Secundines, Sooterkin

▷ **After injury** *may indicate* an anagram

Aftermath Consequence, Fall out, Legacy, Mow(ing), Rawing, Rawn, Rowan, Rowen, Rowing, Sequel(a)

Afternoon A, Arvo, PM, Postmeridian, Undern

Afterpiece, Afterthought Addendum, Codicil, Epimetheus, Exode, Footnote, Note, PS, Supplement

Again Afresh, Agen, Anew, Back, Bis, De novo, Ditto, Do, Eft, Eftsoons, Encore, Iterum, More, Moreover, O(v)er, Re-, Recurrence, Reprise, Than, Then

Against A, Anti, Beside, Con, Counter, Gainsayer, Into, Nigh, On, Opposing, To, V, Versus

Agape Feast, Hiant, Ringent, Yawning

Agate Chalcedonyx, Moss, Murr(h)a, Onyx, Ruin

Agave Henequen, Lily, Maenad, Maguey

Age(d), Ages, Aging Achievement, Ae, Aeon, Aet, Alcheringa, Anno domini, Antique, Archaise, Atomic, Augustan, Azilian, Calpa, Century, Chellean, Coon's, Copper, Cycle, Dark, Day, Doddery, Eld, Elizabethan, Eon, Epact, Epoch(a), Era, Eternity, Generation, Gerontic, Golden, Grey, Heroic, Hoar, Hore, Ice, Information, Iron, Jazz, Jurassic, Kaliyuga, Kalpa, La Tene, Lias, Magdalenian, Maglemosian, Mature, Mental, Middle, Millennium, Neolithic, New, New Stone, Of, Old, Oligocene, Paleolithic, Passé, Periclean, Period, Phanerozoic, Progeria, Reindeer, S(a)eculum, Saros, Senescence, Silver, Solera, Space, Stone, Third, Villanovan, Yellow, Yonks, Yug(a)

Agency, Agent Agitator, Ambassador, Art, Bailiff, Barm, Bond, Broker, BSI, Bureau, Catalyst, Cat's paw, Cause, Commis, Complexone, Comprador(e), Consul, Countryside, Crown, Customs, Dating, Delcredere, Developing, Disclosing, Distributor, Doer, Double, Emissary, Environment, Envoy, Enzyme, Escort, Estate, Exciseman, Executor, Factor, Fed, Finger, Flack, Forwarding, Free, G-man, Go-between, Hand, Hirudin, House, Implement, Indian, Influence, Institorial, Instrument, Intermediary, Kinase, Law, Legate, Literary, Magic bullet, Man, Means, Medium, Mercantile, Mole, Mutagen, Narc, Narco, Nerve, Ninja, OO, -or, Order paper, Oxidizing, Parliamentaire, Parliamentary, Patent, Penetration, Pinkerton, Press, Procurator, Proxy, Realtor, Reducing, Rep(resentative), Resident, Reuters, Riot, Road, Runner, Salesman, Secret (service), Setter, Shipping, Sleeper, Solvent, Spy, Syndic, Tass, Teratogen, Third party, Ticket, Training, Travel, UNESCO, Vakeel, Vakil, Virino, Voice, Wetting, Wire service

Agenda Business, Hidden, Programme, Remit, Schedule

Aggie Agnes, Ines, Nessa, Nesta

Aggravate Annoy, Inflame, Irk, Needle, Nettle, Provoke, Try, Vex

Aggregate, Aggregation Ballast, Congeries, Detritus, Etaerio, Granulite, Gravel, Omnium, Ore, Sum, Total

Aggression, Aggressive, Aggressor Arsey, Attack, Belligerent, Bullish, Butch,

Defiant, Enemy, Feisty, Foe, Gungho, Hawk, Invader, In-your-face, Militant, On-setter, Pushing, Rambo, Rampant, Road rage, Shirty, Truculent, Wild

Agile Acrobatic, Deft, Lissom(e), Nifty, Nimble, Quick, Spry, Supple, Swank

Agitate(d), **Agitation**, **Agitator** Activist, Ado, Agitprop, Betoss, Boil, Bolshie, Bother, Chartist, Churn, Commotion, Commove, Convulse, Demagogue, Discompose, Distraught, > **DISTURB**, Doodah, Ebullient, Emotion, Excite, Extremist, Fan, Fantad, Fanteeg, Fantigue, Fantod, Ferment, Firebrand, Flurry, Fluster, Flutter, Fraught, Frenzy, Fuss, Goad, Heat, Hectic, Jabble, Lather, Militant, Panicky, Pedetic, Perturb, Poss, Pother, Rattle, Restless, Rouse, Ruffle, Seethed, Sod, Stir(-up), Swivet, Tailspin, Taking, Tew, Thermal, Tizzy, Toss, Tremor, Trepidation, Trouble, Turmoil, Tweak, Twitchy, Upset, Welter, Whisk, Wrought up, Ytost

▷ **Agitate** *may indicate* an anagram

Agley Awry, Unevenly

Aglow Alight, Tipsy

▶ **Agnes** *see* AGGIE

Agnostic Laodicean

Ago Lang syne

Agog Astir, Athirst, Eager, Keen, Pop-eyed

Agonise, **Agony** Ache, Anguish, Brood, Dread, Ecstasy, Heartache, > **PAIN**, Throe(s), Torment, Torture

Agree(ing), **Agreed**, **Agreement** Accede, Accept, Accord, Acquiescence, Allow, Amen, Analog(ue), Analogy, Apply, As one, Assent, Assort, Atone, Ausgleich, Aye, Bilateral, Bipartite, Bond, Cartel, Champerty, Chime, Closing, Coincide, Collective, Comart, Community, Compact, Comply, Comport, Concert, Concord(at), Concur, Conform, Congree, Congruent, Consension, Consensus, > **CONSENT**, Consonant, Contract, Contrahent, Convection, Correspond, Cotton, Covenant, Cushty, Dayton Accords, Deal, Deffo, Deign, Done, Entente, Equate, Escrow, Fadge, Gatt, Gentleman's, Handfast, Harmony, Homologous, Indenture, Jibe, Knock-for-knock, League, Like-minded, Mercosur, National, Net Book, Nod, Nudum pactum, Okay, Pact, Pair, Placet, Plant, Prenuptial, Procedural, Productivity, Rabat(te), Repurchase, Right(o), Right on, Roger, Sanction, Schengen, Service, Side, Sort(ance), Specialty, Sponsion, Square, Standstill, Substantive, Suit, Sweetheart, Sympathy, Synchronise, Synesis, Syntony, Tally, Technology, Threshold, Trade, Treaty, Uh-huh, Union, Unison, Unspoken, Wilco, Yea, Yes

Agreeable Amene, Harmonious, Pleasant, Sapid, Sweet, Well-disposed, Willing, Winsome

Agriculture, **Agricultural(ist)** Arval, Geoponic, Georgic, Inari, Permaculture, Smallholding, Tull

Aground Ashore, Beached, Sew, Stranded

Ague Dumb

▷ **Ague(ish)** *may indicate* an anagram

Ah Ach, Ay

Ahead Anterior, Before, Foreship, Forward, Frontwards, In store, Onward, Up

Aiblins Perhap, Perhaps, Yibbles

Aid(s), **Aide** Accessory, Adjutant, Assist, Decca, > **DEPUTY**, First, Foreign, Galloper, Grant, Hearing, Help, Key, Legal, Lend-lease, Monitor, Optophone, Orthosis, PA, Realia, Relief, Serve, Slim, Subsidy, Subvention, Succour, Support, Teaching, Visual, Yeoman('s) service

Ail(ment) Affect, Afflict(ion), Complaint, Croup, Disease, Malady, Narks, Pink-eye, Pip, Sickness

Aim Approach, Aspire, Bead, Bend, End, Ettle, Eye, Goal, Hub, Intent, Level, Mark, Mission, Object, Plan, Plank, Point, Purpose, Reason, Sake, Seek, Sight(s), Target, Tee, Telos, Train, View, Visie, Vizy, Vizzie, Zero-in

Aimless Adrift, Drifting, Erratic, Haphazard, Random, Unmotivated

Air(s), Airer, Airy Aerate, Aerial, Aero, Allure, Ambiance, Ambience, Aquarius, Arietta, Atmosphere, Attitude, Aura, Bearing, Calypso, Canzona, Canzone, Cavatina, Compressed, Dead, Demaine, Descant, Ditty, Draught, Dry, Emphysema, Ether(eal), Expose, Fan, Filmy, Front, Gemini, Heaven, Horse, Inflate, Libra, Lift, Light, Liquid, Look, Lullaby, Madrigal, Manner, Melody, Mien, Nitre, Oat, Open, Ozone, Parade, Periptery, Pneumatic, Radio, Screen, Scuba, Serenade, Serenata, Serene, Shanty, Side, Sky, Slipstream, Solo, Song, Strain, Swank, Thin, Trigon, > TUNE, Vent, Ventilate, Vital, Wake, Wind

Airborne Ab

Air-conditioning Plenum system

Aircraft, Airship Aerodyne, Aerostat, Angels, AST, Auster, Autoflare, Autogiro, Autogyro, Aviette, Avion, Biplane, Blimp, Brabazon, Bronco, Camel, Canard, Canberra, Chaser, Chopper, Coleopter, Comet, Concorde, Convertiplane, Corsair, Crate, Cropduster, Cyclogiro, Delta-wing, Dirigible, Doodlebug, Drone, Eagle, F, Ferret, Fixed-wing, Flying wing, Fokker, Freedom-fighter, Freighter, Galaxy, Glider, Gotha, Gyrodyne, Gyroplane, Hang-glider, Harrier, Hawkeeze, Heinkel, Helicopter, Hercules, Hunter, Hurricane, Interceptor, Intruder, Jet star, Jumbo, Jump-jet, Kite, Lancaster, Liberator, Lifting-body, Messerschmitt, Microlight, Microlite, MIG, Mirage, Monoplane, Mosquito, Moth, Multiplane, Nightfighter, Nightfinder, Oerlikon, Orion, Ornithopter, Orthopter, Parasol, Penguin, Phantom, > PLANE, Provider, Prowler, Ramjet, Rigid, Rotaplane, Runabout, Scramjet, Semi-rigid, Skyhawk, Sopwith, Sopwith Camel, Spitfire, SST, Starfighter, Starlifter, Stealth bomber, STOL, Stratocruiser, Stratotanker, Stuka, Super Sabre, Sweptwing, Swing-wing, Tankbuster, Taube, Taxiplane, Thunderbolt, Thunderchief, Tomcat, Tornado, Tracker, Trident, Tri-jet, Triplane, Tube, Turbo-jet, Turbo-prop, Turboramjet, Vigilante, Viking, Viscount, Voodoo, VTOL, Wild weasel, Zeppelin

Aircraftsman, Airman AC, Aeronaut, Erk, Fokker, Kiwi, LAC, RAF

Aircraftswoman Penguin, Pinguin

▶ **Airfield** see AIRPORT

Air force Luftwaffe

Airlift Thermal

Airline, Airway Aeroflot, Anthem, BAC, BEA, Duct, Larynx, Lot, Lyric, Qantas, SAS, S(ch)norkel, TWA, Weasand(-pipe), Windpipe

▶ **Airman** see AIRCRAFTSMAN, FLIER

Airport Drome, Entebbe, Faro, Gander, Gatwick, Heliport, Idlewild, Kennedy, Landing strip, Lod, Luton, Lydda, Lympne, Orly, Prestwick, Runway, Shannon, Stansted, Stolport, Vertiport, Wick

Air-raid Blitz, Mission

Air-tight Hermetic, Indisputable, Sealed

Aisle Gangway

Aitch Ache, Aspirate, H

Ajax Loo

Aka Alias

Akin Alike, Cognate, Congener, Kindred

Alarm Alert, Arouse, Bell, Bleep, Caution, Concern, Dismay, Eek, False, Fire, Fricht, Fright, Ghast, Larum, Panic, Perturb, Rock, Rouse, Siren, Smoke, Startle, Tirrit, Tocsin, Warn, Yike(s)

Alas Ah, Alack, Ay, Eheu, Ha, Haro, Harrow, Io, Lackadaisy, Lackaday, O, Oh, Ohone, O me, Ou, Sadly, Waesucks, Waly, Well-a-day, Wellanear, Wel(l)away, Woe

Alaskan AK, Sourdough

Alban Berg

Albanian Arna(o)ut

Albatross Alcatras, Golf, Gooney(-bird), Omen, Onus, Wandering

Albeit Tho(ugh)

Albert Chain, Chevalier, Consort, Hall, Herring, Slang

Album Autograph, Looseleaf, Photo, Record, Stamp

Albumen, Albumin Chalaza, Glair, Leucosin, Mucin, Myogen, Protein, Ricin, Serum, White

Alchemic, Alchemist, Alchemy Adept, Brimstone, Faust(us), Hermetic(s), Multiplier, Orpiment, Paracelsus, Quicksilver, Sal ammoniac, Sorcery, Spagyric, Spagyrist, Witchcraft

Alcides Hercules

Alcohol(ic) Absolute, Acrolein, Aldehyde, Amyl, Bibulous, Booze, Borneol, Catechol, Cetyl, Chaptalise, Cholesterol, Choline, Citronellol, Cresol, Denatured, Diol, Dipsomaniac, Drinker, Ethal, Ethanol, Ethyl, Farnesol, Feni, Fenny, Firewater, Fusel-oil, Geraniol, Glycerin(e), Grain, Hard, Hard stuff, Inebriate, Inositol, Isopropyl, Jungle juice, Lauryl, Linalool, Lush, Mahua, Mahwa, Mannite, Mannitol, Mercaptan, Mescal, Methanol, Meths, Methyl, Mow(r)a, Nerol, Phytol, Plonko, Propyl, Rotgut, Rubbing, Rubby, Secondary, Snake juice, Sorbitol, Sphingosine, Spirits, Spirits of wine, Spirituous, Sterol, Terpineol, Tincture, Tocapherol, Triol, Wino, Wood, Xylitol

Alcove Apse, Bay, Bole, Carrel(l), Dinette, Inglenook, Lunette, Niche, Recess, Tokonoma

Alcyonarian Sea-feather

Aldehyde Acrolein, Aldol

Alder Fothergilla

Alderman Bail(l)ie, CA

Alderney CI, Cow

Ale, Alehouse Audit, Barleybree, Barley wine, Beer, Church, Four, Heather, Humpty-dumpty, Lamb's wool, Light, Morocco, Nappy, Nog, Nogg, October, Pale, Plain, Purl, Real, Small, Stout, Swats, Tiddleywink, Tipper, White, Whitsun, Wort, Yard, Yill, Yorkshire stingo

Alert Arrect, Astir, Attentive, Aware, Gleg, Gogo, Intelligent, Open-eyed, Qui vive, Red, Scramble, Sharp, Sprack, Sprag, Stand-to, Vigilant, Volable, Wary, Watchful, Wide-awake

Alewife Barkeeper, Gaspereau

Alexander, Alexandrine Alex, Arius, Macedonian, Pope, Sandy, Sasha, Sawn(e)y, Selkirk, Senarius

Alfalfa Lucern(e), Luzern

Alfred Dreyfus, Garnet, Jingle

Alfresco Barbecue, Plein-air

Alga(e) Anabaena, Blanketweed, Chlorella, Conferva, Desmid, Diatom, Dulse, Heterocontae, Isokont, Jelly, Nostoc, Periphyton, Phycology, Pleuston, Pond scum, Prokaryon, Protococcus, Red, Seaweed, Spirogyra, Star-jelly, Stonewort, Ulothrix, Ulotrichales, Valonia, Volvox, Witches' butter, Zooxanthella

Algebra Boolean, Linear, Quadratics

Algerian Kabyle, Nimidian

Algonquin Innu

Alias Aka, Epithet, Moni(c)ker, Pen-name, Pseudonym

Alibi Excuse, Watertight

Alien(ate), Alienation A-effect, Amortise, Disaffect, Ecstasy, Estrange, ET, Exotic, External, Foreign, Forinsecal, Fremd, Hostile, Martian, Metic, Outlandish, Outsider, Philistine, Repugnant, Strange(r)

Alight Alowe, Availe, Detrain, Disembark, Dismount, In, Lambent, Land, Lit, Perch, Pitch, Rest, Settle

Align Arrange, Associate, Collimate, Dress, Juxtapose, Marshal, Orient, Straighten

▸ **Alike** *see* LIKE

Aliquot Submultiple

Alive Alert, Animated, Breathing, Extant, Quick

Alkali(ne), Alkaloid Antacid, Apomorphine, Atropine, Base, Bebeerine, Berberine, Betaine, Borax, Brucine, Capsaicin, Choline, Cinchon(id)ine, Codeine, Colchicine, Corydaline, Emetin(e), Ephedrine, Gelsemin(in)e, Guanidine, Harmaline, Harmin(e), Hyoscine, Lixivium, Lobeline, Lye, Mescalin, Narceen, Narceine, Nicotine, Papaverine, Pilocarpin, Piperine, Potash, Potass, Quinine, Reserpine, Rhoeadine, Scopolamine, Soda, Solanine, Sparteine, Thebaine, Theobromine, Theophylline, Tropine, Veratridine, Veratrin(e), Vinblastine, Vinca, Vincristine, Volatile, Yohimbine

Alkane Hexane

All A, > ENTIRE, Entity, Finis, Omni, Pan, Quite, Sum, > TOTAL, Toto, Tutti, Whole

Allah Bismillah, God

Allay Alleviate, Calm, Disarm, Lessen, Quieten, Soothe

Allegation, Allege Accuse, Assert, Aver, Claim, Obtend, Plead, Purport, Represent, Smear

Allegiance Faith, Foy, Loyalty

Allegory, Allegorical Apologue, Fable, Mystic, Myth, Parable

Allergy Atopy, Aversion, Bagassosis, Hay fever, Hives

Alleviate Allay, Allege, Calm, Mitigate, Mollify, Palliate, > RELIEVE, Temper

Alley Aisle, Blind, Bonce, Bowling, Corridor, Enning, Ginnel, Lane, Laura, Marble, Passage, Silicon, Tin Pan, Twitten, Vennel, Walk, Wynd

Alliance Agnation, Axis, Bloc, Cartel, Coalition, Combine, Compact, Confederation, Dreibund, Dual, Federacy, > LEAGUE, Marriage, NATO, Quadruple, Syndicate, Triple, Union

Alligator Al(l)igarta, Avocado, Cayman

Alliteration Head-rhyme

Allocate, Allocation Allot, Apportion(ment), Assign, Designate, Earmark, Placement, Priorate, Ration, Share, Zone

Allot(ment), Allow(ance), Allowed, Allowing Admit, Affect, Alimony, Allocation, Although, Aret(t), Assign, Award, Batta, Beteem(e), Budget, Charter, Cloff, Confess, Cor(r)ody, Diet, Discount, Dole, Enable, Entitle, Excuse, Expenses, Feod, Give, Grant, House-bote, Husbandage, Indulge, Jobseekers', Latitude, Legit(imate), Let, Licit, Luit(en), Machining, Mag, Mobility, Okay, Palimony, Parcel, Pension, Percentage, > PERMIT, Personal, Pittance, Plot, Portion, Quarterage, Quota, Ratio, Ration, Rebate, Rood, Salt-money, Sanction, Separation, Sequel, Share(-out), Shrinkage, Sizings, Stint, Stipend, Subsistence, Suffer, Tare, Tax, Teene, Though, Tolerance, Tolerate, Tret, Weighting, Yield

Allotment-holder Cleruch

▸ **Allow** *see* ALLOT

Alloy Albata, Alnico®, Amalgam, Babbit, Bell-metal, Billon, Brass, Britannia

metal, Bronze, Cermet, Chrome(l), Compound, Constantan, Cupronickel, Duralumin®, Electron, Electrum, Eutectoid, Ferrochrome, Gunmetal, Invar®, Iridosmine, Kamacite, Latten, Magnalium, Magnox, Manganin®, Marmem, Mischmetal, Mix, Monel®, Nichrome®, Nickel-silver, Nicrosilal, Nimonic, Nitinol, Occamy, Oreide, Orichalc, Ormolu, Oroide, Osmiridium, Paktong, Pewter, Pinchbeck, Platinoid, Porous, Potin, Pot metal, Prince's metal, Shakudo, Shibuichi, Similor, Solder, Spelter, Steel, Stellite®, Tambac, Terne, Tombac, Tombak, Tutenag, Zircal(l)oy, Zircoloy
▷ **Alloy** *may indicate* an anagram
Allright A1, Assuredly, Fit, Hale, Hunky(-dory), Jake, OK, Safe, Tickety-boo, Well
All-round Overhead, Versatile
All-seeing Panoptic
Allspice Jamaica pepper, Pimiento
Allude, Allusion Hint, Imply, Innuendo, Mention, Refer, Reference, Suggest
Allure, Alluring Agaçant(e), Charm, Circe, Decoy, Entice, Femme fatale, Glam, Glamour, Inviting, Magnet(ic), SA, Seduce, Seductive, Tempt, Trap, Trepan, Vamp
Ally, Allied Accomplice, Agnate, Aide, Alley, Alliance, Backer, Belamy, Cognate, Colleague, Dual, German(e), Holy, Marble, Marmoreal, Partner, Plonker, Related, Taw, Unholy
Almanac Calendar, Clog, Ephemeris, Nautical, Nostradamus, Whitaker's, Wisden, Zadkiel
Almighty Creator, Dollar, God, Jehovah, Omnipotent
Almond Amygdal, Emulsion, Jordan, Marchpane, Marzipan, Orgeat, Praline, Ratafia, Sugared, Valencia
Almost Anear, Anigh, Most, Near, Nigh(ly), Practically, Ripe, Une(a)th, Virtually, Well-nigh, Welly
Alms Awmous, Charity, Dole, Handout, Zakat
Aloe Agave, Pita
Alone Hat, Jack, Lee-lane, Onely, Pat, Secco, Separate, Single, Singly, Sola, Solo, Solus, Tod, Unaccompanied, Unaided, Unattended, Unholpen
Along, Alongside Abeam, Aboard, Abreast, Apposed, Beside, By, Parallel
Aloof Abeigh, Apart, Asocial, Cool, Detached, Distant, Hou inch, Indrawn, Mugwump, Offish, Remote, Reserved, Reticent, Skeigh, Snooty, Stand-offish, Toffee-nosed, Unapproachable
Alpaca Paco
Alphabet ABC, Black-out, Brahmi, Braille, Cyrillic, Deaf, Devanagari, Estrang(h)elo, Futhark, Futhorc, Futhork, Glagol, Glagolitic, Glossic, Grantha, Hangul, Horn-book, International, ITA, Kana, Kanji, Katakana, Kufic, Latin, Manual, Nagari, Og(h)am, Pangram, Phonetic, Pinyin, Romaji, Roman, Runic, Signary, Syllabary
Alpine, Alps Australian, Bernese, Cottian, Dinaric, Gentian, Graian, Julian, Laburnum, Lepontine, Maritime, Matterhorn, Pennine, Rhaetian, Savoy, Southern, Transylvanian, Tyrol
Also Add, And, Eke, Item, Likewise, Moreover, Too, Und
Altar, Altar-cloth, Altarpiece Butsudan, Dossal, Dossel, High, Polyptych, Retable, Shrine, Tabula
Alter Adapt, Adjust, Bushel, Change, Cook, Correct, Customise, Distort, Evolve, Falsify, Lib, Modify, Modulate, Mutate, Recast, Revise, Transpose, Up-end, >**VARY**
Altercation Barney, Brawl, Fracas, Row, Words, Wrangle
Alternate, Alternating, Alternation, Alternative Boustrophedon, Bypass,

Exchange, Instead, Metagenesis, > OPTION, Ossia, Other, Rotate, Second
string, Solidus, Staggered, Systaltic, Tertian, Variant

▷ **Alter(native)** *may indicate* an anagram

▷ **Alternately** *may indicate* every other letter

Althaea Mallow, Malva

Although Admitting, Albe(e), All-be, But, Even, Howsoever, Howsomever,
Whereas, While

Altitude Elevation, Height

Alto Countertenor

Altogether Algate(s), All-to-one, Completely, Entirely, Holus-bolus, Idea, In all,
Nude, Nudity, Purely, Slick, Tout, Uncut, Wholly

▷ **Altogether** *may indicate* words to be joined

Altruistic Heroic, Humane, Philanthropic, Selfless, Unselfish

Alum Potash

Aluminium, Alumino-silicate Al, Bauxite, Sillimanite, Stilbite

Alumnus Graduate, OB

Always Algate(s), Ay(e), Constant, E'er, Eternal, Ever(more), Forever, I, Immer,
Semper, Sempre, Still

Amalgamate Coalesce, Consolidate, Fuse, Merge, Unite

Amalthea Cornucopia

Amarylli(d)s Leocojum, Lily, Polianthes

Amass Accumulate, Assemble, Collect, Heap, Hoard, Pile, Upheap

Amateur(s) A, AA, Armchair, Beginner, Corinthian, Dilettante, Diy, Enthusiast,
Ham, Inexpert, L, Laic, Lay, Neophyte, Novice, Sunday painter, Tiro, Tyro

Amatory Eros, Erotic, Fervent

Amaze(d), Amazement, Amazing Astonish, Astound, Awe, Awhape, Cor,
Criv(v)ens, Dumbfound, Far out, Flabbergast, Gee-whiz, Gobsmack, Goodnow,
Grace, Incredible, Jesus wept, Magical, Monumental, O, Open-eyed,
Open-mouthed, Perplex, Poleaxe, Pop-eyed, Stagger, Stupefaction,
Stupendous, Thunderstruck

Amazon Ant, ATS, Brimstone, Britannia, Dragon, Hippolyta, Orellana,
Penthesilea, Thalestris, Tupi, Virago

Ambassador Diplomat, Elchee, Elchi, Eltchi, Envoy, HE, Internuncio, Leaguer,
Ledger, Legate, Leiger, Minister, Nuncio, Plenipo, Plenipotentiary

Amber Colophony, Lammer, Ligure, Resin, Retinite, Succinum

Ambience Aura, Milieu, Setting

Ambiguous, Ambiguity Amphibology, Cryptic, Delphic, Double, Double
entendre, Enigmatic, Epicene, Equivocal, Loophole, Weasel words

Ambition, Ambitious Aim, Arrivisme, Aspiring, Careerism, Drive, Emulate,
Goal, Go-getter, High-flier, Keen, Office-hunter, Purpose, Pushy, Rome-runner

Amble Meander, Mosey, Pace, Poddle, Saunter, Stroll

Ambrose Emrys

Ambrosia(l) Beebread, Fragrant, Odorant, Ragweed, Savoury

Ambulance, Ambulanceman Blood-wagon, Field, Pannier, Paramedic, Van,
Yellow-flag, Zambu(c)k

Ambulatory Stoa

Ambush(ed) Ambuscade, Bushwhack, Embusque, Latitant, Lurch, Perdu(e),
Trap, Waylay

Amelia Bloomer

Ameliorate Amend, Ease, Improve, Remedy

Amen Ammon, Approval, Inshallah, Verify

Amenable Putty

Amend(ment) Alter, Change, Expiate, Expurgate, Fifth, Redress, Reform, Repair, Restore, > REVISE, Satisfy

▷ **Amend** *may indicate* an anagram

Ament Catkin, Idiot

America(n) Algonki(a)n, Algonqu(i)an, Am, Caddo, Cajun, Carib, Chicano, Chickasaw, Copperskin, Digger, Doughface, Down-easter, Federalist, Flathead, Fox, Gringo, Interior, Joe, Jonathan, Latino, Mistec, Mixtec, Native, Norteno, Olmec, Paisano, Salish, Stateside, Statesman, Statist, Tar-heel, Tico, Tupi, Uncle Sam, US(A), WASP, Yankee, Yanqui

Americium Am

Amiable Friendly, Genial, Gentle, Inquiline, Sweet, Warm

Amid(st) Among, Atween, Between, Inter, Twixt

Amide Asparagine

Amino-acid Dopa, Tyrosine, Valine

Amiss Awry, Ill, Up, Wrong

Ammonia(c) Amide, Amine, Choline, Ethylamine, Hartshorn, Oshac

Ammonite Serpent-stone

Ammunition Ammo, Bandoleer, Bandolier, Buckshot, Bullets, Chain-shot, Dum-dum, Grape(shot), Grenade, Round, Shot, Slug, Tracer

Amnesia Fugal, Fugue, Lethe, Retrograde

Amnesty Oblivion

Amoeba Melboean

Amok Rampaging

Among Amid(st), In, Within

Amorous(ly) Casanova, Erotic, Fervent, Lustful, Smickly, Spoony, Warm

Amorphous Formless, Shapeless, Vague

Amount Come, Dose, Element, Figure, Lashings, Levy, Lot, Number, Ocean, Pot(s), Premium, Price, Quantity, Quantum, Span, Stint, Throughput, Volume, Whale, Wheel

Amour Affair(e), Intrigue, Love

Ampersand Tironian sign

Amphetamine Benny, Benzedrine, Speed

Amphibian, Amphibious Amb(l)ystoma, Amtrack, Anura, Axolotl, Batrachian, Caecilia, Caecilian, Desman, Eft, Frog, Guana, Hassar, Labyrinthodont, Mermaid, Mudpuppy, Newt, Olm, Proteus, Rana, Salamander, Salientia, Seal, Tadpole, Toad, Urodela(n), Urodele, Weasel

Amphipod Sand-screw, Shrimp

Amphitheatre Bowl, Circus Maximus, Coliseum, Colosseum, Ring, Stage

Ample Bellyful, Copious, Enough, Generous, Good, Large, Opulent, Profuse, Rich, Roomy, Round, Uberous, Voluminous

Amplifier, Amplify Booster, Double, Eke, Enlarge, Hailer, Laser, Loud hailer, Maser, Megaphone, Push-pull, Solion, Tannoy®, Transistor, Treble

Amulet Abraxas, Charm, Churinga, Fetish, Greegree, Grigri, Grisgris, Haemon, Pentacle, Periapt, Phylactery, Sea-bean, Talisman, Tiki, Toadstone, Token

Amuse(ment), Amusing(ly) Caution, Cottabus, Disport, Diversion, Divert, Divertimento, Divertissement, Drole, Droll, Game, Gas, Giocoso, Glee, Hoot, Killing, Levity, Light, Occupy, Pleasure, Popjoy, Priceless, Regale, Rich, Scream, Slay, Solace, > SPORT, Tickle, Titillate, Wacky

Amy Johnson, Robsart

▶ **An** *see* A

Ana(s) Story, Teal

Anabaptist Abecedarian, Dipper, Dopper, Hutterite, Knipperdolling

Anableps Four-eyes
Anachronism Archaism, Solecism
Anaconda Water boa
Anacreon Te(i)an
Anaemia Aplastic, Cooley's, Favism, Haemolytic, Megaloblastic, Pernicious, Sickle-cell, Thalassaemia
Anaesthetic, Anaesthetise, Anaesthetist Analgesic, Avertin®, Benzocaine, Bupivacaine, Caudal, Chloroform, Cocaine, Endotracheal, Epidural, Ether, Eucain(e), Freeze, Gas, General, Halothane, Infiltrate, Intravenous, Jabber, Ketamine, Lidocaine, Lignocaine, Local, Metopryl, Morphia, Novocaine, Number, Opium, Orthocaine, Pentothal, Procaine, Rhigolene, Special K, Spinal, Stovaine, Topical, Trike, Urethan(e)
Anagram Jumble
Anal Proctal, Tewel
Analgesic Aspirin, Bute, Codeine, Disprin, Ketamine, Menthol, Methadone, Morphia, Moxa, Painkiller, Pethidine, Phencyclidine, Quina, Salicin(e), Sedative
Analogous, Analogy Akin, Corresponding, Like, Parallel, Similar
Analyse(r), Analysis Alligate, Anagoge, Anatomy, Assess, Breakdown, Construe, Diagnosis, Emic, Eudiometer, Examine, Explication, Factor, Force-field, Fourier, Gravimetric, Harmonic, Input-output, Job, Kicksorter, Miscue, Parse, Pollen, Process, Psych out, Qualitative, Quantative, Quantitative, Risk, Rundown, Scan(sion), Semantics, Sift, Spectral, Spectroscopic, Spectrum, Systems, Test, Transactional, Volumetric
▷ **Analysis** *may indicate* an anagram
Analyst Alienist, Investment, Jung, Psychiatrist, Shrink, Trick cyclist
Anarchist, Anarchy Black Hand, Bolshevist, Chaos, Kropotkin, Nihilism, Provo, Rebel, Revolutionary, Trotskyite
Anathema Ban, Curse, Execration, Oath, Warling
Anatole, Anatolian France, Hittite
Anatomy, Anatomist Bones, Framework, Herophilus, Histology, Morbid, Worm
Ancestor, Ancestral, Ancestry Adam, Avital, Descent, Extraction, For(e)bear, Forefather, Gastraea, Humanoid, Lin(e)age, Parent, Predecessor, Proband, Profectitious, Progenitor, Propositus, Roots, Sire, Tipuna, Tree, Tupina
Anchor(age) Atrip, Bower, Cell, Deadman, Drag, Drift, Drogue, Eremite, Grapnel, Hawse, Hermit, Kedge, Kedger, Killick, Killock, Laura, Moor, Mud-hook, Mushroom, Nail, Ride, Roads(tead), Rode, Root, Scapa Flow, Sea, Sheet, Spithead, Stock, Stream, Toehold, Waist, Weather
Anchorite Recluse
Anchovy Fish, Pear
Ancient Antediluvian, Archaic, Auld-warld, Bygone, Early, Gonfanoner, Historic, Hoary, Iago, Immemorial, Lights, Neolithic, Ogygian, > **OLD(ER)**, Old-world, Primeval, Primitive, Pristine, Ur, Veteran
Ancient city Carthage, Ur
Ancillary Adjunct, Secondary, Subservient
And Als(o), Ampassy, Ampersand, Amperzand, Ampussyand, Besides, Et, Furthermore, Item, 'n', Plus, Tironian sign, Und
Andalusite Macle
Andiron Chenet, Dog, Firedog
Andrew(es) Aguecheek, Lancelot, Merry
Androgynous Epicene

Android Automaton, Golem, Robot
Anecdote(s) Ana, Exemplum, Story, Tale, Yarn
Anemometer Wind-sleeve, Windsock
Anemone Actinia, Pasque-flower, Windflower
Angel(s) Abdiel, Adramelech, Apollyon, Archangel, Ariel, Arioch, Asmadai,
Azrael, Backer, Banker, Beelzebub, Belial, Benefactor, Cake, Cherub, Clare,
Destroying, Deva, Dominion, Dust, Eblis, Falls, Fuzzy-wuzzy, Gabriel,
Guardian, Hierarchy, Host, Iblis, Investor, Israfel, Ithuriel, Lucifer, Michael,
Power, Principality, Raphael, Recording, Rimmon, Seraph, Spirit, St, Throne,
Uriel, Uzziel, Virtue, Watcher, Zadkiel, Zephiel
Angela Brazil
Angel's wings Begonia
Anger, Angry > ANNOY, Bile, Black, Bristle, Choler(ic), Conniption, Cross,
Dander, Displeased, Dudgeon, Enrage, Exasperation, Face, Fury, Gram, Heat,
Horn-mad, Incense, Inflame, Infuriate, Iracund, Irascible, Ire, Kippage, Livid,
Mad, Monkey, Moody, Nettle, Pique, Provoke, Radge, Rage, Rampant, Ratty,
Renfierst, Rile, Roil, Rouse, Sore, Spleen, Steam, Stroppy, Tamping, Tantrum,
Tarnation, Teen(e), Temper, Tene, Tooshie, Vex, Vies, Waspish, Waxy, Wound
up, Wrath, Wroth, Yond
Angina Sternalgia, Vincent's
Angle(d), Angular Acute, Altitude, Argument, Aspect, Axil, Azimuthal,
Canthus, Cast, Catch, Chiliagon, Coign, Complementary, Conjugate,
Contrapposto, Corner, Cos, Critical, Deidre, Diedral, Diedre, Dihedral, Elbow,
Elevation, Ell, Fish, Fish-hook, Fork, Geometry, Gonion, Hade, Hip, In, L,
Laggen, Laggin, Mitre, Oblique, Obtuse, Parallax, Pediculate, Perigon, Piend,
Pitch, Plane, Quoin, Radian, Rake, Re-entrant, Reflex, Right, Sally, Sine,
Sinical, Solid, Steeve, Steradian, Supplementary, Sweepback, Trotline, Vertical,
Viewpoint, Washin, Weather
Angle(r) Attitude, Exterior, Facial, Hour, Hyzer, Interior, Mung, Negative,
Peterman, Pitch-cone, Polyhedral, Position, Positive, Rodster, Round,
Saltchucker, Spherical, Stalling, Straight, Visual, Walton, Wide-gab
Anglesey Mona
Anglican(s) CE-men, Conformist, Episcopal
Anglo-Catholic High-church
Anglo-Indian Qui-hi, Qui-hye, Topi-wallah
Angora Goat, Mohair, Rabbit
Angst Dread
Anguish(ed) Agony, Distress, Gip, Grief, Gyp, Hag-ridden, Heartache, Misery,
> PAIN, Pang, Sorrow, Throes, > TORMENT, Torture, Woe
Angus Aberdeen
Animal(s) Acrita, Anoa, Armadillo, Atoc, Bag, Bandog, Barbastel, Beast,
Bestial, Brute, Cariacou, Carnal, Chalicothere, Coati, Creature, Criollo, Critter,
Ethology, Fauna, Felis, Gerbil, Herd, Ichneumon, Jacchus, Jerboa, Kinkajou,
Klipdas, Mammal, Marmoset, Marmot, Menagerie, Moose, Noctule, Oribi,
Pack, Parazoon, Pet, Protozoa, Pudu, Quagga, Rac(c)oon, Rhesus, Sensual,
Sloth, Stud, Symphile, Tarsier, Teledu, Urson, Waler, Xenurus, Yapock, Zerda,
Zoo
Animal-catcher Utricularia
Animate(d), Animation Activate, Actuate, Arouse, Biophor, Ensoul, Excite,
Fire, Hortatory, Hot, Inspire, Live, Morph, Mosso, Pixil(l)ation, Rouse, Spritely,
Suspended, Verve, Vivify
Animosity Enmity, Friction, Hostility, Ill-will, Malice, Pique, Rancour

Ankle Coot, Cuit, Cute, Hock, Hucklebone, Knee, Malleolus, Talus
Ankle(t), Ankle covering Cootikin, Cuitikin, Cutikin, Gaiter, Jess
Anna, Anne, Annie Boleyn, Hathaway, Laurie, Oakley, Page, Pavlova, Pice,
Sewell, Sister
Annal(s) Acta, Archives, Chronicles, Register
Annatto Roucou
Annex(e) Acquire, Add, Affiliate, Attach, Codicil, Extension, Subjoin
Annihilate Destroy, Erase, Exterminate, Obliterate, Slay
Anniversary Birthday, Feast, Jubilee, Obit, Triennial, Wedding, Yahrzeit
Annotate, Annotator Comment, Interpret, Note, Postil, Scholiast
Announce(r), Announcement Banns, Bellman, Biil(ing), Blazon, Bulletin,
Communiqué, Declare, Decree, Divulgate, Gazette, Herald, Hermes, Inform,
Intimate, Meld, Newsflash, Noise, Post, Preconise, Proclaim, Promulgate,
Pronunciamento, Publish, Release, > REPORT, Rescript, Speaker(ine), State,
Toastmaster, Town crier, Trumpet
Annoy(ance), Annoyed, Annoying Aggravate, Aggrieve, Anger, Antagonise,
Badger, Blight, Bother, Bug, Bugbear, Chagrin, Deuce(d), Disturb, Doggone,
Doh, Drat, Fash, Fleabite, Frab, Fumed, Gall, Harass, Hatter, Hector, Hip,
Huff, Hump, Humph, Incense, Irk, > IRRITATE, Mickey-taking, Miff, Mischief,
Molest, Moryah, Nag, Nark, Nettle, Noisome, Peeve, Pesky, Pester, Pipsqueak,
Pique, Rankle, Rats, Ratty, Resentful, Ride, Rile, Roil, Rub, Shirty, Tiresome,
Tracasserie, Try, Vex, Wazzock
Annual, Annuity Book, Etesian, > FLOWER, Half-hardy, Hardy, Life, Pension,
Perpetuity, Rente, Tontine, Yearbook, Yearly
Annul(ment) Abolish, Abrogate, Cashier, Cassation, Dissolution, Irritate,
Negate, Recision, Repeal, Rescind, Reversal, Revoke, Vacatur, > VOID
Annular Toric
Anodyne Balm, Narcotic, Paregoric, Sedative
Anoint(ing) Anele, Cerate, Chrism, Embrocate, Grease, Hallow, Nard, Smear
Anomaly Eccentric, Gravity, Magnetic, Mean, True
▷ **Anomaly** *may indicate* an anagram
Anon Again, Anew, Later, Soon
Anonymous Adespota, Anon, A.N.Other, Faceless, Grey, Impersonal, Somebody,
Unnamed
Anorak Wonk
Another Extra
Answer(ing), Answer(s) Account, Acknowledge, Amoebaean, Ans, Antiphon,
Because, Comeback, Crib (sheet), Defence, Echo, Key, Lemon, Light, No, Oracle,
Rebuttal, Rebutter, Rein, Rejoin(der), Repartee, Reply, Rescript, Respond,
Response, Responsum, Retort, Return, Riposte, Serve, Sol, Solution, Solve,
Verdict, Yes
Ant(s), Anthill Amazon, Army, Bull(dog), Carpenter, Colony, Driver, Dulosis,
Emmet, Ergataner, Ergates, Ergatomorph, Fire, Formic, Formicary, Leafcutter,
Legionary, Myrmecoid, Myrmidon, Nasute, Neuter, Pharaoh, Pismire, Sauba,
Slave, Soldier, Termite, Thief, Umbrella, Velvet, White, Wood
Antacid Magnesia, Peptic
Antagonist(ic), Antagonise Estrange, Oppugnant, Peare, Peer
Antarctica Amelie Land, Graham land, Wilkes Land
Ant-bear Tamanoir
Ante Bet, Punt, Stake
Ant-eater Aardvark, Echidna, Edental, Manis, Numbat, Pangolin, S(e)ladang,
Spiny, Tamandu, Tamandua, Tapir

Antelope Addax, Antilope, Blackbuck, Blaubok, Blesbok, Bloubok, Bluebuck, Bongo, Bontebok, Bubal(is), Bushbuck, Cabric, Chamois, Chikara, Chiru, Dikdik, Duiker, Duyker, Dzeren, Eland, Elk, Gazelle, Gemsbok, Gerenuk, Gnu, Goral, Grysbok, Harnessed, Hartbees, Hartebeest, Impala, Inyala, Kaama, Kid, Klipspringer, Kob, Kongoni, Koodoo, Kudu, Lechwe, Madoqua, Marshbuck, Mhorr, Mohr, Nagor, Nilgai, Nilgau, Nyala, Nylghau, Oribi, Oryx, Ourebi, Ox, Pale-buck, Pallah, Prongbuck, Pronghorn, Pronk, Puku, Pygarg, Reebok, Reedbuck, Rhebok, Sable, Saiga, Sasin, Sassaby, Serow, Sitatunga, Situtunga, Springbok, Steenbok, Steinbock, Stemback, Stembok, Suni, Takin, Thar, Topi, Tragelaph, Tsessebe, Waterbuck, Wildebeest

Antenna Aerial, Dipole, Dish, Horn, Sensillum, TVRO

Anterior Anticous, Earlier, Front, Prior

Anthelmintic Worm

Anthem Chant, Hymn, Introit, Isodica, Marseillaise, Motet(t), National, Psalm, Responsory, Song, Star Spangled Banner, Stem, Theme, Tract, Troparion

Anthology Album, Ana, Chrestomathy, Digest, Divan, Florilegium, Garland, Pick, Spicilege

Anthony Absolute, Adverse, Trollope

Anthracite Blind-coal

Anthrax Sang

Anthropo(i)d Peripatus, Sivapithecus

Anthropologist Mead

Anti Against, Agin, Con, Hostile

Anti-aircraft AA

Anti-bacterial, Antibiotic Actinomycin, Amoxicillin, Ampicillin, Aureomycin®, Bacitracin, Bacteriostat, Cephalosporin, Ciprofloxacin, Cloxacillin, Colistin, Cortisone, Co-trimoxazole, Doxorubicin, Doxycycline, Drug, Erythromycin, Gentamicin, Gramicidin, Griseofulvin, Interferon, Interleukin, Kanamycin, Lincomycin, Lineomycin, Methicillin, Mitomycin, Neomycin, Nystatin, Opsonin, Oxacillin, Oxytetracycline, Penicillin, Polymixin, Quinolone, Rifampicin, Rifamycin, Spectinomycin, Streptomycin, Streptothricin, Terramycin®, Tetracycline, Tyrocidine, Tyrothricin, Vancomycin, Wide-spectrum

Antibody Agglutinin, Amboceptor, Antitoxin, Blocker, Hybroid, Isoagglutinin, Lysin, Monoclonal, Opsonin, Precipitin, Reagin

Antic(s) Caper, Dido, Frolic, Gambado, Hay, Prank, Shenanigan, Stunt

Anti-carlist Queenite

Anticipate, Anticipation Antedate, Augur, Await, Drool, > EXPECT, Forecast, Foresee, Foresight, Forestall, Foretaste, Hope, Intuition, Prevenancy, Prolepsis, Prospect, Second-guess, Type

Anticlimax Bathos, Damp squib, Deflation, Letdown

Anticline Upwrap

Anticlockwise Dextrorse, Laevorotatory, Widdershins, Withershins

Anticoagulant C(o)umarin, Heparin, Hirudin, Prostacyclin, Warfarin

Anti-Communist McCarthyism

Anticyclone High

Antidote Adder's wort, Alexipharmic, Angelica, Antivenin, Arrowroot, Bezoar, Contrayerva, Cure, Dimercaprol, Emetic, Guaco, Interleukin, Mithridate, Nostrum, Orvietan, Remedy, Ribavirin, Senega, Theriac(a), (Venice)-Treacle

Anti-freeze Glycerol, Lagging

Antigen Hapten(e)

Antihistamine Dimenhydrinate

Anti-imperialist Guelf, Guelph
Antimacassar Tidy
Antimony Kohl, Sb, Stibium
Antioxidant Lycopene
Anti-parliamentarian Poujadist
Antipathy Allergy, Aversion, Detest, > DISLIKE, Enmity, Repugnance
Anti-perfectionist Cobden
Antiphon The Reproaches
Antipodean Abo, Antarctic, Antichthon, Enzed, Underworld
Antipope Novatian(us)
Anti-protectionist Cobden
Antiquated, Antique, Antiquarian Ancient, Archaic, A(u)stringer, Bibelot,
  Curio, Dryasdust, FAS, Fog(e)y, Fogram(ite), Fossil, Old-fangled, Ostreger, Relic
Anti-reformer Obscurant
Anti-revolutionary White
Anti-Roman Ghibel(l)ine
Anti-royalist Whig
Anti-semitic Pamyat
Antiseptic Acriflavine, Carbolic, Cassareep, Creosote, Disinfectant, Eupad,
  Eusol, Formaldehyde, Guaiacol, Iodine, Lysol®, Phenol, Sterile, Tar, Thymol,
  Tutty
Anti-slavery Free-soil, Wilberforce
Anti-smoker ASH, Misocapnic
Antisocial Hostile, Ishmaelitish, Misanthropic
Antithesis Contrary, Converse, Opposite
Anti-three Noetian
Antitoxin Antibody, Antivenin, Guaco, Serum, Vaccine
Anti-union Secesher
Antler(s) Bosset, Crown, Horn, Palm, Rights, Staghorn, Surroyal, Tine
Ant-proof Bilian
▸ **Anus** *see* ANAL
Anvil Bick-iron, Block, Incus, Stiddie, Stithy
Anxiety, Anxious Angst, Brood, Care(ful), Cark, Concern, Disquiet, Dysthymia,
  Fanteeg, Fantigue, Fantod, Fraught, Grave, Heebie-jeebies, Hypochondria,
  Inquietude, Jimjams, Jumpy, Reck, Restless, Scruple, Solicitous, Stress,
  Suspense, Sweat, Tension, Trepidation, Twitchy, Unease, Unquiet, Upset,
  Uptight, White-knuckle, Worriment
Any Arrow, Ary, Some
Anybody, Anyone Everyman, One, Whoso, You
Anyhow Anyway, Leastways
Anything Aught, Diddly-squat, Oucht, Owt, Whatnot
▷ **Anyway** *may indicate* an anagram
Apache Arizona, AZ
Apart Aloof, Aside, Asunder, Atwain, Beside, Separate
Apartheid Racism, Verkrampte
Apartment Ben, Condominium, Digs, Duplex, Efficiency, Flat, Insula, Mansion,
  Pad, Paradise, Penthouse, Pied-a-terre, Quarters, Room, Simplex, Solitude,
  Suite, Tenement, Unit, Walk-up
Apathetic, Apathy Accidie, Acedia, Incurious, Languid, Lethargic, Listless,
  Lobotomized, Pococurante, Torpid
Ape(-like), Apeman Anthropoid, Barbary, Big-foot, Bonobo, Catarrhine, Copy,
  Dryopithecine, Gelada, Gibbon, Gorilla, > IMITATE, Magot, Mimic, Orang,

Paranthropus, Pithecoid, Pongo, Proconsul, Sacred, Simian, Simulate, Yowie
Aperient Cascara, Laxative, Senna
Aperitif > DRINK, Pernod®
Aperture Balistraria, Chink, Fenestella, Hole, Keyhole, Osculum, Relative, Spiracle, Window
Apex Acme, Culmen, Keystone, Knoll, Knowe, Solar, Summit, Vortex
Aphid Ant-cow, Phylloxera
Aphorism Adage, Epigram, Gnome, Proverb, Sutra
Aphrodisiac, Aphrodite Cytherean, Erotic, Idalian, Paphian, Philter, Philtre, Spanish fly, Urania, Yohimbine
Aplomb Assurance, Cool, Equanimity, Poise, Sangfroid, Serenity
Apocryphal Spurious, Tobit
Apograph Roneo®
Apollo Belvedere, Pythian, Sun
Apology Excuse, Justifier, Mockery, Oops, Pardon, Scuse
Apostate Citer, > HERETIC, Pervert, Rat, Recreant, Renegade, Runagate, Turncoat
Apostle, Apostolic Cuthbert, > DISCIPLE, Evangelist, Johannine, Jude, Matthew, Pauline, Spoon, Twelve
Apostrophe, Apostrophise Elision, O(h), Soliloquy, Tuism
Apothegm Dictum, Maxim, Motto
Appal(ling) Abysmal, Affear(e), Dire, Dismay, Egregious, Frighten, Horrify, Piacular, Shock, Tragic
▷ **Appallingly** *may indicate* an anagram
Apparatus Alembic, Appliance, Autoclave, Caisson, Chemostat, Clinostat, Coherer, Colorimeter, Condenser, Cosmotron, Cryostat, Davis, Defibrillator, Device, Digester, Ebullioscope, Effusiometer, Electrograph, Electrophorus, Electroscope, Eprouvette, Equipment, Eudiometer, Exciter, Fixings, Gadget, Golgi, Graith, Helioscope, Hemocytometer, Hodoscope, Holophote, Hydrophone, Incubator, Injector, Instrument, Jacquard, Kipps, Kymograph, Lease-rod, Masora(h), Microreader, Mimeograph, Multi-gym, Oscillograph, Oxygenator, Pasteuriser, Percolator, Phonometer, Phytotron, Potometer, Proto®, Pulmotor®, Radiosonde, Replenisher, Respirator, Respirometer, Resuscitator, Retort, Rounce, Scintiscanner, Scuba, Set, Snorkel, Sphygmograph, Spirophore, Stellarotor, Steriliser, Still, Switchgear, Tackle, Tackling, Talk-you-down, Teleprinter, Thermopile, Tokamak, Transformer, Transmitter, Tromp(e), Ventouse, Wheatstone's bridge, Whip-and-derry
Apparel Attire, Besee, > COSTUME, Garb, Raiment, Wardrobe, Wardrop
Apparent(ly) Ap, Clear, Detectable, Manifest, Ostensible, Outward, Overt, Plain, Prima facie, Semblance, Visible
▷ **Apparent** *may indicate* a hidden word
Apparition Dream, Eidolon, Fetch, Ghost, > ILLUSION, Phantom, Shade, Spectre, Visitant, Wraith
Appeal(ing) Ad, Beg, Cachet, Catchpenny, Charisma, Charm, Cri de coeur, Cry, Entreat, Entreaty, Epirrhema, Fetching, Invocation, It, O, Oomph, Plead, SA, Screeve, Solicit, SOS, Suit
Appear(ance) Advent, Air, Apport, Arrival, Aspect, Broo, Brow, Burst, Cast, Compear, Debut, Emerge, Enter, Exterior, Eye, Facade, Facies, Far(r)and, Farrant, Fa(s)cia, Feature, Format, Garb, Guise, Habitus, Hue, Image, Kithe, Kythe, Loom, > MANNER, Mien, Occur, Ostensibly, Outward, Person, Phase, Phenomenon, Physiognomy, Presence, Prosopon, Represent, Rig, Rise, Seem, Semblance, Show, Spring, Superficies, Theophany, View, Visitation, Wraith

Appease(ment) Allay, Alleviate, Calm, Danegeld, Mitigate, > MOLLIFY, Munichism, Pacify, Placate, Propitiate, Satisfy, Soothe, Sop

Append(age) Adjunct, Affix, Aglet, Allantois, Aril, Arista, Cercus, Chelicera, Codpiece, Ctene, Fang, Flagellum, Hanger-on, Lobe, Lug, Palp(us), Paraglossa, Parapodium, Pedipalp, Stipel, Suffix, Swimmeret, Tail, Tailpiece, Tentacle, Ugly, Uropod, Uvula

Appendix Addendum, Apocrypha, Codicil, Grumbling, Label, Pendant, Pendent, Rider, Schedule, Vermiform

Appetite, Appetitive, Appetise(r) Antepast, Antipasto, Aperitif, Appestat, Bhagee, Bhajee, Bulimia, Bulimy, Canapé, Concupiscence, Concupy, Crudités, Desire, Dim-sum, Entremes(se), Entremets, Flesh, Hunger, Limosis, Malacia, Meze, Mezze, Nacho, Orectic, Orexis, Passion, Pica, Polyphagia, Relish, Tapa(s), Titillate, Twist, Yerd-hunger, Yird-hunger

Applaud, Applause Acclaim, Bravo, > CHEER, Clap, Claque, Eclat, Encore, Extol, Hum, Kentish fire, Olé, Ovation, Praise, Root, Ruff, Tribute

Apple Adam's, Alligator, Baldwin, Balsam, Biffin, Blenheim orange, Braeburn, Bramley, Charlotte, Codlin(g), Cooker, Costard, Crab, Custard, Dead Sea, Discord, Eater, Granny Smith, Greening, Jenneting, John, Jonathan, Leather-coat, Love, Mammee, May, McIntosh (red), Medlar, Nonpareil, Oak, Pacific Rose, Pearmain, Pippin, Pomace, Pome(roy), Pom(e)water, Pomroy, Potato, Punic, Pyrus, Quarantine, Quarenden, Quar(r)ender, Quarrington, Quodlin, Redstreak, Reinette, Rennet, Ribston(e), Ruddock, Russet, Seek-no-further, Snow, Sops-in-wine, Sorb, Sturmer, Sugar, Sweeting, Thorn, Toffee, Windfall, Winesap

Apple juice Malic

Apple-picker Atalanta

Applicant Ordinand, Postulant

Application, Apply, Appliance(s) Address, Adhibit, Appeal, Appose, Assiduity, Barrage, Blender, Devote, Diligence, Dressing, Exercise, Foment, Give, Implement, Inlay, Lay, Lotion, Mixer, Ointment, Opodeldoc, Petition, Plaster, Poultice, Put, Request, Resort, Respirator, Rub, Sinapism, Stupe, Truss, > USE, Vice, White goods

Appliqué Hawaiian

Appoint(ee), Appointment Advowson, Assign, Berth, Date, Delegate, Depute, Designate, Dew, Due, Executor, Induction, Installation, Make, Name, > NOMINATE, Nominee, Office, Ordain, Position, Post, Posting, Rendezvous, Room, Set, Tryst

▷ **Appointed** *may indicate* an anagram

Apportion(ment) Allocate, Allot, Mete, Parcel, Ration, Share, Weigh

Apposite Apt, Cogent, Germane, Pat, Pertinent, Relevant, Suitable

Appraise, Appraisal Analyse, > EVALUATE, Gauge, Guesstimate, Judge, Tape, > VALUE, Vet

Appreciate, Appreciation Acknowledgement, Cherish, Clap, Dig, Endear, Esteem, Gratefulness, Increase, Prize, Realise, Regard, Relish, Rise, Sense, Stock, Taste, Thank you, Treasure, > VALUE

Apprehend, Apprehension Afears, Alarm, Arrest, > CATCH, Collar, Fear, Grasp, Insight, Intuit, Perceive, Quailing, See, Take, Toey, Trepidation, Uh-oh, Unease, Uptake

Apprehensive Jumpy, Nervous, Uneasy

Apprentice(ship) Article, Commis, Cub, Devil, Garzone, Improver, Indent(ure), Jockey, L, Learner, Lehrjahre, Novice, Noviciate, Novitiate, Printer's devil, Pupillage, Snob, Tiro, Trainee, Turnover, Tyro(ne)

Approach(ing), **Approachable** Abord, Access, Accost, Advance, Affable, Anear, Appropinquate, Appulse, Avenue, Close, Come, Converge, Cost(e), Drive, Driveway, Fairway, Feeler, Gate, Imminent, Line, Near, Nie, Overture, Pitch, Procedure, Road, Run-up, Towards, Verge

Appropriate Abduct, Abstract, Annex, Apposite, Apt, Asport, Assign, Bag, Borrow, Collar, Commandeer, Commensurate, Confiscate, Convenient, Due, Embezzle, Expedient, Fit, Germane, Good, Happy, Hijack, Hog, Jump, Just, Meet, Nick, Pilfer, Plagiarise, Pocket, Pre-empt, Proper, Purloin, Right, Seize, Sequester, Sink, Snaffle, Steal, Suit, Swipe, Take, Timely, Trouser, Usurp

Approval, **Approve(d)** Adopt, Allow, Amen, Applaud, Attaboy, Aye, Blessing, Bravo, > COUNTENANCE, Credit, Dig, Endorse, Favour, Hear hear, Homologate, Hubba-hubba, Imprimatur, Initial, Kitemark, Laud, Nod, Okay, Olé, Orthodox, Plaudit, Rah, Ratify, Rubber-stamp, Sanction, Stotter, Thumbs-up, Tick, Tribute, Yay, Yes, Zindabad

Approximate(ly), **Approximation** Almost, Circa, Close, Coarse, Estimate, Guess, Imprecise, Near, Roughly

Apricot Mebos

April, **April fool** Apr, Hunt-the-gowk

Apron Barm-cloth, Bib, Blacktop, Brat, Bunt, Canvas, Dick(e)y, Ephod, Fig-leaf, Gremial, Ice, Pinafore, Pinner, Pinny, Placket, Stage, Tablier, Tier, Waist

Apse Concha, Exedra, Niche, Recess, Tribune

Apt(ly) Apposite, Appropriate, Apropos, Ben trovato, Capable, Evincive, Fit, Gleg, Happy, Liable, Pat, Prone, Suitable, Tends

Aptitude Ability, Bent, Faculty, Flair, Gift, Skill, Talent, Tendency

Aqua(tic) Euglena, Flustra, Lentic, Lotic, Regia, Zizania

Aqualung Scuba

Aqueduct Canal, Channel, Conduit, Hadrome, Xylem

Arab(ian), **Arabia**, **Arabic** Abdul, Adeni, Algorism, Ali, Baathist, Bahraini, Bahrein, Bedouin, Druse, Druz(e), Effendi, Fedayee(n), Gamin, Geber, Hashemite, Himyarite, Horse, Iraqi, Jawi, Lawrence, Mudlark, Nabat(a)ean, Nes(h)ki, Omani, PLO, Qatari, Rag(head), Saba, Sab(a)ean, Saracen, Saudi, Semitic, Sheikh, Street, UAR, Urchin, Yemen

Arabis Cress

Arachnid Podogona, Ricinulei, > SPIDER

Arbiter, **Arbitrator** ACAS, Censor, Daysman, Judge, Ombudsman, Ref(eree), Umpire

Arbitrary Despotic, Haphazard, Random, Wanton

Arboreal, **Arbour** Bower, Dendroid, Pergola, Trellis

Arc Azimuth, Bow, Carbon, > CURVE, Flashover, Fogbow, Halo, Island, Mercury, Octant, Quadrant, Rainbow, Reflex, Seadog, Trajectory, White rainbow

Arcade Amusement, Burlington, Cloister, Gallery, Loggia, Mall, Penny, Triforium

Arcadia(n) Idyllic, Nemoral, Sylvan

Arcane Esoteric, Obscure, Occult, Orphism, Recherché, Rune, Secret

Arch(ed) Acute, Admiralty, Arblaster, Arcade, Archivolt, Arcuate, Camber, Chief, Coom, Counterfort, Crafty, Cross-rib, Crown-green, Ctesiphon, > CUNNING, Curve, Elfin, Embow, Espiegle, Fallen, Flying buttress, Fog-bow, Fornicate, Fornix, Gill, Gothic, Hance, Haunch, Hog, Horseshoe, Instep, Intrados, Keel, Keystone, Lancet, Leery, Lierne, Limb-girdle, Marble, Norman, Ogee, Ogive, Order, Parthian, Pectoral, Pelvic, Portal, Proscenium, Relieving, Roach, Roguish, Roman, Safety, Saucy, Segmental, Shouldered, Skew, Soffit, Span, Squinch, Stilted, Trajan, Triumphal, Vault, Zygoma

Archaeological, Archaeologist Carter, Dater, Dig, Evans, Layard, Leakey, Mycenae, Petrie, Pothunter, Wheeler, Woolley

Archangel Azrael, Gabriel, Israfeel, Israfel, Israfil, Jerahmeel, Michael, Raguel, Raphael, Sariel, Satan, Uriel

Arch-binder Voussoir

Archbishop Anselm, Augustine, Cosmo, Cranmer, Davidson, Dunstan, Ebor, Elector, Hatto, Lanfranc, Lang, Langton, Laud, Metropolitan, Primate, Temple, Trench, Tutu, Whitgift

Archdeacon Ven

Archduke Trio

Archer Acestes, Bow-boy, > BOWMAN, Cupid, Eros, Hood, Philoctetes, Sagittary, Tell, Toxophilite

Archetype Avatar, Form, Model, Pattern

Archibald, Archie, Archy Ack-ack, Cockroach, Oerlikon, Rice, Roach

Archilochian Epode

Archipelago Alexander, Antarctic, Azores, Bismarck, Camaguey, Fiji, Franz Josef Land, Gulag, Japan, Kerguelen, Malay, Marquesas, Mergui, Novaya Zemlya, Palmer, Paumotu, St Pierre and Miquelon, Severmaya Zemlya, Spitsbergen, Sulu, Svalbard, Tierra del Fuego, Tonga, Tuamoto, West Indies

Architect(ure), Architectural Arcology, Baroque, Bauhaus, Bricolage, Brutalism, Byzantine, Churrigueresque, Composite, Corinthian, Creator, Data-flow, Decorated, Designer, Domestic, Doric, Early English, Entablature, Federation, Flamboyant, Georgian, Gothic, Ionic, Jacobean, Landscape, Lombard, Mission, Moderne, Moorish, Moresque, Mudejar, Naval, Neoclassical, Neo-gothic, Norman, Palladian, Perpendicular, Planner, Plateresque, Prostyle, Romanesque, Saxon, Spandrel, Spandril, Tectonic, Tudor, Tuscan

● **ARCHITECTS**
●
●

4 letters:	Soane	Columbo	Vitruvius
Adam	Utzon	Gropius	
Kent	Wyatt	Lutyens	10 letters:
Loos		Venturi	Inigo Jones
Nash	6 letters:	Vignola	Mackintosh
Shaw	Casson		Trophonius
Webb	Foster	8 letters:	Van der Rohe
Wood	Nissen	Bramante	
Wren	Repton	Palladio	11 letters:
	Spence	Piranesi	Abercrombie
5 letters:	Street	Saarinen	Butterfield
Gaudi	Wright	Vanbrugh	Le Corbusier
Inigo			
Nervi	7 letters:	9 letters:	12 letters:
Pugin	Behrens	Hawksmoor	Brunelleschi
Scott	Bernini	Macquarie	

Architrave Epistyle, Platband

Archive(s) Backfile, Muniment, PRO, Records, Register

Archon Draco

Arch-villain Ringleader

Arctic Estotiland, Frigid, Hyperborean, In(n)uit, Inupiat, Polar, Tundra

Ardent, Ardour Aflame, Aglow, Boil, Broiling, Burning, Fervent, Fervid, Fiery, Fire, Flagrant, Heat, Het, > **HOT**, Hot-brained, In, Mettled, Mettlesome, Passion(ate), Perfervid, Rage, Spiritous, Vehement, Warm-blooded, Zealous, Zeloso

Arduous Laborious, Uphill

Are A, 're

Area Acre, Aleolar, Apron, Are, Bailiwick, Belt, Bovate, Broca's, Carucate, Catchment, Centare, Centiare, Centre, Curtilage, Dec(i)are, Dedans, Development, Disaster, District, Domain, Endemic, Eruv, Extent, Farthingland, Gau, Goal, Grey, Growth, Heartland, Hectare, Henge, Hide, Husbandland, Imperium, Input, Karst, Landmass, Lathe, Latitude, Lek, Locality, Manor, Metroplex, Milieu, Morgen, Mush, No-go, Orb, Oxgang, Oxgate, Oxland, Parish, Patch, Penalty, Place, Pleasance, Plot, Precinct, Province, Purlieu, Quad, Quadrat, Quarter, Range, Redevelopment, Refugium, > **REGION**, Rest, Retrochoir, Rood, Sector, Service, Shire, Sterling, Subtopia, Support, Target, Technical, Terrain, Territory, Theatre, Tie, Tract, Tundra, Tye, Urban, White, Yard, Zone

Arena Circus, Cockpit, Dohyo, Field, Lists, Maidan, Olympia, > **RING**, Rink, Stadium, Tiltyard, Velodrome, Venue

Argal Ergo

Argent Ag, Silver

Argentina RA

Argon Ar

Argonaut Acastus, Jason, Lynceus, Meleager, Nautilus

Argot Flash, Idiom, Jargon, Lingo, Shelta

Argue, Argument Altercation, Antistrophon, Argie-bargie, Argle-bargle, Argy-bargy, Bandy, Beef, Blue, Brush, Case, Casuism, Choplogic, Conflict, Contend, Contest, Cosmological, Debate, Deprecate, Diallage, Difference, Dilemma, Dispute, Dissent, Elenchus, Elenctic, Enthymeme, Eristic, Exchange, Expostulate, Forensic, Free-for-all, Generalisation, Logic, Logomachy, Moot, Ob and soller, Ontological, Paralogism, Patter, Pettifog, Plead, Polemic, Polylemma, Premiss, Propound, Quarrel, Quibble, Quodlibet, Rammy, Ratiocinate, > **REASON**, Remonstrate, Row, Run-in, Sophism, Sorites, Spar, Stickle, Straw man, Summation, Syllogism, Teleological, Theme, Thetic, Tiff, Transcendental, Trilemma, Wrangle, Yike

Argyle Argathelian

Aria Ballad, Cabaletta, Melody, Song

Arid Dry, Parched

Ariel Pen

Arise Appear, Be, Develop, Emanate, Emerge, Upgo, Wax

Aristocracy, Aristocrat(ic) Blood, Boyar, Buckeen, Classy, Debrett, Duc, Elite, Eupatrid, Gentry, Grandee, High-hat, Junker, Nob, Noble, Optimate, Patrician, Thane, Tony, U-men, Upper-crust, Well-born

Aristotle Peripatetic, Stagirite, Stagyrite

Arithmetic(ian) Algorism, Algorith, Arsmetrick, Cocker, Euclid, Logistic, Modular, Sums

Ark(wright) Chest, Noah

Arly Thicket

Arm(ed), Arms Akimbo, Arsenal, Bearing, Brachial, Branch, Bundooks, Canting, Cove, Crest, Embattle, Equip, Escutcheon, Fin, Firth, Frith, Gnomon, Halbert, Hatchment, Heel, Heraldic, Inlet, Jib, Krupp, Limb, Loch, Long, Member, Olecranon, Pick-up, Quillon, Radius, Ramous, Rocker, Rotor, SAA,

Secular, Side, Small, Spiral, Tappet, Tentacle, Timer, Tone, Transept, Tremolo, Ulnar, > WEAPON, Whip

▷ **Arm** *may indicate* an army regiment, etc.

Armada Spanish

Armadillo Dasypod, Dasypus, Pangolin, Peba, Pichiciago, Tatou(ay), Xenurus

Armature Shuttle

Armenian Haikh

Armistice Truce

Armour(ed) Ailette, Armature, Armet, Barbette, Beaver, Besagew, Bevor, Brasset, Breastplate, Brigandine, Buckler, Byrnie, Camail, Cannon, Casspir, Cataphract, Chaffron, Chain, Chamfrain, Chamfron, Character, Chausses, Corium, Cors(e)let, Couter, Cuirass, Cuish, Cuisse, Culet, Curat, Curiet, Cush, Defence, Fauld, Garniture, Gear, Genouillère, Gere, Gorget, Greave, Habergeon, Hauberk, Hoplology, Jack, Jambeau, Jazerant, Jesserant, Lamboys, Loricate, Mail, Male, Mentonnière, Nasal, Nosepiece, Panoply, Panzer, Pauldron, Petta, Placcat, Placket, Plastron, Plate, Poitrel, Poleyn, Pouldron, Sabaton, Scale, Secret, > SHIELD, Solleret, Spaudler, Tace, Tank, Taslet, Tasse(t), Thorax, Tonlet, Tuille, Vambrace, Vantbrass, Ventail, Visor, Voider, Weed

Armpit Axilla, Oxter

Armstrong Satchmo

Army Arrière-ban, BEF, Church, Colours, Confederate, Crowd, Federal, Field, Fyrd, Golden (Horde), Horde, Host, IRA, Land, Landwehr, Lashkar, Legion, Line, Military, Militia, Multitude, New Model, Para-military, Red, SA, Sabaoth, Salvation, Sena, Service, Soldiers, Standing, Swarm, TA, Territorial, Volunteer, War, Wehrmacht

▷ **Army** *may indicate* having arms

Aroma(tic) Allspice, Aniseed, Aryl, Balmy, Coriander, Fenugreek, Fragrant, Odorous, Pomander, Spicy, Stilbene, Vanillin, Wintergreen

Around About, Ambient, Circa, Near, Peri-, Skirt, Tour

▷ **Around** *may indicate* one word around another

Arouse, Arousal Alarm, > EXCITE, Fan, Fire, Incite, Inflame, Must(h), Needle, Provoke, Stole, Touch up, Urolagnia, Waken

Arrange(r), Arrangement Adjust, Array, Attune, Bandobast, Bundobust, Concert, Concinnity, Configuration, Design, Display, Dispose, Do, Edit, Engineer, Fix, Foreordain, Formation, Grade, Ikebana, Layout, Marshal, Modus vivendi, Orchestrate, Orchestration, Ordain, > ORDER, Ordnance, Organise, Pack, Pattern, Perm, Permutation, Plan, Position, Prepare, Prepense, Quincunx, Redactor, Regulate, Run, Schedule, Schema, Scheme, Set, Settle, Sort, Spacing, Stereoisomerism, Stow, Straighten, Style, System, Tactic, Taxis, Transcribe

▷ **Arrange** *may indicate* an anagram

Arras Tapestry

Array(ed) Attire, Bedight, Deck, Herse, Marshal, Muster, Panoply, Phased, Seismic

Arrear(s) Aft, Ahint, Backlog, Behind, Debt, Owing

Arrest(ed), Arresting Abort, Alguacil, Alguazil, Ament, Apprehend, Attach, Attract, Blin, Book, Bust, Caption, Capture, Cardiac, Catch, Check, Citizen's, Collar, Detain, False, Furthcoming, Hold, House, Knock, Lift, Nab, Nail, Nick, Nip, Nobble, Pinch, Pull, Restrain, Retard, Riveting, Round-up, Run-in, Salient, Sease, Seize, Stasis, Stop, Sus(s)

Arris Groin

Arrival, Arrive, Arriving Accede, Advent, Attain, Come, Get, Happen, Hit,

Inbound, Influx, Johnny-come-lately, Land, Latecomer, Natal, Nativity, Reach, Show, Strike

Arrogance, Arrogant Assumption, Bold, Bravado, Cavalier, Cocksure, Disdain, Dogmatic, Effrontery, Haughty, Haut(eur), High, Hogen-mogen, Hoity-toity, Hubris, Imperious, Morgue, Overweening, Presumption, Proud, Side, Stuck-up, Surquedry, Toploftical, Turkeycock, Uppish, Uppity, Upstart

Arrogate Appropriate, Assume, Claim, Impute, Usurp

Arrow, Arrow-head Acestes, Any, Ary, Blunt, Bolt, Broad(head), Dart, Dogbolt, Filter, Flechette, Flight, Missile, Pheon, Pointer, Quarrel, Reed, Sagittate, Shaft, Sheaf

Arrowroot Kuzu, Maranta, Pia

Arsenal Ammo, Armo(u)ry, Depot, Magazine, Side

Arsenate, Arsenic(al), Arsenide As, Erythrite, Realgar, Resalgar, Rosaker, Salvarsan, Scorodite, Skutterudite, Smaltite, Speiss, Zarnich

Arson(ist) Firebug, Pyromania

Art(s), Arty, Art school, Art style Abstract, Applied, Ars, Arte Povera, Bauhaus, Bloomsbury, Bonsai, Bricart, Brut, Chiaroscuro, Clair-obscure, Clare-obscure, Clip, Cobra, Commercial, Conceptual, Constructivism, Contrapposto, Craft, Cubism, Cunning, Dada, Daedal(e), Deco, Decorative, Dedal, De Stijl, Die Brucke, Diptych, Divisionism, Earth, Ekphrasis, Environmental, Es, Expressionism, Fauvism, Feat, Fine, Finesse, Flemish, Folk, Fugue, Futurism, Genre, Graphic, Guile, Impressionist, Jugendstil, Kakemono, Kano, Ka pai, Kinetic, Kirigami, Kitsch, Knack, Liberal, Mandorla, Mannerism, Martial, Minimal, Montage, Motivated, Music, Mystery, Nabis, Nazarene, Neoclassical, Neo-impressionism, New Wave, Norwich, Nouveau, Optical, Origami, Orphic cubism, Orphism, Outsider, Performance, Performing, Perigordian, Plastic, Pointillism, Pop, Postimpressionism, Postmodern, Practical, Pre-Raphaelite, Primitive, Psychedelic, Public, Quadratura, Quadrivium, Relievo, Sienese, > SKILL, Still-life, Supremation, Surrealism, Synchronism, Tachism(e), Tatum, Tenebrism, Toreutics, Trecento, Trivium, Trompe l'oeil, Trouvé, Tsutsumu, Useful, Verism, Virtu, Visual, Vorticism

▷ **Art** *may indicate* an -est ending

Artefact(s) Neolith, Tartanalia, Tartanry, Xoanon

▷ **Artefact** *may indicate* an anagram

Artemis Selene

Artemus Ward

Artery Aorta, Carotid, Coronary, Duct, Femoral, Frontal, Iliac, Innominate, M1, Maxillary, Phrenic, Pulmonary, Radial, Route, Spermatic, Temporal

Artful Cute, Dodger, Foxy, Ingenious, Quirky, Sly, Subtle, Tactician

Arthropod Limulus, Tardigrade, Water-bear

Artichoke Cardoon, Jerusalem

Article(s) A, An, Apprentice, Column, Commodity, Definite, Feature, Five, Indefinite, Indenture, Item, Leader, Paper, Piece, Pot-boiler, Sidebar, Specify, The, Thing, Thinkpiece, Thirty-nine, Treatise, Ware

Articulation, Articulate(d) Clear, Coherent, Coudé, Diarthrosis, Distinct, Eloquent, Enounce, Express, Fluent, Fortis, Gimmal, Gomphosis, Hinged, Jointed, Jymold, Lenis, Limbed, Lisp, Pretty-spoken, Pronounce, Schindylesis, Trapezial, Utter, Vertebrae, Voice

Artifice(r), Artificial Bogus, Chouse, Dodge, Ersatz, Factitious, Finesse, Guile, Hoax, In vitro, Logodaedaly, Man-made, Mannered, Opificer, Pretence, Prosthetic, Pseudo, Reach, Ruse, Sell, Sham, Spurious, Stratagem, > STRATEGY, Synthetic, Theatric, > TRICK, Unnatural, Wile, Wright

Artificial respiration Kiss of life, Schafer's method
Artillery Battery, Cannon, Field, Fougade, Fougasse, Guns, Mortar, Ordnance,
  Pyroballogy, RA, Rafale, Ramose, Ramus, Train
Artiodactyl Camel, Chevrotain, Deerlet
Artisan Craftsman, Joiner, Journeyman, Mechanic, Peon, Pioner, Pyoner,
  Shipwright, Workman
Artist(ic) Barbizon, Bohemian, Cartoonist, Colourist, Cubist, Dadaist,
  Daedal(e), Deccie, Decorator, Die Brucke, Etcher, Fauve, Fine, Gentle, Gilder,
  ICA, Impressionist, Left Bank, Limner, Linear, Maestro, Master, Miniaturist,
  > MUSICIAN, Nazarene, Oeuvre, Orphism, > PAINTER, Pavement, Paysagist,
  Piss, Plein-airist, Primitive, RA, Romantic, Screever, > SCULPTOR, Sien(n)ese,
  Tachisme, Trapeze, Trecentist, Virtuose, Virtuoso

● **ARTISTS**
●
● **3 letters:**
● Arp
● Cox
● Rap
●
● **4 letters:**
● Cuyp
● Dadd
● Dali
● Doré
● Etty
● Goya
● Hals
● John
● Klee
● Lely
● Miró
● Opie
● Phiz
●
● **5 letters:**
● Aiken
● Appel
● Bacon
● Bakst
● Bosch
● Corot
● Crome
● Degas
● Dulac
● Dürer
● Ensor
● Ernst
● Hoare
● Hooch
● Klimt
● Leech

Léger
Lippi
Lotto
Lowry
Manet
Monet
Munch
Nabis
Orpen
Redon
Riley
Rodin
Seago
Steen
Steer
Tatum
Watts

6 letters:
Boudin
Braque
Brucke
Calder
Callot
Derain
D'Orsay
Escher
Fuseli
Giotto
Greuze
Guardi
Haydon
Ingres
Knight
Le Nain
Millet
Renoir

Ribera
Rivera
Romney
Rothko
Rubens
Seurat
Signac
Sisley
Stubbs
Tissot
Titian
Turner
Warhol

7 letters:
Apelles
Audubon
Bellini
Bernini
Bonnard
Cézanne
Chagall
Chardin
Cimabue
Collier
Courbet
Cranach
Da Vinci
El Greco
Epstein
Gauguin
Hobbema
Hockney
Hogarth
Hokusai
Holbein
Hoppner

Kneller
Matisse
Millais
Morisot
Morland
Murillo
Nattier
Picasso
Pissaro
Poussin
Prudhon
Raeburn
Raphael
Rouault
Sargent
Sickert
Spencer
Tiepolo
Uccello
Utamaro
Utrillo
Van Dyke
Van Eyck
Van Gogh
Vermeer
Watteau
Zeuxian
Zoffany

8 letters:
Daubigny
Eastlake
Kirchner
Landseer
Leonardo
Magritte
Mantegna

- Masaccio
- Mondrian
- Nevinson
- Perugino
- Piranesi
- Reynolds
- Rousseau
- Topolski
- Veronese
- Whistler
- **9 letters:**
- Beardsley
- Bonington

Canaletto
Carpaccio
Constable
Correggio
Delacroix
Donatello
Fragonard
Gericault
Giorgione
Grunewald
Hiroshige
Kandinsky
Rembrandt
Velasquez

10 letters:
Alma-Tadema
Botticelli
Burne-Jones
Guillaumin
Madox Brown
Modigliani
Rowlandson
Signorelli
Sutherland
Tintoretto
Van der Goes

12 letters:
Gainsborough
Lichtenstein
Michelangelo
Winterhalter

14 letters:
Jackson Pollock

15 letters:
Hieronymus
Bosch
Toulouse-Lautrec

Artless Candid, Ingenuous, Innocent, Naive, Open, Seely, Simple
Arturo Toscanini
Arum Acorus, Green-dragon, Lily, Taro
As Aesir, Als, Arsenic, Coin, Eg, Forasmuch, Kame, Qua, Ridge, 's, Since, So, Thus, Ut, While
As above US
Asafoetida Hing
As before Anew, Ditto, Do, Stet
Asbestos Amiant(h)us, Amosite, Chrysolite, Crocidolite, Earthflax, Fireproof, Rockwood
Ascend(ant), Ascent Anabasis, Climb, Dominant, Escalate, Gradient, Lift, Pull, Ramp, Rise, Sclim, Sklim, Slope, Up, Upgang, Uphill, Uprise, Zoom
Ascertain Determine, Discover, > ESTABLISH, Prove
Ascetic Agapetae, Anchor(et), Anchorite, Ancress, Ashramite, Austere, Dervish, Diogenes, Encratite, Eremital, Essene, Fakir, Faquir, Gymnosophist, Hermit, Jain(ite), Monk, Nazarite, Nazirite, Nun's flesh, Sad(d)hu, Simeon Stylites, Stylite, Sufic, Therapeutae, Yogi(n)
Ascidian Chordate, Urochordate
Asclepiad Stapelia
Ascribe Assign, > ATTRIBUTE, Blame, Imply, Impute
Asdic Sonar
As far as Quoad
As good as Equal, Tantamount
Ash(es), Ashy Aesc, Aizle, Cinders, Cinereal, Clinker(s), Easle, Embers, Fly, Kali, Lahar, Pallor, Pearl, Pozz(u)olana, Prickly, Rowan, Ruins, Soda, Sorb, Spodo-, Tephra, Urn, Varec, Wednesday, Weeping, Witchen, Yg(g)drasil(l)
Ashamed Abashed, Embarrassed, Hangdog, Mortified, Repentant, Shent
Ashore Aland, Beached, Grounded, Stranded
Ash-pan Backet
Asia(n), Asiatic Altaic, Azari, Balinese, Bangladeshi, Bengali, Cantonese, E, Evenki, Ewenki, Gook, Hun, Hyksos, Indian, Kashmir, Korean, Kurd, Lao, Malay, Mongol, Naga, Negrito, Nepalese, Phrygian, Pushtu, Samo(y)ed, Shan, Siamese, Sogdian, Tamil, Tartar, Tibetan, Tocharian, Tokharian, Turanian, Turk(o)man
Asia Minor Anatolia, Ionic
Aside Apart, By, Despite, Private, Separate, Shelved, Sotto voce
Asinine Crass, Dull, Idiotic, Puerile, Stupid

Ask Beg, Beseech, Cadge, Demand, Desire, Enquire, Entreat, Evet, Implore, Intreat, Invite, Newt, Petition, Prithee, Pump, Quiz, Request, Rogation, Seek, Solicit, Speer, Speir, Touch

Askance Asconce, Askew, Oblique, Sideways

Askew Agee, Aglee, Agley, Ajee, Aslant, Awry, Crooked, Skivie

Asleep Dormant, Inactive, Napping

Asparagus Asperge, Sparrow-grass, Spear, Sprew, Sprue

Aspect Angle, Bearing, Brow, Face, Facet, Facies, Feature, Look, Mien, Nature, Outlook, Perfective, Perspective, Side, > VIEW, Visage, Vista

Aspersion Calumny, Innuendo, Libel, Slander, Slur, Smear

Asphalt Bitumen, Blacktop, Gilsonite®, Pitch, Pitch Lake, Uinta(h)ite

Aspirant, Aspirate, Aspiration, Aspire Ambition, Breath, Buckeen, Challenger, Desire, Dream, Endeavour, Ettle, Goal, H, Hope(ful), Pretend, Pursue, Rough, Spiritus, Wannabe(e), Yearn

Ass Buridan's, Burnell, Burro, Cardophagus, Chigetai, Clot, Couscous, Cuddie, Dick(e)y, Donkey, Dziggetai, Funnel, Golden, Hemione, Hemionus, Hinny, Jack, Jenny, Jerusalem pony, Kiang, K(o)ulan, Kourbash, Kourmiss, Kouskous, Kumiss, Kurbash, Kyang, Liripipe, Liripoop, Moke, Neddy, Nitwit, Onager, Quagga, Sesterce, Simp, > STUPID PERSON

Assail(ant) Assault, Attack, Batter, Bego, Belabour, Bepelt, Beset, Bombard, Impugn, Onsetter, Oppugn, Pillory, Ply, Revile

Assassin(ate), Assassination Booth, Brave, Bravo, Brutus, Casca, Character, Frag, Gunman, Highbinder, Hitman, Killer, Ninja, Sword, Thuggee, Tyrannicide

Assault Assail, Assay, Attack, Battery, Bombard, Hamesucken, Indecent, Invasion, Mug, > RAID, Scalade, Stoor, Storm, Stour, Stowre

Assay Cupel, Examine, Proof, Test, Wet

Assemble, Assembly Agora, Audience, Ball, Bundestag, Chapter, Chatuaqua, Cho(u)ltry, Co, Collation, > COLLECTION, Comitia, Company, Conclave, Concourse, Congeries, Congress, Consistory, Constituent, Convene, Conventicle, Convention, Convocation, Convoke, Cortes, Council, Court, Curia, Dail Eireann, Dewain, Diet, Divan, Donnybrook, Ecclesia, Eisteddfod, Erect, Feis(anna), Folkmoot, Folkmote, Force, Forgather, Gather(ing), Gemot(e), General, Gorsedd, Group, Headstock, Hoi polloi, Kgotla, Knesset, Landtag, Legislative, Levee, Loya jirga, Majlis, Make, Mass, > MEETING, Mejlis, Moot, Muster, National, Panegyry, Panoply, Parishad, Parliament, Patron, Pattern, Plenum, Pnyx, Powwow, Presence, Primary, Quorum, Rally, Rechate, Recheate, Reichstag, Repair, Resort, Sanghat, Sanhedrin, Sanhedron, Sejm, Senate, Skupshtina, Sobranje, Soc, Society, Stort(h)ing, Synagogue, Synedrion, Synod, T(h)ing, Tribunal, Troop, Unlawful, Vidhan Sabha, Volksraad, Wapens(c)haw, Wapins(c)haw, Wappens(c)haw, Wardmote, Weapon-s(c)haw, Witan, Witenagemot, Zemstvo

Assent Accede, Acquiesce, Agree, Amen, Aye, Comply, Concur, Nod, Placet, Royal, Sanction, Yea, Yield

Assert(ing), Assertion Affirm, Allege, Constate, Contend, > DECLARE, Ipse-dixit, > MAINTAIN, Pose, Predicate, Proclaim, Pronounce, Protest, Rumour, Thetical

Assess(ment) Affeer, Appraise, Audition, Cense, Estimate, Evaluate, Gauge, Guesstimate, > JUDGE, Levy, Means test, Measure, Perspective, Rating, Referee, Scot and lot, Special, Stent, Tax, Value, Weigh

Asset(s) Advantage, Capital, Chattel, Fixed, Floating, Goodwill, Intangible, Liquid, Net, Plant, Property, Resource, Talent, Virtue, Wasting

Assiduous Attentive, Busy, Constant, Diligent, Studious, Thorough

Assign(ation), **Assignment** Allocate, > **ALLOT**, Apply, Appoint, Aret, Ascribe, Attribute, Award, Date, Dedicate, Duty, Errand, Fix, Grant, Impute, Point, Quota, Refer, Transfer, Tryst

Assimilate(d) Absorb, Blend, Digest, Esculent, Fuse, Imbibe, Incorporate, Merge

Assist(ance), **Assistant** Acolyte, Adjunct, Aid(e), Aide-de-camp, Ally, Alms, Attaché, Best boy, Busboy, Cad, Chainman, Collaborate, Counterhand, Counter-jumper, Dresser, Ex parte, Facilitate, Factotum, Famulus, Feldschar, Felds(c)her, Gofer, > **HAND**, Headlanger, Help, Henchman, Legal aid, Mentor, National, Offsider, Omnibus, Public, Reinforce, Relief, Second, Server, Servitor, Shill, Sidesman, Smallboy, Social, Stead, Subsidiary, Subsidy, Suffragan, Supernumerary, > **SUPPORT**, Usher

Assize Botley, Circuit, Court, Maiden, Oyer

Associate, **Association** Accomplice, Affiliate, Alliance, Amphictyony, Ass, Attach, Bedfellow, Brotherhood, Cartel, Chapel, Chum, Clang, Club, Cohort, Combine, Comecon, Compeer, Complice, Comrade, Concomitant, Confrère, > **CONNECT**, Consort(ium), Co-partner, Correlate, Crony, Enclisis, Fellow, Fraternise, Free, Gesellschaft, Guild, Hobnob, Housing, Intime, Join, Kabele, Kebele, League, Liaison, Lloyds, Mell, Member, Mess, Mix, Moshav, Oddfellows, Pal, Parent teacher, Partner, Phoresy, Press, Professional, Relate, Residents', Ring, Round Table, Samit(h)i, Sangh(at), Sidekick, Sodality, Stablemate, Symbiosis, Syndicate, Toc H, Toenadering, Trade, Union, Verein, Whiteboy, Word, Yoke-mate

Assort(ed), **Assortment** Paraphernalia, Pick-'n'-mix, Various

▷ **Assorted** *may indicate* an anagram

Assuage Allay, Appease, Beet, Calm, Ease, Mease, Mitigate, Mollify, Slake, Soften

As such Qua

Assume, **Assuming**, **Assumption** Adopt, Affect, Arrogate, Attire, Axiom, Believe, Don, Donné(e), Feign, Hypothesis, Lemma, Occam's Razor, Posit, Postulate, Preconception, Premise, Premiss, Presuppose, Pretentious, Principle, Putative, Saltus, Suppose, Surmise, Take

▷ **Assumption** *may mean* attire

Assure(d), **Assurance** Aplomb, Aver, Belief, Calm, > **CERTAIN**, Confidence, Confirm, Earnest, Gall, Guarantee, Pledge, Poise, Warranty

Assuredly Indeed, Perdie, Verily, Yea

Astatine At

Astern Abaft, Apoop, Rear

Asteroid Ceres, Eros, Eros 433, Hermes, Hygiea, Juno, Pallas, Phaethon, Pholus, Star, Starfish, Trojan, Vesta

Astir Afoot, Agate, Agog

Astonish(ed), **Astonishing**, **Astonishment**, **Astound** Abash, Admiraunce, Amaze, Banjax, Bewilder, Confound, Corker, Crikey, Daze, Donnert, Dum(b)found, Dumbstruck, Eye-popping, Flabbergast, Gobsmack, Heavens, Mind-boggling, Open-eyed, Open-mouthed, Phew, Pop-eyed, Prodigious, Rouse, Singular, Stagger, Startle, Stun, Stupefaction, Stupefy, Stupendous, Surprise, Thunderstruck, Wow

Astray Abord, Amiss, Errant, Lost, Will, Wull

Astride Athwart, Spanning, Straddle-back

Astringent Acerbic, Alum, Catechu, Dhak, Gambi(e)r, Harsh, Kino, Krameria, Rhatany, Sept-foil, Severe, Sour, Styptic, Tormentil, Witch-hazel

Astrologer, **Astrology** Archgenethliac, Chaldean, Culpeper, Faust, Figure-caster, Genethliac, Judicial, Lilly, Moore, Nostradamus, Soothsayer,

Starmonger, Zadkiel

Astronaut Cosmonaut, Gagarin, Glenn, Lunarnaut, Spaceman, Spacer, Taikonaut

Astronomer, Astronomy, Astronomical Almagest, Aristarchus, Bessel, Bradley, Brahe, Callipic, Cassini, Celsius, Copernicus, Eddington, Encke, Eratosthenes, Eudoxus, Flamsteed, Galileo, Hale, Halley, Herschel, Hewish, Hipparchus, Hoyle, Hubble, Huggins, Infra red, Jeans, Kepler, Laplace, Leverrier, Lockyer, Lovell, Meton, Neutrino, Omar Khayyam, Oort, Physical, Planetology, Ptolemy, Radar, Radio, Reber, Roche, Schwarzschild, Selenography, Selenology, Sosigenes, Stargazer, Star read, Telescopy, Tycho Brahe, Ultraviolet, Urania, Uranic, X-ray, Zwicky

Astrophel Penthia

Astrophysicist Seifert

Astute Acute, Canny, Crafty, Cunning, Downy, Perspicacious, Shrewd, Subtle, Wide, Wily

As usual Solito

As well Additionally, Also, Both, Even, Forby, Too

Asylum Bedlam, Bin, Bughouse, Frithsoken, Funny-farm, Girth, Grith, Haven, Institution, Lunatic, Madhouse, Magdalene, Nuthouse, Political, Rathouse, Refuge, Retreat, Sanctuary, Shelter, Snake-pit

Asymmetric(al) Lopsided, Skew

At Astatine, In, To, Up-bye

Atahualpa Inca

At all Ava, Ever, Oughtlings

At all events Algate

Atavistic Reversion, Throw-back

Atheist Doubter, Godless, Infidel, Sceptic

Athenian, Athene Attic, Cleruch, Pallas, Pericles, Solon, Timon

Athlete, Athletic(s) Agile, Agonist, Blue, Coe, Discobolus, Field, Gymnast, Jock, Leish, Miler, Milo, Nurmi, Olympian, Pacemaker, Quarter-miler, Runner, Sportsman, Sprinter, Track

Athodyd Ram-jet

Athwart Across, Awry, Oblique, Traverse

Atlantic Pond

Atlas Dialect, Linguistic, Maps, Range, Silk

▷ **At last** *may indicate* a cobbler

Atmosphere Aeropause, Air, Ambience, Aura, Chemosphere, Elements, Epedaphic, Ether, F-layer, Geocorona, Ionosphere, Lid, Magnetosphere, Mesophere, Meteorology, Miasma, Ozone, Standard, Thermosphere, Tropopause, Troposphere, Upper, Vibe(s)

At most Al piu

Atoll Bikini, Eniwetok, Kwajalein, Male, Motu, Tarawa

Atom(ic), Atoms Boson, Electron, Excimer, Free, Gram, Ion, Iota, Isobare, Isotone, Isotope, Labelled, Ligand, Molecule, Monad, Monovalent, Muonic, Nuclide, Odoriphore, Particle, Pile, Primeval, Radionuclide, Recoil, Sellafield, Side-chain, Steric, Stripped, Substituent, Tagged, Windscale, Xylyl

At once Ek dum, Holus-bolus, Immediate, Instanter, Presto, Statim, Straight away, Swith, Tight, Tit(e), Titely, Tyte

Atone(ment) Aby(e), Acceptilation, Appease, Expiate, Penance, Redeem, Redemption, Yom Kippur

Atop Upon

▷ **At random** *may indicate* an anagram

Atrocious, Atrocity Abominable, Brutal, Diabolical, Flagitious, Heinous, Horrible, Monstrous, Outrage, Vile

Atrophy Degeneration, Marasmus, Sudeck's, Sweeny, Wasting

▷ **At sea** *may indicate* an anagram

Attach(ed), Attachment Accessory, Accrete, Adhesion, Adhibition, Adnate, Adnation, Adscript, Affix, Allonge, Annexe, Bolt, Bro, Byssus, Cleat, Covermount, Devotement, Devotion, Distrain, Garnish, Glom, Glue, > JOIN, Netsuke, Obconic, Pin, Snell, Stick, Tie, Weld

Attack(ing), Attacker Access, Affect, Airstrike, Alert, Anti, Apoplexy, Asperse, Assail, Assault, At, Batten, Bego, Belabour, Beset, Bestorm, Blitz(krieg), Bodrag(ing), Bombard, Bordraging, Bout, Broadside, Bushwhack, Camisade, Camisado, Campaign, Cannonade, Charge, Clobber, Club, Counteroffensive, Coup de main, Denounce, Descent, Diatribe, Feint, Fit, Flèche, Foray, Get, Handbag, Iconoclast, Ictus, Impugn, Incursion, Inroad, Invade, Inveigh, Lampoon, Lese-majesty, Let fly, Maraud, Molest, Mug, Offensive, Onding, Onfall, Onrush, Onset, Onslaught, Oppugn, Panic, Pillage, Polemic, Predacious, Pre-emptive, Push, Quart(e), Raid, Rough, Sandbag, Savage, Seizure, Sic(k), Siege, Skitch, Snipe, Sortie, Storm, Strafe, Strike, Swoop, Thrust, Tilt, Vilify, Vituperate, Wage, Warison, Wolf-pack, Zap

Attain(ment) Accomplish, Arrive, Earn, Fruition, Get, Land, Reach

Attempt Bash, Bid, Burl, Crack, Debut, Effort, Endeavour, Essay, Go, Mint, Nisus, Seek, Shot, Show, Shy, Stab, Strive, > TRY, Venture, Whack, Whirl

Attend(ance), Attendant Accompany, Apple-squire, Await, Batman, Bearer, Be at, Behold, Bulldog, Caddy, Cavass, Chaperone, Chasseur, Checker, Corybant, Courtier, Cuadrilla, Cupbearer, Custrel, Entourage, Equerry, Escort, Esquire, Famulus, Footman, Gillie, Hand-maiden, Harken, Hear, > HEED, Hello, Holla, Iras, Kavass, Led captain, > LISTEN, Maenad, Marshal, Mute, Note, Outrider, Outrunner, Page, Panisc, Panisk, Paranymph, People, Presence, Pursuivant, Respect, Roll-up, Satellite, Second, Server, Sowar, Steward, Trainbearer, Turn-out, Valet, Varlet, Visit, Wait, Watch, Whiffler, Zambuck

Attention, Attentive Achtung, Assiduity, Court, Coverage, Dutiful, Ear, Gallant, Gaum, Gorm, Heed, Interest, Mind, Notice, Present, Psst, Punctilio, Qui vive, > REGARD, Selective, Solicitous, Spellbound, Tenty, Thought

Attenuate, Attenuation Lessen, Neper, Rarefy, Thin, Weaken

Attest Affirm, Certify, Depose, Guarantee, Notarise, Swear, > WITNESS

Attic Bee-bird, Cockloft, Garret, Greek, Koine, Loft, Mansard, Muse, Salt, Solar, Soler, Sollar, Soller, Tallat, Tallet, Tallot

Attila Etzel, Hun

Attire Accoutre, Adorn, Apparel, Clobber, > DRESS, Garb, Habit

Attitude Air, Aspect, Behaviour, Demeanour, Light, > MANNER, Mindset, Nimby, Outlook, Pose, Posture, Propositional, Sense, Song, Stance, Tone, Viewpoint

Attorney Advocate, Counsellor, DA, District, Lawyer, Proctor, Prosecutor

▷ **Attract(ion), Attractive** Attrahent, Bait, Barrie, Becoming, Bewitch, Bonny, Bootylicious, Catchy, Charisma, > CHARM, Cheesecake, Clou, Crowd puller, Cute, Cynosure, Dipolar, Dish(y), Draught, > DRAW, Dreamboat, Duende, Engaging, Entice, Epigamic, Eye candy, Eye-catching, Eyeful, Fanciable, Fascinate, Feature, Fetching, Fox(y), Gravity, Groovy, Heartthrob, Himbo, Hunky, Inducement, Inviting, It, Loadstone, Lodestone, Looker, Lovable, Lovely, Lure, Luscious, Magnes, Magnet(ism), Mecca, Mediagenic, Meretricious, Nubile, Photogenic, Picturesque, Pull, Sematic, Sexpot, Shagtastic, Sideshow, Sightly, Slick, Soote, Speciosity, Spunk, Stotter, Striking,

Studmuffin, Taking, Taky, Tasteful, Theme-park, Weber, Winning, Winsome, Zaftig, Zoftig

Attribute Accredit, Allot, Ap(p)anage, Ascribe, Asset, Credit, Gift, Impute, Lay, Metonym, Owe, Quality, Refer, Shtick

Attune Accord, Adapt, Temper

Atypical Aberrant

Aubergine Brinjal, Brown Jolly, Egg-plant, Mad-apple

Aubrey Beardsley

Auburn Abram, Chestnut, Copper, Titian, Vill(age)

Auction(eer) Barter, Bridge, Cant, Dutch, Hammer, Knock out, Outcry, Outro(o)per, Roup, Sale, Subhastation, Tattersall, Vendue

Audacious, Audacity Bald-headed, Bold, Brash, Cheek, Chutspah, Der-doing, Devil-may-care, Effrontery, Face, Hardihood, Indiscreet, Insolence, Intrepid, Neck, Nerve, Rash, Sauce

Audience, Auditorium Assembly, Court, Durbar, Gate, Hearing, House, Interview, Pit, Sphendone, Tribunal

Audiovisual AV

Audit(or) Accountant, Check, Ear, Environmental, Examine, Green, Inspect, Listener, Position

Audition Cattle-call, Screen-test

Auditory Acoustic, Oral

Audrey Hoyden

Augment(ed) Boost, Eche, Eke, Ich, Increase, Supplement, Swell, Tritone

August Awe-inspiring, Grand, Imperial, Imposing, Lammas, Majestic, Noble, Solemn, Stately, Stern

Augustine, Augustus Austin, Hippo, John

Auk Guillemot, Ice-bird, Roch, Rotch(e)

Aunt(ie) Agony, Augusta, Beeb, Giddy, Maiden, Naunt, Sainted, Tia

Aura Aroma, Emanation, Mystique, Nimbus, Odour, Vibrations

Aureole Coronary, Halo, Nimbus

Auricle Ear, Otic

Aurora Eos, Leigh, Matutinal, Merry dancers, Northern lights

Auspice(s) Aegis, Patronage

Auster S-wind

Austere, Austerity Ascetic, Astringent, Bleak, Dantean, Hard, > HARSH, Moral, Plain, Rigour, Severe, Spartan, Stern, Stoic, Stoor, Strict, Vaudois, Waldensian

Austin Friar

Australia(n) Alf, Antipodean, Aussie, Balt, Banana-bender, Bananalander, Billjim, Canecutter, Cobber, Currency, Current, Darwinian, Digger, Gin, Godzone, Gumsucker, Gurindji, Jackie, Jacky, Koori, Larrikin, Lucky Country, Murree, Murri, Myall, Norm, Ocker, Oz, Pintupi, Roy, Sandgroper, Strine, Wallaby, Yarra-yabbies

Austrian Cisleithan, Tyrolean

Authentic(ate) Certify, Echt, Genuine, Honest, Notarise, Official, Real, Sign, Test, True, Validate

Author(ess) Anarch, Auctorial, Inventor, Me, Parent, Volumist, Wordsmith, > WRITER

▷ **Author** *may refer to* author of puzzle

Authorise(d), Authorisation Accredit, Clearance, Countersign, Delegate, Empower, Enable, Exequatur, Imprimatur, Legal, Legit, > LICENCE, Official, OK, Passport, > PERMIT, Plenipotentiary, Retainer, Sanction, Sign, Stamp, Warrant

Authority, Authoritarian, Authoritative Canon, Charter, Circar, Cocker, Commission, Commune, Crisp, Definitive, Domineering, Dominion, Establishment, Ex cathedra, Expert, Fascist, Free hand, Gravitas, Hegemony, Inquirendo, Jackboot, Licence, Magisterial, Mandate, Mantle, Mastery, Name, Oracle, Permit, > **POWER**, Prefect, Prestige, Pundit, Remit, Right, Rod, Say-so, Sceptre, Sircar, Sirkar, Source, Supremacy, Unitary, Warrant

Autobiography Memoir

Autocrat(ic) Absolute, Caesar, Cham, Despot, Khan, Neronian, Tsar, Tyrant

Autograph Signature

Autolycus Scrapman

Automatic, Automaton Android, Aut, Browning, Deskill, Instinctive, Machine, Mechanical, Pistol, Quarter-boy, Quarter-jack, Reflex, Robot, RUR, Zombi

Auto-pilot George

Autopsy Necropsy

Auto-suggestion Coueism

Autumn(al) Fall, Filemot, Leaf-fall, Libra, Philamot

Auxiliary Adjunct, Adjuvant, Adminicle, Aide, Be, Feldsher, Have, Helper, Ido, Subsidiary

Avail(able) Benefit, Dow, Eligible, Going, Handy, Off-the-shelf, On call, Open, Pickings, > **READY**, Serve, Use, Utilise

Avalanche Bergfall, Deluge, Landfall, Landslide, Landslip, Lauwine, Slide, Slip, Snowdrop

Avant-garde Modernistic, Spearhead

Avarice, Avaricious Cupidity, Golddigger, Greed, Money-grubbing, Pleonexia, Sordid

Avatar Epiphany, Incarnation, Rama

Avaunt Away, Go

Avenge(r) Eriny(e)s, Eumenides, Goel, Kurdaitcha, Nightrider, Punish, Redress, Requite, > **REVENGE**, Steed, Wreak

Avenue Alley, Arcade, Boulevard, Channel, Corso, Cradle-walk, Hall, Madison, Mall, Midway, Passage, Vista, Way, Xyst(us)

Aver Affirm, Asseverate, Depose, Swear, Vouch

Average Adjustment, Av, Batting, Dow Jones, Mean, Mediocre, Middle-brow, Middling, Moderate, Moving, Norm, Par, Particular, Run, Run-of-the-mill, Soso, Standard, Weighted

Averse, Aversion, Avert Against, Antipathy, Apositia, Disgust, Dislike, Distaste, Hatred, Horror, Opposed, Phobic, Scunner, Stave off

Avert Avoid, > **DEFLECT**, Forfend, Parry, Ward

Aviary Volary

Aviator Airman, Alcock, Bleriot, Brown, Byrd, Earhart, Flier, Hinkler, Icarus, Johnson, Lindbergh, Pilot, Red Baron, Richthofen

Avid Agog, > **EAGER**, Greedy, Keen

Avifauna Ornis

Avignon Pont

Avocado Aguacate, Guac(h)amole, Pear

Avocet Scooper

Avoid(er), Avoidance Abstain, Ba(u)lk, Boycott, Bypass, Cop-out, Cut, Dodge, Duck, Elude, Escape, Eschew, Evade, Evitate, Evite, Fly, Forbear, Gallio, Hedge, Miss, Obviate, Parry, Prevaricate, Scutage, Secede, Shelve, Shun, Sidestep, Skirt, Spare, Spurn, Waive

Avoirdupois Size, Weight

Avow(ed) Acknowledged, Affirm, Declare, Own, Swear

Await Abide, Bide, Expect, Tarry

Awake(ning) Aware, Conscious, Conversion, Fly, Rouse, Vigilant

Award Academy, Accolade, Addoom, Allot, Alpha, Aret(t), Bafta, Bestow, Bursary, Cap, Clasp, Clio, Crown, Emmy, Exhibition, Golden Raspberry, Golden Starfish, Grammy, Grant, Honours, Logie, Medal, Meed, Mete, Oscar, Padma Shri, Palme d'or, Premium, Present(ation), Prix Goncourt, > **PRIZE**, Queen's, Razzie, Scholarship, Tony, Trophy, Vir Chakra, Yuko

Aware(ness) Alert, C(o)enesthesis, Cognisant, Conscious, Conversant, ESP, Est, Hep, Hip, Informed, Liminal, Onto, Panaesthesia, Prajna, Presentiment, Samadhi, Scienter, Sensible, Sensile, Sensitive, Sentience, Streetwise, Switched on, Vigilant, Wot

Away Absent, Afield, Apage, Avaunt, By, For-, Fro(m), Go, Hence, Off, Out, Past

▷ **Away** *may indicate* a word to be omitted

Awe(d) D(o)ulia, Dread, Fear, Intimidate, Loch, Overcome, Popeyed, Regard, Respect, Reverent, Scare, Solemn

Awe-inspiring Numinous

Awful(ly) Alas, Deare, Dere, Dire, Fearful, Horrendous, O so, Piacular, Terrible

▷ **Awfully** *may indicate* an anagram

Awkward Angular, Bolshy, Bumpkin, Clumsy, Complicated, Corner, Crabby, Cubbish, Cumbersome, Cussed, Embarrassing, Farouche, Fiddly, Fix, Gangly, Gauche, Gawky, Handless, Howdy-do, Inconvenient, Inept, Kittle-cattle, Lanky, Loutish, Lurdan(e), Lurden, Maladdress, Mauther, Mawr, Naff, Nasty, Ornery, Perverse, Refractory, Slummock, Spot, Sticky, Stiff, Stroppy, Stumblebum, Swainish, Uneasy, Ungainly, Unwieldy, Wry

Awl(-shaped) Brog, Els(h)in, Nail, Stob, Subulate

Awn(ing) Barb, Beard, Canopy, Ear, Shade, Velarium

Awry Agley, Askew, Cam, Kam(me), Wonky

Axe Abolish, Adz(e), Bardiche, Bill, Celt, Chop(per), Cleaver, Curtal, Eatche, Gisarme, Gurlet, Halberd, Halbert, Hatchet, Ice, Jeddart staff, Jethart-staff, Labrys, Lochaber, Mattock, Palstaff, Palstave, Partisan, Piolet, Retrench, Sax, Slate, Sparth(e), Sperthe, Spontoon, Stone, Thunderbolt, Tomahawk, Twibill

Axiom Adage, Motto, Peano's, Proverb, Saw, Saying

Axis Alliance, Anorthic, Anticous, Axle, Caulome, Chital, Cob, Columella, Epaxial, Henge, Hinge, Major, Minor, Modiolus, Myelon, Neutral, Optic, Pivot, Polar, Principal, Rachis, Radical, Spindle, Sympodium, Visual, X, Y, Z

Axle, Axle-shoulder Arbor, Axis, Fulcrum, Hurter, Journal, Live, Mandrel, Mandril, Pivot, Stub

Ay I

Aye Always, Eer, Ever, Yea, Yes

Ayesha She

Azo-dye Para-red

Aztec Nahuatl

Bb

B Bachelor, Black, Book, Born, Boron, Bowled, Bravo

Babble(r) Blather, Brook, Chatter, Gibber, Haver, Lallation, Lurry, Prate, Prattle, Runnel, Tonguester, Twattle, Waffle

Babel Charivari, Confusion, Din, Dovercourt, Medley

Baboon Ape, Bobbejaan, Chacma, Dog-ape, Drill, Gelada, Hamadryas, Mandrill, Sphinx

Baby Bairn, Blue, Bub, Bunting, Changeling, Designer, Duck, Grand, Infant, Jelly, Neonate, Nursling, Pamper, Papoose, Plunket, Preverbal, Rhesus, Sis, Small, Sook, Suckling, Tar, Test tube, Thalidomide, Tot, War, Wean

Babylonian Mandaean, Semiramis, Sumerian

Bacchanalian, Bacchus Ivied, Upsee, Ups(e)y

Bacchantes Maenads

Bachelor BA, Bach, Benedict, Budge, Celibate, En garçon, Pantagamy, Parti, Seal, Single, Stag

Bacillus Comma, Germ, Klebs-Loffler, Micrococcus, Virus

Back(ing), Backward Abet, Accompany, Addorse, Again, Ago, Anticlockwise, Antimacassar, Arear, Arrear, Arrière, Assist, Baccare, Backare, Bankroll, Buckram, Champion, Chorus, Consent, Defender, Dorsal, Dorse, Dorsum, Dos, Ebb, Empatron, Encourage, Endorse, Finance, Frae, Fro, Fund, Gaff, Help, Hind, Historic, La-la, Late, Notaeum, Notal, Notum, On, Patronise, Poop, Pronotum, Punt, Rear(most), Retral, Retro(grade), Retrogress, Retrorse, Return, Rev, Reverse, Ridge, Root, Shy, Spinal, Sponsor, Stern, > SUPPORT, Sweeper, Tail, Telson, Tergum, Third, Thrae, Tonneau, Ulu, Uphold, Verso, Vie, Vo, Wager, Watteau

▷ **Back(ing)** *may indicate* a word spelt backwards

Back and forth Boustrophedon

Backbiter, Backbiting Catty, Defame, Detract, Libel, Molar, Slander

Backbone Chine, Grit, Guts, Mettle

Backchat Lip, Mouth, Sass

Backer Angel, Benefactor, Patron, Punter, Seconder, Sponsor

Backfire Boomerang

Backgammon Acey-deucy, Lurch, Tick-tack, Trick-track, Tric-trac, Verquere

Background Antecedence, Field, Fond, History, Horizon, Microwave, Muzak, Setting, Ulterior

Backhander Bribe, Payola, Reverso, Sweetener

Backroom Boffin, Boy, Moor

Backslide(r), Backsliding Apostate, Lapse, Regress, Relapse, Revert

Backwash Rift

Backwater Bogan, Ebb, Logan, Retreat, Slough, Wake

Backwoods Boondocks, Boonies, Hinterland

Backyard Court, Patio

Bacon Bard, Canadian, Collar, Danish, Essayist, Flitch, Francis, Gammon, Lardo(o)n, Pancetta, Pig, Pork, Rasher, Roger, Spec(k), Streaky, Verulam

Bacteria, Bacterium Aerobe, Amphitrica, Bacilli, Bacteriological, Botulinum, > **BUG**, Campylobacter, Chlamydia, Clostridia, Cocci, Coliform, Culture, Detritivore, Diplococcus, Escherichia, > **GERM**, Gonococcus, Gram-negative, Gram-positive, Intestinal flora, Klebsiella, Listeria, Lysogen, Meningococcus, Microbe, Mother, MRSA, Mycoplasma, Nitrous, Packet, Pasteurella, Pathogen, Probiotic, Prokaryote, Proteus, Pseudomonas, Pus, Ray-fungus, Rhizobium, Rickettsia, Salmonella, Schizomycete, Septic, Serotype, Serum, Shigella, Spirilla, Spirochaete, Spore, Staph, Staphylococcus, Strep(tococcus), Streptobacillus, Streptomyces, Sulphur, Superbug, Thermophil(e), Treponemata, Vibrio, Vinegar-plant, Yersinia, Zoogloea

Bad, Badness Addled, Chronic, Crook, Defective, Diabolic, Dud, Duff, Egregious, Execrable, Faulty, God-awful, Heinous, Ill, Immoral, Inferior, Injurious, Lither, Mal, Naughty, Nefandrous, Nefarious, Nice, Off, Ominous, Oncus, Onkus, Piacular, Poor, Rancid, Rank, Ropy, Scampish, Scoundrel, Sinful, Spoiled, Turpitude, Useless, Wack, Wick, > **WICKED**

▷ **Bad(ly)** *may indicate* an anagram

Badge Brassard, Brooch, Button, Chevron, Cockade, Cockleshell, Cordon, Crest, Emblem, Ensign, Epaulet, Episemon, Fáinne, Film, Flash, Garter, Gorget, ID, Insignia, Kikumon, Mark, Mon, Rosette, Scallop, Shield, Shouldermark, > **SIGN**, Symbol, Tiger, Token, Vernicle, Vine-rod, Wings

Badger > **ANNOY**, Bait, Bedevil, Beset, Brock, Browbeat, Bug, Bullyrag, Cete, Dassi(e), Ferret, Gray, Grey, > **HARASS**, Hassle, Heckle, Hog, Honey, Hound, Nag, Pester, Plague, Provoke, Ratel, Ride, Roil, Sow, Stinking, Teledu, Wisconsin

Bad habit Cacoethes, Vice

Badinage Banter, Chaff, Raillery

Bad luck Ambs-ace, Ames-ace, Deuce-ace, Hard cheese, Hard lines, Hoodoo, Jinx, Jonah, Shame, Voodoo

Bad-tempered Carnaptious, Curmudgeon, Curnaptious, Curst, Grouchy, Grum(py), Irritable, Moody, Nowty, Patch, Splenetic, Stroppy

Bad woman Harridan, Loose, Mort

Baffle(d), Baffling Anan, Balk, Bemuse, Bewilder, Confound, Confuse, Elude, Evade, Floor, Flummox, Foil, Fox, Get, Hush-kit, Mate, Muse, Mystify, Nark, Nonplus, Pose, Puzzle, Stump, Throw, Thwart

Bag(gage), Bags Acquire, Alforja, Allantois, Amaut, Amowt, Ascus, Ballonet, Besom, Bladder, Blue, Body, Bulse, Buoyancy, Caba(s), Caecum, Callet, Capture, Carpet, Carrier, Carryall, Case, Cecum, Clutch, Cly, Cod, Cool, Corduroy, Crone, Crumenal, Cyst, Daypack, Dilli, Dilly, Dime, Diplomatic, Ditty, Doggy, Dorothy, Douche, Duffel, Dunnage, > **EFFECTS**, Excess, Flannels, Flotation, Follicle, Galligaskins, Game, > **GEAR**, Gladstone, Grab, Grip, Gripsack, Grow, Holdall, Ice, Impedimenta, Jelly, Jiffy®, Kill, Lavender, Lithocyst, Marsupium, Meal-poke, Minx, Mixed, Monkey, Musette, Muzzle, Mystery, Nap, Net, Nunny, Overnight, Oxford, Packsack, Pantaloons, Plastic, Plus fours, Pochette, Pock(et), Pocketbook, Pockmanky, Pockmantie, Poke, Politzer's, Poly(thene), Port(manteau), Portmantle, Portmantua, Post, Pot, Pouch, Pounce, Pudding, Punch, Purse, Rake, Red, Reticule, Ridicule, Rucksack, Sabretache, Sac(cule), Sachet, Sack, Saddle, Sag, Satchel, Scent, Scrip, Scrotum, Sea, Shopper, Sick, Slattern, Sleeping, Sponge, Sporran, Stacks, Strossers, Sugar, Survival, Tea, Tote, > **TRAP**, Trews, Trollop, Trouse(r), Tucker (box), Udder, Unmentionables, Utricle, Valise, Vanity, Viaticals, Waist, Wallet, Water, Weekend, Win, Woolpack, Work, Ziplock

Bagatelle Bauble, Fico, Trifle, Trinket

Bagpipe Biniou, Chorus, Cornemuse, Drone, Musette, Pibroch, Piffero, Skirl,

Sourdeline, Uillean, Zampogna
Bahamas BS
Bail(er), Bailment Bond, Ladle, Mainpernor, Mainprise, Mutuum, Scoop
Bailey Bridge, Castle wall, Ward
Bailiff Adam, Bandog, Beagle, Bum, Factor, Foud, Grieve, Huissier, Hundreder, Hundredor, Land-agent, Nuthook, Philistine, Reeve, Shoulder-clapper, Shoulder-knot, Steward, Tipstaff, Water
Bairn Baby, > CHILD, Infant, Wean
Bait Badger, Berley, Brandling, Burley, Capelin, Chum, Dap, Decoy, Entice, Gentle, Gudgeon, Harass, Hellgram(m)ite, Incentive, Lobworm, Lug(worm), Lure, Mawk, > RAG, Ragworm, Sledge, Teagle, Tease
Bake(r), Baked, Baking Alaska, Batch, Baxter, > COOK, Fire, Kiln-dry, Roast, Scorch, Shirr
Baker's daughter Own
Baker Street Irregular
Balance Account, Beam, Compensation, Counterpoise, Counterweight, Equate, Equilibrium, Equipoise, Equiponderate, Even, Funambulate, Gyroscope, Gyrostat, Invisible, Isostasy, Launce, Libra, Librate, Meet, Otolith, Peise, Perch, Peyse, Poise, > REMAINDER, Remnant, Residual, Rest, Running, Scale, Sea-legs, Spring, Stand, Steelyard, Symmetry, Torsion, > TOTAL, Trial, Trim, Tron(e), Visible
Balcony Circle, Gallery, Loggia, Mirador, Moucharaby, Porch, Quarter-gallery, Sundeck, Tarras, Terrace, Veranda(h)
Bald, Baldness Alopecia, Apterium, Awnless, Barren, Calvities, Coot, Crude, Egghead, Fox-evil, Glabrous, Hairless, Madarosis, Open, Peelgarlic, Pilgarlic(k), Pollard, Psilosis, Slaphead, Smoothpate, Stark, Tonsured
Balderdash Drivel, Flapdoodle, Nonsense, Rot
Baldmoney Emeu, Meu, Spignel
Bale Bl, Bundle, Evil, Lave, Pack, Sero(o)n, Truss
Baleful Evil, Malefic, Malignant
▶ **Balk** *see* BAULK
Balkan Albanian, Bulgarian, Macedon, Rumanian, Serb, Vlach
Ball(s) Aelopile, Aelopyle, Aeolipile, Aeolipyle, Agglomerate, Alley, Ally, Ammo, Aniseed, Apple, Beach, Bead, Beamer, Birthing, Bobble, Boll, Bolus, Bosey, Bouncer, Break, Buzzer, Caltrap, Caltrop, Camphor, Cap, Cherry, Chin, Chinaman, Chopper, Clew, Clue, Condyle, Cotill(i)on, Cramp, Creeper, Croquette, Crystal, Cue, Curve, Daisy-cutter, > DANCE, Delivery, Dodge, Dollydrop, Dot, Dribbler, Eight, Ensphere, Eolipile, Eolipyle, Eolopile, Eolopyle, Falafel, Felafel, Gazunder, > GLOBE, Glomerate, Googly, Gool(e)ys, Goolies, Grub, Gutta, Gutter, Hank, Hop, Hummer, Inswinger, Ivory, Jump, Knur(r), Leather, Leg-break, Lob, Long-hop, Marble, Masked, Masque(rade), Matzo, Medicine, Minié, Mirror, Moth, Nur(r), O, Object, Off-break, Off-cutter, Off-spin, Orb, Outswinger, Overarm, Pakora, Pea, Pellet, Pill, Poi, Pomander, Pompom, Prom, Puck, Punch, Quenelle, Rabbit, Rissole, Round, Rover, Rundle, Seamer, Shooter, Shot, Sliotar, Sneak, Sphere, Spinner, Stress, Swinger, Taw, Testes, Thenar, Three, Tice, Track(er), Witches, Wood, Yorker
Ballad Bab, Bothy, Broadside, Bush, Calypso, Carol, Folk-song, Lay, Lillibullero, Lilliburlero, > SONG, Torch-song
Ballast Kentledge, Makeweight, Stabiliser, Trim, Weight
Ball-boy Dry-bob
Ballerina Coryphee, Dancer, Pavlova, Prima
Ballet, Ballet movement, Ballet-system Bharat Natyam, Bolshoi, Checkmate,

Développé, Don Pasquale, Écarté, Firebird, Giselle, Kirov, Laban, Labanotation, Leg business, Plie, Pointer, Swan Lake

Ballet-interlude Divertimento

Balloon(ist) Aeronaut, Aerostat, Airship, Bag, Barrage, Billow, Blimp, Bloat, Dirigible, Dumont, Fumetto, Hot air, Lead, Montgolfier, Pilot, Rawinsonde, Sonde, Trial, Weather, Zeppelin

Ballot Butterfly, Election, > POLL, Referendum, Suffrage, Ticket, Vote

Ballot-box Urn

Ballpoint Bic®, Biro®

Balm(y) Anetic, Arnica, Balsam, Calamint, Fragrant, Garjan, Gilead, Gurjun, Lemon, Lenitive, Lotion, > MILD, Mirbane, Myrbane, Nard, Oil, Opobalsam, Ottar, Redolent, Remedy, Soothe, Spikenard, Tiger, Tolu, Unguent

Balmoral Bonnet

Baloney Bunk, Hooey

Balsam Canada, Copaiba, Copaiva, Friar's, Nard, Peruvian, Resin, Spikenard, Tamanu, Tolu(ic), Touch-me-not, Tous-les-mois, Turpentine

Balt Esth, Lett

Baltic Estonian

Bamboo Split cane, Tabasheer, Whangee

Bamboozle(d) Cheat, Dupe, Flummox, Hoodwink, Mystify, Nose-led, Perplex, Trick

Ban Abolish, Accurse, Anathema, Black(ing), Censor, Debar, D-notice, Embargo, Estop, Excommunicate, Forbid, For(e)say, For(e)speak, Gate, Green, Moratorium, No, Outlaw, Prohibit, Proscribe, Taboo, Tabu, Test, Veto

Banal Corny, Dreary, Flat, Hackneyed, Jejune, Mundane, Platitudinous, > TRITE, Trivial

Banana(s) Abaca, Hand, > MAD, Matoke, Musa, Plantain, Scitamineae, Split, Strelitzia

Band(s) Alice, Ambulacrum, Anadem, Armlet, Barrulet, Belt, Border, Braid, Brake, Brass, Brassard, Brassart, Caravan, CB, Channel, Chromosome, Cingulum, Circlet, Citizen's, Clarain, Cohort, Collar, Collet, Combo, Company, Conduction, Corslet, Coterie, Crew, Deely boppers, Elastic, Endorse, Energy, Enomoty, Facia, Falling, Fascia, Fasciole, Ferret, Ferrule, Fess, Filament, Fillet, Frequency, Frieze, Frog, Frontlet, Galloon, Gamelan, > GANG, Garage, Garland, Garter, Gasket, Gaskin, Geneva, Gird, Girth, Guard, > HOOP, Hope, Iron, Jazz, Jug, Kitchen, Label, Laticlave, Lytta, Maniple, Mariachi, Massed, Military, Mourning, Myrmidon, Noise, One-man, Orchestra, Orchestrina, Pack, Parral, Parrel, Parsal, Parsel, Pass, Patte, Pipe, Plinth, Property, Purfle, Puttee, Retinaculum, Rib, Ribbon, Rigwiddie, Rigwoodie, Rim, Ring, Robbers, Rubber, Rymme, Sash, Scarf, Screed, Scrunchie, Scrunchy, Sect, Shadow, Shallal, Shash, Sheet, Shoe, Snood, Steel, Strake, Strap, Stratum, String, Stripe, Swath(e), Tambu-bambu, Tape, Tendon, Throat-latch, Tie, Tippet, Torques, Tourniquet, Train, Troop, Troupe, Tumpline, Turm, Tyre, Unite, Valence, Vinculum, Virl, Vitrain, Vitta, Wanty, Wedding, Weeper, Welt, With(e), Wristlet, Zona, Zone

Bandage Bind, Blindfold, Capeline, Dressing, Fillet, Ligature, Lint, Pledget, Roller, Scapular, Sling, Spica, Suspensor, Swaddle, Swathe, T, Tape, Truss, Tubigrip®, Wadding

Bandicoot Pig-rat

Bandit Apache, Bravo, Brigand, Desperado, Fruit-machine, Gunslinger, Klepht, Moss-trooper, Outlaw, Pirate, Rapparee, > ROBBER, Squeegee, Turpin

Bandsman, Band-leader Alexander, Bugler, Conductor, Maestro, Miller, Wait

Bandy Vie

Bane Curse, Evil, Harm, Poison

Bang(er) Amorce, Big, Cap, Chipolata, Clap, Cracker, Crock, Explode, Flivver, Fringe, Haircut, Heap, Implode, Jalopy, Maroon, Rattletrap, Report, Sausage, Sizzler, Slam, Sonic, Thrill, Wurst

Bangle Anklet, Armlet, Bracelet, Kara

Banish(ment) Ban, Deport, Depose, Exile, Expatriate, Expel, Extradition, Forsay, Maroon, Ostracise, > OUTLAW, Relegate, Rusticate

Banjo Ukulele

Bank(ing) An(n)icut, Asar, Backs, Bar, Bay, Bk, Blood, Bluff, Bottle, Brae, Brim, Bund, Camber, Cay, Central, Chesil, Clearing, Cloud, Commercial, Cooperative, Data, Depend, Deposit, Dogger, Down, Dune, Dyke, Earthwork, Escarp, Fog, Gene, Giro, Glacis, Gradient, Gradin(e), Hele, Hill, Home, Incline, Jodrell, Land, Left, Lender, Levee, Link, Memory, Merchant, Mound, Nap, National, Nore, Overslaugh, Parapet, Penny, Piggy, Pot, Private, Rake, Ramp, Rampart, Reef, > RELY, Reserve, Rivage, Riverside, Rodham, Row, Sandbar, Savings, Shallow, Shelf, Side, Slope, Soil, Sperm, Staithe, State, Sunk, Telephone, Terrace, Terreplein, Tier, Vault, West, World

Banker Agent, Financial, Fugger, Gnome, Lombard, Medici, > RIVER, Rothschild, Shroff

▷ **Banker** *may indicate* a river

Banknote Flimsy, Greenback

Bankrupt(cy) Break, Broke, Bung, Bust, Cadaver, Carey Street, Crash, Debtor, Deplete, Duck, Dyvour, Fail, Fold, Insolvent, Lame duck, Notour, Receivership, Ruin, Rump, Scat, Sequestration, Skatt, Smash

▷ **Bankrupt** *may indicate* 'red' around another word

Bank System Giro

Bann(s) Out-ask

Banner Banderol(e), Bandrol, Bannerol, > FLAG, Gumphion, Labarum, Oriflamme, Sign, Streamer

Banquet Beanfeast, Dine, Feast, Junket, Spread

Banquette Firestep

Bant Diet, Reduce

Banter Badinage, Borak, Chaff, Dicacity, Dieter, Jest, > JOKE, Persiflage, Picong, Rag, > RAILLERY, Rally, Ribaldry, Roast, Tease

Bantu Bosotho, Gazankulu, Herero, Qwaqwa, Shangaan, Sotho, Transkei, Tutsi, X(h)osa

Bap Bread, Roll, Tommy

Baptise(d), Baptism, Baptist Affusion, Amrit, Christen, Dip, Dipper, Dopper, Dunker, Illuminati, Immersion, Sabbatarian, Sprinkle, Tinker

Bar(s) Angle-iron, Anti-roll, Astragal, Asymmetric, Axletree, Bail, Ban, Barrelhouse, Baulk, Beam, Bierkeller, Bilboes, Billet, Bistro, Blackball, Blacklist, Block(ade), Bloom, Bolt, Boom, Bottega, Brasserie, Buffet, Bull, Bumper, But, Buvette, Café(-chantant), Café-concert, > CAGE, Came, Cantina, Capo, Capstan, Cocktail, Coffee, Colour, Counter, Cramp(on), Crow, Crush, Currency, Dive, Double-tree, Draw, Drift, Dumbbell, Espresso, Estop(pel), Except, Exclude, Fen, Fid, Flinders, Forbid, Foreclose, Forestall, Fret, Gad, Gemel, Grate, Grid, Grog-shop, Hame, Handspike, Heck, > HINDRANCE, Horizontal, Hound, Impediment, Ingoes, Ingot, Ingowes, Inn, Inner, Judder, Juice, Karaoke, Kickstand, Knuckleduster, Latch, Let, Lever, Limbo, Line, Local, Lounge, Macron, Mandrel, Mandril, Measure, Menu, Milk, Mousing, Muesli, Mullion, Nail, Nanaimo, No-go, Norman, Obstacle, Onely, Orgue, Outer,

Overslaugh, Oxygen, Parallel, Perch, Pile, Pinch, Pole, Private, Prohibit, Pub, Public, Putlog, Rabble, Rack, Rail, Ramrod, Rance, Randle-balk, Randle-perch, Randle-tree, Reach, Restrict, Rib, Risp, Rod, Roll, Roo, Rung, Saddle, Salad, Saloon, Sans, Save, Saving, Scroll, Semantron, Shaft, Shanty, Shet, Shut, Singles, Skewer, Slice, Slot, Snack, Snug, Spacer, Spar, Speakeasy, Sperre, Spina, Spit, Splinter, Sprag, Stancher, Stanchion, Status, Stave, Sternson, Stick, Stirre, Stretcher, Stripe, Sway, Swee, T, Tael, Tap(-room), Tapas, Taphouse, Tavern(a), Temple, Toll, Tombolo, Tommy, Tool, Torsion, Tow, Trace, Trangle, Transom, Trapeze, Triblet, Trundle, Type, Vinculum, Wall, Ward, Wet, Whisker, Window, Wine, Wire, Wrecking, Z, Zed, Zygon

Barabbas Robber

Barb(ed) Bur(r), Fluke, Harl, Herl, > HOOK, Jag(g), Jibe, Pheon, Prickle, Ramus, Tang, Vexillum

Barbados, Barbadian Bajan, Bim(m)

Barbara Allen, Major

Barbarian, Barbaric Boor, Crude, Fifteen, Foreigner, Goth, Heathen, Hottentot, Hun, Inhuman, Lowbrow, Outlandish, Philistine, Rude, Savage, Tartar, Tatar(ic)

Barbary Ape, Roan

Barbecue Braai vleis, Cook-out, Flame-grill, Grill, Hangi, Hibachi, Roast, Spit

Barbel Beard

Barber Epilate, Figaro, Scrape(r), Shaver, Strap, Todd, Tonsor, Trimmer

Barbiturate Goofball

Bard Ariosto, Griot, Heine, Meat, Minstrel, Muse, Ossian, Scald, Scop, Skald, Taliesin

Bare, Bare-headed Adamic, Aphyllous, Bald, Barren, Blank, Bodkin, Cere, Décolleté, Denude, Hush, Lewd, Marginal, Moon, > NAKED, Open, Plain, Scant, Sear, Stark, Uncase, Uncover, Unveil

Barefoot Discalced, Unshod

Barely At a pinch, At a stretch, Hand-to-mouth, Hardly, Just, Merely, Scarcely, Scrimp

Bargain(ing) Barter, Braata, Chaffer, Champerty, > CHEAP, Collective, Contract, Coup, Deal, Dicker, Distributive, Effort, Find, Go, Haggle, Higgle, Horse-trade, Huckster, Integrative, Option, > PACT, Plea, Productivity, Scoop, Snip, Steal, Supersaver, Time, Trade, Trock, Troke, Truck, Wanworth, Wheeler-dealing

Barge Birlinn, Bucentaur, Budgero(w), Butty, Gabbard, Gabbart, Galley-foist, Hopper, Intrude, Jostle, Keel, Lighter, Nudge, Obtrude, Pra(a)m, Ram, Scow, > SHIP, Trow, Wherry

▷ **Barge** *may indicate* an anagram

Bargee, Bargeman Keeler, Keelman, Legger, Lighterman, Ram, Trow

Barium Ba, Witherite

Bark Angostura, Ayelp, Azedarach, Bass, Bast, Bay, Bowwow, Calisaya, Cambium, Canella, Caribbee, Cascara, Cascarilla, Cassia, China, Cinchona, Cinnamon, Cork, Cortex, Cusparia, Honduras, Jesuit's, Kina, Kinakina, Latration, Liber, Myrica, Peel, Pereira, Peruvian, Phloem, Quebracho, Quest, Quillai, Quina, Quinquina, Red, Rind, Sagrada, Salian, Sassafras, Scrape, Scurf, > SHIP, Skin, Slippery elm, Tan, Tap(p)a, Totaquine, Waff, Waugh, Woof, Wow, Yaff, > YAP, Yellow, Yelp, Yip

Bar-keeper, Barmaid, Barman Advocate, Ale-wife, Bencher, Hebe, Luckie, Lucky, Tapster, Underskinker

Barley (water) Awn, Bear, Bere, Bigg, Hordeum, Malt, Orgeat, Pearl, Pot, Truce, Tsamba

Barm(y) Yeast
Barmecide, Barmecidal Imaginary
Barn Bank, Byre, Cowshed, Dutch, Farm, Grange, Mow, Perchery, Skipper, Tithe
Barnaby Rudge
Barnacle Acorn, Cypris, Goose(neck), Limpet
Barometer Aneroid, Glass, Orometer, Statoscope, Sympiesometer, Torricellian tube, Weatherglass
Baron B, Corvo, Drug, Munchausen, Noble, Thyssen, Tycoon
Baronet Bart
Baronne Dudevant Sand
Baroque Fancy, Gothic, Ornate, Rococo
▷ **Baroque** *may indicate* an anagram
Barrack(s), Barracking Asteism, Boo, Cantonment, Casern(e), Cat-call, Garrison, Heckle, Irony, Quarters
Barrage Balloon, Fusillade, Heat, Salvo
Barred Banned, Edh, Trabeculated
Barrel Bl, Butt, Cade, Capstan, Cascabel, Cask, Clavie, Drum, Hogshead, Keg, Kibble, Morris-tube, Oildrum, Organ, Pièce, Pork, Run(d)let, Tan-vat, Thrall, Tierce, Tun, Vat, Water, Wood
Barrel-organ Apollonicum, Hurdy-gurdy, Street piano
Barren Addle, Arid, Badlands, Blind, Blunt, Clear, Dry, Eild, > EMPTY, Farrow, Hirstie, Jejune, Sterile, Unbearing, Waste, Wasteland, Wilderness, Yeld, Yell
Barrier Bail, Barrage, Bayle, Block, Breakwater, Cauld, Checkrail, Cheval de frise, Chicane, Cordon (sanitaire), Crash, Crush, > DAM, Defence, Drawgate, Dyke, Fence, Fraise, Gate, Heat, Hedge, Hurdle, Mach, Obstruct, Pain, Rail(-fence), Rampart, Restraint, Revetment, Roadblock, Screen, Skreen, Sonic, Sound, Spina, Stockade, Thermal, Tollgate, Trade, Transonic, Turnpike, Turnstile, > WALL
Barrister Advocate, Attorney, Counsel, Devil, Lawyer, Rumpole, Sergeant (at law), Serjeant(-at-law), Silk, Templar, Utter
Barrow Dolly, Handcart, Henge, How, Hurley, Kurgan, Molehill, Mound, Pushcart, Tram, Trolley, Truck, Tumulus
Barrow-boy Coster, Trader
Bar-tail Scamel, Staniel, Stannel
Barter Chaffer, Chop, Coup, Dicker, > EXCHANGE, Haggle, Hawk, Niffer, Sco(u)rse, Swap, > TRADE, Traffic, Truck
Basalt Diabase, Tachylite, Tephrite, Toadstone, Traprock, Wacke
Base Adenine, Alkali, Bed, Beggarly, Billon, Bottom, Caitiff, Camp, Codon, Cytosine, Degenerate, Degraded, Dog, Down, E, Erinite, > ESTABLISH, First, Floor, Foot, Foothold, Footstall, Found, Fundus, Guanine, Harlot, Histamine, Ignoble, Indamine, Infamous, Install, Lewis, > LOW, > MEAN, Nefarious, Nook, Parasaniline, Partite, Patten, Platform, Plinth, Podium, Premise, Ptomaine, Purin(e), Pyrimidine, Pyrrolidine, Radix, Rascally, Rests, Ribald, Root, Rosaniline, Schiff, Servile, Shameful, Shand, Sheeny, Socle, Soda, Spaceport, Staddle, > STAND, Station, Substrate, Ten, Thymine, Torus, Triacid, Turpitude, Unworthy, Uracil, Vile
Baseball Apple, Nine
Baseless Idle, Unfounded, Ungrounded
Base-line Datum
Basement Bargain
Bash Belt, Clout, Go, Hit, Rave, Shot, Slog, Strike, Swat, Swipe
Bashful Awed, Blate, Coy, Modest, Retiring, Shamefast, Sheep-faced, Sheepish,

> **SHY**

Basic, Basis ABC, Abcee, Alkaline, Aquamanale, Aquamanile, Crude,
> **ESSENTIAL**, Fiducial, Fond, Fundamental, Ground(work), Gut, Integral,
Intrinsic, Logic, Nitty-gritty, No-frills, No-nonsense, Pou sto, Primordial,
Principle, Radical, Rudimentary, Spit-and-sawdust, Staple, Substance,
Underlying, Uracil

Basilica St Peter's

Basilisk Cannon, Lizard

Basin Aquamanale, Aquamanile, Artesian, Benitier, Bidet, Bowl, Canning,
Catch, Catchment, Cirque, Corrie, Cwm, Dish, Dock, Doline, Donets, Drainage,
Foxe, Geosyncline, Great, Impluvium, Kuzbass, Kuznetsk, Lavabo, Laver,
Minas, Monteith, Pan, Park, Piscina, Playa, Porringer, Reservoir, River, Scapa
Flow, Slop, Stoop, Stoup, Sugar, Tank, Tarim, Tidal

Bask Apricate, Revel, Sun, Sunbathe, > **WALLOW**

Basket, Basket-work Baalam, Bass, Bassinet, Bread, Buck, Cabas, Calathus,
Canephorus, Car, Cesta, Cob, Coop, Corbeil(le), Corbicula, Corf, Creel, Cresset,
Dosser, Fan, Flasket, Flax kit, Frail, Gabian, Hamper, Hask, Junket, Kago,
Kajawah, Kipe, Kit, Leap, Maund, Mocock, Mocuck, Moses, Murlain, Murlan,
Murlin, Osiery, Pannier, Ped, Petara, Pitara(h), Pollen, Pottle, Punnet, Rip,
Scull, Scuttle, Seed-lip, Skep, Skull, Trolley, Trug, Van, Wagger-pagger(-bagger),
Waste(-paper), Wattlework, Whisket, Wicker(-work), Will(e), Wisket, Work

Basket-bearer Canephor(a), Canephore, Canephorus

Basket-maker Alfa, Cane, Halfa, Wicker

Basque Euskarian

Bass Alberti, Ale, Alfie, B, Continuo, Deep, El-a-mi, Figured, Fish, Largemouth,
Low, Ostinato, Serran, Smallmouth, Thorough, Walking

Bast Liber

Bastard, Bastard-wing Alula, Base, By-blow, Filius nullius, Git, Illegitimate,
Mamzer, Momzer, Mongrel, Sassaby, Side-slip, Slink, Spuriae, Spurious,
Whoreson

▷ **Bastard** *may indicate* an anagram

Baste Enlard, Sew, Stitch, Tack

Bastion Citadel, Lunette, Moineau

Bat, Batter, Batting, Batsman, Batty Aliped, Ames, Assail, Barbastelle, Baton,
Belfry, Blink, Chiroptera, Close, Cosh, Crackers, Dad, Die Fledermaus, Eyelid,
False vampire, Flittermouse, Flying fox, Fruit, Grace, Hammerhead, Hatter,
Haywire, Hit, Hobbs, Hook, Horseshoe, In, Ink mouse, Insectivorous, Kalong,
Language, Leisler, Man, Mastiff, Maul, May, Mormops, Mouse-eared, Myopic,
Nictate, Nictitate, Night, Nightwatchman, Noctilio, Nora, Nurdle, Opener,
Pinch-hit, Pipistrel(le), Poke, Pummel, Racket, Racquet, Ram, Rearmouse,
Reremice, Reremouse, Roussette, Ruin, Sauch, Saugh, Scotch hand, Serotine,
Sledge, Stick, Stonewall, Straight, Striker, Swat, Trap-stick, Vampire,
Vespertilionid, Viv, Whacky, Willow, Wood

Batch Bake, Bunch

Bath(room) Aerotone, Aeson's, Bagnio, Bain-marie, Bed, Blanket, Blood,
Bubble, Caldarium, Cor, Dip, En suite, Epha, Foam, Hammam, Hip,
Hummaum, Hummum, Jacuzzi®, Laver, Mikvah, Mud, Mustard, Piscina,
Plunge, Salt, Sauna, Shower, Sitz, Slipper, Soak, Spa, Sponge, Steam, Stew,
Stop, Tepidarium, Therm, Tub, Turkish, Tye, Vapour, Whirlpool, Wife

Bathe, Bathing Balneal, Balneation, Balneology, Bay(e), Beath, Bogey, Bogie,
Dip, Dook, Douk, Embay, Foment, Immerse, Lave, Lip, Skinny-dip, Souse,
Splash, Stupe, > **SWIM**, Tub, > **WASH**

Batman Valet
Baton Mace, Rod, Sceptre, Staff, Truncheon
Batrachian Frog, Toad
▷ **Bats**, **Batting** *may indicate* an anagram
Battalion Bn, Corps, Troop
Batten Fasten, Tie
Batter(ed) Bombard, Bruise, Buffet, Decrepit, Pound
Battery Accumulator, Artillery, Drycell, Field, Galvanic, Henhouse, Nicad, Penlight, Pra(a)m, Primary, Solar, Storage, Troop, Voltaic, Waffle, Water
Battle(s), **Battleground** Action, Affair, Ben, Clash, Cockpit, Combat, > CONFLICT, Encounter, Engagement, Field, > FIGHT, Fray, Front, Hosting, Joust, Pitched, Royal, Sarah, Sciamachy, Skiamachy, Spurs, Stoor, Stour, Stowre, Theatre, Wage, > WAR

● **BATTLES**

3 letters:
Kut
Ulm

4 letters:
Alma
Ivry
Jena
Laon
Loos
Mons
Nile
Zama

5 letters:
Accra
Alamo
Allia
Arcot
Arras
Boyne
Bulge
Crecy
Ipsus
Issus
Lewes
Marne
Parma
Sedan
Somme
Ypres

6 letters:
Actium
Argyle
Arnhem

Barnet
Camlan
Cannae
Cressy
Crimea
Maldon
Naseby
Sadowa
Senlac
Shiloh
Tobruk
Varese
Verdun
Vigrid
Wagram
Wipers

7 letters:
Aboukir
Alamein
Beaches
Britain
Bull Run
Cambrai
Colenso
Coronel
Corunna
Dunkirk
Flodden
Flowers
Glencoe
Jericho
Jutland
Lepanto
Magenta
Marengo

Nations
Picardy
Plassey
Salamis
Warburg

8 letters:
Antietam
Ardennes
Blenheim
Borodino
Bosworth
Clontarf
Culloden
Edgehill
Flanders
Fontenay
Hastings
Inkerman
Jemappes
Manassas
Marathon
Navarino
Omdurman
Philippi
Poitiers
Ragnarok
Saratoga
Talavera
Waterloo

9 letters:
Agincourt
Balaclava
Caporetto
El Alemein

Gallipoli
Ladysmith
Otterburn
Oudenarde
Pharsalia
Ramillies
Sedgemoor
Solferino
Theomachy
Trafalgar
Worcester

10 letters:
Armageddon
Austerlitz
Bunker Hill
Camperdown
Gettysburg
Lundy's Lane
Stalingrad
Steenkerke

11 letters:
Bannockburn
Hohenlinden
Marston Moor
Prestonpans
Thermopylae
Wounded Knee

12 letters:
Flodden Field
Roncesvalles

13 letters:
Bosworth Field

Little Bighorn   **14 letters:**   **15 letters:**
Passchendaele   Stamford Bridge   Missionary Ridge

Battle-axe Amazon, Bill, Gorgon, Halberd, Ogress, Sparth(e), Termagant, Termagent, Turmagant, Turmagent
Battlement Barmkin, Crenellate, Merlon, Rampart
Battle-order Phalanx
Battleship Carrier, Destroyer, Dreadnought, Gunboat, Man-o'-war, Pocket, Potemkin
Bauble Bagatelle, Gaud, Gewgaw, Trifle
Bauhaus Gropius
Baulk Demur, Gib, Hen, Impede, Jib, Reest, Reist, Shy, Thwart
Bavardage Fadaise
Bawdy Raunchy, Sculdudd(e)ry, Skulduddery
Bawl Bellow, Gollar, Howl, Weep
Bay Ab(o)ukir, Aere, Arm, Baffin, Bantry, Bark, Bell, Bengal, Bight, Biscay, Bonny, Botany, Broken, Byron, Cardigan, Chesapeake, Cienfuegos, Cleveland, Colwyn, Corpus Christi, Cove, Covelet, Creek, Daphne, Delagoa, Delaware, Discovery, Dublin, Dvina, False, Famagusta, Fleet, Frobisher, Fundy, Galway, Gdansk, Georgian, Glace, Golden, Great Australian Bight, Green, Guantanamo, Gulf, Hangzhou, Harbour, Hawke's, Herne, Horse, > **HOWL**, Hudson, Inlet, James, Jervis, Jiazhou, Kavalla, Kuskokwim, Laura, Laurel, Layby, Loading, Lobito, MA, Manila, Massachusetts, Montego, Morton, Narragansett, New York, Niche, Oleander, Omaha, Oriel, Passamaquoddy, Pegasus, Pigs, Plenty, Port Phillip, Poverty, Recess, Red, Roan, St Michel, San Francisco, Santiago, Setubal, Shark, Sick, Sligo, Suvla, Table, Tampa, Tasman, Thunder, Tor, Toyama, Tralee, Ungava, Vae, Vlore, Voe, Waff, Walfish, Walvis, Wash, Whitley, Yowl
Bayonet Jab, Skewer, Stab, Sword
Bazaar Alcaiceria, Emporium, Fair, Fete, Market, Pantechnicon, Sale, Sook, Souk
BBC Auntie
Be Exist, Live, Occur
Beach Bondi, Coast, Daytona, Ground, Hard, Lido, Littoral, Machair, Miami, Omaha, Palm, Plage, Raised, Sand, Seaside, Shingle, Shore, Storm, Strand, Waikiki
Beachcomber Arenaria
Beacon Belisha, Fanal, Landing, Lightship, Need-fire, Pharos, Racon, Radar, Radio, Robot, Signal
Bead(s), Beaded Aggri, Aggry, Baily's, Ballotini, Bauble, Blob, Bugle, Cabling, Chaplet, Crab-stones, Drop, Droplet, Gadroon, Gaud, Kubaloi, Mala, Moniliform, Ojime, Passament, Passement, Paternoster, Poppet, Poppit, Prayer, Rosary, Se(a)wan, Subha, Sweat, Tear, Wampum(peag), Worry
Beadle Apparitor, Bederal, Bedral, Bumble, Herald, Paritor, Verger
Beagle Spy
Beak AMA, Bailie, Bill, Cad, Cere, Coronoid, Egg-tooth, Gar, JP, Kip(p), Magistrate, Master, Metagnathous, Mittimus, Nasute, Neb, Nose, Pecker, Prow, Ram, Rostellum, Rostrum, Shovel
Beaker Cup, Goblet
Beakless Erostrate
Beak-shaped Coracoid
Beam(ing) Arbor, Balance, Bar, Ba(u)lk, Binder, Boom, Bowstring, Box,

Beamish | 50

Breastsummer, Bressummer, Broadcast, Bum(p)kin, Cantilever, Carline, Carling, Cathead, Collar, Crosshead, Crosspiece, Deck, Girder, Grin, Hammer, Hatch, Herisson, Holophote, I, Irradiate, Joist, Ke(e)lson, Landing, Laser, Lentel, Lintel, Manteltree, Molecular, Needle, Outrigger, Particle, Pencil, Principal, Purlin, Putlock, Putlog, Radio, > **RAFTER**, > **RAY**, Rayon, Refulgent, Rident, Ridgepole, Rood, Roof-tree, Sandwich, Scantling, Searchlight, Shaft, Shine, Shore, Sleeper, Smile, Solive, Stanchion, Stemson, Sternpost, Straining, Streamer, Stringer, Stringpiece, Summer, Support, Tailing, Tie, Timber, Trabeate, Trabecula, Transom, Trave, Trimmer, Truss, Universal, Viga, Walking, Weigh-bauk, Yard, Yardarm

Beamish Galumphing, Nephew

Bean Abrus, Adsuki, Arabica, Asparagus pea, Baked, Berry, Black, Black-eye, Borlotti, Broad, Bush, Butter, Cacao, Calabar, Castor, Cocoa, Coffee, Cow-pea, Dwarf, Fabaceous, Fava, Flageolet, French, Frijol(e), Garbanzo, Goa, Gram, Green, Haricot, Harmala, Head, Horse, Jack, Jumping, Kachang putch, Kidney, Lablab, Lentil, Lima, Locust, Molucca, Moong, Moth, Mung, Nelumbo, Nib, Noddle, Ordeal, Pichurim, Pinto, Runner, Scarlet runner, Shell, Snap, Soy(a), String, Sugar, Sword, Tonga, Tonka, Tonquin, Urd, Wax, Winged, Yard-long

Beanfeast > **PARTY**, Spree, Wayzgoose

Bear(er), Bear lover Abide, Abrooke, Andean, Arctic, Arctophile, Baloo, Balu, Beer, Bigg, Breed, Brook, Brown, Bruin, Brunt, > **CARRY**, Cave, Churl, Cinnamon, Coati-mondi, Coati-mundi, Cub, Demean, Dree, Ean, > **ENDURE**, Engender, Exert, Fur-seal, Gonfalonier, Great, Grizzly, Hack, Ham(m)al, Harbinger, Have, Hold, Honey, Humf, Hump(h), Jampani, Keb, Kinkajou, Koala, Kodiak, Koolah, Lioncel(le), Lionel, Lug, Mother, Nandi, Nanook, Owe, Paddington, Panda, Polar, Pooh, Rac(c)oon, Roller, Rupert, Russia, Sackerson, Seller, Shoulder, Sit, Sloth, Spectacled, Stand, Stay, Stomach, > **SUFFER**, Sunbear, Sustain, Targeteer, Teddy, Teem, Thole, Throw, Tolerate, Tote, Transport, Undergo, Upstay, Ursine, Water, Whelp, White, Wield, Woolly, Yield

Bearberry Manzanita, Uva-ursi

Beard(ed) Aaron, Alfalfa, Anchor, Arista, Assyrian, Aureole, Awn, Balaclava, Barb, Barbiche, Beaver, Belgrave, Cadiz, Cathedral, Charley, Charlie, Confront, Defy, Ducktail, Face, Five o'clock shadow, Forked, Fungus, Goatee, Hair(ie), Hairy, Hear(ie), Imperial, Jewish, Kesh, Lincolnesque, Mephistopheles, Old Dutch, Olympian, Outface, Peak, Pencil, Raleigh, Rivet, Roman T, Screw, Shenandoah, Spade, Stibble, Stiletto, Stubble, Swallowtail, Tile, Trojan, Tuft, Uncle Sam, Vandyke, Whiskerando, Whiskery, Ziff

Beardless Callow, Clean, Tahr, Tehr

▷ **Bearhug** *may indicate* Teddy or similar around a word

Bearing(s) Air, Allure, Amenaunce, Armorial, Aspect, Azimuth, Babbitt, Ball, Behaviour, Bush, Carriage, Deportment, Direction, E, Endurance, Gait, Hatchment, Haviour, Hugger-mugger, Lioncel(le), Lionel, Manner, Mascle, Middy, Mien, N, Needle, Nor, Pheon, Port, Presence, Reference, Relevant, Roller, S, Tenue, Thrust, W, Yielding

▷ **Bearing** *may indicate* compass points

Beast > **ANIMAL**, Arna, Behemoth, Brute, Caliban, Caribou, Chimera, > **CREATURE**, Dieb, Dragon, Dzeren, Gayal, Genet, Grampus, Hippogriff, Hodog, Hog, Hy(a)ena, Hydra, Jumart, Kinkajou, Lion, Mammoth, Marmot, Mastodon, Mhorr, Monoceros, Oliphant, Opinicus, Oryx, Panda, Potto, Quagga, Rac(c)oon, Rhytina, Rother, Rumptifusel, Sassaby, Steer, Sumpter, Tarand, Teg, Theroid, Triceratops, Triton, Wart-hog, Whangam, Yahoo, Yak, Yale, Zizel

Beat(ing), Beaten, Beater Anoint, Arsis, Athrob, Bandy, Bang, Baste, Bastinado, Batter, Battue, Belabour, Belt, Bepat, Best, Blatter, Bless, Bo Diddley, Bubble, Cadence, Cane, Cat, Chastise, Clobber, Club, Clump, Conquer, Cream, Cudgel, Cuff, Curry, Debel, > **DEFEAT**, Ding, Donder, Dress, Drub, Duff up, Excel, Fatigue, Faze, Feague, Feeze, Fibbed, Firk, Flagellate, Flail, Flam, Float, Flog, Floor, Flush, Fly, Fustigate, Hipster, Hollow, Horsewhip, Ictus, Inteneration, Knock, Knubble, Lace, Laidie, Laidy, Lambast(e), Larrup, Lash, Laveer, Lay, Lick, Lilt, Lounder, Mall, Malleate, Mersey, Nubble, Outclass, Outdo, Outflank, Outstrip, Paik, Palpitate, Pash, Paste, Pommel, Pound, Prat, Pug, Pulsate, Pulse, Pulsedge, Pummel, Pun, Quop, Raddle, Ram, Ratten, Resolve, Retreat, Rhythm, Ribroast, Round, Rowstow, Ruff(le), Scourge, Scutch, Slat, Smight, Smite, Soak, Sock, Strap, Strap-oil, Strike, Swinge, Systole, Taber, Tabor, Tabrere, Tachycardia, Tact, Tala, Tattoo, Thesis, Thrash, Thresh, Throb, Thud, Thump, Thwack, Tick, Tired, Top, Torture, Tricrotic, Trounce, Tuck, Tund, Verberate, Vibrate, Wallop, Wappend, Welt, Wham, Whip, Whisk, Whitewash, Wraught, Ybet, Yerk, Yirk

▷ **Beaten-up** *may indicate* an anagram

Beat it Skedaddle, Vamo(o)se

Beatitude Macarism

Beau Admirer, Blade, Brummel, Cat, Damoiseau, Dandy, Flame, Geste, Lair, Lover, Masher, Nash, Spark, Tibbs

Beaufort Scale, Windscale

Beaut(y) Advantage, Bathing, Belle, Bombshell, Camberwell, Charmer, Colleen, Comeliness, Corker, Dish, Doll, Glory, Houri, Hyperion, Lana, Monism, Picture, Pride, Pulchritude, Purler, Sheen, Smasher, Stunner

Beautiful, Beautify Bonny, Bright, Embellish, Enhance, Fair, Fine, Gorgeous, Ornament, Pink, Radiant, Smicker, Specious, To kalon

Beauty spot Patch, Tempe, Tika

Beaver Beard, Castor, Eager, Grind, Mountain, Oregon, Rodent, Sewellel

Because (of) As, Forasmuch, Forwhy, Hence, In, Inasmuch, Sens, Since

Beckon Gesture, Nod, Summons, Waft, Wave

Become, Becoming Apt, Besort, Decent, Decorous, Enter, Fall, Fit, Flatter, Get, Go, Grow, Happen, Occur, Seemly, Suit, Wax, Worth

Bed(ding), Bedstead Air, Allotment, Amenity, Apple-pie, Arroyo, Base, Bassinet, > **BEDCOVER**, Berth, Bottom, Box, Bundle, Bunk, Caliche, Camp, Carrycot, Channel, Charpoy, Cill, Cot(t), Couch(ette), Counterpane, Couvade, Coverlet, Cradle, Crib, Cross, Cul(t)ch, Day, Divan, Doona, Doss, Duvet, Erf, False, Feather, Filter, Fluidized, Flying, Four-poster, Futon, Gault, Greensand, Hammock, Inlay, Kago, Kang, Kip, Knot, Knot garden, Layer, Lazy, Lilo®, Litter, Marriage, Mat, Matrix, Mattress, Murphy, Nap, Nest, Nookie, Oyster, Pad, Paillasse, Pallet, Palliasse, Pan, Parterre, Patch, Pavement, Pay, Pig, Plank, Plant, Plot, Procrustean, Puff, Quilt, Retire, Rollaway, Roost, Rota, Sack, Scalp, Settle, Shakedown, Sill, Sitter, Sleep, Sofa, Standing, Stratum, Stretcher, Sun, Tanning, Test, Thill, Trough, Truckle, Trundle, Twin, Wadi, Wady, Ware, Water, Wealden, Wedding

Bedaub Cake, Deck, Smear

Bed-bug B, B flat, Chinch, Flea, Louse, Vermin

Bedchamber, Bedroom Boudoir, Chamber, Cubicle, Dorm(itory), Dormer, Dorter, Ruelle, Ward

Bedcover Palampore, Palempore

Bedeck Adonise, Adorn, Array, Festoon

▷ **Bedevilled** *may indicate* an anagram

Bedjacket Nightingale

Bedlam Chaos, Furore, Madness, Nuthouse, Tumult, Uproar

Bed-rest Dutch-wife

Bedwetting Enuresis

Bee Athenia, Bumble, Carpenter, Cuckoo, Deseret, Drone, Drumbledor, Dumbledore, Group, Hiver, Honey, Humble, Killer, King, Lapidary, Leaf-cutter, Mason, Mining, Nurse, Queen, Quilting, Raising, Solitary, Spell, Spell-down, Spelling, Swarm, Worker, Working

Beech Antarctic, Copper, Fagus, Hornbeam, Mast, Taw(h)ai, Tree

Bee-eater Merops, Rainbow-bird

Beef(y) Baron, Bleat, Brawny, Bresaola, Bull(y), Bullock, Carpaccio, Charqui, Chateaubriand, Chuck, Complain, Corned, Filet mignon, Groan, Grouse, Hough, Jerk, Kobe, Liebig, Mart, Mice, Mousepiece, Muscle, Neat, Ox, Pastrami, Peeve, Porterhouse, Rother, Salt-junk, Sauerbraten, Sey, Silverside, Sirloin, Stolid, Stroganoff, Tournedos, Tranche, Undercut, Vaccine, Wellington

Beefeater Billman, Exon, Gin, Oxpecker, Warder, Yeoman

Bee-glue Propolis

Beehive Alveary, Apiary, Ball, Gum, Skep

Beelzebub Devil

Beer Ale, Alegar, Amber fluid, Bantu, Bitter, Black, Bock, Chaser, Draught, Drink, Dry, Entire, Export, Gill, Ginger, Granny, Grog, Guest, Heavy, Herb, Home-brew, Kaffir, Keg, Kvass, Lager, Lambic, Lite, Lush, Malt, March, Middy, Mild, Mum, Near, Nog, October, Pils(e)ner, Pint, Pony, Porter, Real, Root, Saki, Scoobs, Sherbet, Skeechan, Small, Spruce, Stingo, Stout, Swanky, Swats, Swipes, Switchel, Table, Taplash, Tinnie, Tipper, Tshwala, Tube, Wallop, Wheat, Zythum

Beer garden Brasserie

Bee's nest Bink

Beet Blite, Chard, Fat-hen, Goosefoot, Mangel(wurzel), Spinach, Sugar

Beetle Ambrosia, Anobiid, Argos tortoise, Asiatic, Bacon, Bark, Batler, Bee, Blister, Bloody-nosed, Boll weevil, Bombardier, Bruchid, Bug, Bum-clock, Buprestidae, Buprestus, Burying, Bustle, Buzzard-clock, Cabinet, Cadelle, Cane, Cantharis, Carabid, Cardinal, Carpet, Carrion, Chafer, Christmas, Churchyard, Cicindela, Click, Clock, Cockchafer, Cockroach, Coleoptera, Colorado, Coprophagan, Curculio, Darkling, Deathwatch, Dermestid, Devil's coach-horse, Diving, Dor(r), Dor-fly, Dumbledore, Dung, Dyticus, Dytiscus, Elater, Elytron, Elytrum, Firefly, Flea, Furniture, Glow-worm, Gold(smith), Goliath, Gregor, Ground, Hammer, Hangover, Hercules, Hop-flea, Hornbug, Huhu, Humbuzz, Impend, Japanese, Jewel, June, Khapra, Ladybird, Ladybug, Lamellicorn, Larder, Leaf, Leather, Longhorn, Longicorn, Mall(et), Maul, May-bug, Meloid, Museum, Musk, Oakpruner, Oil, Overhang, Pill, Pinchbuck, Pine, Potato, Project, Protrude, Race(-bug), Rhinoceros, Rhynchophora, Roach, Rosechafer, Rove, Sacred, Scamper, Scarab(ee), Scavenger, Scolytus, Scurry, Sexton, Shard, Skelter, Sledge(-hammer), Snapping, Snout, Soldier, Spanish fly, Spider, Spring, Stag, Tenebrio, Tiger, Toktokkie, Tortoise, Tumble-bug, Tumble-dung, Turnip-flea, Typographer, Vedalia, VW, Water, Weevil, Whirligig, Wireworm, Woodborer, Wood-engraver

Beetle-crushers Cops

Befall Happen, Occur

Before(hand) A, Advance, Ante, Avant, By, Coram, Earlier, Early, Ere, Erst(while), > **FORMER**, Or, Pre, Previously, Prior, Pro, Sooner, Till, To, Until, Van, Zeroth

Before food Ac
Befriend Assist, Cotton, Fraternise, Support
Befuddle Bemuse, Inebriate, Stupefy
Beg(gar), Beggarly, Begging Abr(ah)am-man, Ask, Badgeman, Beseech,
 Besognio, Bey, Bezonian, Blighter, Blue-gown, Cadge, Calendar,
 Clapper-dudgeon, Crave, > ENTREAT, Exoration, Flagitate, Fleech, Gaberlunzie,
 Gangrel, Hallan-shaker, Implore, Impoverish, Irus, Jarkman, Lackall,
 Lazar(us), Lazzarone, Lumpenproletariat, Maund, Mendicant, Mump,
 Niggardly, Obtest, Palliard, Panhandle, Pauper, Penelophon, Penniless,
 > PLEAD, Pled, Pray, Prig, Prog, Ptochocracy, Rag, Randie, Randy, Ruffler,
 Ruin(ate), Sadhu, Schnorr(er), Screeve, Scrounge, Shool(e), Skelder, Skell,
 Solicit, Sue, Supplicate, Thig(ger), Toe-rag, Touch, Undo, Whipjack
Beget Gender
Beggar rule Ptochocracy
Begging bowl Clackdish, Clapdish
Begin(ner), Beginning Ab ovo, Alpha, Author, B, Babyhood, Black, Cause,
 Clapdash, Commence, Daw, Dawn, Deb, Debut, Embryo, Enter, Exordium,
 Fall-to, Fledgling, Genesis, Germ, Go, Greenhorn, Inaugural, Inception,
 Inchoate, Incipient, Incipit, Initial, Initiate, Intro, L, Lead, Learn, Learner,
 Logos, Nascent, Neophyte, > NOVICE, Oncome, Onset, Ope(n), Ord, > ORIGIN,
 Outbreak, Pose, Prelim(inary), Presidium, Primer, Rookie, Seed, Set, > START,
 Startup, Takeoff, Tenderfoot, Tiro, To-fall, Tyro, Tyro(ne), Yearn
Begone Aroint, Aroynt, Avaunt, Scram, Shoo, Vamo(o)se
Begonia Elephant's-ear(s)
Begorrah Bedad, Musha
Begrudge Envy, Resent
Beguile(r) Charm, Coax, Divert, Enchant, Ensnare, Flatter, Gull, Intrigue,
 Jack-a-lantern, Wile
Behalf Ex parte, For, Part, Sake
Behave, Behaviour, Behaving Acquired, Act, Conduct, Convenance, Decorum,
 Demean, Deportment, Do, Epimeletic, Etepimeletic, Ethics, Goings-on,
 Horme, > MANNER, Nature, Netiquette, Noblesse oblige, Obey, Praxeology,
 Quit, React, Response, Satisficing, Strong meat, Tribalism, Unreasonable
Behead Decapitate, Decollate, Guillotine
Behind(hand) Abaft, Aft(er), Ahind, Ahint, Apoop, Arear, Arere, Arrear, Arse,
 Astern, Beneath, Bottom, Bum, Buttocks, Croup, Derrière, Fud, Late, Overdue,
 Post, Prat, > REAR, Slow, Tushie
Behold(en) Affine, Ecce, Eye, Here's, Indebted, La, Lo, Look, Observe, See, View
Beige Greige, Tan
Being Cratur, Creature, Ens, Entia, Entity, Esse, Essence, Existence, Human,
 Man, Metaphysics, Mode, Nature, Omneity, Ontology, > PERSON, Saul, Soul,
 Subsistent, Substance, Supreme, Ubiety, Wight
Bejabers Arrah
Belch Boak, Boke, Brash, Burp, Emit, Eruct, Rift, Spew, Yex
Belcher Foulard, Handkerchief, Toby
Beldam(e) Crone, Hag, Harridan, Scold
Belfry Campanile, Tower
Belgian Flemish, Walloon
Belief, Believe, Believed, Believer, Believing Accredit, Anata, Ativism, Bigot,
 Buy, Christian, Conviction, Credence, Credit, Creed, Cult, Culture, Deem, Deist,
 Doctrine, Doxastic, Doxy, Dukkha, Faith, Formulism, Gnostic, Heterodoxy,
 Hold, Holist, Idea, Islam, Ism, Ludism, Manichaeism, Meme, Messianist,

Methink, Notion, > **OPINION**, Orthopraxy, Ovist, Pacifism, Pantheism, Persuasion, Physicism, Pluralism, Presumption, Religion, Reputed, Seeing, Shema, Solfidian, Superstition, Suspect, Tenet, Theist, Think, Threap, Threep, Transcendentalism, Trinitarian, Trow, Trust, Ubiquitarianism, Unitarian, Universalism, Wear, Wis(t)

Belittle Cheapen, Cry down, Decry, Depreciate, Derogate, Discredit, Disparage, Downgrade, Humble, Pooh-pooh, Slight

Bell(s) Angelus, Ben, Big Ben, Bob, Bow, Bronte, Cachecope, Canterbury, Carillon, Chime, Chinese pavilion, Crotal, Curfew, Daisy, Diving, Division, Gong, Grandsire, Jar, Low, Lutine, Minute, Mort, Pancake, Passing, Pavilion, Peal, Peter, Pinger, Pudding, Ring, Roar, Sacring, Sanctus, Shark, Sleigh, Tailor, Tantony, Tenor, Tent, Tintinnabulum, Tocsin, Toll, Tom, Triple, Tubular, Vair, Vaire, Verry

Bell-bird Arapunga, Campanero

Belle Beauty, Starr, Toast, Venus

Bell-founder Belleter

Bellicose, **Belligerent** Chippy, Combatant, Gung-ho, Hostile, Jingoist, Martial, Militant, Truculent, Warmonger

Bellow(s) Buller, Holla, Holler, Moo, Rant, Rave, Roar, Rout, Saul, Thunder, Troat, Tromp(e), Trumpet, Windbag

Bell-ringer, **Bell-ringing** Bob, Campanology, Changes, Clapper, Course, Grandsire, Handstroke, Hunting, Maximus, Quasimodo, Rope, Sally, Tocsin, Toller

Belly Abdomen, Alvine, Bag, Beer, Bunt, Calipee, Celiac, Coeliac, Kite, Kyte, Pod, > **STOMACH**, Swell, Tum(my), Venter, Wame, Weamb, Wem(b), Womb

Belong, **Belonging(s)** Apply, Appurtenant, Chattels, Effects, Incident, Inhere, Intrinsic, Paraphernalia, Pertain, > **PROPERTY**, Relate, Traps

Beloved Acushla, Alder-lief, Boyfriend, David, Dear, Doy, Esme, Inamorata, Joy, Lief, Pet, Popular, Precious

Below Beneath, Inf(erior), Infra, Nether, Sub, Under, Unneath

Belt(ed) Baldric(k), Band, Bandoleer, Bandolier, Baudric(k), Bible, Black, Cartridge, Chastity, Clitellum, Clobber, Commuter, Conveyor, Copper, Cotton, Crios, Demolition, Equator, Fan, Fold and thrust, Gird(le), Girt, Great, Green, Hip, Inertial, Judoka, Kuiper, Larrup, Life, Lonsdale, Mitre, Money, Muesli, Orion's, Orogenic, Polt, Pound, Radiation, Roller, Rust, Safety, Sam Browne, Sanitary, Sash, Seat, Speed, Stockbroker, Storm, Strap, Stratosphere, Sun, Surcingle, Suspender, Swipe, Sword, Taiga, Tear, Tore, Tract, Van Allen, Wanty, Webbing, Wing, Zodiac, Zone, Zoster

Belt up Sh

Belvedere Gazebo, Mirador

Bemoan > **LAMENT**, Mourn, Sigh, Wail

Bemuse Infatuate, Stonn(e), Stun, Stupefy, Throw

Ben Battle, Hur, Jonson, Mountain, Nevis, Spence

Bench Banc, Banker, Bink, Bleachers, Counter, Court, Cross, Exedra, Form, Front, King's, Knifeboard, Magistrates, Optical, Pew, Queen's, Rusbank, > **SEAT**, Settle, Siege, Stillage, Thoft, Thwart, Treasury, Trestle, Widow's

Benchmark Criteria, Yardstick

Bend(er), **Bending**, **Bends** Angle, Arc, Arch, Articular, Becket, Bight, Binge, Buck(le), Bust, Camber, Carrick, Chicane, Circumflect, Corner, Crank(le), Cringe, > **CROOK**, Curl, Curve, Diffraction, Dog-leg, Double up, Elbow, Engouled, Epinasty, Es(s), Expansion, Falcate, Fawn, Flex(ural), Flexion, Flexure, Fold, Geller, Geniculate, Genu, Genuflect, Grecian, Hairpin, Hinge,

Hook, Horseshoe, Hunch, Incline, Inflect, Kink, Knee(cap), Kneel, Knot, Kowtow, Meander, Mould, Nutant, Ox-bow, Plash, Plié, Ply, Recline, Reflex, Retorsion, Retortion, Retroflex, Riband, S, Scarp, Sheet, Souse, Spree, Spring, Stave, Stoop, Swan-neck, Twist, U, Ups(e)y, Uri, Wale, Warp, > YIELD, Z
▷ **Bendy** *may indicate* an anagram
Beneath Below, Sub, Under, Unworthy
Benedict(ine) Black Monk, Cluniac, Dom, Eggs, Maurist, Olivetan, OSB, Tironensian, Tyronensian
Benediction Blessing, God-speed
Benefactor Angel, Backer, Barmecide, Carnegie, Donor, Maecenas, > PATRON, Promoter
Beneficial, **Beneficiary**, **Benefit**, **Benefice** > AID, Alms, Avail, Behalf, Behoof, Behove, Bonus, Boon, Boot, Charity, Collature, Commendam, Commensal, Devisee, Disablement, Dole, Donee, Endorsee, Enure, FIS, Fringe, Housing, Incapacity, Incumbent, Inheritor, Injury, Inure, Invalidity, Living, Manna, Maternity, Ménage, Neckverse, Pay, Perk, Perquisite, Plus, Portioner, Postulate, Prebend, Profit, Sake, Salutary, Sanative, Sickness, Sinecure, Spin-off, Stipend, Supplementary, Symbiotic, Unemployment, Use, Usufruct
Benevolence, **Benevolent** Charitable, Clement, Humanitarian, Kind, Liberal, Pecksniffian, Philanthropy
Benighted Ignorant
Benign Affable, Altruistic, Gracious, Kindly, Trinal
Benin DY
Benito Duce, Mussolini
Benjamin Franklin
Bennett Alan, Phil
Bent Akimbo, Bowed, Brae, Coudé, Courb, Crooked, Curb, Determined, Dorsiflex, Falcate, Fiorin, Flair, Geniculate, Habit, Heath, Inclination, Ingenium, Intent, Leant, Peccant, Penchant, Ply, Reclinate, Redtop, Round-shouldered, Scoliotic, Talent, Taute
▷ **Bent** *may indicate* an anagram
Bent grass Fiorin, Redtop
Bentham Utilitarian
Benzine Kinone, Phene, Toluene, Toluol
Bequeath, **Bequest** Bestow, Chantr(e)y, Demise, Endow, Heirloom, > LEAVE, Legacy, Mortification, Pittance, Transmit, Will
Berate(d) Censure, Chide, Jaw, Reproach, Scold, Shent, Slate, Vilify
Berber Almoravide, Kabyle, Rif(i), Riff, Shluh, Tuareg
Bereave(d), **Bereavement** Deprive, Loss, Mourning, Orb, Sorrow, Strip, Widow
Beret Green
Berg Alban, Floe
Bermuda Shorts
Bernard Levin, Shaw
Bernini Baroque
Berry Allspice, Bacca, Cubeb, Fruit, Goosegog, Haw, Pepo, Peppercorn, Pigeon, Pimento, Pottage, Rhein, Rhine, Sal(l)al, Slae, Sloe, Sop, Tomatillo
Berserk Amok, Ape-shit, Baresark, Frenzy, Gungho, Rage
Berth Anchorage, Bunk, Cabin, Couchette, Dock, Moor, Seat, Space
Beryl Aquamarine, Emerald, Heliodor, Morganite, Silica
Beryllium Be
Beseech Beg, Crave, Entreat, Implore, Invoke, Obsecrate
Beset Amidst, Assail, Assiege, Badger, Bego, Environ, Harry, Perplex, Scabrid,

Siege

Beside(s) Adjacent, Alone, And, At, Au reste, Else, Forby(e), Further(more), Moreover, Next, On, Withal, Yet

Besiege(d) Beset, Best(ed), Blockade, Gherao, Girt, Invest, Obsess, Plague, Surround

▷ **Besiege** *may indicate* one word around another

Besmirch Smear, Soil, Sully

Besom Cow, Kow

Besot(ted) Dotard, Infatuate, Intoxicate, Lovesick, Stupefy

Bespangle Adorn, Gem

Bespeak, Bespoken Address, Bee, Beta, Engage, Hint

Best A1, Ace, Aristocrat, Beat, Choice, Cream, Creme, Damnedest, Deluxe, Elite, Eximious, Finest, Flagship, Flower, Foremost, Greatest, Ideal, Optima, Outdo, Outwit, Overcome, Peak, Peerless, Pick, Pièce de résistance, Pink, Plum, Purler, Quintessence, Ream, Super, The, The tops, Tiptop, Top, Topper, Transcend, Wale

Bestiality Zoophalia

Bestiary Physiologus

Best man Paranymph

Bestow Accord, Bequeath, Donate, > GIVE, Impart, Present

Bestride Cross

Bet(ting), Betting System A cheval, Ante, Back, Banco, Chance, Double, Each way, Flutter, Gaff, Gamble, Go, Hedge, Impone, Lay, Long shot, Martingale, Mise, Note, Pari-mutuel, Perfecta, Pip, Punt, Quadrella, Quinella, Ring, Risk, Roll up, Saver, Set, Spec, Sport, Spread, Stake, Superfecta, Tattersalls, Tatts, Totalisator, Totalise, Tote, Treble, Treble chance, Triella, Trifecta, > WAGER, Yankee

Betel Catechu, Pan, Pawn, Siri(h)

Betimes Anon, Early, Soon

Betise Solecism

Betray(al), Betrayer Abandon, Abuse, Belewe, Cornuto, Desert, Divulge, Dob, Double-cross, Gethsemane, Giveaway, Grass, Judas, Renegade, Renege, Rumble, Sell, Sellout, Shop, Sing, Sinon, Stab, Traditor, Traitor, Treachery, Treason, Turncoat

Betroth(ed), Betrothal Assure, Engage, Ensure, Espouse, Fiancé(e), Pledge, Subarr(h)ation

Better Abler, Amend, Apter, Bigger, Buck, Cap, Convalescent, Fairer, Finer, Gambler, Gamester, Imponent, Improve, Meliorate, Mend, Outdo, Outpoint, Outshine, Outsmart, Outstrip, Outwit, Preponderate, Punter, Race-goer, Reform, Superior, Surpass, Throw, Top, Turfite, Worst

Between Amid, Bet, Betwixt, Inter, Interjacent, Linking, Mesne, Twixt

Bevel Angle, Cant, Oblique, Slope, Splay

Beverage Ale, Cocoa, Coffee, Cordial, Cup, > DRINK, Hydromel, Nectar, Tea

Bevy Flock, Group, Herd, Host

Beware Cave, Fore, Heed, Mind, Mistrust, Pas op

Bewilder(ed), Bewilderment Amaze, At sea, Baffle, Buffalo, Confuse, Consternation, Daze, Flummox, Mate, Maze, Mystify, Perplex, Stun, Taivert, Will, Wull

Bewitch(ed), Bewitching Charm, Delight, Elf-shot, Enchant, Ensorcell, Glam(orous), Hex, Hoodoo, Jinx, Obeah, Obiah, Strike

Beyond Above, Ayont, Besides, Farther, Outwith, Over, Thule, Trans, Ulterior

Bias(ed) Angle, Aslant, Bent, Chauvinism, Discriminatory, Grid, Imbalance,

Loaded, One-sided, Partial, Parti pris, Partisan, Penchant, Predilection,
> **PREJUDICE**, Prepossess, Sexism, Skew, Slope, Tendency, Unjust, Warp

Bib, Bibulous Apron, Beery, Feeder, Pout, Tope, Tucker

Bibelot Objet d'art

Bible Adulterous, Alcoran, Alkoran, Antilegomena, Apocrypha, Authority, AV,
Avesta, Bamberg, Book, Breeches, Bug, Coverdale, Cranmer, Cromwell, Douai,
Douay, Family, Ferrara, Fool, Forgotten sins, Gemara, Geneva, Gideon, Good
book, Goose, Gospel, Gutenberg, Hagiographa, Hexapla, Holy, Idle, Isagogic,
Itala, Italic, King James (version), Leda, Matthew Parker, Mazarin(e), Midrash,
Missal, Murderer, New English, NT, Omasum, Ostrog, OT, Pentateuch,
Peshito, Peshitta, Peshitto, Polyglot, Psalter, Revised Version, RSV, RV,
Scriptures, Septuagint, Stomach, Talmud, Tanach, Tantra, Targum, Taverner,
Taverners, Thirty-six-line, Treacle, Tyndale, Unrighteous, Vinegar, Vulgate,
Whig, Wicked, Wife-hater, Wyclif(fe), Zurich

Biblical scholar Rechabite, USPG, Wycliffe

Bibliophagist, Bibliophile Bookworm

Bicarb Saleratus

Bicker Argue, Bowl, Brawl, Coggie, Dispute, Tiff, Wrangle

Bicycle, Bike(r) Bambi, Bone-shaker, Coaster, Dandy-horse, Dirt, Draisene,
Draisine, Exercise, Fixed-wheel, Hobby, Hobbyhorse, Mixte, Moped, Mount,
Mountain, Multicycle, Ordinary, Pedal, Penny-farthing, Quad, Raleigh®,
Recumbent, Roadster, Safety, Scooter, Spin, Tandem, Trail, Tree, Velocipede

Bid(der), Bidding system Acol, Apply, Call, Canape, Command, Contract,
Declare, Double, Forcing, Gone, Hostile, Invite, Jump, Misère, Nod, NT,
> **OFFER**, Order, Pass, Pre-empt, Proposal, Psychic, Puffer, Redouble, Shut-out,
Summon, Take-over, Tell, Tender, Vied, White bonnet

Biddy Gammer

Biennial Trieteric

Bier Hearse, Litter

Big Beamy, Bulky, Bumper, Burly, Cob, Enormous, Fat, Ginormous, Gross,
> **LARGE**, Loud, Mansize, Massive, Mighty, Obese, Skookum, Slockdoliger,
Slockdologer, Soc(k)dologer, Sogdolager, Sogdoliger, Stonker, Thumping, Tidy,
Vast, Whacker, Whopper

Bigamy, Bigamist, Bigamous Bluebeard, Diandrous

Bight Canterbury, Heligoland

Bigot(ed) Chauvinist, Dogmatist, Fanatic, Hide-bound, Intolerant,
Narrow-minded, Racialist, Sexist, Wowser, Zealot

Bigshot, Bigwig Cheese, Law lord, Nib, Nob, Oner, Oneyer, Oneyre, Swell, > **VIP**

Bijou Doll-like

▶ **Bike** *see* **BICYCLE**

Bikini Atoll, Tanga

Bile, Bilious(ness) Cholaemia, Choler, Gall, Icteric, Melancholy, Scholaemia,
Venom, Yellow

Bilge Leak, Pump, Rot, Waste

Bilingual Diglot

Bilk Default

Bill(y) Ac(c), Accommodation, Accompt, Account, Act, Ad, Addition, Barnacle,
Beak, Becke, Budd, Buffalo, Can, Carte, Chit(ty), Cody, Coo, Coronoid, Demand,
Dixy, Docket, Double, Due, Exactment, Fin, Finance, Foreign, Gates, Goat,
Hybrid, Invoice, Kaiser, > **LAW**, Lawin(g), Legislation, Liam, Liar, List, Measure,
Menu, Neb, Ness, Nib, > **NOTE**, Notice, Pork barrel, Portland, Poster, Private,
Programme, Public, Reckoning, Reform, Remanet, Rhamphotheca, Rostral,

Rostrum, Score, Short, Shot, Show, Sickle, Silly, Sparth(e), Sperthe, Spoon, Sticker, Tab, Tomium, Trade, Treasury, True, Twin, Victualling, Willy
Billet Berth, Casern, Cess, Chit, Coupon, Note, Quarter
Billet doux Capon, Valentine
Billiards, Billiards player, Billiards stroke Bar, Cannon-game, Cueist, Jenny, Long jenny, Massé, Pocket, Pool, Potter, Pyramids, Snooker, Whitechapel
Billion Gillion, Milliard, Tera
Bill of sale Bs
Billow Roil, Roller, Rule, Surge, Swell, Wave
Bin Bing, Box, Container, Crib, Dump, Hell, Receptacle, Sin, Snake-pit, Stall, Wagger-pagger, Wheelie, Wheely
Binary ASCII, Semidetached
Bind(er), Binding Adherent, Adhesive, Akedah, Alligate, Apprentice, Astrict, Astringent, Bale, Bandage, Bandeau, Bandster, Bias, Bibliopegist, Brail, Burst, Calf, Chain, Cinch, Circuit, Clamp, Colligate, Complain, Cord, Cummerbund, Deligation, Drag, Edge, Embale, Enchain, Engage, > **FASTEN**, Fetter, Galloon, Gird, Girdle, Grolier, Hay-wire, Hold, Incumbent, Indenture, Iron, Keckle, Lash(er), Law-calf, Leash, Ligament, Ligature, Mail, Marl, Morocco, Muslin, Obi, Obligate, Oblige, Oop, Organdie, Oup, Parpen, Perfect, Pinion, Raffia, Restrict, Ring, > **ROPE**, Roxburghe, Sheaf, Spiral, Strap, Stringent, Stygian, Swathe, Syndesis, Tape, Tether, Thirl, Thong, Three-quarter, Tie, Tree-calf, Truss, Twine, Valid, Whip, Withe, Yapp, Yerk, Yoke
Bindweed Bearbine, Convolvulus, With(y)wind
Bing Crosby, Go, Heap
Binge Bat, Beano, Bend(er), Blind, Carouse, > **DRINK**, Drinking-bout, Party, Riot, Soak, Souse, Splore, Spree, Toot, Tout
Bingo Beano, Housey-housey, Keno, Lotto, Tombola
Binocular(s) Glasses, OO, Stereoscope
Biochemical, Biochemist(ry) Ames, DNA, Proteomics
Biographer, Biography Boswell, CV, Hagiography, History, Life, Memoir, Plutarch, Potted, Prosopography, Suetonius, Vita
Biology, Biologist Cladistics, Mendel, Phenetics, Photodynamics, Somatology, Teratology
Bioscope Kinema
Birch Birk, Cane, Cow, Flog, Hazel, Kow, Larch, Reis, Rice, Rod, Silver, Swish, Twig, Weeping, Whip, White, Withe
Bird(s) Al(l)erion, Aves, Avian, Bertram, Brood, Damsel, Doll, Early, Flier, Fowl, Gal, > **GIRL**, Grip, Hen, Jail, Left, Ornis, Pecker, Pen, Poultry, Quod, Raptor, Roaster, Sis, Skirt, Time

BIRDS

2 letters:	Jay	Ree	Cobb
Ka	Kae	Roc	Coly
	Kea	Ruc	Coot
3 letters:	Maw	Tit	Crax
Ani	Mew	Tui	Crow
Auk	Moa		Dodo
Boo	Nun	4 letters:	Dove
Cob	Owl	Barb	> DUCK
Emu	Pea	Chat	Emeu
Fum	Pie	Cirl	Erne

- Eyas
- Fung
- Gled
- Gnow
- Guan
- Guga
- Gull
- Hawk
- Hern
- Huia
- Huma
- Ibis
- Iynx
- Jynx
- Kagu
- Kaka
- Kite
- Kiwi
- Knot
- Kora
- Lark
- Loom
- Loon
- Lory
- Mina
- Monk
- Myna
- Nene
- Otis
- Pavo
- Pawn
- Pern
- Piet
- Pink
- Pown
- Pyot
- Rail
- Rhea
- Roch
- Rook
- Ruff
- Ruru
- Rype
- Shag
- Smee
- Sora
- Swan
- Taha
- Teal
- Tern
- Tick
- Tody

Tuli
Weka
Wren
Xema
Yale
Yite

5 letters:
Agami
Ardea
Ariel
Bennu
Booby
Bosun
Capon
Colin
Colly
Crake
Crane
Diver
Egret
Finch
Fleet
Galah
Glede
Goose
Goura
Grebe
Heron
Hobby
Homer
Isaac
Junco
Kight
Liver
Lowan
Macaw
Madge
Manch
Mavis
Merle
Mimus
Monal
Murre
Mynah
Nandu
Nelly
Noddy
Ousel
Ox-eye
Peggy
Pekan

Pewit
Picus
Pilot
Piper
Pipit
Pitta
Poaka
Poker
Potoo
Prion
Quail
Quest
Quist
Raven
Reeve
Rifle
Robin
Rotch
Ryper
Saker
Scape
Scart
Scaup
Scops
Scray
Scrub
Serin
Shama
Sitta
Skart
Snipe
Solan
Soree
Spink
Sprug
Squab
Stare
Stilt
Stint
Stork
Swift
Sylph
Terek
Tewit
Topaz
Twite
Umber
Umbre
Urubu
Veery
Vireo
Wader

Whaup
Widow
Wonga
Yaffa

6 letters:
Aquila
Avocet
Avoset
Bantam
Barbet
Bishop
Bittor
Bittur
Bonxie
Boubou
Brolga
Bulbul
Canary
Chough
Chukar
Condor
Corbie
Coucal
Cuckoo
Curlew
Cushat
Darter
Dikkop
Dipper
Drongo
Duiker
Dunlin
Duyker
Elanet
Evejar
Falcon
Fulmar
Gambet
Gander
Gannet
Garuda
Gentle
Gentoo
Go-away
Godwit
Gooney
Goslet
Grakle
Hagden
Hagdon
Haglet

- Hermit
- Hoopoe
- Houdan
- Jabiru
- Jacana
- Jaegar
- Kakapo
- Kotuku
- Lanner
- Leipoa
- Linnet
- Lintie
- Loerie
- Loriot
- Lourie
- Lungie
- Magpie
- Martin
- Menura
- Merlin
- Merops
- Missel
- Mistle
- Monaul
- Mopoke
- Mossie
- Motmot
- Musket
- Mutton
- Nandoo
- Oriole
- Oscine
- Osprey
- Oxbird
- Parrot
- Parson
- Pavone
- Peahen
- Peewee
- Peewit
- Pernis
- Petrel
- Phoebe
- Pigeon
- Plover
- Pouter
- Progne
- Puffin
- Pukeko
- Pullet
- Queest
- Quelea

Quoist
Redcap
Reeler
Roller
Scamel
Scarth
Scaury
Scraye
Sea-cob
Sea-mew
Seapie
Shrike
Simara
Simorg
Simurg
Siskin
Skarth
Smeath
Soland
Sorage
Strich
Sultan
Sylvia
Tailor
Takahe
Tarcel
Tassel
Tewhit
Thrush
Tom-tit
Toucan
Towhee
Trogon
Turaco
Turbit
Tyrant
Tystie
Verdin
Walker
Waxeye
Whidah
Whydah
Willet
Woosel
Yaffle
Ynambu
Yucker
Zoozoo

7 letters:
Anhinga
Antbird

Apteryx
Babbler
Bécasse
Bee-kite
Bittern
Bittour
Bluecap
Blue-eye
Blue jay
Bluetit
Boobook
Bullbat
Bunting
Buphaga
Bush-tit
Bustard
Buzzard
Cacique
Cariama
Cheeper
Chewink
Coal-tit
Cole-tit
Colibri
Corella
Cotinga
Courlan
Courser
Cow-bird
Creeper
Crombec
Cropper
Diamond
Dinorus
Dottrel
Dovekie
Dunnock
Emu-wren
Fantail
Fern-owl
Figbird
Finfoot
Flicker
Frigate
Gobbler
Goburra
Gorcrow
Goshawk
Grackle
Grallae
Hacklet
Hadedah

Hagbolt
Hagdown
Halcyon
Harrier
Hemipod
Hoatzin
Humming
Ice-bird
Jacamar
Kamichi
Kestrel
Killdee
Kinglet
Lapwing
Leghorn
Limpkin
Manakin
Maribou
Martlet
Mesites
Minivet
Oilbird
Ortolan
Oscires
Ostrich
Pandion
Peacock
Pelican
Penguin
Phoenix
Pickmaw
Piculet
Pinnock
Pintado
Pintail
Pochard
Pockard
Poe-bird
Poy-bird
Quetzal
Rainbow
Rasores
Redpoll
Redwing
Regulus
Rooster
Rosella
Rotchie
Ruddock
Sakeret
Sawbill
Scooper

Scourie
Sea-mell
Simurgh
Sirgang
Sitella
Skimmer
Skylark
Snow-cap
Spadger
Sparrow
Squacco
Staniel
Stinker
Sturnus
Sunbird
Swallow
Tanager
Tanagra
Tarrock
Tattler
Teacher
Teuchat
Tiercel
Tinamou
Titanis
Titlark
Titling
Tokahea
Totanus
Touraco
Tumbler
Tweeter
Vulture
Vulturn
Wagtail
Warbler
Waxbill
Waxwing
Whooper
Widgeon
Wimbrel
Witwall
Woosell
Wren-tit
Wrybill
Wryneck
Yang-win

8 letters:
Aasvogel
Accentor
Adjutant

Aigrette
Alcatras
Altrices
Amadavat
Aquiline
Arapunga
Avadavat
Barnacle
Bellbird
Blackcap
Bluebird
Blue-wing
Boatbill
Boattail
Bobolink
Bob-white
Buln-buln
Caracara
Cardinal
Cargoose
Cheewink
Chirn-owl
Cockatoo
Cockerel
Coquette
Curassow
Dabchick
Didapper
Dip-chick
Dobchick
Dotterel
Estridge
Fauvette
Fernbird
Fish-hawk
Flamingo
Gambetta
Gang-gang
Garefowl
Garganey
Greenlet
Grosbeak
Guacharo
Hackbolt
Hangbird
Hangnest
Hawfinch
Hazelhen
Hemipode
Hernshaw
Hoactzin
Hornbill

Killdeer
Kingbird
Kiskadee
Landrail
Lanneret
Laverock
Longspur
Lorikeet
Lyrebird
Magotpie
Megapode
Mire-drum
Morepork
Murrelet
Nightjar
Notornis
Nuthatch
Ovenbird
Oxpecker
Paradise
Parakeet
Peetweet
Percolin
Petchary
Pheasant
Philomel
Podargus
Poorwill
Prunella
Puffbird
Quarrian
Quarrion
Rainbird
Rallidae
Redshank
Redstart
Reedling
Reed-wren
Rice-bird
Rifleman
Ringtail
Riroriro
Sandpeep
Scolopar
Screamer
Shake-bag
Shoebill
Silktail
Skua-gull
Snowbird
Stanniel
Struthio

Surfbird
Swiftlet
Tantalus
Tapacolo
Tapaculo
Teru-tero
Thrasher
Thresher
Throstle
Ticklace
Titmouse
Tom-noddy
Toucanet
Tragopan
Trembler
Troopial
Troupial
Tubenose
Umbrella
Umbrette
Water-hen
Wheatear
Whimbrel
Whinchat
Whipbird
Whitecap
White-eye
Wildfowl
Wirebird
Woodchat
Woodcock
Woodlark
Woodwale
Yoldring

9 letters:
Accipiter
Aepyornis
Albatross
Aylesbury
Baldicoot
Baltimore
Beccaccia
Beccafico
Bergander
Blackbird
Blackhead
Blackpoll
Bower-bird
Brambling
Broadbill
Bullfinch

- Campanero
- Cassowary
- Chaffinch
- Chatterer
- Chickadee
- Coachwhip
- Cockatiel
- Cormorant
- Corncrake
- Cross-bill
- Currawong
- Dowitcher
- Estreldid
- Fieldfare
- Fig-pecker
- Fire-crest
- Fledgling
- Francolin
- Friarbird
- Frogmouth
- Gallinule
- Gerfalcon
- Gier-eagle
- Goldcrest
- Goldfinch
- Goosander
- Grassquit
- Grenadier
- Guillemot
- Happy Jack
- Helldiver
- Heronshaw
- Hornywink
- Icteridae
- Impundulu
- Jack-snipe
- Kittiwake
- Lintwhite
- Mallemuck
- Merganser
- Mistletoe
- Mollymawk
- Mousebird
- Night-hawk
- Nutjobber
- Olive-back
- Ossifraga
- Ossifrage
- Pardalote
- Peaseweep
- Peregrine
- Phalarope

Pictarnie
Porphyrio
Ptarmigan
Razorbill
Rosy-finch
Salangane
Sandpiper
Sapsucker
Satinbird
Scansores
Sea-turtle
Secretary
Seedeater
Sheldrake
Shoveller
Skunk-bird
Solitaire
Spoonbill
Standgale
Stonechat
Stormbird
Storm-cock
Sugarbird
Swart-back
Sword-bill
Talegalla
Thickhead
Thick-knee
Thornbill
Trochilus
Trumpeter
Turnstone
Volucrine
Water-rail
Wind-hover
Woodspite
Xanthoura

10 letters:
Aberdevine
Bearded tit
Bluebreast
Bluethroat
Brain-fever
Bubbly-jock
Budgerigar
Butter-bump
Chiff-chaff
Demoiselle
Dickcissel
Didunculus
Dive-dapper

Dollarbird
Ember-goose
Eyas-musket
Fallow-chat
Fly-catcher
Fringillid
Goatsucker
Gobemouche
Grassfinch
Greenfinch
Greenshank
Hen-harrier
Honey-eater
Honey guide
Kingfisher
Kookaburra
Locust-bird
Mallee fowl
Marsh-robin
Meadowlark
Night-churr
Noisy miner
Nutcracker
Peckerwood
Pettichaps
Pettychaps
Pratincole
Quaker-bird
Racket-tail
Rafter-bird
Regent-bird
Rhampastos
Rhinoceros
Roadrunner
Ruby-throat
Saddleback
Saddlebill
Sanderling
Sandgrouse
Shearwater
Sheathbill
Sicklebill
Silverbill
Spatchcock
Stone-snipe
Tanagridae
Tropicbird
Wattlebird
Weaver bird
Whisky-jack
Whisky-john
Wonga-wonga

Woodpecker
Woodpigeon
Yaffingale
Yellowbird
Yellowhead
Yellowlegs
Yellowyite

11 letters:
Apostlebird
Bokmakierie
Bristlebird
Butcherbird
Fallow-finch
Fringilline
Gnatcatcher
Grallatores
Happy-family
Honey-sucker
Humming-bird
Ichthyornis
Java sparrow
Leatherhead
Mockingbird
Moss-bluiter
Moss-cheeper
Nightingale
Pied wagtail
Plantcutter
Pyrrhuloxia
Reed-warbler
Scissortail
Snowbunting
Sparrow-hawk
Stilt-plover
Stone-curlew
Storm petrel
Stymphalian
Thunderbird
Tree-creeper
Wall creeper
Whitethroat
Woodcreeper
Woodswallow
Woodwarbler
Yellow-ammer

12 letters:
Bronze-pigeon
Drongo-cuckoo
Drongo-shrike
Flowerpecker

- Hedge-warbler
- Honey creeper
- Peppershrike
- Ring-dotterel
- Sage-thrasher
- Sedge-warbler
- Serpent-eater
- Standard-wing
- Stonechatter

Stormy petrel
Throstle-cock
Whippoorwill
Willy wagtail
Yellow-hammer
Yellow-yowley

13 letters:
Archaeopteryx

Cetti's warbler
Cock-of-the-rock
Oyster-catcher
Pipiwharauroa
Plantain-eater
Willow-wagtail
Willow warbler
Wilson's petrel

14 letters:
Manx shearwater
Tawny frogmouth

16 letters:
Tyrant flycatcher

17 letters:
Pectoral sandpiper

▷ **Bird** *may indicate* a prison sentence
Bird-catcher Avicularia, Fowler, Papageno
Bird-like Hirundine, Sturnine
Bird's nest(ing) Caliology, Monotropa, Soup
Bird-watcher Augur, Twitcher
Birkenhead F.E.Smith
Birmingham Brum(magem)
Birth Burden, Congenital, Delivery, Drop, Extraction, Genesis, Happy event, Jataka, Lineage, Nativity, Natural, Origin, Parage, Parity, Virgin
Birthday Anniversary, Genethliac
Birthmark Blemish, Mole, Mother-spot, Naevus, Stigmata, Strawberry
Birthright Heritage, Mess, Patrimony
Birthwort Aristolochia
Biscuit Abernethy, Bath-oliver, Bourbon, Brandysnap, Butterbake, Captain's, Charcoal, Cookie, Cracker, Cracknel, Crispbread, Dandyfunk, Digestive, Dog, Dunderfunk, Fairing, Flapjack, Florentine, Fortune cookies, Four-by-two, Garibaldi, Ginger nut, Gingersnap, Hardtack, Kiss, Langue de chat, Lebkuchen, Macaroon, Marie, Mattress, Matza(h), Matzo(h), Nut, Oatcake, Oliver, Osborne, Parkin, Perkin, Petit four, Petticoat tails, Pig's ear, Pilot, Poppadom, Poppadum, Pretzel, Ratafia, Rusk, Rye roll, Shortbread, Soda, Sweetmeal, Tack, Tararua, Tea, Wafer, Water, Wine, Zwieback
Bisexual AC/DC, Freemartin, Switch-hitter
Bishop Aaronic, Abba, Aidan, Ambrose, Bench, Berkeley, Bp, Cambrensis, Cantuar, Chad, Coverdale, Diocesan, Dunelm, Ely, Eparch, Episcopate, Eusebian, Exon, Golias, Hatto, Henson, Latimer, Lord, Magpie, Metropolitan, Norvic, Odo, Ordainer, Patriarch, Peter, Piece, Polycarp, Pontiff, Prelate, Priest, Primate, Primus, Proudie, RR, Sleeve, Suffragan, Titular, Tulchan, Weaver, Weed
Bismarck Otto
Bismuth Bi
Bison Bonas(s)us, Buffalo, Ox, Wisent
Bit Baud, Cantle(t), Centre, Chad, Cheesecake, Chip, Crumb, Curb, Curn, Drib, Excerpt, Flibbert, Fraction, Gag, Haet, Hate, Ion, Jaw, Jot, Mite, Modicum, Morsel, Mote, Mu, Nit, Ort, Ounce, Pelham, Peni, Penny, > PIECE, Port, Rap, Rare, Ratherish, Scintilla, Scrap, Section, Shaving, Shiver, Shred, Smidgen, Snaffle, Snatch, Snippet, Some, Soupcon, Spale, Speck, Splinter, Spot, Spudding, Suspicion, Tad, Tait, Tate, Threepenny, Trace, Unce, Whit
Bite(r), Biting, Bitten Caustic, Chelicera, Chew, Eat, Engouled, Erose, Etch, Gnash, Gnat, Hickey, Hickie, Incisor, Knap, Masticate, Midge, Molar, Mordacious, Mordant, Morsel, Morsure, Nibble, Nip(py), Occlude, Peck, Pium, Rabid, Remorse, Sarcastic, Sharp, Shrewd, Snap, Sound, Spammie, Tart
Bitter(ness) Absinth, Acerb, Acid, Acrid, Acrimonious, Ale, Aloe, Angostura,

Bile, Cassareep, Caustic, Eager, Ers, Fell, Gall, Keen, Marah, Maror, Myrrh, Pique, Rancorous, Rankle, Resentful, Sarcastic, Sardonic, Snell, Sore, Spleen, Tart(aric), Venom, Verjuice, Virulent, Vitriolic, Wersh, Wormwood

Bittern Boomer, Bull-of the-bog, Butterbump, Heron, Sedge, Siege

Bittersweet Dulcamara

Bitumen Albertite, Asphalt, Blacktop, Elaterite, Gilsonite®, Maltha, Mineral tar, Pissasphalt, Pitch, Tar, Uintaite

Bivalve Clam, Cockle, Lamellibranch, Mollusc, Muscle, Mussel, Oyster, Pelecypod, Piddock, Razorshell, Scallop, Whelk

Bivouac Camp

Bizarre Antic, Curious, Eccentric, Exotic, Fantastic, Far-out, Freaky, Gonzo, Grotesque, Odd, Off-the-wall, Outlandish, Outré, Pythonesque, Queer, Strange, Surreal, Weird

▷ **Bizarre** *may indicate* an anagram

Blab Babble, Gossip, Prate, Squeal

Black(en), **Blackness**, **Black-out** Amadoda, Atramental, B, BB, Bess, Blae, Boong, Cape Coloured, Carbon, Char, Charcoal, Cilla, Coloured, Coon, Cypress, Darkie, Darky, Death, Denigrate, Dinge, Dwale, Ebon(y), Eclipse, Ethiop, Fuzzy-wuzzy, Geechee, Gladwellise, Graphite, Heben, Hole, Ink(y), Ivory, Japan, Jeat, Jet, Jim Crow, Kohl, Lepidomelane, Malign, Market, Melanic, Melano, Moke, Moor, Muntu, Myall, Negritude, Negro, Niello, Niger, Nigrescent, Nigritude, Obliterate, Obscure, Outage, Oxford, Piceous, Pitch, Platinum, Pongo, Prince, Pudding, Puke, Quashee, Quashie, Raven, Sable, Sambo, Scab, School, Sericon, Sheep, Slae, Sloe, Snowball, Sodium, Solvent, Sombre, Soot, Sooterkin, Spode, Spook, Stygian, Swart(y), Swarth(y), Tar, Uncle Tom, Weeds

Black art Necromancy, Nigromancy

Blackball Ban, Exclude, Pip, Reject

Blackberry Acini, Bramble, Mooch, Mouch

Blackbird Crow, Jackdaw, Ousel, Raven, Woosel

Blackcurrant Quinsy-berry

Black eye(d) Half-mourning, Mouse, Shiner, Susan

Blackguard Leg, Nithing, Raff, Revile, Rotter, Scoundrel, Sweep

Blackhead Comedo

Black hole Collapsar

Blackjack Billie, Billy, Cosh, Flag, Sphalerite, Tankard, Truncheon, Vingt(-et)-un

Blackleg Fink, Scab, Snob

Black-letter Gothic

Black magic Goety

Blackmail(er) Bleed, Chantage, Chout, Exact, Extort, Ransom, Shakedown, Strike, Vampire

Blackout ARP, Eclipse, Faint, Swoon

Black Sea Pontic

Black sheep Neer-do-well, Reprobate

Blacksmith Brontes, Burn-the-wind, Farrier, Forger, Harmonious, Shoer, Vulcan

Blackthorn Sloe

Bladder Air, Balloon, Blister, Cholecyst, Cyst, Gall, Hydatid, Isinglass, Sac, Sound, Swim, Urinary, Utricle, Varec(h), Vesica, Vesicle

Blade Acrospire, Bilbo, Brand, Brown Bill, Cleaver, Co(u)lter, Cutlass, Dandy, Espada, Faible, Foible, Forte, Gleave, Gouge, Guillotine, Hydrofoil, Knife, Lance, Leaf, Man, Mouldboard, Oar, Omoplate, Palmetto, Peel, Propellor,

Rachilla, Rapier, Razor, Rip, Rotor, Scimitar, Scull, Scythe, Skate, Spade-, Spatula, Spatule, Spear, Spoon, Stiletto, Stock, Strigil, > **SWORD**, Symitar, Toledo, Turbine, Vane, Vorpal, Web

Blair Eric, Tony

Blame(worthy) Accuse, Censure, Condemn, Confound, Decry, Dispraise, Fault, Guilt, Inculpate, Odium, Rap, Reprehensible, Reproach, Reprove, Stick, Thank, Twit, Wight, Wite, Wyte

Blameless Innocent, Irreproachable, Unimpeachable

Blanch Bleach, Etiolate, Scaud, Whiten

Blancmange Carrageen, Flummery, Mould, Shape, Timbale

Bland Anodyne, Glop, Mild, Pigling, Sleek, Smooth, Spammy, Suave, Tame, Unctuous

Blandish(ment) Agremens, Agrement, Cajole, > **COAX**, Flatter, Treacle, Wheedle

Blank Cartridge, Empty, Erase, Flan, Lacuna, Mistigris, Planchet, Shot, Space, Tabula rasa, > **VACANT**

Blanket Afghan, Bluey, Chilkat, Counterpane, Cover, Electric, Fire, General, Hudson's Bay, Kaross, Mackinaw, Manta, Obscure, Overall, Poncho, Quilt, Rug, Saddle, Sarape, Security, Serape, Shabrack, Smog, Space, Stroud, Wagga, Wet, Whittle

Blare Horn, Trumpet

Blarney Cajolery, Flattery, Nonsense, Sawder, Taffy

Blasé Worldly

Blaspheme, Blasphemous Abuse, > **CURSE**, Defame, Profanity, Revile

Blast(ed) Blight, Blore, Blow, Bombard, Dang, Darn, Dee, Drat, Dynamite, Explode, Fanfare, Flaming, Flurry, Fo(e)hn, Gale, Gust, Noser, Oath, Parp, Pryse, Rats, Scarth, Scath(e), Sere, Shot, Sideration, Skarth, Tantara, Toot, Tromp(e), Trump(et), Volley

Blatant Flagrant, Hard-core, Noticeable, Open, Strident, Vulgar

Blather Baloney, Gabble

Blaze(r) Beacon, Bonfire, Burn, Cannel, Conflagration, Firestorm, > **FLAME**, Flare, Glare, Jacket, Low(e), Lunt, Palatinate, Race, Ratch, Star, Sun, Tead(e)

Bleach Agene, Blanch, Chemic, Chloride, Decolorate, Etiolate, Janola®, Keir, Kier, Peroxide, Whiten, Whitster

Bleak Ablet, Bare, Blay, Bley, Cheerless, Dour, Dreary, Dreich, Raw, Wintry

Bleary Blurred, Smudged

Bleat Baa, Blat, Bluster, Maa

Bleed(er), Bleeding Cup, Ecchymosis, Epistaxis, Extravasate, Fleam, Haemorrhage, Leech, Menorrhagia, Menorrh(o)ea, Metrorrhagia, Milk, Purpura, Root-pressure

Bleep Earcon, Pager

Blefuscudian Big-endian, Little-endian

Blemish Birthmark, Blot, Blotch, Blur, Botch, Defect, Flaw, Mackle, Mark, Mote, Naevus, Scar, Smirch, Spot, Stain, Sully, Taint, Tash, Vice, Wart, Wen

Blench Flinch, Recoil, Wince

Blend(ing) Amalgam, Coalesce, Commix, Contemper, Contrapuntal, Counterpoint, Electrum, Fuse, Go, Harmonize, Hydrate, Interfuse, Interlace, Liquidise, Meld, Melt, > **MERGE**, Mingle, Mix, Osmose, Portmanteau, Scumble, Sfumato, Synalepha

▷ **Blend** *may indicate* an anagram

Blenny Eel-pout, Gunnel, Shanny

Bless(ing), Blessed(ness) Amen, Approval, Asset, Beatitude, Benedicite, Benediction, Benison, Benitier, Bensh, Bismillah, Boon, Brachah, Brocho,

Consecrate, Cup, Damosel, Darshan, Elysium, Ethereal, Felicity, Gesundheit, Godsend, Grace, Gwyneth, Holy (dam), Kiddush, Luck, Macarise, Mercy, Mixed, Sain, Saint, Sanctify, Sanctity, Sheva Brachoth, Sheva Brochos, Toronto, Urbi et orbi, Xenium

Bless me Lawk(s)

Blight Afflict, Ague, Bespot, Blast, Destroy, Eyesore, Fire, Planning, Potato, Rot, > RUIN, Rust, Shadow, Viticide, Wither

Blighter Cuss, Perisher, Varment, Varmint

Blimey Coo, Cor, Crimini, O'Riley, Strewth

Blimp Airship, Colonel

Blind(ness), Blind spot Amaurosis, Amblyopia, Artifice, Austrian, Beesome, Bisson, Blend, Blotto, Carousal, Cecity, Chi(c)k, Cog, Concealed, Dazzle, Eyeless, Feint, Festoon, Gravel, Hemeralopia, Hood, Jalousie, Legless, Meropia, Mole, Night, Nyctalopia, Onchocerciasis, Persian, Persiennes, Pew, Prestriction, Rash, Roller, Roman, Scotoma, Seel, Shade, Shutter, Snow, Stimie, Stimy, Stymie, Sun, Teichopsia, Typhlology, Venetian, Window, Word, Yblent

Blindfish Amblyopsis

Blindfold Bandage, Hoodwink, Muffle, Seal, Wimple

Blindworm Anguis

Blink(er), Blinkered, Blinking Bat, Blepharism, Bluff, Broken, Eye-flap, Flash, Haw, Idiot, Insular, Nictate, Owl-eyed, Owly, Twink, Wapper, Wink

Bliss(ful) Beatitude, Bouyan, Composer, Delight, > ECSTASY, Eden, Happy, Idyll, Ignorance, Married, Millenium, Nirvana, Paradise, Rapture, Sion, Tir-na-nog, Valhalla, Walhalla, Wedded

Blister(ed), Blistering Blab, Blain, Bleb, Bubble, Bullate, Cold sore, Epispastic, Herpes, Pemphigus, Phlyctena, Scorching, Tetter, Vesicant, Vesicle, Visicate, Water

Blitz Attack, Bombard, Onslaught, Raid

Blizzard Buran, Gale, Snowstorm, Whiteout

Bloat(er) Buckling, Puff, Strout, Swell, Tumefy

Blob Bead, Bioblast, Drop, Globule, O, Spot, Tear

Bloc Alliance, Cabal, Cartel, Party

Block(er), Blockage, Blocked, Blocking Altar, Anvil, Ashlar, Atresia, > BAR, Barricade, Barrier, Brake, Breeze, Brick, Briquette, Building, Bung, Bunt, Catasta, Cavity, Chinese, Choke, Chunk, Clint, Clog, Clot, Cloy, Compass, Congest, Constipated, Cut-off, Cyclopean, Cylinder, > DAM, Dead-eye, Debar, Dentel, Dentil, Die, Dit, Domino, Electrotint, Embolism, Emphractic, Encompass, Euphroe, Fipple, Hack-log, High-rise, Hunk, Ice, Ileus, Impasse, Impede, Impost, Ingot, Insula, Interclude, Interrupt, Investment, Jam, Line, Lingot, Lodgment, Log-jam, Lump, Mental, Ministroke, Mitre, Mutule, Nerve, Nifedipine, Nog, Notepad, Oasis®, Obstacle, > OBSTRUCT, Occlude, Office, Opossum, Oppilate, Pad, Page, Parry, Perched, Pile-cap, Pile-up, Pillow, Plinth, Plummer, Power, Pre-empt, Prevent, Process, Psychological, Quad, Ram, Saddle, Scotch, Sett, Siege, Snatch, Stalemate, Stap, Starting, Stenosis, Stimie, Stimy, Stone, Stonewall, Stop, Stumbling, Stymie, Swage, Tamp, Thwart, Tower, Tranche, Trig, Triglyph, Uphroe, Upping-stock, Wood(cut), Wrest, Writer's, Zinco, Zugzwang

Blockbuster Epic

Blockhead Jolterhead, Mome, Nitwit, Noodle, Pig sconce, Stupid

Bloke Beggar, Chap, Cove, Fellow, Gent, Man, Oik

Blond(e) Ash, Cendré, Fair, Flaxen, Goldilocks, Peroxide, Platinised, Platinum, Strawberry, Tallent, Tow-haired, Towhead

Blood(y) Ancestry, Bad, Bally, Blue, Blut, Claret, Clot, Cruor, Cup, Ecchymosis, Ensanguine, Epigons, Factor, First, Full, > GORE, Haemal, Haemorrhage, Ichor, Internecine, Introduce, Kin, Kinship, Knut, Menses, New, Nut, Opsonin, Parentage, Persue, Pigeon's, Plasma, Platelet, Plurry, Properdin, Pup, Race, Rare, Red, Rh negative, Rh positive, Ruby, Sang, Serum, Show, Stroma, Toff, Welter, Whole, Young

Blood disease, Blood-poisoning Hypinosis, Isch(a)emia, Leukemia, Lipaemia, Purpura, Pyaemia, Sapraemia, Septicemia, Spanaemia, Thalassemia, Thrombocytopenia, Toxaemia, Uraemia

Bloodhound Lime, Lyam, Sleuth, Spartan

Bloodless Anaemic, Isch(a)emic, Wan, White

Blood-letter Leech, Phlebotomist, Sangrado

▸ **Blood-poisoning** *see* BLOOD DISEASE

Blood-pressure Hypertension, Hypotension

Bloodshot Red-eyed

Blood-sport Hunting, Shooting, Venery

Blood-sucker Asp, Dracula, Flea, Gnat, Ked, Leech, Louse, Mosquito, Parasite, Reduviid, Sponger, Tick, Vampire(-bat)

Bloom(er), Blooming Anthesis, Bally, Blossom, Blow, Blush, Boner, Dew, Effloresce, Error, Film, Florescent, Flowery, Flush, Gaffe, Glaucous, Heyday, Knickers, Loaf, Miscalculation, Out, Pruina, Rationals, Reh, Remontant, Rosy, Underwear

▷ **Bloomer** *may indicate* a flower

Blossom Blow, Burgeon, Festoon, Flourish, Flower, May, Orange, Pip

Blot Atomy, Blob, Cartel, Delete, Disgrace, Dry, Eyesore, Obscure, Smear, Smudge, Southern, Splodge, Splotch

Blotch(y) Blemish, Giraffe, Monk, Mottle(d), Spot, Stain

Blotto Legless

Blouse Choli, Garibaldi, Gimp, Guimpe, Kerbaya, Middy, Pneumonia, Sailor, Shirtwaist, Smock, Tunic, Windjammer

Blow(er) Appel, Bang, Bash, Bat, Bellows, Biff, Billow, Blip, Bloom, Brag, Breeze, Buckhorse, Buffet, Burst, Calamity, Clap, Clat, Claut, Clip, Clout, Clump, Conk, Coup, Cuff, Dad, Daud, Dev(v)el, Dinnyhayser, Dint, Douse, Dowse, Estramacon, Etesian, Facer, Fan, Fillip, Gale, Grampus, Gust, Hammer, Haymaker, Hit, Hook, Ictus, Impact, Insufflate, Karate, Kibosh, Knuckle sandwich, KO, Lame, Lander, Lick, Lounder, Muff, Neck-herring, Northerly, Noser, Oner, One-two, Paddywhack, Paik, Pash, Phone, Piledriver, Plague, Plug, Plump(er), Polt, Pow, Puff, Punch, Purler, Rats, Rattler, Rib-roaster, Roundhouse, Sas(s)arara, Scat, Settler, Short, Sideswipe, Side-winder, Sis(s)erary, Skiff, Skite, Skyte, Slat, Slog, Slug, Snot, Sock, Sockdolager, Sockdologer, Southwester, Spanking, Spat, Spout, Squall, Squander, Stripe, Stroke, Strooke, Stunning, Sufflate, Supercharger, Swash, Swat, Swinger, Telephone, Thump, Thwack, Tingler, Tootle, Trump(et), Tuck, Undercut, Upper-cut, Waft, Wallop, Wap, Waste, Welt, Whammy, Whample, Whang, Whap, Wheeze, Wherret, Whiffle, Whirret, > WIND, Winder, Wipe, Wuther

Blown-up Elated, Enlarged, Exploded

Blow-out Binge, Bloat, Exhale, Feast, Feed, Flat, Lava, Nosh-up, Snuff, Spiracle, > SPREAD

Blowpipe Hod, Peashooter, Sarbacane, Sumpit(an)

Blub(ber) Cry, Fat, Snotter, Sob, Speck, > WEEP, Whimper

Bludge Sinecure

Bludgeon Bully, Club, Cosh, Cudgel, Sap

Blue(s) Abattu, Accablé, Adult, Anil, Aquamarine, Azure, Beard, Berlin, Bice, Bleuâtre, Blow, Bottle, Butterfly, C, Caesious, Cafard, Cambridge, Cantab, Celeste, Cerulean, Clair de lune, Cobalt, Coomassia, Copenhagen, Cornflower, Coventry, Cyan, Danish, Danube, Dejected, Dirty, Disconsolate, Doldrums, > **DOWN**, Duck-egg, Eatanswill, Eggshell, Electric, Facetiae, Firmament, Fritter, Gentian, Germander, Glaucous, Glum, Hauyne, Heliotrope, Hump, Indecent, Indigo, Indol(e), Iron, Isatin(e), Lapis lazuli, Lavender, Lewd, Lionel, Low, Mazarine, Methylene, Midnight, Monastral®, Mope, Morose, Murder, Nattier, Naughty, Navy, Nile, Ocean, Off-colour, Oxford, Peacock, Periwinkle, Perse, Petrol, Phycocyan, Porn, Powder, Prussian, Rabbi, Ribald, Riband, Right, Ripe, Robin's egg, Royal, Sad, Sapphire, Saxe, Saxon(y), Scurrilous, > **SEA**, Shocking, Sky, Slate, Smalt(o), Smutty, Sordid, Spirit, Splurge, Squander, Stafford, Steel, Stocking, Teal, Thenard's, Tony, Tory, Trist, True, Trypan, Turnbull's, Turquoise, Ultramarine, Unhappy, Urban, Verditer, Washing, Watchet, Wedgwood®, Welkin, Woad, Zaffer, Zaffre

▷ **Blue** *may indicate* an anagram

Bluebell Blawort, Blewart, Campanula, Harebell

Bluebottle Blawort, Blewart, Blowfly, Blowie, Brommer, Brummer, Cop, Cornflower, Fly, Policeman

▸ **Blue-legged** *see* **BLUESTOCKING**

Blueprint Cyanotype, Draft, Plan, Recipe

Bluestocking, Blue-legged Basbleu, Carter, Erudite, Femme savante, Hamburg(h), Mrs Montagu, Précieuse, Sheba

Bluff(ing) Blunt, Cle(e)ve, Cliff, Clift, Crag, Fake, Flannel, Frank, Hal, Headland, Height, Hoodwink, Kidology, Pose, Precipice, Steep, Trick

Blunder(er), Blundering Betise, Bévue, Bish, Bloomer, Blooper, Boob, Break, Bull, Bumble, Clanger, Clinker, Cock-up, Err, Faux pas, Floater, Flub, Fluff, Gaff(e), Goof, Howler, Inexactitude, Irish, Josser, Malapropism, > **MISTAKE**, Muddle, Mumpsimus, Slip, Solecism, Stumble, Trip

Blunt(ed), Bluntly Abrupt, Alleviate, Bate, Bayt, Brash, Brusque, Candid, Deaden, Disedge, Downright, Forthright, Frank, Hebetate, Mole, Morned, Obtund, Obtuse, Outspoken, Pointblank, Rebate, Retund, Retuse, Roundly, Snub, Straight-out, Stubby

Blur(ring) Cloud, Confuse, Fog, Fuzz, Halation, Mackle, Macule, Pixilation, > **SMUDGE**, Stump, Tortillon

Blurb Ad, Puff

Blush(ing) Colour, Cramoisy, Crimson, Erubescent, Erythema, Incarnadine, Mantle, > **REDDEN**, Rouge, Rubescent, Ruby, Rufescent, Rutilant

Bluster(ing), Blusterer, Blustery Arrogance, Bellow, Blore, Hector, Rage, Rant, Rodomontade, Roister, Sabre-rattler, Squash, Swagger, Vapour, Windbag, Wuthering

Boar Barrow, Calydonian, Erymanthian, Hog, Pentheus, Sanglier, Sounder, Tusker, Wild

Board(s), Boarding Abat-voix, Admiralty, Banker, Barge, Beaver, Billet, Bristol, Bulletin, Catchment, Centre, Cheese, Chevron, Circuit, Collegium, Committee, Contignation, Counter, Cribbage, Dagger, Dart, Daughter, Deal, Directors, Diving, Draft, Draining, Drawing, Embark, Embus, Emery, Enter, Entrain, Fare, Fascia, Featheredge, Fibro, Flannelgraph, Full, Gibraltar, Gutter, Hack, Half, Half-royal, Hawk, Hoarding, Idiot, Instrument, Ironing, Kip, Lag, Ledger, Lodge, Magnetic, Malibu, Masonite®, Match, Mill, Mortar, Moulding, Notice, Otter, Ouija, Palette, Pallet, Panel, Parochial, Particle, Patch, Pedal, Peg(board), Pension, Planch(ette), Plank, Ply(wood), Quango, Running,

Sandwich, Sarking, Scaleboard, School, Screed, Sheathing, Shelf, Shingle, Side-table, Sign, Skirting, Sleeve, Snow, Sounding, Splasher, Spring, Stage, Strickle, Stringboard, Supervisory, Surf, > TABLE, Telegraph, Thatch, Theatre, Trencher, Verge, Wainscot, Wobble

▷ **Board** *may refer to* chess or draughts

Boarder Interne, PG, Roomer

Boarding house Digs, Lodgings, Pension

Boast(er), Boasting Big-note, Blew, Blow, Blowhard, Bluster, Bobadil, Bounce, Brag, Braggadocio, Breeze, Crake, Crow, Fanfaronade, Gas, Gascon(nade), Glory, Hot air, Jactitation, Line, Ostent(atious), Prate, Rodomontade, Scaramouch, Skite, Swagger, Swank, Tall, Thrasonic, Vainglory, Vaunt, Yelp

Boat Ark, Barge, Bark, Canal, Cat, Coaster, Codder, Corvette, Cott, Cruiser, Curragh, Dragon, Eight, Flagship, Flatboat, Fly(ing), Fore-and-after, Four, Foyboat, Goldie, Gravy, Hooker, Isis, Jolly, Keel, Kit, Lapstrake, Launch, Long, Lymphad, Mackinaw, Monkey, Monohull, Mosquito, Motor, Narrow, Outrigger, Pair-oar, Pedalo, Pont, Privateer, PT, Pucan, Puffer, Sailer, Sauce, Sculler, Shallop, She, > SHIP, Skiff, Slogger, Smack, Swing, Tangle-netter, Tanker, Tender, Torpid, Trek-ox, Vaporetto, Vedette, > VESSEL, Wager, Weekender

Boater > HAT, Punter, Straw

Boatman Bargee, Charon, Cockswain, Coxswain, George, Gondolier, Harris, Hoveller, Phaon, Voyageur, Waterman, Wet-bob

Boat population Tank(i)a

Boat-shaped Carina, Scaphoid

Boatswain Bosun, Serang, Smee

Bob Acres, Beck, Curtsey, Deaner, Dip, Dock, Dop, Duck, Float, Hod, Hog, Jerk, Page-boy, Peal, Plumb, Plummet, Popple, Rob, S, Shingle, Sled(ge), Sleigh

Bobbin Reel, Shuttle, Spindle, Spool

Bobble Pompom

Bobby Bluebottle, Busy, Copper, Flatfoot, Patrolman, Peeler, Pig, > POLICEMAN

Bobby-dazzler Dinger, Stunner

Bock Stein

Bode Augur

Bodice Basque, Bolero, Bustier, Chemise, Chemisette, Choli, Corsage, Gilet, Halter, Jirkinet, Liberty, Plastron, Polonie, Polony, Spencer, Tucker, Watteau

Bodkin Eyeleteer, Needle, Poniard, Stilet(to)

Body, Bodies, Bodily Administration, Amount, Anatomic, Astral, Barr, Board, Bouk, Buik, Buke, Bulk, Cadaver, Cadre, Carcase, Carcass, Carnal, Caucas, Centrosome, Chapel, Chapter, Chassis, Chondriosome, Ciliary, Clay, Coachwork, Coccolite, Cohort, Column, Comet, Committee, Contingent, Cormus, Corpor(e)al, Corps, Corpse, Corpus, Corse, Cytode, Detail, Earth, Flesh, Food, Frame, Fuselage, Gazo(o)n, Golgi, Goner, Grey, > GROUP, Heavenly, Hull, Incarnate, Inclusion, Ketone, Lewy, Lich, Like, Lithites, Malpighian, > MASS, Militia, Moit, Mote, Mummy, Nacelle, Nucleole, Nucleolus, Pack, Personal, Phalanx, Pineal, Plant, Platelet, Platoon, Polar, Politic, Posse, Purview, Quango, Relic(t), Ruck, Senate, Solid, Soma, Soredium, Sound-box, Soyle, Spinar, Spore, Squadron, Square, Staff, Statoblast, Stiff, Syndicate, Tagma, Testis, Thallus, Torse, Torso, Trunk, Turm, Ulema, Vitreous, Wolffian, X

▷ **Body** *may indicate* an anagram

Body builder Steroid

Bodyguard Amulet, > ESCORT, Gentleman-at-arms, House-carl, Minder, Praetorian, Protector, Retinue, Schutzstaffel, > SHIELD, SS, Triggerman,

Varangian, Yeomen

Body segment Arthromere, Metamere

Boer Afrikaner, Kruger

Bog(gy) Allen, Blanket, Can, Carr, Clabber, Fen, Gents, Glaur, Hag, Lair, Latrine, Loo, Machair, Marsh, Merse, Mire, Morass, Moss(-flow), Mud, Muskeg, Peat, Petary, Quag, Raised, Serbonian, Slack, Slade, Slough, Spew, Spouty, Stodge, Sump, Vlei, Washroom, WC, Yarfa, Yarpha

Bog(e)y Boggart, Bug(aboo), Bugbear, Chimera, Eagle, Mumbo jumbo, Nis(se), Par, Poker, Rawhead, Scarer, Spectre, Troll

Boggle Astonish, Bungle, Demur, Hesitate, Perplex, Shy

Bog-trotter Tory

Bogus Assumed, Counterfeit, Fake, False, Histrionic, Phoney, > SHAM, Snide, Snobbish, Spoof, Spurious

Bohemian Arty, Beatnik, Gypsy, Hippy, Hussite, Mimi, Offbeat, Taborite, Trustafarian

Boil(er), Boiled, Boiling (point) Angry, Anthrax, Blain, Botch, Brew, Bubble, C, Carbuncle, Coction, Cook, Cree, Dartre, Decoct, Ebullient, Foam, Furuncle, Gathering, Hen, Herpes, Kettle, Leep, Ligroin, Pimple, Pinswell, Poach, Poule, Rage, Reflux, Samovar, Seethe, Simmer, Sod, Sore, Steam, Stew, Stye, Tea-kettle

Boisterous Gilp(e)y, Goustrous, Gusty, Hoo, Knockabout, Noisy, Rambunctious, Randy, Riotous, Rorty, Rough, Stormy, Strepitoso, Termagant, Turbulent, Wild

Bold(ly), Boldness Assumptive, Brash, Brass, Bravado, Bravery, Bravura, Brazen, Brussen, Caleb, Crust, Daredevil, Defiant, Derring-do, Diastaltic, Familiar, Free, Gallus, Hardihood, Heroics, High-spirited, Impudent, Intrepid, Malapert, Mature, Outspoken, Parrhesia, Pert, Plucky, Presumptive, Rash, Risoluto, Sassy, Temerity, Unshrinking

Bole Stem, Trunk

Bolivar Liberator

Bollard Cone, Kevel

Bolshevik Communist, Maximalist, Soviet

Bolster Cushion, Dutch wife, Pillow, > PROP

Bolt Arrow, Coach, Cuphead, Dash, Dead, Eat, Elope, Expansion, Explosive, Fish, Flee, Gobble, Gollop, Gorge, Gulp, Latch, Levant, Levin, Lightning, Lock, Machine, Missile, Panic, Pig, Pintle, Ragbolt, Rivet, Roll, Scoff, Slot, Snib, Sperre, Stud, Tap, Thunder, Toggle, U, Wing, Wolf

Bolus Ball

Bomb(er), Bombing Atom, Attack, B, Blitz, Blockbuster, Borer, Buzz, Candle, Carpet, Cluster, Cobalt, Daisycutter, Depth charge, Deterrent, Dirty, Doodlebug, Egg, Fission, Flop, Flying, Fragmentation, Fusion, Glide, Greek fire, Grenade, H, Harris, Hydrogen, Lancaster, Land-mine, Letter, Liberator, Loft, Logic, Megaton, Millennium, Mills, Minnie, Mint, Molotov cocktail, Mortar, Nail, Napalm, Neutron, Nuclear, Nuke, Parcel, Petar, Petard, Petrol, Pineapple, Pipe, Plaster, Plastic, Prang, Precision, Radium, Ransom, Robot, Shell, Skip, Smart, Smoke, Sneak-raid, Stealth, Stick, Stink, Stratofortress, Stuka, Tactical, Terrorist, Thermonuclear, Time, Torpedo, Turkey, V1, Volcanic, Walleye

Bombard(ment) Attack, Battery, Blitz, Cannonade, Drum-fire, Mortar, Pelt, Shell, Stone, Stonk, Strafe, Straff

Bombardon Tuba

Bombast(ic) Euphuism, Fustian, Grandiose, Hot air, Magniloquence, Orotund, Pomp, Rant, Timid, Tumid, Turgent

Bombay Nasik
Bombay duck Bum(m)alo
▶ **Bomber** *see* **BOMB**
Bonanza Luck, Windfall
Bonaparte Boney, > **NAPOLEON**, Plon-plon
Bond(age) Adhesive, Agent, Assignat, Bail, Cedula, Cement, Chain, Compact, Connect, Copula, Corporate, Duty, Escrow, Flemish, Gilt, Hyphen, Ionic, James, Knot, Liaise, Ligament, Link(age), Manacle, Mortar, Nexus, Noose, > **PLEDGE**, Rapport, Shackle, Starr, Thral(l)dom, > **TIE**, Valence, Vinculum, Yearling, Yoke
Bond(s), Bondsman Affinity, Baby, Bail, Bearer, Consols, Coordinate, Covalent, Covenant, Daimyo, Dative, Debenture, Deep-discount, Double, Electrovalent, English, Ernie, Esne, Fetter, Fleming, Flemish, Geasa, Grammy, Granny, Heart, Herringbone, Hydrogen, Income, Investment, Ionic, Junk, Long, Managed, Metallic, Municipal, Nexus, Pair, Peptide, Performance, Post-obit, Premium, Property, Recognisance, Relationship, Revenue, Running, Samurai, Security, Semipolar, Serf, Shogun, Single, Slave, Solder, Stacked, Superglue, Surety, Thete, Treasury, Triple, Vassal, Zebra
Bone(s), Bony Acromion, Anableps, Apatite, Astragalus, Atlas, Axis, Baculum, Calcaneus, Caluarium, Cannon, Capitate, Capitellum, Carina, Carpel, Carpus, Catacomb, Centrum, Chine, Clavicle, Cly, Coccyx, Coffin, Columella, Concha, Condyle, Coracoid, Coral, Costa, Coxa, Crane, Cranium, Cuboid, Cunciform, Dentary, Diaphysis, Dib, Dice, Diploe, Endosteal, Ethmoid, Femur, Fetter, Fibula, Fillet, Frontal, Funny, Ganoid, Gaunt, Haunch, Hause-bane, Horn, Humerus, Hyoid, Ilium, Incus, Innominate, Involucrum, Ischium, Ivory, Jugal, Kneecap, Knuckle, Lacrimal, Lamella, Luez, Luz, Malar, Malleolus, Malleus, Mandible, Manubrium, Marrow, Mastoid, Maxilla, Medulla, Membrane, Metacarpal, Metatarsal, Napier's, Nasal, Navicular, Occipital, Olecranon, Omoplate, Orthopaedics, Os, Ossicle, Palatine, Parasphenoid, Parietal, Patella, Pecten, Pectoral, Pedal, Pelvis, Pen, Percoid, Perone, Petrous, Phalanx, Pisiform, Premaxilla, Pubis, Pygostyle, Quadrate, Rachial, Rack, Radialla, Radius, Relic, Rib, Sacrum, Scaphold, Scapula, Sclere, Sepium, Sequestrum, Sesamoid, Skeleton, Skull, Sphenoid, Splint, Splinter, Spur, Squamosal, Stapes, > **STEAL**, Sternebra, Sternum, Stifle, Stirrup, Suboperculum, T, Talus, Tarsus, Temporal, Tibia, Tibiotarsus, Tot, Trapezium, Triquetral, Trochanter, Trochlea, True-rib, Tympanic, Ulna, Vertebrae, Vomer, Whirl, Wish, Wormian, Zygomatic
Bone-head Capitellum, Capitulum
Bonehouse Ossuary
Boneshaker Dandy-horse, Draisene, Draisine
Bonfire Bale-fire, Beltane, Blaze, Chumping, Clavie, Feu de joie, Pyre
Boniface Inn-keeper, Landlord, Taverner
Bonne-bouche Cate
Bonnet Balmoral, Bongrace, Cap, Cornette, Cowl, Easter, Glengarry, Hood, Hummel, Hummle, Kiss-me, Mobcap, Mutch, Poke, Scotch, Sun, Toorie, War
Bonny Blithe, Gay, Merry, Sonsy, Weelfar'd
Bonsai Saikei
Bonus Bounty, Bye, Christmas box, Danger money, Dividend, Escalator, Extra, Hand-out, Lagniappe, No-claim, > **PREMIUM**, Reversionary, Reward, Scrip, Spin-off, Windfall
Boob Gaffe, Nork, Simpleton, Stumer
Booby Dunce, Hick, Patch, Patchcocke, Patchoke, > **STUPID**
Boojum Snark

Book(s), Bookish, Bookwork Academic, Acts, Album, Amos, Antilegomena,
Antiphonary, Apocalypse, Apocrypha, Atlas, Audio, B, Backlist, Baruch,
Bestiary, Bestseller, Bible, Black, Blotter, Blue, Bodice-ripper, Breviary,
Caxton, Chrestomathy, Chron(icles), Chumash, Classic, Closed, Coffee-table,
Commonplace, Compendium, Concordance, Cookery, Corinthians,
Course, Cyclopedia, Dan(iel), Deuteronomy, Diary, Dictionary, Digest,
Directory, Domesday, Doomsday, Eccles, Ecclesiastes, Edda, Ench(e)iridion,
Encyclopedia, Engage, Enter, Eph, Ephesians, Erudite, Esdras, Esther,
Exercise, Exeter, Exodus, Ezek(iel), Ezra, Facetiae, Folio, Gal, Galatians,
Gazetteer, Genesis, Good, Gradual, Gradus, Grimoire, Grolier, Guide, Hag(gai),
Haggadah, Haggadoh, Hagliographa, Hardback, Heptameron, Herbal,
Hitopodesa, Hosea, Hymnal, I Ching, Imprint, Incunabula, Isaiah, Issue,
Jashar, Jasher, Joel, John, Joshua, Jud(ges), Jude, Kama Sutra, Kells, Kings,
Lam(entations), Lectionary, Ledger, Leviticus, Lib, Liber, Libretto, Literary, Log,
Luke, Macc, Maccabees, Malachi, Manga, Manual, Mark, Martyrs, Matthew,
Micah, Missal, Monograph, Mook, Nahum, Nomenclator, NT, Numbers,
Octavo, Octodecimo, Omnibus, Open, Orarium, Order, Ordinal, Ordinary, OT,
Page-turner, Paperback, Paralipomena, Pass, Passionary, Pedantic, Penny
dreadful, Pharmacopoeia, Philemon, Philippians, Phrase, Pica, Plug, Polyglot,
Pop-up, Porteous, Portesse, Potboiler, Prayer, Primer, Prompt, Prophet,
Proverbs, Psalms, Psalter, Pseudepigraphia, Publication, Quair, Quarto, Quire,
Rag, Ration, Reader, Red, Reference, Remainder, > **RESERVE**, Responsorial,
Revelations, Road, Rom, Romans, Satyricon, Script, Scroll, Sext, Sextodecimo,
Sibylline, Sir, Sixteenmo, Sketch, Snobs, Softback, Spelling, Statute, Studious,
Study, Style, Sus, Susanna, Sutra, Table, Tablet, Talking, Telephone, Teratology,
Text(ual), Thriller, Title, Titule, To-bit, Tome, Trade, Transfer, Triodion,
Tripitaka, Twelvemo, Twelve Tables, Vade-mecum, Veda, Vercelli, Vesperal,
Visiting, Visitor's, Vol(ume), Waste, White, Work, Year, Zephadiah
Bookbinder, Bookbinding Fanfare, Grolier, Mutton-thumper, Organdie
Book-case Credenza, Press, Satchel
Bookie(s), Bookmaker John, Layer, Librettist, Luke, Mark, Matthew, Printer,
Ringman, To-bit
Booking Reservation
Bookkeeper, Bookkeeping Clerk, Double entry, Librarian, Posting, Recorder,
Satchel, Single-entry
Booklet B, Brochure, Folder
Book-like Solander
Book-lover Incunabulist
Bookmark Tassel
Book-scorpion Chelifer
Bookseller Bibliopole, Colporteur, Conger, Sibyl, Stallman
Bookworm Sap, Scholar
Boom(ing) Baby, Beam, Boost, Bowsprit, Bump, Fishpole, Increase, Jib,
Orotund, Prosper, Resound, Roar, Sonic, Spar, Supersonic, Swinging, Thrive,
Torpedo, Wishbone
Boomer Bittern, Bull-of the-bog, Butter-bump, Kangaroo, Mire-drum
Boomerang Backfire, Kiley, Kyley, Kylie, Recoil, Ricochet, Throwstick, Woomera
Boon Bene, Benefit, Blessing, Bounty, Cumshaw, Gift, Godsend, Mills, Mitzvah,
Prayer, Windfall
Boor(ish) Bosthoon, Chuffy, Churl, Clodhopper, Crass, Goth, Grobian, Hog,
Ill-bred, Jack, Keelie, Kern(e), Kernish, Kill-courtesy, Lob, Lout, Lumpen, Ocker,
Peasant, Philistine, Trog, Uncouth, Yahoo, Yob, Yokel

Boost(er) Afterburner, Bolster, Ego, Encourage, Fillip, Help, Hoist, Impetus, Increase, Injection, Lift, Promote, Raise, Rap, Reheat, Reinforce, Reinvigorate, Spike, Supercharge, Tonic, Wrap

Boot(s) Addition, Adelaide, Ankle-jack, Avail, Balmoral, Beetle-crushers, Benefit, Blucher, Bottine, Bovver, Brogan, Brogue, Buskin, Cerne, Chukka, Cockers, Cold, Combat, Concern, Cothurn(us), Cowboy, Cracowe, Crowboot, Denver, Derby, Desert, Dismiss, Field, Finn(e)sko, Finsko, Fire, Football, Galage, Galosh, Gambado, Go-go, Granny, Gum, Hessian, High shoe, Hip, Jack, Jemima, Jodhpur, Kamik, Kletterschuh, Lace-up, Larrigan, Last, Mitten, Moon, Muchie, Muc(k)luc(k), Mukluk, Pac, Para, Profit, Riding, Rock, Russian, Sabot, > SACK, Seven league, > SHOE, Surgical, Thigh, Toe, Tonneau, Tops, Trunk, Ugh, Vibram®, Vibs, Wader, Warm, Weller, Wellie, Wellington, Welly

Booth Assassin, Crame, Kiosk, Polling, Stall, Stand, Telephone, Voting

Bootlegger Cooper, Coper, Runner

Bootless Futile, Idle, Vain

Booty Creach, Creagh, Haul, Loot, Prey, Prize, Spoil(s), Spolia optima, Swag

Booze(r) > DRINK, Liquor, Pub, Spree, Tipple

Borage Bugloss, Comfrey, Gromwell, Myosote

Borax Tincal

Border(s), Borderland, Borderline Abut, Adjoin, Apron, Bed, Bind, Bound, Braid, Checkpoint, Coast, Cot(t)ise, Dado, Dentelle, > EDGE, Engrail, Fimbria, Frieze, Fringe, Frontier, Furbelow, Guilloche, Head-rig, Hedgerow, Hem, Herbaceous, Impale, Kerb, Lambrequin, Limb, Limbo, Limen, Limes, Limit, Limitrophe, Lip, List, March, Marchland, > MARGIN, Mat, Mattoid, Meith, Mete, Mount, Neighbour, Orle, Pand, Pelmet, Penumbra, Perimeter, Purfle, Purlieu, Rand, Rim, Roadside, Roon, Royne, Rubicon, Rund, Rymme, Scottish, Selvage, Selvedge, Side, Skirt, Skirting, Strand, Strip, Surround, Swage, The Marches, Trench, Tressure, Valance, Valence, > VERGE

▷ **Borders** *may indicate* first and last letters

Bore(d), Boredom, Borer, Boring Aiguille, Anobium, Anorak, Apathy, Aspergillum, Aspergillus, Aspersoir, Auger, Awl, Beetle, Bind, Bit, Broach, Brog, Bromide, Calibre, Chokebore, Deadly, Drag, > DRILL, Dry, Dusty, Dweeb, Eagre, Eat, Eger, Elshin, Elsin, Endured, Ennui, Ennuye, Foozle, Gim(b)let, Gouge, Gribble, Grind, Had, Heigh-ho, Ho-hum, Irk, Jumper, Listless, Longicorn, Longueur, Miser, Mole, Nerd, Noyance, Nudni(c)k, Nuisance, Nyaff, Oporose, Pain, Pall, Penetrate, Perforate, Pest, Pholas, Pierce, Pill, Probe, Prosaic, Prosy, Punch, Ream(ingbit), Rime, Sat, Schmoe, Scolytus, Screw, Severn, Shothole, Snooze, Snore, Sondage, Spleen, Sting, Stob, Stupid, Tediosity, Tedious, Tedisome, Tedium, Tedy, Terebra, Teredo, Termes, Termite, Thirl, Tire, Trepan, Trocar, Tunnel, > WEARY, Well, Wimble, Windbag, Wonk, Woodworm, Worldweary, Xylophoga, Yawn

Borgia Cesare, Lucretia

Boric Sassolin, Sassolite

Born B, Free, Great, Nascent, Nat(us), Né(e)

Boron B

Borough Borgo, Pocket, Port, Quarter, Rotten, Township, Wick

Borrow(ed), Borrowing Adopt, Appropriate, Cadge, Copy, Derivative, Eclectic, George, Hum, Leverage, Scunge, Straunge, > TAKE, Touch

Bosh Humbug, Nonsense, Rot

Bosom Abraham's, Breast, Close, Gremial, Inarm, Intimate, Poitrine

Boss(ed), Bossy Blooper, Burr, Cacique, Director, Dominate, Gadroon, Governor, Headman, Honcho, Hump, Inian, Inion, Jewel, Knob, Knop, Knot, Leader,

Maestro, > **MANAGER**, Massa, > **MISTAKE**, Mistress, Netsuke, Noop, Nose-led, Omphalos, Overlord, Overseer, Owner, Pannikin, Pellet, Protuberance, Ruler, Run, Sherang, Straw, Stud, Superintendent, Taskmaster, Umbo(nate)

Boston Hub

Bot Oestrus

Botanist, Botany Banks, Bryology, Candolle, Carpology, Cockayne, Dendrologist, Frees, Garden, Godet, Herbist, Linnaeus, Phytology, Tradescant, Weigel

Botch(ed) Bungle, Clamper, Cock-up, Flub, Fudge, Mismanage, Pig's ear, Spoil, Tink

Both Together, Two

Bother(some) Ado, Aggro, Care, Deave, Deeve, Disturb, Drat, Fash, Fluster, Fuss, Get, Hassle, Hector, Incommode, Irk, Irritate, Moither, Nuisance, Perturb, Pesky, Pest(er), Pickle, Reke, Todo, > **TROUBLE**

Bottle(s) Ampul(la), Bacbuc, Balthasar, Balthazar, Belshazzar, Borachio, Bundle, Carafe, Carboy, Cock, Cork, Costrel, Courage, Cruet, Cruse, Cucurbital, Cutter, Dead-men, Decanter, Demijohn, Fearlessness, Feeding, Fiasco, Flacket, Flacon, Flagon, Flask, Goatskin, Gourd, Guts, Half-jack, Hen, Imperial, Jeroboam, Klein, Lachrymal, Lagena, Magnetic, Magnum, Marie-Jeanne, Matrass, Medicine, Methuselah, Mettle, Mickey, Nansen, Nebuchadnezzar, > **NERVE**, Nursing, Phial, Pilgrim, Pitcher, Pooter, Pycnometer, Rehoboam, Resource, Retort, Salmanaser, Salmanazar, Screwtop, Siphon, Smelling, Split, Squeeze, Squeezy, Sucking, Tear, Tube, Twenty-sixer, Vial, Vinaigret(te), Wad, Water, Weighing, Winchester, Wine, Woulfe

▷ **Bottle(d)** *may indicate* an anagram or a hidden word

Bottom Anus, Aris, Arse, Ass, Base, Beauty, Bed, Benthos, Bilge, Breech, Bum, Butt, Buttocks, Croup(e), Croupon, Demersal, Derrière, Doup, End, Fanny, Floor, Foot, Foundation, Fud, Fundus, Haunches, Hunkers, Hurdies, Keel(son), Kick, Lumbar, Nadir, Nates, Podex, Posterior, Pottle-deep, Prat, Pyramus, Rear, Rock, Root, Rump, Seat, Ship, Sill, Sole, Staddle, Tail, Tush, Weaver

Bottom drawer Glory box

Bottomless Subjacent

Botulism Limberneck

Boudoir Bower, Room

Bouffant Pouf

Bough Branch, Limb

Bought Coft

Boulder Gibber, Niggerhead, Rock, > **STONE**

Boule Senate

Bounce(r), Bouncing, Bouncy Bang, Blague, Bound, Caper, Dap, Dead-cat, Doorman, Dop, Dud, Eject, Evict, Fib, Jounce, Keepy-uppy, Kite, Lie, Lilt, Resilient, Ricochet, Spiccato, Spring, Stot, Tale, Tamp, Verve, Vitality, Yorker, Yump

▷ **Bouncing** *may indicate* an anagram

Bound(er), Boundary Adipose, Apprenticed, Articled, Bad, Barrier, Beholden, Border, Bourn(e), Bubalis, Cad, Cavort, Certain, Circumference, Curvet, Decreed, Demarcation, Demarkation, Dool, Dule, Duty, End, Engirt, Entrechat, Erub, Eruv, Event horizon, Exciton, Fence, Four, Frape, Galumph, Gambado, Gambol, Girt, Harestane, Hedge, Heel, Held, Hoarstone, Hops, Hourstone, Ibex, Interface, Izard, Jump, Kangaroo, K/T, > **LEAP**, Limes, Limit, Linch, Lollop, Lope, March-stone, Meare, Meer, Meith, Mere, Merestone, Mete, Moho, Muscle, Obliged, Ourebi, Outward, Pale, Parameter, Perimeter, Periphery,

Plate, Prance, Precinct, Prometheus, Purlieu, Redound, Ring-fence, Roller, Roo, Roped, Rubicon, Scoup, Scowp, Serf, Side, Sideline, Six(er), Skelp, Skip, Spang, Spring, Sten(d), Stoit, Stylolite, Terminator, T(h)alweg, Tied, Touchline, Upstart, Vault, Verge, Wallaby

▷ **Bounds** *may indicate* outside letters

Bounty, Bountiful Aid, Bligh, Boon, Christian, Generosity, > **GIFT**, Goodness, Grant, Head money, Honorarium, Largess(e), Lavish, Queen Anne's

Bouquet Aroma, Attar, Aura, Compliment, Corsage, Fragrancy, Garni, Nose, Nosegay, Plaudit, Posy, Spiritual, Spray

Bourbon Alfonso

Bourgeois Biedermeier, Common, Pleb(ian), Pooter(ish)

Bout Bender, Bust, Contest, Dose, Go, Jag, Match, Spell, Spree, Turn, Venery, Venewe, Venue

Boutique Shop

Bovine Stolid

Bow(ing), Bower, Bowman Alcove, Arbour, Arc, Arch, > **ARCHER**, Arco, Arson, Bandy, Beck, Bend, Boudoir, Butterfly, Clara, Congé(e), Crescent, Crook, Cupid, > **CURVE**, Defer, Dicky, Drail, Droop, Duck, Echelles, Eros, Eugh, Eye, Fiddle(r), Fiddlestick, Foredeck, Halse, Hawse, Jook, Jouk, Kneel, Kotow, Laval(l)ière, Lean, Long, Lout, Lowt, Martellato, Moulinet, Namaste, Nameste, Nod, Nutate, Obeisance, Obtemper, Paganini, Pergola, Prore, Quarrel, Reverence, Salaam, Seamer, Shelter, Slope, Sound, Spiccato, Stick, > **SUBMIT**, Tie, Yew, Yield

Bowdler(ize) Edit(or), Water

Bowels Entrails, Guts, Innards, Viscera

▷ **Bower** *may indicate* using a bow

Bowl(ing), Bowler, Bowl over, Bowls B, Basin, Begging, Bicker, Bocce, Bocci(a), Boccie, Bodyline, Bool, Bosey, Bouncer, Cage-cup, Calabash, Candlepins, Cap, Carpet, Caup, Chalice, Cheese, Chinaman, Christie, Christy, Cog(g)ie, Coolamon, Crater, Cup, Deliver, Derby, > **DISH**, Dismiss, Dome, Drake, Dumbfound, Dust, Ecuelle, End, Finger, Fivepin, Goldfish, Googly, Grub, Hog, Hoop, Jack, Jeroboam, Jorum, Kegler, Krater, Lavabo, Laver, Leg-spin, Lightweight, Lob, Locke, Mazer, Monteith, Night, Offbreak, Old, Over-arm, Pace, Pan, Pétanque, Piggin, Porringer, Pot-hat, Pottinger, Punch, Raku, Rice, Rink, Roll, Roundarm, Seam(er), Skip, Skittle(s), Spare, Speed, Spinner, Spofforth, Stadium, Stagger, Stummel, Sucrier, Super, Ten-pin, Tom, Underarm, Underhand, Underwood, Voce, Wassail, Wood, York(er)

Box(ing) Baignoire, Ballot, Bandbox, Bareknuckle, Bento, Bijou, Bimble, Binnacle, Black, Blue, Bonk, Buist, Bunk, Bush, Caddy, Call, Camera, Canister, Case, Cash, Casket, Cassolette, Chest, Chinese, Christmas, Ciborium, Clog, Coach, Coffer, Coffin, Coffret, Coin, Confessional, Cool, Crate, Cuff, Deed, Dialog(ue), Dispatch, Ditty, Dog, Drawer, Encase, Enclose, > **FIGHT**, File, Fist, Fund, Fuse, Fuzz, Glory, Glove, Go-kart, Grass, Hat, Hay, Hedge, Honesty, Humidor, Hutch, Ice, Idiot, Inro, Jewel, Journal, Junction, Jury, Keister, Kick, Kiosk, Kite, Knevell, Ladle, Letter, Light, Live, Locker, Lodge, Loge, Match, Mill, Mitre, Mocock, Mocuck, Musical, Nest(ing), Omnibus, Orgone, Package, Paint, Pandora's, Papeterie, Patch, Peepshow, Peg, Penalty, Petara, Pew, Phylactery, Pill, Pillar, Pitara, Pix, Poor, Post, Pouncet, Powder, Press, Prompt, Protector, Puff, Pugilism, Pyxis, Register, Ring, Royal, Saggar(d), Sagger, Sand, Savate, Scrap, Seggar, Sentry, Set-top, Shadow, Shoe, Shooting, Signal, Skinner, Skip(pet), Slipcase, Smudge, Soap, Solander, Sound, > **SPAR**, Spice, Spring, Squeeze, Strong, Stuffing, Swell, Tabernacle, Tefillin, Telephone, Telly, Thai, Tin, Tinder, Tool, Touch, Trunk, Tube, Tuck, TV, Vanity, Vasculum, Vinaigrette,

Voice, Weather, Window, Wine, Witness, Yakhdan

Boxer Ali, Amycus, Babyweight, Bantamweight, Bruiser, Bruno, Canine, Carnera, Carpentier, Carthorse, Chinaman, Cooper, Crater, Cruiserweight, Dog, Eryx, Farr, Featherweight, Flyweight, Ham, Heavyweight, Lightweight, McCoy, Middleweight, Mosquito-weight, Pandora, Pollux, Pug, Pugil(ist), Rebellion, Rocky, Shadow, Southpaw, Strawweight, Welterweight, Wilde

Boxing-glove Hurlbat, Muffle, Whirlbat, Whorlbat

Boy(s) Amoretto, Apprentice, Ball, Bevin, Blue-eyed, Breeches, Bub(by), Cabin, Callant, Catamite, Champagne, Chiel(d), > CHILD, Chokra, Chummy, Cub, Cupid, Dandiprat, Errant, Galopin, Garçon, Gorsoon, Gossoon, Green Mountain, Groom, Ha, Hansel, Jack, Kid, Klonkie, Knave, Knave-bairn, Kwedien, Lackbeard, > LAD, Loblolly, Loon(ie), Minstrel, Nibs, Nipper, Office, Page, Pot, Prentice, Principal, Putto, Rent, Roaring, Shaver, Son, Spalpeen, Sprig, Stripling, Tad, Tar, Ted(dy), Tiger, Toy, Urchin, Whipping, Wide, > YOUTH

▷ **Boy** *may indicate* an abbreviated name

Boycott Avoid, Ban, Bat, Black, Blacklist, Exclude, Hartal, Isolate, Ostracise, Shun, Swadeshi

Boyfriend Beau, Date, Fella, Fellow, Steady

Boyle Juno

Bp Bishop, DD, RR

Brace(s), Bracing Accolade, Couple, Crosstree, Fortify, Gallace, Gallows, Gallus(es), Gird, Hound, Invigorate, Pair, Pr, Rear-arch, Rere-arch, Skeg, Spider, Splint, Steady, Stiffener, Strut, > SUPPORT, Suspenders, Tauten, Thorough, Tone, Tonic, Two

Bracelet Armil(la), Armlet, Bangle, Cuff, Darbies, Handcuff, Identity, Manacle, Manilla

Brachiopod Ecardines, Lamp-shell, Spirifer

Bracken Brake, Fern, Pteridium, Tara

Bracket Angle-iron, Bibb, Brace, Cantilever, Console, Corbel, Couple, Cripple, Lance rest, Misericord(e), Modillion, Mutule, Parenthesis, Potence, Pylon, Rigger, Sconce, Square, Straddle, Strata, > STRUT, Trivet, Truss

Bract Glume(lla), Involucel, Involucre, Leaf, Lemma, Palea, Palet, Phyllary, Spathe

Brad Nail, Pin, Rivet, Sprig

Brag(gart), Bragging Basilisco, Birkie, Bluster, Boast, Bobadil, Braggadocio, Bull, Cockalorum, Crow, Falstaff, Fanfaronade, Gab, Gascon, Hot-air, Loudmouth, Parolles, Puckfist, Puff, Rodomontader, Skite, Slam, Swagger, Thrason, Thrasonic, Tongue-doubtie, Tongue-doughty, Vainglorious, Vaunt

Brahma(n) Sannyasi(n)

Braid A(i)glet, Aiguillette, Fishbone, French, Frog, Galloon, Lacet, Plait, Plat, Rickrack, Rick-rack, Ricrac, Seaming-lace, Sennet, Sennit, Sinnet, Soutache, Tress, Trim, Twist, Weave

Braille (system) Moon

Brain(s), Brainy, Brain disease, Brain-power Amygdala, Appestat, Bean, Bright, Cerebellum, Cerebrum, Cortex, Diencephalon, Dura mater, Encephalon, Epencephalon, Fornix, Genius, Gyrus, Harn(s), Head, Hippocampus, Hydrocephalus, Hypothalamus, Insula, Intelligence, IQ, Kuru, Left, Limbic, Loaf, Lobe, Mastermind, Mater, Medulla, Medulla oblongata, Metencephalon, Mind, Noddle, Noesis, Nous, Peduncle, Pericranium, Pia mater, Pons, Pontile, Prosencephalon, Rhinencephalon, Rhombencephalon, Sconce, Sense, Sensorium, Striatum, Subcortex, Tapagnosia, Tectum, Telencephalon, Thalamencephalon, Thalamus, Upper stor(e)y, Vermis, Wetware

▷ **Brain(s)** *may indicate* an anagram

Brainless Anencephaly, Bimbo, Stupid, Thick

Brainwash(ing) Indoctrinate, Menticide, Propaganda

Brake ABS, Adiantum, Air, Antilock, Bracken, Curb, Disc, Dive, Drag, Drum, Fern, Foot, Grove, Hand, Hydraulic, Nemoral, Overrun, Ratchet, Rein, Shoe, Shooting, > SLOW, Spinney, Sprag, Tara, Thicket, Vacuum, Westinghouse

Bramble, Brambly Batology, Blackberry, Boysenberry, Brier, Cloudberry, Rubus, Thorn, Wait-a-bit, Youngberry

Bran Cereal, Chesil, Chisel, Oats, Pollard

Branch(ed), Branches, Branching, Branch Office Affiliate, Antler, Arm, BO, Bough, Cladode, Cow, Dendron, Dept, Diversify, Diverticulum, Divide, Filiate, Fork, Grain, Jump, Kow, Lateral, Leaf-trace, Limb, Lobe, Loop, Lye, Lylum, Offshoot, Olive, Patulous, Raguly, Ramate, Ramulus, Reis, Rice, Shroud, Special, Spray(ey), Sprig, Spur, Tributary, Turning, Turn-off, Twig, Wattle, Yard

Branch-rib Lierne

Brand Broadsword, Buist, Burn, Cauterise, Chop, Class, Denounce, Earmark, Ember, Excalibur, Falchion, Faulchin, Faulchion, Idiograph, Inust, Iron, Label, Line, > MARK, Marque, Own, Power, Sear, Sere, Stigma, Sweard, Sword, Torch, Wipe

Brandish Bless, Flaunt, Flourish, Waffle, Wampish, Wave

Brandy Aguardiente, Applejack, Apricot, Aqua vitae, Armagnac, Bingo, Calvados, Cape Smoke, Cold without, Dop, Eau de vie, Fine, Framboise, Grappa, Mampoer, Marc, Mobbie, Mobby, Nantes, Nantz, Napoleon, Palinka, Peach, Quetsch, Slivovic(a), Slivovitz, Smoke

Bras Arms

Brash Impudent, Jumped-up, Pushy, Rain, Rash

Brass(y), Brassware Benares, Brazen, Cheek, Club, Corinthian, Cornet, Dinanderie, Face, Front, Harsh, High, Horn, Horse, Latten, Lip, Loot, Lota(h), Loud, Matrix, > MONEY, Moola(h), Oof, Oricalche, Orichalc, Pyrites, Sass, Snash, Sopranino, Talus, Top, Trombone, Wood

Brassard Armlet

Brass hat Brig

Brassica Brussels (sprout), > CABBAGE, Colza, Turnip

Brat Bairn, Enfant terrible, Gait(t), Gamin, Geit, Git, Gyte, Imp, Lad, Terror, Urchin

Brave(ry) Amerind, Apache, Bold, Conan, Corragio, Courage, Creek, Dare, > DEFY, Doughty, Dress, Face, Fearless, Gallant, Game, Gamy, Gutsy, Hardy, Heroism, Indian, Injun, Intrepid, Lion, Manful, Manly, Nannup, Plucky, Prow(ess), Sannup, Skookum, Spunk, Stout, Uncas, Valiant, Valour, Wight

Bravo Acclaim, B, Bandit, Bully, Desperado, Euge, Murderer, Olé, Spadassin, Villain

Brawl(er) Affray, Bagarre, Bicker, Brabble, Donnybrook, Dust, Fight, Flite, Flyte, Fracas, Fratch, Fray, Melee, Prawl, Rammy, Roarer, Roughhouse, Row, Scuffle, Set-to, Shindig, Stoush, Tar, Wrangle

Brawn Beef, Burliness, Headcheese, He-man, Might, Muscle, Power, Rillettes, Sinew

Bray Cry, Heehaw, Stamp, Vicar, Whinny

Brazen Bold, Brassy, Flagrant, Impudent, Shameless, Unabashed

Brazier Brasero, Fire, Hibachi, Mangal, Scaldino

Brazil(ian) Caboclo, Carioca, Para

Breach Assault, Break, Chasm, Cleft, Gap(e), Infraction, Redan, Rupture, Saltus, Schism, Solution, Trespass, Violate

Bread, Bread crumbs Afrikomen, Azym(e), Bagel, Baguette, Bannock, Bap, Barmbrack, Batch, Baton, Brewis, Brioche, Brownie, Bun, Cash, Chal(l)ah, Chametz, Chapati, Cheat, Ciabatta, Cob, Coburg, Corn, Corsned, Croissant, Crostini, Croute, Crouton, Crumpet, Crust, Damper, Dibs, Dika, Doorstep, Elephant's-foot, Eulogia, Flatbread, Focaccia, French, Garlic, Gluten, Graham, Granary, Grissino, Guarana, Hallah, Hametz, Hometz, Horse, Host, Indian, Injera, Jannock, Johnny-cake, Kaffir, Laver, Leavened, Loaf, Long tin, Manchet, Maori, Milk-sop, > **MONEY**, Monkey, Na(a)n, Pain, Panada, Panary, Pane, Paneity, Paratha, Pikelet, Pit(t)a, Pone, Poppadom, Poultice, Pumpernickel, Puree, Puri, Raspings, Ravel, Roll, Rooty, Roti, Round, Rusk, Rye, Sally Lunn, Schnecken, Shive, Simnel, Sippet, Smor(re)brod, Soda, Soft-tommy, Sourdough, Staff of life, Standard, Stollen, Stottie, Sugar, Sweet, Tartine, Tea, Tommy, Tortoise-plant, Twist, Wastel, Zakuski, Zwieback

Breadfruit Ja(c)k

Breadwinner Earner, Pa

Break, Break-down, Break-in, Break-up, Broken Adjourn, Aposiopesis, Bait, Breach, Caesura, Caesure, Cantle, Cark, Cesure, Chinaman, Chip, Cleave, Coffee, Comb, Comma, Commercial, Comminute, Compost, Conk, Crack, Crock, Crumble, Deave, Debacle, Deeve, Demob, Destroy, Diffract, Disintegrate, Disperse, Disrupt, Erupt, Exeat, Fast, Fault, Four, > **FRACTURE**, Fragment, Fritter, Frush, Gaffe, Give, Greenstick, Half-term, Half-time, Hernia, Hiatus, Holiday, Infringe, Interim, Interlude, Intermission, Interrupt, > **INTERVAL**, Irrupt, Knap, Knickpoint, Lacuna, Lapse, Leave, Lysis, Moratorium, Nickpoint, Nooner, Outage, Part, Pause, Phreak, Playtime, Poach, Polarise, Price, Reave, Recess, Recrudescent, Relief, Rend, Resorption, Respite, Rest, Rift, Ruin, Rupture, Saltus, Schism(a), Secede, Shatter, Shiver, Smash, Smokeho, Smoko, Snap, Split, Stave, Stop, Stop-over, Stove, Sunder, Tame, Tea-ho, Tear, Time-out, Torn, Transgress, Truce, Vacation, Violate

Breakable Brittle, Delicate, Fissile, Frail, Friable

Breakdown Analyse, Autolysis, Cataclasm, Collapse, Conk, Glitch, Glycolosis, Histolysis, Hydrolysis, Lyse, Lysis, Nervous, Ruin

Breaker Billow, Comber, Ice, Roller, Smasher, Surf

Breakfast B, Brunch, Chota-hazri, Continental, Disjune, English, Kipper, Petit déjeuner, Power, Wedding

Breakneck Headlong

Breakwater Groyne, Jetty, Mole, Pier, Tetrapod

Bream Fish, Porgy, Sar(gus), Tai

Breast(s), Breastbone, Breastwork Bazuma, Blob, Bosom, Brave, Brisket, Bristols, Bust, Counter, Diddy, Duddy, Dug, Falsies, Garbonza, Gazunga, Heart-spoon, Jubbies, Jugs, Knockers, Norg, Nork, Pigeon, Rampart, Redan, Sangar, Stem, Sternum, Sungar, Supreme, Tit, Xiphisternum

Breastplate Armour, Byrnie, Curat, Curiet, Pectoral, Plastron, Rational, Rest, Shield, Thorax, Xiphiplastron

Breath(e), Breathing, Breather Aerobe, Aspirate, Branchia, Caesural, Cheyne-Stokes, Circular, Cypress-knee, Eupnoea, Exhalation, Expiration, Flatus, Gasp, Gill, H, Halitosis, Hauriant, Haurient, Hobday, Hypernoea, Hyperventilation, Hypopnoea, Inhale, Inspiration, Lung, Nares, Nostril, Orthopnoea, Oxygenator, Pant, Pneuma, Prana, Pulmo, Rale, Respire, Respite, Rest, Rhonchus, Rough, Scuba, Snore, Snorkel, Snortmast, Snuffle, Spiracle, Spirit, Spiritus, Stertor, Stridor, Vent, Wheeze, Whiff, Whift, Whisper, Whist, Wind, Windpipe

Breathless(ness) Anhelation, Apnoea, Asthma, Dyspnoea, Emphysema,

Orthopnoea, Puffed-out, Tachypnoea, Wheezing

Breathtaking Amazing, Asphyxia

Breech(es) Bible, Buckskin, Chaps, Flog, Galligaskins, Hose, Jodhpurs, Kneecords, Knickerbockers, Plushes, Riding, Smallclothes, Smalls, Trews, Trouse(rs), Trusses

Breed(er), Breeding(-place) Bear, Beget, Cleck, Endogamous, Engender, Engend(r)ure, Eugenics, Fast, Generation, Gentilesse, Gentrice, Hetero, Hotbed, In-and-in, Lineage, > MANNERS, Origin, Panmixia, Procreate, Propagate, Pullulate, Race, Raise, Rear, Seminary, Sire, Species, Stock, Strain, Stud, Telegony, Thremmatology, Tribe, Voltinism

Breeze, Breezy Air, Breath, Brisk, Catspaw, Chipper, Doctor, Fresh, Gentle, Gust, Light, Mackerel, Moderate, Sea, Slant, Sniffler, Tiff, Zephyr

Brethren Bohemian, Darbyite, Elder, Exclusive, Herrnhuter, Kin, Open, Plymouth, Trinity

Breton Armoric, Brezonek

Breve Minim, Note, O

Breviary Portesse, Portous

▶ **Brevity** *see* BRIEF

Brew(ery), Brewer, Brewing Ale, Billycan, Brose, Browst, Bummock, > CONCOCT, Contrive, Dictionary, Distillery, Ferment, Infusion, Liquor, Malt, Potion, Steep, Witches', Yeast, Yill, Zymurgy

Briar Bramble, Canker, Lawyer

Bribe(ry) Backhander, Bonus, Boodle, Bung, Carrot, Dash, Embracery, Get at, Graft, Grease, Hush-money, Insult, Kickback, Oil, Palm, Palm-grease, Palm-oil, Payola, Schmear, Slush, Soap, Sop, Square, Straightener, Suborn, Sweeten(er), Tamper, Tempt, Tenderloin, Vail, Vales

Bric-a-brac Bibelot, Curio, Rattle-trap, Smytrie, Tatt, Virtu

Brick(s), Brickwork Adobe, Air, Bat, Bath, Boob, Bullnose, Bur(r), Clanger, Clinker, Closer, Course, Dutch clinker, Fletton, Gaffe, Gault, Gold, Hard stocks, Header, Ingot, Klinker, Lateritious, Lego®, Malm, Nogging, Red, Soldier, Sport, Stalwart, Stretcher, Terra-cotta, Testaceous, Tile, Trojan, Trump

Brickbat Missile

Bricklayer Churchill

Bride(s) Bartered, Danaides, Ellen, Hen, Spouse, War, Wife, Ximena

Bridesmaid Paranymph

Bridge(head), Bridge player Acol, Al Sirat, Aqueduct, Auction, Bailey, Balance, Barre, Bascule, Bestride, Bifrost, Biritch, Bridle-chord, Brig, Brooklyn, Cantilever, Capo, Capodastro, Capotasto, Catwalk, Chevalet, Chicago, Chicane, Clapper, Clifton, Contract, Counterpoise, Cross, Cut-throat, Deck, Declarer, Drawbridge, Duplicate, Flying, Foot, Four-deal, Gangplank, Gangway, Gantry, Girder, Hog's back, Humber, Humpback, Humpbacked, Ice, Irish, Jigger, Land, Lattice, Leaf, Lifting, Ligger, Link, London, Menai, Nasion, Overpass, Pivot, Plafond, Ponceau, Ponticello, Pontifice, Pont Levis, Pontoon, Rainbow, Rialto, Rubber, Sighs, Sinvat, Skew, Snow, > SPAN, Spanner, Stamford, Straddle, Suspension, Swing, Tay, Temper, Tête-de-pont, Through, Transporter, Traversing, Trestle, Truss, Turn, Vertical lift, Viaduct, Vint, Waterloo, Weigh, Wheatstone, Wire

Bridge pair EW, NS, SN, WE

Bridge protector Ice-apron

Bridge system Acol

Bridle Bit, Branks, Bridoon, Bristle, Browband, Crownpiece, Curb, Hackamore, Halter, Headstall, Musrol, Noseband, Rein, Scold's

Bridle path Orbit, Track

Brief(s), Briefing, Briefly, Brevity Awhile, Barristerial, Bluette, Brachyology, Breviate, Cape, Compact, > **CONCISE**, Conspectus, Crisp, Curt, Dossier, Fill in, Fleeting, Instruct, Laconic, Nearly, Pants, Pennorth, Pithy, Prime, Scant, > **SHORT(EN)**, Short-term, Short-winded, Sitrep, Succinct, Summing, Tanga, Terse, Transient, Undies, Update, Watching

Brig Br, Hermaphrodite, Jail, Nancy Bell, > **SHIP**, Snow

Brigade Boys', Corps, Fire, Fur, Girls', Green-ink, International, Naval, Red, Troop

Brigand Bandit, Bandolero, Cateran, Haiduck, Heiduc, Heyduck, Klepht, Pillager, Pirate, > **ROBBER**, Rob Roy, Trailbaston

Bright, Brightness Afterglow, Alert, Ashine, Brainy, Breezy, Brilliant, Brisk, Cheery, Cla(i)re, Clear, Clever, Effulgent, Elaine, Facula, Fair, Floodlit, Florid, Garish, Gay, Glad, Glow, Helen, Hono(u)r, Light, Lit, Loud, Lucid, Luculent, Lustre, Net(t), Nit, Radiant, Rorie, Rosy, Scintillating, Sematic, Sharp, Sheeny, Sheer, Shere, Skyre, Smart, Spark(y), Stilb, Sunlit, Sunny, Vive, Vivid, White

Bright spot Facula

Brilliant, Brilliance Ace, Blaze, Brainy, Def, Effulgent, Flashy, Galaxy, Gay, Gemmy, Glossy, Inspired, Lambent, Lucent, Lustre, Mega-, Meteoric, Nitid, Pear, > **RADIANT**, Refulgent, Resplendent, Shiny, Spangle, Splendour, Star, Virtuoso, > **VIVID**, Water

Brim Edge, Lip, Rim, Ugly

Brimstone Hellfire, S, Sulphur

Brindisi Skolion, Toast

Brindled Piebald, Tabby, Tawny

Brine Muriatic, Ozone, Pickle, Saline, Salt

Bring Afferent, Bear, Carry, Cause, Conduct, Convey, Earn, Evoke, Fet, Fetch, Foist, Hatch, Induce, Land, Produce, Wreak

Bring up Breed, Educate, Exhume, Foster, Nurture, Raise, > **REAR**

Brink > **EDGE**, Lip, Rim, Shore, > **VERGE**

Brio Elan

Brisk(ness) Active, Alacrity, Alert, Allegro, Breezy, Busy, Chipper, Crank, Crisp, Crouse, Fresh, Gaillard, Galliard, Jaunty, Kedge, Kedgy, Kidge, Lively, Peart, Perk, Pert, Rattling, Roaring, Scherzo, Sharp, Smart, Snappy, Spanking, Spirited, Sprightly, Vivace, Yare, Zippy

Bristle, Bristling, Bristly Aciculum, Arista, Awn, Barb, Birse, Bridle, Campodeiform, Chaeta, Flurry, Fraught, Frenulum, Glochidium, Gooseflesh, Hackles, Hair, Hérissé, Hispid, Horrent, Horripilation, Nereid, Polychaete, Seta, Setose, Striga, Strigose, Stubble, Styloid, Vibraculum, Villus, Whisker

Bristle-tail Campodea

Brit Silt

Brit(ish), Briton(s), Briton All-red, Anglo, Herring, Iceni, Insular, Isles, Kipper, Limey, Pict, Pom, Rooinek, Saxon, Silurian, UK

Britain Alban(y), Albion, GB

Britannia, Britannia metal Tutania

Brittany Armorica

Brittle Bruckle, Crackly, Crimp, Crisp, Delicate, > **FRAGILE**, Frush, Hot-short, Redsear, Red-share, Red-shire, Redshort, Shivery, Spall, Spalt

▷ **Brittle** *may indicate* an anagram

Broach Approach, Open, Raise, Spit, Suggest, Tap, Widen

Broad(ly) Crumpet, Dame, Doll, Doxy, Drab, General, Generic, Largo, Latitudinous, Loose, Outspoken, Ovate, Pro, Roomy, Spatulate, Thick, Tolerant,

Wide, Woman

Broad-beaked Latirostrate

Broadcast(ing), **Broadcaster** Ad(vertise), Air, Announce, Beam, Breaker, CB, Disperse, Disseminate, Downlink, Emission, Ham, IBA, Network, Newscast, OB, On, Outside, Pirate, Programme, Promulgate, Radiate, Radio, Relay, Satellite, > **SCATTER**, Scattershot, Screen(ed), SECAM, Seed, Simulcast, Sky, Sow, Sperse, Spread, Sprinkle, Transmission, Ventilate, Wavelength

Broad-nosed Platyrrhine

Broadside Barrage, Criticism, Salvo, Tire

Broadway Boulevard, Esplanade, Motorway

Brocade Arrasene, Baldachin, Baldaquin, Baudekin, Bawdkin, Kincob, Zari

Brochure Leaflet, Pamphlet, Programme, Tract

Brogue Accent, > **SHOE**

Broke(n) Bankrupt, Bust(ed), Duff, Evans, Fritz, Impoverished, Insolvent, Kaput, On the rocks, Puckeroo, Shattered, Skint, Stony, Stove, Strapped

▷ **Broken** *may indicate* an anagram

Broken off Prerupt

Broker Agent, Banian, Banyan, Go-between, Jobber, Mediator, > **MERCHANT**, Shadchan, Uncle

Bromide Halide, Haloid, Truism

Bromine Br

Bronchitis, **Bronchitic** Chesty, Husk

Bronte(s) Bell, Cyclops

Brontosaurus Apatosaurus

Bronze, **Bronze age** Bell, Bras(s), Brown, Eugubine, Gunmetal, Hallstatt(ian), Helladic, Kamakura, Manganese, Minoan, Mycenean, Ormolu, Phosphor, Schillerspar, Sextans, Talos, Tan, Third

Brooch Cameo, Clasp, Fibula, Luckenbooth, Ouch, Owche, Pin, Preen, Prop, Spang, Sunburst

Brood(y) Clock, Clucky, Clutch, Cogitate, Covey, Eye, Lyrie, Hatch, Hover, Incubate, Introspect, Kindle, Litter, Meditate, Mill, Mull, Nest, Nid, Perch, Pet, > **PONDER**, Repine, Roost, Sit, Sulk, Team

Brook Abide, Babbling, Becher's, Beck, Branch, Burn, Countenance, Creek, Endure, Ghyll, Gill, Kerith, Kill, Pirl, Purl, Rill(et), River, Rivulet, Runlet, Runnel, Stand, Stomach, Stream, Suffer, Tolerate

Broom Besom, Brush, Cow, Cytisus, Genista, Gorse, Greenweed, Knee-holly, Kow, New, Orobranche, Retama, Spart, Sweeper, Whisk

Broth Bouillon, Brew(is), Cullis, Dashi, Kail, Kale, Muslin-kale, Pot liquor, Pottage, Scotch, Skilly, > **SOUP**, Stock

Brothel Bagnio, Bordel(lo), Cathouse, Corinth, Crib, Den, Flash-house, Honkytonk, Hothouse, Kip, Knocking shop, Red-light, Seraglio, Stew, Vaulting-house

Brother(hood) Ally, Bhai, Billie, Billy, Blood, Boet, Brethren, Bro, Bud, Comrade, Fellow, Fra, Freemason, Lay, > **MONK**, Moose, Pre-Raphaelite, Sib(ling), Theatine, Trappist, Worker

Brow Crest, Forehead, Glabella, Ridge, Sinciput, Tump-line

Browbeat Badger, Bully, Butt, Hector, Nut

Brown(ed) Abram, Adust, Amber, Apricate, Auburn, Au gratin, Bay, Biscuit, Bisque, Bister, Bistre, Bole, Br, Braise, Brindle, Bronzed, Brunette, Burnet, Burnt umber, Capability, Caramel, Caromel, Chamois, Cinnamon, Cook, Coromandel, Dun, Fallow, Filemot, Fulvous, Fusc(ous), Grill, Hazel, Infuscate, Ivor, John, Khaki, Liver, March, Meadow, Mocha, Mousy, Ochre, Olive,

Oxblood, Philamot, Rufous, Rugbeian, Russet, Rust, Scorch, Seal, Sepia, Sienna, Soare, Sore, Sorrel, Tan, Tawny, Tenné, Testaceous, Toast, Tom, Umber, Vandyke, Wholemeal, Windsor

Browne Sam

Brownie Dobbie, Dobby, Dobie, Goblin, Hob, Kobold, Leprechaun, Nis(se), Rosebud, Sprite

Browse(r) Graze, Netscape®, Pasture, Read, Scan, Stall-read, Surf

Bruce Robert

Bruise Contund, Contuse, Crush, Damage, Ding, Ecchymosis, Frush, Golp(e), Hurt, Intuse, Livedo, Lividity, Mark, Mouse, Pound, Purpure, Rainbow, Shiner, Ston(n), Stun, Surbate

Brummagen Tatty

Brunette Dark, Latin

Brush (off), Brushwood Bavin, Bottle, Brake, Broom, Carbon, Chaparral, Clash, Dandy, Dismiss, Dust, Encounter, Fan, Filbert, Filecard, Firth, Fitch, Frith, Grainer, Hag, Hog, Kiss, Liner, Loofah, Mop, Paint, Pig, Pope's head, Putois, Rebuff, Rice, Rigger, Sable, Scrub, Scuff, Skim, Striper, Thicket, Touch, Whisk, Wire

Brusque Abrupt, Blunt, Curt, Downright, Pithy, Short

Brussels Carpet, Lace

Brutal, Brute Animal, Barbaric, Beast, Bête, Caesar, Caliban, Cruel, Hun, Iguanodon, Inhuman, Nazi, Nero, Ostrogoth, Pitiless, Quagga, Rambo, Roughshod, Ruffian, Thresher-whale, Yahoo

Brutus Wig

Bryophyte Moss, Tree-moss

Bubble(s), Bubbly Air-bell, Air-lock, Barmy, Bead(ed), Bell, Bleb, Blister, Boil, Buller, Cavitate, Champagne, Cissing, Ebullition, Effervesce, Embolus, Enthuse, Espumoso, Foam, > **FROTH**, Gassy, Globule, Gurgle, Head, Magnetic, Mantle, Mississippi, Popple, Rale, Reputation, Roundel, Rowndell, Seed, Seethe, Simmer, South Sea, Vesicle, Widow

Bubble and squeak Colcannon

Buccaneer Corsair, Dampier, Drake, Freebooter, Morgan, Picaroon, Pirate

Buck (up) Bongo, Brace, Cheer, Dandy, Deer, Dollar, Elate, Encheer, Hart, Jerk, Leash, Male, Ourebi, Pitch, Pricket, Ram, Rusa, Sore, Sorel(l), Sorrel, Spade, Spay(a)d, > **STAG**, Staggard, Stud, Water, Wheel

Buckaroo Cowboy, Cowpoke

Bucket(s) Bail, Bale, Clamshell, Ice, Jacob's ladder, Kibble, Noria, Pail, Piggin, Rust, Scuttle, Situla, Slop, Stoop(e), Stope, Stoup, Tub

Buckeye Ohio

Buckle Artois, Clasp, Contort, Crumple, Deform, Dent, Fasten, Warp

▷ **Buckle** *may indicate* an anagram

Buckle-beggar Patrico

Buckler Ancile, Rondache, > **SHIELD**, Targe

▷ **Bucks** *may indicate* an anagram

Buckshee Free

Buckthorn Cascara, Wahoo

Buckwheat Brank, Sarrasin, Sarrazin

Bucolic Aeglogue, Eglogue, Idyllic, Pastoral, Rural, Rustic

Bud(ding), Buddy Botoné, Bottony, Bulbil, Burgeon, Clove, Cobber, Deb, Eye, Gem(ma), Germinate, Holly, Knop, Knosp, Knot, Nascent, Pal, Scion, Serial, Shoot, Sprout, Taste, Turion

Buddha, Buddhism, Buddhist Abhidhamma, Ahimsa, Amitabha, Anata,

Anatta, Anicca, Arhat, Asoka, Bodhisattva, Dalai Lama, Dukkha, Esoteric, Foism, Gautama, Hinayana, Jain, Jataka, Jodo, Kagyu, Mahatma, Mahayana, Maya, Nichiren, Pali, Pitaka, Pure Land, Rinzai, Ryobu, Sakya-muni, Sangha, Shinto, Siddhartha Gautama, Sila, Soka Gakkai, Soto, Theravada, Tripitaka, Triratna, Vajrayana, Zen(o)

Budge Jee, Move, Stir, Submit

Budget Allocation, Estimate, Operating, Plan, Programme, Shoestring

Buff Beige, Birthday suit, Eatanswill, Fan, Fawn, Nankeen, Nude, Nut, Polish, > RUB, Streak

Buffalo African, Anoa, Arna, Asiatic, Bison, Bonasus, Bugle, Cap, Cape, Carabao, Ox, Perplex, Takin, Tamarao, Tamarau, Timarau, Water, Zamouse

Buffer Bootblack, Cofferdam, Cutwater, Fender, Sleek-stone

Buffet Bang, Blow, Box, Carvery, Counter, Cuff, Finger-food, Hit, Lam, Maltreat, Perpendicular, Shove, Sideboard, Smorgasborg, Strike, Strook(e)

Buffoon(ery) Antic, Clown, Droll, Goliard, Harlequin, Horseplay, Iniquity, Jester, Mime(r), Mome, Mummer, Nutter, Pantagruel, Pantaloon(ery), Pickle-herring, Pierrot, Punchinello, Scaramouch, Scogan, Scoggin, Scurrile, Slouch, Tomfool, Vice, Wag, Zany

Bug(s) Anoplura, Arthropod, Assassin, Bacteria, Bedevil, Beetle, Berry, Capsid, Chinch, Cimex, Coccidae, Cockchafer, Corixid, Croton, Damsel, Debris, Dictograph®, Eavesdrop, Germ, Ground, Harlequin, Hassle, Hemiptera, > INSECT, Jitter, June, Kissing, Lace, Lightning, Listeria, Maori, May, Mealy, Micrococcus, Mike, Milkweed, Millennium, Mite, Nettle, Pill, Reduviid, Rhododendron, Shield, Skeeter, Squash, Tap, Vex, Wheel, Wiretap

Bugbear Anathema, Bogey, Bogle, Bogy, Eten, Ettin, Poker, Rawhead

Buggy Beach, Car, Cart, Pushchair, Shay, Tipcart, Trap

Bughouse Fleapit, Loco

Bugle, Bugle call Chamade, Clarion, Cornet, Hallali, Last post, Ox, Reveille, Taps, > TRUMPET, Urus

Build(ing), Building site Accrue, Anabolism, Ar(a)eostyle, Assemble, Bhavan, Big, Bricks and mortar, Capitol, Chapterhouse, Colosseum, Commons, Corncrib, Cot, > CREATE, Cruck, Curia, Develop, Dipteros, Drystone, Duplex, Edifice, Edify, Erect, Fabric, High-rise, Hut, Infill, Insula, Kaaba, Ken, Linhay, Listed, Low-rise, Lyceum, Minaret, Monopteron, Mould, Observatory, Outhouse, Palazzo, Phalanstery, Phalanx, Pile, Portakabin®, Premises, Prytaneum, Quonset®, Raise, Ribbon, Rotunda, Skyscraper, Stance, Structure, Synthesis, System, Tectonic, Telecottage, Temple, Tenement, Tholos, Tower, Triplex®

Builder Brick, Constructor, Engineer, Mason, Millwright, Stonemason, Waller

▷ **Building** *may indicate* an anagram

Bulb Camas(h), Camass, Chive, Cive, Corm, Flash, Globe, Lamp, Light, Olfactory, Pearl, Rupert's drop, Scallion, Set, Shallot, Squill

Bulge, Bulging Astrut, Bag, Bias, Biconvex, Bug, Bulbous, Bunchy, Cockle, Entasis, Expand, Exsert, Inion, Protrude, Protuberant, Relievo, Rotund, Strout, Strut, > SWELL, Tumid

Bulk(y) Aggregate, Ample, Big, Body, Corpulent, Density, Extent, Gross, Hull, Massive, Preponderance, Roughage, Scalar, > SIZE, Stout, Vol(ume), Weight

Bull(s), Bullock, Bully Anoa, Apis, Bakha, Beef, Blarney, Bludgeon, Bluster, Bovine, Brag, Brave, Browbeat, Buchis, Bucko, Despot, Dragoon, Drawcansir, Encierro, Englishman, Eretrian, Fancyman, Farnese, Flashman, Flatter, Gold, Gosh, Hapi, Harass, Hawcubite, Haze(r), Hector, Hoodlum, Huff, Intimidate, Investor, Iricism, Irish(ism), John, Killcow, Lambast, Maltreat, Merwer,

Mick(e)(y), Mistake, Mithraism, Mohock, Nandi, Neat, Pamplona, Papal, Piker, Pistol, Placet, Poler, Rhodian, Roarer, Rot, Ruffian, Sitting, Souteneur, Stag, Stale, Strong-arm, Swash-buckler, Taurine, Taurus, Toitoi, Tommy-rot, Tosh, Trash, Twaddle, Tyran(ne), Tyrannise, Tyrant, Unigenitus, Winged, Zo(bo)

Bulldog Marshal, Tenacious

Bulldoze(r) Angledozer, Coerce, Earthmover, Leveller, Overturn

Bullet Ammo, Balata, Ball, Baton round, Biscayan, Dumdum, Fusillade, Magic, Minié, Minié ball, Missile, Pellet, Percussio, Plastic, Round, Rubber, Shot, Slug, Soft-nosed, Tracer

Bulletin Memo, Message, Newsletter, Report, Summary

Bull-fight(er) Banderillero, Banderillo, Corrida, Cuadrilla, Escamillo, Matador, Picador, Rejoneador, Tauromachy, Toreador, Torero

Bull-head Cottoid, Father-lasher, Pogge, Sea-poacher

Bull-rider Europa

Bull-roarer Rhombos, Tu(r)ndun

Bull's eye Carton, God, Humbug, Target

Bulrush Pandanaceous, Reed, Reed-mace, Tule

Bulwark Bastion, Defence, Rampart, Resistor

Bum Ass, Beg, Prat, Sponge, Thumb, Tramp, Vagabond

Bumble Beadle, Bedel(l)

▷ **Bumble** *may indicate* an anagram

Bumboat woman Buttercup

Bumf Spam

Bump(er), Bumps Big, Blow, Bradyseism, Bucket, Clour, Collide, Dunch, Encephalocele, Fender, Hillock, Immense, Inian, Inion, Joll, Jo(u)le, Jowl, Keltie, Kelty, Knar, Knock, Mamilla, Mogul, Organ, Overrider®, Phrenology, Reveille, Rouse, Speed, Thump

Bumpkin Bucolic, Bushwhacker, Clodhopper, Hawbuck, Hayseed, Hick, Jock, Lout, Oaf, Put(t), Rube, Rustic, Yokel, Zany

Bumptious Arrogant, Brash, Randie, Randy, Uppity

Bun Barmbrack, Bath, Black, Chelsea, Chignon, Chou, Currant, Devonshire split, Hot-cross, Huffkin, Mosbolletjie, Roll, Teacake, Toorie, Wad

Bunch Acinus, Anthology, Bob, Botryoid, Bouquet, Byndle, Cluster, Fascicle, Finial, Flock, > GROUP, Hand, Handful, Lot, Lump, Nosegay, Panicle, Raceme, Spray, Staphyline, Tassel, Tee, Truss, Tuft

Bundle Axoneme, Bale, Bavin, Bluey, Bottle, Byssus, Desmoid, Dorlach, Drum, Fag(g)ot, Fascicle, Fascine, Fibre, Fibrovascular, Kemple, Knitch, Lemniscus, Matilda, > PACK(AGE), Parcel, Sack, Sheaf, Shiralee, Shock, Shook, Stook, Swag, Tie, Top, Trousseau, Truss, Vascular, Wad, Wadge, Wap

Bung Cork, Dook, Obturate, Plug, Stopgap, Stopper

Bungalow Dak

Bungle(r) Blunder, Blunk, Bodge, Boob, Botch, Bumble, Bummle, Dub, Duff, Fluff, Foozle, Foul, Foul up, Goof, Mash, Mess, Mis(h)guggle, Muddle, Muff, Mull, Prat, Screw, Spoil

Bunk(er), Bunkum Abscond, Absquatulate, Balderdash, Baloney, Berth, Blah, Bolt, Casemate, Claptrap, Clio, Entrap, Guy, Hazard, History, Hokum, Humbug, Malarky, Nonsense, Rot, Sandtrap, Scuttle, Stokehold, Tosh, Trap, Tripe

Bunter Billy, Owl

Bunthorne Aesthete, Poet

Bunting Bird, Cirl, Flag, Fringilline, Ortolan, Snow, Streamer, Yellow-hammer, Yowley

Buoy Bell, Breeches, Can, Dan, Daymark, Dolphin, Float, Life, Marker, Nun,

Raft, Ring, Seamark, Sonar, Sonobuoy, Spar, Sustain, Wreck

Buoyant Afloat, Blithe, Floaty, Resilient

Burble Blat, Gibber

Burden Albatross, Beare, Bob, Cargo, Cark, Chant, Chorus, Cross, Cumber, Deadweight, Drone, Droore, Encumber, Encumbrance, Fa-la, Fardel, Folderol, Fraught, Freight, Gist, Handicap, Hum, Lade, > **LOAD**, Lumber, Millstone, Monkey, Oercome, Onus, Oppress, Put-upon, Refrain, Rumbelow, Saddle, Servitude, Shanty, Substance, Tax, Tenor, Torch, Trouble, Weight, Woe, Yoke

Burdensome Irksome, Onerous, Oppressive, Weighty

Burdock Clote(-bar), Clothur, Cockle-bar, Weed

Bureau Agency, Agitprop, Cominform, Davenport, Desk, Interpol, Kominform, Marriage, > **OFFICE**, Volunteer

Bureaucracy, Bureaucrat(ic) CS, Impersonal, Jack-in-office, Mandarin, Red tape, Tapist, Wallah

Burgeon(ing) Asprout, Blossom, Bud, Grow, Sprout

Burgess, Burgher Citizen, Freeman

Burglar, Burgle Area-sneak, Cat, Crack(sman), House-breaker, Intruder, Peterman, Picklock, Raffles, Robber, Screw, Thief, Yegg

Burgundy Macon, Vin

Burial(place) Catacomb, Charnel, Committal, Crypt, Cubiculum, Darga, Funeral, God's acre, Golgotha, Grave, Interment, Kurgan, Lair, Last rites, Sepulchre, Sepulture, Tomb, Tumulus, Vault, Zoothapsis

Burin Graver

Burlesque Caricatura, Caricature, Comedy, Farce, Heroicomical, Hudibrastic(s), Hurlo-thrumbo, Lampoon, Macaronic, Parody, Satire, Skimmington, Skit, Spoof, Travesty

Burlington RA

Burly Bluff, Stout, Strapping

Burmese Karen(ni), Naga, Shan

Burn(er), Burning, Burnt Adust, Afire, Alow(e), Ardent, Argand, Arson, Ash, Auto-da-fé, Bats-wing, Beck, Bishop, Blaze, Blister, Blowtorch, Brand, Bren(ne), Brent, Brook, Bunsen, Causalgia, Caustic, Cauterise, Char, Chark, Chinese, Cinder, Coal, Coke, Combust, Conflagration, Cremate, Crozzled, Crucial, Deflagrate, Destruct, Eilding, Ember, Emboil, Empyreuma, Fervid, Fircone, > **FIRE**, Fishtail, Flagrant, Flare, Flash, Fresh(et), Gleed, Gut, Holocaust, Ignite, In, Incendiary, Incense, Incinerate, Inure, Inust(ion), Kill, Live, Lunt, Offering, On, Oxidise, Oxyacetylene, Plo(a)t, Powder, Pyric, Pyromania, Rill, Sati, Scald, Scorch, Scouther, Scowder, Scowther, Sear, Sienna, Sike, Singe, Sizzle, Smart, Smoulder, Suttee, Swale, Third-degree, Thurible, Torch, Umber, Urent, Ustion, Ustulation, Weeke, Welsbach, Wick

Burp Belch

Burr(ing) Brei, Brey, Clote, Croup, Dialect, Knob, Rhotacism

Burrow(er), Burrowing Dig, Earth, Fossorial, Gopher, Groundhog, Hole, How, Howk, Mole, Nuzzle, Root, Sett, Tunnel, Viscacha, Warren, Wombat, Worm

Bursar(y) Camerlengo, Camerlingo, Coffers, Grant, Purser, Scholarship, Treasurer

Bursitis Beat

Burst(ing) Blowout, Brast, Break, Dehisce, Disrupt, Dissilient, Ebullient, Erumpent, Erupt, > **EXPLODE**, Flare-up, Fly, Implode, Pop, Sforzato, Shatter, Spasm, Spirt, Split, Sprint, Spurt, Stave, Tetterous

Bury Cover, Eard, Earth, Embowel, Engrave, Enhearse, Graff, Graft, Imbed, Inearth, Inhearse, Inhume, Inter, Inurn, Landfill, Repress, Sepulture, Sink,

Ye(a)rd, Yird

Bus Aero, Bandwagon, Car, Charabanc, Coach, Double-decker, Greyhound, Hondey, Hopper, ISA, Jitney, Mammy-wagon, Rattletrap, Single-decker, Tramcar, Trolley, Walking

Bus conductor Cad, Clippy

Bush(y) Bramble, Brier, Bullace, Busket, Calico, Clump, Cotton, Dumose, Firethorn, Hawthorn, Hibiscus, Kapok, Mallee, Matagouri, Mulberry, Outback, Poinsettia, Poly-poly, President, Sallee, Shepherd, Shrub, Sugar, Thicket, Tire, Tod(de)

Bush-baby Durukuli, Galago, Nagapie, Night-ape

Bushel Ardeb, Bu, Co(o)mb, Cor, Ephah, Fou, Homer, Peck, Weight, Wey

Business Affair, Agency, Biz, Bus, Cartel, Cerne, Co, Commerce, Company, Concern, Conglomerate, Craft, Duty, Enterprise, Ergon, Establishment, Exchange, Fasti, Firm, Funny, Game, Gear, Hong, Industry, Line, Métier, Monkey, Office, Palaver, Pi(d)geon, Pidgin, Practice, Professional, Racket, Shebang, Shop, Show, To-do, Trade, Traffic, Transaction, Tread, Turnover, Unincorporated, Vocation, Zaikai

Businessman Babbitt, Capitalist, City, Entrepreneur, Financier, Realtor, Taipan, Trader, Tycoon

Busk(er) Bodice, Corset, Entertainer, German-band

Buskin(s) Brod(e)kin, Cothurn(us), Shoe

Buss Kiss, Osculate, Smack

Bussu Troelie, Troely, Troolie

Bust Beano, Boob, Brast, Break, Chest, Falsies, Figurehead, Herm(a), Insolvent, Sculp, Shatter(ed), Spree, Statue, Term(inus), To-tear, To-torne, Ups(e)y

▷ **Bust** *may indicate* an anagram

Bustard Bird, Otis, Turkey

Buster Keaton

Bustle Ado, Beetle, Do, Dress-improver, Flap, Pad, Scurry, > **STIR**, Swarm, Tournure, Whew

Busy Active, At (it), Deedy, > **DETECTIVE**, Dick, Eident, Employ, Ergate, Eye, Goer, Hectic, Hive, Humming, Occupied, Ornate, Prodnose, Stir, Tec, Throng, Worksome

Busybody Bustler, Meddler, Noser, Pragmatic, Snooper, Trout, Yenta

But Aber, Bar, Except, However, Keg, Merely, Nay, Only, Save, Sed, Simply, Tun

Butch He-man, Macho

Butcher(y) Cumberland, Decko, Dekko, Flesher, Kill, Killcow, Look, Massacre, Ovicide, Sever, Shambles, Shochet, Shufti, Slaughter, Slay

Butler Bedivere, Bread-chipper, Jeeves, Khansama(h), Major-domo, RAB, Rhett, Samuel, Servant, Sewer, Sommelier, Steward

Butt (in) Aris, Barrel, Bumper, Bunt, Clara, Dimp, Dunch, Enter, Geck, Glasgow kiss, Goat, Header, Horn, Jesting-stock, Laughing-stock, Mark, Nut, Outspeckle, Pantaloon, Pipe, Push, Ram, Roach, Scapegoat, Snipe, Stompie, > **STOOGE**, Straight man, Stump, Target, Tun, Ups

Butter Adulation, Billy, Brandy, Butyric, Cocoa, Coconut, Drawn, Flatter, Galam, Garcinia, Ghee, Ghi, Goa, Goat, Illipi, Illupi, Kokum, Mahua, Mahwa, Maitre d'hotel, Mow(r)a, Nut, Nutter, Pat, Peanut, Print, Ram, Scrape, Shea, Spread, Vegetable

▷ **Butter** *may indicate* a goat or such

Buttercup Bumboat woman, Crow-foot, Crow-toe, Goldilocks, Ranunculus, Reate, Thalictrum

Butterfingers Muff

Butterfish Nine-eyes
Butterfly Apollo, Argus, Birdwing, Blue, Brimstone, Brown, Cabbage white, Camberwell beauty, Cardinal, Chequered skipper, Cleopatra, Clouded yellow, Comma, Common blue, Dilettante, Eclosion, Emperor, Fritillary, Gate-keeper, Grayling, Hair-streak, Heath, Hesperid, Imaginal, Kallima, Large copper, Large white, Leaf, Lycaena, Marbled-white, Meadow brown, Milk-weed, Monarch, Morpho, Mourning-cloak, Nerves, Nymphalid, Nymphean, Orange-tip, Owl, Painted lady, Papilionidae, Peacock, Pieris, Psyche, Purple emperor, Red admiral, Rhopalocera, Ringlet, Satyr(idae), Satyrinae, Silverspot, Skipper, Small white, Speckled wood, Stamper, Sulphur, Swallow-tail, Thecla, Thistle, Tiger swallowtail, Tortoiseshell, Two-tailed pasha, Vanessa, Wall brown, White admiral
Buttermilk Bland, Lassi
Butternut Souari
Butter-tree Mahua, Mahwa, Mow(r)a
Buttocks Arse, Ass, Bahookie, Booty, Bottom, Can, Coit, Derrière, Doup, Duff, Fanny, Fundament, Gluteus maximus, Hinder-end, Hinderlan(d)s, Hurdies, Jacksie, Jacksy, Keester, Keister, Mooning, Nache, Nates, Prat, Quoit, Seat, Tush
Button(s) Barrel, Bellboy, Fastener, Frog, Hot, Knob, Mute, Netsuke, Olivet, Page(boy), Panic, Pearl, Push, Snooze, Stud, Switch, Toggle
Buttonhole Accost, Boutonniere, Detain, Eye, Flower
Buttress Brace, Counterfort, Flying, Hanging, Pier, Prop, Stay, Support, Tambour
Buxom Bonnie, Busty, Plump, Sonsy
Buy(ing), Buyer Believe, Bribe, Coff, Corner, Customer, Emption, Engross, Impulse, Monopsonist, Oligopsony, Panic, Purchase, Regrate, Shop, Shout, Spend, Take, Trade, Vendee
▷ **Buyer** *may indicate* money
Buzz(er) Bee, Bombilate, Bombinate, Button, Fly, Hum, Rumour, Scram, Whirr, Whisper, Zed, Zing, Zoom
Buzzard Bee-kite, Bird, Buteo, Hawk, Pern, Puttock, Vulture
By Alongside, At, Gin, Gone, In, Near, Neighbouring, Nigh, Of, Past, Per, Through, With, X
Bye Extra
Bye-bye Adieu, Farewell, Tata
Bygone B.C., Dead, Departed, Past, Yore
By Jove Egad
Bypass Avoid, Circuit, Coronary, > DETOUR, Evade, Ignore, Omit, Shunt, Skirt
By-product Epiphenomenon, Spin-off
Byre Cowshed, Manger, Stable, Trough
By so much The
By the way Apropos, Incidentally, Obiter
Byway Alley, Lane, Path
Byword Ayword, Phrase, Proverb, Slogan
Byzantine Catapan, Complicated, Exarch, Intricate, Intrince, Theme

Cc

C Around, Caught, Celsius, Cent, Centigrade, Charlie, Conservative, San

Cab Boneshaker, Crawler, Drosky, Fiacre, Four-wheeler, Growler, Gurney, Hackney, Hansom, Mini, Noddy, Taxi, Vettura

Cabal(ler) Arlington, Ashley, Buckingham, Clifford, Clique, Conspiracy, Coterie, Faction, Junto, Lauderdale, Party, Plot

Cab(b)alistic Abraxis, Mystic, Notarikon, Occult

Cabaret Burlesque, Floorshow

Cabbage(-head), Cabbage soup Book choy, Borecole, Brassica, Castock, Cauliflower, Cavalo nero, Chinese, Choucroute, Cole, Collard, Crout, Custock, Drumhead, Kerguelen, Kohlrabi, Kraut, Loaf, Loave, Pak-choi, Pamphrey, Pe-tsai, Sauerkraut, Savoy, Shchi, Shtchi, Skunk, Thieve, Turnip, Wild, Wort

Caber Fir, Janker, Log, Sting

Cabin Berth, Bibby, Bothy, Box, Cabana, Caboose, Camboose, Coach, Cottage, Crannog, Crib, Cuddy, Den, Gondola, Hovel, Hut, Izba, Lodge, Loghouse, Long-house, Pod, Pressure, Room, Roundhouse, Saloon, Shanty, Stateroom, Trunk

Cabin-boy Grummet

Cabinet Bahut, Cabale, Case, Closet, Commode, Console, Cupboard, Filing, Kitchen, Ministry, Secretaire, Shadow, Shrinal, Vitrine

Cabinet maker Chippendale, Ebeniste, Hepplewhite, Joiner, PM

Cable(way), Cable-car Chain, Coax(ial), Extension, Flex, Halser, Hawser, Jumper, Jump leads, Junk, Landline, Lead, Lead-in, Lifeline, Null-modern, Oil-filled, Outhaul, Rope, Slatch, Snake, Téléférique, > **TELEGRAM**, Telegraph, Telepherique, Telpher(age), Topping lift, Trunking, Wire, Yoke

Cache Deposit, Hidlin(g)s, > **HOARD**, Inter, Stash, Store, Treasure

Cachet Prestige

Cackle Cluck, Gaggle, Gas, Haw, Snicker, Titter

Cacography Scrawl

Cacophony Babel, Caterwaul, Charivari, Discord, Jangle

Cactus, Cactus-like Alhagi, Barel, Cereus, Cholla, Christmas, Dildo, Easter, Echino-, Hedgehog, Jojoba, Maguey, Mescal, Nopal, Ocotillo, Opuntia, Organ-pipe, Peyote, Prickly pear, Retama, Saguaro, Stapella, Star, Strawberry, Torch-thistle, Tuna, Xerophytic

Cad Base, Boor, Bounder, Churl, Cocoa, Heel, Oik, Rascal, Rotter, Skunk

Cadaver(ous) Body, Corpse, Deathly, Ghastly, Goner, Haggard, Stiff

Caddy Porter, Tea, Teapoy

Cadence Beat, Close, Euouae, Evovae, Fa-do, Flow, Lilt, Meter, Perfect, Plagal, Rhythm

Cadenza Fireworks

Cadet(s) Junior, OTC, Scion, Syen, Trainee, Younger

Cadge(r) Bludge, Bot, Bum, Impose, > **SCROUNGE**, Sponge

Cadmium Cd

Caesar Nero

Caesium Cs

Cafe(teria) Automat, Bistro, Brasserie, Buvette, Canteen, Commissary, Cybercafe, Diner, Dinette, Donko, Eatery, Estaminet, Filtré, Greasy spoon, Hashhouse, Internet, Juke joint, Pizzeria, Pull-in, Tearoom, Transport

Cage Bar, Battery, Box, Cavie, Confine, Coop, Corf, Dray, Drey, Enmew, Faraday, Fold, Frame, Grate, Hutch, Keavie, Mew, Pen, > PRISON, Safety, Squirrel, Trave

Cahoots Hugger-mugger

Cairn Barp, Dog, Horned, Man, Mound, Raise

Caisson Bends

Caitiff Meanie

Cajole(ry) Beflum, Beguile, Blandish, Blarney, Carn(e)y, > COAX, Cuittle, Humbug, Inveigle, Jolly, Persuade, Wheedle

Cake Agnus dei, Angel, Baba, Babka, Baklava, Banbury, Bannock, Bara brith, Barmbrack, Battenberg, Birthday, Brioche, Brownie, Buckwheat bun, Carcake, Cattle, Chapat(t)i, Chillada, Chupati, Chupattie, Chupatty, Clapbread, Clot, Coburg, Corn dodger, Cotton, Croquette, Cruller, Crumpet, Dainty, Devil's food, Drizzle, Dundee, Eccles, Eclair, Fancy, Farl(e), Filter, Fish, Flapjack, Frangipane, Frangipani, Fritter, Galette, Genoa, Gingerbread, Girdle, > HARDEN, Hockey, Hoe, Idli, Jannock, Jumbal, Jumbles, Koeksister, Kruller, Kuchen, Kueh, Lamington, Lardy, Latke, Layer, Linseed, Macaroon, Madeira, Madeleine, Maid of honour, Marble, Meringue, Millefeuille, Mud, Muffin, Napoleon, Nut, Oatmeal, Oil, Pan, Panettone, Paratha, Parkin, Parliament, Pat, Patty, Pavlova, Petit four, Pikelet, > PLASTER, Pomfret, Pone, Pontefract, Poori, Popover, Pound, Profiterole, Puff, Puftaloon(a), Puri, Queencake, Ratafia, Ready-mix, Religieuse, Rice, Rock, Rosti, Roti, Rout, Rum baba, Rusk, Sachertorte, Saffron, Sally Lunn, Salt, Sandwich, Savarin, Scone, Seed, Set, Simnel, Singing-hinny, Slab, Slapjack, Soul, Spawn, Spice, Sponge, Stollen, Stottie, Sushi, Swiss roll, Tablet, Tansy, Tea(bread), Tipsy, Torte, Tortilla, Twelfth, Upside down, Vetkoek, Wad, Wafer, Waffle, Wedding, Wonder, Yeast

▷ **Cake** *may indicate an anagram*

Cake-shaped Placentiform

Cakestand Curate

Cakewalk Doddle

Calaboose Jail, Loghouse

Calamitous, Calamity Blow, Catastrophe, Dire, > DISASTER, Distress, Fatal, Ill, Jane, Ruth, Storm, Tragic, Unlucky, Visitation, Woe

Calcareous Ganoin, Lithite

Calcium Ca, Colemanite, Dogger, Dripstone, Otolith, Quicklime, Scawtite, Whewellite

Calculate(d), Calculation, Calculator Abacus, Actuary, Compute(r), Cost, Design, Estimate, Extrapolate, Log, Napier's bones, Prorate, Quip(p)u, Rate, > RECKON, Slide-rule, Sofar, Soroban, Tactical, Tell

Calculus Cholelith, Differential, Functional, Infinitesimal, Integral, Lambda, Lith, Lithiasis, Predicate, Propositional, Science, Sentential, Sialolith, Stone, Tartar, Urolith

Caledonian Kanak

Calendar Advent, Agenda, Almanac, Chinese, Diary, Fasti, Gregorian, Hebrew, Intercalary, Jewish, Journal, Julian, Luach, Lunisolar, Menology, Newgate, New Style, Ordo, Perpetual, Revolutionary, Roman, Sothic

Calender(ing) Dervish, Mangle, Swissing

Calf Ass, Bobby, Box, Cf, Deacon, Dogie, Dogy, Freemartin, Golden, Leg, Maverick, Poddy, Sleeper, Stirk, Sural, Tollie, Tolly, Tree, Veal, Vitular

Caliban Moon-calf
Calibrate, Calibre Bore, Capacity, Graduate, Mark, > QUALITY, Text
Californium Cf
Caliph Abbasid(e), Vathek
Call(ed), Calling, Call on, Call up Adhan, Appeal, Arraign, Art, Awaken, Azan, Banco, Bawl, Beck, Behote, Bevy, Bid, Boots and saddles, Business, Buzz, Career, Chamade, Cite, Claim, Clang, Clarion, Cleep, Clepe, Close, Cold, Conference, Conscript, Convene, Convoke, Cooee, Cry, Curtain, Dial, Drift, Dub, Evoke, Gam, Go, Hail, Hallali, Haro, Heads, Heave-ho, Hech, Hete, Hey, Hight, Ho, Hot(e), Howzat, Huddup, Hurra(h), Job, Junk, Last (post), Line, Local, Métier, Misère, Mobilise, Mot, Name, Nap, Need, Nemn, Nempt, Nominate, Olé, Page, Phone, Photo, Post, Proo, Pruh, Pursuit, Rechate, Recheat, Retreat, Reveille, Ring, Roll, Rort, Rouse, Route, Sa-sa, Sennet, > SHOUT, Shut-out, Slam, Slander, Slogan, Soho, Sola, SOS, STD, Style, Subpoena, Summon(s), Tails, Tantivy, Taps, Telephone, Term, Toho, Toll, Trumpet, Trunk, Visit, Vocation, Waken, Wake-up, Whoa-ho-ho, Wo ha ho, Yell, Yo, Yodel, Yodle, Yo-ho(-ho), Yoicks, Yoo-hoo
Calla(s) Aroid, Lily, Maria
Caller Fresh, Guest, Herring, Inspector, Muezzin, Rep, Traveller, > VISITOR
Calligraphy Kakemono
Callipers Odd legs
Callosity, Call(o)us Bunion, Cold, Corn, Hard, Horny, Obtuse, Ringbone, Seg, Thylose, Tough, Tylosis, Unfeeling
Callow Crude, Green, Immature, Jejune
Calm Abate, Alegge, Aleye, Allay, Allege, Appease, Ataraxy, Composed, Cool, Doldrums, Easy, Easy-osy, Eevn, Equable, Equanimity, Even, Eye, Flat, Glassy, Halcyon, Loun(d), Lown(d), Lull, Mellow, Mild, Milden, Millpond, Nonchalant, Pacify, Peaceful, Philosophical, Phlegmatic, Placate, Placid, Quell, Quiet, Relax(ed), Repose, Seraphic, Serene, Settle, Simmer down, Sleek, > SOOTHE, Sopite, Still, Stilly, Subside, Tranquil(lise), Unturbid, Windless
Calorie Gram, Kilogram
Calumniate, Calumny Aspersion, Backbite, Defame, Libel, Malign, Slander, Slur
Calvary Golgotha
Calvin(ist) Accusative, Coolidge, Genevan, Hopkins, Huguenot, Infralapsarian, Predestination, Sublapsarian, Supralapsarian
Calydonian Boar
Calypso Ogygia, Siren, > SONG
Cam Cog, River, Snail, Tappet
Camaraderie Fellowship, Rapport, Team spirit
Camber Hog, Slope
Cambium Phellogen
Cambodian Khmer (Rouge)
Cambria(n) Menevian, Wales
Cambridge Cantab, Squat, Uni
Came Arrived
Camel, Camel train Aeroplane, Arabian, Artiodactyla, Bactrian, Caisson, Colt, Dromedary, Kafila, Llama, Oont, Sopwith, Tulu
Cameo Anaglyph, Camaieu, Carving
Camera, Camera man Box, Brownie®, Camcorder, Candid, Chambers, Cine, Compact, Digital, Disc, Electron, Flash, Gamma, Grip(s), Iconoscope, Kodak®, Miniature, Minicam, Movie, Obscura, Orthicon, Palmcorder, Panoramic,

Pantoscope, Pinhole, Polaroid®, Process, Programmed, Reflex, Retina, Schmidt, SLR, Somascope, Speed, Steadicam®, Stop-frame, Video, Vidicon, Viewfinder, Webcam

Camouflage Conceal, > DISGUISE, Mark, Maskirovka, War-dress

▷ **Camouflaged** *may indicate* an anagram

Camp(er) Affectation, Aldershot, Banal, Base, Belsen, Bivouac, Boma, Boot, Caerleon, Cantonment, Castral, Colditz, Concentration, David, Death, Depot, D(o)uar, Dumdum, Epicene, Faction, Fat, Flaunt, Gulag, Happy, Health, High, Holiday, L(a)ager, Labour, Lashkar, Leaguer, Low, Manyat(t)a, Oflag, Outlie, Peace, Prison, Side, Siwash, Stagey, Stalag, Stative, Swagman, Tent, Theatrical, Transit, Treblinka, Valley Forge, Work, Zare(e)ba, Zariba, Zereba, Zeriba

Campaign(er) Barnstorm, Battle, Blitz, Blitzkreig, Canvass, Crusade, Doorknock, Drive, Field, Jihad, Lobby, Mission, Promotion, Run, Satyagraha, Smear, Stint, Strategist, Tree-hugger, Venture, Veteran, War, Warray, Warrey, Whispering, Whistle-stop, Witchhunt

Campanula Rampion

Campeador Chief, Cid

Camp-follower Lascar, Leaguer-lady, Leaguer-lass, Sutler

Camphor Menthol

Campion Knap-bottle, Lychnis, Ragged robin, Silene

▷ **Camptown** *may indicate* de-

Can(s) Able, Billy, Bog, Capable, Churn, Cooler, Dow, Gaol, Garbage, Gents, Headphones, Is able, Jerry, Jug, Karsy, Loo, May, Nick, Pail, Pot, Preserve, > PRISON, Privy, Stir, Tank, Tin, Trash, Watering

Canada, Canadian Abenaki, Acadian, Canuck, Comox, Dene, Dogrib, Hare, Herring choker, Inuit, Johnny Canuck, Maliseet, Montagnais, Naskapi, Nuxalk, Péquiste, Quebeccer, Quebecker, Québecois, Salteaux, Slavey, Stoney, Tsimshian, Ungava, Yukon

Canal Alimentary, Ampul, Anal, Birth, Caledonian, Channel, Conduit, Corinth, Duct, Duodenum, Fa, Enteron, Erie, Foss(e), Gota, Grand (Trunk), Grande Terre, Grand Union, Groove, Gut, Haversian, Kiel, Klong, Labyrinth, Lode, Manchester Ship, Meatus, Midi, Mitelland, Navigation, New York State Barge, Oesophagus, Panama, Pharynx, Pipe, Pound, Resin, Ring, Root, Scala, Schlemm's, Semi-circular, Ship, Shipway, Spinal, Stone, Suez, Suo, Urethra, Waterway, Welland, Zanja

Canal-boat Barge, Fly-boat, Gondola, Vaporetto

Canapé Cate, Snack, Titbit

Canary Bird, Grass, Roller, Serin, Singer, Yellow

Cancel Abrogate, Adeem, Annul, Counteract, Countermand, Cross, Delete, Destroy, Erase, Kill, Negate, Nullify, Obliterate, Override, Remit, Repeal, Rescind, Retrait, Revoke, Scrub, Undo, Unmake, Void, Wipe, Write off

Cancer(ian) Moon Child

Cancer(ous) Big C, Carcinoma, Crab, Curse, Kaposi's Sarcoma, Leukaemia, Oat-cell, Tropic, Tumour, Wolf

Candela Cd

▸ **Candelabra** *see* CANDLE(STICK)

Candid, Candour Albedo, Blunt, Camera, Franchise, Frank, Honesty, Open, Outspoken, Plain(-spoken), Round, Upfront

Candida Fungus

Candidate(s) Agrege, Applicant, Aspirant, Contestant, Entrant, Field, Nominee, Ordinand, Postulant, Running mate, Stalking horse, Testee

Candied, Candy Angelica, Caramel, Cotton, Eryngo, Eye, Glace, Maple, Rock,

Snow, Succade, Sugar, > **SWEET**

Candle(stick), Candelabra Amandine, Bougie, C(i)erge, Dip, Fetch, Girandole, Hanukiah, International, Jesse, Lampadary, Light, Long-sixes, Menorah, Mould, Padella, Paschal, Pricket, Roman, Rushlight, Sconce, Serge, Shammash, Shammes, Slut, Sperm, Standard, Tace, Tallow, Tallow-dip, Taper, Torchère, Tricerion, Wax, Waxlight

Candlefish Eulachon, Oolakon, Oulachon, Oulakon, Ulic(h)an, Ulic(h)on, Ulikon

▶ **Candy** *see* **CANDIED**

Cane Arrow, Baculine, Bamboo, Baste, Beat, Birk, Crabstick, Dari, Dhurra, Doura, Dur(r)a, Ferula, Ferule, Goor, Gur, Jambee, Malacca, Narthex, Penang-lawyer, Pointer, Raspberry, Rat(t)an, Rod, Stick, Sugar, Swagger-stick, Swish, Switch, Swordstick, Tan, Tickler, Vare, Wand, Whangee, Wicker(-work)

Canine Biter, C, Dog, Eye-tooth

Canker Corrosion, Curse, Lesion, Ulcer

Cannabis Benj, Bhang, Bifter, Boneset, Durban poison, Ganja, Ganny, Grass, Hash, Hemp, Henry, Louie, Pot, Skunk, Zol

Cannibal Anthropophagus, Heathen, Long pig, Man-eater, Ogre, Thyestean, Wendigo

Cannon Amusette, Barrage, Basilisk, Bombard, Breechloader, Carom, Carronade, Chaser, Collide, Criterion, Culverin, Drake, Drop, Falcon, Gun, Howitzer, Kiss, Long-tom, Loose, Monkey, Mons Meg, Nursery, Saker, Stern-chaser, Water, Zamboorak, Zomboruk, Zumbooru(c)k

Cannot Canna, Cant, Downa(e), Downay

Canny Careful, Frugal, Prudent, Scot, Shrewd, Slee, Sly, Thrifty, Wice, Wily, Wise

Canoe(ist) Bidarka, Bidarkee, Canader, Dugout, Faltboat, Kayak, Log, Mokoru, Monoxylon, Montaria, Oomiack, Paddler, Peterborough, Piragua, Pirogue, Rob Roy, Surf, Waka, Woodskin

Canon(ise) Austin, Besaint, Brocard, Camera, Cancrizans, Chapter, Chasuble, Code, Crab, Infinite, Isidorian, > **LAW**, Line, Mathurin(e), Minor, Nocturn, Norbertine, Nursery, Pitaka, Polyphony, Prebendary, Precept, Premonstratensian, Retrograde, Rota, Round, Rule, Square, Squier, Squire, Standard, Tenet, Unity, White

Canopy Awning, Baldachin, Baldaquin, Chuppah, Ciborium, Clamshell, Dais, He(a)rse, Huppah, Majesty, Marquee, Marquise, Pavilion, Shamiana(h), State, Tabernacle, Tent, Tester

Cant Argot, Bevel, Heel, Incline, Jargon, Mummery, Patois, Patter, Rogue's Latin, Shelta, Slang, Slope, Snivel, Snuffle, Tip

Cantankerous Cussed, Fire-eater, Ornery, Querulous, Testy, Tetchy

Cantata Kinderspiel, Motet, Tobacco

Canteen Chuck-wagon, Mess, Munga, Naafi

Canter Amble, Hypocrite, Jog, Lope, Tit(t)up, Tripple

Canto Air, Fit(te), Fitt, Fytte, Melody, Verse

Canton Aargau, Appenzell, Basle, District, Eyalet, Fribourg, Glarus, Graubunden, Jura, Lucerne, Neuchatel, Quarter, St Gall, Schaffhausen, Schwyz, Solothurn, Thurgau, Ticino, Unterwalden, Uri, Valais, Vaud, Zug, Zurich

Cantred Commot(e)

Canvas Awning, Burlap, Dra(b)bler, Fly-sheet, Lug-sail, Mainsail, Marquee, Oil-cloth, Paint, Raven's-duck, Reef, > **SAIL**, Staysail, Stuns(ai)l, Tent, Trysail, Wigan

Canvass(er) Agent, Doorstep, Drum, Poll, Solicit

▷ **Canvasser** *may indicate* a painter or a camper

Canyon Box, Canada, Defile, Grand, Grand Coulee, Nal(l)a, Nallah, Submarine

Cap(ped) Abacot, Amorce, Balaclava, Balmoral, Barret, Baseball, Bathing, Bellhop, Bendigo, Ber(r)et, Biggin, Biretta, Blakey, Blue, Blue-bonnet, Bonnet-rouge, Bycoket, Call, Calotte, Calpac(k), Calyptrate, Capeline, Caul, Chaco, Chape, Chapeau, Chaperon, Chapka, Chechia, Cheese-cutter, Cloth, Cockernony, Coif, Cope, Cornet, Cowl, Cradle, > **CROWN**, Czapka, Davy Crockett, Deerstalker, Dunce's, Dutch, Fatigue, Ferrule, Filler, Flat, Fool's, Forage, Gandhi, Garrison, Gimme, Glengarry, Grannie, Granny, > **HAT**, Havelock, Hummel bonnet, Iceberg, International, Jockey, Juliet, Kalpak, Kepi, Kilmarnock, Kippa, Kippoth, Kipput, Kiss-me(-quick), Knee, Liberty, Lid, Mob, Monmouth, Monteer, Montero, Mor(r)ion, Mortar-board, Muffin, Mutch, Newsboy, Night, Outdo, Pagri, Patellar, Percussion, Perplex, Phrygian, Pile, Pileus, Pinner, Polar, Puggaree, Quoif, Root, Schapska, Shako, Skullcap, Square, Statute, Stocking, Summit, > **SURPASS**, Taj, Tam(-o'-shanter), Thimble, Thinking, Thrum, Toe, Toorie, Top, Toque, Toy, Trenchard, Trencher, Tuque, Turk's, Watch, Wishing, Yarmulka, Yarmulke, Zuchetto

Capable, **Capability** Able, Brown, Capacity, Competent, Deft, Effectual, Efficient, Firepower, Qualified, Skilled, Susceptible, Up to

Capacitance, **Capacity** Ability, Aptitude, C, Cab, Competence, Content, Cor, Cubic, Endowment, Function, Gift, Limit, Log, Power, Qua, Receipt, Scope, Size, Skinful, Tankage, Thermal, Tonnage, Valence, Vital, Volume

Caparison Robe, Trap(pings)

Cape Agulhas, Almuce, Bon, Burnouse, Byron, Calimere Point, Canaveral, Canso, Cloak, Cod, Comorin, Delgado, Dezhnev, Domino, Dungeness, East(ern), Fairweather, Faldetta, Fanion, Fanon, Farewell, Fear, Fichu, Finisterre, Flattery, Good Hope, Guardafui, Harp, Hatteras, Head(land), Helles, Hoe, Hogh, Hook of Holland, Horn, Inverness, Kennedy, Leeuwin, Lindesnes, Lizard, Manteel, Mant(e)let, Mantilla, Mantle, Matapan, May, Miseno, Mo(z)zetta, Muleta, Naze, Ness, Nordkyn, North, Northern, Ortegal, Palatine, Parry, Pelerine, Peninsula, Point, Poncho, Promontory, Race, Ras, Ray, Reinga, Roca, Ruana, Runaway, Sable, St Vincent, Sandy, Scaw, Skagen, Skaw, Sontag, Southwest, Talma, Tippet, Trafalgar, Ushant, Verde, Waterproof, Western, Wrath

Caper(ing) Antic, Bean, Boer, Capparis, Capriole, Cavort, Dance, Dido, Flisk, Frisk, Frolic, Gambado, Gambol, Harmala, Harmalin(e), Harmel, Harmin(e), Prance, Prank, Saltant, Scoup, Scowp, Skip, Tit(t)up

Capet Marie Antoinette

Cape Town SA

Capitalist Financier, Moneyer, Sloane

▷ **Capitalist** *may indicate* one living in a capital

Capitals A1, Assets, Block, Boodle, Bravo, Bully, Cap, Chapiter, Chaptrel, Doric, Equity, Euge, Excellent, Fixed, Flight, Float, Floating, Fonds, Great, Helix, Human, Initial, Ionic, Lethal, Lulu, Metropolis, Principal, Risk, Rustic, Seat, Seed, Social, Splendid, Sport, Stellar, Stock, Super, Topping, UC, Upper case, Venture, Working

● **CAPITALS**
●
●

●	**3 letters:**	Ufa	**4 letters:**	Baku
●	Jos		Acra	Bari
●	Rio		Apia	Bern

Bida	Enugu	Bangui	Moroni
Bonn	Hanoi	Banjul	Moscow
Brno	Harar	Bastia	Munich
Caen	Jammu	Batumi	Muscat
Cali	Jinan	Beirut	Nagpur
Chur	Kabul	Berlin	Nassau
Cork	Kazan	Bhopal	Nevers
Dili	Konia	Bogota	Niamey
Doha	Konya	Bruges	Nouméa
Faro	Lagos	Brunei	Ottawa
Graz	Lassa	Colima	Oviedo
Homs	Lhasa	Cracow	Owerri
Hums	Lille	Darwin	Palmas
Ipoh	Lyons	Denver	Pamjin
Kiel	Macao	Dessau	Panaji
Kiev	Meroe	Dodoma	Peking
Kobe	Minsk	Dublin	Pierre
Laos	Monza	Geneva	Prague
Lima	Nancy	Giyani	Ranchi
Lomé	Nukus	Gondar	Regina
Male	Palma	Habana	Riyadh
Metz	Paris	Harare	Roseau
Nuuk	Patna	Havana	Ryazan
Oslo	Pella	Hobart	Sendai
Pegu	Perth	Hohhot	Skopje
Riga	Pinsk	Ibadan	Sokoto
Rome	Poona	Ilorin	St Paul
San'a	Praha	Imphal	Taipei
Sion	Praia	Jaipur	Tallin
Susa	Quito	Jalapa	Tehran
Suva	Rabat	Johore	Thebes
Xian	Salem	Kaduna	Thimbu
	Sanaa	Kigali	Tirana
5 letters:	Seoul	Kohima	Tobruk
Abiya	Simla	Lahore	Topeka
Abuja	Sofia	Lisbon	Umtata
Accra	Sucré	Loanda	Vienna
Agana	Tokyo	London	Warsaw
Amman	Tunis	Luanda	Xining
Berne	Turin	Lusaka	Yangon
Bisho	Vaduz	Macapá	Zagreb
Boise	Zomba	Maceió	
Cairo		Madrid	**7 letters:**
Cuzev	**6 letters:**	Maikop	Abidjan
Dacca	Abakan	Malabo	Ajaccio
Dakar	Albany	Manama	Algiers
Delhi	Ankara	Manila	Antioch
Dhaka	Asmara	Maputo	Atlanta
Dijon	Astana	Maseru	Baghdad
Dilli	Athens	Mekele	Bangkok
Dutse	Austin	Merano	Barnaul
Emisa	Bamako	Merida	Beijing

- Belfast
- Bikaner
- Bishkek
- Caracas
- Cardiff
- Cayenne
- Colombo
- Conakry
- Cordoba
- Cuttack
- Douglas
- Funchal
- Gangtok
- Goiania
- Hanover
- Honiara
- Huhenot
- Isfahan
- Jackson
- Jakarta
- Kaesong
- Kampala
- Karachi
- Khartum
- Konakri
- Lansing
- Louvain
- Lucknow
- Madison
- Malacca
- Managua
- Mathura
- Mbabane
- Memphis
- Morelia
- Munster
- Nairobi
- Nicosia
- Nineveh
- Palermo
- Papeete
- Pishpek
- Plovdiv
- Potsdam
- Rangoon
- San José
- San Juan
- Stanley
- Taiyuan
- Tallinn
- Tbilisi
- Teheran

Tel Aviv
Thimphu
Toronto
Trieste
Tripoli
Vilnius
Vilnyus
Xanthus
Yaounde
Yerevan

8 letters:
Abu Dhabi
Adelaide
Agartala
Asuncion
Belgrade
Belmopan
Beyrouth
Boa Vista
Brasilia
Brisbane
Brussels
Budapest
Cagliari
Calcutta
Canberra
Cape Town
Castries
Columbia
Columbus
Culiacan
Curitiba
Djibouti
Edmonton
Eraklion
Florence
Freetown
Gaborone
Godthaab
Golconda
Hannover
Hargeisa
Hartford
Helsinki
Honolulu
Istanbul
Jayapura
Katmandu
Khartoum
Kingston
Kinshasa

Kirkwall
Kishinev
Lausanne
Lilongwe
Mandalay
Monrovia
Monterey
Narbonne
Ndjamena
Pamplona
Pergamum
Port Said
Pretoria
Saltillo
Salzburg
Santiago
Sarajevo
Shanghai
Shenyang
St Helier
Tashkent
Usumbura
Valletta
Victoria
Windhoek
Winnipeg

9 letters:
Amsterdam
Annapolis
Ashkhabad
Bangalore
Benin City
Bucharest
Bujumbura
Cartagena
Chihuahua
Des Moines
Edinburgh
Fongafale
Heraklion
Innsbruck
Islamabad
Jerusalem
Kathmandu
Leningrad
Ljubljana
Magdeburg
Maiduguri
Melbourne
Mogadishu
Nashville

Nuku'alofa
Perigueux
Perpignan
Port Blair
Port Louis
Porto Novo
Port Royal
Putrajaya
Pyongyang
Reykjavik
Samarkand
St Georges
Stockholm
Stuttgart
Thorshavn
Trebizond
Ulan Bator
Vientiane

10 letters:
Addis Ababa
Basse-terre
Baton Rouge
Bratislava
Bridgetown
Charleston
Copenhagen
Eisenstadt
Frauenfeld
Georgetown
Kragujevac
Libreville
Little Rock
Mexico City
Montevideo
Montgomery
Montpelier
Nouakchott
Panama City
Paramaribo
Persepolis
Porto Velho
Providence
Rawalpindi
Trivandrum
Valladolid
Washington
Wellington
Whitehorse
Willemstad
Yashkar-Ola

- **11 letters:**
- Brazzaville
- Buenos Aires
- Campo Grande
- Charlestown
- Guadalajara
- Johore Bahru
- Kuala Lumpur
- Nakhichevan
- Ouagadougou
- Pandemonium
- Pondicherry

Port Moresby
Port of Spain
Saarbruchen
San Salvador
Tegucigalpa
Yellowknife

12 letters:
Antananaviro
Bloemfontein
Fort-de-France
Pandaemonium

Port-au-Prince
Port Harcourt
Salt Lake City
Santo Domingo
Tenochtitian
Williamsburg
Yamoussoukro

13 letters:
Hertogenbosch
Jefferson City

14 letters:
Constantinople

15 letters:
Charlotte Amalie

16 letters:
Pietermaritzburg

Capitulate Acquiesce, Comply, > SURRENDER
Capless Bare
▷ **Capless** *may indicate* first letter missing
Capone Al, Scarface
▷ **Capriccioso** *may indicate* an anagram
Caprice, **Capricious** Arbitrary, Boutade, Capernoitie, Conceit, Desultory, Erratic, Fancy, Fitful, Freak, Humoresk, Humoresque, Irony, Megrim, Mood, Perverse, Quirk, Vagary, Wayward, Whim(sy)
Capsize Crank, Overbalance, Purl, Tip, Turn turtle, Upset, Whemmle, Whomble
▷ **Capsized** *may indicate* a word upside down
Capstan Sprocket, Windlass
Capsule Amp(o)ule, Bowman's, Cachet, Habitat, Internal, Ootheca, Orbiter, Ovisac, Pill, Space, Spacecraft, Spansule, Spermatophore, Suppository, Time, Urn
Captain Ahab, Bligh, Bobadil, Bones, Brassbound, Capt, Channel, Chief, Cid, Commander, Condottiere, Cook, Copper, Cuttle, Flint, Group, Hornblower, Kettle, Kidd, Leader, Macheath, Master, Nemo, Old man, Owner, Patron, Patroon, Post, Privateer, Protospatharius, Skip(per), Standish, Subah(dar), Subedar, Swing, Trierarch
Caption Cutline, Heading, Headline, Inscription, Masthead, Roller, Sub-title, Title
Captious Critical, Peevish
Captivate(d), **Captivating** Beguile, Bewitch, Charm, Enamour, Enthrall, Epris(e), Take, Winsome
Captive, **Captivity** Bonds, Duress, POW, Prisoner, Slave
Capture Abduct, Annex, Bag, Catch, Collar, Cop, Electron, Enchain, Enthral(l), Grab, Land, Motion, Net, Prize, Rush, Seize, Snabble, Snaffle, Snare, > TAKE
Capuchin Cebus, Monkey, Sajou
Car Astra, Audi, Auto, Banger, Beetle, Berlin, Biza, BL, Bluebird, Bomb, Brake, Bubble, Buffet, Bugatti, Buick, Bumper, Bus, Cab(riolet), Cadillac, Catafalco, Catafalque, Chariot, Classic, Clunker, Coach, Company, Concept, Convertible, Cortina, Coupé, Courtesy, Crate, Daimler, Diner, Dodgem®, Drag(ster), Drophead, Dunger, Elf, Estate, E-type, Fastback, Fiat, Flivver, Ford, Formula, Freight, Ghost, Gondola, Griddle, GT, Hardtop, Hatchback, Heap, Hearse, Hillman, Hot-rod, Irish, Jalop(p)y, Jamjar, Jammy, Jaunting, Jim Crow, Kart, Kit, Knockabout, Lada, Lagonda, Lancia, Landaulet, Landrover, Lift-back, Limo, Limousine, Merc(edes), MG, Mini, Model T, Morris, Nacelle, Notchback, Observation, Opel, Panda, Parlour, Patrol, Popemobile, Prowl, Racer, Ragtop, Railroad, Rattletrap, Restaurant, Roadster, Roller, Rolls, RR,

Runabout, Rust bucket, Saloon, Scout, Sedan, Service, Shooting-brake, Skoda, Sleeper, Sleeping, Soft-top, Speedster, Sports, Squad, Station wagon, Steam, Stock, Stretch-limo, Subcompact, Sunbeam, Tank, Telepherique, Telpher, Three-wheeler, Tin Lizzie, Tonneau, Tourer, Tram, Trolley, Turbo, Two-seater, Vehicle, Veteran, Vintage, Voiture, VW, Wheeler, Wheels

Caramel Brûlé

Carat Point

Caravan Caf(f)ila, Convoy, Fleet, Kafila, Safari, Trailer

Caravanserai Choltry, Choutry, Inn, Khan

Caraway Aj(o)wan, Carvy, Seed

Car-back Boot, Dick(e)y, Tonneau

Carbamide Urea

Carbide Silicon

Carbine Gun, Musket

Carbohydrate Agarose, Carrageenan, Cellulose, Chitin, Dextran, Disaccharide, Glycogen, Heptose, Hexose, Inulin, Ketose, Laminarin, Mannan, Mucilage, Pectin, Pectose, Pentosan(e), Pentose, Saccharide, Sorbitol, Starch, Sucrose, Sugar

Carbolic Orcin

Carbon(ate) Activated, Ankerite, Austenite, Buckminsterfullerene, Buckyball, C, Charcoal, Coke, Dialogite, Diamond, Flame, Flimsy, Fullerene, Gas black, Graphite, Lampblack, Natron, Scawtite, Soot, Spode, Spodium, Urao, Witherite, Zaratite

Carbon deficiency Acapnia

Carboy Demijohn

Carbuncle Anthrax, Ruby

Carcase, Carcass Body, Cadaver, Carrion, Corpse, Cutter, Krang, Kreng, Morkin, Mor(t)ling

Card(s), Cardboard Ace, Affinity, Amex®, Baccarat, Basto, Bill, Birthday, Bower, Business, Calling, Canasta, Cartes, Cash, Caution, Charge, Cheque, Chicane, Cigarette, Club, Comb, Compass, Court(esy), Credit, Cue, Curse of Scotland, Dance, Debit, Deck, Deuce, Devil's (picture) books, Diamond, Donor, Drawing, Ecarté, Eccentric, Euchre, Expansion, Face, False, Flash, Flaught, Flush, > **GAME**, Gold, Green, Hand, Hard, Health, Heart, Hole, Honour, ID, Identification, Identity, Intelligent, Jack, Jambone, Jamboree, Joker, Kanban, Key, King, Laser, Leading, Letter, Loo, Loyalty, Magnetic, Manille, Master, Matador, Maximum, Meishi, Meld, Memory, Mise, Mistigris, Mogul, Mournival, Oddity, Ombre, Pack, Past, Pasteboard, Payment, PC, Picture, Placard, Place, Plastic, Playing, Proximity, Punch(ed), Quatorze, Quatre, Queen, Queer, Quiz, Race, Rail, Red, Rippler, Rove, Scraperboard, Scribble, Shade, Show, Sim, Singleton, Smart, Soda, Solo, Sound, Spade, Spadille, Squeezer, Stiffener, Store, Strawboard, Swab, Swipe, Swish, Switch, Swob, Swot, Talon, Tarok, Tarot, Tease(r), Tenace, Test, Thaumatrope, Ticket, Tiddy, Time, Tose, Toze, Trading, Trey, Trump, Union, Valentine, Visa, Visiting, Wag, Weirdie, Wild, Yellow, Zener

Cardigan Jacket, Wam(m)us, Wampus, Woolly

Cardinal Camerlingo, Chief, College, Eight, Eminence, Eminent, Grosbeak, Hat, HE, Hume, Legate, Manning, Mazarin, Newman, Number, Pivotal, Polar, Prelate, Radical, Red, Red-hat, Richelieu, Sacred college, Sin, Spellman, Virtue, Vital, Wolsey, Ximenes

Card-player Dealer, Pone

Care(r), Caring Attention, Burden, Cark, Caution, Cerne, Cherish, Community,

> **CONCERN**, Cosset, Grief, Heed, Intensive, Kaugh, Keep, Kiaugh, Maternal, Mind, Pains, Palliative, Parabolanus, Providence, Reck(e), Reke, Residential, Respite, Retch, Solicitude, > **TEND**, Tenty, Worry

Careen(ing) Parliament-heel

Career Course, Hurtle, Life, Line, Run, Rush, Speed, Start, Tear, Vocation

▷ **Career** *may indicate* an anagram

Carefree > **CARELESS**, Irresponsible, > **NEGLIGENT**, Oops, Perfunctory, Rollicking, Thoughtless

Careful(ly) Canny, Chary, Discreet, Gentle, Hooly, Meticulous, Mindful, Painstaking, Pernickety, Provident, Prudent, Scrimp, Studious, Tentie, Tenty, Thorough, Vigilant, Ware, Wary

Careless(ly) Casual, Cheery, Debonair, Easy, Free-minded, Gallio, Improvident, Imprudent, Inadvertent, Insouciance, Irresponsible, Lax, Lighthearted, Négligé, > **NEGLIGENT**, Nonchalant, Oops, Oversight, Perfunctory, Raffish, Rash, Remiss, Resigned, Riley, Rollicking, Slam-bang, Slapdash, Slaphappy, Slipshod, Sloven(ly), Slubber, Taupie, Tawpie, Thoughtless, Unguarded, Unmindful, Untenty, Unwary

▷ **Carelessly** *may indicate* an anagram

Caress Bill, Coy, Embrace, Fondle, Kiss, Lallygag, Lollygag, Noursle, Nursle, Pet, Touch

Caretaker Concierge, Curator, Custodian, Granthi, Guardian, Interim, Janitor, Nightwatchman, Sexton, Shammash, Shammes, Superintendent, Verger, Warden

Careworn Haggard, Lined, Tired, Weary

Cargo Bulk, Burden, Fraught, Freight, Lading, Last, > **LOAD**, Payload, Shipload, Shipment

Caribbean Belonger, Puerto Rican, Soca, Sokah, Taino, WI

Caribou Tuktoo, Tuktu

Caricature, Caricaturist Ape, Beerbohm, Burlesque, Caron d'Ache, Cartoon, Cruikshank, Doyle, Farce, Gillray, Rowlandson, Skit, Spy, Tenniel, Travesty

Carlin Pug

Carmelite Barefoot, White (Friar)

Carmen AA, BL, Chai, RAC

Carnage Butchery, Massacre, Slaughter

Carnal Bestial, Lewd, Sensual, Sexual, Worldly

Carnation Clove pink, Dianthus, Gillyflower, Malmaison, Picotee, Pink

Carnival Fair, Fasching, Festival, Fete, Mas, Moomba, Revelry

Carnivore Cacomistle, Cacomixl, Creodont, Fo(u)ssa, Genet, Glutton, Grison, Meerkat, Ratel, Suricate, Viverridae, Wolverine

Carob Algarroba, Locust, St John's bread

Carol Noel, Sing, Song, Wassail, Yodel

Carousal, Carouse Bend, Birl(e), Bouse, Bride-ale, Compotation, Drink, Mallemaroking, Mollie, Orge, Orgy, > **REVEL**, Roist, Screed, Spree, Upsee, Upsey, Upsy, Wassail

Carp(er) Beef, Censure, Complain, Crab, Critic, Crucian, Crusian, Gibel, Goldfish, Id(e), Koi, Kvetch, Mirror, Mome, Nag, Nibble, Nitpick, Roach, Roundfish, Scold, Twitch, Yerk, Yirk

Carpenter Cabinet-maker, Carfindo, Chips, Fitter, Joiner, Joseph, Menuisier, Quince, Tenoner, Woodworker, Wright

▷ **Carpenter** *may indicate* an anagram

Carpet Aubusson, Axminster, Beetle, Berate, Bessarabian, Broadloom, Brussels, Castigate, Chide, Dhurrie, Drugget, Durrie, Dutch, Kali, Kelim, Khilim,

Kidderminster, Kilim, Kirman, Lecture, Lino, Magic, Mat, Moquette, Persian, Rate, Red, Reprimand, Reproach, Rug, Runner, Shagpile, Shark, Shiraz, Stair, Turkey, Wall-to-wall, Wig, Wilton

Carrageen Sea-moss

Carriage Air, Bandy, Barouche, Bearing, Berlin(e), Bier, Brake, Brit(sch)ka, Britska, Britzka, Brougham, Buckboard, Buggy, Cab, Calash, Calèche, Car, Cariole, Caroche, Carriole, Carryall, Cartage, Chaise, Charet, Chariot, Chassis, Chay, Clarence, Coach, Coch, Composite, Conveyance, Coupé, Curricle, Demeanour, Dennet, Deportment, Désobligeante, Diner, Dormeuse, Dos-a-dos, Do-si-do, Drag, Dros(h)ky, Ekka, Equipage, Fiacre, Fly, Four-in-hand, Gait, Gig, Gladstone, Go-cart, Growler, Gun, Haulage, Herdic, Horseless, Hurly-hacket, Landau(let), Limber, Mien, Non-smoker, Norimon, Observation-car, Phaeton, Pick-a-back, Pochaise, Pochay, Poise, Port(age), Portance, Postchaise, Posture, Poyse, Pram, Pullman, Railcar, Railway, Random, Ratha, Remise, Rickshaw, Rockaway, Shay, Sled, Sleeper, Smoker, Sociable, Spider, Stanhope, Sulky, Surrey, Tarantas(s), Taxi, Tender, Tenue, Tilbury, Tim-whiskey, Tonga, Trail, Trap, Vetture, Victoria, Voiture, Wagonette, Waterage, Whirligig, Whisk(e)y

Carrier Airline, Arm, Baldric, Barkis, Barrow, Bomb-ketch, Caddy, Cadge, Camel, Coaster, Conveyor, Escort, Fomes, Fomites, Frog, Grid, Hamper, Haversack, Hod, Janker, Jill, Minority, Nosebag, Noyade, Obo, Packhorse, Pigeon, Porter, Rucksack, Satchel, Schistosoma, Semantide, Sling, Straddle, Stretcher, > **TRAY**, Vector

Carrion Cadaver, Carcase, Carcass, Flesh, Ket, Stapelia

Carrots Seseli, Titian

Carry(ing) Bear, Chair, Convey, Enlevé, Escort, Ferry, Frogmarch, Hawk, Hent, Hump, Kurvey, Land, Pack, Pickaback, Port, Stock, Sustain, Tide over, Tote, > **TRANSPORT**, Trant, Wage, With, Yank

Carry on Continue, Create, Wage

Carry out Execute, Pursue

Cart Bandy, Barrow, Bogey, Buck, Cape, Car(r)iole, Chapel, Democrat, Dog, Dolly, Dray, Furphy, Gambo, Gill, Golf, Governess, Gurney, Hackery, Jag, Jill, Lead, Mail, Pie, Rickshaw, Scotch, Shandry, T, Tax(ed), Telega, Trolley, Tumbrel, Tumbril, Village, Wag(g)on, Wain, Whitechapel

Cartel Duopoly, Ring, Syndicate

Carthaginian Punic

Carthorse Shire

Carthusian Bruno

Cartilage Antitragus, Arytenoid, Chondrin, Chondrus, Cricoid, Darwin's tubercle, Disc, Epiglottis, Gristle, Hyaline, Lytta, Meniscus, Semilunar, Tendron, Thyroid, Tragus, Worm, Xiphoid

Cartload Seam

Cartographer Cabot, Chartist, Mercator, OS, Speed

Carton Box, Case, Crate, Sydney, Tub

Cartoon(ist) Animated, Bairnsfather, Caricature, Comic, Disney, Drawn, Emmet, Fougasse, Fumetto, Garland, Goldberg, Leech, Low, Manga, Mel, Partridge, Popeye, Robinson, Short, Spy, Strip, Tenniel, Thurber, Tidy, Tintin, Trog

Cartridge Blank, Bullet, Cartouche, Cassette, Doppie, Magazine, QIC, Shell

Cart-track Rut

Cartwheel Handspring

Caruncle Aril, Carnosity

Carve(d), Carver, Carving Alcimedon, Armchair, Bas relief, Camaieu, Cameo, Chisel, Cilery, Crocket, Cut, Dismember, Doone, Enchase, Engrave, Entail, Entayle, Fiddlehead, Gibbons, Glyptic, Hew, Incise, Inscribe, Insculp, Intaglio, Knotwork, Netsuke, Nick, Petroglyph, Scrimshaw, Sculp(t), Slice, Tondo, Truncheon, Whittle

Caryatid Column, Telamon

Casanova Heartbreaker, Leman

Cascade Cataract, Fall, Lin(n), Stream, Waterfall

Cascara Buckthorn, Honduras bark, Rhamnus, Wahoo

Case(s), Casing Abessive, Ablative, Accusative, Action, Adessive, Allative, Altered, Appeal, Aril, Ascus, Assumpsit, Attaché, Basket, Beer, Bere, Bittacle, Blimp, Box, Brief, Bundwall, Burse, C, Ca, Cabinet, Calyx, Canister, Canterbury, Capsule, Cartouch(e), Cartridge, Cause celebre, Cellaret, Chase, Chitin, Chrysalis, Cocoon, Compact, Crate, Croustade, Crust, Dative, Declension, Detinue, Dispatch, Dossier, Dressing, Elative, Elytron, Enallage, Essive, Etui, Etwee, Example, Flan, Flapjack, Frame, Genitive, Grip, Hanaper, Hard, Hatbox, Hold-all, Housewife, Hull, Humidor, Husk, > IN CASE, Index, Indusium, Inessive, Instance, Keister, Locative, Locket, Lorica, Manche, Matter, Mezuzah, Nacelle, Nominative, Non-suit, Nutshell, Objective, Oblique, Ochrea, Ocrea, Papeterie, Patient, Pencil, Penner, Phylactery, Plight, Plummer-block, Pod, Port, Possessive, Prima facie, Quiver, Recce, Reconnoitre, Sabretache, Sad, Scabbard, Sheath(e), Shell, Situation, Six-pack, Sporran, Stead, Sted, Subjunctive, Suit, Tantalus, Tea-chest, Telium, Test, Theca, Tichborne, Trial, Trunk, Valise, Vasculum, Vocative, Volva, Walise, Walking, Wallet, Wardian, Wing, Writing

Case-harden Nitrode

Casein Curd

Casement Frame, Roger, Sash, Window

Cash Blunt, Bonus, Bounty, Change, Coin, Dosh, Dot, Float, Hard, Imprest, Lolly, > MONEY, Needful, Ochre, Oscar, Pence, Petty, Ready, Realise, Rhino, Spondulicks, Spot, Stumpy, Tender, Tin, Wampum, Wherewithal

Cashier Annul, Break, Depose, Disbar, Dismiss, Oust, Teller, Treasurer

Cashmere Circassienne

Cask(et) Armet, Barrel, Barrico, Bas(i)net, Box, Breaker, Butt, Cade, Casque, Cassette, Drum, Firkin, Galeate, Harness, Heaume, Hogshead, Keg, Leaguer, Octave, Pin, Pipe, Puncheon, Pyxis, Run(d)let, Salade, Sallet, Sarcophagus, Scuttlebutt, Shrine, Solera, Tierce, Tun, Wine

Cask-stand Stillion

Cassava Manioc, Tapioca, Yucca

Casserole Diable, Osso bucco, Pot, Salmi, Terrine, Tzimmes

Cassette Cartridge, Tape, Video

Cassia Cleanser, Senna

Cassio Lieutenant

Cassiterite Needle-tin, Tinstone

Cassock Gown, Soutane, Subucula

Cast (down, off, out), Casting Abattu, Actors, Add, Appearance, Bung, Die, Discard, Ecdysis, Ectype, Eject, Endocranial, Exorcise, Exuviae, Exuvial, Fling, Found, Fusil, Grape, Heave, Hob, Hue, Hurl, Impression, Ingo(w)es, Keb, Look, Lose, Mew, Molt, Moulage, Mould, Pick, Plaster(stone), Players, Put, Reject, Shed, Shoot, Sling, Slive, Slough, Spoil, Stookie, Tailstock, > THROW, Toss, Tot, Warp, Wax, Ytost

▷ **Cast** *may indicate* an anagram or a piece of a word missing

Castanet Crotal(um), Knackers
Castaway Adrift, Crusoe, Gunn, Left, Outcast, Selkirk, Stranded, Weft
▷ **Cast by** *may indicate* surrounded by
Caste Brahmin, Class, Dalit, Group, Harijan, Hova, Kshatriya, Rajpoot, Rajpout, Rank, Scheduled, Sect, Sudra, Vaisya, Varna
Caster Truckle
Castigate Berate, Chastise, Criticise, Denounce, Keelhaul, Lash, Punish
Cast-iron Spiegeleisen
Castle(d) Adamant, Arundel, Balmoral, Bamburgh, Bastille, Belvoir, Berkeley, Bouncy, Braemar, Broch, C, Calzean, Canossa, Carbonek, Carisbrooke, Casbah, Chateau, Chepstow, Chillon, Citadel, Colditz, Conwy, Corfe, Culzean, Dangerous, Despair, Doubting, Dunsinane, Edinburgh, Egremont, Eileen Donan, Elephant, Elsinore, Fastness, Fort, Fotheringhay, Glamis, Gormenghast, Harlech, Herstmonceux, Hever, Howard, Kasba(h), Kenilworth, Lancaster, Leeds, Lincoln, Ludlow, Maiden, Malperdy, Man, More, Mot(t)e, Motte and bailey, Otranto, Perilous, Rackrent, Raglan, Rook, Sand, Schloss, Sherborne, Sissinghurst, Spain, Stirling, Stokesay, Stormont, Stronghold, Tintagel, Trim, Urquhart, Villa, Wartburg, Warwick, Windsor
Castor-oil Ricinus
Castrate(d) Alter, Cut, Doctor, Emasculate, Eunuch, Evirate, Geld, Glib, Lib, Mutilate, Neuter, Spado, Spay, Swig
Castro Fidel
Casual Accidental, Adventitious, Airy, Blasé, Chance, Flippant, Grass, Haphazard, Idle, Incidental, Informal, Jaunty, Lackadaisical, Nochalant, Odd(ment), Offhand, Off-the-cuff, Orra, Passing, Promiscuous, Random, Scratch, Sporadic, Stray, Temp, Throwaway
Casualty Caduac, Chance-medley, > VICTIM
Casuist Jesuit
Cat Abyssinian, Alley, American curl, American wirehair, Angora, Asian shorthair, Asparagus, Australian mist, Balinese, Baudrons, Binturong, Birman, Bluepoint, Bobcat, Burmese, Cacomistle, Cacomixl, Caracal, Chantilly, Chartreux, Cheetah, Cheshire, Civet, Clowder, Colourpoint, Cop, Cornish Rex, Cougar, Dandy, Dasyure, Delundung, Devon Rex, Domestic, Egyptian Mau, Eyra, Fat, Felid, Feline, Felix, Flog, Foss(a), Foumart, Foussa, Genet(te), Gib, Gossip, Grimalkin, Gus, Havana Brown, Himalayan, Hipster, Hodge, Jaguar(ondi), Jaguarundi, Jazzer, Kilkenny, Kit, Korat, Lair, La Perm, Lash, Leopard, Linsang, Lion, Long-hair, Lynx, Maine coon, Malkin, Maltese, Manul, Manx, Margay, Marmalade, Mehitabel, Mewer, Mog, Mountain, Mouser, Munchkin, Musang, Musk, Nandine, Neuter, Nib, Norwegian Forest, Ocelot, Ocicat, Oriental, Ounce, Painter, Pallas's, Palm, Panther, Pard, Pardal, Persian, Pharaoh, Polecat, Practical, Puma, Puss, Quoll, Ragdoll, Rasse, Rex, Ringtail, Rumpy, Russian blue, Sacred, Scottish Fold, Scourge, Sealpoint, Selkirk Rex, Serval, Shorthair, Siamese, Siberian Forest, Sick, Singed, Snowshoe, Somali, Spew, Sphynx, Spue, Swinger, Tabby, Tibert, Tiffanie, Tiffany, Tiger, Tigon, Tigress, Tobermory, Tom, Top, Tortoise-shell, Turkish Angora, Turkish Van, Tybalt, Viverra, Weasel, Zibet(h)
Catacomb Cemetery, Crypt, Hypogeum, Vault
Catalepsy Catatony, Trance
Catalogue Cattle dog, Dewey, Dictionary, Index, Inventory, List, Litany, Magalog, Messier, Ragman, Ragment, Raisonné, Record, Register, Specialogue, Subject, Table, Tabulate, Union
Catalyst Accelerator, Agent, Influence, Unicase, Ziegler

Catamite Ingle

Catapult Ballista, Ging, Launch, Mangon(el), Perrier, Petrary, Propel, Scorpion, Shanghai, Sling, Slingshot, Stone-bow, Tormentum, Trebuchet, Wye, Y

Cataract Cascade, Film, Pearl, Pearl-eye, Torrent, Waterfall, Web and pin

Catarrh Coryza, Rheum

Catastrophe Apocalypse, Calamity, > DISASTER, Doom, Epitasis, Fiasco, Meltdown

Catatonia Stupor

Cat-call Boo, Mew, Miaow, Miaul, Razz, Wawl, Wrawl

Catch(y), Caught Air, Apprehend, Attract, Bag, Benet, Bone, C, Capture, Chape, Clasp, Cog, Collar, Contract, Cop, Corner, Cotton on, Ct, Deprehend, Detent, Dolly, Engage, Enmesh, Ensnare, Entoil, Entrap, Fang, Field, Fumble, Gaper, Get, Glee(some), Grasp, Had, Hank, Haud, Haul, Hear, Hitch, Hold, Hook, Inmesh, Keddah, Keight, Kep(pit), Kheda, Kill, Land, Lapse, Lasso, Latch, Lime, Lock, Morse, Nab, Nail, Net, Nick, Nim, Nobble, Noose, Overhear, Overhent, Overtake, Parti, Pawl, Rap, Release, Rope, Round, Rub, Safety, Sean, Sear, See(n), Seize, > SNAG, Snap, Snare, Snib, Snig, > SONG, Surprise, Swindle, Tack, Take, Tickle, Trammel, Trap, Trawl, Trick, Tripwire, Troll, Twig, Understand, Wrestle

Catchword Motto, Shibboleth, Slogan, Tag

Catechism Carritch, Test

Categorise, Category > CLASS, Etic, Genre, Genus, Label, Order, Pigeonhole, Range, Taxon

Cater(er) Acatour, Cellarer, Feed, Manciple, > PROVIDE, Purveyor, Serve, Steward, Supply, Victualler, Vivandière

Caterpillar Army worm, Aweto, Boll worm, Cotton-worm, Cutworm, Eruciform, Geometer, Gooseberry, Hop-dog, Hornworm, Inchworm, Larva, Looper, Osmeterium, Palmer, Tent, Webworm, Woolly-bear

Catfish Hassar, Woof

Cathartic Turbeth

Cathedral Basilica, Chartres, Chester, Cologne, Dome, Duomo, Ely, Guildford, Lateran, Lichfield, Lincoln, Minster, Notre Dame, Rheims, Ripon, St Paul's, Salisbury, Sens, Up(p)sala, Wells, Westminster, Winchester, Worcester, York

Catherine Braganza, Parr

Catherine-wheel Girandole

Cathode Electrode, Filament, Ray

Catholic Broad, Defenders, Doolan, Eclectic, Ecumenical, Fenian, General, Irvingism, Jebusite, Latin, Left-footer, Liberal, Marian, Opus Dei, Ostiary, Papalist, Papaprelatist, Papist, Passionist, Recusant, Redemptionist, Roman, Salesian, Spike, Taig, Te(a)gue, Teigue, Thomist, Tike, Tory, Tridentine, Tyke, Universal, Ursuline, Waldenses, Wide

Catkin Amentum, Chat, Lamb's tail, Pussy-willow, Salicaceous

Cat-lover Ailurophile

Catmint Nep, Nepeta

Cato Porcian, Uticensis

Cats-eye Chatoyant, Cymophane

Catsmeat Lights

Catspaw Pawn, Tool

Cat's tail Reed-mace, Typha

Cat's whiskers Vibrissa

Cattle(pen) Aberdeen Angus, Africander, Ankole, Aver, Ayrshire, Beefalo, Bestial, Brahman, British white, Buffalo, Carabao, Charbray, Charol(l)ais,

Chillingham, Dexter, Drove, Durham, Fee, Friesland, Galloway, Gaur, Gayal, Guernsey, Gyal, Heard, Herd, Hereford, Highland, Holstein (Friesian), Illawara, Jersey, Kerry, Kine, Kouprey, Kraal, Ky(e), Kyloe, Lairage, Limousin, Lincoln, Longhorn, Luing, Neat, Nout, Nowt, Owsen, Oxen, Piemontese, Rabble, Redpoll, Rother, Santa Gertrudis, Shorthorn, Simment(h)al, Soum, Sowm, Steer, Stock, Store, Stot, Sussex, Tamarao, Tamarau, Teeswater, Welsh black

Cattle disease Anthrax, Black water, Footrot, Hoove, Johne's, Listeriosis, Lumpy jaw, Mange, Mastitis, Milk lameness, Moorill, Quarter-ill, Red-water, Rinderpest, Scours, Scrapie, Texas fever, Wire-heel, Woody-tongue

Cattle food Fodder

Cattleman Cowboy, Herder, Maverick, Rancher, Ringer, Stock-rider

Catty Kin, Spiteful

Caucasian Aryan, Azabaijani, European, Melanochroi, Paleface, Semite, Shemite, White, Yezdi, Yezidee, Zezidee

Caucus Assembly, Cell, Gathering, Race

▸ **Caught** see CATCH

Caul Baby-hood, Kell, Membrane, Sillyhow

Cauldron Kettle, Pot

Cauliflower Curd, Ear, Floret

Caulk Fill, Pitch, Snooze

Causation, Cause(d), Causes Aetiology, Agent, Beget, Breed, Bring, Compel, Create, Crusade, Determinant, Due, Effect, Efficient, Encheason, Engender, Factor, Final, First, Flag-day, Formal, Gar(re), Generate, Ideal, Induce, Lead, Lost, Make, Material, Motive, Movement, > OCCASION, Parent, Probable, Provoke, Reason, Root, Sake, Source, Teleology, Topic, Ultimate, Wreak

Causeway Tombolo

Caustic Acid, Acrimonious, Alkaline, Burning, Erodent, Escharotic, Lime, Moxa, Pungent, Sarcastic, Scathing, Seare, Tart, Vitriol, Waspish, Withering

Cauterise Brand, Burn, Disinfect, Inustion, Sear

Caution, Cautious (person) Achitophel, Admonish, Ahithophel, Alert, Amber, Awarn, Beware, Cagey, Card, Care, Cave, Caveat, Chary, Circumspect, Credence, Cure, Defensive, Deliberate, Discretion, Fabian, Gingerly, Guard(ed), Heedful, Leery, Prudent, Rum, Scream, Skite, Tentative, Vigilant, Ware, > WARN, Wary, Yellow card

Cavalcade Pageant, Parade, Procession, Sowarree, Sowarry

Cavalier Brusque, Cicisbeo, Devil-may-care, Gallant, Lively, Malignant, Offhand, Peart, Rider, Royalist

Cavalry(man) Blues, Car(a)bineer, Car(a)binier, Cornet, Cossack, Dragoon, Equites, Heavies, Horse, Household, Hussar, Ironsides, Knights, Lancers, Light-horse, Plunger, Ressaldar, Risaldar, Rough-rider, Rutter, Sabres, Silladar, Spahi, Uhlan, Yeomanry

Cave(rn), Caves, Cave-dwelling Acherusia, Alert, Altamira, Antar, Antre, Beware, Cellar, Collapse, Corycian, Den, Domdaniel, Erebus, Fingal's, Fore, Grot(to), Hollow, Jenolan, Lascaux, Look-out, Lupercal, Mammoth, Nix, Pot-hole, Proteus, Sepulchre, Snow, Spel(a)ean, Speleology, Spelunker, Speos, Tassili, Vault, Waitomo, Ware, Weem

Cave-dweller Troglodyte

Caveman Adullam, Aladdin, Fingal, Neanderthal, Primitive, Troglodyte, Troll

Caviare Beluga, Roe, Sevruga, Sturgeon

Cavil Carp, Haggle, Quibble

Cavity Acetabulum, Amygdale, Amygdule, Androclinium, Atrial, Camera,

Cavort(ing) | 104

Camouflet, Celom, Chamber, Clinandrium, Coelenteron, Coelom(e), Concepticle, Concha, Countermark, Crater, Crypt, Dent, Domatium, Druse, Enteron, Follicle, Foss, Gap, Geode, Glenoid, Hold, Hole, Lacuna, Locule, Mediastinum, Orbita, Orifice, Pocket, Resonant, Segmentation, Sinus, Tear, Tympanum, Vacuole, Vein, Ventricle, Vesicle, Vitta, Vomica, Vug, Vugg, Vugh, Well

Cavort(ing) Jag

Cavy Agouti, Capybara, Hograt, Paca

Cease(fire) Abate, Blin, Cut, Desist, Die, Disappear, Halt, Intermit, Lin, Lose, Pass, Refrain, Remit, Sessa, > STOP, Truce

Ceaseless Eternal, Incessant

Cecil Rhodes

Cedar(wood) Arolla, Atlas, Deodar, Incense, Japanese, Toon

Cede Grant, Yield

Ceiling Absolute, Barrel, Coffered, Cove, Cupola, Dome, Glass, Lacunar, Laquearia, Limit, Plafond, Roof, Service, Soffit

Celebrate(d), Celebration, Celebrity Ale, Beanfeast, Besung, Bigwig, Binge, Carnival, Cel, Chant, Commemorate, Distinguished, Do, Emblazon, Encaenia, Epithalamion, Epithalamium, Fame, Feast, Fest, Festivity, Fete, Fiesta, Gala, Gaudeamus, Gaudy, Glorify, Grog-up, Harvest home, Hold, Holiday, Honour, Jamboree, Jollifications, Jollities, Jubilee, Keep, Laud, Legend, Lion, Loosing, Lowsening, Maffick, Mardi gras, Mass, Mawlid al-Nabi, Megastar, Monstre sacre, Name, Noted, Nuptials, Observe, Occasion, Orgy, Panathenaea, Praise, Randan, Rejoice, Renown, Repute, Revel, Roister, Saturnalia, Sing, Spree, Star, Storied, Sung, Superstar, Treat, Triumph, Wassail, Wet

Celerity Dispatch, Haste, Speed, Velocity

Celery Alexanders, Smallage, Stick

Celestial Chinese, Divine, Ethereal, Heavenly, Supernal, Uranic

Celibate, Celibacy Bachelor, Chaste, Paterin(e), Rappist, Rappite, Shakers, Single, Spinster

Cell(s), Cellular Battery, Bullpen, Cadre, Chamber, Chapel, Condemned, Crypt, Cubicle, Death, Dungeon, Group, Laura, Padded, Peter, > PRISON, Strip, Tank, Unit

● **CELLS**
●
● **1 letter:**
● T
●
● **3 letters:**
● Dry
● Pec
● Sex
● Wet
●
● **4 letters:**
● Axon
● Comb
● Cone
● Cyte
● Fuel
● Germ

Hair	Guard	Cybrid
HeLa	Linin	Cytoid
Mast	Lymph	Diaxon
Oxum	Nerve	Gamete
Soma	Nicad	Goblet
Stem	Solar	Killer
Zeta	Spore	Morula
	Stone	Neuron
5 letters:	Swarm	Oocyte
Ascus	Water	Plasma
Basal	X-body	Sensor
Canal		Sickle
Clark	**6 letters:**	Somite
Flame	Button	Target
Giant	Censor	Zygote
Gland	Collar	

7 letters:
Cadmium
Cambium
Cathode
Daniell
Energid
Gemmule
Gravity
Helper T
Lithite
Myotome
Myotube
Neurite
Neurone
Neutron
Plastid
Primary
Schwann
Sertoli
Somatic
Spireme
Sporule
Storage
Tapetum
Vesicle
Voltaic

8 letters:
Akaryote
Auxocyte
Basidium
Basophil
Blasteme
Blastula
Congenic
Cytology
Daughter
Defensin
Ectomere
Endoderm
Endosarc
Epiblast
Eukaryon
Galvanic
Gonidium
Gonocyte
Hapteron
Hemocyte

Meiocyte
Meristem
Monocyte
Myoblast
Neoblast
Palisade
Parietal
Platelet
Purkinje
Receptor
Retinula
Schizont
Selenium
Seredium
Squamous
Standard
Sweatbox
Symplast
Synergid
Tracheid
Unipolar
Zoosperm
Zoospore

9 letters:
Adipocyte
Antipodal
Astrocyte
Athrocyte
Auxospore
Basophile
Coenocyte
Companion
Corpuscle
Desmosome
Ectoplasm
Embryo-sac
Fibrocyte
Haemocyte
Hybridoma
Idioblast
Internode
Iridocyte
Karyology
Laticifer
Leclanché
Leucocyte
Macromere

Merozoite
Microcyte
Myelocyte
Myofibril
Organelle
Periplasm
Periplast
Phagocyte
Phellogen
Proembryo
Secondary
Spermatid
Sporocyte
Suspensor
Syncytium
Synkaryon
Thymocyte
Trabecula
Tracheide

10 letters:
Ameloblast
Archespore
Blastoderm
Blastomere
Centrosome
Choanocyte
Chromaffin
Chromosome
Cnidoblast
Eosinophil
Epithelium
Fibroblast
Gametocyte
Histiocyte
Leucoblast
Leukoblast
Lymphocyte
Macrophage
Melanocyte
Mesenchyme
Myeloblast
Neuroblast
Neutrophil
Normoblast
Osteoblast
Osteoclast
Perikaryon

Phelloderm
Protoplast
Spermatium
Spherocyte
Totipotent

11 letters:
Aplanospore
Arthrospore
Endothelium
Erythrocyte
Granulocyte
Interneuron
Kinetoplast
Megaloblast
Melanoblast
Microgamete
Microvillus
Motor neuron
Odontoblast
Poikilocyte
Propoceptor
Schistocyte
Spheroplast

12 letters:
Aplanogamete
Chondroblast
Electrolytic
Haematoblast
Interstitial
Paraphysisis
Photovoltaic
Reticulocyte
Spermatocyte
Spermatozoid
Spermatozoon
Spongioblast

13 letters:
Chromatophore
Mitochondroin
Photoelectric
Photoreceptor

14 letters:
Spermatogonium
Weston standard

Cellar Basement, Bodega, Coalhole, Dunny, Hypogeum, Ratskeller, Storm, Vault, Vaut, Wine
Cell division Amitosis

Cellist, Cello Hermit, Prisoner, Tortelier

Celluloid, Cellulose Acetate, Cel, Viscose, Xylonite

Celt(ic) Belgic, Breton, Brython, Druid, Gadhel, Gael, Goidel, Helvetii, Kelt, Taffy, Welsh

Cement Araldite®, Compo, Concrete, Fix, Flaunch, Glue, Grout, High-alumina, Hydraulic, Lute, Maltha, Mastic, Mortar, Paste, Pointing, Porcelain, Portland, Putty, Rice-glue, Roman, Rubber, Slurry, > STICK, Trass, Water

Cemetery Aceldama, Arenarium, Arlington, Boneyard, Boot Hill, Campo santo, Catacomb, Churchyard, God's Acre, Golgotha, Graveyard, Musall, Necropolis, Père Lachaise, Potter's field, Saqqara, Urnfield

Censer Cassolette, Navicula, Thurible

Censor(ious), Censure Accuse, Admonition, Animadvert, Appeach, Ban, Banner, Berate, Blame, Blue-pencil, Bowdler, Braid, Cato, Comstockery, > CONDEMN, Critical, Criticise, Damn, Dang, Decry, Dispraise, Edit, Excommunicate, Excoriate, Expurgate, Gag, Obloquy, Opprobrium, Rap, Repress, Reprimand, Reproach, Reprobate, Reprove, Satirise, Scold, Scrub, Slam, Slate, Stricture, Suppress, Tax, Tirade, Traduce, Wig

Census Count, Poll

Cent Bean, Coin, Ct, Penny, Red

Centaur Ch(e)iron, Horseman, Nessus, Sagittary, Therianthropic

Centenary, Centennial Anniversary, Colorado

Centipede Chilopoda, Earwig, Polypod, Scolopendra, Scutiger

Central, Centre Active, Amid, Attendance, Axis, Broca's, Bunt, Call, Cardinal, Chakra, Civic, Community, Contact, Core, Cost, Day, Daycare, Dead, Detention, Detoxification, Deuteron, Deuton, Downtown, Drop-in, Epergne, Eye, Field, Focus, Frontal, Garden, Health, Heart, Hotbed, Hothouse, Hub, Incident, Inmost, Internal, Interpretive, Kernel, Kingpin, Law, Leisure, Lincoln, Live, Main, Mecca, Median, Medulla, Mid(st), Music, Nave, Nerve, Nucleus, Omphalus, Pompidou, Profit, Property, Reception, Rehabilitation, Remand, Shopping, Social Education, Storm, Teachers', Trauma, Visitor, Waist, Weather

Central heating Cen, CH

▷ **Centre** *may indicate* middle letters

Centrepiece Epergne

Century Age, C, Era, Magdeburg, Period, Ton

Cephalopod Ammonite, Calamary, Cuttle, Loligo, Nautilus, Octopus, Sepia, Squid

Ceramic(s) Agateware, Arcanist, China, Earthen, Ferrite, Porcelain, Pottery, Sialon, Tiles

Cereal Amelcorn, Barley, Blé, Bran, Buckwheat, Bulgar, Bulg(h)ur, Cassava, Corn, Cornflakes, Couscous, Emmer, Farina, Gnocchi, Grain, Granola, Groats, Hominy, Maize, Mandioc(a), Mandiocca, Mani(h)oc, Manihot, Mealie, Millet, Muesli, Oats, Paddy, Popcorn, Rye(corn), Sago, Samp, Sarassin, Seed, Semolina, Sorghum, Spelt, Tapioca, Tef(f), Triticale, Triticum, Wheat, Zea

Cerebrate, Cerebration Pore, Thought

Ceremonial, Ceremony Amrit, Barmitzvah, Chado, Chanoyu, Common Riding, Coronation, Doseh, Durbar, Encaenia, Enthronement, Etiquette, Eucharist, Flypast, Form(al), Gongyo, Habdalah, Havdalah, Havdoloh, Heraldry, Investiture, Matsuri, Maundy, Mummery, Observance, Occasion, Ordination, Pageantry, Parade, Pomp, Powwow, Protocol, Rite, Ritual, Sacrament, Sado, Seder, Service, State, Tea, Unveiling, Usage

Cerium Ce

Cert(ain), Certainty Absolute, Actual, Assured, Banker, Bound, Cast-iron,

Cinch, Cocksure, Confident, Convinced, Decided, Exact, Fact, Fate, Indubitable, Inevitable, Infallible, Keen, Monte, Moral, Nap, One, Positive, Poz, Precise, Shoo-in, Siccar, Sicker, Snip, Some, > **SURE**, Sure-fire, Truth, Yes

Certainly Agreed, Ay, Certes, Fegs, Forsooth, Indeed, Iwis, Jokol, OK, Oke, Pardi(e), Pardy, Perdie, Siccar, Sicker, > **SURE**, Truly, Verily, Yea, Yes, Yokul, Ywis

Certificate, Certified, Certify Affirm, Attest, Bene decessit, Bond, Chit, Cocket, Confirm, Credential, Death, Debenture, Depose, Diploma, Docket, Document, Enseal, Gold, Guarantee, Landscrip, Licence, Lines, Medical, MOT, Notarise, Paper, Patent, Proven, Savings, School, Scrip, Scripophily, Share, Stock, Sworn, Talon, Testamur, Testimonial, Treasury, U, Unruly, Voucher, Warrant

Cesspit Bog, Dungmere, Sinkhole, Slurry

Cetacean Dolphin, Porpoise, Whale

Ceylon(ese) Serendip, Vedda(h)

Chafe, Chafing Chunter, Fray, Fret, Harass, Intertrigo, Irritate, > **RUB**, Seethe, Worry

Chaff(y) Badinage, Banter, Bran, Chip, Dross, Hay, Husk, Rag, Raillery, Rally, Ramentum, Refuse, Roast, Rot, Tease, Twit

Chaffer(ing) Bandy, Bargain, Haggle, Higgle, Hucksterage, Traffic

Chaffinch Whitewing

Chagrin Envy, Mortify, Spite, Vexation

Chain(ed) Acre's-breadth, Albert, Anklet, Band, Bind, Bond, Bracelet, Branched, Bucket, Cable, Catena, Chatelaine, Choke, Cistron, Cordillera, Cyclic, Daisy, Decca, Dixie, Drive, Duplex, Dynasty, Engineer's, Esses, Fanfarona, Fetter, Fob, Food, Furlong, Gleipnir, Golden, Grand, Gunter's, Gyve, Heavy, Learner's, Markov, Mayor, Micella(r), Micelle, > **MOUNTAIN**, Noria, Open, Pennine, Pitch, Range, Rockies, Roller, Safety, Seal, > **SERIES**, Shackle, Side, Slang, Snigging, Sprocket, Straight, String, Strobila, Supply, Surveyor's, Suspensor, Team, Tug, Voluntary, Watch

Chain-gang Coffle

Chair Basket, Bath, Bench, Bentwood, Berbice, Bergère, Birthing, Bosun's, Butterfly, Camp, Cane, Captain's, Carver, Club, Curule, Deck, Dining, Director's, Easy, Electric, Emeritus, Estate, Fauteuil, Fiddle-back, Folding, Frithstool, Garden, Gestatorial, Guérite, High, Jampan, Jampanee, Jampani, Ladder-back, Lounger, Love-seat, Merlin, Morris, Musical, Personal, Pew, Preside, Recliner, Rocker, > **SEAT**, Sedan, Stool, Sugan, Swivel, Throne, Wainscot, Wheel, Windsor, Wing

Chair-back Ladder, Splat

Chairman Convener, Emeritus, Landammann, Mao, MC, Pr(a)eses, Prof, Prolocutor, Sheraton, Speaker

Chalaza Albumen, Treadle, Treddle

Chaldean Babylonian, Ur

Chalet Cabana, Cot, Skio

Chalice Poisoned

Chalk(y) Calcareous, Cauk, Cawk, Crayon, Credit, Cretaceous, French, Senonian, Soapstone, Spanish, Steatite, Tailor's, White(n), Whit(en)ing

Challenge(r), Challenging Acock, Assay, Call, Cartel, Champion, Confront, Contest, Dare, Defy, Gage, Gauntlet, Glove, Hazard, Hen(ner), Iconoclasm, Impugn, Oppugn, Provoke, Query, Question, Recuse, Sconce, Shuttle, Tackle, Taker, Tall order, Tank, Threat, Vie, Wero, Whynot

Chamber(s) Airlock, Atrium, Auricle, Bubble, Camarilla, Camera, Casemate, Cavern, Cavitation, Cavity, Cell(a), Chanty, Close-stool, Cloud, Cofferdam, Combustion, Cubicle, Decompression, Dene-hole, Dolmen, Echo, Float,

Fumatorium, Gas, Gazunder, Gilded, Hall, Horrors, Hypogea, Inspection, Ionization, Jerry, Jordan, Kiva, Lethal, Locule, Lok Sabha, Lower, Magma, Mattamore, Mesoscaphe, Plenum, Po(t), Presence, Privy, Reaction, Resonance-box, Roum, Second, Serdab, Silo, Spark, Star, Swell-box, Synod, Thalamus, Undercroft, Upper, Utricle, Vault, Ventricle, Wilson cloud, Zeta

Chamberlain Camerlengo, Camerlingo, Censor

Chameleon Ethiopian, Lizard, Tarand

Chamfer Bevel, Groove

Chamois Ibex, Izard, Shammy

Champ Bite, Chafe, Chew, Chomp, Eat, Gnash, Gnaw, Hero, Mash, Morsure, Munch

Champagne Boy, Bubbly, Charlie, Fizz, Gigglewater, Pop, Sillery, Simkin, Simpkin, Stillery, Troyes, Widow

Champion(s) Ace, Adopt, Ali, Apostle, Belt, Campeador, Cid, Cock, Crusader, Cupholder, Defend, Don Quixote, Doucepere, Douzeper, Dymoke, Enoch, Espouse, Gladiator, Harry, > **HERO**, Horse, Kemp, Kemper(yman), King, Knight, Maintain, Matchless, Messiah, Messias, Neil, Paladin, Palmerin, Peerless, Perseus, Promachos, Proponent, Protagonist, Roland, St Anthony, St David, St Denis, St George, St James, St Patrick, Spiffing, Spokesman, Star, Support, Tribune, Upholder, Victor, Wardog, > **WINNER**, Yokozuna

Championship Open, Seven, Super Bowl, Title

Chance (upon), Chancy Accident, Aleatory, Aunter, Bet, Break, Buckley's, Cast, Casual, Cavel, Coincidence, Contingent, Dice, Earthly, Even, Fat, > **FATE**, Fighting, First refusal, Fluke, Fortuitous, Fortuity, Fortune, > **GAMBLE**, Game, Hap, Happenstance, Hobnob, Iffy, Kevel, Light, Loaves and fishes, Look-in, Lot, > **LOTTERY**, Luck, Main, Meet, Mercy, Occur, Odds, Odds-on, Opening, Opportunity, Outside, Posse, Potluck, Probability, Prospect, Random, Rise, Risk, Run into, Russian roulette, Serendipity, Slant, Spec, Sporting, Stake, Stochastic, Sweep, Toss-up, Treble, Turn, Tychism, Ventre, Venture, Wager

Chancel Adytum, Bema, Nave

Chancellor Adolf, Bismarck, Dollfuss, Kohl, Logothete, Minister, More

Chancery Court, Hanaper

Chandelier Candlestick, Corona, Drop, Electrolier, Gasolier, Girandole, Lustre, Pendant

Chandler Acater, Raymond

Chaney Lon

Change(able), Changes, Changing Adàpt, Adjust, Agio, > **ALTER**, Amendment, Attorn, Backtrack, Barter, Become, Bob-major, Capricious, Cash, Catalysis, Chameleon, Chop, Cline, Commute, Convert, Coppers, Denature, Departure, Dichrony, Edit, Enallage, Esterify, Eustatic, Evolve, Exchange, Fickle, Find, Flighty, Float, Fluctuate, Flux, Guard, Gybe, Inflect, Innovate, Kembla, Killcrop, Labile, Loose, Make-over, Menopause, Metabolic, Metabolise, Metamorphose, Metamorphosis, Mobile, Modify, Mutable, Mutalis mutandis, Mutanda, Mutation, Parallax, Peal, Peripet(e)ia, Permute, Port, Prophase, Protean, Quantum leap, Realise, Recant, Rectify, Reform, Refraction, Regime, Rejig, Resipiscence, Rest, Reverse, Revise, Revolutionise, Rework, Sandhi, Scourse, Sd, Sea, Seesaw, Sere, Sex, Shake-out, Shake-up, Shift, Silver, Small, Sublimation, Substitute, Swap, Swing, Switch, Tempolabile, Tolsel, Tolsey, Tolzey, Transfer, Transfiguration, Transform, Transition, Transmogrify, Transmute, Transpose, Transubstantial, Turn, Uncertain, Upheaval, U-turn, Vagary, Variant, Variation, Vary, Veer, Vicissitude, Volatile, Volte-face, Wankle, Washers, Waver, Wheel, Wow

▷ **Change(d)** *may indicate* an anagram
Changeling Auf, Killcrop, Oaf, Turncoat
Channel Access, Aflaj, Aqueduct, Artery, Beagle, Bed, Billabong, Bristol, Canal, Canaliculus, Chimb, Chime, Chine, Chute, Conduit, Culvert, Cut, Cutting, Distribution, Ditch, Drain, Duct, Dyke, Ea, English, Estuary, Euripus, Fairway, Falaj, Flume, Foss, Funnel, Furrow, Gat, Geo, Gio, Glyph, Grough, Gully, Gut, Gutter, Head-race, Ingate, Katabothron, Katavothron, Khor, Kill, Kos, Lane, Leat, Leet, Limber, Major, Meatus, Medium, Minch, Moat, Mozambique, Multiplex, Narrows, North, Penstock, Pentland Firth, Pescadores, Pipeline, Qanat, Race, Rebate, Rigol(l), Rivulet, St George's, Sea-gate, Seaway, Sewer, Shunt, Sinus, Sky, Sloot, Sluice, Sluit, Sny(e), Solent, Solway Firth, Sound, Sow, Spillway, Sprue, Strait, Suez, Sure, Swash, Tailrace, Tideway, Tracheole, Trough, Ureter, Vallecula, Watercourse, Wireway, Yucatan
Chant Anthem, Antiphon, Canticle, Cantillate, Cantus, Chaunt, Daimoku, Decantate, Euouae, Evovae, Gregorian, Haka, Harambee, Hymn, Intone, Introit, Motet, Pennillion-singing, Plainsong, Psalm, Sing, Slogan, Te deum, Yell
Chantilly Cream, Lace
Chaos, Chaotic Abyss, Anarchy, Confusion, Disorder, Fractal, Hun-tun, Jumble, Mess, Mixter-maxter, Muss, Shambles, Shambolic, Snafu, Tohu bohu
▷ **Chaotic** *may indicate* an anagram
Chap(s) Beezer, Bloke, Bo, Bod, Bor, Chafe, Cheek, Chilblain, Chop, Cleft, Cod, Codger, Cove, Crack, Customer, Dog, Fella, Fellow, Flews, Genal, Gent, Gink, Guy, Hack, Joll, Jowl, Kibe, Lad, > **MAN**, Mouth, Mum, Ocker, Rent, Rime, Spray, Spreathe, Spreaze, Spreethe, Spreeze, Wang
Chapel Bethel, Bethesda, Beulah, Cha(u)ntry, Ebenezer, Feretory, Galilee, Lady, Oratory, Parabema, Prothesis, Sacellum, Sistine
Chaperon(e) Beard, Cap, Duenna, Escort, Gooseberry, Griffin, Griffon, Gryphon, Muffin
Chaplain CF, Ordinary, Padre, Priest, Skypilot, Slope
Chaplet Anadem, Coronet, Fillet, Garland, Wreath
▷ **Chaps** *may indicate* an anagram
Chapter Accidents, C, Canon, Cap, Capitular, Ch, Chap, Cr, Division, Episode, Lodge, Phase, Section, Social, Sura(h), Verse
Char(woman) Adust, Burn, Cleaner, Coal, Daily, Duster, Mop(p), Mrs Mop(p), Scorch, Sear, Singe, Smoulder, Toast, Togue, Torgoch
Charabanc Bus, Chara, Coach
Character(s) Aesc, Alphabet, Ampersand, Ampussyand, Atmosphere, Aura, Backslash, Brand, Calibre, Case, Cipher, Clef, Cliff, Climate, Coloration, Complexion, Contour, Credit, Delimiter, Deuteragonist, Devanagari, Digamma, Digit, Dramatis personae, Eta, Ethos, > **FEATURE**, Fish, Fist, Form, Grain, Graphics, Grit, Hieroglyphic, Homophone, Ideogram, Ideograph, Italic, Kanji, Kern, Kind, La(m)bda, Letter, Logogram, Make-up, Mark, Mu, Nagari, > **NATURE**, Non-person, Nu, Ogam, Ogham, Pahlavi, Pantaloon, Part, Pehlevi, Person(a), Personage, > **PERSONALITY**, Phonogram, Physiognomy, Pi, Polyphone, Protagonist, Psi, Raisonneur, Reference, Repute, Rho, Role, Rune, Runic, Sampi, San, Self, Sirvente, Slash, Sonancy, Space, Sphenogram, Stamp, Subscript, Superscript(ion), Swung dash, Syllabary, Symbol, Testimonial, Ton(e), Trait, Uncial, Unit, Vav, Vee, Waw, Wen, Wild card, Wyn(n), Yogh, Zeta
Characterise(d), Characterism, Characteristic(s) Acquired, Attribute, Aura, Cast, Colour, Distinctive, Ethos, Facies, Feature, Hair, Hallmark, Has, Headmark, Idiomatic, Idiosyncrasy, Jizz, Lineament, Mien, Nature, Notate,

Peculiar, Persona, Phenotype, Point, Property, Quality, Signature, Stigma, Strangeness, Streak, Style, > TRAIT, Transfer, Typical, Vein

Characterless Anon, Inane, Wet

Charade Enigma, Pretence, Riddle

Charcoal Carbon, Coke, Fusain, Sugar

Charge(s), Charged, Charger Accusal, Accuse, Aerate, Agist, Allege, Annulet, Arraign, Ascribe, Assault, Baton, Bear, Behest, Blame, Brassage, Brush, Buckshot, Bum rap, Care, Cathexis, Commission, Community, Complaint, Congestion, Cost, Count, Cover, Criminate, Damage, Debit, Delate, Delf, Delph, Demurrage, Depth, Depute, Directive, Dittay, Dockage, Due, Duty, Electric, Electron, Entrust, Entry, Exit, Expense, Fare, Fee, Fill, Fixed, Fleur-de-lis, Floating, Flock, Freight, Fullage, Fuse, Fuze, Gazump, Gravamen, > HERALDIC, Hot, Hypothec, Impeach, Impute, Indict, Inescutcheon, Inform, Instinct, Ion, Isoelectric, Last, Lien, Lioncel(le), Lionel, Live, Load, Mandate, Mine, Mount, Objure, Obtest, Onrush, Onslaught, Onus, Ordinary, Orle, Overhead, Pervade, Pew-rent, Plaint, Positive, Premium, Prime, Prix fixe, Q, Rack-rent, Rap, Rate, Red-dog, Rent, Report, Reprise, Roundel, Run, > RUSH, Saddle, Service, Specific, Steed, Tariff, Tax, Tear, Terms, Tilt, > TRAY, Tressure, Trickle, Trust, Tutorage, Upfill, Vaire, Vairy, Verdoy, Vigorish, Ward, Warhead, Wharfage

Chariot(eer) Auriga, Automedon, Biga, Cart, Curricle, Hur, Phaethon, Quadriga, Vimana, Wagon, Wain

Charisma Oomph, Personality

Charitable, Charity Alms, Awmous, Benign, Caritas, Cause, Dole, Dorcas, Eleemosynary, Largesse, Leniency, Liberal, Lion, Love, Mercy, Oddfellow, Openhanded, Oxfam, Pelican, Zakat

Charivari Rough music, Uproar

Charlatan Cheat, Crocus, Empiric, Escroc, Faker, Imposter, Katerfelto, Mountebank, Poseur, Quack(salver), Saltimbanco

Charlemagne Carlovingian

Charles, Charley, Charlie Beard, Car, Champagne, Chan, Chaplin, Checkpoint, Elia, Lamb, (Old) Rowley, Pretender, Rug-gown, Sap, Tail-end, Watchman

Charles de Gaulle Airport

Charlotte Bronte, Russe, Yonge

Charm(er), Charming Abracadabra, Abrasax, Abraxas, Allure, Amulet, Appeal, Aroma, Attraction, Beguile, Bewitch, Captivate, Charisma, Circe, Comether, Cute, Cutie, Delectable, Emerods, Enamour, Enchant, Engaging, > ENTRANCE, Fascinate, Fay, Fetish, Grace, Greegree, Gri(s)gris, Hand of glory, Houri, Juju, Magnetic, Mascot, Mojo, Obeah, Obi(a), Periapt, Phylactery, Porte-bonheur, Pretty, Prince, Quaint, Quark, Ravish, Siren, Smoothie, Spellbind, Suave, Sweetness, Taking, Talisman, Tefillah, Telesm, Tephillah, Tiki, Trinket, Unction, Voodoo, Winning, Winsome

▷ **Charming** *may indicate* an anagram

Chart(ed), Charting Abac, Bar, Breakeven, Card, Control, Diagram, Eye, Flip, Flow, Gantt, Graph, Histogram, Hydrography, Isogram, Isopleth, List, Magna Carta, > MAP, Mappemond, Nomogram, Organisation, Pie, Plane, Plot, Portolano, Ringelmann, Social, Table, Timetable, Waggoner, Weather, Z

Charta, Charter Atlantic, Book, Citizen's, Covenant, Hire, Lease, Novodamus, Rent, Social (chapter), Tenants', Time, Voyage

Chary Cagey, Careful, Cautious, Frugal, Shy, Wary

Charybdis Maelstrom, Whirlpool

Chase(r), Chasing Cannock, Chace, Chevy, Chivy, Ciseleur, Ciselure, Course, Cranbome, Decorate, Drink, Game, Harass, Hound, > HUNT, Jumper, Oxo,

Pursuit, Race, Scorse, Sic(k), Steeple, Sue, Suit, Wild-goose

Chasm Abyss, Crevasse, Fissure, Gap, Gorge, Gulf, Schism, Yawn

Chaste, Chastity Agnes, Attic, Celibate, Classic, Clean, Florimell, Ines, Innocent, Modesty, Nessa, > PURE, Vestal, Virginal, Virtue

Chasten, Chastise(d), Chastisement Beat, Correct, Discipline, Disple, Lash, Rib-roast, Rollicking, Scold, Scourge, Shame-faced, Spank, Strap, Whip

Chat, Chatter(box) Babble, Bavardage, Blab(ber), Blether, Campanero, Causerie, Chelp, Chinwag, Clack, Clishmaclaver, Confab(ulate), Converse, Cosher, Coze, Crack, Dialogue, Froth, Gab(ble), Gas, Gossip, Gup, Hobnob, Jabber, Jargon, Jaw, Kilfud, Madge, Mag(pie), Natter, Patter, Pie, Pourparler, Prate, Prattle, Rabbit, Rabble, Rap, Rattle, Scuttlebutt, Shmoose, Talk, Talkee-talkee, Tattle, Tongue-work, Twattle, Waffle, Windbag, Witter, Wongi, Yacketyyak, Yak, Yap, Yarn, Yatter, Yoking

Chateau Castle, Cru, Malmaison, Schloss

Chateaubriand René

Chattel Asset, Chose, Deodand

Chaucer(ian) Dan, OE

Chauffeur Cabby, Coachy, Driver, Sice, Syce

Chauvinist Alf, Bigot, Jingo, MCP, Partisan, Patriot, Sexist

Cheap Bargain, Base, Catchpenny, Cheesy, Chintzy, Cut-price, Downmarket, Giveaway, Ignoble, Knockdown, Low, Off-peak, Poor, Sacrifice, Shoddy, Stingy, Tatty, Tawdry, Ticky-tacky, Tinhorn, Tinpot, Tinselly, Trivial, Tuppenny, Two-bit, Twopenny, Undear, Vile

▷ **Cheap** *may indicate* a d- or p- start to a word

Cheapside Bow

Cheat(ers), Cheating Bam, Bamboozle, Beguile, Bilk, Bite(r), Bob, Bonnet, Bucket, Bullock, Cardsharp(er), Charlatan, Chiaus, Chicane(ry), Chisel, Chouse, Clip, Cod, Cog(ger), Colt, Con, Cozen, Crib, Cross, Cross-bite(r), Cuckold, Cully, Defraud, Delude, Diddle, Dingo, Dish, Do, Doublecross, Duckshove, Dupe, Escroc, Faitor, Fiddle, Finagle, Flam, Fleece, Fob, Foister, Fox, Fraud, Gaff, Gip, Glasses, Gull-catcher, Gum, Gyp, Hoax, Hocus, Hoodwink, Hornswoggle, Horse, Intake, Jockey, Leg, Magsman, Mulct, Mump, Nick, Pasteboard, Picaro(on), Poop, Queer, Rib, Rig, Rogue, Rook, Rush, Scam, Screw, Shaft, Sharper, Short-change, Slur, Smouch, Snap, Stack, Stiff, Sting, Swindle, Thimble-rigging, Trepan, Trim, Two-time, Welsh, Wheedle

Check Arrest, Audit, Bauk, Ba(u)lk, Bill, Bridle, Collate, Compesce, Control, Count, Cramp, Cross-index, Curb, Dam, Damp, Detain, Detent, Discovered, Dogs-tooth, Examine, Foil, Frustrate, Halt, Hamper, Hobble, Houndstooth, Inhibit, Jerk, Jerque, Let, Limit, Mate, Monitor, Observe, Overhaul, Party, Perpetual, Prevent, Rain, Reality, Rebuff, Rebuke, Rein, Repress, Reprime, Repulse, Reread, > RESTRAIN, Revoke, Saccade, Screen, Service, Setback, Shepherd's, Shorten, Sit-upon, Sneap, Sneb, Snib, Snub, Sound, Spot, > STEM, Stop, Stunt, Tab, Tally, Tartan, Tattersall, Test, Thwart, Tick, Trash, Verify, Vet

Checkers Chinese, Piece

Check-out Till

Cheddar Cheese, Gorge

Cheek(y) Alforja, Audacity, Brass-neck, Buccal, Chap, Chollers, Chutzpah, Cool, Crust, Flippant, Fresh, Gum, Hard-faced, Hussy, Impertinent, Impudent, Joll, Jowl, Lip, Malapert, Malar, Masseter, Neck, Nerve, Noma, Pert, Presumption, Quean, Sass, Sauce, Sideburns, Wang, Yankie, Zygoma

Cheep Chirp, Chirrup, Peep

Cheer(s), Cheerful(ness), Cheering Acclaim, Agrin, Applaud, Banzai, Barrack,

Blithe, Bonnie, Bravo, Bright, Bronx, Bubbly, Buck, Buoy, Cadgy, Canty, Carefree, Cherry, Chin-chin, Chipper, Chirpy, > **COMFORT**, Crouse, Debonair, Drink, Ease, Elate, Elevate, Enliven, Exhilarate, Festive, Genial, Gladden, Happy-go-lucky, Hearten, Hilarity, Holiday, Hooch, Hoorah, Hurra(h), Huzzah, Insouciance, Jocund, Jovial, Kia-ora, Light-hearted, Lightsome, Lively, Meal, Ovate, Peart, Perky, Please, Praise, Prosit, Rah, Riant, Rivo, Root, Rumbustious, Shout, Sko(a)l, Slainte, Sonsie, Sunny, Ta, Tata, Thanks, Three, Tiger, Tiggerish, Toodle-oo, Warm, Winsome, Yell

Cheerless Dismal, Drab, Drear, Gloomy, Glum

Cheese, Cheesy American, Amsterdam, Appenzell, Asiago, Bel Paese, Blue, Boursin, Brie, Caboc, Caerphilly, Camembert, Cantal, Casein, Caseous, Cheddar, Cheshire, Chessel, Chèvre, Colby, Cottage, Coulommiers, Cream, Crowdie, Curd, Damson, Danish blue, Derby, Dolcelatte, Double Gloucester, Dunlop, Edam, Emmental(er), Emmenthal(er), Ermite, Esrom, Ewe, Fet(a), Fontina, Fromage frais, Fynbo, Gloucester, Goat, Gorgonzola, Gouda, Grand Panjandrum, Gruyère, Halloumi, Hard, Havarti, Huntsman, Ilchester, Islay, Jarlsberg®, Junket, Kebbock, Kebbuck, Kenno, Killarney, Lancashire, Leicester, Limburg(er), Lymeswold®, Macaroni, Mascarpone, Mousetrap, Mozzarella, Mu(e)nster, Mycella, Neufchatel, Oka, Orkney, Paneer, Parmesan, Pecorino, Pont l'Eveque, Port Salut, Pot, Provolone, Quark, Raclette, Rarebit, Reblochon, Rennet, Ricotta, Romano, Roquefort, Sage Derby, Samso, Sapsago, Skyr, Stilton®, Stone, Stracchino, Swiss, Tilsit, Tofu, Truckle, Vacherin, VIP, Wensleydale

Cheesecake Pin-up, Talmouse

Cheese-scoop Pale

Chef Commis, Escoffier

Chekhov Anton

Chemical Acanthin, Acid, Acrolein, Adrenalin®, Agent orange, Alar, Aldehyde, Alkali, Allomone, Alum, Amide, Anabolic, Barilla, Bradykinin, Bute, Carbide, Carnallite, Caseose, Catalyst, Cephalin, Cerebroside, Depside, Developer, Dopamine, Encephalin, Enkephalin(e), Enol, Fixer, Fluoride, Formyl, Freon, Fungicide, Gamone, Glutamine, Glycol, Halon, Harmin, Heavy, Hecogenin, Heptane, Hexylene, Hexylresorcinol, Histamine, Hypo, ICI, Imine, Imipramine, Indican, Interleukin, Larvicide, Morphactin, Natron, Nitre, Oestregen, Olefin, Olein, Oxide, Oxysalt, Pentane, Pentene, Pentyl, Peptide, Periclase, Phenol, Phenyl, Pheromone, Potash, Potassa, Psoralen, Ptomaine, Reagent, Resorcin, Resorcinol, Restrainer, Serotonin, Soman, Soup, Strontia, Sulphide, Thio-salt, Toner, Trimer, Weedicide, Weedkiller

Chemise Cymar, Sark, Serk, Shift, Shirt, Simar(re), Smock, Symar

Chemist(ry) Alchemy, Alchymy, Analyst, Apothecary, Bunsen, Butenandt, Cavendish, Cleve, Davy, Debye, Dewar, Dispenser, Druggist, Drugstore, FCS, Gahn, Hevesy, Inorganic, Lavoisier, Liebig, LSA, MPS, Nernst, Newlands, Nobel, Nuclear, Organic, Paracelsus, Pasteur, Pharmacist, Physical, Pothecary, Pottingar, Proust, Prout, Redwood, RIC, Sabatier, Sanger, Schiff, Spageric, Spagiric, Spagyric, Spicer, Stinks, Stoich(e)iometry, Technical, Urey, Zymurgy

Cheops Khufu

Cheque Blank, Giro, Gregory, Open, Rubber, Stumer, Tab, Traveller's

Chequer Dice

Cherish(ed) Dear, Dote, Enshrine, Entertain, Esteem, Foment, Foster, Harbour, Inshrine, Nestle, Nurse, Pamper, Pet, Precious, Treasure

Cheroot Cigar, Manil(l)a

Cherry (tree) Amarelle, Ball, Bigaroon, Bigarreau, Bird, Blackheart, Cerise,

Cornelian, Gean, Ground, Heart, Jerusalem, Kearton, Kermes, Kermesite, Malpighia, Marasca, Maraschino, May-duke, Maz(z)ard, Merry, Morel(lo), Red, Sweet, Whiteheart

Cherry-pie Heliotrope

Cherub Angel, Putto, Seraph

Chess (move), Chess player, Chess term Black, Blindfold, Endgame, Euwe, Fianchetto, FIDE, J'adoube, Karpov, Lightning, Miranda, Patzer, Plank, Shogi, Speed, White, Zugzwang, Zwischenzug

Chessman Bishop, Black, Castle, Horse, King, Knight, Pawn, Pin, Queen, Rook, White

Chest(y) Ark, Bahut, Bosom, Box, Breast, Buist, Bunker, Bureau, Bust, Caisson, Cap-case, Case, Cassone, Chapel, Chiffonier, Coffer, Coffin, Coffret, Commode, Community, Cub, Dresser, Hope, Inro, Kist, Larnax, Locker, Lowboy, Meal-ark, Medicine, Ottoman, Pectoral, Pereion, Pigeon, Pleural, Safe, Scrine, Scryne, Sea, Shrine, Slop, Steam, Sternum, Tallboy, Tea, Thorax, Toolbox, Trunk, Wangan, Wangun, Wanigan, War, Wind

Chester Deva

Chestnut Auburn, Badious, Ch, Chincapin, Chinese, Chinkapin, Chinquapin, Cliché, Conker, Dwarf, Favel(l), Hoary, Horse, Marron, Marron glacé, Moreton Bay, Russet, Saligot, Soare, Sorrel, Spanish, Sweet, Water

Chest protector > ARMOUR, Bib

Chevalier Bayard, Knight, Pretender

Chevron Dancette, Stripe

Chew(ing) Bite, Champ, Chaw, Cud, Eat, Fletcherism, Gnaw, Gum, Manducate, Masticate, Maul, Meditate, Moop, Mou(p), Munch, Ruminate, Siri(h), Spearmint

Chewink Ground-robin

Chiastolite Macle

Chic Dapper, Elegant, In, Kick, Modish, Posh, Radical, Smart, Soigné, Stylish, Swish, Tonish, Trim

Chicago Windy City

Chicane(ry) Artifice, Deception, Fraud, Wile

Chichester Yachtsman

Chichi Precious

Chick(en) Australorp, Battery, Biddy, Boiler, Broiler, Capon, Cheeper, Chittagong, Chuckie, Clutch, Cochin, Coronation, Coward, Cowherd, Eirack, Gutless, Hen, Howtowdie, Kiev, Layer, Marengo, Minorca, Mother Carey's, Niderling, Poltroon, Poot, Poult, Pout, Prairie, Precocial, Pullus, Quitter, Roaster, Spatchcock, Spring, Squab, Supreme, Timorous, Unheroic, Windy, Wyandotte, Yellow

Chickenfeed Maize

Chickenpox Varicella

Chickpea Garbanzo

Chickweed Snow-in-summer

Chicory Endive, Radiccio, Succory, Witloof

Chide Admonish, Berate, Objurgate, Rate, Rebuke, Reprove, Row, Scold, Tick off, Twit, Upbraid

Chief(tain) Arch, Ardrigh, Ariki, Boss, Caboceer, Cacique, Calif, Caliph, Capital, Capitan, Capitayn, Capo, Caradoc, Cazique, Ch, Chagan, Dat(t)o, Dominant, Emir, Finn (MacCool), First, Foremost, Geronimo, Grand, Haggis, > HEAD, Hereward, Jarl, Kaid, King, Leader, > MAIN, Mass, Mugwump, Nizam, Oba, Overlord, Paramount, Pendragon, Premier, Primal, Prime, Principal, Quanah,

Raja(h), Rajpramukh, Rangatira, Rangatiratanga, Ratoo, Ratu, Sachem, Sagamore, Sarpanch, Sudder, Supreme, Tanist, Tank, Top

Chiffonier Cabinet, Commode

Chilblain Kibe

Child(ish), Childhood, Children Aerie, Alannah, Ankle biter, Babe, Baby, Badger, Bairn, Bambino, Bantling, Boy, Brat, Brood, Butter-print, Ch, Changeling, Cherub, Chick, Chickabiddy, Chit, Collop, Cub, Dream, Elfin, Eyas, Foster, Foundling, Gait, Gangrel, Ge(i)t, Girl, Gyte, Heir, Hellion, Hurcheon, Imp, Infancy, Infant, Inner, Issue, It, Jailbait, Jejune, Juvenile, Kid(die), Kiddie(wink), Kiddy, Kinder, Lad, Latchkey, Limb, Litter, Littlie, Littling, Love, Mamzer, Mardy, Minion, Minor, Mite, Munchkin, Naive, Nipper, Nursling, Offspring, Papoose, Piccaninny, Pickin, Progeny, Puerile, Puss, Putto, Ragamuffin, Rip, Rug rat, Scion, Second, Small fry, Smout, Smowt, Sprog, Street arab, Subteen, Tacker, Ted, Teeny-bopper, Tike, Toddle(r), Tot(tie), Totty, Trot, Tweenager, Tyke, Urchin, Waif, Wean, Weanel, Weanling, Weeny-bopper, Whelp, Younker, Youth

Childbearing, Childbirth Couvade, Intrapartum, Lamaze, Parity, Puerperal, Tocology, Tokology

Child-killer Herod

Childless Atocous, Atokous, Barren, Nullipara, Sp

Chill(er), Chilly Bleak, Cauldrife, > **COLD**, Frappé, Freeze, Freon®, Frigid, Frosty, Gelid, Ice, Iciness, Mimi, Oorie, Ourie, Owrie, Parky, Raw, Refrigerate, Rigor, Scare

Chilli Bird's eye

Chime(s) Bell, Cymar, Jingle, Peal, Semantron, Tink, > **TOLL**, Wind

Chimera Graft

Chimney (pot), Chimney corner Can, Cow(l), Femerall, Flare stack, Flue, Funnel, Lamp, Lug, Lum, Smokestack, Stack, Stalk, Steeplejack, Tallboy, Tunnel

Chimp Ape, Jocko

Chin, Chinwag Chitchat, Double, Genial, Jaw, Jowl, Mentum

China(man), Chinese Ami, Amoy, Boxer, Cameoware, Cantonese, Cathay, Celestial, Ch, Chelsea, Chink(y), Chow, Coalport, Cochin, Cock, Communist, Confucius, Crackle, Crockery, Delft, Derby, Dresden, Eggshell, Etrurian, Flowery land, Friend, Fukien, Google, Googly, Goss, Hakka, Han, Hizen, Hmong, Imari, Kanji, Kaolin, Kuo-yu, Limoges, Manchu, Mandarin, Mangi, Maoist, Mate, Meissen, Min, Ming, Minton, National, Oppo, Pal, Pareoean, Pekingese, Pe-tsai, Pinyin, Porcelain, > **POTTERY**, Putonghua, Queensware, Red, Rockingham, Royal Worcester, Seric, Sèvres, Shanghai, Sinic, Spode®, Sun Yat-sen, Tai-ping, Taoist, Teng, Tocharian, Tungus, Uigur, Wal(l)y, Ware, Wedgwood®, Whiteware, Willowware, Worcester, Wu

Chine Chink, Chynd, Ridge

Chink Chinaman, Chop, Cleft, Clink, Cloff, Crack, Cranny, Crevice, Gap, Rent, Rift, Rima, Sinic, Window

Chintz Kalamkari

Chip(s) Blue, Bo(a)st, Carpenter, Counter, Cut, Deep-fried, EPROM, EROM, Fish, Flake, Fragment, Game, Hack, Knap, Log, Nacho(s), Neural, Nick, Pin, Potato, Shaving, Silicon, Spale, Spall, Span, Teraflop, Tortilla, Transputer

▷ **Chip** *may indicate* an anagram

Chipmunk Gopher, Hackee, Suslik, Zizel

Chipper Jaunty, Spry, Wedge

Chiron Centaur

Chiropody Podiatry
Chiropractic McTimoney
Chirp(y), Chirrup Cheep, Cherup, Chirm, Chirr, Cicada, Peep, Pip, Pipe, Pitter, Stridulate, Trill, Tweet, Twitter
Chisel(ler), Chisel-like Bam, Boaster, Bolster, Bur, Burin, Carve, Cheat, Clip, Drove, Firmer, Gad, > GOUGE, Half-round, Mason, Paring, Scalpriform, Scauper, Scorper, Sculpt, Socket, Sting
Chit Docket, Girl, Note, Voucher
Chivalry, Chivalrous Brave, Bushido, Courtly, Gallant, Quixotic
Chivvy Badger, Harass, Pursue
Chloride, Chlorine Calomel
Chlorophyll Leaf-green
Chock Trig
Chocolate Aero, Brown, Cacao, Carob, Cocoa, Dragee, Ganache, Milk, Neapolitan, Noisette, Pinole, Plain, Theobroma, Truffle, Vegelate
Choice, Choose, Choosy, Chosen Adopt, Anthology, Appoint, Aryan, Cherry-pick, Cull, Dainty, Decide, Druthers, Eclectic, Elect, Elite, Esnecy, Fine, Fork, Free will, Hobson's, Leet, Leve, Lief, List, Multiple, Opt, Option, Or, Ossian, Peach, Peculiar, > PICK, Picking, Plum(p), Precious, Predilect, Prefer, Proairesis, Rare, Recherché, > SELECT, Superb, Try(e), Via media, Volition, Wale
Choiceless Beggar
Choir, Choral, Chorister, Chorus Antiphony, Antistrophe, Anvil, Apse, Burden, Choragus, Choregus, Dawn, Decani, Faburden, Fauxbourdon, Group, Hallelujah, Harmony, Hymeneal, Motet, Ninth, Parabasis, Precentor, > REFRAIN, Ritual, Singing, Stop, Strophe, Treble, Triad, > UNISON
Choir-master Choragus, Choregus, Precentor
Choke(r) Block, Clog, Gag, Garotte, Glut, Silence, Smoor, Smore, Smother, Stap, Stifle, Stop, Strangle(hold), Strangulate, > THROTTLE
Choky Can, Prison
Cholera Hog
Cholesterol Squalene
Choliamb Scazon
▶ **Choose** *see* CHOICE
Chop(per), Chops, Chopper(s), Choppy Adze, Ax(e), Celt, Charge, Cheek, Chump, Cleave, Côtelette, Cuff, Cutlet, Dice, Fell(er), Flew, Hack, Helicopter, Hew, Ivory, Karate, Lop, Mince, Mouth, Rotaplane, Rough, Suey, Teeth, To-rend, Wang
Chopin Pantoufle, Shoe
Chopstick(s) Waribishi
Chord(s) Arpeggio, Barré, Broken, Common, Diameter, Eleventh, Harmony, Intonator, Latus rectum, Neapolitan sixth, Nerve, Ninth, Picardy third, Riff, Seventh, Submediant, Thirteenth, Triad, Vocal
Chore Darg, Duty, Fag, Task
Choreographer Arranger, Ashton, Balanchine, Cecchetti, Cranko, Fokine, Laban, Massine
Chorus Antistrophe, Dawn, Ninth, Stop, Strophe
Chosen Korea
Chough Chewet
Chowder Bouillabaisse, Skink, Soup
Christ > CHRIST, Ecce homo, Messiah, Pantocrator, Prince of Peace, Saviour, The Good Shepherd, The Redeemer, X, Xt
Christen(ing) Baptise, Launch, Name-day

Christian(ity) Abcee, Abecedarian, Absey, Adventist, Albigenses, Anabaptist, Beghard, Believer, Cathar(ist), Charismatic, Coptic, Dior, Donatist, D(o)ukhobor, Ebionite, Galilean, Giaour, Gilbertine, Gnostic, Godsquad, Goy, Heteroousian, Holy roller, Homo(i)ousian, Hutterite, Jehovah's Witness, Lutheran, Marrano, Melchite, Melkite, Methodist, Moral, Mozarab, Muscular, Mutineer, Nazarene, Nestorian, Phalange, Pilgrim, Presbyterian, Protestant, Quaker, Quartodeciman, RC, Sabotier, Scientist, SCM, Shambe, Traditor, Uniat(e), Unitarian, Valdenses, Waldensian, Wesleyan, Xian, Zwinglian

Christian Scientist Eddy

Christmas(time) C(h)rimbo, Dec, Island, Nativity, Noel, Yuletide

Christopher Kit, Robin, Sly, Wren

Chromatin Karyotin

Chromium Cr

Chromosome Aneuploid, Autosome, Centromere, Cistron, Euchromatin, Genome, Haploid, Homologous, Id(ant), Karyotype, Lampbrush, Operon, Philadelphia, Ploid(y), Polytene, Prophage, Trisomy, X, Y

Chronicle(r) Anglo-Saxon, Annal, Brut, Calendar, Diary, Froissart, Hall, History, Holinshed, Logographer, Moblog, Paralipomena, Parian, Paris, > **RECORD**, Register, Stow

Chrysalis Nymph, Pupa

Chrysanthemum Corn-marigold, Feverfew

Chrysolite Olivine, Peridot

Chub Cheven, Chevin, Fish

Chubby Butterball, Plump

Chuck (out) Berry, Buzz, Chook(ie), Discard, Eject, Food, Grub, Pat, Pitch, Shy, Sling, Three-jaw, Toss, Turf

Chuckle Chortle, Giggle, Gurgle

Chukka Polo

Chum(my) Buddy, Cobber, Cock, Companion, Crony, Mate, Pal, Sociable, Sodality

Chump Mug(gins), Noddle, Sap, Stupid

Chunk(y) Boxy, Chubby, Gob, Piece, Slab, Squat, Wad

Church Abbey, Armenian, Autocephalous, Basilica, Bethel, Bethesda, Broad, Brood, Byzantine, CE, Ch, Chapel, Chevet, Clergy, Collegiate, Congregational, Coptic, Delubrum, Eastern, EC, Ecumenical, Episcopal, Episcopalian, Established, Faith, Fold, Free, Greek, High, House, Kirk, Lateran, Latin, Low, Lutheran, Maronite, Methodist, Minster, Moravian, Mormon, New, New Jerusalem, Orthodox, Pentecostal, Preaching-house, Prebendal, Presbyterian, RC, Reformed, Relief, Rome, Russian Orthodox, Shrine, Smyrna, Station, Stave, Steeple, Temple, Triumphant, Unification, Unitarian, United Reformed, Visible, Wee Free, Western, Wool

Churchgoer, Churchman, Churchwarden Antiburgher, Azymite, Baptist, Believer, Classis, Clay, Cleric, Clerk, Congregation, Deacon, Dom, Dopper, Elder, Evangelist, Hatto, Ignorantine, Incumbent, Invisible, Knox, Lector, Lutheran, Methodist, Militant, Moderator, Moonie, Mormon, MU, Newman, Oncer, Parson, PE, Pipe, Pontiff, Prebendary, Precentor, Predicant, Predikant, Prelate, Presbyterian, Priest, Protestant, Puritan, Rector, Ruridecanal, Sacristan, Sidesman, Sim, Simeonite, Subdeacon, Succentor, Swedenborgian, Tantivy, Triumphant, Ubiquitarian, Unitarian, Verger, Visible, Wesleyan, Worshipper, Wren

Church house Deanery, Manse, Parsonage, Presbytery, Rectory, Vicarage

Churchill Tank, Winston

Churchyard God's acre
Churl(ish) Attercop, Boor, Crabby, Curmudgeonly, Cynical, Ethercap, Ettercap, Gruff, Ill-natured, Nabal, Peasant, Rustic, Serf, Surly
Churn Bubble, Kirn, Seethe
Chute Flume, Runway
CIC Shogun, Sirdar
Cicada Greengrocer, Locust, Tettix
Cicatrix Scar
Cicely Myrrh, Sweet
Cicero Cic, Tully
Cid Campeador, Chief, Hero
Cider Drink, Perry, Scrumpy
Ci-devant Ex
Cigar(ette), Cigarette cards Beedi(e), Bumper, Burn, Cancer stick, Caporal, Cartophily, Cheroot, Cigarillo, Claro, Coffin nail, Conch, Concha, Corona, Dog-end, Doob, Durry, Fag, Filter-tip, Gasper, Giggle(-stick), Havana, Joint, Locofoco, Long-nine, Loosies, Maduro, Manilla, Panatella, Paper-cigar, Perfecto, Puritano, Reefer, Regalia, Roach, Roll-up, Smoke, Snout, Splif(f), Stog(e)y, Stogie, Stompie, Twist, Weed, Whiff, Zol
Cinch Belt, Certainty, Duck soup, Girth
Cinchona Kina, Quina
Cinder(s) Ash, Breeze, Clinker, Dander, Embers, Slag
Cinderella Drudge, Stepdaughter
Cinema(s) Art house, Big screen, Biograph, Bioscope, Circuit, Drive-in, Films, Fleapit, Flicks, Megaplex, Movies, Multiplex, Mutoscope, New Wave, Nickelodeon, Nouvelle Vague, Odeon, Plaza, Theatre, Tivoli
Cinnabar Vermilion
Cinnamon, Cinnamon stone Canella, Cassia(bark), Essonite, Hessonite, Spice
Cipher Chi-rho, Code, Cryptogram, Nihil, Nobody, > NOTHING, Number, O, Steganogram, Zero
Circle Almacantar, Almucantar, Annulet, Antarctic, Arctic, Circassian, Co, Colure, Company, Compass, Corn, Corolla, Coterie, Cromlech, Crop, Cycloid, Cyclolith, Dip, Disc, Dress, Druidical, Eccentric, Ecliptic, Embail, Enclose, Epicyclic, Equant, Equator, Equinoctial, Euler's, Family, Fraternity, Full, Galactic, Girdle, Gloriole, Great, Gyre, Halo, Hoop, Horizon, Hour, Hut, Inner, Inorb, Lap, Longitude, Loop, Magic, Malebolge, Mandala, Meridian, Mohr's, Nimbus, O, Orb, Orbit, Parhelic, Parquet, Parterre, Penannular, Peristalith, Pitch, Polar, Quality, Rigol, > RING, Rondure, Rotate, Roundlet, Sentencing, Set, Setting, Small, Sphere, Stemme, Stone, Striking, Surround, Tinchel, Traffic, Transit, Tropic, Turning, Umbel, Upper, Vertical, Vicious, Vienna, Virtuous, Volt, Wheel
Circuit(ous) Ambit, AND, Autodyne, Bypass, Closed, Comparator, Daughterboard, Diocese, Discriminator, Dolby®, Equivalent, Eyre, Gyrator, IC, Integrated, Interface, Lap, Limiter, Logic, Loop, Microprocessor, Motherboard, NAND, NOR, NOT, Open, OR, Perimeter, Phantom, Phase, Printed, Quadripole, Reactance, Ring, Round, Scaler, Series, Short, Smoothing, Three-phase, Tour, Windlass
Circuit-breaker Fuse
Circular Annular, Court, Folder, Leaflet, Mailshot, Orby, Round, Spiral, Unending, Wheely
Circulate, Circulation Astir, Bloodstream, Cyclosis, Disseminate, Flow, Gyre, Issue, Mingle, Mix, Orbit, Pass, Publish, Report, Revolve, Rotate, Scope, Spread,

Stir, Troll, Utter

▷ **Circulating** *may indicate* an anagram

Circumcise(r), Circumcision Bris, Brith, Brit milah, Infibulate, Milah, Mohel, Pharaonic

Circumference Boundary, Girth, Perimeter, Size

Circumlocution Periphrasis, Tautology

Circumnavigation Periplus

Circumscribe Define, Demarcate, Enclose, Restrain

Circumspect Chary, Guarded, Prudential, Wary

Circumstance(s), Circumstantial Case, Detail, Event, Fact, Formal, > INCIDENT, Mitigating, Precise, Shebang, Situation

Circumvent Bypass, Dish, Evade, Outflank, Outwit, Usurp

Circus, Circus boy Arena, Big top, Eros, Flea, Flying, Harrier, Hippodrome, Marquee, Maximus, Media, Monty Python, Ring, Sanger, Slang, Three-ring

Cistercian Trappist

Cistern Feed-head, Flush-box, Sump, Tank, Tub, Vat

Citadel Acropolis, Alhambra, Castle, Fort(ress), Keep, Kremlin

Citation, Cite Adduce, Allegation, Mention, Name, Quote, Recall, Reference, Repeat, Sist, Summon

Citizen(s), Citizenship Burgess, Burgher, Civism, Cleruch, Denizen, Dicast, Ephebe, Franchise, Freeman, Jus sanguinis, Jus soli, Kane, National, Oppidan, Patrial, People, Quirites, Resident, Roman, Second-class, Senior, Snob, Subject, Trainband, Trierarch, Venireman, Voter

Citroen DS

Citron, Citrous Bergamot

Citrus Acid, Calamondin, Cedrate, Lemon, Lime, Mandarin, Min(n)eola, Orange, Pomelo, Tangerine, Ugli

City Agra, Athens, Atlantis, Babylon, Burgh, Carthage, Cosmopolis, Ctesiphon, Dodge, EC, Empire, Eternal, Forbidden, Free, Garden, Gath, Hilversum, Holy, Imperial, Inner, LA, Leonine, Medina, Megalopolis, Metropolis, Micropolis, Mycenae, NY, Persepolis, Petra, Pompeii, Rhodes, Salem, Smoke, Sparta, Tech, Teheran, Town, Ur, Vatican, Weldstadt, Wen

Civet Binturong, Cat, Fo(u)ssa, Genet(te), Herpestes, Linsang, Musang, Nandine, Palm, Paradoxine, Paradoxure, Rasse, Suricate, Toddy-cat, Viverra, Zibet

Civil(ian), Civilisation, Civilised, Civility Amenity, Christian, Cit, Citizen, Civ(vy), Comity, Courtesy, Culture, Fertile crescent, Humane, Indus Valley, Kultur, Maya, Municipal, Nok, Non-combatant, Polite, Politesse, Secular, Temporal, Urbane

Civil Service CS

Clad(ding) Sarking, Weatherboard

Clag(gy) Stickjaw

Claim Appeal, Arrogate, Assert, Asseverate, Bag, Challenge, Charge, Darraign(e), Darrain(e), Darrayn, Demand, Deraign, Droit, Encumbrance, Haro, Harrow, Lien, List, Maintain, Nochel, Plea, Pose, Posit, Postulate, Pretence, Pretend, Profess, Pulture, Purport, Puture, Revendicate, Right, Set-off, Sue, Title

Claimant Irredentist, Petitioner, Pot-waller, Pretender, Prospector, Tichborne, Usurper

Clairvoyance, Clairvoyancy ESP, Fey, Insight, Lucidity, Psiphenomena, Taisch, Taish, Tel(a)esthesia, Telegnosis

Clam Bivalve, Cohog, Geoduck, Giant, Gweduc, Littleneck, Mollusc, Mya,

Quahang, Quahog, Soft-shell, Tridacna, Venus

Clamant Vociferous

Clamber Climb, Crawl, Scramble, Spra(i)ckle, Sprauchle

Clammy Algid, Damp, Dank, Moist, Sticky, Sweaty

Clamour(ing), **Clamorous** Blatant, Brouhaha, Din, Hubbub, Hue, Outcry, Racket, Raird, Reird, Rout, Shout, Strepitant, Uproar, Utis, Vociferate

Clamp Beartrap, Clinch, Coupler, Denver boot, Fasten, Grip, Holdfast, Jumar, Pinchcock, Potato-pit, Serrefine, Stirrup, Tread, Vice, Wheel

Clan(sman) Cameron, Clique, Gens, Gentile, Group, Horde, Kiltie, Kindred, Name, Phratry, Phyle, Sect, Sept, Society, Stewart, Stuart, Tribe

Clandestine Covert, Furtive, Secret, Underhand

Clang(er), **Clanging**, **Clank** Bell, Belleter, Boob, Boo-boo, Clash, Gong, Jangle, Plangent, Ring

Clap(per), **Clapping** Applaud, Blow, Castanet, Chop, Crotal, Dose, Jinglet, Peal, Thunder, Tonant

Claptrap Bilge, Blab, Bombast, Bunkum, Eyewash, Hokum, Rot, Tripe

Claque(ur) Fans, Hat, Laudator, Sycophant

Clara Bow, Butt

Claret Blood, Loll-shraub, Loll-shrob, Vin

Clarify, **Clarifier** Clear, Despumate, Dilucidate, Explain, Explicate, Finings, Purge, Refine, Render, Simplify

Clarinet Reed

Clarion Brassy, Clear, Trumpet

Clary Orval, Sage

Clash(ing) Bang, Clangour, Clank, Claver, Coincide, Collide, Conflict, Friction, Gossip, > IMPACT, Incident, Irreconcilable, Jar, Loud, Missuit, Shock, Showdown, Strike, Swash

Clasp(ing) Adpress, Agraffe, Amplexus, Barrette, Brooch, Button, Catch, Chape, Clip, Embrace, Fibula, Grasp, Hasp, Hesp, Hook, Hug, Inarm, Interdigitate, Link, Morse, Ochreate, Ouch, Tach(e), Tie, Unite

Class(ification), **Classify**, **Classy** Acorn, Arrange, Assort, Bourgeois(ie), Bracket, Brand, Breed, Business, Cabin, Canaille, Caste, > CATEGORY, Chattering, Cheder, Cl, Clan, Clerisy, Clinic, Club, Course, Criminal, Dewey, Digest, Division, Economy, Estate, Evening, Faction, First, Form, Genera, Gentry, Genus, > GRADE, Group, Harvard, Heder, Hubble, Ilk, Keep-fit, Kohanga Reo, League, Life, Linn(a)ean, List, Lower, Mammal, Master, Middle, Number, Order, Phonetics, Phylum, Pigeon-hole, Pleb(eian), Proper, Race, Range, Rank, Rate, Rating, Reception, Remove, Salariat, Second, Seminar, Shell, Siege, Social, Sort(ation), Spectral, Steerage, Stratum, Stream, Syntax, Taxonomy, Teach-in, Third, Tony, Tourist, Tribe, Tutorial, > TYPE, U, Universal, Upper, Varna, Water, Working, World, Year

Classic(al), **Classics**, **Classicist** Ageless, Ancient, Basic, Derby, Elzevir, Grecian, Greek, Humane, Leger, Literature, Pliny, Purist, Roman, Standard, Traditional, Vintage

Clatch Blunk, Smear, Spoil

Clatter Bicker, Charivari, Clack, Din, Noise, Rattle

Clause Apodosis, Article, Basket, Condition, Conscience, Coordinate, Dependent, Disability, Endorsement, Escalator, Escape, Exclusion, Exemption, Filioque, Four, Golden parachute, Grandfather, Independent, Main, Member, Omnibus, Option, Poison-pill, Principal, Protasis, Proviso, Reddendum, Reported, Reservation, Rider, Salvo, Saving, Sentence, Subordinate, Tenendum, Testatum, Testing, Warrandice

Claw Chela, Claut, Crab, Dewclaw, Edate, Falcula, Grapple, Griff(e), Hook, Nail, Nipper, Pounce, Scrab, Scramb, Sere, Talent, > **TALON**, Tear, Telson, Tokay, Unguis

Clay Allophane, Argil, Argillite, Barbotine, B(e)auxite, Bentonite, Blaes, Blaise, Blaize, Bole, Calm, Cam, Caum, Ceramic, Charoset(h), China, Cimolite, Cloam, Clunch, Cob, Cornish, Earth, Engobe, Fango, Figuline, Fire, Fuller's earth, Gault, Glei, Gley, Gumbotil, Hardpan, Haroset(h), Illite, Kaolin, Laterite, Lithomarge, Loam, Lute, Malm, Marl, Meerschaum, Mire, Mortal, Mud, Papa, Pipeclay, Pipestone, Pise, Plastic, Plastilina, Porcelain, Potter's, Pottery, Puddle, Pug, Saggar(d), Sagger, Scroddle(d), Seggar, Sepiolite, Slip, Slurry, Smectite, Thill, Till(ite), Tumphy, Varve, Warrant, Warren, Wax

Clean(er), Cleaning Absterge, Bathbrick, Besom, Bleach, Bream, Broom, Careen, Catharise, Catharsis, Chaste, Clear, Daily, Debride, Decontaminate, Dentifrice, Depurate, Deterge(nt), Dhobi, Dialysis, Dicht, Douche, Dust(er), Eluant, Emunge, Enema, Erase, Ethnic, Evacuant, Evacuate, Expurgate, Fay, Fettle, Fey, Floss, Flush, Full, Grave, Groom, Gut, Heels, Hoover®, Hygienic, Immaculate, Innocent, Launder, Lave, Lustrum, Lye, Mouthwash, Mrs Mop(p), Mundify, Net, Overhaul, Porge, Pull-through, Pumice, Pure, Purgative, Purge, Ramrod, Rebite, Rub, Rump, Sandblast, Scaffie, Scavenge, Scour, Scrub, Shampoo, Snow-white, Soap, Soogee, Soogie, Soojey, Sponge, Spotless, Squeaky, Squeegee, Sterile, Sujee, Swab, Sweep, Tidy, Toothpick, Ultrasonic, Vac(uum), Valet, > **WASH**, Whistle, Wipe

Clear(ance), Clearly Absolve, Acquit, Aloof, Apparent, Bell, Berth, Bold, Bore, Brighten, Bus, Categorical, Clarify, Crystal, Decode, Definite, Delouse, Diaphanous, Dispel, Distinct, Downright, Earn, Eidetic, Evacuate, Evident, Exculpate, Exonerate, Explicit, Fair, Five-by-five, Gain, Headroom, Hyaline, Intelligible, Iron, Laund, Leap, Legible, Limpid, Lucid, Luculent, Manifest, Mop, Neat, Negotiate, Net(t), > **NOT CLEAR**, Observable, Obvious, Ope(n), Overleap, Palpable, Pellucid, Perspicuous, Plain, Play, Pratique, Predy, Pure, Quit, Rack, Realise, Remble, Rid, Ripple, Serene, Sheer, Shere, Slum, Sweep, Thro(ugh), Thwaite, Transire, Translucent, Transparent, Unblock, Vault, Vivid, Well, Windage, Wipe

Clearing Assart, Glade, Opening, Shire, Slash

Cleat Bitt, Wedge

Cleave, Cleavage, Cleft Adhere, Bisulcate, Chimney, Chine, Cling, Cloff, Cohere, Cut, Divide, Division, Divorce(ment), Gap, Ghaut, Goose-grass, Grike, Gryke, Pharynx, Rift, Riva, Scissure, Severance, Slack, Space, Spathose, Split

Clef Treble

Clematis Montana, Old man's beard, Traveller's joy, Virgin's-bower

Clemenceau Tiger

Clemency, Clement Ahimsa, Grace, Lenience, Lenity, Mercy, Mildness, Quarter, Temperate

Cleopatra Needle

Clergy(man), Cleric(al) Abbé, Canon, Cantor, Cardinal, Chaplain, Cleric, Clerk, Cloth, Curate, Curé, Deacon, Dean, Ecclesiast(ic), Goliard, Incumbent, Josser, Levite, Ministerial, Ministry, Non-juror, Non-usager, Notarial, Paperwork, Parson, Pastor, Pontifex, Pontiff, Preacher, Prebendary, Precentor, Prelate, Presbyter, Presenter, Priest, Primate, Prior, Proctor, Rabbi, Rector, Red-hat, Reverend, Rome-runner, Scribal, Secretarial, Shaveling, Shepherd, Sky pilot, Slope, Spin-text, Spirituality, Squarson, Subdeacon, Theologian, Vartabed, Vicar

Clergy-hater Misoclere

Clerk(s) Actuary, Baboo, Babu, Basoche, Cleric, Cratchit, Cursitor, Filing, Heep, Lay, Limb, Notary, Parish, Pen-driver, Penman, Penpusher, Poster, Prot(h)onotary, Protocolist, Recorder, Salaryman, Scribe, Secretariat, Shipping, Tally, Vicar, Writer

Clever(ness) Able, Adroit, Astute, Brainy, Bright, Canny, Cool, Cute, Daedal(e), Deep-browed, Deft, Genius, Gleg, Ingenious, Intellectual, Jackeen, Know-all, Natty, Nimblewit, Sage(ness), Shrewd, Skilful, Smart(y), Smarty-pants, Souple, Subtle

Clevis Becket

Cliché Banality, Boilerplate, Commonplace, Corn, Platitude, Saying, Tag

Click(er), Clicking Castanet, Catch, Forge, Pawl, Rale, Ratch(et), Snick, Succeed, Tchick, Ticktack

Client Customer, Gonk, John, Patron, Trick

Cliff(s) Beachy Head, Bluff, Cleve, Corniche, Crag, Craig, Escarp, Palisade, Precipice, Sca(u)r

Cliffhanger Samphire, Serial, Thriller

Climate Atmosphere, Attitude, Continental, Mood, Sun, Temperament, Temperature, Weather

Climax Apex, Apogee, Catastasis, Come, Crescendo, Crest, Crisis, Edaphic, End, Head, Heyday, Orgasm, Top, Zenith

Climb(er) Alpinist, Aralia, Aristolochia, Ascend, Breast, Briony, Bryony, Clamber, Clematis, Clusia, Cowage, Cowhage, Cowitch, Crampon, Creeper, Cucumber, Dodder, Heart-pea, Hedera, Ivy, Kie-kie, Kudzu, Lawyer, Layback, Liana, Liane, > **MOUNT**, Munro-bagger, Pareira, Parvenu, Prusik, Rat(t)an, Rise, Root, Scale, Scan, Scandent, Scansores, Sclim, Scramble, Shin, Shinny, Sklim, Smilax, Social, Speel, Steeplejack, Sty(e), Swarm, Timbo, Tuft-hunter, Udo, Up(hill), Uprun, Vine, Wistaria, With(y)wind, Woodbine, Zoom

Clinch Attach, Carriwitchet, Ensure, Fix, Quibble, Rivet, Secure, Settle

Cling(er), Clinging Adhere, Bur(r), Cherish, Cleave, Embrace, Hold, Hug, Ring, Tendril

Clinic Dental, Dispensary, Hospital, Hospitium, Mayo, Well-woman

Clink Gingle, Jail, Jingle, Lock up, Prison, Stir, Ting, Tinkle

Clinker Ash, Slag

Clip(ped), Clipper, Clipping Banana, Barrette, Brash, Bulldog, Butterfly, Cartridge, Clasp, Crocodile, Crop-ear, Crutch, Curt, Curtail, Cut, Cutty Sark, Dag, Dock, Dod, Excerpt, Fleece, Jubilee, Jumar, Krab, Lop, Pace, Paper, Pare, Peg, Prerupt, Prune, Roach, Scissel, Secateur, Shear, Ship, Shore, Shorn, Snip, Spring, Staccato, Tie, Tie-tack, Tinsnips, Topiarist, Trim

Clippy Cad, Conductor

Clique Cabal, Clan, Club, Coterie, Faction, Gang, Junta, Ring, Set

Clive Arcot

Cloak(room), Cloaks Aba, Abaya, Abba, Abolla, Amice, Bathroom, Buffalo-robe, Burnous, Capa, Cape, Capote, Caracalla, Cardinal, Cassock, Chasuble, Chimer(e), Chlamydes, Chlamys, Chuddah, Chuddar, Conceal, Cope, Cover, Disguise, Dissemble, Djellaba(h), Domino, Gabardine, Gaberdine, Gal(l)abea(h), Gal(l)abi(y)a(h), Gal(l)abi(y)eh, Gentlemen, Gents, Grego, Hall-robe, Heal, Hele, Himation, Hood, Inverness, Jelab, Jellaba, Joseph, Kaross, Manta, Manteel, Mant(e)let, Mantle, > **MASK**, Mourning, Mousquetaire, Mozetta, Opera, Paenula, Paletot, Pallium, Paludamentum, Pelisse, Pilch, Poncho, Powder-room, Rail, Revestry, Rocklay, Rokelay, Roquelaure, Sagum, Sarafan, Scapular, > **SCREEN**, Shroud, Swathe, Talma, Toga, Vestiary, Vestry, Visite

Clobber Anoint, Dress, Garb, Habiliments, Lam, Tack

Clock Alarm, Ammonia, Analogue, Astronomical, Atomic, Beetle, Big Ben, Biological, Blowball, Body, Bracket, Bundy, Caesium, Carriage, Clepsydra, Cuckoo, Dandelion, Digital, Doomsday, Floral, Grandfather, Grandmother, Hit, Knock, Long case, Meter, Parliament, Quartz, Repeater, Sandglass, Solarium, Speaking, Speedo, Strike, Sundial, Tell-tale, Time(r), Turret, Wag at the wa', Water

Clockmaker Fromanteel, Graham, Harrison, Knibb, Mudge, Tompion

Clockwise Deasil, Deasiul, Deasoil, Deiseal, Deisheal

Clockwork Precision, Regular

Clod Clumsy, Divot, Glebe, Lump, Mool, Mould, Put(t), Scraw, Sod, Stupid, Turf

Clog Accloy, Ball, Block, Clam, Crowd, Dance, Fur, Galosh, Golosh, Hamper, Jam, Lump, Mire, Obstruct, Overshoe, Patten, Sabot

Cloisonné Shippo

Cloister Arcade, Confine, Cortile, Immure, Monastery, Mure, Refuge

Clone, Cloning Ramet, Reproduce, Therapeutic

Cloots Worricow

Close(d), Closing, Closure Airless, Alongside, Atresia, Block, Boon, By, Cadence, Clammy, Clap, Clench, Complete, Cone off, Court, Dear, Debar, Dense, > END, Epilogue, Ewest, Finale, Gare, Grapple, Handy, Hard, Hard by, Imminent, Inbye, Infibulate, Intent, Intimate, Lock, Lucken, Marginal, Mean, Miserly, Muggy, Mure, Narre, Narrow, Near, Nearhand, Neist, Nie, Niggardly, Nigh, Nip and tuck, Obturate, Occlude, Occlusion, Oppressive, Parochial, Precinct, Reserved, Reticent, Seal, Secret, Serre, Serried, Serry, Shet, Shut(ter), Shutdown, Silly, Slam, Snug, Stap, Sticky, Stuffy, Sultry, Tailgate, Temenos, Tight, Uproll, Warm, Yard

Close-cropped Crewcut, Not-pated

Close-fitting Skintight, Slinky, Tight

Closet Cabinet, Confine, Cubicle, Cupboard, Dooket, Earth, Locker, Safe, Wardrobe, WC, Zeta

Close-up Detail, Fill, Shut, Stop, Zoom

Closing-time Eleven, End

Clot(ting) Agglutinate, Ass, Clag, Clump, Coagulate, Congeal, Crassamentum, Cruor, Curdle, Dag, Embolism, Embolus, Gel, Globule, Gob, Gout, Grume, Incrassate, Incrust, Jell, Lapper, Lopper, > LUMP, Mass, Prothrombin, Splatch, Stupid, Thicken, Thrombosis, Thrombus

Cloth Antependium, Carmelite, Clergy, Cloot, Clout, Dishrag, Duster, > FABRIC, > FELT, Frocking, Frontal, Gremial, Loin, Lungi, > MATERIAL, Nap, Napery, Napje, Nappie, Needlework, Netting, Pall, Pane, Pilch, Priesthood, Print(er), Purificator, Puttee, Putty, Rag, Raiment, Roll, Sashing, Scarlet, Serviette, Sheet, Sheeting, Shoddy, Stripe, Stuff, Sudarium, Supper, Sweatband, T, Tapestry, Tea, > TEXTILE, Throw, Tissue, Vernicle, Veronica, Washrag, Whole

- **CLOTHS**
-
-

1 letter:	Web	Drab	Ikat
J®		Duck	Kelt
	4 letters:	Fent	Knit
3 letters:	Aida	Gair	Lamé
Abb	Baft	Haik	Lawn
Rep	Ciré	Harn	Leno
Say	Doek	Hyke	Line

Mull	Panne	Coutil	Russel
Nude	Perse	Covert	Samite
Pina	Pilot	Crepon	Satara
Puke	Piqué	Cubica	Sateen
Rund	Plaid	Cyprus	Saxony
Shag	Plush	Damask	Sendal
Slop	Poult	Devoré	Shalli
Sulu	Rayon	Dialon®	Sherpa
Wire	Scrim	Dimity	Sindon
Wool	Serge	Domett	Soneri
	Slops	Dossal	Stroud
5 letters:	Stupe	Dossel	Tamine
Atlas	Surah	Dowlas	Tartan
Baize	Surat	Duffel	Tencel®
Beige	Surge	Duffle	Thibet
Binca	Tabby	Dupion	Tricot
Budge	Tamin	Durrie	Velour
Chino	Tammy	Etamin	Velure
Crash	Terry	Faille	Velvet
Crepe	Tibet	Fannel	Vicuna
Denim	Toile	Frieze	Wadmal
Dobby	Towel	Gloria	Wincey
Drill	Tulle	Greige	Winsey
Duroy	Tweed	Gurrah	
Fanon	Tweel	Haique	**7 letters:**
Foulé	Twill	Harden	Abattre
Frisé	Union	Herden	Alamode
Gauze	Voile	Hodden	Alepine
Gazar	Wigan	Hoddin	Baracan
Grass		Humhum	Batiste
Gunny	**6 letters:**	Hurden	Brocade
Haick	Aertex®	Jersey	Cabbage
Honan	Alpaca	Kersey	Cambric
Jaspe	Angora	Khanga	Camelot
Kanga	Armure	Kincob	Challie
Kente	Barège	Lampas	Challis
Khadi	Beaver	Madras	Cheviot
Khaki	Bouclé	Medley	Chiffon
Kikoi	Broche	Melton	Crombie
Linen	Burlap	Merino	Cypress
Llama	Burnet	Mohair	Delaine
Loden	Burrel	Mongoe	Dhurrie
Lurex®	Byssus	Moreen	Doeskin
Lycra®	Caddis	Muleta	Dorneck
Moiré	Calico	Muslin	Dornick
Mongo	Camlet	Mutton	Drabbet
Monks	Camlot	Nankin	Drapery
Mummy	Canvas	Oxford	Droguet
Mungo	Chintz	Pongee	Drugget
Ninon	Cilice	Rateen	Duvetyn
Orlon®	Cloqué	Ratine	Etamine
Panel	Coburg	Runner	Faconné

- Fannell
- Fishnet
- Flannel
- Foulard
- Fustian
- Galatea
- Genappe
- Gingham
- Gore-tex®
- Grogram
- Hessian
- Holland
- Hopsack
- Jaconet
- Jamdani
- Khaddar
- Kitenge
- Lockram
- Mockado
- Nankeen
- Oilskin
- Organza
- Orleans
- Ottoman
- Paisley
- Percale
- Rabanna
- Raploch
- Raschel
- Ratteen
- Rattine
- Sacking
- Sagathy
- Schappe
- Silesia
- Sinamay
- Spandex®
- Stammel
- Tabaret
- Tabinet
- Taffeta
- Tiffany
- Tussore
- Viyella®
- Wadmaal
- Webbing
- Woolsey
- Worsted
- Zanella

- **8 letters:**
- Aircraft

Algerine
American
Armozeen
Armozine
Arresine
Bagheera
Barathea
Barracan
Bayadere
Bobbinet
Brocatel
Cameline
Cashmere
Casimere
Celanese
Chambray
Chamelot
Chenille
Ciclaton
Corduroy
Corporal
Coteline
Coutille
Cretonne
Drabette
Duchesse
Dungaree
Duvetine
Duvetyne
Eolienne
Gambroon
Gossamer
Homespun
Jacquard
Jeanette
Lava-lava
Lustring
Mackinaw
Mantling
Marcella
Marocain
Mazarine
Moleskin
Moquette
Nainsook
Organdie
Osnaburg
Pashmina
Prunella
Rodevore
Sarcenet
Sarsenet

Shabrack
Shalloon
Shantung
Sicilian
Swanskin
Tabbinet
Tarlatan
Toilinet
Whipcord
Wild silk
Zibeline

9 letters:
Aeroplane
Balzarine
Bengaline
Bombasine
Calamanco
Cassimere
Cerecloth
Charmeuse®
Ciclatoun
Corporale
Cottonade
Crepoline
Crimplene®
Crinoline
Evenweave
Fabrikoid®
Farandine
Filoselle
Folk-weave
Gaberdine
Georgette
Grenadine
Grosgrain
Haircloth
Horsehair
Indiennes
Levantine
Longcloth
Mandilion
Mandylion
Marseille
Matelassé
Messaline
Open-weave
Overcheck
Paramatta
Penistone
Percaline
Persienne

Pinstripe
Polyester
Ravenduck
Sailcloth
Sharkskin
Silkaline
Stockinet
Swansdown
Tarpaulin
Tricotine
Velveteen
Wire gauze
Worcester
Zibelline

10 letters:
Balbriggan
Broadcloth
Brocatelle
Candlewick
Farrandine
Fearnought
Ferrandine
Florentine
Geotextile
Kerseymere
Lutestring
Mousseline
Needlecord
Parramatta
Polycotton
Ravensduck
Seersucker
Shabracque
Sicilienne
Tattersall
Toilinette
Tuftaffeta
Winceyette

11 letters:
Abercrombie
Cloth of gold
Dotted Swiss
Drap-de-berry
Dreadnought
Hammercloth
Interfacing
Kendal green
Marquisette
Nun's veiling
Sempiternum

- Stockinette
- Stretch knit
- Swiss muslin

12 letters:
Brilliantine
Crepe de chine

Leather-cloth

13 letters:
Linsey-woolsey

Cloth-designing Batik
Clothe(s), Clothing, Clothed Apparel, Array, Attire, Baggies, Besee, Bib and
tucker, Cape, Casuals, Chasuble, Choli, Cits, Clad, Clericals, Clobber, Coat,
Combinations, Coordinates, Costume, Cour, Cover, Croptop, Dicht, Dight,
Don, Drag, > **DRESS**, Duds, Emboss, Endue, Finery, Frippery, Garb, Garments,
Gear, Gere, Get-up, Glad rags, Grave, Habit, Haute couture, Innerwear, Judogi,
Jumps, Kimono, Layette, Mocker, Outfit, Pannicle, Plain, Raggery, Rag
trade, Raiment, Rami, Rigout, Robes, Samfoo, Samfu, Schmutter, Scungies,
Shmatte, Shroud, Slops, Sunday best, Swaddling, Swathe, Swothling, Tackle,
Togs, Tracksuit, Trappings, Trousseau, Tweeds, Two-piece, Vernicle, Vestiary,
Vestiture, Vestment, Wardrobe, Watteau, Weeds, Widow's weeds, Workwear,
Yclad, Ycled
Clothes horse Airer, Winterhedge
Cloud(ing), Clouded, Cloudiness, Cloudy Altocumulus, Altostratus, Banner,
Benight, C, Cataract, Cirrocumulus, Cirrostratus, Cirrus, Coalsack, Coma,
Contrail, Crab Nebula, Cumulonimbus, Cumulus, Dim, Dull, Emission nebula,
Fog, Fractocumulus, Fractostratus, Funnel, Goat's hair, Haze, Horsehead
Nebula, Infuscate, Magellanic, Mare's tail, Milky, Mist, Molecular, Mushroom,
Nacreous, Nephele, Nephelometer, Nepho-, Nimbostratus, Nimbus, Nubecula,
Nubilous, Nuée ardente, Obscure, Octa, Okta, Oort, Overcast, Pall, Pother,
Rack, Stain, Storm, Stratocumulus, Stratus, Thunderhead, Turbid, Virga, War,
Water-dog, Woolpack, Zero-zero
Cloudberry Mountain bramble
Cloudless Serene
Clough Dale, Gorge, Ravine
Clout Belt, Cloth, Hit, Influence, Lap(pie), Lapje, Pull, Raddle
Clove Chive, Eugenia, Rose-apple, Split
Clover Alfalfa, Alsike, Berseem, Calvary, Cinque, Cow-grass, Four-leaf, Hare's
foot, Japan, Ladino, Lespedeza, Medic(k), Melilot, Owl's, Pin, Rabbit-foot, Red,
Serradella, Serradilla, Shamrock, Souple, Sucklers, Sweet, Trefoil, Trilobe,
White
Clown(ish) Antic, Antick, August(e), Boor, Bor(r)el, Buffoon, Carl, Chough,
Chuff, Clout-shoe, Coco, > **COMEDIAN**, Comic, Costard, Daff, Feste, Froth,
Girner, Gobbo, Goon, Gracioso, Grimaldi, Harlequin, Hob, Idiot, Jack-pudding,
Jester, Joey, Joker, Joskin, Leno, Merry Andrew, Mountebank, Nedda, Nervo,
Peasant, Pickle-herring, Pierrot, Put, Rustic, Slouch, Thalian, Touchstone,
Trinculo, Wag, Zany
Cloy(ing) Choke, Clog, Glut, Pall, Satiate, Surfeit, Sweet
Club(s), Club-like Adelphi, Airn, Almack's, Alpeen, Apex, Army and Navy,
Artel, Association, Athen(a)eum, Baffy, Band(y), Basto, Bat, Bath, Beefsteak,
Blackjack, Blaster, Bludgeon, Boodles, Bourdon, Brassie, Brook's, Bulger,
C, Card, Carlton, Caterpillar, Cavalry, Chigiriki, Clavate, Cleek, Clip-joint,
Combine, Conservative, Constitutional, Cordeliers, Cosh, Cotton, Country,
Crockford's, Cudgel, Devonshire, Disco(theque), Driver, Driving iron, Drones,
Fan, Fascio, Feuillant, Fustigate, Garrick, Glee, Golf, Guards, Guild, Hampden,
Hell-fire, Honky-tonk, Indian, Investment, Iron, Jacobin, Jigger, Jockey, Junior
Carlton, Kennel, Kierie, Kiri, Kitcat, Kiwanis, Knobkerrie, Landsdowne, Lathi,
League, Leander, Lions, Lofter, Luncheon, Mace, Mallet, Mashie, Maul, Mell,

Mere, Meri, Mess, Midiron, Monday, National Liberal, Niblick, Night(stick), Nightspot, Nitery, Nulla(-nulla), Oddfellows, Patu, Pitching wedge, Polt, Priest, Provident, Pudding, Putter, Quarterstaff, RAC, Reform, Ring, Rota, Rotarian, Rotary, Round Table, Sand wedge, Savage, Savile, Shillelagh, Slate, Society, Soroptimist, Sorosis, Spoon, Spot, Spurs, Strike, Strip, Thatched House, Tong, Travellers, Trefoil, Truncheon, Trunnion, Union, United Services, Variety, Waddy, Wedge, White's, Wood, Youth

Club-foot Kyllosis, Polt-foot, Talipes, Varus

Clubman Member

Club-rush Deer-hair, Scirpus, Sedge

Cluck Chirrup, Dent

Clue Across, Anagram, Ball, Charade, Clave, Dabs, Down, > HINT, Inkling, Key, Lead, Light, Rebus, Scent, Scooby(doo), Signpost, Thread, Tip

Clueless Ignorant

Clump Cluster, Finial, Knot, Mass, Mot(te), Patch, Plump, Tread, Tuft, Tump, Tussock

▷ **Clumsily** *may indicate* an anagram

Clumsy Artless, Awkward, Bauchle, Bungling, Butterfingers, Cack-handed, Calf, Chuckle, Clatch, Clodhopper, Cumbersome, Dub, Dutch, Galoot, Gauche, Gimp, Ham(-fisted), Heavy-handed, Horse-godmother, Inapt, Inelegant, Inept, Inexpert, Klutz, Lob, Loutish, Lubbard, Lubber, Lummox, Lumpish, Maladroit, Mauther, Mawr, Mawther, Messy, Mor, Nerd, Nurd, Off-ox, Palooka, Plonking, Rough, S(c)hlemiel, Schlemihl, Spastic, Spaz(zy), Squab, Stot, Swab, Swob, Taupie, Tawpie, Two-fisted, Ungain, Unskilful, Unwieldy

Cluster Assemble, Bunch, Clump, Collection, Constellate, Conurbation, Corymb, Cyme, Gather, Globular, Glomeration, Knot, Oakleaf, Packet, Plump, Raceme, Sheaf, Sorus, Strap, Thyrse, Truss, Tuffe, Tuft, Umbel, Verticillaster

Clutch Battery, Brood, Chickens, Clasp, Cling, Eggs, Friction, Glaum, Grab, > GRASP, Gripe, Nest, Seize, Sitting, Squeeze

Clutter Confusion, Litter, Mess, Rummage

Coach Battlebus, Berlin, Bogie, Bus, Car, Carriage, Chara, Clerestory, Crammer, Diligence, Dilly, Double-decker, Drag, Edifier, Fly, Four-in-hand, Gig, Hackney, Landau(let), Life, Microbus, Phaeton, Post chaise, Pullman, Railcar, Rattler, Repetiteur, Saloon, Shay, Sleeper, Slip, Sobriety, Stage, Surrey, Tally(-ho), Teach(er), Thoroughbrace, Train(er), Tutor, Voiture

Coach-horse Rove-beetle

Coachman Automedon, Bunene, Coachy, Dragsman, Jarvey, Jehu, John

Coagulant, Coagulate, Coagulation Cautery, Clot, Congeal, Curds, Jell, Rennet, Run, Runnet, Set, Solidify

Coal Anthracite, Bituminous, Black diamonds, Brown, Burgee, Cannel, Cherry, Clinker, Coom, Crow, Culm, Dice, Eldin, Ember, Fusain, Gas, Gathering, Hard, Jud, Knob, Lignite, Maceral, Mineral, Nut, Open-cast, Paper, Purse, Sapropelite, Score, Slack, Soft, Splint, Steam, Vitrain, Wallsend, White, Wood

Coalesce(nce) Amalgamate, Concrete, Fuse, Merge, Sintery, Synaloepha, Unite

Coalfish Saith

Coalition Alliance, Bloc, Janata, Merger, Rainbow, Tie

Coal-tar Cresol, Indene

Coal-tub Corf, Dan, Scuttle

Coarse(ness) Base, Blowzy, Bran, Broad, Common, Crude, Dowlas, Earthy, Fisherman, Foul, Grained, Grobian, Gross, Grossièreté, Haggery, Ham, Illbred, Indelicate, Low-bred, Plebeian, Rabelaisian, Rank, Rappee, Raunchy, Ribald, Rough, Rudas, Rude, Sackcloth, Semple, Slob, Sotadic, Unrefined, Vulgar

Coast(al) Barbary, Beach, Bight, Caird, Causeway, Coromandel, Costa, Drift, Freewheel, Glide, Gold, Hard, Ivory, Littoral, Longshore, Malabar, Maritime, Murman(sk), Orarian, Riviera, Seaboard, Seafront, Seaside, > **SHORE**, Slave, Sledge, Strand, Toboggan

Coaster Beermat, Drog(h)er, Mat, Roller, Ship

Coastguard CG, Gobby

Coastline Watermark

Coast-road Corniche

Coat(ing) Abaya, Ab(b)a, Achkan, Acton, Admiral, Anarak, Anodise, Anorak, Balmacaan, Barathea, Bathrobe, Belton, Benjamin, Blazer, Box, British warm, Buff, Buff-jerkin, Calcimine, Car, Chesterfield, Cladding, Claw-hammer, Clearcole, Cloak, Clutch, Cocoon, Coolie, Cover, Covert, Creosote, Crust(a), Cutaway, Doggett's, Dress, Duffel, Duster, Electroplate, Enamel, Encrust, Exine, Extine, Fearnought, Film, Fleece, Frock, Fur, Gabardine, Galvanise, Gambeson, Ganoin, Glaze, Grego, Ground, Ha(c)queton, Hair, Happi, Impasto, Integument, Inverness, Jack(et), Jemmy, Jerkin, Jodhpuri, Joseph, Jump, Jupon, Lacquer, Lammie, Lammy, Layer, Loden, Mac, Mackinaw, Matinee, Metallise, Morning, Newmarket, > **OVERCOAT**, Paint, Paletot, Palla, Parka, Parkee, Passivate, Patinate, Pebbledash, Pelage, Pelisse, Perfuse, Peridium, Petersham, Plate, Polo, Pos(h)teen, Primer, Primine, Prince Albert, Raglan, Redingote, Resin, Resist, Riding, Roquelaure, Sack, Saque, Sclera, Seal, Sheepskin, Shellac, Sherardise, Sherwani, Silver, Skinwork, Spencer, Sports, Stadium, Surtout, Swagger, Swallowtail(ed), Tabard, Taglioni, Tail, Tar, Teflon, Tent, Top, Trench, Truss, Trusty, Tunic, Tuxedo, Ulster(ette), Underseal, Veneer, Verdigris, Warm, Wash, Windjammer, Wool, Wrap-rascal, Zamarra, Zamarro, Zinc

Coat of arms Crest, Hatchment

Coat-tail Flap

Coax Blandish, Blarney, Cajole, Carn(e)y, Cuittle, Flatter, Lure, Persuade, Wheedle, Whilly(wha), Whillywhaw

Cob Hazel(nut), Horse

Cobalt Co, Zaffer, Zaffre

Cobble(s), Cobblers Claptrap, Cosier, Cozier, Mend, Patch, Rot, Snob, Soutar, Souter, Sowter, Stone, Sutor, Twaddle, Vamp

Cobra King

Cobweb(by) Arachnoid, Araneous, Gossamer, Snare, Trap

Cocaine Basuco, C, Charlie, Coke, Crystal, Freebase, Moonrock, Nose candy, Number, Ready-wash, Snow

Coccid Wax-insect

Cock(y) Alectryon, Ball, Capon, Chanticleer, Chaparral, Erect, Escape, Fighting, Flip, Fowl, France, Fugie, Half, Hay, Heath, Jack-the-lad, Jaunty, Midden, Penis, Roadrunner, Robin, Rooster, Shake-bag, Snook, Strut, Swaggering, Tilt, Turkey, Vain, Valve, Vane

Cock-a-hoop Crowing, Elated

Cockatoo Bird, Corella, Galah, Leadbeater's, Major Mitchell, Parrot

Cockboat Cog

Cockchafer Humbuzz, Maybug

Cocker Blenheim, Cuiter, Spaniel

Cockeyed Agee, Askew, Skewwhiff

Cockfight Main

Cockle Bulge, Crease, Wrinkle

▷ **Cockle(s)** *may indicate* an anagram

Cockney 'Arriet, 'Arry, Bow, Eastender, Londoner, Londonese
▷ **Cockney** *may indicate* a missing h
Cockpit Greenhouse, Well
Cockroach Archy, Beetle, Black beetle, Croton bug, German, Oriental, Orthoptera
▶ **Cockscomb** *see* COXCOMB
Cocktail Alexander, Aperitif, Atomic, Bellini, Bloody Mary, Buck's fizz, Bumbo, Cobbler, Cold duck, Crusta, Daiquiri, > DRINK, Egg-flip, Fruit, Fustian, Gibson, Gimlet, Harvey Wallbanger, Highball, > HORSE, Julep, Manhattan, Margarita, Martini®, Melange, Mix, Molotov, Old-fashioned, Piña colada, Pink lady, Prawn, Punch, Rickey, Rusty nail, Sangaree, Sangria, Sazerac®, Screwdriver, Sherry cobbler, Side-car, Snowball, Spritzer, Stengah, Stinger, Swizzle, Tom Collins, Twist, White-lady
Cocoa Criollo, Nib(s)
Coconut Coco-de-mer, Coir, Copra, Head, Madafu, Toddy-palm
Cocoon Dupion, Mother, Swathe, Trehala
Cod Bag, Cape, Coalfish, Fish, Gade, Gadus, Haberdine, Keeling, Kid, Lob, Man, Morrhua, Murray, Red, Saith, Saltfish, Stockfish, Torsk, Tusk, Whiting
Coda End(ing), Epilogue, Rondo, Tail
Coddle Cosset, Molly, Nancy, Pamper, Pet, Poach
Code, Coding Access, Alphanumeric, Amalfitan, Area, Bar, Binary, Bushido, Canon, Character, Cipher, City, Civil, Clarendon, Codex, Colour, Computing, Condition, Country, Cryptogram, Cryptograph, Dialling, Disciplinary, Dogma, Dress, DX, EBCDIC, Enigma, Error, Escape, Ethics, Fuero, Genetic, Gray, Green Cross, Hammurabic, Highway, Hollerith, Iddy-umpty, Justinian, MAC, Machine, Morse, Napoleon(ic), Object, Omerta, Opcode, Penal, PGP, Pindaric, Postal, Price, Rulebook, Scytale, Signal, Sort, Source, STD, Talmud, Time, Twelve Tables, Zip
Code-breaker Malpractitioner
Codger Buffer, Fellow
Codicil Addition, Label, PS
Codon Initiator
Coefficient Correlation, Diffusion, Partition, Pearson's correlation, Spearman's rank-order, Transmission, Young modulus
Coelacanth Latimeria
Coerce, Coercion Bully, Compel, Dragoon, Gherao, Pressure, Railroad, Restrain, Threaten
Coffee, Coffee beans, Coffee pot Arabica, Brazil, Cafetiere, Cappuccino, Decaff, Demi-tasse, Espresso, Expresso, Filter, Gaelic, Gloria, Granules, Instant, Irish, Java, Latte, Macchiato, Mocha, Peaberry, Robusta, Rye, Tan, Triage, Turkish
Coffee-house Lloyd's
Coffer Ark, Box, Casket, Cassone, Chest, Lacunar, Locker
Coffin Bier, Casket, Hearse, Kist, Larnax, Sarcophagus, Shell, Wooden kimono, Wooden overcoat
Cog(ged) Contrate, Mitre-wheel, Nog, Pinion, Tooth
Cogent Compelling, Forceful, Good, Sound, Telling
Cogitate Deliberate, Mull, Muse, Ponder
Cognate Paronym
Cohabit Bed, Indwell, Share
Co-heir Parcener
Cohere(nt) Agglutinate, Clear, Cleave, Cling, Logical, Stick
Cohort Colleague, Crony, Soldier

Coif Calotte, Cap, Hood
Coiffure Hairdo, Pompadour, Tête
Coil(s), Coiled Armature, Bight, Bought, Choke, Clew, Clue, Curl, Fake, Fank, Furl, Hank, Helix, Ignition, Induction, Loading, Mortal, Moving, Primary, Rouleau, Scorpioid, Solenoid, Spark, Spiral, Spiraster, Spire, Tesla, Tickler, Toroid, Twine, Twirl, > WIND, Wound, Wreath, Writhe, Yoke
Coin Base, Bean, Bit, Cash, Change, Coign(e), Copper, Create, Doctor, Double-header, Dump(s), Fiver, Han(d)sel, Imperial, Invent, Make, Mill, Mint, Mite, > MONEY, Neoterise, Numismatic, Nummary, Piece, Plate, Proof, Shiner, Slip, Smelt, Specie, Stamp, Sterling, Strike, Tenner, Thick'un, Thin'un, Touchpiece, Unite, Unity

COINS

1 letter:
D

2 letters:
As
DM
Kr
Rd
Xu

3 letters:
Ban
Bar
Bob
Cob
Dam
Ecu
Fen
Fil
Fin
Flu
Hao
Jun
Kip
Lat
Lei
Lek
Leu
Lev
Lew
Mil
Mna
Moy
Ore
Pul
Pya
Red
Sen

Sol
Som
Sou
Won
Yen
Zuz

4 letters:
Anna
Baht
Bani
Birr
Buck
Cedi
Cent
Chon
Dibs
Dime
Doit
Dong
Dram
Duro
Euro
Fiat
Fils
Inti
Jack
Jane
Jiao
Kina
Kobo
Kuna
Kyat
Lari
Lion
Lira
Loti
Maik

Mark
Merk
Mina
Obol
Para
Paul
Peag
Peni
Peso
Pice
Pula
Puli
Punt
Rand
Real
Reis
Rial
Riel
Rock
Ryal
Sene
Sent
Slog
Tael
Taka
Tala
Toea
Tray
Trey
Vatu
Yuan
Zack

5 letters:
Agora
Angel
Asper
Aurar

Baiza
Bekah
Belga
Bodle
Broad
Brown
Butat
Butut
Chiao
Colon
Conto
Crore
Crown
Daric
Dibbs
Dinar
Dobra
Ducat
Eagle
Eyrir
Franc
Fugio
Gazet
Gerah
Groat
Grosz
Haler
Krona
Krone
Kroon
Kurus
Laari
Laree
Leone
Liard
Litas
Livre
Louis

Lyart	Bender	Peseta	Milreis
Maile	Bezant	Pesewa	Moidore
Manat	Boddle	Qintar	Ostmark
Maneh	Byzant	Rappen	Ouguiya
Mohur	Canary	Rouble	Patrick
Mongo	Centas	Rupiah	Piastre
Mopus	Colone	Santum	Piefort
Naira	Copeck	Satang	Pistole
Nakfa	Couter	Sceatt	Pollard
Ngwee	Dalasi	Seniti	Quarter
Noble	Danace	Sequin	Quetzal
Obang	Deaner	Shekel	Ringgit
Oscar	Décime	Sickle	Ruddock
Paisa	Denier	Siglos	Rufiyaa
Paolo	Derham	Somoni	Sextans
Pence	Dirham	Stater	Solidus
Pengo	Dirhem	Stiver	Spanker
Penie	Dodkin	Stotin	Tambala
Penni	Dollar	Talent	Testoon
Penny	Double	Tanner	Testril
Plack	Drachm	Tester	Thrimsa
Pound	Ekuele	Teston	Thrymsa
Razoo	Escudo	Thaler	Tughrik
Rider	Filler	Tickey	Unicorn
Royal	Florin	Toonie	Xerafin
Ruble	Forint	Tugrik	
Rupee	Gilder	Turner	**8 letters:**
Sceat	Gourde	Vellon	Brockage
Scudo	Guinea	Wakiki	Cardecue
Scute	Gulden		Cruzeiro
Semis	Halala	**7 letters:**	Denarius
Sente	Heller	Afghani	Doubloon
Shand	Hryvna	Austral	Ducatoon
Soldo	Jitney	Bolivar	Emalengi
Souon	Kobang	Cardecu	Farthing
Sucre	Koruna	Carolus	Groschen
Sycee	Kroner	Centavo	Johannes
Tenge	Kroona	Chetrum	Kreutzer
Thebe	Kruger	Cordoba	Llangeni
Tical	Kwacha	Crusado	Louis d'or
Ticky	Kwanza	Drachma	Maravedi
Tolar	Lepton	Ekpwele	Millieme
Toman	Likuta	Guarani	Napoleon
Tyiyn	Loonie	Guilder	Ngultrum
Zaire	Makuta	Hryvnya	Picayune
Zimbi	Mancus	Jacobus	Pistolet
Zloty	Markka	Joannes	Planchet
	Mawpus	Kopiyka	Portague
6 letters:	Pa'anga	Kreuzer	Portigue
Aureus	Pagoda	Lemoira	Quadrans
Balboa	Pataca	Metical	Rigmarie
Bawbee	Pennia	Millime	Semuncia

- Sesterce
- Shilling
- Skilling
- Solidare
- Spur-rial
- Spur-ryal
- Stotinka
- Xeraphim
- Zecchino
-
- **9 letters:**
- Boliviano
- Britannia
- Centesimo
- Dandiprat

Dandyprat
Didrachma
Dupondius
Half-eagle
Luckpenny
Pistareen
Rennminbi
Rix-dollar
Rose noble
Schilling
Sou marque
Sovereign
Spur-royal
Yellowboy
Zwanziger

10 letters:
Broadpiece
Chervonets
Krugerrand
Portcullis
Reichsmark
Siege-piece

11 letters:
Bonnet-piece
Deutschmark
Double eagle
Sword-dollar
Tetradrachm

12 letters:
Antoninianus

13 letters:
Rennminbi yuan

14 letters:
Three-farthings

18 letters:
Maria Theresa
dollar

Coinage Currency, Invention, Nonce-word
Coincide(nt), Coincidence Accident, Chance, Consilience, Fit, Fluke, Homotaxis, Overlap, Rabat(to), Simultaneous, Synastry, Synchronise, Tally
Coke Chark, Coal, Cocaine, Kola
Col Pass, Poort, Saddle
Cold(-blooded) Ague, Algid, Arctic, Austere, Biting, Bitter, Bleak, C, Catarrh, Cauld(rife), Charity, Chill(y), Colubrine, Common, Coryza, Ectotherm, Frem(d), Fremit, Frigid, Frost(y), Gelid, Glacial, Hiemal, Icy, Impersonal, Jeel, Nippy, Nirlit, Parky, Passionless, Perishing, Piercing, Poikilotherm(ic), Polar, Psychro-, Remote, Rheumy, Rigor, Rume, Snap, Snell, Sniffles, Sour, Standoffish, Streamer, Subzero, Taters, Weed, Wintry
Cold sore Herpes, Shiver
Coldstream Borderer, Guard
Cole Colza, King, Nat, Porter
Colic Batts, Bots, Botts, Gripe, Lead, Painter's, Upset, Zinc
Collaborate, Collaborator, Collaboration Assist, Combine, > **COOPERATE**, Quisling, Synergy, Vichy
Collapse Apoplexy, Buckle, Cave, Conk, Crash, Crumble, Crumple, Debacle, Downfall, Fail(ure), Fall, Fold, Founder, Give, Implode, Inburst, Landslide, Meltdown, Phut, Purler, Rack, Rot, Ruin, Scat(ter), Sink, Slump, Stroke, Subside, Sunstroke, Swoon, Telescope, Tumble, Wilt, Wrack, Zonk
▷ **Collapsing** *may indicate* an anagram
Collar(ed) Arrest, Astrakhan, Bermuda, Bertha, Berthe, Bib, Bishop, Blue, Brecham, Buster, Butterfly, Button-down, Buttonhole, Capture, Carcanet, Chevesaile, Choke(r), Clerical, Collet, Dog, Esses, Eton, Falling-band, Flea, Gorget, Grandad, Hame, Head(stall), Holderbat, Horse, Jabot, Jampot, Karenni, Mandarin, Moran, Mousquetaire, Nab, Nail, Neckband, Necklet, Ox-bow, Peter Pan, Piccadell, Piccadillo, Piccadilly, Pikadell, Pink, Polo, Puritan, Rabato, Rebater, Rebato, Revers, Rollneck, Roman, Ruff, Sailor, Seize, Shawl, Steel, Storm, Tackle, Tappet, Tie-neck, Torque, Turndown, Turtleneck, Vandyke, Whisk, White, Wing, Yoke
Collation Comparison, Meal, Repast
Colleague Ally, Associate, Bedfellow, Confrère, Mate, Oppo, Partner
Collect(ion), Collective(ly), Collector Accrue, Agglomerate, Aggregate, Album, Alms, Amass, Amildar, Ana, Anthology, Arcana, Assemble, Aumil, Bank, Bow, Budget, Bunch, Bundle, Burrell, Caboodle, Calm, Cap, Cete, Clowder,

Compendium, Compile, Congeries, Conglomerate, Covey, Cull, Dossier, Dustman, Earn, Egger, Exaltation, Exordial, Fest, (Fest)schrift, Florilegium, Gaggle, Garner, Gather, Gilbert, Glean, Glossary, Grice, Heap, Herd, Hive, Idant, In all, Jingbang, Job lot, Kit, Kitty, Levy, Loan, Magpie, Meal, Meet, Mein(e)y, Meinie, Menagerie, Menyie, Miscellany, Mish-mash, Montem, Murmuration, Museum, Muster, Nide, Offertory, Omnibus, Omnium-gatherum, Paddling, Pile, Plate, Pod, Post, Prayer, Quest, Raft, Raise, Recheat, Sedge, Serene, Set, Shoe, Siege, Skein, Smytrie, Sord, Sottisier, Sounder, Spring, Stand, Tahsildar, Team, Troop, Unkindness, Watch, Whipround, Wisp

▷ **Collection** *may indicate* an anagram

Collection-box Brod, Ladle, Rammle

Collectorate Taluk

College(s) Academy, All Souls, Alma Mater, Ampleforth, Balliol, Brasenose, Business, C, Caius, Campus, CAT, Cheltenham, Clare, Classical, Coed, Commercial, Community, Corpus, Cow, Cranwell, Downing, Electoral, Emmanuel, Eton, Exeter, Foundation, Girton, Hall, Herald's, Jail, Junior, Keble, King's, Lancing, Linacre, Lincoln, LSE, Lycée, Lyceum, Madras(s)a(h), Madressah, Magdalen(e), Medrese, Medresseh, Merton, Newnham, Nuffield, Open, Oriel, Poly, Polytechnic, Pontifical, Protonotariat, Queen's, Ruskin, Sacred, St Johns, Saliens, Sandhurst, Selwyn, Seminary, Sixth-form, Somerville, Sorbonne, Staff, Tech(nical), Technikon, Tertiary, Theologate, Training, Trinity, Tug, UMIST, Up, Village, Wadham, Winchester, Yeshwa(h)

Collide, Collision Afoul, Barge, Bird-strike, Bump, Cannon, Carom(bole), Clash, Dash, Fender-bender, Foul, Head-on, Impact, Into, Kiss, Meet, Pile-up, Rencounter, Strike, Thwack

Collie Bearded, Border, Dog, Kelpie, Kelpy, Rough, Sheepdog

Collier Geordie, Hoastman, Miner, Necklace, Patience, Ship

Colloid Gel, Lyophil(e), Sol

Collude, Collusive Abet, Cahoots, Conspire, Deceive

Colon Aspinwall, Sigmoid, Spastic, Transverse

Colonel Blimp, Bogey, Chinstrap, Col, Everard, Goldstick, Newcome, Nissen, Pride

Colonial, Colonist Ant, Antenatal, Boer, Creole, Emigré, Oecist, Oikist, Overseas, Phoenician, Pioneer, Planter, Polyp(e), Settler, Sicel(iot), Sikel(ian), Sikeliot, Stuyvesant, Swarm, Territorial

Colonnade Eustyle, File, Gallery, Porch, Portico, Stoa

Colony Aden, Charter, Cleruchy, Crown, Dependency, Hive, Hongkong, Nudist, Penal, Presidio, Proprietary, Rookery, Settlement, Swarm, Termitarium, Warren, Zambia

Colophony Rosin

Colossal > ENORMOUS, Epochal, Gigantic, Huge, Vast

Colosseum Amphitheatre

Colour(ed), Colouring, Colours Achromatic, Alizarin(e), Anil, An(n)atta, An(n)atto, Anthocyan, Aquamarine, Arnotto, Auburn, Bay, Bedye, Bice, Bisque, Bister, Bistre, Blee, Blue, Blush, Buff, Burgundy, C, Camel, Cap, Cappagh-brown, Cardinal, Cerise, Chica, Chromatic, Chrome, Complementary, Complexion, Coral, Crayon, Criant, Cyan, Day-Glo®, Distort, Dye, Ecru, Eosin, False, Filemot, Film, Flag, Florid, Flying, French navy, Gamboge, Gouache, Gules, Haem, > HUE, Ink, Irised, Isabel, Jet, Kalamkari, Lake, Leer, Lemon, Lilac, Lime, Local, Lovat, Lutein, Magenta, Maroon, Mauve, Metif, Nankeen, Navy, Oatmeal, Ochre, Olive, Or, Orange, Orpiment, Palette, Pastel, Peach, Philamot, Philomot, Pied, Pigment, Pochoir, Polychrome,

Primary, Prism, Prismatic, Process, Puke, Queen's, Reddle, Regimental, Reseda, Rince, Riot, Roucou, Rouge, Ruddle, Sand, Secondary, Sematic, Sepia, Shade, Sienna, Solferino, Solid, Spectrum, Startle, Tartrazine, Taupe, Teal, Tenne, Tenny, Tertiary, Tie-dye, Tinc(ture), Tinge, Tint, Titian, Tone, Ultramarine, Umber, Umbrage, Uvea, Vert

Colour blindness Daltonism, Deuteranopia, Dichrom(at)ism, Monochromatic, Protanomaly, Protanopia, Protanopic, Tritanopia

▷ **Coloured** *may indicate* an anagram

Colourful Abloom, Brave, Flamboyant, Flowery, Iridescent, Kaleidoscope, Opalescent, Splashy, Vivid

Colourless Albino, Bleak, Drab, Dull, Hyalite, Pallid, Pallor, Wan, White

Colt Cade, Foal, Gun, Sta(i)g, Teenager, Two-year-old

Columbine Aquilegia

Column(s), **Column foot** Agony, Anta, Atlantes, Clustered, Commentary, Control, Corinthian, Correspondence, Cylinder, Decastyle, Diastyle, Doric, Editorial, Eustyle, Fifth, File, Geological, Gossip, Hypostyle, Impost, Lat, Lonelyhearts, Monolith, Nelson's, Newel, Obelisk, Pericycle, Peristyle, Persian, Personal, Pilaster, > **PILLAR**, Pilotis, Prostyle, Rouleau, Row, Short, Spina, Spinal, Spine, Stalactite, Stalagmite, Steering, Stylobate, Systyle, Tabulate, Telamone, Third, Tige, Tore, Torus, Trajan's, Vertebral

Columnist Advertiser, Caryatid, Newsman, Stylite, Telamon, Writer

Coma(tose) Apoplexy, Crown, Sedated, Sleep, Torpor, Trance

Comb(er), **Combed**, **Combing** Alveolate, Beehive, Breaker, Card, Copple, Crest, Curry, Dredge, Fine-tooth, Hackle, Heckle, Hot, Kaim, Kame, Kangha, Kemb, Noils, Pecten, Rake, Red(d), Ripple(r), Scribble, Search, Small tooth, Smooth, Tease(l), Toaze, Tooth, Tose, Toze, Trawl, Wave

Combat(ant), **Combative** Argument, > **BATTLE**, Competitor, Conflict, Contest, Dispute, Duel, > **FIGHT**, Gladiator, Joust, Jujitsu, Just, Karate, Kendo, List, Mêlée, Militant, Oppose, Paintball, Protagonist, Spear-running, Unarmed, War

Combination, **Combine(d)**, **Combining** Accrete, Alligate, Ally, Amalgam, Associate, Axis, Bloc, Cartel, Cleave, Clique, Coalesce, Coalition, Composite, Concoction, Conflated, Conglomerate, Consortium, Coordinate, Crasis, Fuse, Group, Harvester, Integration, Join, Junta, Kartell, League, Meld, Merge(r), Mingle, Mixture, Perm(utation), Piece, Pool, Quill, Ring, Solvate, Splice, Syncretize, Synthesis, Terrace, Trona, Unite, Valency, Wed, Zaibatsu

Comb-like Ctenoid, Pecten

Combustible, **Combustion** Ardent, Fiery, Inflammable, Phlogistic, Phlogiston, Spontaneous, Wildfire

▷ **Combustible** *may indicate* an anagram

Come, **Coming (back)**, **Coming out** Advent, Anear, Anon, Appear, Approach, Ar(r), Arise, Arrive, Attend, Debouch, Derive, Emerge, Future, Happen, Iceman, Issue, Millenarian, Orgasm, Parousia, Pass, Pop, Respond, Second, Via

Comeback Boomerang, Bounce, Echo, Homer, Quip, Rally, Rearise, Rebound, Recovery, Repartee, Reply, Retort, Retour, Return, Reversion, Riposte

Comedian Benny, Buffoon, Chaplin, > **CLOWN**, Comic, Durante, Emery, Goon, Groucho, Hope, Joker, Karno, Leno, Quipster, Robey, Scream, Screwball, Tate, Tati, Tummler, Wag, Wise, Yell

Comedo Blackhead

Comedown Avale, Bathetic, Bathos, Disappointment, Drop, Letdown, Shower

Comedy Black, Com, Drama, Errors, Farce, High, Humour, Keystone, Knockabout, Lazzo, Low, Millamant, Musical, Situation, Slapstick, Thalia,

Travesty

Comely Beseen, Bonny, Fair, Goodly, Graceful, Jolly, Likely, Pleasing, Pretty, Proper

Comestible(s) Cate, Eats, Fare

Comet Geminid, Halley's, Kohoutek, Meteor, Oort cloud, Reindeer, Shoemaker-Levy 9, Vomet, Xiphias

Come through Weather

Comfort(er), Comforting Amenity, Analeptic, Balm, Bildad, Calm, Cheer, Cherish, Clover, Cold, Consolation, Console, Creature, Crumb, Dummy, Ease, Eliphaz, Featherbed, Reassure, Relief, Relieve, Scarf, Solace, Soothe, Succour, Zophar

Comfortable, Comfy Armchair, Bein, Canny, Cose, Cosh, Cosy, Couthie, Couthy, Cushy, Easy, Gemutlich, Heeled, Homely, Mumsy, Plum, Plushy, Relaxed, Rug, Snug, There, Tosh, Trig, Warm, Well, Well-to-do

Comic(al) Beano, Buff, Buffo(on), Bumpkin, Buster, Chaplin, Clown, > COMEDIAN, Dandy, Droll, Eagle, Facetious, Fields, > FUNNY, Gagster, Hardy, Horror, Jester, Knock-about, Laurel, Leno, Mag, Manga, Quizzical, Rich, Robey, Strip, Tati, Trial, Zany

Comma Inverted

Command(eer), Commanding, Commandment(s) Behest, Bid, Categorical imperative, Charge, Coerce, Control, Decalogue, Direction, Dominate, Domineer, Easy, Edict, Fiat, Fighter, Firman, Haw, Hest, High, Imperious, Impress, Instruction, Jussive, Mandate, Maritime, Mastery, Mitzvah, Mobile, > ORDER, Precept, Press, Requisition, Rule, Seize, Ukase, Warn, Warrant, Will, Wish, Writ

Commander Admiral, Ag(h)a, Barleycorn, Bey, Bloke, Blucher, Boss, Brennus, Brig, Caliph, Centurion, Cid, Decurion, Emir, Emperor, Field cornet, Generalissimo, Hetman, Hipparch, Imperator, Killadar, Leader, Manager, Marshal, Master, Meer, Mir, Moore, Officer, Overlord, Pendragon, Raglan, Seraskier, Shogun, Sirdar, Taxiarch, Trierarch, Turcopolier, Vaivode, Voivode, Waivode, Warlord, Wing

Commando Chindit(s), Fedayee(n), Green Beret, Raider, Ranger, SAS

Commemorate, Commemoration Encaenia, Epitaph, Eulogy, Keep, Memorial, Monument, Plaque, Remember

Commence Begin, Initiate, Open, Start

Commend(ation) Belaud, Bestow, Encomium, Entrust, Laud, Panegyric, > PRAISE, Roose, Tribute

Commensal Epizoon, Messmate

Commensurate Adequate, Enough, Equivalent, Relevant

Comment(ary), Commentator Analyst, Animadvert, Annotate, Apercu, Comm, Coryphaeus, Critic, Critique, Descant, Discuss, Editorial, Essay, Explain, Exposition, Expound, Footnote, Gemara, Gloss(ographer), Glosser, Hakam, Kibitz, Margin, Midrashim, Note, Par, Platitude, Postil, Remark, Running, Scholiast, Zohar

Commerce, Commercial Ad, Barter, Cabotage, Jingle, Marketable, Mercantile, Mercenary, Merchant, Shoppy, Simony, Trade, Traffic

Commercial traveller Drummer, Rep

Commiserate, Commiseration Compassion, Pity, Sympathise

Commission(er), Commissioned Authorise, Brevet, Brokerage, Charge, Charity, Countryside, Delegation, Depute, ECE, Employ, Engage, Envoy, Errand, European, Factor, High, Husbandage, Job, Kickback, Law, Magistrate, Mandate, Office(r), Official, Ombudsman, Order, Percentage, Perpetration,

Place, Poundage, Price, Rake-off, Resident, Roskill, Roving, Royal, Task, Task force, Trust, Wreck

Commit(al), Commitment Consign, Contract, Decision, Dedication, Delegate, Devotion, Do, Engage, Entrust, Enure, Impeachment, Perpetrate, Pledge, Rubicon

Committee Board, Body, Commission, Council, Group, Joint, Junta, Politburo, Presidium, Propaganda, Review body, Samiti, School, Select, Standing, Steering, Syndicate, Table, Vigilance, Watch, Works

Commode, Commodious Ample, Closestool, Roomy, Spacious

Commodities, Commodity Article, Futures, Gapeseed, Item, Physicals, Soft, Staple, Ware

Common(ly), Commoner, Commons As per usual, Average, Cad, Conventional, Diet, Dirt, Doctor's, Ealing, Eatables, Enclosure, Epicene, Everyday, Familiar, Fare, Folk, General, Green, Greenham, House, Law, Lay, Low, Lower House, Mark, Mere, MP, Mutual, Naff, Non-U, Normal, People, Pleb, Prevalent, Prole, Public, Related, Rife, Roturier, Ryfe, Scran, Sense, Shared, Stray, Tie, Tiers d'état, Trite, Tritical, Tuft, Tye, Use, > USUAL, Vile, Vul(gar), Vulgo, Vulgus, Widespread, Wimbledon

Commonplace Banal, Copybook, Hackneyed, Homely, Humdrum, Idée reçue, Mot, Ordinary, Philistine, Plain, Platitude, Prosaic, Quotidian, Trite, Workaday

Commonsense Gumption, Nous, Smeddum, Wit

Commonwealth Puerto Rico

Commotion Bluster, Bustle, Carfuffle, Clangour, Clatter, Curfuffle, Dirdam, Dirdum, Do, Dust, Ferment, Flap, Flurry, Fraise, Fuss, Hell, Hoo-ha(h), Hurry, Pother, Racket, Romage, Rort, Ruckus, Ruction, Rumpus, Shemozzle, Shindig, Shindy, Shivaree, Steery, Stir, Storm, Stushie, Tirrivee, Tirrivie, To-do, Toss, Tumult, Turmoil, Upheaval, Uproar, Whirl, Wroth

Communal, Commune Agapemone, Collective, Com, Meditate, Mir, Paris, Phalanstery, Public, Talk, Township

Communicate, Communication Ampex, Announce, Baud, Boyau, Cable, Channelling, Conversation, Convey, Cybernetic, E-mail, Expansive, Impart, Infobahn, Inform, Intelpost, Intelsat, Internet, Message, Nonverbal, Note, Oracy, Prestel®, Proxemics, Reach, Road, Semiotics, Signal, Tannoy®, Telepathy, Telex, Telstar, Tieline, Transmit, Utraquist, Viewdata

Communion Creed, Fellowship, Host, Housel, Intinction, Lord's Supper, Species, Viaticum

Communiqué Announcement, Statement

Communism, Communist Apparat(chik), Aspheterism, Bolshevist, Com, Comecon, Cominform, Comintern, Commo, Comsomol, Deviationist, Essene, Fourier, Khmer Rouge, Komsomol, Leninite, Maoist, Nomenklatura, Perfectionist, Pinko, Politburo, Populist, Red, Revisionism, Soviet, Spartacist, Stalinism, Tanky, Titoist, Trot, Vietcong, Vietminh

Communities, Community Alterne, Ashram, Biome, Body, Brook Farm, Brotherhood, Clachan, Climax, Coenobitism, Coenobium, Colonia, Colony, Consocies, Ecosystem, EEC, Enclave, European, Frat(e)ry, Global, Kahal, Kibbutz, Mesarch, Neighbourhood, People, Phyle, Public, Pueblo, Seral, Sere, Shtetl, Sisterhood, Society, Street, Toon, Town, Tribe, Ujamaa, Village, Virtual, Volost, Zupa

Commute(r) Change, Convert, Reduce, Straphanger, Travel

Como Lake, Perry

Compact Agreement, Cement, Concise, Conglobe, Covenant, Covin, Coyne, Dense, Entente, Fast, Firm, Flapjack, Hard, Knit, League, Match, Neat, Pledge,

Powder, Solid, Terse, Tight, Treaty, Well-knit

Companion(able) Achates, Arm candy, Associate, Attender, Barnacle, Bedfellow, Bonhomie, Bud(dy), Butty, CH, China, Comate, Comrade, Consort, Contubernal, Crony, Cupman, Duenna, Ephesian, Escort, Felibre, > **FELLOW**, Fere, Handbook, Helpmate, Mate, Pal, Pard, Playmate, Sidekick, Skaines mate, Stable, Thane, Thegn, Trojan, Vade-mecum

Company, Companies Actors, Artel, Ass, Assembly, Band, Bank, Battalion, Bevy, > **BUSINESS**, Bv, Cahoot, Cartel, Cast, Cavalcade, Chartered, CIA, Circle, City, Close, Club, Co, Conger, Consort, Cordwainers, Core, Corporation, Corps, Coy, Crew, Crowd, Decury, Dotcom, East India, Enterprise, Entourage, Faction, Finance, Fire, > **FIRM**, Flock, Free, Gang, Garrison, Ging, Guild, Haberdashers, Heap, Holding, Hudson's Bay, ICI, Inc, Indie, In-house, Intercourse, Investment, Jingbang, Joint-stock, Limited, Listed, Livery, Management, Maniple, Muster, Order, Organisation, Parent, Plc, Private, Public, Quoted, Rep(ertory), Room, SA, Sedge, Set, Set out, Shell, Siege, Sort, SpA, Stock, Subsidiary, Syndicate, Table, Team, Thiasus, Touring, Troop, Troupe, Trust, Twa, Two(some), Visitor, White

Compare(d), Comparison Analogy, Balance, Beside, Bracket, Collate, Confront, Contrast, Correspond, Cp, Equate, Liken, Match, Odious, Parallel, Relation, Simile, Weigh

Compartment Ballonet, Bay, Booth, Box, Carriage, Casemate, Cell, Chamber, Cofferdam, Cubbyhole, Cubicle, Dog box, Locellate, Loculament, Loculus, Panel, Partition, Pigeonhole, Pocket, Pod, Room, Room(ette), Severy, Stall, Till, Watertight

Compass Ambit, Area, Beam, Binnacle, Bounds, Bow, Gamut, Goniometer, Gyro, Gyromagnetic, Gyroscope, Infold, Magnetic, Mariner's, Needle, Orbit, Pelorus, Perimeter, Prismatic, Radio, > **RANGE**, Reach, Rhumb, Room, Scale, Sweep, Tessitura, Width

Compassion(ate) Aroha, Bleed(ing), Clemency, Commiseration, Empathy, Humane, Mercy, Pity, Samaritan, Sympathy

Compatible Consistent, Fit, Harmonious

Compatriot National

Compel(led), Compulsion, Compulsive, Compulsory Addiction, Coact, Coerce, Command, Constrain, Dragoon, Duress, Enforce, Extort, Fain, > **FORCE**, Gar, Make, Mandatory, Oblige, Pathological, Steamroller, Strongarm, Tyrannise

Compendium Breviate

Compensate, Compensation Amend(s), Balance, Boot, Comp, Counterbalance, Counterpoise, Damages, Demurrage, Guerdon, Offset, Payment, Recoup, Redress, Reparation, Reprisal, Requital, Restitution, Restore, Retaliation, Salvage, Satisfaction, Solatium, Wergild, X-factor

Compère Emcee, Host, MC, Presenter

Compete Contend, Emulate, Enter, Match, Outvie, Play, Rival, Vie

Competence, Competent Ability, Able, Adequate, Can, Capacity, Dab, Efficient, Fit, Responsible, Sui juris, Worthy

Competition, Competitive, Competitor Agonist, Backmarker, Bee, Biathlon, Candidate, Comper, Contest, Cup, Drive, Entrant, Event, Field, Freestyle, Gymkhana, Head-to-head, Heptathlon, Imperfect, Judoka, Karateka, Knockout, Match, Match-play, Open, Opponent, Pairs, Panellist, Pentathlon, Perfect, Player, Pro-am, Puissance, Race, Rally, Regatta, Repechage, Rival(ise), Rodeo, Show-jumping, Super G, Tension, Test, Tiger, Tournament, Tourney, Trial, Triallist, Wap(p)enshaw

Compile(r), Compilation Anthology, Arrange, Collect, Edit, Prepare, Segue,

Zadkiel

Complacent Babbitt, Fatuous, Joco, Pleasant, Self-satisfied, Smug

Complain(t), Complainer Adenoids, Affection, Affliction, Alas, Alastrim, Alopecia, Anaemia, Angashore, Angina, Asthma, Barrack, Beef, Bellyache, Bitch, Bleat, BSE, Carp, Cavil, Charge, Chorea, Colic, Crab, Cramp, Criticise, Diatribe, Disorder, Dropsy, Epidemic, Ergot, Exanthema, Girn, Gout, Gravamen, Groan, Grouch, Grouse, Growl, Grudge, Grumble, Grutch, Harangue, Hives, Hone, Hypochondria, > ILLNESS, Jeremiad, Kvetch, Lupus, Malady, Mange, Mean(e), Mein, Mene, Moan, Morphew, Mumps, Murmur, Nag, Natter, Neuralgia, Ologoan, Pertussis, Plica, Poor-mouth, Protest, Pule, Pyelitis, Querimony, Rail, Remonstrate, Repine, Rickets, Sapego, Sciatica, Scold, Sigh, Silicosis, Squawk, Staggers, Thrush, Tic, Tinea, Upset, Wheenge, Whimper, Whine, Whinge, Yammer, Yawp

Complaisant Agreeable, Flexible, Suave, Supple

Complement Alexin, Amount, Balance, Finish, Gang, Lot, Reciprocate

Complete(ly), Completion Absolute, Accomplish, Achieve, All, Arrant, Attain, Clean, Congenital, Consummate, Crown, Do, End, Entire, Finalise, Finish, Follow through, Fruition, Fulfil, Full, Full-blown, Hollow, Incept, Integral, In toto, One, Ouroboros, Out, Out and out, Perfect, Plenary, Quite, Ready, Sew-up, Sheer, Spang, Sum, Teetotal, Thorough, Total, Unanimous, Uncut, Unequivocal, Unmitigated, Whole (hog)

Complex(ity) Abstruse, Arcane, Castration, Compound, Difficult, Electra, Golgi, Hard, Heath Robinson, Immune, Inferiority, Intricate, Intrince, Involute, Knot, Manifold, Mixed, Multinucleate, Nest, Network, Obsession, Oedipus, Paranoid, Persecution, Phaedra, Superiority, Syndrome, Web

Complexion Aspect, Blee, Hue, Leer, Temper, Tint, View

Compliance, Compliant, Comply Agree, Assent, Conform, Deference, Docile, Follow, Hand-in-glove, Obey, Observe, Obtemper, Sequacious, Surrender, Wilco, Yield

Complicate(d), Complication Bewilder, Complex, Deep, Elaborate, Embroil, Implex, Intricate, Involve, Inweave, Node, Nodus, Perplex, Ramification, Rigmarole, Sequela, Snarl, Tangle, Tirlie-wirlie

▷ **Complicated** *may indicate* an anagram

Compliment(s) Baisemain, Bouquet, Congratulate, Devoirs, Douceur, Encomium, Flatter, Flummery, Praise, Soap, Trade-last, Tribute

Component Coherer, Constituent, Contact, CRT, Element, Factor, Guidance, Impedor, Inductor, Ingredient, Longeron, > PART, Pre-amp, Subunit, Tensor

Compose(d), Composure Aplomb, Arrange, Calm, Choreograph, Consist, Cool, > CREATE, Equanimity, Even, Face, Improvise, Indite, Lull, Notate, Orchestrate, Placid, Poise, Produce, Reconcile, Sangfroid, Sedate, Serenity, Settle, Soothe, Tranquil, Unruffled, Write

Composer Contrapunt(al)ist, Hymnist, Inditer, Inventor, Maker, Melodist, Musician, > POET, Serialist, Six, Songwriter, Symphonist, Triadist, Tunesmith, Writer

● **COMPOSERS**
●
●

● **3 letters:**	Arne	Bull	Ives
● Bax	Bach	Byrd	Kern
●	Berg	Cage	Lalo
● **4 letters:**	Blow	Dima	Monk
● Adam	Brel	Graf	Nono

- Orff
- Peri
- Raff
- Wolf
-

5 letters:
- Auber
- Auric
- Balfe
- Berio
- Bizet
- Bliss
- Bloch
- Boito
- Boyce
- Brian
- Bruch
- Crumb
- D'Indy
- Dukas
- Elgar
- Fauré
- Field
- Finzi
- Glass
- Gluck
- Grieg
- Harty
- Haydn
- Henze
- Holst
- Ibert
- Lasso
- Lehar
- Liszt
- Loewe
- Lully
- Parry
- Prout
- Ravel
- Reger
- Rossi
- Satie
- Sousa
- Suppe
- Tosti
- Verdi
- Watts
- Weber
- Weill
- Zappa
-

6 letters:
Alfven
Arnold
Azione
Barber
Bartók
Berlin
Boulez
Brahms
Bridge
Burney
Busoni
Chopin
Coates
Delius
Duparc
Dvořák
Flotow
Franck
German
Glière
Glinka
Gounod
Handel
Hummel
Joplin
Kodaly
Lassus
Ligeti
Mahler
Mingus
Morley
Mozart
Ogolon
Pierne
Rameau
Rubbra
Schutz
Tallis
Varese
Wagner
Walton
Webern

7 letters:
Albeniz
Alberti
Allegri
Bantock
Bellini
Berlioz
Berners

Borodin
Britten
Brubeck
Copland
Corelli
Debussy
De Falla
Delibes
Dohnany
Dowland
Gibbons
Ireland
Janácek
Lambert
Mancini
Martinu
Milhaud
Nielsen
Novello
Ormandy
Poulenc
Puccini
Purcell
Purnell
Quilter
Rodgers
Rodrigo
Romberg
Rossini
Roussel
Salieri
Smetana
Stainer
Strauss
Tartini
Tippett
Vivaldi
Warlock
Xenakis
Youmans

8 letters:
Alaleona
Albinoni
Boughton
Bruckner
Chabrier
Chausson
Couperin
Gershwin
Gesualdo
Glazunov

Grainger
Granados
Honegger
Kreutzer
Marcello
Mascagni
Massenet
Messager
Messiaen
Paganini
Respighi
Schubert
Schumann
Scriabin
Sessions
Sibelius
Sondheim
Sullivan
Taverner
Telemann

9 letters:
Bacharach
Balakirev
Beethoven
Bernstein
Boulanger
Broughton
Buxtehude
Chaminade
Cherubini
Donizetti
Dunstable
Hindemith
Meyerbeer
Offenbach
Pachelbel
Pergolesi
Prokofiev
Scarlatti
Schnittke
Zemlinsky

10 letters:
Birtwistle
Boccherini
Carmichael
Cole Porter
Monteverdi
Mussorgsky
Palestrina
Ponchielli

- Rawsthorne
- Saint-Saëns
- Schoenberg
- Stravinsky
- Villa-Lobos
- Williamson

11 letters:
- Charpentier

Frescobaldi
Humperdinck
Leoncavallo
Mendelssohn
Stockhausen
Tchaikovsky
Wolf Ferrari

12 letters:
Khachaturian
Rachmaninoff
Shostakovich

13 letters:
Havergal Brian
Maxwell Davies

14 letters:
Rimsky-Korsakov

15 letters:
Vaughan
    Williams

▷ **Composing** *may indicate* an anagram
  Composite Aster, Costmary, Foalfoot, Gerbera, Groundsel, Hybrid, Integral,
    Motley, Opinicus, Rag(weed), Sphinx, Synthesized, Thistle
  Composition, Compositor Albumblatt, Aleatory, Azione, Bagatelle,
    Beaumontage, Beaumontague, Canon, Capriccio, Caprice, Cob, Concerto,
    Creation, Dite, Essay, Etude, Exaration, Fantasia, Inditement, Ingredient,
    Line, Loam, Met, Montage, Morceau, Nonet(te), Opus, Oratorio, Part-writing,
    Pastiche, Piece, Pieta, Poem, Polyphony, Printer, Quartette, Raga, Rhapsody,
    Round, Ship, Sing, Smoot, Sonata, Sonatina, Structure, Suite, Symphony,
    Synthesis, Terracotta, Texture, Toccata, Treatise, Typesetter, Verismo,
    Voluntary, Work
  Compost Dressing, Fertilizer, Humus, Vraic, Zoo doo
  Compound, Compound stop Admixture, Amalgam, Bahuvrihi, Blend, > **CAMP**,
    Composite, Constitute, Coordination, Cpd, Cutting, Derivative, Ethiops, Mix,
    Mixture, Multiply, Racemate, Rooting, Type

COMPOUNDS

3 letters:
- Azo

4 letters:
- Alum
- EDTA
- Enol
- Haem
- Heme
- TEPP
- Urea

5 letters:
- Allyl
- Aloin
- Amide
- Amino
- Azide
- Azine
- Azole
- Diazo
- Diene
- Dimer
- Diode

Erbia
Ester
Furan
Halon
Imide
Imine
Lipid
Nitro
Olein
Oxide
Oxime
Potin
Pyran
Salol
Sarin
Tabun
Thiol
Trona
Vinyl

6 letters:
Acetal
Alkane
Alkene

Ammine
Arsine
Baryta
Borane
Calque
Cetane
Chrome
Cresol
Epimer
Fluate
Glycol
Halide
Haloid
Hexene
Isatin
Isomer
Ketone
Kinone
Lithia
Niello
Octane
Phenol
Pinene
Potash

Purine
Pyrone
Retene
Silane
Speiss
Tannin
Tartar
Tetryl
Thymol
Triene
Trimer
Uranyl

7 letters:
Acetone
Acridin
Aglycon
Ammonia
Benzene
Betaine
Bromide
Caliche
Calomel
Camphor

- Carbide
- Chelate
- Choline
- Cinerin
- Creatin
- Cumarin
- Cyanide
- Diamine
- Diazine
- Diazole
- Dioxide
- Dvandva
- Epoxide
- Erinite
- Ethanol
- Eugenol
- Fenuron
- Ferrite
- Flavone
- Hormone
- Hydrate
- Hydride
- Indican
- Indoxyl
- Lactate
- Lactone
- Menthol
- Metamer
- Monomer
- Niobite
- Nitride
- Nitrite
- Oxazine
- Oxonian
- Pentane
- Peptone
- Polyene
- Polymer
- Protein
- Quassia
- Quinoid
- Quinone
- Realgar
- Skatole
- Steroid
- Sulfide
- Syncarp
- Taurine
- Terpene
- Toluene
- Tritide
- Uridine

Wolfram
Zymogen

8 letters:
Acridine
Aglycone
Aldehyde
Alizarin
Arginine
Astatide
Butyrate
Catenane
Chloride
Chromene
Coenzyme
Coumarin
Creatine
Cyanogen
Datolite
Dieldrin
Dopamine
Ethoxide
Farnesol
Fluoride
Furfuran
Glycogen
Hydroxyl
Indoform
Isologue
Ketoxime
Lecithin
Luteolin
Massicot
Melamine
Monoxide
Oligomer
Pentosan
Peroxide
Piperine
Ptomaine
Purpurin
Pyrazole
Rock-alum
Rotenone
Selenate
Silicide
Siloxane
Sodamide
Stilbene
Sulphide
Sulphone
Tautomer

Tetroxid
Thiazide
Thiazine
Thiazole
Thiophen
Thiotepa
Thiourea
Titanate
Tolidine
Triazine
Triazole
Trilling
Tyramine
Urethane
Xanthate
Xanthine
Zirconia

9 letters:
Aflatoxin
Alicyclic
Aliphatic
Anhydride
Biguanide
Carbazole
Carnitine
Celloidin
Cellulose
Cementite
Cetrimide
Chromogen
Copolymer
Cortisone
Deuteride
Dibromide
Dipeptide
Disulfram
Endorshin
Ferrocene
Flavanone
Fulleride
Glycoside
Greek fire
Guanosine
Haematein
Histamine
Hydrazide
Hydroxide
Imidazole
Impsonite
Ionophore
Menadione

Merbromin
Methoxide
Monoamine
Organotin
Pentoxide
Phenazine
Phenoxide
Pheromone
Phosphide
Piperonal
Polyamine
Porphyrin
Qinghaosu
Quercetus
Quinidine
Serotonin
Tetroxide
Veratrine

10 letters:
Amphoteric
Argyrodite
Cellosolve®
Cytochroma
Dichloride
Dimethoate
Disulphide
Enkephalin
Ethambutol
Isocyanate
Lumisterol
Mercaptide
Nitrazepam
Nucleoside
Phenocaine
Picrotoxin
Piperazine
Piperidine
Propionate
Putrescine
Pyrimidine
Tatpurusha
Thimerosal
Tocopherol

11 letters:
Acetanilide
Amphetamine
Coprosterol
Dimercaprol
Electrolyte
Fluorescein

Ghitathione
Hydrocarbon
Neostigmine
Sesquioxide
Sphingosine

12 letters:
Carbohydrate
Formaldehyde
Haematoxylin

Hydroquinone
Permanganate
Phenanthrine
Polyurethane
Thiosinamine
Triglyceride
Trimethadine

13 letters:
Catecholamine

Cycloheximide
Isoproterenol
Metronidazole
Nortriptyline
Phenothiazine
Trinucleotide

14 letters:
Cyanocobalamin
Oxyhaemoglobin

Phenolphthalin
Polycarboxylic
Polyunsaturate
Trohalomethane

17 letters:
Pentachloro-
    phenol

▷ **Compound(ed)** *may indicate* an anagram
  Comprehend, Comprehensive All-in, Catch-all, Catholic, Compass,
    Compendious, Contain, Exhaustive, Fathom, Follow, Full-scale, General,
    Global, Grasp, Include, Indepth, Ken, Large, Omnibus, Panoramic, Perceive,
    School, Sweeping, Thoroughgoing, > **UNDERSTAND**, Wide
  Compress(ed), Compression, Compressor Astrict, Astringe, Bale, Coarctate,
    Contract, Pack, Solidify, Squeeze, Stupe, Thlipsis, Turbocharger
  Comprise Contain, Embody, Embrace, Include
  Compromise Avoision, Brule, Commit, Concession, Endanger, Give and take,
    Happy medium, Involve, Settlement, Time-server, Trade off
▶ **Compulsion** *see* **COMPEL**
  Compunction Hesitation, Regret, Remorse, Scruple, Sorrow
  Computation, Computer (language), Computer term, Computer user ActiveX,
    Ada, Algol, Algorism, Analog(ue), Anorak, Antialising, Apple, Arpa, ASCII,
    Authoring, Autosave, Basic, Bloatware, Boot, Bootstrap, Brain, Browser,
    Busbar, C, CADMAT, Calculate, Calculus, Cast(er), Checksum, Chiphead,
    Clickstream, Clipboard, COBOL, COL, CORAL, Counter, Crippleware,
    Cyber(netics), Cyberpunk, Cybersurfer, Desktop, Digerati, Digital, DRAM,
    Earcon, Earom, Eniac, EPROM, ERNIE, Estimate, Ethernet, E-wallet, Extranet,
    FAT, Figure, Fileserver, Firewall, Floptical, Fortran, Freenet, GIGO, Gopher,
    Groupware, Hacker, HAL, Hardware, High-end, Holmes, Hybrid, Hypermedia,
    ICL, IDE, Integrator, Interface, Internet, IT, JANET, Java®, Kludge, Laptop,
    Linker, Linux, LISP, Luser, Macro, Mail merge, Mainframe, MARC, Measure,
    Micro, MIDI, Modem, Morphing, Mouse potato, Nerd, Network, Neural,
    Notebook, Number-cruncher, Numlock, OCCAM, OCR, On-line, Otaku,
    Palmtop, PASCAL, Patch, PC, Peer-to-peer, Perl, Personal, Pixel, Platform,
    Processor, Program, PROM, Pushdown, RAM, README file, Read-out,
    Realtime, Reboot, Reckoner, RISC, ROM, Scratchpad, Server, Shareware,
    SNOBOL, Software, Spreadsheet, Sprite, Stand-alone, String, Subroutine,
    Superserver, TALISMAN, Tally, Tape streamer, TAURUS, Thick client, Thin
    client, Toggle, Tower, Track(er)ball, Turing machine, Unix, Vaccine, Voxel,
    WIMP, WORM, Wysiwyg
  Comrade Achates, Ally, Buddy, Butty, China, Fellow, Friend, Kamerad, Mate,
    Oliver, Pal, Pard, Roland, Tovarich, Tovaris(c)h
  Con(man) Against, Anti, Bunco, Diddle, Dupe, Fleece, Hornswoggle, Jacob, Lag,
    Learn, Peruse, Read, Scam, Scan, Steer, Sucker, Swindle, Tweedler
  Concave Dished, Invexed
  Conceal(ed), Concealment Blanket, Blind, Closet, Clothe, Cover, Curtain,
    Dissemble, Doggo, Drown, Feal, Heal, Heel, Hele, > **HIDE**, Latent, Misprision,
    Occult, Palm, Perdu(e), Recondite, Screen, Scriene, Secrete, Shroud, Sleeve,
    Smother, Snow job, Stash, Subreption, Ulterior, Wrap

Concede, Concession Acknowledge, Admit, Allow, Budge, Carta, Charter, Compromise, Confess, Favour, Forfeit, Franchise, Munich, Ou, Owe, Own, Privilege, Ship, Sop, Synchoresis

Conceit(ed) Bumptious, Caprice, Carriwitchet, Cat-witted, Concetto, Crank, Crotchet, Device, Dicty, Egomania, Fancy, Fastuous, Figjam, Flory, Fop, Fume, Hauteur, Idea, Mugwump, Notion, Podsnappery, Prig, Princock, Princox, Puppyism, Quiblin, Self-assumption, Side, Snotty, Stuck-up, Swellhead, Toffee-nose, Vain(glory), Wind

Conceive, Conceivable Beget, Create, Credible, Imagine, Possible, Surmise

Concentrate(d), Concentration Aim, Attend, Bunch, Cathexis, Centre, Collect, Condense, Dephlegmate, Distil, Elliptical, Essence, Extract, Focalise, Focus, Intense, Kurtosis, Listen, Major, Mantra, Mass, Molality, Molarity, Navel-gazing, Potted, Rivet, Samadhi, Titrate, Titre

Concept(ion) Brain, Hent, Ideal, Ideation, Image, Immaculate, Myth, Notion, Stereotype

Concern(ing) About, After, Ail, Altruism, Anent, As to, Bother, Business, Care, Cerne, Company, Disturb, Firm, Going, Heed, In re, Intéressé, Interest, Into, Lookout, > MATTER, Mell, Misease, Over, Part, Pidgin, Pigeon, Re, Reck, Regard, Reke, Respect, Retch, Solicitude, Touch, Trouble, Worry

▷ **Concerned** *may indicate* an anagram

Concert (place) Agreement, Benefit, Chamber, Charivari, Cooperation, Device, Dutch, Gig, Hootananny, Hootenanny, Hootnannie, Odeon, Odeum, Pop, Prom(enade), Recital, Singsong, Smoker, Symphony, Together, Unison, Unity, Wit

Concertina Bandoneon, Pleat, Squeezebox, Squiffer

Concerto Brandenburg, Emperor, Grosso

▶ **Concession** *see* CONCEDE

Conch Shell, Strombus

Conchie CO

Conciliate Allay, Calm, Disarm, Ease, Mollify, Placate, Reconcile

Concise Compact, Curt, Encapsulated, Laconic, Short, Succinct, Terse, Tight

Conclave Assembly, Caucus, Confab, Meeting

Conclude(d), Conclusion, Conclusive Achieve, A fortiori, Afterword, Amen, Binding, Cease, Clinch, Close, Complete, Dead, Decide, Deduce, > END, Envoi, Explicit, Finding, Fine, Finis, > FINISH, Foregone, Gather, Illation, Infer, Lastly, Limit, Omega, Peroration, Point, Postlude, Punchline, Reason, Resolve, Settle, Summary, Upshot, Uptie

Conclusive Cogent, Convincing, Estoppel, Final

Concoct(ion) Brew, Compound, Creation, Plan, Trump (up)

Concord Consonance, Harmony, Peace, Plane, Sympathy, Treaty, Unity

Concorde SST

Concourse Assembly, Confluence, Esplanade, Throng

Concrete, Concretion Actual, Aggregate, Beton, Bezoar, Cake, Calculus, Clot, Dogger, Gunite, Hard, Lean, Mass, Minkstone, No-fines, Pile-cap, Positive, Prestressed, Reify, Reinforced, Siporex, Solid, Tangible, Tremie

Concubine Apple-squire, Campaspe, Harem, Hetaria, Madam, Mistress, Odalisk

Concur Accord, Agree, Coincide, Comply, > CONSENT, Gree

Concurrent(ly) Meantime

Concuss(ion) Clash, Shock, Stun

Condemn(ation) Accuse, Blame, Blast, Cast, Censor, Censure, Convict, Damn, Decry, Denounce, Deprecate, Doom, Judge, Kest, Obelise, Proscribe, Revile,

Sentence, Theta, Upbraid

Condense(d), Condenser Abbe, Abbreviate, Abridge, Brief, Capacitator, Compress, Contract, Distil, Encapsulate, Epitomise, Jet, Liebig, Précis, Rectifier, Reduce, Shorten, Shrink, Summarise, Vernier, Vinifactor

Condescend Deign, Patronise, Stoop, Vouchsafe

Condiment Caraway, Cayenne, Chutney, Cum(m)in, Flavour, Horse radish, Kava, Relish, Sambal, Sambol, Sauce, Tracklement, Turmeric, Vinegar

Condition(al), Conditioning Circ(s), Congenital, Connote, Fettle, Going, Hammertoe, Hood, If, > **IN GOOD CONDITION**, Kelter, Kilter, Necessary, Nick, Order, Pass, Pavlovian, Plight, Pliskie, Ply, Point, Position, Predicament, Prepare, Prerequisite, Presupposition, Protasis, Proviso, Provisory, Repair, Reservation, Reserve, Rider, Ropes, Sine qua non, Sis, Standing, State, Sted, Stipulation, String, Sufficient, Term, Tid, Tox(a)emia, Trim, Trisomy, Unless

Condom Blob, Cap, Franger, French letter, Gumboot, Johnny, Letter, Prophylactic, Rubber, Safe, Scumbag, Sheath

Condone Absolve, Excuse, Forgive, Overlook

Conduct(or), Conductress Accompany, Anode, Arm, Arrester, Barbirolli, Bearing, Beecham, Behaviour, Bulow, Bus-bar, Cad, Chobdar, Clippie, Coil, Comport, Demean(our), Deportment, Direct, Disorderly, Drive, Editor, Electrode, Escort, Feedthrough, Fetch, Goings-on, Haitink, Hallé, Ignitron, Karajan, Kempe, Klemperer, Lark, Lead, Liber, Lightning, Maestro, Mho, Microchip, Nerve, N-type, Officiate, Outer, Parts, Photodiode, > **PILOT**, Previn, Probe, Prosecute, Protocol, Psychopomp, P-type, Rattle, Safe, Sargent, Scudaller, Scudler, Shunt, Skudler, Solicit, Solti, Tao, Thermistor, Toscanini, Transact, > **USHER**, Varactor, Varistor, Wave guide, Wire, Wood, Zener diode

▷ **Conducting** *may indicate* an '-ic' ending

Conduit Aqueduct, Canal, Carrier, Duct, Main, Penstock, Pipe, Tube, Utilidor

Cone(s), Conical Cappie, Circular, Female, Fir, Fusion, Moxa, Nose, Pastille, Peeoy, Pineal, Pingo, Pioy(e), Puy, Pyramid, Retinal, Seger, Spire, Storm, Strobilus, Taper, Tee, Traffic, Volcanic, Wind, Windsock

Coney Daman, Doe, Hyrax

Confection(er) Candy, Caramel, Chocolate, Concoction, Conserve, Countline, Ice, Kiss, Marzipan, Noisette, Nougat, Quiddery, Rock, Sweet, Sweetmeat, Tablet

Confederal, Confederacy, Confederate, Confederation Accessory, Alliance, Ally, Association, Body, Bund, Bunkosteerer, Cover, Illinois, League, Partner, Senegambia, Union

Confer(ence) Bestow, Bretton Woods, Cf, Collogue, Colloqium, Colloquy, Congress, Council, Diet, Do, Dub, Fest, Forum, Grant, Huddle, Hui, Imparlance, Imperial, Indaba, Intercommune, Lambeth, Meeting, Munich, Negotiate, News, Palaver, Parley, Pawaw, Pear, Potsdam, Pourparler, Powwow, Press, Pugwash, Quadrant, Seminar, Settle, Summit, Symposium, Synod, > **TALK**, Teach-in, Video, Vouchsafe, Yalta

Confess(ion), Confessor Acknowledge, Admit, Agnise, Avowal, Concede, Declare, Disclose, Edward, Own, Peccavi, Recant, Shrift, Shriver, Sing, Whittle

Confide(nce), Confident(ial), Confidant Aplomb, Aside, Assertive, Assured, Bedpost, Belief, Bottle, Certitude, Cocksure, Cocky, Cred, Crouse, Entre nous, Entrust, Faith, Feisty, Gatepost, Hardy, Hope, Hush-hush, Intimate, Morale, Nerve, Pack, Private, Privy, Sanguine, Secret, Secure, Self-possessed, Sub rosa, Sure, Tell, Trust, Unbosom, Under the rose, Vaulting

Confine(d), Confines, Confinement Ambit, Bail, Bale, Cage, CB, Chain, Constrain, Cramp, Crib, Detain, Emmew, Encase, Enclose, Endemic, Enmew,

Ensheath, Gaol, Gate, House arrest, Immanacle, Immew, Immure, Impound, > **IMPRISON**, Incage, Incarcerate, Incommunicado, Inhoop, Intern, Local, Mail, March, Mew, Mure, Narrow, Pen, Pent, Pinion, Poky, Restrict, Rule 43, Rules, Section, Solitary, Tether, Thirl, Trammel

Confirm(ed), **Confirmation** Addict, Ascertain, Assure, Attest, Bear, Certify, Chrisom, Christen, Chronic, Clinch, Corroborate, Endorse, Homologate, Obsign, OK, Ratify, Sacrament, Sanction, Seal, Strengthen, Ten-four, Tie, Validate, Vouch

Confiscate, **Confiscation** Attainder, Deprive, Dispossess, Distrain, Escheat, Garnishee, Impound, Infangenethef, Raupatu, Seize, Sequestrate

Conflagration Blaze, Holocaust, Inferno, Wildfire

Conflict(ing) Agon, Armageddon, Battle, Camp, Clash, Close, Contend, Contravene, Controversy, Disharmony, Encounter, Feud, Fray, Inconsistent, Jar, Lists, Mêlée, Muss, Oppose, Rift, Scrape, Strife, > **STRUGGLE**, Tergiversate, War

Conform(ity) Accord, Adjust, Comply, Consistence, Correspond, Normalise, Obey, Observe, Propriety, Standardize, Stereotype(d), Suit, Trimmer, Yield

Confound(ed) Abash, Amaze, Astound, Awhape, Baffle, Bewilder, Blamed, Blasted, Blest, Blinking, Bumbaze, Contradict, Darn, Drat, Dumbfound, Elude, Floor, Jigger, Mate, Murrain, Nonplus, Perishing, Perplex, Rabbit, Spif(f)licate, Stump, Throw

▷ **Confound** *may indicate* an anagram

Confrère Ally

Confront(ation) Appose, Beard, Breast, Eyeball, Face, Loggerheads, Mau-mau, Meet, Nose, Oppose, Showdown, Tackle

Confuse(d), **Confusedly**, **Confusion** Addle, Anarchy, Astonishment, Babel, Baffle, Bazodee, Bedevil, Befog, Befuddle, Bemuse, Bewilder, Blur, Bobby-die, Burble, Bustle, Chaos, Cloud, Clutter, Complicate, Debacle, Didder, Discombobulate, Disconcert, Disorient, Distract, Dither, Dizzy, Dudder, Dust, Egarement, Embrangle, Embroglio, Embroil, Farrago, Flap, Flat spin, Flummox, Flurry, Fluster, Fog, Fox, Fuddle, Galley-west, Hash, Havoc, Hazy, Helter-skelter, Hubble-bubble, Huddle, Hugger-mugger, Hurly-burly, Hurry-scurry, Hurry-skurry, Imbrangle, Imbroglio, > **IN CONFUSION**, Indistinct, Litter, Lost, Lurry, Maelstrom, Maffled, Mayhem, Maze, Melange, Melee, Mess, Mingle, Mish-mash, Mixtie-maxtie, Mix-up, Mizzle, Mizzy maze, Moider, Moither, Moonstruck, Morass, > **MUDDLE**, Mudge, Muzzy, Overset, Pellmell, Perplex, Pi(e), Pose, Ravel, Razzle-dazzle, Razzmatazz, Rout, S(c)hemozzle, Scramble, Skimble-skamble, Snafu, Spin, Stump, Stupefy, Synchysis, Tangle, Throw, Tizzy, Topsy-turvy, Tzimmes, Welter, Whemmle, Whomble, Whummle, Woolly, Woozy

▷ **Confuse(d)** *may indicate* an anagram

Confute Confound, Contradict, Deny, Disprove, Infringe, Redargue, Refel

Congeal Coagulate, Freeze, Gel, Gunge, Set, Solidify

Congenial Agreeable, Amiable, Compatible, Connate, Couthie, Couthy, Happy, Kindred, Simpatico, Sympathique

Congenital Connate, Inborn, Innate, Inveterate

Congest(ed), **Congestion** Coryza, Cram, Crowd, Engorge, Impact, Jam, Logjam, Turgid

Conglomerate, **Conglomeration** Aggregate, Banket, Gather, Heap, Mass

Congo(u) Shaba, Tea

Congratulate, **Congratulation** Applaud, Felicitate, Laud, Mazeltov, Preen, Salute

Congregate, Congregation(alist) Assembly, Barnabite, Body, Brownist, Class, Community, Conclave, Ecclesia, Flock, Fold, Gathering, Host, Laity, Oratory, Propaganda, Synagogue

Congress(man) ANC, Assembly, Conclave, Continental, Council, Eisteddfod, Intercourse, Legislature, Pan-Africanist, Rally, Senator, Solon, Synod, Vienna

Conifer(ous) Araucaria, Cedar, Cypress, Cyrus, Evergreen, Larch, Picea, Pine, Spruce, Taiga, Taxus, Thuja, Yew

Conject(ure) Fancy, Goldbach's, Guess, Speculate, Surmise, Theory, View

Conjoin Alligate, Ally, Connect, Knit

Conjugate, Conjugation Couple, Hermitian, Join, Nuptial, Synopsis, Typto, Zygosis

Conjunction Alligation, Ampersand, And, Combination, Consort, Nor, Polysyndeton, Synod, Syzygy, Together, Union, Unless

Conjure, Conjuror Angekkok, Charm, Contrive, Heypass, Heypresto, Hocus-pocus, Illusionist, Imagine, Invoke, Mage, Magic, Palmer, Prestidigitator, Prestigiator, Thaumaturgus

Connect(ed), Connection, Connector About, Accolade, Adaptor, Affinity, Agnate, Anastomosis, And, Associate, Attach, Band, Bind, Bridge, Bridle, Cable, Clientele, Coherent, Colligate, Conjugate, Couple, Cross-link, Delta, Dovetail, Drawbar, Fishplate, Fistula, Hook-up, > IN CONNECTION WITH, Interlink, Interlock, Join, Jumper, Kinship, Liaison, Lifeline, Link, Marry, Merge, Mesh, Nexus, On, Online, Patch, Pons, Raphe, Rapport, Relate, Relative, Respect, Shuttle, Splice, S-R, Synapse, Syntenosis, Syssarcosis, Tendon, Through, Tie, Tie-in, Union, Y, Yoke, Zygon

Connecticut Ct

Connive, Connivance Abet, Cahoots, Collude, Condone, Conspire, Plot

Connoisseur Aesthete, Cognoscente, Epicure, Expert, Fancier, Gourmet, Judge, Maven, Mavin, Oenophil

Connotate, Connotation Imply, Infer, Intent, Meaning

Conquer(or), Conquest Beat, Conquistador, Crush, Debel, Genghis Khan, Hereward, > MASTER, Moor, Norman, Ostrogoth, Overcome, Overpower, Overrun, Pizarro, Subjugate, Tame, Tamerlane, Vanquish, Victor

Conquistador Cortes, Cortez

Conscience, Conscientious Casuistic, Duteous, Heart, Inwit, Morals, Painstaking, Pang, Remorse, Scruple(s), Sense, Superego, Syneidesis, Synteresis, Thorough, Twinge

Conscious(ness) Awake, Aware, Chit, Limen, Mindful, On to, Persona, Sensible, Sentient

Conscript(ion) Blood-tax, Choco, Commandeer, Draft(ee), Impress, Landsturm, Levy, Nasho, > RECRUIT, Register

Consecrate, Consecration Bless, Hallow, Noint, Oint, Sacring, Sanctify, Venerate

Consecutive Sequential, Successive

Consensus Agreement, Harmony, Unanimity

Consent Accord, Acquiesce, Affo(o)rd, Agree, Approbate, Comply, Concur, Grant, Informed, Permit, Ratify, Volens, Yes-but, Yield

Consequence, Consequent(ial) Aftermath, Consectaneous, Corollary, Effect, End, Importance, Issue, Karma, Knock-on, Logical, Moment, Outcome, Ramification, Repercussion, > RESULT, Sequel, Upshot

Conservative Blimpish, Blue, C, Cautious, Diehard, Disraeli, Fabian, Hard-hat, Hidebound, Hunker, Neanderthal, Old guard, Old-line, Preppy, Progressive, Rearguard, Redneck, Right(-wing), Safe, Square, Thrifty, Tory, True blue,

Unionist, Verkramp

Conservatory Hothouse, Orangery, Solarium

Conserve, Conservation(ist) Can, Comfiture, Husband(ry), Jam, Jelly, Maintain, Maintenance, Noah, NT, Protect, Save

Consider(able), Consideration Animadvert, Attention, Avizandum, By-end, Case, Cerebrate, Chew over, Cogitate, Contemplate, Count, Courtesy, Debate, Deem, Deliberate, Entertain, Envisage, Factor, Fair, Feel, Forethought, Heed, Importance, Inasmuch, Judge, Many, Meditate, Muse, Pay, Perpend, Poise, Ponder, Premeditate, Pretty, Rate, Reckon, Reflect, Regard, Respect, See, Several, Shortlist, Solicitous, Song, Speculate, Steem, Study, Substantial, Think, Tidy, Vast, View, Ween, Weigh

Consign(ment) Allot, Award, Batch, Bequeath, Delegate, Deliver, Drop shipment, Entrust, Lading, Ship, Transfer

Consist(ent), Consistency Agree, Coherent, Comprise, Enduring, Even, Liaison, Rely, Steady

Consolation, Console Ancon, Appease, Balm, Comfort, Relief, Solace, Sop

Consolidate Coalesce, Combine, Compact, Gel, Merge, Pun, Unify

Consommé Julienne, Soup

Consonant(s) Affricate, Agma, Agreeing, Cacuminal, Cerebral, Explosive, Fortis, Fricative, Harmonious, Implosive, Labial, Lateral, Lenis, Media, Mouillé, Plosive, Sonorant, Spirant, Surd, Tenuis, Velar

Consort Ally, Associate, Maik, Mate, Moop, Moup, Partner, Spouse

Consortium Coalition, Combine, Ring

Conspicuous Arresting, Blatant, Clear, Eminent, Glaring, Kenspeck(le), Landmark, Light, Manifest, Patent, Salient, Signal, Striking

Conspiracy, Conspirator, Conspire, Conspiring Cabal, Casca, Cassius, Catiline, Cato St, Champerty, Cinna, Collaborate, Colleague, Collogue, Collude, Complot, Connive, Covin, Covyne, Guy, Highbinder, In cahoots, Intrigue, Oates, Omerta, > **PLOT**, Ring, Scheme

Constable Beck, Catchpole, Cop, Dogberry, Dull, Elbow, Harman(-beck), Headborough, High, John, Officer, Painter, Petty, Pointsman, Posse, Special, Thirdborough, Tipstaff, Verges

Constancy, Constant Abiding, Boltzmann, C, Changeless, Chronic, Coefficient, Devotion, Dielectric, Diffusion, Dirac, Eccentricity, Eternal, Faith, Firm, Fundamental, G, Gas, Gravitational, H, Honesty, Hubble's, K, Lambert, Leal(ty), Logical, Loyal, Magnetic, Often, Parameter, > **PERPETUAL**, Planck's, Pole star, Resolute, Sad, Solar, Staunch, Steadfast, Steady, Time, True, Unfailing, Uniform, Usual

Constellation Andromeda, Antlia, Apus, Aquarius, Aquila, Ara, Argo, Aries, Auriga, Bootes, Caelum, Canis major, Canis minor, Carina, Cassiopeia, Centaurus, Cepheus, Cetus, Cham(a)eleon, Circinus, Columba, Coma Berenices, Coma Cluster, Corvus, Crater, Cygnus, Cynosure, Delphinus, Dolphin, Dorado, Draco, Equuleus, Eridanus, Fornax, Galaxy, Gemini, Gru(i)s, Hercules, Horologium, Hydra, Hydrus, Indus, Lacerta, Leo, Leo minor, Lepus, Libra, Lupus, Lynx, Lyra, Mensa, Monoceros, Musca, Norma, Octans, Ophiuchus, Orion, Pavo, Pegasus, Perseus, Phoenix, Pictor, Piscus Austrinus, > **PLANET**, Puppis, Pyxis, Reticulum, Sagitta, Sagittarius, Scorpius, Sculptor, Scutum, Serpens, Sextans, Southern Cross, Spica, > **STAR**, Telescopium, Triangulum (Australe), Tucana, Twins, Unicorn, Vela, Virgin, Virgo, Volans, Vulpecula, Wag(g)oner, Whale, Zodiacal

Consternation Alarm, Dismay, Doodah, Fear, Horror

Constipate(d), Constipation Astrict, Bind, Block, Costive, Stegnotic, Stenosis

Constituency, Constituent Borough, Component, Element, Immediate, Part, Principle, Seat, Voter

▷ **Constituents** *may indicate* an anagram

Constitute, Constitution(al) Appoint, Charter, Compose, Comprise, Congenital, Creature, Establishment, Form, Fuero, Health, Physique, Policy, Polity, Seat, State, Synthesis, Upmake, Walk

Constrain(ed), Constraint Bind, Bondage, Boundary, Coerce, Confine, Coop, Curb, Duress(e), Hard, Oblige, Pressure, Repress, Stenosis, Taboo, Trammel

Constrict(ed), Constriction Bottleneck, Choke, Coarctate, Contract, Cramp, Hour-glass, Impede, Limit, Phimosis, Squeeze, Stegnosis, Stenosis, Strangulate, Thlipsis, Tighten, Venturi

Construct(ion), Constructor, Constructive Build, Compile, Engineer, Erect, Fabricate, Facture, Fashion, Form, Frame, Idolum, Make, Manufacture, Seabee, Tectonic, Weave

Construe Deduce, Explain, Expound, Infer

Consul Ambassador, Attaché, Horse, Praetor

Consult(ant), Consultation Confer, Deliberate, Discuss, Emparl, Imparl, Joint, Peritus, See, Surgery, Vide

Consume(r), Consumption, Consumptive Bolt, Burn, Caterpillar®, Decay, Devour, Diner, Eat, Engross, Exhaust, Expend, Feed, Glutton, Hectic, Mainline, Scoff, Spend, Swallow, TB, Use, Waste, Wear

Consummate, Consummation Keystone, Seal

Contact Abut, Adpress, Contingence, Hook-up, Lens, Liaise, Liaison, Meet, Reach, Shoe, Taction, > **TOUCH**, Touchy-feely, Wiper

Contagious, Contagion Infection, Noxious, Poison, Taint, Variola, Viral

Contain(er) Amphora, Ampulla, Aquafer, Aquifer, Barrel, Bass, Bidon, Bin, Bottle, Box, Buddle, Cachepot, Can, Canakin, Canikin, Canister, Cannikin, Cantharus, Capsule, Carafe, Carboy, Carry, Carton, Case, Cask, Cassette, Chase, Chest, Churn, Coffer, Comprise, Coolamon, Crate, Crater, Crucible, Cup, Cupel, Decanter, Dracone, Dredger, Enclose, Encompass, Enseam, Esky®, Feretory, Flagon, Flask, Gourd, > **HOLD**, House, Igloo, Include, Incubator, Intray, Jar, Jeroboam, Jerrican, Jerrycan, Jug, Keg, Kirbeh, Leaguer, Lekythos, Monkey, Monstrance, Mould, Olpe, Pail, Pinata, Piscina, Pitcher, Pithos, Pod, Pottle, Reliquary, Repository, Restrain, Sac(k), Saggar, Scyphus, Shaker, Situla, Skin, Skip, Snaptin, Spittoon, Stamnos, Tank, Tantalus, Terrarium, Tinaja, Trough, Tub, Tun, Tupperware®, Urn, Vessel, Vinaigrette, Wineskin, Woolpack, Workbag

Contaminate(d) Adulterate, Corrupt, Defile, Denature, Flyblown, Impure, Infect, Pollute, Soil, Stain, Tarnish

Contemplate, Contemplation Consider, Ecce, Envisage, Hesychasm, Meditate, Muse, Ponder, Reflect, Retrospection, Rue, Samadhi, Spell, Study, Think, Watch

Contemporary AD, Coetaneous, Current, Equal, Fellow, Modern, Present, Verism

Contempt(ible), Contemptuous Abject, Ageism, Aha, Arsehole, Bah, BEF, Cheap, Contumely, Crud, Crumb, Cullion, Cynical, Derision, Despisal, Disparaging, Dog-bolt, Fig, Hangdog, Ignominious, Insect, Low, Mean, Measly, Misprision, Odious, Paltry, Phooey, Pish, Poxy, Pshaw, Ratfink, Rats, Razoo, Scabby, Scarab, Schlub, > **SCORN**, Scumbag, Sexism, Shabby, Shithead, Slimeball, Sneeze, Sniff, Snooty, Snot, Soldier, Sorry, Squirt, Squit, Supercilious, Toad, Toerag, Vilipend, Weed, Whipster, Wretched

Contend(er) Argue, Candidate, Claim, Clash, Compete, Cope, Debate, Dispute,

Fight, Grapple, Oppose, Stickle, > **STRIVE**, Struggle, Submit, > **VIE**, Wrestle

Content Apaid, Apay, Appay, Blissful, Happy, Inside, Please, Satisfy, Volume

▷ **Content** *may indicate* a hidden word

Contention, **Contentious** Argument, Bellicose, Cantankerous, Case, Combat, Competitive, Perverse, Polemical, Rivalry, Strife, Struggle, Sturt

Contest(ant) Agon, Battle, Beauty, Biathlon, Bout, Catchweight, Challenge, Championship, Combat, Competition, Concours, Darraign, Decathlon, Defend, Deraign, Dogfight, Duel(lo), Entrant, Eurovision, Event, Examinee, Free-for-all, Fronde, Handicap, Heptathlon, Kriegspiel, Lampadephoria, Match, Matchplay, Olympiad, Pancratium, Paralympics, Pentathlon, Pingle, Play-off, Prizer, Race, Rival, Roadeo, Rodeo, Set-to, Skirmish, Slam, Slugfest, Strife, Struggle, Tenson, Tetrathlon, Tournament, Triathlon, Vie, War, With

Context Opaque, Transparent

Continent(al) Abstinent, Asia, Atlantis, Austere, Chaste, Dark, Epeirogeny, Euro, European, Gallic, Gondwanaland, Laurasia, Lemuria, Mainland, Moderate, Pang(a)ea, Shelf, Teetotal, Temperate, Walloon

Contingency, **Contingent** Accident, Arm, Casual, Chance, Conditional, Dependent, Event, Fluke, Group, Prospect

Continual(ly), **Continuous** Adjoining, Away, Chronic, Connected, Eer, Endlong, Eternal, Ever, Frequent, Incessant, Non-stop, On(going)

Continue, **Continuation**, **Continuing**, **Continuity** Abye, Duration, Dure, During, Enduring, Enjamb(e)ment, Follow-on, Go on, Hold, Keep, Last, Link, Ongoing, Onward, Persevere, Persist, Proceed, Prolong, Remain, Resume, Sequence, Stand, Subsist, Survive, Sustain, Synaphe(i)a, Tenor

▷ **Continuously** *may indicate* previous words to be linked

Contort(ion) Deform, Gnarl, Jib, Twist, Warp, Wry

Contour Curve, Graph, Isallobar, Isobase, Isocheim, Isochime, Isogeothermal, Line, Profile, Silhouette, Streamline, Tournure

Contraband Hot, Illicit, Prohibited, Smuggled

Contraception, **Contraceptive** Cap, Coil, Condom, Diaphragm, Dutch cap, IU(C)D, Loop, Minipill, Oral, Pessary, Pill, Prophylactic, Rubber(s), Sheath, Vimule®

Contract(ion), **Contractor** Abbreviate, Abridge, Agreement, Appalto, Astringency, Bargain, Biceps, Bottomry, Braxton-Hicks, Bridge, Builder, Catch, Champerty, Charter, Clonus, Condense, Consensual, Constringe, Contrahent, Covenant, Cramp, Crasis, Curtail, Debt, Diastalsis, Dupuytren's, Dwindle, Engage, Entrepreneur, Escrow, Fitzgerald-Lorentz, Flex, Gainsay, Gooseflesh, Guarantee, Hand-promise, Hire, Incur, Indenture, Jerk, Ketubah, Knit, Lease, Levator, Lorentz-Fitzgerald, Make, Miosis, Myosis, Narrow, Obligee, Party, Peristalsis, Promise, Pucker, Purse, Restriction, Risus (sardonicus), Service, Shrink, Shrivel, Sign, Slam, Social, Spasm, Specialty, Steelbow, Stenosis, Stipulation, Supplier, Sweetheart, Syngraph, Systole, Tetanise, Tetanus, Tic, Tighten, Time bargain, Tonicity, Treaty, Triceps, Wrinkle, Yellow-dog, Z

Contradict(ion), **Contradictory** Ambivalent, Antilogy, Antinomy, Belie, Bull, Contrary, Counter, Dementi, Deny, Disaffirm, Disprove, Dissent, > **GAINSAY**, Negate, Oxymoron, Paradox, Sot, Stultify, Sublate, Threap, Threep, Traverse

Contrarily, **Contrary** Adverse, A rebours, Arsy-versy, But, Captious, Converse, Counter, Counterfleury, Crosscurrent, Cross-grained, Cross-purpose, Froward, Hostile, Inverse, Mary, Opposite, Ornery, Perverse, Rebuttal, Retrograde, Wayward, Withershins

Contrast Chiaroscuro, Clash, Colour, Compare, Differ, Foil, Relief

Contravene Infringe, Oppose, Thwart, Violate

Contribute, Contribution Abet, Add, Assist, Chip in, Conduce, Donate, Dub, Furnish, Go, Help, Input, Kick in, Mite, Offering, Share, Sub, Subscribe, Whack, Widow's mite

▷ **Contributing to** *may indicate* a hidden word

Contrite, Contrition Penance, Penitent, Remorse, Repentant, Rue, > SORRY

Contrivance, Contrive Art, Contraption, Deckle, Deus ex machina, Device, Dodge, Engine, Finesse, Gadget, Gin, Hokey, Invention, Page, Plot, Rest, Wangle

Contrive(r) Chicaner, Cook, Devise, Engineer, Frame, Hatch, Intrigue, Machinate, Manage, Manoeuvre, Plan, Procure, Scheme, Secure, Stage, Trump, Weave

Control(ler), Controllable Ada, Appestat, Big Brother, Birth, Boss, Bridle, Cabotage, Chair, Check, Christmas tree, Corner, Corset, Cybernetics, Descendeur, Dirigible, Dirigism(e), Dominate, Dominion, Dynamic, Etatiste, Fast-forward, Fet(ch), Finger, Flood, Fly-by-wire, Gain, Gar, Gerent, Govern, Ground, Gubernation, Harness, Have, Heck, Helm, Influence, Influx, Joystick, Knee-swell, Lead, Lever, > MANAGE, Martinet, Mastery, Moderate, Mouse, Nipple, Numerical, Operate, Override, Pilot, Placebo, Police, Population, Possess, Power, Preside, Price, Process, Puppeteer, Quality, Radio, Regulate, Regulo®, Rein, Remote, Rent, Repress, Restrain, Rheostat, Ride, Ripple, Rule, Run, School, Servo, Snail, Solion, Steady, Steer, Stop, Stranglehold, Stringent, Subdue, Subject, Subjugate, Supervise, Suzerain, Sway, Takeover, Thermostat, Throttle, Tiller, Tone, Valve, Weld, Wield, Zapper

Controversial, Controversy Argument, Contention, Debate, Dispute, Eristic(al), Furore, Hot potato, Polemic(al), Tendentious

Conundrum Acrostic, Egma, Enigma, Puzzle, Riddle, Teaser

Convalesce(nt), Convalescence Anastatic, Mend, Rally, Recover, Recuperate, Rest-cure

▶ **Convene** *see* CONVOKE

Convenience, Convenient Behoof, Commode, Eft, Expedient, Facility, Gain, Gents, > HANDY, Hend, Lav, Leisure, Near, Opportune, Pat, Privy, Public, Suitable, Toilet, Use, Well

Convent Cloister, Fratry, Friary, House, > MONASTERY, Motherhouse, Nunnery, Port-royal, Priory, Retreat

Convention(al) Academic, Accepted, Babbitt, Blackwood, Bourgeois, Caucus, Conclave, Conformity, > CUSTOMARY, Diet, Done, Formal, Geneva, Habitude, Iconic, Lingua franca, Meeting, Middlebrow, Middle-of-the-road, More, National, Nomic, Orthodox, Pompier, Proper, Schengen, Staid, Starchy, Stereotyped, Stock, Synod, Uptight, Usage, Warsaw

Converge Approach, Focus, Meet

Conversation(alist), Converse, Conversant Abreast, Antithesis, Board, Buck, Cackle, Causerie, Chat, Chitchat, Colloquy, Commune, Confab, Crosstalk, Deipnosophist, Dialogue, Discourse, Eutrapelia, Eutrapely, Hobnob, Interlocution, Jaw-jaw, Natter, Opposite, Palaver, Parley, Persiflage, Rap, Rhubarb, Shop, Socialise, > TALK, Transpose, Wongi, Word

Conversion, Converter, Convert(ible) Adapt, Alter, Assimilate, Azotobacter, Bessemer, Catalytic, Catechumen, Change, Commute, Cyanise, Diagenesis, Disciple, Encash, Etherify, Exchange, Expropriate, Fixation, Gummosis, Hodja, Kho(d)ja, L-D, Liquid, Marrano, Metanoia, Neophyte, Noviciate, Novitiate, Persuade, Prill, Proselyte, Put, Ragtop, Realise, Rebirth, Recycle, Revamp, Souper, Tablet, Taw, Torque, Transduce, Transform, Transmute, Try

▷ **Conversion, Converted** *may indicate* an anagram

Convex(ity) Arched, Bowed, Camber, Curved, Entasis, Extrados, Gibbous, Lenticle, Nowy

Convey(ance) Assign, BS, Carousel, Carriage, Carry, Charter, Coach, Conduct, Cycle, Deed, Eloi(g)n, Enfeoffment, Giggit, Grant, Guide, Lease, Litter, Lorry, Mailcar(t), Pneumatic, Re-lease, Sac and soc, Screw, Tip, Title deed, Tote, Tram, Transfer, Transit, Transmit, Transport, Vehicle

Convict(ion) Attaint, Belief, Bushranger, Certitude, Cockatoo, Cogence, Crawler, Credo, Creed, Criminal, Demon, Dogma, Faith, Felon, Forçat, Lag, Magwitch, Old chum, > **PERSUASION**, Plerophory, Ring, Trusty, Vehemence, Yardbird

Convince(d), Convincing Assure, Cogent, Doubtless, Luculent, Persuade, Satisfy, Sold, Sure

Convivial(ity) Boon, Bowl, Festive, Gay, Genial, Jovial, Social

Convoke Assemble, Call, Convene, Summon

Convolute(d), Convolution Coiled, Gyrus, Helical, Intricate, Spiral, Tortuous, Twisty, Whorl, Writhen

Convolvulus Bindweed, Dodder

Convoy Caravan, Column, Conduct, Escort, Pilot, Train, Wagon-train

Convulsion(s), Convulsive Agitate, Clonic, Commotion, Disturb, DT, Eclampsia, > **FIT**, Galvanic, Paroxysm, Spasm, Throe, Tic

Cook(s), Cooker, Cooking Aga®, Babbler, Bake, Balti, Beeton, Benghazi, Bhindi, Bouche, Braise, Broil, Cacciatore, Calabash, Captain, Charbroil, Chargrill, Chef, Coddle, Concoct, Cordon bleu, Cuisine, Deep-fry, Devil, Do, Doctor, Dumple, Edit, Escoffier, Fake, Falsify, Fiddle, Flambé, Forge, Fricassee, Fry, Fudge, Greasy, Grill, Haute cuisine, Haybox, Marinière, Meunière, Microwave, Nouvelle cuisine, Poach, Prepare, Pressure, Provencale, Ribroast, Rig, Ring, Roast, Roger, Sous-chef, Spit, Steam, Stew, Stir-fry, Tandoori, Tikka, Tire

▷ **Cook** *may indicate* an anagram

Cool(er), Cooling, Coolness Aloof, Aplomb, Calm, Can, Chill, Collected, Composed, Cryogen, Cryostat, Defervescence, Desert, Dispassionate, Distant, Esky®, Fan, Frappé, Fridge, Frigid, Frosty, Gaol, Goglet, Ice(box), Jail, Jug, Keel, La Nina, Phlegm, Prison, Quad, Quod, Reefer, Refresh, Regenerative, Reserved, Sangfroid, Serene, Skeigh, Stir, Temperate, Thou(sand), Trendy, Unruffled, Wint(e)ry

Coop Cage, Cavie, Confine, Gaol, Hutch, Mew, Pen, Rip

Cooper Gary, Henry, Tubman

Cooperate, Cooperation, Cooperative Collaborate, Combine, Conspire, Contribute, Coop, Give and take, Liaise, Play, Synergy, Teamwork, Together, Worker's

Coordinate(d), Coordination Abscissa, Abscisse, Agile, Arrange, Cartesian, Ensemble, Harmony, Nabla, Orchestrate, Ordonnance, Peer, Polar, Right ascension, Spherical, Synergy, Teamwork, X, Y, Z

Coot Stupid, Sultan

Cop(s) Bag, Bull, Catch, Dick, Keystone, Peeler, Peon, > **POLICEMAN**, Silent

Copal Dammar, Resin

Cope Chlamys, Deal, Face, Handle, Make do, > **MANAGE**, Mantle, Meet, Negotiate, Pallium, Poncho

Coping (stone) Balustrade, Capstone, Skew

Copious Abundant, Affluent, Ample, Fecund, Fluent, Fruitful, Fulsome, Plentiful, Profuse

Copper As, Atacamite, Blister, Bluebottle, Bobby, Bornite, Busy, Cash, Cent, Chessylite, > **COIN**, Cu, D, Dam, Double, Erinite, Flatfoot, Lawman, Lota(h),

Malachite, Mountain-blue, Ormolu, Peacock, Pence, Penny, Pfennig, Pie, Pig, Plack, Policeman, Red, Rosser, Rozzer, S, Sen(s), Slop, Special, Traybit, Venus, Verdet, Washer, Washtub, Wire bar

Copse Thicket

Copulate Intercourse, Line, Mate, Roger, Tup

Copy(ing), Copier, Copyist Aemule, Ape, Apograph, Autotype, Calk, Calque, Camera-ready, Carbon, Clerk, Clone, Counterpart, Crib, Cyclostyle, Diazo, Ditto, Download, Dyeline, Echo, Echopraxia, Ectype, Edition, Eidograph, Electro, Emulate, Engross, Estreat, Example, Facsimile, Fair, Fax, Flimsy, Forge, Hard, Hectograph, > IMITATE, Issue, Jellygraph, Knocking, Manifold, Manuscript, Match, Me-tooer, Milline, Mimeograph®, Mimic, Mirror, MS, Offprint, Parrot, Photostat®, Plagiarism, Polygraph, Read-out, Replica, Repro, Reproduce, Review, Roneo®, Scribe, Script, Scrivener, Sedulous, Show, Simulate, Spit, Stencil, Stuff, Telautograph®, Tenor, Tenure, Trace, Transcribe, Transume, Vidimus, Xerox®

Copyright C

Coquette Agacerie, Flirt, Rosina, Tease, Vamp

Cor Bath, Crumbs, Ephah, Homer

Coracle Currach, Curragh

Coral (reef) Alcyonaria, Aldabra, Atoll, Brain, Cup, Deadman's fingers, Gorgonia(n), Laccadives, Madrepore, Millepore, Pink, Precious, Red, Reef, Sea fan, Sea ginger, Sea-pen, Sea whip, Seed, Stony, Zoothome

Cord, Cord-like Aiguillette, Band, Bedford, Bind, Boondoggle, Cat-gut, Chenille, Communication, Creance, Drawstring, Flex, Fourragère, Funicle, Gasket, Heddle, Lace, Laniard, Lanyard, Ligature, Line, Moreen, Myelon, Net, Ocnus, Piping, Quipo, Quipu, Rep(s), Restiform, Rip, Rope, Sash, Sennit, Service, Shroudline, Spermatic, Spinal, > STRING, Tendon, Tie, Torsade, Twine, Umbilical, Vocal, Wick

Cordial Anise(ed), Anisette, Benedictine, Cassis, Drink, Gracious, Grenadine, Hearty, Hippocras, Kind, Neighbourly, Oporice, Orangeade, Persico(t), Pleasant, Ratafia, Rosa-solis, Roso(g)lio, Shrub, Tar-water, Warm

Cordon Picket, Ring, Sanitaire, Surround

Corduroy Rep(p)

Cordyline Ti-tree

Core Barysphere, Calandria, Campana, Centre, Chog, Essence, Filament, Hard, Heart, Hub, Kernel, Nife, Nitty-gritty, Plerome, Quintessence, Slug

Co-religionist Brother

Coriander Cilantro

Corinthian(s) Casuals, Caulis, Epistolaters

Cork(ed), Corker Balsa, Bouché, Bung, Float(er), Humdinger, Mountain, Oner, Phellem, Phellogen, Plug, Seal, Shive, Stopper, Suber(ate)

Corkscrew Bore, Opening, Spiral

Cormorant Duiker, Duyker, Scart(h), Skart(h)

Corn(y) Bajr(a), Banal, Blé, Cereal, Cob, Emmer, Epha, Flint, Gait, Graddan, Grain, Green, Grist, Guinea, Icker, Indian, Kaffir, Mabela, Maize, Mealie, Muid, Negro, Nubbin, Pickle, Pinole, Posho, Rabi, Rye, Seed, Shock, Stitch, Straw, Sugar, Sweet, Thrave, Trite, Zea

Corncrake Landrail

Cornel Dogberry, Tree

Corner Amen, Angle, Bend, Cantle, Canton, Cranny, Dangerous, Diêdre, Elbow, Entrap, Hole, Hospital, Lug, Monopoly, NE, Niche, Nook, NW, Penalty, Predicament, Quoin, SE, Short, Speakers', Spot, SW, Tack, Tight, Trap, Tree,

Vertex
Cornerstone Coi(g)n, Encoignure, Skew-corbel, Skew-put, Skew-table
Cornet Cone, Cornopean, Field, Horn
Cornice Surbase
Cornish(man) Cousin Jack
Cornstalks Strammel, Straw, Strummel, Stubble
Cornucopia Amalthea, Horn
Cornwall SW
Corollary Conclusion, Dogma, Porism, Rider, Theory, Truism
Corona Aureole, Cigar, Larmier, Nimbus, Wreath
Coroner Procurator fiscal
Corporal Bardolph, Bodily, Bombardier, Brig(adier), Lance-pesade,
    Lance-prisade, Lance-prisado, Lance-speisade, Naik, NCO, Nym, Pall, Physical,
    Trim
Corporation Belly, Body, Close, Commune, Company, Conglomerate, Guild,
    Kite, Kyte, Paunch, Public, Stomach, Swag-belly, Tum, Wame, Wem
Corps Body, C, Crew, Diplomatic, Peace, RAC, REME, Unit
Corpse Blob, Body, Cadaver, Carcass, Carrion, Goner, Like, Mort, Relic, Remains,
    Stiff, Zombi(e)
Corpulence, Corpulent Adipose, Fat, Gross, Obese, Stout, Tubby
Corpuscle Cell, Erythrocyte, Malpighian, Meissner's, Microcyte, Neutrophil,
    Pacinian, Phagocyte
Correct(ing), Correctly, Correctness, Correction, Corrector Accurate,
    Alexander, Align, Amend, Aright, Blue-pencil, Bodkin, Castigate, Chasten,
    Chastise, Check, Decorous, Diorthortic, Emend, Exact, Fair, Grammatical,
    Legit, Mend, Politically, Preterition, Probity, Proofread, Proper, Propriety,
    Punctilious, Punish, Purism, Rebuke, Rectify, Rectitude, Redress, Remedial,
    Reprove, Revise, Right(en), Scold, Spot-on, Sumpsimus, Trew, True, U
▷ **Corrected** *may indicate* an anagram
Correspond(ence), Correspondent, Corresponding Accord, Agree, Analogy,
    Assonance, Coincident, Communicate, Congruence, Counterpart, Equate,
    Equivalence, Eye-rhyme, Fit, Foreign, Hate mail, Homolog(ue), Identical,
    Match, On all fours, One to one, Par, Parallel, Relate, Snail mail, Symmetry,
    Tally, Veridical, War, Write
Corridor Air, Aisle, Berlin, Entry, Gallery, Lobby, Passage, Polish, Re-entry
Corroborate Confirm, Support, Verify
Corrode(d), Corrosion, Corrosive Acid, Brinelling, Burn, Canker, Decay, Eat,
    Erode, Etch, Fret, Gnaw, Hydrazine, Mordant, > **ROT**, Rubiginous, Rust, Waste
Corrugate Gimp
Corrupt(er), Corrupting, Corruption Abuse, Adulterate, Bastardise, Bent, Bobol,
    Bribable, Canker, Debase, Debauch, Debosh, Decadent, Defile, Degenerate,
    Depravity, Dissolute, Dry rot, Emancipate, Embrace(o)r, Embrasor, Empoison,
    Etch, Fester, Gangrene, Graft(er), Immoral, Impure, Inquinate, Jobbery,
    Leprosy, Malversation, Nefarious, Obelus, Payola, Perverse, Poison, Pollute,
    Power, Putrid, Ret(t), Rigged, Rot, Scrofulous, Seduce, Sepsis, Septic, Sleaze,
    Sodom, Sophisticate, Spoil, Suborn, Tammany, Twist, Venal, Vice, Vitiate
Corsage Buttonhole, Pompadour, Posy, Spray
Corsair Barbary, Picaroon, Pirate, Privateer, Robber, Rover
Corset, Corslet Belt, Bodice, Busk, Girdle, Lorica, Roll-on, Stays, Thorax, Waspie
Corsican Napoleon
Cortege Parade, Retinue, Train
Cortex Cerebral, Renal

Cortisone Hecogenin
Corundum Emery, Sapphire
Corvo Rolfe
Corybant Roisterer
Cosh Sap
Cosmetic Beautifier, Blusher, Bronzer, Eye-black, Eyeliner, Eye-shadow, Face-pack, Foundation, Fucus, Highlighter, Kohl, Liner, Lip gloss, Lip liner, Lipstick, Lotion, Maquillage, Mascara, Mousse, Mudpack, Paint, Pearl-powder, Powder, Reface, Rouge, Talcum, Toner
▸ **Cosmic** *see* **COSMOS**
Cosmonaut Gagarin, Spaceman, Tereshkova
Cosmopolitan International, Urban
Cosmos, Cosmic Globe, Heaven, Infinite, Nature, Universe, World
Cossack Ataman, Hetman, Mazeppa, Russian, Tartar, Zaporogian
Cosset Caress, Coddle, Fondle, Pamper
Cost(s), Costly Bomb, Carriage, Charge, Damage, Direct, Earth, Escuage, Estimate, Exes, > **EXPENSE**, Factor, Fixed, Hire, Indirect, Loss, Marginal, Opportunity, Outlay, Overhead, Precious, Price, Prime, Quotation, Rate, Sacrifice, Sumptuous, Toll, Unit, Upkeep, Usurious, Variable
Costa Rica(n) Tico
Costermonger Barrow-boy, Kerb-merchant, Pearly
Costume Apparel, Attire, Camagnole, Cossie, Dress, Ensemble, Get-up, Gi(e), Guise, Judogi, Livery, Maillot, Motley, Nebris, Polonaise, Rig, Surcoat, Tanga, Togs, Uniform, Wear
Cosy Cosh, Intime, Snug
Cot Moses basket
Coterie Cell, Cenacle, Circle, Clan, Clique, Club, Ring, Set, Society
Cottage(r) Bach, Bordar, Bothie, Bothy, Box, Bungalow, Cabin, Chalet, Cot, Crib, Dacha, Home-croft, Hut, Lodge, Mailer
Cotton Agree, AL, Alabama, Balbriggan, Batiste, Batting, Bengal, Calico, Candlewick, Ceiba, Chambray, Chino, Chintz, Collodion, Coutil(le), Cretonne, Denim, Dho(o)ti, Dimity, Ducks, Fustian, Galatea, Gossypine, Gossypium, Humhum, Ihram, Jaconet, Lavender, Lawn, Lea, Lille, Lint, Lisle, Manchester, Marcella, Muslin, Nainsook, Nankeen, Nankin, Osnaburg, Pongee, Sea-island, Seersucker, Silesia, Stranded, Surat, T-cloth, Thread, Twig, Upland
Cotton soil Regar, Regur
Cotyledon Seed-leaf
Couch Bed, Casting, Davenport, Daybed, > **DIVAN**, Express, Grass, Lurk, Palanquin, Palkee, Palki, Quick, Recamier, Sedan, Settee, Sofa, Studio, Triclinium, Winnipeg, Word
Coué Auto-suggestion
Cougar Cat, Painter
Cough(ing) Bark, Croup, Expectorate, Hack, Hawk, Hem, Hoast, Hooping, Kink, Pertussis, Phthisis, Rale, Tisick, Tussis, Ugh, Whooping
Could Couth
Council (meeting), Councillor, Counsel(lor) Achitophel, Admonish, Admonitor, Advice, Advocate, Ahithophel, Alfred, Amphictryon, Anziani, Aread, A(r)re(e)de, Assembly, Attorney, Aulic, Aunt, Ayuntamiento, Board, Body, Boule, Bundesrat, Burgess, Cabinet, Casemate, Committee, Consistory, Corporation, County, Cr, Decurion, Dergue, Devil, Dietine, Divan, Douma, Duma, Ecumenical, Egeria, European, Executive, Exhort, Great, Greenbag, Hebdomadal, Indaba, Induna, Industrial, Info, Islands, Jirga, Junta, Kabele,

Kebele, King's, Kite, Landst(h)ing, Lateran, Leader, Legislative, Loan, Majlis, Mentor, Nestor, Nicaean, Nicene, Panchayat, Paraclete, Parish, Powwow, Press, Privy, Provincial, Queen's, Rede, Regional, Reichsrat, Robber, Samaritan, Sanhedrim, Sanhedrin, Security, Senate, Shoora, Shura, Sobranje, Sobranye, Soviet, Syndicate, Synedrion, Synod, Thing, Town, Trades, Trent, Tridentine, Trullan, Vatican, Volost, Wages, Whitley, Witan, Witenagemot, Works, Zemstvo, Zila, Zillah

Count(ed), **Counter**, **Counting** Abacus, Add, Algoriam, Anti, Bar, Basie, Blood, Buck, Buffet, Calculate, Cavour, Census, Chip, Compute, Coost, Desk, Dracula, Dump, Earl, Enumerate, Fish, Geiger, Geiger-Muller, Graf(in), Grave, Itemise, Jet(t)on, Landgrave, Margrave, Marker, Matter, Merel(l), Meril, Milton Work, Nobleman, Number, Obviate, Olivia, Oppose, Palatine, Palsgrave, Paris, Pollen, Presume, Proportional, Rebut, > **RECKON**, Refute, Rejoinder, Rely, Retaliate, Retort, Rhinegrave, Scintillation, Score, Sperm, Squail, Statistician, Stop, Sum, Table, Tally, Tell, Tiddleywink, Ugolino, Weigh, Zeppelin

Countenance Approve, Brow, Endorse, Face, Favour, Mug, Sanction, Support, Visage

Counteract(ing) Ant-, Antidote, Cancel, Correct, Frustrate, Offset, Talion

Counterbalance Bascule, Offset, Undo, Weigh

Counter-charge Recrimination

Counterclockwise L(a)evorotatory

Counterfeit(er) Belie, Bogus, Boodle, Brum, Coiner, Duffer, Dummy, Fantasm, Flash, Forge, Imitant, Phantasm, Phoney, Pinchbeck, Postiche, Pseudo, Queer, Rap, Schlenter, Sham, Shan(d), Simulate, Slang, Slip, Smasher, Snide, Spurious, Stumer

Counterfoil Stub

Counterglow Gegenschein

Counter-irritant Seton

Countermand Abrogate, Annul, Cancel, Override, Rescind, Retract, Revoke

Counterpart Copy, Double, Obverse, Oppo, Parallel, Shadow, Similar, Spit(ting), Tally, Twin

Counterpoint Contrapuntal, Descant

Countersign Endorse, Password

Counterthrust Riposte

Counties, **County** Antrim, Armagh, Avon, Barset, Beds, Berkshire, Buteshire, Carlow, Cavan, Ceredigion, Champagne, Clare, Cleveland, Co, Comital, Cork, Cornwall, District, Donegal, Dorset, Down, Dublin, Durham, Dyfed, Fermanagh, Fife, Flint, Gwent, Gwynedd, Hampshire, Herefordshire, Herts, Hunts, Kent, Kerry, Kesteven, Kildare, Kilkenny, Kincardineshire, Kinrossshire, Kirkcudbrightshire, Lanarkshire, Laois, Leicestershire, Leitrim, Limerick, Lincolnshire, Loamshire, Londonderry, Longford, Louth, Mayo, Meath, Merionithshire, Merseyside, Metropolitan, Midlothian, Monaghan, Monmouthshire, Montgomeryshire, Moray, Nairnshire, Neath Port Talbot, NI, Norfolk, Northamptonshire, Northumberland, North Yorkshire, Notts, Offaly, Omagh, Oxfordshire, Palatine, Parish, Peeblesshire, Pembrokeshire, Perth(shire), Powys, Radnorshire, Renfrewshire, Roscommon, Ross, Ross and Cromarty, Rutland, Seat, Selkirkshire, Shire, Shropshire, Six, Som(erset), South Glamorgan, Staffordshire, Stirlingshire, Suffolk, Surrey, Sussex, Sutherland, Sy, The Mearns, Tipperary, Torfaen, Tyne and Wear, Tyrone, Vale of Glamorgan, Warwickshire, Waterford, West Glamorgan, West Lothian, Westmeath, West Midlands, Westmoreland, West Sussex, West Yorkshire, Wexford, Wicklow, Wigtownshire, Wilts, Worcs, Yorkshire

Countless Infinite, Innumerable, Myriad, Umpteen, Untold
Country(side), Countrified Annam, Bangladesh, Boondocks, Bucolic,
  Champaign, Clime, Colchis, Edom, Enchorial, Fatherland, Greenwood, High,
  Karoo, Karroo, > LAND, Lea, Lee, Low, Mongolia, Motherland, Nation, Parish,
  Paysage, People, Province, Realm, Region, Republic, Rural, Satellite, Scenery,
  Soil, State, Sultanate, Thrace, Tundra, Tweedy, Weald, Wold, Yemen
Country girl Amaryllis
Country house Hall, Manor, Quinta
Countryman Arcadian, Bacon, Boor, Culchie, Hick, Hillbilly, Hodge, National,
  Native, Peasant, Un, Yokel
Coup Blow, Deal, KO, Move, Putsch, Scoop, Stroke
Coupé Cabriolet, Landaulet
Couple(r), Coupling Ally, Band, Brace, Bracket, Connect, Direct, Duet, Duo,
  Dyad, Fishplate, Flange, Galvanic, Gemini, Geminy, Hitch, Item, > JOIN,
  Marrow, Marry, Mate, Meng(e), Ment, Ming, Octave, Pair, Pr, Relate, Shackle,
  Tie, Tirasse, Turnbuckle, Tway, Union, Universal, Voltaic, Wed, Yoke
Couple of ducks Spectacles
Couplet Distich, Heroic
Coupon(s) Ration, Ticket, Voucher
Courage(ous) Balls, Bottle, Bravado, Bravery, Bulldog, Cojones, Dutch,
  Fortitude, Gallantry, Game, Gimp, Grit, Gumption, Guts, Hardihood, Heart,
  Heroism, Lion-heart, Macho, Mettle, Moxie, Nerve, Pluck, Prowess, Rum,
  Spirit, Spunk, Stalwart, Steel, Valiant, Valour, Wight
Courgette Zucchini
Courier Estafette, Guide, Harbinger, Herald, > MESSENGER, Postillion, Postman
Course(s) Access, Afters, Aim, Aintree, Antipasto, Appetiser, Arroyo, Ascot,
  Assault, Atlantic, Barge, Bearing, Beat, Belt, Canal, Career, Chantilly, Chase,
  Circuit, Collision, Consommé, Correspondence, Crash, Current, Curriculum,
  Cursus, Daltonism, Dessert, Diadrom, Dish, Dromic, Entrée, Epsom, Fish,
  Food, Foundation, Going, Golf, Goodwood, Greats, Heat, Isodomon, Lane,
  Lap, Layer, Leat, Leet, Line, Lingfield, Links, Longchamp, Magnetic, Main,
  Meal, Meat, Mess, Newbury, Newmarket, Nine-hole, Nulla, > OF COURSE,
  Orbit, Period, Policy, PPE, Procedure, Process, Programme, Progress, Pursue,
  Quadrivium, Race, Raik, Refresher, Regimen, Rhumb, Ride, Ring, Rink, Road,
  Rota, Route, Routine, Run, Rut, Sandown, Sandwich, Semester, Seminar,
  Series, Sorbet, Soup, Stadium, Starter, Stearage, Steerage, Step(s), Stratum,
  Streak, Stretch, Stretching, String, Syllabus, Tack, Tanride, Tenor, Track, Trade,
  Trend, Troon, Vector, Via media, Water table, Way, Wearing, Wentworth
Court(ier) Address, Admiralty, Appellate, Arches, Areopagus, Atrium,
  Attention, Audience, Audiencia, Aula, Banc, Bar, Basecourt, Bench, Beth Din,
  Bishop's, Boondock, Camelot, Caravanserai, Cassation, Centre, Chancery,
  Chase, Clay, Consistory, County, Criminal, Crown, CS, Ct, Curia, Curia Regis,
  Curtilage, Cutcher(r)y, Date, Dedans, Dicastery, Diplock, District, Doctor's
  Commons, Domestic, Duchy, Durbar, Dusty Feet, En tout cas, Evora, Eyre,
  Federal, Fehm(gericht), Fehmgerichte, Forensic, Forest, Forum, Friars,
  Fronton, Galleria, Garth, Go steady, Grass, Guildenstern, Halimot(e),
  Hampton, Hard, High, Hof, Holy See, Hustings, Hypaethron, Inferior,
  Intermediate, Invite, Jack, Justice, Juvenile, Kachahri, Kacheri, Kangaroo,
  Keys, King, King's Bench, Kirk Session, Knave, Law, Leet, Lobby, Lyon,
  Magistrate's, Majlis, Marshalsea, Mash, Moot, Old Bailey, Open, Parvis, Patio,
  Peristyle, Petty Sessions, Philander, Piepowder, Police, Porte, Praetorium,
  Presbytery, Prize, Probate, Provincial, Provost, Quad, Quarter Sessions, Queen,

Queen's Bench, Retinue, Rosenkrantz, Royal, Sanhedrim, Sanhedrin, See, Service, Session, Sheriff, Shire-moot, Spoon, Stannary, Star Chamber, Sue, Superior, Supreme, Swanimote, Sweetheart, Thane, Thegn, Traffic, Trial, Tribunal, Vehm, Vehmgericht(e), Vestibulum, Walk out, Ward, Wench, Woo, World, Wow, Yard, Youth

Courteous, Courtesy Affable, Agrement, Bow, Chivalry, Civil, Comity, Devoir, Etiquette, Genteel, Gracious, Hend, Polite, Refined, Urbanity

Courtesan Aspasia, Bona-roba, Delilah, Demi-monde, Demi-rep, Geisha, Hetaera, Lais, Lampadion, Lorette, Madam, Phryne, Plover, Pornocracy, Prostitute, Stallion, Thais

Courtly Chivalrous, Cringing, Dignified, Flattering, Refined

Court-martial Drumhead

Courtyard Area, Cortile, Enceinte, Garth, Marae, Patio, Quad

Cousin(s) Bette, Cater, Country, Coz, Cross, German, Kin, Kissing, Robin, Skater

Couturier Dior, Dressmaker

Cove Abraham's, Arm, Bay, Bight, Buffer, Creek, Cure, Gink, Grot, Guy, Hithe, Hythe, Inlet, Lulworth, Nook

Covenant(er) Abrahamic, Alliance, Appurtenant, Bond, Contract, Hillmen, Pledge, Restrictive, Warranty, Whiggamore

Coventry Isolation

Cover(ed), Covering Adventitia, A l'abri, Amnion, Antependium, Antimacassar, Apron, Aril, Attire, Awning, Barb, Bard(s), Bark, Bedspread, Bestrew, Bind, Blanket, Bodice, Brood, Bubblewrap, Bury, Camouflage, Canopy, Cap, Caparison, Cape, Capsule, Casing, Casque, Catch-all, Caul, Ceil, Ciborium, Cladding, Clapboard, Cleithral, Clithral, Coat, Cocoon, Coleorhiza, Conceal, Cope, Copyright, Cosy, Counterpane, Cour, Covert, Cowl, Curtain, Deadlight, Deck, Deputise, Dividend, Dome, Drape(t), Dripstone, Duchesse, Dust-sheet, Duvet, Eiderdown, Encase, Endue, Enguard, Enlace, Enshroud, Envelop(e), Enwrap, Exoderm(is), Exoskeleton, Extra, Face, Falx, Fanfare, Felting, Fielder, Figleaf, Fingerstall, First-day, Flashing, Fother, Front, Gaiter, Gambado, Grolier, Ground, Hap, Harl, Hat, Hatch, Havelock, Heal, Heel, Hejab, Hele, Hell, Helmet, Hijab, Hood, Housing, Hubcap, Immerse, Incase, Indusium, Inmask, Insulate, Insurance, Insure, Jacket, Lag, Lay, Leap, Leep, Legging, Legwarmer, Lid, Liner, Loose, Manche, Mantle, Mask, Metal, Mount, Muffle, Mulch, Notum, Numnah, Obscure, OC, Occlude, On, Operculum, Orillion, Orlop, Overlay, Palampore, Palempore, Pall, Pand, Parcel, Pasties, Patch, Pebbledash, Pelmet, Periderm, Pillow sham, Plaster, Plate, Pleura, Point, Pseudonym, Pullover, Quilt, Radome, Regolith, Robe, Roof, Roughcast, Rug, Sally, Screen, Serviette, Setting, Sheath, Sheet, Shell, Shelter, Shield, Shrink-wrap, Shroud, Shuck, Skin, Smokescreen, Solleret, Span, Spat, Stand-by, Stifle, Swathe, Tampian, Tampion, Tapadera, Tapis, Tarpaulin, Teacosy, Tectorial, Tegmen, Tegument, Tent, Test(a), Tester, Thatch, Thimble, Thumbstall, Tick(ing), Tile, Tilt, Tonneau, Top, Trapper, Trench, Trip, Turtleback, Twill, Twilt, Umbrella, Upholster, Valance, Veil, Vele, Veneer, Ventail, Vesperal, Vest, Visor, Volva, Wainscot, Waterdeck, Whelm, Whitewash, Wrap, Wrapper, Yapp

Covert(ly) Clandestine, Copse, Privy, > SECRET, Shy, Sidelong, Sub rosa, Surreptitious, Tectrix, Ulterior

Covet(ed), Covetous Avaricious, Crave, Desiderata, Desire, Eager, Envy, Greedy, Hanker, Yearn

Cow Adaw, Alderney, Amate, Appal, Awe, Ayrshire, Bovine, Brahmin, Browbeat, Cash, Charolais, Colly, Crummy, Danton, Daunt, Dexter, Dsomo, Dun, Galloway, Gally, Goujal, Guernsey, Hawkey, Hawkie, Heifer, Hereford,

Intimidate, Jersey, Kouprey, Kyloe, Mart, Milch, Mog(gie), Moggy, Mooly, Muley, Mulley, Overawe, Redpoll, Red Sindhi, Rother(-beast), Sacred, Santa Gertrudis, Scare, Simmental, Springing, Stirk, Subact, Teeswater, Threaten, Unnerve, Vaccine, Zebu, Z(h)o

Coward(ly) Bessus, Cat, Chicken, Cocoa, Craven, Cuthbert, Dastard, Dingo, Dunghill, Fraidy-cat, Fugie, Funk, Gutless, Hen, Hilding, Jessie, Lily-livered, Meacock, Milk-livered, Niddering, Nidderling, Nidering, Niderling, Niding, Nithing, Noel, Panty-waist, Poltroon, Pusillanimous, Recreant, Scaramouch, Sganarelle, Slag, Sook, Squib, Viliaco, Viliago, Villagio, Villiago, Yellow, Yellow-belly

Cowboy, Cowgirl Broncobuster, Buckaroo, Cowpoke, Cowpuncher, Gaucho, Inexpert, Io, Jerrybuilder, Leger, Llanero, Puncher, Ranchero, Ritter, Roper, Vaquero, Waddie, Waddy, Wrangler

Cow-catcher Fender, Reata

Cower Croodle, Crouch, Fawn, Quail, Skulk, Wince

Cowl Bonnet, Capuchin, Granny, Hood, Kilmarnock

Cowpox Vaccinia

Cowshed, Cowstall Byre, Crib, Shippen, Shippon, Stable, Stall, Staw

Cowslip Culver-key, Pa(i)gle

Cox Steerer

Coxcomb Copple, Crest, Dandy, Dude, Fop, Jackanapes, Popinjay, Yellow-rattle

Coy Arch, Coquettish, Demure, Laithfu', Mim, Shamefast, > SHY, Skeigh, Skittish

Coyote SD

CPRS Think tank

Crab(by), Crablike Apple, Attercop, Blue swimmer, Calling, Cancer, Cancroid, Cantankerous, Capernoity, Cock, Coconut, Daddy, Decapoda, Diogenes, Ethercap, Ettercap, Fiddler, Ghost, Grouch, Hard-shell, Hermit, Horseman, Horseshoe, King, Land, Limulus, Mantis, Mitten, Mud, Nebula, Ochidore, Oyster, Pagurian, Partan, Pea, Perveroe, Podite, Roast, Robber, Rock, Sand, Saucepan-fish, Scrawl, Sentinel, Sidle, Soft-shell, Soldier, Spectre, Spider, Velvet, Woolly-hand, Xiphosura, Zoea

▷ **Crab** *may indicate* an anagram

Crab-apple Scrog-bush, Scrog-buss

Crab-eater Urva

Crabs-eye Abrus

Crack(ed), Cracker(s), Cracking Ad-lib, Admirable, Bananas, Biscuit, Bonbon, Break, Cat, Catalytic, Chap, Chasm, Chat, Chink, Chip, Chop, Clap, Cleave, Cleft, Cloff, Confab, Cranny, Craquelure, Craqueture, Craze, Cream, Crepitate, Crevasse, Crevice, Crispbread, Dawn, Decode, Doom, Dunt, Elite, Expert, Fatiscent, Fent, Firework, First-rate, Fisgig, Fissure, Fizgig, Flaw, Flip-flop, Fracture, Go, Graham, Grike, Gryke, Gully, Hairline, Hit, Jibe, Joint, Knacker, Leak, Liar, Little-endian, Matzo, Moulin, Oner, Peterman, Pore, Praise, Prawn, Quarter, Quip, Rap, Report, Rhagades, Rictus, Rift, Rille, Rima, Rime, Rimous, Rive, Rock, Saltine, Sand, Seam, Shake, Snap, Soda, Solve, Split, Squib, Sulcus, Toe, Top, Try, Waterloo, Yegg

Crackerjack Ace, Nailer, Trump

Crackle, Crackling Craze, Crepitation, Crepitus, Crinkle, Decrepitate, Fizz, Glaze, Rale, Skin

Crackpot Nutter

Cracksman Burglar, Peterman, Raffles

Cradle Bassinet, Berceau, Cat's, Cot, Crib, Cunabula, Hammock, Knife, Nestle,

Newton's, Rocker

Craft(y) Arch, Art, Aviette, Barbola, Boat, Canal boat, Cautel, Cunning, Disingenuous, Finesse, Fly, Guile, Hydroplane, Ice-breaker, Insidious, Kontiki, Landing, Machiavellian, Mister, Mystery, Oomiack, Reynard, Saic, Shallop, Ship, Shuttle, > SKILL, Slee, Sleeveen, Slim, Slippy, Sly, Slyboots, State, Subdolous, Subtil(e), Subtle, Suttle, Triphibian, Umiak, Underhand, Versute, > VESSEL, Wile, Workmanship

▷ **Craft** *may indicate* an anagram

Craftsman AB, Artificer, Artisan, Artist, Chippy, Cutler, Ebonist, Fabergé, Finisher, Gondolier, Guild, Hand, Joiner, Journeyman, Mason, Mechanic, Morris, Opificer, Wainwright, Wright

Crag(gy) Eyrie, Height, Heuch, Heugh, Krantz, Noup, Rock

Cram(mer) Bag, Candle-waster, Cluster, Craig, Fill, Gag, Gavage, Neck, Pang, Prime, Rugged, Scar(p), Shoehorn, Spur, Stap, Stodge, Stow, Swat, Tuck

Cramp(ed) Agraffe, Charleyhorse, Confine, Constrict, Crick, Hamper, Hamstring, Incommodious, Myalgia, Pinch, Poky, Potbound, Restrict, Rigor, Squeeze, Stunt, Tetany, Writer's

Crane Brolga, Cherry picker, Davit, Deck, Demoiselle, Derrick, Dragline, Gantry, Gooseneck, Grabbing, Herd, Heron, Hooper, Ichabod, Jib, Jigger, Kenworthy, Luffing-jib, Rail, Sarus, Sedge, Shears, Sheer, Siege, Stork, Stretch, Tower, Tulip, Whooper, Whooping, Winch

Crane-fly Leatherjacket, Tipulidae

Crank(y) Eccentric, Grouch, Handle, Lever, Mot, Perverse, Whim, Wince, Winch, Wind

Crash Bingle, Collapse, Disk, Dush, Fail, Fall, Fragor, Intrude, Linen, Nosedive, Pile up, Prang, Rack, Ram, Rote, Shunt, Slam, Smash, Thunderclap, Topple

▷ **Crashes** *may indicate* an anagram

Crass Coarse, Crude, Rough, Rude

Crate Biplane, Box, Case, Ceroon, Crib, Hamper, Sero(o)n, Soapbox, Tube

Crater Alphonsus, Aristarchus, Aristotle, Askja, Autolycus, Bail(l)y, Blowhole, Caldera, Cavity, Cissing, Clavius, Copernicus, Fra Mauro, Grimaldo, Hipparchus, Hole, Hollow, Kepler, Kilauea, Maar, Meteor, Newton, Plato, Ptolemaeus, Pythagoras, Schickard, Sinus iridium, Theophilus, Tycho

Cravat Ascot, Neckatee, Neck-cloth, Oerlay, Overlay, Scarf, Soubise, Steenkirk, Tie

Crave, Craving Appetite, Aspire, Beg, Beseech, Covet, Desire, Entreat, Gasp, Greed, Hanker, Hunger, Itch, Libido, Long, Lust, Malacia, Methomania, Munchies, Opsomania, Orexis, Pica, Polyphagia, Sitomania, The munchies, Thirst, Yearn, Yen

Craven Abject, Coward, Dastard, Hen, Recreant

Crawl(er) All fours, Clamber, Creep, Cringe, Drag, Grovel, Lag, Lickspittle, Pub, Reptile, Scramble, Scrome, Skulk, Snail, Swim, Sycophant, Tantony, Trail, Trudgen, Yes-man

Crayfish Astacology, Gilgie, Jilgie, Yabbie, Yabby

Crayon Chalk, Colour, Conté®, Pastel, Pencil, Sauce

Craze(d), Crazy Absurd, Ape, Barmy, Bats, Batty, Berserk, Bonkers, Break, Cornflake, Crack(ers), Crackpot, Cult, Daffy, Dement, Derange, Dingbats, Dippy, Distraught, Doiled, Doilt, Doolally, Dottle, Dotty, Fad, Flake, Flaw, Folie, Frantic, Furious, Furore, Gaga, Geld, Gonzo, Gyte, Haywire, Headbanger, Insane, Loco, Loony, Lunatic, Madden, Maenad(ic), Mania, Manic, Mattoid, Melomania, Meshug(g)a, Nuts, Porangi, Potty, Psycho(path), Rage, Rave, Scatty, Screwball, Skivie, Slatey, Stunt, Unhinge, Wacko, Wacky, Wet,

W(h)acky, Whim, Wowf, Zany
▷ **Crazy** *may indicate* an anagram
Creak(y) Cry, Grate, Grind, Rheumatic, Scraich, Scraigh, Scroop, Seam, Squeak
Cream(y) Barrier, Bavarian, Best, Chantilly, Clotted, Cold, Cornish, Crème
fraiche, Devonshire, Double, Elite, Foundation, Glacier, Ivory, Jollop, Lanolin,
Liniment, Lotion, Mousse, Off-white, Ointment, Opal, Paragon, Pick,
Ream, Rich, Salad, Salve, Sillabub, Single, Skim, Smitane, Sour, Sun(screen),
Syllabub, Vanishing, Whipped, Whipping
Crease Crumple, > FOLD, Lirk, Pitch, Pleat, Popping, Return, Ridge, Ruck(le),
Ruga, Rugose, Wrinkle
Create, Creation, Creative Arty, Build, Coin, Compose, Continuous, Devise,
Dreamtime, Engender, Establish, Fabricate, Forgetive, Form, Found, Generate,
Genesis, Godhead, Ideate, Imaginative, > INVENT, Oratorio, Originate, Produce,
Shape, Universe
Creator Ahura Mazda, Author, Demiurge, God, Inventor, Maker, Ormazd,
Ormuzd
Creature Animal, Ankole, Basilisk, Beast, Being, Chevrotain, Cratur, Critter,
Crittur, Man, Nekton, Saprobe, Sasquatch, Sphinx, Whiskey, Wight
Credence, Credential(s) Certificate, Document, Papers, Qualifications, Shelf,
Testimonial
Credibility Street
Credible, Credit(s), Creditor Ascribe, Attribute, Belief, Billboard, Byline,
Carbon, Crawl, Esteem, Extended, Family, Honour, HP, Kite, Kudos, LC, Lender,
Mense, Post-war, Probable, Reliable, Renown, Revolving, Shylock, Social,
Strap, Street, Tally, Tick, Title, Trust, Weight, Youth
Credulous Charlie, Gullible, Naive, Simple, Trusting
Creed Apostle's, Athanasian, Belief, Doctrine, Faith, Ism, Nicene, Ophism,
Outworn, Sect, Tenet
Creek Bay, Breaches, Cooper, Cove, Crick, Dawson, Estuary, Fleet, Geo, Goe,
Indian, Inlet, Kill, Pow, Slough, Vac, Voe, Wick
Creel Basket, Hask, Scull, Skull
Creep(er), Creeping, Creeps Ai, Ampelopsis, Arbutus, Aseismic, Boston ivy,
Cleavers, Crawl, Grew, Grovel, Grue, Heebie-jeebies, Heeby-jeebies, Herpetic,
Honey, Inch, Insect, Ivy, Mission, Nerd, Nuthatch, Pussyfoot, Repent, Reptant,
Sarmentous, Sittine, Skulk, Slink, Snake, Sneak(sby), Sobole(s), Soil, Toad,
Tropaeolum, Truckle, Vinca, Vine, Virginia, Wickthing, Willies
Creeping Jenny Moneywort
Cremate, Cremation, Crematorium Burn, Char, Cinerarium, Ghat, Ghaut,
Incinerate, Pyre, Sati, Suttee, Ustrinium
Creole Gullah, Haitian, Kriol, Papiamento, Tok Pisin
Crepe Blini, Blintz(e), Canton, Pancake
Crescent Barchan(e), Bark(h)an, Fertile, Growing, Lune(tte), Lunulate, Lunule,
Meniscus, Moon, Red, Sickle, Waxing
Cress Cardamine, Garden, Hoary, Isatis, Pepperwort, Wart, Water, Yellow
Crest(ed) Acme, Chine, Cimier, Cockscomb, Comb, Copple, Crista, Height,
Kirimon, Knap, Mon, Peak, Pileate, Pinnacle, Plume, Ridge, Summit, Tappit,
Tee, > TOP, Tufty
Cretaceous Chalky, Senonian
Cretan Candiot(e), Minoan, Teucer
Crevasse Bergschrund, Chasm, Gorge, Rimaye
Crew Boasted, Company, Core, Eight, Equipage, Four, Lot, Manners, Men, Oars,
Prize, Sailors, Salts, Seamen, Team, Teme, Torpid

Crew-cut Not(t)

Crib Cheat, Cot, Cowhouse, Cratch, Filch, Horse, > **KEY**, Manger, Pony, Purloin, Putz, Shack, Stall, Steal, Trot

Crick Cramp, Kink, Spasm

Cricket(ers) Balm, Bat, Botham, Bowler, Bradman, CC, Cicada, Dry-bob, French, Grade, Grasshopper, Grig, Hopper, Jerusalem, Katydid, Keeper, Knott, Leg, Long-leg, Long-off, Long-on, Longstop, March, May, Mid-on, Mole, Muggleton, Nightwatchman, Opener, Packer, Point, Pyjama, Shield, Single-wicket, Slip, Stool, Stridulate, Tate, Test, Tettix, Tip and run, Vigoro, Warner, Windball, Windies, Wisden, XI(gent)

Crier Bellman, Herald, Muezzin, Niobe, Outrooper

Crime Attentat, Barratry, Caper, Chantage, Chaud-mellé, Computer, Corpus delicti, Ecocide, Fact, Felony, Fraud, Graft, Hate, Heist, Iniquity, Inside job, Malefaction, Mayhem, Misdeed, Misdemeanour, > **OFFENCE**, Organised, Ovicide, Peccadillo, Perjury, Pilferage, Ram raid, Rap, Rape, Rebellion, > **SIN**, Tort, Transgression, Treason, Victimless, War, Wrong

Crimea Balaclava

Criminal Bandit, Bent, Bushranger, Chummy, Con, Cosa Nostra, Counterfeiter, Crack-rope, > **CROOK**, Culpable, Culprit, Delinquent, Escroc, Felon, Flagitious, Forensic, Gangster, Heavy, Heinous, Highbinder, Hitman, Hood(lum), Jailbird, Ladrone, Lag, Larcener, Lifer, Looter, Lowlife, Maf(f)ia, Malefactor, Maleficent, Malfeasant, Mob(ster), Mobster, Ndrangheta, Nefarious, Nefast, Outlaw, Perp(etrator), Racketeer, Receiver, Recidivist, Reprehensible, Rustler, Sinner, Snakehead, Thug, Triad, Underworld, Villain, Wicked, Wire, Yakuza, Yardie, Yegg

▷ **Criminal** *may indicate* an anagram

Crimp Pleat

Crimson Carmine, Incarnadine, Modena, Red, Scarlet

Cringe, Cringing Cower, Creep, Crouch, Fawn, Grovel, Shrink, Sneaksby, Truckle

Crinkle, Crinkly Rugate, Rugose

Crinoline Farthingale, Hoop

Cripple(d) Damage, Debilitate, Disable, Game, Hamstring, Handicap, Injure, > **LAME**, Lameter, Lamiter, Maim, Paralyse, Polio, Scotch, Spoil

Crisis Acme, Crunch, Drama, Emergency, Exigency, Fastigium, Fit, Flap, Head, Identity, Make or break, Midlife, Panic, Pass, Quarterlife, Shake-out, Solution, Test

Crisp Brisk, Clear, Crimp, Crunchy, Fresh, Potato, Sharp, Short, Succinct, Terse

Crispin Sutor(ial)

Criss-cross Alternate, Fret, Interchange, Vein

Criteria, Criterion Benchmark, Gauge, Koch's postulates, Measure, Precedent, Proof, Rayleigh, Rule, Shibboleth, > **STANDARD**, Test, Touchstone

Critic(al), Criticise, Criticism Acute, Agate, Animadversion, Archer, Aristarch, Armchair, Arnold, Attack, Badmouth, Bagehot, Barrack, Bellettrist, Berate, Bird, Blame, Boileau, Boo, Captious, Carp, Castigate, Cavil, Censor(ious), > **CENSURE**, Climacteric, Clobber, Comment, Condemn, Connoisseur, Crab, Criticaster, > **CRUCIAL**, Crunch, Dangle, Decisive, Denigrate, Denounce, Deprecate, Desperate, Diatribe, Dutch uncle, Earful, Etain, Exacting, Excoriate, Fastidious, Fateful, Feuilleton, Flak, Flay, Fulminous, Gosse, Harrumph, Important, Impugn, Inge, Inveigh, Judge, Judgemental, Knife-edge, Knock(er), Lash, Leavis, Literary, Masora(h), Mas(s)orete, Mordacious, Nag, Nasute, Nibble, Nice, Niggle, Overseer, Pan, Pater, Puff, Pundit, Quibble, Rap, Rebuke, Reprehend, Review(er), Rip, Roast, Ruskin,

Scalp, Scarify, Scathe, Scorn, Second guess, Serious, Severe, Shaw, Sideswipe, Slag, Slam, Slashing, Slate, Sneer, Snipe, Stick, Stricture, Strop, Tense, Textual, Threap, Touch and go, Ultracrepidate, Urgent, Vet, Vitriol, Vituperation, Watershed, Zoilism

Croak Creak, Crow, Die, Grumble, Gutturalise

Croatian Cravates, Glagolitic, Serb

Crochet Lace, Weave

Crock Chorrie, Crate, Jar, Mug, Pig, Pitcher, Pot, Potshard, Potshare, Potsherd, Stean(e)

Crockery Ceramics, China, Dishes, Earthenware, Oddment, Sunbeam, Ware

▷ **Crocks** *may indicate* an anagram

Crocodile Cayman, File, Flat dog, Garial, Gavial, Gharial, Line, Mud gecko, Mugger, River-dragon, Saltwater, Sebek, Teleosaur(ian)

Crocus Autumn, Naked lady, Prairie, Saffron

Croesus Lydia

Cromwell Ironside, Lord Protector, Noll, Oliver, Protector, Richard, Roundhead

Crone(s) Beldam(e), Ewe, Graeae, Hag, Mawkin, Ribibe, Rudas, Sibyl, Sybil, Trot, Trout, > WITCH

Crony Anile, Chum, Intimate, Mate, Pal, Sidekick

Crook(ed) Adunc, Ajee, Aslant, Awry, Bad, Bend, Bow, Cam, Camsheugh, Camsho(ch), Criminal, Cromb, Crome, Crosier, Crummack, Crummock, Crump, Curve, Elbow, Fraud, Heister, Hook, Indirect, Kam(me), Kebbie, Lituus, Malpractitioner, Operator, Shyster, Sick, Skew(whiff), Slick(er), Squint, Staff, Swindler, Thraward, Thrawart, Thrawn, Twister, Wonky, Yeggman

▷ **Crooked** *may indicate* an anagram

Croon(er), Crooning Bing, Como, Lament, Lull, Monody, Murmur, Sing

Crop(s), Cropped Basset, Browse, Cash, Catch, Clip, Cover, Craw, Cut, Distress, Dock, Emblements, Energy, Epilate, Eton, Foison, Forage, Harvest, Hog, Ingluvies, Kharif, Milo, Not(t), Plant, Poll, Produce, Rabi, Riding, Rod, Root, Shingle, Silage, Stow, Subsistence, Succession, Top, Truncate, White

Cropper Downfall, Header, Purler

Croquet (term) Peel, Rover

Croquette Kromesky, Quenelle, Rissole

Cross(ing), Crossbred Angry, Ankh, Ansate, Archiepiscopal, Banbury, Basta(a)rd, Beefalo, Bois-brule, Boton(n)e, Burden, Calvary, Cantankerous, Canterbury, Capital, Cattalo, Celtic, Channel, Chi, Chiasm(a), Cleche, Clover-leaf, Compital, Constantine, Crosslet, Crotchety, Crucifix, Crux, Decussate, Demi-wolf, Dihybrid, Double, Dso(mo), Dzobo, Eleanor, Encolpion, Faun, Fiery, Fitché, Fleury, Foil, Footbridge, Ford, Frabbit, Fractious, Frampold, Franzy, Funnel, Fylfot, Geneva, George, Grade, Greek, Holy rood, Humette, Hybrid, Ill, Imp, Indignant, Interbreed, Intersect, Intervein, Iona, Iracund, Irate, Irked, Iron, Jerusalem, Jomo, Jumart, Kiss, Krest, Ladino, Latin, Level, Liger, Lorraine, Lurcher, Maltese, Mameluco, Market, Mermaid, Military, Mix, Moline, Mongrel, Mule, Narky, Nattery, Node, Norman, Northern, Nuisance, Obverse, Ordinary, Orthodox, Overpass, Overthwart, Papal, Patonce, Patriarchal, Pattée, Pectoral, Pedestrian, Pelican, Plumcot, Plus, Pommé, Potence, Potent, Preaching, Puffin, Quadrate, Ratty, Reciprocal, Red, Roman, Rood, Rose, Rouen, Rouge, Rubicon, Ruthwell, Sain, St Andrew's, St Anthony's, St George's, St Patrick's, St Peter's, Saltier, Saltire, Satyr, Shirty, Sign, Snappy, Southern, Strid, Svastika, Swastika, T, Tangelo, Tau, Tayberry, Ten, Testy, Thraw, Thwart, Tiglon, Tigon, Times, Transit, Transom, Transverse, Traverse, Tree, Urdé, Vexed, Vext, Victoria, > VOTE, Weeping, Whippet, Wry, X,

Yakow, Zambo, Zebra(ss), Zebrinny, Zebroid, Zebrula, Zebrule, Zedonk, Z(h)o,
Zobu

▷ **Cross** *may indicate* an anagram

▶ **Cross-bar** *see* CROSSPIECE

Cross-bearer Crucifer

Cross-bill Metagnathous

Cross-bones Marrowbones

Cross-bow Arbalest, Bal(l)ista

Cross-country Langlauf, Overland

Cross-dressing Eonism

Cross-examine Grill, Interrogate, Question, Targe

Cross-eyed Skelly(-eyed), Squint

Crossfertilisation Allogamy, Heterosis, Hybrid vigour, Xenogamy

Cross-grained Ill-haired, Mashlam, Mashlim, Mas(h)lin, Mashlock, Mashlum,
Stubborn

Crosspiece, **Cross-bar**, **Cross-timber** Bar, Cancelli, Footrail, Inter-tie, Lierne,
Phillipsite, Putlock, Putlog, Quillon, Serif, Seriph, Stempel, Stemple, Stretcher,
Stull, Swingle-tree, Toggle, Transom, Whiffle-tree, Whipple-tree, Yoke

Crossroads Carfax, Carfox, Carrefour, Compital, Soap

Crossword Cryptic, Grid, Puzzle, Quickie

Crotchet(y) Eccentric, Fad, Fancy, Grouch, Kink, Quarter-note, Toy

Crouch Bend, Cringe, Falcade, Fancy, Lordosis, Ruck, Set, Squat, Squinch

Croup Angina, Cough, Kink, Rump

Crow Boast, Brag, Carrion, Chewet, Chough, Corbie, Corvus, Crake, Currawong,
Daw, Flute-bird, Gorcrow, Hooded, Hoodie, Huia, Jackdaw, Jim(my), Murder,
Piping, Raven, Rook, Saddleback, Skite, Squawk, Swagger, Vaunt

Crowbar Gavelock, James, Jemmy, Lever

Crowd(ed) Abound, Army, Bike, Boodle, Bumper, Bunch, Byke, Caboodle,
Clutter, Concourse, Congest(ed), Cram, Crush, Crwth, Dedans, Doughnut,
Drove, Fill, Flock, Galere, Gate, Gathering, Herd, Horde, > HOST, Huddle,
Hustle, Jam, Lot, Mein(e)y, Meinie, Menyie, Mob, Mong, Multitude, Ochlo-,
Pack, Pang, Press, Rabble, Raft, Ram, Ratpack, Ring, Ruck, Scrooge, Scrouge,
Scrowdge, Scrum, Serr(é), Shoal, Shove, Slew, Slue, Squeeze, Stuff, Swarm,
Swell, Three, Throng, Trinity, Varletry

Crowfoot Gilcup, Reate

Crown Acme, Bays, Bull, Camp, Cantle, Cap, Capernoity, Cidaris, Civic, Coma,
Corona, Cr, Diadem, Ecu, Engarland, Enthrone, Fillet, Garland, Gloria, Haku,
Head, Headdress, Instal, Iron, Ivy, Krantz, Laurel, Monarch, Mural, Naval,
Nole, Noll, Noul(e), Nowl, Olive, Optical, Ore, Ovation, Pate, Peak, Pschent,
Sconce, Taj, Tiara, > TOP, Triple, Triumphal, Trophy, Vallary, Vertex

Crucial Acute, Critical, Essential, Key, Pivotal, Quintessential, Vital, Watershed

Crucible Cruset, Melting-pot, Vessel

Crucifix(ion), **Crucify** Calvary, Cross, Golgotha, Mortify, Rood, Torment, Torture

Crude(ness) Bald, Brash, Brute, Coarse, Earthy, Halfbaked, Immature,
Incondite, Primitive, Raunch, Raw, Rough, Rough and ready, Rough-hewn,
Rough-wrought, Tutty, Uncouth, Vulgar, Yahoo

Cruel(ty) Barbarous, Bloody, Brutal, Dastardly, De Sade, Draconian, Fell,
Fiendish, Flinty, Hard, Heartless, Immane, Inhuman, Machiavellian, Mental,
Neronic, Pitiless, Raw, Remorseless, Sadistic, Stern, Tormentor, Vicious

▷ **Cruel** *may indicate* an anagram

Cruet Ampulla, Condiments, Decanter

Cruise(r) Booze, Busk, Cabin, Nuke, Prowl, Rove, Sail, Ship, Tom, Travel, Trip,

Voyager

Crumb(le), Crumbly, Crumbs Coo, Decay, Disintegrate, Ee, Fragment, Friable, Law, Leavings, Moulder, Mull, Murl, Nesh, Nirl, Ort, Particle, Ped, Raspings, Rot, Rotter

Crumpet Dish, Girl, Muffin, Nooky, Pash, Pikelet

Crumple Collapse, Crunkle, Crush, Raffle, Scrunch, Wrinkle

Crunch(y) Chew, Craunch, Crisp, Gnash, Graunch, Grind, Munch, Occlude, Scranch

Crusade(r) Baldwin, Campaign, Cause, Pilgrim, Tancred, Templar

Crush(ed), Crusher Acis, Anaconda, Annihilate, Bow, Champ, Comminute, Conquer, Contuse, Cranch, Crunch, Defeat, Destroy, Graunch, Grind, Hug, Jam, Knapper, Levigate, Mangle, Mash, Mill, Molar, Mortify, Oppress, Overcome, Overwhelm, Pash, Policeman, Pound, Press, Pulp, Pulverise, Quash, Ruin, Schwarmerei, Scotch, Scrum, Scrumple, Smash, Squabash, Squash, Squeeze, Squelch, Squish, Stamp, Stave, Steam-roll, Stove, Suppress, Telescope, Trample, Tread

Crust(y) Argol, Beeswing, Cake, Coating, Coffin, Continental, Cover, Crabby, Craton, Fur, Gratin, Heel, Horst, Kissing, Kraton, Lithosphere, Oceanic, Osteocolla, Pie, Reh, Rind, Rine, Sal, Salband, Scab, Shell, Sial, Sima, Sinter, Sordes, Surly, Tartar, Teachie, Terrane, Tetchy, Upper, Wine-stone

Crustacea(n) Amphipod, Barnacle, Brachyuran, Branchiopoda, Camaron, Cirriped, Cirripede, Cirripid, Cladoceran, Copepod, Crab, Crayfish, Cumacean, Cyclops, Cyprid, Cypris, Decapod(a), Entomostraca, Euphausia, Fishlouse, Foot-jaw, Gribble, Isopod, Krill, Langoustine, Lobster, Macrura, Malacostracan, Marron, Nauplius, Ostracoda, Pagurian, Phyllopod, Prawn, Rhizocephalan, Sand-hopper, Scampi, Scampo, Schizopod, Sea slater, Shellfish, Shrimp, Slater, Squilla, Stomatopod, Woodlouse, Yabbie, Yabby

Crutch Morton's, Potant

Crux Essence, Nub

Cry(ing) Aha, Alalagmus, Alew, Banzai, Bark, Battle, Bawl, Bell, Blat, Bleat, Bleb, Blub(ber), Boo, Boohoo, Bray, Bump, Caramba, Caw, Cheer, Chevy, Chirm, Chivy, Clang, Crake, Croak, Crow, Dire, Euoi, Eureka, Evoe, Exclaim, Fall, Field-holler, Gardyloo, Gathering, Geronimo, Gowl, Greet, Halloo, Harambee, Haro, Harrow, Havoc, Heigh, Hemitrope, Herald, Hinny, Hoicks, Holler, Honk, Hoo, Hoop, Hosanna, Hout(s)-tout(s), Howl, Humph, Io, Kaw, Low, Mewl, Miaou, Miau(l), Miserere, Mourn, Night-shriek, O(c)hone, Oi, Olé, Ow, Pugh, Rallying, Rivo, Sab, Scape, Scream, Screech, Sell, Sese(y), Sessa, > **SHOUT**, Shriek, Slogan, Snivel, Snotter, Sob, Soho, Sola, Squall, Squawk, Street, Tally-ho, Tantivy, Umph, Vagitus, View-halloo, Vivat, Vociferate, Wail, War, Watchword, Waul, Wawl, Weep, Westward ho, Whee(ple), Whimper, Whine, Whinny, Whoa, Whoop, Winge, Wolf, Yammer, Yelp, Yicker, Yikker, Yip, Yippee, Yodel, Yo-heave-ho, Yo-ho-ho, Yoick, Yoop, Yowl

Crypt(ic) Catacomb, Cavern, Chamber, Crowde, Encoded, Favissa, Grotto, Hidden, Obscure, Occult, Secret, Sepulchre, Short, Steganographic, Tomb, Unclear, Undercroft, Vault

Cryptogam Acotyledon, Acrogen, Fern(-ally), Moss, Pteridophyte

Cryptographer Decoder, Ventris

Crystal(lise), Crystal-gazer, Crystalline Allotriomorphic, Axinite, Baccara(t), Beryl, Candy, Citrine, Clathrate, Clear, Copperas, Coumarin, Cumarin, Dendrite, Druse, Effloresce, Elaterin, Enantiomorph, Epitaxy, Erionite, Fuchsin(e), Geode, Glass, Hemihedron, Hemimorphic, Hemitrope, Ice-stone, Ideal, Imazadole, Jarosite, Lead, Liquid, Lithium, Love-arrow, Macle,

Macro-axis, Melamine, Mixed, Nicol, Orthogonal, Orthorhombic, Pellucid, Phenocryst, Piezo, Piezoelectric, Pinacoid, Pinakoid, Prism, Pseudomorph, Purin(e), Quartz, R(h)aphide, R(h)aphis, Rhinestone, Rock, Rotenone, Rubicelle, Scryer, Shoot, Skryer, Smectic, Snowflake, Sorbitol, Spar, Spicule, Table, Trichite, Trilling, Twin(ned), Watch-glass, Xanthene, Xenocryst

Cub Baby, Kit, Novice, Pup, Whelp, Wolf

Cube, Cubic, Cubist Bath, Braque, Cu, Die, Necker, Nosean, Quadrate, Rubik's®, Serac, Smalto, Snub, Solid, Stere, Stock, Tesseract

Cubicle Alcove, Booth, Carrel(l), Stall

Cuckold Actaeon, Cornute, Graft, Homer, Lenocinium, Vulcan's badge, Wittol

Cuckoo Ament, Ani, April fool, Bird, Brain-fever bird, Gouk, Gowk, Inquiline, Insane, Koel, > **MAD**, Mental, Piet-my-vrou, Stupid

▷ **Cuckoo** *may indicate* an anagram

Cuckoopint Arum

Cucumber Bitter-apple, Choko, Colocynth, Coloquintida, Dill, Elaterium, Gherkin, Pickle, Sea-slug, Squirting, Trepang, Wolly

Cuddle Canoodle, Caress, Clinch, Embrace, Fondle, Hug, Nooky, Smooch, Smuggle, Snuggle

Cudgel Alpeen, Ballow, Bludgeon, Brain, Club, Cosh, Drub, Fustigate, Plant, Rack, Shillelagh, Souple, Stick, Swipple, Tan, Towel, Truncheon

Cue Cannonade, Catchword, Feed, Feed-line, Half-butt, Hint, Mace, > **PROMPT**, Reminder, Rod, Sign, Signal, Wink

Cuff Box, Buffet, Clout, French, Iron, Muffettee, Strike, Swat

Cuirass Armour, Corselet, Lorica

Cuisine Bourgeoise, Cookery, Food, Lean, Menu, Minceur, Nouvelle

Cul-de-sac Blind, Dead-end, Impasse, Loke

Cull Gather, Pick, Select, Thin, Weed

Culminate, Culmination Apogean, Apogee, Climax, Conclusion, Crest, End, Head

Culpable Blameworthy, Guilty

Cult Aum Shinrikyo, Cabiri, Candombie, Cargo, Creed, Fertility, Macumba, Personality, Rastafarian, Sect, Shango, Shinto, Wicca, Worship

Cultivate(d), Cultivation Agronomy, Arty, Civilise, Dig, Dress, Ear, Ere, Farm, Genteel, Grow, Hoe, Hydroponics, Improve, Labour, Pursue, Raise, Refine, Sative, Sophisticated, Tame, Tasteful, Till, Tilth

Culture(d), Cultural Acheulean, Acheulian, Agar, Art(y), Aurignacian, Azilian, Bel esprit, Brahmin, Capsian, Civil(isation), Corporate, Ethnic, Experiment, Explant, Gel, Grecian, Hallstatt, Hip-hop, Humanism, Kultur(kreis), La Tène, Learning, Maglemosean, Maglemosian, Minoan, Mousterian, Organisational, Perigordian, Polish, Pure, Refinement, Solutrean, Sophisticated, Starter, Strepyan, Suspension, Tardenoisian, Tissue, Villanovan, Water

Cumbersome Clumsy, Heavy, Lumbering, > **UNWIELDY**

Cunctator Dilatory

Cuneiform Wedge(d)

Cunning Arch, Art, Artifice, Cautel, Craft(y), Deceit, Deep, Devious, Down, Finesse, Foxy, Insidious, Leery, Machiavellian, Quaint, Skill, Slee(kit), Sleight, Slim, Sly(boots), Smart, Sneaky, Subtle, Vulpine, Wile

Cup(s), Cupped Aecidium, America's, Beaker, Calcutta, Calix, Calyculus, Cantharus, Chalice, Claret, Cotyle, Cruse, Cupule, Cyathus, Cylix, Davis, Demitasse, Deoch-an-doruis, Deuch-an-doris, Dish, Doch-an-dorach, Dop, Egg, European, FA, Fairs, Final, Fingan, Finjan, Fruit, Gemma, Glenoid, Goblet, Grace, Grease, Hanap, Horn, Kylix, Loving, Melbourne, Merry, Monstrance,

Moustache, Mug, Noggin, Nut, Pannikin, Parting, Planchet, Plate, Poley, Posset, Pot, Procoelous, Quaff, Quaich, Quaigh, Rhyton, Rider, Ryder, Sangrado, Scyphus, Stem, Stirrup, Tantalus, Tass(ie), Tastevin, Tazza, Tea-dish, Tig, Tot, > **TROPHY**, Tyg, UEFA, Volva, Waterloo, World

Cup-bearer Ganymede, Hebe

Cupboard Almery, Almirah, A(u)mbry, Beauf(f)et, Cabinet, Chiffonier, Chiff(o)robe, Closet, Court, Credenza, Dresser, Fume, Livery, Locker, Meat-safe, Press, Walk-in

Cup-holder Hanaper, Hebe, Plinth, Saucer, Zarf, Zurf

Cupid Amoretto, Amorino, Archer, Blind, Cherub, Dan, Eros, Love, Putto

Cupola Belfry, Dome, Tholos

Cup-shaped Poculiform

Cur Dog, Messan, Mongrel, Mutt, Pi-dog, Scab, Scoundrel, Wretch, Yap

Curare, Curari Ourali, Poison, Wourali

Curassow Crax

Curate Minister, Nathaniel, Padré, Priest

Curb Bit, Brake, Bridle, Check, Clamp, Coaming, Dam, Edge, Puteal, Rein, Restrain, Rim, Snub, Well

Curd(s) Bean, Cheese, Junket, Lapper(ed)-milk, Lemon, Skyr, Tofu

Curdle Clot, Congeal, Earn, Erne, Lopper, Posset, Ren, Rennet, Run, Set, Sour, > **TURN**, Whig, Yearn

Cure(d), Curative Ameliorate, Amend, Antidote, Antirachitic, Bloater, Cold turkey, Dry-salt, Dun, Euphrasy, Ginseng, Heal, Hobday, Hydropathy, Jadeite, Jerk, Kipper, Laetrile, Medicinal, Nature, Nostrum, Panacea, Park-leaves, Prairie oyster, > **PRESERVE**, Reast, Recover, Recower, Reest, Remede, Remedy, Restore, Salt, Salve, Serum, Smoke, Smoke-dry, Tan, > **TREATMENT**, Tutsan, Water

▷ **Cure** *may indicate* an anagram

Curfew Gate, Prohibit, Proscribe

Curie Ci

Curio, Curiosity, Curious Agog, Bibelot, Freak, Inquisitive, Into, Meddlesome, Nos(e)y, Objet d'art, Objet de vertu, Odd, Peculiar, Prurience, Rarity, Rum, > **STRANGE**

▷ **Curious(ly)** *may indicate* an anagram

Curium Cm

Curl(s), Curler, Curling, Curly Bev, Bonspiel, Cirrus, Coil, Crimp, Crimple, Crinkle, Crisp, Crocket, Dildo, Earlock, Friz(z), Frizzle, Heart-breaker, Hog, Inwick, Kiss, Leaf, Loop, Love-lock, Outwick, Perm, Pin, Quiff, Repenter, Ringlet, Roll, Roulette, Scroll, Shaving, Spiral, Spit, Tong, Trunk, Twiddle, > **TWIST**, Ulotrichous, Wave, Wind

Curlew Bird, Whaup, Whimbrel

Curmudgeon Boor, Churl, Grouch, Route, Runt

Currant Berry, Flowering, Raisin, Rizard, Rizzar(t), Rizzer

Currency Cash, Circulation, > **COIN**, Coinage, Decimal, Euro, Finance, Fractional, Jiao, Kip, Koruna, Monetary, > **MONEY**, Prevalence, Reserve, Soft

▷ **Currency** *may indicate* a river

Current Abroad, AC, Actual, Alternating, Amp(ere), Amperage, California, Canary, Contemporaneous, Cromwell, DC, Direct, Draught, Drift, Dynamo, Ebbtide, Eddy, Electric, El Nino, Equatorial, Euripus, Existent, Flow, Foucault, Going, Gyre, Humboldt, Hummock, I, Immediate, Inst, Intermittent, Japan, Kuroshio, Labrador, Millrace, Modern, Newsy, North Atlantic, Now, Ongoing, Output, Peru, Present, Prevalent, Pulsating, Race, Rapid, Rife, Rip, Roost,

Running, Stream, Thames, Thermal, Thermionic, Tide, Tideway, Topical, Torrent, Turbidity, Underset, Undertow, Updraught

Curriculum Cursal, National, Programme

Curry Bhuna, Brush, Comb, Cuittle, Dhansak, Fawn, Groom, Ingratiate, Korma, Madras, Spice, Tan, Tandoori, Turmeric, Vindaloo

Curse Abuse, Anathema, Badmouth, Ban, Bane, Beshrew, > **BLASPHEME**, Blast, Chide, Dam(me), Damn, Dee, Drat, Ecod, Egad, Excommunicate, Execrate, Heck, Hex, Imprecate, Jinx, Malison, Maranatha, Mau(l)gré, Mockers, Moz(z), Mozzle, Nine (of diamonds), Oath, Paterson's, Pize, Plague, Rant, Rats, Scourge, 'Snails, Spell, Swear, Upbraid, Weary, Winze, Wo(e)

Cursive Estrang(h)elo, Run

Cursor Mouse, Turtle

Cursorily, Cursory Casual, Hasty, Lax, Obiter, Passing, Sketchy, Speedy, Superficial

Curt Abrupt, Blunt, Crusty, Laconic, Offhand, Short, Snappy

Curtail(ment) Apocope, Crop, Cut, Reduce, Shorten

Curtain(s), Curtain-rod Arras, Backdrop, Bamboo, Canopy, Caudle, Cloth, Cyclorama, Death, Demise, Drape, Drop, Dropcloth, Dropscene, Fatal, Hanging, Iron, Louvre, Net, Pall, Portière, Purdah, Safety, Scene, Screen, Scrim, Shower, Tab, Tormentor, Tringle, Upholstery, Vail, Valance, Veil, Vitrage, Window

Curtsey Bob, Bow, Dip, Dop

Curvature, Curve(d), Curvaceous, Curvy Adiabatic, Aduncate, Anticlastic, Apophyge, Arc, Arch, Archivolt, Axoid, Bend, Bight, Bow, Camber, Cardioid, Catacaustic, Catenary, Caustic, Characteristic, Cissoid, Conchoid, Contrapposto, Crescent, Cycloid, Diacaustic, Dogleg, Entasis, Epicycloid, Epinastic, Epitrochoid, Ess, Evolute, Exponental, Extrados, Felloe, Felly, Folium, French, Gaussian, Geodesic, Gooseneck, Growth, Hance, Helix, Hodograph, Hollow-back, Hook, Hyperbola, Hypocycloid, Inswing, Intrados, Isochor, J, Jordan, Kyphosis, Laffer, Learning, Lemniscate, Limacon, Liquidus, Lituus, Lordosis, Loxodrome, Normal, Nowy, Ogee, Parabola, Phillips, Pothook, Pott's disease, Pulvinate, Reclinate, Record, Rhumb, Roach, Rotundate, Scoliosis, Sheer, Sinuate, Sinusoid, Slice, Spiral, Spiric, Strophoid, Survival, Swayback, Synclastic, Tautochrone, Tie, Tractrix, Trajectory, Trochoid, Tumble-home, Twist, Undulose, U-turn, Volute, Witch (of Agnesi)

Cushion(s) Air, Allege, Bolster, Buffer, Frog, Ham, Hassock, Kneeler, > **PAD**, Pillow, Pin, Pouf(fe), Pulvillus, Scatter, Soften, Squab, Upholster, Whoopee

Cusp Horn, Spinode, Tine

Custard (apple) Creme caramel, Flam(m), Flan, Flaune, Flawn, Flummery, Pa(w)paw, Zabaglione

Custodian, Custody Care, Claviger, Guard, Hold, Janitor, Keeping, Sacrist, Steward, Trust, Ward

Custom(ised), Customs (officer), Customary Agriology, Coast-waiters, Consuetude, Conventional, Couvade, Dedicated, De règle, Dhamma, Dharma, Douane, Exciseman, Familiar, Fashion, Folklore, > **HABIT**, Land-waiter, Lore, Manner, Montem, Mores, Nomic, Octroi, Ordinary, Practice, Praxis, Relic, Rite, Routine, Rule, Sororate, Spanish, Sunna, Tax, Thew, Tidesman, Tide-waiter, Tikanga, Tradition, Unwritten, Usance, Used, Usual, Won, Wont, Woon, Zollverein

Customer Client, Cove, Patron, Prospect, Purchaser, Shillaber, Shopper, Smooth, Stiff, Trade, Trick, Ugly

Cut(ter), Cutting Abate, Abjoint, Abridge, Abscission, Abscond, Acute, Adeem,

Adze, Aftermath, Ali Baba, Amputate, Apocope, Axe, Bang, Bisect, Bit, Bite, Bowdlerise, Boycott, Brilliant, Broach, Caesarean, Caique, Canal, Cantle, Caper, Carver, Castrate, Caustic, Censor, Chap, Chisel, Chopper, Chynd, Circumscribe, Cleaver, Clinker-built, Clip, Colter, Commission, Concise, Coppice, Coulter, Coupé, Crew, Crop, Cruel, Culebra, Curtail, Deadhead, Decrease, Dedekind, Dicer, Die, Director's, Discide, Disengage, Dismember, Dissect, Division, Divorce, Dock, Dod, Edge, Edit, Emarginate, Embankment, Engraver, Entail, Entayle, Epistolary, Epitomise, Eschew, Estrepe, Excalibur, Excide, Excise, Exscind, Exsect, Exude, Fashion, Fell, Fillet, Flench, Flense, Flinch, Form, Froe, Frow, Gaillard, Garb, Gash, Go-down, Grater, Graven, Gride, Gryde, Hack, Handsaw, Hew(er), Ignore, Incision, Incisor, Indent, Intersect, Jigsaw, Joint, Junk, Kerf, Kern, Kirn, Lacerate, Lance, Leat, Lesion, Lin, Lop, Math, Medaillon, Microtome, Milling, Mohel, Mortice, Mortise, Mower, Nache, Nick, Not, Notch, Nott, Occlude, Omit, Open, Operate, Osteotome, Oxyacetylene, Padsaw, Pare, Pink, Plant, Pliers, Ploughshare, Pollard, Pone, Power, Precivise, Press, Proin, Quota, Race, Rake off, Rase, Razor, Reap, Rebate, Reduction, Re-enter, Resect, Retrench, Revenue, Ring, Ripsaw, Roach, Rose, Rout, Saddle, Sarcastic, Sarky, Saw(n), Scarf, Scathing, Scion, Scission, Scissor, Score, Sculpt, Scye, Scythe, Secant, Secateurs, Sect, Section, Sever, Sey, Share(out), Shaver, Shears, Shingle, Ship, Shorn, Short, Shred, Shun, Sickle, Sirloin, Skin, Skip, Slane, Slash, Slicer, Slip, Slit, Sloop, Sned, Snee, Snib, Snick, Snip, Snub, Spade, Speedy, Spin, Spud, Steak, Stencil, Stereotomy, Stir, Stramac, Stramazon, Strimmer®, Style, Surgeon, Swath(e), Tailor(ess), Tart, Tenderloin, Tenotomy, Tomial, Tomium, Tonsure, Tooth, Topside, Transect, Trash, Trench, Trenchant, Trepan, Trim, Truant, Truncate, Urchin, Whang, Whittle, Winey

▷ **Cut** *may indicate* an anagram
▷ **Cutback** *may indicate* a reversed word
  Cute Ankle, Pert, Pretty, Taking
  Cuticle Epidermis, Eponychium, Periplast, Pleuron, Skin
  Cut in Interpose, Interrupt
  Cutlass Machete, Sword
  Cutlery Canteen, Flatware, Fork, Knife, Setting, Silver, Spoon, Tableware, Trifid
  Cutlet Schnitzel
  Cut off Elide, Enisle, Estrange, Inisle, Insulate, Intercept, > ISOLATE, Lop, Prune
  Cut-throat Razor, Ruinous
  Cuttlebone, Cuttlefish Octopus, Pen, Polyp(e)s, Polypus, Sea-sleeve, Sepia, Sepiost(aire), Sepium, Squid
  CV Biodata
  Cyanide Acrylonitrile, Nitrile, Prussiate
  Cycad Coontie, Coonty
  Cyclamen Sow-bread
  Cycle, Cyclist Anicca, Arthurian, Bike, Biorhythm, Cal(l)ippic, Calvin, Carbon, Carnot, Cell, Circadian, Closed, Daisy, Diesel, Eon, Era, Fairy, Four-stroke, Freewheel, Frequency, Geological, Gigahertz, Heterogony, Hydrologic, Indiction, Ko, Krebs, Life, Light-year, Lunar, Metonic, Moped, Nitrogen, Oestrus, Orb, Otto, Pedal, Peloton, Period, Rankine, Repulp, Revolution, Ride, Roadster, Rock, Rota, Round, Samsara, Saros, Scorch, Series, Sheng, Solar, Song, Sonnet, Sothic, Spin, Sunspot, TCA, Trade, Trick, Trike, Turn, UCI, Urea, Water, Wheeler, Wheelman, Wu
  Cyclone Cockeye(d) bob, Storm, Tornado, Typhoon, Willy-willy
  Cyclops Arges, Arimasp(i), Brontes, Polyphemus, Steropes

Cylinder, Cylindrical Clave, Column, Drum, Master, Pipe, Pitch, Roll, Rotor, Slave, Spool, Steal, Stele, Terete, Torose, Treadmill, Tube

Cymbal(s) High-hat, Hi-hat, Zel

Cynic(al) Crab, Diogenes, Doubter, Hard-bitten, Hard-boiled, Menippus, Pessimist, Sardonic, Sceptic, Thersites, Timon

Cynosure Centre, Focus

Cynthia Artemis, Moon

Cypress Bald, Leyland(ii), Monterey, Retinospora, Swamp, Tree

Cypriot Enosis, Eoka

Cyst Atheroma, Bag, Blister, Chalazion, Dermoid, Hydatid, Impost(h)ume, Meibomian, Ranula, Sac, Sebaceous, Vesicle, Wen

Czechoslovakia CZ, Sudetenland

Dd

D Daughter, Delta, Died, Edh, Eth, Penny

Dab(s) Bit, Daub, Fish, Flounder, Pat, Print, Ringer, Smear, Spot, Stupe, Whorl

Dabble(r) Clatch, Dally, Dilettante, Plouter, Plowter, Potter, Smatter, Splash, Stipple, Trifle

Dachshund Teckel

Dactyl Anapaest

Dad(dy) Blow, Dev(v)el, Father, Generator, Hit, Male, Pa(pa), Pater, Polt, Pop, Slam, Sugar, Thump

Daddy-longlegs Crane-fly, Jennyspinner, Leather-jacket, Spinning-jenny, Tipula

Daffodil Asphodel, Jonquil, Lent-lily, Narcissus

Daft Absurd, Crazy, Potty, Ridiculous, Silly, Simple, Stupid

Dag Jag, Pierce, Pistol, Prick, Stab, Tag, Wool

Dagger(s) An(e)lace, Ataghan, Baselard, Bayonet, Bodkin, Crease, Creese, Da(h), Diesis, Dirk, Double, Dudgeon, Han(d)jar, Hanger, Jambiya(h), Katar, Khanjar, Kindjahl, Kirpan, Kreese, Kris, Lath, Misericord(e), Obelisk, Obelus, Poi(g)nado, Poniard, Pugio, Puncheon, Pusser's, Quillon, Rondel, Sgian-dubh, Skean, Skene(-occle), Spanish, Stiletto, Swordbreaker, W(h)inger, Whiniard, Whinyard, Yatag(h)an

Dahlia Cosmea

Daily Adays, Char, Circadian, Diurnal, Domestic, Guardian, Help, Journal, Mail, Mirror, Paper, Per diem, Quotidian, Rag, Regular, Scotsman, Sun, Tabloid

Dainty Cate(s), Cute, Delicacy, Elegant, Elfin, Entremesse, Entremets, Exquisite, Junket, Lickerish, Liquorish, Mignon(ne), > **MORSEL**, Neat, Nice, Particular, Petite, Pussy, Sunket, Twee

Dairy Creamery, Loan, Parlour

Dairymaid Dey, Patience

Dais Estate, Machan, Platform, Podium, Pulpit, Stage, Tribune

Daisy African, Barberton, Bell, Felicia, Gowan, Hen and chickens, Livingstone, Marguerite, Marigold, Michaelmas, Moon, Ox-eye, Shasta, Transvaal, Vegetable sheep

Dale(s) Dell, Dene, Dingle, Glen, Vale, Valley, Yorkshire

Dally Coquet(te), Dawdle, Finger, Flirt, Play, Spoon, Sport, Toy, Trifle, Wait

Dam An(n)icut, Arch, Aswan, Bar, Barrage, Barrier, Block, Boulder, Bund, Cabora Bassa, Cauld, Check, Gravity, Hoover, Kariba, Kielder, Ma, Mater, Obstacle, Obstruct, Pen, Stank, > **STEM**, Sudd, Turkey nest, Weir, Yangtze

Damage(d), Damages, Damaging Bane, Banjax, Bruise, Buckle, Charge, Chip, Collateral, Contuse, Cost, Cripple, Dent, Desecrate, Detriment, Devastate, Devastavit, Estrepe, Exemplary, Fault, Flea-bite, Foobar, Fubar, Fuck up, Harm, Havoc, Hit, Hole, Hurt, Impair, Injury, Insidious, Loss, Mar, Mayhem, Moth-eaten, Mutilate, Nobble, Prang, Price, Punitive, Ratten, Ravage, Retree, Sabotage, Scaith, Scath(e), Scotch, Scratch, Skaith, Smirch, Solatium, > **SPOIL**, Tangle, Toll, Value, Vandalise, Violate, Wear and tear, Wing, Wound, Wreak,

Wreck

▷ **Damage(d)** *may indicate* an anagram

Dambuster Ondatra

Dame Crone, Dowager, Edna, Gammer, Lady, Matron, Nature, Naunt, Partlet, Peacherino, Sis, Title(d), Trot, Woman

Damn(ation), Damned Accurst, Attack, Blame, Condemn, Curse, Cuss, Darn, Dee, Execrate, Faust, Hell, Hoot, Jigger, Malgre, Perdition, Predoom, Sink, Swear, Tarnal, Tarnation, Tinker's, Very

Damp(en), Damping Aslake, Black, Blight, Check, Clam(my), Dank, Dewy, Fousty, Fusty, Humid, Moist, Muggy, Raw, Rheumy, Rising, Roric, Soggy, Sordo, Sultry, Unaired, Viscous, > WET, White

Damper Barrier, Check, Dashpot, Killjoy, Mute

Damsel Girl, Lass, Maiden, Wench

Damson Plumdamas

Dan Box, Cupid, Leno, Olivetan, Scuttle, Tribe

Dance(r), Dancing Astaire, Baladin(e), Ballabile, Ballant, Ballerina, Ballroom, Bayadère, Bob, Body-popping, Caper, Chorus-girl, Contredanse, Corybant, Coryphee, Dervish, Diaghilev, Dinner, Dolin, Exotic, Figurant, Foot, Gandy, Gigolo, Hetaera, Hetaira, Hoofer, Kick-up, Knees-up, Leap, Maenad, Modern, Nautch-girl, Night, Nijinsky, Nureyev, Oberek, Old-time, Partner, Pavlova, Petipa, Pierette, Raver, Ring, St Vitus, Salome, Saltatorious, Skipper, Spring, Step, Strut, Table, Tea, Terpsichore, Tread, Trip(pant), Vogue(ing), Whirl

DANCES

3 letters:	Go-go	5 letters:	Ragga
Bop	Haka	Bamba	Robot
Fan	Hora	Belly	Round
Gig	Hula	Bogle	Rumba
Hay	Jive	Brawl	Salsa
Hey	Jota	Carol	Samba
Hop	Juba	Ceroc®	Shake
Ice	Juke	Conga	Skank
Jig	Kolo	Disco	Snake
Lap	Line	Fling	Stomp
Pas	Lion	Furry	Sword
Poi	Loup	Galop	Tango
Sun	Nach	Ghost	Twist
Tap	Pogo	Gigue	Valse
Toe	Polo	Glide	Volta
War	Reel	Gopak	Waltz
	Rope	Horah	
4 letters:	Sand	Limbo	6 letters:
Alma	Shag	Loure	Almain
Ball	Slam	Mambo	Apache
Barn	Spin	Mooch	Ballet
Clog	Spot	Natch	Bolero
Dump	Stag	Paspy	Boogie
Fado	Taxi	Pavan	Boston
Folk	Wire	Paven	Branle
Frug		Pavin	Bubble
Giga		Polka	Canary

- Can-can
- Cha-cha
- Fading
- Floral
- German
- Hustle
- Jump-up
- Kathak
- Lavolt
- Maxixe
- Minuet
- Morris
- Pavane
- Redowa
- Shimmy
- Smooch
- Square
- Toy-toy
- Trophe
- Valeta
- Veleta
- Waggle

7 letters:
- Bambuca
- Beguine
- Bourrée
- Bransle
- Brantle
- Cantico
- Capuera
- Carioca
- Coranto
- Cossack
- Country
- Courant
- Csardas
- Farruca
- Forlana
- Foxtrot
- Furlana
- Gavotte
- Halling
- Hoe-down
- Lambada
- Lancers
- Landler
- Lavolta
- Macabre
- Mazurka
- Measure
- Moresco

- Morisco
- Morrice
- Moshing
- One-step
- Pericon
- Planxty
- Polacca
- Pyrrhic
- Ridotto
- Ringlet
- Romaika
- Roundel
- Roundle
- Routine
- Sardana
- Sashaya
- Shuffle
- Tanagra
- Tordion
- Toyi-toy
- Toy-toyi
- Trenise
- Two-step
- Ziganka

8 letters:
- Alegrias
- Bunnyhop
- Bunnyhug
- Cachucha
- Cakewalk
- Canticoy
- Capoeira
- Chaconne
- Cotillon
- Courante
- Egg-dance
- Excuse-me
- Fandango
- Flamenco
- Flip-flop
- Galliard
- Habanera
- Hay-de-guy
- Haymaker
- Headbang
- Hey-de-guy
- Heythrop
- Hoolican
- Hornpipe
- Hula-hula
- Irish jig

- Joncanoe
- Junkanoo
- Kantikoy
- Kazachok
- Kazatzka
- Lindy hop
- Macarena
- Marinera
- Matachin
- Medicine
- Merengue
- Murciana
- Orchesis
- Rigadoon
- Robotics
- Ronggeng
- Saraband
- Snowball
- Soft-shoe
- Taglioni
- Toyi-toyi
- Trucking

9 letters:
- Allemande
- Bergamask
- Bergomask
- Bossanova
- Caballero
- Cha-cha-cha
- Chipaneca
- Cotillion
- Ecossaise
- Eightsome
- Farandole
- Formation
- Gallopade
- Hoolachan
- Jitterbug
- Kathakali
- Malaguena
- Pas de deux
- Paso doble
- Passepied
- Paul Jones
- Polonaise
- Poussette
- Quadrille
- Quickstep
- Ring-shout
- Roundelay
- Siciliano

- Sink-a-pace
- Tambourin
- Tripudium
- Variation
- Zapateado

10 letters:
- Antimasque
- Breakdance
- Carmagnole
- Charleston
- Cinque-pace
- Corroboree
- Gay Gordon's
- Hay-de-guise
- Hay-de-guyes
- Hey-de-guise
- Hey-de-guyes
- Hokey-cokey
- Passamezzo
- Petronella
- Rug-cutting
- Saltarello
- Seguidilla
- Sicilienne
- Sinke-a-pace
- Strathspey
- Tarantella
- Thé dansant
- Tripudiate
- Turkey trot
- Tyrolienne
- Walk-around

11 letters:
- Antistrophe
- Black bottom
- Buck and wing
- Comprimario
- Cracovienne
- Lambeth walk
- Palais glide
- Passacaglia
- Pastourelle
- Progressive
- Schottische
- Shimmy-shake
- Varsovienne

12 letters:
- Bharat Natyam
- Labanotation

Passemeasure
Passy-measure
Virginia reel

13 letters:
Highland fling

14 letters:
Divertissement
Jack-in-the-green

18 letters:
Sir Roger de
Coverley

Dance movement Arabesque, Balancé, Battement, Batterie, Brisé, Chassé, Dos-à-dos, Dosido, Entrechat, Fishtail, Fouetté, Glissade, Jeté, Lassu, Pantalon, Pas de basque, Pas de chat, Pas seul, Pigeonwing, Pirouette, Plié, Poule, Poussette, Routine, Sauté, Step

Dance tune Toy

▷ **Dancing** *may indicate* an anagram

Dancing party Ball, Ridotto

Dandelion Kok-saghyz, Piss-a-bed, Scorzonera, Taraxacum

Dander Anger, Gee, Passion, Saunter, Temper

Dandle Dance, Doodle, Fondle, Pet

Dandruff Furfur, Scurf

Dandy Adonis, Beau, Blood, Boulevardier, Buck(een), Cat, Coxcomb, Dapper, > DUDE, Exquisite, Fantastico, Fop, Gem, Jay, Jessamy, Johnny, Kiddy, Knut, Lair, Macaroni, Masher, Modist, Monarcho, Muscadin, Nash, Nut, Posh, Roy, Smart, Spark, Spiff, Swell, Ted, Toff, U, Yankee-doodle

Dandy-horse Draisene, Draisine

Dane(s) Clemence, Dansker, Ogier, Ostmen

Danger(ous) Apperil, Breakneck, Chancy, Crisis, Dic(e)y, Dire, Dodgy, Emprise, Fear, Hairy, Hazard, Hearie, High-risk, Hot, Insecure, Jeopardy, Lethal, Menace, Mine, Nettle, Nocuous, Objective, Parlous, Periculous, > PERIL, Pitfall, Precarious, Quicksand, Risk, Serious, Severe, Snag, Snare, Tight, Trap, Wonchancy

Dangle A(i)glet, Aiguillette, Critic, Flourish, Hang, Loll, Swing

Daniel Dan, Defoe, Deronda, Lion-tamer, Portia, Quilp

Dank Clammy, Damp, Humid, Moist, Wet, Wormy

Daphne Agalloch, Agila, Eaglewood, Lace-bark, Laura, Laurel, Mezereon

Dapper Dressy, Natty, Neat, Smart, Spiff, Spruce, Sprush, Spry, > TRIM

Darbies Cuffs, Irons, Snaps

Dare, **Dare-devil**, **Daring** Adventure, Bold, Brave, Challenge, Courage, Da(u)nton, Defy, Durst, Emprise, Face, Gallant, Gallus, Hardihood, Hazard, Hen, Intrepid, Moxie, Neck, Prowess, Racy, Stuntman, Taunt, Venture

Dark(en), **Darkie**, **Darkness** Aphelia, Aphotic, Apophis, Black, Blind, Cimmerian, Cloud, Depth, Dim, Dingy, Dirk(e), Dusky, Eclipse, Erebus, Evil, Gloom, Glum, Inumbrate, Mare, Maria, Melanous, Mulatto, Murk(y), Negro, Night, Obfuscate, Obscure, Ominous, Ousel, Ouzel, Pall, Phaeic, Pitch-black, Pit-mirk, Rooky, Sable, Sad, Secret, Shady, Shuttered, Sinister, Solein, Sombre, Sooty, Sphacelate, Stygian, Sullen, Swarthy, Tar, Tenebr(i)ous, Tenebrose, Unfair, Unlit, Wog, Woosel, Yellowboy, Yellowgirl

Darling Acushla, Alannah, Asthore, Beloved, Charlie, Cher, Chéri(e), Chick-a-biddy, Chick-a-diddle, Chuck-a-diddle, Dear, Dilling, Do(a)ting-piece, Duck(s), Favourite, Grace, Honey, Idol, Jarta, Jo(e), Lal, Love, Luv, Mavourneen, Mavournin, Minikin, Minion, Oarswoman, Own, Peat, Pet, Poppet, Precious, Sugar, Sweetheart, Yarta, Yarto

Darn Begorra, Blow, Doggone, Hang, Mend, Repair, Sew

Dart(er) Abaris, Arrow, Banderilla, Dace, Dash, Deadener, Dodge, Fleat, Fléchette, Flit, Harpoon, Javelin, Launch, Leap, Scoot, Skrim, Speck, Spiculum, Sprint, Strike, Thrust, Wheech

Dash(ing), **Dashed** Backhander, Bally, Blade, Blight, Blow, Buck, Charge,

Collide, Cut, Dad, Dah, Damn, Dapper, Dart(le), Daud, Debonair, Ding, Elan, En, Fa(s)cia, Flair, Fly, Go-ahead, Hang, Hurl, > HURRY, Hustle, Hyphen, Impetuous, Jabble, Jaw, Jigger, Lace, Line, Minus, Morse, Natty, Nip, Panache, Pebble, Rakish, Ramp, Rash, Rule, Run, Rush, Sally, Scamp(er), Scart, Scoot, Scrattle, Scurry, Scuttle, Shatter, Showy, Soupçon, Souse, Spang, Speed, Splash, Splatter, Sprint, Strack, Streak, Stroke, > STYLE, Swung, Throw, Touch, Viretot

Dashboard Fascia

Dashwood Hell-fire club

Dastard(ly) Base, Coward, Craven, Nid(d)erling, Poltroon

Data(base), Datum Archie, Cyberspace, Donne(e), Evidence, Facts, Fiche, File, Floating-point, Gen, HOLMES, Info, Input, Material, Matrix, News, Soft copy

Date(d), Dates, Dating AD, Age, AH, Almanac, Appointment, Blind, Boyfriend, Calendar, Carbon, Carbon-14, Computer, Court, Deadline, Engagement, Epoch, Equinox, Era, Escort, Exergue, Expiry, Fixture, Girlfriend, Ides, Julian, Meet, Outmoded, > OUT OF DATE, Passé, Past, Radioactive, Radio-carbon, Radiometric, Rubidium-strontium, See, System, > TRYST, Ult(imo), Value

Daub Begrime, Blob, Dab, Gaum, Mess, Moil, Noint, Plaister, Plaster, > SMEAR, Smudge, Splodge, Teer, Wattle

Daughter (in law) Child, D, Elect, Girl, Jephthah's, Niece, Offspring, Skevington's

Daunt Adaw, Amate, Awe, Deter, Dishearten, Intimidate, Overawe, Quail, Stun, Stupefy, Subdue

Dauphin Delphin

David Dai, Psalmist

Davit Crane, Derrick, Hoist

Davy Crockett, Jones

Daw Bird, Magpie, Margery

Dawdle(r) Dally, Draggle, Drawl, Idle, Lag(gard), > LOITER, Potter, Shirk, Slowcoach, Tarry, Troke, Truck

Dawn Aurora, Cockcrow, Daw, Daybreak, Daylight, Day-peep, Dayspring, Loan, Eos, False, Light, Morrow, Occur, Prime, Roxane, Start, Sunrise, Ushas

Day(s) Account, Ahemeral, All Fools', All Hallows', All Saints', All Souls', Anniversary, Annunciation, Anzac, April Fool's, Armistice, Ascension, Australia, Bad hair, Baker, Banian, Bastille, Boxing, Calendar, Calends, Calpa, Canada, Civil, Columbus, Commonwealth, Contango, D, Daft, Date, Decoration, Degree, Distaff, Dog, Dominion, Duvet, Early, Ember, Empire, Epact, Fast, Fasti, Father's, Feast, Ferial, Field, Flag, Fri, Gang, Gaudy, Groundhog, Guy Fawkes', Halcyon, High, Hogmanay, Holy, Holy Innocents', Holy-rood, Hundred, Ides, Inauguration, Independence, Intercalary, Judgment, Judicial, Kalends, Kalpa, Labo(u)r, Lady, Laetare, Lammas, Law(ful), Lay, Leap, Mardi, May, Memorial, Michaelmas, Midsummer, Mon, Morrow, Mother's, Muck-up, Mufti, Mumping, Name, New year's, Nones, Nychthemeron, Oak-apple, Octave, Open, Orangeman, Pancake, Paper, Pay, Poppy, Pound, Present, Primrose, Pulvering, Quarter, Rag, Rainy, Red-letter, Remembrance, Rest, Robin, Rock, Rogation, Rood(-mas), Rosh Chodesh, Sabbath, Saint's, St Swithin's, St Valentine's, Salad, Sat, Settling, Shick-shack, Show, Sidereal, Snow, Solar, Solstice, Speech, Sports, Station, Sun, Supply, Tag, Term, Thanksgiving, Thurs, Ticket, Time, Transfer, Trial, Tues, Twelfth, Utas, Valentine's, Varnishing, VE, Veterans', Victoria, Visiting, VJ, Waitangi, Wed, Wedding, Working

Daybreak Cockcrow

Daydream(er) Brown study, Dwam, Fancy, Imagine, Muse, Reverie, Rêveur,

Walter Mitty

Daylight Artificial, Dawn, Space, Sun

Daze(d) Amaze, Bemuse, Confuse, Dwaal, Gally, Muddle, Muzzy, Punch drunk, Reeling, Spaced out, > **STUN**, Stupefy, Stupor, Trance

Dazzle(d), Dazzling Bewilder, Blend, Blind, Eclipse, Foudroyant, Glare, Meteoric, Outshine, Radiance, Resplendent, Splendour, Yblent

Deacon Cleric, Doctor, Minister

Deactivate Unarm

Dead(en) Abrupt, Accurate, Alamort, Asgard, Asleep, Blunt, Brown bread, Bung, Cert, Cold, Complete, D, Deceased, Defunct, Doggo, Expired, Extinct, Gone(r), Inert, Infarct, Late, Lifeless, Morkin, Muffle, Mute, Napoo, Niflheim, Numb, Obsolete, Obtund, Ringer, She'ol, Slain, Smother, Stillborn, True, Utter, Waned

Dead end, Deadlock Blind alley, Cut-off, Dilemma, Impasse, Logjam, Stalemate, Stoppage

Dead-leaf colour Filemot, Philamot, Philomot

Deadline Date, Epitaph, Limit

Deadlock Stand-off, Sticking-point

Deadly Baleful, Dull, Fell, Funest, Internecine, > **LETHAL**, Malign, Mortal, Mortific, Pestilent, Unerring, Venomous

Deadly Nightshade Belladonna, Dwale

Deadpan Expressionless

Dead reckoning Dr

Dead tree Rampick, Rampike

Deaf(en), Deafness Adder, Asonia, Deave, Deeve, Dunny, Heedless, Paracusis, Presbyc(o)usis, Surd(ity)

Deal(er), Dealings, Deal with Address, Agent, Agreement, Allot(ment), Arb, Arbitrageur, Bargain, Breadhead, Brinjarry, Broker, Business, Cambist, Chandler, Chapman, Commerce, Cope, Coup, Cover, Croupier, Dispense, Distributor, Do, Dole, Eggler, Exchange, Fripper, Goulash, Hand(le), Help, Inflict, Insider, Interbroker, Jiggery-pokery, Jobber, Lashing, Lay on, Lay out, Let, Manage, Mercer, Merchant, Mickle, Middleman, Monger, Mort, Negotiate, New, Operator, Package, Pine, Productivity, Pusher, Raft, Raw, Sale, Serve, Side, Sort, Spicer, Square, Stockist, Stockjobber, Takeover, Tape, Timber, Tout(er), > **TRADE**, Traffic, Transaction, Treat, Truck, Wheeler, Wholesaler, Wield, Woolstapler, Yardie

Dean Acheson, Arabin, Colet, Decani, Doyen, Forest, Head, Inge, Nellie, Provost, RD, Rural, Rusk, Slade, Spooner, Swift, Vale, Vicar-forane

Dear(er), Dearest, Dear me Ay, Bach, Beloved, Cara, Caro, Cher(e), Cherie, Chou, Chuckie, Darling, Duck(s), Expensive, High, Honey(bun), Lamb, Leve, Lief, Lieve, Loor, Love, Machree, Mouse, My, Pet, Pigsney, Pigsnie, Pigsny, Steep, Sweet, Sweetie, Toots(ie), Up

Dearth Famine, Lack, Paucity, Scantity, Scarcity, > **SHORTAGE**

Deaspiration Psilosis

Death(ly) Auto-da-fe, Bane, Bargaist, Barg(h)est, Biolysis, Black, Cataplexis, Charnel, Clinical, Cot, Curtains, Cypress, Demise, Departure, Dormition, End, Eschatology, Euthanasia, Exit, Extinction, Fatality, Funeral, Fusillation, Gangrene, Grim Reaper, Hallal, Heat, Infarction, Jordan, Karoshi, Lead colic, Lethee, Leveller, Living, Mors, Napoo, Necrosis, Nemesis, Night, Obit, Quietus, Reaper, Sati, Sergeant, SIDS, Small-back, Strae, Sudden, Suttee, Terminal, Thanatism, Thanatopsis, Thanatos

Death-flood Styx

Deathless(ness) Athanasy, Eternal, Eterne, Immortal, Struldberg, Timeless,

Undying
Debacle Cataclysm, Collapse, Disaster, Fiasco
Debar Deny, Exclude, Forbid, > **PREVENT**, Prohibit
Debase(d) Adulterate, Allay, Bemean, Cheapen, Corrupt, Demean, Depreciate, Dialectician, Dirty, Grotesque, Hedge, Lower, Pervert, Traduce, Vitiate
Debate Argue, Combat, Contention, Contest, Deliberate, Dialectic, Discept, Discuss(ion), > **DISPUTE**, Flyte, Forensics, Full-dress, Moot, Polemics, Powwow, Reason, Teach-in, Warsle, Wrangle, Wrestle
Debauch(ed), **Debauchee**, **Debauchery** Corrupt, Decadent, Defile, Degenerate, Dissipate, Dissolute, Heliogabalus, Libertine, Licence, Orgy, Profligate, Rake-hell, Riot, Roist, Royst, Seduce, Spree, Stuprate, Wet, Whore
Debenture Bond, Security
Debilitate(d), **Debility** Asthenia, Atonic, Cachexia, Feeble, Languid, Weak
Debit Charge, Debt, Direct
Debonair Cavalier, Gay, Gracious, Jaunty
Debris Bahada, Bajada, Detritus, Eluvium, Moraine, Moslings, Refuse, > **RUBBLE**, Ruins, Tephra, Waste
▷ **Debris** *may indicate* an anagram
Debt(or) Alsatia, Arrears, Arrestee, Dr, Due, Floating, Funded, Insolvent, IOU, Liability, Moratoria, National, Obligation, Poultice, Public, Queer Street, Score, Tie, Unfunded
Debt-collector Bailiff, Forfaiter, Remembrancer
Debut Launch, Opening, Outset, Presentation
Debutante Bud, Deb
Decade Rosary, Ten
Decadence, **Decadent** Babylonian, Decaying, Degeneration, Dissolute, Effete, Fin-de-siècle, Libertine
Decamp Abscond, Absquatulate, Bolt, Bunk, Depart, Flee, Guy, Levant, Mizzle, Slide, Slope, Vamoose
Decant Pour, Unload
Decapitate, **Decapitation** Aphesis, > **BEHEAD**, Guillotine
▷ **Decapitated** *may indicate* first letter removed
Decay(ed), **Decaying** Alpha, Appair, Beta, Biodegrade, Blet, Canker, Caries, Caseation, Consenescence, Crumble, Decadent, Declension, Decline, Decompose, Decrepit, Dieback, Disintegrate, Dissolution, Doat, Doddard, Doddered, Dote, Dricksie, Druxy, Dry rot, Fail, F(o)etid, Forfair, Gangrene, Heart-rot, Impair, Moulder, Pair(e), Perish, Plaque, Putrefy, Radioactive, Ret, Rot, Saprogenic, Sap-rot, Seedy, Sepsis, Spoil, Tabes, Wet-rot
Decease(d) Death, Decedent, Demise, Die, Stiff
Deceit(ful), **Deceive(r)** Abuse, Artifice, Bamboozle, Barrat, Befool, Bitten, Blind, Bluff, Braide, > **CHEAT**, Chicane, Chouse, Con, Cozen, Cuckold, Defraud, Delude, Diddle, Dike, Dissemble, Do brown, Double-cross, Double-tongued, Dupe, Duplicity, False(r), Fastie, Fast-talk, Fiddle, Flam, Fox, Fraud, Gag, Gerrymander, Gloze, Guile, Gull, Hoax, Hoodwink, Hornswoggle, Humbug, Hype, Illusion, Imposition, Inveigle, Invention, Jiggery-pokery, Kid, Malengine, Mata Hari, Mendacious, Mislead, Mislippen, Phenakism, Poop, Poupe, Pretence, Punic, Rig, Ruse, Sell, Sham, Sinon, Sleekit, Snow job, Spruce, Stratagem, Subreption, Swindle, Swizzle, Tregetour, Trick, Trump, Two-faced, Two-time, Wile
Decency, **Decent** Chaste, Decorum, Fitting, Healsome, Honest, Kind, Modest, Passable, Seemly, Sporting, Wholesome
Decentralise Disperse

Deception, Deceptive Artifice, Bluff, Catchpenny, Catchy, Cheat, Chicanery, Codology, > **DECEIT**, Disguise, Dupe, Duplicity, Eyewash, Fallacious, False, Flam, Fraud, Gag, Gammon, Guile, Have-on, Hocus-pocus, Hokey-pokey, Hum, Hunt-the-gowks, Hype, Ignes-fatui, Ignis-fatuus, Illusion, Insidious, Lie, Moodies, Runaround, Ruse, Sell, Sleight, Smoke and mirrors, Specious, Sting, The moodies, > **TRICK**, Trompe l'oeil, Two-timing, Underhand

Decide(r), Decided Addeem, Agree, Ballot, Barrage, Cast, Clinch, Conclude, > **DECISION**, Deem, Definite, Determine, Distinct, Engrenage, Firm, Fix, Jump-off, Mediate, Opt, Parti, Predestination, Pronounced, Rescript, > **RESOLVE**, Rule, Run-off, See, Settle, Sudden death, Tiebreaker, Try

Decimal Mantissa, Recurring, Repeating, Terminating

Decimate Destroy, Lessen, Weaken

Decipher(ing) Cryptanalysis, Decode, Decrypt, Descramble, Discover, Interpret

▷ **Decipher(ed)** *may indicate* an 'o' removed

Decision Arbitrium, Arrêt, Crossroads, Crunch, Decree, Engrenage, Fatwa, Fetwa, Firman, Judg(e)ment, Placit(um), Referendum, Resolution, Resolve, Responsa, Ruling, Sentence, Sudden death, Verdict

Decisive Climactic, Clincher, Critical, Crux, Definite, Final, Pivotal

Deck Adorn, Array, Attrap, Bejewel, Boat, Cards, Clad, Daiker, Daub, Decorate, Dizen, Embellish, Equip, Flight, Focsle, Forecastle, Garland, Hang, Helideck, Hurricane, Lower, Main, Monkey poop, Orlop, Ornament, Pack, Platform, Poop, Prim, Promenade, Quarter, Saloon, Spar, Sun, Tape, Upper, Void, Well

Declare, Declaration, Declaim, Decree Absolute, Affidavit, Affirm, Air, Allege, Announce, Annunciate, Assert, Asseverate, Aver, Avow, Balfour, Bann(s), Breda, Dictum, Diktat, Doom, Edict, Elocute, Enact, Fatwa(h), Fiat, Firman, Go, Grace, Harangue, Hatti-sherif, Independence, Indulgence, Insist, Interlocutory, Irade, Law, Mandate, Manifesto, Mecklenburg, Meld, Motu proprio, Mou(th), Nisi, Noncupate, Novel(la), Nullity, Nuncupate, Orate, Ordain, Order, Ordinance, Parlando, Pontificate, Predicate, Proclaim, Profess, Promulgate, Pronounce, Protest, Psephism, Publish, Rant, Recite, Rescript, Resolve, Rights, Rule, Ruling, SC, Sed, Senecan, Shahada, Signify, Speak, Spout, State, Statutory, Testify, Testimony, UDI, Ultimatum, Unilateral, Vie, Voice, Vouch, Word

▷ **Declaring** *may indicate* a word beginning 'Im'

Decline, Declining Age, Ail, Atrophy, Catabasis, Comedown, Decadent, Degeneration, Degringoler, Deny, Descend, Deteriorate, Devall, Die, Dip, Dissent, Downhill, Downtrend, Downturn, Droop, Dwindle, Ebb, Fade, Fall, Flag, Forbear, Paracme, Quail, Recede, Recession, Refuse, Retrogression, Rot, Rust, Sag, Senile, Set, Sink, Slide, Slump, Stoop, Wane, Welke, > **WILT**, Withdraw, Wither

Decoct(ion) Apozem, Cook, Devise, Ptisan, Tisane

Decode(d) En clair

Decolleté Low, Neckline

Decompose, Decomposition Biodegradable, Crumble, Decay, Disintegrate, Hydrolysis, Mor, Pyrolysis, Rot, Wither

Decompression Bends

Decor Background, Scenery

Decorate(d), Decoration, Decorative Adorn, Angelica, Aogai, Arpillera, Attrap, Award, Baroque, Beaux-arts, Biedermeier, Bordure, Braid, Brattishing, Braze, Brooch, Cartouche, Centrepiece, Chambranle, Champlevé, Chinoiserie, Christingle, Cinquefoil, Cloissoné, Cresting, Crocket, Cul-de-lampe, Dentelle, Diamante, Doodad, Dragée, Dragging, Emblazon, Emboss, Embrave, Engrail,

Enrich, Epergne, Etch, Fancy, Festoon, Filigree, Finial, Fleuret(te), Fleuron,
Floriated, Flushwork, Fluting, Fourragère, Frieze, Frill, Frog, Furbish,
Gammadion, Garniture, Gaud, Gild, Goffer, Gradino, Grecque key, Guilloche,
Historiated, Ice, Illuminate, Impearl, Inlay, Intarsia, Intarsio, Interior,
Knotwork, Linen-fold, Linen-scroll, Marquetry, MC, Medal(lion), Mola, Motif,
Moulding, Oath, OBE, Order, > ORNAMENT, Ornate, Orphrey, Ovolo, Paint,
Paper, Parament, Pâté-sur-pâté, Pinata, Pipe, Pokerwork, Pompom, Prettify,
Prink, Purfle, Purple heart, Quilling, Rag-rolling, Rangoli, Repoussé, Rich,
Rosemaling, Ruche, Scallop, Schwarzlot, Scrimshander, Scrimshaw, Serif,
Set-off, Sgraffito, Skeuomorph, Soutache, Spangle, Staffage, Stomacher,
Storiated, Strapwork, Studwork, Tailpiece, Tattoo, TD, Titivate, Tool, Topiary,
Trim, Veneer, Wallpaper, Well-dressing

Decorous, **Decorum** Becoming, Demure, Etiquette, Fitness, Parliamentary,
Prim, > PROPER, Propriety, Seemlihe(a)d, > SEEMLY, Staid

Decoy Allure, Bait, Bonnet, Button, Call-bird, Coach, Crimp, Entice, Lure, Piper,
Roper, Ruse, Shill, Stale, Stalking-horse, Stool-pigeon, Tole, Toll, Trap, Trepan

Decrease Decrew, Diminish, Dwindle, Iron, Lessen, Press, Reduce, Rollback,
Slim, Step-down, Subside, Wane, Wanze

Decree > DECLAIM, Saw

Decrepit Dilapidated, Doddery, Failing, Feeble, Frail, Moth-eaten, Time-worn,
Tumbledown, Warby, Weak

Decry Condemn, Crab, Denounce, Derogate, Detract, Downgrade

Dedicate(d), **Dedication** Corban, Devote, Endoss, Hallow, Inscribe, Oblate,
Pious, Sacred, Votive

Deduce, **Deduction**, **Deductive** A priori, Assume, Conclude, Consectary,
Corollary, Derive, Discount, Dockage, Gather, Illation, Infer(ence), Obvert,
Off-reckoning, Reason, Rebate, Recoup, Reprise, Stoppage, Surmise, Syllogism

Deed(s) Achievement, Act(ion), Atweel, Backbond, Charta, Charter, Derring-do,
Disposition, Escrol(l), Escrow, Exploit, Fact(um), Feat, Indeed, Indenture,
Manoeuvre, Mitzvah, Muniments, Premises, Specialty, Starr, > TITLE, Trust

Deem Consider, Opine, Ordain, Proclaim, Repute, Think

Deep(en), **Deeply** Abstruse, Bass(o), Brine, Briny, Enhance, Excavate, Grum,
Gulf, Hadal, Intense, Low, Mindanao, Mysterious, > OCEAN, Profound,
Re-enter, Rich, Sea, Sonorous, Throaty, Upsee, Ups(e)y

Deep-rooted Inveterate

Deer(-like) Axis, Bambi, Barasing(h)a, Barking, Blacktail, Brocket, Buck,
Cariacou, Caribou, Carjacou, Cervine, Chevrotain, Chital, Doe, Elaphine, Elk,
Fallow, Gazelle, Hart, Hog, Moose, Mouse, Mule, Muntjac, Muntjak, Musk,
Père David's, Pricket, Pudu, Pygarg, Red, Rein, Roe, Rusa, Sambar, Sambur,
Selenodont, Sika, Sorel(l), Spade, Spay(d), Spayad, Spitter, Spottie, Stag(gard),
Tragule, Ungulate, Virginia, Wapiti, Water, White-tailed

Deer-hunter Tinchel

Deface Disfigure, Spoil

▷ **Defaced** may indicate first letter missing

Defame, **Defamatory**, **Defamation** Abase, Bad mouth, Blacken, Calumny,
Cloud, Denigrate, Detract, Dishonour, Impugn, Libel, Malign, Mud,
Mudslinging, Scurrilous, Slander, Smear, Stigmatise, Traduce, Vilify

Default(er) Absentee, Bilk, Dando, Delinquent, Flit, Levant, Neglect, Omission,
Waddle, Welsh

Defeat(ed), **Defeatist** Beat, Best, Caning, Capot, Codille, Conquer, Counteract,
Debel, Defeasance, Demolish, Discomfit, Dish, Ditch, Fatalist, Floor, Foil,
Foyle, Hammer, Hiding, Kippered, Laipse, Lick, Loss, Lurch, Marmelize,

Master, Mate, Negative, Out, Outclass, Outdo, Outplay, Outvote, Outwit, > **OVERCOME**, Overpower, Overreach, Overthrow, Overwhelm, Pip, Reverse, Rout, Rubicon, Scupper, Set, Shellacking, Sisera, Squabash, Stump, Tank, Thrash, Thwart, Tonk, Trounce, Vanquish, War, Waterloo, Whap, Whip, Whitewash, Whop, Whup, Wipe-out, Worst

Defecate, Defecation Horse, Mute, Poop, Shit, Tenesmus

Defect(ion), Defective, Defector Abandon, Amateur, Apostasy, Bug, Coma, Crack, Faulty, Flaw, > **FORSAKE**, Frenkel, Halt, Hamartia, Kink, Manky, Mote, Natural, Paralexia, Point, Psellism, Rachischisis, Renegade, Renegate, Ridgel, Ridgil, Rig, Rogue, Runagate, Schottky, Shortcoming, Spina bifida, Terrace, Treason, Trick, Want, Weakness, Wreath

Defence, Defend(er), Defensible Abat(t)is, Alibi, Antibody, Antidote, Antihistamine, Apologia, Back, Back four, Bailey, Barbican, Barmkin, Barricade, Bastion, Battery, Battlement, Berm, Bestride, Bridgehead, Bulwark, Calt(h)rop, Catenaccio, CD, Champion, Chapparal, Civil, Curtain, Demibastion, Ditch, Embrasure, Hedgehog, Herisson, Hold, J(i)u-jitsu, Justify, Kaim, Keeper, Laager, Laer, Last-ditch, Linebacker, Maintain, Martello Tower, MIDAS, Miniment, Moat, Muniment, Outwork, Palisade, Parapet, Perceptual, Propugnation, Rampart, Redan, Redoubt, Resist, Ringwall, > **SHELTER**, Shield, Stonewall, Support, Sweeper, Tenable, Tenail(le), Testudo, Tower, Trench, Trou-de-loup, Uphold, Vallation, Vallum, Vindicate, Wall, Warran(t), Zonal

Defenceless Helpless, Inerm, Naked, Sitting duck, Vulnerable

Defendant Accused, Apologist, Respondent, Richard Roe

Defer(ence), Deferential Bow, Complaisance, Delay, Dutiful, Homage, Morigerous, Obeisant, Pace, Polite, Postpone, Procrastinate, Protocol, Respect, Shelve, Submit, Suspend, Waive, Yield

Defiance, Defiant, Defy Acock, Bold, Brave, Contumacy, Dare, Daring, Disregard, Do or die, Outbrave, Outdare, Recusant, Resist, Stubborn, Titanism, Truculent, Unruly

Deficiency, Deficient Absence, Acapnia, Anaemia, Beriberi, Defect, Inadequate, Incomplete, Kwashiorkor, Lack, Osteomalacia, Scant, Scarcity, SCID, Shortage, Shortfall, Spanaemia, Want

▷ **Deficient** *may indicate* an anagram

Deficit Anaplerotic, Arrears, Defective, Ischemia, Loss, Poor, Shortfall

Defile(ment) Abuse, Array, Barranca, Barranco, Besmear, Col, Conspurcation, Desecrate, Dishonour, Donga, Enseam, > **FOUL**, Gate, Gorge, Gully, Inquinate, Inseem, Kloof, Moil, Pass, Pollute, Poort, Ravine, Ray, Roncesvalles, Smear, Spoil, > **SULLY**

Define(d), Definition, Definitive Decide, Demarcate, Determine, Diorism, Distinct, Explain, Fix, Limit, Parameter, Set, Tangible, Term

Definite(ly) Classic, Clear, Emphatic, Firm, Hard, Pos, Positive, Precise, Specific, Sure, Yes

Deflate Burst, Collapse, Flatten, Lower, Prick, Puncture

Deflect(or), Deflection Avert, Bend, Detour, Diverge, Divert, Glance, Otter, Paravane, Refract, Snick, Swerve, Throw, Trochotron, Veer, Windage

Deform(ed), Deformity Anamorphosis, Blemish, Crooked, Disfigure, Distort, Gammy, Hammer-toe, Harelip, Misborn, Mishapt, Mooncalf, Mutilate, Phocomelia, Phocomely, Polt-foot, Saddle-nose, Stenosed, Talipes, Valgus, Varus, Warp

▷ **Deformed** *may indicate* an anagram

Defraud Bilk, Cheat, Cozen, Gull, Gyp, Mulct, Shoulder, Sting, Swindle, Trick

Defray Bear, Cover, Meet

Defrost Thaw

Deft Adept, Agile, Dab, Dexterous, Elegant, Handy, Nimble

Defunct Deceased, Extinct, Obsolete

▶ **Defy** *see* DEFIANCE

Degenerate, Degeneration, Degenerative Acorn-shell, Ascidian, Atrophy, Balanus, Base, Cirrhipedea, Cirrhipedia, Cirrhopod(a), Cirripedea, Cirripedia, Decadent, Deprave, Descend, Deteriorate, Eburnation, Fatty, Kaliyuga, Necrobiosis, Pejorate, Pervert, Rakehell, Relapse, Retrogress, Salp, Tunicate

Degrade, Degradation Abase, Cheapen, Culvertage, Debase, Demote, Depose, Diminish, Disennoble, Embase, Humble, Imbase, Lessen, Lower, > SHAME, Waterloo

Degree(s) Aegrotat, As, Azimuthal, BA, Baccalaureate, BCom, BD, B es S, C, Class, D, Desmond (Tutu), Doctoral, Douglas (Hurd), Engler, Extent, External, F, First, German, Gradation, Grade, Grece, Gree(s), Greece, Gre(e)se, Grice, Griece, Grize, > IN A HIGH DEGREE, K, Lambeth, Latitude, Letters, Level, Levitical, Licentiate, MA, Measure, Mediant, Nth, Nuance, Peg, PhD, Pin, Poll, Rate, Remove, Second, Stage, Status, Step, Third, Trevor (Nunn), Water

Dehiscence Suture

Dehydrate Exsiccate

Deification, Deify Apotheosis

Deign Condescend, Stoop

Deity Avatar, Demogorgon, Divine, Faun, > GOD, > GODDESS, Idolise, Immortalise, Numen, Pan, Satyr, Zombi(e)

Deject(ed), Dejection Abase, Abattu, Alamort, Amort, Blue, Chap-fallen, Crab, Crestfallen, Despondent, Dismay, Dispirited, Down, Downcast, Gloomy, Hangdog, Humble, Melancholy

Delay(ed) Ambage, Avizandum, Behindhand, Check, Cunctator, Defer, Demurrage, Detention, Fabian, Filibuster, For(e)slow, Forsloe, Frist, Hesitate, Hinder, Hitch, Hold up, Hysteresis, Impede, Laches, Lag, Late, Laten, Let, Linger, Loiter, Mora(torium), Obstruct, Procrastinate, Prolong, Prorogue, Remanet, Reprieve, Respite, Retard, Setback, Slippage, Sloth, Slow, > STALL, Stand-over, Stay, Stonewall, Temporise, Wait

Delectable Delicious, Luscious, Tasty

Delegate, Delegation Agent, Amphictyon, Apostolic, Appoint, Assign, Decentralise, Depute, Devolution, Mission, Nuncio, Offload, Representative, Secondary, Transfer, Vicarial, Walking

Delete Cancel, Cut, Erase, Excise, Expunge, Purge, Rase, Scratch, Scrub, Twink out

Deliberate(ly) Adagio, Consider, Debate, Intentional, Meditate, Moderate, Ponder, Prepensely, Studied, Voulu, Weigh, Witting

Delicacy, Delicate Airy-fairy, Beccafico, Blini, Canape, Cate, Caviare, Dainty, Difficult, Discreet, Ectomorph, Eggshell, Elfin, Ethereal, Fastidious, Fine, Finespun, Finesse, Flimsy, Fragile, > FRAIL, Friand, Gossamer, Guga, Hothouse, Inconie, Incony, Kickshaw, Kidglove, Ladylike, Light, Lobster, Morbidezza, Nesh, Nicety, Niminy-piminy, Ortolan, Oyster, Reedy, Roe, Sensitive, Soft, Subtle(ty), Sunket, Sweetmeat, Taste, Tender, Tenuous, Ticklish, Tidbit, Titbit, Truffle

Delicious Ambrosia, Delectable, Exquisite, Fragrant, Goloptious, Goluptious, Gorgeous, Lekker, Lip-smacking, Mor(e)ish, Mouthwatering, Scrummy, Scrumptious, Tasty, Toothsome, Yummo, Yummy, Yum-yum

▷ **Delight** *may indicate* 'darken'

Delight(ed), Delightful Bliss, Chuff, Delice, Dreamy, Elated, Elysian, Enamour,

Enjoyable, Enrapture, Exuberant, Felicity, Fetching, Frabjous, Gas, Glad, Glee, Gratify, Honey, Joy, Nice, Overjoy, Over the moon, Please, Pleasure, > **RAPTURE**, Regale, Scrummy, Super, Taking, Tickle, Turkish, Whacko, Whee, Whoopee, Wizard, Yippee, Yum-yum

Delineate Draft, Sketch, Trace

Delinquent Bodgie, Criminal, Halbstarker, Juvenile, Negligent, Offender, Ted

Delirious, Delirium Deranged, DT, Frenetic, Frenzy, Insanity, Mania, Phrenetic, Spazz, Wild

Deliver(ance), Deliverer, Delivery Accouchement, Ball, Birth, Bowl, Breech, Caesarean, Consign, Convey, Deal, Drop, Elocution, Escape, Express, Extradition, Give, Jail, Lead, Liberate, Lob, Orate, Over, Pronounce, Recorded, Redeem, Release, Relieve, Render, Rendition, > **RESCUE**, Rid, Round(sman), Salvation, Save, Say, Seamer, Sell, Shipment, Speak, Special, Tice, Transfer, Underarm, Underhand, Utter, Wide, Yorker

Dell Dale, Dargle, Dene, Dimble, Dingle, Dingl(e)y, Glen, Valley

Delphic Pythian

Delphinium Larkspur

Delta Camargue, D, Del, Flood-plain, Kronecker, Nabla, Nile, Oil Rivers, Triangle

Delude, Delusion Bilk, Cheat, Deceive, Fallacy, Fool, Hoax, > **MISLEAD**, Paranoia, Schizothymia, Trick

Deluge Avalanche, Flood, Ogygian, Saturate, Submerge, > **SWAMP**

De luxe Extra, Plush, Special

Delve Burrow, Dig, Excavate, Exhume, Explore, Probe, Search

Demagogue Agitator, Fanariot, Leader, Mobsman, Phanariot, Speaker, Tribune

Demand(ing) Appetite, Call, Claim, Cry, Dun, Exact, Excess, Exigent, Fastidious, Final, Hest, > **INSIST**, Mandate, Market, Need, Order, Postulate, Pressure, Request, Requisition, Rush, Sale, Stern, Stipulate, Stringent, Summon, Ultimatum, Want

Demean(ing) Belittle, Comport, Debase, Degrade, Humble, Infra dig, Lower, Maltreat

Demeanour Air, Bearing, Conduct, Expression, Front, Gravitas, Mien, Port

Dement(ed) Crazy, Hysterical, Insane, Mad, Wacko

Demi-god Aitu, Daemon, Garuda, Hero

Demi-mondaine Cocotte, > **LOOSE WOMAN**, Prostitute

Demise Death, Decease, Finish

Demo March, Parade, Protest, Rally, Sit-in

Democracy, Democrat D, Hunker, Industrial, Locofoco, Montagnard, Popular, Republic, Sansculotte, Social, Tammany

Demoiselle Crane, Damselfish

Demolish, Demolition Bulldoze, Devastate, Devour, Dismantle, Floor, KO, Level, Rack, > **RAZE**, Smash, Wreck

▶ **Demon** *see* **DEVIL**

Demoness Lilith

Demonstrate, Demonstration, Demonstrator Agitate, Barrack, Display, Endeictic, Evènement, Evince, Explain, Hunger march, Maffick, Manifest, March, Morcha, Ostensive, Portray, Protest, Prove, Provo, Send-off, > **SHOW**, Sit-in, Touchy-feely

Demoralize Bewilder, Corrupt, Destroy, Shatter, Unman, Weaken

Demote, Demotion Comedown, Degrade, Disbench, Disrate, Embace, Embase, Reduce, Relegate, Stellenbosch

Demur Hesitate, Jib, Object

Demure Coy, Mim, Modest, Prenzie, Primsie, Sedate, Shy

Den Dive, Domdaniel, Earth, Hell, Hide-away, Holt, Home, Lair, Lie, Opium, Room, Shebeen, Study, Sty, Wurley

Denial, Deny, Denier Abnegate, Antinomian, Aspheterism, Bar, Contradict, Démenti, Disavow, Disenfranchise, Disown, Forswear, > GAINSAY, Nay, Negate, Nick, Protest, Refuse, Refute, Renague, Renay, Reneg(e), Renegue, Reney, Renig, Renounce, Reny, Repudiate, Sublate, Traverse, Withhold

Denigrate Besmirch, Blacken, Defame, Tar

Denim Jeans

Denizen Diehard, Inhabitant, Resident

Denomination Category, Cult, Sect, Variety

Denote Import, Indicate, Mean, Signify

Denouement Anagnorisis, Climax, Coda, Exposure, Outcome, Showdown

Denounce, Denunciation Ban, Commination, Condemn, Criticise, Decry, Delate, Diatribe, Hatchet job, Hereticate, Proclaim, Proscribe, Shop, Stigmatise, Upbraid

Denry Card

Density Compact, Current, D, Double, Firm, Flux, Neutral, Opaque, Optical, Reflection, Relative, Solid, Spissitude, Tesla, Thick, Transmission, Vapour, Woofy

Dent(ed) Batter, Concave, Dancette, Depress, Dimple, Dinge, Dint, Nock, V

Dental, Dentist(ry) DDS, Entodontics, Extractor, Kindhart, LDS, Odontic, Periodontic, Toothy

Dentures Biteplate, Bridge, Bridgework, False teeth, Plate, Store teeth, Wallies

▸ **Deny** *see* DENIAL

Deodorant Anti-perspirant

Deoxidise Outgas, Reduce

Depart(ed), Departing, Departure Abscond, Absquatulate, Bunk, D, Dead, Decession, Defunct, Die, Digress, Divergence, Exit, Exodus, Flight, > GO, Leave, Lucky, Outbound, Rack off, Remue, Vade, Vamoose, Walkout

Department Achaea, Ain, Aisne, Allier, Alpes Maritimes, Angers, Arcadia, Ardeche, Ardennes, Argo, Argolis, Ariege, Arrondissement, Arta, Attica, Aube, Aude, Aveyron, Bas-Rhin, Belfort, Beziers, Bouches-du-Rhone, Branch, Bureau, Calvados, Cantal, Charente, Cher, Commissariat, Corrèze, Cote d'Or, Cotes d'Armor, Cotes du Nord, Creuse, DEFRA, Deme, Deux-Sevres, Division, Dordogne, Doubs, Drôme, El(e)ia, Essonne, Eure, Eure-et-Loir, Faculty, Finistere, Fire, FO, Gard, Gers, Gironde, Greencloth, Guadeloupe, Gulag, Hanaper, Haute-Garonne, Haute-Loire, Haute-Marne, Haute-Normandie, Hautes-Alpes, Hautes-Saône, Hautes-Savoie, Haute-Vienne, Haut-Rhin, Hauts-de-Seine, Herault, Home, Ille-et-Vilaine, Indre, Indre-et-Loire, Isere, Jura, Landes, Loire, Loir-et-Cher, Lot, Lot-et-Garonne, Lozere, Maine-et-Loire, Manche, Mayenne, Meurthe-et-Moselle, Meuse, Ministry, Morbihan, Moselle, Nièvre, Nome, Nomos, Nord, Office, Oise, Orne, Pas-de-Calais, Province, Puy de Dôme, Pyrénées(-Atlantique), Pyrénées-Orientales, Region, Rehabilitation, Rhône, Sanjak, Saône-et-Loire, Sarthe, Savoie, Secretariat(e), Section, Seine-et-Marne, Seine Maritime, Seine St Denis, Somme, Sphere, State, Tarn(-et-Garonne), Treasury, Tuscany, Val de Marne, Val d'Oise, Var, Vaucluse, Vendée, Vienne, Voiotia, War, Wardrobe, Yonne, Yvelines

Depend(ant), Dependency, Dependent Addicted, Child, Client, Colony, Conditional, Contingent, Count, Dangle, Fief, Habit, Hang, Hinge, Icicle, Lean, Minion, Pensioner, Relier, Rely, Retainer, Ross, Sponge, Subject, Trust, Turn on, Vassal

Dependable Reliable, Reliant, Secure, Sheet-anchor, Solid, Sound, Staunch, Sure, > TRUSTWORTHY
Depict Delineate, Display, Draw, Limn, Paint, Portray, Present, Represent
Depilate, Depilatory Grain, Rusma, Slate
Deplete Diminish, Drain, Exhaust, Reduce
Deplorable, Deplore Base, Bemoan, Chronic, Complain, Deprecate, Dolorous, Grieve, Lament, Mourn, Piteous, Regret, Rue
Deploy(ment) Extend, Herse, Unfold, Use
▷ **Deploy(ment)** *may indicate* an anagram
Depopulate Deracinate
Deport(ment) Address, Air, Banish, > BEARING, Carriage, Demeanour, Mien, Renvoi, Renvoy
Depose, Deposition Affirm, Banish, Dethrone, Displace, Dispossess, Overthrow, Pieta, Testify
Deposit Alluvial, Alluvium, Arcus, Argol, Atheroma, Bank, Bathybius, Bergmehl, Calc-sinter, Calc-tuff, Caliche, Cave-earth, Coral, Crag, Delta, Depone, Diluvium, Drift, Evaporite, Fan, File, Firn, Fur, Gyttja, Kieselguhr, Land, Lay, Lodge(ment), Loess, Löss, Measure, Moraine, Natron, Outwatch, Park, Pay dirt, Placer, Plank, Plaque, Precipitate, Put, Repose, Residuum, Saburra, Saprolite, > SEDIMENT, Silt, Sinter, Sludge, Stockwork, Stratum, Surety, Tartar, Terramara, Terramare, Till, Time, Tophus, Turbidite
Depot Barracoon, Base, Camp, Depository, Station, Terminus, Treasure-city, Warehouse
Deprav(ed), Depravity Bestial, Cachexia, Cachexy, > CORRUPT, Dissolute, Evil, Immoral, Low, Reprobate, Rotten, Sodom, Total, Turpitude, Ugly, Vice, Vicious, Vile
Deprecate Censure, Deplore, Expostulate, Reproach
Depreciate Abase, Belittle, Derogate, Detract, Discount
Depredate, Depredation Pillage, Plunder, Rob
Depress(ed), Depressing, Depression Accablé, Alamort, Alveolus, Amort, Astrobleme, Attrist, Black dog, Blight, Blues, Cafard, Caldron, Canada, Canyon, Chill, Col, Combe, Couch, Crab, Crush, Cyclone, Dampen, Deject, Dell, Dene, Dent, Despair, > DIMPLE, Dip, Dismal, Dispirit, Dolina, Doline, Doomy, Downlifting, Drear, Drere, Dumpish, Endogenous, Exanimate, Flatten, Fonticulus, Foss(ula), Fossa, Fovea, Frog, Geosyncline, Ghilgai, Gilgai, Gilgie, Glen, Gloom, Graben, Grinch, Ha-ha, Hammer, Hilar, Hilum, Hilus, Hollow, Howe, Hyp, Joes, Kettle, Kick(-up), Lacuna, Leaden, Low(ness), Low-spirited, Moping, Neck, Ocean basin, Pan, Pit, Polje, Postnatal, Prostrate, Qattara, Recession, Re-entrant, Sad, Saddle, Salt-cellar, Salt-pan, Scrobicule, Sink, Sinkhole, Sinus, Sitzmark, Slot, > SLUMP, Slumpflation, Soakaway, Spiritless, Stomodaeum, Sump, Swag, Swale, Swallowhole, Trench, Trough, Umbilication, Vale, Vallecula, Valley, Wallow, Weigh down, Wet blanket
Deprivation, Deprive(d) Bereft, Deny, Disenfranchise, Disfrock, Disseise, Disseize, Expropriate, Famine, Foreclose, Geld, Have-not, Hunger, Reduce, Remove, Rob, Withhold
Depth Draught, Draw, F, Fathom, Gravity, Intensity, Isobath, Pit, Profundity
Deputise, Deputy Act, Agent, Aide, Assistant, Commis(sary), Delegate, Legate, Lieutenant, Locum, Loot, Mate, Number two, Prior, Proxy, Represent, Secondary, Standby, Sub, Substitute, Succentor, Surrogate, Vicar, Vice, Viceregent, Vidame
Derange(d) Craze, Détraqué, Disturb, Insane, Manic, Troppo, Unhinge, Unsettle
Derby Demolition, Donkey, Eponym, Hat, Kentucky, Kiplingcotes, Race, Roller

Derek Bo

Derelict Abandoned, > DECREPIT, Deserted, Negligent, Outcast, Ramshackle

Deride, Derision, Derisive Contempt, Gup, Guy, Hoot, Jeer, Mock, Nominal, Raspberry, > RIDICULE, Sardonic, Scoff, Scorn, Snifty, Snort, Yah, Ya(h)boo

Derive, Derivation, Derivative Ancestry, Creosote, Deduce, Descend, Extract, Get, Kinone, Of, Offshoot, Origin, Pedigree, Secondary

▶ **Dermatitis** *see* SKIN DISEASE

Derogate, Derogatory Belittle, Decry, Defamatory, Demeaning, Detract, Discredit, Pejorative, Personal, Slighting, Snide

Deronda Daniel

Derrick Crane, Davit, Hoist, Jib, Spar, Steeve

Dervish Calender, Doseh, Mawlawi, Mevlevi, Revolver, Santon, Whirling

Descant Comment, Discourse, Faburden, Melody, Song

Descartes René

Descend(ant), Descent Ancestry, Avail, Avale, Bathos, Blood, Chute, Cion, Decline, Degenerate, Derive, Dismount, Dive, Drop, Epigon, Extraction, Heir, Heraclid, > LINEAGE, Offspring, Pedigree, Prone, Rappel, Said, Say(y)id, Scarp, Scion, Seed, Shelve, Sien(t), Sink, Stock, Syen, Vest, Volplane

Describe, Description, Descriptive Blurb, Define, Delineate, Depict, Designate, Draw, Epithet, Exposition, Expound, Graphic, Job, Narrate, Outline, Paint, Portray, Rapportage, Recount, Relate, Report, Sea-letter, Sketch, Specification, Synopsis, Term, Trace

▷ **Describing** *may indicate* 'around'

Descry Behold, Discern, Get, Notice, Perceive

Desecrate, Desecration Abuse, Defile, Dishallow, Profane, Sacrilege, Unhallow

▷ **Desecrated** *may indicate* an anagram

Desert(er), Deserted, Desert(s) Abandon, Apostasy, Arabian, Arid, Ar Rimal, Arunta, Atacama, AWOL, Badland, Barren, Bledowska, Bug, Bunk, Colorado, Come-uppance, D, Dahna, Defect, Desolate, Dissident, Due, Empty, Eremic, Etosha Pan, Factious, Fail, Fezzan, Foresay, Forhoo, Forhow, Forlorn, Forsake, Forsay, Frondeur, Garagum, Gibson, Gila, Gobi, Great Basin, Great Indian, Great Sandy, Great Victoria, Heterodox, Indian, Jump ship, Kalahari, Kara Kum, Kavir, Kyzyl Kum, Libyan, Lurch, Meeds, Merit, Mohave, Mojave, Nafud, Namib, Negev, Nubian, Ogaden, Painted, Pategonian, Pindan, Rat, Refus(e)nik, Reg, > RENEGADE, Reward, Rub'al-Khali, Run, Runaway, Sahara, Sahel, Sands, Secede, Shamo, Simpson, Sinai, Sonoran, Sturt, Syrian, Tacna-Arica, Tergiversate, Thar, Turncoat, Ust(y)urt, Victoria, Void, Wadi, Waste, Western Sahara, Wilderness, Worthiness

Deserve(d) Condign, Earn, > MERIT, Well-earned, Worthy

Desiccate(d) Dry, Sere

Design(er) Adam, Aim, Architect, Ashley, Batik, Broider, Cardin, Cartoon, Castrametation, Chop, Cloisonné, Create, Cul de lampe, Damascene, Decal(comania), Decor, Depict, Devise, Dévoré, Dior, Draft, Embroidery, End, Engender, Engine(r), Engineer, Erté, Etch, Fashion, Feng-shui, Former, Hepplewhite, Hitech, Iconic, Impresa, Imprese, Industrial, Intend(ment), Intent(ion), Interior, Issigonis, Layout, Linocut, Logo, Marquetry, Mascle, Mean, Meander, Millefleurs, Modiste, Monogram, Morris, Mosaic, Motif, Pattern, > PLAN, Plot, Propose, Pyrography, Quant, Retro, Ruse, Schema, Scheme, Seal, Sheraton, Sketch, Specification, Stencil, Stubble, Stylist, Sunburst, Tatow, Tattoo, Tattow, Tatu, Think, Tooling, Trigram, Versace, Vignette, Watermark, Whittle

Designate Earmark, Note, Style, Title

Desirable, Desire, Desirous Ambition, Appetite, Aspire, Avid, Best, Cama, Conation, Concupiscence, Covet, Crave, Cupidity, Dreamboat, Earn, Eligible, Epithymetic, Fancy, Gasp, Hanker, Hope, Hots, Hunger, Itch, Kama(deva), Le(t)ch, Libido, List, Long, Luscious, Lust, Mania, Nymphomania, Orectic, Owlcar, Plum, Reck, Request, Residence, Salt, Streetcar, Thirst, Velleity, Vote, Wanderlust, Want, Whim, Will, Wish, Yearn, Yen

Desist Abandon, Cease, Curb, Pretermit, Quit, Stop

Desk Almemar, Ambo, Bureau, Carrel(l), Cash, Check-in, Cheveret, City, Copy, Davenport, Desse, Devonport, Enquiry, E(s)critoire, Faldstool, Lectern, Lettern, Litany, Pay, Pedestal, Prie-dieu, Pulpit, Reading, Roll-top, Scrutoire, Secretaire, Vargueno, Writing

Desman Pyrenean

Desolate, Desolation Bare, Barren, Desert, Devastate, Disconsolate, Forlorn, Gaunt, Godforsaken, Gousty, Moonscape, Waste, Woebegone

Despair, Desperate, Desperation Acharne, Anomy, De profundis, Despond, Dire, Dismay, Extreme, Frantic, Gagging, Giant, Gloom, Hairless, Headlong, Last-ditch, Last-gasp, Life and death, Reckless, Unhopeful, Urgent, Wanhope

▶ **Despatch** *see* DISPATCH

Desperado Bandit, Bravo, Ruffian, Terrorist

Despicable Abject, Base, Caitiff, Cheap, Churl, Contemptible, Heinous, Ignoble, Ignominious, Mean, Moer, Puke, Ratfink, Scumbag, Shabby, Toerag, Wretched

Despise Condemn, Contemn, Forhow, Hate, Ignore, Scorn, Spurn, Vilify, Vilipend

Despite For, Malgré, Notwithstanding, Pace, Though, Venom

Despoil Mar, Ravage, Vandalise

Despondent Dejected, Downcast, Forlorn, Gloomy, Sad

Despot(ism) Autarchy, Autocrat, Caesar, Darius, Dictator, Napoleon, Nero, Satrap, Stratocrat, Tsar, Tyrant, Tzar

Dessert Afters, Baked Alaska, Baklava, Bavarian Cream, Bavarois, Bombe, Charlotte, Charlotte russe, Cobbler, Compote, Coupe, Crème brulée, Crème caramel, Entremets, Flummery, Fool, Junket, Kissel, Knickerbocker glory, Kulfi, Marquise, Mousse, Mud pie, Nesselrode, Parfait, Pashka, Pavlova, Peach Melba, Pud(ding) Sawine, Sabayon, Semifreddo, Shoofly pie, Strudel, Sundae, Syllabub, Tiramisu, Tortoni, Trifle, Vacherin, Zabaglione

Destine(d), Destination Design, End, Fate, Foredoom, Goal, Home, Intend, Joss, Meant, Port, Purpose, Weird

Destiny Doom, > FATE, Karma, Kismet, Lot, Manifest, Moira, Yang, Yin

Destitute Bankrupt, Bare, Broke, Devoid, Dirt-poor, Helpless, Indigent, Needy, Poor, Sterile

Destroy(er) Annihilate, Antineutrino, Antineutron, Antiparticle, Apollyon, Atomise, Blight, D, Decimate, Deep-six, Deface, Delete, Demolish, Denature, Destruct, Dish, Dismember, Dissolve, Eat, Efface, End, Eradicate, Erase, Estrepe, Exterminate, Extirpate, Flivver, Fordo, Harry, Iconoclast, > KILL, Murder, Obliterate, Overkill, Perish, Predator, Ravage, Raze, Ruin, Saboteur, Scuttle, Slash, Smash, Spif(f)licate, Spoil, Sterilize, Stew-can, Stonker, Subvert, Trash, Undo, Uproot, Vandal, Vitiate, Whelm, Wreck, Zap

Destruction, Destructive Adverse, Autolysis, Bane, Can, Collapse, Deathblow, Deleterious, Devastation, Doom, Downfall, End, Götterdämmerung, Grave, Havoc, Holocaust, Insidious, Internecine, Kali, Lethal, Loss, Pernicious, Quelea, Rack, Ragnarok, Ravage, Sabotage, Speciocide, Stroy, Wrack

Desultory Aimless, Cursory, Fitful, Idle

Detach(ed), Detachment Abstract, Alienate, Aloof, Body, Calve, Clinical, Cut,

Detail, Discrete, Insular, Isle, Isolate, Loose, Outlying, Outpost, Patrol, Picket, Picquet, Separate, Sever, Staccato, Stoic, Unfasten, Unhinge

Detached work Ravelin

Detail(s), Detailed Annotate, Dock, Elaborate, Embroider, Expatiate, Explicit, Expound, Instance, > ITEM, Itemise, Minutiae, Nicety, Particular(ise), Pedantry, Point, Recite, Relate, Respect, Send, Spec, Special, Specification, Technicality

▷ **Detailed** *may indicate* last letter missing

Detain(ee), Detention Arrest, Buttonhole, Collar, Custody, Delay, Detinue, Gate, Glasshouse, Hinder, Intern, Keep, POW, Preventive, Retard, Stay, > WITHHOLD

Detect(or), Detective Agent, Arsène, Asdic, Bloodhound, Brown, Bucket, Busy, Catch, Chan, CID, Cuff, Dick, Discover, Divine, Doodlebug, Dupin, Espy, Eye, Fed, Find, Flambeau, Flic, Fortune, French, Geigercounter, Geophone, Gumshoe, Hanaud, Hercule, Holmes, Interpol, Investigator, Jack, Lecoq, Lupin, Maigret, Metal, Microwave, Mine, Minitrack®, Nose, Peeper, PI, Pinkerton, Plant, Poirot, Private eye, Prodnose, Radar, Reagent, Rumble, Scent, Scerne, Sense, Sensor, Shadow, Shamus, Sherlock, > SLEUTH, Sofar, Sonar, Sonobuoy, Spot, Tabaret, Take, Tec, Thorndyke, Toff, Trace, Trent, Vance, Wimsey, Yard

Detent Pawl, Trigger

Deter(rent) Block, Check, Daunt, Dehort, Delay, Dissuade, Prevent, Restrain, Turn-off

Detergent Cationic, Cleaner, Solvent, Surfactant, Syndet, Tepol, Whitener

Deteriorate, Deterioration Decadence, Degenerate, Derogate, Entropy, Pejoration, Rust, Worsen

▷ **Deterioration** *may indicate* an anagram

▷ **Determination** *may indicate* 'last letter'

Determine(d), Determination Arbitrament, Ardent, Ascertain, Assign, Assoil, Bent, Condition, Dead-set, > DECIDE, Define, Doctrinaire, Dogged, Dour, Drive, Earnest, Fix, Govern, Grit(ty), Headstrong, Hell-bent, Indomitable, Influence, Intent, Judgement, Law, Out, Point, Purpose, Quantify, > RESOLUTE, Resolve, Rigwiddie, Rigwoodie, Self-will, Set, Settle, Shape, Stalwart, Steely, Type, Weigh

Detest(able) Abhor, Despise, Execrable, Execrate, Hate, Loathsome, Pestful, Vile

Detonate, Detonator Blast, Explode, Fire, Fuse, Fuze, Ignite, Kindle, Plunger, Primer, Saucisse, Saucisson, Tetryl, Trip-wire

Detour Bypass, Deviate, Divert

Detract Belittle, Decry, Diminish, Discount, Disparage

Detriment(al) Adverse, Damage, Harm, Injury, Loss, Mischief

Deuce Dickens, Old Harry, Twoer

Deuteron Diplon

Devalue Debase, Reduce, Undermine

Devastate Demolish, Destroy, Lay waste, Overwhelm, Ravage, Ruin, Sack, Traumatise, Waste, Wreck

Develop(er), Developed, Developing, Development Advance, Amidol®, Aplasia, Breakthrough, Breed, Bud, Build, Burgeon, Catechol, Creep, Educe, Elaborate, Enlarge, Epigenetic, Escalate, Evolve, Expand, Expatriate, Foetus, Full-fledged, Fulminant, Genesis, Germinate, Gestate, Grow, Hatch, Hydroquinone, Hypo, Imago, Improve, Incipient, Incubate, Lamarckism, Larva, Mature, Metamorphose, Metol, Morphogenesis, Oidium, Ontogenesis, Pathogeny, Pullulate, Pupa, Pyro, Pyrogallol, Quinol, Ribbon, Ripe(n), Shape, Soup, Speciation, Sprawl, Teens, Tone, Unfold, Upgrow

▷ **Develop** *may indicate* an anagram

Deviant, **Deviate**, **Deviation** Aberrance, Abnormal, Anomaly, Average, Brisure, Deflect, Depart, Derogate, Digress, Diverge, Divert, Error, Kinky, Kurtosis, List, Mean, Pervert, Quartile, Sheer, Solecism, Sport, Standard, Stray, Swerve, Transvestite, > **TURN**, Valgus, Varus, Veer, Wander, Wend

Device Appliance, Artifice, Contraption, Contrivance, Deus ex machina, Dodge, Emblem, Expedient, Gadget, Gimmick, Gubbins, Instrument, Logo, Mnemonic, Pattern, Plan, > **STRATAGEM**, Subterfuge, Tactic, Tag, Trademark, Trick

DEVICES

3 letters:
Bug
FET
LED
Mux
Zip

4 letters:
Capo
Fret
Fuse
Gobo
Orle
Plug
Rest
Tram
Trap

5 letters:
Audio
Balun
Chaff
Cleat
Cramp
Diode
Frame
Gizmo
Gland
Input
Maser
Meter
Mixer
Modem
Mouse
Optic®
Pager
Petar
Prism
Probe
Quipu

Relay
Saser
Scart
Servo
Shear
Sonde
Sprag
SQUID
Timer
Tromp
Valve
V-clip
Waldo

6 letters:
Atlatl
Biodot
Bungee
Buzzer
Charge
Cotter
Cut-out
Dasher
Deckle
De-icer
Detent
Dimmer
Dongle
Elevon
Engine
Etalon
Filter
Friend®
Kludge
Petard
Pick-up
Pinger®
Possum
Quippu
Rabble

Reverb
Roller
Router
Selsyn
Sensor
Switch
Swivel
Temple
Tipple
Tracer
Tremie
Triode
Trompe
Turtle
Tympan
Viewer
Wafter
Widget

7 letters:
Bearing
Bendlet
Cleaver
Clicker
Compass
Counter
Coupler
Dashpot
Digibox®
Divider
Doubler
Fuzzbox
Genlock
Gimbals
Grapnel
Imprese
Inhaler
Isotron
Jetpack
Krytron

Lighter
Machine
Minicom
Monitor
Pelorus
Pickoff
Plunger
Ratchet
Rotator
Scanner
Shut-off
Shuttle
Sniffer
Snorkel
Snuffer
Sounder
Spoiler
Stinger
Storage
Sundial
Swatter
Synchro
Tokamak
Tonepad
Vernier
Vocoder

8 letters:
Atomiser
Autodial
Barostat
Betatron
Bootjack
Calutron
Conveyor
Demister
Detector
Diestock
Ecraseur
Enlarger

Episcope
Episemon
Geophone
Ignitron
Monogram
Odograph
Paravane
Pulsator
Pyrostat
Resister
Shoehorn
Snow-eyes
Snowshoe
Solenoid
Spreader
Squeegee
Sweatbox
Swellbox
Terminal
Thin-film
Trembler
Varactor
Vibrator

9 letters:
Aspirator
Capacitor
Compasses
Converter
Delayline
Detonator
Dynamotor
Eccentric
Excelsior
Exerciser
Generator
Gyroscope
Hendiadys
Hodoscope
Hydrofoil
Hydrostat
Hygrostat
Konimeter
Kymograph
Megaphone

Mekometer
Metronome
Nebuliser
Octophone
Optophone
Overdrive
Pacemaker
Parachute
Periscope
Photocell
Pitchbend
Polygraph
Propeller
Rectifier
Regulator
Remontoir
Resonator
Responsor
Rheotrope
Rotachute
Rotameter
Satellite
Scrambler
Separator
Sequencer
Simulator
Smokejack
Sonograph
Sprinkler
Steadicam
Tabulator
Tasimeter
Telemeter
Thyristor
Tonometer
Trackball
Tremulant

10 letters:
Applicator
Autowinder
Centrifuge
Chronotron
Commutator
Comparator

Cyclometer
Derailleur
Descendeur
Groundprox
Humidistat
Hygroscope
Jawbreaker
Jaws of Life
Metrostyle
Microphone
Microscope
Peripheral
Phonoscope
Phonospore
Remontoire
Respirator
Siderostat
Snowplough
Spirograph
Stabiliser
Stimpmeter
Suppressor
Switchgear
Tachograph
Tachometer
Telewriter
Thermistor
Thermopile
Thermostat
Tourniquet
Transducer
Transistor
Turnbuckle
Ventilator
Vertoscope®
Videophone
Viewfinder
Viscometer

11 letters:
Afterburner
Autochanger
Baffle-plate
Carburettor
Epidiascope

Fluoroscope
Insufflator
Multiplexer
Smokerlyzer
Snickometer
Spectograph
Speedometer
Swingometer
Trackerball
Transceiver
Transformer
Transponder

12 letters:
Breathalyser
Concentrator
Intrauterine
Lithotripter
Oscillograph
Sensitometer
Snooperscope
Spectroscope
Supercharger
Teleprompter
Thermocouple
Turbidimeter
Viscosimeter

13 letters:
Baton-sinister
Phonendoscope
Rack and pinion

14 letters:
Anamorphoscope
Dead man's
   handle
Interferometer
Intervalometer
Plethysmograph
Scintillometer
Spinthariscope

Devil(ish), Demon Abaddon, Afree, Afrit, Ahriman, Amaimon, Apollyon, Asmodeus, Atua, Auld Hornie, Azazel, Barbason, Beelzebub, Belial, Buckra, Clootie, Cloots, Dasyure, Davy Jones, Deev, Deil, Demogorgon, Demon, Deuce, Devling, Diable, Diabolic, Dickens, Div, Drudge, Dust, Eblis, Falin, Familiar, Fend, Fiend, Fient, Ghoul, Goodman, Goodyear, Grill, Hangie, Hornie, Iblis, Imp, Incubus, Infernal, Lamia, Legion, Lilith, Lord of the Flies, Lori, Lucifer,

Mahoun(d), Manta, Mara, Maxwell's, Mazikeen, Mephisto(pheles), Mischief, Nick, Old Bendy, Old Nick, Old One, Old Pandemonium, Old Poker, Old Roger, Old Split-foot, Old Toast, Printer's, Ragamuffin, Rahu, Ralph, Satan, Sathanas, Satyr, Scour, Scratch, Screwtape, Season, Setebos, Shaitan, Shedeem, Snow, Sorra, Succubine, Succubus, Tailard, Tasmanian, Tempter, Titivil, Tutivillus, Wendigo, Wicked, Wicked One, Wirricow, Worricow, Worrycow, Zernebock

Devious Braide, Cunning, Deep, Eel(y), Erroneous, Evasive, Implex, Indirect, Scheming, Shifty, Stealthy, Subtle, Tortuous, Tricky

Devise(d) Arrange, Contrive, Decoct, Hatch, Hit-on, Imagine, Invenit, Invent, Plot, Thermette

Devitrified Ambitty

Devoid Barren, Destitute, Empty, Vacant, Wanting

Devolve Occur, Result, Transmit

Devote(e), Devotion(al), Devoted Addiction, Aficionado, Angelus, Attached, Bhakti, Consecrate, Corban, Dedicate, Employ, Fan, Fervid, Fiend, Holy, Hound, Loyalty, Novena, Ophism, Passion, Pious, Puja, Religioso, Sea-green incorruptible, S(h)akta, Solemn, True, Zealous

Devour(ing) Consume, Eat, Engorge, Engulf, Manducate, Moth-eat, Scarf, Scoff, > SWALLOW, Vorant

▷ **Devour** *may indicate* one word inside another

Devout Holy, Pia, Pious, Reverent, Sant, Sincere

Dew(y) Bloom, Moist, Mountain, Rime, Roral, Roric, Rorid, Roscid, Serein, Serene, Tranter

Dexterity, Dexterous Adept, Adroit, Aptitude, Cleverness, Craft, Deft, Feat(e)ous, Featuous, > HANDY, Knack, Shrewd, Sleight, Slick

Diabolic Cruel, > DEVILISH, Infernal

Diacritic (mark) Acute, Angstrom, Cedilla, Circumflex, Diaresis, Eth, Grave, Háček, Thorn, Tilde, Umlaut

Diadem Coronet, Fillet, Garland, Tiara

Diagnose, Diagnosis Fetal, Findings, Identify, Scan, Scintigraphy

Diagonal(ly) Bend(wise), Bias, Cater(-corner), Catty-cornered, Counter, Oblique, Slant, Solidus, Twill

Diagram Argand, Block, Butterfly, Chart, Compass rose, Decision tree, Dendogram, Drawing, Fault-tree, Feynman, Figure, Flow, Graph, Graphics, Grid, Hertzsprung-Russell, Indicator, Logic, Map, Plan, Plat, Run-chart, Scatter, Schema, Stem-and-leaf, Stemma, Stereogram, Tephigram, Venn, Wind rose

Dial(ling) Card, Face, Mug, Phiz, Phone, Pulse, STD, Visage

Dialect Accent, Aeolic, Alemannic, Arcadic, Attic, Basuto, Burr, Doric, Eldin, Eolic, Erse, Eye, Franconian, Friulian, Gallo-Romance, Gascon, Geechee, Geordie, Greenlander, Hegelian, Idiom, Ionic, Isogloss, Jargon, Jockney, Joual, Khalka, Koine, Konkani, Ladin, Lallans, Landsmaal, Langobardic, Langue d'oc, Langue d'oil, Langue d'oui, Lingo, Low German, Mackem, Norman, Norn, Parsee, Patois, Prakrit, Riffian, Romansch, Scouse, Sesotho, Syriac, Taal, Talkee-talkee, Tongue, Tshi, Twi, Vernacular, Wu, Yealdon, Yenglish, Yinglish

Dialogue Colloquy, Conversation, Critias, Discussion, Exchange, Interlocution, Lazzo, Pastourelle, Speech, Stichomythia, Talk, Upspeak

Dialysis Kidney, Peritoneal

Diameter Breadth, Calibre, Gauge, Systyle, Tactical, Width

Diamond(s), Diamond-shaped Adamant, Black, Boart, Brilliant, Bristol, Carbonado, Cullinan, D, DE, Delaware, Eustace, Florentine, Hope, Ice, Industrial, Isomer, Jim, Koh-i-noor, Lasque, Lattice, Lozenge, Paragon, Pick,

Pitch, Pitt, Quarry, Rhinestone, Rhomb, Rock, Rose-cut, Rosser, Rough, Rustre, Sancy, Solitaire, Spark, Sparklers, Squarial, Suit

Diana Artemis, Di

Diapason Normal, Open, Ottava, Stopped

Diaphanous Clear, Sheer, Translucent

Diaphoretic Sweater

Diaphragm Cap, Iris, Mid-riff, Phrenic, Stop

Diaresis Trema

▶ **Diarist** *see* DIARY

Diarrhoea Collywobbles, Gippy tummy, Lientery, Montezuma's revenge, Runs, Scours, Squitters, The shits, Trots, Verbal, Weaning-brash, Wood-evil

Diary, Diarist Chronicle, Dale, Day-book, Evelyn, Hickey, Journal, Kilvert, Log, Nobody, Pepys, Pooter, Record, Video

Diaspora Exodus, Galuth

Diatribe Harangue, Invective, Philippic, Tirade

Dice(r), Dicey Aleatory, Astragals, Bale, Bones, Chop, Craps, Cube, Doctor, Dodgy, Fulham, Fullams, Fullans, Gourd(s), Highman, Jeff, Mandoline, Poker, Shoot, Snake-eyes, Tallmen

Dichotomy Split

Dick(y), Dickey Clever, Deadeye, Front, Moby, OED, Policeman, Rumble, Shaky, Shirt, Spotted, Tec, Tonneau, Tucker, Tumbledown, Unstable, Wankle, Weak, Whittington

▷ **Dick** *may indicate* a dictionary

Dickens Boz, Deuce, Devil, Mephistopheles

Dicker Bargain, Barter, Haggle, Trade

▷ **Dicky** *may indicate* an anagram

Dictate, Dictator(ial) Amin, Authoritarian, Autocrat, Big Brother, Caesar, Castro, Cham, Command, Czar, Decree, Demagogue, Despot, Duce, Franco, Fu(e)hrer, Gauleiter, Hitler, Impose, Lenin, Ordain, Overbearing, Peremptory, Peron, Salazar, Shogun, Stalin, Tell, Tito, Totalitarian, Tsai, Tyrant, Tzar

Diction Language, Lexis, Speech, Style

Dictionary Alveary, Calepin, Chambers, Data, Etymologicon, Fowler, Gazetteer, Glossary, Gradus, Hobson-Jobson, Idioticon, Johnson's, Larousse, Lexicon, Lexis, OED, Onomasticon, Thesaurus, Vocabulary, Webster, Wordbook

Dictum Obiter

Did Began, Couth, Fec(it), Gan

Didactic Sermonical

Diddle Cheat, Con, Hoax

Dido Antic, Caper, Carthaginian, Elissa

Die(d), Dying Ache, Cark, Choke, Crater, Croak, Cube, D, Decadent, Desire, End, Evanish, Exit, Expire, Fade, Fail, Flatline, Forfair, Fulham, Fulhan, Fullam, Go, Go west, Highman, Hop, Kark, Long, Morendo, Moribund, Ob(iit), Orb, Pass, Peg out, Perdendosi, Perish, Peter, Snuff, Snuff it, Solidum, Sphacelation, Stamp, Sterve, Succumb, Suffer, Swage, Swelt, Tine, Wane

Diehard Blimp, Fanatic, Intransigent, Reactionary, Standpatter, Zealot

Diet(er) Assembly, Bant(ing), Cacatrophy, Council, Dail, Eat, Fare, Hay, Intake, Kashrut(h), Ketogenic, Landtag, Lent, Macrobiotic, Parliament, Pleading, Reduce, Regimen, Reichstag, Slim, Solid, Sprat, Staple, Strict, Tynwald, Vegan, Vegetarian, Weightwatcher, Worms

Dietetics Sit(i)ology

Differ(ence), Differing, Different(ly) Allo, Barney, Change, Cline, Contrast, Deviant, Diesis, Disagree, Discord, Discrepant, Disparate, Dispute,

Dissent, Dissimilitude, Distinct, Diverge, Diverse, Else, Elsewise, Nuance, Omnifarious, Other, Othergates, Otherguess, Otherness, Otherwise, Potential, Separate, Several, Symmetric, Tiff, Unlike, Variform, Various, Vary

Differential, Differentiate Calculus, Del, Distinguish, Nabla, Secern, Taxeme, Wage

Difficult(y) Abstruseness, Ado, Aporia, Arduous, Augean, Badass, Balky, Ballbuster, Bitter, Block, Bolshie, Bother, Catch, Choosy, Complication, Corner, Deep, Depth, Dysphagia, Extreme, Fiddly, Formidable, Gordian, > **HARD**, Hassle, Hazard, Hiccup, Hobble, Hole, Ill, Impasse, Indocile, Intractable, Jam, Kink, Knot, Lurch, Mulish, Net, Nodus, Obstacle, Parlous, Pig, Pitfall, Plight, Predicament, Quandary, Queer St, Recalcitrant, Rough, Rub, Scrape, Scrub, Setaceous, Shlep, Snag, Soup, Steep, Stick, Sticky, Stiff, Strait, Stubborn, Stymie, Ticklish, Tight spot, Trial, Tricky, Troublous, Une(a)th, Uphill, Via dolorosa

Diffident Bashful, Meek, Modest, Reserved, Shy

Diffuse, Diffusion Barophoresis, Disperse, Disseminate, Endosmosis, Exude, Osmosis, Pervade, Radiate, Spread, Thermal

Dig(s), Digger, Digging, Dig up Antipodean, Australian, Backhoe, Beadle, Bed(e)ral, Bedsit, Billet, Bot, Burrow, Costean, Delve, Enjoy, Excavate, Flea-bag, Fossorial, Gaulter, Gibe, Gird, Graip, Grub, Howk, Jab, Kip, Lair, Like, Lodgings, Mine, Navvy, Nervy, Nudge, Pad, Pioneer, Probe, Prod, Raddleman, Resurrect, Root, Ruddleman, Sap, See, Spade, Spit, Spud, Star-nose, Taunt, Tonnell, Trench, Tunnel, Undermine, Unearth

Digest(ible), Digestion, Digestive Abridgement, Absorb, Abstract, Aperçu, Archenteron, Assimilate, Codify, Concoct, Endue, Epitome, Eupepsia, Eupepsy, Gastric, Indew, Indue, Light, Pandect, Pem(m)ican, Pepsin(e), Peptic, Précis, Salt-cat, > **SUMMARY**

Digit(s) Binary, Bit, Byte, Dactyl, Finger, Hallux, Mantissa, Number, Pollex, Prehallux, Thumb, Toe

Dignified, Dignify August, Elevate, Exalt, Handsome, Honour, Lordly, Majestic, Manly, Proud, Solemn, Stately

Dignitary Bigwig, Dean, Name, Personage, Provost, > **VIP**

Dignity Aplomb, Bearing, Cathedra, Decorum, Face, Glory, Grandeur, Maestoso, Majesty, Nobility, Poise, Pontificate, Presence, Scarf, Tiara

Digraph Eng, Ng

Digress(ion) Apostrophe, Deviate, Diverge, Ecbole, Episode, Excurse, Excursus, Maunder, Veer, Wander

Dike Bank, Channel, Cludgie, Dam, Ditch, > **DYKE**, Embank(ment), Estacade, Lav(atory), Levee, Wall

Dilapidated, Dilapidation Decrepit, Desolate, Disrepair, Eroded, Ruined, Rust bucket, Tumbledown

Dilate, Dilation, Dilatation Amplify, Develop, Diastole, Ecstasis, Enlarge, Expand, Increase, Mydriasis, Sinus, Swell, Telangiectasia, Tent, Varix

Dilatory Protracting, Slow, Sluggish, Tardy

Dilemma Casuistry, Choice, Cleft, Dulcarnon, Fix, Horn, Predicament, Quandary, Why-not

Dilettante Aesthete, Amateur, Butterfly, Dabbler, Playboy

Diligence, Diligent Active, Application, Assiduous, Coach, Conscience, Eident, Industry, Intent, Painstaking, Sedulous, Studious

Dill Anise, Pickle

Dilute, Dilution Adulterate, Delay, Diluent, Lavage, Simpson, Thin, Water, Weaken

Dim(ness), Dimming, Dimwit Becloud, Blear, Blur, Brownout, Caligo, Clueless, Crepuscular, Dense, Dusk, Eclipse, Fade, Faint, Feint, Gormless, Ill-lit, Indistinct, Mist, Nebulous, Ninny, Obscure, Overcast, Owl, Pale, Shadow, Unsmart

Dimension Area, Breadth, Extent, Fourth, Height, Length, Measure, Size, Volume, Width

Diminish(ed), Diminuendo, Diminution, Diminutive Abatement, Assuage, Baby, Bate, Calando, Contract, Cot(t)ise, Deactivate, Decrease, Détente, Detract, Disparage, Dissipate, Dwarf, Dwindle, Erode, Fourth, Hypocorism(a), Lessen, Lilliputian, Minify, Minus, Mitigate, Petite, Pigmy, Scarp, Small, Stultify, Subside, Toy, Trangle, Wane, Whittle

Dimple(d) Dent, Depression, Hollow, Orange-peel

Din Babel, Charivary, Chirm, Commotion, Deen, Discord, Gunga, Hubbub, > NOISE, Rackct, Racket, Raird, Randan, Reel, Reird, Uproar, Utis

Dine(r), Dining Aristology, Eat, Feast, Refect, Sup, Trat(toria)

Dingbat Doodad

Dinghy Pram, Shallop, Ship, Skiff

Dingo Warrigal

Dingy Crummy, Dark, Dirty, Drear, Dun, Fusc(ous), Grimy, Isabel(la), Isabelline, Lurid, Oorie, Ourie, Owrie, Shabby, Smoky

Dining-room Cafeteria, Cenacle, Commons, Frater, Hall, Langar, Refectory, Restaurant, Triclinium

Dinner Banquet, Collation, Feast, Hall, Kail, Kale, Meal, Prandial, Progressive, Repast, Spread

Dinosaur Allosaurus, Ankylosaur, Apatosaurus, Brachiosaurus, Brontosaurus, Ceratopsian, Chalicothere, Coelurosaur, Cotylosaur, Cynodont, Dinothere, Diplodocus, Dolichosaurus, Duck-billed, Elasmosaur, Glyptodon, Hadrosaur, Ichthyosaur(us), Iguanodon, Megalosaur, Mosasaur, Omithosaur, Ornithischian, Ornithopod, Oviraptor, Pelycosaur, Placoderm, Plesiosaur, Prehistoric, Prosauropod, Pteranodon, Pterodactyl, Pterosaur, Saurischian, Sauropod, Smilodon, Stegadon(t), Stegosaur, Teleosaurus, Theropod, Titanosaurus, Titanothere, Triceratops, Tyrannosaurus, Uintothere, Velociraptor

Dint Brunt, Dent, Depression, Force, Means, Power

Diocese Bishopric, District, Eparchate, See

Diode Zener

Diogenes Cynic

Dioxide Cassiterite, Needle-tin

Dip(per) Bagna cauda, Baptise, Basin, Bathe, Bob, Brantub, Dabble, Dap, Dean, Dib, Diver, Dop, Double, Duck, Dunk, Foveola, Geosyncline, Guacomole, H(o)ummus, Houmous, Hum(m)us, Immerse, Intinction, Ladle, Lucky, Magnetic, Ouzel, Paddle, Rinse, Rollercoaster, Sag, Salute, Star, Submerge, Tapenade, Taramasalata, Tzatziki, Ursa

Diphthong Synaeresis, Synizesis

Diploma Charter, Parchment, Qualification, Scroll, Sheepskin

Diplomacy, Diplomat(ic) Altemat, Ambassador, Attaché, CD, Chargé d'affaires, Chateaubriand, Cheque-book, Consul, DA, Dean, Dollar, Doyen, El(t)chi, Envoy, Fanariot, Finesse, Gunboat, Legation, Lei(d)ger, Megaphone, Phanariot, Plenipotentiary, Shuttle, Suave, > TACT

▷ **Dippy** *may indicate* a bather

Dipsomania Oenomania

Dire Dreadful, Fatal, Fell, Hateful, Ominous, Urgent

Direct(or), Directly Administer, Advert, Aim, Airt, Auteur, Aventre, Board, Boss, Cann, Channel, Charge, Command, Compere, Con(n), Conduct, Control, Cox, Dead, Due, Eisenstein, Enjoin, Executive, Explicit, Fast-track, Fellini, First-hand, Forthright, Frontal, Guide, Helm, Hitchcock, Immediate, Impresario, Instruct, Intendant, Kappelmeister, Lead, Lean, Manager, Mastermind, Navigate, Nonexecutive, Outright, Pagnol, Pilot, Play, Point-blank, Ready, Refer, Régisseur, Rudder, Set, Signpost, Stear, > STEER, Straight, Teach, Tell, Truffaut, Unvarnished, Vector, Welles

Direction Aim, Airt, Arrow, Astern, Bearings, Course, Cross-reference, E, End-on, Guidance, Guide, Heading, Keblah, L, Line, N, Orders, Passim, R, Route, Rubric, S, Sanction, Send, Sense, Side, Slap, Tack, Tenor, Thataway, Tre corde, Trend, W, Way, Wedelns

Direction-finder Asdic, Compass, Decca, Quadrant, Radar, Sextant, Sonar

Directory Crockford, Debrett, Encyclop(a)edia, Kelly, List, Red book, Register, Yellow pages®

Dirge Ballant, Coronach, Dirige, Epicedium, Knell, Monody, Requiem, Song, Threnody

Dirigible Airship, Balloon, Blimp, Zeppelin

Dirk Anelace, Dagger, Skean, Whinger, Whiniard, Whinyard

Dirt(y) Begrime, Bemoil, Cacky, Chatty, Clag, Clarty, Colly, Contaminate, Coom, Crock, Crud, Draggle, Dung, Dust, Earth, Festy, Filth, Foul, Gore, Grime, Grufted, Grungy, Impure, Manky, Moit, Mote, Muck, Obscene, Ordure, Pay, Pollute, Ray, Sculdudd(e)ry, Scum, Scungy, Scuzzy, Skanky, Skulduddery, Smirch, Smut(ch), Soil, Sooty, Sordes, Sordor, Squalid, Stain, Trash, Unclean, Unsatisfactory, Warb, Yucky, Yukky

Dis Hades, Hell

Disability, Disable Cripple, Incapacitate, Lame, Maim, Paralyse, Scissor-leg, Scotch, Wreck

Disadvantage Detriment, Downside, Drawback, Handicap, Mischief, Out, Penalise, Penalty, Supercherie, Upstage, Wrongfoot, Zugswang

Disagree(ing), Disagreeable, Disagreement Argue, Argy-bargy, Bad, Clash, Conflict, Contest, Debate, Differ, Discrepant, Dispute, Dissent, Dissonant, Evil, Fiddlesticks, Friction, Heterodoxy, Pace, Plagu(e)y, Rift, Unpleasing

Disallow Forbid, Overrule

Disappear(ing) Cook, Dispel, Evanesce, Evanish, Evaporate, Fade, Kook, Latescent, Melt, Occult, Pass, Skedaddle, Slope, > VANISH

Disappoint(ment), Disappointed Anticlimax, Balk, Bombshell, Bummer, Chagrin, Comedown, Crestfallen, Delude, Disgruntle, Frustrate, Gutted, Heartsick, Lemon, Letdown, Regret, Sell, Shucks, Sick, Suck-in, Sucks, Swiz(zle), Thwart

Disapproval, Disapprove Ach, Animadvert, Boo, Catcall, Censure, Deplore, Deprecate, Discountenance, Expostulate, Frown, Harrumph, Hiss, Napoo, Object, Pejorative, Po-faced, Raspberry, Razz, Reject, Reproach, Reprobate, Squint, Tush, Tut, Tut-tut, Umph, Veto, Whiss

Disarm(ament), Disarming Bluff, Defuse, Demobilise, Nuclear, Winsome

Disarrange Disturb, Muddle, Ruffle, Tousle, Unsettle

Disarray Disorder, Mess, Rifle, Tash, Undress

Disaster, Disastrous Adversity, Apocalypse, Bale, Calamity, Cataclysm(ic), Catastrophe, Debacle, Dire, Doom, Evil, Fatal, Fiasco, Flop, Impostor, Meltdown, Mishap, Pitfall, Rout, Ruin, Screw-up, Seism, Shipwreck, Titanic, Tragedy, Wipeout

Disavow Abjure, Deny, Disclaim, Recant, Retract

Disbelief, Disbelieve(r) Acosmism, Anythingarian, Atheism, Gawp, Incredulity, Mistrust, Nothingarianism, Occamist, Phew, Phooey, Puh-lease, Puh-leeze, Question, Sceptic, Shoot, Voetsak

Disburse Distribute, Expend, Outlay, Spend

Disc, Disk Bursting, Button, CD, Cheese, Compact, Coulter, Counter, Diaphragm, Dogtag, EP, Epiphragm, Flexible, Floppy, Frisbee®, Gold, Gong, Hard, Harrow, Intervertebral, Laser, LP, Magnetic, Mono, O, Optical, Parking, Paten, Patin, Planchet, Plate, Platinum, Puck, RAM, Rayleigh, Record, Rosette, Roundel, Roundlet, Rowel, Sealed unit, Silver, Slipped, Slug, Stereo, Stylopodium, Swash plate, System, Tax, Token, Video, Wafer, Whorl, Winchester, Wink, WORM

Discard(ed) Abandon, Burn, Crib, Defy, Dele, Jettison, Kill, Leave, Obsolete, Off, Offload, Oust, > REJECT, Scrap, Shed, Shuck, Slough, Sluff, Supersede, Trash

Discern(ing), Discernment Acumen, Acute, Descry, Discrimination, Eagle-eyed, Flair, Insight, Perceive, Percipient, Perspicacity, Realise, Sapient, Scry, See, Skry, > TASTE, Tell, Wate

Discharge Absolve, Acquit, Arc, Assoil, Blennorrhoea, Brush, Cashier, Catamenia, Catarrh, Conditional, Corona, Dejecta, Deliver, Demob, Disembogue, Disgorge, Dismiss, Disruptive, Dump, Efflux, Effusion, Egest, Ejaculate, Eject, Embogue, Emission, Emit, Encopresis, Enfilade, Evacuate, Excrete, Execute, Exemption, Expulsion, Exude, Fire, Flashover, Flower, Flux, Frass, Free, Gleet, Glow, Lava, Lay off, Leak, Let off, Leucorrhoea, Lochia, Loose, Maturate, Menses, Mitimus, Mute, Offload, Otorrhoea, Oust, Ozaena, Pay, Perform, Period, Planuria, Purulence, Pus, Pyorrhoea, Quietus, Rheum, Rhinorrhoeal, Sack, Salvo, Sanies, Secretion, Show, Shrive, Snarler, Spark, Suppurate, Teem, Unload, Vent, Void, Water, Whites

Disciple(s) Adherent, Apostle, Baruch, Catechumen, Follower, John, Judas, Luke, Mark, Matthew, Peter, Simon, Son, Student, The Seventy, Thomist, Votary

Disciplinarian, Discipline Apollonian, Ascesis, Chasten, Chastise, Correct, Despot, Drill, Exercise, Feng Shui, Inure, Martinet, Mathesis, Punish, Regimentation, Regulate, Sadhana, School, Science, Spartan, Stickler, Subject, Taskmaster, Train, Tutor

▸ **Disc jockey** *see* DJ

Disclaim(er) Deny, Disown, No(t)chel, Recant, Renounce, > REPUDIATE, Voetstoots

Disclose, Disclosure Apocalypse, Confess, Divulge, Expose, Impart, Leak, Manifest, Propale, > PUBLISH, Report, Reveal, Spill, Tell, Unheal, Unhele, Unrip, Unveil

Discoloration, Discolour(ed) Bruise, Cyanosis, Dyschroa, Ecchymosis, Livid, Livor, Stain, Streak, Tarnish, Tinge, Weather

Discomfit(ure) Abash, Confuse, Disconcert, Disturb, Frustrate, Lurch, Shend

Discomfort Ache, Angst, Dysphoria, Gyp, Heartburn, Pain, Unease

Disconcert(ing) Abash, Confuse, Disturb, Embarrass, Faze, Feeze, Flurry, Fluster, Nonplus, Off-putting, Phase, Pheese, Pheeze, Phese, > RATTLE, Shatter, Throw, Upset, Wrong-foot

▷ **Disconcert(ed)** *may indicate* an anagram

Disconnect(ed) Asynartete, Detach, Disjointed, Off-line, Sever, Staccato, Uncouple, Undo, Unplug

Disconsolate Desolate, Doleful, Downcast, > GLOOMY

Discontent(ed) Disquiet, Dissatisfied, Humph, Repined, Sour, Umph

Discontinuance, Discontinue Abandon, Cease, Desist, Desuetude, Drop,

Prorogue, Stop, Terminate

Discord(ant) Absonant, Ajar, Conflict, Din, Dispute, Eris, Faction, Hoarse, Jangle, Jar, Raucous, Ruction, Strife

▷ **Discord(ant)** *may indicate* an anagram

Discount Agio, Cashback, Deduct, Disregard, Forfaiting, Invalidate, > REBATE, Trade

Discountenance Disfavour, Efface, Embarrass

Discourage(ment) Caution, Chill, Dampen, Dash, Daunt, Demoralise, Deter, Dishearten, Disincentive, Dismay, Dissuade, Enervate, Frustrate, Opposition, Stifle, Unman

Discourse Address, Argument, Conversation, Descant, Diatribe, Dissertate, Eulogy, Expound, Homily, Lecture, Lucubrate, Orate, Preach, Relate, Rigmarole, Sermon, Wash

Discourteous, Discourtesy Impolite, Insult, Rude, Slight, Uncivil, Unmannerly

Discover(y), Discoverer Amundsen, Anagnorisis, Ascertain, Betray, Breakthrough, Columbus, Cook, Descry, Detect, Discern, Discure, Eureka, > FIND, Heureka, Heuristic, Learn, Locate, Manifest, Moresby, Protege, Rumble, Serendip, Serendipity, Spy, Tasman, Trace, Treasure trove, Unearth, Unhale, Unmask, Unveil

▷ **Discovered in** *may indicate* an anagram or a hidden word

Discredit(able) Debunk, Decry, Disgrace, Explode, Infamy, Scandal, Smear, Unworthy

Discreet, Discretion Cautious, Circumspect, Freedom, Option, Polite, Politic, Prudence, Prudent, Trait, Wise

Discrepancy Difference, Gap, Lack, Shortfall, Variance

Discrete Distinct, Separate, Unrelated

Discriminate, Discriminating, Discrimination Ag(e)ism, Colour bar, Diacritic, Differentiate, Discern, Distinguish, Elitism, Invidious, Nasute, Racism, Secern, Segregate, Select, Sexism, Siz(e)ism, Speciesism, Subtle, Taste

Discursive Roving

Discuss(ed), Discussion Agitate, Air, Canvass, Commune, Conf(erence), Debate, Dialectic, Dialogue, Dicker, Disquisition, En l'air, Examine, Excursus, Expatiate, Handle, Hob and nob, Interlocution, Korero, Moot, Over, Palaver, Parley, Pourparler, Prolegomenon, Quodlibet, Rap, Re, Symposium, Talk, Tapis, Treatment, Ventilate, Vex

Disdain(ful) Belittle, Contempt, Coy, Deride, Despise, Geck, Poof, Pooh-pooh, Puh, Sassy, > SCORN, Scout, Sdei(g)n, Sniffy, Spurn, Supercilious, Ugh

Disease(d) Affection, Ailment, Epidemic, Fever, Functional, Industrial, Infection, Malady, Noso-, Nosocomial, Organic, Pest(ilence), Rot, Scourge, Sickness

● **DISEASES**
●
● **2 letters:**
● CD
● MS
● TB
● VD
●
● **3 letters:**
● BSE
● Flu

Haw
Pip
Pox
> STD
TSE
Wog

4 letters:
Aids

Boba
Bunt
Clap
Conk
Gout
Keel
Kuru
Loco
Lues

Lyme
Roup
Yaws

5 letters:
Bang's
Black
Borna
Brand

Dread
Dutch
Ebola
Edema
Ergot
Favus
Fifth
Gapes
Lupus
Lurgi
Lurgy
Mesel
Mumps
Ngana
Palsy
Pinta
Polio
Pott's
Rabid
Scall
Sprue
Surra
Tinea
Virus
Weil's
Worms

6 letters:
Anbury
Blight
Blotch
Border
Canker
Chagas'
Chorea
Cowpox
Crohn's
Cruels
Dartre
Dengue
Eczema
Farcin
Graves'
Income
Johne's
Mad cow
Marck's
Meazel
Mildew
Morbus
Mosaic
Nagana

Oedema
Paget's
Rabies
Sapego
Scurvy
Social
Still's
Thrush
Tunnel
Typhus
Ulitis
Urosis
Yuppie
Zoster

7 letters:
Ascites
Batten's
Bright's
British
Caisson
Cholera
Coeliac
Crewels
Dieback
Dourine
Endemic
English
Frounce
Hansen's
Hardpad
Hydatid
Icterus
Leprosy
Maidism
Malaria
Marburg
Moor-ill
Murrain
Mycosis
Myiasis
Pébrine
Podagra
Porrigo
Purples
Rickets
Rosette
Scabies
Sequela
Serpigo
Tetanus
Tetters

Typhoid
Variola
Wilson's
Zymosis

8 letters:
Addison's
Alastrim
Beri-beri
Bornholm
Clubroot
Cushing's
Cynanche
Diabetes
Dutch elm
Economo's
Fishskin
Gaucher's
Glanders
Glaucoma
Gummosis
Hodgkin's
Hookworm
Impetigo
Jaundice
Kala-azar
Leaf-roll
Loose-cut
Menières
Minamata
Myxedema
Nosology
Pandemic
Pathogen
Pellagra
Phthisis
Phytosis
Progeria
Pullorum
Rachitis
Raynaud's
Rose-rash
Scrofula
Shingles
Smallpox
Suppeago
Swayback
Swinepox
Syphilis
Tay-Sachs
The bends
Venereal

Vincent's
Zoonosis

9 letters:
Brown lung
Chancroid
Chlorosis
Christmas
Cirrhosis
Contagion
Diathesis
Distemper
Dysentery
Enteritis
Exanthema
Filanders
Gonorrhea
Ideopathy
Ixodiasis
Kawasaki's
Lathyrism
Leucaemia
Leukaemia
Loose smut
Myxoedema
Nephritis
Nephrosis
Newcastle
New Forest
Pellagrin
Pemphigus
Porphyria
Seborrhea
Siderosis
Silicosis
Toxicosis
Trichosis
Tularemia

10 letters:
Acromegaly
Alzheimer's
Amoebiasis
Asbestosis
Autoimmune
Babesiosis
Bagassosis
Bluetongue
Byssinosis
Chickenpox
Dandy-fever
Deficiency

- Diphtheria
- Erysipelas
- Filariasis
- Framboesia
- Gonorrhoea
- Heartwater
- Hemophilia
- Iatrogenic
- Ichthyosis
- Impaludism
- Leuchaemia
- Limber-neck
- Lou Gehrig's
- Louping ill
- Moniliasis
- Muscardine
- Nosography
- Ornithosis
- Parkinson's
- Scarlatina
- Seborrhoea
- Tularaemia

11 letters:
Anthracosis
Brittle-bone
Cardiopathy
Consumption
Green Monkey
Haemophilia
Hebephrenia
Huntington's
Kwashiorkor
Listeriosis
Myxomatosis
Parasitosis
Psittacosis
Rickettsial
Septicaemia
Thalassemia
Trichinosis
Yellow-fever

12 letters:
Enterobiasis
Fascioliasis
Finger and toe

Foot and mouth
Furunculosis
Legionnaires'
Molybdenosis
Motor neurone
Osteomalacia
Osteoporosis
Scheuermann's
Shaking palsy
Slapped cheek
Thalassaemia
Tuberculosis
Uncinariasis

13 letters:
Elephantiasis
Leichmaniasis
Leptospirosis
Osteomyelitis
Poliomyelitis
Sclerodermata
Syringomyelia
Toxoplasmosis
Tsutsugamushi

14 letters:
Cystic fibrosis
Histoplasmosis
Leucodystrophy
Onchocerciasis
Pneumoconiosis
Sporotrichosis
Trichomoniasis
Trichophytosis

15 letters:
Schistosomiasis
Trypanosomiasis

16 letters:
Pneumonoco-
niosis
Sleeping sickness
Sweating sickness

17 letters:
Multiple sclerosis

▷ **Diseased** *may indicate* an anagram
Disembark Alight, Detrain, Land
Disembarrass Extricate, Rid, Unthread
Disembowel Eviscerate, Exenterate, Gralloch, Gut
Disenchant Disabuse, Dismay, Embitter
Disencumber Free, Rid, Unburden
Disengage(d), Disengagement Clear, Divorce, Liberate, Loosen, Release, Untie
Disentangle Debarrass, Extricate, Red(d), Solve, Unravel, Unsnarl
Disestablishmentarian Cosmist
Disfavour Maugre
Disfigure(ment), Disfigured Agrise, Agryze, Camsho, Deface, Deform, Goitre, Mutilate, Scar, Spoil, Tash, Ugly
▷ **Disfigured** *may indicate* an anagram
Disgorge Discharge, Spew, Spill, Vent, Void
Disgrace Atimy, Attaint, Baffle, Blot, Contempt, Contumely, Degrade, Discredit, Dishonour, Dog-house, Ignominy, Indignity, Infamy, Obloquy, Opprobrium, Scandal, Shame, Shend, Slur, Soil, Stain, Stigma, Yshend
Disgraceful Diabolical, Fie, Ignoble, Ignominious, Indign, Infamous, Mean, Notorious, Shameful, Turpitude
Disgruntled Malcontent, Resentful, Sore
▷ **Disgruntled** *may indicate* an anagram
Disguise(d) Alias, Blessing, Camouflage, Cloak, Colour, Conceal, Cover, Covert, Dissemble, Hide, Hood, Incog(nito), Mantle, Mask, Masquerade, Obscure, Peruke, Pretence, Pseudonym, Ring, Shades, Travesty, Veil, Vele, Veneer, Visagiste, Visor, Vizard
▷ **Disguised** *may indicate* an anagram
Disgust(ing) Ach-y-fi, Ad nauseam, Aversion, Aw, Bah, Cloy, Discomfort,

Execrable, Faugh, Fie, Foh, Fulsome, Grody, Irk, Loathsome, Manky, Mawkish, Minging, Nauseous, Noisome, Obscene, Odium, Oughly, Ouglie, Pah, Pho(h), Pish, Pshaw, Pugh, Repel, Repugnant, > **REVOLT**, Revulsion, Scomfish, Scumfish, Scunner, Scuzz, > **SICKEN**, Si(e)s, Squalid, Tush, Ugsome, Vile, Yech, Yu(c)k, Yucko, Yukky

Dish(y) Allot, Apollo, Ashet, Basin, Belle, Bowl, Chafing, Charger, Cocotte, Cook-up, Cutie, Dent, Dole, Dreamboat, Epergne, Flasket, Grail, Kitchen, Laggen, Laggin, Lanx, Luggie, Muffineer, Ovenware, Pan, Pannikin, Paten, Patera, Patin(e), Petri, Plate, Platter, Porringer, Ramekin, Ramequin, Receptacle, Sangraal, Sangrail, Sangreal, Satellite, Saucer, Scallop, Serve, Service, Side, Smasher, Special, Watchglass

DISHES

3 letters:
Poi

4 letters:
Fool
Mess
Olla
Puri
Sate
Soss
Taco
Toll

5 letters:
Adobo
Balti
Bhaji
Bitok
Brose
Champ
Curry
Dolma
Gomer
Kasha
Kibbe
Kofta
Korma
Laksa
Maror
Pilau
Pilow
Poori
Raita
Ramen
Salmi
Satay
Sushi
Tamal

Tikka

6 letters:
Bhagee
Bharta
Cou-cou
Cuscus
Diable
Entrée
Fondue
Haggis
Hotpot
Kimchi
Kishke
Mornay
Mousse
Muesli
Nachos
Paella
Pakora
Panada
Quiche
Ragout
Regale
Salmis
Sowans
Sowens
Subgum
Surimi
Tamale
Tsamba

7 letters:
Biriani
Bobotie
Burrito
Calzone
Cassava

Ceviche
Comport
Compote
Crowdie
Crubeen
Crumble
Custard
Cuvette
Dariole
Dhansak
Dopiaza
Egg roll
Fajitas
Fal-a-fel
Fel-a-fel
Foo Yung
Friture
Grav lax
Marengo
Mousaka
Padella
Poutine
Rarebit
Ravioli
Sashimi
Seviche
Soufflé
Stovies
Tempura
Terrine
Timbale
Tostada

8 letters:
Brandade
Caponata
Chop suey
Chow mein

Coolamon
Coq au vin
Coquille
Couscous
Crostini
Dog's-body
Entremes
Feijoada
Flummery
Frittata
Gado-gado
Halloumi
Kedgeree
Keftedes
Kickshaw
Kouskous
Kreplach
Mazarine
Meuniere
Moussaka
Pandowdy
Pastrami
Porridge
Pot-au-feu
Pot-roast
Raclette
Shashlik
Sillabub
Souvlaki
Squarial
Sukiyaki
Syllabub
Teriyaki
Tzatziki
White-pot
Yakimono
Yakitori

- **9 letters:**
- Carbonara
- Carpaccio
- Compotier
- Egg-fo-yang
- Enchilada
- Entremets
- Fricassee
- Galantine
- Gravad lax
- Guacamole
- Howtowdie
- Jambalaya
- Manicotti
- Pastitsio
- Pepper-pot
- Reistafel
- Rijstafel
- Shashlick

Souvlakia
Succotash

10 letters:
Blanquette
Cacciatore
Couscousou
Doner kebab
Egg-foo-yung
Jugged hare
Koulibiaca
Mousseline
Nasi goreng
Parmigiana
Plat du jour
Provencale
Quesadilla
Rijsttafel
Salmagundi

Sauerkraut
Shish kebab
Spitchcock
Spring roll
Stroganoff

11 letters:
Buck-rarebit
Fritto misto
Saltimbocca
Sauerbraten
Spanakopita
Surf and turf
Welsh rabbit

12 letters:
Eggs Benedict
Shepherd's pie
Steak tartare

Sweet and sour
Taramasalata
Welsh rarebit

13 letters:
Rumbledethump
Solomon Grundy
Toad-in-the-hole

14 letters:
Chilli con carne
Rumbledethumps
Scotch woodcock

15 letters:
Bubble and
  squeak

Dishabille Disarray, Négligé, Undress
Dishearten Appal, Core(r), Cow, Daunt, Depress, Discourage, Dispirit
Dishevel(led) Blowsy, Blowzy, Daggy, Mess, Rumpled, Touse, Tousle, Touzle, Tumble, Uncombed, Unkempt, Windswept
Dishonest(y) Bent, Crooked, Cross, Dodgy, False, Fraud, Graft, Hooky, Hot, Improbity, Jiggery-pokery, Knavery, Malpractice, Malversation, Shonky, Stink, Twister, Underhand, Venal
Dishonour Defile, Disgrace, Disparage, Ignominy, Seduce, > SHAME, Violate, Wrong
Disillusion Disenchant, Sour
Disincline(d), Disinclination Apathy, Loth, Off, Reluctant
Disinfect(ant) Acriflavin(e), Carbolic, Cineol(e), Cleanse, Eucalyptole, Formalin, Formol, Fuchsine, Fumigate, Lysol®, Phenol, Purify, Sheep-dip, TCP, Terebene
Disingenuous Insincere, Mask, Oblique, Two-faced
Disinherit Deprive, Dispossess
Disintegrate, Disintegration Break, Collapse, Crumble, Decay, Erode, Fragment, Lyse, Lysis, Osteoclasis, Rd, Rutherford
Disinter Exhume, Unearth
Disinterested Apathetic, Impartial, Incurious, Mugwump, Unbiased
Disjointed Bitty, Incoherent, Rambling, Scrappy
▸ **Disk** *see* DISC
Dislike Allergy, Animosity, Animus, Antipathy, Aversion, Derry, Disesteem, Displeasure, Distaste, Lump, Mind, Needle, Scunner, Warling
Dislocate, Dislocation Break, Diastasis, Displace, Fault, Luxate, Slip
Dislodge Budge, Displace, Expel, Luxate, Oust, Rear, Tuft, Unship, Uproot
Disloyal(ty) False, Treason, Unfaithful, Untrue
Dismal Black, Bleak, Cheerless, Dark, Dowie, Dowly, Drack, Dreary, Funereal, > GLOOMY, Grey, Long-faced, Morne, Obital, Sepulchral, Sombre, Sullen, Trist(e), Wae
Dismantle(d), Dismantling Decommission, Derig, Divest, Get-out, Sheer-hulk, Strike, Strip, Unrig

Dismast Unstep

Dismay Amate, Appal, Confound, Consternation, Coo, Daunt, Fie, Ha, Horrify, Lumme, Qualms

Dismiss(al) Annul, Ax, Boot, Bounce, Bowl(er), Bum's rush, Cancel, Cashier, Catch, Chuck, Congé, Constructive, Daff, Discard, Discharge, Expulsion, Fire, Heave-ho, Kiss-off, Lay off, Marching orders, Mitten, Och, Prorogue, Push, Recall, Reform, Remove, R.O., Road, Sack, Scout, Send, Shoo, Spit, Spurn, Stump, Via, Voetsak, Voetsek, Walking papers, York

Dismount Alight, Hecht

Disobedience, Disobedient, Disobey Contumacy, Defy, Flout, Insubordination, Rebel, Wayward

Disorder(ly), Disordered Ague, Ailment, Anarchy, Ariot, Asthma, Ataxia, Catatonia, Chaos, Chlorosis, Clutter, Confuse, Contracture, Defuse, Derange, Deray, Diabetes, Dishevel, Dissociative, Dysthymic, Dystrophy, Echolalia, Entropy, Epilepsy, Farrago, Grippe, Haemophilia, Hallucinosis, Huntingdon's chorea, Hypallage, Inordinate, Irregular, Mange, ME, Mental, Mess, Mistemper, > MUDDLE, Muss(y), Neurosis, Oncus, Onkus, Pandemonium, Panic, Para-, Pell-mell, Personality, Porphyria, Psychomatic, Psychosis, Ragmatical, Rile, Roughhouse, Rowdy, SAD, St Vitus' Dance, Schizophrenia, Seborrh(o)ea, Shell-shock, Slovenly, Sydenham's chorea, Tarantism, Thalass(a)emia, Tousle, Turbulence, Unhinge, Unruly, Upset, Virilism

▷ **Disorder(ed)** *may indicate* an anagram

Disorganised At sea, Deranged, Scatterbrain, Shambolic, Structureless

Disown Deny, Disclaim, Disinherit, Renounce, Repudiate, Unget

Disparage, Disparaging Abuse, Belittle, Decry, Defame, Denigrate, Depreciate, Detract, Discredit, Lessen, Pejorative, > SLANDER, Slur, Snide, Traduce, Vilify

Dispassionate Calm, Clinical, Composed, Cool, Impartial, Objective, Serene

Dispatch Bowl, Celerity, Consign, Destroy, Dismiss, Expede, Expedite, Express, Gazette, Kibosh, Kill, Missive, Post, Pronto, Remit, Report, > SEND, Ship, Slaughter, Slay

Dispel Disperse, Scatter

Dispensation, Dispense(r), Dispense with Absolve, Administer, Aerosol, Apothecary, Automat, Ax(e), Cashpoint, Chemist, Container, Distribute, Dose, Dropper, Exempt, Handout, Indult, Scrap, Visitation

Dispersable, Disperse, Dispersion Diaspora, Diffract, Diffuse, Disband, Dissolve, Lyophil(e), Scail, Scale, > SCATTER, Skail, Sow, Strew

Dispirit(ed) Dampen, Dash, Daunt, Discourage, Dishearten, Exorcism, Listless, Sackless

Displace(ment), Displaced Antevert, Blueshift, Depose, Disturb, Ectopia, Ectopy, Fault, Heterotopia, Lateroversion, Luxate, Move, Oust, Proptosis, Ptosis, Reffo, Shift, Stir, Subluxation, Unseat, Unsettle, Uproot, Valgus, Varus, Volumetric

Display, Display ground Air, Array, Blaze, Blazon, Brandish, Bravura, Depict, Eclat, Epideictic, Etalage, Evidence, Evince, Exhibition, Exposition, Express, Extend, Extravaganza, Exude, Fireworks, Flaunt, Float, Gondola, Hang, Head-down, Head-up, Heroics, LED, Lek, Liquid crystal, Manifest, Mount, Muster, Ostentation, Outlay, Overdress, Pageant, Parade, Paraf(f)le, Peepshow, Pixel, Pomp, Propale, Pyrotechnics, Rode, Rodeo, Roll-out, Scene, Shaw, > SHOW, Sight, Spectacle, Splash, Splurge, Sport, Spree, State, Stunt, Tableau, Tattoo, Tournament, Up, Vaunt, Wear

Displease(d), Displeasure Anger, Dischuffed, Humph, Irritate, Provoke, Umbrage

Disport Amuse, Divert, Play

Dispose(d), **Disposal**, **Disposition** Apt, Arrange, Bestow, Cast, Despatch, Dump, Eighty-six, Kibosh, Lay(-out), Ordonnance, Prone, Sale, Sell, Service, Settle, Stagger

▷ **Disposed**, **Disposition** *may indicate* an anagram

Disposition Affectation, Attitude, Bent, Bias, Humour, Inclination, Kidney, Lie, Nature, Penchant, Talent, Temper(ament), Trim

Dispossess(ed) Abate, Attaint, Bereft, Depose, Deprive, Evict, Oust

Disproportion(ate) Asymmetric, Extreme, Imbalance, Unequal

Disprove, **Disproof** Debunk, Discredit, Negate, Rebut, Rebuttal, Redargue, Refel, Refute

Dispute(d), **Disputant** Argue, Barney, Brangle, Cangle, Case, Chaffer, Challenge, Chorizont(ist), Contend, Contest, Contravene, Contretemps, Controversy, Debate, Deny, Differ, Discept, Discuss, Eristic, Fray, Haggle, Kilfud-yoking, Lock-out, Militate, Ob and soller, Odds, Oppugn, Plea, Polemic, Pro-and-con, > QUESTION, Quibble, Rag, Resist, Spar, Stickle, Threap(it), Threep(it), Tiff, Tissue, Variance, Wrangle

Disqualify Debar, Incapacitate, Recuse, Reject, Unfit

Disquiet(ed) Agitate, Concern, Discomboberate, Discombobulate, > DISTURB, Pain, Perturb(ation), Solicit, Turmoil, Uneasy, Unnerve, Vex

Disraeli Dizzy, Tancred

Disregard(ed) Anomie, Anomy, Contempt, Defy, Disfavour, Flout, Forget, Ignore, Oblivion, Omit, Overlook, Oversee, Pass, Pretermit, Slight, Spare, Violate, Waive

Disrepair Dilapidation, Ruin

Disreputable, **Disrepute** Base, Disgrace, Grubby, Louche, Low, Lowlife, Raffish, Ragamuffin, Reprobate, Rip, Scuzz(ball), Seamy, Shady, Shameful, Shy, Sleazy

Disrespect(ful) Contempt, Derogatory, Discourtesy, Flip(pant), Impiety, Impolite, Irreverent, Profane, Slight, Uncivil

Disrupt(ion) Breach, Cataclasm, Disorder, Distract, Hamper, Interrupt, Jetlag, Mayhem, Perturb, Quonk, Screw, Upheaval

▷ **Disruption** *may indicate* an anagram

Dissatisfaction Displeasure, Distaste, Humph, Umph

Dissect(ion) Analyse, Dismember, Examine, Necrotomy, Zootomy

Dissemble(r) Conceal, Feign, Fox, Hypocrite, Impostor

Dissension, **Dissent(er)**, **Dissenting** Contend, Differ, Disagree, Discord, Dissident, Faction, Heretic, Jain, Lollard, Noes, Non-CE, Non-con(formist), Pantile, Protest, Raskolnik, Recusant, Separat(ion)ist, Splinter group, > STRIFE, Vary

Dissertation Essay, Excursus, Lecture, Thesis, Treatise

▶ **Dissident** *see* DESERTER

Dissimilar Different, Diverse, Heterogeneous, Unlike

Dissipate(d) Debauch, Diffuse, Disperse, Dissolute, Gay, Revel, Scatter, Shatter, Squander, Waste

▷ **Dissipated** *may indicate* an anagram

Dissociate Separate, Sever, Withdraw

Dissolute Degenerate, Demirep, Falstaffian, Hell, Lax, Libertine, Licentious, Loose, Rake-helly, Rakish, Rip, Roué, Wanton

▷ **Dissolute** *may indicate* an anagram

Dissolution Dismissal, Divorce, End, Repeal, Separation

Dissolve Deliquesce, Digest, Disband, Disunite, Liquesce, Melt, Repeal, Terminate, Thaw

Dissonance Wolf
Dissuade Dehort, Deter, Discourage
Distaff Clotho, Female, Lady, Rock, Stick
Distance Absciss(a), Afield, Apothem, Breadth, Coss, Declination, Eloi(g)n,
   Farness, Foot, Headreach, Height, Hyperfocal, Interval, Klick, Kos(s), Latitude,
   League, Length, Mean, Mean free path, Mileage, Northing, Outland,
   Parasang, Parsec, Range, Reserve, Rod, Span, Spitting, Stade, Striking, Way,
   Yojan, Zenith
Distant Aloof, Far, Frosty, Hyperfocal, Icy, Long, Northing, Offish, Outland,
   Polar, Remote, Tele-, Timbuctoo, Yonder
Distaste(ful) Gross-out, Repugnant, Ropy, Scunner, Unpalatable, Unpleasant,
   Unsavoury
Distemper Ailment, Colourwash, Hard-pad, Paint, Panleucopenia, Tempera
Distend(ed), Distension Bloat, Dilate, Ectasia, Emphysema, Expand, Hoove,
   Inflate, > STRETCH, Swell, Turgid, Tympanites, Varicocele, Varicose
Distil(late), Distillation, Distiller, Distilling Alcohol, Alembic, Anthracine,
   Azeotrope, Brew, Condense, Drip, Pelican, Pyrene, Pyroligneous, Rosin, Turps,
   Vapour
▷ **Distillation** *may indicate* an anagram
Distinct(ive) Apparent, Characteristic, Clear, Determinate, Different, Evident,
   Grand, Individual, Peculiar, Plain, Separate, Several, Signal, > SPECIAL,
   Stylistic, Vivid
Distinction Beaut(y), Blue, Cachet, Credit, Diacritic, Difference, Dignity,
   Diorism, Disparity, Division, Eclat, Eminence, Honour, Lustre, Mark,
   Mystique, Note, Nuance, OM, Prominence, Quiddity, Rank, Renown,
   Speciality, Style, Title
Distinguish(ed), Distinguishing Classify, Demarcate, Denote, Diacritic,
   Different(iate), Discern, Discriminate, Divide, Elevate, Mark, Notable,
   Perceive, Prestigious, Prominent, Signal, Stamp
Distort(ion), Distorted Anamorphosis, Bend, Colour, Contort, Deface, Deform,
   Dent, Fudge, Garble, Helium speech, Jaundiced, Mangle, Misshapen, Pervert,
   Rubato, Thraw, Travesty, Twist, > WARP, Wow, Wrest, Wring, Wry
▷ **Distort(ed)** *may indicate* an anagram
Distract(ed), Distraction Absent, Agitate, Amuse, Avocation, Bewilder, Divert,
   Embroil, Éperdu, Forhaile, Frenetic, Lost, Madden, Mental, Nepenthe, Perplex,
   Sidetrack, Sledge, Upstage
▷ **Distract(ed)** *may indicate* an anagram
Distrain(t) Na(a)m, Poind, Sequestrate, Stress
Distraught Deranged, Elfish, Elvan, Frantic, Mad, Troubled
Distress(ed), Distressing Afflict, Ail, Alack, Anger, Anguish, Antique, Distraint,
   Dolour, Exigence, Extremity, Grieve, Harass, Harrow, Heartbreak, Hurt, Ill, > IN
   DISTRESS, Irk, Misease, Misfortune, Need, Oppress, Pain, Poignant, Prey, Sad,
   Shorn, Sore, SOS, Straits, Traumatic, Tribulation, > TROUBLE, Une(a)th
Distribute(d), Distribution Allocate, Allot, Binomial, Busbar, Carve, Chi-square,
   Colportage, Deal, Deliver(y), Deploy, Dish, Dispense, Dispose, Exponential, F,
   Frequency, Gamma, Gaussian, Geometric, Issue, Lie, Lot, Mete, Normal, Out,
   Pattern, Poisson's, Prorate, Repartition, Serve, Share
▷ **Distributed** *may indicate* an anagram
District Alsatia, Amhara, Arcadia, Ards, Area, Arrondissement, Bail(l)iwick,
   Banat, Barrio, Belt, Canton, Cantred, Classis, Community, Diocese, End,
   Exurb, Federal, Gau, Ghetto, Hundred, Lathe, Liberty, Locality, Loin, Manor,
   Metropolitan, > NEIGHBOURHOOD, Oblast, Pachalic, Pale, Parish(en), Paroch,

Pashalik, Patch, Phocis, Province, Quarter, Quartier, Rape, > REGION, Ride, Riding, Ruhr, Rural, Sanjak, Section, Sheading, Sircar, Soc, Soke(n), Stannary, Suburb, Sucken, Talooka, Taluk, Tenderloin, Township, Venue, Vicinage, Walk, Wapentake, Way, Wealden, Zila, Zillah, Zone

Distrust Caution, Doubt, Suspect, Wariness

Disturb(ance), Disturbed Ado, Aerate, Affray, Agitate, Atmospherics, Autism, Betoss, Brabble, Brainstorm, Brash, Brawl, Broil, Carfuffle, Collieshangie, Concuss, Delirium, Dementia, Derange, Desecrate, Disquiet, Dust, Dysfunction, Feeze, Firestorm, Fracas, Fray, Fret, Harass, Hoopla, Incommode, Infest, Interrupt, Jee, Kerfuffle, Kick-up, Kurfuffle, Muss, Outbreak, Perturb(ation), Prabble, Rammy, Ramp, Ripple, Romage, Rook, Roughhouse, Rouse, Ruckus, Ruction, Ruffle, Rumpus, Shake, Shellshock, Shindy, Shook-up, Stashie, Static, Steer, Stir, Sturt, Tremor, Trouble, Turbulent, Unquiet, Unrest, Unsettle, Upheaval, Uproot, > UPSET, Vex

▷ **Disturb(ed)** *may indicate* an anagram

Disunite Alienate, Dissever, Divide, Divorce, Split

Disuse Abandon, Abeyance, Desuetude, Discard, Lapse

Ditch Barathron, Barathrum, Channel, Crash-land, Cunette, Delf, Delph, Dike, Discard, Donga, Drainage, Drop, Dyke, Euripus, Foss(e), Graft, Grip, Gully, Ha(w)-ha(w), Haw-haw, Jettison, Khor, Level, Lode, Moat, Na(l)la(h), Nulla(h), Rean, Reen, Rhine, Rid, Sea, Sheuch, Sheugh, Sike, Sloot, Sluit, Spruit, Stank, Syke, Trench

Dither(ing) Agitato, Bother, Faff, Hesitate, Indecisive, Pussyfoot, Twitter

Dittany Gas-plant

Ditty, Ditties Air, Arietta, Canzonet, Departmental, Jingle, Lay, Song

Diuretic Frusemide, Furosemide

Diva Callas, Patti, Singer

Divan Compilement, Congress, Couch, Council, Settee, Sofa

Dive(r), Diving Armstand, Backflip, Belly-flop, Crash, Dart, Den, Duck, Full-gainer, Half-gainer, Header, Honkytonk, Jackknife, Joint, Ken, Nitery, Nose, Pass, Plummet, Plunge, Plutocrat, Power, Saturation, Scoter, Skin, Sound, Stage, Stoop, Submerge, Swallow, Swan, Swoop, Tailspin, Urinant

Diver(s) Didapper, Duck, Embergoose, Flop, Frogman, Gainer, Grebe, Guillemot, Loom, Loon, Lungie, Many, Merganser, Pearl, Pike, Plong(e), Pochard, Poker, Puffin, Sawbill, Scuba, Snake-bird, Speakeasy, Sundry, Urinator, Various, Zoom

Diverge(nce) Branch, Deviate, Divaricate, Spread, Swerve, Variant, Veer

Divers Miscellaneous, Some

Diverse, Diversify Alter, Chequer, Dapple, Different, Eclectic, Interlard, Intersperse, Manifold, Motley, Multifarious, Separate, Variegate, Various, Vary

Diversion, Divert(ing) Amuse, Avocation, Beguile, Deflect, Detour, Disport, Dissuade, Distract, Entertain, Game, Hare, Hobby, Interlude, Pastime, Pleasure, Prolepsis, Ramp, Red-herring, Refract, Reroute, Ruse, Shunt, Sideshow, Sidetrack, Sport, Stalking-horse, Steer, Stratagem, Sway, Switch, Tickle, Upstage, Yaw

▷ **Diverting** *may indicate* an anagram

Divest Denude, Rid, Strip, Undeck, Undress

Divide(d) Apportion, Balk, Band, Bipartite, Bisect, Branch, Cantle, Cleft, Comminute, Commot(e), Continental, Counter-pale, Cut, Deal, Demerge, Digital, Dimidiate, Dissever, Estrange, Fork, Great, Indent, Parcel, Part, Partitive, Polarise, Rend, Rift, Separate, Sever, Share, > SPLIT, Sunder, Watershed, Zone

Dividend Bonus, Div, Interim, Into, Peace, Share

Divination, Diviner Augury, Auspices, Axinomancy, Belomancy, Bibliomancy, Botanomancy, Capnomancy, Cartomancy, Ceromancy, Chiromancy, Cleromancy, Coscinomancy, Crithomancy, Crystal-gazing, Crystallomancy, Doodlebug, Dowser, Empyromancy, Geomancy, Gyromancy, Hariolation, Haruspex, Hepatoscopy, Hieromancy, Hieroscopy, Hydromancy, I Ching, Intuition, Lampadomancy, Lithomancy, Magic, Mantic, Myomancy, Omphalomancy, Oneiromancy, Ornithomancy, Ornithoscopy, Palmistry, Pyromancy, Rhabdomancy, Scapulimancy, Sciomancy, Seer, Sibyl, Sortes, Sortilege, Spae(man), Spodomancy, Taghairm, Tais(c)h, Theomancy, Tripudiary, Vaticanator, Xylomancy

Divine, Divine presence, Divinity Acoemeti, Atman, Avatar, Beatific, Clergyman, Conjecture, Curate, DD, Deduce, Deity, Douse, Dowse, Ecclesiastic, Forecast, Foretell, Fuller, > **GOD**, > **GODDESS**, Godhead, Guess, Hariolate, Heavenly, Holy, Immortal, Inge, Isiac, Kami, Mantic, Numen, Numinous, Olympian, Pontiff, Predestinate, Predict, Presage, Priest, RE, Rector, RI, Rimmon, Scry, Sense, Seraphic, Shechinah, Shekinah, Spae, Superhuman, Supernal, Theanthropic, Theologise, Theology, Triune

Division, Divisible Amitosis, Angiosperm, Arcana, Arm, Arrondissement, Bajocian, Banat(e), Bannet, Bar, Bizone, Branch, Brome, Caesura, Canton, Cantred, Cantref, Cassini's, Caste, Category, Cell, Champart, Chapter, Classification, Cleft, Cloison, Clove, Comitatus, Commot(e), Commune, Compartment, Coralline Crag, Corps, County, Crevasse, Curia, Department, Dichotomy, Disagreement, Disunity, Duan, Eyalet, Family, Farren, Fissile, Fork, Grisons, Guberniya, Gulf, Gulph, Hedge, Hide, Hundred, Inning, Isogloss, Keuper, Kim(m)eridgian, Lathe, Leet, Legion, Lindsey, List, Lobe, Long, M(e)iosis, Mitosis, Mofussil, Nome, Pachytene, Pargana, Part, Partition, Passus, Pergunnah, Period, Phratry, Phyle, Phylum, Pipe, Pitaka, Platoon, Polarisation, Presidency, Queen's Bench, Quotition, Rape, Red Crag, Reduction, Region, Replum, Reservation, Riding, Sanjak, Schism, Section, Sector, Segment, Semeion, Sept(ate), Sever, Share, Sheading, Shed, Shire, Short, Stage, Subheading, Tahsil, Tanach, Taxis, Telophase, Tepal, Thanet, Trichotomy, Trio, Trivium, Troop, Tuath, Unit, Vilayet, Volost, Wapentake, Ward, Watershed

Divisor Aliquant, Aliquot

Divorce(d) Diffarreation, Disaffiliate, Dissolve, Disunion, Div, Estrange, Get(t), Part, Separate, Sequester, > **SUNDER**, Talak, Talaq

Divot Clod, Sod, Turf

Divulge Confess, Disclose, Expose, Publish, Reveal, Split, Tell, Unveil, Utter

DIY Flatpack

Dizziness, Dizzy Beaconsfield, Ben, Capricious, Dinic, Disraeli, Giddy, Giglot, Lightheaded, Mazey, Mirligoes, Swimming, Vertiginous, > **VERTIGO**, Woozy

DJ Deejay, Monkey-suit, Selecta, Shockjock, Tuxedo, Veejay

DNA Antisense, Centromere, Chromatin, Cistron, Codon, Complementary, Cytosine, Exon, Gene, Heteroduplex, Homopolymer, Intron, Junk, Microsatellite, Muton, Nucleosome, Plasmid, Procaryote, Profiling, Prokaryote, Purine, Recombinant, Replicon, RNA, Satellite, Selfish, Southern blot, Telomere, Thymidine, Transposon, Vector, Watson-Crick model

Do(es), Doing Accomplish, Achieve, Act, Anent, Banquet, Beano, Begin, Char, Cheat, Chisel, Cod, Con, Cozen, Deed, Dich, Dish, Div, Doth, Dupe, Effectuate, Enact, Execute, Function, Gull, Handiwork, Hoax, Mill, Perform, Same, Serve, Settle, Shindig, Spif(f)licate, Suffice, Thrash, Ut

▷ **Do** *may indicate* an anagram

Do away Abolish, Banish, Demolish, Kill

Docile Agreeable, Amenable, Biddable, Dutiful, Facile, Meek, Submissive, Tame, Tractable, Yielding

Dock(er), Docked, Docks Abridge, Barber, Basin, Bistort, Bob, Camber, Canaigre, Clip, Curta(i)l, Cut, Deduct, De-tail, Dry, Floating, Grapetree, Graving, Knotweed, Lop, Marina, Moor, Off-end, Pare, Patience, Pen, Pier, Quay, Rhubarb, Rumex, Rump, Scene, Seagull, Shorten, Snakeweed, Sorrel, Sourock, Stevedore, Tilbury, Watersider, Wet, Wharf, Wharfie, Yard

Docket Invoice, Label, Tag

Dockyard Arsenal, Rosyth

Doctor(s) Allopath, Alter, Arnold, Asclepiad, Barefoot, Barnardo, Bleeder, BMA, Bones, Breeze, Bright, Brighton, Brown, Caius, Castrate, Chapitalize, Clinician, Cook, Cup(per), Cure(r), Dale, Diagnose, Dr, Dryasdust, Erasmus, Extern(e), Fake, Falsify, Family, Faustus, Feldsher, Fell, Finlay, Flying, Foster, Fundholder, Galen, Geriatrician, Geropiga, GP, Hakeem, Hakim, Healer, Homeopath, Houseman, Hyde, Imhotep, Intern, Internist, Jekyll, Jenner, Johnson, Kildare, Lace, Leach, Leech, Linacre, Load, Locum, Luke, Manette, Massage, MB, MD, Medicate, Medico, Middleton, Mindererus, Minister, Misrepresent, MO, MOH, Molla(h), Moreau, Mulla(h), Neuter, No, Ollamh, Ollav, Paean, Panel, Pangloss, Paracelsus, Paramedic, Pedro, PhD, Physician, Pill(s), Practitioner, Quack, Quacksalver, Rabbi, RAMC, Registrar, Resident, Rig, Salk, Sangrado, Saw, Sawbones, School, Shaman, Slammer, Slop, Spin, Stum, Surgeon, Syn, Syntax, Thorne, Treat, Vaidya, Vet, Water, Watson, Who, Witch

▷ **Doctor(ed)** *may indicate* an anagram

Doctrine Adoptianism, Adoptionism, Antinomian, Apollinarian, Archology, Arianism, Averr(h)oism, Bonism, Brezhnev, Cab(b)ala, Calvanism, Chiliasm, Consubstantiation, Credo, Creed, Determinism, Ditheletism, Docetism, Dogma, Doxie, Doxy, Esotery, Federalism, Fideism, Finalism, Functionalism, Gnosticism, Gospel, Holism, Infralapsarianism, Islam, Ism, Jansenism, Krypsis, Laches, Lore, Malthusian, Manich(a)eism, Metempsychosis, Molinism, Monergism, Monism, Monroe, Nestorianism, Neutral monism, Nihilism, Pragmatism, Predestination, Pythagorean(ism), Reformism, Satyagrahi, Sharia, Sheria, Shibboleth, Strong meat, Subjectivism, Sublapsarianism, Subpanation, Substantialism, Swedenborgianism, Syndicalism, Synergism, System, Teleology, > TENET, Terminism, Theory, Theravada, Thomism, Transubstantiation, Tutiorism, Utilitarianism, Voluntarism, Wasm, Weismannism, Whiteboyism, Zoism, Zwinglian

Document(s), Documentary Bumf, Bumph, Carta, Certificate, Charter, Contract, Conveyance, Covenant, Daftar, Deed, Diploma, Docket, Doco, Dompass, Dossier, Fiat, Form, Grand Remonstrance, Holograph, Latitat, Logbook, Mandamus, Offer, Papers, Precept, Production, Public, Ragman, Ragment, Record, Resort, Roll, Roul(e), Screed, Source, Stamp note, Warrant, Waybill, Writ, Write up

Dod Pet, Poll

Dodder(y) Old, Shake, Stagger, Strangleweed, Totter, Tremble

Doddle Easy

Dodge, Dodgy Artful, Avoid, Bell-ringing, Column, Elude, Evade, Evasion, Iffy, Jink, Jook, Jouk, Racket, Ruse, Shirk, Sidestep, Skip, Slalom, Slinter, Tip, Trick, Twist, Urchin, Weave, Welsh, Wheeze, Wire, Wrinkle

Doe(s) Deer, Faun, Hind

Doff Avail(e), Avale, Remove, Rouse, Shed, Tip

Dog(s) Bowwow, Canes, Canidae, Canine, Feet, Fire, Fog, Heading, Hot, Hunter, Kennel, Leading, Nodding, Pursue, Sea, Search, Seeing-eye, Shadow, Sleeve, Spotted, Stalk, Sun, Tag, Tail, Top, Tracker, Trail, Wammul, Water, Yellow

DOGS

3 letters:
Cur
Eye
Gun
Pig
Pom
Pug
Rab
Yap

4 letters:
Barb
Bird
Brak
Bran
Bush
Cant
Chow
Dane
Fido
Heel
Iron
Kuri
Mutt
Oath
Peke
Puli
Rach
Sled
Stag
Tike
Toby
Tosa
Tray
Tyke
Wolf

5 letters:
Alans
Apsos
Argos
Boots
Boxer
Brach
Cairn
Coach

Dhole
Dingo
Guard
Guide
Haunt
Hound
Husky
Hyena
Kurre
Laika
Lorel
Luath
Moera
Pidog
Pluto
Pooch
Rache
Rover
Shock
Spitz
Spoor
Whelp
Zorro

6 letters:
Afghan
Bandog
Barbet
Barker
Basset
Beagle
Bitser
Blanch
Borzoi
Bounce
Bowler
Briard
Caesar
Canaan
Chenet
Cocker
Collie
Dangle
Eskimo
Gelert
Goorie

Heeler
Jackal
Katmir
Kelpie
Kennet
Ketmir
Kratim
Lassie
Mauthe
Messan
Moppet
Pariah
Piedog
Police
Poodle
Pye-dog
Ranger
Saluki
Setter
Shaggy
Shough
Sirius
Sothic
Talbot
Teckel
Touser
Towser
Vizsla
Westie
Yapper
Yorkie

7 letters:
Andiron
Basenji
Bobbery
Boerbul
Bouvier
Brachet
Bulldog
Courser
Griffon
Harrier
Hearing
Iceland
Lurcher

Maltese
Maremma
Mastiff
Mongrel
Orthrus
Pointer
Prairie
Raccoon
Reynard
Samoyed
Sapling
Sausage
Shar-Pei
Sheltie
Shih tzu
Showghe
Sniffer
Spaniel
Starter
> **TERRIER**
Volpino
Whiffet
Whippet
Yapster

8 letters:
Aardwolf
Aberdeen
Airedale
Alsatian
Blenheim
Bouvrier
Bratchet
Brittany
Carriage
Cerberus
Chow-chow
Doberman
Elkhound
Hovawart
Huntaway
Kangaroo
Keeshond
Komondor
Labrador
Landseer

- Malamute
- Malemute
- Papillon
- Pekinese
- Pembroke
- Pinscher
- Samoyede
- Sealyham
- Sheepdog
- Springer
- Turnspit
- Warragal
- Warrigal

9 letters:
- Buckhound
- Chihuahua
- Coonhound
- Dachshund
- Dalmatian
- Deerhound
- Dobermann
- Gazehound
- Great Dane
- Greyhound
- Harlequin
- Kerry blue
- Lhasa apso
- Molossian
- Pekingese

Retriever
Schnauzer
Staghound
Strong-eye
Wolfhound

10 letters:
Bedlington
Bloodhound
Blueheeler
Fox terrier
Otterhound
Pomeranian
Rottweiler
Schipperke
Shin-barker
Tripehound
Weimaraner

11 letters:
Bichon frise
Jack Russell
Montmorency
Skye terrier
Sleuthhound
Tibetan apso
Trendle-tail
Trindle-tail
Trundle-tail
Wishtonwish

12 letters:
Border collie
Gazelle hound
Japanese chin
Newfoundland
Saint Bernard
West Highland

13 letters:
Affenpinscher
Dandie Dinmont
Scotch terrier
Sussex spaniel

14 letters:
Italian spinone
Tibetan mastiff

15 letters:
Bernese Mountain
Estrela Mountain
Mexican hairless
Norwegian
  buhund
Portuguese water
Swedish vallhund

16 letters:
Doberman-
  pinscher

Pyrenean
  mountain
Russian
  wolfhound
Shetland
  sheepdog

17 letters:
Anatolian
  Shepherd
Dobermann-
  pinscher

18 letters:
Large
  Munsterlander
Old English
  sheepdog
Rhodesian
  ridgeback

20 letters:
Landseer
  Newfoundland

21 letters:
Polish Lowland
  sheepdog

Dog-bane Apocynum
Doge Dandolo
Dogfish Huss, Rigg
Dogged Determined, Die-hard, Dour, Indefatigable, Pertinacious, Stubborn, Sullen
Doggerel Crambo, Jingle, Laisse, Rat-rhyme
Dog Letter R
Dogma(tic) Assertive, Belief, Conviction, Creed, Doctrinal, Ideology, Ipse dixit, Opinionative, Pedagogic, Peremptory, Pontifical, Positive, > **TENET**
Do-gooder Piarist, Reformer, Salvationist, Samaritan, Scout
Dogsbody Bottle-washer, Gofer, Skivvy
Dog star Canicula, Lassie, Sirius, Sothic
Do it Dich
Dolce Stop, Sweet
Dole Alms, Batta, B(u)roo, Give, Grief, Maundy, Payment, Pittance, Pog(e)y, Ration, > **SHARE**, Tichborne, Vail, Vales
Doll(y) Barbie®, Bimbo, Common, Corn, Creeper, Crumpet, Dress, Dutch, Golliwog, Kachina, Kewpie®, Maiden, Marionette, Matryoshka, Maumet, Mommet, Mummet, Ookpik®, Ornament, Paris, Parton, Poppet, Puppet, Ragdoll, Russian, Sis(ter), Sitter, Tearsheet, Toy, Trolley, Varden, Washboard, Wax

Dollar(s) Balboa, Boliviano, Buck, Cob, Cob money, Euro, Fin, Greenback, Iron man, Peso, Petrol, Piastre, Pink, S, Sand, Sawbuck, Sawhorse, Scrip, Smacker, Spin, Sword, Top, Wheel

Dollop Glob, Helping, Share

▷ **Dolly** *may indicate* an anagram

Dolly-bird Dish

Dolour Grief, Pain, Sorrow

Dolphin Amazon, Arion, Beluga, Bottlenose, Cetacean, Coryphene, Delphinus, Grampus, Lampuka, Lampuki, Meer-swine, Porpess(e), Risso's, River, Sea-pig

Dolt Ass, Blockhead, Clodhopper, Noodle, Oaf, Owl, > STUPID

Domain Archaea, Bacteria, Bourn(e), Demain, Demesne, Eminent, Emirate, Empire, Estate, Eukarya, Manor, Predicant, Public, Rain, Realm, Region, Reign

Dome(-shaped) Al-Aqsa, Cap, Cupola, Cupula, Dagoba, Geodesic, Head, Imperial, Louvre, Millennium, Onion, Periclinal, Rotunda, Salt, Stupa, Tee, Tholos, Tholus, Tope, Vault, Xanadu

Domestic(ate) Char, Cleaner, Dom, Esne, Familiar, Home-keeping, Homely, House, Housetrain, Humanise, Interior, Internal, Intestine, Maid, Menial, > SERVANT, Tame, Woman

Domicile Abode, Dwelling, Hearth, Home, Ménage

Dominate, Dominance, Dominant Ascendancy, Baasskap, Ballbreaker, Bethrall, Clou, Coerce, Control, Hegemony, Henpeck, Maisterdome, Mesmerise, Monopolise, O(v)ergang, Override, Overshadow, Power, Preponderant, Preside, Rule, Soh, > SUBDUE, Subjugate, Tower

Domineer Boss, Henpeck, Lord, Ride, Swagger, Tyrannize

Dominica(n) Jacobite, Monk, OP, Preaching friar, Predicant, Savonarola, WD

Dominie Maister, Master, Pastor, Sampson, Schoolmaster

Dominion Dom, Empire, Khanate, NZ, Realm, Reame, Reign, > RULE, Supremacy, Sway, Territory

Domino(es) Card, Fats, Mask, Matador

Don Academic, Address, Assume, Caballero, Camorrist, Endue, Fellow, Garb, Giovanni, Indew, Juan, Lecturer, Mafia, Prof, Quixote, Reader, Senor, Spaniard, Tutor, Wear

Dona(h) Duckie, Love

Donate, Donation Aid, Bestow, Contribution, Gift, Give, Peter's pence, Present, Wakf, Waqf

Done Achieved, Complete, Crisp, Ended, Executed, Had, Over, Spitcher, Tired, Weary

Donjon Dungeon, Keep

Donkey Ass, Burro, Cardophagus, Cuddie, Cuddy, Dapple, Dick(e)y, Dunce, Eeyore, Fussock, Genet(te), Jennet, Jerusalem pony, Kulan, Modestine, Moke, Mule, Neddy, Nodding, Onager, Stupid, Years

Donor Benefactor, Bestower, Settlor, Universal

Doo Dove

Doodle(r) Scribble, Yankee

Doodlebug Antlion, Larva, V1

Doom(ed) Condemned, Damnation, Date, Destine, Destiny, > FATE, Fay, Fey, Fie, Goner, Ill-starred, Lot, Predestine, Preordain, Ragnarok, Ruined, Sentence, Spitcher, Star-crossed, Weird

Doone Carver, Lorna

Door(s), Doorstep, Doorway Aperture, Communicating, Damnation, Drecksill, Dutch, Elephant, Entry, Exit, Fire, Folding, Front, Haik, Hake, Hatch, Heck, Ingress, Jib, Lintel, Louver, Louvre, Muntin, Oak, Open, Overhead, Portal,

Postern, Revolving, Rory, Screen, Sliding, Stable, Stage, Storm, Street, Swing, Trap, Up and over, Vomitory, Wicket, Yett

Doorkeeper, Doorman Bouncer, Commissionaire, Guardian, Janitor, Ostiary, Porter, Tiler, Tyler, Usher

Doormat Subservient, Weakling

Doorpost Architrave, Dern, Durn, Jamb, Yate, Yett

Dope Acid, Amulet, Bang, Coke, Crack, > **DRUG**, Gen, Goose, Info, Lowdown, Narcotic, Nobble, Rutin, Sedate, Soup, > **STUPID PERSON**, Tea

Dorcas Gazelle, Needle, Shepherdess

Dorian, Doric Metope, Mutule

Doris Day, Lessing, Mollusc

Dormant Abed, Comatose, Hibernating, Inactive, Inert, Joist, Latent, Resting, > **SLEEPING**, Torpescent

Dormitory Barrack, Dorter, Dortour, Hall, Hostel, Quarters

Dormouse Loir

Dorothy Bag, Dot, Sayers

Dorsal Back, Neural, Notal

Dory Fish, John

Dosage, Dose Acute, Administer, Booster, Cascara, Cumulative, Drachm, Draught, Drench, Drug, Hit, Kilogray, > **MEASURE**, Physic, Posology, Potion, Powder, Rem, Threshold, Tolerance

Doss (house) Dharmsala, Dharmshala, Kip, Padding-ken, Spike

Dossier File, Record

Dot(s), Dotted, Dotty Absurd, Bind(h)i, Bullet, Centred, Criblé, Dit, Dower, Dowry, Ellipsis, Engrailed, Leader, Lentiginose, Limp, Micro, Morse, Occult, Or, Particle, Pixel, > **POINT**, Polka, Precise, Punctuate, Punctulate, Punctum, Schwa, Semé(e), Set, Speck, Spot, Sprinkle, Stigme, Stipple, Stud, Tap, Tittle, Trema, Umlaut

Dote, Dotage, Doting, Dotard Adore, Anile, Anility, Cocker, Dobbie, Idolise, Imbecile, Pet, Prize, Senile, Tendre, Twichild

Double(s) Amphibious, Ancipital, Bi-, Bifold, Binate, Clone, Counterpart, Crease, Dimeric, Doppel-ganger, Doppio, Dual, Duo, Duple(x), Duplicate, Equivocal, Fetch, Fold, Foursome, Geminate, Gimp, Image, Ingeminate, Ka, Look-alike, Loop, Martingale, Pair, Parlay, Polyseme, Reflex, Replica, Ringer, Run, Similitude, Spit, Trot, Turnback, Twae, > **TWIN**, Two(fold)

Double-barrelled Tautonym

Double-cross, Double dealing Ambidext(e)rous, Two-time

Double-entendre Polyseme, Polysemy

Doublet Peascod, Pourpoint, TT

Doubt(ful), Doubter Ambiguous, Aporia, Askance, But, Debatable, Distrust, Dubiety, Dubitate, Hesitate, Hum, Iffy, Incertitude, Misgiving, Mistrust, > **NO DOUBT**, Precarious, Qualm, Query, > **QUESTION**, Rack, Scepsis, Sceptic, Scruple, Shady, Shy, Sic, Skepsis, Sus, Suspect, Suspicious, Suss, Thomas, Thos, Umph, Uncertain, Unsure, Waver

Doubtless Probably, Sure, Truly

Douceur Bonus, Sop, Sweetener

Douche Bath, Gush, Rinse, Shower, Wash

Dough(y) Boodle, Cake, Calzone, Cash, Duff, Hush-puppy, Knish, Loot, Magma, Masa, Money, Paste, Pop(p)adum, Ready, Sad, Sour, Spondulicks, Strudel

Doughboy Dumpling, Soldier

Doughnut Beavertail®, Cruller, Knish, Koeksister, Olycook, Olykoek, Sinker, Torus

Doughty Brave, Intrepid, Resolute, Stalwart, Valiant
Dour Glum, Hard, Mirthless, Morose, Reest, Reist, Sinister, Sullen, Taciturn
Douse Dip, Drench, Extinguish, Snuff, Splash
Dove Collared, Columbine, Culver, Cushat, Diamond, Doo, Ice-bird, Mourning, Pacifist, > PIGEON, Queest, Quoist, Ring, Rock, Stock, Turtle
Dove-cot(e) Columbarium, Columbary, Louver, Louvre, Lover
Dovetail Fit, Lewis(son), Mortise, Tally, Tenon
Dowager Elder, Widow
Dowdy Frumpish, Mums(e)y, Shabby, Sloppy, Slovenly
Dowel Peg, Pin
Down(s)s, Down(beat), Downsize, Downward, Downy A bas, Abase, Abattu, Alow, Amort, Bank, Below, Berkshire, Blue, Cast, Catabasis, Chapfallen, Comous, Cottony, Crouch, Darling, Dejected, Dowl(e), Drink, Epsom, Feather, Fledge, Floccus, Flue, Fluff, Fly, Fuzz, Goonhilly, Ground, Hair, Hill, Humble, Humiliate, Jeff, Kennet, Lanugo, Losing, Low, Lower, Nap, Oose, Ooze, Owing, Pappus, Pennae, Pile, Plumage, Powder, Quash, Repress, Sebum, Slim, Thesis, Thistle, Tomentum, Unserviceable, Urinant, Vail, Wold, Wretched
Downcast Abject, Chapfallen, Despondent, Disconsolate, Dumpish, Hangdog, Hopeless, Melancholy, Woebegone
Downfall, Downpour Cataract, Collapse, Deluge, Fate, Flood, Hail, Onding, Overthrow, Rain, Ruin, Shower, Thunder-plump, Torrent, Undoing, Waterspout
Downgrade(d) Déclassé, Disrate
Downright Absolute, Arrant, Bluff, Candid, Clear, Complete, Flat, Plumb, Plump, Pure, Rank, Sheer, Stark, Utter
Downstairs Below
Dowry Dot, Dower, Lobola, Lobolo, Merchet, Portion, Settlement, Tocher
Dowse(r), Dowsing Divine, Enew, Fireman, Rhabdomancy, Water-witch
Doxology Gloria, Glory
Doxy Harlot, Loose woman, Wench
Doyen Dean, Senior
Doze Ca(u)lk, Dove(r), Nap, Nod, Semi-coma, Sleep, Slip, Slumber
Dozen(s) Baker's, Long, Round, Thr(e)ave, Twal, Twelve
Dr Debtor, Doctor, Dram
Drab Ash-grey, Cloth, Dell, Dingy, Dull, Dun, Isabel(line), Lifeless, Livor, Mumsy, Prosaic, Pussel, Quaker-colour, Rig, Road, Slattern, Sloven, Subfusc, Tart, Trull, Wanton, Whore
Drabble Bemoil, Draggle
Dracula Bat, Count, Vampire
Draft Cheque, Draw, Ebauche, Essay, Landsturm, Minute, MS, Outline, Plan, Press, Projet, Rough, Scheme, Scroll, Scrowle, > SKETCH
Drag Car, Drail, Dredge, Drogue, Elicit, Eonism, Epicene, Extort, Fiscal, Form, Hale, Harl, > HAUL, Induced, Keelhaul, La Rue, Lug, Parasite, Pressure, Profile, Puff, Pull, Rash, Sag, Schlep, Shoe, Skidpan, Sled, Snig, Sweep, Toke, Tote, Trail, Train, Travail, Travois, Trawl, Treck, Trek, Tump, Vortex
Draggle Drail, Lag, Straggle
Dragon Basilisk, Bel, Bellemère, Chaperon(e), Chindit, Draco, Drake, Fafnir, Fire-drake, Gargouille, Komodo, Kung-kung, Ladon, Lindworm, Opinicus, Peist, Puk, Python, Rouge, Safat, Shrew, Typhoeus, Wantley, Wivern, Worm, Wyvern
Dragonfly Aeschna, Demoiselle, Devil's darning needle, Nymph, Odonata
Dragon's teeth Cadmus, Spartae, Sparti

Dragoon Coerce, Force, Press, Trooper

Drain(ed), Drainage, Draining, Drainpipe Bleed, Brain, Buzz, Catchment, Catchwater, Channel, Cloaca, Cundy, Delf, Delph, Dewater, Ditch, Dry, Ea(u), > EMPTY, Emulge(nt), Exhaust, Field, Fleet, Grating, Grip, Gully, Gutter, Ketavothron, Kotabothron, Lade, Leach, Leech, Limber, Lose, Milk, Mole, Nala, Nulla(h), Penrose, Pump, Rack, Rone, Sap, Scupper, Seton, Sew(er), Sheuch, Sheugh, Silver, Sink, Siver, Sluice, Sluse, Soakaway, Sough, Spend, Stank, Storm, Sump, Sure, Syver, Tile, Trench, Trocar, Unwater, Ureter, U-trap, Weary, Well

Dram Drink, Drop, Nipperkin, Nobbler, Portion, Snifter, Tickler, Tiff, Tot, Wet

Drama(tic), Drama school Auto, Catastasis, Charade, Closet, Comedy, Drastic, ER, Farce, Heroic, Histrionic, Kabuki, Kathakali, Kitchen sink, Legit, Mask, Masque, Mime, Moralities, No, Nogaku, Noh, Piece, Play, RADA, Scenic, Sensational, Singspiel, Stagy, Striking, Tetralogy, Theatric, Thespian, Tragedy, Unities, Wagnerian, Wild

Dramatist Adamov, Aeschylus, Albee, Aristophanes, Beaumarchais, Beaumont, Brecht, Bridie, Calderon, Congreve, Corneille, Coward, Drinkwater, Eumenides, Euripides, Fletcher, Frisch, Fry, Gay, Genet, Goldoni, Havel, Ibsen, Ionesco, Jarry, Kyd, Lyly, Massinger, Menander, Middleton, Molière, Odets, O'Neill, Osborne, Otway, Pinero, Pirandello, Plautus, > PLAYWRIGHT, Racine, Rostand, Rowe, Rowley, Schiller, Seneca, Shadwell, Shaffer, Sherriff, Sophocles, Stoppard, Strindberg, Synge, Terence, Udall, Vanbrugh, Voltaire, Webster, Wedekind, Wesker, Wilde, Wilder, Will, > WRITER, Yeats

Dram-shop Bar, Boozingken, Bousingken

Drape(ry) Adorn, Coverlet, Coverlid, Curtain, Festoon, Fold, Hang, Mantling, Swathe, Valance, Veil, Vest

Draper Gilpin, Hosier, Mercer, Ruth, Scotch cuddy

Drastic Dire, Dramatic, Extreme, Harsh, Purge, Senna, > SEVERE, Violent

Drat Bother, Dang, Darn

Draught(s), Draughtsman Aloetic, Aver, Breeze, Dam, Design, Drench, Drink, Fish, Gulp, Gust, Haal, Hippocrene, King, Men, Nightcap, Outline, Plan, Potation, Potion, Pull, Quaff, Sketch, Sleeping, Slug, Swig, Tracer, Up-current, Veronal, Waucht, Waught, Williewaught

▷ **Draught** *may refer to* fishing

Draught-board Dam-board, Dambrod

Dravidian Tamil

Draw (off), Drawer(s), Drawing, Drawn Adduct, Allure, Attract, Bleed, Bottom, Cock, Crayon, Dead-heat, Delineate, Derivation, Describe, Dis(em)bowel, Doodle, Dr, Draft, Drag, Dress, Educe, Entice, Equalise, Evaginate, Extract, Fetch, Gather, Gaunt, Glorybox, Gut, Haggard, Hale, Halve, Haul, Induce, Indue, Inhale, Lengthen, Limn, Longbow, Lottery, Pantalet(te)s, Panty, Perpetual check, Petroglyph, Protract, Pull, Rack, Raffle, Remark, Scent, Score, Sesquipedalian, Shottle, Shuttle, Siphon, Sketch, Slub, Snig, Spin, Stalemate, Stumps, Sweepstake, Syphon, Tap, Taut, Technical, Tempt, Tenniel, Tie, Till, Toke, Tole, Tombola, Top, Tose, Tow(age), Toze, Trice, Troll, Tug, Unsheathe, Uplift

▷ **Draw** *may indicate* something to smoke

Drawback Catch, Downside, Ebb, Impediment, > OBSTACLE, Rebate, Retraction, Shrink, Snag

Drawbridge Bascule, Pontlevis

Drawing Cartoon, Charcoal, Crayon, Dentistry, Detail, Diagram, Elevation, Freehand, Fusain, Graphics, Indraft, Line, Mechanical, Monotint,

Orthograph, Pastel, Petroglyph, Profile, Seductive, Sepia, Silverpoint, Study, Technical, Traction, Wash, Working

Drawl Dra(u)nt, Haw, Slur, Twang

▷ **Drawn** *may indicate* an anagram

Drawn up Atrip, Drafted

Dray Cart, Lorry, Wagon

Dread(ed) Angst, Anxiety, Awe, Fear, > HORROR, Rasta, Redoubt, Thing

Dreadful Awful, Chronic, Dearn, Dire, Formidable, Ghastly, Horrendous, Penny, Sorry, Terrible

Dream(er), Dream home, Dream state, Dreamy Alchera, Alcheringa, Aspire, Castle, Desire, Drowsy, Dwalm, Dwa(u)m, Fantast, Fantasy, Faraway, Gerontius, Idealise, Illusion, Imagine, Languor, Long, Mare, Mirth, Moon, Morpheus, Muse, Nightmare, On(e)iric, Pensive, Phantasmagoria, Pipe, > REVERIE, Rêveur, Romantic, Somniate, Spac(e)y, Stargazer, Surreal, Sweven, Trance, Trauma, Vague, Vision, Walter Mitty, Wet

Dreary Bleak, Desolate, Dismal, Doleful, Dreich, Dull, Gloom, Gray, Grey, Oorie, Ourie, Owrie, Sad

Dredger Caster

Dregs Bottom, Draff, Dunder, F(a)eces, Fecula, Gr(e)aves, Grounds, Lees, Legge, Mother, Mud, Riffraff, Scaff, Sediment, Settlings, Silt, Snuff, Ullage

Dreikanter Ventifact

Drench Dowse, Soak, Souse, Steep, Submerge

Dress(ing), Dressed Academic, Accoutre, Adorn, Aguise, Align, Ao dai, Array, Attire, Attrap, Bandage, Bandoline, Bedizen, Black-tie, Bloomer, Blouson, Boast, Bodice, Boun, Bowne, Brilliantine, Busk, Caftan, Cataplasm, Charpie, Cheongsam, Chimer, Cimar, Clad, > CLOTHING, Coat, Cocktail, Comb, Compost, Compress, Corsage, Corset, Costume, Court, Curry, Cymar, Dandify, Dashiki, Deck, Deshabille, Dight, Dirndl, Dizen, Doll, Dolly Varden, Dolman, Don, Drag, Dub, Dubbin, Elastoplast®, Empire, Endue, Enrobe, Evening, Fancy, Far(r)andine, Farthingale, Fatigues, Ferrandine, Fertiliser, Fig, Finery, Flamenco, French, Frock, Full, Gamgee tissue, Garb, Garnish, Gauze, Girt, Gown, Graith, Granny, Guise, Gymslip, > HABIT, Highland, Ihram, Italian, Jaconet, Kabuki, Ketchup, K(h)anga, Kimono, Kirtle, Kitenge, Line, Lint, Lounger, Maxi, Mayonnaise, Merveilleuse, Midi, Mineral, Mob, Morning, Mother Hubbard, Mufti, Mulch, Muu-muu, Oil, Ore, Patch, Peplos, Pinafore, Plaster, Pledget, Plumage, Polonaise, Pomade, Poultice, Power, Prank, Preen, Prepare, Princess (line), Rag, Raiment, Rainbow, Ranch, Ray, Rehearsal, Rémoulade, Rig, Robe, Russet, Russian, Rybat, Sack, Sacque, Salad, Samfoo, Samfu, Sari, Sarong, Sartorial, Sauce, Scutch, Seloso, Separates, Sheath, Shift, Shirt, Shirtwaister, Simar(re), Smock, Sterile, Stole, Stupe, Subfusc, Subfusk, Suit, Sundress, Symar, Tartan, Tasar, Taw, Tent, Tenue, Tew, Thousand Island, Tiff, Tire, Tog, Toga, Toilet, Tonic, Top, Treat, Trick, Trim, Trollopee, Tunic, Tusser, Tussore, Tuxedo, Uniform, Vest, Vinaigrette, Wear, Wedding, Well, White-tie, Wig, Yclad, Ycled

Dressage Demivolt(e), Manège, Passade, Passage, Pesade, Piaffe

▷ **Dressed up, Dressing** *may indicate* an anagram

Dresser Adze, Almery, Bureau, Chest, Couturier, Deuddarn, Dior, Lair, Lowboy, Sideboard, Transvestite, Tridarn, Welsh

Dressing-gown Bathrobe, Negligee, Peignoir

Dressing-room Apodyterium, Vestiary, Vestry

Dressmaker Costumier, Dorcas, Modiste, Seamstress, Tailor

Drew Steeld, Stelled

Dribble Drip, Drivel, Drop, Seep, Slaver, Slobber, Slop, Trickle

Dried Fish Bum(m)alo, Bummaloti, Haberdine, Speld(r)in(g), Stockfish

▸ **Dried Fruit** *see* DRY FRUIT

Drift(ing), **Drifter** Becalmed, Continental, Cruise, Current, Digress, Diluvium, Float, Genetic, Heap, Impulse, Longshore, Maunder, Natant, North Atlantic, Plankton, Purport, Rorke, Slide, Tendence, Tendency, > TENOR, Waft, Wander, Zooplankton

Drill(ing) Appraisal, Auger, Bore, Burr, Close order, Directional, Educate, Exercise, Fire, Form, Hammer, Jackhammer, Jerks, Kerb, Monkey, Pack, PE, Pierce, Pneumatic, Power, PT, Radial, Reamer, Ridge, Rimer, Seeder, Sow, Square-bashing, Teach, Train, Twill, Twist, Usage, Wildcat

Drink(er), **Drunk(enness)** AA, Absorb, Adrian Quist, Alkie, Alky, Babalas, Bacchian, Barfly, Bender, Beverage, Bev(v)y, Bezzle, Bib(ite), Binge, Birl(e), Bland, Blatted, Blind, Blitzed, Bloat, Blotto, Bombed, Boose, Booze, Bosky, Bottled, Bouse, Bowl, Bracer, Brandy, Bumper, Burst, Carafe, Carousal, Cat-lap, Chaser, Compotation, > CORDIAL, Corked, Crapulent, Crapulous, Cratur, Crocked, Cuppa, Cut, Demitasse, Digestif, Dipsomaniac, Double, Down, Drain, Draught, Drop, Ebriate, Ebriose, Elixir, Entire, Eye-opener, Finger, Fleein', Flying, Fou, Fuddle-cap, Fuddled, Full, Glug, Half-seas-over, Heart-starter, High, Hogshead, Honkers, Hophead, Imbibe, Indulge, Inhaust, Intemperate, Irrigate, Ivresse, Jag, Jar, Juice, Juicehead, Knock back, Lap, Legless, Lethean, Libation, Lit, Loaded, Lord, Lower, Lush(y), Maggoty, Maltworm, Maudlin, Merry, Methomania, Methysis, Mixer, Moony, Mortal, Mug, Nog(gin), Obfuscated, Oenomania, Oiled, One, Oppignorate, Overshot, Paid, Paint, Partake, Particular, Peg, Pickled, Pick-me-up, Pie-eyed, Pint(a), Piss-artist, Pissed, Pisshead, Pisspot, Pixil(l)ated, Plonk(o), Plottie, Potation, Poteen, Potion, Primed, Quaff, Rat-arsed, Ratted, Roaring, Rolling, Rotten, Round, Rouse, Rumfustian, Rummer, Screwed, Sea, Shebeen, Shicker, Shotover, Silenus, Sip(ple), Skinned, Slake, Slewed, Sloshed, Slued, Slug, Slurp, Smashed, Smoothie, Snort, Soak, Soused, Sozzled, Sponge, Spongy, Spunge, Squiffy, Steaming, Stewed, Stimulant, Stinko, Stocious, Stoned, Stonkered, Stotious, Stuporous, Sup, Swacked, Swallow, Swig, Swill, Tank, Temulence, Tiddl(e)y, Tiff, Tift, Tight, Tipper, Tipple, Tipsy, Tope, Toss, Tossicated, Tost, Two-pot screamer, Usual, Wash, Wat, Wauch, Waught, Well-oiled, Wet, Whiffled, Williewaught, Winebag, Wino, Wrecked, Zonked

● **DRINKS**
●

2 letters:	Kir	Coke®	Sack
It	L&P	Flip	Sake
	Mum	Grog	Saki
3 letters:	Pop	Homa	Soda
Ale	Rum	Kava	Soft
Ava	Rye	Kola	Soma
Bub	Tea	Malt	Sour
Cha	Tot	Mead	Sura
Cup	Vin	Neck	Tape
Dop		Nipa	Tass
Fap	**4 letters:**	Ouzo	Tent
Gin	Asti	Port	Yill
G&T	Bock	Purl	
Hom	Bull	Raki	

5 letters:

Assai
Bingo
Bombo
Bumbo
Cider
Cocoa
Copus
Crush
Doris
Float
Glogg
Haoma
Hogan
Hooch
Joram
Jorum
Julep
Kefir
Kelty
Kvass
Lassi
Mâcon
Malwa
Mauby
Meath
Medoc
Meths
Mobby
Morat
Mulse
Nappy
Negus
Pekoe
Pepsi®
Perry
Pimms
Polly
Pombe
Punch
Rakee
Rummy
Sarsa
Sarza
Shake
Short
Shrub
Skink
Sling
Smile
Stout
Toddy
Tonic
Totty
Vodka
Xeres

6 letters:

Amrita
Apozem
Arrack
Bishop
Burton
Busera
Cassis
Caudle
Cauker
Chasse
Coffee
Cognac
Cooler
Cooper
Doctor
Eggnog
Enzian
Gimlet
Grappa
Gutrot
Hobnob
Hootch
Kalied
Keltic
Kephir
Kirsch
Kumiss
Kümmel
Maotai
Meathe
Mescal
Mickey
Mobbie
Nectar
Obarni
Old Tom
Oolong
Orgeat
Oulong
Pastis
Pernod®
Plotty
Porter
Posset
Pulque
Rickey
Rotgut
Saloop
Samshu
Shandy
Sherry
Smiler
Squash
Stingo
Strega
Strunt
Taffia
Tisane
Waragi
Yaqona
Zythum

7 letters:

Absinth
Akvavit
Alcopop
Amoroso
Aquavit
Bacardi®
Bitters
Campari®
Caribou
Chablis
Chianti
Cobbler
Curaçao
Curaçoa
Daquiri
Eggflip
Fairish
Fustian
Guarana
Italian
Koumiss
Malmsey
Mineral
Nobbler
Oenomel
Oloroso
Persico
Philter
Philtre
Pilsner
Pink gin
Quickie
Ratafia
Reviver
Rosiner

Rosolio
Sangria
Sazerac
Screech
Scrumpy
Sherbet
Sherris
Sloe gin
Snifter
Stengah
Swizzle
Tequila
Tio Pepe®
Wassail

8 letters:

Absinthe
Aleberry
Ambrosia
Anisette
Aperitif
Armagnac
Borachio
Bordeaux
Brown cow
Burgundy
Calvados
Champers
Charneco
Ciderkin
Coca-cola®
Cold duck
Daiquiri
Dog's nose
Dubonnet®
Eau de vie
Geropiga
Ginsling
Gluhwein
Highball
Hollands
Homebrew
Hydromel
Lemonade
Mahogany
Nepenthe
Nightcap
Persicot
Pilsener
Ragmaker
Red biddy
Regmaker

- Resinata
- Resinate
- Rice beer
- Riesling
- Rosoglio
- Sangaree
- Schnapps
- Skokiaan
- Snowball
- Spritzer
- Switchel
- Tequilla
- Tincture
- Vermouth
- Witblits
-
- **9 letters:**
- Applejack
- Aqua-vitae
- Ayahuasco
- Badminton
- Buck's fizz
- Calabogus
- Champagne
- Chocolate

Claret cup
Cream soda
Cuba libre
Eccoccino
Febrifuge
Firewater
Gingerade
Grenadine
Hippocras
Lambswool
Manhattan
Metheglin
Milk punch
Milkshake
Mint julep
Moose milk
Nipperkin
Refresher
Sauternes
Slivovica
Slivovitz
Snakebite
Stiffener
Sundowner
The cratur

Whisky mac

10 letters:
Blackstone
Bloody Mary
Buttermilk
Chartreuse®
Lolly water
Maraschino
Mickey Finn
Piña colada
Pousse-café
Shandygaff
Tom Collins

11 letters:
Aguardiente
Amontillado
Benedictine
Black and tan
Black velvet
Boiler-maker
Doch-an-doris
Half-and-half
Niersteiner

Screwdriver
Soapolallie
Tom and Jerry
Whiskey sour

12 letters:
Deoch-an-doris
Doch-an-dorach
Doch-an-doruis
Humpty-dumpty
Jimmy Woodser
Marcobrunner
Old-fashioned
Sarsaparilla

13 letters:
Deoch-an-doruis
Mops and brooms
Prairie oyster

14 letters:
John Barleycorn

Drink store Cellar

Drip Bore, Dew-drop, Dribble, Drop, Gutter, IV, Leak, Post-nasal, Saline, Seep, Splatter, Stillicide, Trickle, Wimp

Dripstone Label, Larmier

Drive(r), **Driving**, **Drive out** AA, Acquired, Actuate, Amber gambler, Ambition, Backseat, Banish, Beetle, Bullocky, Ca', Cabby, Campaign, Carman, Chain, Charioteer, Chauffeur, Coachee, Coact, Crankshaft, Crew, Crowd, Designated, Disk, Dislodge, Dr, Drover, Drum, Economy, Eject, Emboss, Energy, Enew, Enforce, Engine, Expatriate, Faze, Feeze, Ferret, Fire, Firk, Flexible, Fluid, Force, Four-stroke, Four-wheel, Front-wheel, Fuel, Gadsman, Goad, Hack, Hammer, Haste, Heard, Helmsman, Herd, Hie, Hoon, Hoosh, Hot-rod, Hoy, Hunt, Hurl, Impact, Impel, Impetus, Impinge, Impulse, Jarvey, Jehu, Jockey, Juggernaut, Lash, Libido, Locoman, Lunge, Mahout, Make, Mall, Miz(z)en, Motor, Motorman, Offensive, Overland, Peg, Penetrate, Phase, Piston, Power, Powertrain, Propel, Puncher, Put, RAC, Rack, Ram, Rebut, Reinsman, Ride, Road, Roadhog, Run, Scorch, Screw, Scud, Shepherd, Shoo, Spank, Spin, Spur, Start, Stroke, Sumpter-horse, Sunday, Sweep, Tape, Task-master, Teamster, Tee, Test, Thrust, Toad, Tool, Torrential, Trot, Truckie, Tup, Two-stroke, Urge, Urgence, Vetturino, Wagoner, Whist, Wood, Wreak

Drivel Balderdash, Blether(skate), Drip, Drool, Humbug, Maunder, Nonsense, Pabulum, Pap, Rot, Salivate, Slaver

Driving club AA, Iron, RAC

Drizzle Drow, Haze, Mist, Mizzle, Roke, Scouther, Scowther, Serein, Skiffle, Smir(r), Smur, Spit

Droll Bizarre, Comic, Funny, Jocular, Queer, Waggish

Drone Bee, Buzz, Dog-bee, Doodle, Dor(r), Drant, Draunt, Drawl, Hanger-on,

Hum, Idler, Parasite, Tamboura, Thrum, Windbag

Drool Drivel, Gibber, Salivate, Slaver

Droop(y), Drooping Cernuous, Decline, Flaccid, Flag, Languish, Lill, Limp, Lob, Loll, Lop, Nutate, Oorie, Ourie, Owrie, Peak, Ptosis, > SAG, Slink, Slouch, Weeping, Welk(e), Wilt, Wither

Drop(s), Dropping Acid, Airlift, Apraxia, Bag, Bead, Beres, Blob, Cadence, Calve, Cascade, Cast, Chocolate, Cowpat, Dap, Delayed, Descent, Deselect, Dink, Dip, Downturn, Drappie, Drib(let), Ease, Ebb, Escarp(ment), Fall, Floor, Flop, Fruit, Fumet, Gallows, Globule, Gout(te), Guano, Gutta, Guttate, Instil, Knockout, Land, Minim, Modicum, Muff, Mute, Omit, Pilot, Plonk, Plummet, Plump, Plunge, Plunk, Precepit, Precipice, (Prince) Rupert's, Rain, Scat, Scrap, Shed, Sip, Skat, Spraint, Stilliform, Tass, Taste, Tear, Virga, Wrist

Drop-out Beatnik, Hippie, Hippy

Drop-shot Dink

Dropsy Anasarca, Ascites, Edema, Oedema

Dross Chaff, Dregs, Recrement, Scoria, Scorious, Scum, Sinter, Slack, Slag, Waste

Drought Dearth, Drouth, Lack, Thirst

Drove(r) Band, Crowd, Flock, Herd, Host, Masses, Overlander, Puncher

Drown(ed), Drowning Drench, Drent, Drook, Drouk, Engulf, Inundate, Noyade, Overcome, Sorrows, Submerge

Drowse, Drowsiness, Drowsy Blet, Comatose, Doze, Hypnagogic, Hypnopompic, Lethargic, Nap, Narcolepsy, Narcosis, Nod, Snooze

Drub Anoint, Thrash

Drudge(ry) Devil, Dogsbody, Donkey-work, Fag, Grind, Hack, Jackal, Johnson, Plod, Scrub, Slave(y), Snake, Sweat, Swink, Thraldom, Toil, Trauchle, Treadmill

Drug(ged) Acaricide, ACE inhibitor, Anti-depressant, AZT, Bag, Barbiturate, Base, Blow, Bolus, Bomber, Boo, Botanical, Cholagogue, Deck, Depressant, Designer, DET, Diuretic, Dope, Downer, E, Ecbolic, Ecphractic, Elixir, Emmenagogue, Errhine, Euphoriant, Fantasy, Fertility, Fig, Galenical, Gateway, Hallucinogen, Hard, High, Homeopathy, Immunosuppressant, Knockout drops, Largactic, Lifestyle, Line, Load, Mainline, Medicine, Miracle, Nervine, Nobble, OD, Opiate, Painkiller, Paregoric, Parenteral, Peace, Pharmaceutics, Pharmacopoeia, Poison, Popper, Prophylactic, Psychedelic, Psychoactive, Psychodelic, Recreational, Scag, Sedate, Sialogogue, Snort, Soft, Soporific, Sorbefacient, Speedball, Spermicide, Spike, Statin, Stimulant, Stone(d), Stupefacient, Stupefy, Substance, Synthetic, Tranquiliser, Truth, Upper, Vermicide, Weed, White stuff, Wonder, Wrap, Zeolitic

- **DRUGS**

1 letter:	Tea	Soma	Grass
Q		Toot	Hocus
	4 letters:		Intal®
3 letters:	Acid	**5 letters:**	L-dopa
Eve	Adam	Aloes	Mummy
Hop	Bang	Benny	Opium
Ice	Bute	Bhang	Quina
INH	Dopa	Candy	Rutin
LSD	Hemp	Crank	Salep
PCP®	Junk	Dagga	Salop
Tab	Sida	Ganja	Senna

- Speed
- Sugar
- Sulfa
- Taxol
- Zyban

6 letters:
- Amulet
- Ativan®
- Charas
- Curare
- Dragée
- Heroin
- Inulin
- Joypop
- Mescla
- Mummia
- Nubain®
- Peyote
- Pituri
- Prozac®
- Saloop
- Sulpha
- Valium®
- Viagra®

7 letters:
- Atabrin
- Atebrin®
- Botanic
- Cascara
- Charlie
- Churrus
- Codeine
- Damiana
- Dapsone
- Ecstasy
- Eucaine
- Guarana
- Hashish
- Henbane
- Hypnone
- Insulin
- Jellies
- Librium®
- Metopon
- Miltown®
- Mogadon®
- Morphia
- Nebutal®
- Patulin
- Quinine

Relenza®
Ritalin®
Seconal®
Septrin®
Seroxat®
Steroid
Suramin
Trional
Turpeth
Veronal®
Xenical®

8 letters:
Adjuvant
Ataraxic
Banthine
Curarine
Diazepam
Fentanyl
Goofball
Hyoscine
Ketamine
Laetrile
Laudanum
Mersalyl
Mescalin
Methadon
Miticide
Moonrock
Morphine
Naloxone
Narcotic
Nepenthe
Nystatin
Oxytocic
Psilocin
Retrovir®
Rifampin
Roborant
Rohypnol®
Scopolia
Serevent®
Snowball
Tetronal
Thiazide
Varidase
Veratrin
Viricide
Zerumbet

9 letters:
Acyclovir

Analeptic
Angel-dust
Anovulant
Antrycide
Augmentin
Barbitone
Biguanide
Busulphan
Captopril
Carbachol
Cisplatin
Clozapine
Compound Q
Corticoid
Cyclizine
Digitalis
Dramamine®
Electuary
Ephedrine
Foscarnet
Frusemide
Ibuprofen
Iprindole
Isoniazid
Jaborandi
Lorazepam
Mepacrine
Methadone
Mydriasis
Novocaine
Nux vomica
Oxycontin®
Paludrine®
Pethidine
Phenytoin
Practolol
Quinidine
Quinquina
Reserpine
Sudorific
Synergist
Tamoxifen
Temazepam
Teniacide
Totaquine
Trinitrum
Verapamil
Veratrine
Vermifuge
Wobbly egg

10 letters:
Amantadine
Ampicillin
Antagonist
Anxiolytic
Atracurium
Belladonna
Benzedrine
Bufotenine
Cimetidine
Clofibrate
Clomiphene
Colestipol
Disulfiram
Ergotamine
Ethambutol
Fluoxetine
Formestane
Imipramine
Indapamide
Isoniazide
Ivermectin
Mefloquine
Nalbuphine
Nifedipine
Nitrazepam
Papaverine
Paroxetine
Penicillin
Pentaquine
Phenacetin
Prednisone
Primaquine
Probenecid
Propanolol
Psilocybin
Rifampicin
Salbutamol
Selegiline
Stramonium
Sucralfate
Taeniacide
Zidovudine

11 letters:
Aminobutene
Amphetamine
Beta-blocker
Carbimazole
Chloroquine
Ciclosporin
Cinnarizine

- Clenbuterol
- Clindamycin
- Cyclosporin
- Deserpidine
- Distalgesic
- Fluconazole
- Fluvoxamine
- Galantamine
- Gemfibrozil
- Haloperidol
- Ipratropium
- Isoxsuprine
- Magic bullet
- Meprobamate
- Nikethamide
- Paracetamol
- Pentamidine
- Pentazocine
- Pravastatin

Purple heart
Succedaneum
Thalidomide
Theobromine
Tolbutamide
Tous-les-mois
Tropomyosin
Vinblastine
Vincristine

12 letters:
Alpha-blocker
Anthelmintic
Antiperiodic
Arsphenamine
Azathioprine
Chlorambucil
Fluphenazine
Gonadotropin

Guanethidine
Indomethacin
Methaqualone
Methotrexate
Mifepristone
Perphenazine
Physotigmine
Promethazine
Salicylamide
Streptomycin
Trimethoprim

13 letters:
Amitriptyline
Anthelminthic
Antihistamine
Carbamazepine
Flunitrazepam
Materia medica

Nitroglycerin
Penicillamine
Phencyclidine
Pyrimethamine
Sulphadiazine
Thiabendazole
Triamcinolone

14 letters:
Bendrofluozide
Butyrhophenone
Flucloxacillin
Norethisterone
Pentobarbitone
Phenacyclidine
Phenobarbitone
Phenylbutazone
Sulphanilamide

Druid Gorsedd

Drum(mer), Drumming, Drumbeat Arête, Atabal, Barrel, Beatbox, Bodhran, Bongo, Brake, Carousel, Chamade, Conga, Dash-wheel, Devil's tattoo, Dhol, Djembe, Dr, Drub, Ear, Flam, Gran cassa, Kettle, Lambeg, Mridamgam, Mridang(a), Mridangam, Myringa, Naker, Ngoma, Oil, Pan, Paradiddle, Percussion, Rappel, Rataplan, Reel, Rep, Ridge, Rigger, Roll, Ruff, Ruffle, Salesman, Side, Skin, Snare, Steel, Tabla, Tabour, Tabret, Tambourine, Tam-tam, Tap, Tattoo, Thrum, Timbal, Timp(ano), Tom-tom, Touk, Traps, Traveller, Tuck, Tymbal, Tympanist, Tympano, Whim, Winding, Work

Drum-belly Hoven

Drumstick Attorney, Leg, Rute

▶ **Drunk(ard)** *see* DRINK

▷ **Drunken** *may indicate* an anagram

Drupe Tryma

Druse Crystal

Dry(ing), Drier Air, Anhydrous, Arefaction, Arefy, Arid, Blot, Bone, Brut, Corpse, Crine, Dehydrate, Desiccate, Detox, Drain, Dull, Ensear, Evaporate, Exsiccator, Firlot, Fork, Harmattan, Hasky, Hi(r)stie, Humidor, Hydrate, Jejune, Jerk, Khor, Kiln, Mummify, Oast, > PARCH, Prosaic, Reast, Reist, Rizzar, Rizzer, Rizzor, Sciroc, Scorch, Sear, Sec(co), Seco, Sere, Shrivel, Siccative, Siroc(co), Sober, Sponge, Steme, Stove, Ted, Thirsty, Thristy, Toasted, Torrefy, Torrid, Towel, Tribble, Trocken, TT, Unwatery, Watertight, Welt, Wilt, Win(n), Wipe, Wither, Wizened, Xeransis, Xerasia, Xero(sis), Xerostomia

Dryad Eurydice, Nymph

Dry fruit, Dried fruit Achene, Akene, Currant, Mebos, Prune, Raisin, Samara, Silicula, Siliqua, Silique, Sultana

Dry mouth Xerostoma

DT's Dingbats, Hallucinations, Zooscopic

Dual Double, Twin, Twofold

Dub Array, > CALL, Entitle, Hete, Knight, Name

Dubious Doubtful, Equivocal, Fishy, Fly-by-night, Hesitant, Iffy, Improbable, Questionable, Scepsis, Sceptical, Sesey, Sessa, > SHADY, Shonky, Suspect, Touch and go, Unlikely

▷ **Dubious** *may indicate* an anagram

Dubliner Jackeen

Duce Leader, Musso(lini)

Duchess Anastasia, Malfi, Peeress, Titled

Duchy Brabant, Cornwall, Dukedom, Franconia, Grand, Limburg, Luxembourg, Nassu, Omnium, Realm, Swabia, Valois, Westphalian

Duck(ling), Ducked Amphibian, Avoid, Aylesbury, Bald-pate, Bargander, Bergander, Blob, Blue, Bluebill, Bob, Broadbill, Bufflehead, Bum(m)alo, Canard, Canvasback, > **COUPLE OF DUCKS**, Dead, Dearie, Decoy, Dip, Diving, Dodge, Dodo, Douse, Drook, Drouk, Dunk(er), Eider, Enew, Escape, Evade, Ferruginous, Flapper, Gadwall, Garganey, Garrot, Golden-eye, Goosander, Greenhead, Hareld, Harlequin, Heads, Herald, Immerse, Indian runner, Jook, Jouk, Lame, Long-tailed, Mallard, Mandarin, Muscovy, Musk, Nil, Nodding, Nun, O, Oldsquaw, Old Tom, Orpington, Paddling, Palmated, Paradise, Pekin(g), Pintail, Plunge, Pochard, Poker, Redhead, Ruddy, Runner, Rush, Scaup, Scoter, Sheld(d)uck, Shieldrake, Shovel(l)er, Shun, Sitting, Smeath, Smee(th), Smew, Sord, Spatula, Spirit, Sprigtail, Steamer, Surf(scoter), Teal, Team, Tufted, Tunker, Ugly, Velvet scoter, Whistling, Widgeon, Wigeon, Wood, Zero

Duckbill Ornithorhynchus, Platypus

Duckwalk Waddle

Duckweed Lemna

Ducky Sweet, Twee

Duct Bile, Canal(iculus), Channel, Conduit, Diffuser, Diffusor, Emunctory, Epididymus, Fistula, Gland, Lachrymal, Lacrimal, Laticifer, Lumen, Parotid, Pipe, Tear, Thoracic, Tube, Ureter, Vas deferens

Dud Bouncer, Failure, Flop, Shan(d), Stumer

Dude Cat, Coxcomb, Dandy, Fop, Lair, Macaroni, Popinjay, Roy

Dudgeon Anger, Hilt, Huff, Pique

Due(s) Adequate, Arrearage, Claim, Debt, Deserts, Forinsec, Geld, Heriot, Just, Lot, Mature, Owing, Reddendo, Rent, Right, > **SUITABLE**, Thereanent, Toll, Tribute, Worthy

Duel(list) Mensur, Monomachy, Principal, Tilt

Duenna Chaperone, Dragon

Duff Bungle, Dough, Nelly, NG, Plum, Pudding, Rustle

Duffer Bungler, Rabbit, Useless

Dug Ploughed, Teat, Titty, Udder

Dugong Halicore, Sea-cow, Sea-pig, Sirenian

Dug-out Abri, Canoe, Piragua, Pirogue, Shelter, Trench, Trough

Duke(dom) Alva, Clarence, D, Ellington, Fist, Iron, Milan, Orsino, Peer, Prospero, Rohan, Wellington

Dulcimer Cembalo, Citole, Cymbalo, Santir, Sant(o)ur

Dull(ard), Dullness Anorak, Bald, Banal, Barren, Besot, Bland, Blear, Blunt, Boeotian, Boring, Cloudy, Commonplace, Dead (and alive), Deadhead, Dense, Dim, Dinge, Dingy, Ditchwater, Doldrums, Dowf, Dowie, Drab, Drear, Dreich, Dry, Dunce, Faded, Flat, Fozy, Grey, Heavy, Hebetate, Ho-hum, Humdrum, Illustrious, Insipid, Jejune, Lacklustre, Lifeless, Log(y), Lowlight, Mat(t), Matte, Monotonous, Mopish, Mull, Obtund, Obtuse, Opacity, Opiate, Ordinary, Overcast, Owlish, Pall, Pedestrian, Perstringe, Podunk, Prosaic, Prose, Prosy, Rebate, Rust, Slow, Sopite, Staid, Stick, Stodger, Stodgy, Stolid, Stuffy, Stultify, > **STUPID**, Sunless, Tame, Tarnish, Tedious, Ticky-tacky,

Toneless, Torpor, Treadmill, Tubby, Vapid, Wonk, Wooden, Zoid

Dumb(ness) Alalia, Aphonic, Crambo, Hobbididance, Inarticulate, Mute, Silent, Stupid

Dumbfound(ed) Amaze, Astound, Flabbergast, Stun, Stupefy, Stupent

Dumb ox Aquinas

Dummy Comforter, Copy, Effigy, Fathead, Flathead, Mannequin, Mannikin, Mock-up, Model, Pacifier, Quintain, Soother, Table, Teat, Waxwork

Dump(ing), Dumps Abandon, Blue, Core, Dejection, Dispirited, Doldrums, Empty, Fly-tipping, Hole, Jettison, Junk, Mine, Scrap, Shoot, Store(house), Tip, Unlade, Unload

Dumpling Dim sum, Dough(boy), Gnocchi, Knaidel, Knaidloch, Kneidlach, Knish, Kreplach, Matzoball, Norfolk, Quenelle, Ribaude, Suet, Won ton

Dumpy Pudgy, Squat

Dun Annoy, Cow, Importune, Pester, > SUE, Tan

Duncan Isadora

Dunce Analphabet, Booby, Dolt, Donkey, Dullard, Fathead, Schmo, Schmuck, Schnook, Stupid

Dune Areg, Bar, Barchan(e), Bark(h)an, Erg, Sandbank, Seif, Star, Whaleback

Dung(hill) Argol, Buttons, Chip, Coprolite, Cowpat, Droppings, Fewmet, Fumet, Fumiculous, Guano, Hing, Manure, Midden, Mixen, Mute, Ordure, Puer, Pure, Scat, Scumber, Shard, Sharn, Siege, Skat, Skummer, Sombrerite, Sombrero, Spraint, Stercoraceous, Tath

Dungarees Overalls

Dung-eating Merdiverous

Dungeon Bastille, Cell, Confine, Donjon, Durance, Oubliette, Souterrain

Dunk Immerse, Sop, Steep

Dunnock Accentor

Duo Couple, Pair, Twosome

Dupe Catspaw, Chiaus, Chouse, Cony, Cully, Delude, Geck, Gull, Hoax, Hoodwink, Mug, Pawn, Pigeon, Plover, Sitter, Sucker, Swindle, > TRICK, Victim

Duplex Twofold

Duplicate, Duplicator Clone, Copy, Cyclostyle, Double, Facsimile, Match, Ozalid®, Replica, Reproduce, Roneo®, Spare

Durable Enduring, Eternal, Eterne, Hardy, Lasting, Permanent, Stout, Tough

Duralumin® Y-alloy

Duration Extent, Period, Span

Duress Coercion, Pressure, Restraint

Durham Palatine

During Amid, Dia-, For, In, Over, Throughout, While, Whilst

Dusk(y) Dark, Dewfall, Dun, Eve, Gloaming, Gloom, Owl-light, Phaeic, Twilight, Umbrose

Dust(y) Arid, Ash, Bo(a)rt, Calima, Clean, Coom, Cosmic, Culm, Derris, Devil, Duff, Earth, Fuss, Khaki, Lemel, Limail, Lo(e)ss, Miller, Nebula, Pellum, Pollen, Pother, Pouder, Poudre, Powder, Pozz(u)olana, Pudder, Rouge, Seed, Shaitan, Slack, Stour, Talc, Volcanic, Wipe

▷ **Dusted** *may indicate* an anagram

Duster Cloth, Feather, Red, Talcum, Torchon

Dustman Doolittle, Garbo(logist), Scaffie

Dust measure Konimeter, Koniscope

Dutch(man), Dutchwoman Batavian, Boor, Cape, Courage, D(u), Double, Elm, Erasmus, Flying, Frow, Kitchen, Knickerbocker, Middle, Mynheer, Parnell shout, Patron, Pennsylvania, Sooterkin, Taal, Wife

Dutiful, Duty Active, Ahimsa, Average, Blench, Bond, Charge, Corvee, Customs, Death, Debt, Deontology, Devoir, Docile, Drow, Due, Duplicand, End, Estate, Excise, Fatigue, Feu, Function, Heriot, Homage, Imposition, Impost, Incumbent, Lastage, Likin, Mission, Mistery, Mystery, Obedient, Obligation, Octroi, Office, Onus, Pia, Picket, Pious, Point, Prisage, Probate, Rota, Sentry-go, Shift, Stamp, Stillicide, Stint, Succession, Tariff, > TASK, Tax, Toll, Transit, Trow, Watch, Zabeta

Duvet Doona, Quilt

Dwarf(ism) Achondroplasia, Agate, Alberich, Andvari, Ateleiosis, Bashful, Belittle, Bes, Black, Bonsai, Brown, Doc, Dopey, Droich, Drow, Durgan, Elf, Gnome, Grumpy, Happy, Hobbit, Homuncle, Hop o' my thumb, Knurl, Laurin, Little man, Man(n)ikin, > MIDGET, Mime, Minikin, Minim, Nanism, Nectabanus, Ni(e)belung, Nurl, Overshadow, Pacolet, Pigmy, Pygmy, Red, Regin, Ront, Rumpelstiltskin, Runt, Skrimp, Sleepy, Sneezy, > STUNT, Tiddler, Titch, Tokoloshe, Tom Thumb, Toy, Troll, Trow, White

Dwell(er), Dwelling Abide, Be, Bungalow, Cabin, Cell, Cot(tage), Descant, Discourse, Domicile, Habitation, Harp, Heteroscian, Hogan, House, Hut, Laura, Lavra, Live, Lodge, Longhouse, Maison(n)ette, Mansion, Messuage, Palafitte, Pied-à-terre, Pueblo, Reside, Roof, Tenement, Tepee, Terramara, Tipi, Weem, Wigwam, Won(ing), Woon

Dwindle Decline, Diminish, Fade, Lessen, Peter, Shrink, Wane

Dye(ing), Dyestuff Acid, Alkanet, Amaranth, Anil, Anthracene, Anthraquinone, Archil, Azo(benzine), Azurine, Bat(t)ik, Brazil(e)in, Burnt umber, Camwood, Canthaxanthin, Carthamine, Catechin, Chay(a), Chica, Chicha, Chico, Choy, Cinnabar, Cobalt, Cochineal, Colour, Congo, Corkir, Crocein, Crotal, Crottle, Cudbear, Dinitrobenzene, Direct, Embrue, Engrain, Envermeil, Eosin, Flavin(e), Fluoxene, Fuchsin(e), Fustic, Fustoc, Gambi(e)r, Gentian violet, Grain, Haematoxylin, Henna, Hue, Ikat, Imbrue, Imbue, Incardine, Indamine, Indican, Indigo, Indigocarmine, Indirubin, Indoxyl, Indulin(e), Ingrain, Kalamkari, Kamala, Kermes, Kohl, Korkir, Madder, Magenta, Mauvein(e), Methyl violet, Murex, Myrobalan, Nigrosin(e), Orcein, Orchel(la), Orchil, Para-red, Phenolphthalein, Phthalein, > PIGMENT, Primuline, Puccoon, Purpurin, Pyronine, Quercitron, Quinoline, Raddle, Resorcinol, Rhodamine, Rosanilin(e), Safranin(e), Shaya, > STAIN, Stone-rag, Stone-raw, Sumac(h), Sunfast, Tannin, Tartrazine, Tie-dye, Tinct, Tint, Tropaeolin, Turnsole, Valonia, Vat, Wald, Weld, Woad, Woald, Wold, Xanthium, Xylidine

▶ **Dying** *see* DIE

Dyke Aboideau, Aboiteau, Bund, Devil's, > DIKE, Gall, Offa's

Dynamic Ballistics, Energetic, Forceful, Gogo, High-powered, Potent

Dynamite Blast, Explode, Gelignite, Giant-powder, TNT, Trotyl

Dynamo Alternator, Armature

Dynasty Angevin, Bourbon, Capetian, Carolingian, Chin(g), Ch'ing, Chou, Era, Gupta, Habsburg, Han, Hapsburg, Honan, House(hold), Hyksos, Khan, Manchu, Maurya, Merovingian, Ming, Pahlavi, Ptolemy, Qajar, Q'ing, Rameses, Romanov, Rule, Safavid, Saga, Sassanid, Seleucid, Seljuk, Shang, Song, Sui, Sung, Tai-ping, Tang, Tudor, Wei, Yi, Yuan, Zhou

Dysentery Bloody flux, Slugellosis

Dyslexia Strephosymbolia

Dyspeptic Cacogastric

Dysprosium Dy

Dystrophy Duchenne's, Muscular

Ee

E Boat, East, Echo, Energy, English, Spain

Each All, Apiece, Ea, > **EVERY**, Ilka, Per, Severally

Eager(ly) Agog, Antsy, Ardent, Avid, Beaver, Bore, Earnest, Enthusiastic, Fain, Fervent, Fervid, Frack, Gung-ho, Hot, Intent, > **KEEN**, Perfervid, Race, Raring, Rath(e), Ready, Roost, Sharp-set, Sore, Spoiling, Thirsty, Toey, Wishing, Yare

Eagle Al(l)erion, American, Aquila, Bald, Bateleur, Berghaan, Bird, Double, Erne, Ethon, Fish, Gier, Golden, Harpy, Hawk, Legal, Lettern, Nisus, Ossifrage, Sea, Spread, Tawny, Wedge-tailed

Ear(drum), Ear trouble Ant(i)helix, Attention, Audience, Auricle, Barotitis, Cauliflower, Cochlea, Concha, Conchitis, Deafness, Dionysius, Dolichotus, External, Glue, Hearing, Helix, Icker, Incus, Inner, Internal, Jenkins, Kieselguhr, Labyrinth, Labyrinthitis, Listen, Locusta, Lop, Lug, Malleus, Middle, Modiolus, Myringa, Myringitis, Nubbin, Otalgia, Otalgy, Otic, Paracusis, Paramastoid, Parotic, Pavilion, Periotic, Petrosal, Phonic, Pinna, Prootic, Spike, Thick, Tin, Tragus, Tympanitis, Utricle

Earl(dom) Belted, Mar, Peer, Sandwich

Earlier, Early Above, Ago, Ahead, Alsoon, AM, Antelucan, Auld, Betimes, Cockcrow, Daybreak, Ere-now, Ex, Germinal, Incipient, Or, Precocious, Precursor, Prehistoric, Premature, Prevernal, Previous, Primeval, Primordial, Prior, Rath(e), Rath(e)ripe, Rear, Rudimentary, Soon, Timely, Tim(e)ous

▷ **Early** *may indicate* belonging to an earl

Early man Eoanthropus, Flat-earther

▷ **Early stages of** *may indicate* first one or two letters of the word(s) following

Earmark Allocate, Bag, Book, Characteristic, > **RESERVE**, Tag, Target

Earn(er), Earnings Achieve, Addle, Breadwinner, Deserve, Digerati, Gain, Income, Invisible, Make, Merit, O.T.E., Win

Earnest Ardent, Arle(s)(-penny), Deposit, Fervent, Imprest, Intent, Promise, Serious, Token, Zealous

Earring Drop, Hoop, Keeper, Pendant, Sleeper, Snap, Stud

Earshot Hail, Hearing

Earth(y) Alkaline, Antichthon, Art, Asthenosphere, Brown, Capricorn, Clay, Cloam, Cologne, Craton, Diatomite, Dirt, Drey, Dust, E, Eard, Edaphic, Epigene, Foxhole, Friable, Fuller's, Gaea, Gaia, Gault, Ge, Globe, Ground, Horst, Infusiorial, Kadi, Lair, Leaf-mould, Lemnian, Lithosphere, Loam, Malm, Mankind, Mantle, Mools, Mould, Mouls, Papa, Pise, Planet, Rabelaisian, Racy, Rare, Red, Seat, Sett, Sod, > **SOIL**, Subsoil, Taurus, Telluric, Tellus, Terra, Terrain, Terramara, Terrene, Topsoil, Tripoli, Virgo, Wad, Ye(a)rd, Yellow, Yird

Earth-bound Chthonian

Earthenware Arretine, Biscuit, Ceramic, Creamware, Crock(ery), Delf(t), Della-robbia, Delph, Faience, Figuline, Maiolica, Majolica, Pig, Pot, Queen's ware, Raku, Samian, Terracotta

Earthquake Aftershock, Bradyseism, Foreshock, Mercalli, Richter, Seism, Shake, Shock, Temblor, Tremor

Earth's surface Sal, Sial

Earthwork Agger, Bank, Cursus, Gazon, Parados, Rampart, Remblai, Vallum

Earthworm Angledug, Angletwitch, Angleworm, Annelid, Bait, Night-crawler

Earwig Clipshear(s), Forkit-tail, Forky-tail

Ease, Easing, Easygoing Alleviate, Carefree, Clear, Clover, Comfort, Content, Defuse, Deregulate, Détente, Facility, Hands down, Informal, Lax, Mellow, Mid(dy), Mitigate, Palliate, Peace, Pococurante, Quiet, Relieve, Reposal, Repose, Soothe

East(erly), Eastward Anglia, Asia, Chevet, E, Eassel, Eassil, Eothen, Eurus, Levant, Middle, Near, Orient, Ost, Sunrise

Easter Festival, Island, Pace, Pasch, Pasque

Eastern(er), Eastern language Asian, Kolarian, Oriental, Virginian

East European Lettic, Slovene

Easy, Easily ABC, Breeze, Cakewalk, Carefree, Child's play, Cinch, Cushy, Dagage, Doddle, Eath(e), Ethe, Facile, Free, Gift, Glib, Hands down, Independent, Jammy, Lax, Light, Midshipman, Natural, Nimps, Oldster, Picnic, Pie, Pushover, Simple, Sitter, Snotty, Soft, Tolerant, User-friendly, Walk-over, Well, Yare

▷ **Easy** *may indicate* an anagram

Eat(able), Eater, Eating Bite, Bolt, Champ, Chop, Commensal, Consume, Corrode, Edible, Edite, Endew, Endue, Erode, Esculent, Etch, Fare, Feast, > FEED, Fret, Gastronome, Gnaw, Go, Gobble, Graze, Grub, Hog, Hyperphagia, Ingest, Manducate, Munch, Nosh, Nutritive, Omnivore, Partake, Phagophobia, Predate, Refect, Scoff, Stuff, Sup, Swallow, Syssitia, Take, Taste, Trencherman, Trophesy, Whale

Eavesdrop(per) Cowan, Earwig, Icicle, Listen, Overhear, Pry, Snoop, Stillicide, Tab-hag, Tap, Wiretap

Ebb(ing) Abate, Decline, Recede, Refluent, Sink, > WANE

Ebony Black, Cocus-wood, Coromandel, Hebenon, Jamaican

Ebullient Brash, Effervescent, Exuberant, Fervid

Eccentric Abnormal, Cam, Card, Character, Crank, Curious, Daffy, Dag, Deviant, Dingbat, Ditsy, Ditzy, E, Farouche, Fey, Fie, Freak, Fruitcake, Geek, Gonzo, Iffish, Irregular, Kinky, Kook(y), Mattoid, Nutcase, Nutter, Odd(ball), Offbeat, Off-centre, Off the wall, Original, Outré, > PECULIAR, Phantasime, Pixil(l)ated, Queer, Quirky, Quiz, Rake, Raky, Recondite, Rum, Scatty, Screwball, Screwy, Squirrelly, Wack(y), Way-out, Weird(o), W(h)acko

▷ **Eccentric** *may indicate* an anagram

Ecclesiastic Abbé, Clergyman, Clerical, Lector, Secular, Theologian

Echelon Formation

Echinoderm Asteroidea, Basket-star, Brittle-star, Comatulid, Crinoid, Heart-urchin, Sea-egg, Sea-lily, Sea-urchin, Starfish

Echo Angel, Answer, Ditto, E, Imitate, Iterate, Rebound, Repeat, Repercussion, Reply, Resonant, > RESOUND, Respeak, Reverb(erate), Revoice, Ring, Rote, Tape

Eclat Flourish, Glory, Prestige, Renown

Eclectic Babist, Broad, Complex, Liberal

Eclipse Annular, Block, Cloud, Deliquium, Hide, Lunar, Obscure, Occultation, Outmatch, Outweigh, Overshadow, Partial, Penumbra, Solar, Total, Transcend

Eclogue Bucolic, Idyll, Pastoral

Eco-community Seral

Economic(s), Economise Budget, Conserve, Dismal science, Eke, Entrench, Husband, Intrench, Pinch, Retrench, Scrimp, Skimp, Spare, Sparing, Stagflation, > STINT, Supply-side, Welfare

Economist Angell, Bentham, Chrematist, Cole, Friedman, Keynes, Malthus, Marginalist, Meade, Mill, Pareto, Physiocrat, Ricardo, Tinbergen, Toynbee, Veblen, Webb

Economy, Economic(al), Economics Agronomy, Black, Careful, Cliometrics, Command, Conversation, Frugal, Knowledge, Market, Mixed, Neat, New, Parsimony, Planned, Political, Retrenchment, Shoestring, Siege, Stakeholder, Thrift, Tiger, Token

Ecstasy, Ecstatic Bliss, Delight, Delirious, Dove, E, Exultant, Joy, Liquid, Lyrical, Nympholepsy, Rapture, Rhapsodic, Sent, Trance, Transport

Ecumenical Catholic, Lateran

Eczema Pompholyx

Eddy Backset, Curl, Gurge, Maelstrom, Nelson, Pirl, Purl, Rotor, Sousehole, Swelchie, Swirl, Vortex, Weel, Well, Whirlpool, Wiel

Eden Bliss, Fall, Heaven, Paradise, PM, Utopia

Edentate Ant-eater, Armadillo, Sloth, Tatou, Xenarthra

Edge, Edging, Edgy Advantage, Arris, Border, Bordure, Brim, Brink, Brittle, Brown, Burr, Chamfer, Chimb, Chime, Chine, Coaming, Costa, Cutting, Dag, Deckle, End, Flange, Flounce, Frill, Fringe, Frontier, Furbelow, Gunnel, Gunwale, Hem, Hone, Inch, Inside, Kerb, Knife, Leading, Leech, Limb(ate), Limbus, Limit, Lip, List, Lute, Marge(nt), Margin, Nosing, Orle, Outside, Parapet, Periphery, Picot, Pikadell, Piping, Rand, Rim, Rund, Rymme, Selvage, Selvedge, Sidle, Skirt, Strand, Trailing, Trim, Tyre, Verge, Wear

▸ **Edible** *see* EAT(ABLE)

Edict Ban, Bull, Decree, Decretal, Extravagantes, Fatwa, Firman, Interim, Irade, Nantes, Notice, Pragmatic, Proclamation, Pronunciamento, Rescript, Ukase

Edifice Booth, Building, Structure

Edify Instruct, Teach

Edinburgh Auld Reekie

Edit(or), Editorial Abridge, Article, City, Copy (read), Cut, Dele, Emend, Expurgate, Garble, Leader, Prepare, Recense, Redact, Revise, Seaman

▷ **Edited** *may indicate* an anagram

Edition Aldine, Bulldog, Bullpup, Ed, Extra, Ghost, Hexapla(r), Impression, Issue, Library, Limited, Number, Omnibus, Trade, Variorium, Version

Edmond, Edmund Burke, Gosse, Ironside(s), Rostand, Spenser

Educate(d) Baboo, Babu, Enlighten, Evolué, Informed, Instruct, Learned, Noursle, Nousell, Nousle, Nurture, Nuzzle, Polymath, Preppy, Scholarly, School, > TEACH, Train, Yuppie

Education(alist) Adult, B.Ed, Classical, Conductive, Didactics, Further, Heurism, Learning, Mainstream, Montessori, Paedotrophy, Pedagogue, Pestalozzi, Physical, Piarist, Primary, Schooling, Steiner, Teacher, Tertiary, Upbringing

Educe Elicit, Evoke, Extract, Infer

Edward Confessor, Ed, Elder, Lear, Martyr, Ned, Ted

Eel Conger, Congo, Electric, Elver, Glass, Grig, Gulper, Gunnel, Hagfish, Kingklip, Lamper, Lamprey, Lant, Launce, Leptocephalus, Moray, Murray, Murr(e)y, Olm, Paste, Sand(ling), Silver belly, Snig, Spitchcock, Tuna, Vinegar, Wheat, Wolf

Eerie Spooky, Uncanny, Unked, Weird

Efface Cancel, Delete, Dislimn, > ERASE, Expunge, Obliterate

Effect(s), Effective(ness), Effectual Able, Achieve, Acting, Auger, Babinski, Bags, Barkhausen, Belongings, Bit, Bohr, Border, Bricolage, Butterfly, Causal, C(h)erenkov, Chromakey, Coanda, Competent, Compton, Consequence,

Coriolis, Domino, Doppler, Dr(y)ice, Eclat, Efficacious, Enact, End, Estate, Experimenter, Foley, Fringe, Functional, Fungibles, Gear, Goods, Greenhouse, Ground, Gunn, Halo, Hawthorne, Home, Horns and halo, Impact, Implement(al), Impression, Introgenic, Josephson, Joule(-Thomson), Kerr, Keystone, Knock-on, Magnus, Meissner, Moire, Mossbauer, Neat, Nisi, Notch, Operant, Optical, Outcome, Ovshinsky, Oxygen, Parallax, Peltier, Perficient, Personal, Phi, Photoelectric, Photovoltaic, Piezoelectric, Piezomagnetic, Pinch, Placebo, Pogo, Position, Potent, Primary, Promulgate, Raman, Ratchet, Recency, Repercussion, > **RESULT**, Ripple, Schottky, Seebeck, Side, Skin, Sound, Sovereign, Special, Spectrum, Spin-off, Stark, Striking, Stroop, Submarine, Tableau, Teeth, Telling, Thermoelectric, Thomson's, Toxic, Tunnel, Tyndall, Upshot, Valid, Viable, Virtual, Win, Withdrawal, Work, Zeeman

Effeminate Camp, Carpet-knight, Carpet-monger, Cissy, Cookie-pusher, Dildo, Epicene, Female, Gussie, Jessie, Milksop, (Miss) Nancy, Molly(coddle), Panty-waist, Poovy, Prissy, Punce, Sissy, Swish, Tender, Tenderling, Tonk, Unman, Wuss(y)

Effervescence, **Effervescent** Bubbling, Ebullient, Fizz, Frizzante, Pétillant, Soda

▷ **Effervescent** *may indicate* an anagram

Effete Camp, Epigon(e)

Efficacious, **Efficacy** Effective, Operative, Potent, Sovereign, Value

Efficiency, **Efficient** Able, Capable, Competent, Current, Despatch, Electrode, Ergonomics, Luminous, Productivity, Quantum, Smart, Streamlined, Strong, Thermal, Volumetric

Effigy Figure, Guy, Idol, Image, Statua, Statue

Efflorescence Bloom, Blossom, Reh

Effluence, **Effluent**, **Effluvia** Air, Aura, Billabong, Discharge, Fume, Gas, Halitus, Miasma, Odour, Outflow, Outrush

Effort Achievement, Attempt, Best, Conatus, Drive, Essay, Exertion, Fit, Herculean, Labour, Molimen, Nisus, Pains, Rally, Spurt, Stab, Strain, Struggle, > **TRY**, Work, Yo

Effortless Lenis

Effrontery Audacity, Brass, Cheek, Face, Gall, Neck, Nerve, Temerity

Effulgent Bright, Radiant, Shining

Effuse, **Effusion**, **Effusive** Emanate, Exuberant, Exude, Gush, Lyric, Ode, Outburst, Prattle, Rhapsody, Sanies, Screed, Spill

Eft After

Eg As, Example

Egest Eliminate, Evacuate, Excrete, Void

Egg(s) Abet, Benedict, Berry, Bomb, Caviar(e), Chalaza, Cleidoic, Clutch, Cockney, Collop, Coral, Curate's, Darning, Easter, Edge, Fabergé, Fetus, Flyblow, Foetus, Free-range, Glair(e), Goad, Goog, Graine, Hoy, Incite, Instigate, Layings, Mine, Nest, Nidamentum, Nit, Oocyte, Oophoron, Ostrich, Ova, Ovum, Pace, Plover's, Prairie oyster, Press, Raun, Roe, Scotch, Scrambled, Seed, Spat, Spawn, Spur(ne), Tar(re), Thunder, Tooth, Tread(le), Urge, Whore's, Wind, Yelk, Yolk, Zygote

Egghead Don, Highbrow, Intellectual, Mensa, Pedant

Egg-plant Aubergine, Brinjal

Egg-producer Gametophyte, Hen, Ovipositor

Egg-shaped Obovate, Oval, Ovate

Egg-white Albumen, Glair

Ego(ism), **Egoist** Che, Conceit, I, Narcissism, Not-I, Pride, Self, Solipsism, Ubu,

Vanity

Egocentric Solipsistic

Egregious Eminent, Flagrant, Glaring, Shocking

Egypt(ian), Egyptologist Arab, Cairene, Carter, Cheops, Chephren, Copt(ic), ET, Gippo, Goshen, Gyppo, Imhotep, Nasser, Nefertiti, Nilote, Nitrian, Osiris, Ptolemy, Rameses, Syene, UAR, Wafd, Wog

Eiderdown Bedspread, Duvet, Quilt

Eight(h), Eighth day Acht, Byte, Crew, Cube, Middle, Nundine, Octa, Octad, Octal, Octastrophic, Octave, Octet, Ogdoad, Okta, Ottava, Ure

Eighteen Majority

Eighty R

Einsteinium Es

Either Also, Both, O(u)ther, Such

Ejaculate Blurt, Discharge, Emit, Exclaim

Eject Bounce, Disgorge, Dismiss, Emit, Erupt, Expel, Oust, Propel, Spew, Spit, Spue, Vent

Eke Augment, Eche, Enlarge, Husband, Supplement

Elaborate Detail, Develop, Dressy, Enlarge, Evolve, Florid, Imago, Improve, Intricate, Ornate, Rich, Stretch

Elan Dash, Drive, Esprit, > **FLAIR**, Gusto, Lotus, Panache, Spirit, Vigour

Elapse Glide, Intervene, Pass

Elastic(ity) Adaptable, Bungee, Buoyant, Dopplerite, Elater, Flexible, Give, Resilient, Rubber, Spandex®, Springy, Stretchy, Tone, Tonus

Elate(d), Elation Cheer, Euphoric, Exalt, Exhilarate, Gladden, Hault, Ruff(e), Uplift

Elbow, Elbow tip Akimbo, Ancon, Angle, Bender, Cubital, Hustle, Joint, Jostle, Justle, Kimbo, Noop, Nudge, Olecranon, Tennis

Elder(ly), Eldest Ancestor, Ancient, Bourtree, Chief, Classis, Eigne, Geriatric, Guru, Kaumatua, Kuia, OAP, Presbyter, > **SENIOR**, Sire, Susanna, Wallwort

Eldorado Ophir

Eleanor(a) Bron, Duse, Nora(h)

Elect(ed), Election(eer), Electoral Choice, Choose, Chosen, Eatanswill, Elite, General, Gerrymander, Hustings, In, Israelite, Khaki, Off-year, Opt, Pick, PR, Primary, Psephology, Rectorial, Return, Select, Stump

Electrical discharge Corposant, Ion, Zwitterion

Electrical instrument Battery, Charger, Galvaniser, Mains, Resistor, Rheostat, Shoe

Electrical unit Amp(ere), Coulomb, Farad, Kilowatt, Ohm, Volt, Watt

Electric eye Pec

Electrician Gaffer, Lineman, Ohm, Siemens, Sparks, Tesla

Electricity Galvanism, HT, Juice, Mains, Negative, Positive, Power, Static, Vitreous

Electrify Astonish, Galvanise, Startle, Stir, Thrill

Electrode Anode, Cathode, Dynode, Element, Photocathode

Electrolyte Ampholyte

Electromagnet(ic) Abampere, Armature, Oersted, Solenoid, Weber

Electron(ics), Electronic device Cooper pairs, Exciton, FET, Linac, Lone pair, Martenot, Polaron, Quantum, Thermionics, Valence, Valency

Elegance, Elegant Artistic, Bijou, Chic, Classy, Debonair, Fancy, Feat, Finesse, Gainly, Galant, Grace, Jimp, Luxurious, Polished, Recherche, Refined, Ritzy, > **SMART**, Soigné(e), Suave, Swish, Tall, Urbane

Elegy Dirge, Lament, Poem

Element(s), Elementary Abcee, Abecedarian, Absey, Barebones, > COMPONENT, Detail, > ESSENCE, Essential, Factor, Feature, Fuel, Heating, Ideal, Identity, Milieu, Pixel, Primary, Principle, Rare Earth, Simple, Trace, Transition, Weather

ELEMENTS

3 letters:
Air
Tin (Sn)

4 letters:
Atom
Fire
Gold (Au)
Iron (Fe)
Lead (Pb)
Neon (Ne)
Ylem
Zinc (Zn)

5 letters:
Alloy
Argon (Ar)
Boron (B)
Earth
Morph(eme)
Niton
Radon (Rn)
Terra
Water
Xenon (Xe)

6 letters:
Barium (Ba)
Carbon (C)
Cerium (Ce)
Cesium
Cobalt (Co)
Copper (Cu)
Curium (Cm)
Erbium (Er)
Helium (He)
Indium (In)
Iodine (I)
Nickel (Ni)
Osmium (Os)
Oxygen (O)
Radium (Ra)
Silver (Ag)
Sodium (Na)

7 letters:
Arsenic (As)
Bismuth (Bi)
Bromine (Br)
Cadmium (Cd)
Caesium (Cs)
Calcium (Ca)
Dubnium (Db)
Fermium (Fm)
Gallium (Ga)
Hafnium (Hf)
Hahnium (Hn)
Halogen
Hassium (Hs)
Holmium (Ho)
Iridium (Ir)
Isotope
Krypton (Kr)
Lithium (Li)
Mercury (Hg)
Niobium (Nb)
Peltier
Rhenium (Re)
Rhodium (Rh)
Silicon (Si)
Sulphur (S)
Terbium (Tb)
Thorium (Th)
Thulium (Tm)
Uranide
Uranium (U)
Wolfram
Yttrium (Y)

8 letters:
Actinide
Actinium (Ac)
Antimony (Sb)
Astatine (At)
Chlorine (Cl)
Chromium (Cr)
Didymium
Europium (Eu)
Fluorine (F)
Francium (Fr)

Hydrogen (H)
Illinium
Inchoate
Lutetium (Lu)
Masurium
Nebulium
Nitrogen (N)
Nobelium (No)
Platinum (Pt)
Polonium (Po)
Rubidium (Rb)
Samarium (Sm)
Scandium (Sc)
Selenium (Se)
Tantalum (Ta)
Thallium (Tl)
Titanium (Ti)
Tungsten (W)
Vanadium (V)

9 letters:
Alabamine
Aluminium (Al)
Americium (Am)
Berkelium (Bk)
Beryllium (Be)
Brimstone
Columbium
Germanium (Ge)
Joliotium
Lanthanum (La)
Magnesium (Mg)
Manganese (Mn)
Metalloid
Neodymium (Nd)
Neptunium (Np)
Palladium (Pd)
Plutonium (Pu)
Potassium (K)
Ruthenium (Ru)
Strontium (Sr)
Tellurium (Te)
Virginium
Ytterbium (Yb)
Zirconium (Zr)

10 letters:
Dysprosium (D)
Gadolinium (Gd)
Lanthanide
Lawrencium (Lr)
Meitnerium (Mt)
Molybdenum (Mo)
Phlogiston
Phosphorus (P)
Promethium (Pm)
Rudimental
Seaborgium (Sg)
Technetium (Tc)

11 letters:
Californium (Cf)
Einsteinium (Es)
Mendelevium (Md)
Transuranic
Unnilennium (Une)
Unnilhexium (Unh)
Unniloctium (Uno)
Ununquadium (Uuq)

12 letters:
Kurchatovium
Nielsbohrium
Praseodymium (Pr)
Protactinium (Pa)
Unnilpentium (Unp)
Unnilseptium (Uns)

13 letters:
Rutherfordium
Transactinide
Unniliquadium (Unq)

Elephant African, Babar, Hathi, Indian, Jumbo, Kheda, Mammoth, Mastodon, Oliphant, Pachyderm, Pad, Pink, Rogue, Subungulata, Trumpeter, Tusker, White

Elephant-headed Ganesa

Elephant's ears Begonia

Elevate(d), Elevation, Elevator Agger, Attitude, Cheer, Colliculus, El, Eminence, Ennoble, Foothill, Grain, Heighten, Hoist, Jack, Lift, Machan, Montic(u)le, Monticulus, Promote, > RAISE, Random, Relievo, Ridge, Rise, Steeve, Sublimate, Up(lift), Uplying, Upraise, Wallclimber

Eleven Elf, Hendeca-, Legs, Side, Tail-ender, Team, XI

Elf, Elves Alfar, Chiricaune, Fairy, Goblin, Imp, Kobold, Ouph, Pigwiggen, Pixie, Ribhus, Sprite

Elicit Evoke, Extract, Toase, Toaze, Tose, Toze

Eligible Available, Catch, Fit, Nubile, Parti, Qualified, Worthy

Eliminate, Elimination Cull, Delete, Discard, Exclude, Execute, Extirpate, Heat, Liquidate, Omit, Preclude, Purge, Red-line, Rid, Separate, Slay, Void, Zap

Elision Synal(o)epha, Syncope

Elite Best, Choice, Crack, > CREAM, Elect, Flower, Liberal, Meritocracy, Ton, U, Zaibatsu

Elixir Amrita, Arcanum, Bufo, Cordial, Daffy, Essence, Medicine, Panacea, Quintessence, Tinct

Elizabeth Bess(ie), Gloriana, Oriano

Elk Deer, Gang, Irish, Moose

Elkoshite Nahum

Ellipse, Elliptic Conic, Oblong, Oval

Elm Dutch, Slippery, Wahoo, Weeping, Wich, Winged, Wych

Elmer Gantry

Elongate Extend, Lengthen, Protract, Stretch

Elope Abscond, Decamp

Eloquence, Eloquent Articulate, Demosthenic, Facundity, Fluent, Honey-tongued, Oracy, Rhetoric, Vocal

Else(where) Absent, Alibi, Aliunde, Other

Elucidate Explain, Expose, Interpret

Elude, Elusive Avoid, Dodge, Escape, > EVADE, Evasive, Foil, Intangible, Jink, Slippy, Subt(i)le, Will o' the wisp

▶ **Elves** see ELF

Elysium Tir-nan-Og

Em Mut(ton), Pica

Emaciated, Emaciation Atrophy, Erasmus, Gaunt, Haggard, Lean, Skinny, Sweeny, Tabid, Thin, Wanthriven, Wasted

Emanate, Emanation Arise, Aura, Discharge, Exude, Issue, Miasma, Radiate, Spring

Emancipate, Emancipation Deliver, Forisfamiliate, Free, > LIBERATE, Manumission, Uhuru

Emasculate Castrate, Debilitate, Evirate, Geld, Unsex

Embalm Anoint, Mummify, Preserve

Embankment Berm, Bund, Causeway, Dam, Dyke, Earthwork, Levee, Mattress, Mound, Rampart, Remblai, Sconce, Staith(e), Stopbank, Terreplein

Embargo > BAN, Blockade, Edict, Restraint

Embark Begin, Board, Enter, Inship, Launch, Sail

Embarrass(ed), Embarrassing, Embarrassment Abash, Ablush, Barro, Chagrin, Cheap, Disconcert, Gêne, Haw, Mess, Mortify, Pose, Predicament, Shame,

Sheepish, Squirming, Straitened, Toe-curling, Upset, Writhing

▷ **Embarrassed** *may indicate* an anagram

Embassy Consulate, Embassade, Legation, Mission

Embed(ded) Fix, Immerse, Inlaid, Set

Embellish(ed), Embellishment Adorn, Beautify, Bedeck, Deck, Decorate, Dress, Embroider, Enrich, Frill, Garnish, Garniture, Mordent, > ORNAMENT, Ornate, Rel(l)ish, Roulade, Turn

Ember(s) Ash, Cinder, Clinker, Gleed

Embezzle(ment) Defalcate, Malversation, Peculate, Purloin, > STEAL

Embitter(ed) Acerbate, Aggravate, Enfested, Rankle, Sour

Emblem(atic) Badge, Bear, Colophon, Daffodil, Device, Figure, Ichthys, Impresa, Insignia, Kikumon, Leek, Lis, Maple leaf, Oak, Rose, Roundel, Shamrock, Sign, Spear-thistle, > SYMBOL, Tau-cross, Thistle, Token, Totem(ic), Triskelion, Wheel

Embody, Embodied, Embodiment Epitome, Fuse, Incarnation, Incorporate, Personify, Quintessence

Embolism Clot, Infarct

Emboss(ed) Adorn, Chase, Cloqué, Engrave, Matelassé, Pounce, Raise, Repoussé, Toreutic

Embrace(d) Abrazo, Accolade, Arm, Canoodle, Clasp, Clinch, Clip, Coll, Complect, Comprise, Cuddle, Embosom, Encircle, Enclasp, Enclose, Enfold, Enlacement, Envelop, Espouse, Fold, Grab, Halse, Haulst, Hause, Hesp, Hug, Imbrast, Inarm, Inclasp, Inclip, Include, Kiss, Lasso, Neck, Press, Stemme, Twine, Welcome, Wrap

▷ **Embraces, Embracing** *may indicate* a hidden word

Embrocate, Embrocation Anoint, Arnica, Liniment

Embroider(y) Appliqué, Arrasene, Assisi, Battalia-pie, Braid, Brede, Couching, Crewel-work, Cross-stitch, Cutwork, Drawn threadwork, Embellish, Exaggerate, Eyelet, Fag(g)oting, Fancywork, Featherstitch, Filet, Framework, Gros point, Handiwork, Knotting, Lace(t), Mola, Needlepoint, Needlework, Open-work, Opus anglicanum, Orfray, Ornament, Orphrey, Orris, Petit point, Pinwork, Pulled threadwork, Purl, Sampler, Sew, Smocking, Stitch, Stumpwork, Tambour, Tent, Wrap

Embroideress Mimi

Embroil Confuse, Entangle, Involve, Trouble

Embryo(nic) Blastocyst, Blastula, Conceptus, Epicotyl, Fo(e)tus, Gastrula, Germ, Mesoblast, Morula, Nepionic, Neurula, Origin, Rudiment, Undeveloped

Emend Adjust, Alter, Edit, Reform

Emerald Beryl, Gem, Green, Oriental, Smaragd, Uralian

Emerge(ncy), Emerging Anadyomene, Arise, Craunch, Crise, Crisis, Crunch, Debouch, Eclose, Emanate, Enation, Erupt, Exigency, Issue, Lash-up, Last-ditch, Loom, Need, Outcrop, Pinch, Spring, Stand-by, Stand-in, Strait, Surface

▷ **Emerge from** *may indicate* an anagram or a hidden word

Emerson Waldo

Emetic Apomorphine, Cacoon, Epicac, Evacuant, Ipecacuanha, Puke, Sanguinaria, Stavesacre, Tartar, Vomitory

Emigrant, Emigration Chozrim, Colonist, Italiot, Jordim, Redemptioner, Settler, When-we, Yordim

Emile Zola

Emily Ellis

Eminence, Eminent Alp, Altitude, Cardinal, Distinguished, Eximious, Grand,

Height, Hill, Inselberg, Knoll, Light, Lion, Lofty, Luminary, Noble, > **NOTABLE**, Note, Palatine, Prominence, Renown, Repute, Stature, Tor, Trochanter, > **VIP**, Wallah

Emissary Agent, Envoy, Legate, Marco Polo

Emission, Emit Discharge, Emanate, Field, Give, Issue, Spallation, Thermionic, Utter

Emmer Amelcorn, Wheat

Emollient Paregoric

Emolument Income, Perk, Remuneration, Salary, Stipend, Tip, Wages

Emotion(al) Affection, Anger, Anoesis, Atmosphere, Breast, Chord, Ecstasy, Empathy, Excitable, Feeling, Freak-out, Gusty, Hysteria, Joy, Limbic, Passion, Reins, Roar, Sensibility, Sensitive, Sentiment, Spirit, Torrid, Transport, Weepy

Emotionless Deadpan, Glassy

Empathy Identifying, Rapport, Rapprochement, Sympathy

Emperor Agramant(e), Akbar, Akihito, Antoninus, Augustus, Babur, Barbarossa, Bonaparte, Caligula, Caracalla, Charlemagne, Claudius, Commodus, Concerto, Constantine, Diocletian, Domitian, Ferdinand, Gaius, Genghis Khan, Gratian, Hadrian, Heraclius, Hirohito, Imp, Imperator, Inca, Jimmu, Justinian, Kaiser, Keasar, Kesar, King, Maximilian, Menelik, Mikado, Ming, Mogul, Montezuma, Mpret, Napoleon, Negus, Nero, Nerva, Otho, Otto, Penguin, Peter the Great, Purple, Pu-yi, Rex, Rosco, Ruler, Severus, Shah Jahan, Shang, Sovereign, Sultan, Tenno, Theodore, Theodosius, Tiberius, Titus, Trajan, Tsar, Valens, Valentinian, Valerian, Vespasian, Vitellius, Wenceslaus

Emphasis, Emphasize, Emphatic Accent, Birr, Bold, Dramatise, Forcible, Foreground, Forzando, Hendiadys, Italic, Marcato, Positive, Sforzando, > **STRESS**, Underline, Underscore, Vehement

Empire Assyria, British, Byzantine, Celestial, Chain, Chinese, Domain, Empery, First, Georgia, Holy Roman, Indian, Kingdom, NY, Ottoman, Parthia, Persian, Principate, Realm, Reich, Roman, Russian, Second, Turkish, Western

Empiricism Positivism

Emplacement Battery, Platform

Employ(ment) Business, Calling, Designated, Engage, Exercitation, Hire, Occupy, Pay, Place, Portfolio, Practice, Pursuit, Service, Shiftwork, Trade, Use, Using, Utilise, Vocation

Employee(s) Factotum, Hand, Help, Hireling, Intrapreneur, Minion, Munchkin, Networker, Payroll, Pennyboy, Personnel, Rainmaker, Servant, Staff, Staffer, Valet, Walla(h), Worker

Employer Baas, Boss, Malik, Master, Melik, Padrone, User

▷ **Employs** *may indicate* an anagram

Emporium Bazaar, Shop, Store

Empower Authorise, Enable, Entitle, Permit

Empress Eugenie, Josephine, Messalina, Queen, Sultana, Tsarina

Empty Addle, Bare, Barren, Blank, Boss, Buzz, Claptrap, Clear, Deplete, Deserted, Devoid, Disembowel, Drain, Exhaust, Expel, Forsaken, Futile, Gousty, Gut, Hent, Hollow, Inane, Jejune, Lade, Lave, Null, Phrasy, Pump, Shallow, Teem, Toom, Tume, Unfurnished, Unoccupied, Unpeople, Vacant, Vacate, Vacuous, Vain, Viduous, > **VOID**

▷ **Empty** *may indicate* an 'o' in the word or an anagram

Emulate Ape, Copy, Envy, Equal, Imitate, Match

Emulsion Pseudosolution, Tempera

Enable Authorise, Empower, Potentiate, Qualify, Sanction

Enact Adopt, Effect, Ordain, Personate, Portray

Enamel(led), Enamel work Aumail, Champlevé, Cloisonné, Della-robbia, Dentine, Fabergé, Ganion, Lacquer, Polish, Porcelain, Schwarzlot, Shippo, Smalto, Stoved, Vitreous

Encampment Bivouac, Douar, Dowar, Duar, Laager, Laer, Settlement

Encase(d), Encasement Box, Crate, Emboîtement, Encapsulate, Enclose, Obtect

Enchant(ing), Enchanted, Enchantment Bewitch, Captivate, Charm, Delight, Gramary(e), Incantation, Magic, Necromancy, Orphean, Rapt, Sorcery, Spellbind, Thrill

Enchanter, Enchantress Archimage, Archimago, Armida, Circe, Comus, Fairy, Lorelei, Magician, Medea, Mermaid, Prospero, Reim-kennar, Sorcerer, Vivien, Witch

Encircle(d) Belt, Enclose, Encompass, Enlace, Entrold, Gird, Inorb, Introld, Orbit, Pale, Ring, > SURROUND, Wreathe

Enclave Cabinda, Ceuta, > ENCLOSURE, Melilla, Pocket, San Marino

Enclose(d), Enclosing, Enclosure Bawn, Beset, Boma, Box, Cage, Carol, Carrel, Case, Common, Compound, Corral, Court, Embale, Embowel, Embower, Enceinte, Encircle, Enclave, Enshrine, Fence, Fold, Forecourt, Garth, Haggard, Haw, Hem, Henge, Hope, Impound, In, Incapsulate, Infibulate, Insert, Interclude, Lairage, Pale, Peel, Pele, Pen(t), Petavius, Pightle, Pin, Pinfold, Pit, Playpen, Plenum, Rail, Rath, Recluse, Ree(d), Ring, Run, Saddling, Seal, Sekos, Sept, Seraglio, Serail, Several, Sin bin, Steeld, Stell, Stockade, Sty, > SURROUND, Tine, Unsaddling, Vibarium, Ward, Winner's, Wrap, Yard

Encode Cipher, Scramble

Encomium Eulogy, Praise, Sanction, Tribute

Encompass Bathe, Begird, Beset, Environ, Include, Surround

Encore Again, Agen, Ancora, Bis, Ditto, Do, Iterum, Leitmotiv, Recall, Repeat

Encounter Battle, Brush, Combat, Contend, Cope, Dogfight, Face, Hit, Incur, Intersect, Interview, > MEET, One-one, Rencontre, Ruffle, Skirmish, Tilt

Encourage(ment), Encouraging Abet, Acco(u)rage, Alley-oop, Animate, Attaboy, Bolster, Boost, Brighten, Buck, Cheer, Cohortative, Comfort, Commend, Dangle, Egg, Elate, Embolden, Empatron, Exhort, Fillip, Fire, Fortify, Foster, Fuel, Gee, Hearten, Heigh, Help, Hope, Hortatory, Incite, Inspirit, Nourish, Pat, Patronise, Proceleusmatic, Prod, Protreptic, Push, Reassure, Root, Support, Tally-ho, Train, Upcheer, Uplift, Urge, Wean, Yo

Encroach(ment) Impinge, Infringe, Inroad, Intrude, Invade, Overlap, Overstep, Poach, Purpresture, Trespass, Usurp

Encrypt(ion) CODING, Public key

Encumber, Encumbrance Burden, Charge, Clog, Deadwood, Dependent, > HANDICAP, Impede, Load, Obstruct, Saddle

Encyclopaedic Comprehensive, Diderot, Extensive, Universal, Vast

End(ing) Abolish, Abut, Aim, Ambition, Amen, Anus, Arse, Big, Bitter, Bourn(e), Butt, Cease, Climax, Close, Closure, Cloture, Coda, Conclude, Crust, Culminate, Curtain, Curtains, Cut off, Dead, Death, Decease, Denouement, Desinence, Desistance, Destroy, Determine, Dissolve, Domino, Effect, Envoi, Envoy, Epilogue, Exigent, Expire, Explicit, Extremity, Fatal, Fattrels, Feminine, Final(e), Fine, Finis, > FINISH, Finite, Gable, Grave, Heel, Ish, Izzard, Izzet, Kill, Kybosh, Last, Let up, Little, Loose, Masculine, Mill, Nirvana, No side, Ort, Outro, Period, Peter, Pine, Point, Purpose, Quench, Receiving, Remnant, Rescind, Result, Roach, Scotch, Scrag, Shank, Slaughter, Sopite, Split, Sticky, Stub, Supernaculum, Surcease, Swansong, Tag, Tail, Tailpiece, Telesis, Telic, Telos, Term, Terminal, Terminate, Terminus, Thrum, Tip, Toe, Top, Ultimate, Up, Upshot, West, Z

Endanger Hazard, Imperil, Periclitate, Risk

Endear(ing), Endearment Adorable, Affection, Asthore, Caress, Cariad, Ducky, Enamour, Hinny, Honey (-bunch), Honey-chile, Ingratiate, Jarta, Luv, Machree, Mavourneen, Peat, Pet

Endeavour Aim, Effort, Enterprise, Morse, Strive, Struggle, Try, Venture

Endemic Local, Prevalent

Endive Escarole

Endless Continuous, Ecaudate, Eternal, Eterne, Infinite, Interminable, Perpetual, Undated

▷ **Endlessly** *may indicate* a last letter missing

End of the world Ragnarok

Endorse(ment) Adopt, Affirm, Allonge, Approve, Assurance, Back, Confirmation, Initial, Okay, Oke, Ratify, Rubber stamp, Sanction, Second, Sign, Subscript, > **SUPPORT**, Underwrite, Visa

Endow(ment) Assign, Bequeath, Bestow, Bless, Cha(u)ntry, Dot, Dotation, Enrich, Foundation, Gift, Leave, Patrimony, State, Vest, Wakf, Waqf

Endurance, Endure(d), Enduring Abought, Aby(e), Bear, Bide, Brook, Dree, Face, Fortitude, Have, Hold, > **LAST**, Livelong, Lump, Patience, Perseverance, Pluck, Ride, Stamina, Stand, Stay, Stomach, Stout, Support, Sustain, Swallow, Tether, Thole, Timeless, Tolerance, Undergo, Wear

Endymion Bluebell

Enema Catharsis, Clyster, Purge

Enemy Adversary, Antagonist, Boer, Devil, Fifth column, Foe(n), Fone, Opponent, Public, Time

Energetic, Energise, Energy Active, Alternative, Amp, Animation, Arduous, Atomic, Cathexis, Chakra, Chi, Dash, Drive, Dynamic, Dynamo, E, Enthalpy, Entropy, EV, Fermi, Fireball, Firebrand, Firecracker, Force, Fossil, Free, Fructan, Geothermal, Gism, Go, Graviton, Hartree, H.D.R., Horme, Input, Instress, Internal, > **JET**, Jism, Jissom, Joie de vivre, Joule, Kinetic, Kundalini, Lattice, Libido, Lossy, Luminous, Magnon, Moxie, Nuclear, Orgone, Pep, Phonon, Potency, Potential, > **POWER**, Powerhouse, Prana, QI, Quantum, Rad, Radiant, Radiatory, Renewable, Roton, Rydberg, Sappy, Solar, Stamina, Steam, Sthenic, Stingo, Tidal, Trans-uranic, Vehement, Verve, Vibrational, Vigour, Vim, Vital, Wave, Wind (-farm), Zappy, Zing, Zip

Enfold Clasp, Embrace, Envelop, Stemme, Swathe, Wrap

Enforce(ment) Administer, Coerce, Control, Exact, Implement, Impose

Eng Agma

Engage(d), Engagement, Engaging Absorb, Accept, Appointment, At, Attach, Bespoken, Betrothal, Bind, Book, Busy, Contract, Date, Embark, Employ, Engross, Enlist, Enmesh, Enter, Fascinate, Gear, Gig, Hire, Hold, Interest, Interlock, Lock, Mesh, Met, Occupy, Pledge, Promise, Prosecute, Reserve, Residency, Skirmish, Sponsal, Sponsion, Spousal, Sprocket, Trip, Wage, Winsome

▷ **Engagement** *may indicate* a battle

Engender Beget, Breed, Cause, Occasion, Produce

Engine, Engine part Athodyd, Beam, Booster, Bricole, Bypass, Carburettor, Catapult, Compound, Diesel, Donkey, Dynamo, Fan-jet, Fire, Four, Gas, Gin, Heat, Ion, Jet, Lean-burn, Light, Locomotive, Machine, Mangonel, > **MOTOR**, Nacelle, Onager, Orbital, Outboard, Petard, Petrary, Petrol, Petter, Pilot, Plasma, Podded, Pony, Pug, Pulp, Pulsejet, Push-pull, Put-put, Radial, Ramjet, Reaction, Reciprocating, Retrorocket, Rocket, Rotary, Scorpion, Scramjet, Search, Side-valve, Stationary, Steam, Stirling, Tank, Terebra, Testudo,

Traction, Trompe, Turbine, Turbofan, Turbojet, Turbo-prop, Turboprop, Two-handed, Two-stroke, V, Vernier, Wankel, Warwolf, Water, Winch, Winding

Engineer(ing), Engineers AEU, Arrange, Barnes Wallis, BE, Brindley, Brinell, Brunel, CE, De Lessops, Genetic, Greaser, Ground, Heinkel, Junkers, Kennelly, Manoeuvre, Marconi, Marine, Mastermind, McAdam, Mechanical, Mechatronics, Military, Mime, Operator, Organise, Otto, Planner, Process, RE, Repairman, Rig, Sapper, Scheme, Siemens, Smeaton, Social, Stage, Stephenson, Strauss, Systems, Telford, Tesla, Traffic, Wangle, Wankel, Watt, Whittle, Whitworth

England Albany, Albion, Blighty, Demi-paradise, Eden, John Bull, Merrie, Merry, Middle, The Old Dart

English(man) Anglican, Anglice, Baboo, Babu, Basic, Brit, Bro talk, Choom, E, Eng, Estuary, Gringo, Hawaiian, Hong Kong, Indian, Irish, Jackeroo, John Bull, King's, Kipper, Limey, Middle, Mister, Modern, Newspeak, Norman, Officialese, Oxford, Philippine, Pidgin, Pom(my), Pommie, Pongo, Pork-pudding, Queen's, Qui-hi, Qui-hye, Rock, Rooinek, Sassenach, Saxon, Scotic, Shopkeeper, Side, Singapore, Singlish, South African, South Asian, Southron, Standard, Strine, Wardour Street, Woodbine, Yanqui, Yinglish

Engorge Devour, Glut, Swallow

Engraft Inset

Engrave(r), Engraving Aquatint, Blake, Carve, Cerography, Cerotype, Chalcography, Character, Chase, Cut, Die-sinker, Dry-point, Durer, Enchase, Eng, Etch, Glyptic, Glyptograph, Hogarth, Impress, Inciser, Inscribe, Insculp, Intagliate, Inter, Lapidary, Line, Mezzotint, Niello, Photoglyphic, Plate, Scalp, Scrimshander, Scrimshandy, Scrimshaw, Steel, Stillet, Stipple, Stylet, Stylography, Turn, Wood, Xylographer

Engross(ed) Absorb, Engage, Enwrap, Immerse, Monopolise, > OCCUPY, Preoccupy, Prepossess, Rapt, Sink, Writ large

Engulf Overwhelm, Swamp, Whelm

Enhance Add, Augment, Better, Elevate, Embellish, Exalt, Heighten, Intensify

Enigma(tic) Charade, Conundrum, Dilemma, Gioconda, Mystery, Oracle, Poser, Problem, > PUZZLE, Quandary, Question, Rebus, Riddle, Secret, Sphinxlike, Teaser

Enjoin Command, Direct, Impose, Prohibit, Require

Enjoy(able), Enjoyment Apolaustic, Appreciate, Ball, Brook, Delectation, Fruition, Glee, Groove, Gusto, Have, Lekker, Like, Own, Possess, Relish, Ripping, Savour, Taste, Wallow

Enlarge(ment), Enlarger Accrue, Acromegaly, Add, Aneurism, Aneurysm, Augment, Blow-up, Diagraph, Dilate, Exostosis, Expand, Expatiate, Explain, Increase, > MAGNIFY, Piece, Ream, Rebore, Sensationalize, Swell, Telescope, Tumefy, Upbuild, Varicosity

Enlighten(ed), Enlightenment Awareness, Bodhisattva, Dewali, Divali, Edify, Educate, Explain, Haskalah, Illumine, Instruct, Nirvana, Revelation, Satori, Verlig(te)

Enlist Attest, Conscript, Draft, Engage, Enrol, Induct, Join, Levy, Muster, Prest, Recruit, Roster, Volunteer

Enliven(ed) Animate, Arouse, Brighten, Cheer, Comfort, Exhilarate, Ginger, Invigorate, Merry, Pep, Refresh, Warm

Enmity Animosity, Aversion, Hatred, Malice, Nee(d)le, Rancour, Spite

Ennoble(ment) Dub, Elevate, Ermine, Exalt, Honour, Raise

Ennui Boredom, Tedium

Enormous Colossal, Exorbitant, Googol, Huge, Humongous, Humungous, > **IMMENSE**, Jumbo, Mammoth, Mega, Plonking, Vast

Enough Adequate, > **AMPLE**, Anow, Basta, Belay, Enow, Fill, Geyan, Nuff, Pax, Plenty, Qs, Sate, Satis, Suffice, Sufficient, Via, When

Enounce Affirm, Declare, State

Enquire, Enquiring, Enquiry Ask, Check, Curious, Eh, Examine, Inquest, Inquire, Organon, Request, Scan, See, Steward's, Trial

Enrage(d) Emboss, Enfelon, Imboss, > **INCENSE**, Inflame, Infuriate, Livid, Madden, Wild

Enrapture(d) Enchant, Ravish, Sent, Transport

Enrich Adorn, Endow, Enhance, Fortify, Fructify, Oxygenate

Enrol(ment) Attest, Empanel, Enlist, Enter, Incept, > **JOIN**, List, Matriculate, Muster, Register

Ensconce(d) Establish, Settle, Shelter, Snug

Ensemble Band, Octet(te), Orchestra, Outfit, Ripieno, Set, Tout, Whole

Enshrine Cherish, Sanctify

Ensign Ancient, Badge, Banner, Duster, > **FLAG**, Gonfalon, Officer, Pennon, Red, White

Enslave(ment) Addiction, Bondage, Captivate, Chain, Enthral, Thrall, Yoke

Ensue Follow, Result, Succeed, Supervene, Transpire

Entail Involve, Necessitate, Require

Entangle(ment) Ball, Cot, Elf, Embrangle, Embroil, Encumber, Ensnarl, Entrail, Fankle, Implicate, > **KNOT**, Mat, Ravel, Retiarius, Taigle, Trammel

Enter Admit, Board, Broach, Come, Enrol, Infiltrate, Ingo, Inscribe, Insert, Invade, Lodge, Log, Penetrate, Pierce, Record, Run, Submit, Table

Enterprise, Enterprising Adventure, Ambition, Aunter, Cash cow, Dash, Emprise, Free, Go ahead, Goey, Go-getter, Gumption, Industry, Minefield, Plan, Private, Public, Push, Spirit, Starship, Stunt, Up and coming, Venture

Entertain(er), Entertaining, Entertainment Accourt, Acrobat, Afterpiece, All-nighter, Amphitryon, Amuse, Balladeer, Ballet, Beguile, Burlesque, Busk, Cabaret, Carnival, Cater, Charade, Cheer, Chout, Circus, Comedian, Comic, Concert, Conjure, Consider, Cottabus, Crack, Craic, Cuddy, Diseur, Diseuse, Distract, Divert, Divertissement, ENSA, Extravaganza, Fete, Fleshpots, Floorshow, Foy, Fun, Gaff, Gala, Gas, Gaudy, Gig, Harbour, Harlequin, Have, Hospitality, Host(ess), Impressionist, Interest, Interlude, Intermezzo, Jester, Juggler, Karaoke, Kidult, Kursaal, Lauder, Levee, Light, Masque, Melodrama, Minstrel, Musical, Olio, Opera, Palladium, Panto, Pap, Party, Peepshow, Performer, Piece, Pierrot, Play, Raree-show, Reception, Regale, Review, Revue, Ridotto, Roadshow, Rodeo, Serenade, Showbiz, Sideshow, Singer, Snake-charmer, Soirée, Son et lumière, Striptease, Table, Tamasha, Tattoo, Treat, Variety, Vaudeville, Ventriloquist, Wattle

Enthral(l) Charm, Enchant, Enslave, Spellbind

Enthuse, Enthusiasm, Enthusiast(ic) Acclamatory, Amateur, Ardent, Ardour, Buff, Bug, Buzz, Cat, Cheerleader, Crazy, Crusader, Delirium, Demon, Devotee, Ebullience, Ecstatic, Estro, Fandom, Fiend, Fire, Flame, Freak, Furor(e), Get-up-and-go, Gung-ho, Gusto, Hacker, Hearty, Hype, Into, Keen, Lyrical, Mad, Mania, Muso, Nethead, Nympholept, Oomph, Outpour, Overboard, Passion, Perfervid, Preoccupation, Rah-rah, Raring, Rave, Rhapsodise, Schwärmerei, Sold, Spirit, Teeny-bopper, Verve, Warmth, Whole-hearted, Wonk, Zealot, Zest

Entice(ment), Enticing Allure, Angle, Cajole, Carrot, Decoy, Lure, Persuade, Seductive, > **TEMPT**, Tole, Toll

Entire(ly), Entirety Absolute, All, Bag and baggage, Clean, Complete, Full Monty, Inly, Intact, Integral, In toto, Livelong, Lot, Purely, Systemic, Thorough, Total, Tout, > WHOLE

Entitle(ment) Empower, Enable, Legitim, Name, Right

Entity Being, Body, Existence, Holon, Monad, Tao, Tensor, Thing, Virino

Entomologist Fabré

Entourage Cortège

Entrail(s) Bowels, Chawdron, Giblets, Gralloch, Guts, Ha(r)slet, Humbles, Lights, Numbles, Offal, Quarry, Tripe, Umbles, Viscera

Entrance(d), Entrant, Entry Access, Adit, Anteroom, Arch, Atrium, Attract, Avernus, Bewitch, Charm, Closehead, Contestant, Door, Doorstop, Double, Dromos, Eye, Fascinate, Foyer, Gate, Ghat, Hypnotise, In-door, Infare, Inflow, Ingress, Inlet, Introitus, Jawhole, Jaws, Jib-door, Mesmerise, Mouth, Narthex, Pend, Porch, Portal, Porte-cochère, Postern, Propylaeum, Propylon, Ravish, Reception, Record, Regest, Registration, Single, Spellbound, Starter, Stem, Stoa, Stoma, Stulm, Torii

Entreat(y) Appeal, Ask, Beg, Beseech, Flagitate, Impetrate, > IMPLORE, Orison, Petition, Plead, Pray, Precatory, Prevail, Prig, Rogation, Solicit, Sue, Supplicate

Entrée Access, Dish, Entry, Ingate

Entrench(ment) Coupure, Encroach, Fortify, Trespass

Entrepreneur Businessman, Executor, Impresario, Wheeler-dealer

Entrust Aret(t), Confide, Consign, Delegate, Give

▶ **Entry** *see* ENTRANCE

Entwine Complect, Impleach, Intervolve, Lace, Twist, Weave

Enumerate, Enumeration Catalogue, Count, Detail, Fansi, List, Tell

Enunciate, Enunciation Articulate, Declare, Deliver, Diction, Proclaim

Envelop(e) Arachnoid, Bangtail, Chorion, Corolla, Corona, Cover(ing), Cuma, Enclose, Entire, First day cover, Floral, Invest, Involucre, Jiffy(bag)®, Muffle, Mulready, Perianth, Sachet, Sae, Serosa, Smother, Surround, Swathe, Window

Envious, Envy Begrudge, Covet, Jaundiced, Jealousy, Penis

Environment(s), Environmental(ist) Ambience, Ecofreak, Econut, Eco-warrior, Element, Entourage, Ergonomics, Green, Greenpeace, Habitat, Milieu, Realo, Setting, Sphere, Surroundings, Umwelt, Vicinity

Envisage Contemplate, Imagine, Suppose

Envoi Farewell, RIP

Envoy Agent, Diplomat, Elchee, El(t)chi, Hermes, Legate, Plenipotentiary

Enzyme ACE, Aldolase, Allosteric, Amylase, Amylopsin, Apyrase, Arginase, Asparaginase, Autolysin, Bromel(a)in, Carbohydrase, Carboxylase, Casease, Catalase, Cathepsin, Cellulase, Chimotrypsin, Cholinesterase, Chymopapain, Coagulase, Collagenase, Constitutive, Cyclase, Cytase, Deaminase, Decarboxylase, Diastase, Dipeptidase, Elastase, Enolase, Enterokinase, Erepsin, Esterase, Fibrinolysin, Flavoprotein, Guanase, Histaminase, Hyaluronidase, Hydrase, Hydrolase, Inducible, Inulase, Invertase, Isomerase, Kallikrein, Kinase, Lactase, Lecithinase, Ligase, Lipase, Luciferase, Lyase, Lysin, Lysozyme, Maltase, Mutase, Neuraminidase, Nuclease, Oxdoreductase, Oxidase, Oxygenase, Papain, Pectase, Pectinesterase, Pepsin(e), Peptidase, Permease, Peroxidase, Phosphatase, Plasmin, Polymerase, Protease, Proteinase, PSA, Ptyalin, Reductase, Ren(n)in, Restriction, Ribonuclease, Saccharase, Steapsin, Streptodornase, Streptokinase, Subtilisin, Sulfatase, Sulphatase, Thrombin, Thrombokinase, Thromboplastin, Transaminase, Transcriptase, Transferase, Trehalase, Trypsin, Tyrosinase, Urease, Urokinase, Zymase

Eon Arch(a)ean

Epaminondas Theban

Ephemera(l) Brief, Day, Drake, Fungous, Mayfly, Momentary, Passing, Transient, Transitory, Trappings

Epic Aeneid, Ben Hur, Beowulf, Calliope, Colossal, Dunciad, Edda, Epopee, Epyllion, Gilgamesh, Heroic, Homeric, Iliad, Kalevala, Lusiad(s), Mahabharata, Nibelungenlied, Odyssey, Ramayana, Rhapsody, Saga

Epicene Hermaphrodite

Epicure(an) Apicius, Apolaustic, Connoisseur, Friand, Gastronome, Gastrosopher, Glutton, > GOURMAND, Gourmet, Hedonist, Sybarite

Epidemic Pandemic, Pestilence, Plague, Prevalent, Rampant, Rash

Epigram Adage, Apophthegm, Gnomic, Mot, Proverb

Epigraph Citation, Inscription, RIP

Epilepsy, Epileptic Clonic, Eclampsia, Falling evil, Falling sickness, Fit, Grand mal, Petit mal, Turn

Epilogue Appendix, Coda, Postscript

Epiphenomenon ESP

Epiphyte Air-plant

Episcopalian PE, Prelatic

Episode, Episodic Chapter, Incident, Page, Picaresque, Scene

Epistle(s) Lesson, Letter, Missive, Pastoral, Titus

Epitaph Ci-git, Hic jacet, Inscription, RIP

Epithet Adj(ective), Antonomasia, Apathaton, Byword, Curse, Expletive, Panomphaean, > TERM, Title

Epitome, Epitomise Abridge, Abstract, Digest, Image, Model, Summary, Typify

Epoch Age, Eocene, Era, Holocene, Magnetic, Miocene, Neogene, Oligocene, Palaeocene, Palaeolithic, Perigordian, Period, Pl(e)iocene, Pleistocene

Epsom salts Kieserite

Equable, Equably Calm, Just, Pari passu, Smooth, Tranquil

Equal(ly), Equality, Equal quantities Alike, A(n)a, As, Balanced, Commensurate, Compeer, Egal(ity), Emulate, Equinox, Equiparate, Equity, Even, Even-steven, Fifty-fifty, For, Identical, Identity, Is, Iso-, Isocracy, Isonomy, Level, Level-pegging, Maik, Make, Match, Mate, Owelty, Par, Pari passu, > PEER, Peregal, Pheer(e), Rise, Rival, > SO, Square, Upsides, Wyoming, Ylike

Equanimity Aplomb, Balance, Poise, Serenity

Equate, Equation(s) Balance, Cubic, Differential, Diophantine, Dirac, Exponential, Gas, Identity, Linear, Logistic, Maxwell, Parametric, Personal, Polar, Quadratic, Reduce, Relate, Rhizic, Schrödinger, Simultaneous, Van der Waals', Wave

Equator(ial) Celestial, Galactic, Line, Magnetic, Thermal, Tropical

Equerry Courtier, Officer, Page

Equilibrium Balance, Composure, Homeostasis, Isostasy, Poise, Punctuated, Stable, Stasis, Steady state, Tautomerism, Thermodynamic

Equinox Autumnal, Vernal

Equip(ment), Equipage Accoutrement, Adorn, Aguise, Aguize, Apparatus, Apparel, Appliance, Armament, Array, Attire, Carriage, Codec, Deadstock, Deck, Dight, Expertise, > FURNISH, Gear, Gere, Get-up, Graith, Habilitate, Kit, Material, Matériel, Mechanise, Muniments, Outfit, Paraphernalia, Retinue, Rig, Sonar, Spikes, Stock, Stuff, Tack(le), Tool, Trampet(te), Trampoline, Turn-out

Equity Actors, Equality, Justice, Law, Negative, Union

Equivalence, Equivalent Correspondent, Equal, Equipollent, Ewe, Formal,

In-kind, Same, Tantamount

Equivocal Ambiguous, Dubious, Evasive, Fishy, Oracular, Vague

Equivocate Flannel, Lie, Palter, Prevaricate, Quibble, Tergiversate, Waffle, Weasel

Er Um

Era Age, Archaean, C(a)enozoic, Christian, Common, Cretaceous, Cryptozoic, Decade, Dynasty, Eozoic, Epoch, Hadean, Hegira, Hej(i)ra, Hijra, Jurassic, Lias, Mesozoic, Palaeozoic, Period, Precambrian, Proterozoic, Republican, Vulgar

Eradicate, Erase Abolish, Delete, Demolish, Destroy, Efface, Expunge, Extirp, Obliterate, Purge, Root, Scrat, Scratch, Stamp-out, Strike off, Uproot, Uptear

Erasmus Humanist

Erbium Er

Erect(ion), Erector Attolent, Build, Construct(ion), Elevate, Hard-on, Henge, Horn, Perpendicular, Priapism, Prick, Rear, Rigger, Stiffy, Straight-pight, Tentigo, Upright, Vertical

Ergo Argal, Hence, Therefore

Erica Heather, Ling

Ermine Fur, Minever, Miniver, Stoat

Ernie Bondsman

Erode, Erosion Abrade, Corrasion, Denude, Destroy, Deteriorate, Etch, Fret, Planation, Spark, Wash, Wear, Yardang

Eros, Erotic(a) Amatory, Amorino, Amorous, Aphrodisiac, Carnal, Cupid, Curiosa, Lascivious, Philtre, Prurient, Salacious, Steamy

Err(or) Aliasing, Anachronism, Bish, Blip, Blooper, Blunder, Boner, Bug, Clanger, Comedy, Corrigendum, EE, Fault, Glaring, Heresy, Human, Jeofail, K'thibh, Lapse, Lapsus, Literal, Mackle, Mesprise, Mesprize, Misgo, Misprint, Misprise, Misprize, Misstep, > **MISTAKE**, Mumpsimus, Out, Probable, Rounding, Rove, Sampling, Semantic, Sin, Slip, Slip-up, Solecism, Standard, Stray, Trip, Truncation, Typo, Typographical, Wander

Errand Chore, Commission, Fool's, Message, Mission, Sleeveless, Task

Errand-boy Cad, Galopin, Page

Erratic Haywire, Temperamental, Unstable, Vagary, Vagrant, Wayward

Erroneous False, Inaccurate, Mistaken, Non-sequitur

Ersatz Artificial, Synthetic

Erudite, Erudition Academic, Didactic, Learned, Savant, Scholar, Well-read, Wisdom

Erupt(ion), Erupture Belch, Brash, Burst, Ecthyma, Eject, Emit, Emphlysis, Exanthem(a), Exanthemata, > **EXPLODE**, Fissure, Flare, Fumarole, Hives, Hornito, Lichen, Mal(l)ander, Mallender, Morphew, Outbreak, Outburst, Papilla, Paroxysm, Pompholyx, Pustule, Rash, Rose-drop, Scissure

Escalate, Escalator Accrescence, Expand, Granary, Grow, Lift, Travolator

Escape(e), Escapade, Escapist Abscond, Atride, Avoid, Bale out, Bolt, Bolthole, Breakout, Caper, Eject, Elope, Elude, Elusion, Esc, Evade, Exit, Fire, Flee, Flight, Frolic, Gaolbreak, Hole, Hoot, Houdini, Hout, Lam, Leakage, Leg-it, Let-off, Levant, Loop(-hole), Meuse, Mews, Muse, Narrow, Near thing, Outlet, Prank, Refuge, Rollick, Runaway, Sauve qui peut, Scapa, Scarper, Seep(age), Shave, Slip, Vent, Walter Mitty, Wilding, Wriggle

Escapement Anchor, Foliot, Recoil

Eschew Abandon, Avoid, For(e)go, Ignore, > **SHUN**

Escort Accompany, Attend, Bodyguard, Chaperone, Comitatus, Conduct, Convoy, Cortege, Corvette, Date, Destroyer, Entourage, Frigate, Gallant, Gigolo, Guide, Lead, Outrider, Protector, Retinue, See, Send, Set, Squire, Take, Tend,

Usher, Walker
Escutcheon Achievement, Crest, Shield
Esker OS
Eskimo Aleut, Caribou, Husky, In(n)uit, Inuk, Inukitut, Thule, Yupik
Esoteric Abstruse, Acroamatic, Arcane, Inner, Mystic, Occult, Orphic, Private, Rarefied, Recondite, Secret
ESP Psi
Especial(ly) Chiefly, Esp, Espec, Outstanding, Particular
Esperanto Ido, Zamenhof
Espionage Industrial, Spying, Surveillance
Esplanade Promenade, Walk
Esprit Insight, Spirit, Understanding, Wit
Esquire Armiger(o), Esq, Gent
Essay(s) Article, Attempt, Causerie, Critique, Dabble, Disquisition, Dissertation, Endeavour, Festschrift, Go, Paper, Prolusion, Stab, Theme, Thesis, Tractate, Treatise, Try
Essayist Addison, Bacon, Carlyle, Columnist, Elia, Ellis, Emerson, Hazlitt, Holmes, Hunt, Huxley, Lamb, Locke, Montaigne, Pater, Prolusion, Ruskin, Scribe, Steele, > **WRITER**
Essence Alma, Atman, Attar, Aura, Being, Core, Element, Entia, Esse, Extract, Fizzen, Flavouring, Foison, Gist, Heart, Hom(e)ousian, Inbeing, Inscape, Kernel, Marrow, Mirbane, Myrbane, Nub, Nutshell, Oil, Ottar, Otto, Perfume, Per-se, Pith, Quiddity, Ratafia, Soul, Ylang-ylang
Essential(ly) Basic, Central, Crucial, Entia, Formal, Fundamental, Imperative, In, Indispensable, Inherent, Integral, Intrinsic, Kernel, Key, Lifeblood, Linch-pin, Marrow, Material, Must, Necessary, Need, Nitty-gritty, Nuts and bolts, Part-parcel, Per-se, Prana, Prerequisite, Quintessence, Radical, Requisite, Sine qua non, Vital, Whatness
Establish(ed) Abide, Anchor, Ascertain, Base, Build, Create, Deploy, Embed, Enact, Endemic, Engrain, Ensconce, Entrench, Evince, Fix, > **FOUND**, Haft, Imbed, Ingrain, Instal(l), Instate, Instil, Institute, Inveterate, Ordain, Pitch, Pre-set, Prove, Raise, Root(ed), Set, Stable, Standing, Substantiate, Trad, Trite, Valorise, Verify
Establishment Building, Business, CE, Church, Co, Concern, Creation, Hacienda, Household, Institution, Lodge, Proving ground, Salon, School, Seat, System, Traditional
Estate Allod(ium), Alod, Assets, Commons, Demesne, Domain, Dominant, Dowry, Fazenda, Fee-simple, Fee-tail, Fen, First, Fourth, General, Hacienda, Hagh, Haugh, Having, Hay, Housing, Industrial, Land-living, Latifundium, Legitim, Life, Manor, Messuage, Odal, Personal(ity), Plantation, Press, > **PROPERTY**, Real, Runrig, Second, Situation, Spiritual, Standing, Talooka, Taluk(a), Temporal, Thanage, Third, Trading, Trust, Udal, Zamindari, Zemindari
Estate agent Realtor
Esteem(ed), Estimable Account, Admiration, Appreciation, Count, Have, Honour, Izzat, Los, Precious, Prestige, Price, Pride, Prize, Rate, > **REGARD**, Reputation, Respect, Store, Value, Venerate, Wonder, Worthy
Ester Depside, Glyceride, Olein, Palmitin, Phthalate, Psilocybin, Urethan(e)
▶ **Estimable** *see* **ESTEEM**
Estimate, Estimation Appraise, Assess, Calculate, Carat, Conceit, Cost, Esteem, Extrapolation, Forecast, Gauge, Guess, Guess(timate), Inexact, Interval, Opinion, Point, Projection, Quotation, Rate, Rating, Reckon, Regard, Sight,

Value, Weigh

Estrange Alienate, Disunite, Wean

Estuary Bay, Creek, Dee, Delta, Firth, Gironde, Humber, Inlet, La Plata, Mouth, Ostial, Para

Esurient Arid, Insatiable

Etc(etera) Et al(ia), So on

Etch(ing) Aquafortis, Aquatint(a), Bite, > **ENGRAVE**, Incise, Inscribe

Eternal, Eternity Aeonian, Ageless, Endless, Everlasting, Eviternal, Ewigkeit, Forever, Immortal, Infinity, Never-ending, Perdurable, Perpetual, Sempiternal, Tarnal, Timeless

Ether Atmosphere, Ch'i, Crown, Gas, Petroleum, Sky, Yang, Yin

Ethereal Airy, Delicate, Fragile, Heavenly, Nymph

Ethic(al), Ethics Deontics, Marcionite, Moral, Principles, Work

Ethiopia(n) African, Amharic, Asmara, Cushitic, Galla, Geez, Kabele, Kebele

Ethnic Racial, Roots

Ethyl ET

Etiquette Code, Conduct, Kawa, > **MANNERS**, Politesse, Propriety, Protocol, Ps and Qs, Punctilio

Etna Empedocles, Vessel, Volcano

Etonian Oppidan, Victim

Etruscan Tyrrhenian

Etymologist Hobson-jobson, Isodore

Eucalyptus Bloodwood, Coolabah, Gum-tree, Ironbark, Jarrah, Mallee, Marri, Morrell, Sallee, Stringybark, Sugar gum, Tewart, Tooart, Tuart, Wandoo, Yate

Eucharist Communion, Housel, Mass, Supper, Viaticum

Eugene Aram, Onegin

Eugenia Jambal, Jambolan(a), Jambu(l)

Eulogy Encomium, Panegyric, Praise, Tribute

Euphausia Krill, Shrimp

Euphemism Fib, Gosh, Gracious, Heck, Hypocorism

Euphoria, Euphoric Cock-a-hoop, Ecstasy, Elation, High, Jubilation, Mindfuck, Rapture, Rush

Euphrasia Eyebright

Eurasian Chee-chee, Chi-chi

Europe(an) Balt, Bohunk, Catalan, Community, Continent, Croat, E, Faringee, Faringhi, Feringhee, Fleming, Hungarian, Hunky, Japhetic, Lapp, Lithuanian, Palagi, Polack, Ruthene, Ruthenian, Serb, Slavonian, Slovene, Topi-Wallah, Transleithan, Tyrolean, Vlach, Yugoslav

Europium Eu

Eustace Diamonds

Euthanasia Exit

Evacuate, Evacuation Excrete, Expel, Getter, Planuria, Planury, Scramble, Stercorate, Stool, Vent, Void, Withdraw

Evade, Evasion, Evasive Ambages, Avoid, Cop-out, Coy, Dodge, Duck, Elude, Equivocate, Escape, Fence, Fudge, Hedge, Loophole, Mealymouthed, Parry, Prevaricate, Quibble, Quillet, Scrimshank, Shack, Shifty, Shirk, Shuffling, Sidestep, Skive, Skrimshank, Slippy, Stall, Subterfuge, Tergiversate, Waive, Weasel, Weasel out, Whiffler

Evaluate, Evaluation Appraise, Assess, Estimate, Gauge, Job, Rate, Review, Waid(e), Weigh

Evanescent Cursory, Fleeting, Fugacious

Evangelical, Evangelist(ical) Converter, Crusader, Fisher, Gospeller,

Happy-clappy, Jesus freak, John, Luke, Marist, Mark, Matthew, Moody,
Morisonian, Peculiar, Preacher, Revivalist, Salvationist, Sankey, Sim(eonite),
Stundist, Wild

Evaporate, Evaporation Condense, Dehydrate, Desorb, Dry, Exhale, Steam,
Steme, Ullage, Vaporise

Evelyn Diarist, Hope

Eve(n), Evening Albe(e), Albeit, All, All Hallow's, Average, Balanced, Clean,
Drawn, Dusk, Een, Ene, Equable, Equal, Erev, Fair, Flush, Forenight, Iron,
J'ouvert, Level, Level-pegging, Meet, Nightfall, Pair, Par, Plain, Plane, Plateau,
Quits, Rib, St Agnes's, Smooth, Soirée, Subfusc, Subfusk, Sunset, Tib(b)s,
Toss-up, Twilight, Vesperal, Vespertinal, Vigil, Yester, Yet

Evening flight Ro(a)ding

Evensong Vespers

Event Case, Circumstance, Contingency, Discus, Encaenia, Episode, Fest, Field,
Gymkhana, Happening, Happy, Heat, Incident, Iron man, Landmark, Leg,
Media, Milestone, Occasion, Occurrence, Ongoing, Outcome, Pass, Regatta,
Result, Stick-on, Three-day, Three-ring circus, Track, Triple

Even-toed Artiodactyl

Eventual(ity), Eventually Case, Contingent, Finally, Future, In time, Nd, Sooner
or later

Ever Always, Ay(e), Constantly, Eternal, Eviternity

Everglade Vlei

Evergreen Abies, Ageless, Arbutus, Cembra, Cypress, Gaultheria, Ivy, Myrtle,
Olearia, Periwinkle, Pinaster, Privet, Thuja, Thuya, Washington, Winterberry,
Yacca

Everlasting Cat's ear, Changeless, Enduring, Eternal, Immortal, Immortelle,
Perdurable, Recurrent, Tarnal

Every(one), Everything All, Complete, Each, Existence, Full Monty, Ilk(a), In
toto, Monty, Sum, The works, To a man, Tout, Tout le monde, Universal, Varsal

Everyday Banal, Informal, Mundane, Natural, Ordinary, Plain

Everywhere Omnipresent, Passim, Rife, Throughout, Ubiquity

Evict Disnest, Eject, Expel, Oust

Evidence, Evident Adminicle, Apparent, Argument, Axiomatic,
Circumstantial, Clear, Confessed, Credentials, Direct, Distinct, Document,
Empirical, Exemplar, Flagrant, Hearsay, Indicate, Internal, King's, Manifest,
Marked, Obvious, Overt, > **PATENT**, Plain, Premise, Prima facie, Probable,
Proof, Queen's, Record, Sign, Smoking gun, State's, Surrebuttal, Testimony,
Understandable

Evil Ahriman, Alastor, Amiss, Badmash, Bale, Beelzebub, Budmash, Corrupt,
Depraved, Eale, Guilty, Harm, Heinous, Hydra, Ill, Immoral, Iniquity, King's,
Malefic, Mare, Mischief, Necessary, Night, Perfidious, Rakshas(a), Shrewd,
Sin, > **SINISTER**, Turpitude, Vice, Wicked

Evil eye Jettatura

Evince Disclose, Exhibit, Indicate, > **MANIFEST**, Show

Eviscerate(d) Debilitate, Disembowel, Drawn, Gralloch

Evoke Arouse, Awaken, Elicit, Move, Stir

Evolution(ary) Countermarch, Development, Emergent, Growth, Holism,
Lamarck, Moner(on), Neo-Lamarckism, Orthogenesis, Phylogeny, Social,
Spencerman, Stellar, Transformism, Turning

▷ **Evolution** *may indicate* an anagram

Ewe Crone, Gimmer, Keb, Sheep, Teg, Theave

Ewer Aquamanale, Aquamanile

Ex Former, Late, Quondam, Ten

Exacerbate Aggravate, Embitter, Exasperate, Irritate, Needle

Exact(ing), Exactitude, Exactly Accurate, Authentic, Careful, Dead, Definite, Due, Elicit, Estreat, Even, Exigent, Extort, Fine, Formal, It, Jump, Literal, Literatim, Mathematical, Meticulous, Nice(ty), Pat, Point-device, > **PRECISE**, Require, Slap-bang, Spang, Specific, Spot-on, Strict, Stringent, T, To a 't', Verbatim

Exaction Blackmail, Extortion, Impost, Montem, Sorelion, Tax

Exaggerate(d), Exaggeration Agonistic, Amplify, Ballyhoo, Boast, Brag, Camp, Colour, Distend, Dramatise, > **EMBROIDER**, Goliathise, Hoke, Hyperbole, Inflate, Lie, Line-shoot, Magnify, Munch(h)ausen, Mythomania, Overdo, Overdraw, Overpaint, Overplay, Overrate, Overstate, Over-the-top, Romance, Steep, Stretch, Tall, Theatrical

Exalt(ed), Exaltation Attitudes, Deify, Dignify, Elation, Enhance, Ennoble, Erect, Extol, Glorify, High, Jubilance, Larks, Lofty, Magnific, > **PRAISE**, Raise, Rapture, Ruff(e), Sama, Sublime, Supernal, Throne

Exam(ination), Examine, Examinee, Examiner Agrégé, A-level, Analyse, Analyst, Appose, Audit, Auscultation, Autopsy, Baccalauréat, Biopsy, Case, Check-out, Check-up, Cognosce, Collate, Comb, Common Entrance, Consideration, Cross-question, CSE, Deposal, Depose, Disquisition, Dissect, Docimasy, Endoscopy, Entrance, Expiscate, Explore, Eyeball, Finals, GCE, GCSE, Going-over, Grade(s), Great-go, Greats, Gulf, Haruspex, Hearing, Inspect, Inter, Interrogate, Interview, Introspection, Jerque, Jury, Little-go, Local, Mark, Matriculation, Medical, Mocks, Moderator, Mods, Mug, O-level, Once-over, Oral, Ordalian, Ordeal, Overhaul, Palp(ate), Paper, Peruse, Physical, Post-mortem, Prelim, Probe, Pry, Psychoanalyse, Pump, > **QUESTION**, Quiz, Ransack, Recce, Reconnaissance, Responsions, Review, Sayer, Scan, Schools, Scrutator, Scrutineer, Scrutinise, Search, Seek, Shroff, Sift, Sit, Smalls, Sus(s), Test, Trial, Tripos, Try, Unseen, Vet, Viva, Voir dire

Example Apotheosis, Assay-piece, Byword, Epitome, Foretaste, > **FOR EXAMPLE**, Illustration, Instance, Lead, Lesson, Model, Paradigm, Paragon, > **PATTERN**, Praxis, Precedent, Prototype, Role model, Say, Shining, Showpiece, Specimen, Standard, Stormer, Such as, Touchstone, Type, Typify

Exasperate, Exasperating, Exasperation Anger, Embitter, Galling, Irk, Irritate, Nettle, Provoke

Excavate, Excavation, Excavator Armadillo, Burrow, Catacomb, Crater, Cutting, Delf, Delph, > **DIG**, Dike, Disinter, Ditch, Dragline, Dredge, Drive, Earthwork, Gaulter, Hollow, JCB, Mine, Pichiciago, Pioneer, Pioner, Pyoner, Quarry, Shaft, Sink, Sondage, Steam-shovel, Stope, Well

Exceed, Exceeding(ly) Amain, Not half, Outdo, Overstep, Surpass, Transcend, Very

Excel(lence), Excellency, Excellent A1, Ace, Admirable, A-per-se, Assay-piece, Bangin(g), Beat, Beaut, Better, Bitchin, Blinder, Bodacious, Boffo, Bonzer, Booshit, Boss, Bottler, Bravo, Brill, Bully, Capital, Castor, Champion, Cheese, Choice, Class(y), Classical, Copacetic, Copesettic, Copybook, Corking, Crack, Crackerjack, Crucial, Daisy, Def, Dic(k)ty, Dilly, Dominate, Doozy, Elegant, Excelsior, Exemplary, Eximious, Exo, Extraordinaire, Fab, Fantastic, Five-star, Great, Grit, Grouse, HE, High, Humdinger, Hunky(-dory), Inimitable, Jake, Jammy, Jim-dandy, Knockout, Lalapalooza, Laudable, Lollapalooza, Lummy, Matchless, Mean, Mega-, Merit, Neat, Noble, Out and outer, Outbrag, Outdo, Outstanding, Outtop, Overdo, Overtop, Paragon, Peachy, Phat, Prime, Pure, Rad, Rare, Rattling, Ring, Rinsin', Ripping, Ripsnorter, Say-piece, > **SHINE**,

Shit-hot, Sick-dog, Sik, Spanking, Spiffing, Stellar, Stonking, Stupendous, Sublime, Superb, Super-duper, Superior, Supreme, Swell, Terrific, Tip-top, Top flight, Top-hole, Topnotch, Topping, Transcend, Transcendant, Triff, Virtue, Wal(l)y, War, Way-out, Wicked, Worth

Except(ion) Bar, But, Else, Exc, Nobbut, Omit, Save, Than, Then, Unless

Exceptional Abnormal, Anomaly, Cracker, Egregious, Especial, Extraordinary, Gas, Rare, Ripsnorter, Select, Singular, Special, Uncommon, Zinger

Excerpt(s) Digest, Extract, Passage, Scrap

Excess(ive), Excessively All-fired, Basinful, Exorbitant, Extortionate, Extravagant, Flood, Fulsome, Glut, Hard, Inordinate, > **LAVISH**, Mountain, Nimiety, OD, Old, OTT, Outrage, Over, Overage, Overblown, Overcome, Overdose, Overkill, Overmuch, Overspill, Over-the-top, Owercome, Plethora, Preponderance, Profuse, Salt, Satiety, Spate, Spilth, Steep, Superabundant, Superfluity, Surfeit, Surplus, Terrific, Troppo, Ultra, Undue, Unequal, Woundily

Exchange Baltic, Bandy, Barter, Bourse, Cambist, Catallactic, Change, Chop, Commute, Contango, Convert, Cope, Corn, Ding-dong, Employment, Enallage, Excambion, Foreign, Inosculate, Interplay, Ion, Labour, Logroll, > **MARKET**, Mart, Needle, Niffer, Paraphrase, PBX, Post, Rally, Rate, Recourse, Rialto, Royal, Scorse, Scourse, Stock, Swap, Switch, Swop, Telephone, Tolsel, Tolsey, Tolzey, > **TRADE**, Traffic, Transfusion, Trophallaxis, Truck

Exchequer Remembrancer

Excise(man), Excise district Ablate, Bobbitt, Crop, Expunge, Gauger, Resect, Ride, Tax

Excitable, Excite(d), Excitement, Exciting Ablaze, Aboil, Abuzz, Aerate, Agitate, Agog, Amove, Animate, Aphrodisiac, Arouse, Athrill, Atwitter, Awaken, Brouhaha, Buck-fever, Climatic, Combustible, Commotion, Delirium, Electrify, Emove, Enthuse, Erethism, Feisty, Fever, Fire, Flap, Flat spin, Frantic, Frenzy, Frisson, Furore, Fuss, Galvanise, Gas, Grip, Headiness, Heat, Hectic, Het, Hey-go-mad, Hilarity, Hobson-Jobson, Hoopla, Hothead, Hyped, Hyper, Hysterical, Impel, Incite, Inebriate, Inflame, Intoxicate, Jimjams, Kick, Kindle, Metastable, Must, Neurotic, Oestrus, Orgasm, Overheat, Overwrought, Panic, Passion, Pride, Prime, Provoke, Racy, Radge, Red-hot, Rile, Roil, > **ROUSE**, Rousement, Ruff(e), Rut, Send, Sexy, Spin, Spur, Startle, Stimulate, Stir(e), Suscitate, Temperamental, Tetany, Tew, Thrill, Titillate, Trickle, Turn-on, Twitter, Upraise, Va-va-voom, Waken, Whee, Whet, Whoopee, Yahoo, Yerk, Yippee, Yoicks

▷ **Excite(d)** *may indicate* an anagram

Exclaim, Exclamation (mark) Ahem, Begorra, Blurt, Bo, Ceas(e), Crikey, Criv(v)ens, Dammit, Ecphonesis, Eina, Ejaculate, Epiphonema, Eureka, Expletive, Fen(s), Good-now, Hadaway, Haith, Halleluiah, Hallelujah, Heigh-ho, Hem, Hip, Hookey Walker, Hosanna, Inshallah, Interjection, Oops, Pling, Protest, Pshaw, Sasa, Screamer, Sese(y), Sessa, Vociferate, Walker, Whau, Whoops, Wow, Yippee, Zounds

Exclude, Excluding, Exclusion Ban, Bar, Block, Debar, Deforcement, Disbar, Drop, Eliminate, Ex, Except, Excommunicate, Freeze out, Omit, Ostracise, Outbar, Outwith, Pauli, Shut out, Social

Exclusive Cliquish, Closed-shop, Complete, Debarment, Elect, Monopoly, Particular, Pure, Rare, Scoop, Select, Single, Sole

Excommunicate Curse

Excoriate Flay, Slam

Excrement, Excretion Dirt, Doo-doo, Dung, Faeces, Frass, Jobbie, Keech,

Meconium, Oliguria, Ordure, Poo(p), Poo-poo, Puer, Pure, Refuse, Scatology, Shit(e), Sir-reverence, Stercoraceous, Strangury, Turd, Urea, Waste

Excrescence Aril, Carnosity, Caruncle, Enate, Gall, Growth, Knob, Knurl, Lump, Nurl, Pimple, Pin, Spavin(e), Strophiole, Talpa, Twitter(-bone), Wart

Excruciate, Excruciating Agonising, Rack, Torment, Torture

Exculpate Acquit, Clear, Forgive

Excursion Airing, Cruise, Dart, Digression, Jaunt, Junket, Outing, Road, Sally, Sashay, Sortie, Tour, Trip

Excusable, Excuse Absolve, Alibi, Amnesty, Bunbury, Condone, Essoin, Essoyne, Evasion, Exempt, Exonerate, Faik, Forgive, Mitigate, Occasion, Off come, Out, Overlook, Palliate, > **PARDON**, Pretext, Release, Salvo, Venial, Viable, Whitewash

Execrate Abhor, Ban, Boo, Curse

Execute(d), Executioner, Executive, Executor Abhorson, Accomplish, Account, Administrate, Behead, Carnifex, Deathsman, Despatch, Discharge, Dispatch, Exor, Finish, Fry, Gan, Gar(r)otte, Gin, Guardian, Hang, Headsman, Implement, Ketch, Kill, Koko, Lynch, Management, Noyade, Official, Perform, Pierrepoint, Politburo, Scamp, Top, Trustee, Tyburn

Exemplar(y) Byword, Impeccable, Laudable, Model, Paragon, St, Warning

Exemplify Cite, Epitomise, Illustrate, Instantiate, Satisfy

Exempt(ion) Dispensation, Exclude, Exeem, Fainites, Fains, Free, Immune, Impunity, Indemnity, Overslaugh, Quarter, Spare, Vains

Exercise(s) Aerobics, Air, Antic, Apply, Callanetics®, Cal(l)isthenics, Chi kung, Cloze, Constitutional, Drill, Employ, Enure, Eurhythmics, Exert, Floor, Gradus, Inure, Isometrics, Kata, Kegel, Krav Maga, Lesson, Limber, Manual, Medau, Op, Operation, PE, Physical jerks, Pilates, Ply, Popmobility, Practice, Practise, Press-up, PT, Pump iron, Push-up, Qigong, Shintaido, Sit-up, Solfeggi(o), Step (aerobics), Stretch, Tai chi (ch'uan), Thema, Theme, Thesis, Train, Trampoline, Use, Vocalise, Warm-up, Wield, Work, Work-out, Xyst(us), Yomp

▷ **Exercise(d)** *may indicate* an anagram

Exert(ion) Conatus, > **EFFORT**, Exercise, Labour, Operate, Strain, Strive, Struggle, Trouble, Wield

Ex-European Japhetic

Exhalation, Exhale Breath, Fume, Miasma, Reek, Steam, Transpire, Vapour

Exhaust(ed), Exhausting, Exhaustion, Exhaustive All-in, Beaten, Beggar, Bugger(ed), Burn, Burn-out, Bushed, Clapped out, Consume, Deadbeat, Debility, Deplete, Detailed, Dissipate, Do, Done, Drain, Eduction, Effete, Emission, Empty, End, Enervate, Fatigue, Forfeuchen, Forfochen, Forfoughen, Forfoughten, Forjaskit, Forjeskit, Forspent, Forswink, Frazzle, Gruelling, Heat, Heatstroke, Inanition, Jet-lagged, Jet-stream, Jiggered, Knacker, Mate, Milk, Out, Outwear, Poop, Powfagged, Puckerood, Puggled, Rag, Ramfeezle, Rundown, Sap, Shatter, Shot, Shotten, Spend, Spent, Stonkered, Tailpipe, Tire, Trauchled, Use, Used up, Wabbit, Wappend, Warby, Washed-up, Wasted, Waygone, > **WEARY**, Wind, Worn, Zonked

Exhibit(ion), Exhibitioner Circus, Concours, Demo, Demonstrate, Demy, Diorama, Discover, Display, Evince, Expo, Expose, Fair, Hang, Indicate, > **MANIFEST**, Olympia, Pageant, Panopticon, Parade, Present, Retrospective, Salon, Scene, Set forth, Show(piece), Showcase, Viewing

Exhilarate(d) Bubble, Cheer, Elate, Enliven

Exhort(ation) Admonish, Allocution, Caution, Counsel, Incite, Lecture, Par(a)enesis, Persuade, Urge

Exhume Delve, Disinter, Resurrect, Unearth

Exigency, Exigent Emergency, Pressing, Taxing, Urgent, Vital

Exile Adam, Babylon, Banish, Deport, Emigré, Eve, Expatriate, Exul, Galut(h), Ostracise, Outlaw, Relegate, Tax, Wretch

Exist(ence), Existing Be(ing), Corporeity, Dwell, Enhypostasia, Entelechy, Esse, Extant, Identity, In esse, Life, Live, Ontology, Perseity, Solipsism, Substantial, Ubiety

Existentialist Camus, Sartre

Exit Débouché, Door, Egress, Gate, Leave, Log off, Log out, Outlet

Exodus Book, Departure, Flight, Hegira, Hejira

Ex-official Outler

Exogamous Outbred

Exonerate(d) Absolve, Acquit, Clear, Excuse, Exempt, Shriven

Exorbitant Excessive, Expensive, Steep, Tall, Undue

Exorcise, Exorcist Benet, Lay

Exordium Opening, Preface, Prelude

Exotic Alien, Ethnic, Fancy, Foreign, Free, Outlandish, Strange

Expand, Expanse, Expansion Amplify, Boom, Branch out, Develop, Diastole, Dilate, Distend, Ectasis, Elaborate, > **ENLARGE**, Escalate, Flesh out, Grow, Increase, Magnify, Ocean, Outspread, Snowball, Spread, Stretch, Swell, Wax, Wire-draw

Expatiate Amplify, Descant, Dwell, Enlarge, Perorate

Expatriate Banish, Colonial, Emigrate, Émigré, Exile, Outcast

Expect(ant), Expectation, Expected, Expecting Agog, Anticipate, Ask, Await, Due, Foresee, Gravid, Hope, Lippen, Look, Natural, Par, Pip, Pregnant, Presume, Prim, Prospect, Require, > **SUPPOSE**, Tendance, Think, Thought, Usual, Ween

Expectorant, Expectorate Expel, Guaiacol, Hawk, Spit

Expedient Advisable, Artifice, Contrivance, Fend, Make-do, Makeshift, Measure, Politic, Resort, Resource, Shift, Stopgap, Suitable, Wise

Expedite, Expedition, Expeditious Advance, Alacrity, Anabasis, Celerity, Crusade, Dispatch, Excursion, Fastness, Field trip, Hasten, Hurry, Kon-tiki, Pilgrimage, Post-haste, Quest, Safari, Short cut, Speed, Trek, Trip, Voyage

Expel Amove, Dispossess, Drum out, Egest, Evacuate, Evict, Exile, Exorcize, Hoof, Oust, Out(cast), Read out, Void

Expend(iture) Budget, Consume, Cost, Dues, Gavel, Goings-out, Mise, Occupy, Oncost, Outgo(ing), Outlay, Poll, Squander, Tithe, Toll, Use, Waste

Expendable Cannon-fodder

Expense(s) Charge, Cost, Current, Exes, Fee, Law, Oncost, Outgoing, Outlay, Overhead, Price, Sumptuary

Expensive Chargeful, Costly, Dear, Executive, High, Salt, Steep, Upmarket, Valuable

Experience(d) Accomplished, A posteriori, Assay, Blasé, Discovery, Empiric, Encounter, Expert, > **FEEL**, Felt, Find, Freak-out, Gust, Hands-on, Have, Incur, Know, Learn, Live, Mature, Meet, Mneme, Near-death, Old hand, Old-stager, Ordeal, Out-of-body, Pass, Plumb, Seasoned, See, Senior, Sense, Sensory, Stager, Stand, Street-smart, Streetwise, Taste, Transference, Trial, Trip, Trocinium, Try, Undergo, Versed, Work

Experiment(al) Attempt, Avant-garde, Control, Empirical, Essay, Peirastic, Pilot, Sample, Taste, Tentative, > **TRIAL**, Try, Venture, Vivisection

Expert(ise) Accomplished, Ace, Adept, Adroit, Arch, Authority, Boffin, Buff, Cambist, Cocker, Cognoscente, Connoisseur, Crack, Craft, Dab(ster), Dan, Deft, Don, Egghead, Finesse, Fundi, Gourmet, Gun, Hotshot, Karateka, Know-all, Know-how, Luminary, Maestro, Masterly, Maven, Mavin, Meister, Nark, Oner,

Oneyer, Oneyre, Peritus, Practised, Pro, Proficient, Pundit, Ringer, Savvy, Science, Shroff, Skill(y), Sly, Specialist, Technique, Technocrat, Troubleshooter, Ulema, Used, W(h)iz

Expiate, Expiation, Expiatory Amends, Atone, Penance, Piacular

Expire(d), Expiry Blow, Collapse, Croak, > DIE, End, Exhale, Invalid, Ish, Lapse, Neese, Pant, Sneeze, Terminate

Explain(able) Account, Annotate, Aread, Arede, Arreede, Clarify, Conster, Construe, Decline, Define, Describe, Elucidate, Explicate, Exponible, Expose, Expound, Extenuate, Gloss, Gloze, Justify, Parabolize, Salve, Solve, Upknit

Explanation, Explanatory Apology, Commentary, Exegesis, Exegetic, Exposition, Farse, Gloss, Gloze, Hypothesis, Key, Note, Preface, Reading, Rigmarole, Solution, Theory

Expletive Arrah, Darn, Exclamation, Oath, Ruddy, Sapperment

Explicit Clean-cut, Clear, Definite, Express, Frank, Full-on, Outspoken, > PRECISE, Specific

Explode, Explosion, Explosive Agene, Airburst, Amatol, Ammonal, ANFO, Antimatter, Aquafortis, Backfire, Bang, Bangalore torpedo, Big bang, Blast, Burst, Cap, Cheddite, Chug, Cordite, Cramp, Crump, Cyclonite, Debunk, Detonate, Dualin, Dunnite, Dust, Egg, Erupt, Euchloric, Euchlorine, Fireball, Firecracker, Firedamp, Firework, Fulminant, Fulminate, Gasohol, Gelatine, Gelignite, Grenade, Guncotton, Gunpaper, Gunpowder, HE, High, Iracund, Jelly, Landmine, Low, Lyddite, Megaton, Melinite, Mine, Nail-bomb, Napalm, Nitroglycerine, Outburst, Ozonide, Paravane, Payload, Petar(d), Petre, Phut, Plastic, Plastique, Pluff, Pop, Population, Pow, Priming, Propellant, Ptarmic, Pustular, Report, Roburite, SAM, Semtex®, Sheet, Shrapnel, Snake, Sneeze, Soup, Squib, Supernova, Tetryl, Thunderflash, Tinderbox, TNT, Tonite, Trinitrobenzene, Trotyl, Volatile, Volcanic, Warhead, Xyloidin(e)

Exploit(s), Exploiter, Exploitation Act, Adventure, Deed, Develop, Escapade, Feat, Gest, Harness, Ill-use, Impose, Kulak, Manoeuvre, Milk, Mission, Parlay, Rachmanism, Ramp, Res gestae, Stunt, Sweat, Tap, Use, Utilise

Explore(r), Exploration Amerigo, Amundsen, Baffin, Balboa, Bandeirante, Banks, Barents, Bering, Boone, Burton, Cabot, Cartier, Chart, Columbus, Cook, Cortes, Da Gama, Dampier, Darwin, De Soto, Dias, Diaz, Discover, Dredge, Eric, Eriksson, Examine, Feel, Field trip, Frobisher, Fuchs, Humboldt, Investigate, Livingstone, Magellan, Map, Marco Polo, Mungo Park, Nansen, Navigator, Pathfinder, Peary, Pioneer, Potholer, Probe, Przewalski, Rale(i)gh, Research, Rhodes, Ross, Scott, Scout, Search, Shackleton, Spaceship, Speke, Stanley, Sturt, Tasman, Vancouver, Vasco da Gama, Vespucci

▷ **Explosive** *may indicate* an anagram

Exponent Advocate, Example, Index, Interpreter, Logarithm

Export(s) Despatch, Invisible, Klondike, Klondyke, Ship, Visible

Expose(d), Exposure Air, Anagogic, Bare, Bleak, Blot, Blow, Burn, Debag, Debunk, Denude, Desert, Disclose, Double, Endanger, En prisé, Exhibit, Flashing, Glareal, Indecent, Insolate, Moon, Nude, Object, Open, Out, Over, Propale, Reveal, Showdown, Snapshot, Streak, Strip, Subject, Sun, Time, Uncover, Unmask, Windswept

Exposition Aperçu

Expostulate, Expostulation Argue, Arrah, Protest, Remonstrate

Expound(er) Discourse, Discuss, Exegete, Explain, Open, Prelict, Red, Scribe, Ulema

Express(ed), Expression, Expressive Air, APT, Aspect, Breathe, Cacophemism, Circumbendimus, Cliché, Colloquialism, Conceive, Concetto, Couch,

Countenance, Declare, Denote, Eloquent, Embodiment, Epithet, Explicit, Face, Fargo, Formulate, Good-luck, Gup, Hang-dog, Hell's bells, Idiom, Limited, Locution, Lyrical, Manifest, Metonym, Mien, Mot (juste), Neologism, Non-stop, Orient, Paraphrase, Phrase, Pleonasm, Pony, Precise, Pronto, Put, Quep, Register, Say(ne), Show, Soulful, > SPEAK, State, Strain, Succus, Term, Token, Tone, Topos, Utterance, Vent, > VOICE

Expressionless Aphasia, Blank, Boot-faced, Deadpan, Impassive, Inscrutable, Po(ker)-faced, Vacant, Wooden

Expressman Fargo

Expropriate Dispossess, Pirate, Seize

Expulsion Discharge, Eccrisis, Ejection, Eviction, Exile, Sacking, Synaeresis

Expunge Cancel, Delete, Erase, Obliterate

Expurgate Bowdlerize, Castrate, Censor, Purge

Exquisite Beautiful, Choice, Ethereal, Fine, Intense, Lair, Macaroni, Pink, Princox, Refined, Soigné(e), Too-too

Ex-serviceman Vet

Extemporise Ad lib, Improvise, Pong

Extend(ed), **Extension** Add, Aspread, Augment, Conservative, Cremaster, Draw, Eke, Elapse, Ell, Elongate, Enlarge, Escalate, Expand, Exsert, Fermata, Grow, Increase, Jumboise, Length, Long, Long-range, Long-stay, Long-term, Offer, Outgrowth, Overbite, Overlap, Porrect, Proffer, Prolong, Propagate, Protract, Reach, Retrochoir, Span, Spread, Steso, > STRETCH, Substantial, Widen

Extensive, **Extent** Ambit, Area, Capacious, Catch-all, Compass, Comprehensive, Distance, Duration, Large, Latitude, Length, Limit, > MAGNITUDE, Panoramic, Range, Reach, Scale, Size, Spacious, Span, Spread-eagle, Sweeping, Wide, Widespread

Extenuate Diminish, Lessen, Mitigate, Palliate

Exterior Aspect, Crust, Derm, Facade, Outer, > OUTSIDE, Shell, Surface, Veneer

Exterminate, **Extermination** Abolish, Annihilate, Destroy, Holocaust, Uproot

External Exoteric, Exterior, Extraneous, Foreign, Outer

Extinct(ion) Archaeopteryx, Bygone, Chalicothere, Creodont, Dead, Death, Defunct, D(e)inothere, Dodo, Obsolete, Quagga, Rasure, Saururae, Theodont

Extinguish Douse, Dout, Dowse, Dowt, Extirpate, Obscure, Quash, Quell, Quench, Slake, Smother, Snuff, Stamp out, Stifle, Suppress

Extirpate End, Erase, Excise, Obliterate, Root, Uproot

Extol Commend, Enhance, Eulogise, Exalt, Laud, Puff

Extort(ion), **Extortioner** Barathrum, Blackmail, Bleed, Bloodsucker, Chantage, Chout, Churn, Compel, Exact, Force, Gombeen, Montem, Rachman, Rack, Racketeer, Ransom, Screw, Shank, Squeeze, Sweat, Urge, Vampire, Wrest, Wring

Extra Accessory, Additament, Addition(al), Additive, Adjunct, And, Annexe, Attachment, Bisque, Bonus, By(e), Debauchery, Encore, Etcetera, Further, Gash, Lagniappe, Left-over, Leg bye, Make-weight, More, Nimiety, Odd, Optional, Out, Over, Overtime, Perk, Plus, Plusage, Reserve, Ripieno, > SPARE, Spilth, Staffage, Sundry, Super, Supernumerary, Supplementary, Suppletive, Surplus, Trop, Undue, Walking-gentleman, Walking-lady, Wide, Woundy

Extract(ion), **Extractor** Apozem, Bleed, Breeding, Catechu, Clip, Corkscrew, Decoction, Descent, Distil, Draw, Educe, Elicit, Emulsin, Enucleate, Essence, Estreat, Excerpt, Exodontics, Extort, Gist, Gobbet, Insulin, Kino, Liver, Milk, Mine, Oust, Parentage, Passage, Pericope, Pick, Piece, Pituitary, Pry, Pyrene, Pyrethrin, Quintessence, Retour, Smelt, Squeeze, Stope, Suck, Summary, Tap, Trie, Try, Vanilla, Ventouse, Winkle, Worm, Wring, Yohimbine

Extradition Renvoi

Extraneous Extrinsic, Foreign, Irrelevant, Outlying, Spurious

Extraordinary Amazing, By-ordinar, Case, Curious, Humdinger, Important, Phenomenal, Preternatural, Rare, Singular, Startling, Strange, Unusual

Extravagance, Extravagant, Extravaganza Bombastic, Excessive, Fancy, Feerie, Glitzy, Heroic, High-flown, Hyperbole, Lavish, Luxury, Outré, Prodigal, Profligate, Profuse, Rampant, Reckless, Riotise, Romantic, Splash, Splurge, Squander, Sumptuous, Superfluous, Waste

Extreme(ly), Extremist Acute, Almighty, Butt, Deep-dyed, Desperate, Die-hard, Drastic, Edge, Exceptional, Farthermost, Gross, In spades, > **INTENSE**, Jacobin, Mega-, Mondo, Nazi, Opposite, Parlous, Pretty, Radical, Root and branch, Steep, Thule, Too, Tremendous, Ultimate, Ultima thule, Ultra, Unco, Utmost, Utter, > **VERY**, Vitally, Wing

▷ **Extreme** *may indicate* a first or last letter

Extremity Bourn(e), Crisis, Digit, Ending, Finger(-tip), Limb, Limit, Outrance, Pole, Tip, Toe, Utterance

Extricate Liberate, Loose, Rescue, Untangle

Extrinsic Aliunde, External, Irrelevant, Outward

Extrovert Lad, Outgoing

Extrude Debar, Eject, Project

Exuberance, Exuberant Brio, Copious, Ebullient, Effusive, Gusto, Hearty, Lavish, Mad, Profuse, Rambunctious, Rumbustious, Skippy, Streamered

Exudation, Exude Bleed, Ectoplasm, Emit, Extravasate, Guttate, Ooze, Secrete, Still, Sweat, Swelter, Ulmin, Weep

Exult(ant) Crow, Elated, > **GLOAT**, Glorify, Jubilant, Paeonic, Rejoice, Triumphant, Whoop

Eye(ful), Eye-ball, Eyes, Eyepiece Beady, Canthus, Compound, Cringle, Eagle, Ee, Eine, Electric, Emmetropia, Evil, Glad, Glass, Glim, Glom, Goggles, Hurricane, Huygen's, Iris, Jack, Keek, Klieg, Lamp, Lazy, Lens, London, Magic, Mincepie, Mind's, Mongoloid, Naked, > **OBSERVE**, Ocellar, Ocular, Ogle, Ommateum, Ommatidium, Optic, Orb, Pedicel, Peeper, PI, Pigsn(e)y, Pigsnie, Pineal, Pupil, Regard, Retina, Rhabdom, Roving, Sclera, Screw, Shufti, Shufty, Sight, Spy, Storm-centre, Tec, Third, Uvea, Watch, Water-pump, Weather, Whally, Windows, Winker

Eyebright Euphrasy

Eyebrow Bree, Brent-hill, Glib, Penthouse, Superciliary

Eyeglass Loupe

Eyelash Cilium

Eyelet Cringle, Grommet, Hole

Eyelid Canthus, Ectropion, Haw, Palpebral

Eye-rod Rhabdom

Eye-shadow Kohl

Eyesore Blot, Disfigurement, Sty(e)

Eye-stalk Ommatophore, Stipes

Eye trouble Amblyopia, Ametropia, Aniseikonia, Anisomatropia, Aphakia, Asthenopia, Astigmatism, Cataract, Ceratitis, Coloboma, Cycloplegia, Diplopia, Entropion, Erythropsia, Exophthalmus, Glaucoma, Hemeralopia, Hemi(an)op(s)ia, Hypermetropia, Hyperopia, Iritis, Keratitis, Leucoma, Lippitude, Micropsia, Miosis, Monoblepsis, Muscae volitantes, Myosis, Nebula, Nyctalopia, Nystagmus, Ommateum, Palinop(s)ia, Photophobia, Photopsia, Pink-eye, Presbyopia, Private, Retinitis, Retinoblastoma, Scotoma(ta), Seeing, Shiner, Stigmatism, Strabismus, Strephosymbolia,

Strong, Stye, Synechia, Teichopsia, Thylose, Thylosis, Trachoma, Trichiasis, Tritanopia, Tylosis, Wall-eye, Xeroma, Xerophthalmia

Eye-wash Collyrium

Eyrie Nest

Ezra Pound

Ff

F Fahrenheit, Fellow, Feminine, Fluorine, Following, Force, Foxtrot

Fab Super

Fabian, Fabius Dilatory, Washington

Fable(s) Aesop, Allegory, Apologue, Exemplum, Fiction, Hitopadesa, La Fontaine, Legend, Marchen, Milesian, Myth, Panchatantra, Parable, Romance, Tale, Tarand

Fabric > CLOTH, Contexture, Framework

Fabricate, Fabrication Artefact, Concoct, Construct, Contrive, Cook, Fake, Fangle, Figment, Forge, > INVENT, Lie, Porky, Trump, Weave, Web

Fabulous (beast), Fabulous place Apocryphal, Apologue, Chichevache, Chimera, Cockatrice, Eldorado, Fictitious, Fung, Gear, Griffin, Hippogriff, Hippogryph, Huma, Incredible, Jabberwock(y), Kylin, Legendary, Magic, Manticora, Manticore, Merman, Monoceros, Mythical, Opinicus, Orc, Phoenix, Roc, Romantic, Simorg, Simurg(h), Snark, Sphinx, Tarand, Tragelaph, Unicorn, Unreal, Utopia, Wivern, Wyvern, Yale

Facade Front(age), Frontal, Mask, Pretence

Face, Facing Abide, Affront, Ashlar, Ashler, Aspect, Audacity, Brave, Brazen, Caboched, Caboshed, Cheek, Chiv(v)y, Coal, Countenance, Culet, Dalle, Dare, Dartle, Deadpan, Dial, Eek, Elevation, Encounter, Facade, Fat, Favour, Features, Fineer, Fortune, > FRONT, Gardant, Girn, Gonium, Grid, Groof, Groue, Grouf, Gurn, Hatchet, Head-on, Jib, Kisser, Light, Lining, Look, Lore, Mascaron, Meet, Metope, Moe, Mug, Mush, Obverse, Opposite, Outstare, Outward, Pan, Paper tiger, Phisnomy, Phiz(og), Physiognomy, Poker, Puss, Revet, Revetment, Roughcast, Rud, Rybat, Side, Snoot, Socle, Straight, Stucco, Type, Veneer, Vis(age), Visnomy, Withstand, Zocco(lo)

Face-ache Noli-me-tangere

Face-lift Rhytidectomy

Face-saving Redeeming, Salvo

Facet(ed) Angle, Aspect, Bezel, Culet, Face, Pavilion, Polyhedron

Facetious Frivolous, Jocular, Waggish, Witty

Facile Able, Adept, Complaisant, Ductile, Easy, Fluent, Glib

Facilitate, Facility Amenity, Assist, Benefit, Capability, > EASE, Expedite, Fluency, Gift, ISO, Knack, Skill

Facsimile Copy, Photostat®, Replica, Repro

Fact(s), Factual Actual, Case, Corpus delicti, Correct, Data, Datum, Detail, Griff, Info, Literal, Mainor, Nay, Really, Truism, Truth, Veridical, Yes

Faction Bloc, Cabal, Camp, Caucus, Clique, Contingent, Ghibelline, Guelph, Junto, Red Army, Schism, Sect, Tendency, Wing

Factor Agent, Aliquot, Broker, Cause, Chill, Clotting, Coagulation, Co-efficient, Common, > COMPONENT, Divisor, Edaphic, Element, F, Feel-good, Growth, House, Intrinsic, Load, Modulus, Power, Q, Quality, Representative, Rh, Rhesus, Risk, Safety, Steward, Wind chill, X

Factory Cannery, Gasworks, Glassworks, Hacienda, Maquiladora, Mill, Plant,

Refinery, Sawmill, Steelworks, Sweatshop, Tinworks, Works, Workshop

Factotum Circar, Handyman, Servant, Sircar, Sirkar

Faculty Aptitude, Arts, Capacity, Department, Ear, Ease, Indult, Knack, Power, School, Sense, Speech, > **TALENT**, Teachers, Wits

Fad(dish) Crank, Craze, Cult, Fashion, Foible, Ismy, Thing, Vogue, Whim

Fade(d), Fading Blanch, Die, Diminuendo, Dinge, Elapsion, Etiolate, Evanescent, Fall, Filemot, Lessen, Mancando, Pale, Passé, Perdendo(si), Peter, Smorzando, Smorzato, Stonewashed, Vade, Vanish, Wallow, Wilt, Wither

Faeces Dingleberry, Dung, Kak, Meconium, Motion, Mute, Scybalum, Skatole, Stercoraceous, Stools

Fag(ging) Chore, Cigarette, Drag, Drudge, Fatigue, Gasper, Homosexual, Menial, Pennalism, Quean, Reefer, Snout, Tire, Toil, Weary

Fag-end Ash, Butt, Dout, Lag, Snipe, Stub

Fag(g)ot(s) Bavin, Bundle, Fascine, Firewood, Homosexual, Kid, Knitch, Twigs

Fail(ing), Failure Ademption, Anile, Anuria, Blemish, Blow, Bomb, Bummer, Cark, > **COLLAPSE**, Conk, Crack up, Crash, Cropper, Debacle, Decline, Defalcation, Default, Defect, Demerit, Die, Dog, Dry, Dud, Fault, Feal, Fiasco, Fink out, Flame out, Flivver, Flop, Flow, Flunk, Fold, Founder, Frost, Glitch, Gutser, Infraction, Lapse, Lemon, Lose, Malfunction, Manqué, Mis-, Miscarry, Miss, Muff, Nerd, No-hoper, No-no, Omit, Outage, Oversight, Pip, Plough, Pluck, Pratfall, Reciprocity, Refer, Refusal, Respiratory, Shambles, Short(coming), Short circuit, Slippage, Smash, Spin, Stumer, Turkey, Vice, Wash-out, Weakness, White elephant, Wipeout

Fain Lief

Faineant Gallio

Faint(ness) Black-out, Conk, Darkle, Dim, Dizzy, Dwalm, Fade, Lassitude, Pale, Stanck, Swarf, Swarve, Swelt, Swerf, Swerve, Swoon, Swound, Syncope, Unclear, Wan, Whitish

Faint-heart Coward, Craven, Timid, Wet

Fair Adequate, A(e)fald, Aefauld, Acfwld, Darnet, Bartholomew, Bazaar, Beauteous, Beautiful, Belle, Blond, Bon(n)ie, Bonny, Brigg, Decent, Dishy, Donnybrook, Equal, Equitable, Evenhanded, Exhibition, Expo(sition), Feeing-market, > **FESTIVAL**, Fine, Funfair, Gaff, Gala, Gey, Goose, Gwyn, Hiring, Honest, Hopping, Isle, > **JUST**, Kermess, Kermis, Kirmess, Market, Mart, Mediocre, Mela, Mop, Nundinal, Objective, OK, Paddington, Passable, Play, Pro rata, Rosamond, Sabrina, Sporting, Square, Statute, Steeple, Straight, Tavistock, Tidy, Tolerable, Tow-headed, Trade, Tryst, Unbias(s)ed, Vanity, Wake, Widdicombe

Fair-buttocked Callipygean

Fairing Ornament, Spat

Fairly Clearly, Enough, Evenly, Midway, Moderately, Pari passu, Pretty, Properly, Quite, Ratherish

Fairway Dog-leg, Pretty

Fairy, Fairies Banshee, Befana, Cobweb, Dobbie, Dobby, Elf(in), Fay, Gloriana, Good people, Hob, Hop o' my thumb, Leprechaun, Lilian, Little people, Mab, Morgane(tta), Morgan le Fay, Moth, Nis, Peri, Pigwidgin, Pigwiggen, Pisky, Pixie, Pouf, Puck, Punce, Sandman, Seelie, Sidhe, Spirit, Sprite, Sugar-plum, Tink(erbell), Titania, Tooth, Unseelie, Urchin-shows

Faith(ful) Accurate, Achates, Belief, Constant, Creed, Devoted, Doctrine, Faix, Fay, Feal, Fegs, Fideism, Fiducial, Haith, Implicit, Islam, Lay, Loyal, Plerophory, Punic, Puritanism, Quaker, Religion, Shahada, Shema, Solifidian, Staunch, Strict, Troth, > **TRUE**, True-blue, Trust, Truth, Umma(h)

Faithless Atheist, Disloyal, False, Hollow, Nullifidian, Perfidious, Punic

Fake(r), **Faking** Bodgie, Bogus, Copy, Counterfeit, Duff(er), Ersatz, False, Fold, Fraud, Fudge, Imitation, Imposter, Impostor, Paste, Phoney, Postiche, Pretend, Sham, Spurious, Trucage, Truquage, Truqueur, Unreal

Falcon Gentle, Hawk, Hobby, Iceland, Kestrel, Lanner(et), Merlin, Nyas, Peregrine, Prairie, Saker, Sakeret, Spar-hawk, Sparrow-hawk, Stallion, Staniel, Stannel, Stanyel, Tassel-gentle, Tassell-gent, Tercel-gentle, Tercel-jerkin

Falklander Kelper

Fall(s), **Fallen**, **Falling** Abate, Accrue, Angel, Arches, Astart, Autumn, Boyoma, Cadence, Cascade, Cataract, Churchill, Chute, Collapse, Crash, Cropper, Cross press, Declension, Decrease, Degenerate, Descent, Dip, Domino effect, Douse, Downswing, Dowse, > **DROP**, Ebb, Firn, Flag, Flop, Flump, Folding press, Free, Grabble, Grand, Gutser, Gutzer, Horseshoe, Idaho, Iguaçu, Incidence, Kabalega, Kaieteur, Lag, Landslide, Lapse, Lin(n), Niagara, Oct(ober), Onding, Owen, Perish, Plonk, Plummet, Plump, Plunge, Prolapse, Purl(er), Rain, Reaction, Relapse, Ruin, Sheet, Sin, Sleet, Snow, Soss, Spill, Stanley, Sutherland, Tailor, Takakkau, Topple, Toss, Trip, Tugela, Tumble, Victoria, Voluntary, Wipeout, Yellowstone, Yosemite

Fallacious, **Fallacy** Elench(us), Error, Gamblers', Idolum, Ignoratio elenchi, Illogical, Illusion, Material, Naturalistic, Pathetic, Sophism, Specious, Unsound

Fallible Human, Imperfect

▷ **Falling** *may indicate* an anagram or a word backwards

Fallow Barren, Lea, Tan, Uncared, Uncultivated, Untilled

False, **Falsify** Adulterate, Bastard, Bodgie, Bogus, Braide, Canard, Cavil, Charlatan, Cook, Deceitful, Disloyal, Dissemble, Doctor, Fake, Feigned, Fiddle, Forge, Illusory, Knave, Lying, Meretricious, Mock, Perjury, Pinchbeck, Postiche, Pretence, Pseudo, Rap, Roorback, Sham, Specious, Spoof, Spurious, Treacherous, Two-faced, Untrue, Veneer

False notions Idola

Falter Hesitate, Limp, Stoiter, Totter, Waver

Fame, **Famous** Bruit, Celebrity, Distinguished, Eminent, Glitterati, Gloire, Glory, Greatness, History, Humour, Illustrious, Kudos, Legendary, Luminous, Name, Noted, Notorious, Prestige, Reclamé, Renown, Repute, Rumour, Splendent, Spur, Stardom, Word

Familiar(ise), **Familiarity** Accustom, Acquaint, Assuefaction, Au fait, Auld, Chummy, Comrade, Conversant, Crony, Dear, Demon, Easy, Free, Friend, Habitual, Homely, Homey, Incubus, Intimate, Known, Liberty, Maty, Old, Old-hat, Privy, Python, Used, Versed, Warhorse

Family Ancestry, Bairn-team, Blood, Breed, Brood, Clan, Class, Close-knit, Cognate, Consanguine, Descent, Dynasty, Extended, House(hold), Issue, Kin, Kind, Line, Mafia, Medici, Name, Nuclear, One-parent, Orange, People, Phratry, Progeny, Quiverful, Race, Sept, Sib(b), Sibship, Stem, Stirps, Strain, Taffy, Talbot, Tribe, Whanau

Family tree Pedigree, Stemma

Famine Dearth, Lack, Scarcity

Famish(ed) Esurient, Hungry, Ravenous, Starving

▷ **Famished** *may indicate* an 'o' in the middle of a word

Fan(s), **Fan-like** Admirer, Aficionado, Alligator, Alluvial, Arouse, Bajada, Blow, Cat, Clapper, Claque, Colmar, Cone, Cool, Cuscus, Devotee, Diadrom, Dryer, Enthusiast, Extractor, Fiend, Flabellum, Following, Groupie, Hepcat, Khuskhus, Nut, Outspread, Partisan, Punka(h), Rhipidate, Ringsider,

Sail, Spectator, Spread, Supporter, Tail, Tifosi, Ventilate, Votary, Voteen, Washingtonia, Wind machine, Wing, Winnow, Zealot, Zelant

▷ **Fan** *may indicate* an anagram

Fanatic(al) Bigot, Devotee, Energumen, Enthusiastic, Extremist, Fiend, Frenetic, Glutton, Mad, Maniac, Nut, Partisan, Phrenetic, Picard, Rabid, Santon, Ultra, Wowser, Zealot

Fancy, Fanciful Caprice, Chim(a)era, Conceit, Concetto, Crotchet, Daydream, Dream, Dudish, Elaborate, Fangle, Fantasy, Fit, Flam, Florid, Frothy, Guess, Hallo, Idea(te), Idolon, > IMAGINE, Inclination, Lacy, Liking, Maya, Mind, My, Nap, Notion, Ornamental, Ornate, Picture, Pipe dream, Predilection, Reverie, Rococo, Suppose, Thought, Urge, Vagary, Visionary, Ween, Whigmaleerie, Whigmaleery, Whim(sy), Woolgather

▷ **Fancy** *may indicate* an anagram

Fane Banner, Pronaos

Fanfare Flourish, Sennet, Show, Tantara, Trump, Tucket

Fang Tooth, Tusk

Fanny Adams, Bottom, Gas-lit, Price

Fantasist, Fantasy, Fantastic Absurd, Antic, Bizarre, Caprice, Chimera, Cockaigne, Cockayne, Escapism, Fab, Fanciful, Grotesque, Hallucination, Idol, Kickshaw(s), Lucio, Myth, Outré, Phantasmagoria, Queer, Romance, Unreal, Untrue, Walter Mitty, Wannabe(e), > WHIM, Whimsical, Wild

Far Apogean, Away, Distal, Distant, Extreme, Outlying, Remote, Thether, Thither

Farce(ur) Burletta, Charade, Comedy, Exode, Feydeau, Lazzo, Mime, Mockery, Pantomime, Rex, Sham

Fare Apex, Charge, Cheer, Commons, Do, Eat, Excess, Excursion, > FOOD, Go, Passage, Passenger, Rate, Table, Traveller

Farewell Adieu, Adios, Aloha, Apopemptic, Bye, Cheerio, Departure, Godspeed, > GOODBYE, Leave, Prosper, Sayonara, Send off, So long, Toodle-oo, Toodle-pip, Totsiens, Vale, Valediction

Far-fetched Fanciful, Improbable, Recherché

Farm(ing), Farmhouse Agronomy, Arable, Bocage, Bowery, City, Cold Comfort, Collective, Cooperative, Croft, Cultivate, Dairy, Deep-litter, Dry, Emmerdale, Estancia, Extensive, Factory, Fat, Fish(ery), Funny, Geoponical, Grange, Hacienda, Health, Home, Homestead, Husbandry, Intensive, Kibbutz, Kolkhoz, Land, Ley, Loaf, Location, Mailing, Mains, Mas, Mixed, No-tillage, Onstead, Orley, Pen, Plaas, Plough, Poultry, Ranch, Rent, Sewage, Shamba, Sheep station, Smallholding, Sovkhoz, Station, Stead(ing), Sted(d), Stedde, Steed, Stock, Store, Stump, Subsistence, Tank, Till, Toon, Toun, Town, Trash, Tree, Truck, Wick, Wind

Farmer Blockie, Boer, Campesino, Carl, Cockatoo, Cocklaird, Cocky, Collins Street, Colon, Cow cocky, Crofter, Estanciero, Gebur, Gentleman, George, Giles, Hick, Hobby, Macdonald, Metayer, Nester, NFU, Peasant, Pitt Street, Queer St, Ryot, Share-cropper, Smallholder, Sodbuster, Squatter, Stubble-jumper, Tenant, Tiller, Whiteboy, Yeoman, Zeminda(r)

Farmhand Cadet, Cottar, Cotter, Cottier, Ditcher, Hand, He(a)rdsman, Hind, Ploughman, Redneck, Rouseabout, Roustabout, Shearer

▸ **Farmhouse** *see* FARM

Farmyard Barton, Homestall, Villatic

Farouche Awkward, Shy, Sullen

Farrago Hotch-potch, Jumble, Medley, Mélange

Farrier Marshal, Smith

Farrow Litter, Mia, Sow
Far-sighted Presbyte
Fart Poep
Farthing Brass, F, Fadge, Har(r)ington, Mite, Q, Quadragesimal, Rag
Fascia Band, Fillet, Platband
Fascinate, Fascinating Allure, Attract, Bewitch, > **CHARM**, Dare, Enchant,
  Engross, Enthral(l), Fetching, Inthral, Intrigue, Kill, Mesmeric, Rivet, Siren,
  Witch
Fascist Blackshirt, Blue shirt, Brownshirt, Dictator, Falange, Falangist, Iron
  Guard, Lictor, Nazi, Neo-nazi, NF, Rexist, Sinarchist, Sinarquist
Fashion(able), Fashioned Aguise, A la (mode), Bristol, Build, Chic, Construct,
  Convention, Corinthian, Craze, Create, Cult, Custom, Cut, Dernier cri, Design,
  Directoire, Elegant, Entail, Fad, Feat, Feign, Forge, Form, Genteel, Go, Hew,
  High, Hip, Hot, In, Invent, Kitsch, Look, > **MAKE**, Man-about-town, Manière,
  Manners, Mode, Mondain(e), Mould, Newgate, Pink, Preppy, Rage, Rag
  trade, Rate, Roy, Sc, Shape, Smart, Smith, Snappy, Snazzy, Stile, Stylar, Style,
  Swish, Tailor, Ton, Ton(e)y, Tonish, > **TREND(Y)**, Turn, Twig, Vogue, Way, Wear,
  With-it, Work, Wrought
Fast(ing), Faster Abstain, Apace, Ashura, Breakneck, Citigrade, Clem,
  Cracking, Daring, Dharna, Dhurna, Double-quick, Elaphine, Express, Fizzer,
  Fleet, Immobile, Lent, Lightning, Loyal, Maigre, Meteoric, Moharram,
  Muharram, Muharrem, Pac(e)y, Posthaste, Presto, Pronto, Quadragesimal,
  Quick, Raffish, Raking, Ramadan, Ramadhan, Rash, Relay, Siyam, Spanking,
  Speedy, Stretta, Stretto, Stuck, Supersonic, Swift, Tachyon, Thick, Tight, Tisha
  b'Av, TishaBov, Tishah-Baav, Tishah-b(e)Ab, Tishah-b(e)Av, Whistle-stop,
  Yarer, Yom Kippur
Fast and loose Fickle, Pick-the-garter, Strap-game
Fasten(er), Fastening Anchor, Attach, Bar, Belay, Bind, Bolt, Buckle, Button,
  Chain, Clamp, Clasp, Click, Clinch, Clip, Cramp, Cufflink, Dead-eye,
  Diamond-hitch, Dome, Espagnolette, Eye-bolt, Frog, Gammon, Hasp, Hesp,
  Hook, Lace, Latch, Lock, Moor, Morse, Nail, Netsuke, Nut, Padlock, Parral,
  Patent, Pectoral, Pin, Preen, Press stud, Reeve, Rivet, Rope, Rove, Seal,
  > **SECURE**, Sew up, Shut, Spar, Sprig, Staple, Stitch, Tach(e), Tag, Tape, Tassel,
  Tether, Tintack, Toggle, U-bolt, Velcro®, Wedge, Zip
Fastidious Chary, Critical, Dainty, Fussy, Neat, Nice, Particular, Precieuse,
  Precious, Squeamish
Fat(s), Fatten, Fatty Adipic, Adipocere, Adipose, Aldermanly, Aliphatic, Arcus,
  Atheroma, Bard, Batten, Battle, Blubber, Brown, Butter, Calipash, Calipee,
  Cellulite, Cholesterol, Chubbed, Chubby, Corpulent, Creesh, Degras, Dika-oil,
  Dosh, Dripping, Embonpoint, Enarm, Endomorph, Flab, Flesh, Flick, Fozy,
  Fubsy, Galam-butter, Grease, Gross, Keech, Kitchen-fee, Lanolin, Lard, Leaf,
  Lipaemia, Lipid, Lipoma, Love handles, Margarine, Marge, Marrow, Obese,
  Oil, OS, Palmitin, Pinguid, Plump, Poddy, Podgy, Polyunsaturated, Portly,
  Puppy, Pursy, Rich, Rolypoly, Rotund, Saddlebags, Saginate, Saim, Saturated,
  Schmal(t)z, Seam(e), Sebacic, Sebum, Shortening, Soil, Spare tyre, Spe(c)k,
  Squab, Stearic, Steatopygia, Steatorrhea, Suberin, Suet, Tallow, Tin, Tomalley,
  Triglyceride, Tub, Unsaturated, Vanaspati, Waller, Wool
Fatal(ism), Fate(s), Fated, Fateful Apnoea, Atropos, Cavel, Chance, Clotho,
  Deadly, Death, Decuma, Destiny, Doom, End, Fay, Fell, Joss, Karma, Kismet,
  Lachesis, Lethal, Lot, Meant, Moira, Mortal, Mortiferous, Nemesis, Norn(a),
  Parca, Pernicious, Portion, Predestination, Skuld, Urd, Verdande, Waterloo,
  Weird, Weird sisters

Father(ly) Abba, Abbot, Abuna, Adopt, Apostolic, Bapu, Begetter, Breadwinner, Brown, City, Curé, Dad, Engender, Foster, Founding, Fr, Generator, Genitor, Getter, Gov, Governor, Guv, Male, Pa, Padre, Papa, Pappy, Parent, Pater(nal), Paterfamilias, Patriarch, Père, Pilgrim, Pop(pa), Popper, Priest, Rev, Sire, Stud, Thames, Tiber, William

Father-lasher Sea-scorpion

Fathom Delve, Depth, Dig, F, Plumb, Plummet, Understand

Fatigue Battle, Combat, Exhaust, Fag, Jade, Jet lag, ME, Metal, Neurosthenia, Overdo, Tire, Weariness, Weary

Fatuous Gaga, Idiotic, Silly, Stupid

Faucet Cock, Spigot, Tap

Fault(y) Arraign, Bad, Beam, Blame(worthy), Blunder, Bug, Cacology, Carp, Culpable, Defect, Demerit, Dip, Dip-slip, Drop-out, Duff, > ERROR, Failing, Flaw, Frailty, Gall, Glitch, Gravity, Henpeck, Hitch, Imperfect, Literal, Massif, > MISTAKE, Nag, Nibble, Niggle, Nit-pick, Oblique, Out, Outcrop, Overthrust, Para, Peccadillo, Rate, Reprehend, Rift, Rupes Recta, San Andreas, Sclaff, Set-off, Short, Slip, Step, Strike, Strike-slip, Technical, Thrust, Trap, Underthrust, Upbraid, Vice

Faultless Immaculate, Impeccable, Lily-white, Perfect

Fauna Mesobenthos, Wild life

Fauvist Matisse

Faux pas Blunder, Boner, Gaffe, Leglen-girth, Solecism

Favour(able), Favoured, Favourite Advance, Advantage(ous), Aggrace, Agraste, Alder-liefest, Approval, Back, Befriend, Behalf, Benign, Bless, Boon, Bribe, Cert, Chosen, Cockade, Curry, Darling, Ex gratia, Fancy, Favodian, Form horse, Good turn, Grace, Graste, Gratify, Gree, Hackle, Hot, In, Indulge, Kickback, Minion, Odour, Particular, Peat, Persona grata, Pet, Pettle, Popular, > PREFER, Promising, Propitious, Resemble, Rib(b)and, Roseate, Rose-knot, Rosette, Smile, Toast, Token, Win-win

Fawn(er), Fawning Adulate, Bambi, Beige, Blandish, Brown-nose, Crawl, Creep, Cringe, Deer, Ecru, Flatter, Fleech, Grovel, Ko(w)tow, Lickspittle, Obsequious, Servile, Smarm, Smoo(d)ge, Subservient, Sycophant, Tasar, Toady, Truckle, Tussah, Tusseh, Tusser, Tussore

Fay Fairy, Korrigan, Peri

FBI G-men

Fear Aichmophobia, Angst, Apprehension, Awe, Bête noire, Bugbear, Claustrophobia, Cold sweat, Crap, Creeps, Cyberphobia, Dismay, Doubt, Drad, Dread, Foreboding, > FOR FEAR, Fright, Funk, Hang-up, Horror, Kenophobia, Mysophobia, Nyctophobia, Ochlophobia, > PHOBIA, Photophobia, Redoubt, Revere, Taphephobia, Taphophobia, Terror, Thalassophobia, Trepidation, Willies

Fearful Afraid, Cowardly, Dire, Horrific, Nervous, Pavid, Rad, Redoubtable, Timorous, Tremulous, Windy

Fearless Bold, Brave, Courageous, Gallant, Impavid, Intrepid

Fearsome Dire, Formidable

Feasible Goer, Likely, On, Possible, Practical, Probable, Viable

Feast Adonia, Agape, Assumption, Banquet, Barmecide, Beano, Belshazzar's, Blow-out, Candlemas, Carousal, Celebration, Dine, Do, Double, Eat, Encaenia, Epiphany, Epulation, Festival, Fleshpots, Fool's, Gaudeamus, Gaudy, Halloween, Hallowmas, Hockey, Hogmanay, Holy Innocents, Id-al-Adha, Id-al-Fitr, Immaculate Conception, Isodia, Junket, Kai-kai, Lady Day, Lamb-ale, Lammas, Love, Luau, Lucullus, Martinmas, Michaelmas, Midnight, Movable,

Noel, Passover, Pentecost, Pig, Potlatch, Purim, Regale, Revel, Roodmas, Seder, Shindig, Spread, Succoth, Sukkot(h), Tabernacles, Tuck-in, Wake, Wayzgoose, Weeks, Yule, Zagmuk

Feast-day Mass

Feat Achievement, Deed, Effort, Exploit, Gambado, Handspring, Stunt, Trick

Feather(ed), Feathers Alula, Barbicel, Boa, Braccate, Cock, Contour, Covert, Crissum, Down, Duster, Filoplume, Flags, Fledged, Fletch, Flight, Gemmule, Hackle, Harl, Hatchel, Herl, Lei, Lure, Macaroni, Manual, Oar, Ostrich, Pen(na), Pin, Pinna, Pith, Plumage, Plume, Plumule, Pteryla, Ptilosis, > QUILL, Rectrix, Remex, Remiges, Rocket-tail, Saddle-hackle, Scapular, Scapus, Secondary, Semiplume, Shaft, Shag, Sickle, Standard, Stipa, Swansdown, Tectrix, Tertial, Vibrissa, White, Wing covert

Feather-worker Plumassier

Feature(s) Acoustic, Amenity, Appurtenance, Article, Aspect, Attribute, Brow, Character, Chin, Depict, Double, Eye, Eyebrow, Face, Figure, Hallmark, Highlight, Item, Jizz, Landmark, Lineament, Neotery, Nose, Nucleus, Overfold, Phiz(og), Physiognomy, Spandrel, Star, Temple, Trait, Underlip

Featureless Flat

Febrifuge Atabrin, Atebrin®, Mepacrine, Quina

February Fill-dyke

Fecund(ity) Fertile, Fruitful, Prolific, Uberty

Federal, Federation Alliance, Axis, Bund, Commonwealth, Interstate, League, Russian, Statal, Union

Fee Charge, Chummage, Commitment, Common, Contingency, Corkage, Drop-dead, Dues, Duty, Faldage, Fine, Groundage, Hire, Honorarium, Interchange, Mortuary, Mouter, Multure, Obvention, Pay, Premium, Refresher, Retainer, Sub, Subscription, Transfer, Tribute

Feeble Banal, Characterless, Daidling, Debile, Decrepit, Droob, Effete, Feckless, Fizzenless, Flaccid, Foisonless, Footling, Fragile, Fus(h)ionless, Geld, Ineffective, Infirm, Jessie, Namby-pamby, Pale, Puny, Sassy, Sickly, Slender, Slight, Tailor, Tame, Thin, Tootle, Wallydrag, Wallydraigle, Washy, Wastrel, Weak, Weak-kneed, Weak-minded, Weed, Weedy, Wersh, Wet, Wimpish, Worn

Feed(er), Feeding Battle, Bib, Break, Browse, Cake, Cater, Cibation, Clover, Cowfeteria, Cram, Cue, Demand, Dine, Dressing, Drip, > EAT, Fatten, Filter, Fire, Fishmeal, Flushing, Fodder, Food, Force, Gavage, Graze, Hay, Lunch, Meal, Nourish, Paid, Pecten, Provender, Refect, Repast, Sate, Soil, Stoke, Stooge, Stover, Sustain, Tire, Tractor, Wean, Wet nurse

Feedback Negative, Positive

Feel, Feeling(s) Aesthesia, Affetuoso, Artificial, Atmosphere, Ballottement, Compassion, Darshan, Déja vu, > EMOTION, Empathy, Empfindung, Euphoria, > EXPERIENCE, Fellow, Finger, Flaw, Frisk, Grope, Groundswell, Handle, Heart, Heartstrings, Hunch, Intuit, Knock, Know, Palp, Passible, Passion, Phatic, Pity, Premonition, Presentiment, Probe, Realise, Sensate, Sensation, > SENSE, Sensitive, Sentiment, Somesthesis, Spirit, Tactual, Touch, Turn, Undercurrent, Vehemence, Vibes, Vibrations, Zeal

Feeler Antenna, Barbel, Exploratory, Overture, Palp, Sensillum, Tentacle

▶ **Feet** *see* FOOT

Feign Act, Affect, Colour, Fake, Malinger, Mime, Mock, > PRETEND, Sham, Simulate

Feint Deke, Disguise, Dodge, Faint, Fake, Spoof, Trick

Fel(d)spar Adularia, Albite, Anorthite, Gneiss, Hyalophane, Moonstone, Orthoclase, Petuntse, Petuntze, Plagioclase, Sun-stone

Felicity Bliss, Happiness, Joy, Relevance
▶ **Feline** *see* CAT
Fell Axe, Chop, Cruel, Deadly, Dire, Dread, Fierce, Heath, Hew, Hide, Hill,
 Inhuman, Knock-down, KO, Lit, Log, Malign, Moor, Pelt, Poleaxe, Ruthless,
 Sca, Shap, Skittle
Fellow(s), Fellowship Academic, Associate, Bawcock, Birkie, Bloke, Bo, Bro,
 Buffer, Carlot, Cat, Chal, Chap, Chi, China, Cock, Cod(ger), Collaborator,
 Co-mate, Communion, Companion, Comrade, Confrère, Cove, Cully, Cuss,
 Dandy, Dean, Dog, Don, Dude, Equal, F, Fogey, Fop, Gadgie, Gadje, Gaudgie,
 Gauje, Gink, Guy, Joe, Joker, Josser, Kerel, Lad, Like, M, Mall, Man, Mate,
 Member, Mister, Mun, Partner, Peer, Professor, Rival, Seniority, Sister, Sociate,
 Sodality, Swab, Twin, Waghalter, Wallah
Felon(y) Bandit, Convict, Crime, Gangster, Offence, Villain
Felt Bat(t), Drugget, Knew, Met, Numdah, Numnah, Pannose, Roofing, Sensed,
 Tactile, Underlay, Velour
Female (bodies), Feminine, Feminist Anima, Bint, Bit, Dame, Distaff, Doe,
 F, Filly, Girl, Harem, Hen, Her, Kermes, Lady, Libber, Maiden, Muliebriety,
 Pen, Petticoated, Riot girl, Sakti, Shakti, She, Sheila, Shidder, Soft, Spindle,
 Thelytoky, -trix, > WOMAN, Yin
▷ **Female, Feminine** *may indicate* an -ess ending
Fen Bog, Carr, Ea, Jiao, Marsh, Morass
Fence(r), Fencing (position) Balestra, Bar, Barrier, Botte, Carte, Croisé,
 Cyclone®, Derobement, Dogleg, Enclose, Epee, Feint, Flanconade, Flèche,
 Foils, Fraise, Froissement, Haha, Hay, Hedge, Hot, Hurdle, Iaido, Imbrocate,
 Inquartata, Kendo, Link, Mensur, Molinello, Montant, Netting, Obstacle, Ox,
 Oxer, Pale, Paling, Palisade, Palisado, Parry, Passado, Pen, Picket, Post and rail,
 Quart(e), Quinte, Rabbit-fence, Raddle, Rail, Rasper, Receiver, Reset, Ring,
 Scrimure, Seconde, Sept(um), Septime, Singlestick, Sixte, Snow, Stacket,
 Stockade, Stramac, Stramazon, Sunk, Swordplay, Tac-au-tac, Tierce, Touché,
 Trellis, Virginia, Wattle, Wear, Weir, Weldmesh®, Wire, Worm
Fend(er) Buffer, Bumper, Cowcatcher, Curb, Mudguard, Parry, Provide, Resist,
 Skid, Ward, Wing
Fennel Finnochio, Finoc(c)hio, Herb, Love-in-a-mist, Narthex, Ragged lady
Fent Offcut, Remnant, Slit
Feral Brutal, Fierce, Savage, Wild
Ferdinand Archduke, Bull
Ferment(ation) Barm, Enzym(e), Leaven, Mowburn, Protease, Ptyalin, Seethe,
 Solera, Storm, Stum, Trypsin, Turn, Vinify, Working, Ye(a)st, Zyme, Zymo-,
 Zymology, Zymosis, Zymurgy
Fermium Fm
Fern Acrogenous, Adder's-tongue, Adiantum, Archegonial, Asparagus,
 Aspidium, Asplenium, Azolla, Barometz, Bird's nest, Bladder, Bracken, Brake,
 Bristle, Buckler, Bungwall, Ceterach, Cinnamon, Coral, Cryptogam, Cyathea,
 Cycad, Dicksonia, Door, Elkhorn, Fairy moss, Filicales, Filices, Filmy, Fishbone,
 Grape, Hard, Hart's-tongue, Ice, Isoetes, Lady, Maidenhair, Male, Marattia,
 Marsh, Marsilea, Marsilia, Meadow, Moonwort, Mosquito, Mulewort, Nardoo,
 Nephrolepis, Oak, Ophioglossum, Osmunda, Parsley, Pepperwort, Pig,
 Pillwort, Polypod, Polystichum, Ponga, Pteridology, Pteris, Punga, Rachilla,
 Rhizocarp, Rockbrake, Royal, Salvinia, Schizaea, Scolopendrium, Seed, Shield,
 Silver, Snowbrake, Spleenwort, Staghorn, Sword, Tara, Tree, Venus's hair,
 Walking, Wall rue, Water, Woodsia
Ferocious Brutal, Cruel, Fell, Predatory, Rambunctious

Ferret Albin, Black-footed, Business, Fesnyng, Gill, Hob, Jill, Nose, Polecat, Ribbon, Rootle, Snoop, Trace, Unearth

Ferry(man) Charon, Convey, Hovercraft, Passage, Plier, Pont, Roll-on, RORO, Sealink, Shuttle, Soyuz, Train, Traject, Tranect

Fertile, **Fertility (symbol)** Battle, Fat, Fecund, Fruitful, Linga, Priapus, Productive, Prolific, Rhiannon, Rich, Uberous

Fertilise(r), **Fertilisation** Ammonia, Auxin, Bee, Bone-ash, Bone-earth, Bone-meal, Caliche, Caprify, Compost, Cross, Fishmeal, Guano, Heterosis, Humogen, Humus, In-vitro, IVF, Kainite, Manure, Marl, Nitrate, Nitre, Nitro-chalk, Pearl-ash, Phosphate, Pollen, Pollinator, Potash, Potassa, Self, Sham, Stamen, Superphosphate, Top dressing

Fervent, Fervid, Fervour Ardent, Burning, Earnest, Heartfelt, Heat, Hwyl, Intense, Keen, Passionate, White-hot, Zeal, Zeloso

Fester Beal, Putrefy, Rankle, Rot, Suppurate

Festival, Festive, Festivity Adonia, Aldeburgh, Ale, Al Hijra(h), All Saints' Day, Ambarvalia, Anniversary, Anthesteria, Ashora, Bairam, Baisak(h)i, Bayreuth, Beano, Beltane, Biennale, Candlemas, Carnival, Celebration, Cerealia, Chanuk(k)ah, Childermas, Church-ale, Circumcision, Commemoration, Convivial, Corpus Christi, Corroboree, Crouchmas, Dassehra, Dewali, Dionysia, Divali, Diwali, Doseh, Druid, Easter, Eisteddfod, Encaenia, En fête, Epiphany, > FAIR, Feast, Feis, Fete, Fête-champêtre, Fete-Dieu, Fete-galante, Fiesta, Fringe, Gaff, > GALA, Gaudy, Gregory, Hallowmas, Hanukkah, Harvest, Harvest home, Hock-tide, Hogmanay, Holi, > HOLIDAY, Holy-ale, Hosay, Hosein, Id-al-fitr, Imbolc, Imbolg, Kermess, Kermiss, Kirmess, Kumbh Mela, Kwanzaa, Lady-day, Lailat-ul-Qadr, Lammas, Laylat-al-Miraj, Lemural, Lemuria, Lesser Bairam, Let-off, Lughnasadh, Lupercalia, Matsuri, Mayday, Mela, Merry-night, Michaelmas, Miraj, Mod, Moombah, Navaratra, Navaratri, Noel, Obon, Palilia, Panathenaean, Panegyry, Pardon, Pasch, Passover, Pentecost, Pesa(c)h, Play, Pongal, Pooja(h), Pop, Potlach, Puja, Purim, Quirinalia, Revel, Rosh Hashanah, Rush-bearing, Samhain, Saturnalia, Seder, Semi-double, Shabuath, Shavuath, Shemini Atseres, Shrove(tide), Simchas Torah, Simchat(h) Torah, Simchat Torah, Slugfest, Terminalia, Tet, Thargelia, Thesmophoria, Tide, Transfiguration, Up-Helly-Aa, Utas, Vesak, Vinalia, Visitation, Vulcanalia, Wake, Wesak, Yom Tob, Yomtov, Yuan Tan, Yule(tide)

Festoon Deck, Decorate, Encarpus, Garland, Swag, Wreathe

Fetch(ing) Arrive, Attract, Bring, Charming, Fet(t), Get, Gofer, Realise

Fete Bazaar, Champetre, Entertain, > FESTIVITY, Gala, Honour, Tattoo

Fetish(ist) Charm, Compulsion, Gimp, Idol, Ju-ju, Obeah, Obi(a), Talisman, Totem, Voodoo

Fetter Basil, Bilboes, Chain, Gyve, Hamshackle, Hopple, Iron, Leg-iron, Manacle, Shackle

Fettle Arrange, Condition, Frig, Potter, Repair

Feud Affray, Blood, Clash, Feoff, Fief, Quarrel, Strife, > VENDETTA

Feudal (service) Arriage, Auld-farrant, Forinsec, Old

Fever(ish) African coast, Ague, Beaver, Blackwater, Brain, Breakbone, Buck, Cabin, Calenture, Cat-scratch, Cerebrospinal, Childbed, Dengue, East coast, Enteric, Ferment, Fog, Frenetic, Gastric, Gate, Glandular, Haemorrhagic, Hay, Heatstroke, Hectic, Hyperpyretic, Insolation, Intense, Intermittent, Jail, Japanese river, Jungle, Kala-azar, Lassa, Malaria, Malta, Marsh, Mediterranean, Miliary, Milk, Mono, Mud, Paratyphoid, Parrot, Parturient, Passion, Puerperal, Putrid, Pyretic, Pyrexia, Pyrogenic, Q, Quartan, Quintan, Quotidian, Rabbit, Ratbite, Recurrent, Relapsing, Remittent, Rheumatic, Rift

Valley, Rock, Rocky mountain spotted, Roseola, Sandfly, Scarlatina, Scarlet, Sextan, Spotted, Spring, Sunstroke, Swamp, Swine, Tap, Temperature, Tertian, Texas, Tick, Trench, Typhoid, Typhus, Undulant, Verruga, Vomito, West Nile, Whot, Worm, Yellow(jack)

Few(er) Handful, Infrequent, > LESS, Limited, Scarce, Some, Wheen

Fey Clairvoyant, Eccentric, Elfin, Weird

Fez Tarboosh, Tarboush, Tarbush

Fiancé(e) Betrothed, Intended, Promised

Fiasco Bomb, Debacle, Disaster, Failure, Flask, Flop, Lash-up, Wash-out

Fiat Command, Decree, Edict, Order, Ukase

Fib Gag, > LIE, Prevaricate, Story, Taradiddle, Untruth

Fibre, Fibrous Abaca, Acrilan®, Acrylic, Aramid, Arghan, Backbone, Bass, Bast, Beta, Buaze, Bwazi, Cantala, Carbon, Coir, Constitution, Cotton, Courtelle®, Cuscus, Dietary, Dralon®, Elastane, Elastin, Filament, Filasse, Flax, Funicle, Gore-Tex®, Graded-index, Hair, Hemp, Henequen, Henequin, Herl, Hypha, Ispaghula, Istle, Ixtle, Jute, Kapok, Kenaf, Kevlar®, Kittul, Lemniscus, Manilla, Monkey-grass, Monofil, Monomode, Multimode, Mungo, Muscle, Myotube, Nap, Natural, Nerve, Noil(s), Nylon, Oakum, Olefin(e), Optic(al), Orlon®, Peduncle, Piassaba, Piassava, Pina, Pita, Polyarch, Pons, Pontine, Pulu, Raffia, Ramee, Rami, Rhea, Rock-cork, Roughage, Rove, Sida, Silk, Sisal, Slagwool, Sleave, Slub(b), Spandex, Splenium, Staple, Sterculia, Strand, Strick, Sunn-hemp, Tampico, Toquilla, Tow, Uralite, Viver, Vulcanized, Wallboard, Watap, Whisker, Wood pulp

Fibula Bone, Brooch, Perone

Fickle(ness) Capricious, Change, False, Inconstant, Light, Mutable, Protean, Shifty, Varying, Volage, Volatile

Fiction(al), Fictitious Bogus, Cyberpunk, Fable, Fabrication, Legal, Pap, Phoney, Picaresque, Romance, Science, Slash, Splatterpunk, > STORY

Fiddle(r), Fiddling Amati, Bow, Calling-crab, Cello, Cheat, Crab, Cremona, Croud, Crouth, Crowd, Crwth, Fidget, Fix, Gju, Ground, Gu(e), Jerrymander, Kit, Launder, Nero, Peculate, Petty, Potter, Racket, Rebec(k), Rig, Rote, Sarangi, Saw, Sawah, Scam, Scotch, Scrape, Scrapegut, Second, Spiel, Strad, Sultana, > TAMPER, Tinker, Toy, Trifle, Tweedle(-dee), Twiddle, Viola, > VIOLIN, Wangle

Fidelity Accuracy, Faith, Fealty, Loyalty, Troth

Fidget(y) Fantad, Fanteeg, Fantigue, Fantod, Fike, Fuss, Fyke, Hirsle, Hotch, Jimjams, Jittery, Niggle, Trifle, Twiddle, Twitch, Uneasy

Fiduciary Trustee

Fief Benefice, Fee

Field(er), Fielding, Fields(man) Aalu, Aaru, Abroad, Aceldama, Aerodrome, Area, Arena, Arish, Arpent, Arrish, Campestral, Campestrian, Catch, Champ(s), Close, Coulomb, Cover, Domain, Electric, Electromagnetic, Electrostatic, Elysian, Entry, Fid, Flodden, Flying, Forte, Fylde, Glebe, Gracie, Gravitational, Grid(iron), Gully, Hop-yard, Ice, Keep wicket, Killing, Land, Landing, Lare, Lay, Lea(-rig), Leg slip, Ley, Line, Long leg, Long-off, Long-on, Longstop, Lords, Magnetic, Mead(ow), Mid-off, Mid-on, Mid-wicket, Mine, Oil, Padang, Paddock, Paddy, Parrock, Pasture, Pitch, Playing, Point, Potter's, Province, Realm, Runners, Salting, Sawah, Scarecrow, Scope, Scout, Shamba, Short leg, Shortstop, Short stop, Silly, Slip, Sphere, Square leg, Stage, Stray, Stubble, Territory, Tract, Unified, Vector, Visual, W.C., World

▷ **Field** *may indicate* cricket

Field marshal Allenby, Bulow, French, Haig, Ironside, Kesselring, Kitchener, Montgomery, Roberts, Robertson, Rommel, Slim, Wavell

Fieldwork Lunette, Ravelin, Redan, Redoubt, Tenaillon

Fiend Barbason, Demon, > **DEVIL**, Enthusiast, Flibbertigibbet, Frateretto, Hellhound, Hobbididance, Mahn, Modo, Obidicut, Smulkin, Succubus

Fierce(ly) Billyo, Breem, Breme, Cruel, Draconic, Dragon, Grim, Hard-fought, Intense, Ogreish, Rampant, Renfierst, > **SAVAGE**, Severe, Tigerish, Tigrish, Violent, Wild, Wood, Wud

Fiery Ardent, Argand, Aries, Con fuoco, Dry, Fervent, Hot, Igneous, Leo, Mettlesome, Phlogiston, Sagittarius, Salamander, Zealous

Fiesta Festival, Fete, Gala, Holiday

Fife Piffero

Fifth Column, Diapente, Hemiol(i)a, Nones, Perfect, Quint, Sesquialtera, Sextans

Fifty Demi-c, Jubilee, L

Fig Bania, Benjamin-tree, Caprifig, Fico, Figo, Footra, Fouter, Foutra, Foutre, Hottentot, Indian, Moreton Bay, Mouldy, Sycamore, Sycomore, Syncomium, Trifle

Fight(er), Fighting Affray, Agonistics, Aikido, Alpino, Altercate, Bandy, Barney, > **BATTLE**, Bicker, Biffo, Blue, Bout, Box, Brave, Brawl, Bruiser, Bundeswehr, Bush-whack, Campaign, Chaud-mellé, Chindit, Combat, Conflict, Contest, Crusader, Cuirassier, Defender, Dog, Donnybrook, Duel, Encounter, Engagement, Extremes, Faction, Fecht, Fence, Fisticuffs, Flyting, Fray, Freedom, Free-for-all, Fund, Ghazi, Gladiator, Grap(p)le, Gunslinger, Gurkha, Hurricane, Kite, Kumite, Lapith, Marine, Med(d)le, Medley, Mêlée, Mercenary, MIG, Militate, Mill, Mujahed(d)in, Mujahidin, Naumachy, Night, Partisan, Pellmell, Pillow, PLO, Prawle, Press, Pugilist, Pugnacity, Punch up, Rammy, Repugn, Resist, Ring, Ruck, Ruction, Rumble, Savate, Sciamachy, Scold, Scrap, Scrimmage, Scuffle, Shadow, Shine, Skiamachy, Skirmish, Slam, Soldier, Spar, Spitfire, Squabble, Stoush, Straight, Strife, Struggle, Sumo, Swordsman, Tar, Tatar, Thersites, Toreador, Tuilyie, Tuilzie, Tussle, Umbrella, War(-dog), War-horse, War-man, Warrior, Wraxle, Wrestle, Yike, Zero

Figment Delusion, Fiction, Invention

Figure(s), Figurine Arabic, Aumail, Bas-relief, Body, Build, Caganer, Canephorus, Caryatid, Cast, Chladni, Cinque, Cipher, Cone, Cube, Cypher, Decahedron, Digit, Ecorché, Effigy, Eight, Ellipse, Enneagon, Enneahedron, Epanadiplosis, Escher, > **FORM**, Fusil, Girth, Gnomon, Graph, Heptagon, Hexagon, Hour-glass, Icon, Icosahedron, Idol, Ikon, Image, Impossible, Insect, Intaglio, Integer, Interference, Lay, Lissajous, Magot, Matchstick, Moai, Motif, Nonagon, Number, Numeral, Numeric, Octagon, Octahedron, Orant, Outline, Parallelogram, Pentacle, Pentalpha, Plane, Polygon, Poussette, Prism, Puppet, Pyramid, Reckon, Repetend, Repoussoir, Rhomboid, See, > **SHAPE**, Sheela-na-gig, Significant, Simplex, Solid, Sonorous, Statistics, Statue(tte), String, Tanagra, Telamon, Tetragon, Torus, Triangle, Trihedron, Triskele, Triskelion, Ushabti, Waxwork

Figure of speech Allegory, Alliteration, Analogy, Antimask, Antimasque, Antimetabole, Antithesis, Asyndeton, Catachresis, Chiasmus, Deixis, Diallage, Ellipsis, Euphemism, Hendiadys, Hypallage, Hyperbaton, Hyperbole, Hysteron proteron, Irony, Litotes, Meiosis, Metalepsis, Metaphor, Metonymy, Onomatopoeia, Oxymoron, Paral(e)ipsis, Prosopoea, Simile, Solecism, Syllepsis, Synecdoche, Taxeme, Tmesis, Trope, Tropology, Zeugma

Figure study Arithmetic, Mathematics, Numeration

Figure-weaver Draw-boy

Filament Barbule, Byssus, Cirrus, Fibre, Fimbria, Floss, Gossamer, Hair, Hypha,

Mycor(r)hiza, Myofibril, Paraphysis, Protonema, > **THREAD**, Whisker, Wreath

Filch Appropriate, Drib, Pilfer, Pinch, Prig, Purloin, Smouch, > **STEAL**

File, Filing(s) Abrade, Archive, Back up, Batch, Binary, Box, Burr, Clyfaker, Coffle, Croc(odile), Crosscut, Database, Data set, Disc, Disk, Dossier, Enter, Floatcut, Generation, Half-round, Index, Indian, Limation, Line, Lodge, Nail, Pigeon-hole, Pollute, Quannet, Rank, Rasp, Rat-tail, README, Riffler, Risp, Row, Scalprum, Scratch, Single, Single-cut, String, Swarf, Text, Tickler, TIF(F)

Filial generation F1

Filibuster Freebooter, Hinder, Obstruct, Run on, Stonewall

Filigree Delicate, Fretwork, Sheer

Filipino Igorot, Moro, > **PHILIPPINE(S)**

Fill(ing), Filler Anaplerosis, Balaam, Banoffee, Banoffi, Beaumontag(u)e, Beaumontique, Billow, Bishop, Bloat, Brick-nog, Brim, Bump, Centre, Charge, Cram, Fat-lute, Gather, Gorge, Heart, Imbue, Impregnate, Inlay, Instill, Jampack, Line, Mastic, Occupy, Pabulous, Packing, Permeate, Plug, Repletive, Salpicon, Sate, Satisfy, Shim, Stack, Stock, Stocking, Stopping, > **STUFF**, Tales, Tank-up, Teem, Top up, Ullage

Fillet(s) Anadem, Annulet, Band, Bandeau, Bandelet, Bone, Cloisonné, Flaunching, Fret, Goujons, Grenadine, Headband, Infula, Label, Lemniscus, List(el), Mitre, Moulding, Reglet, Regula, Ribbon, Rollmop, Slice, Snood, Sphendone, Stria, Striga, Taeniate, Tape, Teniate, Tilting, Tournedos, Vitta

Fillip Boost, Kick, Snap, Stimulus

Filly Colt, Foal, She

Film(s), Filmmaker, Filmy, Filming Acetate, Actioner, Amnion, Biopic, Blaxploitation, Blockbuster, Bollywood, Buddy, Carry On, Casablanca, Caul, Cel, Chick-flick, Chiller, Cine, Cinema vérité, Cinerama®, Circlorama®, Cliffhanger, Cling, Clip, Coat, Compilation, Creature feature, Deepie, Dew, Diorama, Docudrama, Documentary, Dogma, Dust, Epic, ET, Exposure, Feature, Fiche, Flick, Floaty, Footage, Gigi, Gossamer, Hammer, Haze, Hollywood, Horror, Horse opera, Infomercial, Kell, Kidult, Lacquer, Layer, Loid, Mask, Membrane, Microfiche, Mist, Molecular, Montage, Movie, Neo-noir, Newsreel, Noddy, Noir, Non-flam, Oater, Omnimax®, Outtake, Panchromatic, Patina, Pellicle, Photo, Pilot, Plaque, Prequel, Psycho, Quickie, Quota-quickie, Reel, Release, Reversal, Roll, Romcom, Rush, Safety, Scale, Scent-scale, Screen, Scum, Sheet, Shoot-'em-up, Short, Shot, Silent, Skin, Skin flick, Slasher-movie, Slick, Slo-mo, Snuff, Spaghetti western, Splatter, Studio, Talkie, Tear-jerker, Technicolor, Titanic, Trailer, Travelogue, Trippy, Two-shot, Ultrafiche, Varnish, Video, Video-nasty, Vitaphone®, Web, Weepie, Weepy, Weft, Western

Film star Extra, Vedette

Filter(ing) Band-pass, Clarify, Colour, Dialysis, Dichroic, Leach, Low-pass, Percolate, Perk, Seep, Sieve, > **SIFT**, Skylight, Strain

Filth(y) Addle, Augean, Bilge, Colluvies, Crock, Crud, Defile, Dirt, Dung, Feculent, Foul, Grime, Lucre, Mire, Muck, Obscene, Pythogenic, Refuse, Slime, Smut(ch), Soil, Squalor, Stercoral, Sullage, Yuck

Fin Adipose, Anal, Caudal, Ctene, Dollars, Dorsal, Fluke, Pectoral, Pelvic, Pinna, Pinnule, Rib, Skeg, Skegg, Stabiliser, Ventral

Final(e), Finalise Absolute, Closing, Coda, Conclusive, Cup, Decider, End, End-all, Eventual, Exam, Extreme, Grand, Last, Net(t), Peremptory, Sew up, Swansong, Terminal, Ultimate, Utter

Finance, Financial, Financier Ad crumenan, Angel, Back, Banian, Banker, Bankroll, Banyan, Bottomry, Cambism, Chrematistic, Equity, Exchequer,

Fiscal, Gnome, Grubstake, Mezzanine, Monetary, Revenue, Sponsor, Subsidise, Treasurer, Underwrite

Finch Bird, Brambling, Bunting, Canary, Charm, Chewink, Crossbill, Darwin's, Fringillid, Gouldian, Grosbeak, Linnet, Marsh-robin, Peter, Redpoll, Rosy, Serin, Siskin, Spink, Twite, Zebra

Find(er), Finding Ascertain, Come across, Detect, Direction, Discover(y), Get, Hit, Inquest, > LOCATE, Meet, Provide, Rumble, Trace, Track down, Trouvaille, Unearth, Verdict

Fine, Fine words Amende, Amerce, Amerciament, Arts, Assess, Beau(t), Bender, Blood-wit(e), Bonny, Boshta, Boshter, Boss, Brandy, Brave, Braw, Champion, Dainty, Dandy, Dick, End, Eriach, Eric(k), Estreat, F, Fair, Famous, Forfeit, Gate, Godly, Good(ly), Gossamer, Gradely, Graithly, Grand, Grassum, Hair, Hairline, Handsome, Heriot, Hunkydory, Immense, Impalpable, Inconie, Incony, Infangthief, Issue, Keen, Leirwite, Log, Maritage, Merchet, Mooi, Mulct, Nifty, Niminy-piminy, Noble, OK, Oke, Outfangthief, > PENALTY, Phat, Precise, Pure, Relief, Safe, Sconce, Sheer, Sicker, Slender, Spanking, Subtle, Summery, Super, Tax, Thin, Ticket(t)y-boo, Tiptop, Topping, Unlaw, Wally, Waly, Wer(e)gild

Fine-collector Cheater

Finery Braws, Fallal, Frills, Frippery, Gaudery, Ornament, Trinket, Wally, Warpaint

Finesse Artifice, Artistry, Delicacy, Skill, Strategy

Fine-weather All-hallond, All-hallow(e)n, All-hollown

Finger(s), Fingernail Dactyl, Digit, Fork, Green, Handle, Index, Lunula, Medius, Name, Nip, Piggy, Pinky, Pointer, Potato, Prepollex, Pusher, Ring(man), Shop, Sponge, Talaunt, Talon, Tot, Trigger, White

Finger-hole Lill, Ring

Fingerprint(ing) Dabs, Dactylogram, DNA, Genetic, Loop, Whorl

Fingerstall Hutkin

Finial Bunch, Knob, Ornament, Tee

Finical, Finicky Faddy, Fastidious, Fussy, Particular, Pernickety, Precise

Finis, Finish(ed), Finishing touch Arch, Blanket, Calendar, Close, Coating, Coda, Complete, > CONCLUDE, Crown, Die, Dish, Do, Dope, Dress, > END, Epilog(ue), Epiphenomena, Exact, Full, Grandstand, Kibosh, Lacquer, Log off, Matt, Mirror, Neat, Outgo, Outwork, Pebbledash, Peg out, Perfect, Photo, Refine, Ripe, Round, Satin, Settle, Shot, Spitcher, Surface, Terminate, Through, Top out, Up (tie), Veneer, Wau(l)k, Wind-up

Finite Bounded, Limited

Finn(ish) Esth, Huck(leberry), Karelian, Lapp, Mickey, Mordvin, Suomic, Udmurt, Votyak

Fiord Bay, Hardanger, Inlet, Oslo, Randers, Trondheim

Fir Abies, Balsam, Douglas, Larch, Oregon, Scotch, Silver, Spruce, Umbrella

Fire(side) Accend, Agni, Animate, Ardour, Arouse, Arson, Atar, Axe, Bake, Bale, Barbecue, Barrage, Beacon, Behram, Blaze, Boot, Brand, Brazier, Brush, Burn, Bush, Chassé, Conflagration, Corposant, Covering, Delope, Discharge, Dismiss, Elan, Electric, Element, Embolden, Ena, Energy, Enfilade, Enkindle, Enthuse, Flak, Flame, Friendly, Furnace, Greek, Gun, Hearth, Hob, Ignite, Inferno, Ingle, Inspire, Kentish, Kiln, Kindle, Launch, Let off, Light, Liquid, Lowe, Pop, Prime, Prometheus, Pull, Pyre, Quick, Rake, Rapid, Red, Red cock, Sack, St Anthony's, St Elmo's, Scorch, Shell, Shoot, Smudge, Spark, Spirit, Spunk, Stoke, Stove, Strafe, Tracer, Trial, Wake, Watch, Wisp, Zeal

▸ **Firearm** see GUN

Fireback Reredos

Fireball Bolide
Firebird Phoenix
Fire-break Epaulement, Greenstrip
Fire-dog Andiron
Fire engine Green Goddess
Fire-extinguisher Halon, Hell-bender, Salamander
Firefly Glow-worm, Lightning-bug, Luciferin, Pyrophorus
Fire-guard Fender
Fireman Abednego, Brigade, Deputy, Prometheus, Stoker, Visiting
Fire-opal Girasol
Fireplace Camboose, Chimney, Grate, Hearth, Hob, Ingle, Loop-hole, Range
Fireplug H, Hydrant
Fireproof Abednego, Asbestos, Incombustible, Inflammable, Meshach,
　　Salamander, Shadrach, Uralite
Firewalker Salamander
Firewood Billet, Faggot, Knitch, Tinder
Firework(s) Banger, Bengal-light, Bunger, Cherry bomb, Cracker, Devil, Fisgig,
　　Fizgig, Flip-flop, Fountain, Gerbe, Girandole, Iron sand, Jumping Jack, Maroon,
　　Pastille, Peeoy, Petard, Pharaoh's serpent, Pinwheel, Pioy(e), Pyrotechnics,
　　Realgar, Rocket, Roman candle, Serpent, Skyrocket, Sparkler, Squib, Tantrum,
　　Throwdown, Tourbill(i)on, Volcano, Wheel, Whizzbang
Fire-worshipper Parsee
Firing Baking, Fusillade, Mitten, Salvo, Touchpaper
Firm Adamant, Agency, Binding, Business, Collected, Compact, Company,
　　Concern, Concrete, Conglomerate, Constant, Crisp, Decided, Determined,
　　Duro, Faithful, Fast, Fixed, Hard, Inc, Oaky, Obdurate, Obstinate, > **RESOLUTE**,
　　Sclerotal, Secure, Set, Siccar, Sicker, > **SOLID**, Stable, Stalwart, Staunch,
　　Ste(a)dfast, Steady, Steely, Steeve, Stern, Stieve, Stiff, Strict, Sturdy, Sure, Tight,
　　Tough, Well-knit
Firmament Canopy, Empyrean, Heaven, Sky
First Ab initio, Alpha, Arch, Archetype, Best, Calends, Champion, Chief,
　　Earliest, E(a)rst, Foremost, Former, Front, Head, I, Ideal, Imprimis, Initial,
　　1st, Kalends, Led, Maiden, No 1, One, Opener, Or, Original, Pioneer, Pole,
　　Pole position, Premier, Prima, Primal, Prime, Primo, Principal, Prototype,
　　Rudimentary, Senior, Starters, Top, Uppermost, Victor, Yama
First-aid(ers) Zambu(c)k
First born Ariki, Eigne, Eldest, Heir, Major, Senior
First class, First rate A1, Crack, Prime, Supreme, Tiptop, Top(notch)
First day Calends
First fruits Annat, Arles, Primitiae, Windfalls
First man Adam, Ask, Gayomart, Premier, President, Yama, Ymer, Ymir
First offender Eve, Probationer
▶ **First rate** *see* FIRST CLASS
First woman Embla, Eve, Pandora, Premier
Firth Estuary, Forth, Inlet, Moray, Pentland, Solway, Tay
Fish(ing) Angle, Bob, Bottom, Cast, Catch, Chowder, Coarse, Cran, Creel, Dredge,
　　Dry, Dry-fly, Episcate, Fly, Flying, Frozen, Fry, Game, Gefilte, Goujons, Guddle,
　　Halieutics, Haul, Inshore, Ledger, Mess, Net, Otterboard, Overnet, Piscine,
　　Queer, Roe, Rough, Sashimi, Shoal, Snigger, Sniggle, Spin, Spot, Trawl, Troll,
　　Tub, Walking, Wet, White
Fish-basket Creel, Hask, Kipe
Fish disease Argulus

FISH

2 letters:
- Ai
- Id

3 letters:
- Ayu
- Bar
- Bib
- But
- Cat
- Cod
- Cow
- Dab
- Dib
- Dog
- Eel
- Gar
- Ged
- Hag
- Ide
- Koi
- Lax
- Lob
- Par
- Pod
- Ray
- Rig
- Sar
- Tai
- Top

4 letters:
- Bass
- Blay
- Bley
- Brit
- Butt
- Carp
- Cero
- Chad
- Char
- Chub
- Chum
- Coho
- Cray
- Cusk
- Dace
- Dare
- Dart
- Dory

Fugu
Gade
Goby
Gump
Hake
Harl
Hoki
Huso
Huss
Ikan
Jack
Kelt
Keta
Lant
Leaf
Ling
Luce
Lump
Maid
Maze
Moki
Mola
Mort
Opah
Orfe
Parr
Peal
Peel
Pike
Pope
Pout
Raun
Rawn
Rigg
Rudd
Ruff
Scad
Scar
Scat
Scup
Seer
Seir
Shad
Sild
Slip
Snig
Sole
Star
Tope
Trot

Tuna
Tusk
Woof

5 letters:
- Ablet
- Allis
- Angel
- Apode
- Aspro-
- Basse
- Blain
- Bleak
- Bream
- Brill
- Bully
- Capon
- Charr
- Cisco
- Clown
- Cobia
- Cohoe
- Coley
- Cuddy
- Danio
- Dorad
- Doras
- Doree
- Dorse
- Elops
- Elver
- Fluke
- Gadus
- Gibel
- Grunt
- Jewie
- Jurel
- Laker
- Lance
- Loach
- Lythe
- Maise
- Maize
- Manta
- Masus
- Mease
- Molly
- Murre
- Murry
- Nerka

Padle
Perai
Perca
Perch
Pilot
Piper
Pirai
Platy
Pogge
Powan
Prawn
Roach
Roker
Royal
Ruffe
Saith
Sargo
Saury
Scrod
Sewen
Sewin
Shark
Sheat
Skate
Slope
Smelt
Snoek
Snook
Solen
Speck
Sprat
Sprod
Tench
Tetra
Togue
Torsk
Trout
Tunny
Umber
Wahoo
Whiff
Wirra
Witch
Yabby
Zebra

6 letters:
- Alevin
- Allice
- Anabas

- Angler
- Archer
- Ballan
- Barbel
- Belone
- Beluga
- Big-eye
- Blenny
- Bonito
- Bounce
- Bowfin
- Braise
- Braize
- Bumalo
- Burbot
- Callop
- Caplin
- Caranx
- Caribe
- Cheven
- Clupea
- Cockle
- Comber
- Conger
- Conner
- Cottus
- Cudden
- Cuddie
- Cuddin
- Cunner
- Cuttle
- Darter
- Dentex
- Diodon
- Dipnoi
- Discus
- Doctor
- Dorado
- Dun-cow
- Espada
- Finnac
- Finnan
- Fogash
- Fumado
- Gadoid
- Garvie
- Gilgie
- Goboid
- Goramy
- Grilse
- Groper
- Gulper

Gunnel
Gurami
Gurnet
Haddie
Hapuka
Hassar
Inanga
Jerker
Jilgie
Kipper
Labrus
Lancet
Launce
Lizard
Louvar
Lunker
Mad Tom
Mahsir
Maigre
Marlin
Meagre
Medaka
Medusa
Megrim
Milter
Minnow
Morgay
Mudcat
Mullet
Murena
Nerite
Oyster
Paddle
Paidle
Pakoko
Parrot
Pholas
Piraya
Plaice
Podley
Pollan
Porgie
Puffer
Redfin
Remora
Robalo
Roughy
Saithe
Salmon
Samlet
Sander
Sardel

Sargus
Sauger
Saurel
Scampi
Sea-bat
Sea-owl
Seeder
Serran
Shanny
Sheath
Shiner
Skelly
Sparid
Splake
Sucker
Tailor
Tarpon
Tautog
Tinker
Toitoi
Tomcod
Trygon
Twaite
Ulicon
Ulikon
Vendis
Weever
Wirrah
Wrasse
Yabbie
Zander
Zingel

7 letters:
Ale-wife
Anchovy
Anemone
Asterid
Azurine
Batfish
Bellows
Bergylt
Bloater
Bluecap
Boxfish
Brassie
Buffalo
Bummalo
Cabezon
Capelin
Cavalla
Cavally

Ceviche
Cichlid
Codfish
Copepod
Cottoid
Crappie
Croaker
Crucian
Crusian
Cutlass
Dogfish
Eelfare
Eel-pout
Escolar
Findram
Finnack
Finnock
Flattie
Garfish
Garvock
Geelbek
Gemfish
Goldeye
Gourami
Grouper
Growler
Grunion
Gudgeon
Gurnard
Gwiniad
Gwyniad
Haddock
Hagdown
Hagfish
Halibut
Herling
Herring
Hirling
Hogfish
Homelyn
Houting
Ichthys
Inconnu
Jewfish
Kahawai
Keeling
Koi carp
Lampern
Lamprey
Lampuki
Lantern
Lingcod

- Lobster
- Lyomeri
- Mahseer
- Matelot
- Medacca
- Merling
- Mojarra
- Moon-eye
- Morwong
- Muraena
- Oarfish
- Old-wife
- Oolakan
- Opaleye
- Osseter
- Oulakan
- Oulicon
- Panchax
- Pandora
- Peacock
- Pegasus
- Pigfish
- Pinfish
- Piranha
- Pollack
- Pomfret
- Pompano
- Ragfish
- Rasbora
- Ratfish
- Rat-tail
- Redfish
- Rorqual
- Roughie
- Sand dab
- Sardine
- Scalare
- Scallop
- Sculpin
- Sea-bass
- Sea-cock
- Sea-dace
- Sea-moth
- Sea-pike
- Sea-star
- Sea-wife
- Sevruga
- Sillock
- Silurid
- Skegger
- Skitter
- Snapper

Sock-eye
Sparoid
Speldin
Sterlet
Sunfish
Sunstar
Surgeon
Teleost
Tiddler
Tilapia
Titling
Torgoch
Torpedo
Tubfish
Ulichon
Vendace
Wall-eye
Whipray
Whistle
Whiting
Wide-gab

8 letters:
Albacore
Anableps
Arapaima
Asteroid
Atherine
Billfish
Blennius
Bloodfin
Blowfish
Blueback
Bluefish
Bluegill
Brisling
Bullhead
Bullhorn
Cabezone
Cabrilla
Carangid
Cardinal
Cavefish
Characid
Characin
Chimaera
Coalfish
Corkwing
Cucumber
Cyprinid
Dealfish
Dragonet

Drumfish
Eagle-ray
Escallop
Eulachon
Fallfish
Fighting
Filefish
Flathead
Flounder
Four-eyes
Frogfish
Ganoidei
Gillaroo
Gilthead
Goatfish
Gobiidae
Graining
Grayling
Hackbolt
Hair-tail
Half-beak
Hard-head
Holostei
Hornbeak
Hornpout
Kabeljou
Killfish
Kingfish
Kingklip
Kukukuma
Lionfish
Luderick
Lumpfish
Lungfish
Mackerel
Mahi-mahi
Mata Hari
Menhaden
Milkfish
Monkfish
Moonfish
Mosquito
Mulloway
Nannygai
Nennigai
Nine-eyes
Oulachon
Paradise
Patutuki
Pickerel
Pilchard
Pipefish

Pirarucu
Redbelly
Rock-cook
Rockfish
Rockling
Roncador
Rosefish
Saibling
Sailfish
Saltfish
Sardelle
Scabbard
Sciaenid
Scorpion
Scuppaug
Sea-devil
Seahorse
Sea-lemon
Sea-raven
Sea-robin
Sergeant
Serranus
Skipjack
Smear-dab
Snake-eel
Sparling
Spelding
Speldrin
Stenlock
Sting-ray
Stonecat
Sturgeon
Tarakihi
Tarwhine
Teraglin
Terakihi
Tile-fish
Toadfish
Trevally
Tropical
Tubenose
Tullibee
Weakfish
Whitling
Wolffish

9 letters:
Amberjack
Anchoveta
Barracuda
Blackfish
Butterfly

Carangoid
Cascadura
Ceratodus
Chaetodon
Chavender
Clingfish
Clupeidae
Coregonus
Coryphene
Devilfish
Gaspereau
Glassfish
Globefish
Goldfinny
Goldsinny
Golomynka
Goosefish
Greenbone
Greenling
Grenadier
Haberdine
Hornyhead
Hottentot
Houndfish
Ichthyoid
Jacksmelt
Jewelfish
Kabeljouw
Killifish
Labyrinth
Latimeria
Matelotte
Menominee
Mudhopper
Neon tetra
Pikeperch
Porbeagle
Porcupine
Quillback
Roussette
Scaldfish
Scalefish
Schnapper

Scorpaena
Selachian
Shubunkin
Siluridae
Slickhead
Snailfish
Snakehead
Snipefish
Spadefish
Spearfish
Speldring
Stargazer
Steenbras
Stingaree
Stockfish
Stonefish
Surfperch
Surmullet
Swellfish
Swordfish
Sword-tail
Thornback
Threadfin
Tittlebat
Topminnow
Trachinus
Troutfish
Trunkfish
Whitebait
White bass
Wreckfish

10 letters:
Barracoota
Barracouta
Barramunda
Bitterling
Bombay duck
Bottlehead
Butterfish
Candlefish
Cockabully
Cornetfish

Cyclostome
Damselfish
Demoiselle
Dollarfish
Etheostoma
Fingerling
Flutemouth
Groundling
Horned pout
Lumpsucker
Maskalonge
Maskanonge
Maskinonge
Midshipman
Mossbunker
Mudskipper
Needlefish
Nurse-hound
Rabbitfish
Red emperor
Red-snapper
Ribbonfish
Rudderfish
Scopelidae
Sea-poacher
Sea-surgeon
Serrasalmo
Sheepshead
Ship-holder
Shovelnose
Silverside
Springfish
Squeteague
Teleostome
Titarakura
Tripletail
Yellowtail

11 letters:
Chondrostei
Dolly Varden
Istiophorus
Lapidosteus

Lepidosiren
Lophobranch
Maskallonge
Moorish idol
Muskellunge
Ostracoderm
Oxyrhynchus
Plagiostome
Plectognath
Scolopendra
Seventy-four
Soldierfish
Stickleback
Stoneroller
Surgeonfish
Triggerfish
Trumpetfish
Water souchy
Yellowbelly

12 letters:
Ballan-wrasse
Elasmobranch
Father-lasher
Heterosomata
Histiophorus
Mangrove Jack
Miller's thumb
Mouthbreeder
Orange roughy
Plectognathi
Rainbow-trout
Squirrelfish

13 letters:
Leatherjacket
Musselcracker
Sailor's choice
Sergeant Baker

15 letters:
Crossopterygian

Fisher(man) Ahab, Andrew, Angler, Black cat, Caper, Codder, Dragman, High-liner, Liner, Pedro, Peter, Piscator, Rodster, Sharesman, Walton
▸ **Fisherwoman** *see* FISHSELLER
Fish-hawk Osprey
Fishing-ground Haaf
Fishing-line G(u)imp, Gymp, Paternoster
Fishpond Ocean, Stew, Vivarium
Fishseller, Fisherwoman Fishwife, Molly Malone, Ripp(i)er, Shawley, Shawlie

Fishy Botargo, Suspicious, Vacant

Fission Multiple, Nuclear

Fissure Chasm, Cleft, Crack, Crevasse, Crevice, Gap, Grike, Gryke, Lode, Rent, Rolando, Sand-crack, Scam, Sylvian, Sylvius, Vallecula, Vein, Zygon

Fist Clench, Dukes, Hand, Iron, Join-hand, Mailed, Neaf(fe), Neif, Neive, Nief, Nieve, Pud, Punch, Thump

Fit(s), Fitful, Fitting(s), Fitness Able, Access, Adapt, Ague, Appointment, Appropriate, Apropos, Apt, Babbitt, Bout, Canto, Capable, Cataleptic, Cataplexy, Click, Concinnous, Condign, Congruous, Conniption, Convulsion, Culver-tail, Darwinian, Decent, Decorous, Desultory, Dod, Dove-tail, Due, Eclampsia, Egal, Eligible, Ensconce, Epilepsy, Equip, Exies, Expedient, Fairing, Fay, Fiddle, Furniment, Furnishing, Fytte, Gee, Germane, Habile, Hale, Hang, Health, Hinge, Huff, Hysterics, Ictus, Inclusive, In-form, Interference, Intermittent, In trim, Just, Kashrut(h), Lune, Marry, Mate, Meet, Mood, Nest, Paroxysm, Passus, Pertinent, Prepared, Press, > **PROPER**, Queme, Ready, Rig, Rind, Ripe, Rynd, Seemly, Seizure, Set, Shrink, Sit, Snotter, Sort, Sound, Spasm, Spell, Start, Suit(able), Syncope, Tantrum, Throe, To prepon, Turn, Up to, Well, Wobbler, Wobbly, Worthy, Wrath

▷ **Fit(ting)** *may indicate* a 't'

Fitment Adaptor, Unit

Fitzgerald Edward, Ella, Scott

Five(s) Cinque, Mashie, Pallone, Pedro, Pentad, Quinary, Quintet, Sextan, Towns, V

Five years Lustre, Lustrum

Fix(ed), Fixer, Fixative Affeer, Anchor, Appoint, Appraise, > **ARRANGE**, Assess, Assign, Attach, Bind, Brand, Cement, Clamp, Clew, Clue, Constant, Corking-pin, Cure, Decide, Destinate, Destine, Determine, Do, Embed, Empight, Encastré, Engrain, Establish, Fast, Firm, Fit, Freeze, Gammon, Hold, Hypo(sulphite), Immutable, Impaction, Imprint, Inculcate, Ingrain, Jag, Jam, Locate, Lodge, Nail, Name, Narcotic, Nobble, Orientate, Peg, Persistent, Pin, Point, Quantify, Repair, Resolute, Rig, Rigid, Rivet, Rove, Rut, Scrape, Screw, Seat, Seize, Set, Settle, Ship, Shoo, Skatole, Skewer, Splice, Stage, Staple, Static, Stell, Step, Stew, Stuck, Tie, Valorize, Weld

Fixture Attachment, Event, Match, Permanence, Rawlplug®, Unit

Fizz(ed), Fizzy Buck's, Effervesce, Gas, Hiss, Pop, Sherbet, Sod, Soda

Fizzle Failure, Flop, Hiss, Washout

▸ **Fjord** *see* **FIORD**

Flabbergast(ed) Amaze, Astound, Floor, Thunderstruck

Flabby Flaccid, Lank, Lax, Limp, Pendulous, Saggy

Flaccid Flabby, Lank, Limp, Soft

Flag(gy), Flags Acorus, Ancient, Ashlar, Banderol, Banner, Black, Blackjack, Blue (ensign), Blue Peter, Bunting, Burgee, Calamus, Chequered, Colour(s), Dan(n)ebrog, Decline, Droop, Duster, Ensign, Fail, Falter, Fane, Fanion, Field colours, Gladdon, Gonfalon, Green, Guidon, Hail, Hoist, Irideal, Iris, Jack, Jade, Jolly Roger, Kerbstone, Languish, Lis, Old Glory, Orris, Pave(ment), Pavilion, Pencel, Pennant, Pennon, Penoncel(le), Pensel, Pensil, Peter, Pilot, Pin, Prayer, Quarantine, Rag, Red, Red Duster, Red Ensign, Sag, Sedge, Semaphore, Sick, Sink, Slab(stone), Slack, Standard, Stars and bars, Stars and stripes, Streamer, Tire, Tricolour, Union (Jack), Vane, Vexillology, Waif, Whift, White (ensign), Wilt, Wither, Yellow (Jack)

Flagday Tagday

Flagellate Beat, Mastigophora, Scourge, Trypanosome, Whip

Flagon Bottle, Carafe, Jug, Stoop, Stoup, Vessel
Flagpole Pin, Staff
Flagrant Egregious, Glaring, Heinous, Patent, Wanton
Flagship Admiral, Victory
Flail Beat, Drub, Swingle, Swip(p)le, Threshel
Flair Art, Bent, Elan, Gift, Knack, Panache, Style, > TALENT
Flak AA, Attack, Criticism
Flake Chip, Flame, Flaught, Flaw, Floccule, Flocculus, Fragment, Peel, Scale, Smut, Snow
Flam Impose
Flamboyant Baroque, Brilliant, Florid, Garish, Grandiose, Ornate, Ostentatious, Paz(z)azz, Piz(z)azz, Swash-buckler
Flame, Flaming Ardent, Blaze, Fire, Flake, Flambé, Flammule, Glow, Kindle, Leman, Lover, Lowe, Musical, Olympic, Oxyacetylene, Sensitive, Sweetheart
Flan Pastry, Quiche, Tart
Flanders Mare, Moll
Flange Border, Collar, Collet, Lip, Rim
Flank(s) Accompany, Anta, Flange, Flitch, Ilia, Lisk, Loin, Side, Spur
Flannel Blather, Canton, Cloth, Cotton, Face, Outing, Soft-soap, Waffle, Zephyr
Flap(ped), Flapper, Flapping Agnail, Aileron, Alar, Alarm(ist), Aventail(e), Bate, Beat, Bird, Bobbysoxer, Bustle, Chit, Dither, Elevon, Epiglottis, Fipple, Flacker, Flaff, Flag, Flaught, Flutter, Fly, Fuss, Giglet, Giglot, Hover, > IN A FLAP, Labium, Labrum, Lapel, Loma, Louvre, Lug, Operculum, Panic, Spin, Spoiler, Tab, Tag, Tailboard, Tailgate, Tiswas, To-do, Tongue, TRAM, Volucrine, Wave, Whisk
Flare(d), Flare up Bell, Fishtail, Flame, Flanch, Flaunch, Godet, Magnesium, Scene, Signal, Solar, Spread, Spunk, Ver(e)y, Widen
Flash(y), Flasher Coruscate, Cursor, Electronic, Essex man, Fire-flag, Flare, Flaught, Fulgid, Fulgural, Garish, Gaudy, Glaik, Gleam, Glisten, Glitzy, Green, Green ray, Helium, Indicate, Instant, Jay, Lairy, Levin, Lightning, Loud, Magnesium, Meretricious, Mo, Ostentatious, Photopsy, Raffish, Ribbon, Ring, Roary, Scintillation, Second, Sequin, Showy, Sluice, Snazzy, Spark, Streak, Strobe, Swank(e)y, Tick, Tigrish, Trice, Twinkle, Vivid, Wire
▷ **Flashing** *may indicate* an anagram
Flask(-shaped) Ampulla, Aryballos, Bottle, Canteen, Carafe, Conceptacle, Costrel, Cucurbit, Dewar, Erlenmeyer, Fiasco, Flacket, Flacon, Florence, Goatskin, Hip, Lekythos, Matrass, Mick(e)(y), Pocket-pistol, Powder, Reform, Retort, Thermos®, Vacuum, Vial
Flat(s), Flatten(ed), Flattener Ancipital, Apartment, Bachelor, Bald, Banal, Beat, Bed-sit, Blow-out, Bulldoze, Callow, Complanate, Compress, Condominium, Corymb(ose), Cottage, Coulisse, Dead, Demolish, Dorsiventral, Double, Dress, Dull, Even, Feeble, Flew, Floor, Flue, Fool, Gaff, Garden, Granny, Guyot, Haugh, High-rise, Homaloid, Home-unit, Horizontal, Insipid, Ironed, Jacent, Key, KO, Law, Level, Lifeless, Llano, Marsh, Monotonous, Mud, Nitwit, Norfolk, Oblate, Pad, Pancake, Pedestrian, Peneplain, Peneplane, Penthouse, Pentice, Pied-à-terre, Plain, Planar, Plane, Planish, Plat, Plateau, Press, Prone, Prostrate, Recumbent, Rooms, Salt, Scenery, Service, Smooth, Splayfoot, Spread-edged, Squash, Studio, Tableland, Tabular, Tame, Tasteless, Tenement, True, Vapid, Walk-up
Flat-chested Cithara
Flat-faced Socle
Flat-foot(ed) Policeman, Splay
Flat-nosed Camus

Flatter(ing), **Flatterer**, **Flattery** Adulate, Becoming, Beslaver, Blandish, Blarney, Bootlick, Butter, Cajole, Candied, Carn(e)y, Claw(back), Complimentary, Comprabatio, Earwiggy, En beau, Eyewash, Fawn, Fillibrush, Flannel, Flannen, Fleech, Flummery, Fulsome, Gloze, Gnathonic(al), Honey, Imitation, Lip-salve, Moody, Palp, Phrase, Poodle-faker, Proneur, Puffery, Sawder, Smarm, Snow job, Soap, Soft soap, Soother, Souk, Spaniel, Stroke, Sugar, Sweet talk, Sycophant, Taffy, Toady, Treacle, Unction, Wheedle, Word

Flatulence Belch, Borborygmus, Burp, Carminative, Colic, Gas, Wind

Flaunt Brandish, Flourish, Gibe, Parade, Skyre, Strout, Strut, Wave

Flavour(ed), **Flavouring** Absinth(e), Alecost, Anethole, Angostura, Anise, Aniseed, Aroma, Benne, Bold, Borage, Bouquet garni, Clove, Coriander, Cumin, Dill, Essence, Fenugreek, Flor, Garlic, Garni, Gingili, Marinate, Mint, Orgeat, Piperonal, Quark, Race, Ratafia, Relish, Rocambole, Sair, Sassafras, Sesame, Tack, Tang, Tarragon, > TASTE, Til, Tincture, Twang, Vanilla

Flaw Blemish, Brack, Bug, Chip, Crack, Defect, Fallacy, > FAULT, Gall, Hamartia, Imperfection, Kink, Knothole, Lophole, Red-eye, Rima, Spot, Taint, Tear, Thief, Tragic, Windshake

Flawless Impeccable

Flax(en) Aleseed, Blonde, Codilla, Harden, Hards, Herden, Herl, Hurden, Line, Linseed, Lint, Lint-white, Linum, Mill-mountain, Poi, Tow

Flay Excoriate, Fleece, Flense, Scourge, Skin, Strip, Uncase, Whip

Flea Aphaniptera, Chigger, Chigoe, Chigre, Daphnid, Hopper, Itch-mite, Lop, Pulex, Sand, Turnip, Water

Flea-bane Erigeron

Fleabite Denier

Fleck Dash, Freak, Spot, Streak

Fledgling Aerie, Eyas, Sorage

Flee Abscond, Bolt, Decamp, Escape, Eschew, Fly, Lam, Loup, Run, Scapa, Scarper, Scram

Fleece, **Fleecy** Bleed, Coat, Despoil, Flocculent, Golden, Jib, Lambskin, Lanose, Pash(i)m, Pashmina, Plot, Pluck, Rifte, Ring, Rob, Rook, Shave, Shear, Sheepskin, Skin, > SWINDLE, Toison

Fleer Ogle

Fleet(ing) Armada, Brief, Camilla, Ephemeral, Evanescent, Fast, First, Flit, Flota, Flotilla, Fugacious, Fugitive, Hasty, Hollow, Lightfoot, Navy, Pacy, Passing, Prison, Spry, Street, Transient, Velocipede

Flesh(y) Beefy, Body, Carneous, Carrion, Corporeal, Corpulent, Creatic, Dead-meat, Digastric, Finish, Goose, Gum, Hypersarcoma, Joint, Longpig, Lush, Meat, Mons, Mummy, Muscle, Proud, Pulp, Sarcous, Spare tyre, Tissue

Flesh-eating Cannibalism, Carnassial, Creophagus, Omophagic

Fleshless Dry, Maigre, Pem(m)ican

Flex(ible), **Flexibility** Adaptable, Bend(y), Compliant, Double-jointed, Elastic, Genu, Limber, Lissom(e), Lithe, Pliant, > RESILIENT, Rubato, Rubbery, Squeezy, Supple, Tensile, Tonus, Wieldy, Willing, Wiry

▷ **Flexible**, **Flexuous** *may indicate* an anagram

Flick(er), **Flicks** Bioscope, Cinema, Fillip, Film, Flip, Flirt, Flutter, Glimmer, Gutter, Movie, Movy, Snap, Snow, Spang-cockle, Switch, Talkie, Twinkle, Waver

Flickertail ND

Flier Aerostat, Airman, Alcock, Amy, Aviator, Bleriot, Blimp, Brown, Crow, Daedalus, Erk, Fur, George, Gotha, Handout, Icarus, Leaflet, Lindbergh, Montgolfier, Pilot, RAF, Scotsman, Spec, Speedy

▷ **Flier** *may indicate* a bird

Flight(y) Backfisch, Birdbrain, Bolt, Bubble-headed, Capricious, Charter, Contact, Dart, Departure, Escalier, Escape, Exaltation, Exodus, Fast, Fickle, Flaught, Flibbertigibbet, Flip, Flock, Flyby, Fly-past, Free, Fugue, Giddy, Grese, Gris(e), Guy, Hegira, Hejira, Hejra, Hellicat, Hijra, Lam, Mercy, Milk-run, Mission, Open-jaw, Pair, R(a)iser, Redeye, Ro(a)ding, Rode, Rout, Skein, Sortie, Stairs, > **STAMPEDE**, Stayre, Steps, Swarm, Test, Top, Tower, Trap, Vol(age), Volatile, Volley, Whisky-frisky, Wing

Flightless Kakapo, Ostrich, Rhea, Struthious

▷ **Flighty** *may indicate* an anagram

Flimsy Finespun, Gimcrack, Gossamer, Jimcrack, Lacy, Sleazy, Sleezy, Tenuous, Thin, Weak, Wispy

Flinch Blench, Cringe, Funk, Quail, Recoil, Shrink, Shudder, Start, Wince

Fling Dance, Flounce, Highland, Hurl, Pitch, Shy, Slat, Slug, Slump, Spanghew, Spree, Throw, > **TOSS**

Flint Chert, Firestone, Granite, Hag-stone, Hornstone, Microlith, Mischmetal, Optical, Pirate, Rock, Silex, Silica, Stone, Touchstone

Flip(pant), Flipping Airy, Bally, Brash, Cocky, Flick, Frivolous, Impudent, Jerk, Nog, Pert, Purl, Sassy, Saucy, Toss, Turn

Flipper(s) Fin-toed

Flirt(ation), Flirting, Flirtatious Bill, Buaya, Carve, Chippy, Cockteaser, Come-hither, Come-on, Coquet(te), Dalliance, Demivierge, Footsie, Gallivant, Heart-breaker, Lumber, Mash, Minx, Neck, Philander(er), Prick-teaser, Rig, Toy, Trifle, Vamp, Wow

Flit Dart, Decamp, Flicker, Flutter, Moonlight, Scoot

Float(er), Floating, Flotation Balsa, Bob, Buoy, Caisson, Camel, Carley, Clanger, Drift, Fleet, Flotsam, Flutterboard, Froth, Fucus, Jetsam, Jetson, Levitate, Lifebuoy, Milk, Natant, Neuston, Oropesa, Outrigger, Planula, Pontoon, Pram, Quill, Raft, Ride, Sail, Skim, Sponson, Stick, Trimmer, Vacillate, Waft, Waggler, Waterwings

Floating garden Chinampa

Flock(s) Assemble, Bevy, Charm, Chirm, Company, Congregation, Drove, Flight, Fold, Forgather, Gaggle, Gather, Gregatim, Herd, Mob, Rally, Sedge, Sord, Spring, Trip, Troop, Tuft, Vulgar, Wing, Wisp, Wool

Flog(ger), Flogging Beat, Birch, Breech, Cane, Cat, Exert, Flay, Hawk, Hide, Knout, Lace, Lambast, Larrup, Lash, Lather, Lick, Orbilius, Rope's end, Scourge, Sell, Strap, Tat, > **THRASH**, Thwack, Tout, Vapulate, Welt, Whip

Flood(ed) Awash, Bore, Cataclysm, Deluge, Deucalion's, Diffuse, Diluvium, Drown, Dump, Eger, Flash, Freshet, Gush, Inundate, Irrigate, Noachic, Overflow, Overwhelm, Pour, Rage, Smurf, Spate, Speat, Swamp, Tide, > **TORRENT**, Undam

Floodgate St(a)unch

Floodlight Ashcan, Blond(e), One-key

Floor(ing) Area, Astound, Baffle, Barbecue, Beat, Benthos, Chess, Deck, Dev(v)el, Down, Entresol, Etage, Fell, Flags(tone), Flatten, Flight, Gravel, Ground, Kayo, KO, Mezzanine, Parquet, Pelvic, Piano nobile, Pit, Planch, Platform, Puncheon, Screed, Shop, Stage, Story, Stump, Terrazzo, Tessella, Tessera, Thill, Woodblock

Flop Belly-landing, Bomb, Collapse, Dud, Failure, Fizzer, Fosbury, Lollop, Mare's-nest, Misgo, Phut, Plump, Purler, Washout, Whap, Whitewash

Flora Benthos, Biota, Cybele, Flowers, Intestinal

Florence, Florentine Tuscan

Florid Coloratura, Cultism, Flamboyant, Fresh, Gongorism, High, Red, Rococo, Rubicund, Ruddy, Taffeta

Florida Fa

Floss(y) Dental, Flashy, Florence, Ornate, Silk

▶ **Flotation** *see* FLOAT

Flotilla Armada, Escadrille

Flotsam Detritus, Driftwood, Flotage, Waift, Waveson, Weft

Flounce Falbala, Frill, Furbelow, Huff, Prance, Ruffle, Sashay, Toss

Flounder Blunder, Fluke, Reel, Slosh, Struggle, Stumble, Tolter, Toss, Wallow

Flour Cassava, Couscous(ou), Cribble, Crible, Farina, Graham, Gram, Kouskous, Meal, Middlings, Pinole, Plain, Powder, Red-dog, Rock, Rye, Self-raising, Soy(a), Wheatmeal, White, Wholegrain, Wholemeal, Wholewheat, Wood

Flourish(ed), Flourishing Blague, Bless, Bloom, Blossom, Boast, Brandish, Bravura, Burgeon, Cadenza, Epiphonema, Fanfare, Fiorita, Fl, Flare, Floreat, Grow, Kicking, Lick, Melisma, Mort, Omar, Palmy, Paraph, Prosper, Rubric, Scroll, Swash, Tantara, Thrive, Tucket, Veronica, Vigorous, Wampish, Wave, Welfare

Flout Disdain, Disobey, Insult, Malign, Mock, Profane, Scorn, Scout

Flow(ing) Abound, Afflux, Cantabile, Cash, Current, Cursive, Cusec, Distil, Ebb, Emanate, Estrang(h)elo, Fleet, Fluent, Fluid, Flush, Flux, Freeform, Gene, Gush, Knickpoint, Laminar, Liquid, Loose-bodied, Nappe, Nickpoint, Obsequent, Onrush, Ooze, Popple, Pour, Purl, Rail(e), Rayle, Rill, Rin, Run, Scapa, Seamless, Setter, Slip, Slur, Spate, Spurt, Stream, Streamline, Teem, Tidal, Torrent, Trickle, Turbulent, Viscous

Flower (part), Flowering, Flowers, Flower bed Best, Bloom, Bloosme, Blossom, Cream, Develop, Efflorescence, Elite, Inflorescence, Parterre, Passion, Plant, Pre-vernal, Prime, Remontant, > RIVER, Spray, Square, Stalked, Stream, Trumpet, Vernal, Wreath

● **FLOWERS**
●
●

● **4 letters:**	Daisy	Gollan	Alyssum
● Arum	Enemy	Henbit	Anemone
● Cyme	Hosta	Madder	Astilbe
● Disc	Padma	Maguey	Bugloss
● Flag	Phlox	Nuphar	Campion
● Gold	Poppy	Onagra	Cowslip
● Gool	Spink	Orchid	Freesia
● Gule	Tansy	Paeony	Fumaria
● Irid	Toran	Pompom	Gentian
● Iris	Tulip	Pompon	Gilt-cup
● Knot	Umbel	Protea	Glacier
● Lily	Yulan	Scilla	Gladdon
● Pink		Sesame	Godetia
● Rose	**6 letters:**	Silene	Golland
●	Adonis	Smilax	Gowland
● **5 letters:**	Arabis	Spadix	Ipomoea
● Agave	Camash	Tassel	Kikumon
● Aster	Camass	Torana	Melilot
● Brook	Corymb		Nosegay
● Bugle	Crants	**7 letters:**	Petunia
● Camas	Dahlia	Aconite	Picotee

- Quamash
- Rampion
- Sulphur
- Verbena
-
- **8 letters:**
- Abutilon
- Amaranth
- Argemone
- Asphodel
- Bindi-eye
- Bluebell
- Carolina
- Clematis
- Cyclamen
- Daffodil
- Floscule
- Foxglove
- Gardenia
- Geranium
- Gillyvor
- Glory-pea

Hepatica
Hibiscus
Kok-sagyz
Larkspur
Leucojum
Magnolia
Marigold
Myosotis
Oleander
Primrose
Scabious
Stapelia
Trollius
Tuberose
Turnsole
Valerian

9 letters:
Bald-money
Belamoure
Buttercup
Columbine

Edelweiss
Eglantine
Galingale
Gessamine
Hellebore
Hydrangea
Jessamine
Melampode
Pimpernel
Rudbeckia
Santonica
Saxifrage
Speedwell
Strobilus

10 letters:
Bellamoure
Buttonhole
Coronation
Granadilla
Heliotrope
Immortelle

Nasturtium
Pentstemon
Poinsettia
Snapdragon
Stavesacre
Tibouchine
Touch-me-not

11 letters:
Boutonniere
Bur-marigold
Gillyflower
Loose-strife
Meadow-sweet

12 letters:
Hortus siccus
None-so-pretty
Tradescantia

▷ **Flower** *may indicate* a river
Flower arrangement, Flower work Barbola, Ikebana, Lei
Flowery Anthemia, Damassin, Orchideous, > ORNATE, Pseudocarp, Verbose
Flu Asian, Gastric, Grippe, Lurgi, Yuppie
Fluctuate(r), Fluctuation Ambivalence, Balance, Seiche, Trimmer, Unsteady, Vacillate, Vary, Waver
Flue Chimney, Duct, Funnel, Pipe, Tewel, Uptake, Vent
Fluent(ly) Eloquent, Facile, Flowing, Glib, Liquid, Oracy, Verbose, Voluble
Fluff(y) Bungle, Dowl(e), Down, Dust, Feathery, Flocculent, Floss, Flue, Fug, Fuzz, Girl, Lint, Mess-up, Muff, Noil, Oose, Ooze, Thistledown
Fluid Amniotic, Anasarca, Ascites, Broo, Chyle, Cisterna, Colostrum, Condy's, Coolant, Edema, Enema, Fixative, Fl, Humour, Joint-oil, Juice, Latex, > LIQUID, Lymph, Movable, Mucus, Oedema, Perfect, Perilymph, Plasma, Sap, Seminal, Serous, Serum, Shifting, Spermatic, Spittle, Succus, Synovia, Vitreum, Vril, Water
▷ **Fluid** *may indicate* an anagram
Fluke Accident, Anchor, Chance, Fan, Flounder, Ga(u)nch, Grapnel, Killock, Liver, Lobe, Redia, Schistosome, Scratch
Flummox Baffle, Bamboozle, Floor, Nonplus
Flunk Fail
Flunkey Chasseur, Clawback, Haiduck, Heyduck, Jeames, Lackey, Servant, Toady
Fluorescence, Fluorescent Bloom, Day-glo, Epipolism, Glow, Phosphorescence
Fluorine F
Flurry Bustle, Fluster, Haste, Hoo-ha, Shower
Flush(ed) Affluent, Beat, Busted, Even, Ferret, Florid, Flow, Gild, Hectic, Heyday, Hot, Level, Red, Rolling, Rose, Royal, Rud, Scour, Sluice, Spaniel, Start, Straight, Sypher, Thrill, Tierce, Vigour, Wash
Fluster Befuddle, Confuse, Disconcert, Faze, Flap, Pother, Rattle, Shake

Flute (player) Bellows-maker, Bohm, Channel, Claribel(la), Crimp, Fife, Fipple, Flageolet, German, Glass, Glyph, Groove, Marsyas, Nose, Ocarina, Piccolo, Pipe, Poogye(e), Quena, Shakuhachi, Sulcus, Thisbe, Tibia, Toot, Transverse, Whistle

Flutter Bat, Bet, Fan, Fibrillate, Flacker, Flaffer, Flaught, Flichter, Flicker, Flitter, Fly, > GAMBLE, Hover, Palpitate, Play, Pulse, Sensation, Twitter, Waft, Winnow

Flux D, Electric, Flow, Fusion, Luminous, Magnetic, Maxwell, Melt, Neutron, Panta rhei, Radiant, Tesla, Weber

Fly(ing), Flies Abscond, Agaric, Airborne, Alder, Alert, Antlion, Assassin, Astute, Aviation, Awake, A-wing, Baker, Bedstead, Bee, Blister, Blowfly, Blue-arsed, Bluebottle, Bolt, Bot, Breese, Breeze, Brize, Brommer, Bulb, Bush, Cab, Caddis, Carriage, Carrot, Cecidomyia, Chalcid, Cheesehopper, Cheese skipper, Cleg, Cluster, Cock-a-bondy, Crane, Cuckoo, > CUNNING, Decamp, Deer, Diptera, Dobson, Doctor, Dolphin, Doodlebug, Dragon, Drake, Drone, Drosophila, Dry, Dung, Dutchman, Escape, Face, Fiacre, Flee, Flesh, Flit, Fox, Frit, Fruit, Glide, Glossina, Gnat, Grannom, Greenbottle, Greenhead, Hackle, Harvest, Hedge-hop, Hessian, Homoptera, Hop, Horn, Horse, Hover, Hurtle, Ichneumon, Instrument, Jenny-spinner, Jock Scott, Lace-wing, Lamp, Lantern, Laputan, March brown, Mosquito, Moth, Motuca, Murragh, Musca, Mutuca, Needle, New Forest, Nymph, Onion, Opening, Ox-warble, Palmer, Para, Pilot, Pium, Plecopteran, Pomace, Rapid, Robber, Saucer, Sciaridae, Scorpion, Scotsman, Screwworm, Scud, Sedge, Silverhorn, Simulium, Smart, Smother, Snake, Snipe, Soar, Spanish, Speed, Spinner, Stable, Stream, Syrphidae, Tabanid, Tachina, Tear, Thrips, Tipula, Trichopteran, Tsetse, Tube, Turkey brown, Vamoose, Vinegar, Volatic, Volitate, Warble, Watchet, Water, Welshman's button, Wet, Wheat, Wide-awake, Willow, Wily, Wing, Yellow sally, Yogic, Zebub, Zimb, Zipper

Fly-catcher Attercop, Cobweb, Darlingtonia, Dionaea, King-bird, Phoebe, Spider, Tanrec, Tyrant

Flying-fox Fruit-bat, Kalong

Flying saucer UFO

Fly-killer Chowri, Chowry, DDT, Swat

Foam(ing) Barm, Bubble, Froth, Lather, Mousse, Oasis®, Polystyrene, Ream, Scum, Seethe, Spindrift, Spooming, Spume, Sud(s), Surf, Wake, Wild water, Yeast, Yest

Fob Chain, Defer, Fub, Pocket, Slang

Focal, Focus Centre, Converge, Fix, Hinge, Hub, Narrow, Pinpoint, Point, Prime, Principal, Spotlight, Train

Fodder Alfalfa, Browsing, Buckwheat, Cannon, Clover, Eatage, Emmer, Ensilage, Foon, Forage, Gama-grass, Grama, Guar, Hay, Lucerne, Oats, Oilcake, Pasture, Provender, Rye-grass, Sainfoin, Silage, Soilage, Stover

Foe Contender, > ENEMY, Opponent, Rival

Foetus Embryo

Fog Aerosol, Brume, Cloud, Damp, Fret, Haar, (London) Particular, Miasm(a), Mist, Murk, Obscure, Pea-soup(er), Roke, Sea-fret, Sea-haar, Smog, Smoke, Soup, Thick, Vapour, Yorkshire

Fogey Die-hard

Fogg Phileas, Solicitor

Foible Failing, Flaw, Idiosyncrasy, Quirk, Weakness

Foil(ed) Ba(u)lk, Chaff, Cross, Dupe, Epée, Fleurette, Frustrate, Gold, Lametta, Leaf, Offset, Paillon, Pip, Scotch, Scupper, Silver, Stooge, Stump, Tain, Thwart, Touché

Foist Fob, Insert, Suborn, Wish

Fold(er), Folding, Folded, Folds Anticline, Bend, Binder, Close, Collapse, Concertina, Convolution, Corrugate, Cote, Crash, Crease, Crimp, Crinkle, Crunkle, Diapir, Diptych, Dog-ear, Double, Duo-tang®, Epicanthus, Epiploon, Fake, Fan, File, Fr(a)enum, Frill, Furl, Gather, Groin, Gyrus, Jack-knife, Lap, Lapel, Lap(p)et, Lirk, Mesentery, Monocline, Nappe, Nympha, Obvolute, Octuple, Omentum, Origami, Pastigium, Pen, Pericline, Pintuck, Pleach, > PLEAT, Plica, Plunging, Ply, Pran(c)k, Prancke, Ptyxis, Recumbent, Ruck(le), Ruga, Sheep-pen, Syncline, Triptych, Tuck, Vocal, Wrap

Foliage Coma, Finial, Frond, Greenery, Leafage

Folio(s) Elephant, F(f), File, Percy

Folk(sy) Beaker, Homespun, Kin, People, Public

Follicle Graafian

Follow(er), Following Adhere, After, Agree, And, Anthony, Attend(ant), Believer, Clientele, Consequence, Copy, Dangle, Disciple, Dog, Echo, Ensew, Ensue, Entourage, Epigon(e), Equipage, F, Fan, Groupie, Heel(er), Henchman, Hereon, Hunt, Man, Merry men, Muggletonian, Myrmidon, Neist, Next, Obey, Pan, Post, Pursue, Rake, Road, Run, Satellite, School, Secundum, Seewing, Segue, Sequel, Seriation, Servitor, Shadow, Sheep, Sidekick, Stag, Stalk, Stear, Steer, Subsequent, Succeed, Sue, Suivez, Supervene, Tag, Tail, Tantony, Trace, Track, Trail, Train, Use, Vocation, Votary

▷ **Follower** 'a follower' *may indicate* B

Folly Antic, Bêtise, Idiocy, Idiotcy, Imprudence, Lunacy, Mistake, Moria, Unwisdom, Vanity

Foment(ation) Arouse, Brew, Embrocation, Excite, Poultice, Stupe

Fond(ness) Amatory, Ardour, Dote, Keen, Loving, Partial, Penchant, Tender, Tendre

Fondant Ice, Sweet

Fondle Canoodle, Caress, Dandle, Grope, Hug, Nurse, Pet, Snuggle

Font Aspersorium, Bénitier, Delubrum, Ennage, Source

Food Aliment, Ambrosia, Bakemeat, Balti, Batten, Battill, Battle, Bellytimber, Board, Bolus, Bord, Broth, Browse, Bully, Burger, Cate, Chametz, Cheer, Cheese, Chop, Chow, Chuck, Chyme, Cocoyam, Collation, Comestible, Comfort, Commons, Convenience, Course, Curd, Deutoplasm, Dietetics, > DISH, Dodger, Dog's body, Dunderfunk, Eats, Esculents, Eutrophy, Falafel, Fare, Fast, Fast casual, Felafel, Fodder, Forage, Frankenstein, Freedom, Fuel, Functional, Grub, Hangi, Hometz, Incaparina, Ingesta, Jootha, Jorts, Junk, Kai, Keep, Langar, Leben, Lerp, Long-pig, Maigre, Manna, Mato(o)ke, Matzoon, Meal, Meat, Muckamuck, Nacho, Nardoo, Nosebag, Nosh, Nourishment, Nourriture, Oven-ready, Pabulum, Pannage, Pap, Parev(e), Parve, Pasta, Peck, Pemmican, Pizza, Prog, Provender, Provision, Ration(s), Rysttafel, Sambal, Sap, Sashimi, Scaff, Scoff, Sitology, Sizings, Skin, Slow, Snack, Soil, Soul, Staple, Stodge, Sushi, Table, Tack, Takeaway, Tamale, Taro, Tempura, Teriyake, Tofu, Trimmings, Trophallaxis, Tuck(er), Vegeburger, Veggie-burger, Viand, Victuals, Vivers, Waffle, Yantia, Yittles, Yog(h)urt

Food-plant Laser, Silphium

Foodstore Delicatessen, Grocery, Larder, Pantry, Silo

Fool(hardy), Foolish(ness) Air-head, Anserine, April, Assot, Berk, BF, Bob, Brainless, Brash, Buffoon, Cake, Capocchia, Chump, Clot, Clown, Cockeyed, Coxcomb, Cully, Daft, Dagonet, Daw, Delude, Dessert, Dummy, Dunce, Empty, Etourdi, Fatuous, Feste, Flannel(led), Fol, Fon, Fond, Fox, Gaby, Gaga, Galah, Git, Glaikit, Goat, Gobbo, Goon, Goose, Gooseberry, Groserts, Gubbins, Gull,

Gullible, Halfwit, Hanky-panky, Hare-brained, Highland, Huntiegowk, Hunt-the-gowk, Idiotic, Imbecile, Inane, Ineptitude, Injudicious, Jest, Joke, Kid, Kissel, Lark, Loon, Mamba, Mislead, Mome, Moron, Muggins, Niaiserie, Nignog, Ni(n)compoop, Ninny, Nong, Oanshagh, Omadhaun, Patch, Poop, Poupe, Punk, Rash, Sawney, Scogan, Scoggin, Senseless, Shallow, Snipe, Soft, Sot, Spoony, > **STUPID**, Sucker, Tom (noddy), Trifle, Unwitty, Vice, Wantwit, Yorick, Yoyo, Zany

Foolproof Fail-safe

Foot(ing), **Footwork**, **Feet** Amphibrach, Amphimace, Anap(a)est, Antibacchius, Antispast, Athlete's, Bacchius, Ball, Base, Choliamb, Choree, Choriamb, Club, Cold, Cretic, Dactyl, Dance, Dochmii, Dochmius, Epitrite, F, Hephthemimer, Hoof, Hoppus, Iamb(us), Immersion, Infantry, Ionic, Molossus, Ockodols, Pad, Paeon, Palama, Pastern, Paw, Pay, Pedate, Pedicure, Pes, Plates, Podium, Proceleusmatic, Pyrrhic, Roothold, Scazon, Semeia, Serif, Shanks's mare, Shanks's pony, Spade, Spondee, Standing, Syzygy, Tarsus, Terms, Tootsie, Tootsy, Tootsy-wootsy, Tread, Trench, Tribrach, Trilbies, Triseme, Trochee, Trotter, Tube, Verse, Wrong

Football(er) Aerial pingpong, Australian Rules, Back, Barbarian, Ba'spiel, Camp, Canadian, Centre, Fantasy, FIFA, Five-a-side, Flanker(back), Fly-half, Gaelic, Goalie, Gridder, Keeper, Kicker, League, Libero, Lineman, Lock, Midfield, Pack, Pele, Pigskin, RU, Rugby, Rugger, Rules, Safety, Seven-a-side, Sevens, Soccer(oos), Sport, Stand-off, Striker, Subbuteo®, Sweeper, Table, Tight-end, Togger, Total, Touch(back), Wallgame, Wing, Wingman

Footboard Stretcher

Foot-fault Bunion, Corn, Hammer-toe, Verruca

Foothold Lodgement, Purchase, Stirrup

Footlights Floats

Footloose Peripatetic

Footman Attendant, Flunkey, Lackey, Pedestrian, Pompey, Yellowplush

Footnote Addendum, PS

Footpad Land-rat, Mugger, Robber

Footpath, **Footway** Banquette, Catwalk, Clapper, Track

Footplate Horseshoe

Footprint Ecological, Ichnite, Ichnolite, Pad, Prick, Pug, Seal, Slot, Trace, Track, Tread, Vestige

Footrest, **Footstool** Coaster, Cricket, Hassock, Stirrup, Stool, Tramp

Footrot, **Footsore** Blister, Bunion, Corn, Halt, Surbate, Surbet, Weary, Wire-heel

Footslogger Infantryman

Footwashing Maundy, Nipter

Footwear Gumboot, > **SHOE**, Slipper, Sock, Spats, Stocking

Fop(pish) Apery, Barbermonger, Beau, Buck, Cat, Coxcomb, Dandy, Dude, Exquisite, Fallal, Fangled, Fantastico, Finical, La-di-da, Macaroni, Monarcho, Muscadin, Popinjay, Skipjack, Toff

For Ayes, Because, Concerning, Cos, Pro, Since, To

Forage Alfalfa, Fodder, Graze, Greenfeed, Ladino, Lucern(e), Pickeer, Prog, Raid, Rummage, Sainfoin, Search

Foray Attack, Creach, Creagh, Raid, Sortie, Spreagh

Forbear(ance), **Forbearing** Abstain, Clement, Endure, Indulgent, Lenience, Lineage, Longanimity, Mercy, Pardon, Parent, Patient, Quarter, > **REFRAIN**, Suffer, Tolerant, Withhold

Forbid(den), **Forbidding** Ban, Bar, City, Denied, Don't, Dour, Enjoin,

For(e)speak, Gaunt, Grim, Haram, Hostile, Loury, NL, Prohibit, Stern, Taboo, Tabu, Tapu, Tref(a), Verboten, Veto

Force(d), Forceful, Forces, Forcible Activist, Agency, Air-arm, Army, Back emf, Bathmism, Bind, Birr, Bludgeon, Body, Bounce, Brigade, Bring, Brunt, Bulldoze, Cadre, Capillary, Cascade, Centrifugal, Centripetal, Chi, Coerce, Cogency, Commando, Compel, Constrain, Coriolis, Cram, Delta, Detachment, Dint, Domineer, Downflow, Dragoon, Drive, Duress(e), Dynamic, Dyne, E, Edge, Electromotive, Emphatic, Energetic, Equilibrant, Erdgeist, Erg, Exchange, Expeditionary, Extort, Extrude, F, Farci, Fifth, Fire brigade, Frogmarch, G, Gar, Gendarmerie, Gilbert, Gism, Gouge, Gravitational, Hale, Host, Hurricane, Impetus, Impose, Impress, Inertial, Instress, Intense, Irgun, Irrupt, Jism, Juggernaut, Kinetic, Kundalini, Labour, Land, Lashkar, Legion, Life, Linn, Lorentz, Magnetomotive, Magnus, Make, Mana, Manpower, Market, Militia, Moment, Momentum, Muscle, Navy, Newton, Numen, Oblige, Od, Odyl(e), OGPU, Old Contemptibles, Orgone, Orotund, Personnel, Phrenism, Physical, Pigs, Pion, Pithy, Plastic, Police, Posse, Potent, Pound, Poundal, Prana, Press(gang), Pressure, Prise, Procrustean, Psyche, Pull, Put, Qi, Railroad, Rape, Ravish, Reave, Regular, Require, Restem, Route, Rush, SAS, Sforzando, Shear, Snorting, Spetsnaz, Squirt, Steam(roller), Stick, Stiction, Strained, > **STRESS**, Strong-arm, Subject, TA, Task, Telergy, Telling, Thrust, Torque, Tractive, Troops, Van der Waals', Vehement, Vigorous, Vim, Violence, Vires, Vis, Vis visa, Vital, Vively, Vociferous, Vril, Wrench, Wrest, Wring, Zap

▷ **Force(d)** *may indicate* an anagram

Forced labour Begar

Force-feeding Gavage

Forceps Bulldog, Capsule, Crow(s)bill, Hemostatic, Mosquito, Obstetrical, Pedicellaria, Pincers, Rongeur, Tenaculum, Thumb, Vulsella

Ford Anglia, Car, Crossing, Drift, Escort, Sierra, Strid, Tin Lizzy, Wade

Forearm Cubital, Radius, Ulna

▸ **Forebear** *see* **FORBEAR**

Foreboding Anxiety, Augury, Cloudage, Croak, Feeling, Freet, > **OMEN**, Ominous, Premonition, Presage, Presentiment, Sinister, Zoomantic

Forecast(er), Forecasting Augury, Auspice, Divine, Extrapolation, Horoscope, Metcast, Numerical, Perm, Portend, Precurse, Predict, Presage, Prescience, Prognosis, Prognosticate, Prophesy, Rainbird, Shipping, Soothsay, Spae, Tip, Weather

Foreclose Bar, Block, Obstruct, Preclude

Forefather(s) Ancestor, Elder, Forebear, Parent, Rude

Forefront Van

Forehead Brow, Front(let), Glabella(r), Sincipitum, Temple

Foreign(er) Alien, Amakwerekwere, Arab, Auslander, Barbarian, Easterling, Ecdemic, Eleanor, Ethnic, Exclave, Exotic, External, Extraneous, Extrinsic, Forane, Forinsecal, Forren, Fraim, Fremit, Gaijin, German, Gringo, Gweilo, Malihini, Metic, Moit, Mote, Outlander, Outside, Oversea, Peregrine, Remote, > **STRANGE**, Stranger, Taipan, Tramontane, Uitlander, Unfamiliar, Wog

Foreman Baas, Boss, Bosun, Chancellor, Gaffer, Ganger, Manager, Overseer, Steward, Superintendent, Topsman

Foremost First, Front, Leading, Primary, Prime, Supreme, Van

▷ **Foremost** *may indicate* first letters of words following

Forenoon Undern

Forepart Cutwater, Front

Forerunner Augury, Harbinger, Herald, Messenger, Omen, Pioneer, Precursor,

Prequel, Trailer, Vaunt-courier

Foresee Anticipate, Divine, Preview, Prophesy, Scry

Foreshadow Adumbrate, Augur, Bode, Forebode, Hint, Portend, Prefigure, Presage, Type

Foreshow Betoken, Bode, Signify

Foresight Ganesa, Prescience, Prophecy, Prospect, Providence, Prudence, Taish, Vision

Foreskin Prepuce

Forest(ry) Arden, Ashdown, Black, Bracknell, Bush, Caatinga, Charnwood, Chase, Cloud, Dean, Epping, Fontainebleau, Gallery, Gapo, Glade, Greenwood, Igapo, Jungle, Managed, Monte, Nandi, Nemoral, New, Petrified, Rain, Savernake, Selva, Sherwood, Silviculture, Taiga, Thuringian, Urman, Virgin, Waltham, > **WOOD**, Woodcraft

Forestall Anticipate, Head-off, Obviate, Pip, Pre-empt, Prevent, Queer, Scoop

Forester Foster, Lumberjack, Verderer, Walker, Woodman, Woodward

Foretaste Antepast, Antipasto, Appetiser, Pregustation, Prelibation, Preview, Sample, Trailer

Foretell(ing), Forewarn Augur, Bode, Caution, Divine, Fatidic, Forecast, Portend, Predict, Premonish, Presage, Prognosticate, Prophecy, Soothsay, Spae

Forethought Anticipation, Caution, Prometheus, Provision, Prudence

Forever Always, Amber, Ay(e), Eternal, Evermore, Keeps

▸ **Forewarn** *see* **FORETELL**

Foreword Introduction, Preamble, Preface, Proem, Prologue

For example Eg, Say, Vg, ZB

For fear Lest

Forfeit Deodand, Fine, Forgo, > **PENALTY**, Relinquish, Rue-bargain, Sconce

Forge(d), Forger(y) Blacksmith, Copy, Counterfeit, Drop, Dud, Fabricate, Fashion, Foundry, Hammer, Heater, Horseshoe, Ireland, Lauder, Mint, Paper-hanger, Pigott, Progress, Rivet-hearth, Smith(y), Smithery, Spurious, Stiff, Stithy, Stumer, Tilt, Trucage, Truquage, Utter, Valley, Vermeer, Vulcan

Forget(ful), Forget-me-not Amnesia, Dry, Fluff, Lethe, Myosotis, Neglect, Oblivious, Omit, Overlook

Forgive(ness), Forgiving Absolution, Amnesty, Clement, Condone, Merciful, Overlook, Pardon, Placable, Remission, Remittal

Forgo(ne) Abstain, Expected, Refrain, Renounce, Waive

Forgotten Bygone, Missed, Sad

Forjeskit Overscutched

Fork(ed) Bifurcate, Biramous, Branch, Caudine, Cleft, Crotch, Crutch, Divaricate, Forficate, Fourchette, Grain, Graip, Morton's, Osmeterium, Prong, Replication, Runcible, Sucket, Tine, Toaster, Tormenter, Tormentor, Trident, Trifid, Tuner, Tuning, Y

Forlorn(ness) Abject, Aidless, Desolate, Destitute, Drearisome, Miserable, Nightingale, Sad, Woebegone

Form(s) Alumni, Bench, Bumf, Cast, Ceremonial, Class, Constitute, Coupon, Create, Document, Dress, Experience, Fashion, Feature, Fig, > **FIGURE**, Formula, Free, Game, Gestalt, Hare, Image, Keto, Lexicalise, Logical, Mode, Mood, Morph(ic), Morphology, Mould, Order, Originate, > **OUT OF FORM**, P45, Physique, Protocol, Questionnaire, Redia, Remove, Rite, Ritual, Schedule, Shape, Shell, Stage, Stamp, State, Stereotype, Structure, Style, Symmetry, Ternary, Version

Formal Ceremonious, Conventional, Dry, Exact, Fit, Literal, Methodic, Official, Pedantic, Precise, Prim, Routine, Set, Solemn, Starched, Stiff, Stodgy, Tails

Formality Ceremony, Ice, Pedantry, Protocol, Punctilio, Starch
Formation Battalion, Configuration, Diapyesis, Echelon, Eocene, Fours, Growth, Line, Manufacture, Origin, Pattern, Phalanx, Prophase, Reaction, Riss, Wedge
▷ **Former** *may indicate* something that forms
Former(ly) Ance, Auld, Before, Ci-devant, Earlier, Ere-now, Erst(while), Ex, Late, Maker, Matrix, Old, Once, One-time, Past, Previous, Prior, Pristine, Quondam, Sometime, Then, Umquhile, Whilom
Formidable Alarming, Armipotent, Battleaxe, Fearful, Forbidding, Gorgon, Powerful, Shrewd, Stoor, Stour, Stowre, Sture, Tiger
Formless Amorphous, Invertebrate, Nebulous, Shapeless
▷ **Form of, Forming** *may indicate* an anagram
Formosan Tai
Formula(te) Define, Devise, Doctrine, Empirical, Equation, Frame, Incantation, Invent, Kekule, Lurry, Molecular, Paternoster, Prescription, Protocol, > RECIPE, Reduction, Rite, Ritual, Stirling's, Structural
Forsake Abandon, Desert, Quit, Renounce
Forsooth Certes, Certy, Even, Marry, Quotha
Forswear Abandon, Abjure, Disavow, Renounce, Reny
Forsyte Fleur, Saga
Fort(ification), Fortress Acropolis, Alamo, Alhambra, Balclutha, Bastille, Bastion, Battlement, Bawn, Blockhouse, Bonnet, Breastwork, Bridgehead, Burg, Casbah, Castellated, Castellum, Castle, Citadel, Contravallation, Crémaillère, Demilune, Deva, Dun, Earthwork, Edinburgh, Enceinte, Epaule, Escarpment, Fastness, Fieldwork, Flanker, Flèche, Fortalice, Fortilage, Fortlet, Fraise, Ft, Gabion(ade), Garrison, Golconda, Haven, Hedgehog, Hornwork, Kaim, Kame, Kasba(h), Keep, Knox, La(a)ger, Lauderdale, Louisbourg, Maiden, Malakoff, Martello tower, Masada, Merlon, Mile-castle, Moineau, Motte and bailey, Orillion, Pa(h), Peel, Pele, Pentagon, Place, Rampart, Rath, Ravelin, Redoubt, Reduit, Ring, Salient, Sallyport, Sangar, Sconce, Stronghold, Sumter, Talus, Tenaille, Terreplein, Tete-du-pont, Tower, Trench, Vallation, Vitrified, William, Worth
Forte F, Metier, Specialty, Strength
Forth Away, From, Hence, Out
Forthright Candid, Direct, Frank, Prompt
Forthwith Anon, Directly, Eft(soons), Immediately
Fortify Arm, Augment, Brace, Casemate, Embattle, Lace, Munify, Steel, > STRENGTHEN
Fortitude Endurance, Grit, Mettle, Patience, Pluck, > STAMINA
Fortunate Auspicious, Blessed, Blest, Godsend, Happy, > LUCKY, Opportune, Providential, Well
Fortune (teller), Fortune-telling Auspicious, Bonanza, Bumby, Cartomancy, Chaldee, Cha(u)nce, Destiny, Dukkeripen, Fame, Fate, Felicity, Genethliac, Geomancy, Hap, Hydromancy, I Ching, Lot, Luck, Mint, Motser, Motza, Oracle, Packet, Palmist, Peripety, Pile, Prescience, Pyromancy, Sibyl, Soothsayer, Sortilege, Spaewife, Success, Taroc, Tarok, Tarot, Tyche, Wealth, Windfall
Forty, Forties Capot, F, Hungry, Kemple, Roaring
Forty-ninth Parallel
Forum Arena, Assembly, Debate, Platform, Tribunal
Forward(s) Accede, Advanced, Ahead, Along, Anterior, Arch, Assertive, Assuming, Bright, Early, Flanker, Forrad, Forrit, Forth, Fresh, Future, Hasten, Hooker, Immodest, Impudent, Insolent, Lock, Malapert, On(wards), Pack, Pert,

Petulant, Porrect, Precocious, > **PROGRESS**, Promote, Prop, Readdress, Redirect, Scrum, Send, Stem, To(ward), Van, Wing

Fossil(ised), Fossils Amber, Ammonite, Baculite, Belemnite, Blastoid(ea), Calamite, Ceratodus, Chondrite, Conodont, Corallian, Cordaites, Derived, Encrinite, Eohippus, Eozoon, Eurypterus, Exuviae, Fairy stone, Florula, Florule, Fogy, Goniatite, Graptolite, Hipparion, Ichnite, Ichnolite, Ichthyodurolite, Ichthyolite, Index, Jew's stone, Lepidostrobus, Lingulella, Living, Mosasauros, Nummulite, Odontolite, Olenus, Oligocene, Orthoceras, Osteolepis, Ostracoderm, Oxfordian, Pal(a)eo-, Pentacrinus, Petrifaction, Phytolite, Plesiosaur, Pliohippus, Pliosaur, Psilophyton, Pteridosperm, Pterodactyl(e), Pterygotus, Pythonomorph, Relics, Reliquiae, Remanié, Reworked, Sigillaria, Sinanthropus, Sivatherium, Snakestone, Stigmaria, Stromatolite, Taphonomy, Teleosaurus, Titanotherium, Trace, Trilobite, Uintatherium, Wood-opal, Zinganthropus, Zoolite

Foster (child, mother), Fostering Adopt, Cherish, Da(u)lt, Develop, Farm out, Feed, Fornent, Further, Harbour, Incubation, Metapelet, Metaplot, Nourish, Nourse(l), Noursle, Nousell, Nurse, Nurture, Nuzzle, > **REAR**

Foul, Foul-smelling Base, Beray, Besmirch, Besmutch, Bewray, Bungle, > **DEFILE**, Dreggy, Drevill, Enseam, Evil, Feculent, Funky, Gross, Hassle, Hing, Mephitic, Mud, Noisome, Olid, Osmeterium, Professional, Putid, Putrid, > **RANK**, Reekie, Rotten, Sewage, Soiled, Squalid, Stagnant, Stain, Stapelia, Technical, Unclean, Unfair, Vile, Violation, Virose

▷ **Foul** *may indicate* an anagram

Found (in) Among, Base, Bed, Bottom, Build, Cast, Caught, Emong, Endow, > **ESTABLISH**, Eureka, Institute, Introduce, Met, Occur, Plant, Recovered, Rest, Start, Table

Foundation(s) Base, Bedrock, Corset, Cribwork, Establishment, Footing, Girdle, Grillage, Ground, Groundwork, Hard-core, Hypostasis, Infrastructure, Institution, Matrix, Panty girdle, Pile, Roadbed, Rockefeller, Root, Scholarship, Stays, Stereobate, Substrata, Substructure, Trackbed, Underlie, Underlinen

▷ **Foundations** *may indicate* last letters

Founder Author, Collapse, Crumple, Fail, Inventor, Iron-master, Miscarry, Oecist, Oekist, Patriarch, Perish, Settle, Sink, Steelman, Stumble

Fount Aonian, Digital, Source, Springlet, Wrong

Fountain Acadine, Aganippe, Arethusa, Bubbler, Castalian, Cause, Conduit, Drinking, Fauwara, Forts, Gerbe, Head, Hippocrene, Jet, Pant, Pirene, Salmacis, Scuttlebutt, Soda, Spring, Trevi, Youth

Fountain basin Laver

Four(times), Foursome Cater, Georges, Horsemen, IV, Mess, Qid, Quartet, Quaternary, Quaternion, Reel, Tessara, Tessera, Tetrad, Tetralogy, Tiddy, Warp

Fourpence Groat

Fourteenth Bastille, Trecento, Valentine

Fourth Deltaic, Estate, Fardel, Firlot, Forpet, Forpit, July, Perfect, Quarter, Quartet, Quaternary, Quintan, Sesquitertia, Tritone

Fowl Barnyard, Biddy, Boiler, Brahma, Brissle-cock, Burrow-duck, Capon, Chicken, Chittagong, Cob, Cock, Coot, Domestic, Dorking, Duck, Ember, Gallinaceous, Gallinule, Game, Gleenie, Guinea, Hamburg(h), Heather-bleat(er), > **HEN**, Houdan, Jungle, Kora, Leghorn, Mallee, Moorhen, Orpington, Partridge, Pheasant, Pintado, Plymouth Rock, Poultry, Quail, Rooster, Rumkin, Rumpy, Solan, Spanish, Spatchcock, Spitchcock, Sultan, Sussex, Teal, Turkey, Wyandotte

Fox(y) Alopecoid, Arctic, Baffle, Blue, Charley, Charlie, Corsac, Cunning, Desert,

Fennec, Flying, Fool, Friend, Fur, Grey, Kit, Lowrie(-tod), Outwit, Pug, Puzzle, Quaker, Red, Reynard, Rommel, Russel, Silver, Skulk, > **SLY**, Swift, Tod, Uffa, Uneatable, Vixen, White, Zerda, Zoril(le), Zorro

Foxglove Cowflop, Deadmen's bells, Digitalis, Witches-thimble

Foxhole Earth

Foyer Hall, Lobby

Fracas Brawl, Dispute, Mêlée, Prawle, Riot, Rumpus, Scrum, Shindig, Uproar

Fraction Common, Complex, Compound, Continued, Improper, Ligroin, Mantissa, Packing, Part, Partial, Piece, Proper, Scrap, Simple, Some, Vulgar

Fracture Break, Colles, Comminuted, Complicated, Compound, Crack, Fatigue, Fault, Fissure, Greenstick, Hairline, Impacted, Pathological, Pott's, Rupture, Simple, Split, Stress

Fragile Brittle, Crisp, Delicate, Frail, Frangible, Nesh, Slender, Tender, Vulnerable, Weak

Fragment(s) Atom, Bit, Bla(u)d, Brash, Breccia, Brockram, Cantlet, Clastic, Crumb, End, Flinder, Fritter, Frust, Graile, Lapilli, Mammock, Mite, Morceau, Morsel, Ort, > **PARTICLE**, Piece, Potshard, Potsherd, Relic, Restriction, Rubble, Scrap, Segment, Shard, Shatter, Sheave, Shiver, Shrapnel, Shred, Skerrick, Sliver, Smithereens, Smithers, Snatch, Splinter

▷ **Fragment of** *may indicate* a hidden word

Fragrance, Fragrant Aromatic, Attar, Bouquet, Conima, Nosy, Odour, Olent, > **PERFUME**, Pot-pourri, Redolent, > **SCENT**, Sent, Spicy, Suaveolent

Frail Brittle, Creaky, Delicate, Feeble, Flimsy, > **FRAGILE**, Puny, Slight, Slimsy, Weak

Framboesia Morula, Yaws

Frame(work) Adjust, Airer, Angle, Armature, Bail, Bayle, Body, Bow, Brickbat, Build, Cadge, Cadre, Cage, Case, Casement, Casing, Cent(e)ring, Centreing, Chase, Chassis, Clamper, Climbing, Cold, Compages, Companion, Cowcatcher, Cradle, Cratch, Cribwork, Deckel, Deckle, Draw, Entablature, Everest pack, Fabric, Fiddley, Flake, Form, Frisket, Gallows, Gambrel, Gantry, Garden, Gate, Gauntry, Grid-iron, Heck, Horse, Hull, Jungle gym, Lattice, Limit, Louvre, Mantel, Mixter, Mood, Mount, Mullion, Muntin(g), Newsreel, Ossature, Outrigger, Oxford, Pannier, Pantograph, Parameter, Partners, Passe-partout, Pergola, Physique, Pillory, Plant, Plot, Plummer-block, Poppet head, Portal, Puncheon, Rack, Rave, Redact, Retable, Rib(bing), Rim, Sampling, Sash, Scaffold, Scuncheon, Sect(ion), Set, Setting, Skeleton, Spring-box, Stanchion, Still(age), Stocking, Stocks, Straddle, Stretcher, Stretching, Stroma, > **STRUCTURE**, Studwork, Surround, Tabernacle, Taboret, Tambour, Tent(er), Tepee, Time, Trave, Trellis, Tress, Tressel, Trestle, Tribble, Trussing, Vacuum, Victimize, Walking, Wattle, Ways, Window, Yoke, Zarf, Zimmer®

Framley Parsonage

Franc Fr, Leu, Lev, Lew

France Anatole, Marianne, RF, Thibault

Franchise Charter, Contract, Liberty, Privilege, Right, Suffrage, Vote, Warrant

Franciscan Custos, Minorite, Observant, Salesian, Scotist, Tertiaries

Francium Fr

Franck Cesar

Frank(ish) Artless, Austrasia, Blunt, > **CANDID**, Direct, Easy, Free, Free-spoken, Honest, Ingenuous, Man-to-man, Merovingian, Natural, Open, Outspoken, Overt, Postage, Postmark, Ripuarian, Salian, Sincere, Stamp, Straight, Straightforward, Sty, Upfront

Frankincense Laser, Olibanum, Thus

Frans, Franz Hals, Lehar

Frantic Demoniac, Deranged, Distraught, Frenzied, Hectic, Mad, Overwrought, Phrenetic, Rabid, Violent, Whirl(ing)

▷ **Frantic** *may indicate* an anagram

Frappé Iced

Fraternise, Fraternity Affiliate, Brotherhood, Burschenschaft, Consort, Elk, Fellowship, Lodge, Mingle, Moose, Order

Fratricide Cain

Fraud(ulent) Barratry, Bobol, Bubble, Charlatan, Cheat, Chisel, Collusion, Covin, Cronk, Deceit, Diddle, Do, Fineer, Gyp, Humbug, Hypocrite, > IMPOSTOR, Imposture, Jiggery-pokery, Jobbery, Knavery, Liar, Peculator, Piltdown, Pious, Pseud(o), Put-up, Ringer, Rip-off, Roguery, Rort, Scam, South Sea Bubble, Stellionate, Supercherie, Swindle, Swiz(z), Swizzle, Tartuffe, Trick

Fraught Perilous

Fray(ed) Bagarre, Brawl, Contest, Feaze, Frazzle, Fret, Fridge, Ravel, Riot, Scrimmage

Freak Cantrip, Caprice, Chimera, Control, Deviant, Geek, Jesus, Mooncalf, Sport, Teras, Whim, Whimsy

Freckle Ephelis, Fern(i)tickle, Fern(i)ticle, Heatspot, Lentigines, Lentigo, Spot, Sunspot

Frederick Barbarossa, Carno, Great

Free(d), Freely Acquit, Assoil, Buckshee, Candid, Canny, Church, Clear, Complimentary, Cuffo, Dead-head, Deregulate, Devoid, Disburden, Disburthen, Disengage, Disentangle, Eleutherian, Emancipate, Enfranchise, Enlarge, Excuse, Exeem, Exeme, Exempt, Exonerate, Extricate, Familiar, Footloose, Frank, French, Gratis, House, Idle, Immune, Independent, Kick, Large, Lavish, Lax, Leisure, Let, Liberate, Loose, Manumit, Open, Parole, Pro bono, Quit(e), Range, Ransom, Redeem, > RELEASE, Relieve, Rescue, Reskew, Rick, Rid, Sciolto, Scot, Solute, Spare, Spring, Stald, Stall, Trade, Unlock, Unloosen, Unmew, Unmuzzle, Unshackle, Unsnarl, Untangle, Untie, Untwist, Vacant, Verse, Voluntary

▷ **Free** *may indicate* an anagram

Freebooter Cateran, Corsair, Franklin, Marauder, Moss-trooper, Pad, Pindaree, Pindari, Pirate, Rapparee, Snapha(u)nce, Snaphaunch, Thief, Viking

Freedom Abandon, Autonomy, Breadth, Carte blanche, Eleutherian, Exemption, Fear, Fling, Four, Immunity, Impunity, Laisser aller, Laisser faire, Laissez aller, Laissez faire, Latitude, Liberty, Licence, Moksha, Play, Range, Releasement, Speech, Uhuru, UNITA, Want, Worship

Free gift Bonus, Charism, Perk

Freehold(er) Enfeoff, Franklin, Frank tenement, Odal(l)er, Seisin, Udal(ler), Yeoman

Freelance Eclectic, Independent, Mercenary, Stringer

Freeloader Sponge

▷ **Freely** *may indicate* an anagram

Freeman Burgess, Ceorl, Churl, Franklin, Liveryman, Thegn, Thete, Villein

Freemason(ry), Freemason's son Craft, Lewis, Lodge, Moose, Templar

Free-range Eggs, Outler

Free State Orange

Freethinker Agnostic, Bradlaugh, Cynic, Libertine, Sceptic

Free-trade(r) Cobdenism, Wright

Free-wheel Coast

Freeze(s), Freezer, Freezing Alcarrazo, Benumb, Congeal, Cool, Cryogenic,

Cryonics, Eutectic, Freon®, Frost, Harden, Ice, Lyophilize, Moratoria, Nip, Numb, Paralyse, Regelate, Riss, Stiffen, Wage

Freight Cargo, Carriage, Fraught, Goods, Load

French(man), Frenchwoman Alsatian, Aristo, Basque, Breton, Cajun, Crapaud, Creole, Dawn, Dreyfus, Frog, Gallic(e), Gaston, Gaul, Gombo, Grisette, Gumbo, Huguenot, Joual, Jules, M, Mamselle, Marianne, Midi, Monsieur, Mounseer, Neo-Latin, Norman, Parleyvoo, Pierre, René, Rhemish, Savoyard

Frenetic Deranged, Frantic, Overwrought

Frenzied, Frenzy Amok, Berserk, Corybantic, Deliration, Delirium, Demoniac, Enrage, Enrapt, Euhoe, Euoi, Evoe, Feeding, Fit, Fury, Hectic, Hysteric, Lune, Maenad, Mania, Must, Nympholepsy, Oestrus, Phrenetic, Rage

Frequency, Frequent(er), Frequently Angular, Attend, Audio, Bandwidth, Channel, Common, Constant, Expected, Familiar, Forcing, Formant, FR, Fresnel, Gene, Habitué, Hang-out, Haunt, Hertz, High, Incidence, Intermediate, Medium, Megahertz, Natural, Often, Penetrance, Pulsatance, Radio, Recurrent, Regular, Relative, Resort, Spatial, Spectrum, Superhigh, Thick, Ultrahigh, Video

Fresco Intonaco, Sinopia, Tempera

Fresh(en), Freshness Airy, Aurorean, Brash, Caller, Chilly, Clean, Crisp, Dewy, Entire, Forward, Green, Hot, Insolent, Lively, Maiden, New, Novel, Quick, Rebite, Recent, Roral, Roric, Rorid, Smart, Span-new, Spick, Sweet, Tangy, Uncured, Verdure, Vernal, Virent

Freshman Bajan, Bejan(t), Fresher, Pennal, Recruit, Student

Fret(ful) Chafe, Filigree, Fray, Grate, Grecque, Haze, Impatient, Irritate, Ornament, Peevish, Repine, Rile, Ripple, Roil, Rub, Stop, Tetchy, Tracery, Whittle, Worry

Friable Crisp, Crumbling, Powdery

Friar(s) Augustinian, Austin, Bacon, Barefoot, Black, Brother, Bungay, Capuchin, Carmelite, Conventual, Cordelier, Crutched, Curtal, Dervish, Dominican, Fra(ter), Franciscan, Frate, Grey, Jacobin, Laurence, Limiter, Lymiter, Minim, Minor, Minorite, > MONK, Observant, Observantine, Predicant, Recollect, Recollet, Redemptionist, Rush, Tuck, White

Friction Attrition, Conflict, Dissent, Drag, Rift, Rub, Skin, Sliding, Stiction, Stridulation, Tribology, Tripsis, Wear, Xerotripsis

Friday Black, Girl, Golden, Good, Holy, Man, Savage

Fridge Esky®, Freezer, Icebox, Rub

Fried cake Croquette, Cruller

Friend(ly), Friends Achates, Affable, Ally, Alter ego, Ami(cable), Amigo, Approachable, Associate, Avuncular, Belamy, Benign, Boet(ie), Bosom, Bud(dy), Buster, Butty, Cackermander, Cater-cousin, China, Choma, Chum, Circle, Cobber, Cock, Cohort, Compadre, Companion, Companionable, Comrade, Confidant, Cordial, Couthie, Crony, Cully, Damon, Downhome, Edwin, En ami, Fairweather, False, Familiar, Feare, Feathered, Feer, Fere, Fiere, Gemütlich, Gossib, Gossip, Gregarious, Hail-fellow-well-met, Ingle, Intimate, Inward, Jong, Kith, Litigation, Marrow, Mate, Mentor, Mucker, Near, Outgoing, Paisano, Pal, Paranymph, Pen, Penn, Pheere, Privado, Prochain ami, Prochein ami, Pythias, Quaker, Sidekick, Sociable, Societal, Sport, Steady, Tillicum, Tonga, Tosh, Wack(er), Warm, Well-wisher, Wus(s)

Friendliness, Friendship Amity, Bonhomie, Camaraderie, Contesseration, Entente, Platonic, Sodality

Frieze Dado, Metope, Zoophorus

Fright(en), Frightened, Frightful Afear, Affear(e), Agrise, Agrize, Agryze,

Alarm, Aroint, Aroynt, Ashake, Chilling, Cow, Dare, Da(u)nt, Deter, Eek, Eerie, Faceache, Fear(some), Flay, Fleg, Fleme, Fley, Flush, Gallow, Gally, Ghast, Gliff, Glift, Grim, Grisly, Hairy, Horrid, Horrific, Intimidate, Ordeal, Panic, Scar, > **SCARE**, Scarre, Scaur, Schrecklich, Shocking, Sight, Skear, Skeer, Skrik, Spine-chilling, Spook, Stage, Startle, Terrible, Terrify, Terror, Tirrit, Unco, White-knuckle, Windy, Yitten

Frigid Bleak, Cold, Dry, Frory, Frosty, Ice, Indifferent, Serac, Stiff

Frill Armil, Armilla, Bavolet, Falbala, Furbelow, Jabot, Oriental, Ornament, Papillote, Ruche, Ruff(le), Tucker, Valance

▷ **Frilly** *may indicate* an anagram

Fringe(s), Fringed Bang, Border, Bullion, Ciliated, Ciliolate, Edge, Fall, Fimbria, Frisette, Interference, Laciniate, Loma, Lunatic, Macramé, Macrami, Pelmet, Peripheral, Robin, Ruff, Run, Thrum, Toupee, Toupit, Tsitsith, Tzitzith, Valance, Verge, Zizith

Frisian Holstein

Frisk(y) Caper, Cavort, Curvet, Fisk, Flimp, Frolic, Gambol, Search, Skip, Wanton

Fritillary Snake's-head

Fritter Batter, Beignet, Dribble, Dwindle, Fragment, Fribble, Pakora, Piddle, Potter, Puf(f)taloon, Squander, Waste

Frivolous Butterfly, Empty(-headed), Featherbrain, Flighty, Flippant, Frothy, Futile, Giddy, Idle, Inane, Light, Light-minded, Lightweight, Playboy, Skittish, Trifling, Trivial

Frizz(le), Frizzly Afro, Crape, Crimp, Crinkle, Curly, Fry, Fuzz, Hiss

Frock Dress, Gown, Ordain, Robe, Smock

Frog Anoura, Anura, Batrachia(n), Braid, Bullfrog, Crapaud, Depression, Flying, Fourchette, Frenchman, Frush, Goliath, Hairy, Hyla, Marsupial, Mounseer, Nic, Nototrema, Paddock, Paradoxical, Peeper, Pelobatid, Platanna, Puddock, Puttock, Rana, Ranidae, Tree, Wood, Xenopus

Frogman Diver

Frogmouth Mo(re)poke, Podargus

Frog spawn Redd, Tadpole

Frolic(some) Bender, Bust(er), Cabriole, Caper, Cavort, Curvet, Disport, Escapade, > **FRISK(Y)**, Fun, Galravage, Galravitch, Gambol, Gammock, Gil(l)ravage, Jink, Kittenish, Lark, Play, Pollick, Prank, Rag, Rand, Rig, Romp, Scamper, Skylark, Splore, Sport, Spree, Tittup, Wanton

From A, Against, Ex, For, Frae, Off, Thrae

Frond Fern, Leaf, Tendril

Front(al), Frontman Antependium, Anterior, Bow, Brass, Brow, Cold, Cover, Dead, Dickey, Dicky, Esplanade, Facade, Face, Fore(head), Forecourt, Foreground, Groof, Grouf, Head, Home, Metope, National, Newscaster, Occluded, Paravant, People's, Plastron, Polar, Popular, Pose, Preface, Pro, Prom, Prow, Sector, Sinciput, Stationary, Tabula, Temerity, Van, Vaward, Ventral, Warm, Western

Frontier(sman) Afghan, Barrier, Border, Boundary, Checkpoint, Limit, Limitrophe, List, March, North-west, Pathan, Wild West

Front page P1

Front-ranker Pawn

Frost(ing), Frosty Alcorza, Chill, Cranreuch, Cryo-, Freon®, Frigid, Frore(n), Frorne, Glacé, Ground, Hoar, Hore, Ice, Icing, Jack, Mat, Nip, Rime, White

Froth(y) Barm, Bubble, Cuckoospit, Cuckoospit(tle), Despumate, Foam, Frogspit, Gas, Head, Lather, Mantle, Off-scum, Ream, Saponin, Scum, Seethe, Shallow, Spoom, Spoon, Spume, Sud, Yeasty, Yest, Zephir

Frown Glower, Lour, Lower, Scowl
Frozen Froren, Gelid, Glacé, Graupel, Ice-bound, Static, Tundra
Fructification, **Fructify**, **Fructose** Aeci(di)um, Basidium, Fertilise, Flower,
    Fruit, Inulin
Frugal Meagre, Parsimonious, Provident, Prudent, Scant, Skimpy, Spare,
    Spartan, Thrifty
Fruit(ing), **Fruit tree**, **Fruity** Accessory, Achene, Acinus, Akene, Autocarp,
    Bacciform, Cedrate, Coccus, Compot(e), Confect, Conserve, Crop, Dessert,
    Drupe, Eater, Encarpus, Etaerio, First, Follicle, Forbidden, Fritter, Harvest,
    Issue, Orchard, Poof, Product(ion), Pseudocarp, Result, Return, Rich, Ripe,
    Schizocarp, Seed, Soft, Stoneless, Sweetie, Sweety, Syconium, Syncarp, Utricle,
    Valve, Wall, Xylocarp, Yield

FRUIT

3 letters:
Fig
Haw
Hep
Hip
Hop
Jak
Key
Nut

4 letters:
Akee
Bael
Bito
Date
Gage
Gean
Jack
Kaki
Lime
Pepo
Pome
Sloe
Sorb
Star
Tuna
Ugli

5 letters:
Ackee
Anana
Anona
Apple
Assai
Berry
Bread
Choko

Genip
Gourd
Guava
Jaffa
Lotus
Mango
Nancy
Naras
Nashi
Nelis
Olive
Papaw
Prune
Regma
Rowan
Whort

6 letters:
Almond
Ananas
Babaco
Banana
Banian
Banyan
Carica
Cherry
Chocho
Citron
Citrus
Comice
Durian
Durion
Emblic
Feijoa
Lichee
Litchi
Longan

Lychee
Mammee
Medlar
Narras
Nelies
Papaya
Pawpaw
Pepino
Pomace
Pomelo
Pruine
Quince
Raisin
Rennet
Replum
Russet
Samara
Sapota
Sharon
Squash
Tomato
Wampee

7 letters:
Apricot
Avocado
Bullace
Chayote
Crab-nut
Cypsela
Geebung
Genipap
Gherkin
Kumquat
Leechee
Litchee
Manjack

Morello
Passion
Pimento
Pinguin
Poperin
Pupunha
Regmata
Ruddock
Satsuma
Silicle
Siliqua
Silique
Sorosis
Soursop
Succade
Tangelo
Winesap

8 letters:
Abricock
Apricock
Bergamot
Bilberry
Blimbing
Calabash
Dewberry
Fraughan
Goosegog
Hagberry
Hastings
Hedgehog
Kalumpit
Minneola
Mulberry
Plantain
Prunello
Rambutan

- Rathripe
- Sebesten
- Shaddock
- Silicula
- Sunberry
- Tamarind
- Tayberry
- Waxberry

9 letters:
- Algarroba
- Allocarpy
- Apple-john
- Aubergine
- Bakeapple
- Blueberry
- Canteloup
- Carambola
- Caryopsis
- Cherimoya
- Cranberry
- Cremocarp

Freestone
Haanepoot
Hackberry
Mirabelle
Myrobalan
Naseberry
Nectarine
Neesberry
Ortanique
Persimmon
Plumdamas
Poppering
Ratheripe
Saskatoon
Shadberry
Sorb-apple
Star-apple
Tomatillo
Victorine
Whimberry
Whinberry

10 letters:
Apothecium
Blackberry
Canteloupe
Cherimoyer
Clementine
Clingstone
Elderberry
Granadilla
Grenadilla
Jargonelle
Mangosteen
Pick-cheese
Punicaceae
Scaldberry
Watermelon
Youngberry

11 letters:
Boysenberry
Hesperidium
Huckleberry

Marionberry
Pampelmoose
Pampelmouse
Pomegranate
Pompelmoose
Pompelmouse
Salmonberry

12 letters:
Blackcurrant
Checkerberry
Custard-apple
Service-berry
Whortleberry

13 letters:
Bullock's heart

14 letters:
Worcesterberry

Fruitful(ness) Calathus, Ephraim, Fat, Fecund, Feracious, Fertile, Productive, Prolific, Uberty, Worthwhile

Fruitless Bare, Futile, Sisyphean, Sterile, Useless, Vain

Frump(ish) Dowdy, Judy, Shabby, Unkempt

Frustrate Baffle, Ba(u)lk, Beat, Blight, Bugger, Check, Confound, Dash, Disappoint, Discomfit, Dish, Foil, Hogtie, Outwit, Scotch, Stymie, Tantalise, Thwart

Fry, Fried Blot, Brit, Christopher, Elizabeth, Fricassee, Fritter, Frizzle, Parr, Sauté, Sizzle, Small, Spawn, Whippersnapper, Whitebait

Fuddle(d) Drunk, Fluster, Fuzzle, Maudlin, Ta(i)vert, Tosticated, Woozy

▷ **Fuddle(d)** *may indicate* an anagram

Fudge Cook, Doctor, Dodge, Drivel, Evade, Fiddlesticks, Nonsense, Rot, Stop-press

Fuel Anthracite, Argol, Astatki, Atomic, Avgas, Biodiesel, Biogas, Briquet(te), Bunker, Butane, Candle-coal, Cannel, Carbonette, Charcoal, Coal, Coke, Derv, Diesel, Eilding, Eldin(g), Ethane, Faggot, Fire(wood), Fossil, Gasohol, Gasoline, Go-juice, Haxamine, Hydrazine, Hydyne, Kerosene, Kerosine, Kindling, Knitch, Lignite, Mox, Napalm, Naphtha, Nuclear, Orimulsion, Paraffin, Peat, Propane, Propellant, Smokeless, Solid, Stoke, Triptane, Unleaded, Yealdon

Fug Frowst

Fugitive Absconder, Ephemeral, Escapee, Fleeting, Hideaway, Lot, Outlaw, Refugee, Runaway, Runner, Transient

Fugue Ricercar(e), Ricercata

Fulcrum Key-pin, Pivot

Fulfil(ment) Accomplish, Complete, Fruition, Honour, Implementation, Meet, Pass, Realise, > SATISFY, Steed, Subrogation

Fulgent Bright, Shining

Full(ness), Fully Abrim, Ample, Arrant, Bouffant, Capacity, Chock-a-block, Chocker, Complete, Copious, Embonpoint, Engorged, Entire, Fat, Fed, Flush,

Fou, Frontal, German, High, Hoatching, Hotch, Mill, Plein, Plenary, Plenitude, Pleroma, Plethora, Replete, Rich, Sated, Satiated, Thorough, Toss, Turgid, Turgor, Ullage, Up, Wau(l)k, Wholly

Full-faced Caboched, Caboshed

Full-throated Goitred

Fulminate, Fulmination Detonate, Explode, Levin, Lightning, Rail, Renounce, Thunder

Fumarole Mofette

Fumble Blunder, Faff, Grope, Misfield, Muff

Fume(s) Bluster, Gas, Halitus, Nidor, Rage, Reech, Reek, Settle, Smoke, Stum, Vapours

Fumigate Disinfect, Smoke

Fun(ny), Funny bone Amusing, Antic, Boat, Buffo, Caper, Clownery, Comedy, Comic(al), Delight, Droll, Frolic, Gammock, Gig, Giocoso, Glaik, Guy, Hilarity, Humerus, Humorous, Hysterical, Ill, Jest, Jouisance, Jouysaunce, Killing, Kinky, Lark, Music, Play, Pleasure, Priceless, Rag, Rich, Rummy, Scream, Sidesplitting, Skylark, Sport, Uproarious, Weird(o), Yell

Funambulist Blondin, Equilibrist, Tight-rope

Function(al) Act, Algebraic, Antilog, Apparatchik, Arccos, Arcsine, Arctan, Bunfight, Ceremony, Characteristic, Cosec, Cosh, Cotangent, Coth, Density, Discriminant, Distribution, Dynamic, Exponential, Gamma, Gibbs, Hamilton(ian), Helmholtz, Hyperbolic, Integrand, Inverse, Jacobian, Job, Logarithm, Map(ping), > OPERATE, Periodic, Polymorphic, Probability, Propositional, Quadric, Quantical, Recursive, Role, Run, Secant, Sech, Sentential, Service, Sine, Sinh, State, Ste(a)d, Step, Surjection, Tan(h), Tick, Transcendental, Trigonometric, Use, Utensil, Utility, Versin, Vital, Wave, > WORK

Functionless Otiose

Fund(s), Funding, Fundraising Bank, Bankroll, Barrel, Capital, Chest, Consolidated, Emendals, Endow, Evergreen, Finance, Fisc, Fisk, Gild, Hedge, Imprest, Index, Jackpot, Kitty, Managed, Mutual, Nest-egg, Pension, Pool, Pork-barrel, Prebend, Private, Public, Purse, Revolving, Roll-up, Sinking, Slush, Social, Sou-sou, Stabilisation, Stock, Subsidise, Sustentation, Susu, Telethon, Treasury, Trust, Vulture, Wage(s), War chest, Wherewithal

Fundamental(ist) Basic(s), Bedrock, Cardinal, Essence, Grass-roots, Hamas, Missing, Nitty-gritty, Organic, Prime, Principle, Radical, Rudimentary, Taliba(a)n, Ultimate

Fund-holder Rentier

Funeral, Funereal Charnel, Cortege, Dismal, Exequy, Feral, Hearse, Obit, Obsequy, Sad-coloured, Solemn, Tangi

Fungicide Biphenyl, Bordeaux mixture, Burgundy mixture, Captan, Diphenyl, Ferbam, Menadione, PCP, Thiram, Zineb

Fungoid, Fungus Agaric, Amadou, Amanita, Ambrosia, Anthersmut, Anthracnose, Apothecium, Asci(us), Asomycete, Aspergillus, Barm, Basidium, Beefsteak, Black, Blackknot, Blewits, Blue-mould, Blue-rot, Boletus, Bootlace, Botrytis, Bracket, Bread-mould, Bunt, Candida, Ceps, Chantarelle, Chanterelle, Cladosporum, Clubroot, Conk, Coral spot, Corn smut, Craterellus, Cryptococcus, Cup, Death-cap, Death-cup, Dermatophytosis, Destroying angel, Discomycetes, Dutch elm, Earth-star, Elf-cup, Empusa, Endophyte, Ergot, Eumycetes, Favus, Funnel-cap, Fuss-ball, Fuzz-ball, Gall, Gibberella, Gill, Honey, Horsehair, Hypersarcoma, Hypha, Imperfect, Ink-cap, Ithyphallus, Jelly, Jew's ear, Liberty cap, Lichen, Magic mushroom, Merulius,

Mildew, Milk cap, Monilia, Morel, Mould, Mucor(ales), Mushroom, Mycelium, Mycetes, Mycology, Noble rot, Oak-leather, Oidium, Orange-peel, Penicillium, Pest, Peziza, Phallus, Phycomycete, Pileum, Plica, Polonica, Porcino, Pore, Prototroph, Puccinia, Puckfist, Puffball, Pythium, Rhizopus, Rhytisma, Russula, Rust, Saccharomyces, Saprolegnia, Saprophyte, Sariodes, Scab, Shaggy cap, Shaggy mane, Shoestring, Slime, Smut, Sooty mould, Spunk, Stinkhorn, Stipe, Stromata, Sulphur tuft, Tarspot, Thalline, Thallophyte, Toadstool, Torula, Tremella, Trichophyton, Truffle, Tuckahoe, Uredine, Ustilago, Velvetshank, Wax cap, Wheat rust, Witches' butter, Wood hedgehog, Yeast, Yellow brain, Yellow rust, Yellows, Zygomycete, Zygospore

Fungus-eater Mycophagist

Funicular Cable-car

Funk(y) Blue, Dodge, Dread, Fear, Scared, Stylish

Funnel Buchner, Chimney, Choana, Drogue, Flue, Hopper, Infundibulum, Separating, Smokestack, Stack, Stovepipe, Tun-dish, Wine

Fur Astrakhan, Astrex, Beaver(skin), Boa, Broadtail, Budge, Calabre, Caracul, Castor, Chinchilla, Coonskin, Crimmer, Ermelin, Ermine, Fitchew, Flix, Flue, Fun, Galyac, Galyak, Genet, Kolinsky, Krimmer, Lettice, Minever, Miniver, Mink, Mouton, Musquash, Ocelot, Otter, Pashm, Pean, Pekan, Rac(c)oon, Roskyn, Sable, Sealskin, Sea-otter, Stole, Tincture, Tippet, Vair(e), Victorine, Wolverine, Zibeline, Zorino

Furbish Polish, Renovate, Spruce, Vamp

Furl Fold, Roll, Stow, Wrap

Furlough Congé, Leave

Furnace Arc, Athanor, Blast, Bloomery, Bosh, Calcar, Cockle, Cremator, Cupola, Destructor, Devil, Electric, Finery, Firebox, Forge, Glory-hole, Kiln, Lear, Lehr, Lime-kiln, Oast, Oon, Open-hearth, Oven, Pot, Producer, Reverberatory, Scaldino, Solar, Tank, Wind

Furnish(ing) Appoint, Array, Deck, Decorate, Endow, Endue, Equip, Feed, Fledge, Gird, Lend, Produce, Provision, Soft, Stock, Supply, Tabaret, Upholster

Furniture Biedermeier, Chattels, Chippendale, Duncan Phyfe, Encoignure, Escritoire, Etagère, Flatpack, Hepplewhite, Insight, Lumber, Moveable, Queen Anne, Sheraton, Sideboard, Sticks, Stoutherie, Street, Tire, Unit, Washstand, Whatnot

Furore Brouhaha, Commotion, Outburst, Stink, Storm, Uproar

Furrier Trapper

Furrow(ed) Crease, Feer, Feerin(g), Furr, Groove, Gutter, Plough, Pucker, Rill(e), Rugose, Rut, Stria, Sulcus, Vallecula, Wrinkle

Fur-seal Seecatch(ie)

Further(more), Furthest Additional, Advance, Again, Aid, Also, Besides, Deeper, Else, Expedite, Extend, Extra, Extreme, Fresh, Infra, Longer, Mo(e), Mow, Other, Promote, Serve, Speed, Subserve, Then

Furtive(ly) Clandestine, Cunning, Hole and corner, Secret, Sly, Sneaky, Stealthy, Stowlins, Stownlins

Fury, Furies, Furious Acharné, Agitato, Alecto, > ANGER, Apoplexy, Atropos, Avenger, Eriny(e)s, Eumenides, Exasperation, Frantic, Frenzied, Furor, Hectic, Incensed, > IRE, Livid, Maenad, Megaera, Rabid, Rage, Savage, Seething, Tisiphone, Virago, Wood, Wrath, Yond

Furze Gorse, Whin

Fuse(d), Fusion Anchylosis, Ankylosis, Blend, Coalesce, Cohere, Colliquate, Conflate, Encaustic, Endosmosis, Flow, Flux, Match, Merge, Merit, Nuclear, Percussion, Portfire, Proximity, Rigelation, Run, Safety, Saucisson, Short,

Slow-match, Syncretism, Syngamy, Time, Tokamak, Unite

Fuselage Body, Monocoque, Structure

Fuss(y) Ado, Agitation, Anile, Ballyho, Bobsie-die, Bother, Br(o)uhaha, Bustle, Carfuffle, Chichi, Coil, Commotion, Complain, Cosset, Create, Cu(r)fuffle, Dust, Faff, Fantad, Fantod, Fiddle-faddle, Finical, Finikin, Hairsplitter, Hoohah, Hoopla, Mither, Niggle, Nit-pick, Old-womanish, Overexact, Overnice, Overwrought, Palaver, Particular, Perjink, Pernickety, Picky, Pother, Precise, Prejink, Primp, Prissy, Racket, Razzmatazz, Rout, Song, Song and dance, Spoffish, Spoffy, Spruce, Stashie, Stickler, Stink, > STIR, Stishie, Stooshie, Stushie, Tamasha, To-do, Tracasserie

Fustian Bombast, Gas, Pompous, Rant

Futile Empty, Feckless, Idle, Inept, No-go, Nugatory, Null, Otiose, Pointless, Sleeveless, Stultified, Trivial, Useless, > VAIN

Future(s), Futurist Again, Be-all, Coming, Demain, Financial, Hence, Horoscope, Index, Interest-rate, Later, Long-range, Offing, Ovist, Paragogic, Posterity, Prospect, To-be, Tomorrow

Fuzz(y) Blur, Crepe, Fluff, Foggy, Lint, Pig, Policeman

Gg

G George, Golf, Gravity

Gab(ble), Gabbler Chatter, Dovercourt, Jabber, Pie, Prattle, Talkative, Yabber

Gable Clark, Corbie, Jerkinhead, Pediment, Pine end

Gabriel Angel, Walter

Gad(about), Gadzooks Gallivant, Lud, Rover, Sbuddikins, Sdeath, Traipse, Trape(s), Viretot

Gadfly Breese, Breeze, Brize

Gadget Appliance, Artifice, Device, Dingbat, Dingus, Doodad, Doodah, Doofer, Doohickey, Gismo, Gizmo, Gubbins, Hickey, Jimjam, Notion, Possum, Tool, Utility, Waldo, Widget

Gadolinium Gd

Gadzooks Odsbobs

Gaekwar Baroda

Gael(ic) Celt, Erse, Goidel, Scottish, Teague

Gaff(e), Gaffer Bêtise, Blague, Bloomer, Error, Floater, Foreman, Gamble, Game, Solecism, Spar, Throat, Trysail, Yokel

Gag Brank, Choke, Estoppel, Joke, Pong, Prank, Retch, Silence(r), Smother, Wheeze

Gage Challenge, Pawn, Pledge, Plum

▸ **Gaiety** *see* GAY

Gain(s), Gained Acquire, Appreciate, Attain, Avail, Boodle, Boot, Bunce, Capital, Carry, Catch, Chevisance, Clean-up, Derive, Earn, Edge, Fruit, > GET, Good, Gravy, Land, Lucre, Obtain, Plus, Profit, Purchase, Rake-off, Reap, Thrift, Use, Velvet, Wan, Win, Windfall, Winnings

Gainsay Contradict, Deny

Gait Bearing, Canter, Pace, Piaffer, Rack, Trot

Gaiter(s) Cootikin, Cu(i)tikin, Gambado, Hogger, Legging(s), Puttee, Spat(s), Spattee, Spatterdash, Vamp

Gala Banquet, Festival

Galaxies, Galaxy Active, Andromeda, Great Attractor, Heaven, Magellanic cloud, Milky Way, Radio, Seyfert, Spiral, Stars

Galbanum Ferula

Gale(s) Backfielder, Equinoctial, Fresh, Moderate, Peal, Ripsnorter, Sea turn, Snorter, Squall, Storm, Tempest, Whole, Winder

Gall Aleppo, Bedeguar, Bitterness, Canker, Ellagic, Enrage, Fell, Irritate, Mad-apple, Maugre, Maulgre, Oak(nut), Saddle, Sage-apple, Sandiver, > SAUCE, Tacahout, Vine

Gallant(ry) Admirer, Amorist, Beau, Blade, Buck, Cavalier, Chevalier, Cicisbeo, Courtliness, Lover, Prow, Romeo, Sigisbeo, Spark, Valiance

Galleon Galloon, Ghostly, Ship

Gallery Accademia, Alure, Amphitheatre, Arcade, Assommoir, Belvedere, Brattice, Bretasche, Bretesse, Brettice, Brow, Catacomb, Celestials, Cupola, Dedans, Fly, Gods, Hayward, Hermitage, Jube, Ladies', Loft, Loggia, Louvre,

Machicolation, Mine, Minstrel, National, Organ, Pawn, Pinacotheca, Pinakothek, Pitti, Prado, Press, Public, Rogues', Serpentine, Shooting, Strangers', Tate, Terrace, Tribune, Triforium, Uffizi, Veranda(h), Whispering, Whitechapel, Winning

Galley Bireme, Bucentaur, Caboose, Drake, Galliot, Kitchen, Lymphad, Penteconter, Proof

Gallimaufry Macedoine, Mishmash, Stew

Gallium Ga

Gallon(s) Bushel, Cong(ius), Cran, Hin, Imperial, Tierce

Galloon Lace, Osiris

Gallop(er) Aide, Canter, Career, Lope, Trot, Wallop

Gallows Bough, Cheat, Drop, Dule-tree, Forks, Gibbet, Nub, Nubbing-cheat, Patibulary, Three-legged mare, Tree, Tyburn, Tyburn-tree, Widow, Woodie

Gallows-bird Crack-halter, Crack-hemp, Crack-rope

Gall-stone Cholelith

Galore Abundance, A gogo, Plenty, Whisky

Galosh Overshoe, Rubber

Galvanise Buck up, Ginger, Rouse, Zinc

Gam Pod

Gambit Manoeuvre, Ploy, Stratagem

Gamble(r), Gambling (place) Adventure, Ante, Back, Bet, Casino, Chance, Dice(-play), Flutter, Gaff, Hold, Jeff, Martingale, Mise, Pari-mutuel, Parlay, Partingale, Piker, Plunge, Policy, Punter, Raffle, Reno, Risk, Roulette, School, Spec, Speculate, Speculator, Sweep(stake), Throw(ster), Tinhorn, Tombola, Tontine, Treble chance, Two-up, > WAGER

Gambol Frisk, Frolic

Game(s) Away, Closed, Commonwealth, Computer, Decider, Electronic, Frame, Gallant, Gammy, Ground, Gutsy, High-jinks, Highland, Home, Intrepid, Isthmian, Jeu, > LAME, Match, Middle, Nemean, Numbers, Olympic, On, Open, Panel, Paralympic, Parlour, Perfect, Platform, Play, Plaything, Preference, Pythian, Raffle, Road, Round, Rubber, Saving, Secular, Spoof, Sport, Square, String, Table, Tie-break, Vie, Waiting, Willing

GAMES

2 letters:	Swy	I-spy	Solo
Eo	Tag	Keno	Taws
Go	Tig	Kino	Vint
PE	War	Laik	Wall
RU		Loto	Word
	4 letters:	Ludo	
3 letters:	Base	Main	**5 letters:**
Cat	Brag	Mora	Bingo
Hob	Bull	Palm	Bocce
Loo	Crap	Polo	Bowls
Maw	Dibs	Pool	Cards
Nap	Fa-fi	Putt	Catch
Nim	Fair	Ruff	Chess
Pam	Faro	Scat	Cinch
Pit	Goff	Skat	Craps
Put	Golf	Slam	Darts
Sim	Grab	Snap	Fives

- Gleek
- Goose
- Halma
- House
- Jacks
- Keeno
- Lotto
- Lurch
- Merel
- Meril
- Monte
- Morra
- Noddy
- Novum
- Omber
- Ombre
- Poker
- Quino
- Roque
- Rummy
- Shogi
- Tarok
- Tarot
- Trugo
- Two-up
- Video
- Whisk
- Whist

6 letters:
- Basset
- Beetle
- Boston
- Boules
- Casino
- Chemmy
- Clumps
- Crambo
- Ecarté
- Euchre
- Fantan
- Footer
- Gammon
- Gobang
- Gomoku
- Hockey
- Hoopla
- Hurley
- Kitcat
- Merell
- Pelota
- Piquet

Quinze
Quoits
Shinny
Shinty
Soccer
Socker
Squash
Tenpin
Tipcat
Uckers
Vigoro

7 letters:
Ba'spiel
Bezique
Braemar
Camogie
Canasta
Cassino
Charade
Chicken
Codille
Conkers
Coon-can
Croquet
Curling
Diabolo
Doubles
Hangman
Hurling
In-and-In
Jai Alai
Jukskei
Kabaddi
Lottery
Mahjong
Mancala
Marbles
Matador
Muggins
Murphy's
Netball
Old Maid
Pachisi
Pallone
Passage
Peekabo
Pharaoh
Pinball
Plafond
Pontoon
Primero

Push-pun
Pyramid
Rackets
Reversi
Ring-taw
Seven-up
Singles
Snooker
Squails
Tenpins
Vingt-un

8 letters:
All-fives
All-fours
Baccarat
Bumpball
Buzkashi
Canfield
Chouette
Conquian
Cottabus
Cribbage
Dominoes
Draughts
Fivepins
Football
Forfeits
Four-ball
Foursome
Gin rummy
Goalball
Handball
Handicap
Hardball
Kickball
Klondike
Klondyke
Korfball
Leapfrog
Mahjongg
Monopoly®
Napoleon
Ninepins
Nintendo®
Octopush
Pachinko
Pall-mall
Pastance
Patience
Peekaboo
Penneech

Penneeck
Penuchle
Petanque
Ping-pong
Pinochle
Pintable
Pope Joan
Push-ball
Reversis
Rolypoly
Roulette
Rounders
Scrabble®
Skittles
Slapjack
Softball
Sphairee
Subbuteo®
Teetotum
Trap-ball
Tray-trip
Tredille
Tric-trac
Verquere
Verquire

9 letters:
Acey-deucy
Badminton
Bagatelle
Billiards
Black-cock
Black-jack
Broomball
Cutthroat
Duplicate
Fillipeen
Hopscotch
Jingo-ring
Lanterloo
Level-coil
Matrimony
Mistigris
Mournival
Mumchance
Newmarket
Paintball
Parcheesi®
Pelmanism
Punchball
Quadrille
Quidditch®

- Shoot'em-up
- Solitaire
- Spoilfive
- Stoolball
- Tip-and-run
- Tredrille
- Trick-trac
- Tric-track
- Twenty-one
- Vingt-et-un
- Water polo

10 letters:
- Angel-beast
- Basketball
- Battledore
- Bouillotte
- Candlepins
- Cat's cradle
- Deck tennis
- Dumb Crambo
- Five-stones
- Flapdragon
- Handy-dandy
- Horseshoes
- Hot cockles
- Jackstones
- Jackstraws
- Knurr-spell
- Lansquenet

Paddleball
Phillipina
Phillipine
Philopoena
Punto-banco
Put and take
Snapdragon
Spillikins
Strip poker
Tablanette
Tchoukball
Thimblerig
Trick-track
Troll-madam
Trou-madame
Volley-ball

11 letters:
Barley-brake
Bumble-puppy
Catch-the-ten
Chemin de fer
Fox and geese
General post
Gerrymander
Mumbletypeg
Puncto-banco
Racquetball
Rouge et noir
Sancho-pedro

Shovelboard
Speculation
Tick-tack-toe
Tiddlywinks
Troll-my-dame

12 letters:
Consequences
Fast and loose
Hoodman-blind
Knucklebones
One-and-thirty
Pitch and putt
Pitch and toss
Shuffleboard
Span-farthing
Troll-my-dames

13 letters:
Blind Man's Buff
Chicken-hazard
Double or quits
French cricket
Musical chairs
Postman's knock
Prisoner's base
Space Invaders
Tenpin bowling
Tickly-benders

14 letters:
Crown and anchor
Ducks and drakes
Fives and threes
Follow-my-leader
Hunt-the-slipper
Pig-in-the-middle
Prick-the-garter
Shove-halfpenny
Snip-snap-
snorum
Tenpins bowling
Three-card monte

15 letters:
Chinese Whispers

16 letters:
Piggy-in-the-
middle
Snakes and
ladders
Trente-et-
quarante

20 letters:
Kiss-me-quick-in-
the-ring

Game, Game birds Bag, Fowl, Grouse, Guan, Hare, Meat, Partridge, Pheasant, Prairie chicken, Ptarmigan, Quail, > QUARRY, Rype(r), Snipe, Spatchcock, Woodcock

Gamekeeper Mellors, Velveteen, Venerer, Warrener

Gaming place Bucket-shop, Casino, Saloon, Table

Gammerstang Taupie, Tawpie

Gammon Baloney, Bilge, Tosh

Gamut Compass, Range

Gander Airport, Look-see

Gandhi Mahatma

Gang Band(itti), Bing, Bunch, Canaille, Chain, Coffle, Core, Crew, Crue, Droog, Elk, Go, Horde, Mob, Mods, Nest, Outfit, Pack, Posse, Press, Push, Ratpack, Rockers, Triad, Tribulation, Troop, Yardie

Ganglia Basal

Gangrene Canker, Gas, Noma, Phaged(a)ena, Sphacelate, Thanatosis

Gangster Al, Bandit, Capone, Crook, Dacoit, Dakoit, Hatchet-man, Highbinder, Hood, Mafioso, Mobster, Ochlocrat, Scarface, Skollie, Skolly, Tsotsi, Yakuza, Yardie

Gangway Brow, Catwalk, Road

Gannet Booby, Guga, Solan(d)

Gantry Elmer

Ganymede Cupper

▶ **Gaol(er)** *see* JAIL(ER)

Gap Aperture, Belfort, Breach, Chasm, Chink, Credibility, Day, Deflationary, Diastema, Dollar, Embrasure, Energy, F-hole, Financing, Flaw, Fontanel(le), Gender, Generation, Gulf, Gulph, Hair-space, Hiatus, Hole, Inflationary, Interlude, Interstice, Kirkwood, Lacunae, Leaf, Lin(n), Loophole, M(e)use, Mews, Muset, Musit, Opening, Ostiole, Pass, Rest, Rima, Shard, Sherd, Skills, Slap, > SPACE, Spark, Street, Synapse, Trade, Truth-value, Water, Wind

Gape(r), **Gaping** Comber, Dehisce, Fatiscent, Gant, Ga(u)p, Gerne, Hiant, Mya, Outstare, Rictal, Rictus, Ringent, Rubberneck, Stare, Yawn, Yawp

Garage Carport, Chopshop, Hangar, Lock-up

Garb Apparel, Costume, Gear, Gere, Guise, Ihram, Invest, Leotard, Raiment, Toilet

Garbage Bunkum, Junk, Refuse, Rubbish, Trash

Garble Edit, Jumble, Muddle

▷ **Garble** *may indicate* an anagram

Garden(ing), **Gardens** Arbour, Area, Babylon(ian), Bagh, Bear, Beer, Botanic, Chinampa, Colegarth, Cottage, Covent, Cremorne, Dig, Eden, Erf, Floriculture, Garth, Gethsemane, Hanging, Hesperides, Hoe, Italian, Kailyard, Kew, Kitchen, Knot, Landscape, Lyceum, Market, Monastery, NJ, Olitory, Paradise, Parterre, Physic, Pleasance, Plot, Potager, Ranelagh, Rockery, Roji, Roof, Rosary, Rosery, Tea, Tilth, Topiary, Tuileries, Vauxhall, Welwyn, Window, Winter, Yard, Zoological

Gardener Adam, Capability Brown, Fuchs, Jekyll, Landscape, Mali, Mallee, Mary, Nurseryman, Topiarist, Tradescant, Trucker

Gargantuan Enormous, Huge, Pantagruel, Vast

Gargle Gargarism, Mouthwash

Gargoyle Waterspout

Garish Criant, Flashy, Gaudy, Glitzy, Jazzy, Painty, Roary, Rorie, Rory, Technicolour

Garland Anadem, Anthology, Chaplet, Coronal, Crants, Festoon, Lei, Stemma, Toran(a), Vallar(y), Wreath

Garlic Clove, Elephant, Hedge, Rams(on), Rocambole

Garment Aba(ya), Abba, Alb, Ao dai, Barrow, Blouse, Blouson, Bodice, Body warmer, Bolero, B(o)ub(o)u, B(o)urk(h)a, Breeks, Burnous, Burqa, Busuuti, Caftan, Catsuit, Cerements, Chador, Chasuble, Chimer, Cilice, Cimar, Clout, Cote-hardie, Cotta, Cover-slut, Dalmatic, Dashiki, Dirndl, Djibbah, Doublet, Dreadnought, Ephod, Exomion, Exomis, Fanon, Foundation, Gambeson, G-suit, Habiliment, Habit, Hand-me-down, Himation, Hug-me-tight, Ihram, Izar, Jeistiecor, Jibbah, Jubbah, Jumpsuit, Kaftan, Kanzu, Kaross, K(h)anga, Kittel, Levis, Lingerie, Mandilion, Mandylion, Mantle, Negligee, One-piece, Pallium, Pantihose, Pantyhose, Partlet, Pelerine, Pelisse, Penitential, Peplos, Pilch, Popover, Rail, Ramée, Rami(e), Reach-me-down, Rochet, Rompers, Ruana, Sackcloth, Salopettes, Sanbenito, Sari, Sarong, Scapular, Shroud, Singlet, Slop, Soutane, Step-in, Stola, Stole, Sulu, Surcoat, Surplice, Swimsuit, Tabard, Tank-top, Thong, Toga, Togs, Tunic(le), Unitard, Vestment, Vesture, Waistcoat, Weed, Woolly, Wrapper, Zephyr

Garnet Alabandine, Almandine, Andradite, Carbuncle, Demantoid, Essonite, Grossular(ite), Hessonite, Melanite, Pyrenite, Pyrope, Rhodolite, Spessartite, Topazolite, Uvarovite

Garnish Adorn, Attach, Crouton, Decorate, Gremolata, Lard, Parsley, Sippet, Staffage

Garret Attic, Loft, Sol(l)ar, Sol(l)er
Garrison Fort, Man, Presidial
Garrulity, Garrulous Babbling, Gas, Gushy, Windbag
Garter Bowyang, Crewel, Flash, G(r)amash, Gramosh, Nicky-tam
Gary Glitter, Player
Gas(sy) Acetylene, Afterdamp, Air, Ammonia, Argon, Argonon, Arsine, Azote,
  Blah(-blah), Blather, Blether, Bottle(d), Butadiene, Butane, Butene, BZ,
  Calor®, Carrier, Chat, Chlorine, Chokedamp, Chrom(at)osphere, CN, Coal(-oil),
  Crypton, CS, Cyanogen, Damp, Diphosgene, Dispersant, Electrolytic,
  Emanation, Ethane, Ethene, Ether(ion), Ethine, Ethylene, Firedamp, Fizz,
  Flatulence, Flatus, Flocculus, Flue, Fluorin(e), Formaldehyde, Fugacity,
  Gabnash, Greenhouse, H, Halitus, He, Helium, Hot-air, Hydrogen, Ideal, Inert,
  Jaw, Ketene, Kr(ypton), Laughing, Lewisite, Lurgi, Mace®, Marsh, Methane,
  Mofette, Mustard, Napalm, Natural, Ne, Neon, Nerve, Nitrogen, Noble, North
  Sea, Nox, O, Oil, Olefin(e), Orotund, Oxyacetylene, Oxygen, Perfect, Petrol,
  Phosgene, Phosphine, Plasma, Poison, Prate, Producer, Propane, Propellant,
  Propene, Propylene, Protostar, Radon, Rare, RN, Sarin, Sewage, Sewer, Silane,
  Solfatara, Soman, Sour, Stibine, Sulphur dioxide, Swamp, Synthesis, Tabun,
  > TALK, Taraniki wind, Tear, Tetrafluoroethene, Therm, Thoron, Town, V-agent,
  Vapour, Waffle, War, Water, Whitedamp, > WIND, Xenon, Yackety-yak
Gasbag Blimp, Envelope, Prattler
Gascon(ade) Boast, Braggart, Skite
Gash Incise, Rift, Score, Scotch, > SLASH
Gas-mask Inhaler
Gasp(ing) Anhelation, Apn(o)ea, Chink, Exhale, Kink, Oh, Pant, Puff, Singult,
  Sob
Gast(e)ropod Conch, Cowrie, Cowry, Dog-whelk, Dorididae, Euthyneura,
  Fusus, Glaucus, Haliotis, Harp-shell, Limpet, Mitre, Mollusc, Murex, Nerita,
  Nerite, Nudibranch, Opisthobranch, Ormer, Pelican's foot, Periwinkle,
  Pteropod, Purpura, Sea-ear, Sea-hare, Slug, Snail, Spindle-shell, Stromb, Top,
  Triton, Turbo, Turritello, Wentletrap, Whelk
Gate(s), Gateway Alley, Attendance, Brandenburg, Caisson, Cilician, Crowd,
  Decuman, Entry, Erpingham, Golden, Head, Ivory, Kissing, Lock, Lych,
  Mallee, Menin, Moravian, Nor, Pearly, Portal, Portcullis, Postern, Praetorian,
  Propylaeum, Propylon, Pylon, Starting, Tail, Taranaki, Toran(a), Torii,
  Traitor's, Turnout, Turnstile, Waste, Water, Wicket, Yate, Yet(t)
Gatecrash(er) Interloper, Intrude, Ligger, Sorn, Unasked
Gatepost Sconcheon, Scontion, Scuncheon
▷ **Gateshead** *may indicate* 'g'
Gather(ed), Gathering Accrue, Amass, Assemble, Bee, Braemar, Cluster, Collate,
  > COLLECT, Colloquium, Concourse, Conglomerate, Congregate, Conventicle,
  Corral, Corroboree, Crop, Crowd, Cull, Derive, Eve, Fest, Function, Gabfest,
  Galaxy, Get together, Glean, Glomerate, Harvest, Hootenanny, Hotchpot, Hui,
  Husking, In, Infer, Jamboree, Kommers, Learn, Lek, Lirk, Love-in, Meinie,
  Menyie, Pleat, Plica, Plissé, Pucker, Purse, Raft, Rake, Rally, Reef, Reunion,
  Round-up, Rout, Ruche, Ruff(le), Salon, Shindig, Shir(r), Shoal, Shovel,
  Singsong, Social, Spree, Take, Tuck, Vindemiate, Vintage, Wappensc(h)aw
Gauche Awkward, Clumsy, Farouche, Graceless
Gaudy Criant, Fantoosh, Flash, Garish, Glitz(y), Meretricious, Tacky, Tinsel
Gauge Absolute, Alidad(e), Anemometer, > ASSESS, Bourdon, Broad, Calibre,
  Denier, Dial, Estimate, Etalon, Evaluate, Feeler, Judge, Lee, Limit, Loading,
  Manometer, Marigraph, Measure, Meter, Narrow, Ombrometer, Oncometer,

Perforation, Plug, Pressure, Rain, Rate, Ring, Scantle, Size, Slip, Standard, Strain, Tape, Template, Tonometer, Tram, Tread, Tyre, Udometer, Vacuum, Water, Weather, Wind, Wire

Gauguin Paul

Gaul Asterix, Cisalpine, Vercingetorix

Gaunt Haggard, Lancaster, Lean, Randletree, Ranneltree, Rannletree, Rantletree, Rawbone, > **THIN**, Wasted

Gauntlet C(a)estus, Gantlope

Gauss G

Gautama Buddha

Gauze, Gauzy Gas mantle, Gossamer, Muslin, Sheer, Tiffany, Wire

Gawky Clumsy, Cow, Gammerstang

Gawp Rubberneck

Gay, Gaiety Blithe, Bonny, Boon, Buxom, Camp, Canty, Daffing, Debonair, Festal, Frolic, Gallant, Gladsome, Glee, Gordon, Grisette, Inverted, Jolly, Lightsome, May, Merry, Nitid, Out, Rackety, Riant, Rorty, Tit(t)upy, Volatile

Gaze Moon, Pore, Regard, Stare

Gazelle Ariel, Gerenuk, Goa, Mhorr, Mohr, Tabitha, Thomson's

Gazette London, Paper

Gear(ing) Angel, Arrester, Attire, Bags, Bevel, Capital, Clobber, Dérailleur, Differential, Draw, Duds, Engrenage, Epicyclic, Fab, Finery, Granny, Harness, Helical, Herringbone, Hypoid, Involute, Kit, Landing, Lay-shaft, Mesh, Mess, Mitre, Neutral, Overdrive, Ratio, Reverse, Rig, Riot, Rudder, Spur, Steering, Sun and planet, Synchromesh, > **TACKLE**, Timing, Top, Trim, Tumbler, Valve, Worm(-wheel)

Gecko Tokay

Gee Horse, Hump, My, Reist, Sulk, Tout, Towt, Urge

Geiger-counter Scintillator

Geisha Maiko

Gel Hair, Pectin, Pectose, Silica

Gelatine, Gelatinous Calipash, Collagen, Glutinous, Isinglass, Size, Tunicin

Geld(ing) Castrate, Lib, Neuter, Spado

Gelignite Jelly

Geller Uri

Gem Abraxas, Agate, Alexandrite, Almandine, Amazonite, Andradite, Asteria, Baguette, Birthstone, Bloodstone, Boule, Brilliant, Briolette, Cabochon, Cachalong, Cairngorm, Carnelian, Cat's eye, Chrysolite, Chrysoprase, Cornelian, Cymophane, Demantoid, Diamante, Diamond, Dumortierite, Emerald, Girasol(e), Girosol, Grossular(ite), Hawk's eye, Heliodor, Heliotrope, Hessonite, Hiddenite, Hyacinth, ID, Idaho, Indicolite, Iolite, Jacinth, Jargo(o)n, Jasper, Jaspis, > **JEWEL**, Kunzite, Lapis lazuli, Ligure, Marquise, Melanite, Menilite, Moonstone, Morganite, Onyx, Pearl, Peridot(e), Plasma, Prase, Pyrope, Rhinestone, Rhodolite, Rose-cut, Rubellite, Ruby, Sapphire, Sard, Sardius, Sardonyx, Scarab, Scarabaeoid, Smaragd, Solitaire, Sparkler, Spessartite, Starstone, Stone, Tiger's eye, Tourmaline, Turquoise, Uvarovite, Verd antique, Zircon

Gemination, Gemini Diplogenesis, Twins

Gen Info

Gendarme Flic

Gender Form, Natural, Sex

Gene(tics) Allel(e), Allelomorph, Anticodon, Codon, Complementary, Creation, Designer, Disomic, Episome, Exon, Factor, Gay, Genome, Hereditary,

Heterogamy, Holandric, Hologynic, Intron, Jumping, Lysenkoism, Mendel, Michurinism, Molecular, Muton, Oncogene, Operon, Regulatory, Selfish, Structural, Telegony, Terminator, Transposon, Weismannism

Genealogist, Genealogy Armory, Family, Heraldry, Line, Pedigree, Seannachie, Seannachy, Sennachie, Whakapapa

General Agamemnon, Agricola, Agrippa, Alcibiades, Allenby, Antigonus, Antipater, Antony, Ataman, Banquo, Blucher, Booth, Boulanger, Broad, C in C, Clive, Common, Communal, Conde, Cornwallis, Crassus, Current, Custer, De Gaulle, De Wet, Diadochi, Eclectic, Ecumenical, Election, Fairfax, Franco, Gamelin, Gen, GOC, Gordon, Grant, Hadrian, Hannibal, Holofernes, Ike, Inspector, Joshua, Kitchener, Lafayette, Lee, Leslie, Macarthur, Main, Marshall, Massena, Montcalm, Napier, Napoleon, Omnify, Overall, Overhead, Patton, Pershing, Pompey, Prevailing, Raglan, Regulus, Rife, Rommel, Scipio, Sherman, Shrapnel, Smuts, Stilwell, Strategist, Structural, Sulla, Tom Thumb, Turenne, > UNIVERSAL, Vague, Wide, Wolfe

Generate, Generation, Generator Abiogenetic, Age, Beat, Beget, Boomerang, Breeder, Charger, Create, Dynamo, Electrostatic, Epigon, Father, Fuel-cell, House, Kipp, Lost, Magneto, Motor, Noise, Olds, Powerhouse, Signal, Sire, Spawn, Spontaneous, Stallion, Van de Graaff, Windmill, X, Yield

Generosity, Generous Bounty, Charitable, Free-handed, Free-hearted, Handsome, Kind, Largess(e), > LAVISH, Liberal, Magnanimous, Munificent, Noble(-minded), Open, Open-handed, Open-hearted, Philanthropic, Plump, Profuse, Selfless, Sporting, Unstinting

▶ **Genetic** see GENE

Geneva(n) Calvinist, Gin, Hollands

Genial(ity) Affable, Amiable, Benign, Bluff, Bonhomie, Chin, Human, Kindly, Mellow

Genie Mazikeen, Shedeem

Genipap Lana

Genital(s) Ballocks, Bol(l)ix, Bollocks, Box, Crack, Crotch, Cunt, Fanny, Minge, Muff, Naff, Private parts, Privates, Pubes, Pudendum, Pussy, Quim, Secrets, Tackle, Tail, Twat, Vagina, Vulva, Yoni

Genius Agathodaimon, Brain, Daemon, Einstein, Engine, Flash, Inspiration, Ka, Michaelangelo, Numen, Prodigy

Genteel Conish, Polite, Proper, Refined

Gentian European, Felwort, Violet, Yellow

Gentile(s) Aryan, Ethnic, Goy, Nations, Shi(c)ksa

Gentle Amenable, Amenage, Bland, Clement, Delicate, Gradual, Grub, Light, Maggot, Mansuete, Mild, Tame, Tender

Gentleman(ly), Gentlemen Amateur, Baboo, Babu, Caballero, Cavalier, Duni(e)wassal, Dunniewassal, Esq(uire), Gemman, Gemmen, Ja(u)nty, Knight, Messrs, Milord, Mister, Mr, Nob, Proteus, Ritter, Runner, Rye, Sahib, Senor, Signor, Sir, Sirra(h), Smuggler, Squire, Sri, Stalko, Stir(rah), Swell, Tea, Toff, Tuan, Von, Yeoman

Gentry County, Landed, Quality, Squir(e)age

Gents Bog, John, Lav, Loo

Genuflexion Bend, Curts(e)y, Kowtow, Salaam

Genuine Authentic, Bona-fide, Dinkum, Dinky-di, Echt, Frank, Heartfelt, Honest, Intrinsic, Jannock, Jonnock, Kosher, Legit(imate), McCoy, Nain, Proper, Pucka, Pukka, Pure, Pusser, > REAL, Real McCoy, Right, Simon-Pure, Sincere, Square, Sterling, True, Veritable

Genus Class, Form, -ia, Mustela

Geode Druse

Geographer, Geography Chorography, Dialect, Economic, Hakluyt, Linguistic, Mercator, Pausanias, Physical, Political, Strabo

Geology Economic, Isotope, Seismology, Self-rock, Tectonics

Geometer, Geometrician, Geometry Analytical, Conics, Descriptive, Differential, Elliptic, Euclid(ean), Hyperbolic, Moth, Non-Euclidean, Plane, Porism, Projective, Riemannian, Solid, Spherics, Topologist

Geordie Guinea, Tynesider

George(s) Autopilot, Best, Borrow, Eliot, Farmer, Lloyd, Orwell, Pilot, Sand

Georgia(n) Ga, Hanover, Iberian

Geraint Knight

Geranium Dove's foot, Rose, Stork's bill, Yellow

Gerbil Jird

Germ(s) Bacteria, Bug, Culture, Klebsiella, Seed, Spirilla, Strep, Virus, Wheat, Zyme

German(y) Al(e)main(e), Alemannic, Angle, Anglo-Saxon, Bavarian, Berliner, Blood-brother, Boche, Cimbri, Composer, Cousin, Denglish, Franconian, Frank, Fritz, G, Goth, Habsburg, Hans, Hapsburg, Herr, Hessian, High, Hun, Jerry, Jute, Kaiser, Kraut, Landgrave, Low, Lusatian, Neanderthal, Ossi, Ostrogoth, Otto, Palsgrave, Plattdeutsch, Pruce, Prussian, Salic, Saxon, Squarehead, Tedesco, Teuton(ic), Vandal, Visigoth, Wessi, Wolfgang

Germane Apt, > **PERTINENT**, Relevant

Germanium Ge

Germ-free Aseptic

Germinate Grow, Pullulate, Sprout

Gesticulate, Gesticulation, Gesture(s) Ameslan, Beck(on), Ch(e)ironomy, Fico, Gest(e), Harvey Smith, Mime, Motion, Mudra, Salute, > **SIGN**, Signal, Snook, Token

Get, Get by, Get On Acquire, Advance, Aggravate, Annoy, Attain, Bag, Become, Brat, Bring, Capture, Cop, Cope, Derive, Fet(ch), Fette, Gain, Gee, Learn, Make, Manage, Milk, Net, Noy, > **OBTAIN**, Peeve, Procure, Progress, Reach, Realise, Rile, Roil, Secure, See, Sire, Twig, Understand, Win

Getaway Escape, Vamoose

▷ **Getting** *may indicate* an anagram

Getting better Convalescing, Improving, Lysis

Get-up Tog(s)

Geum Avens

Gewgaw Bagatelle, Bauble, Doit, Tat, Trifle

Geyser Soffioni, Therm

Ghanaian Ashanti, Fantee, Fanti, Tshi, Twi

Ghastly Gash, Grim, Hideous, Lurid, Macabre, Pallid, Ugsome, Welladay, White

Gherkin Cornichon

Ghetto Barrio, Slum

Ghost(ly) Acheri, Apparition, Apport, Caddy, Chthonic, Duende, Duppy, Eerie, Eery, Fantasm, Fetch, Gytrash, Haunt, Hint, Holy, Jumbie, Jumby, Larva(e), Lemur, Malmag, No'canny, Paraclete, Pepper's, Phantasm(agoria), Phantom, Revenant, Sampford, Shade, Shadow, Spectre, > **SPIRIT**, Spook, Trace, Truepenny, Umbra, Vision, Visitant, Waff, Wraith

Ghoul Fiend

GI Joe, Yankee

Giant(ess) Alcyoneus, Alifanfaron, Anak, Antaeus, Archiloro, Argus, Ascapart, Atlas, Balan, Balor, Bellerus, Blunderbore, Bran, Briareus, Brobdingnagian,

Cacus, Colbrand, Colbronde, Colossus, Coltys, Cormoran, Cottus, Cyclop(e)s, Despair, Enceladus, Ephialtes, Eten, Ettin, Ferragus, Gabbara, Galligantus, Gargantua, Géant, Gefion, Geirred, Gigantic, Gog, Goliath, Grim, Harapha, Hrungnir, Hymir, Idris, Irus, Jotun(n), Jumbo, Krasir, Lestrigon, Leviathan, Magog, Mammoth, Mimir, Monster, Oak, Og, Ogre, Otus, Pallas, Pantagruel, Patagonian, Polyphemus, Pope, Red, Rounceval, Skrymir, Slaygood, Talos, Talus, Thrym, Titan, Tityus, Tregeagle, Triton, Troll, Tryphoeus, Typhon, Urizen, Utgard, Ymir, Yowie

Gibberish Claptrap, Double Dutch, Greek, Jargon

Gibbet Gallows, Patibulary, Potence, Ravenstone, Tree

Gibbon(s) Hoolock, Hylobate, Orlando, Siamang, Stanley, Wou-wou, Wow-wow

Gibe Barb, Brocard, Chaff, Fleer, Glike, Jeer, Jibe, Shy, Slant, Wisecrack

Gibraltar Calpe

Giddy (girl), Giddiness Dizzy, Fisgig, Fishgig, Fizgig, Giglot, Glaikit, Glaky, Haverel, Hellicat, Hoity-toity, Jillet, Light, Light-headed, Skipping, Staggers, Sturdy, Turn, Vertigo, Volage(ous), Wheel, Woozy

Gift(s), Gifted Ability, Alms, Aptitude, Bef(f)ana, Bequest, Blessing, Blest, Bonbon, Bonsel(l)a, Boon, Bounty, Charism(a), Congiary, Corban, Covermount, Cumshaw, Dash, Deodate, > DONATION, Etrenne, Fairing, Flair, Foy, Freebie, Gab, Garnish, Godsend, Grant, Greek, Handout, Han(d)sel, Hogmanay, Indian, Knack, Koha, Kula, Lagniappe, Largesse, Legacy, Manna, Ne'erday, Nuzzer, Offering, Parting, Peace-offering, PET, Potlatch, > PRESENT, Presentation, Prezzie, Propine, Reward, Sop, Talent, Tongues, Treat, Wakf, Waqf, Windfall, Xenium

Gig Cart, Dennet, Moze, Whisk(e)y

Gigantic Atlantean, Briarean, Colossal, Goliath, > HUGE, Immense, Mammoth, Monster, Patagonian, Rounceval, Titan, Vast

Giggle Cackle, Ha, Keckle, Simper, Snicker, Snigger, Tehee, Titter

Gigolo Gallant, Ladykiller, Pimp

Gilbert Bab, Gb, White, WS

Gild(ed), Gilding Checklaton, Embellish, Enhance, Inaurate, Ormolu, S(c)hecklaton, Vermeil

Gill(s) Beard, Branchia, Cart, Ctenidium, Jill, Noggin, Spiracle

Gillman's Aqualung

Gilpin Draper, John, Renowned

Gilt Elt, Sow

Gimcrack Gewgaw, Tawdry, Trangam

Gimmick Doodad, Doodah, Hype, Ploy, Ruse, Stunt

Gin Bathtub, Geneva, Genever, Hollands, Juniper, Lubra, Max, Mother's ruin, Noose, Old Tom, Pink, Ruin, Schiedam, Schnapp(s), Sloe, Snare, Springe, Toil, Trap, Trepan, Twankay

Ginger Activist, Amomum, Asarum, Cassumunar, Costus, Curcuma, Galanga(l), Galengale, Galingale, Gar, Malaguetta, Nut, Pachak, Pep, Pop, Putchock, Putchuk, Race, Rase, Red(head), Root, Spice, Stem, Turmeric, Zedoary, Zingiber

Gingerbread D(o)um-palm, Lebkuchen, Parkin, Parliament(-cake), Pepper-cake

Gingivitis Ulitis

▶ **Gipsy** *see* GYPSY

Giraffe Camelopard, Okapi

Gird Accinge, Belt, Equip, Gibe, Jibe, Quip

Girder Beam, Binder, H-beam, I-beam, Lattice, Loincloth, Spar

Girdle Baldric, Center, Cestus, Chastity, Cincture, Cingulum, Corset, Enzone, Hippolyte, Hoop, Mitre, Pectoral, Pelvic, Sash, Shoulder, Surcingle, Surround,

Zona, Zone, Zonulet

Girl(s) Backfisch, Ball, Bimbo, Bint, Bird, Bit, Bobby-dazzler, Bobby-soxer, Bohemian, Broad, Burd, Call, Charlie, Chit, Chorus, Coed, Colleen, Cover, Crumpet, Cummer, Cutey, Cutie, Cutty, Dam(o)sel, Deb, Dell, Demoiselle, Dish, Doll, Dollybird, Essex, Filly, Fisgig, Fizgig, Flapper, Fluff, Fraulein, Frippet, Gaiety, Gal, Gammerstang, Geisha, Gibson, Gill(et), Gilp(e)y, Gouge, Gretel, Grisette, Hen, Hoiden, Hoyden, Hussy, Italian, Judy, Kimmer, Kinchinmort, Land, Lass(ock), Lorette, Maid(en), Mauther, Mawr, Mawther, May, Miss(y), Moppet, Mor, Mot, Mousmé, Mousmee, Mystery, Nautch, Number, Nymph(et), Oanshagh, Peach, Petticoat, Piece, Pigeon, Popsy, Principal, Puss, Quean, Queyn, Quin(i)e, Randy, Senorita, Sheila, Shi(c)ksa, Sis(s), Smock, Sweater, Tabby, Taupie, Tawpie, Teddy, Tiller, Tit, Trull, Weeny-bopper, Wench, Widgie, Wimp

▷ **Girl** *may indicate* a female name

Girl friend Baby, Chérie, Confidante, Date, Flame, Hinny, Leman, Moll, Peat

Girth Cinch, Compass, Exploitable, Size, Surcingle

Gist Essence, Kernel, > **NUB**, Pith, Substance

Give, Give up, Giving Abandon, Abstain, Accord, Administer, Afford, Award, Bend, Bestow, Buckle, Cede, Confiscate, Dative, Dispense, Dole, > **DONATE**, Duck, Elasticity, Enable, Enfeoff, Forswear, Gie, Grant, Impart, Jack, Largition, Render, Resign, Sacrifice, Sag, Spring, Stop, Tip, Vacate, Vouchsafe, Yeve

Give-away Freebie, Gift-horse

Given If

Give out Bestow, Dispense, Emit, Exude, Peter

Give over Cease, Lin

Glacial, Glaciation Gunz, Mindel, Riss, Wurm

Glacier Aletsch, Crevasse, Drumline, Fox, Franz-Josef, Hanging, Iceberg, Ice-cap, Icefall, Moraine, Muir, Rhône, Riss, Serac, Stadial, Tasman

Glad(ly), Gladden Cheer, Fain, > **HAPPY**, Lief, Willing

Glade La(u)nd

Gladiator Retiarius, Spartacus

Glamour(ise), Glamorous Charm, Glitter(ati), Glitz, Halo, It, Prestige, SA, Sexy, Spell

Glamour girl Cheesecake, Odalisk, Odalisque, Pin-up

Glance Allusion, Amoret, Argentite, Blink, Browse, Carom(bole), Coup d'oeil, Dekko, Draw, Eld, Eliad, Eye-beam, Galena, Glimpse, Illiad, Inwick, Lustre, Oeillade, Once-over, Peek, > **PEEP**, Ray, Redruthite, Ricochet, Scan, Sheep's eyes, Shufti, Shufty, Skellie, Skelly, Snick, Squint, Squiz, Twire, Vision

Gland Acinus, Adenoid, Adenoma, Adrenal, Apocrine, Bartholin's, Bulbourethral, Colleterial, Conarium, Cowper's, Crypt, Digestive, Ductless, Duodenal, Eccrine, Endocrine, Epiphysis, Exocrine, Goitre, Green, Helocrine, Hypophysis, Hypothalamus, Ink-sac, Lachrymal, Lacrimal, Liver, Lymph, Mammary, Meibomian, Musk-sac, Nectary, Oil, Osmeterium, Ovary, Pancreas, Paranephros, Parathyroid, Parotid, Parotis, Parotoid, Perineal, Pineal, Pituitary, Pope's eye, Preen, Prostate, Prothoracic, Salivary, Scent, Sebaceous, Shell, Silk, Sublingual, Submaxillary, Suprarenal, Sweat, Sweetbread, Tarsel, Tear, Testicle, Testis, Thymus, Thyroid, Tonsil, Uropygial, Vesicle, Zeiss

Glanders Farcy

Glandular (trouble) Adenitis

Glare, Glaring Astare, Blare, Dazzle, Flagrant, Garish, Gleam, Glower, Holophotal, Iceblink, Lour, Low(e), Naked, Shine, Vivid, Whally

Glass(es), Glassware, Glassy Amen, Ampul(la), Aneroid, Avanturine,

Aventurine, Baccara(t), Barometer, Bifocals, Bins, Bottle, Brimmer, Bumper, Burmese, Burning, Calcedonio, Case, Cheval, Cloche, Cocktail, Cooler, Copita, Cordial, Coupe, Cover, Crookes, Crown, Crystal, Cullet, Cupping, Cut, Dark, Delmonico, Diminishing, Eden, Euphon, Favrile, Fibre, Field, Flint, Float, Flute, Frigger, Frit, Fulgurite, Gauge, Glare, Goblet, Goggles, Granny, Green, Ground, Hand, Highball, Horn-rims, Humpen, Hyaline, Iceland agate, Jar, Jena, Jigger, Lace, Lalique, Laminated, Lanthanum, Latticinio, Lead, Lens, Liqueur, Liquid, Log, Lorgnette, Loupe, Lozen(ge), Lunette, Magma, Magnifying, Metal, Mica, Middy, Milk, Millefiori, Minimizing, Mirror, Moldavite, Monocle, Mousseline, Multiplying, Murr(h)ine, Musical, Object, Obsidian, One-way, Opal, Opal(ine), Opera, Optical, Pane, Parison, Paste, Pearlite, Pebble, Peeper, Pele, Pele's hair, Perlite, Perspective, Pier, Pince-nez, Pinhole, Pitchstone, Plate, Pon(e)y, Pressed, Prospective, Prunt, Psyche, Pyrex®, Quarrel-pane, Quarry, Quartz, Reducing, Roemer, Ruby, Rummer, Safety, Schmelz, Schooner, Seam, Seidel, Sheet, Silex, Silica, Sleever, Slide, Smalt(o), Snifter, Soluble, Specs, > **SPECTACLES**, Spun, Stained, Stein, Stemware, Stone, Storm, Strass, Sun, Supernaculum, Tachilite, Tachylite, Tachylyte, Tektite, Telescope, Tiffany, Tiring, Toilet, Trifocals, Triplex®, Tumbler, Uranium, Varifocals, Venetian, Venice, Vernal, Vita, Vitrail, Vitreous, Vitrescent, Vitro-di-trina, Volcanic, Watch, Water, Waterford, Weather, Window (pane), Wine, Wire

Glass-gall Sandiver

Glass-house Conservatory, Orangery

Glassite Sandemania

Glass-maker Annealer, Blower, Glazier, Lalique, Pontie, Pontil, Ponty, Puntee, Punty

Glaze(d), Glazing Aspic, Ciré, Coat, Double, Eggwash, Film, Flambé, Frit, Glost, Ice, Majolica, Peach-blow, Sancai, Slip, Tammy, Temmoku, Velatura

Gleam(ing) Blink, Flash, Glint, Glisten, Glitter, Gloss, Leme, Light, Ray, Relucent, Sheen, Shimmer, > **SHINE**

Glean(er) Gather, Harvest, Lease, Stibbler

Glee Exuberance, Joy, Mirth, Song

Glen Affric, Ghyll, Gill, Rushy, Silicon, Vale

Glib Flip, Slick, Smooth

Glide(away), Glider, Gliding Aquaplane, Coast, Elapse, Float, Illapse, Lapse, Luge, Microlight, Off, On, Portamento, Rogallo, Sail, Sailplane, Sashay, Scorrendo, Scrieve, Skate, Ski, Skim, Sleek, Slide, Slip, Slur, Swim, Volplane

Glimmer(ing) Gleam, Glent, Glint, Glow, Inkling, Light, Stime, Styme, Twinkle, Wink

Glimpse Aperçu, Flash, Glance, Glisk, Stime, Styme, Waff, Whiff

Glint Flash, Shimmer, > **SPARKLE**, Trace, Twinkle

Glisten(ing) Ganoid, Glint, Sheen, Shimmer, > **SHINE**, Sparkle

Glitter(ing) Clinquant, Garish, Gemmeous, Glee, Paillon, Sequin, Spang(le), Sparkle, Tinsel

Gloat(ing) Crow, Drool, Enjoy, Exult, Schadenfreude

Globe, Globule Artichoke, Ball, Bead, Celestial, Drop, Earth, Orb, Shot, Sphear, Sphere

Globulin Legumin, Protein

Gloom(y) Atrabilious, Benight, Blues, Cheerless, Cimmerian, Cloud, Crepuscular, Damp, Dark, > **DESPAIR**, Dingy, Disconsolate, Dismal, Dool(e), Downbeat, Drab, Drear, Drumly, Dump(s), Dyspeptic, Feral, Funereal, Glum, Grey, Louring, Mirk, Misery, Mopish, Morne, Morose, Mumps, Murk,

Obscurity, Overcast, Sable, Sad, Saturnine, Sepulchral, Solein, Solemn,
> **SOMBRE**, Stygian, Sullen, Tenebrous, Unlit

Glorification, **Glorify** Aggrandise, Apotheosis, Avatar, Bless, > **EXALT**, Extol, Halo,
Laud, Lionise, Praise, Radiance, Splendour

Glorious, **Gloria**, **Glory** Chorale, Grand, Halo, Hosanna, Ichabod, Knickerbocker,
Kudos, Lustre, Magnificent, Nimbus, Strut, Sublime, Twelfth

Glory-pea Kaka-beak, Kaka-bill, Kowhai

Gloss(y) Ciré, Enamel, Gild, Glacé, Japan, Lustre, Patina, > **POLISH**, Postillate,
Sheen, Sleek, Slick, Slide, Slur, Supercalendered, Veneer, Wetlook, Whitewash

Glossary Catalogue, Clavis, Index, K'thibh

Gloucester Cheese

Glove Boxing, Cestus, Dannock, Gage, Gauntlet, Kid, Mermaid's, Mitten,
Mousquetaire, Muffle, Oven, Velvet

Glow(er), **Glowing** Aflame, Ashine, Aura, Bloom, Burn, Calescence, Candent,
Candescence, Firefly, Flush, Foxfire, Gegenschein, Gleam, Halation, Iceblink,
Incandescence, Lambent, Leam, Leme, Luculent, Luminesce, Lustre, Perspire,
Phosphorescence, Radiant, Reflet, Rushlight, Shine, Snowblink, Translucent,
> **WARMTH**

Glucin(i)um Gl

Glucose, **Glucoside** Aesculin, Amygdalin, Dextrose, Digitalin, Indican,
Saponin, Solanine

Glue(y) Alkyd, Araldite®, Bee, Cement, Colloidal, Gelatin(e), Ichthyocolla,
Isinglass, Marine, Paste, Propolis, Size, Spetch

Glum Dour, Livery, Lugubrious, Moody, Morose, Ron, Sombre

Glut Choke, Gorge, Sate, Satiate, Saturate, Surfeit

Gluten, **Glutinous** Goo, Ropy, Seiten, Sticky, Tar, Viscid, Zymome

Glutton(ous), **Gluttony** Bellygod, Carcajou, Cormorant, Edacity, Gannet, Gorb,
Gourmand, Greedyguts, Gulosity, Gutser, Gutsy, Gutzer, Lurcher, Pig, Ratel,
Scoffer, Sin, Trencherman, Trimalchio, Wolverine

Glyceride, **Glycerine** Ester, Olein

Glycoside Hesperidin

Gnarl(ed) Knot, Knuckly, Knur, Nob

Gnash(ing) Bruxism, Champ, Grate

Gnat Culex, Culicidae, Midge, Mosquito

Gnaw(ing) Corrode, Erode, Fret, Lagomorph, Rodent

Gnome Adage, Bank-man, Chad, Cobalt, Financier, Kobold, Motto, Proverb, Saw,
Sprite

Gnostic Archontic, Cainite, Mand(a)ean, Marcionism, Ophite, Sabian, Tsabian,
Zabian

Gnu Wildebeest

Go, **Going (after, for, off, on, up, etc)** Advance, Afoot, Anabasis, Animation,
Assail, Attempt, Bash, Betake, Bing, Brio, Choof, Clamber, Continuance,
Crack, Depart, Die, Do, Energy, Fare, Gae, Gang, Gee, Gonna, Green, Hamba,
Hark, Hence, Hie, Imshi, Imshy, Ish, > **LEAVE**, March, Match, Off, Path, Pep,
Perpetual, Ply, Quit, Raik, Repair, Resort, Resume, Run, Scat, Scram, Segue,
Shoo, Skedaddle, Snick-up, Sour, Spank, Stab, Success, Transitory, Trine, Try,
Turn, Vam(o)ose, Verve, Via, Viable, Wend, Work, Yead, Yede, Yeed, Zap, Zing,
Zip

Goad Ankus, Brod, Gad, Impel, Incite, > **NEEDLE**, Prod, Rowel, Spur, Stimulate,
Stimulus, Taunt

Goal(posts) Ambition, Basket, Bourn(e), Destination, Dool, Dream, Drop, Dule,
End, Ettle, Field, Golden, Grail, Hail, Home, Horme, Hunk, Limit, Mission,

Moksha, Own, Score, Target, Tip-in, Touch-in, Ultima Thule, Uprights

Goat(-like) Alpine, Amalthea, Angora, Antelope, Antilope, Billy, Bok, Buck, Caprine, Cashmere, Gait, Gate, Giddy, Goral, Hircine, Ibex, Izard, Kashmir, Kid, Libido, Markhor, Mountain, Nan(ny), Nubian, Rocky mountain, Saanen, Sassaby, Serow, Serpent-eater, Steenbok, Steinbock, Tahr, Takin, Tehr, Thar, Toggenburg

Goatsucker Fern-owl, Nightjar

Gob Clot, Mouth, Yap

Gobble Bolt, Devour, Gorge, Gulp, Slubber, Wolf

Gobelin Tapestry

Go-between Broker, Factor, Intermediate, Link, Mediate, Middleman, Pandarus, Pander, Shuttle

Goblet Chalice, Hanap

Goblin Bargaist, Barg(h)est, Bodach, Bogey, Bogle, Bogy, Brownie, Bucca, Croquemitaine, Empusa, Erl-king, Esprit follet, Genie, Gnome, Gremlin, Knocker, Kobold, Lutin, Nis(se), Phooka, Phynnodderree, Pooka, Pouke, Puca, Pug, Red-cap, Red-cowl, Shellycoat, > SPRITE, Troll, Trow

Goby Dragonet

God(s) All-seer, Divine, Gallery, Gracious, Holy One, Household, Immortals, Light, Maker, Od(d), Olympian, Prime Mover, Principle, Providence, Serpent, The Creator, Trinity, Truth, Unknown, War

- **GODS**
-
-

1 letter:	Tyr	Mors	Khnum
D		Nebo	Liber
	4 letters:	Odin	Lludd
2 letters:	Abba	Ptah	Mimir
An	Agni	Rama	Momus
As	Aitu	Seth	Njord
Ra	Amun	Siva	Numen
Re	Apis	Soma	Orcus
	Ares	Thor	Orixa
3 letters:	Asur	Tyrr	Pales
Anu	Aten	Yama	Picus
Bel	Atum	Zeus	Pluto
Bes	Baal		Rudra
Dis	Brag	**5 letters:**	Satyr
Gad	Bran	Aesir	Sebek
Geb	Cama	Ammon	Shiva
Jah	Deva	Bragi	Sinis
Lar	Dieu	Comus	Surya
Lir	Eros	Cupid	Thoth
Lug	Faun	Dagan	Titan
Mot	Frey	Dagon	Vanir
Pan	Joss	Donar	Woden
Set	Kama	Freyr	Yahve
Sol	Kami	Haoma	Yahwe
Tin	Llyr	Horus	
Tiu	Loki	Hymen	**6 letters:**
Tiw	Lugh	Indra	Adonai
Tum	Mars	Janus	Aeolus

- Amen-ra
- Amon-ra
- Anubis
- Apollo
- Ashtar
- Asshur
- Avatar
- Balder
- Boreas
- Brahma
- Cabiri
- Chemos
- Cronus
- Delian
- Elohim
- Faunus
- Ganesa
- Garuda
- HaShem
- Helios
- Hermes
- Hughie
- Hypnos
- Kronos
- Mammon
- Marduk
- Mexitl
- Mextli
- Mithra
- Molech
- Moloch
- Nereus
- Njorth
- Oannes
- Orisha
- Ormazd
- Ormuzd

Osiris
Panisc
Panisk
Plutus
Rimmon
Saturn
Somnus
Tammuz
Teraph
Teshup
Thamiz
Thunor
Triton
Uranus
Varuna
Vishnu
Vulcan
Yahweh
Zombie

7 letters:
Alastor
Alpheus
Angus Og
Anteros
Bacchus
Chemosh
Daikoku
Ganesha
Hanuman
Heimdal
Jehovah
Jupiter
Krishna
Kuan Yin
Kwan Yin
Mercury

Mithras
Neptune
Nisroch
Oceanus
Penates
Phoebus
Priapus
Proteus
Rameses
Sarapis
Sat guru
Serapis
Setebos
Shamash
Silenus
Thammuz
Zagreus

8 letters:
Achelous
Dionysus
Heimdall
Hyperion
Kamadeva
Mahadeva
Morpheus
Mulciber
Nataraja
Pantheon
Poseidon
Quirinus
Silvanus
Sylvanus
Terminus
Trimurti
Wahiguru
Zephyrus

9 letters:
All-father
Asclepius
Fabulinus
Heimdallr
Jagganath
Promachos
Tetragram
Thunderer
Vertumnus
Zernebock

10 letters:
Demogorgon
Elegabalus
Hephaistos
Juggernaut
Karttikaya
Mumbo-jumbo
Prometheus
Trophonius

11 letters:
Adrammelech
Aesculapius
Bodhisattva

12 letters:
Quetzalcoati
Supreme Being

14 letters:
Tetragrammaton

God-bearing Deiparous
Goddess(es) Divine, Green, Muse

- **GODDESSES**

2 letters:
Ge

3 letters:
Ate
Eos
Hel
Mut
Nox

Nut
Nyx
Ops
Pax

4 letters:
Dian
Eris
Gaea

Gaia
Hera
Idun
Iris
Isis
Juno
Kali
Leda
Leto

Luna
Maat
Maut
Nike
Norn
Pele
Rhea
Sita
Thea

- **5 letters:**
- Aruru
- Ceres
- Diana
- Dione
- Durga
- Erato
- Flora
- Freya
- Grace
- Horae
- Houri
- Hulda
- Iduna
- Irene
- Kotys
- Pales
- Tanit
- Terra
- Tyche
- Ushas
- Venus
- Vesta

6 letters:
Aglaia
Ashnan
Athene
Aurora
Bastet
Cybele
Cyrene
Eastre
Freyja
Frigga
Graeae
Graiae
Hathor
Hecate
Hertha
Hestia
Huldar
Hyaeia
Idalia
Ishtar
Ithunn
Lucina
Pallas
Parcae

Phoebe
Pomona
Satyra
Selene
Semele
Tellus
Tethys
Themis
Thetis

7 letters:
Artemis
Astarte
Astraea
Bellona
Cotytto
Cynthia
Demeter
Fortuna
Kotytto
Lakshmi
Megaera
Minerva
Nemesis
Nepthys

Parvati
Sabrina
Strenia
Victory

8 letters:
Cloacina
Libitina
Valkyrie
Victoria
Walkyrie

9 letters:
Aphrodite
Ashtaroth
Ashtoreth
Eumenides
Mnemosyne
Sarasvati

10 letters:
Amphitrite
Proserpina
Proserpine

Godfather, Godmother Capo, Cummer, Fairy, Gossip, Kimmer, Rama, Sponsor, Woden

Godless Agnostic, Atheistic, Atheous, Impious, Profane

Godly Deist, Devout, Holy, Pious

Godown Hong

God-willing Deo volente, DV, Mashallah

Go-getter Arriviste, Hustler

Goggle(s) Snow-eyes, Stare

Going wrong Aglee, Agley, Misfiring

▷ **Going wrong** *may indicate* an anagram

Goitre Derbyshire neck, Exophthalmic, Graves' disease, Struma

Gold(en) Age, Amber, Apple, Ass, Au, Aureate, Auriferous, Bendigo, Bough, Bull, Bullion, California, Doubloon, Dutch, Eagle, Electron, Electrum, Emerods, Filigree, Filled, Fleece, Fool's, Free, Fulminating, Gate, Gule, Handshake, Hind, Horde, Horn, Ingot, Leaf, Lingot, Moidore, Mosaic, Muck, Nugget, Oaker, Obang, Ochre, Ophir, Or, Oreide, Ormolu, Oroide, Pistole, Placer, Pyrites, Red, Reef, Rolled, Silence, Silver-gilt, Sol, Standard, Stream, Stubborn, Talmi, Tolosa, Treasury, Venice, Virgin, White, Witwatersrand, Yellow

Gold-digger Forty-niner, Prospector

Golden Fleece Phrixus

Goldfield Rand

Goldfinch Charm, Chirm, Redcap

Gold leaf Ormolu

Gold rush Kalgoorlie, Klondike

Goldsmith Cellini, Fabergé, Oliver

Golf (ball) Better-ball, Clock, Crazy, Foursome, Gutta, Matchplay, Medal play,

Repaint, Round, Stableford
Golfer Alliss, Braid, Cotton, Els, Faldo, Hogan, Pivoter, Rees, Roundsman, Seve, Snead, Teer, Trevino, Wolstenholme, Yipper
Golly Crumbs, Gosh
Gondolier Balloonist, Bargee
Gone Ago, Dead, Defunct, Napoo, Out, Past, Ygo(e), Yod
▷ **Gone off** *may indicate* an anagram
Gone west Had it
Gong Bell, DSO, Medal, Tam-tam, VC
Gonorrhoea Clap
Goo Gleet, Gunge, Poise, Ulmin
Goober Monkey nut
Good(ness), Goody-goody Agatha, Agathodaimon, Altruism, Angelic, Bad, Bein, Benefit, Blesses, Bon, Bonzer, Bosker, Bounty, Brod, Budgeree, Canny, Castor, Civil, Clinker, Common, Coo, Cool, Crack(ing), Credit, Dab, Dandy, Def, Dow, Enid, Estimable, Fantabulous, Finger lickin', First-class, G, Gear, Giffen, Gosh, Guid, Humdinger, Lois, Lor, Ma foi, Nobility, > **NO GOOD**, Pi, Plum, Proper, Purler, Rattling, Rectitude, Riddance, Right, Rum, Sake, Salutary, Samaritan, Sanctity, Slap-up, Smashing, Spiffing, St, Suitable, Super, Taut, Tollol, Topping, Valid, Virtue, Virtuous, Weal, Welfare, Whacko, Wholesome, Worthy
Goodbye Addio, Adieu, Adios, Aloha, Apopemptic, Arrivederci, Cheerio, Ciao, Congé, Farewell, Hooray, Hooroo, Sayonara, Tata, Toodle-oo, Toodle-pip, Vale
Good evening Den
Goodfellow Brick, Puck, Robin, Samaritan, Worthy
Good-for-nothing Bum, Donnat, Donnot, Dud, Idler, Layabout, Lorel, Lorrell, Losel, Napoo, Sca(l)lawag, Scallywag, Scant o'grace, Sculpin, Shot-clog, Useless, Vaurien, Waff, Waster, Wastrel
Good Friday Parasceve
Good-humour(ed), Good-natured Amiable, Bonhomie, Gruntled, Kind
Good-looking Bon(n)ie, Bonny, Bonwie, Comely, Fair, Handsome, Personable, Pretty, Wally
Good news Evangel
Good number Thr(e)ave
Good order Eutaxy, Shipshape
Goods Bona, Brown, Cargo, Consumer, Disposable, Durables, Fancy, Flotsam, Freight, Futures, Gear, Hardware, Insight, Ironware, Lagan, Lay-away, Line, Piece, Products, Property, Schlock, Soft, Sparterie, Truck, Wares, White
Goodwill Amity, Bonhom(m)ie, Favour, Gree
Goody Wrong'un
Goon Secombe, Sellers
Goose, Geese Anserine, Barnacle, Bernicle, Blue, Brent, Canada, Capr Barren, Colonial, Daftie, Ember, Gander, Gannet, Golden, Greylag, Grope, Harvest, Hawaiian, Idiot, Juggins, MacFarlane's, Magpie, Michaelmas, Mother, Nana, Nene, Pink-footed, Quink, Roger, Saddleback, Silly, Simpleton, Skein, Snow, Solan, Strasbourg, Stubble, > **STUPID PERSON**, Swan, Team, Wav(e)y, Wawa, Whitehead
Gooseberry Cape, Chaperon(e), Chinese, Detrop, Fool, Gog, Groser(t), Groset, Grossart, Grozer, Honey blob, Kiwi, Physalis, Tomato
Gooseflesh Horripilation
Goosefoot Allgood, Amarantaceae, Beet, Blite, Fat-hen, Mercury, Orache, Saltbush

Gooseherd Quill-driver

Gopher Camass-rat, Minnesota

Gordian Knot

Gordon Chinese, Flash, Rioter

Gore Blood, Cloy, Gair, Horn, Toss

Gorge(s) Abyss, Arroyo, Barranca, Barranco, Canyon, Chasm, Cheddar, Cleft, Couloir, Cram, Defile, Donga, Flume, Gap, Ghyll, Glut, Grand Canyon, Grand Coulee, Gulch, Iron Gate, Khor, Kloof, Lin(n), Nala, Nalla(h), Nulla(h), Olduvai, Overeat, Overfeed, Pass, Ravine, Snarf, Staw, > **STUFF**, Throat, Tire, Tums, Valley, Yosemite

Gorgeous Delectable, Grand, Splendid, Superb

Gorgon Euryale, Medusa, Ogress, Stheno

▸ **Gorilla** *see* **MONKEY**

Gorse Broom, Furze, Gosse, Ulex, Whin

Gosh Begad, Begorra, Blimey, Coo, Cor, Gadzooks, Gee, Gum, Heavens, Lor, My, Och, Odsbobs, Odso

Gospel(s), **Gospeller** Apocryphal, Creed, Diatessaron, Evangel, Fact, John, Kerygma, Luke, Mark, Matthew, Nicodemus, Prosperity, Protevangelium, Synoptic, Truth, Waldensian

Gossamer(y) Araneous, Byssoid, Cobwebby, Gauzy

Gossip Ana(s), Aunt, Backbite, Blether, Cackle, Cat, Causerie, Chat, Chin, Chitchat, Clash, Claver, Cleck, Clish-clash, Clishmaclaver, Confab, Coze, Crack, Cummer, Dirt, Flibbertigibbet, Gab(nash), Gabfest, Gas, Goster, Gup, Hen, Jaw, Loose-tongued, Maundrel, Nashgab, Natter, Noise, On dit, Pal, Personalist, Prattle, Quidnunc, Reportage, Rumour, Scandal(monger), Schmooze, Scuttlebutt, Shmoose, Shmooze, Sweetie-wife, Tabby(cat), Talk(er), Tattle, Tibby, Tittle(-tattle), Twattle, Yatter, Yenta

Got Gat, Obtained

Goth(ic) Alaric, Moesia

Gothamite Abderian, New Yorker

Gouge Chisel, Groove, Scoop

Gourd Bottle, Calabash, Courgette, Dishcloth, Guiro, Hercules' club, Loofa, Melon, Monkeybread, Pumpkin, Squash, Zucchini

Gourmand, **Gourmet** Apicius, > **EPICURE**, Gastronome, Gastrosopher, Lickerish, Table, Trencherman, Ventripotent

Gout Chiragra, Hamarthritis, Podagra, Taste, Tophus

Govern(or), **Government** Adelantado, Administer, Ag(h)a, Agricola, Alderman, Amban, Amman, Amtman, ANC, Autarchy, Autocrat, Autonomy, Bahram, Ban, Beehive, Beg, Beglerbeg, Bencher, Bey, Bridler, Bureaucracy, Burgrave, Cabinet, Caretaker, Castellan, Catapan, Cham, Circar, Classics, Coalition, Command, Commonweal, Condiminium, Congress, Constable, Constitution, Consulate, Cybernetic, Darogha, Democracy, Dergue, Despotism, Dey, Diarchy, Dictatorship, Dinarchy, Directoire, Directory, Dominate, Downing St, Duarchy, Dulocracy, Duumvirate, Dyarchy, Dynast, Earl, Empery, Eparch, Ergatocracy, Escapement, Ethnarch, Exarch, Fascism, Federal, G, Gauleiter, Gerontocracy, Gov, Grieve, Gubernator, Hagiocracy, Hague, Hajjaz, Hakim, Haptarchy, Harmost, HE, Helm, Hexarchy, Hierocracy, Honcho, Hospodar, Imperialism, Ins, Inspector, Isocracy, Junta, Kaimakam, Kakistocracy, Kamalism, Kebele, Khalifate, Khan, Kremlin, Legate, Local, Majlis, Majorism, Monarchy, Monocracy, Mudir, Nabob, Naik, Nomarch, Nomocracy, Ochlocracy, Oireachtas, Oligarchy, Optic®, Pa, Pacha, Padishah, Pasha, Pater, Pentarch, Père, Petticoat, Physiocracy, Pilate, Placemen, Plutocracy, Podesta, Polity,

Polyarchy, Porte, Power, Priest-king, Proconsul, Propraetor, Proveditor, Provedor(e), Providor, Ptochocracy, Quadrumvirate, Quirinal, Raj, Realpolitik, Rection, Rector, Rectrix, Regency, Regié, Regime(n), Reign, Rein, Ride, > **RULE**, Satrap, Senate, Serkali, Shogun, Signoria, Sircar, Sirkar, Stad(t)holder, Stakhanovism, Statecraft, Steer, Stratocracy, Subadar, Sway, Technocracy, Tetrarchy, Thatcherism, Thearchy, Theonomy, Timocracy, Totalitarianism, Triumvirate, Tuchun, Tyranny, Vali, Viceregal, Viceroy, Vichy, Wali, Warden, Wealsman, Whitehall, White House, Witan

Governess Duenna, Eyre, Fraulein, Griffin, Mademoiselle, Prism, Vicereine

Government revenue Jaghir(e), Jagir

Gown Banian, Banyan, Dressing, Empire, Geneva, Green, Johnny, Kirtle, Manteau, Manto, Mantua, Morning, Mother Hubbard, Peignoir, Polonaise, Robe, Silk, Slammakin, Slammerkin, Slop, Stola, Stuff, Tea, Wrap(per)

Grab Annexe, Bag, Clutch, Cly, Collar, Glaum, Grapnel, Hold, Holt, Rap, Seise, Seize, > **SNATCH**, Steal, Swipe

Gracchi Jewels

Grace(s), Graceful Aglaia, Airy, Amnesty, Anna, Bad, Beauty, Become, Benediction, Bethankit, Blessing, Charis(ma), Charites, Charity, Darling, Dr, Elegance, Euphrosyne, Fluent, Gainly, Genteel, Genty, Godliness, Grazioso, Light, Mense, Mercy, Molinism, Mordent, Omnium, Ornament, Pralltriller, Sacrament, Saving, Streamlined, Style, Thalia, Thanks, WG, Willowy

Gracious Benign, By George, Charismatic, Generous, Good, Handsome, Hend, Merciful, Polite

Gradation Cline, Degree, Nuance, Stage

Grade, Gradient Alpha, Analyse, Angle, Assort, Beta, Class(ify), Dan, Degree, Delta, Echelon, Gamma, Geothermal, Gon, Gride, Hierarchy, Inclination, Kyu, Lapse, Measure, Order, Ordinary, Pressure, Rank, Score, Seed, Slope, Stage, Standard, Status, Temperature

Gradual Gentle, Grail, Imperceptible, Inchmeal, Piecemeal, Slow

Graduate, Graduation Alumnus, BA, Bachelor, Calibrate, Capping, Classman, Incept, Laureateship, Licentiate, LlB, MA, Master, Nuance, Optime, Ovate

Graffiti Bomb, Doodle, Tag, Tagger

Graft Anaplasty, Autoplasty, Boodle, Bribery, Bud, Bypass, Crown, Dub, Enarch, Enrace, Flap, Hard, Heteroplasty, Imp, Implant, Inarch, Inoculate, Payola, Pomato, Racket, Scion, Shoot, Skin, Slip, Transplant, Whip, Ympe

Grail Chalice, Cup, Sangraal, Sangrail, Sangreal

Grain(y) Bajra, Bajree, Bajri, Bear, Bere, Boll, Bran, Cereal, Corn, Couscous, Crop, Curn, Curn(e)y, Cuscus, Distiller's, D(o)urra, Extine, Frumentation, Gr, Graddan, Granule, Groats, Grumose, Intine, Kaoliang, Knaveship, Malt, Mashlam, Mashlin, Mashloch, Mashlum, Maslin, Mealie, Millet, Milo, Minim, Mongcorn, Oats, Panic(k), Pannick, Pickle, Pinole, Pollen, Polynology, Popcorn, Puckle, Quarter, Rabi, Raggee, Raggy, Ragi, Rhy, Rye, Sand, Scruple, Seed, Semsem, Sorghum, Thirlage, Tola, Touch, Wheat, Wholemeal

Gram Black, Chich, Chick-pea, Green, Teen, Tene, Urd

Grammar(ian), Grammatical Ablative absolute, Accidence, Amphibology, Anacoluthia, Anacoluthon, Anaphora, Anastrophe, Case, Cataphora, Categorical, Donat, Donet, Generative, Gr, Linguistics, Montague, Paradigm, Pivot, Primer, Priscianist, Scholiast, Stratificational, Syndetic, Syndeton, Synectics, Synesis, Syntax, Systemics, Tagmeme, Transformational, Trivium, Typto, Universal, Valency

Gramophone Record player, Victrolla®

Grampus Orc, Thresher-whale, Whale

Granary Barn, Girnel, Silo
Grand(eur), Grandiose Canyon, Epical, Flugel, G, Gorgeous, Guignol,
 High-faluting, Hotel, Imposing, La(h)-di-da(h), Long, Lordly, Magnificent,
 Majestic, Megalomania, Palatial, Piano(forte), Pompous, Regal, Splendid,
 Stately, Stoor, Stour, Stowre, Sture, Sublime, Swell, Tour
Grandchild Mokopuna, Niece, Oe, Oy(e)
Grandee Adelantado, Don, Magnifico
Grandfather Ancient, Avital, Clock, Goodsire, Gramps, Gudesire, Gutcher,
 Luckie-dad, Oldster, Old-timer, Oupa
Grandmother Babushka, Beldam, Gran(nie), Granny, Moses, Nan(a), Ouma
Grandparent(al) Aval, Avital
Grand Prix Race(-cup)
Grandsire Peal
Grange Moated
Granite Aberdeen, Chinastone, Graphic, Greisen, Luxul(l)ianite, Luxulyanite,
 NH, Pegmatite, Protogine
Grannie Forebear, Knot, Nan(a)
Grant(ed) Accord, Aid, Award, Bestow, Beteem(e), Bounty, Bursary, Carta, Cary,
 Charta, Charter, Concession, > **CONFER**, Cy, Datum, Endow, Exhibition, Feoff,
 Give, Land, Lend, Let, Munich, Obreption, Patent, President, Regium donum,
 Send, Sop, Subsidy, Subvention, Teene, Vouchsafe, Yeven, Yield
Granule, Granulate(d) Kern, Otolith, Pearl, Plastid, Pound, Prill
Grape(s) Aligoté, Botros, Botryoid, Cabernet, Cabernet Sauvignon, Catawba,
 Chardonnay, Chenin blanc, Concord, Delaware, Diamond, Fox, Gamay,
 Gewurztraminer, Grenache, Haanepoot, Hamburg(h), Hanepoot, Honeypot,
 Hyacinth, Lambrusco, Malmsey, Malvasia, Malvesie, Malvoisie, Merlot,
 Muscadel, Muscadine, Muscat(el), Noble rot, Oregon, Petite Syrah, Pinot,
 Pinot Blanc, Pinot Chardonnay, Ptisan, Racemose, Raisin, Rape, Riesling,
 Sauvignon, Scuppernong, Sémillon, Sercial, Shiraz, Sour, Staphyline, Steen,
 Sultana, Sweet-water, Sylvaner, Syrah, Tokay, Uva, Verdelho, Véronique, Vino,
 Wineberry, Zinfandel
Grapefruit Pampelmoose, Pomelo, Pompelmouse, Pompelo, Pumple-nose, Ugli
Grapeshot Mitraille
Grape-sugar Glucose
Grapevine Hearsay, Moccasin telegraph
Graph(ic) Bar, Chart, Contour, Diagram, Histogram, Learning curve,
 Nomograph, Ogive, Picturesque, Pie (chart), Profile, Sonogram, Table, Vivid
Graphite Kish, Plumbago
Grapple Clinch, Close, Hook, Lock, Struggle, Wrestle
Grasp(ing) Apprehend, Catch, Clat, Claut, Clinch, > **CLUTCH**, Compass,
 Comprehend, Fathom, Get, Grab, Grapple, Greedy, Grip(e), Hent, Hug, Prehend,
 Prehensile, Raptorial, Realise, Rumble, Sense, Snap, Snatch, Twig, Uptak(e)
Grass(land), Grass roots, Grassy Agrostology, Alang, Alfa(lfa), Arrow, Avena,
 Bahia, Bamboo, Bang, Barbed wire, Barley, Barnyard, Beard, Bennet, Bent,
 Bermuda, Bhang, Blade, Blady, Blue(-eyed), Bristle, Brome-grass, Bromus,
 Buffalo, Buffel, Bunch, Bush, Canary, Cane, Canna, Cannach, Carpet, Cat's
 tail, Chess, China, Citronella, Cleavers, Clivers, Clover, Cochlearia, Cocksfoot,
 Cockspur, Cogon, Cord, Cortaderia, Cotton, Couch, Cow, Crab, Culm, Cuscus,
 Cutty, Dactylis, Danthonia, Dari, Darnel, Deergrass, Dhur(r)a, Diss, Divot,
 Dogstail, Dog's tooth, Dogwheat, Doob, Doura, Dura, Durra, Eddish, Eel,
 Eelwrack, Elephant, Emmer, Esparto, Feather, Fescue, Finger, Fiorin, Flinders,
 Floating, Flote, Fog, Foggage, Foxtail, Gage, Gama-grass, Ganja, Glume,

Glumella, Goose, Grama, Green(sward), Hair, Halfa, Harestail, Hassock, Haulm, Hay, Haycock, Heath(er), Hemp, Herbage, High veld, Holy, > **INFORM**, Jawar(i), Job's tears, Johnson, Jowar(i), Kangaroo, Kans, Kentucky blue, Khuskhus, Kikuyu, Knoll, Knot, Lalang, Laund, Lawn, Lemon, Locusta, Lolium, Lop, Lucern(e), Lyme, Machair, Manna, Marram, Marrum, Mary Jane, Mat, Materass, Matweed, Mead, Meadow (-fescue), Melic, Melick, Millet, Milo, Miscanthus, Monkey, Moor, Nark, Nassella tussock, Nose, Oat, Orchard, Oryza, Painted, Palet, Pamir, Pampas, Panic, Paspalum, Pasturage, Peach, Pennisetum, Pepper, Persicaria, Phleum, Plume, Poa, Porcupine, Pot, Puszta, Quack, Quaking, Quick, Quitch, Ramee, Rami(e), Rat, Rat on, Redtop, Reed, Rescue, Rhodes, Rib, Ribbon, Rice, Rips, Roosa, Rough, Rumble(r), Rusa, Rye, Rye (-brome), Sacaton, Sago, Salt, Savanna(h), Saw, Scorpion, Scraw, Scurvy, Scutch, Sea-reed, Sedge, Seg, Sesame, Sheep's fescue, Shop, Sing, Sinsemilla, Sisal, Sneak(er), Snitch, Snout, Snow, Sorghum, Sour-gourd, Sourveld, Spanish, Spear, Spelt, Spike, Spinifex, Splay, Split, Squeal, Squirrel-tail, Squitch, Stag, Star(r), Stipa, Stool-pigeon, Storm, Sudan, Sugar, Sward, Swath(e), Sword, Tape, Tath, Tea, Tef(f), Tell, Teosinte, Timothy, Toad, Toetoe, Toitoi, Triticale, Triticum, Tuffet, Turf, Tussac, Tussock, Twitch, Veld(t), Vernal, Vetiver, Whangee, Wheat, Whitlow, Windlestraw, Wire, Witch, Wood melick, Worm, Yard, Yellow-eyed, Yorkshire fog, Zizania, Zostera, Zoysia

Grasshopper Cicada, Cricket, Grig, Katydid, Locust, Long-horned, Meadow, Tettix, Wart-biter, Weta

Grate(r), Grating Abrade, Burr, Cancelli, Chirk, Crepitus, > **FRET**, Graticule, Gravelly, Grid, Grill, Guichet, Guttural, Hack, Hearth, Heck, Hoarse, Ingle, Jar, Mort-safe, Portcullis, Rasp, Risp, Rub, Ruling, Scrannel, > **SCRAPE**, Scrat, Shred, Siver, Strident, Syver

Grateful Beholden, Cinders, Indebted, Obliged

Gratification, Gratify(ing) Aggrate, Indulge, Kick, Masochism, Oblige, Pleasure, Regale, Reward, Sadism

Gratitude God 'a mercy, Ta, Thanks

Gratuitous, Gratuity Baksheesh, Beer-money, Bonsella, Bonus, Bounty, Cumshaw, Free, Glove-money, Gratis, Tip

Grave(yard) Accent, Arlington, Bass, Bier, Burial, Charnel, Chase, Darga, Demure, Dust, God's acre, Heavy, Heinous, Important, Ingroove, Kistvaen, Kurgan, Long home, Mound, Passage, Pit, Sad, Saturnine, Serious, Sober, Sombre, Speos, Staid, Stern, Tomb, Watery

Grave-digger Bederal, Fossor, Sexton

Gravel(ly) Calculus, Channel, Chesil, Chisel, Eskar, Esker, Glareous, Grail(e), Grit, Hoggin(g), Murram, Nonplus, Pay, Pea, Pingo, Shingle

Gravity Barycentric, G, Geotaxis, Geotropism, Great Attraction, Magnitude, Mascon, Quantum, Specific, Weight, Zero

Gravy Baster, Browning, Coin, Jus, Sauce

Gravy-boat Argyle, Argyll

▶ **Gray** *see* **GREY**

Grayling Umber

Graze, Grazing Abrade, Agist, Bark, Brush, Crease, Crop, Feed, Herdwick, Leasow(e), Machair, Pascual, Pasture, Rake, Rangeland, Scrape, Scrawn, Shave, Shieling, Zero

Grease, Greasy Bribe, Creesh, Dope, Dubbing, Elaeolite, Elbow, Enseam, Glit, Lanolin, Lard, Lubricate, Seam(e), Shearer, Sheep-shearer, Smarm, Suint, Unctuous

Great(s), Greater, Greatest Ali, Astronomical, Bully, Colossus, Extreme,

Gargantuan, Gay, Gey, Gran(d), Grit, Gt, Guns, Helluva, Immortal, Important, Lion, Macro, Main, Major, Massive, Mega, Mickle, Mochell, Modern, Much, Muchel(l), Muckle, OS, Profound, Rousing, Stoor, Stour, Stupendous, Sture, Sublime, Super, Superb, Swingeing, Synergy, Tall, Titan(ic), Tremendous, Unco, Untold, Utmost, Vast, Voluminous, Zenith

Great deal Mort

Grebe Cargoose

Grecian Bend, Nose

Greed(y) Avarice, Avid, Bulimia, Bulimy, Cupidity, Edacious, Esurient, Gannet, Gare, Gulosity, Harpy, Killcrop, Lickerish, Mercenary, Piggery, Pleonexia, Rapacity, Selfish, Solan, Voracity, Wolfish

Greek(s) Achaean, Achaian, Achilles, Aeolic, Agamemnon, Ajax, Aonian, Arcadia, Archimedes, Argive, Aristides, Athenian, Attic, Cadmean, Cleruch, Corinthian, Cretan, Cumae, Cyzicus, Delphian, Demotic, Ding, Diomedes, Dorian, Doric, Eoka, Eolic, Epaminondas, Ephebe, Epirus, Euclid, Evzone, Fanariot, Gr, Helladic, Hellene, Hellenic, Homer, Hoplite, Ionian, Isocrates, Italiot(e), Javan, Katharevousa, Klepht, Koine, Laconian, Lapith, Leonidas, Linear B, Locrian, Lucian, Macedonia, Middle, Modern, Molossian, Momus, Nestor, Nike, Nostos, Orestes, Paestum, Patroclus, Pelasgic, Pelopid, Perseus, Phanariot, Pythagoras, Romaic, Samiot, Seminole, Spartacus, Spartan, Stagirite, Strabo, Sybarite, Tean, Teian, Theban, Thersites, Theseus, Thessal(on)ian, Thracian, Timon, Typto, Uniat, Xenophon, Zorba

Green(ery) Almond, Apple, Avocado, Baggy, Bice, Biliverdin, Bottle, Bowling, Caesious, Callow, Celadon, Cerulein, Chard, Chartreuse, Chlorophyll, Chrome, Citron, Cole, Collard, Common, Copper, Corbeau, Crown, Cyan, Dioptase, Eau de nil, Eco-, Ecofriendly, Emerald, Emerande, Envious, Erin, Fingers, Foliage, Forest, Fundie, Fundy, Gaudy, Glaucous, Go, Goddess, Grass, Gretna, Gull, Immature, Inexpert, Jade, Jungle, Kendal, Kensal, Khaki, Lawn, Leafage, Lime, Lincoln, Loden, Lovat, Mead, Monastral®, Moss, Moulding, Naive, New, Nile, Oasis, Olive, Paris, Pea, Peridot, Pistachio, Porraceous, Putting, Raw, Realo, Reseda, Rifle, Rink, Sage, Scheele's, Sea, Sludge, Smaragdine, Sward, Teal, Tender, Terre-vert, Turacoverdin, Tyro, Unfledged, Uninitiated, Unripe, Uranite, Verdant, Verd antique, Verdigris, Verdure, Vert, Virent, Virid, Vir(id)escent, Young

Greenheart Bebeeru

Greenhorn Baby, Dupe, Put(t), Rookie, Sucker

Greenhouse Conservatory, Orangery, Phytotron, Polytunnel

Greens Broccoli, Cabbage, Calabrese, Cash, Money, Sprout, Vegetable(s)

Greet(ing) Abrazo, Accost, All hail, Arvo, Banzai, Benedicite, Blubber, Chimo, Ciao, Hail, Hallo, Halse, Handclasp, Handshake, Haway, Heil, Heita, Hello, Herald, Hi, High-five, Hiya, Hongi, How, How d'ye do, Howsit, Jai Hind, Jambo, Kia ora, Kiss, Kissagram, Mihi, Namaskar, Namaste, Respects, Salaam, Salam Alaikum, Salute, Salve, Sd, Shalom, Shalom aleichem, Sorry, Strippagram, Strippergram, Tena Koe, Wave, > **WELCOME**, Wotcher, Yo

Gregarious Social

Gregorian Chant, NS, Plagal

▶ **Gremlin** *see* **GOBLIN**

Grenade Bomb, Egg, Hand, Pineapple, Rifle, Stun

Greta Garbo

Grey(ing), Gray Age, Agnes, Argent, Ashen, Ashy, Battleship, Beige, Bloncket, Charcoal, Cinereous, Dapple, Dorian, Dove, Drab, Ecru, Feldgrau, Field, Glaucous, Gloomy, Gr, Gridelin, Griesie, Gries(l)y, Grise, Grisy, Grizzled,

Gunmetal, Gy, Hoary, Hodden, Hore, Inn, Iron, Leaden, Liard, Livid, Lucia, Lyart, Mouse-coloured, Neutral, Olive drab, Oyster, Pearl, Perse, Pewter, Poliosis, Putty, Sclate, Slaty, Steel, Taupe, Zane

Greyfriars Bunter, Magnet

Greyhound Grew, Italian, Longtail, Ocean, Persian, Saluki, Sapling, Whippet

Grey matter Cinerea

Grid(dle), **Gridiron** Bar, Barbecue, Brandreth, Cattle, Control, Dot matrix, Grate, Graticule, Grating, National, Network, Reseau, Reticle, Roo-bar, Screen, Starting, Suppressor, Tava(h), Tawa, Windscale

Gride Creak, Grate

Grief, **Grievance**, **Grieve**, **Grievous** Axe, Bemoan, Bitter, Complaint, Condole, Cry, Dear(e), Deere, Distress, Dole, Dolour, Gram(e), Gravamen, Heartbreak, Hone, Illy, Io, > MISERY, Monody, O(c)hone, Pain, Pathetic, Plaint, Rue, Score, Sore, Sorrow, Teen, Tene, Tragic, Wayment, Weeping, Woe, Wrong

Griffin Gripe, Grype, Novice, Pony

Grill(er), **Grilling** Braai, Brander, Broil, Carbonado, Crisp, Devil, Gridiron, Inquisition, Interrogate, Kebab, Mixed, Pump, Question, Rack, Radiator, Reja, Yakimona

Grim Dire, Dour, Gaunt, Glum, Gurly, Hard, Macabre, Stern

▷ **Grim** *may indicate* an anagram

Grimace Face, Girn, Moe, Mop, Moue, Mouth, Mow, Murgeon, Pout

Grime(s), **Grimy** Colly, Dirt, Peter, Rechie, Reechie, Reechy, Soil, Sweep

Grin Fleer, Girn, Risus, Simper, Smirk, Sneer

Grind(ing), **Grinder** Bray, Bruxism, Chew, Crunch, > CRUSH, Droil, Gnash, Grate, Graunch, Grit, Home, Kern, Kibble, Levigate, Mano, Metate, Mill, Mince, Molar, Muller, Pug, Pulverise, Slog, Stamp, Triturate

Grip(ping), **Gripper** Ascendeur, Bite, Chuck, Clam, Clamp, Clip, Clutch, Craple, Embrace, Enthral, Get, Grapple, > GRASP, Haft, Hair, Hairpin, Hand(fast), Handhold, Hend, Hold, Hug, Key, Kirby®, Lewis, Obsess, Pincer, Pinion, Pistol, Prehensile, Purchase, Raven, Rhine, Sally, Setscrew, Sipe, Strain, Streigne, Twist, Valise, Vice, Walise, Wrestle

Gripe(s) Colic, Complain, Ditch, Grasp, Griffin, Ileus, Pain, Tormina

Grisly Gory

Grist Burden

Gristle, **Gristly** Cartilage, Chondroid, Lytta

Grit(s), **Gritty** Blinding, Clench, Gnash, Granular, Grate, Guts, Hominy, Nerve, Pluck, Resolution, Sabulose, Sand, Shingle, Swarf, Valour, Yorkshire

Grizzle(d) Grey

Groan(er) Bewail, Bing, Moan

Grocer Grasshopper, Jorrocks, Pepperer, Symbol

Groggy Dazed, Shaky

Groin Gnarr, Inguinal, Lisk

Groom(ed) Brush, Coistrel, Coistril, Comb, Curry, Dress, Fettler, Kempt, Ostler, Palfrenier, Paranymph, Preen, Prink, S(a)ice, Smarten, Spouse, Strapper, Syce, Tiger, Tracer, Train, Wrangler

▷ **Groom** *may indicate* an anagram

Groove(d), **Groovy** Bezel, Canal, Cannelure, Chamfer, Channel, Chase, Clevis, Coulisse, Croze, Dièdre, Exarate, Fissure, Flute, Fuller, Furr, Furrow, Glyph, Gouge, Kerf, Key-seat, Keyway, Lead-in, Lead-out, Oche, Pod, Rabbet, Race(way), Raggle, Raphe, Rebate, Rif(f)le, Rigol(l), Rout, > RUT, Scrobe, Sipe, Slot, Sulcus, Throat, Track, Trough, Vallecula

Grope(r) Feel, Fumble, Grabble, Hapuka, Ripe, Scrabble

Gross All-up, Coarse, Complete, Crass, Dense, Earn, Earthy, Flagrant, Frankish, Fustilugs, Gr, Loathsome, Material, Obese, Outsize, Overweight, Pre-tax, Rank, Ribald, Rough, Stupid, Sum, Whole

▷ **Gross** *may indicate* an anagram

Grotesque Antic, Bizarre, Fantastic, Fright, Gargoyle, Magot, Outlandish, Rabelaisian, Rococo, Teras

Grotto Cave, Lupercal

Ground(s) Abthane, Arena, Astroturf, Basis, Bottom, Breeding, Campus, Cause, Common, Criterion, Crushed, Deck, Dregs, Eard, Earth, Edgbaston, Epig(a)eal, Epig(a)ean, Epig(a)eous, Floor, Footing, Gathering, Grated, Grist, Grouts, High, Hunting, Lees, Leeway, Lek, Lords, Lot, Marl, Mealed, Middle, Occasion, Oval, Parade, Piste, Pitch, Plat, Pleasure, Plot, Policy, Proving, Quad, > **REASON**, Recreation, Réseau, Ring, Sediment, Slade, Soil, Solum, Sports, Stadium, Stamping, Terra, Terrain, Tom Tiddler's, Touch, Tract, Turf, Udal, Vantage, Venue, Waste(land), Yard, Yird

▷ **Ground** *may indicate* an anagram

Groundbait Chum

Ground-crew Erk

Ground-rent Crevasse

Groundsheet Hutchie

Groundsman Greenkeeper

Group Abelian, Acyl, 'A'list, Band, Batch, Beatles, Bee, Bevy, Bloc(k), Blood, Bloomsbury, Body, Bracket, Bratpack, Bruges, Caboodle, Cadre, Camarilla, Camp, Cartel, Category, Caucus, Cave, Cell, Chain, Chordata, Circle, Clade, Class(is), Clique, Cluster, Cohort, Colony, Combo, Commune, Community, Concertina, Congregation, Consort(ium), Contact, Contingent, Control, Convoy, Coterie, Covey, Crew, Deme, Demi-monde, Denomination, Detail, Enclave, Encounter, Ensemble, Faction, Fascio, Focus, Fold, Fraternity, Front, Galère, Gang, Gemeinschaft, Gender, Genus, Gesellschaft, Ginger, Globe, Guild, Hapu, Heading, Hexad, Hirsel, House, Income, In-crowd, Ketone, Kit, Knot, League, Marathon, Marshal, Nexus, Order, Outfit, Oxford, Pack(et), Panel, Parti, Party, Passel, Peer, Phalange, Phratry, Phylum, Platoon, Pleiad, Pocket, Pod, Point, Pool, Pop, Pressure, Prosthetic, Push, Quincunx, Raceme, Racemose, Rap, Reading, Ring, Rush, School, Sector, Seminar, Series, Set, Several, Sex, Shower, Society, Sort, Sorus, Splinter, Strain, Stream, String, Study, Sub-general, Sub-order, Support, Syndicate, T, Tales, Taxon, Tetrad, Tithing, Trainband, T-Rex, Tribe, Tribune, Trilogy, Trio, TU, Umbrella, Unit, User, Vigilante, Workshop, Zaibatsu, Zupa

Grouse Black, Blackcock, Bleat, Blue, Caper(caillie), Capercailzie, Covey, Gorcock, Greyhen, Gripe, Growl, Grumble, Hazel-hen, Heath-cock, Heath-hen, Jeremiad, Moan, Moorcock, Moorfowl, Moor-pout, Muir-poot, Muir-pout, Mutter, Natter, Peeve, Pintail, Prairie-hen, Ptarmigan, Red, Resent, Ruffed, Rype(r), Sage, Sharp-tailed, Snarl, Spruce, Twelfth, Wheenge, W(h)inge, Willow

Grove Academy, Arboretum, Bosk, Bosquet, Copse, Glade, Hurst, Lyceum, Motte, Nemoral, Orchard, Orchat, Silva, Tope

Grovel Cheese, Crawl, Creep, Fawn, Ko(w)tow

Grow(ing), Grow out, Growth Accrete, Accrue, Acromegaly, Adenoma, Aggrandisement, Angioma, Apophysis, Arborescence, Auxesis, Bedeguar, Boom, Braird, Breer, Burgeon, Car(b)uncle, Cholelith, Chondroma, Compensatory, Condyloma, Crescendo, Crop, Culture, Cyst, Ectopia, Edema, Ellagic, Enate, Enchondroma, Enlarge, Epinasty, Epitaxy, Excrescence,

Grow(n) |

Exostosis, Expansion, Fibroid, Flor, Flourish, Flush, Gain, Gall, Germinate, Get, Goitre, Hepatocele, Hummie, Hyponasty, Increase, Keratosis, Knur(r), Lichen, Lipoma, Mole, Mushroom, Myoma, Nur(r), Oedema, Oncology, Osselet, Osteoma, Osteophyte, Polyp, Proleg, Proliferate, Rampant, Rank, Scirrhus, Septal, Snowball, Spavin, > **SPROUT**, Stalagmite, Stipule, Sympodial, Tariff, Thrive, Tylosis, Vegetable, Wart, Wax, Wox

▷ **Grow(n)** *may indicate* an anagram

Growl(ing) Fremescent, Gnar, Groin, Grr, Gurl, Roar(e), Roin, Royne, Snar(l)

Grown up Adult, Mature, Risen

Grub(by) Assart, Aweto, Bardy, Bookworm, Caddis, Caterpillar, Cheer, Chow, Chrysalis, Dig, Eats, Fare, Fodder, > **FOOD**, Gentle, Groo-groo, Gru-gru, Larva, Leatherjacket, Mawk, Mess, Nosh, Palmerworm, Peck, Pupa, Root(le), Rout, Rowt, Sap, Slave, Stub, Tired, Wireworm, Witchetty, Wog, Worm

Grudge, Grudging Chip, Derry, Envy, Grutch, Resent, Score, Sparse, Spite, Spleen

Gruel Brochan, Bross, Loblolly, Skilligalee, Skilligolee, Skilly

Gruesome Ghastly, Grisly, Grooly, Horror, Livid, Macaberesque, Macabre, > **MORBID**, Sick

Gruff Guttural, Hoarse, Surly

Grumble Beef, Bellyache, Bitch, Bleat, Chunter, Crab, Croak, Girn, Gripe, Grizzle, Groin, Growl, Moan, Murmur, Mutter, Nark, Natter, Repine, Rumble, Whinge, Yammer

Grump(y) Attercop, Bearish, Cross, Ettercap, Grouchy, Moody, Sore-headed, Surly

Grunt Groin, Grumph, Humph, Oink, Pigfish, Spanish, Ugh, Wheugh

Guano Dung, Sombrerite

Guanoco Llama

Guarantee Accredit, Assure, Avouch, Certify, Ensure, Gage, Hallmark, Insure, Mainprise, Money-back, Pignerate, Pignorate, > **PLEDGE**, Plight, Seal, Secure, Sponsion, Surety, Underwrite, > **VOUCHSAFE**, Warn, Warrandice, Warrant(y)

Guard(ed), Guards Acolouthos, Advance, Apron, Beefeaters, Blues, Bostangi, Bouncer, Bracer, Cabiri, Cage, Cag(e)y, Cerberus, Chaperon(e), Chary, Cheesemongers, Cherry-pickers, Coast, Coldstream, Colour, Cordon, Crinoline, Curator, Custodian, Custos, Diehards, Dragoons, Duenna, Equerry, Escort, Eunuch, Excubant, Exon, Fence, Fender, Gaoler, Grenadiers, Greys, Hedge, Home, Horse, INS, Jaga, Jailer, Keep, Lancers, Life, Lilywhites, Look out, Mask, Mort-safe, National, Nightwatch(man), Nutcrackers, Out-rider, Out-sentry, Pad, Palace, Patrol, Picket, Point, Praetorian, > **PROTECT**, Provost, Quillon, Rail, Red, Ride, Screw, Secure, Security, Sentinel, Sentry, Shadow, Shield, Shopping, Shotgun, SS, Strelitz, Streltzi, Swiss, Switzer, Tapadera, Tapadero, Tile, Toecap, Tsuba, Turnkey, Vambrace, Vamplate, Varangian, Vigilante, Visor, Wage, Wait(e), Ward, Wary, Watch (and ward), Watchdog, Watchman, Wear, Weir, Wire, Yeoman

Guardian Altair, Argus, Curator, Custodian, Custos, Dragon, Gemini, Granthi, Hafiz, Janus, Julius, Miminger, Templar, Trustee, Tutelar(y), Warder, Watchdog, Xerxes

Gudgeon Fish, Pin, Trunnion

Guenon Grivet, Vervet

Gue(r)rilla Bushwhacker, Chetnik, Contra, ETA, Fedayee, Gook, Irregular, Khmer Rouge, Komitaji, Maquis, Mujahadeen, Mujaheddin, Mujahed(d)in, Mujahedeen, Mujahideen, Partisan, Red Brigade, Terrorist, Tupamaro, Urban, Viet cong, Zapata

Guess Aim, Aread, Arede, Arreede, Conjecture, Divine, Estimate, Harp, Hazard,

Imagine, Infer, Level, Mor(r)a, Mull, Shot, Speculate, Suppose, Surmise, Theorise
Guessing game Handy-dandy, Mor(r)a, Quiz
Guest(s) Caller, Company, House-party, Inquiline, Parasite, Paying, PG, Symbion(t), Symphile, Synoecete, Umbra, Visitant, > **VISITOR**, Xenial
Guesthouse Minshuku, Xenodochium
Guff Bosh, Gas
Guianian S(a)ouari
Guidance, Guide, Guideline, Guiding Advice, Antibarbus, Auspice, Baedeker, Bradshaw, Cicerone, Clue, Concordance, Conduct, Counsel, Courier, Curb, Cursor, Director(y), Docent, Dragoman, Drive, > **ESCORT**, Field, Gillie, Graticule, Helm, Heuristic, Index, Inertial, Inspire, Itinerary, Jig, Key, Lad, Landmark, Lead, Lodestar, Map, Mark, Marriage, Mentor, Model, Navaid, Navigate, Nose, Pelorus, Pilot, Pointer, Postil(l)ion, Principle, Queen's, Range, Ranger, Reference, Rein, Relate, Rudder, Sabot, Shepherd, Sherpa, Shikaree, Shikari, Sight, Sign, Sixer, Stear, Steer, Stire, Template, Templet, Terrestrial, Tiller, Train, Travelogue, Tutelage, Vocational, Voyageur, Waymark, Weise, Weize, Wise
Guild Artel, Basoche, Company, Freemason, Gyeld, Hanse, Hoastman, League, Mistery, Mystery, Society, Tong, Union
Guile Art, Cunning, Deceit, Dole, Malengine
Guillotine Closure, Louisiette, Maiden, Marianne
Guilt(y) Angst, Blame, Cognovit, Flagitious, Mea culpa, Nocent, Peccavi, Remorse, Wicked
Guinea(s) Canary, Geordie, Gns, Job, Ls, Meg, Spade
Guinea-fowl Pintado
Guinea-pig Abyssinian, Agoute, Agouti, Cavie, Cavy, Paca
Guinea-worm Dracunculus
Guise Form, Manner, Shape
Guitar(ist) Acoustic, Axe(man), Bottleneck, Cithern, Cittern, Dobro®, Electric, Fender®, Gittarone, Gittern, Hawaiian, Humbucker, Lute, Lyre, Pedal steel, Plankspanker, Samisen, Sancho, Sanko, Shamisen, Sitar, Slide, Spanish, Steel, Uke, Ukulele
Gulf Aden, Aqaba, Bay, Bothnia, California, Cambay, Carpentaria, Chasm, Chihli, Corinth, Cutch, Darien, Dvina, Exmouth, Fonseca, Genoa, Gonaives, Hauraki, Honduras, Joseph Bonaparte, Kutch, Lepanto, Leyte, Lingayen, Lions, Mannar, Martaban, Maw, Mexico, Persian, Queen Maud, Saronic, Siam, Sidra, Spencer, Taganrog, Tongking, Tonkin, Trieste, Tunis, Van Diemen, Vorago
Gull(s) Black-backed, Bonxie, Cheat, Cob(b), Cod, Cony, Cozen, Dupe, Fool, Geck, Glaucous, Have, Hoodwink, Ivory, Kittiwake, Laridae, Larus, Maw, Mew, Mollyhawk, Pickmaw, Pigeon, Queer, Rook, Sabine's, Saddleback, Scaury, Scourie, Scowrie, Sea-cob, Sea-mew, Sell, Simp, Skua, Sucker, Swart-back, Tern, Tystie, Xema
Gullet Crop, Enterate, Maw, Oesophagus, Throat, Weasand-pipe
Gullible Green, Naive, Sucker
Gulliver Lemuel
Gully Couloir, Donga, Geo, Gio, Goe, Grough, Gulch, Pit, Rake, Ravine, Sloot, Sluit, Wadi
Gulp Bolt, Draught, Gollop, Quaff, Slug, Sob, > **SWALLOW**, Swig, Swipe, Wolf
Gum (tree) Acacia, Acajou, Acaroid, Agar, Algin, Angico, Arabic, Arabin, Arar, Arctic, Asafoetida, Bablah, Balata, Balm, Bandoline, Bdellium, Benjamin, Benzoin, Bloodwood, Blue, Boot, Bubble, Cerasin, Chicle, Chuddy, Chutty,

Coolabah, Courbaril, Cow®, Dextrin(e), Dragon's-blood, Ee-by, Eucalyptus, Euphorbium, Flooded, Frankincense, Galbanum, Gamboge, Ghost, Gingival, > **GLUE**, Goat's-thorn, Gosh, Grey, Guar, Ironbark, Karri, Kauri, La(b)danum, Lac, Lentisk, Mastic(h), Mucilage, Myrrh, Nicotine, Olibanum, Opopanax, Oshac, Red, Sagapenum, Sarcocolla, Scribbly, Size, Sleep, Snow, Spearmint, Spirit, Starch, Sterculia, Stringybark, Sugar, Sweet, Tacamahac, Tragacanth, Tupelo, Ulmin, Water, White, Xanthan

Gumbo Okra

Gumboil Parulis

Gumption Nous, Spirit

Gun(fire), Guns Amusette, Archibald, Archie, Arquebus, Automatic, Barker, Baton, Bazooka, Beanbag, Beretta, Big Bertha, Biscayan, Blunderbuss, Bofors, Bombard, Breech(-loader), Bren, Broadside, Brown Bess, Browning, Bulldog, Bullpup, Bundook, Burp, Caliver, Cannonade, Carbine, Carronade, Cement, Chokebore, Coehorn, Colt®, Dag, Derringer, Electron, Elephant, Escopette, Falcon(et), Field, Fieldpiece, Firearm, Fire lock, Flame, Flash, Flintlock, Four-pounder, Fowler, Fowlingpiece, Garand, Gat(ling), Gingal(l), Grease, HA, Hackbut, Half-cock, Harquebus, Heater, Hired, Howitzer, Jezail, Jingal, Kalashnikov, Lewis, Long Tom, Luger®, Machine, Magazine, Magnum, Maroon, Martini-Henry®, Matchlock, Mauser®, Maxim, Metal, Minnie, Minute, Mitrailleuse, Morris Meg, Mortar, Musket(oon), Muzzle-loader, Neutron, Noonday, Oerlikon, Ordnance, Over and under, Owen, Paderero, Paterero, Ped(e)rero, Pelican, Perrier, Petronel, Piece, Pistol(et), Pompom, Pump (action), Punt, Purdey®, Quaker, Radar, Ray, Repeater, Rev, Riot, Rod, Roscoe, Saker, Sarbacane, Self-cocker, Shooter, Sidearm, Siege, Smoothbore, Snapha(u)nce, Spear, Spray, Squirt, Staple, Starting, Sten, Sterculia, Sterling, Stern-cannon, Stern-chaser, Stun, Swivel, Taser®, Tea, Thirty eight, Thompson, Tier, Time, Tommy, Tool, Tupelo, Turret, Uzi, Walther, Wesson, Young, Zip

Gunge Gowl

Gunman Ace, Assassin, Bandit, Earp, Greaser, Pistoleer, Sniper, Starter

Gunner, Gunner's assistant Arquebusier, Arsenal, Artillerist, Cannoneer, Cannonier, Culverineer, Gr, Matross, RA

Gunpowder Charcoal, Pebble-powder, Saucisse, Saucisson

Gunwale Gunnel, Portland, Portlast, Portoise

Guppy Million

Gurgle Clunk, Glug, Gobble, Gollar, Goller, Guggle, Ruckle, Squelch

Gurnard Tubfish

Guru Lifestyle, Sadhu, Teacher

Gush(ing) Blether, Effusive, > **FLOOD**, Flow, Jet, Outpour, Rail, Raile, Regurgitate, Rhapsodize, Scaturient, Spirt, Spout, Spurt, Too-too

Gusset Godet, Gore, Insert, Inset, Mitre

Gust Blast, Blore, Flaught, Flaw, Flurry, Puff, Sar, Waff

Gusto Elan, Relish, Verve, Zest

Gut(s), Gutty Archenteron, Balls, Beer, Bowel(s), Chitterlings, Cloaca, Disembowel, Draw, Duodenum, Enteral, Enteron, Entrails, Gill, Ileum, Insides, Kyle, Mesenteron, Minikin, Omental, Omentum, Purtenance, Remake, Sack, Sand, Snell, Stamina, Staying-power, Strip, Thairm, Tripe, Ventriculus, Viscera

Gutta-percha Jelutong, Pontianac, Pontianak

Gutter(ing) Arris, Channel, Conduit, Coulisse, Cullis, Grip, Kennel, Rhone, Rigol(l), Roan, Rone, Sough, Spout, Strand, Sweal, Sweel

Guttersnipe Arab, Gamin, Thief

Guttural Faucal, Throaty

Guy Backstay, Bo, Burgess, Chaff, Clewline, Decamp, Deride, Effigy, Fall, Fawkes, Fellow, Gink, Josh, Mannering, Parody, Rib, Rope, Scarecrow, Stay, Tease, Vang, Wise

Guzzle(d) Gannet, Gorge, Go(u)rmandize, Overeat

Gwyn Nell

Gym(nasium), Gymnast(ic) Acrobat, Akhara, Arena, Contortionist, Dojo, Jungle, Lyceum, Palaestra, PE, PT, Rhythmic, Sokol, Tumbler, Turner

Gymnosophist Yogi

Gypsum Alabaster, Gesso, Plaster, Satin-stone, Selenite, Terra alba

Gypsy, Gipsy Bohemian, Cagot, Caird, Caqueux, Chai, Chal, Chi, Collibert, Egyptian, Esmeralda, Faw, Gipsen, Gitano, Hayraddin, Lavengro, Meg, Rom(any), Rye, Scholar, Tinker, Traveller, Tsigane, Vagabond, Vlach, Walach, Wanderer, Zigan, Zigeuner, Zincala, Zincalo, Zingaro

Gyrate Revolve, Rotate, > SPIN, Twirl

Hh

H Ache, Aitch, Aspirate, Height, Hospital, Hotel, Hydrant, Hydrogen

Haberdasher(y) Clothier, Ferret, Hosier, Notions

Habit(s), Habitual, Habituate, Habitué Accustom, Addiction, Apparel, Assuefaction, Assuetude, Bent, Cacoethes, Chronic, Clothes, Coat, Consuetude, Crystal, Custom, Diathesis, Dress, Ephod, Frequenter, Garb, Inure, Inveterate, Motley, Mufti, Nature, Outfit, Pathological, Practice, Raiment, Regular, Riding, Robe, Rochet, Routine, Scapular, Schema, Season, Set, Soutane, Suit, Surplice, Toge, Trait, Tway, Usual, Way, Won, Wont, Xerotes

Habitat Element, Environment, Haunt, Home, Locality, Station

Hacienda Ranch

Hack(er) Chip, Chop, Cough, Cut, Drudge, Garble, Gash, Ghost, Grub-street, Hag, Hash, Hedge-writer, Heel, Hew, Horse, Journo, Mangle, Mutilate, Nag, Notch, Pad, Paper-strainer, Penny-a-liner, Pot-boiler, Rosinante, Spurn, Steed, Tadpole, Taper, Tussis, Unseam, White hat

Hackle(s) Comb, Rough

Hackneyed Banal, Cab, Cliché, Corny, Percoct, Stale, Threadbare, Tired, Trite

Haddock Arbroath smokie, Findram, Finnan, Fish, Norway, Rizzered, Smoky, Speldin(g), Speldrin(g), Whitefish

Hades Dis, Hell, Orcus, Pit, Tartarus

Had (to) Moten, Must, Obliged, Threw

Haematite Oligist

Haemorrhoids Farmer Giles, Piles

Hafnium Hf

Hag(-like) Anile, Beldame, Besom, Carlin(e), Crone, Harpy, Harridan, Hell-cat, Hex, Nickneven, Occasion, Rudas, Runnion, Trot, Underwood, Witch

Haggard Drawn, > **GAUNT**, Pale, Rider

Haggis Kishke

Haggle Argue, Badger, > **BARGAIN**, Barter, Chaffer, Dicker, Horse-trade, Niffer, Palter, Prig

Ha-ha Dike, Sunk-fence

Hahnium Hn

Hail(er) Acclaim, Ahoy, Ave, Bull-horn, Cheer, Fusillade, Graupel, Greet, Hi, Ho, Megaphone, Salue, Salute, Shower, Signal, Skoal, Skol, Sola, Stentor, Storm, Trumpet, Whoa-ho-ho

Hair (cut), Hair problem/condition, Hair style, Hairlike, Hairy Afro, Ailes de pigeon, Ainu, Alopecia, Baldy, Bang, Barnet, Beard, Beehive, Bezoar, Bingle, Bob, Bouffant, Braid, Brede, Bristle, Brutus, Bumfluff, Bun, Bunches, Butch, Cadogan, Camel, Capillary, Catogan, Chignon, Cilia, Cleopatra, Coat, Cockernony, Coif, Coiffure, Comal, Comate, Comb-over, Cornrow, Corymbus, Cowlick, Crepe, Crew-cut, Crinal, Cronet, Crop, Cue, Curlicue, DA, Dangerous, Dreadlocks, Dubbing, Duck's arse, Ducktail, Earmuffs, Elf locks, En brosse, Esau, Feather, Feather-cut, Fetlock, Filament, Flat-top, Floccus, Forelock, French pleat, French roll, Frenulum, Fringe, Fur, Garconne, Glib(s),

Glochidium, Guard, Hackles, Heard, Heer(i)e, Hispid, Hog, Indumentum,
Kemp, Kesh, Lanugo, Lash, List, Lock, Lovelock, Lowlights, Madarosis, Mane,
Marcel, Mohican, Mop, Mullet, Muttonchops, Not(t), Number two, Pageboy,
Pappus, Pashm, Pele(s), Pelt, Perm(anent), Pigtail, Pika, Pile, Pilus, Plait,
Plica, Pompadour, Ponytail, Poodle cut, Porcupine, Pouf(fe), Pow, Psilosis,
Puberulent, Pubescent, Pudding basin, Punk, Queue, Quiff, Radicle, Rat-tail,
Red mullet, Rhizoid, Roach, Root, Scalp lock, Scopate, Scopula, Set, Shag,
Shingle, Shock, Sideburns, Sidelock, Snell, Spikes, Stinging, Strammel,
Strand, Strigose, Strummel, Switch, Sycosis, Tête, Thatch, Tomentose,
Tonsure, Topknot, Tragus, Tress, Trichoid, Trichology, Trichome, Trim,
Velutinous, Vibrissi, Villi, Villosity, Villus, Wedge, Widow's peak, Wig, Wisp,
> WOOL, Xerasia
Hair-cream, Hair-oil Conditioner, Pomade
Hairdresser Barber, Coiffeur, Comb, Crimper, Friseur, Marcel, Salon, Stylist,
Trichologist
Hairless Bald, Callow, Glabrate, Glabrescent, Glabrous, Irate
Hairnet Kell, Snood
Hairpiece Frisette, Merkin, Postiche, Strand, Toupee, > WIG
Hairpin Bodkin, Slide, U, U-turn
Hair-shirt Ab(b)a, Cilice
Haiti RH
Hal Prince
Halberd Spontoon
Halcyon Calm, Kingfisher, Mild
Hale(r) Drag, Healthy, Koruna, Robust, Well
Half, Halved Bifid, Demi, Dimidiate, Dirempt, Divide, Hemi, Moiety, Semi,
Share, Split, Stand-off, Term
Half-a-dozen Six, VI
Half-asleep, Half-conscious Dove, Dozy
Half-baked Foolish, Mediocre, Samel, Slack-bake
Half-breed, Half-caste Bastard, Baster, Creole, Eurasian, Mameluco, Mestee,
Mestiza, Mestizo, Metif, Métis(se), Mongrel, Mulatto, Mustee, Octaroon,
Quadroon, Quarteroon, Quintero, Quintroon, Sambo, Yellow-boy, Yellow-girl,
Zambo
Half-guinea Smelt
Half-hearted Reluctant, Tepid
Half-hour Bell
Half-pence, Half-penny Mag, Maik, Mail(e), Make, Obolus, Patrick, Portcullis,
Posh, Rap, Wood's
Half-turn Caracol(e), Demivolt
Half-wit Changeling, Mome, Simpleton, > STUPID
Hall Anteroom, Apadana, Atrium, Auditorium, Aula, Basilica, Carnegie, Casino,
Chamber, Citadel, City, Concourse, Corridor, Dance, Dojo, Domdaniel, Dome,
Dotheboys, Ex(h)edra, Festival, Foyer, Gallen, Hardwick, Holkham, Kedleston,
Liberty, Lobby, Locksley, Megaron, Mess, Moot, Music, Narthex, Newby,
Odeon, Palais, Palais de danse, Passage, Prytaneum, Rathaus, Salle, Saloon,
Stationer's, Tammany, Tara, Tolsel, Town, Valhalla, Vestibule, Walhall(a),
Wildfell
Hallmark(ed) Brand, Contrôlé, Logo, Seal, Stamp
▶ **Hallo** *see* HELLO
Hallow Revere, Worship
Hallucinate, Hallucination, Hallucinogen Autoscopy, DT's, Fantasy,

Formication, Freak, Freak out, Illusion, Image, Mirage, Photism, Psilocin, Psilocybin, Psychedelic, Trip

Halo Antheolion, Areola, Aura, Aureola, Corona, Galactic, Gloria, Gloriole, Mandorla, Nimbus, Rim, Vesica, Vesica piscis

Halogen Iodine

Halt(er) Abort, Arrest, Block, Brake, Bridle, Cavesson, Cease, Check, Full stop, Game, Hackamore, Heave-to, Hilch, Lame(d), Limp, Noose, Prorogue, Rope, Stall, Standstill, Staw, > **STOP**, Stopover, Toho, Tyburn-tippet, Whoa

Ham(s) Amateur, Barnstormer, Flitch, Gammon, Haunch, Hock, Hoke, Hough, Hunker, Jambon, Jay, Nates, Overact, Overplay, Parma, Prat, Prosciutto, Radio, Tiro, Westphalian, York

Hamfisted Maladroit, Unheppen

Hamite Berber, Nilot(e)

Hamlet Aldea, Auburn, Cigar, Clachan, Dane, Dorp, Hero, Kraal, Stead, Thorp(e), Vill(age), Wick

Hammer(ed), **Hammerhead** About-sledge, Ballpeen, Ballpein, Beetle, Bully, Bush, Celt, Claw, Drop, Excudit, Flatten, Fore, Fuller, Gavel, Hack, Incuse, Jack, Kevel, Knap, Knapping, Kusarigama, Lump, Madge, Mall(et), Malleate, Martel, Maul, Mjol(l)nir, Monkey, Nevel, Oliver, Pane, Pean, Peen, Pein, Pene, Percussion, Piledriver, Planish, Plessor, Plexor, Pneumatic, Rawhide, Repoussé, Rip, Sheep's-foot, Shingle, Sledge, Steam, Stone, Strike, Tack, Tenderizer, Tendon, Tilt, Trip, Umbre, Water, Wippen

▷ **Hammered** *may indicate* an anagram

Hammerthrower Thor

Hammock Cott

▷ **Hammy** *may indicate* an anagram

Hamper Basket, Cabin, Ceroon, Cramp, Cumber, Delay, Encumber, Entrammel, Hamstring, Handicap, Hobble, Hog-tie, Obstruct, Pad, Pannier, Ped, Pinch, Restrict, Rub, Sero(o)n, Shackle, Tangle, Trammel, Tuck

Hamster Cricetus, Idea

Hamstring Cramp, Hock, Hox, Lame, Popliteal, Thwart

Hand(s), **Hand over**, **Hand down**, **Hand-like**, **Handwriting** Assist(ance), Bananas, Bequeath, Cacography, Calligraphy, Charge, Chicane, Chirography, Clap(ping), Claque, Club, Clutch, Copperplate, Court, Crew, Cursive, Daddle, Danny, Dawk, Dead, Deal, Deck, Deliver, Devolve, Donny, Dukes, Dummy, Famble, Fin, Fist, Flipper, Flush, Free, Glad, Graphology, Help, Helping, Hond, Hour, Impart, Iron, Israel, Italian, Jambone, Jamboree, Jemmy, Kana, L, Lone, Man, Manual, Manus, Maulers, Medieval, Minute, Mitt(en), Nes(h)ki, Niggle, Operative, Orthography, Pad, Palm(atifid), Part, Pass, Paw, Podium, Post, Pud, R, Referral, Rein (arm), Round, Script, Second, Signature, Span, Spencerian, Stage, Station, Straight, Sweep, Text, Tiger, Upper, Whip, Widow, Worker, Yarborough

Handbag Caba(s), Grip, Indispensable, Pochette, Purse, Reticule, Valise

Handbook Baedeker, Companion, Enchiridion, Guide, Manual, Vade-mecum

Handcuff(s) Bracelet, Darbies, Golden, Irons, Manacle, Mittens, Nippers, Snaps, Wristlet

Handful Few, Gowpen, Grip, Problem, Pugil, Rip(p), V

Handicap Bisque, Burden, Cambridgeshire, Ebor, Encumber, Hamper, Impede, Impost, Lame, Liability, Lincolnshire, Mental, > **OBSTACLE**, Off, Physical, Restrict, Weigh(t), Welter-race

Handicraft Marquetry

Handkerchief, **Hanky** Bandan(n)a, Belcher, Billy, Buffon, Clout, Fogle, Foulard,

Kleenex®, Madam, Madras, Monteith, Mouchoir, Muckender, Napkin, Nose-rag, Orarium, Romal, Rumal, Sudary, Tissue, Wipe(r)

Handle(d) Ansate, Bail, Bale, Behave, Bitstock, Brake, Broomstick, Cope, Crank, Dead man's, Deal, Doorknob, Dudgeon, Ear, Feel, Finger, Forename, Gaum, Gorm, Grab, Grip, Haft, Helve, Hilt, Hold, Knob, Knub, Lug, > **MANAGE**, Manipulate, Manubrium, Maul, Moniker, Name, Nib, Palp, Paw, Pommel, Process, Rounce, Shaft, Snath, Snead, Sneath, Sned, Staff, Staghorn, Stale, Steal(e), Steel, Steil, Stele, Stilt, Stock, Tiller, Title, To-name, Touch, Transact, Treat, Use, Whipstock, Wield, Withe

Handmaid(en) Iras, Manicurist, Valkyrie

Hand-out Alms, Charity, Dole, Gift, Release, Sample

Handshake Golden

Hand-signal Beck(on), Point, Wave

Handsome Adonis, Apollo, Bonny, Brave, Comely, Dashing, Dishy, Featuous, Gracious, Liberal

Handspring, Handstand Cartwheel, Diamodov

Hand-warmer Muff, Pome

Hand-washer Pilate

▶ **Handwriting** *see* **HAND**

Handy(man) Accessible, Close, Convenient, Deft, Dext(e)rous, Digit, Factotum, Jack(-of-all-trades), Near, Nigh, Palmate, Palmist, Ready, Skilful, Spartan, Useful

Hang, Hanger, Hanging(s) Append, Arras, Aweigh, Chick, Chik, Coat, Dangle, Darn, Depend, Dewitt, Dossal, Dossel, Dosser, Drape, Droop, Execute, Frontal, Gobelin, Hinge, Hoove, Hove(r), Kakemono, Kilt, Lime, Lobed, Loll, Lop, Lynch, Mooch, Noose, Nub, Pend(ant), Sag, Scenery, Scrag, Set, Sit, Sling, Suspend, Suspercollate, Swing, Tapestry, Tapet, Tapis, Toran(a)

Hanger-on Bur, Lackey, Leech, Limpet, Liripoop, Parasite, Satellite, Sycophant, Toady

Hangman, Hangmen Bull, Calcraft, Dennis, Derrick, Gregory, Ketch, Marwood, Nubbing-cove, Pierrepoint

Hangnail Agnail

Hangover Canopy, Cornice, Crapulence, Drape, DT's, Head, Hot coppers, Katzenjammer, Mistletoe, Remnant, Tester

Hank Bobbin, Coil, Fake, Skein

Hanker(ing) Desire, Envy, Hunger, Itch, Long, Yearn, Yen

Hannibal Punic

Hansard Minutes

Haphazard Casual, Chance, Helter-skelter, Higgledy-piggledy, Hit and miss, Hitty-missy, Promiscuous, > **RANDOM**, Rough and tumble, Slapdash, Willy-nilly

Happen(ing), Happen to Afoot, Be, Befall, Befortune, Betide, Come, Event(uate), Fall-out, Materialise, > **OCCUR**, Pan, Pass, Prove, Subvene, Thing, Tide, Transpire, Worth

Happiness, Happy Apposite, Ave, Beatific, Beatitude, Blessed, Bliss, Bluebird, Bonny, Carefree, Cheery, Chuffed, Cock-a-hoop, Dwarf, Ecstatic, Elated, Eud(a)emony, Exhilarated, Felicity, Felix, Fool's paradise, Fortunate, Glad(some), Gleeful, Golden, Goshen, Gruntled, Halcyon, Half-cut, Hedonism, Jovial, Joy, Larry, Light-hearted, Merry, Opportune, Radiant, Rapture, Sandboy, Seal, Seel, Sele, Serene, Sunny, Tipsy, Trigger, Warrior

Hara-kiri Eventration, Seppuku, Suicide

Harangue Declaim, Diatribe, Earwigging, Lecture, Oration, Perorate, Philippic,

Sermon, Speech, Spruik, Tirade

Harass(ed) Afflict, Annoy, Badger, Bait, Beleaguer, Bother, Chivvy, Distract, Dun, Gall, Grill, Grind, Grounden, Hassle, Haze, Heckle, Hector, Hound, Irritate, Needle, Persecute, Pester, Plague, Press, Thwart, Trash, Vex

Harbinger Herald, Omen, Precursor, Usher

Harbour(ed) Alee, Anchorage, Basin, Brest, Cherish, Dock, Entertain, Foster, Herd, Hide, Hythe, Lodge, Manukau, Marina, Mulberry, Pearl, PLA, Poole, Port, Quay, Reset, Scapa Flow, > **SHELTER**, Watemata, Wellington

Hard(en), Hardness Abstruse, Adamant(ine), Adularia, Augean, Bony, Brindell, Brinell, Brittle, Bronze, Cake, Calcify, Callous, Caramel, Cast-iron, Chitin, Concrete, Cornute, Crusty, Dentin(e), Difficult, Dour, Draconian, Ebonite, Endure, Enure, Firm, Flint(y), Geal, Granite, Gruelling, H, Hellish, Herculean, HH, Horny, Indurate, Inure, Iron(y), Jasper, Knotty, Liparite, Lithoid, Metallic, Metally, Moh, Moh's scale, Nails, Obdurate, Obdure, Osseous, Ossify, Permafrost, Permanent, Petrify, Picrite, Raw, Rugged, Ruthless, Schist, Scleral, Set, Severe, Solid, Sore, Steel(y), Steep, Stereo, Stern, Stoic, Stony, Teak, Temper, Tough, Wooden

Hardback Case-bound

Hard-core Riprap, Scalpins

Hard-headed Stegochepalian

Harding Warden

Hardliner Hawk

Hardly Borderline, Ill, Just, Scarcely, Uneath(es), Unnethes

Hard-pressed Strait, Taxed

Hardship Affliction, Grief, Mill, Mishap, Penance, Privation, Rigour, Trial, Trouble

Hardware Gear, Ironmongery

Hardy Brave, Dour, Durable, Manful, Oliver, Ollie, Rugged, Spartan, Sturdy, Thomas

Hare Arctic, Baud(rons), Bawd, Belgian, Doe, Dolicholis, Down, Electric, Husk, Jack-rabbit, Jugged, Lam, Leporine, Malkin, Mara, March, Mawkin, Mountain, Ochotona, Pika, Puss, Scut, Snowshoe, Spring, Wat

Hare-brained Giddy, Madcap, Scatty

Harem Gynaeceum, Gynoecium, Seraglio, Serai(l), Zenana

Hark(en) Ear, Hear, List(en)

Harlequin Chequered, Columbine, Pantaloon

Harlot Blue gown, Drab, Hussy, Loon, Loose, Paramour, Plover, Pusle, Pussel, Quail, Rahab, Scrubber, Slut, Strumpet, Whore

Harm(ed), Harmful Aggrieve, Bane, Blight, Deleterious, Detriment, Endamage, Evil, Hurt, Inimical, Injury, Insidious, Maleficent, Malignant, Maltreat, Mischief, Nocuous, Noxious, Pernicious, Sinister, Spoil, Wroken, Wrong

Harmless Benign, Canny, Drudge, Informidable, Innocent, Innocuous, Innoxious, Inoffensive

Harmonica Harp

Harmonious, Harmonise, Harmonist, Harmony Agree(ment), Alan, Assort, Atone, Attune, Balanced, Blend, Chord, Close, Concent, Concentus, Concert, Concinnity, Concord, Congruous, Consonant, Consort, Coordinate, Correspondence, Counterpoint, Descant, Diapason, Diatessaron, Doo-wop, Euphony, Eur(h)ythmy, Faburden, Feng-shui, Go, Jibe, Match, Melody, Mesh, Musical, Rappite, Solidarity, Symmetry, Sympathy, Symphonious, Sync, Thorough-bass, Tone, Tune, Unanimity, Unison, Unity

Harmotome Cross-stone

Harness(maker) Breeching, Bridle, Cinch, Equipage, Frenum, Gear, Girth, Hitch, Inspan, Lorimer, Loriner, Pad-tree, Partnership, Swingletree, Tack(le), Throat-stop, Trace, Whippletree, Yoke

Harp(sichord) Aeolian, Clairschach, Clarsach, Clavier, Drone, Dwell, Irish, Lyre, Nebel, Trigon, Virginal, Welsh, Wind, Zither

Harpagon L'avare, Miser

Harpoon(er) Bart, Fis(h)gig, Fizgig, Grain, Iron, Lily iron, Peg, Spear, Specktioneer, Toggler, Tow-iron, Trident

Harpy Aello, Celeno, Eagle, Ocypete

Harridan Hag, Harpy, Shrew, Xantippe, Zantippe, Zentippe

Harrier Hen, Montagu's

Harriet Hetty, Martineau

Harrow Alas, Appal, Brake, Disc, Frighten, Herse, Pitch-pole, Plough, Rake, Rend, Shock

Harry Aggravate, Badger, Bother, Champion, Chase, Chivvy, Coppernose, Dragoon, Flash, Fret, Hal, Harass, Hassle, Hector, Herry, Houdini, Hound, Lauder, Lime, Maraud, Molest, Nag, Pester, Plague, Rag, Reave, Reive, Rieve, Rile, Tate, Tchick, Torment

▷ **Harry** *may indicate* an anagram

Harsh(ness) Abrasive, Acerbic, Austere, Barbaric, Brassy, Cacophonous, Cruel, Desolate, Discordant, Draconian, Extreme, Glary, Grating, Gravelly, Grim, Gruff, Guttural, Hard, Inclement, Raucle, Raucous, Raw, Rigour, Rude, Scabrid, Screechy, > **SEVERE**, Sharp, Spartan, Stark, Stern, Stoor, Stour, Stowre, Strict, Strident, Unkind

Hart Deer, Spade, Spay, Spay(a)d, Venison

Harte Bret

Hartebeest Bubal, Kaama, Kongoni

Harum-scarum Bayard, Chaotic, Madcap, Rantipole

Harvest(er), Harvest home Combine, Crop, Cull, Fruit, > **GATHER**, Hairst, Hawkey, Hay(sel), Hockey, Horkey, In(ning), Ingather, Kirn, Lease, Nutting, Pick, Produce, Rabi, Random, Reap, Shock, Spatlese, Tattie-howking, Thresh, Vendage, Vendange

Has Habet, Hath, Owns, 's

Has-been Effete, Ex, Outmoded

Hash(ish) Bungle, Charas, Discuss, Garble, Garboil, Hachis, Lobscouse, Mince, Pi(e), Ragout

▷ **Hashed** *may indicate* an anagram

Hasn't Hant, Nas

Hassle Aggro, Bother

Hassock Kneeler, Pouf(fe), Stool, Tuffet

Haste(n), Hastening, Hastily, Hasty Cursory, Despatch, Expedite, Express, Festinately, Fly, Hare, Headlong, Hie, Hotfoot, > **HURRY**, Hurry-scurry, Impetuous, Precipitant, Race, Ramstam, Rash, Rush, Scuttle, Speed, Spur, Stringendo, Subitaneous, Sudden, Tear, Tilt, Urge

Hastings Banda, Bustles, Senlac, Warren

Hat Akuba, Ascot, Astrakhan, Balibuntal, Balmoral, Basher, Beanie, Beany, Bearskin, Beaver, Beret, Billycock, Biretta, Boater, Bollinger, Bonnet, Bowler, Boxer, Brass, Breton, Broad-brim, Busby, Cap, Capotain, Cartwheel, Castor, Chapeau, Cheese-cutter, Chimneypot, Christie, Christy, Claque, Cloche, Cocked, Cockle-hat, Coolie, Cossack, Cowboy, Crusher, Curch, Deerstalker, Derby, Dolly Varden, Dunstable, Envoy, Fedora, Fez, Flat-cap, Fore-and-after, Gaucho, Gibus, Gimme, Glengarry, Hard, Hattock, Headdress, Head-rig,

Hennin, Homburg, Kamelaukion, Kepi, Lamington, Leghorn, Lid, Lum, Matador, Mitre, Mob-cap, Mountie's, Mushroom, Nab, Opera, Pagri, Panama, Petasus, Picture, Pilion, Pill-box, Pilleus, Pilos, Pith, Planter's, Plateau, Plug, Poke(-bonnet), Pork-pie, Potae, Profile, Puggaree, Puritan, Ramil(l)ies, Red, Runcible, Safari, Sailor, Scarlet, Shako, Shovel, Silk, Skimmer, Skull-cap, Slouch, Snap-brim, Snood, Sola(-helmet), Solah, Sola-topi, Sombrero, Songkok, Souwester, Steeple-crown, Stetson®, Stovepipe, Straw, Sugarloaf, Sunbonnet, Sundown, Sunhat, Tam(o'shanter), Tarboosh, Tarb(o)ush, Tarpaulin, Ten-gallon, Terai, Thrummed, Tile, Tin, Tit(fer), Toorie, Top(per), Topee, Topi, Toque, Tricorn(e), Trilby, Turban, Tyrolean, Ugly, Wide-awake, Witch's

Hat-band Weeper

Hatch(ment), Hatching Achievement, Altricial, Booby, Breed, Brood, Cleck, Clutch, Companion, Concoct, Cover, Devise, Eclosion, Emerge, Escape, Incubate, Set, Trap-door

Hatchet(-shaped) Axe, Bill, Chopper, Cleaver, Dolabriform, Tomahawk

▷ **Hatching** *may indicate* an anagram

Hatchway (surround) Companionway, Fiddley, Guichet, Porthole, Scuttle, Service

Hate(ful), Hatred Abhor, Abominable, Abominate, Anims, Aversion, Bugbear, Detest, Enmity, Haterent, Loathe, Misogyny, Odium, Phobia, Racism, Resent, Spite, Ug(h), Vitriol

Hat-plant S(h)ola

Hatter Mad

Hatty Etta

Haughty Aloof, Aristocratic, Arrogant, Bashaw, Cavalier, Disdainful, Fastuous, High, Hogen-mogen, Hoity-toity, Hye, Imperious, Lofty, Orgillous, Orgulous, Paughty, > **PROUD**, Scornful, Sdeignful, Sniffy, Toplofty, Upstage

Haul(age), Haulier Bag, Bouse, Bowse, Brail, Carry, Cart, Catch, Drag, Heave, Hove, Kedge, Loot, Plunder, Pull, Rug, Sally, Scoop, Snig, TIR, Touse, Touze, Tow(se), Towze, Transporter, Trice, Winch, Yank

Haunch Hance, Hip, Huckle, Hunkers, Quarter

Haunt(s) Catchy, Den, Dive, Frequent, Ghost, Hang-out, Honky-tonk, Houf(f), Howf(f), Infest, Obsess, Purlieu, Resort, Spot, Spright

Hauteur Bashawism, Height, Morgue, Vanity

Have, Having Bear, Ha(e), Han, Hoax, Hold, Of, > **OWN**, Possess, Sell

Haven Asylum, Harbour, Hithe, Hythe, Oasis, Port, Refuge, Refugium, Retreat, Shelter, Tax

Haver(s) Blether, Clanjamfray, Dither, Gibber, Nigel

▶ **Haversack** *see* **RUCKSACK**

Havoc Desolation, Devastation, Hell, Ravage, Waste

▷ **Havoc** *may indicate* an anagram

Haw Hip, Sloe

Hawaiian Kanaka

Hawk(er), Hawkish Accipitrine, Auceps, Badger, Bastard, Buzzard, Cadger, Camelot, Caracara, Cast, Cheapjack, Cooper's, Cry, Duck, Eagle, Elanet, Eyas, Falcon, Fish, Gerfalcon, Goshawk, Haggard, Hardliner, Harrier, Harrumph, Hobby, Honey-buzzard, Keelie, Kestrel, Kite, Lammergeier, Lanner(et), Marsh, Merlin, Molla(h), Monger, Moolah, Mosquito, Mullah, Musket, Nyas, Osprey, Ossifrage, Passage, Pearlie, Pearly, Peddle, Pedlar, Peregrine, Pigeon, Ringtail, Sacre(t), Sell, Slab, Slanger, Soar(e), Sorage, Sore(-eagle), Sparrow, Spiv, Staniel, Sutler, Tallyman, Tarsal, Tarsel(l), Tassel, Tercel(et), Tiersel, Trant(er), Trucker,

Warlike
Hawkeye IA, Iowa
Hawk-keeper Austringer, Ostreger
Hawser Line, Rope
Hawthorn Albespine, Albespyne, May(flower), Quickset
Hay(cock), Hey Antic, Cock, Contra-dance, Fodder, Goaf, Hi, Kemple, Math,
  Mow, Pleach, Pook, Salt, Stack, Straw, Windrow
Hayfever Pollenosis
Haymaker Blow, Slog
Hayseed Chaw-bacon, Hodge, Joskin, Rustic
Hazard(ous) Breakneck, Bunker, Chance, Danger, Dare, Die, Dye, Game,
  Gremlin, Guess, Imperil, In-off, Jeopardy, Losing, Main, Moral, Nice,
  Occupational, Peril, Pitfall, Play, Pothole, Queasy, > RISK, Stake, Trap, Venture,
  Vigia, Wage, Winning
Haze, Hazy Blear, Cloud, Filmy, Fog, > MIST, Mock, Muzzy, Nebulous, Smaze,
  Smog, Tease
▷ **Haze** *may indicate* an anagram
Hazel(wort) Amenta, Asarabacca, Catkin, Cob, Corylus, Filbert
HC Encomia, Encomium
He, HE A, Helium, Tag, Tig, > TNT, Tom
Head(s), Heading, Headman, Head shaped, Heady Aim, Apex, Ard-ri(gh),
  Beachy, Bean, Behead, Bill, Block, Bonce, Boss, Brain, Brainpan, Bregma, Brow,
  But(t), Caboceer, Cape, Capitani, Capitate, Capitulum, Capo, Captain, Caption,
  Caput, Caudillo, Cephalic, Chaton, Chief, Coarb, Coconut, Coma, Commander,
  Conk, Cop, Coppin, Costard, Cranium, Crest, Crisis, Crown, Crumpet, Cylinder,
  Director, Dome, Dummy, Each, Ear, Exarch, Figure, Flamborough, Foam,
  Foreland, Froth, General, Glomerate, Grand Mufti, Hegumen(os), Herm(a),
  Hoe, Hogh, Jowl, Karmapa, Knob, Knowledge-box, Lead(er), Lid, Lizard, Loaf,
  Loave, Loo, Lore, Malik, Manager, Mayor, Maz(z)ard, Melik, Mocuddum,
  Mogul, Mokaddam, Mr Big, Mull, Muqaddam, Nab, Nana, Napper, Nappy,
  Ness, Nob, Noddle, Noggin, Noll, Noup, Nowl, Nut, Obverse, Occiput, Onion,
  Panicle, Parietal, Pash, Pate, Pater(familias), Patriarch, Pick-up, Point,
  Poll, Pow, Prefect, President, Pressure, Principal, Promontory, Provost, Ras,
  Read-write, Ream, Rubric, Sarpanch, Scalp, Scaup, Scaw, Scholarch, Scolex,
  Sconce, Short, Sinciput, Skaw, Skull, Sound, Source, Spume, Squeers, Starosta,
  Superior, Taipan, Tanadar, Tete, Thanadar, Throne, Tight, Title, Toilet, Top,
  Topic, Tsantsa, Twopenny, Upperworks, Vaivode, Velocity, Voivode, Yorick,
  Zupan
▷ **Head** *may indicate* the first letter of a word
Headache Cephalalgia, Encephalalgia, Hangover, Megrim, Migraine,
  Neuralgia, Red out, Scotodinia, Splitter
Headband Fillet, Garland, Infula, Sphendone
Headdress, Head cover Ampyx, Balaclava, Bandeau, Bas(i)net, Bonnet,
  Burnous(e), Busby, Calotte, Caul, Chaplet, Circlet, Comb, Cor(o)net, Cowl,
  Coxcomb, Crownet, Curch, Doek, Dopatta, Dupatta, Fascinator, Fontange,
  Fool's cap, Frontlet, Hat(tock), Helm(et), Juliet cap, Kaffiyeh, Kell, Kerchief,
  Kuffiyeh, Kufiah, Kufiya(h), Mantilla, Mitre, Mobcap, Modius, Mortarboard,
  Nubia, Periwig, Pill-box, Plug-hat, Porrenger, Porringer, Romal, Sakkos,
  Ship-tire, Silly-how, Skullcap, Sphendome, Stephane, Taj, Tarbush, Tiara,
  Tower, Tulban, Turban, War bonnet, Wig, Wimple
Header Bonder, Dive, Fall, Rowlock
Headhunter Naga

Headland Beachy Head, Bill, Cape, Cape Horn, Dungeness, Finisterre, Head-rig, Hoe, Hogh, Morro, Naze, Ness, Noup, Promontory, Ras, Ross, St Vincent, Scaw, Skaw

Headless Acephalous

Headlight Beam, Dip, Halo

Headline Banner, Caption, Drophead, Frown, Kicker, Ribbon, Scare-head, Screamer, Streamer, Title

Headlock Chancery

Headlong Breakneck, Pell-mell, Precipitate, Ramstam, Reckless, Steep, Sudden, Tantivy, Tearaway

▸ **Headman** *see* HEAD

Headmaster Principal, Squeers

Headphone(s) Cans, Earpiece, Walkman®

Headquarters Base, Command, Depot, Guildhall, Pentagon, SHAEF, SHAPE, Station

▷ **Heads** *may indicate* a lavatory

Headstrong Obstinate, Rash, Stubborn, Unruly, Wayward, Wilful

Head-to-tail Tête-bêche

Headway Advancement, Headroom, Progress

Head-word Lemma

Heal(ing) Aesculapian, Balsam, Chiropractic, Cicatrise, Cleanse, Cure, Esculapian, G(u)arish, Hele, Hippocratise, Intention, Knit, Mend, Mental, New Thought, Olosis, Osteopathy, Restore, Sain, Salve, Sanitory, Spiritual, Therapeutic, Vulnerary

Healer Asa, Doctor, Homeopath, Naturopath, Osteopath, Sangoma, Shaman, Time

Health(y) Bouncing, Bracing, Chin-chin, Doer, Fit, Flourishing, Gesundheit, Hail, Hale, Hartie-hale, Heart, Holism, Kia-ora, L'chaim, Lustique, Lusty, Medicaid, Medicare, Pink, Prosit, Robust, Rosy, Salubrious, Sane, Slainte, Sound, Toast, Tope, Valetudinarian, Vigour, Well, WHO, Wholesome

Heap(ed) Acervate, Agglomerate, Amass, Bing, Boneshaker, Bulk, Car, Clamp, Coacervate, Cock, Congeries, Cumulus, Drift, Hog, Jalopy, Lot, Pile, Raff, Raft, Rick(le), Ruck, Scrap, Slag, Stash, Tass, Toorie, Up-piled

Hear(ing) Acoustic, Attend, Audience, Audile, Avizandum, Captain's mast, Catch, Clairaudience, Dirdum, Ear, Harken, Learn, List(en), Oyer, Oyez, Panel, Paracusis, Try

▷ **Hear(say)** *may indicate* a word sounding like one given

Hearsay Account, Gossip, Report, Rumour, Surmise

Hearse Bier, Catafalco, Catafalque, Shillibeer

Heart(en), Heartily, Hearty, Heart-shaped AB, Agood, Auricle, Backslapping, Beater, Bleeding, Bluff, Bosom, Bradycardia, Cant, Cardiac, Centre, Cheer, Cockles, Columella, Cordate, Cordial, Core, Courage, Crossed, Daddock, Embolden, Essence, Gist, H, Hale, Herz, Inmost, Jarta, Kernel, Lepid, Lonely, Memoriter, Mesial, Mid(st), Middle, Nub, Nucleus, Obcordate, Purple, Robust, Root, Sacred, Sailor, Seafarer, Seaman, Sinoatrial, Staunch, Tachycardia, Tar, Ticker, Yarta, Yarto

Heart-break Crève-coeur, Grief, Sorrow

Heartburn Brash, Cardialgia, Pyrosis

Heartfelt Deep, Genuine, Real, Sincere

Hearth Cupel, Fireside, Home, Ingle, Killogie

Heartless Callous, Cored, Cruel, Three-suited

Heart's ease Pansy

Heart trouble Bradycardia, Fallot's tetralogy, Fibrillation, Murmur, Tachycardia

Heat(ed), Heater, Heating Anneal, Ardour, Arousal, Atomic, Barrage, Beath, Blood, Brazier, Calcine, Califont, Caloric, Calorifier, Central, Chafe, Convector, Dead, Decay, Dielectric, Dudgeon, Eccaleobion, Element, Eliminator, Endothermic, Enthalpy, Estrus, Etna, Excite, Exothermic, Fan, Ferment, Fever, Fire, Fluster, Fug, Furnace, Het, Hibachi, Hyperthermia, Hypocaust, Immersion, Incalescence, Induction, J, Kindle, Latent, Liquate, Lust, Moxibustion, Normalise, Oestrus, Panel, Prelim, Prickly, Q, Radiant, Radiator, Rankine, Recalescence, Red, Render, Repechage, Rut, Salt, Scald, Sinter, Sizzle, Solar, Space, Specific, Spice, Stew, Storage, Stove, Swelter, Teend, Temperature, Tind, Tine, Torrefy, Total, Tynd(e), Underfloor, Warming-pan, Warmth, White

Heath(land) Bearberry, Bent, Briar, Brier, Egdon, Epacrid, Erica, Geest, Lande, Manoao, Manzanita, Moor, Muir, Stead, Ted

Heathen(s) Ethnic, Gentile, Infidel, Litholatrous, Nations, Pagan, Pa(i)nim, Paynim, Philistine, Primitive, Profane, Proselyte of the gate

Heather Bell, Broom, Calluna, Epacrid, Erica, Ling, Rhodora, Sprig

▷ **Heating** *may indicate* an anagram

Heave(d) Cast, Fling, Frost, Heeze, Hoist, Hump, Hurl, Popple, Retch, Shy, Sigh, Vomit

▷ **Heave** *may indicate* 'discard'

Heaven(s), Heavenly Air, Aloft, Ama, Ambrosial, Asgard, Bliss, Celestial, Celia, Divine, Ecstasy, Elysian, Elysium, Empyrean, Ethereal, Fiddler's Green, Firmament, Hereafter, Himmel, Holy, Land o' the Leaf, Leal, Lift, Mackerel, Olympus, Paradise, Pole, Rapture, Seventh, Shangri-la, Sion, Sky, Supernal, Svarga, Swarga, Swerga, Tur-na-n'og, Uranian, Welkin, Zion

Heavy(weight), Heavily, Heaviness Ali, Clumpy, Dutch, Elephantine, Embonpoint, Endomorph, Grave, Hefty, Last, Leaden, Lumpish, Onerous, Osmium, Pesante, Ponderous, Sad, Scelerate, Stout, Top, Upsee, Ups(e)y, Weighty, Wicked

Hebe Barmaid

Hebrew Aramaic, Eli, Heb, Jesse, Karaism, Levi, Mishnayoth, Modern, Yid

Hebridean Harris

Heckle Badger, Gibe, Harass, Hatchel, Needle, Spruik

Hectic Ding-dong, Feverish, Frenetic

Hector Badger, Bluster, Browbeat, Bully, > **HARASS**, Nag

Hedge, Hedging Box, Bullfinch, Enclosure, Equivocate, Haw, Hay, Lay off, Meuse, Mews, Muse, Pleach, Privet, Quickset, Raddle, Sepiment, Shield, Stonewall, Texas, Thicket, Waffle

Hedgehog Gymnure, Hérisson, Tenrec, Tiggywinkle, Urchin

Hedge-parson Bucklebeggar, Patercove

Hedge-sparrow Accentor

Hedonist Cyreniac, Epicurean, Playboy, Sybarite

Heed(ed), Heedful Attend, Listen, > **MIND**, Notice, Observe, Rear, Reck, Regard(ant), Reke, Respect, Rought, Tent

Heedless Careless, Incautious, Rash, Scapegrace, Scatterbrain

Heel Achilles, Cad, Calcaneum, Cant, Careen, Cuban, Dogbolt, Foot, French, Kitten, List, Louse, Rogue, Seel, Spike, Stacked, Stiletto, Tilt, Wedge

Heel-tap Snuff

Hefty Brawny, Heavy, Solid, Weighty

Heifer Io, Quey, Stirk

Height(en), Heights Abraham, Altitude, Cairngorm, Ceiling, Dimension,

Elevation, Embroider, Eminence, Enhance, Golan, H, Hill, Hypsometry, Level, Might, Peak, Procerity, Spot, Stature, Stud, Sum, > SUMMIT, Tor, X

Heinous Abominable, Atrocious, Flagrant

Heir Alienee, Claimant, Coparcener, Dauphin, Devisee, Distributee, Eigne, H(a)eres, Institute, Intitule, Legatee, Parcener, Scion, Sprig, Tanist

Heirless Escheat, Intestate

Held Captive, Hostage, Sostenuto

▷ **Held by** *may indicate* a hidden word

Helen Elaine, Nell(y)

Helicopter, Heliport Airstop, Chopper, Egg-beater, Gunship, Hover, Iroquois, Medevac, Rotodyne, Sea Cobra, Sea King, Sea Knight, Sea Sprite, Sea Stallion, Sikorsky, Sky-hook, Whirlybird

Helios Hyperion

Heliotrope Cherry-pie

Helium He

Helix Alpha, Double

Hell(ish) Abaddon, Ades, Agony, Amenthes, Annw(yf)n, Avernus, Ayss, Below, Chthonic, Dis, Erebus, Furnace, Gehenna, Hades, Heck, Inferno, Jahannam, Lower regions, Malebolge, Naraka, Orcus, Pandemonium, Perditious, Pit, Ruin, Sheol, Stygian, Tartar(ean), Tartarus, Tophet, Torment

Hellbender Menopome, Mud-puppy

Hellebore Itchweed, Setterwort

Hellespont Dardanelles

Hello, Hallo, Hullo Aloha, Chin-chin, Ciao, Dumela, Golden, Hi, Ho(a), Howdy, Howzit, Yoo-hoo

Helm(sman) Cox, Pilot, Steer, Tiller, Timon(eer)

Helmet Armet, Balaclava, Basinet, Beaver, Burganet, Burgonet, Cask, Casque, Comb, Crash, Galea, Heaume, Knapscal, Knapscull, Knapskull, Montero, Mor(r)ion, Nasal, Pickelhaube, Pith, Plumed, Pot, Pressure, Salade, Sal(l)et, Shako, Skid-lid, Smoke, Topee, Topi

Helot Esne, Slave

Help(er), Helping, Helpful Abet, Accomplice, Adjuvant, Advantage, Aid(ance), Aidant, Aide, Alleviate, Ally, Asset, > ASSIST, Avail, Back, Beet-master, Beet-mister, Befriend, Benefit, Bestead, Boon, Brownie, Char(woman), Coadjutor, Complice, Conducive, Daily, Dollop, Dose, Forward, Further(some), Go, Hand, Henchman, Hint, Home, Instrumental, Leg-up, Life-saver, Maid, Mayday, Monitor, Obliging, Order, Patronage, Ration, Recourse, Relieve, Servant, Serve, Slice, SOS, Stead, Sted, Subserve, Subvention, Succour, Taste, Therapeutic, Use

Helpless(ness) Adynamia, Anomie, Feeble, Impotent, Paralytic, Useless

Helpmate Consort

Hem Border, Fringe, Hoop, List

He-man Adonis, Hunk, Jock, Macho

Hemisphere, Hemispherical Dominant, Magdeburg, Rose-cut, Western

Hemlock Conia, Cowbane, Insane root, Tsuga

Hemp Abaca, Bhang, Boneset, Bowstring, Carl(ot), Choke-weed, Codilla, Dagga, Fimble, Ganja, Hards, Henequen, Hiniquin, Indian, K(a)if, Kef, Love-drug, Manil(l)a, Moorva, Murva, Neckweed, Pita, Sida, Sunn, Tat, Tow

Hen Ancona, Andalusian, Australorp, Biddy, Buff Orpington, Chock, Cochin, Dorking, Eirack, Fowl, Grig, Houdan, Langshan, Layer, Leghorn, Maori, Marsh, Mud, Orpington, Partlet, Pertelote, Plymouth Rock, Poulard, Pullet, Ree(ve), Rhode Island Red, Sitter, Sultan, Tappit, Welsummer, Wyandotte

Hence Apage, Avaunt, Ergo, Go, Hinc, So, Therefore, Thus
Henchman Attendant, Follower, Myrmidon, Satellite
Hen-house Battery, Eggery
Henna Camphire
Hennery Run
Hen-pecked Spineless, Woman-tired
Henry Eighth, H, Hal, Hank, Hooray, Hy, James, Navigator, O
Hep Bacca, Berry, Hip
Hepatic Scale-moss
Hepatitis Favism, Jaundice
Herald(ic), **Heraldry** Abatement, Argent, Armory, Azure, Bagwyn, Bars,
Baton sinister, Bend, Bendwise, Blazonry, Bloody Hand, Blue Mantle,
Bordure, Caboched, Calygreyhound, Chevron, Chief, Cicerone, Cinquefoil,
Clarenc(i)eux, Compone, Compony, Couchant, Coue, Counter-passant, Couped,
Coward, Crest, Crier, Degraded, Difference, Displayed, Dormant, Endorse,
Enfield, Erased, Fecial, Fess(e), Fetial, File, Flory, Forerunner, Gardant, Garter,
Gironny, Golp(e), Gules, Gyronny, Hauriant, Hermes, Issuant, King-of-arms,
Lionel, Lodged, Lyon, Manchet, Martlet, Messenger, Minocaine, Morne,
Mullet, Naiant, Naissant, Nascent, Nombril, Norroy, Nowed, Nowy, Opinicus,
Or, Ordinary, Pale, Pallet, Paly, Passant, Pile, Portcullis, Portend, Potant,
Precursor, Proclaim, Purpure, Pursuivant, Quartering, Rampant, Red Hand,
Regardant, Rouge Croix, Rouge Dragon, Roundel, Roundle, Sable, Salient,
Scarp, Sea lion, Segreant, Sejant, Statant, Stentor, Subordinary, Trangle,
Tressure, Trick, Trippant, Trundle, Umbrated, Urinant, Usher, Vaunt-courier,
Verdoy, Vert, Vol(ant), Vorant, Wivern, Wyvern, Yale
Herb(s) Aconite, Ajowan, Allspice, Angelica, Anise, Aristolochia, Arugula,
Avens, Basil, Bay, Bennet, Bergamot, Borage, Capers, Cardamom, Centaury,
Chamomile, Chervil, C(h)ive, Cilanto, Comfrey, Coriander, Costmary,
Cum(m)in, Dill, Dittany, Echinacea, Eruca, Exacum, Eyebright, Felicia, Fennel,
Fenugreek, Ferula, Feverfew, Fireweed, Fitch, Fluellin, Forb, Garlic, Garnish,
Gentian, Germander, Good-King-Henry, Gunnera, Haworthia, Hyssop, Inula,
Kalanchoe, Knapweed, Lamb's ears, Laserpicium, Laserwort, Lewisia, Lovage,
Madder, Madwort, Mandrake, Marjoram, Maror, Medic, Mint, Moly, Mustard,
Oca, Oleraceous, Oregano, Origan(e), Origanum, Ornithogalum, Orval,
Paprika, Parakeelya, Parakelia, Parsley, Paterson's curse, Pia, Pipsissewa,
Plantain, Purpie, Purslane, Pussytoes, Rest-harrow, Rhizocarp, Rodgersia,
Rosemary, Rue, Saffron, Sage, Salad, Saloop, Salsify, Savory, Senna, Sesame,
Soapwort, Sorrel, Southernwood, Spearmint, Staragen, Sweet cicely, Tacca,
Tansy, Tarragon, Thyme, Tormentil, Turmeric, Typha, Valerian, Vervain,
Vetch, Weed, Willow, Wormwood, Wort, Yarrow, Yerba
Herbert Alan, AP(H), Lom, Spencer
Herbicide Agent Orange, Atrazine, Defoliant, Picloram
Herbivore Iguanodon, Sauropod
Hercules Alcides, Huge, Rustam, Rustem
Herd(er), **Herdsman** Band, Corral, Drive, Drover, Flock, Gang, Marshal, Mob,
Pod, Raggle-taggle, Round-up, Shepherd, Tinchel, Vaquero
Here Adsum, Hi, Hic, Hither, Local, Now, Present
Hereditary, **Heredity** Ancestry, Blood, Breeding, Codon, Dynastic, Eugenics,
Exon, Genetics, Id(ant), Idioplasm, Mendelism
▷ **Herein** *may indicate* a hidden word
Here is laid HS
Heresiarch Nestor

Heresy, Heretic(al) Agnoitae, Albi, Albigensian, Apollinaris, Apostasy, Arian, Bab, Bogomil, Bugger, Cathar, Cerinthus, Docete, Donatist, Dulcinist, Eudoxian, Giaour, Heresearch, Heterodoxy, Lollard, Manichaean, Montanism, Nestorian, Nonconformist, Origen, Patarin(e), Pelagius, Phrygian, Racovian, Rebel, Unitarian, Zendik
Heritage Birthright, Due, Ottilie, Patrimony
Hermaphrodite Androgynous, Gynandromorph, Monochinous, Monoecious
Hermes (rod) Caduceus, Mercury
Hermetic Alchemist, Sealed
Hermit(age) Anchoret, Anchorite, Ascetic, Ashram(a), Augustinian, Austin, Cell, Cloister, Crab, Eremite, Grandmontine, Marabout, Monk, Museum, Nitrian, Peter, Recluse, Retreat, Robber-crab, Sannyasi, Soldier-crab, Solitary, Troglodyte
Hernia Bubonocele, Cystocoele, Diverticulum, Enterocele, Hiatus, Inguinal, Rupture
Hero(ic) Achilles, Agamemnon, Aitu, Ajax, Alcides, Amadis, Bader, Bellerophon, Beowulf, Brave, Bunyan, Champ(ion), Cid, Couplet, Crockett, Cuchulain, Cuchullain, Cyrano, Dambuster, Demigod, Drake, Epic, Eponym, Eric, Everyman, Faust, Fingal, Finn, Finn MacCool, Folk, Garibaldi, Glooscap, Gluscap, Gluskap, God, Goody, Great, Hector, Heracles, Hercules, Hiawatha, Howleglass, Hudibrastic, Icon, Ideal, Idol, Ivanhoe, Jason, Kaleva, Kami, Leonidas, Lion, Lochinvar, Lothair, Marmion, Meleager, Nestor, Noble, Oliver, Onegin, Orion, Owl(e)glass, Ow(l)spiegle, Paladin, Parsifal, Pericles, Perseus, Philoctetes, Priestess, Principal, Rambo, Raven, Resolute, Revere, Rinaldo, Roderego, Roderick, Roland, Rustem, Rustum, Saladin, Sheik, Siegfried, Sigurd, Superman, Tam o' Shanter, Tancred, Tarzan, Tell, Theseus, Tragic, Triptolemus, Tristan, Trist(r)am, Ulysses, Valiant, Vercingetorix, Virago, Volsung, White knight, Zorro
Herod Agrippa, Antipas
Heroin Dogfood, Doojie, Dynamite, Gumball, H, Harry, Henry, Horse, Jack, Junk, Scag, Shit, Skag, Smack, Snow, Snowball, Speedball, Sugar
Heroine Andromeda, Ariadne, Candida, Darling, Hedda, Imogen, Isolde, Juliet, Leda, Leonora, Manon, Mimi, Nana, Norma, Pamela, Star, Tess, Una
Heron(s) Ardea, Bird, Bittern, Butter-bump, Egret, Green, Handsaw, Kotuko, Screamer, Sedge, Siege, Squacco
Herpes Cold sore, Dartre, Shingles, Shiver
Herring Bismarck, Bloater, Brisling, Brit, Buckling, Caller, Cisco, Clupea, Digby chick(en), Gaspereau, Kipper, Lake, Ma(a)tjes, Maise, Maize, Mattie, Maze, Mease, Menhaden, Norfolk capon, Ox eye, Rabbitfish, Red, Rollmop, Sea-stick, Shotten, Sild, Silt, Sparling, Teleost, White
Herringbone Sloping
Hesitant, Hesitate, Hesitation Balance, Boggle, Cunctation, Delay, Demur, Dicker, Dither, Doubtful, Dubitate, Er, Falter, Halting, Haver, Haw, Irresolute, Mammer, > PAUSE, Qualm, Scruple, Shillyshally, Shrink, Stagger, Stammer, Swither, Tarrow, Teeter, Tentative, Um, Ur, Vacillate, Wait, Waver
Hesperus Vesper
Hessian Burlap, Hireling
Heterodoxy Heresy
Heterogeneous Diverse, Motley, Piebald
Heterosexual Straight
Hew Ax, Chop, Cut, Hack, Sever
Hex Bewitch, Jinx, Voodoo

Hexameter Dolichurus
▸ **Hey** *see* HAY
Heyday Prime, Summer
Hi Cooee, Hello, Howdie
Hiatus Caesura, Entr'acte, Gap, Hernia, Interact, Interregnum, Interval, Lacuna, Lull
Hibernate, Hibernating Estivate, Hole up, Latitant, Sleep, Winter
Hibernian Irish
Hibiscus Okra, Roselle, Rozelle
Hiccup Glitch, Singultus, Snag, Spasm, Yex
Hick Jake, Oaf, Podunk, Rube, Yokel
Hickory Black, Jackson, Mockernut, Pecan, Scaly-bark, Shagbark
Hidden Buried, Cabalistic, Covert, De(a)rn, Doggo, Hooded, Latent, Obscure, Occult, Pentimento, Recondite, Screened, Secret, Shuttered, Sly, Ulterior, Unseen, Veiled, Wrapped
▷ **Hidden** *may indicate* a concealed word
Hide, Hiding (place) Abscond, Befog, Bield(y), Box-calf, Burrow, Cache, Camouflage, Ceroon, Coat, > CONCEAL, Cootch, Cordwain, Couch, Cour, Crop, Curtain, Cwtch, Deerskin, Doggo, Earth, Eclipse, Encave, Ensconce, Enshroud, Envelop, Epidermis, Fell, Flaught, Flay, Gloss over, Harbour, Heal, Heel, Hele, Hell, Hole-up, Incave, Inter, Kip, Kipskin, Lair, Leather, Mai-mai, Mask, Mobble, Nebris, > OBSCURE, Parfleche, Pell, Pelt, Plank, Plant, Priest's hole, Robe, Saffian, Screen, Secrete, Shadow, Shellac(k), Shroud, Skin, Spetch, Stash, Strap-oil, Tappice, Thong, Thrashing, Trove, Veil, Wallop, Whang, Wrap
Hideous(ness) Deform(ed), Enormity, Gash, Grotesque, Horrible, Monstrous, Odious, Ugly, Ugsome
Hierarchic, Hierarchy Byzantine, Elite, Theocracy
Hieroglyph Cipher, Pictogram
Higgledy-piggledy Mixtie-maxtie
High(er), Highly, Highness Alt(a), Altesse, Altissimo, Apogee, Atop, Brent, Climax, Doped, Drugged, E-la, Elation, Elevated, Eminent, Exalted, Excelsior, Frequency, Gamy, Haut(e), Intoxicated, Lofty, Maggotty, Mind-blowing, Orthian, Prime, Rancid, Ripe, School, Senior, Sent, Shrill, So, Steep, Stenchy, Stoned, String-out, Strong, Superior, Swollen, Tall, Tension, Tipsy, Top-lofty, Topmost, Treble, Up(per), Very, Wired
▷ **High** *may indicate* an anagram
High and mighty Haughty, Hogen-mogen
Highball Drink, Lob, Loft
Highbrow Brain, Egghead, Intelligentsia, Long-hair
High-class Best, Superior, U
High-crowned Copataine
Highest Best, Climax, Mostwhat, Ne plus ultra, Progressive, Supreme
Highest note E-la
High-flown Bombastic, Euphuism
Highland(er), Highlands Blue-bonnet, Blue-cap, Cameron, Cat(h)eran, Down, Duniwassal, Dun(n)iewassal, Gael, Karoo, Kiltie, Masai, Nainsel(l), Plaid(man), Redshank, Riff, Scot, Seaforth, Shire, Teuchter
Highlight Feature, Focus, Heighten, Stress
▸ **High-pitched** *see* HIGH
High-spirited Extravert, Extrovert
High tension HT
Highway Alaska, Alcan, Autobahn, Autopista, Autostrada, Divided, Flyover,

Freeway, Interstate, Motorway, Overpass, Pass, Queen's, Road, Rode, Tarseal, Thoroughfare, Tightrope

Highwayman, Highway robber(y) Bandit, Bandolero, Duval, Footpad, Fraternity, Gilderoy, Jack Sheppard, Land-pirate, Land-rat, Latrocinium, MacHeath, Motorist, Rank-rider, Road-agent, Scamp, Skyjacker, Toby, Tobyman, Turpin, Twitcher, Wheel

Hijack(er) Abduct, Pirate

Hike(r) Backpack, Bushbash, Bushwalk, Raise, Rambler, Ramp, Rise, Traipse, Tramp, Trape(s), Upraise

Hilarious, Hilarity Hysterical, Jollity, Mirth, Riot

Hilary Term

Hill(ock), Hills, Hillside Arafar, Areopagus, Aventine, Barrow, Beacon, Ben, Bent, Berg, Beverly, Black, Bluff, Bombay, Brae, Breed's, Broken, Bunker, Butte, Caelian, Calvan, Capitol(ine), Cheviots, Chiltern, Chin, Cleve, Cone, Coteau, Crag-and-tail, Crest, Djebel, Drumlin, Dun(e), Dunsinane, Eminence, Esquiline, Fell, Flodden, Gebel, Golan Heights, Golgotha, Gradient, Grampians, Hammock, Height, Helvellyn, Highgate, Holt, Horst, How, Hummock, Incline, Inselberg, Janiculum, Jebel, Kip(p), Knap, Knoll, Knot, Kop(je), Koppie, Lammermuir, Lavender, Law, Loma, Low, Ludgate, Mamelon, Man, Matopo, Mendip, Merrick, Mesa, Monadnock, Monte Cassino, Monticule, Morro, Mound, Mount Lofty Ranges, Nab, Naga, Nanatak, Nilgiri(s), North Downs, Otway Ranges, Palatine, Pennines, Pike, Pingo, Pnyx, Quantocks, Quirinal, Rand, Range, Saddleback, Savoy, Scaur, Seven, Silbury, Sion, Stoss, Tara, Tel(l), Toft, Toot, Tump, Tweedsmuir, Valdai, Viminal, Wolds, Wrekin, Zion

Hillbilly Yap

Hill-dweller Ant

Hillman Areopagite, Nepalese

Hilltop Crest, Knoll, Nab

Hilt Basket, Coquille, Haft, Handle, Hasp, Shaft

Him(self) He, Ipse, Un

Himalaya(n) Nepali, Panda, Sherpa, Tibetan

Hind(most) Back, Deer, Lag, Rear

Hinder, Hindrance Back, Bar, Block, Check, Counteract, Cumber, Debar, > DELAY, Deter, Estop, Hamper, Harass, Holdback, Impeach, Impede, Obstacle, Overslaugh, Posterior, Pull-back, Rear, Rein, Remora, Rump, Shackle, Slow, Stop, Stunt, Taigle, Thwart, Trammel

Hindi, Hindu(ism) Arya Samaj, Babu, Bania(n), Banyan, Brahman, Brahmin, Dalit, Gentoo, Gurkha, Harijan, Jaina, Kshatriya, Maharishi, Nagari, Pundit, Rajpoot, Rajput, Rama, Sad(d)hu, Saiva, Sanatana Dharma, Sankhya, Shaiva, S(h)akta, Sheik(h), Shudra, Smriti, Sudra, Swami, Swinger, Trimurti, Untouchable, Urdu, Vaishnava, Vais(h)ya, Varna, Vedanta

Hindquarters Backside, Crupper, Haunches

Hinge(d) Butt, Cardinal, Cross-garnet, Drop-leaf, Garnet, Gemel, Gimmer, Ginglymus, Joint, Knee, Mount, Parliament, Pivot, Stamp, Strap

▷ **Hinge(s)** *may indicate* a word reversal

Hingeless Ecardinate

Hinny Ass, Donkey, Joe

Hint Allude, Clew, Clue, Cue, Element, Gleam, Hunch, Idea, Imply, Inkle, Inkling, Innuendo, Insinuate, Intimate, Key, Mint, Nuance, Office, Overtone, Pointer, Preview, Scintilla, Shadow, Soupçon, > SUGGEST, Tang, Tip, Touch, Trace, Trick, Wind, Wink, Wisp, Word, Wrinkle

▷ **Hint** *may indicate* a first letter

Hip(pie), **Hippy**, **Hips** Cafard, Cheer, Coxa(l), Drop-out, Huck(le), Hucklebone, Hunkers, Informed, Ischium, Sciatic, Tonish

Hippopotamus Behemoth, River-horse, Sea-cow, Sea horse

Hire(d), **Hiring** Affreightment, Charter, Employ, Engage, Fee, Freightage, Job, Lease, Merc(enary), Never-never, Pensionary, Rent, Shape-up, Ticca, Wage

Hirsute Hairy, Pilose, Shaggy

▷ **His** *may indicate* greetings

Hiss Boo, Fizzle, Goose, Hish, Sibilant, Siffle, Sizzle, Swish

Historian Acton, Adams, Antiquary, Archivist, Arrian, Asellio, Bede, Biographer, Bryant, Buckle, Camden, Carlyle, Centuriator, Chronicler, Etain, Froude, Gibbon, Gildas, Green, Griot, Herodotus, Knickerbocker, Livy, Macaulay, Oman, Paris, Pliny, Plutarch, Ponsonby, Renan, Roper, Sallust, Spengler, Starkey, Strachey, Suetonius, Tacitus, Taylor, Thiers, Thucydides, Toynbee, Trevelyan, Wells, Xenophon

History, **Historical** Account, Anamnesis, Ancient, Annal, Bunk, Case, Chronicle, Clio, Epoch(a), Ere-now, Ever, Heritage, Legend, Life, Living, Mesolithic, Modern, Natural, Ontogency, Oral, Past, Record, Renaissance

Histrionic Operatic, Theatrical

Hit Bang, Bash, Baste, Bat, Bean, Belt, Blip, Blockbuster, Bloop, Blow, Bludgeon, Boast, Bolo, Bonk, Bunt, Clobber, Clock, Clout, Club, Collide, Cuff, Dot, Flail, Flick, Flip, Foul, Fourpenny-one, Fungo, Get, Hay, Head-butt, Home(-thrust), Impact, Knock, Lam, Lob, Magpie, Mug, Pandy, Paste, Pepper, Pistol-whip, Polt, Prang, Punto dritto, Ram, Roundhouse, Sacrifice, Score, Sensation, Six, Skier, Sky, Slam, Slap, Slosh, Smash(eroo), Smit(e), Sock, Spank, Stoush, Straik, Stricken, Strike, Strook, Struck, > **SUCCESS**, Swat, Switch, Thwack, Tip, Tonk, Touché, Undercut, Venewe, Venue, Volley, Wallop, Wham, Wing, Ythundered, Zap, Zonk

Hitch(ed) Catch, Contretemps, Edge, Espouse, Hike, Hirsle, Hoi(c)k, Hotch, Jerk, Lorry-hop, Rub, Sheepshank, Sheet bend, Shrug, Snag, Technical, Thumb, Wed

Hitherto Before, Yet

Hittite Uriah

Hive(s) Nettlerash, Skep, Spread, Swarm, Wheal

Hoar(y) Ashen(-grey), Canescent, Froren, Frost, Gaudy-day, Grizzled, Rime

Hoard(ing) Accumulate, Amass, Bill, Billboard, Cache, Coffer, Eke, Heap, Hoord, Husband, Hutch, Mucker, Plant, Pose, Salt away, Save, Sciurine, Snudge, Squirrel, Stash, Stock, Store, Stow, Treasure

Hoarse(ness) Croupy, Frog, Grating, Gruff, Husky, Raucous, Roar(er), Roopit, Roopy, Throaty

Hoax April-fish, Bam, Canard, Cod, Do, Doff, Fub, Fun, Gag, Gammon, Gull, Hum, Huntie-gowk, Kid, Leg-pull, Piltdown, Put-on, Sell, Skit, Spoof, String, Stuff, Supercherie, > **TRICK**

Hobble, **Hobbling** Game, Hamshackle, Hilch, Hitch, Lame, Limp, Pastern, Picket, Spancel, Stagger, Tether

Hobby Avocation, Fad, Falcon, Interest, Pastance, > **PASTIME**, Predator, Pursuit, Recreation, Scrimshaw

Hobby-horse Dada, Obsession, Play-mare

Hobgoblin Bog(e)y, Puck

Hobnail Clinker, Tacket

Hobnob Chat, Mingle

Hobo Bum, > **TRAMP**, Vagrant

Hock Cambrel, Dip, Gambrel, Gambril, Gammon, Ham, Heel, Hough,

Hypothecate, Pawn, Pledge, Rhenish, Wine

Hockey Grass, Hurling, Pond, Shinny, Shinty

Hod Carrier, Tray

Hodge Peasant, Rustic, Yokel

Hoe Claut, Dutch, Grub, Jembe, Nab, Pecker, Prong, Rake, Scuffle, Thrust, Weed

Hog Babiroussa, Babirussa, Boar, Glutton, Guttle, Peccary, Pig, Porker, Road, Shoat, Shott, Whole

Hogmanay Ne'erday

Hog-rat Hutia

Hogshead Butt, Cask, Muid

Hogwash Bull, Nonsense, Swill, Twaddle

Hoi-polloi Prole(tariat), Rabble

Hoist Boom, Bouse, Crane, Davit, Derrick, Gin, Heft, Hills, Jack, Lewis, Lift, Raise, Shearlegs, Shears, Sheerlegs, Sheers, Sway, Teagle, Trice, Whip-and-derry, Wince, Winch, Windas, Windlass

Hold(er), Holding, Hold back, up, etc Absorb, Anchor, Backbreaker, Belay, Believe, Boston crab, Canister, Cease, Cement, Cinch, Clamp, Clasp, Cling, Clutch, Contain, Cotland, Delay, Detain, Display, Dog, Embrace, Engross, Er, Facebar, Fast, Fief, Fistful, Frog, Full nelson, Garter, > GRASP, Grip, Grovet, Half-nelson, Hammerlock, Handle, Haud, Have, Headlock, Heft, Heist, Hiccup, Hinder, Hitch, Ho(a), Hoy, Hug, Impedance, Impede, Impediment, Impound, Incumbent, Intern, Intray, Japanese stranglehold, Keep, Keepnet, Lease, Maintain, Manure, Nelson, Own, Port, Proffer, Rack, Reluct, Reserve, Rivet, Rob, Rundale, Runrig, Save, Scissors, Shelve, Shore, Sleeve, Sostenuto, Stand, Suplex, Suspend, Tenancy, Tenement, Tenure, Toehold, Toft, Tray, Tripod, Wristlock, Zarf, Zurf

Hole(s), Holed, Holey Agloo, Aglu, Albatross, Antrum, Aubrey, Beam, Birdie, Black, Cat, Cave, Cavity, Cenote, Coal, Coalsack, Crater, Cubby, Dell, Den, Dene, Dog-leg, Dolina, Doline, Dormie, Dormy, Dreamhole, Dry, Dugout, Eagle, Earth, Ethmoid, Eye(let), Faveolate, Finger, Foramen, Funk, Gap, Geat, Glory, Gnamma, Gutta, Hag(g), Hideout, Kettle, Knot, Lenticel, Lill, Limber, Loop, Loup, Lubber's, Lumina, Maar, Mortise, Moulin, Namma, Nineteenth, Oillet, > OPENING, Orifex, Orifice, Ozone, Perforate, Pierce, Pigeon, Pinprick, Pit, Pocket, Pore, Port, Pot, Potato, Priest's, Punctuate, Punctum, Puncture, Rowport, Sallyport, Scupper, Scuttle, Scye, Situation, Slot, Snag, Snow, Soakaway, Socket, Sound, Spandrel, Spider, Spiraculum, Starting, Stead, Stew, Stop, Stove, Swallow, Tear, Thirl, Touch, Trema, Vent, Ventage, Ventige, Voided, Vug, Watering, Well, White, Wookey

Holiday(s) Bank, Benjo, Break, Busman's, Childermas, Ferial, Festa, > FESTIVAL, Fete, Fiesta, Furlough, Gala, Half(term), High, Honeymoon, Lag b'Omer, Laik, Leasure, Leave, Legal, Leisure, Long, Minibreak, Off-day, Off-time, Outing, Packaged, Pink-eye, Play-day, Playtime, Public, Purim, Recess, Repose, Rest, Roman, Seaside, Shabuoth, Shavuot, Sojourn, Statutory, Stay, Sunday, Tax, Trip, > VACATION, Villegiatura, Wake(s), Whitsun

Holinshed Chronicler

Holland(s) Batavia, Genevese, Gin, Hogen-mogen, Netherlands, NL

Hollow Acetabulum, Alveary, Antar, Antre, Antrum, Armpit, Axilla, Blastula, Boss, Bowl, Cave(rn), Cavity, Chasm, Chott, Cirque, Cleché, Comb(e), Concave, Coomb, Corrie, Crater, Cup(mark), Cwm, Deaf, Dean, Dell, Delve, Den(e), Dent, Dimple, Dingle, Dip, Dish(ing), Dolina, Doline, Empty, Fossette, Frost, Gilgai, Glenoid, Gnamma-hole, Gowpen, Grot(to), Hole, How, Igloo, Incavo, Insincere, Keck(sy), Kex, Khud, Lip-deep, Mortise, Namma-hole, Niche, Omphaloid,

Orbita, Pan, Pit, Punt, Redd, Rout, Rut, Scoop, Shott, Sinus, Slade, Sleepy, Slot, Slough, Socket, Swire, Thank-you-ma'am, Trematic, Trough, Vlei, Vola, Wame, Wem

Holly Aquifoliaceae, Eryngo, Ilex, Mate, Yaupon

Hollyhock Althaea, Rose mallow

Hollywood Bowl, Tinseltown

Holm Isle

Holmes Sherlock, Wendell

Holmium Ho

Holocaust Churban, Shoah

Hologram, Holograph Laser, MS

Holothurian Trepang

Holster Sheath

Holy(man), Holiness Adytum, Alliance, Blessed, > DIVINE, Godly, Grail, Halidom, Helga, Hery, Khalif, Loch, Mountain, Orders, Pan(h)agia, Pious, Sacred, Sacrosanct, Sad(d)hu, Saintly, Sanctitude, Sannayasi(n), Santon, Sekos, Sepulchre, Shrine, Starets, Staretz, SV, Tirthankara, War

Holy Books, Holy writing Adigranth, Atharvaveda, Bible, Gemara, Granth, Hadith, Koran, Mishnah, NT, OT, Pia, Purana, Rigveda, Sama-Veda, > SCRIPTURE, Shaster, Shastra, Smriti, Sura(h), Tanach, Writ, Yajur-Veda

Holy building, Holy place Chapel, Church, Kaaba, Penetralia, Synagogue, Temenos, Temple

Holy Ghost Paraclete

Holy water Amrit

Homage Bow, Cense, Honour, Kneel, Manred, Obeisance, Tribute, Vail

Home Abode, Base, Blighty, Burrow, Cheshire, Chez, Clinic, Community, Domal, Domicile, Earth, Eventide, Family, Fireside, Gaff, Goal, Habitat, Harvest, Heame, Hearth, Heme, Hospice, House, In, Lair, Libken, Mental, Mobile, Montacute, Nest, Nursing, Pad, Plas Newydd, Remand, Res(idence), Rest, Starter, Stately, Villa

Homecoming Nostos

Home counties SE

Homeless Outler, Rootless, Skell

Homer(ic) Comatose, Cor, Epic(ist), Nod, Pigeon, Somnolent

Home-rule Parnellism, Swaraj

Homesick(ness) Heimweh, Mal du pays

Homespun Plain, Raploch, Russet, Simple

Homestead Ranch, Toft

Homework Prep, Preparation

Homicidal, Homicide Chance-medley, Justifiable, Killing, Manslaughter

Homily Lecture, Midrash, Pi, Postil, Prone, Sermon, Tract

▷ **Homing** *may indicate* coming back

Hominid Oreopitheous

Homogeneous Indiscrete

Homosexual(ity) Auntie man, Bardash, Batty boy, Bender, Bent, Camp, Cat, Closet queen, Cocksucker, Cottaging, Dike, Dyke, Fag(got), Fairy, Fruit, Gay, Gaydar, Ginger, Homophile, Invert, Lesbian, Moffie, Muscle Mary, Ponce, Poof(tah), Poofter, Poove, Pouf(fe), Poufter, Puff, Quean, Queer, Quiff, Rough trade, Shirt-lifter, Swish(y), Tonk, Tribade, Uranism, Urning, Woofter

Hone Grind, > SHARPEN, Whet

Honest(y) Aboveboard, Afauld, Afawld, Candour, Clean, Fair dinkum, Genuine, Incorruptible, Injun, Jake, Legitimate, Lunaria, Lunary, Open-faced,

Penny, Probity, Rectitude, Reputable, Righteous, Round, Sincere, Square, Squareshooter, Straight, Straight-arrow, Trojan, > TRUE, Upfront, Upright, Upstanding

Honey Comb, Flattery, Hybla, Hymettus, Mel, Melliferous, Nectar, Oenomel, Oxymel, Palm, Peach, Popsy-wopsy, Sis, Sugar, Sweetheart, Sweetie, Wood

Honeycomb(ed) Cellular, Faveolate, Favose, Waxwork

Honey-eater Bear, Blue-eye

Honeypot Haanepoot

Honeysuckle Abelia, Anthemion, Caprifoil, Caprifole, Lonicera, Rewa rewa, Suckling, Woodbind, Woodbine

Honorary, Honour(able), Honours, Honorific Accolade, Ace, Adore, Birthday, Blue, CBE, Commemorate, Credit, Dan, Elate, Emeritus, Ennoble, > ESTEEM, Ethic, Face-card, Fame, Fete, Glory, Grace, Greats, Homage, Insignia, Invest, Izzat, King, Knave, Knight, Kudos, Laudation, Laurels, MBE, Mention, Military, OBE, Pundonor, Queen, Remember, Repute, Respect, Revere, Reward, Ten, Tenace, Titular, Tripos, Venerate, Worship

Honourable companion CH

Honourless Yarborough

Hooch Moonshine

Hood(ed) Almuce, Amaut, Amice, Amowt, Apache, Balaclava, Bashlik, Biggin, Blindfold, Calash, Calèche, Calyptra, Capeline, Capuccio, Capuche, Chaperon(e), Coif, Cope, Cowl, Cucullate(d), Gangster, Jacobin, Kennel, Lens, Liripipe, Liripoop, Mantle, Mazarine, Pixie, Robin, Rowdy, Snood, Trot-cosey, Trot-cozy

Hoodlum Gangster, Roughneck, Thug

Hoodoo Mozz

Hoodwink(ed) Blear, Bluff, Cheat, > DECEIVE, Gull, Nose-led, Seel

Hoof(ed) Artiodactyla, Cloot, Coffin, Frog, Trotter, Ungula

Hoohah Humdudgeon

Hook(er), Hooked, Hooks Addict, Adunc, Aduncous, Barb(icel), Becket, Butcher's, Cant(dog), Catch, Chape, Claw, Cleek, Clip, Corvus, Crampon, Cromb, Crome, Crook, Crotchet, Cup, Drail, Fifi, Fish, Fluke, Fly, Gab, Gaff, Gig, Grapnel, Hamate, Hamose, Hamulus, Heel, Hitch, Inveigle, Kype, Meat, Pot, Prostitute, Pruning, Retinaculum, Sister, Snell, Sniggle, Swivel, Tala(u)nt, Tart, Tenaculum, Tenter, Tie, Trip, Uncus, Wanton, Welsh

Hookah Chillum, Hubble-bubble, Pipe

Hooligan Apache, Casual, Desperado, Droog, Hobbledehoy, Keelie, Larrikin, Lout, Ned, Rough(neck), Ruffian, Skollie, Skolly, Tearaway, Ted, Tough, Tsotsi, Yahoo, Yob(bo)

Hoop Bail, Band, Circle, Farthingale, Garth, Gird, Girr, Hula®, O, > RING, Tire, Trochus

Hooray Whoopee, Yippee

Hoot(er) Conk, Deride, Honk, Madge, Nose, Owl, Riot, Screech-owl, Siren, Ululate

Hoover Dam

Hop(per) An(o)ura, Ball, Bin, Cuscus, Dance, Flight, Jeté, Jump, Kangaroo, Leap, Lilt, Opium, Pogo, Saltate, Scotch, Skip, Spring, Tremié, Vine

Hope(ful) Anticipate, Aspirant, Contender, Daydream, Desire, Dream, Esperance, Evelyn, Expectancy, Forlorn, Gleam, Good, Pipe-dream, Promising, Roseate, Rosy, Sanguine, Trust, Valley, White, Wish

Hopeless(ness), Hopeless quest Abattu, Anomie, Anomy, Black, Buckley's chance, Despair, Despondent, Forlorn, Goner, Perdu, Pessimist

Hopscotch Peever
Horace Flaccus, Ode, Satirist
Horatio Nelson
Horatius Cocles
Horde Golden, Many, Mass, Swarm
Horizon Artificial, B, C, Celestial, Event, Gyro, Rational, Scope, Sea-line, Skyline
Horizontal Advection, Flat, Level, Prone, Supine
Hormone ACTH, Adrenalin®, Adrenaline, Aldosterone, Androgen,
  Androsterone, Angiotensin, Autacoid, Auxin, Biosynthesis, Bursicon,
  Calcitonin, Catecholamine, Corticoid, Corticosteroid, Cortisone, Cytokinin,
  Ecdysone, Endocrine, Erythropoietin, Estrogen, Florigen, Folliculin,
  Gastrin, Gibberellin, Glucagon, Gonadotrophic, Gonadotrop(h)in, Growth,
  Hydrocortisone, IAA, Inhibin, Insulin, Intermedin, Juvenile, Kinin,
  Lipotropin, Luteinizing, Melanotropine, Melatonin, Noradrenalin(e),
  Oestradiol, Oestriol, Oestrogen, Oestrone, Oxytocin, Parathyroid,
  Progesterone, Progestin, Progestogen, Prolactin, Prostaglandin, Relaxin,
  Secretagogue, Secretin, Secretion, Serotonin, Sex, Somatomedin,
  Somatostatin, Somatotrop(h)in, Steroid, Stilboestrol, Testosterone, Thymosin,
  Thyroid, Thyrotrop(h)in, Thyroxine, Triiodothyronine, TSH, Vasopressin
Horn(y) Advancer, Amalthea, Antenna(e), Antler, Baleen, Basset, Bez, Brass,
  Bugle, Cape, Ceratoid, Cor, Cornet, Cornett, Cornopean, Cornu(a), Cornucopia,
  Cromorna, Cromorne, Cusp, Dilemma, Exponential, Flugel-horn, French,
  Frog, Golden, Gore, Hooter, > **HORNBLOWER**, Hunting, Ivory, Keratin, Klaxon,
  Lur, Morsing, Mot, Oliphant, Periostracum, Plenty, Post, Powder, Pryse, Ram's,
  Scur, Shofar, Shophor, Spongin, Tenderling, Trey, Trez, Trumpet, Waldhorn
Hornblower Brain, Horatio, Peel, Triton, Trumpeter
Hornbook Battledoor, Battledore
Horned (sheep) Cabrié, Cabrit, Cornute, Hamate, Lunate, Mouflon, Muflon
Hornless Doddy, Humbel, Humlie, Hummel, Mooly, Mul(l)ey, Poley, Polled
Hornpipe Matelote
Horoscope Figure, Future, Prophecy, Star-map
Horrible, Horror Aw(e)some, Brat, Dire, Dread(ful), Execrable, Ghastly, Grisly,
  Gruesome, Hideous, Loathsome, Odious, Shock, Terror, Ugh, Vile
Horrid, Horrific, Horrify(ing) Dire, Dismay, Dreadful, Frightful, Ghastly, Gothic,
  Grim, Grisly, H, Loathy, Odious, Spiteful, Ugly
Hors d'oeuvres Antipasto, Canapé, Carpaccio, Ceviche, Hoummos, Houmus,
  Hummus, Mez(z)e, Pâté, Smorgasbord, Smor(re)brod, Smør(re)brød,
  Zak(o)uski
Horse Airer, Bidet, Bloodstock, Carriage, Cut, Cutting, Dark, Doer, Dray,
  Drier, Drug, Equine, H, > **HEROIN**, High, Hobby, Iron, Knight, Kt, Light,
  Malt, Outsider, Pack, Pantomime, Plug, Ride, Rocking, Sawbuck, Screen,
  Selling-plate, Sense, Stalking, Standard-bred, Stayer, Steeplechaser, Stock,
  Trestle, Vaulting, Willing, Wooden

- **HORSES**
-
-
- **2 letters:**
- GG
-
- **3 letters:**
- Ass
- Bay

Cob	Rip	Barb
Dun	Tit	Buck
Gee		Cert
Nag	**4 letters:**	Colt
Pad	Arab	Crib
Pot	Aver	Dale

Fell
Foal
Hack
Jade
Mare
Pole
Pony
Post
Prad
Roan
Scag
Snow
Span
Stud
Taki
Trot
Yale
Yaud

5 letters:
Arion
Arkle
Bevis
Borer
Caple
Capul
Favel
Filly
Genet
Morel
Mount
Neddy
Pacer
Pinto
Poler
Punch
Rogue
Screw
Seian
Shire
Steed
Tacky
Takhi
Troop
Waler
Wheel
White

6 letters:
Ambler
Bayard
Bronco

Brumby
Calico
Canuck
Cayuse
Chaser
Cooser
Crollo
Curtal
Cusser
Dobbin
Entire
Exmoor
Favell
Ganger
Garran
Garron
Gennet
Hogget
Hunter
Jennet
Kanuck
Keffel
Lampos
Livery
Morgan
Mudder
Novice
Pad-nag
Plater
Pommel
Poster
Quagga
Randem
Remuda
Roarer
Rouncy
Runner
Sabino
Saddle
Shoo-in
Sorrel
String
Stumer
Summer
Tandem
Tarpan
Tracer
Trojan
Vanner

7 letters:
Bobtail

Breaker
Cavalry
Centaur
Charger
Clipper
Coacher
Courser
Cuisser
Dappled
Draught
Eclipse
Eventer
Gelding
Hackney
Hobbler
Liberty
Marengo
Marocco
Morocco
Mustang
Palfrey
Pegasus
Piebald
Quarter
Remount
Saddler
Sheltie
Spanker
Starter
Sumpter
Swallow
Swinger
Trigger
Trotter
Walking
Wheeler
Xanthos
Xanthus

8 letters:
Aquiline
Bangtail
Bathorse
Boerperd
Buckskin
Camargue
Chestnut
Clay-bank
Cocktail
Dartmoor
Destrier
Eohippus

Friesian
Galloway
Highland
Holstein
Hyperion
Kochlani
Lusitano
Palomino
Schimmel
Shetland
Skewbald
Sleipnir
Springer
Stallion
Stibbler
Warragal
Warragle
Warragul
Warrigal
Welsh cob
Whistler
Yarraman
Yearling

9 letters:
Appaloosa
Black Bess
Caballine
Clavileno
Coldblood
Connemara
Gringolet
Houyhnhnm
Icelandic
Incitatus
Knabstrup
Percheron
Rosinante
Rozinante
Warmblood

10 letters:
Andalusian
Bucephalus
Buckjumper
Buttermilk
Clydesdale
Copenhagen
Lipizzaner
Lippizaner
Pliohippus
Przewalski

- Svadilfari
- Przewalskis   Thoroughbred   **16 letters:**
-                                    Tennessee
- **11 letters:**   **12 letters:**   **13 letters:**   Walking
- Daisy-cutter   Hambletonian   Perissodactyl
- High-stepper   Suffolk punch

Horseback Croup
Horse-box Stable, Stall
Horse-chestnut Aesculus, Conker
Horse collar Brecham, Hame
Horse complaint, Horse disease, Horse trouble Blind staggers, Bogspavin, Cracked heels, Curb, Dourine, Equinia, Eweneck, Farcy, Fives, Founder, Frush, Glanders, Gourdy, Head staggers, Heaves, Hippiatric, Knee spawn, Laminitis, Lampas, Lampers, Malander, Mallander, Mallender, Megrims, Miller's disease, Mooneye, Mud fever, N(a)gana, Poll-evil, Quitter, Quittor, Ringbone, Sallenders, Scratches, Seedy-toe, Spavie, Spavin, Strangles, Stringhalt, Summer sores, Surra, Sway-back, Sween(e)y, Thorough-pin, Thrush, Toe-crack, Vives, Windgall, Wind-sucking, Wire-heel, Yellows
Horse-dealer Buster, Coper
Horse-lover Philip
Horseman Ataman, Caballero, Cavalry, Centaur, Conquest, Cossack, Cowboy, Death, Dragman, Famine, Farrier, Hobbler, Hussar, Knight, Lancer, Nessus, Ostler, Parthian, Picador, Pricker, Quadrille, Revere, > RIDER, Slaughter, Spahi, Stradiot, Tracer
Horsemanship Manège
Horseplay Caper, Chukka, Knockabout, Polo, Rag, Rant, Romp
Horsepower Hp, Ps
Horseradish Ben, Moringa
Horseshoe(-shaped) Henge, Hippocrepian, King-crab, Lunette, Manilla, Oxbow, Plate
Horsetail Equisetum
Horse thief Blanco, Rustler
Horticultural, Horticulture, Horticulturist Grower, Pomology, RHS
Hose Chausses, Fishnet, Galligaskins, Gaskins, Lisle, Netherstock(ing), Nylons, Panty, Sock, Stockings, Tabi, Tights, Trunk, Tube
Hospitable, Hospitality Convivial, Entertainment, Euxine, Lucullan, Open house, Philoxenia, Social, Xenial
Hospital Ambulance, Asylum, Barts, Base, Bedlam, Clinic, Cottage, Day, ENT, Field, General, Guys, H, Home, Hospice, Imaret, Karitane, Lambarene, Lazaretto, Leprosarium, Leprosery, Lock, Loony bin, Lying-in, MASH, Mental, Nosocomial, Ozzie, Pest-house, Polyclinic, San, Scutari, Sick bay, Snake-pit, Special, Spital, Spittle, Teaching, Trust, UCH
Host(s), Hostess Amphitryon, Army, Barmecide, Chatelaine, Compere, Crowd, Definitive, Emcee, Entertainer, Eucharist, Heavenly, Hirsel, Hotelier, Innkeeper, Intermediate, Laban, Landlady, Landlord, Legend, Legion, Lion-hunter, Lot, Mass, Mavin, MC, Publican, Quickly, Sabaoth, Swarm, Taverner, Throng, Trimalchio
Hostage Gherao, Pawn, Pledge, POW
Hostel Asylum, Dharms(h)ala, Dorm, Entry, Halfway house, Inn, YHA, Youth
Hostile, Hostility Adverse, Aggressive, Alien, Animus, Bellicose, Bitter, Chilly, Currish, Diatribe, Feud, Hating, Icy, Ill, Ill-will, Inimical, Inveterate, Oppugnant, Unfriendly, Vitriolic, War

Hot (tempered) Ardent, Big, Blistering, Breem, Breme, Cajun, Calid, Candent, Dog days, Enthusiastic, Facula, Fervid, Feverish, Fiery, Fuggy, Gospeller, In, Incandescent, Irascible, Lewd, Live, Mafted, Mustard, Pepper, Piping, Potato, Randy, Red, Roaster, Scorcher, Sizzling, Spicy, Stewy, Stifling, Stolen, Sultry, Sweaty, Sweltering, Sweltry, Tabasco®, Thermidor, Torrid, Toustie, Tropical, Zealful

Hotchpotch Bricolage, Farrago, Mish-mash, Powsowdy, Welter

Hotel, Hotelkeeper Bo(a)tel, Fleabag, Flophouse, Gasthaus, Gasthof, H, Hilton, Host, Hydro, Inn, Motel, Parador, Patron(ne), Posada, Private, Ritz, Roadhouse, Savoy, Tavern, Temperance, Trust

Hothead(ed) Impetuous, Rash, Spitfire, Volcano

Hot-house Conservatory, Nursery, Orangery, Vinery

Hot plate Salamander

Hot rod Dragster

Hotspur Harry, Hothead, Rantipole

Hottentot Criqua, Khoikhoi, Strandloper

Hot water Soup, Therm

Hound(s) Afghan, Basset, Beagle, Bellman, Brach, Cad, Canine, Cry, > DOG, Entry, Gabriel's, Hamiltonstovare, Harass, Harrier, Hen-harrier, Ibizan, Javel, Kennet, Lyam, Lym(e), Mute, Otter, Pack, Pharaoh, Pursue, Rache, Ranter, Reporter, Saluki, Talbot, True, Tufter

Hound's bane Palay

Hour(s) Canonical, Complin(e), Elder's, Eleventh, Golden, H, Happy, Holy, Hr, Little, Lunch, None(s), Orthros, Peak, Prime, Rush, Sext, Sidereal, Small, Staggered, Terce, Tide, Time, Undern, Vespers, Visiting, Witching, Working, Zero

House(s), Housing, Household(er) Abode, Accepting, Admiralty, Althing, Astrology, Audience, Auditorium, B, Bach, Bastide, Beehive, Beth, Bhavan, Bhawan, Biggin, Bingo, Block, Boarding, Bondage, Bourbon, Broadcasting, Broiler, Brownstone, Bundestag, Burghley, Bush, Casa, Chalet, Chamber, Chapter, Charnel, Chateau, Chatsworth, Chattel, Chez, Clapboard, Clearing, Coffee, Commercial, Commons, Concern, Convent, Cote, Cottage (orne), Council, Counting, Country, Crankcase, Crib, Custom(s), Dacha, Dail, Demain, Demesne, Derry, Des res, Discount, Disorderly, Domal, Domicile, Donga, Door, Dower, Drostdy, Drum, Duplex, Dwelling, Dynasty, Edifice, Entertain, Establishment, Este, Familial, Fashion, Fibro(cement), Finance, Firm, Forcing, Frame, Fraternity, Free, Frontager, Full, Gaff, Gambling, Garage, Gite, Government, Habitat, Habitation, Hacienda, Halfway, Hanover, Harbour, Harewood, Hatfield, Heartbreak, Hearth, HK, Ho, Holyrood, Home, Homestead, Ice, Igloo, Inn, Insula, Isuing, Joss, Ken, Kenwood, Keys, Knebworth, Knesset, Lagthing, Lancaster, Leo, Lockwood home, Lodging, Longleat, Lords, Lot(t)o, Maison(ette), Malting, Manor, Manse, Mansion, Mas, Meeting, Meinie, Meiny, Ménage, Messuage, Mobility, Montagne, Nacelle, Odelst(h)ing, Open (-plan), Opera, Orange, Osborne, Pad, Parliament, Pent, Petworth, Picture, Pilot, Plantagenet, Pole, Pondokkie, Post, Prefab, Public, Quinta, Radome, Ranch, Ratepayer, Register, Residence, Rooming, Rough, Russborough, Safe, Sandringham, Satis, Scala, Schloss, Seanad (Eireann), Seat, Semi, Shanty, Sheltered, Show, Sign, Social, Software, Somerset, Sporting, Stable, Station, Steeple, Stewart, Storey, Stuart, Succession, Syon, Tavern, Tea, Terrace, Theatre, Third, Tied, Toft, Tombola, Tower, Town, Tract, Treasure, Tree, Trinity, Trust, Tudor, Upper, Usher, Vaulting, Vicarage, Villa, Wash, Watch, Weather, Weatherboard, Weigh, Wendy, Whare, Wheel, White,

Wilton, Windsor, Work, York, Zero, Zodiac
House-boat Wangun, Wan(i)gan
House-builder Jack
House-keeper Chatelaine, Matron, Publican
House-leek Sengreen
Housemaid's knee Bursa
Houseman Betty, Doctor, Intern, Peer
House-warming Infare
Housewife Etui, Needlecase
Housework Chore, Diy
Housing Case, Crankcase, Shabrack, Shelter, Slum, Tenement
Hova Malagash
Hove Plim, Swell
Hovel Cru(i)ve, Den, Pigsty, Shack, Shanty
Hover Hang, Levitate, Lurk, Poise
How Hill, Hollow
How'dyedo, How d'ye do Hallo, Pass, Salve
However As, But, Leastwise, Sed, Still, Though, Yet
Howitzer Gun
Howl(er) Banshee, Bawl, Bay, Bloop, Clanger, Hue, Mycetes, Squawk, Ululate, Wow, Yawl, Yowl
How much The
Hoy Bilander, Ship
HP Never-never
HQ Centre, Headquarters, SHAPE
Hub Boss, Centre, Focus, Hob, Nave, Pivot, Tee
Hubbub Charivari, Chirm, Coil, Din, Level-coil, Palaver, Racket, Row, Stir
Hubris Pride
Huckster Hawker, Kidd(i)er, Pedlar
Huddle Cringe, Gather, Hunch, Ruck, Shrink
Hudson River, Rock
Hue Colour, Dye, Outcry, Proscription, Steven, Tincture, Tinge, Utis
Huff Dudgeon, Hector, Pant, Pet, Pique, Snuff, Strunt, Umbrage, Vex
Hug Bear, Cuddle, > **EMBRACE**, Squeeze
Huge (number) Astronomical, Brobdingnag, Colossal, Enorm(ous), Gargantuan, Giant, > **GIGANTIC**, Gillion, Ginormous, Humongous, Humungous, Immane, Immense, Leviathan, Lulu, Mega-, Milliard, Monolithic, Monster, Octillion, Prodigious, Socking, Tall, Titanian, Tremendous, Vast, Whacking
Hugo Victor
Huguenot Camisard
Hulk Lout, Ruin, Shale, Shell, Ship
Hull Bottom, Framework, Husk, Inboard, Monocoque, Pod, Sheal, Sheel, Shell, Shiel, Shill, Shiplap
Hullabaloo Outcry, Razzamatazz, Raz(z)mataz(z)
▶ **Hullo** *see* HELLO
Hum(ming) Bombilate, Bombinate, Bum, Chirm, Drone, Lilt, Moan, Murmur, Nos(e)y, Pong, Ponk, Rank, Reek, Sowf(f), Sowth, Stink, Stir, Whir(r), Zing
Human(e), Humanist, Humanity Anthropoid, Bang, Colet, Earthling, Erasmus, Incarnate, Kindness, Mandom, Merciful, Mortal, Philanthropic, Species, Sympathy, Ubuntu, Virtual, Wight
Humble Abase, Abash, Afflict, Baseborn, Chasten, Cow, Degrade, Demean,

Demiss(ly), Lower, Lowly, Mean, > **MEEK**, Modest, Morigerate, Obscure, Poor, Rude, Small, Truckle

Humbug Berley, Blague, Blarney, Buncombe, Bunk(um), Burley, Cant, Claptrap, Con, Delude, Flam, Flummery, Fraud, Fudge, Gaff, Gammon, Gas, Guff, Gum, Hoax, Hoodwink, Hookey-walker, Kibosh, Liar, Maw-worm, Nonsense, Shenanigan, Wind

Humdinger Lulu

Humdrum Banal, Bourgeois, Monotonous, Mundane, Ordinary, Prosaic, Tedious

Humid(ity) Clammy, Damp, Dank, Machie, Machy, Muggy, Saturation, Steam, Sticky, Sultry

Humiliate, Humiliation, Humility Abase, Abash, Baseness, Degrade, Disbench, Eating crow, Fast, Indignity, Mortify, Put-down, > **SHAME**, Skeleton, Take-down, Wither

Humming-bird Colibri, Hermit, Rainbow, Sabre-wing, Sapphire-wing, Sappho, Sylph, Thornbill, Topaz, Trochilus

Hummock Tump

Humorist Cartoonist, Comedian, Jester, Leacock, Lear, Punster, Twain, Wodehouse

Humour, Humorous Aqueous, Bile, Blood, Caprice, Cardinal, Chaff, Coax, Cocker, Coddle, Cosher, Cuiter, Cuittle, Daut, Dawt, Dry, Facetious, Fun, Gallows, Ichor, Indulge, Irony, Jocose, Jocular, Juice, Kidney, Levity, Light, > **MOOD**, Observe, One-liner, Pamper, Phlegm, Pun, Pythonesque, Ribaldry, Salt, Serum, Temper, Trim, Vein, Vitreum, Wetness, Whim, Wit

Humourless Dry, Po(-faced)

Hump(ed) Boy, Bulge, Dorts, Dowager's, Gibbose, Gibbous, Hog, Huff, Hummock, Hunch, Middelmannetje, Pip, Ramp, Road, Speed bump, Tussock

▸ **Humpback** *see* **HUNCHBACK**

Humphrey Bogart

Humus Compost, Leafmould, Moder, Mor, Mull

Hun Alaric, Atli, Attila, Fritz, German

Hunch, Hunchback Camel, Chum, Crookback, Gobbo, Intuition, Kyphosis, Premonition, Quasimodo, Roundback, Sense, Urchin

Hundred(s), Hundredth Burnham, C, Cantred, Cantref, Cent, Centesimal, Centum, Century, Chiltern, Commot, Days, Desborough, Great, Host, > **IN A HUNDRED**, Long, Northstead, Old, Shire, Stoke, Ton, Wapentake

Hundred and fifty CL, Y

Hundred and sixty T

Hundredweight Centner, Quintal

Hung Displayed, Executed, Framed, High

Hungarian, Hungary Bohunk, Cheremis(s), Csardas, Magyar, Nagy, Szekely, Tzigane, Ugric, Vogul

Hunger, Hungry Appestat, Appetite, Bulimia, Bulimy, Clem, > **CRAVE**, Desire, Edacity, Empty, Esurient, Famine, Famish, Fast, Hanker, Hunter, Pant, Peckish, Rapacious, Raven, Ravin, Sharp-set, Unfed, Yaup, Yearn

▷ **Hungry** *may indicate* an 'o' in another word

Hunk(s) Beefcake, Chunk, Dry-fist, Miser(ly), Slab

Hunt(er), Hunting, Huntress, Huntsman Actaeon, Alew, Archer, Artemis, Atalanta, Battue, Beagle, Bellman, Bounty, Calydon, Chace, Chase(r), Chasseur, Chevy, Cool, Coursing, Crockett, Cynegetic, Dog, Drag(net), Esau, Ferret, Fox, Free-shot, Gun, Halloo, Herne, Hound, Jager, Lamping, Leigh, Lurcher, Montero, National, Nimrod, Orion, Peel, Pig-sticking, Poot, Pout,

Predator, Pursue, Quest, Quorn, Rabbit, Rach(e), Rake, Ran, Rancel, Ranzel, Ride, Rummage, Run, Scavenge(r), Scorse, > **SEARCH**, Seek, Shikar(ee), Shikari, Skirter, Slipper, Stag, Stalk, Sticker, Still, Swiler, Terrier, Thimble, Tinchel, Tower, Trail, Trap, Treasure, Venatic, Venator, Venerer, Venery, > **WATCH**, Whip, Whipper-in, Witch, Wolfer, Woodman, Woodsman, Yager

Hunting-call Rechate, Recheat, Tally-ho, View-halloo

Hunting-ground Forestation, Walk

Hurdle(r) Barrier, Doll, Fence, Flake, Gate, Hemery, Raddle, Sticks, Wattle

Hurdy (gurdy) Barrel-organ, Hainch, Haunch, Vielle

Hurl(ing) Camogie, Cast, Dash, > **FLING**, Heave, Put(t), Throw, > **TOSS**

Hurly-burly Furore, Noise

Hurrah Cheers, Huzza, Io, Whee

Hurricane Baguio, Tornade, Tornado, Typhoon, > **WIND**

Hurry Belt, Bustle, Chivvy, Chop-chop, Dart, Dash, Drive, Festinate, Fisk, Frisk, Gad, Gallop, Giddap, Giddup, Giddy-up, Hadaway, Hare, Haste, Hie, Hightail, Induce, Mosey, Post-haste, Press, Push, Race, Railroad, > **RUSH**, Scamper, Scoot, Scramble, Scur(ry), Scutter, Scuttle, Skelter, Skurry, Spank, Speed, Streak, Tear

Hurt(ful) Abuse, Ache, Ake, Bruise, Cutting, Damage, De(a)re, Disservice, Harrow, Hit, > **INJURE**, Lesion, Maim, Nocent, Nocuous, Noxious, Noyous, Pain, Pang, Prick(le), Scaith, Wound, Wring

Hurtle Rush, Spin, Streak, Streek

Husband(ry), Husbands Add, Baron, Breadwinner, Consort, Darby, Ear, Eche, Economy, Eke, Ere, Farm, Gander-mooner, Georgic, Goodman, Groom, H, Hoddy-doddy, Hodmandod, Hubby, Ideal, Man, Manage, Mate, Partner, Polyandry, Retrench, Save, Scrape, Scrimp, Spouse, Squirrel, > **STORE**, Tillage

Hush(-hush) Bestill, Gag, Sh, Silent, Smug, St, Tace, Wheesh(t), Whisht

Husk(s), Husky Acerose, Bran, Draff, Eskimo, Hoarse, Hull, Malemute, Seed, Sheal, Shuck

Hussar Cherry-picker, Cherubim

Hussite Calixtin(e)

Hussy Besom, Hen, Loose, Minx, Vamp

Hustle(r) Frogmarch, Jostle, Pro, Push, Railroad, Shoulder, Shove, Skelp

Hut(s) Banda, Booth, Bothie, Bothy, Bustee, Cabin, Caboose, Chalet, Choltry, Gunyah, Hogan, Humpy, Igloo, Mia-mia, Nissen, Pondok(kie), Quonset®, Rancheria, Rancho, Rondavel, Shack, Shanty, Sheal(ing), Shebang, Shed, Shiel(ing), Skeo, Skio, Succah, Sukkah, Tilt, Tolsel, Tolsey, Tolzey, Tramping, Wan(n)igan, Whare, Wi(c)kiup, Wigwam, Wil(t)ja, Wurley, Wurlie

Hutch Buddle, Crate, Pen

Hyacinth Cape, Grape, Starch, Wild

Hybrid Bigener, Bois-brûlé, Catalo, Centaur, Chamois, Chichi, Chimera, Citrange, Cockatrice, Cross, Dso, Funnel, Geep, Graft, Hippogriff, Hircocervus, Interbred, Jersian, Jomo, Jumart, Lurcher, Mameluco, Mermaid, Merman, Metis, Mongrel, Mule, Mutation, Opinicus, Ortanique, Ox(s)lip, Percolin, Plumcot, Pomato, Ringed, Tangelo, Tiglon, Tigon, Topaz, Ugli, Zho(mo)

▷ **Hybrid** *may indicate* an anagram

Hydra Polyp

Hydrant Fireplug, H

Hydrocarbon Acetylene, Aldrin, Alkane, Alkene, Alkyl, Alkyne, Amylene, Arene, Asphaltite, Benzene, Butadiene, Butane, Butene, Camphane, Camphene, Carotene, Cetane, Cubane, Cycloalkane, Cyclohexane, Cyclopropane, Cymogene, Decane, Diene, Dioxin, Diphenyl, Ethane, Gutta, Halon, Hatchettite, Hemiterpene, Heptane, Hexane, Hexene, Hexyl(ene), Indene,

Isobutane, Isoprene, Ligroin, Limonene, Mesitylene, Naphtha, Naphthalene, Nonane, Octane, Olefine, Paraffin, Pentane, Pentene, Pentylene, Phenanthrene, Phene, Picene, Polyene, Propane, Pyrene, Retene, Squalene, Stilbene, Styrene, Terpene, Toluene, Triptane, Wax, Xylene, Xylol

Hydrogen Deut(er)on, Diplon, Ethene, H, Muonium, Protium, Replaceable, Tritium

Hydrophobic Rabid

Hydroplane Skid

Hydroponic Soil

Hydrozoa(n) Campanularia, Millepore, Portuguese man-of-war, Siphonophore

Hyena Aard-wolf, Earthwolf, Laughing, Spotted, Strand-wolf, Tiger-wolf

Hygiene, **Hygienic** Aseptic, Oral, Sanitary, Sepsis, Sleep

Hymen Maidenhead

Hymn(s) Anthem, Benedictine, Bhajan, Canticle, Carol, Cathisma, Choral(e), Coronach, Dies Irae, Dithyramb, Doxology, Gloria, Hallel, Introit(us), Ithyphallic, Lay, Magnificat, Mantra, Marseillaise, Nunc dimittis, Ode, P(a)ean, Psalm, Recessional, Rigveda, Sanctus, Secular, Sequence, Stabat mater, Sticheron, Tantum ergo, Te deum, Trisagion, Troparion, Veda

Hymnographer, **Hymnologist** David, Faber, Heber, Moody, Neale, Parry, Sankey, Watts

Hyperbole, **Hyperbolic** Auxesis, Exaggeration, Sech

Hypercritical Captious

Hyperion Titan

Hypersensitive Allergic, Idiosyncratic

Hypha(e) Conidiophore, Stroma

Hyphen(ated) Dash, Parasyntheton, Soft

Hypnosis, **Hypnotise**, **Hypnotic**, **Hypnotism**, **Hypnotist** Braidism, Chloral, Codeine, Enthral, Entrance, Hypotonia, Magnetic, Meprobamate, Mesmerism, Svengali

Hypochondria(c) Hyp, Nosophobia, Phrenesiac, Valetudinarian

Hypocrisy, **Hypocrite**, **Hypocritical** Archimago, Bigot, Byends, Cant, Carper, Chadband, Deceit, Dissembler, Heep, Holy Willie, Humbug, Insincere, Janus-faced, Mucker, Nitouche, Pecksniff, Pharisaic, Pharisee, Prig, Sanctimony, Self-pious, Sepulchre, Tartuf(f)e, Two-faced, Whited sepulchre

Hypothesis, **Hypothetical** Biophor, Continuum, Gluon, Graviton, Nebular, Notional, Null, Plantesimal, Sapir-Whorf, Suppositious, Virtual, Working

Hyrax Cony, Daman, Dassie, Klipdas

Hysteria, **Hysteric(al)** Achiria, Astasia, Conniption, Delirium, Frenzy, Meemie, Mother

Ii

I A, Ch, Cham, Che, Dotted, Ego, Ich, Indeed, India, Iodine, Italy, J, Je, Me, Muggins, One, Self

Ian Scot

Ibex Izard

Ibis Hadedah, Sacred, Waldrapp

Ice(d), Ice-cream, Icing, Icy Alcorza, Anchor, Arctic, Ballicatter, Banana split, Berg, Black, Brash, Camphor, Cassata, Coconut, Cone, Cool, Cornet, Coupe, Cream, Crystal, Diamonds, Drift, Dry, Floe, Frappé, Frazil, Freeze, Frigid, Frore, Frosting, Frosty, Gelato, Gelid, Gems, Glacé, Glacial, Glacier, Glare, Glib, Granita, Graupel, Ground, Growler, Hailstone, Hok(e)y-pok(e)y, Hommock, Hummock, Knickerbocker glory, Kulfi, Lolly, Macallum, Marzipan, Neapolitan, Pack, Pancake, Pingo, Polar, Popsicle®, Rime, Rink, Royal, Sconce, Serac, Shelf, Sherbet, Slay, Slider, Slob, Sludge, Sorbet, Spumone, Spumoni, Stream, Sugar, Tickly-benders, Topping, Tortoni, Tutti-frutti, Verglas, Virga, Wafer, Water, Wintry

Ice-axe Piolet

Iceberg Calf, Floe, Growler

Ice-box Cooler, Freezer, Fridge, Frig, Yakhdan

▸ **Ice-cream** *see* **ICE**

Iceland IS

Ice-skating Choctaw, Figure, Glide

Icicle Tangle

Icon Idol, Image, Madonna, Sprite

Icterus Jaundice

Id(e) Ego, Fish, Orfe

Idea(s) Archetype, Brainchild, Brainwave, Clou, Clue, Conceit, Concept, Fancy, Fixed, Germ, Hunch, Idée fixe, Idolum, Image, Inkling, Inspiration, Interpretation, Keynote, Light, > **NOTION**, Obsession, Plan, Plank, Rationale, Recept, Theory, Thought, Whimsy, Zeitgeist

Ideal(ise) A1, Abstract, Bee's knees, Cat's whiskers, Dream, Eden, Ego, Goal, Halo, Hero, Model, Monist, Nirvana, Notional, Paragon, Pattern, > **PERFECT**, Romantic, Siddhi, Sidha, Sublimate, Transcendental, Utopian, Vision

Idealism, Idealist(ic) Dreamer, More, Perfectionist, Quixotic, Romantic, Visionary

Identical Alike, Clone, Congruent, Equal, Menechmian, Same, Selfsame, Verbatim, Very

Identification, Identify Bertillonage, Codeword, Credentials, Designate, Diagnosis, Differentiate, Discern, Document, Dog-tag, Earmark, Empathy, Espy, Finger(print), ID, Label, Mark, Name-tape, Password, Pin, Pinpoint, Place, Recognise, Reg(g)o, Secern, Spot, Swan-hopping, Swan-upping, Verify

Identikit® E-fit

Identity Alias, Appearance, Corporate, Credentials, Equalness, Likeness, Numerical, Oneness, Qualitative, Seity, Self, Selfhood

Ideologue Hard-liner

Idiom Americanism, Argot, Britishism, Cant, Expression, Idioticon, Jargon, Language, Pahlavi, Parlance, Pehlevi, Syri(a)cism, Syrism

Idiosyncrasy Foible, Mannerism, Nature, Quirk, Way

Idiot(ic), Idiocy Congenital, Dingbat, Dolt, Eejit, Fool, Goose, Half-wit, Imbecile, Inane, Maniac, Moron, Natural, Nerk, Nidget, Noncom, Oaf, Ouph(e), > STUPID (PERSON), Tony, Twit, Zany

Idle(ness), Idler Bludger, Boondoggle, Bum, Bumble, Bummle, Cockaigne, Dally, Deadbeat, Diddle, Dilly-dally, Dole-bludger, Donnat, Donnot, Do-nothingism, Drone, Fainéant, Fallow, Farnarkel, Fester, Flaneur, Flim-flam, Footle, Frivolous, Groundless, Hawm, Inaction, Indolent, Inert, Lackadaisical, Laesie, Lallygag, Layabout, Laze, Lazy, Lead-swinger, Lie, Light, Limer, Loaf, Lollop, Lollygag, Lotophagus, Lounge, Lusk, Micawber, Mike, Mollusc, Mooch, Mouch, Otiose, Otium, Patagonian, Piddle, Ride, Scapegrace, Shiftless, Skive, Sloth, Sluggard, Spiv, Stalko, Stock-still, Stooge, Stroam, Tarry, Transcendental, Trock, Troke, Truant, Truck, Twiddle, Unbusy, Unoccupied, Vain, Vegetate, Veg out, Waste

Idol(ise) Adore, Adulate, Baal(im), Baphomet, Bel, Crush, Fetich(e), Fetish, God, Heartthrob, Hero, Icon, Image, Joss, Juggernaut, Lion, Mammet, Manito, Manitou, Matinee, Maumet, Mawmet, Molech, Moloch, Mommet, Moorish, Mumbo-jumbo, Stotter, Swami, Teraph(im), Termagant, Vision, Wood, Worship

Idyll(ic) Arcady, Eclogue, Pastoral, Peneian

Ie Sc

If, If it All-be, An('t), Condition, Gif, Gin, In case, Pot, Provided, Sobeit, Whether

Igloo Snowden

Ignis-fatuus Elf-fire, Fire-dragon, Fire-drake, Friar's lanthorn, Wildfire

Ignite, Ignition Coil, Electronic, Flare, Kindle, Lightning, Spark, Starter

Ignoble Base, Inferior, Mean, Vile

Ignominious, Ignominy Base, Dishonour, Fiasco, Infamous, Scandal, > SHAME

Ignorance, Ignorant Analphabet, Anan, Artless, Benighted, Blind, Clueless, Darkness, Green, Hick, Illiterate, Inerudite, Ingram, Ingrum, Inscient, Know-nothing, Lewd, Lumpen, Misken, Nescience, Night, Oblivious, Oik, Philistine, Purblind, Red-neck, Unaware, Uneducated, Unlettered, Unread, Unschooled, Untold, Unversed, Unwist

Ignore Ba(u)lk, Blink, Bypass, Connive, Cut, Discount, Disregard, Forget, Neglect, Omit, Overlook, Override, Overslaugh, Pass, Pass-up, Rump, Slight, Snub

Igor Prince

I Know Iwis, Ywis

Ill Adverse, All-overish, Bad, Bilious, Cronk, Crook, Evil, Inauspicious, Income, Off-colour, Poorly, Queer, Sea-sick, > SICK, Unweal, Unwell, Valetudinarian, Wog, Wrong

▷ **Ill** *may indicate* an anagram

Ill-balanced Lop-sided

Ill-bred Churlish, Plebeian, Uncouth, Unmannerly

▷ **Ill-composed** *may indicate* an anagram

Ill-defined Diagnosis, Hazy, Unclear, Vague

Ill-dressed Frumpish

Illegal, Illicit Adulterine, Black, Bootleg, Breach, Furtive, Ill-gotten, Malfeasance, Misbegotten, Pirated, Shonky, Unlawful

Illegitimate Bastard, By-blow, Come-o'-will, Fitz, Irregular, Love-child,

Lucky-piece, Mamzer, Misbegotten, Misborn, Misfortunate, Momzer, Natural, Scarp, Spurious, Unlineal

Ill-favoured Lean, Offensive, Thin, Ugly

Ill-feeling, Ill-humour Bad blood, Bile, Curt, Dudgeon, Glum, Hate, Miff, Peevish, Pique, Rheumatic

Illiberal Insular

▶ **Illicit** *see* ILLEGAL

Illiterate Ignoramus, Unlettered, Unread

Ill-looking Peaky, Poorly

Ill-luck Ambs-ace, Ames-ace, Bad trot, Deuce-ace, Misfortune

Ill-mannered, Ill-natured Attercop, Bitchy, Crabby, Ethercap, Ettercap, Guttersnipe, Huffy, Stingy, Sullen, Ugly, Uncouth, Unkind

Illness Aids, Ailment, Attack, Autism, Brucellosis, Complaint, Croup, Death-bed, Diabetes, Disease, DS, Dwalm, Dwaum, Dyscrasia, Eclampsia, Grippe, Hangover, Hypochondria, Lockjaw, Malady, ME, Scarlatina, Sickness, Terminal, Toxaemia, Urosis, Weed, Weid, Wog

Ill-nourished Emaciated

Illogical Non-sequitur

Ill-smelling F(o)etid, High, Hing, Miasmic, Stinking

▶ **Ill-tempered** *see* ILL-MANNERED

Ill-timed Inopportune, Unseasonable

Illuminate(d), Illumination Brighten, Clarify, Cul-de-lampe, Decorate, Enlighten, Floodlit, Lamplight, Langley, Light, Limn, Miniate, Nernst, Pixel, Radiate, Rushlight

Illusion, Illusory Air, Apparition, Barmecide, Deception, Deja vu, Fallacy, Fancy, Fantasy, Hallucination, Ignis-fatuus, Mare's-nest, Maya, Mirage, Muller-Lyer, Optical, Phantom, Phi-phenomenon, Specious, Trompe l'oeil, Unreality, Will o'the wisp

Illustrate(d), Illustration, Illustrator Case, Centrefold, Collotype, Demonstrate, Drawing, Eg, Elucidate, Epitomise, Exemplify, Explain, Figure, Frontispiece, Grangerize, Graphic, Half-tone, Illume, Illumin(at)e, Instance, Instantiate, Limner, Lithograph, Pictorial, Plate, Show, Sidelight, Spotlight, Tenniel, Vignette

Illustrious Bright, Celebrated, Famous, Legendary, Renowned

Ill-will Animosity, Enmity, Grudge, Hostility, Malice, Maltalent, Spite

I'm I'se

Image(s) Atman, Blip, Brand, Corporate, Discus, Effigy, Eidetic, Eidolon, Eikon, Eiluned, Emotion, Enantiomorph, Graphic, Graven, Hologram, Hypnagogic, Icon, Iconograph, Ident, Idol, Invultuation, Joss, Latent, Likeness, Matte, Mirror, Murti, Paranthelium, Pentimento, Phantasmagoria, Photogram, Photograph, Pic(ture), Pixel(l)ated, Pixil(l)ated, Poetic, Profile, Public, Recept, Representation, Scintigram, Search, Shadowgraph, Simulacrum, Spectrum, Spitting, Split, Stereotype, Symbol, Teraph(im), Tiki, Tomogram, Totem, Video, Virtual, Xoanon

Imaginary (land), Imagination, Imaginative, Imagine(d) Assume, Believe, Boojum, Cloud-cuckoo-land, Cockaigne, Cockayne, Conceive, Conjure, Cyborg, Dystopia, Envisage, Esemplasy, Faery, Faine, Fancy, Feign, Fictional, Fictitious, Fictor, Figment, Figure, Hallucinate, Hobbit, Ideate, Invent, Mind's eye, Oz, Picture, Poetical, Prefigure, Pretend, Recapture, Replicant, Scotch mist, Snark, Straw, > SUPPOSE, Surmise, Think, Vicarious, Visualise, Whangam

Imbecile Anile, Fool, Idiot, > STUPID

▷ **Imbecile** *may indicate* an anagram

Imbibe Absorb, Drink, Lap, Quaff, Suck, Swallow
Imbricate Overlie
Imbroglio Complication, Maze
Imbrue, Imbue Colour, Impregnate, Indoctrinate, Infuse, Inoculate, Permeate, Soak, Steep
Imitate, Imitation, Imitator Act, Ape, Copy(cat), Counterfeit, Dud, Echo, Echopraxia, Emulate, Epigon(e), Ersatz, Fake, False, Faux, Follow, Marinist, Me-too, Mime, Mimetic, Mimic(ry), Mockery, Monkey, Parody, Parrot, Paste, Pastiche, Pinchbeck, Potichomania, Rip-off, Sham, Simulate, Stumer, Take-off, Travesty
Immaculate Conception, Flawless, Lily-white, Perfect, Pristine, Spotless, Virgin
Immanentist Pantheist
Immaterial Insignificant, Spiritual, Trifling
Immature(ly), Immaturity Callow, Crude, Embryo, Ergate(s), Green, Inchoate, Larval, Neotenic, Non-age, Puberal, Puberulent, Pupa, Raw, Sophomoric, Tender, Unbaked, Unripe, Young
▷ **Immature** *may indicate* a word incompleted
Immediate(ly) Alsoon, At once, B(e)live, Direct, Eftsoons, Ekdum, First-time, Forthwith, Imminent, Incontinent, Instantaneous, Instanter, Near, > **NOW**, Outright, Present, Pronto, Right-off, Short-term, Slapbang, Spontaneous, Stat, Straight, Straight off, Sudden, Then, Tout de suite
Immense Brobdingnag, Cosmic, Enormous, > **GIGANTIC**, Huge, Vast, Wide
Immerse Baptise, Demerge, Demerse, Drench, Embathe, Emplonge, Enew, Engage, Imbathe, Plunge, Soak, Steep
Immigrant, Immigration Aliya(h), Aussiedler, Carpet-bagger, Chalutz, Greener, Greenhorn, Halutz, Illegal, Incomer, Issei, Merino, Metic, Nisei, Olim, Outsider, Pilgrim, Pommy, Redemption(er), Reffo, Sanei, Sansei, Settler, Wetback, Whenwe
Imminent Approaching, Close, Immediate, Pending
Immobility, Immobilize Cataplexy, Catatonia, Hog-tie, Inertia, Pinion, Rigidity, Tether
Immoderate Excessive, Extreme, Inordinate, Intemperate, Lavish, Undue
Immodest Brash, Brazen, Forward, Indelicate, Unchaste
Immolation Sacrifice, Sati, Suttee
Immoral(ity) Corrupt, Dissolute, Evil, Lax, Libertine, Licentious, Loose, Nefarious, Peccable, Reprobate, Turpitude, Unsavoury, Wanton
Immortal(ity) Agelong, Amarant(h), Amarantin, Amritattva, Athanasy, Deathless, > **DIVINE**, Enoch, Eternal, Ever-living, Famous, Godlike, Memory, Sin, Struldbrug, Timeless, Undying
Immovable Fast, Firm, Obdurate, Rigid, Stable, Stubborn
Immune, Immunisation, Immunise(r), Immunity Acquired, Anamnestic, Anergy, Bar, Cree, Diplomatic, Free, Inoculate, Klendusic, Natural, Non-specific, Pasteurism, Pax, Premunition, Properdin, Serum, Vaccine
Immure Confine, Encloister, Imprison
Imp(ish) Devilet, Elf, Flibbertigibbet, Gamin(e), Hobgoblin, Limb, Lincoln, Litherly, Nickum, Nis(se), Puck, Ralph, Rascal, Sprite
Impact Bearing, Bump, Clash, Collision, Feeze, Impinge, Jar, Jolt, Pack, Percuss, Pow, Slam, Souse, Wham
Impair(ed), Impairment Cripple, Damage, Disease, Enfeeble, > **HARM**, Injure, Lame, Mar, Mental, Odd, Paralogia, Stale, Vitiate
Impala Pallah
Impale Elance, Ga(u)nch, Skewer, Spike, Transfix

Impart Bestow, Convey, Divulge, Impute, Infect, Shed, Tell
Impartial Candid, Detached, Equitable, Even-handed, Fair, Just, Neutral, Unbiased
Impassable, Impasse Deadlock, Dilemma, Invious, Jam, Snooker, Stalemate, Zugzwang
Impassioned Emotional, Fervid, Fiery, Heated, Zealous
Impassive Apathetic, Deadpan, Stoical, Stolid
Impatience, Impatient Chafing, Chut, Dysphoria, Fiddle-de-dee, Fiddlesticks, Fidgety, Fretful, Hasty, Irritable, Och, Peevish, Peremptory, Petulant, Pish, Till(e)y-vall(e)y, Tilly-fally, Tut
Impeach Accuse, Challenge, Charge, Indict
Impeccable Faultless, Novice
Impecunious Penniless, Poor, Short
Impedance, Impede, Impediment Burr, Clog, Dam, Diriment, Encumber, Halt, Hamstring, Handicap, > HINDER, Hog-tie, Let, Log, Obstacle, Obstruct, Reactance, Rub, Shackle, Snag, Stammer, Stymie, Tongue-tie, Trammel, Veto, Z
Impel(led) Actuate, Coerce, Drave, Drive, Drove, Goad, Inspire, > URGE
Impend(ing) Imminent, Looming, Toward
Impenetrable Adamantine, Air-tight, Dense, Hard, Impervious, Proof
Imperative Categorical, Dire, Jussive, Mood, Need-be, Pressing, Vital
Imperceptible Intangible, Invisible, Latent, Subtle
Imperfect(ion) Aplasia, Aplastic, Blotch, Defect, Deficient, Faculty, Feathering, Flawed, Half-pie, Kink, Kinkle, Lame, Poor, Rough, Second, Unideal
Imperial(ist), Imperious Beard, C(a)esarian, Commanding, Haughty, Majestic, Masterful, Mint, Peremptory, Regal, Rhodes, Royal, Tuft
Imperil Endanger, Risk
Imperishable Eternal, Immortal, Indestructible
Impermeable Airtight, Athermanous, Proof, Resistant
Impersonal Abstract, Cold, Detached, Inhuman
Impersonate, Impersonation, Impersonator Amphitryon, Ape, As, Double, Imitate, Impression, Mimic, Pose, Spoof
Impertinence, Impertinent Crust, Flip(pant), Fresh, Impudent, Irrelevant, Rude, Sass, Sauce
Imperturbable Cool, Placid, Stoic, Tranquil
Impervious(ness) Athermancy, Callous, Hardened, Obdurate, Proof, Tight
Impetigo Scrumpox
Impetuous, Impetuosity Birr, Brash, Bullheaded, Elan, > HASTY, Headstrong, Heady, Hothead, Impulsive, Rash, Tearaway, Vehement, Violent, Young Turk
Impetus Birr, Drift, Incentive, MacGuffin, Momentum, Propulsion, Slancio, Steam, Swing
Impious Blasphemous, Godless, Irreverent, Unholy
Implant(ation) AID, Embed, Engraft, Enroot, Graft, Inset, Instil, Nidation, Sow
Implausible Lame, Off-the-wall
Implement Agent, Celt, Cultivator, Disgorger, Eolith, Execute, Flail, Follow out, Fork, Fulfil, Hacksaw, Harrow, Hayfork, Muller, Pin, Pitchfork, Plectrum, Plough, Pusher, Rest, Ripple, Scarifier, Scythe, Seed drill, Shoehorn, Sickle, Spatula, Spayd®, Squeegee, Strickle, Tongs, > TOOL, Toothpick, Utensil
Implicate, Implication Accuse, Concern, Connotation, Embroil, Incriminate, Innuendo, > INVOLVE, Material, Overtone
Implore Beg, Beseech, Crave, > ENTREAT, Obsecrate, Petition, Plead, Pray
Imply, Implied Hint, Insinuate, Involve, Predicate, Signify, > SUGGEST, Tacit

Impolite Ill-bred, Rude, Uncivil

Import(s) Convey, Denote, Drift, Invisible, Mean, Parallel, Sense, Signify, Spell, Visible

Importance, Important (person) Big, Big cheese, Big wheel, Calibre, Cardinal, Central, Cheese, Cob, Coming, Considerable, Core, Cornerstone, Count, Critical, Crucial, Crux, Earth-shaking, Earth-shattering, Eminent, Epochal, Grave, Gravitas, Greatness, Heavy, High, High-muck-a-muck, Honcho, Hotshot, Huzoor, Key, Keystone, Macher, Magnitude, Main, Major, Material, Matters, Megastar, Mighty, Milestone, Moment(ous), Nabob, Nib, Note, Numero uno, Obbligato, Personage, Pivotal, Pot, Preponderate, Prime, Principal, Salient, Seminal, Serious, Significant, Something, Special, Stature, Status, Stress, Substantive, Tuft, Urgent, VIP, Weight, Weighty, Worth

Importune, Importunate Beg, Coax, Flagitate, Press(ing), Prig, Solicit, Urgent

Impose, Imposing, Imposition Allocate, Assess, August, Burden, Charge, Cheat, Diktat, Dread, Enforce, Enjoin, Epic, Fine, Flam, Foist, Fraud, Grand(iose), Hidage, Homeric, Hum, Impot, Inflict, Kid, Levy, Lumber, Majestic, Obtrude, Pensum, Pole, Scot, Sponge, Stately, Statuesque, Sublime, Whillywhaw

Impossible Hopeless, Incorrigible, Insoluble, Insurmountable, No-go, No-no, Unacceptable

Impost Excise, Levy, Tax, Toll

Imposter, Impostor Bunyip, Charlatan, Disaster, Faitor, Faitour, > FAKE, Fraud, Idol, Pretender, Sham, Triumph, Warbeck

Impotent Barren, Helpless, Spado, Sterile, Weak

Impound(er) Appropriate, Bond, Confiscate, Intern, Pen, Pinder, Poind

Impoverish(ed) Bankrupt, Bare, Beggar, Exhaust, Indigent, Straiten

Impractical Absurd, Academic, Chim(a)era, Idealist, Inoperable, Laputan, Not on, Other-worldly, Quixotic, Useless

Imprecation Oath, Pize

Imprecise Approximate, Inaccurate, Indeterminate, Loose, Nebulous, Rough, Sloppy, Vague

Impregnate Conceive, Enwomb, Imbue, Inseminate, Milt, Permeate, Resinate

Impresario Maestro, Manager, Producer, Showman

Impress(ive), Impression(able) Air, Astonish, Awe, Blur, Blurb, Bowl over, Brand, Cliché, Commanding, Conscript, Crimp, Deboss, Dent, Dramatic, Edition, Effect, Engram(ma), Engrave, Enstamp, Epic, Feel(ing), Fingerprint, Fossil, Frank, Gas, Grab, Grandiose, Heroic, Homeric, Idée, Impinge, Imprint, Incuse, Intaglio, Kick ass, Knock, Let, Niello, Noble, Note, Palimpsest, Plastic, Plate, Pliable, Powerful, Prent, Presence, Press(gang), Print, Proof, Recruit, Repute, Responsive, Ripsnorter, Rotund, Seal, Seize, Sense, Shanghai, Slay, Smite, Soft, Spectacular, Stamp, Stereotype, Strike, Susceptible, Sway, Tableau, Touch, Vibrant, Watermark, Weal, Weighty, Wow

Impressionist Cezanne, Liebermann, Lumin(ar)ist, Manet, Matisse, Monet, Morisot, Renoir

Imprint Edition, Engrave, Etch, Stamp

Imprison(ment) Cape, Committal, Confine, Constrain, Custody, Durance, False, Immure, Incarcerate, Intern, Jail, Penal servitude, Quad, Quod, Time

Improbable Buckley's chance, Buckley's hope, Dubious, Far-fetched, Unlikely

Impromptu Ad lib, Extempore, Improvised, Offhand, Spontaneous, Sudden, Unrehearsed

Improper, Impropriety Abnormal, Blue, Demirep, False, Illegitimate, Indecent, Indecorum, Outré, Prurient, Solecism, Undue, Unmeet, Unseemly, Untoward

▷ **Improperly** *may indicate* an anagram

Improve(ment), Improver, Improving Advance, Ameliorate, Beet, Benefit, Bete, Break, Buck, Cap, Chasten, Conditioner, Cultivate, Détente, Didactic, Ease, Edify, Edutainment, Embellish, Emend, Enhance, Enrich, Eugenic, Euthenics, File, Gentrify, Kaizen, Meliorate, Mend, Potentiate, Promote, Rally, Refine, Reform, Resipiscence, Retouch, Sarvodaya, Slim, Streamline, Surpass, Tart, Tatt, Titivate, Top, Touch-up, Turn round, Tweak, Uptrend, Upturn

Improvident Feckless

Improvise(d), Improvisation Adlib, Break, Devise, Drumhead, Extemporise, Invent, Knock-up, Lash-up, Noodle, Ride, Scratch, Sudden, Vamp, Wing

Imprudent Foolhardy, Foolish, Impetuous, Impolitic, Indiscreet, Injudicious, Rash, Reckless, Unwary, Unwise

Impudence, Impudent Audacious, Backchat, Bardy, Bold, Brash, Brassy, Brazen, Cheeky, Cool, Crust, Effrontery, Forward, Gall, Gallus, Impertinent, Insolent, Jackanapes, Lip, Malapert, Neck, > **NERVE**, Pert, Sass(y), Sauce, Saucebox, Saucy, Temerity, Whippersnapper, Yankie

Impugn Censure, Challenge, Defame, Impeach, Malign

Impulse, Impulsive Compelling, Conatus, Dictate, Drive, Efferent, Headlong, Horme, Ideopraxist, Impetus, Instigation, > **INSTINCT**, Libido, Madcap, Nerve, Nisus, Premature, Premotion, Send, Signal, Snap, Specific, Spontaneous, Tendency, Thrust, Tic, Urge, Whim

Impure, Impurity Adulterated, Donor, Faints, Feints, Indecent, Lees, Lewd, Regulus, Scum, Unclean

Imputation, Impute Ascribe, Attribute, Charge, Scandal, Slander, Slur

In A, Amid, Chic, Home, Hostel, I', Inn, Intil, Occupying, On, Pop(ular), Pub, Trendy, Within

Inability Anosmia, Aphagia, Aphasia, Apraxia

Inaccessible Abaton, Impervious, Remote, Unattainable

Inaccurate Distorted, Erroneous, Faulty, Imprecise, Inexact, Out, Rough, Slipshod, Unfaithful

Inactive, Inaction, Inactivity Acedia, Cabbage, Comatose, Dead, Dormant, Extinct, Fallow, Hibernate, Idle, Inert, Moratorium, Passive, Quiescent, Rusty, Sedentary, Sluggish, Torpid, Veg(etate)

In addition Eke, Else, Further, Moreover, Plus, To boot, Too

Inadequate Derisory, Feeble, Inapt, Inferior, Pathetic, Poor, Ropy, Scanty, Thin

Inadvertent(ly) Accidental, Careless, Chance, Unwitting

▷ **In a flap** *may indicate* an anagram

In a high degree So

In a hundred Percent

Inane Empty, Fatuous, Foolish, Imbecile, Silly, Vacant

Inanimate Abiotic, Lifeless

Inappropriate Amiss, Infelicitous, Malapropos, Off-key, Unapt, Unbecoming, Undue, Unsuitable, Untoward

Inapt Maladroit, Unsuitable

Inarticulate(ness) Indistinct, Mumbling, Psellism

Inartistic Artless, Crude

Inattentive, Inattention Asleep, Deaf, Distrait, Dwaal, Dwa(l)m, Dwaum, Heedless, Loose, Slack, Unheeding, Unobservant

Inaudible Silent, Superhet

Inaugurate Han(d)sel, Initiate, Install, Introduce

Inauspicious Adverse, Ominous, Sinister

▷ **In a whirl** *may indicate* an anagram

▷ **In a word** *may indicate* two clue words linked to form one

Inborn, Inbred Homogamy, Inherent, Innate, Native, Selfed, Sib

Incalculable Endless, Unpredictable, Untold

Incandescent Alight, Bright, Brilliant, Excited

Incantation Charm, Magic, Mantra, Spell

Incapable Can't, Powerless, Unable, Useless

Incarnation Advent, Avatar, Embodiment, Fleshing, Krishna, Rama, Ramachandra

In case Lest, So

Incautious Foolhardy, Rash, Reckless, Unwary

Incendiary Arsonist, Combustible, Firebug, Fire-lighter, Fireship, Napalm

Incense(d), Incenser Anger, Aroma, Elemi, Enfelon, Enrage, Homage, Hot, > INFLAME, Joss-stick, Navicula, Onycha, Outrage, Pastil(le), Provoke, Thurible, Thus, Vex, Wrathful

Incentive Carrot, Carrot and stick, Fillip, Impetus, Motive, Premium, Spur, Stakhanovism, Stimulus, Wage

Incessant Constant, Endless

Incest Backcross

Inch(es) Ait, Column, Edge, Isle, Mil, Sidle, Tenpenny, Uncial

Inchoate Formless, Immature, Incipient

Incident(al) Affair, Baur, Bawr, Carry-on, Chance, Circumstance, Episode, Event, Facultative, Handbags, Negligible, Occasion, Occurrent, Page, Scene, Throwaway

Incinerate, Incinerator Burn, Combust, Cremate, Destructor

Incipient Beginning, Germinal, Inchoate

Incise, Incision, Incisive(ness) Bite, Cut, Engrave, Incavo, Lobotomy, McBurney's, Mordant, Notch, Phlebotomy, Punchy, Scarf, Scribe, Slit, Surgical, Tracheotomy, Trenchant

Incisor Foretooth

Incite(ment) Abet, Drive, Egg, Fillip, Hortative, Hoy, Impassion, Inflame, Instigate, Kindle, Motivate, Prod, Prompt, Provoke, Put, Rouse, Sa sa, Sedition, Set, Sic(k), Sool, > SPUR, Sting, Suborn, Suggest, Tar, Urge

Incline(d), Inclination Acclivity, Angle, Aslope, Atilt, Bank, Batter, Bent, Bias, Bow, Camber, Clinamen, Declivity, Dip, Disposed, Drift, Enclitic, Glacis, > GRADIENT, Grain, Hade, Heel, Hill, Kant, Kip, Lean, Liking, List, Maw, Minded, Nod, On, Partial, Peck, Penchant, Proclivity, Prone, Propensity, Rake, Ramp, Ready, Rollway, Set, Shelve, Slant, > SLOPE, Steep, Steeve, Stomach, Supine, Tend, Tilt, Tip, Trend, Upgrade, Velleity, Verge, Weathering, Will

Include(d) Add, Bracket, Compass, Comprise, Connotate, Contain, Cover, Embody, Embrace, Enclose, Involve, Subsume, Therein

Incognito Anonymous, Disguised, Faceless, Secret, Unnamed

Incoherent Confused, Disconnected, Disjointed, Gabbling, Inarticulate, Rambling, Spluttering

Incombustible Clinker

Income Annuity, Benefice, Disposable, Dividend, Earned, Entry, Fixed, Franked, Livelihood, Living, Meal-ticket, Milch cow, Notional, OTE, Penny-rent, Prebend, Primitiae, Private, Proceeds, Rent, Rente, Rent-roll, Returns, Revenue, Salary, Stipend, Unearned, Unfranked, Wages

Incommunicado Isolated, Silent

Incomparable Supreme, Unequalled, Unmatched

Incompatible, Incompatibility Contradictory, Dyspathy, Incongruous, Inconsistent, Mismatched, Unsuited

Incompetent Bungler, Deadhead, Helpless, Ill, Inefficient, Inept, Palooka,

Unable, Unfit

Incomplete Broadbrush, Cagmag, Catalectic, Deficient, Inchoate, Lacking, Partial, Pendent, Rough, Unfinished

Incomprehensible Double Dutch, Hard, Unbelievable

Inconceivable Impossible, Incredible

▷ **In confusion** *may indicate* an anagram

Incongruous, Incongruity Absurd, Discordant, Heterogenous, Irish, Ironic, Sharawadgi, Sharawaggi

In connection with Re

Inconsiderable Light, Slight

Inconsiderate High-handed, Hog, Petty, Presumptuous, Roughshod, Thoughtless, Unkind

Inconsistency, Inconsistent Alien, Anacoluthon, Anomaly, Contradictory, Discrepant, Oxymoronic, Paradoxical, Unequal, Unsteady, Variance

Inconsolable Heartbroken, Niobe

Inconspicuous Unobtrusive

Inconstant Chameleon, Desultory, Fickle, Light, Mutable, > VARIABLE

Inconvenience, Inconvenient Awkward, Bother, Discommode, Fleabite, Incommodious, > TROUBLE, Unseemly, Untoward

Incorporate(d), Incorporation Absorb, Embody, Inc, Integrate, Introgression, Join, Merge, Subsume

Incorporeal Aery, Airy, Spiritual

Incorrect Catachresis, False, Improper, Invalid, Naughty, Wrong

Incorrigible Hopeless, Obstinate

Incorruptible Copper-bottomed, Honest, Immortal, Pure, Robespierre, Sea-green

Increase, Increasing Accelerando, Accelerate, Accession, Accrue, Add, Additur, Aggrandise, Amplify, Amp up, Appreciate, Approve, Augment, Auxetic, Bolster, Bulge, Crank up, Crescendo, Crescent, Crescive, Deepen, Dilate, Double, Ech(e), Eech, Eik, Eke, Enhance, Enlarge, Escalate, > EXPAND, Explosion, Greaten, > GROW, Heighten, Ich, Increment, Interbreed, Jack, Jack up, Lift, Magnify, Mark up, Mount, Multiply, Plus, Proliferate, Propagate, Ramp up, Redshift, Reflation, Regrate, Rise, Snowball, Swell, Thrive, Up, Upswing, Wax

Incredible Amazing, Cockamamie, Extraordinary, Fantastic, Steep, Stey, Tall

Incredulity, Incredulous Distrust, Infidel, Suspicion, Thunderstruck, Unbelief

Increment Accrual, Augment, Growth, Increase

Incriminate Accuse, Implicate, Inculpate

Incubate, Incubator Brooder, Develop, Eccaleobion, Hatch

Incubus Demon, Load, Nightmare

Inculcate Implant, Infuse

Incumbent Lying, Obligatory, Occupier, Official

Incur Assume, Earn, Involve

Incursion Foray, Inroad, Invasion, Raid, Razzia

Indecent Bare, Blue, Fescennine, Free, Immodest, Immoral, Improper, Lewd, Obscene, Rabelaisian, Racy, Scurril(e), Sotadic, Spicy, Sultry, Unproper, Unseem(ly), X-rated

Indecision, Indecisive Demur, Dithery, Doubt, Hamlet, Havering, Hung jury, Inconclusive, Suspense, Swither, Weakkneed

Indeclinable Aptote

Indecorous Graceless, Immodest, Outré, Unbecoming

Indeed Atweel, Ay, Da, Een, Even, Faith, Haith, Insooth, Ja wohl, La, Marry, Quotha, Truly, Verily, Yah, Yea

Indefensible Implausible, Inexcusable, Vincible

Indefinite(ly) A, An, Any, Evermore, Hazy, Nth, Some, Undecided, Vague

Indelible Fast, Permanent

Indelicate Broad, Coarse, Improper, Vulgar, Warm

Indemnify, Indemnification, Indemnity Assythement, Compensation, Double, Insurance

Indent(ed), Indentation Apprentice, Contract, Crenellate, Dancetty, Dimple, Impress, Niche, Notch, Order, Philtrum, Subentire

Independence, Independent Autocephalous, Autogenous, Autonomy, Crossbencher, Detached, Extraneous, Free(dom), Free-lance, Free spirit, I, Liberty, Maverick, Mugwump, Perseity, Self-sufficient, Separate, Separatist, Sui juris, Swaraj, Udal, UDI, Uhuru

Indescribable Incredible, Ineffable

Indestructible Enduring, Impenetrable, Inextirpable

Indeterminate Borderline, Formless, Incalculable, Open-ended, Unknown

Index Alidad(e), Catalogue, Cephalic, Colour, Cranial, Dial, Dow Jones, Exponent, Facial, Finger, Fist, Fog, Footsie, Forefinger, Gazetteer, Glycaemic, Hang Seng, Kwic, Librorum Prohibitorum, Margin, Nasal, Nikkei, Opsonic, Power, Price, Refractive, > REGISTER, Rotary, Share, Table, Thumb, TPI, UV, Verborum

India(n) Adivisi, Asian, Ayah, Baboo, Babu, Bharat(i), Bihari, Canarese, Carib, Chin, Dard, Dravidian, File, Gond(wanaland), Gujarati, Harijan, Harsha, Hindu, Indic, Ink, Jain, Jat, Jemadar, Kafir, Kanarese, Kannada, Khalsa, Kisan, Kolarian, Kshatriyas, Lepcha, Ma(h)ratta, Maratha, Mazhbi, > MEXICAN, Mofussil, Mogul, Mulki, Munda, Munshi, Naga, Nagari, Nair, Nasik, Nation, Nayar, > NORTH AMERICAN, Nuri, Ocean, Oriya, Pali, Panjabi, Pargana, Parsee, Parsi, Peshwa, Plains, Prakrit, Punjabi, Punja(u)bee, Sanskrit, Sepoy, Shri, Sikh, Sind(h), > SOUTH AMERICAN, Sowar, Summer, Swadeshi, Tamil, Telegu, Vakeel, Vakil

Indiaman Clive

Indicate, Indication, Indicative, Indicator Adumbrate, Allude, Argue, Blinker, Cite, Clue, Cursor, > DENOTE, Design, Desine, Dial, Endeixis, Evidence, Evince, Fluorescein, Gesture, Gnomon, Litmus, Manifest, Mean, Mood, Nod, Notation, Performance, Pinpoint, Point, Portend, Proof, Ray, Register, Remarque, Representative, Reveal, Show, > SIGN, Signify, Specify, Symptom, Tip, Token, Trace, Trafficator, Trait, Winker

Indictment Accusation, Caption, Charge, Dittay, Reproach

Indifference, Indifferent Adiaphoron, Aloof, Apathetic, Apathy, Blasé, Blithe, Callous, Cavalier, Cold, Cool(th), Dead, Detached, Disdain, Easy-osy, Empty, Incurious, Insouciant, Jack easy, Mediocre, Neutral, Nonchalant, Perfunctory, Phlegm, Pococurante, Sangfroid, So-so, Stoical, Supercilious, Supine, Tepid, Unconcerned

Indigence, Indigent Need, Pauper, Penury, Poverty, Want

Indigenous Aboriginal, Endemic, Native

▷ **Indi-gent** *may indicate* Baboo or Babu

Indigestion Apepsia, Apepsy, Dyspepsia, Heartburn

Indignant, Indignation Anger, Annoyed, Incensed, Irate, Pique, Resentful, Wrathful

Indignity Affront, Outrage

Indigo Anil, Blue, Bunting, Carmine, Indole, Isatin(e)

Indirect Back-handed, By(e), Devious, Implicit, Mediate, Oblique, Remote, Roundabout, Sidelong, Zig-zag

Indiscreet, Indiscretion Blabbermouth, Folly, Gaffe, Imprudence, Indelicate, Injudicious, Loose cannon, Rash, Unguarded, Wild oats
Indiscriminate Haphazard, Random, Scattershot, Sweeping
Indispensable Basic, Essential, King-pin, Necessary, Sine qua non, Vital
Indispose(d), Indisposition Adverse, Disincline, Ill, Incapacitate, Sick, Unwell
Indisputable Evident
Indistinct Ambiguous, Bleary, Blur, Bumble, Bummle, Faint, Fuzzy, Hazy, Pale, S(c)hwa, Sfumato, > VAGUE
▷ **In distress** *may indicate* an anagram
Indite Compose, Pen, Write
Indium In
Individual(ist), Individuality Being, Discrete, Exclusive, Free spirit, Gemma, Haecceity, Identity, Ka, Libertarian, Loner, Man, Man-jack, One-to-one, Own, Particular, Person, Poll, Respective, Separate, Single, Singular, Solo, Soul, Special, Unit, Zoon
Indoctrinate Brainwash, Discipline, Instruct
Indo-European Aryan, Jat(s)
Indolence, Indolent Bone idle, Fainéance, Inactive, Languid, Lazy, Otiose, Sloth, Sluggish, Supine
Indomitable Brave, Dauntless, Invincible
Indonesia(n) Batavian, Nesiot, RI
Indoor(s) Within
Indubitably Certainly, Certes, Manifestly, Surely
Induce(ment) Bribe, Carrot, Cause, Coax, Draw, Encourage, Get, Inveigle, Lead, Motivate, > PERSUADE, Prevail, Suasion, Suborn, Tempt
Induct(ion), Inductance Epagoge, Henry, Inaugurate, Initiate, Install, L, Logic, Prelude, Remanence
Indulge(nce), Indulgent Absolution, Binge, Coddle, Drink, Favour, Gratify, Humour, Law, Luxuriate, Oblige, Pamper, Pander, Pardon, Pet, Pettle, Please, ⋗ SATISFY, Splurge, Spoil, Spoonfeed, Surfeit, Tolerant, Venery, Voluptuous, Wallow
Industrial, Industrious, Industry Appliance, Application, Business, Busy, Cottage, Deedy, Diligence, Eident, Energetic, Labour, Ocnus, Operose, Ruhr, Service, Smokestack, Sunrise, Technical, Tourism, Zaibatsu
▶ **Inebriate** *see* INTOXICATE
Inedible Inesculent, Noisome, Rotten
Ineffective, Ineffectual Clumsy, Deadhead, Drippy, Droob, Dud, Empty, Fainéant, Fruitless, Futile, Idle, Ill, Impotent, Mickey Mouse, Neutralised, Null, Powerless, Resty, Sterile, Toothless, > USELESS, Void, Weak, Wet
Inefficient Clumsy, Incompetent, Lame, Shiftless, Slack
Inelegant Awkward, Inconcinnity, Stiff, Turgid, Unneat
Ineligible Unqualified
Inept Absurd, Anorak, Cack-handed, Farouche, Nerd, Otaku, Sad sack, Schlimazel, Unskilled, Wet
Inequality Anomaly, Chebyshev's, Disparity, Injustice, Odds, Tchebyshev's
Inert(ia) Catatonia, Comatose, Dead, Dull, Excipient, Inactive, Leaden, Mollusc, Neon, Oblomovism, Potato, Sluggish, Stagnant, Stagnation, Thowless, Torpid
Inestimable Incalculable, Invaluable, Priceless
Inevitable, Inevitably Automatic, Certain, Fateful, Inexorable, Needs, Perforce, TINA, Unavoidable
Inexact(itude) Cretism, Incorrect, Terminological, Wrong
Inexorable Relentless

Inexpedient Impolitic, Imprudent, Unwise

Inexpensive Bargain, Cheap, Dirt-cheap, Economic

Inexperience(d), Inexpert Amateur, Callow, Colt, Crude, Fresh, > **GREEN**, Greenhorn, Ham, Ingénue, Jejune, Raw, Rookie, Rude, Tender, Unconversant, Unseasoned, Unseen, Unversed, Yardbird, Youthful

Inexplicable Magical, Mysterious, Paranormal, Unaccountable

Infallible Foolproof, Right, Sure-fire, Unerring

Infamous, Infamy Base, Ignominious, Notorious, Opprobrium, Shameful, Villainy

Infant Babe, Baby, Innocent, Lamb, Minor, Oral, Rug rat

Infantry(man) Buff, Foot, Grunt, Jaeger, Phalanx, Pultan, Pulto(o)n, Pultun, > **SOLDIER**, Tercio, Turco, Zouave

▷ **Infantry** *may refer to* babies

Infatuate(d), Infatuating, Infatuation Assot, Besot, Circean, Crush, Enamoured, Engou(e)ment, Entêté, Fanatic, Foolish, Lovesick, > **OBSESSION**, Rave, Turn

Infect(ed), Infecting, Infection, Infectious Angina, Anthrax, Candidiasis, Catching, Catchy, Cholera, Communicable, Contagious, Contaminate, Corrupt, Cowpox, Diseased, Fascioliasis, Fester, Focal, Fomes, Giardiasis, Gonorrhoea, Herpes, Leishmaniasis, Listeria, Lockjaw, NSU, Orf, Overrun, Poison, Polio(myelitis), > **POLLUTE**, Py(a)emia, Quittor, Ringworm, Roup, Salmonella, Sarcoid, Septic, Shingles, Smit(tle), Strongylosis, Taint, Tetanus, Thrush, Tinea, Toxocariasis, Trichuriasis, Typhoid, Typhus, Virion, Virulent, Whitlow, Wog, Yersiniosis, Zymosis

Infeftment Sasine, Seisin

Infer(ence), Inferred Conclude, Conjecture, Deduce, Divine, Educe, Extrapolate, Generalise, Guess, Illation, Imply, Judge, Obversion, Putative, Surmise, Syllogism

▷ **Infer** *may indicate* 'fer' around another word

Inferior Base, Bodgier, Cheap-jack, Cheesy, Coarse, Crummy, Degenerate, Dog, Ersatz, Gimcrack, Grody, Grub-street, Indifferent, Infra, Jerkwater, Less, Lo-fi, Lower, Low-grade, Minor, Naff, Nether, One-horse, Ornery, Paravail, Petty, Poor, Rop(e)y, Schlock, Second, Second-best, Shlock, Shoddy, Sprew, Sprue, Subjacent, Subordinate, Substandard, Surat, Tatty, Tinpot, Trashy, Under(man), Underneath, Understrapper, Untermensch, Waste, Worse

Infernal Demogorgon, Diabolic, Hellish, Phitonian, Tartarean, Unholy

Infertile Barren, Sterile

Infest(ed), Infestation Acariasis, Acrawl, Beset, Blight, Dog, Hoatching, Overrun, Pediculosis, Phthiriasis, > **PLAGUE**, Stylopised, Swarm, Torment, Trombiculiasis, Trombidiasis, Uncinariasis

Infidel Atheist, Caffre, Giaour, Heathen, Heretic, Kafir, Pagan, Paynim, Saracen

Infield Intown

Infiltrate Encroach, Enter, Instil, Intrude, Pervade

Infinite, Infinity Cosmic, Endless, Eternal, N

Infinitive Split

Infirm Decrepit, Doddery, Feeble, Lame, Shaky

▷ **Infirm** *may indicate* 'co' around another word

Infirmary Hospital, Sick bay

Inflame(d), Inflammable, Inflammation Acne, Adenitis, Afire, Ancome, Anger, Angina, Aortisis, Appendicitis, > **AROUSE**, Arteritis, Arthritis, Asbestosis, Balanitis, Blepharitis, Bloodshot, Bronchitis, Bronchopneumonia, Bubonic, Bunion, Bursitis, Carditis, Catarrh, Cellulitis, Cervicitis, Cheilitis,

Colitis, Colpitis, Conjunctivitis, Coryza, Croup, Cystisis, Dermatitis, Diverticulitis, Duodenitis, Ecthyma, Eczema, Enamoured, Encephalitis, Encephalomyelitis, Enchafe, Endocarditis, Endometrisis, Enfire, Enkindle, Enteritis, Enterocolitis, Erysipelas, Farmer's lung, Fasciitis, Felon, Fever, Fibrosis, Fibrositis, Fire, Folliculitis, Founder, Frostbite, Garget, Gastritis, Gastroenteritis, Gingivitis, Gleet, Glossitis, Golfer's elbow, Gout, Hepatitis A, Hepatitis B, Hyalitis, Ignatis, Ignite, Ileitis, Impassion, Incense, Infection, Intertrigo, Ire, Iritis, Keratitis, Labyrinthitis, Laminitis, Laryngitis, Lymphadenitis, Lymphangitis, Mastitis, Mastoiditis, Meningitis, Meningocephalitis, Metritis, Misenteritis, Mycetoma, Myelitis, Myocarditis, Myositis, Napalm, Naphtha, Nephritis, Neuritis, Noma, Onychia, Oophoritis, Ophthalmia, Orchitis, Osteitis, Osteoarthritis, Osteomyelitis, Osteoporosis, Otitis, Ovaritis, Panarthritis, Pancreatitis, Papillitis, Paronychia, Parotitis, Pericarditis, Perihepatitis, Perinephritis, Periodontisis, Peritonitis, Perityphlitis, Pharyngitis, Phlebitis, Phlegmasia, Phlegmon, Phlogistic, Phrenitis, Pinkeye, Pleurisy, Pneumonia, Pneumonitis, Polyneuritis, Proctitis, Prostatitis, Prurigo, Pyelitis, Pyelonephritis, Pyorrhoea, Quinsy, Rachitis, > **RED**, Retinitis, Rhinitis, Rosacea, Salpingitis, Sandy blight, Scleritis, Sclerotitis, Shin splints, Sinusitis, Splenitis, Spondylitis, Stimulate, Stomatitis, Strumitis, Sty(e), Sunburn, Swelling, Swimmer's itch, Sycosis, Synovitis, Tendinitis, Tennis elbow, Tenosynovitis, Thoroughpin, Thrombophilia, Thrombosis, Thrush, Thyroiditis, Tonsillitis, Touchwood, Tracheitis, Trichomoniasis, Tylosis, Tympanitis, Typhlitis, Ulitis, Urethritis, Utriculitis, Uveitis, Uvulitis, Vaginitis, Valvulitis, Vasculitis, Vincent's angina, Vulvitis, Whitlow, Windburn, Woody-tongue

Inflate(d), **Inflation** Aerate, Aggrandise, Bloat, Bombastic, Cost-push, Dilate, Distend, Distent, Exaggerate, Grade, Increase, Pneumatic, Pump, Remonetise, RPI, Spiral, Stagflation, Stagnation, Swell

Inflect(ion) Accidence, Conjugation

Inflexible, **Inflexibility** Adamant(ine), Byzantine, Doctrinaire, Hard-ass, Hard-liner, Iron, Obstinate, Ossified, Relentless, Resolute, Rigid, Rigour, Set, Stubborn, Unbending

Inflict(ion) Deal, Force, Give, Impose, Subject, Trouble, Visit, Wreak

Inflorescence Bostryx, Catkin, Ci(n)cinnus, Drepanium, Glomerule, Panicle, Pleiochasium, Polychasium, Raceme, Umbel, Verticillaster

Inflow Affluence, Influx

Influence(d), **Influential** Act, Affect, After, Backstairs, Charm, Clout, Credit, Determine, Drag, Earwig, Embracery, Eminence grise, Factor, Force, Get at, Govern, Hold, Hypnotise, Impact, Impress, Incubus, Inspire, Interfere, Lead, Leverage, Lobby, Macher, Mastery, Militate, Mogul, Octopus, Operation, Power, Pressure, Prestige, > **PULL**, Push, Reach, Rust, Say, Seminal, Significant, Star, Star-blasting, Stimulus, Suggest, Svengali, Sway, Swing, Telegony, Undue, Will, Work, Wull

Influenza Flu, Grippe, Wog

Inform(ation), **Informed**, **Informer** Acquaint, Advise, Agitprop, Apprise, Au fait, Aware, Beagle, Bit, Burst, Canary, Ceefax®, Clype, Contact, Cookie, Datum, Delate, Dob(ber), Dope, Education, Exposition, Facts, Fact sheet, Feedback, Fink, Fisgig, Fiz(z)gig, Gen, Genome, Grapevine, Grass, Griff, Gunsel, Hep, Input, Inside, Instruct, Izvesti(y)a, Light, Lowdown, Media, Moiser, Nark, Nepit, Nit, Nose, Notify, Occasion, Oracle®, Peach, Pem(m)ican, Pimp, Poop, Prestel®, Prime, Printout, Propaganda, Prospectus, Rat, Read-out, Revelation, Rheme, Rumble, Shelf, Shop, Sidelight, Sing, Sneak, Snitch, Squeak, Squeal,

Stag, Stoolie, Stool-pigeon, Supergrass, Sycophant, Teletext®, Tell, Tidings, Tip-off, Up, Videotext®, Viewdata®, Whistle(-blower), Wire

Informal Casual, Intimate, Irregular, Outgoing, Unofficial

Infra Under

Infra dig Ignominious

Infrequent Casual, Occasional, Rare, Scant, Seldom, Sparse

Infringe Contravene, Violate

Infuriate Anger, Bemad, Bepester, Enrage, Exasperate, Incense, Madden, Pester, Provoke

Infuse(r), Infusion Brew, Distill, Gallise, Instil, Mash, Saloop, Saturate, Steep, Tea, Tea-ball, Tea-egg, Tisane, Toddy, Uva-ursi

Ingenious, Ingenuity Adept, Adroit, Art, Artificial, Clever, Cunning, Cute, Inventive, Natty, Neat, Resourceful, Smart, Subtle, Wit

Ingenuous Artless, Candid, Green, Innocent, Naive, Open

Ingest Eat, Endue, Incept, Indue, Swallow

In good condition Fit, Shipshape, Taut, Trim

Ingot Bar, Billet, Bullion, Lingot, Sycee

Ingrain Fix, Impregnate, Train

Ingrate Thankless, Viper

Ingratiate, Ingratiating Butter, Court, Flatter, Greasy, Silken, Smarm(y)

Ingredient(s) Additive, Admixture, Basis, Content, Element, Factor, Formula, Makings, Staple

Ingrowing, Ingrowth Onychocryptosis, T(h)ylosis

Inhabit(ants) Affect, Children, Denizen, Dweller, Inholder, Inmate, Live, Native, Occupant, People, Resident

Inhale, Inhalation Aspirate, Breath(e), Draw, Gas, Inspire, Sniff, Snort, Snuff, Take

Inharmonious Out, Patchy

Inherent Characteristic, Essential, Immanent, Inbred, Innate, Native

Inherit(ance), Inherited, Inheritor Accede, Birthright, Borough-English, Congenital, Feoffee, Gene, Genom, Heirloom, Inborn, Legacy, Legitim, Meek, Mendelism, Particulate, Patrimony, Portion, Reversion, Succeed, Tichborne, Ultimogenitive

Inhibit(ing), Inhibition, Inhibitor Captopril, Chalone, Chalonic, Deter, Enalapril, Forbid, Hang-up, Protease, Restrain, Retard, Retroactive, Stunt, Suppress

Inhuman Barbarous, Brutal, Merciless

Inimical Adverse, Harmful, Hostile

Iniquity, Iniquitous Diabolical, Evil, Offence, Sin, Vice

Initial Acronym, First, Letter, Monogram, Paraph, Prelim(inary), Primary, Rubric

▷ **Initially** *may indicate* first letters

Initiate(d), Initiation, Initiative Baptism, Begin, Bejesuit, Blood, Bora, Bring, Ceremony, Debut, Demarche, Enter, Enterprise, Epopt, Esoteric, Gumption, Induct, Instigate, Instruct, > **LAUNCH**, Nous, Spark, > **START**

Inject(or), Injection Bang, Booster, Collagen, Enema, Epidural, Fuel, Hypo, Implant, Innerve, Inoculation, Instil, Introduce, Jab, Mainline, Pop, Reheat, Serum, Shoot, Skin-pop, Solid, Syringe, Transfuse, Venipuncture

Injunction Command, Embargo, Mandate, Mareva, Swear, Writ

Injure(d), Injury, Injurious, Injustice ABH, Abuse, Aggrieve, Bale, Bled, Bruise, Concuss, Contrecoup, Damage, De(a)re, Forslack, Frostbite, Gash, GBH, Harm, > **HURT**, Ill-turn, Impair, Iniquity, Lesion, Malign, Mar, Mayhem, Mistreat,

Mutilate, NAI, Nobble, Nocuous, Noxal, Nuisance, Oppression, Outrage, Packet, Paire, Prejudice, Rifle, RSI, Scaith, Scath(e), Scotch, Sore, Sprain, Teen(e), Tene, Tort, Trauma, Umbrage, Whiplash, Wound, Wrong

▶ **Injury** *see* AFTER INJURY

Ink(y) Atramental, Black, Bray, China, Chinese, Cyan, Gall, Gold, Indian, Invisible, Magnetic, Marking, Printer's, Sepia, Stained, Sympathetic, Tusche

Inkling Clue, Glimpse, Hint, Idea

Inkpot Standish

Inlaid, Inlay(er) Boulle, Buhl, Damascene, Emblemata, Empaestic, Enamel, Enchase, Incrust, Intarsia, Intarsio, Koftgar(i), Marquetrie, Marquetry, Pietra-dura, Piqué, Set, Tarsia, Veneer

Inland Hinterland, Interior, Up

Inlet Arm, Bay, Bohai, Cove, Creek, Entry, Estuary, Fiord, Firth, Fjord, Fleet, Geo, Gio, Gusset, Infall, Ingate, McMurdo Sound, Moray Firth, Pamlico Sound, Pearl Harbor, Plymouth Sound, Pohai, Port Jackson, Solway Firth, Sullom Voe, Table Bay, Tor Bay, Wash, Zuyder Zee

▷ **Inlet** *may indicate* 'let' around another word

Inmate Intern(e), Lodger, Patient, Prisoner, Resident

Inn(s), Innkeeper Albergo, Alehouse, Auberge, Barnard's, Boniface, Caravanserai, Chancery, Change-house, Coaching, Court, Gray's, Halfway-house, Host, Hostelry, Hotel, House, Imaret, In, Inner Temple, Jamaica, Khan, Ladin(ity), Law, Licensee, Lincoln's, Lodging, Luckie, Lucky, Middle Temple, Motel, Padrone, Parador, Patron, Porterhouse, Posada, Posthouse, Pothouse, Publican, Roadhouse, Ryokan, Serai, Tabard, Taphouse, Tavern(er), Victualler

▷ **Inn** *may refer to* the law

Innards Entrails, Giblets, Gizzard, Guts, Harigals, Harslet, Haslet, Rein, Viscera

Innate Congenital, Essential, Inborn, Inbred, Inbuilt, Instinctive, Natural

Inner(most) Bencher, Esoteric, Internal, Intima, Intimate, Lining, Man, Medulla, Private, Woman

Innings Chance, Knock, Turn

▶ **Innkeeper** *see* INN

Innocent Absolved, Angelic, Arcadian, Babe, Blameless, Canny, Chaste, Cherub, Childlike, Clean, Doddypoll, Dodipoll, Dove, Encyclical, Green, Idyllic, Ingenue, Lamb, Lily-white, Maiden, Naive, Opsimath, Pope, > PURE, Sackless, Seely, Simple, St, Unwitting, White

Innocuous Harmless, Innocent

Innovate, Innovative, Innovation, Innovator Alteration, Ground-breaking, Newell, Novelty, Pioneer

Inn-sign Bush

Innumerable Countless, Infinite, Myriad, N

Inoculate, Inoculation Engraft, Immunise, Jab, Protect, Vaccine, Variolate

Inoffensive Mild, Pleasant

Inoperative Futile, Nugatory, Silent, Void

Inopportune Inconvenient, Intempestive, Untimely

Inordinate Excessive, Irregular, Undue

▷ **Inordinately** *may indicate* an anagram

In place of For, Qua, Vice, With

Input Direct, OCR

Inquest Debriefing, Hearing, Inquiry, Investigation

Inquire, Inquiring, Inquiry Ask, Demand, Investigation, Maieutic, Nose, Organon, Probe, Query, Question, See, Speer, Speir

Inquisition, Inquisitive, Iniquisitor Curious, Interrogation, Meddlesome, Nosy, Prying, Rubberneck, Snooper, Spanish, Stickybeak, Torquemada

▷ **In revolt, In revolution** *may indicate* an anagram

Inroad(s) Breach, Encroachment, Honeycomb, Invasion

Insane, Insanity Absurd, Batty, Crack-brained, Crazy, Deranged, Headcase, Hebephrenia, Loco, Lune, Mad, Manic, Mattoid, Nutso, Paranoia, Pellagra, Psycho, Schizo, Yarra

Insatiable Greedy, Ravenous, Voracious

Insatiate child Killcrop

Inscribe(d), Inscription Chisel, Chronogram, Colophon, Dedicate, Emblazon, Engrave, Enter, Epigraph, Epitaph, Exergue, Graffiti, Hic jacet, Hierograph, Lapidary, Legend, Lettering, Neum(e), Posy, Writ

Inscrutable Deadpan, Esoteric, Mysterious, Sphinx

Insect(s) Entomic, Nonentity, Non-person

● INSECTS

3 letters:	Nymph	Tettix	Stylops
Ant	Ox-bot	Thrips	Termite
Bee	Scale	Vespid	
Bot	Stick	Walker	**8 letters:**
Bug	Zebub	Weevil	Alderfly
Fly			Bookworm
Ked	**6 letters:**	**7 letters:**	Circutio
Lac	Acarid	Antlion	Coccidae
Nit	Breese	Bristle	Crane-fly
Wax	Breeze	Buzzard	Dipteras
Wog	Capsid	Chalcid	Firebrat
	Chigoe	Chigger	Gall-wasp
4 letters:	Cicada	Cornfly	Glossina
Flea	Cicala	Cricket	Greenfly
Gnat	Day-fly	Culicid	Horntail
Grig	Earwig	Cutworm	Horsefly
Lice	Elater	Daphnid	Itchmite
Mite	Gadfly	Ergates	Lacewing
Moth	Hopper	Firefly	Ladybird
Pium	Hornet	Gallfly	Lygus bug
Pupa	Instar	Girdler	Mealybug
Tick	Locust	Grayfly	Metabola
Wasp	Maggot	Hexapod	Milliped
Weta	Mantid	Hive-bee	Mosquito
Zimb	Mantis	Humbuzz	Myriapod
	Mayfly	Katydid	Puss-moth
5 letters:	Noctua	Ladybug	Reduviid
Aphis	Psocid	Odonata	Ruby-tail
Borer	Psylla	Oestrus	Scarabee
Brise	Punkie	Oniscus	Silkworm
Cimex	Redbug	Phasmid	Snowflea
Emmet	Sawfly	Pill-bug	Stinkbug
Gogga	Scarab	Pyralis	Stonefly
Louse	Slater	Sandfly	Symphile
Midge	Spider	Spectre	Waterbug

Whitefly
Wireworm
Woodworm

9 letters:
Ametabola
Booklouse
Caddis-fly
Centipede
Cochineal
Cockroach
Compodeid
Damselfly
Dobsonfly
Dor-beetle
Dragonfly
Ephemeron
Hemiptera
Homoptera
Leaf-miner
Mecoptera
Millepede
Millipede

Rearhorse
Robber-fly
Songololo
Synoekete
Tabanidae
Tiger-moth
Woodlouse
Xylophage

10 letters:
Apterygota
Bark mantis
Bluebottle
Casebearer
Chironomid
Cockchafer
Coleoptera
Collembola
Fan-cricket
Fen-cricket
Froghopper
Greendrake
Harvestman

Leaf-cutter
Leafhopper
Mallophaga
Orthoptera
Phylloxera
Plant-louse
Pond-skater
Psocoptera
Rhipiptera
Silverfish
Springtail
Thysanuran
Treehopper
Web spinner

11 letters:
Bristletail
Dermapteran
Grasshopper
Greenbottle
Hymenoptera
Mole-cricket
Neuropteran

Tiger-beetle
Trichoptera

12 letters:
Bishop's mitre
Creepy-crawly
Dictyopteran
Heteropteran
Rhipidoptera
San Jose scale
Strepsiptera
Thousand-legs
Thysanoptera
Water boatman

13 letters:
Daddy-long-legs
Jenny-longlegs
Leatherjacket
Praying mantis
Staphylinidae
Water scorpion

Insecticide Allethrin, Aphicide, Carbaryl, Chromene, DDT, Deet, Derris, Dieldrin, Endosulfan, Endrin, Flycatcher, Gammexane®, Ivermectin, Lindane®, Malathion®, Menazon, Methoxychlor, Miticide, Naphthalene, Parathion, Paris green, Pyrethrin, Pyrethrum, Rotenone, Spray, Timbo, Toxaphene, Zineb

Insectivore Agoura, Desman, Donaea, Drosera, Hedgehog, Jacamar, Nepenthaceae, Otter-shrew, Sarracenia, Tanrec, Tenrec(idae), Venus flytrap, Zalambdodont

Insecure Infirm, > LOOSE, Precarious, Shaky, Unsafe, Unstable, Unsteady, Vulnerable

Insensitive, Insensitivity Analgesia, Blunt, Callous, Dead, Log, Numb, Obtuse, Pachyderm, Stolid, Tactless, Thick-skinned

Inseparable Indiscrete, One, United

Insert(ed), Insertion, Inset Cue, Empiecement, Enchase, Enter, Entry, Foist, Fudge, Godet, Gore, Graft, Gusset, Immit, Imp, Implant, Inject, Inlay, Input, Intercalar, Interject, Interpolate, Interpose, Intersperse, Introduce, Intromit, Lexical, Mitre, Pin, Sandwich

Inside(r) Content, Core, Entrails, Gaol, Heart, Indoors, Interior, Internal, Interne, Inward, Inwith, Mole, Tum, > WITHIN

Insidious Artful, Crafty, Sly

Insight Acumen, Anagoge, Aperçu, Enlightenment, Hunch, Inkling, Intuition, > PERCEPTION, Tais(c)h

Insignia Armour, Arms, Badger, Charge, Chevron, Mark, Regalia, Ribbon, Roundel, Tab

Insignificant (person) Dandiprat, Fico, Fiddling, Flea-bite, Fractional, Gnat, Inconsiderable, Insect, Mickey Mouse, Minimus, Miniscule, Minnow, Nebbich, Nobody, Nominal, Nonentity, One-eyed, Petit, Petty, Pipsqueak, Quat, Scoot, Scout, Scrub, Shrimp, Slight, Small potatoes, Small-time,

Squirt, Squit, Tenuous, Trifling, Trivial, Two-bit, Unimportant, Venial, Warb, Whippersnapper

Insincere Affected, Artificial, Barmecide, Cant, Double, Double-faced, Empty, Factitious, Faithless, False, Glib, Greenwash, Hollow, Janus-faced, Lip service, Mealy-mouthed, Meretricious, Mouth-made, Pseudo, Shallow, Synthetic, Two-faced

Insinuate, Insinuating, Insinuation Allude, Hint, Imply, Innuendo, Intimate, Sleek, Sneck-draw

Insipid Banal, Blab, Bland, Drippy, Fade, Flat, Insulse, Jejune, Lash, Mawkish, Shilpit, Tame, Tasteless, Vapid, Weak, Wearish, Wersh

Insist(ent) Assert, Demand, Dogmatic, Exact, > STIPULATE, Stress, Swear, Threap, Threep, Urge

Insolence, Insolent Audacity, Bardy, Brassy, Cheek, Contumely, Effrontery, Gum, Hubris, Hybris, Impudence, Lip, Rude, Snash, Stroppy, Wanton

Insoluble Cerasin, Hard, Irresolvable, Mysterious

Insolvent Bankrupt, Broke, Destitute, Penniless

Insomnia Agrypnotic, Sleeplessness, Wakefulness, White night

Insouciant Carefree, Careless, Cavalier

Inspect(ion), Inspector Alnage(r), Auditor, Case, Comb, Conner, Darogha, Examine, Go-over, Government, Investigator, Jerque, Keeker, Lestrade, Look-see, Morse, Muster, Once-over, Peep, Perlustrate, Proveditor, Rag-fair, Recce, Review, Sanitary, Scrutinise, Spot check, Survey, Test, Vet, Vidimus, Visitation

Inspiration, Inspire(d), Inspiring Actuate, Aerate, Afflatus, Aganippe, Animate, Brainstorm, Brainwave, Breath(e), Castalian, Draw, Duende, Elate, Exalt, Fire, Flash, Hearten, Hunch, Idea, Illuminate, Impulse, Induce, Inflatus, Infuse, Kindle, Move, Muse, Pegasus, Prompt, Prophetic, Satori, Sniff(le), Stimulus, Taghairm, Theopnautic, Theopneust(y), Uplift, Vatic, Verbal

In spite of Augre

Instability Anomie, Anomy

Install(ation) Enchase, Enthrone, Inaugurate, Induction, Infrastructure, Insert, Invest, Put (in)

Instalment Episode, Fascicle, Fascicule, Heft, Insert, Livraison, Never-never, Part, Serial, Tranche

Instance, Instant As, Case, Chronon, Example, Flash, Jiffy, Moment, Present, Say, Shake, Spur, Tick, Trice, Twinkling, Urgent

Instead (of) Deputy, For, Lieu, Locum, Vice

Instigate Arouse, Foment, Impel, Incite, Prompt, Spur

Instil(l) Implant, Inculcate, Infuse, Teach, Transfuse

Instinct(ive) Automatic, Flair, Herd, Id, Impulse, Inbred, Innate, Intuition, Nature, Nose, Pleasure principle, Talent, Tendency, Visceral

Institute, Institution Academy, Activate, Asylum, Bank, Begin, Bring, Broadmoor, Charity, College, Erect, Found(ation), I, Inaugurate, Mechanical, MORI, Orphanage, Poorhouse, Protectory, Raise, Redbrick, Retraict, Retrait(e), Retreat, Royal, Smithsonian, Start, University, Women's, Workhouse

Instruct(ed), Instruction, Instructor ADI, Advice, Apprenticeship, Brief, CAI, Catechism, Clinic, Coach, Course, Didactic, Direct(ive), Document, Edify, Educate, Enjoin, Ground(ing), Inform, Lesson, Loop, Macro, Manual, Mystagogue, Mystagogus, Notify, Order, Percept, Prescription, Program, Recipe, Rubric, Script, Swami, > TEACH, Train, Tutelage, Tutorial, Up

Instrument(al) Ablative, Act, Agent, Dash(board), Helpful, Kit, Mean(s), Mechanical, > MUSICAL INSTRUMENT, Negotiable, > RESPONSIBLE, > TOOL,

Transit, Transposing, > UTENSIL

INSTRUMENTS

3 letters:
Fan
Gad

4 letters:
Celt
Clam
Dupe
Fork
Mike
Prog
Rasp
Rote
Tram

5 letters:
Brake
Curet
Fleam
Float
Gadge
Groma
Meter
Miser
Organ
Probe
Sonde
Wecht

6 letters:
Bougie
Broach
Etalon
Megger®
Opener
Pallet
Pestle
Scythe
Strobe
Trocar

7 letters:
Alidade
Cadrans
Caliper
Caltrop
Cautery
Curette

Diopter
Flesher
Forceps
Organic
Pelican
Plotter
Pointel
Probang
Scriber
Sextant
Spatula
Stapler
Strigil
Swazzle
Swingle
Swozzle
Syringe
Trammel

8 letters:
Barnacle
Burdizzo
Diagraph
Dividers
Ecraseur
Enlarger
Iriscope
Odometer
Ohmmeter
Otoscope
Oximeter
Quadrant
Scalprum
Scissors
Snuffler
Strickle
Trephine
Tweezers
Waywiser

9 letters:
Alphonsin
Arcograph
Astrolabe
Atmometer
Auxometer
Barometer
Baryscope

Bolometer
Coelostat
Crows-bill
Cryoscope
Cymograph
Depressor
Dermatome
Dip-circle
Dosemeter
Dosimeter
Dropsonde
Endoscope
Ergograph
Eriometer
Extractor
Fadometer
Fetoscope
Flowmeter
Fluxmeter
Haemostat
Heliostat
Hodometer
Hourglass
Konimeter
Lysimeter
Machmeter
Manometer
Marigraph
Megascope
Metronome
Microtome
Milometer
Nocturnal
Nut-wrench
Oedometer
Ondograph
Optometer
Optophone
Osmometer
Osteotome
Periscope
Polygraph
Potometer
Pyrometer
Raspatory
Retractor
Rheometer
Skiascope

Sonograph
Tasimeter
Telemeter
Telescope
Tellurian
Tellurion
Tenaculum
Tonometer
Toothpick
Tripmeter
Voltmeter
Wavemeter
Xylometer
Zymometer

10 letters:
Almacantar
Almucantar
Altazimuth
Anemometer
Ceilometer
Clinometer
Colposcope
Comparator
Cryophorus
Cystoscope
Drosometer
Fibrescope
Goniometer
Gonioscope
Gravimeter
Heliograph
Hydrometer
Hydroscope
Hygrometer
Hypsometer
Iconometer
Integrator
Micrograph
Micrometer
Microphone
Mileometer
Nephograph
Nephoscope
Nitrometer
Orthoscope
Oscillator
Osteoclast

- Pantograph
- Photometer
- Piezometer
- Pilliwinks
- Planimeter
- Protractor
- Pulsimeter
- Pulsometer
- Pycnometer
- Radiometer
- Radiophone
- Radioscope
- Radiosonde
- Siderostat
- Spirograph
- Spirometer
- Tachigraph
- Tachometer
- Tensometer
- Theodolite
- Thermopile
- Thorascope
- Tribometer
- Tromometer
- Urinometer
- Variometer

11 letters:
- Auxanometer
- Chronograph
- Chronometer
- Chronoscope
- Coercimeter

Colonoscope
Dilatometer
Fluorometer
Fugitometer
Gastroscope
Gradiometer
Helicograph
Intoximeter
Jacob's staff
Laparoscope
Nephroscope
Opeidoscope
Pinnywinkle
Polarimeter
Polariscope
Proctoscope
Psychograph
Pyranometer
Pyrgeometer
Quantometer
Rangefinder
Rocketsonde
Screwdriver
Seismograph
Seismoscope
Solarimeter
Spherometer
Stactometer
Stadiometer
Stauroscope
Stereometer
Stereoscope
Stethoscope

Stroboscope
Synthesizer
Tacheometer
Tensiometer
Thermometer
Thermoscope
Urethoscope
Vectorscope
Voltammeter

12 letters:
Aethrioscope
Bronchoscope
Camera lucide
Cephalometer
Electrometer
Galactometer
Galvanometer
Galvanoscope
Harmonometer
Inclinometer
Keraunograph
Myringoscope
Nephelometer
Oscilloscope
Penetrometer
Pinniewinkle
Respirometer
Scarificator
Sensitometer
Snooperscope
Spectroscope
Sphygmograph

Synchroscope
Tellurometer
Turbidimeter
Zenith-sector

13 letters:
Phonendoscope
Pneumatograph
Pneumatometer
Potentiometer
Pyrheliometer
Reflectometer
Refractometer
Sigmoidoscope
Stalagmometer
Tachistoscope
Weatherometer

14 letters:
Diffractometer
Interferometer
Ophthalmoscope
Phosphoroscope
Synchronoscope

15 letters:
Phenakestoscope

16 letters:
Sphygmoma-
  nometer

Insubordinate Contumacious, Faction, Mutinous, Rebel, Refractory
Insubstantial Airy, Brief, Flimsy, Frothy, Illusory, Jackstraw, Slight, Thin, Wispy, Ye(a)sty
Insufferable Egregious
Insufficient Exiguous, Inadequate, Poor, Scant, Shortfall
Insular Isolated, Moated, Narrow, Xenophobe
Insulate, Insulation, Insulator Biotite, Dielectric, Electret, Enwind, Grommet, Haybox, Inwind, Lagging, Mica, Non-conductor, Padding, Pugging, Sleeving, Tog
Insult(ing) Abuse, Affront, Aspersion, Barb, Charientism, Contumely, Cut, Dyslogistic, Embarrass, Facer, Fig, Injurious, Lese-majesty, Mud, Mud-pie, Offend, Opprobrious, Rip on, Skit, Slagging, Slight, Slur, Snub, Trauma, Uncomplimentary, Verbal, Yenta, Yente
Insurance, Insure(r) Abandonee, Cover, Fidelity, Fire, Guarantee, Hedge, Indemnity, Knock-for-knock, Life, Lloyds, Marine, Medicare, Mutual, National, Participating, Pluvius, Policy, Reversion, Security, Social, Term, Underwrite, Whole-life
Insurgent, Insurrection Cade, Jacquerie, Mutiny, Outbreak, Pandy, Rebel,

Revolt, Sedition, Whisky
Intact Complete, Entire, Inviolate, Unused, Whole
Intaglio Diaglyph
Intake Absorption, Entry, Fuel
Integer, Integral Component, Definite, Entire, Improper, Inbuilt, Indefinite, Needful, Number, Organic, Unitary
Integrate(d), Integration Amalgamate, Assimilate, Combine, Fuse, Harmonious, Holistic, Large-scale, Mainstream, Merge, Tightknit
Integrity Honesty, Principle, Probity, Rectitude, Strength, Uprightness, Whole
Integument Coat, Sheath, Skin, Velum
Intellect, Intellectual(s) Academic, Aptitude, Brain, Cerebral, Dianoetic, Egghead, Eggmass, Far-out, Genius, Highbrow, Intelligent, Intelligentsia, -ist, Learned, Literati, Luminary, Mastermind, Mental(ity), Mind, Noesis, Noetic, Noology, Nous, Profound, Reason, Titan
Intelligence, Intelligent Advice, Artificial, Boss, Brains, Bright, CIA, Discerning, Dope, Eggmass, Emotional, Esprit, G, Grey matter, GRU, Info, Ingenious, IQ, Knowledgeable, Machiavellian, Machine, MI, Mossad, Mother wit, News, Pate, Pointy-headed, Rational, Sconce, Sense, Sharp, Shrewd, Spetsnaz, Spetznaz, Tidings, Wit
Intelligible Exoteric
Intemperance Acrasia, Crapulent, Excess, Gluttony, Immoderation
Intend(ed), Intending Allot, Betrothed, Contemplate, Design, Destine, Ettle, Fiancé(e), Going, > MEAN, Meditate, Propose, Purpose
Intense, Intensify, Intensity Acute, Aggravate, Ardent, Depth, Earnest, Earthquale, Emotional, Enhance, Escalate, Estro, Excess, Extreme, Fervent, Keen, Luminous, Might, Profound, Radiant, Redouble, Sharpen, Vehement, Vivid
Intent, Intention(al) A dessein, Animus, Deliberate, Dole, Earnest, Hellbent, Manifesto, Mens rea, Mind, Paradoxical, Purpose, Rapt, Resolute, Set, Studious, Systematic, Thought, Tire, Witting, Yrapt
Inter Bury, Entomb
Interaction Chemistry, Enantiodromia, Solvation
Interbreed(ing) Miscegenation
Intercalation Embolism
Intercede, Intercession Mediate, Negotiate, Plead, Prayer
Intercept Absciss(a), Abscisse, Check, Hack, Meet
Interchange(d) Altercation, Alternate, Clover-leaf, Crossing, Equivalent, Mutual, Permute, Reciprocate, Substitute
Intercourse Ball, Bang, Bed, Boff, Bonk, Coition, Coitus, Commerce, Commixture, Congress, Consummation, Converse, Copulation, Cottaging, Cunnilingus, Deflowering, Enjoy, Fluff, Fornication, Gamahuche, Gamaruche, Greens, Hochmagandie, Hochmagandy, Jass, Jazz, Jiggy, Jump, Knee-trembler, Know(ledge), Laying, Leg-over, Lie with, Make, Marriage bed, Naughty, Necrophilia, Nookie, Nooky, Poontang, Pussy, Quickie, Ride, Rim, Roger, Root, Rumpy(-pumpy), Screw, Sexual, Shaft, Shag, Shtup, Sixty-nine, Sociality, Sodomy, Stuff, Swive, Tail, Tie, Trade, Trock, Troilism, Truck, Whoredom
Interdict Ban, Forbid, Prohibit, Taboo
Interest(ed), Interesting Amusive, APR, Attention, Behalf, Benefit, Clou, Compound, Concern, Contango, Coupon, Dividend, Ear-grabbing, Engage, Engross, Enthusiasm, Fad, Fee-simple, Fee-tail, Grab, Hot, Human, Import, Income, Insurable, Int(o), Intrigue, Landed, Life, Line, Negative, Part, Partisan, Percentage, Readable, Rente, Respect, Revenue, Scene, Share, Side, Sideline,

Simple, Spice, Stake, Topical, Usage, Usance, Usure, Usury, Vested, Vig(orish), Warm

Interfere(r), Interference Busybody, Clutter, Disrupt, Hamper, Hinder, Intrude, Mar, > **MEDDLE**, Molest, Officious, Pry, Radio, Shash, Static, Tamper, Teratogen

Interferometer Etalon

Intergrowth Perthite

Interim Break, Meantime, Meanwhile, Temporary

Interior Backblocks, Cyclorama, Domestic, Innards, Innate, Inner, Inside, Outback, Plain, Up-country, Vitals

Interject(ion) Ahem, Begorra(h), Gertcha, Haith, Hoo-oo, Interpolate, Lumme, Nation, Sese(y), Sessa, 'Sheart, 'Slid, Tarnation, Tush

Interlace Mingle, Pleach, Weave, Wreathe

Interlock Dovetail, Engage, Knit, Tangle

Interlocutor Elihu, MC, Questioner

Interloper Gate-crasher, Intruder, Trespasser

Interlude Antimask, Antimasque, Divertimento, Entr'acte, Interruption, Kyogen, Lunch-hour, Meantime, Pause, Verset

Intermediary, Intermediate Agent, Bardo, Comprador(e), Go-between, Instar, Mean, Medial, Mesne, Mezzanine, Middleman, Middle-of-the-road, Thirdsman

Interminable Endless, Infinite, Unending

Intermission Apyrexia, Break, Interval, Pause, Recess

Intermittent Broken, Fitful, Off-on, Periodic, Random, Spasmic, Spasmodic, Sporadic

Intern(e) Confine, Doctor, Impound, Restrict, Trainee

Internal Domestic, Inner, Internecine, Inward, Within

International Cap, Cosmopolitan, Lion, Test, UN, Universal

Internet Infobahn, URL, WWW

Interpolate(r), Interpolation Diaskeuast, Insert, Intercalate, Interrupt, Tmesis

Interpose Butt in, Horn in, Interject, Interlay, Interprone, Intervene, Spatchcock, Stickle

Interpret(er) Conster, Construe, Decipher, Decode, Dobhash, Dragoman, Exegete, Explain, Exponent, Expositor, Expound, Glossator, Hermeneutist, Hierophant, Jehovist, Latiner, Lingster, Linguistic, Linkster, Medium, Moonshee, Moonshi, Munshi, Oneirocritic, Origenist, Prophet, Read, Rede, Render, Represent, Spokesman, Textualist, > **TRANSLATE**, Truchman, Ulema

Interpretation Anagoge, Anagogy, Construction, Copenhagen, Eisegesis, Euhemerism, Exegesis, Exegete, Gematria, Gloss(ary), Gospel, Halacha(h), Halakah, Hermeneutics, Midrash, Portray, Reading, Rede, Rendition, Spin, Targum, Translation, Tropology

Interrogate, Interrogation Catechism, Debrief(ing), Enquire, Examine, Grill, Maieutic, Pump, > **QUESTION**, Quiz

Interrupt(ion), Interrupter Ahem, Aposcopesis, Blip, Break, Butt, Chequer, Chip in, Disturb, Entr'acte, Heckle, Hiatus, Intercept, Interfere, Interpellate, Interpolate, Interpose, Interregnum, Intrusion, Overtalk, Pause, Portage, Rheotome, Stop, Suspend, Time-out

Intersect(ion) Carfax, Carfox, Carrefour, Chiasm(a), Cross, Crunode, Cut, Decussate, Divide, Groin, Metacentre, Orthocentre, Trace

Intersperse Dot, Interpose, Scatter, Sprinkle

Interstice Areole, Interlude, Pore, Space

Intertwine Braid, Impleach, Knit, Lace, Plait, Splice, Twist, Writhe

Interval Between, Break, Breather, Class, Closed, Comma, Contour, Diapente,

Diastaltic, Diatesseron, Diesis, Distance, Ditone, Duodecimo, Entr'acte, Fifth, Gap, Half-time, Hiatus, Hourly, Interim, Interlude, Interregnum, Interspace, Interstice, Lunitidal, Meantime, Meantone, Meanwhile, Microtone, Ninth, Octave, Ottava, Perfect, Pycnon, Respite, Rest, Schisma, Semitone, Sixth, Space, Span, Spell, Tritone, Unison, Wait

Intervene, Intervention Agency, Arbitrate, Interfere, Interjacent, Interrupt, Mediate, Mesne, Theurgy, Up

Interview Audience, Audition, Beeper, Conference, Doorstep, Examine, Hearing, Oral, Press conference, See, Vox pop

Interweave, Interwoven, Interwove Entwine, Interlace, Monogram, Pirnit, Plait, Plash, Pleach, Raddle, Wreathed

Intestate Heirless, Unwilling

Intestinal, Intestine(s) Bowel, Chit(ter)lings, Derma, Duodenum, Enteric, Entrails, Guts, Harigals, Innards, Jejunum, Kishke, Large, Mesenteron, Omenta, Rectum, Small, Splanchnic, Thairm, Viscera

Intimacy, Intimate(ly) Achates, Boon, Bosom, Communion, Connote, Familiar, Friend, Heart-to-heart, Inmost, Innuendo, Intrigue, Nearness, Opine, Pack, Private, Signal, Special, Thick, Throng, Warm, Well

Intimation Clue, Hint, Implication, Inkling, Innuendo, Si quis

Intimidate, Intimidating Awe, Browbeat, Bulldoze, Bully, Cow, Daunt, Dragon, Hector, Niramiai, Psych, Threaten, Tyrannise, Unnerve

Into At, Intil, Within

Intolerable, Intolerant Allergic, Bigotry, Excessive, Illiberal, Impossible, Ombrophobe, Self-righteous

Intone, Intonation Cadence, Just, Twang

In touch Au fait

Intoxicant, Intoxicate(d), Intoxicating, Intoxication Alcoholic, Areca-nut, Benj, Bhang, Coca, Corn, Cup, Disguise, Fuddle, Ganja, Heady, > HIGH, Hocus, Hou high, Inebriate, Jag, Merry, Mescal, Peyote, Pixil(l)ated, Rumbullion, Slewed, Soma, Sozzle, Spirituous, Swacked, Temulent, Whiskeyfied, Whiskified, Zonked

Intractable Disobedient, Kittle, Mulish, Obdurate, Perverse, Surly, Unruly, Wilful

Intransigent Adamant, Inflexible, Rigid, Uncompromising

Intransitive Neuter, Objectless

Intrepid Aweless, Bold, Brave, Dauntless, Doughty, Firm, Gallant, > RESOLUTE, Valiant

Intricate Complex, Daedal(ian), Daedale, Dedal, Gordian, Intrince, Involute, Knotty, Pernickety, Sinuous, Tirlie-wirlie, Tricky, Vitruvian

Intrigue(r), Intriguing Affaire, Artifice, Brigue, Cabal, Camarilla, Cloak and dagger, Collogue, Conspiracy, Fascinate, Hotbed, Ignatian, Jesuit, Jobbery, Liaison, Machinate, Plot, Politic, Rat, > SCHEME, Strategy, Traffic, Trinketer

Intrinsic(ally) Basically, Genuine, Inherent, Innate, Inner, Per se

▷ **Intrinsically** *may indicate* something within a word

Introduce(r), Introduction, Introductory Acquaint, Anacrusis, Curtain-raiser, Emcee, Enseam, Exordial, Foreword, Immit, Import, Induct, Initiate, Inject, Insert, Instil(l), Intercalate, Interpolate, Intrada, Introit, Isagogic, Lead-in, Opening, Phase in, Plant, Preamble, Preface, Preliminary, Prelude, Prelusory, Preparatory, Present, Presentment, Proem, Prolegomena, Prolegomenon, Prologue, Proponent, Referral, Standfirst, Start, Usher

▷ **Introduction** *may indicate* a first letter

Intromission Vicious

Introspective Musing, Reflex, Ruminant

▷ **In trouble** *may indicate* an anagram

Introvert(ed) Cerebrotonic, Ingrow, In-toed, Reserved, Shy

Intrude(r), Intrusion, Intrusive Abate, Aggress, Annoy, Bother, Burglar, Disturb, > ENCROACH, Gatecrash, Hacker, Interloper, Invade, Meddle, Nosey, Porlocking, Presume, Raid, Sorn, Trespass

Intuition, Intuitive Belief, ESP, Hunch, Insight, Instinct, Inwit, Noumenon, Premonition, Presentiment, Seat-of-the-pants, Telepathy, Theosophy, Visceral

▷ **In two words** *may indicate* a word to be split

Inuit Eskimo, Yupik

Inundate, Inundation Flood, Overflow, Overwhelm, Submerge, Swamp

Inure Acclimatise, Accustom, Harden, Season, Steel

Invade(r), Invasion Angle, Attack, Attila, Dane, Descent, Encroach, Hacker, Hengist, Horsa, Hun, Infest, Inroad, Intruder, Irrupt, Jute, Lombard, Martian, Norman, Norsemen, Ostrogoth, Overlord, Overrun, Permeate, Raid, Trespass, Vandal, Visigoth

Invalid(ate), Invalidation Bad, Bogus, Bunbury, Cancel, Chronic, Clinic, Defunct, Diriment, Erroneous, Expired, False, Inauthentic, Inform, Inoperative, Irritate, Lapsed, Nugatory, Null, Nullify, Refute, Shut-in, Terminate, Valetudinarian, Vitiate, Void

Invaluable Essential, Excellent, Precious, Useful

Invariable, Invariably Always, Constant, Eternal, Habitual, Perpetual, Steady, Uniform

Invective Abuse, Billingsgate, Diatribe, Philippic, Reproach, Ribaldry, Tirade

Inveigh Declaim, Denounce, Protest, Rail

Invent(ion), Inventive Adroit, Babe, Baby, Brainchild, Chimera, Coin, Contrive, Cook up, > CREATE, Daedal, Design, Device, Excogitate, Fabricate, Fain, Fantasia, Feign, Figment, Imaginary, Improvise, Ingenuity, Mint, Originate, Patent, Pretence, Resourceful, Synectics, Whittle, Wit

Inventor Archimedes, Arkwright, Artificer, Author, Babbage, Baird, Bell, Biro, Boys, Bramah, Cartwright, Celsius, Coiner, Creator, Crompton, Daedalus, Edison, Engineer, Galileo, Geiger, Hansom, Jubal, Marconi, Maxim, Minié, Mint-master, Morse, Nernst, Newcomen, Nobel, Patentee, Savery, Siemens, Tesla, Torricelli, Tull, Watt, Wheatstone, Whitney

Inventory Account, Index, Itemise, List, Perpetual, Personality, Register, Steelbow, Stock

Inversion, Invert(ed) Anastrophe, Antimetabole, Antimetathesis, Capsize, Chiasmus, Entropion, Entropium, First, Homosexuality, Opposite, Overset, Resupinate, Reverse, Second, Tete-beche, Turn, Upset

Invertebrate Annelida, Anthozoan, Arrowworm, Arthropod, Brachiopod, Coelenterate, Cridarian, Crinoid, Ctenophore, Decapod, Echinoderm, Echinoid, Euripterid, Feather star, Gast(e)ropod, Globigerina, Hydrozoan, Mollusc, Onychophoran, Parazoan, Pauropod, Peritrich, Polyp, Poriferan, Protostome, Rotifer, Roundworm, Scyphozoan, Sea-cucumber, Sea-lily, Spineless, Starfish, Tardigrade, Trepang, Trochelminth, Unio, Water bear, Worm, Zoophyte

Invest(or), Investment Agamemnon, Ambient, Angel, Bate, Beleaguer, Besiege, Bet, Blockade, Blue-chip, Capitalist, Collins Street farmer, Contrarian, Dignify, Dub, Embark, Empanoply, Enclothe, Endow, Enrobe, Ethical, Financier, Flutter, Gilt, Girt, Holding, Infeft, Install, On, Pannicle, Panniculus, Parlay, Place, Portfolio, Put, Ring, Robe, Saver, Share, Siege, Sink, Spec, Speculation, Stag, Stake, Stock, Surround, Tessa, Trust, Trustee, Venture, Zaitech

▷ **Invest** *may indicate* one word surrounding another

Investigate, Investigator, Investigation Canvass, Case, Chart, CID, Delve, Examine, Explore, Fed, Ferret, Fieldwork, Go into, Hunt, Inquest, Inquirendo, Inquiry, Inquisition, McCarthyism, Nose, Organon, Organum, Probe, Pry, Quester, Rapporteur, Research, Scan, Scout, Screen, Scrutinise, Search, Sleuth, Snoop, Study, Suss, Tec, Test, T-man, Track, Try, Zetetic

Investiture Award, Inauguration

Inveterate Chronic, Double-dyed, Dyed-in-the-wool, Engrained, Habitual, Hardened

Invidious Harmful, Hostile, Malign

Invigilator Proctor

Invigorate, Invigorating, Invigoration Analeptic, Brace, Brisk, Cheer, Elixir, Energise, Enliven, Fortify, Insinew, Pep, Refresh, Renew, Stimulate, Tonic, Vital

Invincible Almighty, Brave, Stalwart, Valiant

Inviolatable, Inviolate, Inviolable Intemerate, Sacred, Sacrosanct

Invisible Hidden, Imageless, Infra-red, Secret, Tusche, Unseen

Invite, Invitation, Inviting Ask, Attract, Bid, Call, Card, Overture, > REQUEST, Solicit, Stiffie, Summons, Tempt, Toothsome, Woo

Invocation, Invoke Appeal, Call, Conjure, Curse, Entreat, Epiclesis, Solicit

Invoice Account, Bill, Docket, Itemise, Manifest, Pro forma

Involuntary Automatic, Instinctive, Unwitting

Involve(d), Involvement Commitment, Complicate, Complicit, Concern, Embroil, Engage, Entail, Envelop, Imbroglio, Immerse, > IMPLICATE, Include, Intricate, Meet, Necessitate, Participate, Tangle

▷ **Involved** *may indicate* an anagram

Inward(s) Afferent, Centripuntal, Homefelt, Introrse, Mental, Private, Varus, Within

Iodine I, Kelp, Thyroxin(e)

Ion Ammonium, Anion, Carbanion, Carborium, Hydroxyl, Isomer, Onium, Zwitterion

Ionian Iastic, Te(i)an

Iota Atom, Jot, Subscript, Whit

IOU Cedula, Market, PN, Shinplaster, Vowels

IOW Vectis

IRA Provisional, Provo

Iran(ian) Babist, Kurd, Mede, Osset, Parsee, Ta(d)jik, Tadzhik

Irascible Choleric, Crusty, Fiery, Peevish, Snappy, Tetchy, Toustie

Irate Angry, Cross, Infuriated, Wrathful

Ire Anger, Bait, Cholera, Fury, Rage, Wrath

Ireland Composer, Deirdre, Gaeltacht, Hibernia, Innisfail, Irena, IRL, Iverna

Iridescence, Iridescent Chatoyant, Flambé, Opaline, Reflet, Shimmering, Shot, Water-gall

Iridium Ir

Iris Areola, Eye, Flag, Fleur-de-lis, Gladdon, Ixia, Lily, Lis, Orris, Rainbow, Roast-beef plant, Sedge, Seg, Stinking, Sunbow

Irish(man) Bark, Bog-trotter, Boy, Celt(ic), Clan-na-gael, Defender, Dermot, Dubliner, Eamon(n), Eirann, Erse, Fenian, Gael, Gaeltacht, Goidel, Greek, Keltic, Kern(e), Mick(e)(y), Middle, Milesian, Mulligan, Ogamic, Orange(man), Ostmen, Paddy(-whack), Partholon, Pat(rick), Rapparee, Redshank, Reilly, Riley, Rory, Ryan, Sean, Shoneen, Teague, Temper, Ultonian, Whiteboy, Wildgeese

Irk(some) Annoy, Bother, Irritate, Needle, Tedious
Iron(s), Ironwork(s) Airn, Alpha, Angle, Beta, Carron, Cautery, Chains, Chalybeate, Chancellor, Channel, Climbing, Coquimbite, Corrugated, Cramp(on), Crampon, Crimp, Cross, Curling, Curtain, Delta, Derringer, Dogs, Eagle-stone, Fayalite, Fe, Ferredoxin, Ferrite, Fetter, Fiddley, Flip-dog, Galvanised, Gamma, Gem, Golfclub, Goose, Grappling, Grim, Grozing, > GUN, Gyve, Horse, Ingot, Italian, Kamacite, Laterite, Lily, Maiden, Malleable, Marcasite, Mars, Martensite, Mashie, Mashy, Meteoric, Pea, Pig, > PRESS, Pro-metal, Rabble, Rations, Rod, Sad, Shooting, Smoother, Soft, Soldering, Spiegeleisen, Steam, Stirrup, Stretching, Strong, Taconite, Taggers, Terne, Tin terne, Toggle, Tow, Wafer, Waffle, Wear, Wedge, White, Wrought
Iron age Latene, Villanovan
Ironic, Irony Antiphrasis, Asteism, Dramatic, Meiosis, Metal, Ridicule, Sarcasm, Satire, Socratic, Tongue-in-cheek, Tragic, Trope, Wry
Ironside Edmund
Ironwood Pyengadu
▶ **Ironwork(s)** *see* IRON
Irrational Absurd, Brute, Delirious, Foolish, Illogical, Number, Superstitious, Surd, Wild
Irreconcilable Poles apart
Irrefutable Evident, Positive, Undeniable
Irregular(ity) Abnormal, Alloiostrophus, Anomaly, Aperiodic, A salti, Asymmetric, Atypical, Bashi-bazouk, Blotchy, Crazy, Erratic, Evection, Fitful, Flawed, Formless, Free-form, Guerilla, Heteroclitic, Incondite, Inordinate, Kink, Occasional, Orthotone, Para-military, Partisan, Patchy, Rambling, Random, Scalene, Scrawl, Sebundy, Sharawadgi, Sharawaggi, Snatchy, Solecism, Sporadic, TA, Uneven, Unsteady, Unwonted, Variable, Wayward, Zigzag
▷ **Irregular** *may indicate* an anagram
Irrelevant Academic, Digression, Extraneous, Gratuitous, Immaterial, Inept, Non sequitur, Unrelated
Irreligious Heathen, Impious, Pagan, Profane
Irremedial Hopeless, Incurable, Laches
Irrepressible Resilient
Irreproachable Blameless, Spotless, Stainless
Irresistible Almighty, Endearing, Inevitable, Mesmeric, Overwhelming
Irresolute, Irresolution Aboulia, Doubtful, Hesitant, Timid, Unsure, Weak-willed
Irresponsible Capricious, Feckless, Flighty, Fly-by-night, Slap-happy, Strawen, Trigger-happy, Wanton, Wildcat
Irreverent Blasphemous, Disrespectful, Impious, Profane
Irrigate, Irrigation Canalise, Colonic, Douche, Enema, Flood, Get, Water
Irritable, Irritability, Irritant, Irritate(d), Irritation Acerbate, Anger, Annoy, Bête noire, Blister, Bug, Chafe, Chauff, Chippy, Chocker, Crabby, Cross-grained, Crosspatch, Crotchety, Crusty, Dod, Dyspeptic, Eat, Edgy, Enchafe, Erethism, Ewk, Exasperate, Fantod, Feverish, Fiery, Fleabite, Frabbit, Fractious, Fraught, Fretful, Gall, Get, Goad, Grate, Gravel, Hasty, Heck, Intertrigo, Irk, Itch, Jangle, Livery, Mardy, Narky, Needle, Nettle, Niggly, Ornery, Peckish, Peevish, Peppery, Pesky, Pestilent(ial), Pet, Petulance, Pinprick, Pique, Prickly, Provoke, Rag'd, Ragde, Rankle, Rasp, Rattle, Ratty, Rile, Roil, Rub, Ruffle, Savin(e), Scratchy, Shirty, Snappy, Snit, Snitchy, Splenetic, Sting, Tease, Techy, Testy, Tetchy, Thorn, Tickle, Toey, Touchy, Uptight, > VEX, Waxy, Yuke

▷ **Irritated** *may indicate* an anagram
Irving Actor, Berlin
Is Est, Ist
Isaiah Is
Isinglass Carlock, Fish-glue, Mica, Sturgeon
Islam(ic) Al Queda, Crescent, Druse, Druz(e), Hamas, Kurd(ish), Senus(si),
 Sheriat, Shia(h), Shiite, Sunni(te), Taleban, Taliban, Wah(h)abi
Island, Isle(t) Ait, Archipelago, Atoll, Cay, Char, Desert, Eyot, Floating, Holm, I,
 Inch, Is, Key, Lagoon, Mainland, Motu, Refuge, Traffic

ISLANDS

2 letters:	Hova	Bonin	Oland
TT	Idse	Canna	Ormuz
	Iona	Capri	Palau
3 letters:	Java	Ceram	Panay
Aru	Jolo	Cheju	Paros
Cos	Jura	Chios	Pelew
Diu	Keos	Clare	Pemba
Fyn	King	Cocos	Pines
Hoy	Line	Coney	Qeshm
Kos	Long	Coral	Qishm
Man	Mahe	Corfu	Reil's
May	Maui	Crete	Rhode
Rat	Mazu	Delos	Samar
Rum	Mona	Disko	Samoa
Sea	Muck	Ellis	Samos
Yap	Mull	Faial	Saria
	Niue	Farne	Seram
4 letters:	Oahu	Faroe	South
Amoy	Saba	Fayal	Spice
Aran	Sark	Funen	Sumba
Arru	Skye	Haiti	Sunda
Attu	Spud	Ibiza	Thera
Bali	Truk	Islay	Thule
Biak	Uist	Isola	Timor
Bute	Unst	Jerba	Tiree
Calf	Wake	Kiska	Tonga
Cebu	Yell	Kuril	Upolu
Coll		Lanai	Whale
Cook	5 letters:	Lewis	White
Cuba	Aland	Leyte	Wight
Dogs	Apple	Lundy	Youth
Eigg	Arran	Luzon	Zante
Elba	Aruba	Maewo	
Erin	Banka	Malta	6 letters:
Fair	Banks	Matsu	Achill
Fiji	Barra	Melos	Aegean
Guam	Batan	Nauru	Aegina
Heat	Belle	Naxos	Amager
Herm	Bioko	Nevis	Andros
Holy	Bohol	North	Avalon

- Azores
- Baffin
- Banaba
- Bangka
- Barrow
- Bikini
- Borneo
- Bounty
- Butung
- Caicos
- Canvey
- Cayman
- Ceylon
- Chiloe
- Cyprus
- Devil's
- Diomed
- Djerba
- Easter
- Eelpie
- Ellice
- Euboea
- Flores
- Fraser
- Hainan
- Harris
- Hawaii
- Hobart
- Honshu
- Hormuz
- Imbros
- Indies
- Insula
- Ionian
- Ischia
- Ithaca
- Jersey
- Kodiak
- Kurile
- Kvaloy
- Kyushu
- Labuan
- Laputa
- Lemnos
- Lesbos
- Leucas
- Leukas
- Levkas
- Lipari
- Lizard
- Lombok
- Madura

Majuro
Marajo
Mercer
Midway
Negros
Ogygia
Paphos
Patmos
Penang
Pharos
Philae
Phuket
Pladdy
Quemoy
Ramsey
Rhodes
Rialto
Robben
Ryukyu
Safety
Saipan
Savage
Savaii
Scilly
Sicily
Skerry
Skyros
Snares
Soenda
Staffa
Staten
Tahiti
Taiwan
Thanet
Thasos
Tobago
Tresco
Tubuai
Tuvalu
Unimak
Ushant
Veneti
Virgin

7 letters:
Aeolian
Aldabra
Andaman
Antigua
Austral
Bahamas
Baranof

Barbuda
Basilan
Battery
Bedloe's
Bermuda
Bonaire
Cartier
Celebes
Channel
Chatham
Cipango
Corsica
Crannog
Curacao
Cythera
Diomede
Emerald
Eriskay
Falster
Frisian
Fur Seal
Gambier
Gilbert
Gotland
Grenada
Hawaiki
Iwa Jima
Jamaica
Keeling
Laaland
Ladrone
La Palma
Leeward
Liberty
Lofoten
Lolland
Madeira
Majorca
Mariana
Masbate
Mayotte
Mindoro
Minorca
Molokai
Moreton
Mykonos
Nicobar
Norfolk
Oceania
Okinawa
Orcades
Orkneys

Pacific
Palawan
Phoenix
Rathlin
Reunion
Roanoke
Rockall
Salamis
San Juan
Sheppey
Shikoku
Society
Socotra
Sokotra
Solomon
Stewart
St Kilda
St Kitts
St Lucia
Sumatra
Sumbawa
Suqutra
Surtsey
Tenedos
Tokelau
Tortola
Tortuga
Tutuila
Visayan
Volcano
Waihake
Watling
Western
Wrangel
Zealand
Zetland

8 letters:
Alcatraz
Alderney
Aleutian
Anglesey
Anguilla
Antilles
Atlantis
Auckland
Balearic
Barbados
Bathurst
Billiton
Blefuscu
Bora-Bora

- Bornholm
- Canaries
- Caroline
- Catalina
- Choiseul
- Colonsay
- Cyclades
- Dominica
- Falkland
- Farquhar
- Flinders
- Foulness
- Friendly
- Gothland
- Gottland
- Guernsey
- Hamilton
- Hatteras
- Hebrides
- Hokkaido
- Jan Mayen
- Kangaroo
- Kermadec
- Kiribati
- Ladrones
- Lilliput
- Lord Howe
- Luggnagg
- Mackinac
- Maldives
- Mallorca
- Marianas
- Marquesa
- Marshall
- Melville
- Mindanao
- Miquelon
- Moluccas
- Mustique
- Northern
- Pelagian
- Pitcairn
- Pleasant
- Portland
- Pribilof
- Principe
- Sakhalin
- Sandwich
- Sardinia
- Schouten
- Shetland
- Somerset

South Sea
Sporades
Sri Lanka
St Helena
St Martin
St Thomas
Sulawesi
Svalband
Sverdrup
Tasmania
Tenerife
Terceira
Thousand
Thursday
Trinidad
Tsushima
Unalaska
Venetian
Victoria
Viti Levu
Windward
Zanzibar

9 letters:
Admiralty
Andreanof
Anticosti
Antipodes
Ascension
Barataria
Benbecula
Chichagof
Christmas
Elephanta
Ellesmere
Falklands
Fortunate
Galapagos
Governors
Greenland
Hainan Tao
Halmahera
Innisfree
Jamestown
Kerguelen
Lampedusa
Lanzarote
Macquarie
Manhattan
Margarita
Marquesas
Mascarene

Mauritius
Melanesia
Nantucket
New Guinea
Polynesia
Rangitoto
Rarotonga
Runnymede
Sao Miguel
Shetlands
Sjaelland
Stromboli
St Vincent
Teneriffe
Trobriand
Vancouver
Vanua Levu
Walcheren

10 letters:
Basse-Terre
Bermoothes
Campobello
Cape Barren
Cape Breton
Cephalonia
Corregidor
Dodecanese
Formentera
Grand Manan
Grand Terre
Grenadines
Heligoland
Hispaniola
Isle Royale
Kiritimati
Langerhans
Madagascar
Manitoulin
Marinduque
Martinique
Micronesia
Montsarrat
New Britain
New Georgia
New Ireland
Pescadores
Poor Knight
Puerto Rico
Saint Croix
Samothrace
Sandalwood

Seychelles
Three Kings
Vesteralen
West Indies
Whitsunday

11 letters:
Austronesia
Dry Tortugas
Glubdubdrib
Grand Bahama
Grand Canary
Guadalcanal
Lakshadweep
Lesser Sunda
Lindisfarne
Mount Desert
New Siberian
Pantelleria
Philippines
San Salvador
Southampton
Spitsbergen

12 letters:
Bougainville
Cassiterides
Glubbdubdrib
Greater Sundo
Marie Galante
New Caledonia
Newfoundland
Nusa Tenggara
Prince Edward
San Cristobal
Santa Barbara
Seringapatam
South Georgia
Torres Strait

13 letters:
Espiritu Santo
Forneaux Group
Fuerteventura
Juan Fernandez
New Providence
Prince of Wales
Santa Catalina

14 letters:
Amboina oceanic
D'Entrecasteaux

- Lesser Antilles
- Queen Charlotte
- Queen Elizabeth
- Tristan da Cunha
- Turks and Caicos

Vestmannaeyjar

15 letters:
Greater Antilles

Mont-Saint-
Michel
Wallis and Futuna

16 letters:
Heard and
McDonald

Islander Chian, Cretan, D(a)yak, Filipino, Kanaka, Kelper, Laputan, Madeiran, Maltese, Mauritian, Native, Nesiot, Newfie, Orcadian, Parian, Rhodian, Samiot, Sican, Singalese, Taiwanese

Isle of Wight Vectis

Isn't Aint, Nis, Nys

Isolate(d) Ancress, Apart, Backwater, Cleidoic, Cut off, Enclave, Enisle, Incommunicado, Inisle, In vacuo, Island, Lone, Maroon, Pocket, Quarantine, Sea-girt, Seclude, Secret, Segregate, Separate, Sequester, Solitary, Sporadic, Stray

Isomer Carvacrol, Geranial, Neral, Pinene, Theophylline

Isosceles Triangle

Isotope Actinon, Deuterium, Iodine-131, Muonium, Protium, Strontium-90, Thoron, Tritium

Israel(i) Beulah, IL, Meir, Sabra

Issue(s) Children, Come, Crux, Debouch, Denouement, Derive, Disclose, Dispense, Edition, Effluence, Egress, > **EMANATE**, Emerge, Emit, Escape, Exit, Exodus, Family, Feigned, Fiduciary, Flotation, Fungible, General, Government, Gush, Ish, Litter, Material, Number, Offspring, Outflow, Part, Proof, Publish, Result, Rights, Sally, Seed, Side, Son, Spawn, Special, Spring, Stream, Subject, Topic, Turn, Utter

Istanbul Byzantium, Constantinople

Isthmus Darien, Karelian, Kra, Neck, Panama, San Blas, Tehuantepec

It A, Chic, Hep, Id, Italian, Oomph, SA, 't, Vermouth

Italian, Italy Alpini, Ausonia, Bolognese, Calabrian, Chian, Dago, Ding, Este, Etnean, Etrurian, Etruscan, Eyeti(e), Eytie, Faliscan, Florentine, Genoese, Ghibelline, Guelf, Guelph, Hesperia, Irredentist, It, Latian, Latin, Lombard, Medici, Mezzogiorno, Moro, Oscan, Paduan, Patarin(e), Rocco, Roman, Sabine, Samnite, Sicel, Sienese, Signor(i), Sikel, Spag, Tuscan, Umbrian, Venetian, Vermouth, Volscian, Wop

Italic Swash

Itch(ing), Itchiness Acariasis, Annoy, Cacoethes, Dhobi, Euk, Ewk, Hanker, Jock, Miliaria, Photopsy, Prickle, Prurience, Prurigo, Pruritis, Psora, Scabies, Scrapie, Seven-year, Tickle, > **URGE**, Urtication, Yeuk, Youk, Yuck, Yuke

Item(ise) Also, Article, Bulletin, Detail, Entry, Flash, List, Number, Piece, Point, Spot, Too, Topic

Iterate Repeat

Itinerant, Itinerary Ambulant, Didakai, Didakei, Did(d)icoy, Gipsy, Gypsy, Hobo, Journey, Log, Pedlar, Peripatetic, Pie-powder, Roadman, Roamer, Romany, Rootless, Route, Stroller, Traveller

Itself Per se

Ivan Russian, Terrible

Ivory (tower) Black, Bone, Dentine, Distant, Eburnean, Impractical, Incisor, Key, Solitude, Teeth, Tower, Tusk, Vegetable, Whale's bone

Ivy Ale-hoof, Angelica-tree, Aralia, Boston, Bush, Cat's-foot, Climber, Creeper, Evergreen, Gill, Grape, Ground, Hedera, Helix, Japanese, Panax, Poison, Shield, Udo, Weeping

Jj

J Curve, Juliet, Pen

Jab(ber) Chatter, Foin, Gabble, Immunologist, Inject, Jaw, Jook, Nudge, One-two, Poke, Prattle, Prod, Proke, Punch, Puncture, Sook, Sputter, Stab, Stick, Venepuncture, Yak

Jack(s) AB, Apple, Artocarpus, Ass, Ball, Boot, Bower, Bowl(s), Boy, Card, Cheap, Coatcard, Crevalle, Deckhand, Dibs(tones), Five stones, Flag, Frost, Hoist, Honour, Hopper, Horner, Hydraulic, Idle, J, Jock, Ketch, Kitty, Knave, Knucklebones, London, Lumber, Mark, Matlow, Mistress, Nob, Noddy, Pilot, Point, Pot, Pur, Rabbit, Raise, Rating, Ripper, Robinson, Russell, Sailor, Salt, Screw, Shaun, Sprat, Spring-heeled, Springtail, Steeple, Sticker, Straw, Tar, Tee, Tradesman, Turnspit, Union, Uplift, Wood, Yellow

Jackal Anubis, Dieb, Hack, Stooge

Jackass Aliboron, Goburra, Kookaburra, Stupid

Jackdaw Bird, Chawk, Chough, Daw, Kae, Raven, Rheims, Thief

Jacket Acton, Afghanistan, Amauti(k), Anorak, Bainin, Baju, Bania(n), Banyan, Barbour®, Basque, Battle, Bawneen, Bed, Bellhop, Blazer, Blouson, Body-warmer, Bolero, Bomber, Brigandine, Bumfreezer, Bush, Cagoul(e), Camisole, Can, Caraco, Cardigan, Carmagnole, Casing, > **COAT**, Dinner, Dolman, Donkey, Drape, Dressing, Duffel coat, Duffle coat, Dust-cover, Dustwrapper, Fearnought, Flak, Fleece, Gambeson, Gendarme, Grego, Habergeon, Hacking, Ha(c)queton, Half-kirtle, Hug-me-tight, Jerkin, Jupon, Kagool, Kaross, Life, Life preserver, Lumber, Mackinaw, Mae West, Mandarin, Mandilion, Mao, Matinée, Mess, Monkey, Nehru, Newmarket, Norfolk, Parka, Pea, Petenlair, Pierrot, Pilot, Polka, Potato, Railly, Reefer, Safari, Sayon, Shearling, Shell, Shortgown, Simar(re), Sleeve, Slip-cover, Smoking, Spencer, Sports, Steam, Strait, Tabard, Tailcoat, Toreador, Tunic, Tux(edo), Tweed, Vareuse, Waistcoat, Wam(m)us, Wampus, Water, Windbreaker®, Windcheater, Windjammer, Wrapper, Zouave

Jackknife Dive, Fold, Jockteleg, Pike

Jackpot Cornucopia, Kitty, Pool

Jackson Stonewall

Jackstraw Spellican, Spil(l)ikin

Jacobite(s) Non-compounder, Non juror, Wild Geese

Jacquard Matelasse

Ja(c)ques Melancholy, Tati

Jade(d) Axe-stone, Bidet, Cloy, Crock, Disjaskit, Exhaust, Fatigue, Greenstone, Hack, Hag, Horse, Hussy, Limmer, Minx, Nag, Nephrite, Pounamu, Rip, Rosinante, Sate, Screw, Slut, Spleenstone, Stale, Tired, Trite, Weary, Yaud, Yu(-stone)

Jag(ged) Barbed, Cart, Drinking, Erose, Gimp, Injection, Laciniate, Ragde, Ragged, Serrate, Snag, Spree, Spur, Tooth

Jagger Mick, Pedlar

Jaguar American tiger, Car, Caracal, Cat, E-type, Ounce, Tiger

Jail(er) Adam, Alcaide, Alcatraz, Bedford, Bin, Bridewell, Can, Clink, Commit, Cooler, Gaol, Hoosegow, Imprison, Incarcerate, Jug, Keeper, Kitty, Lockup, Marshalsea, Newgate, Nick, Pen, Pokey, > **PRISON**, Screw, Shop, Slammer, Spandau, Strangeways, Tronk, Turnkey, Warder

Jailbird Con, Lag, Lifer, Trusty

Jain(ism) Mahavira

Jakarta Batavia

Jake Honest, Hunkydory, OK, Rube

Jalopy Banger, Boneshaker, Buggy, Car, Crate, Heap, Shandry(dan), Stock-car

Jam(my) Apple butter, Block, Choke, Clog, Confiture, Crush, Cushy, Dilemma, Gridlock, Hold-up, Jeelie, Jeely, Lock, Log, Plight, > **PREDICAMENT**, Preserve, Press, Quince, Seize, Snarl-up, Spot, Squeeze, Stall, Stick, Tailback, Tangle, Traffic, Vice, Vise, Wedge

Jamaica(n) Rasta(farian), Rastaman, Yardie

Jamb Doorpost, Durn, Sconcheon, Scontion, Scuncheon, Upright

James Agee, Bond, Bothwell, Henry, Jacobite, Jemmy, Jesse, Jim, Joyce, Screw, Seamus, Seumas, Sid, Watt

Jane Austen, Calamity, Eyre, Seymour, Shore, Sian

Jangle Clank, Clapperclaw, Clash, Rattle, Wrangle

Janitor Doorman, Porter, Servitor, Tiler

Jankers KP

Jansky Jy

Janus Two-faced

Japan(ese), Japanese drama Ainu, Burakumin, Daimio, Eta, Geisha, Genro, Gloss, Haiku, Heian, Hondo, Honshu, Issei, Kabuki, Kami, Kana, Kirimon, Lacquer, Mandarin, Meiji, Mikado, Mousmé, Mousmee, Nippon, Nisei, No(h), Resin, Sansei, Satsuma, Shinto, Shogun, Togo, Tycoon, Yamato

Jape Jeer, Joke, Prank, Trick

Jar(ring) Albarello, Amphora, Bell, Canopus, Churr, Clash, Crock, Cruet, Din, Dissonant, Distune, Dolium, Enrough, Gallipot, Grate, Greybeard, Gride, Grind, Gryde, Humidor, Hydria, > **JOLT**, Kalpis, Kang, Kilner®, Leyden, Mason, Off-key, Olla, Pint, Pithos, Pot(iche), Quarrel, Rasp, Shelta, Shock, Stamnos, Start, Stean, Steen, Stein, Tankard, Tinaja, Turn, Vessel, Water-monkey

Jargon Argot, Baragouin, Beach-la-mar, Buzzword, Cant, Chinook, Eurobabble, Eurospeak, Gobbledegook, Gobbledygook, Jive, Kennick, Legalese, Lingo, Lingoa geral, Lingua franca, Mumbo-jumbo, Newspeak, Officialese, Parlance, Patois, Patter, Patter-flash, Psychobabble, Shelta, Shoptalk, > **SLANG**, Technobabble, Technospeak, Vernacular

Jasmine Cape, Frangipani, Gelsemine, Gessamine, Jessamy, Madagascar, Olea

Jasper Basanite, Bloodstone, Egyptian, Porcelain

Jaundice(d) Cynical, Icterus, Prejudiced, Sallow, Yellow

Jaunt Journey, Outing, Sally, Stroll, Swan, Trip

Jaunty Airy, Akimbo, Chipper, Debonair, Perky, Rakish

▷ **Jaunty** *may indicate* an anagram

Java man Pithecanthropus

Javelin Dart, Gavelock, Harpoon, Jereed, Jerid, Pile, Pilum, Spear

Jaw(s), Jawbone Blab, Chaft, Chap, Chat, Chaw, Cheek, Chide, Chin, Entry, Glass, Gnathic, Gnathite, Gonion, Hypognathous, Jobe, Lantern, Lumpy, Mandible, Masseter, Maxilla, Mesial, Muzzle, Mylohyoid, Natter, Opisthognathous, Overshot, Phossy, Pi, Premaxillary, Prognathous, Ramus, Rubber, Shark, Stylet, Underhung, Undershot, Wapper-jaw, Ya(c)kety-Ya(c)k

Jay Bird, J, Sirgang, Whisky-jack, Whisky-john

Jazz(er), Jazzman Acid, Barber, Barrelhouse, Basie, Bebop, Blues, Boogie, Boogie-woogie, Bop, Cat, Cool, Dixieland, Enliven, Gig, Gutbucket, Hardbop, Hipster, Jive, Latin, Lick, Mainstream, Modern, New Orleans, Progressive, Ragtime, Riff, Scat, Skiffle, Stomp, Swinger, Trad, Traditional, West Coast

Jealous(y) Envious, Green(-eyed), Green-eyed monster, Grudging, Zelotypia

Jean(s) Chinos, Denims, Levis®, Pants, Trousers, Wranglers®

Jeer(ing) Ballyrag, Barrack, Belittle, Birl, Boo, Burl, Digs, Fleer, Flout, Gird, Hoot, Jape, Jibe, > **MOCK**, Rail, Razz, Ridicule, Scoff, Sling off, Sneer, Taunt, Twit, Yah

Jeeves Valet

Jehovah God, Lord, Yahve(h), Yahwe(h)

Jehovah's Witness Russellite

Jehu Charioteer, Driver

Jejune Arid, Barren, Dry, Insipid, Juvenile

Jelly Acaleph(a), Acalephe, Agar(-agar), Aspic, Brawn, Calf's foot, Chaudfroid, Comb, Cow-heel, > **EXPLOSIVE**, Flummery, Gel, Isinglass, Jam, Kanten, Macedoine, Medusa, Mineral, Mould, Napalm, Neat's foot, Petroleum, Quiddany, Royal, Shape, Tunicin, Vaseline®, Vitreous humour

▷ **Jelly** *may indicate* an anagram

Jellyfish Acaleph(a), Acalephe, Aurelia, Blubber, Box, Cnidaria, Discomedusae, Discophora, Hydromedusa, Irukandji, Medusa, Mesogloea, Planoblast, Portuguese man-of-war, Quarl, Scyphistoma, Scyphozoan, Sea-blubber, Sea-nettle, Sea-wasp, Strobila

Jemmy Betty, Crowbar, Lever

Jenkins Ear, Roy, Up

Jenny Ass, Lind, Long, Mule, Short, Spinner, Spinning, Spinster, Wren

Jeopardise, Jeopardy Danger, Double, Expose, Hazard, Peril, Risk

Jerboa Desert rat

Jeremiad Lament, Tragedy, Woe

Jeremy Fisher, Jerry

Jerk(y), Jerkily, Jerking, Jerks Aerobics, A salti, Bob, Braid, Cant, Diddle, Ebrillade, Flirt, Flounce, Gym(nastics), Hike, Hitch, Hoi(c)k, Jut, Kant, Knee, PE, Peck, Physical, Saccade, Shove, Spasm, Start, Strobe, Surge, Sydenham's chorea, Tic, Toss(en), Tweak, > **TWITCH**, Wrench, Yank

Jerkin Jacket, Tabard

Jerome Kern, Vulgate

Jerry, Jerry-built Boche, Flimsy, Fritz, Hun, Kraut, Mouse, Po(t)

Jersey(s) CI, Cow, Frock, Gansey, Guernsey, Kine, Lily, Maillot, Polo, Roll-neck, Singlet, > **SWEATER**, Sweatshirt, Yellow, Zephyr

Jerusalem Ariel, Hierosolymitan, Sion, Zion

Jess(e) James, Strap

Jest(er), Jesting Badinage, Barm, Baur, Bawr, Bourd(er), Buffoon, Clown, Cod, Comic, Droll, Goliard, Inficete, Jape, Jig, Joker, Josh, Merryman, Miller, Motley, Patch, Quip, Raillery, Ribaldry, Rigoletto, Scogan, Scoggin, Sport, Toy, Trinculo, Wag, Wit, Yorick

Jesuit Bollandist, Ignatius, Loyola, SJ

Jesus > **CHRIST**, Emmanuel, IHS, Immanuel, INRI, Isa, Jabers, Lord

Jet Airbus®, Aircraft, Beadblast, Black, Burner, Chirt, Douche, Fountain, Geat, Harrier, Ink, Jumbo, Plane, Pump, Soffione, Spirt, Spout, Spray, Spurt, Squirt, Stream, Turbine, Turbo, Vapour, Water

Jettison Discard, Dump, Flotsam, Jetsam, Lagan, Ligan

Jetty Groin, Mole, Pier, Wharf

Jew(ish), Jews Ashkenazi, Chas(s)id, Diaspora, Essene, Falasha, Grecian,

Greek, Has(s)id, Hebrew, Kahal, Karaite, Karta, Landsman, Levite, Lubavitch, Maccabee, Marrano, Misnaged, Mitnag(g)ed, Nazarite, Neturei, Peculiar people, Pharisee, Refusenik, Sabra, Sadducee, Semite, Sephardim, Sheeny, Shemite, Shtetl, Smouch, Smouse, Tobit, Wandering, Yid(dish), Zealot

Jewel(s), Jeweller(y) Agate, Almandine, Artwear, Beryl, Bijouterie, Brilliant, Chrysoprase, Cloisonné, Cornelian, Costume, Crown, Diamond, Earbob, Ear-drop, Emerald, Ewe-lamb, Fabergé, Fashion, Ferron(n)ière, Finery, Garnet, > **GEM**, Girandole, Gracchi, Jade, Junk, Lherzolite, Marcasite, Navette, Olivine, Opal, Parure, Paste, Pavé, Pearl, Pendant, Peridot, Rivière, Rubin(e), Ruby, Sapphire, Sard, Scarab, Smaragd, Solitaire, Stone, Sunburst, Tom, Tomfoolery, Topaz, Torc, Treasure, Trinket

Jezebel Harlot, Loose, Whore

Jib Ba(u)lk, Boggle, Boom, > **DEMUR**, Face, Flying, Foresail, Genoa, Milk, Reest, Reist, Stay-sail, Storm

Jibe Bob, Correspond, Dig, Fling, > **JEER**, Mock, Quip, Sarcasm, Slant, Taunt

Jiffy Mo, Pronto, Twinkling

Jig(gle) Bob, Bounce, Dance, Fling, Frisk, Hornpipe, Jog, Juggle, Morris

Jigger(ed) Beat, Chigoe, Jolley, Ruin

Jill Ferret

Jilt Discard, Reject, Shed, Throw-over

Jim(my) Diamond, Dismal, Jas, Lucky, Pee, Piddle, Riddle

Jingle(r) Clerihew, Clink, Ditty, Doggerel, Rhyme, Tambourine, Tinkle

Jingo(ism) Odzooks, Patriot, War-rant

Jink Elude

Jinn(i) Afreet, Eblis, Genie, Marid, Spirit

Jinx Curse, Hex, Jonah, Kibosh, Moz(z), Spoil, Voodoo, Whammy

Jitter(s), Jittery Coggly, DT, Fidgets, Funk, Jumpy, Nervous, Willies

▷ **Jitter(s)** *may indicate* an anagram

Jo > **LOVER**, Sweetheart

Job(bing) Agiotage, Appointment, Berth, Career, Chore, Comforter, Crib, Darg, Errand, Gig, Hatchet, Homer, Inside, Metier, Nixer, Oratorio, Patient, Pensum, Place(ment), Plum, Position, Post, Problem, Pursuit, Put-up, Sinecure, Snow, Spot, Steady, > **TASK**, Ticket, Trotter, Undertaking, Work

▷ **Job** *may indicate* the biblical character

Jock Deejay, DJ, Mac, Sawn(e)y, Scot

Jockey Carr, Cheat, Diddle, Disc, Jostle, Jump, Lester, Manoeuvre, Rider, Steve, Suicide, Swindle, Trick, Video, Winter

▷ **Jockey** *may indicate* an anagram

Jocose, Jocular, Jocund Cheerful, Debonair, Facete, Facetious, Jesting, Lepid, Scurril(e), Waggish

Joe(y), Joseph Addison, Dogsbody, GI, Kangaroo, Pal, Roo, Sloppy, Stalin, Surface, Trey

Jog(ger), Joggle, Jog-trot Arouse, Canter, Dog-trot, Dunch, Dunsh, Heich-how, Heigh-ho, Hod, Jiggle, Jolt, Jostle, Memo, Mosey, Nudge, Piaffe, Prompt, Ranke, Remind, Run, Shake, Shog, Tickle, Trot, Whig

John(ny) Ajax, Augustus, Barleycorn, Bog, Bright, Brown, Bull, Bunyan, Cloaca, Collins, Doree, Dory, Elton, Evan, Gaunt, Gents, Gilpin, Groats, Halifax, Ia(i)n, Ivan, Lackland, Latecomer, Lav, Little, Loo, Peel, Prester, Stage-door, Throne, Toot, Tout, WC

Johnson Cham, Doctor, Idler

Join(er), Joined, Joining Abut, Accede, Accompany, Add, Ally, And, Annex, Associate, Attach, Braze, Butt-end, Cement, Cleave, Combine, Conflate,

Conglutinate, Conjugate, Connect, Cope, > **COUPLE**, Dovetail, Engraft, Enlist, Enrol, Enter, Federate, Fuse, Glue, Graft, Hasp, Hitch, Hyphen, Include, Inosculate, Jugate, Knit, Link, Marry, Meet, Member, Menuisier, Merge, Mix, Mortar, Mortise, Oop, Oup, Overlaunch, Piece, Piecen, Rebate, Regelation, Rivet, Scarf, Seam, Se-tenant, Sew, Siamize, Snug, Solder, Splice, Spot-weld, Squirrel, Staple, Stylolite, Tenon, Unite, Wed, Weld, Yoke

Joint(ed) Ancon, Ankle, Arthrosis, Articular, Ball and socket, Bar, Baron, Butt, Cardan, Carpus, Chine, Clip, Co, Cogging, Colonial goose, Commissure, Conjunction, Cuit, Cup and ball, Cut, Dive, Dovetail, Drumstick, Elbow, Enarthrosis, Entrecôte, Expansion, Fish, Gambrel, Gimmal, Gimmer, Ginglymus, Hainch, Haunch, Heel, Hinge, Hip, Hough, Huck, Hunker, J, Joggle, Jolly, Junction, Knee, Knuckle, Lap(ped), Lith, Loin, Marijuana, Meat, Mitre, Mortise, Mouse (buttock), Mouse-piece, Mutton, Mutual, Phalange, Phalanx, Pin, Popliteal, Psoas, Rabbet, Rack, Raphe, Reducer, Reefer, Rhaphe, Ribroast, Roast, Saddle, Scarf, Schindylesis, Seam, Shoulder, Silverside, Sirloin, Splice, Spliff, Stifle, Straight, Strip, Symphysis, Syndesmosis, T, Tarsus, T-bone, Tenon, Together, Toggle, Tongue and groove, Topside, Trochanter, Undercut, Universal, Vertebra, Water, Weld, Wrist

Joist Accomplement, Bar, Beam, Dormant, Groundsill, H-beam, I-beam, Rib, Rolled-steel, Sleeper, Solive, String, Trimmer

Joke(r), Joke-book Banter, Bar, Booby-trap, Bourdon, Card, Chaff, Chestnut, > **CLOWN**, Cod, Comedian, Comic, Crack, Cut-up, Farceur, Farceuse, Fool, Fun, Funster, Gab, Gag, Glike, Guy, Have-on, Hazer, Hoax, Hum, Humorist, Jape, Jest, Jig, Lark, Legpull, Merry-andrew, Merryman, Mistigris, One, One-liner, Pleasantry, Practical, Prank(ster), Pun, Punchline, Pundigrion, Quip, Sally, Scherzo, Scogan, Scoggin, Sick, Skylark, Sottisier, Squib, Standing, Wag, Wheeze, Wild, Wisecrack, Wit

Jollity, Jolly 'Arryish, Bally, Convivial, Cordial, Do, Festive, Galoot, Gaucie, Gaucy, Gawcy, Gawsy, Gay, Hilarious, Jocose, Jovial, Marine, Mirth, Rag, RM, Roger, Sandboy, Tar, Very

Jolt Bump, Jar, Jig-a jig, Jostle, Jounce, Shake, Shog, Start

Jonah Hoodoo, Jinx, Moz(z)

Jones Davy, Emperor, Inigo

Jordan Pot, Urinal

Joris Horseman

▸ **Joseph** *see* JOE

Josh Chaff, Kid, Rib, Tease

Josiah Stamp, Wedgewood

Joss Incense, Luck, Stick

Jostle Barge, Bump, Compete, Elbow, Hog-shouther, Hustle, Push, Shoulder, > **SHOVE**

Jot(ter), Jotting(s) Ace, Fig, Iota, Memo, Mite, Note, Pad, Stime, Styme, Tittle, Whit

Journal Daily, Daybook, Diary, Ephemeris, Gazette, Hansard, Lancet, Log, Noctuary, Organ, Paper, Periodical, Pictorial, Punch, Rag, Record, TES, TLS, Trade, Weblog

Journalism, Journalist Cheque-book, Columnist, Commentariat, Contributor, Diarist, Diurnalist, Ed, Fleet St, Freelance, (GA) Sala, Gonzo, Hack, Hackery, Hackette, Hatchetman, Inkslinger, Investigative, Keyhole, Lobby, Muckraker, Newshound, Northcliffe, NUJ, Pepys, Press(man), Reporter, Reviewer, Scribe, Sob sister, Stead, Stringer, Wireman, > **WRITER**, Yellow

Journey Circuit, Cruise, Errand, Expedition, Eyre, Foray, Grand Tour, Hadj, Hop,

Jaunce, Jaunse, Jaunt, Mush, Odyssey, Passage, Periegesis, Ply, Raik, Rake, Red-eye, Ride, Run, Sentimental, Tour, Travel, Trek, Viatical, Walkabout

Journeyman Artisan, Commuter, Craftsman, Sterne, Yeoman

Joust Giust, Tilt, Tournament, Tourney

Jove Egad, Gad, Igad, Jupiter, Thunderer

Jovial Bacchic, Festive, Genial, Jolly

Jowl Cheek, Chops, Jaw

Joy(ful), Joyous Bliss, Blithe, > **DELIGHT**, Dream, Ecstasy, Elation, Exulting, Fain, Felicity, Festal, Frabjous, Glad, Glee, Gloat, Hah, Hey, Jubilant, Nirvana, Rapture, Schadenfreude, Sele, Tra-la, Transport, Treat, Yippee

Joyce Haw Haw, Traitor

JP Beak, Quorum

Jubilant, Jubilation, Jubilee Celebration, Cock-a-hoop, Diamond, Ecstatic, Elated, Exultant, Holiday, Joy, Triumphant

Judaism Semitism

Judas Double-crosser, Iscariot, Traitor, Tree

Judder Put-put, Shake, Vibrate

Jude Obscure

Judge(ment), Judges Addoom, Adjudicator, Agonothetes, Alacus, Alcalde, Arbiter, Areopagite, Aret(t), Arrêt, Assess, Assize, Auto-da-fé, Avizandum, Banc, Brehon, Cadi, Calculate, Censure, Centumvirus, Circuit(eer), Common Serjeant, Comparative, Connoisseur, Consider, Coroner, Court, Critic(ise), Daniel, Daysman, Deborah, Decern(e), Decide, Decision, Decreet, Deem(ster), Dempster, Dicast, Differential, Dikast, Discern(ment), District, Ephor, Ermined, Estimate, Evaluate, Gauge, Gesse, Gideon, Good-sense, Guess, Hakeem, Hakim, Hearing, Hold, Honour, Inky-smudge, Interlocutor, J, Jeffreys, Jephthah, Justice, Justicier, Last, Lud, Lynch, Minos, Mufti, Non prosequitur, Nonsuit, Official Referee, Old Fury, Opine, Opinion, Ordinary, Outfangthief, Panel, Paris, Podesta, Providence, Puisne, Puny, Reckon(ing), Recorder, Ref(eree), Regard, Rhadamanthus, Ruler, Samson, Samuel, Sapience, Scan, See, Sentence, Sentiment, Shallow, Sheriff, Sober, Solomon, Sound, Suppose, Surrogate, Syndic, Tact, Think, Touch, Trior, Try, Umpire, Value, Verdict, Weigh up, Wig, Wik, Wisdom, Worship

Judicious Critical, Discreet, Politic, Rational, Sage, Sensible, Shrewd, Sound

Judo, Judo costume Dojo, Gi(e), Shiai

Jug(s) Amphora, Bellarmine, Bird, Blackjack, Bombard, Breasts, Can, Cooler, Cream(er), Crock, Enghalskrug, Ewer, Gaol, Gotch, Greybeard, Growler, John Roberts, Malling, Measuring, Olpe, Pitcher, Pound, Pourer, Pourie, > **PRISON**, Quad, Quod, Shop, Stir, Tits, Toby, Urceolus

Juggle(r) Conjuror, Cook, Escamotage, Fake

Juice, Juicy Bacca, Cassareep, Cassaripe, Cremor, Current, Fluid, Fruity, Gastric, Hypocist, Ichor, Jungle, La(b)danum, Laser, Latex, Lush, Moist, Must, Oil, Pancreatic, Perry, Rare, Sap, Soma, Spanish, Succ(o)us, Succulent, Tarantula, Thridace, Vril, Walnut, Zest

Juju Charm, Fetish

Jujube Lotus, Padma, Sweet

Jukebox Nickelodeon

Julian Apostate

July Dogdays

Jumble Chaos, Conglomeration, Farrago, Garble, Huddle, Jabble, Lumber, Mass, Medley, Mingle-mangle, Mish-mash, Mixter-maxter, Mixtie-maxtie, Mixture, Mix(t)y-max(t)y, Pastiche, Printer's pie, Raffle, Ragbag, Scramble, Shuffle,

Wuzzle

▷ **Jumbled** *may indicate* an anagram

Jumbo Aircraft, Elephant, Jet, Large-scale, Mammoth, OS

Jump(er), Jumping, Jumpy Aran, Assemble, Axel, Bate, Batterie, Boomer, Bound, Bungee, Bungy, Caper, Capriole, Cicada, Cicata, Crew-neck, Cricket, Croupade, Daffy, Desultory, Entrechat, Euro, Eventer, Flea, Fosbury flop, Gansey, Gazump, Gelande (sprung), Guernsey, Halma, Helicopter, Hurdle, Impala, Itchy, Jersey, Joey, Kangaroo, Katydid, Knight, Lammie, Lammy, Leap(frog), Lep, Lope, Lutz, Nervous, Nervy, Ollie, Parachute, Pig, Pogo, Polo-neck, Pounce, Prance, Prank, Pronking, Puissance, Quantum, Quersprung, Rap, Salchow, Saltatory, Saltigrade, Saltus, Scissors, Scoup, Scowp, Skip, Skipjack, Skydiver, > **SPRING**, Start, Sweater, Toe (-loop), Trampoline, Triple, Turtle-neck, Vau(l)t, Water, Western roll

Jumping jack Pantine

Junction Abutment, Alloyed, Angle, Box, Bregma, Carfax, Close, Clover-leaf, Connection, Crewe, Crossroads, Diffused, Gap, Intersection, Joint, Josephson, Knitting, Meeting, P-n, Point, Raphe, Spaghetti, Suture, T, Tight, Union

Juneberry Saskatoon, Shadbush

Jungle Asphalt, Blackboard, Boondocks, Bush, Concrete, Forest, Shola, Tangle

Junior Cadet, Chota, Cion, Dogsbody, Fils, Minor, Name-son, Petty, Puisne, Scion, Sub(ordinate), Underling, Understrapper, Younger

Juniper Red-cedar, Savin(e)

Junk(shop) Bric-a-brac, Chuck in, Jettison, Litter, Lorcha, Lumber, Refuse, Ship, Tagareen, Tatt, Trash

▷ **Junk** *may indicate* an anagram

Junker Prussian

Junket(ing) Beano, Creel, Custard, Feast, Picnic, Rennet, Spree

Junta Cabal, Council

Jupiter Jove, Newspaper

Jurassic Lias, Rhaetic

Jurisdiction Authority, Bailiwick, Domain, Province, Soke(n)

Juror(s), Jury Assize, Dicast, Grand, Hung, Inquest, Judges, Mickleton, Old Fury, Pais, Panel, Party, Petit, Petty, Sail, Special, Tales, Tribunal, Venire, Venireman, Venue

Just(ice) Alcalde, All, Aristides, Astraea, Balanced, Condign, Cupar, Deserved, Equal, Equity, E(v)en, Fair, Fair-minded, Forensic, Honest, Impartial, J, Jasper, Jeddart, Jethart, Jurat, Mere, Natural, Nemesis, Newly, Nice, Only, Palm-tree, Piso, Poetic, Provost, Puisne, Pure and simple, Recent, Restorative, Right(ful), Righteous, Rightness, Rough, Shallow, Silence, Simply, Sommer, Street, Themis, Tilt, Upright

Justifiable, Justification, Justify Apology, Autotelic, Avenge, Aver, Avowry, Clear, Darraign(e), Darrain(e), Darrayn, Defend, Deraign, Excusable, Explain, Grounds, Rationale, Vindicate, Warrant

Just so Exactly, Sic, Stories

Jut Beetle, Bulge, Overhang, Project, Protrude, Sail

Jute Burlap, Corchorus, Gunny, Hengist, Hessian, Horsa, Urena

Juvenile Childish, Teenage(r), Yonkers, Young, Younkers

Juxtaposition Parataxis

K Kelvin, Kilo, King, Kirkpatrick
K2 Dapsang, Godwin Austen
Kaffir Shares, Xosa
Kail, **Kale** Borecole, Cabbage, Cole, Curly-greens, Ninepins
Kaiser Doorn
Kaleidoscope Dappled, Motley, Myrioscope, Various
Kangaroo Bettong, Boomer, Boongary, Bounder, Brush, Cus-cus, Diprotodont, Euro, Forester, Joey, Macropodidae, Nototherium, Old man, Potoroo, Rat, Red, Steamer, Tree, Troop, Wallaby, Wallaroo
Kansas Sunflower
Kaolin Lithomarge
Karate Kung Fu, Wushu
Karma Destiny, Fate, Predestination
Kate Greenaway, Shrew
Kayak Bidarka
Kebab Cevapcici, Doner, Gyro, Satay, Sate, Shashli(c)k, Sosatie, Souvlakia
Keel Bilge, Bottom, Carina, Centreboard, Faint, False, Fin, List, Overturn, Skeg(g), Sliding
Keen(ness), **Keener** Acid, Acute, Agog, Argute, Aspiring, Astute, Athirst, Avid, Aygre, Bemoan, Bewail, Breem, Breme, Cheap, Coronach, Dash, Devotee, Dirge, Eager, Elegy, Enthusiastic, Fanatical, Fell, Greet, Grieve, Hone, Hot, Howl, Into, Lament, Mourn, Mustard, Mute, Narrow, Ochone, Ohone, Partial, Peachy, Perceant, Persant, Raring, Razor, Ready, Red-hot, Rhapsodic, Sharp, Shrewd, Shrill, Snell, Thirsting, Threnodic, Thrillant, Trenchant, Ululate, Wail, Whet, Zeal(ous)
Keep(er), **Keeping** Ames, Armature, Austringer, Castellan, Castle, Celebrate, Chatelain(e), Citadel, Conceal, Conserve, Curator, Custodian, Custody, Depositary, Depository, Detain, Donjon, Escot, Finder, Fort, Gaoler, Goalie, Guardian, Have, Hoard, > **HOLD**, Maintain, Nab, Net, Observe, Ostreger, Park, Pickle, Preserve, Retain, Safeguard, Stay, Stet, Stock, Store, Stow, Stumper, Support, Sustain, Tower, Warden, Withhold
Keep back Detain, Recoup, Reserve, Retard, Stave
Keepsake Memento, Souvenir, Token
Keep under Cow, Subdue, Submerge
Keg Barrel, Cask, Powder, Tub, Tun, Vat
Kelly('s) Eye, Gene, Ned
Kelvin Absolute, K
Ken Eyeshot, Know(ledge), Purview, Range
Kennel(s) Guard, Home, House, Shelter
Kent Lathe, SE, Superman
Kentuckian, **Kentucky** Chicken, Corn-cracker, Derby, KY
Kenya(n) Masai, Mau Mau
Kerala Nair, Nayar

Kerb Edge, Gutter, Roadside
Kerchief Babushka, Bandan(n)a, Headcloth, Romal, Scarf
Kernel Copra, Core, Corn, Grain, Nucleus, Pine, Praline, Prawlin
Kestrel Bird, Hawk, Keelie, Stallion, Staniel, Stannel, Stanyel, Windhover
Ket Carrion, Wool
Ketch Jack
Ketchup Relish, Sauce, Tomato
Kettle Boiler, Cauldron, Dixie, Dixy, Drum, Fanny, Pot, Tea, Turpin, War, Whistling
Key(s), Keyhole A, Ait, Allen, Alt, Ash, B, Basic, C, Cay, Central, Chip, Church, Cipher, Clavis, Clew, Clink, Clue, Control, Crib, D, Dichotomous, Digital, Dital, Dominant, E, Enter, Esc(ape), Essential, F, Flat, Florida, Fruit, Function, G, Greek, High, Holm, Hot, Ignition, Important, Inch, Index, INS, Instrumental, Islet, Ivory, Kaie, King-pin, Latch, Legend, Linchpin, Locker, Low, Main, Major, Master, Minor, Note, Nut, Octachord, Opener, Oustiti, Outsiders, Pass(word), Passe-partout, Piano, Pipe, Pivot, Pony, Prong, Reef, Return, Semibreve, Shift, Signature, Skeleton, Spanner, Spline, Stimulate, Supertonic, Tab, Table, Tipsy, Tonal, Turning, Vital, Watch, Water, Wedge, Woodruff, Yale®
Keyboard, Keypad Azerty, Console, Digitorium, DVORAK, Electronic, Manual, Martenot, Numeric, Piano, Pianola®, Qwerty, Spinet
Keyholder Occupant, Resident, Tenant, Warder
Key man Islander, Kingpin
Keynote Line, Mese, Theme, Tonic
Keystone Cops, Crux, PA, Pennsylvania, Quoin, Sagitta, Voussoir
Keyword Kwic, Sesame
Khan Aga, Chagan, Cham, Serai, Shere
Kick(ing) Back-heel, Bicycle, Boot, Buzz, Corner, Dribble, Drop, Fling, Flutter, Fly, Free, Frog, Garryowen, Goal, Grub, Hack, Hitch, Hoof, Lash, Nutmeg, Pause, Penalty, Pile, Punce, Punt, Recalcitrate, Recoil, Recoyle, Savate, Scissors, Sixpence, Speculator, Spot, Spur, Spurn, Squib, Stab, Tanner, Tap, Thrill, Toe, Up and under, Vigour, Volley, Wince, Yerk, Zip
Kid(s) Arab, Befool, Billy, Brood, Cheverel, Chevrette, Child, Chit, Cisco, Con, Delude, Goat, Hircosity, Hoax, Hocus, Hoodwink, Hum, Joke, Leather, Misguide, Nipper, Offspring, Outwit, Pretend, Rag, Rib, Spoof, Suede, Sundance, > TEASE, Tot, Trick, Whiz(z), Wiz
Kidnap Abduct, Hijack, Plagium, Shanghai, Snatch, Spirit, Steal
Kidney(-shaped) Character, Mettle, Nature, Reins, Renal, Reniform, Sort
Kill(ed), Killer, Killing Assassin, Attrit, Battue, Behead, Biocidal, Boojum, Butcher, Carnage, Carnifex, Category, Chance-medley, Choke, Comical, Croak, Crucify, Cull, Despatch, Destroy, Electrocute, Euthanasia, Execute, Exterminate, Extirpate, For(e)do, Frag, Garotte, Germicide, Gun, Handsel, Hatchet man, Hilarious, Homicide, Ice, Immolate, K, Knacker, Knock off, Liquidate, Lynch, Mactation, Matador(e), Mercy, Misadventure, Mortify, Murder, Napoo, Necklace, Ninja, NK, Off, Orc(a), Penalty, Pesticide, -phage, Pick off, Pip, Predator, Prolicide, Quell, Quietus, Regrate, Sacrifice, Serial, Settle, Shochet, Slaughter, Slay(er), Slew, Smite, Snuff, Spike, Stifle, Stonker, Strangle, Swat, Tailor, Thagi, Thug(gee), Top, Toreador, Total, Vaticide, Veto, Waste, Zap
Killjoy Crab, Puritan, Sourpuss, Spoilsport, Wowser
Kiln Oast, Oven
Kilometre Km, Verst
Kilt Drape, Filabeg, Fil(l)ibeg, Fustanella, Phil(l)abeg, Phil(l)ibeg, Plaid, Tartan

Kimono Yukata

Kin(sman) Ally, Family, Kith, Like, Nearest, Relation, Sib(b), Sybbe

Kind(ly) Akin, Amiable, Avuncular, Benefic, Benevolent, Benign, Boon, Breed, Brood, Brotherly, Category, Class, Clement, Considerate, Favourable, Gender, Generic, Generous, Genre, Gentle, Genus, Good, Humane, Ilk, Kidney, Kin, Lenient, Manner, Modal, Nature, Nice, Sisterly, > SORT, Species, Strain, Strene, Trine, Type, Understanding, Variety, Well-disposed, Ylke

Kindle, Kindling Accend, Fire, Ignite, Incense, Incite, Inflame, > LIGHT, Litter, Lunt, Stimulate, Teend, Tind, Tine, Touchwood, Tynd(e)

Kindness Aloha, Benevolence, Clemency, Favour, Humanity

Kindred Allied, Blood, Like, Related

King(s), Kingly Coatcard, Cobra, Elvis, English, ER, Evil, Highness, Kong, Majesty, Monarch, Pearly, Penguin, Potentate, R, Ransom, Reigner, Rex, Rial, Roi, Royalet, Ruler, Ryal, Seven, Shilling, Sovereign, Stork

● **KINGS**

2 letters:	5 letters:	Amasis	7 letters:
GR	Apple	Arthur	Acestes
Og	Ard-ri	Atreus	Admetus
Re	Balak	Attila	Ard-righ
	Brute	Baliol	Athamas
3 letters:	Creon	Brutus	Baldwin
Asa	Cyrus	Canute	Balliol
Erl	David	Cheops	Beowulf
Ine	Edgar	Clovis	Busiris
Lir	Edwin	Darius	Butcher
Log	Etzel	Duncan	Caradoc
Lud	Gyges	Edmund	Cecrops
Zog	Herod	Egbert	Cepheus
	Hiram	Farouk	Croesus
4 letters:	Idris	Fergus	Danaiis
Agag	Ixion	Harold	Diomede
Agis	James	Hellen	Elidure
Ahab	Laius	Hyksos	Evander
Brut	Lludd	Josiah	Gunther
Ceyx	Louis	Lucomo	Kenneth
Cnut	Midas	Ludwig	Macbeth
Cole	Minos	Lycaon	Malcolm
Edwy	Mpret	Memnon	Oedipus
Fahd	Negus	Nestor	Peishwa
Inca	Ninus	Oberon	Pharaoh
Jehu	Penda	Ogyges	Porsena
Knut	Priam	Paphos	Ptolemy
Lear	Rufus	Peleus	Pyrrhus
Nudd	Uther	Peshwa	Rameses
Numa		Philip	Servius
Offa	6 letters:	Ramses	Sigmund
Olaf	Aegeus	Rhesus	Solomon
Otto	Alaric	Sailor	Stephen
Saul	Alfred	Xerxes	Tarquin
Shah	Alonso		Telamon

Umberto
Porsenna
Florestan
Erechtheus

Rehoboam
Frederick
Ozymandias

8 letters:
Sarpedon
Gambrinus
Wenceslaus

Adrastus
Sisyphus
Gargantua

Aegyptus
Tantalus
Gilgamesh
11 letters:

Alberich
Thutmose
Idomeneus
Charlemagne

Cambyses
Thyestes
Lionheart
Hardicanute

Cophetua
Tigranes
Nabonidus
Jehoshaphat

Diomedes
Zedekiah
Pygmalion
Melchizedek

Endymion
Ras Tafari
Sennacherib

Ethelred
9 letters:
Rodomonte
Tutenkhamen

Hezekiah
Agamemnon
Sigismund

Jereboam
Ahasuerus
Tarquinus
12 letters:

Jonathan
Alexander
Tyndareus
Wayland Smith

Leonidas
Athelstan
Vortigern

Menander
Bretwalda
Wenceslas
14 letters:

Menelaus
Brian Boru
Nebuchadnezzar

Milesian
Conchobar
10 letters:
Sweyn Forkbeard

Odysseus
Cunobelin
Belshazzar
Uther Pendragon

Peishwah
Cymbeline
Cadwaladar

Pentheus
Ethelbert
Caractacus

Kingdom, Kingship Animal, Aragon, Barataria, Bhutan, Bohemia, Brunel, Castile, Cilicia, Connacht, Connaught, Dalriada, Dominion, Edom, Elam, Fes, Fez, Fife, Granada, Heptarchy, Jordan, Leon, Lesotho, Lydia, Mercia, Meroe, Middle, Mineral, Moab, Morocco, Navarre, Nepal, Netherlands, Neustria, Noricum, Northumbria, Norway, Parthia, Plant, Pontic, Realm, Reame, Reign, Royalty, Ruritania, Saba, Samaria, Saudi Arabia, Sennar, Sheba, Spain, Sphere, Swaziland, Sweden, Thailand, Throne, Tonga, Two Sicilies, Vegetable, Wessex, World

Kingfisher Alcyone, Halcyon

Kingmaker Neville, Warwick

King-of-arms Clarenc(i)eux, Garter, Lyon, Norroy (and Ulster)

King's evil Crewels, Cruels, Scrofula

Kingsley Amis, Charles

King's son Dauphin, Delphin, P, Prince

Kink(y) Bent, Buckle, Crapy, Curl, Enmeshed, Flaw, Gasp, Knurl, Null, Nurl, Odd, Perm, Perverted, Quirk, Twist, Wavy

▷ **Kink(y)** *may indicate* an anagram

Kinkajou Honey-bear, Potto

Kip(per) Cure, Dosser, Doze, Limey, Nap, > SLEEPER, Smoke

Kipling Beetle

Kirkpatrick K

Kismet Destiny, Fate, Karma, Predestination

Kiss(er), Kissing Buss, Butterfly, Caress, Contrecoup, Cross, Deep, French, Lip, Mouth, Neck, Osculate, Pax(-board), Pax-brede, Peck, Pet, Plonker, Pree, Salue, Salute, Smack(er), Smooch, Smouch, Snog, Spoon, Thimble, X, Yap

Kit Accoutrement, Christopher, Clobber, Clothes, Housewife, Layette, Marlowe, Mess, > OUTFIT, Rig, Set, Slops, Sportswear, Tackle, Uniform

Kitchen Caboose, Cookhouse, Cuisine, Galley, Scullery, Soup, Thieves

Kite Belly, Bird, Box, Chil, Crate, Dragon, Elanet, Forktail, Gled(e), Hawk, Milvus, Paunch, Puttock, Rokkaku

Kitten(ish) Cute, Kindle, Sexy
Kittiwake Bird, Gull, Hacklet, Haglet
Kitty Ante, Cat, Fisher, Float, Fund, Jackpot, Pool, Pot, Tronc
Kiwi Apteryx, Chinese gooseberry, NZ, Ratitae
Klu-Klux-Klan Nightrider
Knack Art, Flair, Forte, Gift, Hang, Instinct, > TALENT, Technique, Trick
Knacker Castanet, Exhaust
Knapsack Musette
Knapweed Matfelon
Knave(ry) Bezonian, Bower, Boy, Card, Coatcard, Coistril, Coystril, Custrel, Dog, Drôle, Fripon, Jack(-a-napes), Jock, Loon, Makar, Maker, Nob, Noddy, Pam, Pur, Rapscallion, > RASCAL, Recreant, Ropery, Scoundrel, Taroc, Tarot, Tom, Treachery, Varlet, Villain
Knead Conch, Malax(ate), Massage, Mould, Pug, Pummel, Work
Knee(s), Knee-cap, Knee-pan Genicular, Genu, Hock, Housemaid's, Lap, Marrowbones, Patella, Poleyn, Popliteal, Punch, Rotula, Whirl bone
Kneel(er) Defer, Genuflect, Hassock, Kowtow, Prie-dieu, Truckle
Knell Bell, Curfew, Dirge, Peal, Ring, Toll
Knicker(bocker), Knickers Bloomers, Culottes, Directoire, Irving, Panties, Plus-fours, Shorts, Trousers
Knick-knack Bagatelle, Bibelot, Bric-a-brac, Gewgaw, Pretty(-pretty), Quip, Smytrie, Toy, Trangam, Trifle, Victoriana
Knife Anelace, Barlow, Barong, Bistoury, Blade, Boline, Bolo, Bolster, Bowie, Carver, Carving, Case, Catling, Chakra, Clasp, Cleaver, Couteau, Cradle, Cuttle, Cutto(e), Da(h), Dagger, Fleam, Flick, Fruit, Gull(e)y, Hay, Hunting, Jockteleg, Kard, Keratome, Kukri, Lance(t), Machete, Matchet, Moon, Oyster, Palette, Pallet, Panga, Paper, Parang, Pen, Pigsticker, Pocket, Putty, Scalpel, Scalping, Sgian-dubh, Sheath, Shiv, Simi, Skean-dhu, Slash, Snee, Snickersnee, Spade, Stab, Stanley, Steak, Sticker, Switchblade, Table, Tranchet, Trench
Knight Accolon, Aguecheek, Alphagus, Amfortas, Artegal, Balan, Banneret, Bayard, Bedivere, Black, Bliant, Bors, Britomart, Caballero, Calidore, Cambel, Caradoc, Carpet, Cavalier, Chevalier, Companion, Crusader, Douceper, Douzeper, Dub, Equites, Errant, Galahad, Gallant, Gareth, Garter, Gawain, Geraint, Grey, Guyon, Hospitaller, Kay, KB, KBE, Kemper, KG, La(u)ncelot, Launfal, Lionel, Lochinvar, Lohengrin, Maecenas, Malta, Medjidie, Melius, Modred, Mordred, N, Noble, Orlando, Paladin, Palmerin, Parsifal, Perceforest, Perceval, Percival, Pharamond, Pinel, Precaptory, Preux chevalier, Ritter, Round Table, St Columba, Samurai, Sir, Tannhauser, Templar, Teutonic, Trencher, Tristan, Tristram, Valvassor, Vavasour, White
Knit(ting), Knitwear Aran, Contract, Crochet, Double, Entwine, Fair Isle, Hosiery, Interlock, K, Mesh, Porosis, Purl, Seam, Set, Stockinet, Weave, Wrinkle
Knob(by) Berry, Boll, Boss, Botoné, Bottony, Bouton, Bur(r), Cam, Caput, Cascabel, Croche, Gear, Handle, Hill, Inion, Knub, Knur(r), Node, Noop, Pellet, Pommel, Protuberance, Pulvinar, Push-button, Snib, Snub, Snuff, Stud, Torose, Tuber, Tuner
Knobless Enodal
Knock(er), Knock down, off, out Bang, Beaut, Biff, Blow, Bonk, Bump, Ca(a), Chap, Clash, Clour, Collide, Con, Criticise, Daud, Dawd, Degrade, Denigrate, Deride, Dev(v)el, Ding, Dinnyhauser, Etherise, Eyeful, Floor, Grace-stroke, > HIT, Innings, KO, Lowse, Lowsit, Mickey Finn, Opportunity, Pan, Pink, Quietus, Rap, Rat-tat, Six, Skittle, Spat, Steal, Stop, Strike, Stun(ner), Tap, Technical, Thump, Tonk, Wow

Knock-kneed Valgus
Knot(ted), Knotty Apollo, Baff, Bend, Blackwall hitch, Bow, Bowline, Bur(r), Burl, Carrick-bend, Cat's paw, Clinch, Clove hitch, Cluster, Crochet, Diamond hitch, Englishman's, Entangle, Figure of eight, Fisherman's (bend), Flat, French, Gnar, > **GNARL**, Gordian, Granny, Half-hitch, Harness hitch, Hawser-bend, Herculean, Hitch, Interlace, Knag, Knap, Knar, Knur(r), Loop, Love(r's), Macramé, Macrami, Magnus hitch, Marriage-favour, Matthew Walker, Mouse, Nirl, Node, Nowed, Nub, Nur(r), Overhand, Picot, Porter's, Problem, Prusik, Quipu, Reef, Rolling hitch, Rosette, Running, Seizing, Sheepshank, Sheetbend, Shoulder, Shroud, Sleave, Slip, Slub, Spurr(e)y, Square, Stevedore's, Surgeon's, Sword, Tangle, Tat, Thumb, Tie, Timberhitch, Torose, Truelove, Tubercle, Turk's head, Virgin, Wale, Wall, Weaver's (hitch), Windsor, Witch
Know(how), Knowing(ly), Knowledge(able), Known Acquaintance, Autodidactic, Aware, Carnal, Cognition, Common, Compleat, Comprehend, Cred, Epistemics, Erudite, Expertise, Famous, Fly, Gnosis, Gnostic, Have, Hep, Hip, Info, Information, Insight, Intentional, Intuition, Jnana, Ken, Kith, Kydst, Lare, Light, Lore, Mindful, Omniscience, On, On to, Pansophy, Paragnosis, Party, Polymath, Positivism, Privity, Recherché, > **RECOGNISE**, Sapient, Savvy, Science, Scienter, Scilicet, Sciolism, Shrewd, Smattering, Understand(ing), Up, Versed, Wat(e), Weet(e), Well-informed, Well-read, Wise, Wist, Wit, Wot
Know-all Arrogant, Besserwisser, Bumptious, Cognoscenti, Pansophist, Polymath, Poseur, Smart alec(k), Smart-arse, Smart-ass, Wiseacre
Knuckle (bone) Apply, Dolos, Fist, Joint, Ossein, Submit
Koko List
Kookaburra Laughing jackass, Settler's clock
Kop Spion
Koran Scripture, Sura(h)
Korea(n) Chosen, ROK
Kosher Approved, Genuine, Legitimate, Real
Kremlin Fortress
Kri Masora
Krypton Kr
Kudos Credit, Glory, Praise
Kurd Yezidi
Kyanite Disthene

L1

L Latitude, League, Learner, Left, Length, Liberal, Lima, Litre, Long, Luxembourg, Pound

La Indeed, My

Label Badge, Band, Book-plate, Brand, Crowner, Designer, Docket, File, Identifier, Mark, Own, Seal, Sticker, Style, Tab, Tag, Tally, Ticket, Trace

Labiate Catmint, Hoarhound, Horehound

Laboratory Lab, Language, Skylab, Space-lab, Studio, Workshop

Labour(er), Laboured, Laborious Aesthetic, Arduous, Begar, Birth, Carl, Casual, Chirl, Chore, Coolie, Corvée, Cottager, Cottar, Culchie, Dataller, Day, Direct, Docker, Dwell, Forced, Gandy-dancer, Ganger, Gibeonite, Grecian, Grind, Hard, Hercules, Hodge, Hodman, Ida, Indirect, Job, Journeyman, Kanaka, Katorga, Leaden, Manpower, Militant tendency, Moil, Navvy, Okie, Operose, Opposition, Pain, Peon, Pioneer, Prole, Redneck, Roll, Rouseabout, Roustabout, Rouster, Sisyphean, Slave, Spalpeen, Statute, Stint, Strive, Sudra, Swagman, Sweated, Task, The grip, The lump, > TOIL(S), Toss, Travail, Uphill, Vineyard, > WORK(ER), Workmen, Yakka

Labrador Innu, Retriever, Tea

Labyrinth Daedalus, Maze, Mizmaze, Warren, Web

▷ **Labyrinthine** *may indicate* an anagram

Lac Lacquer, Lakh, Resin, Shellac, Tomans

Lace, Lacy Alençon, Babiche, Beat, Blonde, Bobbin, Bone, Bourdon, Brussels, Chantilly, Cluny, Colbertine, Dash, Dentelle, Duchesse, Filet, Galloon, Guipure, Honiton, Inweave, Irish, Jabot, Lash, Macramé, Malines, Mechlin, Mignonette, Mode, Net, Orris, Pearlin, Picot, Pillow, Point, Reseau, Reticella, Ricrac, Rosaline, Seaming, Shoestring, Shoe-tie, Spike, Stay, Tat(ting), Tawdry, Thrash, Thread, Torchon, Trim, Trol(le)y, Valenciennes, Venise, Weave, Welt, Window-bar

Lacerate(d) Ganch, Gash, Gaunch, Maul, Rent, Rip, Slash, Tear

Lachrymose Maudlin, Niobe, Tearful, Water-standing, > WEEPY

Lack(ing), Lacks Absence, Aplasia, Bereft, Dearth, Famine, Ha'n't, Insufficiency, Manqué, Minus, > NEED, Poverty, Privation, Remiss, Sans, Shortfall, Shy, Void, Want

Lackadaisical Languid, Listless, Torpid

Lackaday Haro

Lackey Boots, Flunkey, Moth, Page, Poodle, Satellite, Skip-kennel

Lacklustre Dull, Insipid, Matt

Lack of confidence Doubt, Scepsis

Laconic Blunt, Close-mouthed, Curt, Spartan, Succinct, Terse

Lacquer Coromandel, Enamel, Hair(spray), Japan, Shellac, > VARNISH

Lad Boy(o), Bucko, Callan(t), Chiel(d), Child, Geit, Gyte, Knight, Loonie, Master, Nipper, Shaver, Stableman, Stripling, Tad, Whipper-snapper

Ladder(y) Accommodation, Aerial, Bucket, Companion, Companionway, Etrier, Fish, Jack, Jacob's, Pompier, Potence, Rope, Run, Salmon, Scalado, Scalar,

Scaling, Sea, Squash, Stie, Sty, Trap, Turntable
Ladle Bail, Dipper, Punch, Scoop, Shank
Lady Baroness, Bevy, Bountiful, Burd, Dame, Dark, Dinner, Don(n)a, Duenna, Female, First, Frau, Frow, Gemma, Godiva, Hen, Khanum, Luck, Maam, Madam(e), Memsahib, Muck, Nicotine, Peeress, Senora, Shopping bag, Signora, Tea, White, Windermere
▷ **Lady** *may indicate* an '-ess' ending
Ladybird Cushcow, Hen, Vedalia
▷ **Ladybird** *may indicate* a female of a bird family
Ladykiller Bluebeard, Lothario, Masher, Wolf
Lady of the lake Vivian
Lady's Fingers Gumbo, Okra
Lady's maid Abigail
Lag(gard) Culture, Dawdle, Delay, Drag, Flag, Hysteresis, Inmate, Jailbird, Jet, Leng, > **LINGER**, Loiter, Prisoner, Retard, Slowcoach, Slowpoke, Time, Tortoise, Trail
Lager Pils(e)ner
Lagoon Barachois, Haff, Pontchartrain, Pool, Salina, Saline
▷ **Laic, Laid** *see* **LAY**
Lair Couch, Den, Earth, Haunt, Hideaway, Kennel, Lodge, Warren
Lake(s) Alkali, Basin, Bayou, Carmine, Cirque, Cowal, Crater, Crimson, Cut off, Finger, L, Lacustrine, Lagoon, Lagune, > **LOCH**, Lochan, Lough, Madder, Mead, Mere, Nyanza, Ox-bow, Poets, Pool, Red, Reservoir, Salina, Salt, Shott, Soda, Tarn, Turlough, Vlei, Wine

LAKES

2 letters:	Chott	Taupo	Nyassa
No	Cowan	Tsana	Oneida
	Frome	Urmia	Peipus
3 letters:	Garda		Poyang
Ewe	Gatun	**6 letters:**	Rudolf
Van	Great	Albert	Saimaa
	Huron	Argyle	Te Anau
4 letters:	Ilmen	Averno	Tekapo
Amin	Leman	Baikal	Vanern
Bala	Leven	Barlee	Zurich
Biel	Lower	Bitter	
Bled	Malar	Broads	**7 letters:**
Chad	Morar	Cayuga	Amadeus
Como	Mungo	Corrib	Aral Sea
Erie	Mweru	Edward	Avernus
Erne	Myall	Geneva	Axolotl
Eyre	Nam Co	Kariba	Balaton
Kivu	Neagh	Kittle	Bizerte
Nyos	Nyasa	Ladoga	Iliamna
Pink	Onega	Lugano	Katrine
Tana	Playa	Malawi	Koko Nor
Thun	Poopo	Miveru	Lucerne
	Pskov	Mobutu	Manapua
5 letters:	Sevan	Nakura	Nipigon
Atlin	Tahoe	Nam Tso	Ontario

Rotonia
Sempach
Toronto
Torrens
Turkana
Vattern

8 letters:
Balkhash
Bodensee
Carnegie
Dongting
Gairdner
Grasmere
Kinneret
Maggiore
Manitoba
Masurian
Menindee
Michigan
Naumachy
Okanagan
Onondaga
Regillus

Reindeer
Superior
Tiberias
Titicaca
Tonle Sap
Tungting
Veronica
Victoria
Wakatipu
Wanawaka
Winnipeg

9 letters:
Athabasca
Bangweulu
Champlain
Constance
Ennerdale
Everglade
Genfersee
Great Bear
Great Salt
Innisfree
Killarney

Macquarie
Manapouri
Maracaibo
Naumachia
Nipissing
Serbonian
Thirlmere
Trasimene
Trasimono
Ullswater
Wairarapa
Wastwater
Winnebago
Ysselmeer

10 letters:
Buttermere
Clearwater
Great Slave
Hawes Water
Ijsselmeer
Miraflores
Mistassini
Okeechobee

Okefenokee
Saint Clair
Serpentine
Tanganyika
Windermere

11 letters:
Lesser Slave
Paralimnion
Stanley Pool

12 letters:
Derwentwater
Memphremagog
Waikaremoana
Winnipegosis

13 letters:
Coniston Water
Crummock Water

14 letters:
Disappointment
Ennerdale Water

Lake-dwelling Crannog
Lakeland Cumbria
Lam Flee, Scram
Lama Dalai, Karmapa, Panchen
Lamb(skin) Baa, Barometz, Budge, Bummer, Cade, Canterbury, Caracul, Cosset, Ean(ling), Elia, Fat, Grit, Innocent, Keb, Larry, Noisette, Paschal, Persian, Rack, Shearling, Target, Yean(ling)
Lambent Flickering, Glowing, Licking
Lambert Constant
Lame(ness) Accloy, Claude, Cripple, Crock, Game, Gammy, Gimp(y), Halt, Hamstring, Hirple, Hors de combat, Maim, Main, Spavined, Springhalt, Stringhalt, Weak
Lament(able), Lamentation, Lamenter Bemoan, Bewail, Beweep, Complain, Croon, Cry, Dirge, Dumka, Dump, Elegy, Funest, Jeremiad, Jeremiah, Keen, Meane, Mein, Mene, Moon, Mourn, Ochone, Paltry, Piteous, Plain, Repine, Sigh, Sorry, Threne, Threnody, Ululate, > WAIL, Welladay, Wel(l)away, Yammer
Lamia Deadnettle
Lamina(te) Film, Flake, Folium, Formica®, Lamella, Layer, Plate, Scale, Table
Lamp(s) Aldis, Anglepoise, Arc, Argand, Bowat, Bowet, Buat, Cru(i)sie, Cru(i)zie, Crusy, Davy, Eye, Eyne, Flame, Fluorescent, Fog, Geordie, Glow, Head, Hurricane, Incandescent, Induction, Kudlik, Lampion, Lantern, Lava, Lucigen, Mercury vapour, Miner's, Moderator, Neon, Nernst, Nightlight, Padella, Photoflood, Pilot, Platinum, Quartz, Reading, Riding, Safety, Sanctuary, Scamper, Searchlight, Signal, Sodium, Sodium-vapour, Spirit, Standard, Street, Stride, Stroboscope, Sun, Tail, Tantalum, Tiffany, Tilley, Torchier(e), Tungsten, Uplight(er), Veilleuse, Xenon
Lamplighter Leerie, Spill

Lampoon Caricature, Parody, Pasquil, Pasquin(ade), Satire, Skit, Squib
Lamprey Hag, Lampern, Sandpride
Lancaster Burt, Osbert
Lance Dart, Harpoon, Morne, Pesade, Pike, Prisade, Prisado, Rejôn, Spear,
Speisade, Thermic, White arm
Lancelet Amphious
Lancer Bengal, Picador, Uhlan
Lancet Fleam
Land(s), Landed Acreage, Aina, Alight, Alluvion, Arpent, Bag, Beach, Bigha,
Bovate, Byrd, Carse, Carucate, Cavel, Conacre, Corridor, Country, Croft, Crown,
Demain, Demesne, Disbark, Disembark, Ditch, Doab, Dock, Earth, Edom,
Enderby, Estate, Fallow, Farren, Farthingland, Fee, Feod, Feoff, Feud, Fief,
Freeboard, Gair, Glebe, Gondwanaland, Gore, Graham, Ground, Hide, Holding,
Holm, Holy, Horst, Ind, Innings, Isthmus, Kingdom, La-la, Laurasia, Lea, Leal,
Ley, Light, Link, Machair, Maidan, Manor, Marginal, Marie Byrd, Mesnalty,
Métairie, Moose pasture, Morgen, Mortmain, Nation, Never-never, Nod, No
man's, Odal, Onshore, Oxgang, Oxgate, Pakahi, Palmer, Pangaea, Panhandle,
Parcel, Pasture, Peneplain, Peneplane, Peninsula, Piste, Plot, Ploughgate,
Point, Polder, Pr(a)edial, Promised, Property, Purlieu, Queen Maud, Real estate,
Realm, Realty, Reservation, Roman candle, Rundale, Rupert's, Savanna(h),
Set-aside, Settle, Spit, Swidden, Tack, Taluk, Terra(e), Terra-firma, Terrain,
Territory, Thwaite, Tie, Tir na n'Og, Touchdown, Turbary, Tye, Udal, Unship,
Ure, Van Diemen's, Veld(t), Victoria, Wainage, Waste, Whenua, Wilkes, Yird
▶ **Landfall** *see* **LANDSLIDE**
Landing (craft, stair, system) Autoflare, Crash, Forced, Gallipoli, Gha(u)t, Half,
Halfpace, Hard, Instrument, LEM, Module, Pancake, Pier, Quay, Soft, Solar,
Splashdown, Three-point, Three-pricker, Touchdown, Undercarriage
Landlock Embay
Landlord, Land owner Absentee, Balt, Boniface, Bonnet laird, Copyholder,
Eupatrid, Fiar, Franklin, Herself, Host, Innkeeper, Junker, Laird, Lessor,
Letter, Licensee, Patron, Patroon, Proprietor, Publican, Rachman, Rentier,
Squattocracy, Squire, Squirearchy, Squireen, Thane, Zamindar(i), Zemindar
Landmark Meith, Watershed
Landmass Laurasia
Land right Emphyteusis
Landscape Karst, Paysage, Picture, Saikei, Scene, Vista
Landslide, Landfall Avalanche, Earthfall, Eboulement, Lahar, Scree, Slip
Landsman Lubber
Land-tenure Frankalmoign, Raiyatwari, Ryotwari
Lane Boreen, Bus, Corridor, Crawler, Drangway, Drury, Express, Fast, Fetter,
Gut, Inside, Loan, Lois, Loke, Memory, Mincing, Outside, Overtaking, Passage,
Petticoat, Pudding, Ruelle, Sea-road, Slow, Twitten, Twitting, Vennel, Wynd
Langerhans Insulin, Islets
Language(s) Argot, Artificial, Assembly, Auxiliary, Basic, Body, Cant,
Command, Dead, Dialect, Formal, Georgian, Hobson-Jobson, Humanities,
Idioglossia, Idiolect, Idiom, Inclusive, Jargon, Langue, Ledden, Lingo, Lingua
franca, Macaroni, Machine code, Mellowspeak, Mixed, Modern, Mother
tongue, Native, Natural, Neo, Newspeak, Novelese, Object, Officialese, Page
description, Parlance, Philology, Pidgin, Polysynthetic, Pragmatics, Private,
Procedural, Programming, Prose, Query, Relay, Rhetoric, Sea-speak, Second,
Sign, Sociolect, > **SPEECH**, Style, Symbolic, Synthetic, Target, Technobabble,
Telegraphese, Tone, > **TONGUE**, Union, Vedic, Verbiage, Vernacular, Vocabulary,

Words, World

LANGUAGES

3 letters:	5 letters:	Sotho	German
Ada	Aleut	Suomi	Gullah
Bat	Aryan	Swazi	Hebrew
Fur	Azeri	Taino	Herero
Giz	Balti	Tajik	Italic
Gur	Bantu	Tamil	Ladino
Ibo	Batak	Te reo	Lahnda
Ido	Cajun	Tigre	Lakota
Kwa	Carib	Tonga	Lu wian
Luo	Chewa	Turki	Lydian
Mon	Cobol	Ugric	Manchu
Reo	Dogon	Vogul	Micmac
Tai	Doric	Welsh	Mishmi
Tiv	Fanti	Wolof	Na-Dene
Twi	Farsi	Xhosa	Nepali
	Ganda	Yakut	Novial
4 letters:	Gondi	Yuman	Nubian
Ainu	Hausa	Yupik	Ostyak
Avar	Hindi		Pahari
Cham	Hokan	**6 letters:**	Paiute
Daru	Indic	Adyahe	Pakhti
Erse	Joual	Adygei	Papuan
Geez	Kafri	Adyghe	Pashto
Igbo	Koine	Altaic	Pashtu
Inca	Kriol	Arabic	Pushto
Komi	Kuo-yu	Aranda	Pushtu
Krio	Ladin	Aymara	Romany
Lozi	Lamba	Basque	Rwanda
Maya	Lamut	Basutu	Salish
Motu	Latin	Bokmal	Shelta
Naga	Lubon	Brahui	Sindhi
Nuba	Lunda	Breton	Siouan
Nupe	Lyele	Celtic	Somali
Pali	Malay	Centum	Strine
Pedi	Maori	Chadic	Tanoan
Pict	Mayan	Coptic	Tartar
Shan	Munda	Creole	Telegu
Taal	Nguni	Cymric	Telugu
Thai	Norse	Dardic	Tuareg
Tshi	Oriya	Divehi	Tungus
Tupi	Oscan	Eskimo	Turkic
Urdu	P-Celt	Evenki	Udmurt
Wawa	Sakai	Fantee	Ugrian
Xosa	Sango	Fijian	Uralic
Zulu	Satem	Finnic	Yoruba
Zuni	Shona	Fulani	Zyrian
	Shono	Gaelic	
	Sioux	Gagauz	

7 letters:
Adamawa
Amerind
Amharic
Aramaic
Austric
Bengali
Bislama
Caddoan
Catalan
Chaldee
Chinook
Chuvash
Cushite
Dzongka
Flemish
Frisian
Gagauzi
Hamitic
Hin Motu
Hittite
Janlish
Japlish
Kannada
Khoisan
Kirundi
Kurdish
Kushite
Lallans
Laotian
Lingala
Luganda
Marathi
Miao-Yao
Mingrel
Nahuatl
Nilotic
Nyungar
Oceanic
Ossetic
Ottoman
Pahlavi
Pehlevi
Pictish
Prakrit
Punjabi
Pushtoo
Quechua
Romance
Romansh
Samnite
Samoyed

Semitic
Sesotho
Sinhala
Sinitic
Slovene
Sornian
Sudanic
Swahili
Swedish
Tagalog
Tahitan
Tibetan
Tlingit
Turkish
Turkmen
Umbrian
Uralian
Venetic
Volapuk
Voltaic
Walloon
Wendish
Yerkish
Yiddish

8 letters:
Akkadian
Albanian
Arawakan
Assamese
Bulgaric
Cherkess
Chibchan
Chichewa
Croatian
Cushitic
Dzongkha
Ethiopic
Etruscan
Faliscan
Fanagalo
Filipino
Frankish
Friesian
Gujarati
Gujerati
Gurkhali
Illyrian
Japhetic
Jugoslav
Kashmiri
Kingwana

Kolarian
Kwakiuti
Landsmal
Mandarin
Mongolic
Mon-Khmer
Nez Perce
Penutian
Pilipino
Polabian
Rhaetian
Romansch
Rumansch
Rumonsch
Sanscrit
Sanskrit
Scythian
Setswana
Shemitic
Slavonic
Sumerian
Tahitian
Teutonic
Thracian
Tigrinya
Tshiluba
Tungusic
Turanian
Turkoman
Ugaritic
Wakashan
Warlpiri
Yugoslav

9 letters:
Abkhazian
Algonkian
Algonquin
Anatolian
Brythonic
Cantonese
Chari-Nile
Diglossia
Dravidian
Esperanto
Esthonian
Euskarian
Franglais
Gujarathi
Gujerathi
Hottentot
Inuktitut

Iroquoian
Kamilaroi
Kiswahili
Landsmaal
Langue d'oc
Leizghian
Malayalam
Messapian
Muskogean
Nostratic
Onondagan
Provencal
Putonghua
Roumansch
Sabellian
Semi-Bantu
Sinhalese
Tocharian
Tokharian
Tokharish
Ukrainian
Winnebago

10 letters:
Algonquian
Athabascan
Azerbayani
Circassian
Diachronic
Eteocretan
Finno-Ugric
Gallo-Roman
Himyaritic
Hindustani
Langue d'oil
Malayalaam
Melanesian
Mingrelian
Muskhogean
Niger-Congo
Papiamento
Proto-Norse
Rajasthani
Serbo-croat
Singhalese
Synchronic
Ural-Altaic
Uto-Aztecan
Vietnamese

11 letters:
Dagestanian

- Interglossa
- Interlingua
- Kordofanian
- Langobardic
- Nilo-Saharan
- Osco-Umbrian
- Pama-Nyungan

Sino-Tibetan
Sranantongo
Tessaraglot
Tupi-Guarani

12 letters:
Billingsgate

Gallo-Romance
Idiom neutral
Indo-European
Platt-deutsch
Tibeto-Burman
Volga-Baltaic

13 letters:
Neo-Melanesian
Semito-Hamitic

14 letters:
Thraco-Phrygian

Languid, Languish Die, Divine, Droop, Feeble, Flagging, Listless, Lukewarm, Lydia, Melancholy, Quail, Torpid, Wilt
Languor Lassitude
Lanky Beanpole, Gangly, Gawky, Spindleshanks, Windlestraw
Lanolin Woolfat, Yolk
Lantern Aristotle's, Bowat, Bowet, Buat, Bull's eye, Chinese, Dark(e)y, Epidiascope, Episcope, Friar's, Glim, Japanese, Jaw, Lanthorn, Magic, Sconce, Stereopticon, Storm, Turnip
Lanthanum La
Laodicean Lukewarm
Lap Circuit, Gremial, Leg, Lick, Lip, Luxury, Override, Pace, Sypher
Lapdog Messan, Shough, Showghe
Lapel Revers
Laplander, Lapp Saam(e), Sabme, Sabmi, Sami
Lappet Infula
Lapse Backslide, Drop, Error, Expire, Fa', Fall, Nod, Sliding, Trip
Lapwing Teru-tero
Larceny Grand
Larch Hackmatack, Tamarack
Lard Enarm, Leaf, Saim, Seam(e)
Larder Buttery, Pantry, Spence, Springhouse
Large(ness), Largest Ample, Astronomical, Big, Boomer, Bulky, Buster, Colossus, Commodious, Decuman, Enormous, Epical, Extensive, Gargantuan, > **GIGANTIC**, Ginormous, Great, Grit, Gross, Hefty, Helluva, Huge, Hulking, Humdinger, Humongous, Humungous, Kingsize, L, Lunker, Macrocephaly, Massive, Maximin, Maximum, Outsize, Plethora, Prodigious, Rounceval, Rouncival, Skookum, Slew, Slue, Sollicker, Spacious, Spanking, Stonker, Stout, Swingeing, Tidy, Titanic, Vast, Voluminous, Whopping
Large number Centillion, Fermi, Giga, Gillion, Googol, Googolplex, Grillion, Infinitude, Jillion, Legion, Mille, Nation, Nonillion, Quadrillion, Quintillion, Raft, Regiment, Ruck, Scads, Sea, Septillion, Sextillion, Slather, Slew, Slue, Squillion, Toman, Trillion, Zillion
Largess Alms, Charity, Frumentation, Generosity
Lariat Lasso, Reata, Riata
Lark Adventure, Aunter, Caper, Dido, Dunstable, Exaltation, Fool, Giggle, Guy, Laverock, Magpie, Mud, Pipit, Prank
Larkspur Stavesacre
Larva Ammacoete, Aphid lion, Army-worm, Augerworm, Axolotl, Bagworm, Bloodworm, Bot(t), Budworm, Cabbage worm, Caddice, Caddis, Cankerworm, Caterpillar, Cercaria, Chigger, Chigoe, Coenurus, Doodlebug, Grub, Hellgram(m)ite, Hydatid, Indusium, Instar, Jigger, Jointworm, Leather-jacket, Leptocephalus, Maggot, Mealworm, Measle, Miracidium, Muckworm, Naiad, Nauplius, Nigger, Nymph, Ox-bot, Planula, Pluteus, Porina, Redia, Screwworm, Shade, Silkworm, Strawworm, Tadpole, Trochophore,

Trochosphere, Veliger, Water penny, Wireworm, Witchetty, Witchetty grub, Woodworm, Zoea

Laryngitis Croup, Hives

Lascar Seacunny, Tindal

Lascivious(ness) Crude, Goaty, Horny, Lewd, Lubric, Paphian, Satyric, Sotadic, Tentigo, Wanton

Lash(ed), Lashings Cat, Cilium, Firk, Flagellum, Frap, Gammon, Knout, Mastigophora, Oodles, Oup, Quirt, Riem, Rope's end, Scourge, Secure, Sjambok, Stripe, Swinge, Tether, Thong, Trice, Whang, > **WHIP**

Lass(ie) Damsel, Maid, Quean, Queyn, Quin(i)e

Lassitude Accidie, Acedie, Languor, Lethargy

Lasso Lariat, Reata, Rope

Last(ing) Abide, Abye, Aftermost, > **AT LAST**, Boot-tree, Bottom, Chronic, Coda, Dernier, Dure, Endurance, Endure, Extend, Extreme, > **FINAL**, Hinder, Latest, Linger, Live, Long-life, Model, Nightcap, Outstay, Perdure, Permanent, Perpetuate, Persist, Spin, Stable, Stay, Supper, Survive, Swan-song, Thiller, Thule, Tree, Trump, Ult(imate), Ultimo, Utmost, Wear, Weight, Whipper-in, Yester, Z

Last drop Supernaculum

Last resort Pis aller

Last syllable Ultima

Last word(s) Amen, Envoi, Farewell, Ultimatum, Zythum

Latch Bar, Clicket, Clink, Espagnolette, Lock, Night, Sneck

Late(r), Latest After(wards), Afterthought, Behindhand, Chit-chat, Dead, Deid, Ex, Former, Gen, Infra, Lag, Lamented, New(s), Overdue, Overrunning, Past, Recent, Sine, Slow, State-of-the-art, Stop-press, Syne, Tardive, Tardy, Top shelf, Trendy, Umquhile

Late-learner Opsimath

Latent Concealed, Delitescent, Dormant, Maieutic, Potential

Lateral Askant, Edgeways, Sideways

Latex Antiar, Gutta-percha, Jelutong, Ule

Lath Lag, Splat

Lathe Capstan, Mandrel, Mandril, Turret

Lather Flap, Foam, Froth, Sapples, Suds, Tan

Latin(ist) Biblical, Criollo, Dago, Dog, Erasmus, Eyeti, Greaseball, High, Humanity, Italiot, L, Late, Law, Low, Medieval, Neapolitan, New, Pig, Romanic, Romish, Scattermouch, Silver, Spic, Vulgar, Wop

Latin-American Criollo, Tico

Latitude Breadth, Celestial, Ecliptic, Free hand, Horse, L, Leeway, Liberty, Licence, Meridian, Parallel, Play, Roaring forties, Scope, Tropic, Width

Latrine Ablutions, Bog, Cloaca, Furphy, Garderobe, Loo, Privy, Rear

Latter Last, Previous

Latter-day Recent, Saints, Young

Lattice Bravais, Clathrate, Espalier, Grille, Space, Treillage, Trellis

Lattice-leaf Ouvirandra

Latvian Lett

Laud(er) Commend, Eulogist, Extol, Harry, Praise

Lauderdale Caballer

Laugh(ing), Laughable, Laughter Belly, Cachinnate, Cackle, Chortle, Chuckle, Cod, Corpse, Democritus, Deride, Derision, Fit, Fou rire, Gelastic, Giggle, Goster, Guffaw, Ha, He-he, Ho-ho, Homeric, Hoot, Horse, Hout, Howl, Irrision, Last, Lauch, Leuch, Levity, Ludicrous, > **MIRTH**, Mock, Nicker, Peal, Present,

Riancy, Riant, Rich, Rident, Ridicule, Risus, Scream, Snigger, Snirt(le), Snort, Tehee, Titter, Yo(c)k

Laughing-stock Outspeckle, Sport

Launcelot Gobbo

Launch(ing), Launch pad Begin, Blast-off, Catapult, Chuck, Cosmodrome, ELV, Fire, Float, Hurl, Initiate, Lift-off, Moonshot, Motoscalp, Opening, Pioneer, Presentation, Release, Roll out, Shipway, Slipway, Start, Steam, Unstock, Upsend, VTO

Launder, Laundry Bagwash, Clean, Lav, Steamie, Tramp, Transfer, Wash, Washhouse, Whites

Laurel(s) Aucuba, Bay, Camphor, Cherry, Daphne, Japan, Kalmia, Kudos, Mountain, Pichurim, Rose (bay), Sassafras, Spicebush, Spotted, Spurge, Stan, Sweet-bay, True

Laurence Sterne

Lava Aa, Block, Bomb, Coulee, Cysticercus, Dacite, Flood basalt, Lahar, Lapilli, Magma, Nuée ardente, Pahoehoe, Palagonite, Pillow, Pitchstone, Plug, Pumice, Pyroclast, Scoria, Tephra, Toadstone

Lavatory Ajax, Bogger, Brasco, Can, Carsey, Carzey, Cludgie, Comfort station, Convenience, Cottage, Dike, Dunnakin, Dunny, Dyke, Earth closet, Elsan®, Facilities, Forica, Furphey, Gents, Heads, Jakes, Jane, John, Kars(e)y, Karzy, K(h)azi, Kleinhuisie, Kybo, Ladies, Lat(rine), Loo, Necessary, Netty, Office, Outhouse, Privy, Rear(s), Reredorter, Shithouse, Shouse, Siege, Smallest room, Throne, Thunderbox, Toot, Tout, Urinal, Washroom, WC

Lave Lip, Wash

Lavender Aspic, Spike

Lavengro Borrow

Laver Moabite, Nori, Ore-weed

Lavish Barmecidal, Copious, Excessive, Exuberant, Flush, Free, Fulsome, Generous, Liberal, Lucullan, Lush, Prodigal, Shower, Slap-up, Sumptuous, Wanton, Waste

Law(s) Abingdon, Act, Agrarian, Anti-trust, Ass, Association, Avogadro's, Babo's, Bar, Barratry, Bernoulli's, > **BILL**, Biogenetic, Bode's, Bonar, Boyle's, Bragg's, Brehon, Brewster's, Brocard, Buys Ballot's, Byelaw, Cain, Canon, Capitulary, Case, Chancery, Charles's, Civil, Code, Common, Constitution, Corn, Coulomb's, Criminal, Cupar, Curie's, Curie-Weiss, Cy pres, Dalton's, Dead-letter, Decree, Decretals, De Morgan's, Deodand, Dharma, Dictate, Digest, Din, Distributive, Dry, Edict, Einstein's, Enact, Excise, Forest, Fuero, Fundamental, Fuzz, Game, Gas, Gay-Lussac's, Gresham's, Grimm's, Grotian, Haeckel's, Halifax, Hardy-Weinberg, Henry's, Homestead, Hooke's, Hubble's, Hume's, International, Irade, Iure, Joule's, Jura, Jure, Jus, Kain, Kashrut(h), Kepler's, Kirchhoff's, Labour, Lay, Leibniz's, Lemon, Lenx's, Lien, Lor(d), Losh, Lydford, Lynch, Magdeburg, Mariotte's, Martial, May, Mendel's, Mercantile, Military, Mishna(h), Mishnic, Moral, Mosaic, Murphy's, Natural, Newton's, Noahide, Nomistic, Nomothetic, Ohm's, Oral, Ordinance, Pandect, Parity, Parkinson's, Pass, Penal, Periodic, Planck's, Plebiscite, Poor, Principle, Private, Public, Roman, Rubric, Rule, Salic, Salique, Scout, Sharia(h), Sheria(t), Shield, Shulchan Aruch, Snell's, Sod's, > **STATUTE**, Stefan's, Stokes, Sumptuary, Sunna, Sus(s), Sword, Table, Talmud, Tenet, Thorah, Thorndike's, Torah, Tort, Tradition, Ulema, Unwritten, Use, Verner's, Vigilante, Written

Lawless(ness) Anarchy, Anomie, Anomy, Antinomian, Piratical

Lawmaker, Lawman, Lawyer Alfaqui, Ambulance chaser, Attorney, AV, Barrack room, Barrister, Bencher, BL, Bluebottle, Bramble, Bush, Canon, Coke,

Counsel, DA, Defence, Doge, Draco, Earp, Enactor, Fiscal, Greenbag, Grotius, Hammurabi, Jurisconsult, Jurist, Legal eagle, Legist, Mooktar, Moses, MP, Mufti, Mukhtar, Nomothete, Notary, Penang, Pettifoggers, Philadelphia, Proctor, Procurator fiscal, Prosecutor, Rabbi, Shirra, Shyster, Silk, Solicitor, Spenlow, Stratopause, Talmudist, Templar, Thesmothete, Vakil, WS

Lawn Cloth, Grass, Green, Linen, Sward, Turf

Lawrence DH, Ross, Shaw, TE

Lawrencium Lr

Lawsuit Case, Cause, Plea, Trover

▸ **Lawyer(s), Lawman** *see* LAWMAKER

▷ **Lax** *may indicate* an anagram

Lax(ity) Freedom, Inexact, Laissez-aller, Latitude, Loose, Remiss, > SLACK, Wide, Wide-open

Laxative Aloin, Aperitive, Cascara, Cathartic, Eccoprotic, Elaterin, Elaterium, Glauber's salt, Gregory (powder), Loosener, Physic, Purgative, > PURGE, Saline, Senna-pod, Taraxacum

Lay(ing), Layman, Laic, Laid Air, Amateur, Aria, Ballad, Bed, Bet, Blow, Chant, Civil, Ditty, Drop, Earthly, Egg, Embed, Fit, Impose, Lied, Lodge, Man, Minstrel, Oat, Oblate, Ode, Ordinary, Outsider, Oviparous, Oviposit, Parabolanus, Secular, Set, Sirvente, > SONG, Sypher, Tertiary, Tribal, Wager, Warp

Layabout Loafer, Lotophagus

Lay-by Rest stop

Layer(s) Abscission, Ancona, Appleton, Battery, Boundary, Cake, Caliche, Cladding, Coating, Crust, D, Depletion, E, Ectoplasm, Ectosarc, Ekman, Epiblast, Epilimnion, Epitaxial, Epithelium, Erathem, Exine, Exocarp, Film, Flake, Friction, Ganoin, Germ, Gossan, Gozzan, Granum, Ground, Heaviside, > HEN, Herb, Kennelly(-Heaviside), Kerf, Lamella, Lamina, Lap, Leghorn, Lie, Malpighian, Media, Miocene, Ozone, Pan, Patina, Paviour, Photosphere, Ply, Retina, Scale, Sclerite, Screed, Skin, Sliver, Spathic, Stratify, Stratum, Substratum, Tabular, Tapetum, Tier, Tremie, Trophoblast, Trophoderm, Varve, Vein, Velamen, Veneer

Lay-off Dismiss, Hedge, Redundance

Lay-out Ante, Design, Fell, Format, Map, Mise, Pattern, Spend, Straucht, Straught, Streak, Streek, Stretch

Laze, Laziness, Lazy (person) Bed-presser, Bummer, Cabbage, Faineant, Hallian, Hallion, Hallyon, Indolent, Inert, Lackadaisical, Languid, Layabout, Lie-abed, Lig(ger), Lime, Lither, Loaf, Lotus-eater, Lusk, Mollusc, Ne'er-do-well, Oblomovism, Resty, Sloth, Slouch, Slug(-a-bed), Sluggard, Susan, Sweer, Sweir, Workshy

▷ **Lazily** *may indicate* an anagram

Lea Grass, Meadow

Leach(ing) Cheluviation, Lixivial, Ooze

Lead(er), Leading, Leadership Ag(h)a, Ahead, Akela, Anglesite, Article, Atabeg, Atabek, Ayatollah, Bab, Bellwether, Black, Bluey, Brand, Cable, Cade, Calif, Caliph, Came, Capitano, Capo, Captain, Castro, Caudillo, Causal, Centre, Ceruse, Cheer, Chieftain, Chiliarch, Chin, China white, Choragus, Choregus, CO, Codder, Condottiere, Conducive, Conduct, Coryphaeus, Coryphee, Demagogue, Dictator, Duce, Dux, Editorial, Escort, Ethnarch, Extension, Figurehead, Floor, Foreman, Foremost, Frontrunner, Fu(e)hrer, Fugleman, Gaffer, Garibaldi, Gerent, Go, Graphite, Guide(r), Halter, Hand, Headman, Headmost, Headnote, Hegemony, Heresiarch, Hero, Hetman, Honcho, Idi, Imam, Imaum, Jason, Jefe, Jump, Juve(nile), Kabir, Kame, King, Ksar, Leam,

Litharge, Livid, Loss, Lost, Lyam, Mahatma, Mahdi, Main, Market, Marshal, Massicot, Masticot, Mayor, Meer, Mehdi, Minium, Mir, Nanak, No 1, Nomarch, Nose, Numero uno, Omrah, Open, Pacemaker, Pacesetter, Padishah, Pb, Pilot, Pioneer, Pit, Plumb(um), Plummet, PM, Precentor, Premier(e), President, Price, Ratoo, Rebbe, Rebecca, Red, Role, Ruler, Sachem, Sagamore, Saturn, Saturn's tree, Scotlandite, Scout, Scuddaler, Scudler, Sharif, Sheik(h), Sixer, Skipper, Skudler, Soaker, Soul, Sounding, Spearhead, Staple, Star, Sultan, Supremo, Taoiseach, Tecumseh, Tetraethyl, Top banana, Trail(blazer), Tribune, Tsaddik, Tsaddiq, Tzaddik, Up, Usher, Vaivode, Van(guard), Vanadinite, Va(u)nt, Vaunt-courier, Voivode, Vozhd, Waivode, Warlord, White, Whitechapel, Wulfenite, Youth, Zaddik, Zia

▷ **Lead(s), Leaders** *may indicate* first letters of words

Leaden Flat, Plumbeous, Saturnine

Lead-glance Galena

Leading to Pre

Leaf(y), Leaves Acanthus, Acrospire, Amphigastrium, Amplexicaul, Betel, Blade, Bract, Carpel, Cataphyll, Cladode, Coca, Consent, Corolla, Costate, Cotyledon, Dolma, Drop, Duff, Fig, Finial, Foil, Foliage, Foliar, Folio(se), Folium, Frond, Glume, Gold, Holiday, Induviae, Jugum, K(h)at, Maple, Megaphyll, Needle, Nervate, Out, P, Pad, Page, Pan, Phyllid, Phyllome, Qat, Repair, Riffle, Rosula, Scale, Sclerophyll, Secede, Sepal, Siri(h), Skip, Spathe, Sporophyll, Stipule, Tea, Title, TTL, Valve, Vert, Vine, Withdraw

Leafhopper Thrip

Leafless Ebracteate, Scape

Leaflet At(t)ap, Bill, Bracteole, Circular, Dodger, Fly-sheet, Foliolose, Handbill, Pinna, Pinnula, Prophyll, Stipel, > **TRACT**

League Achaean, Alliance, Arab, Band, Bund, Compact, Delian, Entente, Federation, Gueux, Guild, Hanse(atic), Holy, Ivy, Land, Major, Minor, Nations, Parasang, Primrose, Redheaded, Rugby, Super, Union, Ypres, Zollverein, Zupa

Leak(y) Bilge, Drip, Escape, Extravasate, Gizzen, Holed, Holey, Ooze, Pee, Porous, Seepage, Sype, Trickle, Wee, Weep, Wee-wee

Leak-proof Airtight

Leamington Spa

Lean(ing) Abut, Barren, Batter, Bend, Careen, Carneous, Carnose, Griskin, Heel, > **INCLINE**, Lie, Lig(ge), Minceur, Prop, Propend, Rake, Rely, Rest, Scraggy, Scrawny, Skinny, Spare, Stoop, Taste, Tend, Tilt, Tip, Walty

Leander Abydos

Lean-to Skillion

Leap(ing), Leapt Assemblé, Bound, Brise, Cabriole, Caper, Capriole, Cavort, Clear, Croupade, Curvet, Echappé, Entrechat, Falcade, Fishdive, Frisk, Galumph, Gambado, Gambol, Jeté, Jump, Loup, Luppen, Ollie, Over, Pigeon-wing, Pronk, Quantum, Sally, Salto, Somersa(u)lt, Somerset, > **SPRING**, Stag, Transilient, Vault, Volte

Leap year Bissextile, Penteteric

Lear Edward, King, Nonsense

Learn(ed), Learner Beginner, Blue, Bluestocking, Chela, Con, Discover, Distance, Doctor, Don, Erudite, Gather, Get, Glean, Hear, Instrumental, Kond, L, Lear(e), Leir, Lere, Literate, Literati, Literato, Lucubrate, Master, Memorise, Mirza, Mug up, > **NOVICE**, Pandit, Polymath, Programmed, Pundit, Pupil, Rookie, Savant, Scan, Scholar, Scient, See, Starter, Student, > **STUDY**, Tiro, Trainee, Tutee, Tyro, Wise

Learning Culture, Discipline, Discrimination, Erudition, Index, Insight, Latent,

Lore, Machine, New, Open, Opsimathy, Rep, Wit

Lease(-holder) Charter, Farm, Feu, Gavel, Hire, Let, > RENT, Set(t), Tack, Tacksman

Leash Lead, Lune, Lyam, Lym(e), Slip, Three, Trash, Triplet

Least Minimum

Leather(y) Artificial, Bouilli, Bouilly, Box-calf, Buckskin, Buff, Cabretta, Calf, Capeskin, Chammy, Chamois, Checklaton, Cheverel, Chevrette, Cordovan, Cordwain, Corium, Cowhide, Crispin, Cuir(-bouilli), Deacon, Deerskin, Diphthera, Doeskin, Dogskin, Durant, Fair, Goatskin, Hide, Hog-skin, Horsehide, Japanned, Kid, Kip(-skin), Lamp, Levant, Marocain, Maroquin, Mocha, Morocco, Mountain, Nap(p)a, Neat, Nubuck®, Ooze, Oxhide, Paste-grain, Patent, Pigskin, Plate, Rand, Rawhide, Rexine®, Riem(pie), Roan, Rock, Rough-out, Russia, Saffian, Shagreen, Shammy, Sharkskin, Shecklaton, Sheepskin, Shoe, Skiver, Slinkskin, Spetch, Split, Spur, Stirrup, Strand, Strap, Suede, Tan, Taw, Thong, Upper, Wallop, Wash, Waxed, White, Whitleather, Yuft

Leatherneck Marine, RM

Leave(r), Leavings, Leave off Abandon, Abiturient, Abscond, Absit, Absquatulate, Acquittal, Adieu, Bequeath, Blessing, Bug, Compassionate, Congé, Congee, Decamp, Depart, Desert, Desist, Devisal, Devise, Ditch, Exeat, Exit, Exodus, Forego, Forgo, Forsake, French, Furlough, Garlandage, > GO, Inspan, Ish, Legate, Liberty, Licence, Maroon, Maternity, Mizzle, Omit, Orts, Pace, Park, Part, Paternity, > PERMISSION, Permit, > QUIT, Residue, Resign, Sabbatical, Scapa, Scat, Scram, Shore, Sick, Skedaddle, Skidoo®, Stick, Strand, Vacate, Vade, Vamo(o)se, Will, Withdraw

Leaven Barm, Ferment, Yeast

Lebanese, Lebanon Druse, RL

Lecher(ous), Lechery Gate, Goaty, Lascivious, Libertine, Lickerish, Lustful, Profligate, Rake, Roué, Salaciousness, Satirisk, Satyr, Silen, Whoremonger, Wolf

Lectern Ambo, Desk, Eagle, Oratory

Lecture(r), Lectures, Lecturing Address, Aristotelian, Chalktalk, Creed, Curtain, Dissert(ator), Don, Earful, Erasmus, Expound, Homily, Hulsean, Jaw, Jawbation, Jobe, L, Lector, Pi-jaw, Prelect, Privatdocent, Prone, Rate, Read(er), Rede, Reith, Scold, Sententious, > SERMON, Spout, Talk, Teacher, Teach-in, Wigging, Yaff

Ledge Altar, Berm, Channel, Fillet, Gradin(e), Linch, Misericord(e), Scarcement, Settle, > SHELF, Window (sill)

Ledger Book, Purchase, Register

Lee(s) Dregs, Dunder, Heeltaps, Sediment, Shelter, Ullage

Leech Bleeder, Gnathobdellida, Horse, Medicinal, Parasite, Rhynchobdellida

Leek Allium, Fouat, Fouet, Porraceous, Rocambole

Leer Eliad, Fleer, Oeillade, Ogle

Leeway Drift

Left(-handed), Left-hander, Left-winger Adrift, Balance, Bolshy, Corrie-fisted, Dolly-push, Gallock, Hie, High, Inherited, L, Laeotropic, Laevorotation, Larboard, Links, Lorn, Near, New, Other, Over, Pink, Port, Portsider, Quit, Rad, Red, Relic, Residuum, Resigned, Sinister, Soc(ialist), Southpaw, Thin, Titoism, Trot, Verso, Vo, Went, West, Wind, Yet

Left-over End, Lave, Oddment, Orra, Remanet, > REMNANT, Waste

Leg(s), Leggings, Leggy, Leg-wear Antigropelo(e)s, Bandy, Barley-sugar, Breeches, Cabriole, Cannon, Chaparajos, Chaparejos, Chaps, Crural, Crus, Dib,

Drumstick, Fine, Fly-sail, Gaiter, Galligaskins, Gam(b), Gamash, Gambado, Garter, Gaskin, Giambeux, Gigot, Gramash, Gramosh, Ham, Haunch, Hest, Hock, Jamb, Jambeau, Knock-knee(d), Limb, Long, Member, Myriapod, Oleo, On(side), Peg, Peraeopod, Periopod, Pestle, Pin, Podite, Proleg, Puttees, Pylon, Relay, Section, Shanks, Shanks's pony, Shaps, Shin, Short, Spats, Spatterdash, Spider, Spindleshanks, Square, Stage, Stump, Thigh, Tights

Legacy Bequest, Cumulative, Demonstrative, Dowry, Entail, General, Heirloom, Residuary, Specific, Substitutional

Legal(ism), Legally, Legitimate Bencher, Forensic, Halacha, Halaka(h), Halakha, Lawful, Licit, Nomism, Scienter, Statutory

Legal book Halacha, Halaka(h), Halakha, Talmud

Leg-armour, Leg-covering Cootikin, Cu(i)tikin, Gambado, Jamb(e), Pad

Legate, Legator Ambassador, Consul, Devisor, Emissary, Envoy, Nuncio

Legend Arthurian, Caption, Edda, Fable, Folklore, Motto, Myth, Saga, Story

▷ **Legend** *may indicate* leg-end, (e.g. foot, talus)

Leger Swindler

Leghorn Livorno

Legible Clear, Lucid, Plain

Legion(ary), Legionnaire Alauda, American, Army, British, Cohort, Countless, Deserter, Foreign, Geste, Honour, > **HOST**, Maniple, Many, Throng, Thundering, Zillions

Legislate, Legislator, Legislature Assemblyman, Congress, Decemvir, Decree, MP, Nomothete, Oireachtas, > **PARLIAMENT**, Persian, Solon, Zemstvo

Legitimate Loyal

Legless Amelia, Blotto, Boozy, Caecilia, Psyche

Leg-pull Chaff, Joke, Rise, Rot

Legume, Leguminous Bean, Guar, Lentil, Pea, Pipi, Pod, Pulse

Leibniz Monadism

Leigh Amyas

Leisure(ly) Adagio, Ease, Lento, Liberty, Moderato, Otium, Respite, Rest, Vacation

Lemon Answer, Cedrate, Citron, Citrus, Smear-dab, Sole, Yellow

Lemur Angwantibo, Aye-aye, Babacoote, Bush-baby, Colugo, Galago, Half-ape, Indri(s), Loris, Macaco, Malmag, Mongoose, > **MONKEY**, Potto, Ringtail, Sifaka, Spectre, Tana, Tarsier

Lend Advance, Loan, Prest, Vaunce

Length(y), Lengthen(ing), Lengthwise Archine, Arsheen, Arshin(e), Aune, Barleycorn, Braccio, Cable, Chain, Cubit, Distance, Eke, Ell, > **ELONGATE**, Endways, Epenthetic, Expand, Extensive, Focal, Foot, Furlong, Inch, Ley, Mile, Nail, Passus, Perch, Piece, Plethron, Pole, Prolate, Prolix, Prolong, Protract, Reach, Remen, Rod, Rope, Slow, Span, Stadium, Toise, Vara, Verbose, Yard

Lenient Clement, Exurable, Lax, Mild, Permissive, Soft, Tolerant

Lens Achromatic, Anamorphic, Anastigmat, Aplanatic, Apochromat(ic), Bifocal, Compound, Contact, Corneal, Crookes, Crown, Crystalline, Dielectric, Diopter, Dioptre, Diverging, Electron, Electrostatic, Eye, Eyeglass, Eye-piece, Facet, Fish-eye, Fresnel, Gravitational, Hard, Immersion, Lentil, Macro, Magnetic, Metallic, Mirror, Object-glass, Optic, Pantoscope, Phacoid, Piano-concave, Piano-convex, Soft, Soft-focus, Stanhope, Sunglass, Telephoto, Toric, Trifocal, Varifocal, Water, Wide-angle, Zoom

Lent Careme, Fast, Laetare, Out, Quadragesimal, Term

Lentil(s) D(h)al, Dholl, Ervalenta, Lens, Phacoid, Pulse, Revalenta

Leonora Overture

Leopard Clouded, Hunting, Leap, Libbard, Ounce, Panther, Pard, Snow, Spots
Leopold Bloom
Leotard Maillot
Leper, **Leprosy**, **Leprous** Gehazi, Lazar, Leontiasis, Lionism, Meazel, Mesel, Outcast, Pariah
Lepidopterist Aurelian, Moth-er, Pendleton, Treacler
Leprechaun Elf, Gremlin, Imp
Lepton Muon
Lesbian Bull dyke, Crunchie, Diesel, Dike, Dyke, Homophile, Lipstick, Sapphist, Tribade
Lesion Cut, Gash, Pannus, Scar, Serpiginous, Sore
Less(en), **Lesser**, **Lessening** Abate, Alaiment, Bate, Contract, Deaden, Decline, Deplete, Derogate, Dilute, > **DWINDLE**, Extenuate, Fewer, Junior, Littler, Minus, Reduce, Relax, Remission, Subordinate, Subsidiary, Under
Lesson Example, Lear(e), Lection, Leir, Lere, Life, Moral, Object, Parashah, Period, Sermon, Shiur, Tutorial
Let (go, off, out), **Letting** Allow, Cap, Charter, Conacre, Displode, Divulge, Enable, Entitle, Explode, Hire, Impediment, Indulge, Lease, Litten, Loot(en), Luit(en), Lutten, Net, Obstacle, Obstruct, > **PERMIT**, Rent, Reprieve, Sett, Tenancy, Unhand, Warrant
Let down Abseil, Betray, Lower, Sell, Vail
Let-down Non-event
Lethal Deadly, Fatal, Fell, Mortal
Lethargic, **Lethargy** Accidie, Apathy, Coma, Drowsy, Ennui, Hebetude, Inertia, Lassitude, Listless, Passive, Sleepy, Sluggish, Stupor, Supine, Torpid
Letter(s) Ache, Aerogam, Aesc, Airgraph, Aleph, Alif, Alpha, Ascender, A(y)in, Bayer, Begging, Beta, Beth, Block, Breve, Cadmean, Caph, Capital, Capon, Casket, Chain, Cheth, Chi, Circular, Col, Collins, Consonant, Covering, Cue, Cuneiform, Daled, Daleth, Dead, Dear John, Delta, Digamma, Digraph, Dominical, Edh, Ef(f), Emma, Encyclical, Ep(isemon), Epistle, Epsilon, Eta, Eth, Fan, Favour, Fraktur, French, Gamma, Gimel, Grapheme, He, Heth, Initial, Iota, Izzard, Jerusalem, Kaph, Kappa, Koppa, Kufic, Labda, Lambda, Lamed(h), Landlady, Landlord, Lessee, Lessor, Literal, Love, Mail, Mail-shot, Majuscule, Mem, Memo, Miniscule, Minuscule, Missive, Monogram, Mu, Night, Note, Notelet, Nu, Nun, Og(h)am, Omega, Omicron, Open, Pahlavi, Paston, Pastoral, Patent, Pe, Pehlevi, Phi, Pi, Plosive, Poison-pen, Polyphone, Postbag, Psi, Pythagorean, Qoph, Resh, Rho, Rom, Runestave, Sad(h)e, Samekh, Samian, Sampi, San, Scarlet, Screed, Screwtape, Script, See, Shin, Siglum, Sigma, Sign, Signal, Sin, Sort, Swash, Tau, Tav, Taw, Teth, Theta, Thorn, Toc, Tsade, Typo, Uncial, Upsilon, Vau, Vav, Versal, Vowel, Waw, Wen, Wyn, Wynn, Xi, Yod(h), Yogh, Ypsilon, Zayin, Zed, Zeta
Lettering Cufic, Kufic
Lettuce Butterhead, Cabbage, Chicon, Corn-salad, Cos, Frog's, Iceberg, Lactuca, Lamb's, Lollo rosso, Mizuna, Romaine, Salad, Thridace
Leucoma Albugo
Levant(ine) Coptic, Go, Israelite, Jew, Ottamite, Ottomite
Levee Bank, Dyke, Embankment, Party
Level(ler) A, Abney, Abreast, Aclinic, Ad eundum, Aim, Awash, Base, Break even, Bulldoze, Champaign, Countersink, Degree, Dumpy, Echelon, Energy, Equal, > **EVEN**, Extent, Flat, Flight, Flush, Fog, Grade, Logic, O, Occupational, Ordinary, Par, Plane, Plat(eau), Point, Price, Race, Rank, Rase, Raze, Reduced, Savanna, Sea, Spirit, Split, > **SQUARE**, Stratum, Street, Strew, Strickle,

Subsistence, Support, Surveyor's, Tier, Top, Trophic, True, Water, Y

Lever(age) Backfall, Bell-crank, Cock, Crampon, Crowbar, Dues, Gear, Handspike, Jemmy, Joystick, Key, Knee-stop, Landsturm, Pawl, Peav(e)y, Pedal, Prise, Prize, Pry, Purchase, Stick, Sweep, Swipe, Tappet, Tiller, Treadle, Tremolo arm, Trigger, Tumbler, Typebar

Leviathan Whale

Levitate Float, Hover, Rise

Levity Flippancy, Glee, Humour, Jollity

Levy Capital, Estreat, Impose, Imposition, Leave, Militia, Octroi, Raise, Scutage, Talliate, Tax, Tithe, Toll

Lewd(ness) Bawdy, Blue, Impure, Libidinous, Lubricity, Obscene, Priapism, Prurient, Silen(us), Unclean

Lewis Carroll, Tenon

Lexicographer, Lexicon Compiler, Craigie, Drudge, Etymologist, Florio, Fowler, Glossarist, Grove, Johnson(ian), Larousse, Liddell, Mental, Murray, OED, Thesaurus, Vocabulist, Webster, Words-man

Liability, Liable Anme, Apt, Current, Debt, Employer's, Incur, Limited, Open, Product, Prone, Subject, Susceptible

Liaison Affair, Amour, Contact, Link

Liana Guarana

Libel(lous) Defamatory, Malign, Slander, Smear, Sully, Vilify

Liberal(ity) Abundant, Adullamites, Ample, Besant, Bounteous, Bountiful, Breadth, Bright, Broad, Free(hander), Free-hearted, > **GENEROUS**, Giver, Grey, Grimond, Grit, Handsome, Indulgent, L, Largesse, Lavish, Octobrist, Open, > **PROFUSE**, Rad(ical), Samuelite, Simonite, Steel, Tolerant, Trivium, Unstinted, Verlig, Verligte, Whig

Liberate(d), Liberation, Liberator Bolivar, Deliver, Emancipate, Fatah, > **FREE**, Inkatha, Intolerant, Messiah, PLO, Release, Save, Sucre, Unfetter, UNITA, Women's

Liberian Kroo, Kru

Libertarian, Libertine Chartered, Corinthian, Debauchee, Laxist, Lecher, Lothario, Lovelace, Playboy, Rake, Rip, Roué, Wencher, Wolf

Liberty Bail, Civil, Discretion, Franchise, Freedom, Hall, Mill, Sauce

Library Bibliothecary, BL, Bodleian, Bookmobile, Circulating, Cottonian, Film, Gene, Harleian, Laurentian, Lending, Mazarin, Mobile, Morgue, PL, Public, Radcliffe, Reference, Subscription, Tauchnitz

Librettist Boito, Gilbert, Lyricist

▸ **Lice** see **LOUSE**

Licence, License Abandon, Allow, Authorisation, Carnet, Charter, Dispensation, Driving, Enable, Exequatur, Fling, Franchise, Free(dom), Gale, Imprimatur, Indult, > **LATITUDE**, Let, Marriage, Occasional, Passport, > **PERMIT**, Poetic, Pratique, Provisional, Road-fund, Rope, Slang, Special, Table

Licentious Artistic, Corinthian, Debauchee, Hot, Immoral, Large, Lax, Liberal, Loose, Prurient, Ribald, Sensual, Wanton

Lichen Apothecia, Archil, Corkir, Crotal, Crottle, Cup, Epiphyte, Epiphytic, Graphis, Korkir, Lecanora, Litmus, Orchel, Orchil(la), Orcine, Orseille, Parella, Parelle, Roccella, Rock tripe, Sea-ivory, Stone-rag, Stone-raw, Tree-moss, Usnea, Wartwort

Lick(ing) Bat, Beat, Deer, Lambent, Lap, Leather, Salt, Slake, Speed, Tongue, Whip

▸ **Licorice** see **LIQUORICE**

Lid Cover, Hat, Kid, Maximum, Opercula, Screwtop, Twist-off

Liddell Alice

Lido Beach, Pool

Lie(s), Liar, Lying Abed, Accubation, Accumbent, Ananias, Bam, Bare-faced, Bask, Billy, Bounce(r), Braide, Cau(l)ker, Cellier, Clipe, Clype, Concoction, Contour, Couchant, Cracker, Cram(mer), Cretism, Cumbent, Deception, Decubitous, Decumbent, Direct, Doggo, Fable, False(r), Falsehood, Falsify, Falsity, Fib, Fiction, Figment, Flam, Gag, Gonk, Incumbent, Invention, Inveracity, Kip, Lair, Leasing, Lee(ar), Lig(ge), Lurk, Mythomania, Obreption, Oner, Perjury, Plumper, Porky, Porky (pie), Procumbent, Prone, Prostrate, Pseudologia, Recline, Recumbent, Repent, Repose, Reptant, Ride, Romance(r), Sham, Sleep, Strapper, Stretcher, Supine, Swinger, Tale, Tappice, Tar(r)adiddle, Thumper, Tissue, Try, Untruth, Whacker, Whid, White, Whopper, Yanker

Lied Art-song, Song

Lie-detector Polygraph

Lien Mortgage, Title

Lieu Locus, Place

Lieutenant Cassio, Flag, Loot, Lt, No 1, Sub(altern)

Life Age, Animation, Being, Bio, Biog(raphy), Brian, Brio, C'est la vie, Clerihew, CV, Esse, Existence, Good, Heart, High, Mean, Pep, Plasma, Private, Real, Shelf, Span, Spirit, Still, Subsistence, Time, True, Useful, Vita, Zoe

Life-blood Essence, Lethee

Lifeboat Ark

Life-cell Energid

Life-cycle Redia

Life-force Ch'i, Chi, Qi

Lifeguard Cheesemonger

Lifeless(ness) Abiosis, Algidity, Amort, Arid, Azoic, Barren, Catatonic, Cauldrife, > **DEAD**, Dull, Flat, Inanimate, Inert, Log, Mineral, Possum, Sterile, Stonen, Wooden

Lifelike Breathing, Speaking

Lifeline Umbilicus

Life-rent Usufruct

Life-saver Preserver, Raft

Lift(ed), Lifter, Lifting Arayse, Arsis, Attollent, Bone, Cable-car, Camel, Chair, Cly, Copy, Crane, Davit, Dead, Dumb waiter, Elate, Elevator, Enhance, Extol, Filch, Fillip, Fireman's, Heave, Heeze, Heezie, Heft, Heist, Hitch, Hoise, Hoist, Hove, Jack, Jigger, Kleptomania, Leaven, Lefte, Lever, Lewis, Nab, Nap, Paternoster, Pilfer, Press, Pulley, > **RAISE**, Ride, Scoop, Ski, Sky, Snatch, Stair, Steal, T-bar, Teagle, Theft, Thumb, Up, Winch, Windlass

Ligament Annular, Fr(a)enum, Paxwax, Spring, Suspensory, Tendon, Urachus

Ligation, Ligature Aesc, Bandage, Bind, Tubal

Light(en), Lighting, Lighter, Lights Aerate, Airy, Albedo, Ale, Alow, Alpenglow, Amber, Ancient, Ans(wer), Arc, Aurora, Batswing, Beacon, Beam, Bengal, Bezel, Bleach, Brake, Bude, Bulb, Candle, Cannel, Casement, Chiaroscuro, Cierge, Clue, Courtesy, Day, Dewali, Diffused, Direct, Diwali, Dream-hole, Drop, Drummond, Earth-shine, Eddystone, Electrolier, Ethereal, Fairy, Fall, Fan, Fantastic, Fastnet, Fetch-candle, Fidibus, Fill, Fire, First, Fixed, Flambeau, Flame, Flare, Flax(y), Flicker, Flippant, Flit(t), Floating, Flood, Fluorescent, Fog (lamp), Frothy, Fuffy, Gegenschein, Gleam, Glim(mer), Glow, Gossamer, Green, Guiding, Gurney, Haggis, Hazard, Head, House, Ignite, Illum(in)e, Incandescence, Indirect, Induction, Inner, Irradiate, Junior, Key, Kindle, Klieg, Lamp, Land, Lantern, Lanthorn, Laser, Leading, Leerie, Leggiero,

Levigate, Lime, Link, Loadstar, Lobuli, Lodestar, Lozen, Lucarne, Lucigen, Luminaire, Lumine, Luminescence, Luminous, Lustre, Lux, Mandorla, Match, Mercurial, Merry-dancers, Mithra(s), Moon, Naphtha, Navigate, Neon, Nit, Northern, Obstruction, Od(yl), Offal, Optics, Pale, Pane, Parhelion, Pavement, Phosphene, Phosphorescence, Phot, Photon, Pilot, Pipe, Polar, Portable, Producer-gas, Range, Rear, Red, Reflex, Relume, Rembrandt, Reversing, Riding, Rocket, Running, Rush, Satori, Scoop, Sea-dog, Search, Shy, Southern-vigil, Spill, Spot, Spry, Steaming, Strip, Strobe, Stroboscope, Subtle, Sun, Sunshine, Suttle, Svelte, Tail, Tally, Taper, Taps, Threshold, Tind, Tine, Torch, Torchère, Touchpaper, Traffic, Trivial, Ultraviolet, Unchaste, Unoppressive, UV, Ver(e)y, Vesica, Vesta, Vigil, Watch, Wax, White, Windock, Window, Winnock, Zodiacal

▷ **Light** *may indicate* an anagram

Lighter Barge, Birlinn, Casco, Gas-poker, Keel, Linstock, Lunt, Match, Pontoon, Pra(a)m, Spill, Taper

Lighthouse Beacon, Caisson, Eddystone, Fanal, Fastnet, Phare, Pharos, Sea-mark, Signal

Lightless Aphotic, Dark, Obscure, Unlit

Lightness Buoyancy, Galant, Levity, Pallor

Lightning Ball, Catequil, Chain, Dry, Eclair, Enfouldered, Fireball, Fire flag, Forked, Fulmination, Heat, Levin, Sheet, Thunderbolt, Wildfire, Zigzag

Lightship Nore

Lightweight Nobody, Oz, Trivial

Lignite Jet, Surtarbrand, Surturbrand

Like(ness), Liking As, Broo, Care, Corpse, Dig, Duplicate, Effigy, Eg, Egal, Enjoy, Equal, Fancy, Fellow, Lich, Palate, Parallel, Peas, Penchant, Please, Predilection, Semblant, Shine, Similar, Simile, Sort, Speaking, Taste, Tiki

Likely, Likelihood Apt, Fair, Maximum, Odds-on, Offchance, On, Plausible, Possible, Probable, Probit, Prone

Likewise Also, Do, Eke, Item, So, Too, Tu quoque

Lilac Laylock, Mauve, Pipe-tree, Syringa

Lilliputian Minute

Lilt Swing

Lily African, Agapanthus, Aloe, Amaryllis, Annunciation, Arum, Asphodel, Aspidistra, Belladonna, Blackberry, Calla, Camas(h), Camass, Canada, Candock, Chincherinchee, Colchicum, Colocasia, Convallaria, Corn, Crinum, Dale, Day, Easter, Elaine, Fawn, Fleur de lys, Fritillary, Galtonia, Guernsey, Haemanthus, Hemerocallis, Herb-paris, Jacob's, Jersey, Kniphofia, Laguna, Lent, Leopard, Lote, Lotos, Lotus, Madonna, Mariposa, Martagon, Meadow, Moorva, Mount Cook, Nelumbo, Nenuphar, Nerine, Nuphar, Orange, Padma, Phormium, Pig, Plantain, Pond, Quamash, Regal, Richardia, Sabadilla, Sansevieria, Sarsa, Scilla, Sego, Skunk cabbage, Smilax, Solomon's seal, Spider, Star of Bethlehem, Stone, Sword, Tiger, Trillium, Tritoma, Turk's cap, Vellozia, Victoria, Water, Yucca, Zephyr

Lily-maid Elaine

Lima Sugar bean

Limb Arm, Bough, Branch, Crural, Exapod, Flipper, Hindleg, Imp, Leg, Leg-end, Member, Phantom, Proleg, Pterygium, Ramus, Scion, Shin, Spald, Spall, Spaul(d), Wing

Limbless Amelia

Limbo Bardo, Isolation

Lime Bass(wood), Beton, Calc, Lind(en), Malm, Mortar, Slaked, Soda, Teil, Tilia,

Trap, Unslaked, Viscum, Whitewash

Limerick Doggerel, Twiner, Verse

Limestone Calp, Ca(u)m, Clint, Coquina, Coral Rag, Cornbrash, Cornstone, Forest Marble, Grike, Karst, Kentish rag, Kunkar, Kunkur, Muschelkalk, Oolite, Pisolite, Rottenstone, Scaglia, Travertin(e)

Limey Rooinek

Limit(ation), Limited, Limiting Ambit, Bind, Border, Borné, Bound, Bourn(e), Brink, Cap, Cash, Ceiling, Chandrasekhar, Circumscribe, Climax, Compass, Confine, Deadline, Define, Demark, Determine, Earshot, Eddington, Edge, End, Entail, Esoteric, > EXTENT, Extreme, Finite, Frontier, Gate, Goal, Gole, Impound, Induciae, Insular, Limes, Lynchet, March, Maximum, Meare, Mete, Minimum, Nth, Outedge, Pale, Parameter, Perimeter, Periphery, Predetermine, Qualify, Range, Rate-cap, Ration, Reservation, Restrict, Rim, Roche, Roof, Scant, Shoestring, Sky, Speed, Stint, String, Sumptuary, Tail(lie), Tailye, Tailzie, Term(inus), Tether, Three-mile, Threshold, Thule, Tie, Time, Tropic, Twelve-mile, Utmost, Utter, Verge

▷ **Limit** *may indicate* 'surrounding'

Limner RA

Limousine Daimler, Rolls, Zil

Limp Claudication, Dot, Droopy, Flabby, Flaccid, Flimsy, Floppy, Hilch, Hirple, Hitch, Hobble, Hop, Lank, Lifeless, Spancel, Tangle

Limpet Keyhole, Patella, Slipper, Streptoneura

Limpid Clear, Lucid, Pure

Linch Terrace

Lincoln(shire) Abe, Poacher, Yellow-belly

Linden Baucis, Lime, Tilia

Line(d), Lines, Lining Abreast, Aclinic, Agate, Agonic, Allan, Anacreontic, > ANCESTRY, Anent, Angle, Apothem, Arew, Asclepiadean, Assembly, Asymptote, Axis, Babbitt, Bakerloo, Bar, Barcode, Battle, Baulk, Becket, Bikini, Bluebell, Bob, Bombast, Bottom, Boundary, BR, Brail, Branch, Bread, Bush, Canal, Carolingian, Carriage, Casing, Cell, Ceriph, Chord, Ciel, Club, Coach, Coffle, Colour, Column, Contour, Cord(on), Coseismal, Course, Crease, Credit, Crocodile, Crowsfoot, Curve, Cushion, Dancette, Date, Datum, Deadball, Delay, Descent, DEW, Diagonal, Diameter, Diffusion, Directrix, Distaff, Dotted, Doublure, Downhaul, Downrigger, Dress, Dynasty, Earing, E-la-mi, Encase, Equator, Equinoctial, Equinox, Faint, Fall(s), Fault, Feint, Fess(e), Fettle, File, Finishing, Firing, Firn, Flex, Flight, Frame, Fraunhofer, Front, Frontier, Frost, Furr(ow), Geodesic, Germ, Gimp, Giron, Goal, Graph, Grass, Green, Gridiron, Gymp, Gyron, Hachure, Halyard, Hard, Hatching, Hawser, Hemistich, Heptameter, Hexameter, Hexapody, High-watermark, Hindenburg, Hockey, Hogscore, Hot, House, Impot, Inbounds, Inbred, Incase, Interfluve, Intima, Isallobar, Isentrope, Isobar, Isobath, Isobront, Isocheim, Isochime, Isochron(e), Isoclude, Isocryme, Isogloss, Isogonal, Isogram, Isohel, Isohyet, Isolex, Isomagnetic, Isonome, Isopach(yte), Isophone, Isophote, Isopiestic, Isopleth, Isopyenal, Isotach, Isothere, Isotherm, Knittle, L, Land, Lane, Lansker, Lap, Lariat, Latitude, Lead, Leash, Le(d)ger, Ley, Lie, Ling, LMS, Load, Log, Longitude, Loxodrome, Lubber, Lye, Macron, Maginot, Main, Mainsheet, Mark, Marriage, Mason-Dixon, Median, Meridian, Mesal, Miurus, Monorail, Multiplet, Naman, Nazca, Nidation, Noose, Norsel, Northern, Number, Oche, Octastichon, Ode, Oder-Meisse, Og(h)am, Omentum, Onedin, Ordinate, Orphan, Painter, Parallel, Parameter, Parastichy, Party, Paternoster, Path, Penalty, Pencil, Phalanx, Picket, Pinstripe, Plimsoll, Plumb, Poetastery, Police,

Policy, Popping-crease, Poverty, Power, Product(ion), Profession, Punch, Pure,
Queue, Race, Radial, Radius, Rail, Rank, Raster, Ratlin(e), Ratling, Rattlin, Ray,
Red, Retinue, Rew, Rhumb, Ripcord, Rope, Route, Row, Rugose, Rugous, Rule,
Ry, Sarking, Scazon, Score, Script, Secant, Seperatrix, Serif, Seriph, Service,
Set, Siding, Siegfried, Sield, Sight, Silver, Slur, Snood, Snow, Soft, Solidus,
Sounding, Spectral, Spring, Spunyarn, Squall, SR, Staff, Stance, Stanza,
Starting, Static, Stave, Stean, Steen, Stein, Stem, Stich(os), Stock, Story, Strap,
Streak, Striate, String, Stripe, Stuff, Subtense, Swifter, Symphysis, Syzygy, Tag,
Tailback, Talweg, Tangent, Teagle, Tea lead, Terminator, Tetrameter, Thalweg,
Thin blue, Thin red, Thread, Throwaway, Tidemark, Tie, Timber, Touch,
Trade, Transmission, Transoceanic, Transversal, Tree, Trimeter, Tropic, Trot,
Trunk, Tudor, Variety, Verse, Vinculum, Virgule, Wad, Wallace's, Washing,
Water(shed), White, Widow, Wire, Wrinkle, Yellow, Zag, Zip, Zollner's
Lineage Ancestry, Descent, Extraction, Parage, Pedigree
Linen Amice, Amis, Barb, Bed, Byssus, Cambric, Crash, Damask, Dornick,
Dowlas, Ecru, Flax Table, Harn, Huckaback, Inkle, Lawn, Lint, Lockram,
Moygashel, Napery, Percale, Seersucker, Sendal, Silesia, Toile
Liner Artist, Bin-bag, Eye, Ocean greyhound, RMS, Ship, Sleeve, Steamer, Steen,
Titanic
Linesman Parodist, > **POET**, Touch-judge
Linger(ing) Chronic, Dawdle, Dwell, Hang, Hove(r), Lag, > **LOITER**, Straggle,
Tarry, Tie
Lingerie Bra, Drawers, Undies
Lingo Argot, Bat, Cant, Jargon, Speech
Linguist(ic), Linguistics Glottic, Historical, Philological, Phonemics, Polyglot,
Semantics, Structural, Stylistics, Syntax, Tagmemics, Taxeme
Liniment Balm, Carron-oil, Embrocation, Ointment, Opodeldoc, Salve
Link(ing), Links Associate, Between, Bond, Bridge, Chain, Cleek, Colligate,
Concatenation, Copula, Couple, Cross-reference, Desmid, Drag, Ess, Flambeau,
Golf, Hookup, Hot, Hotline, Incatenation, Interface, Internet, Intertwine,
Karabiner, Krab, Liaise, Machair, Missing, Nexus, Pons, Preposition, Relate,
Tead(e), > **TIE**, Tie-in, Tie-line, Torch, Unite, Weakest, Yoke
Linkman Lamplighter, Mediator
Linnet Finch, Lintie, Lintwhite, Twite
Linoleum Waxcloth
Lint Charpie, Dossil
Lintel Summer, Transom
Lion(ess) Androcles, Aphid, Chindit, Elsa, Glitterati, Hero, Leo, Maned,
Mountain, Nemean, Opinicus, Personage, Pride, Simba
Lionel Trilling
Lion-tamer Dan(iel)
Lip(py), Lips Beestung, Cheek, Fat, Fipple, Flews, Hare, Helmet, Jib, Labellum,
Labiate, Labret, Labrum, Ligula, Muffle, > **RIM**, Rubies, Sass, Sauce, Slack-jaw,
Submentum
Lipstick Chapstick
Liquefy Dissolve, Fuse, Melt
Liqueur, Liquor Abisante, Absinthe, Advokaat, Ale, Almondrado, Amaretto,
Anise, Anisette, Apry, Benedictine, Bree, Brew, Broo, Broth, Calvados, Cassis,
Cerise, Chartreuse, Chasse, Cherry marnier, Cher-suisse, Chicha, Choclair,
Chococo, Cocoribe, Cointreau®, Creature, Crème, Crème de menthe, Curaçao,
Drambuie®, Eau des creoles, Elixir, Enzian, Feni, Fenny, Fraises, Framboise,
Fumet, Fustian, Galliano, Geropiga, Grand Marnier, Hogan, Hogan-mogen,

Hooch, John Barleycorn, Jungle juice, Kahlua, Kaoliang, Kir, Kirschwasser, Kirsh(wasser), Kummel, Lager, Lap, Malt, Maraschino, Mastic, Metheglin, Mickey Finn, Midori, Mirabelle, Mobbie, Mobby, Noyau, Oedema, Ooze, Ouzo, Parfait d'amour, Pasha, Pastis, Pernod, Persico, Pot, Potation, Pousse-café, Prunelle, Rakee, Raki, Ratafia, Roiano, Roncoco, Rose, Rotgut, Rum, Sabra, Sambuca, Samshoo, Schnapps, Sciarada, Shypoo, Skink, Stingo, Stock, Stout, Strega®, Strunt, Stuff, Supernaculum, Tape, Taplash, Tequila, Tia Maria, Tickle-brain, Tiff, Van der Hum, White lightning, Wine, Witblits, Wort

Liquid(ate), Liquidity, Liquids, Liquefaction Acetal, Amortise, Annihilate, Apprize, Azeotrope, Bittern, Bouillon, Bromine, Butanal, Butanol, Butyraldehide, Butyrin, Cacodyl, Cadaverine, Cash, Cash flow, Chloramine, Cinerin, Clyster, Court-bouillon, Creosol, Creosote, Decoction, Dispersant, Dope, Eluate, Erase, Ethanol, Ether, Eucalyptol, Eugenol, Flow, Fluid, Fural, Furfural, Furol, Halothene, Jaw, Kakodyl, Lewisite, Limonene, Linalool, Lye, Massacre, Mess, Minim, Mouillé, Picamar, Pipe, Potion, Protoplasm, Ptisan, Pyrrole, Pyrrolidine, Raffinate, Rhigolene, Safrole, Serum, Solution, Solvent, Syrup, Terebene, Thixotropy, Titer, Titre, Tuberculin, Tusche, Ullage, Verjuice, Whey, Wort

Liquorice Indian, Jequirity, Nail, Nail-rod, Pomfret, Pontefract-cake, Spanish juice, Sugarallie, Sugarally

Lis Iris, Lily

Lisa Mona

Lisp(er) Ephraimite, Sibilance

Lissom(e) Agile, Lithe, Nimble, Svelte

▷ **List** *may indicate* 'listen'

List(s), Listing Active, Agenda, Antibarbarus, Appendix, Army, Atilt, Barocco, Barrace, Bead-roll, Bibliography, Canon, Cant, Catalog(ue), Categorise, Catelog, Cause, Check, Civil, Class, Compile, Credits, Danger, Debrett, Docket, Entry, Enumerate, Front, Glossary, Hark, Hearken, Heel, Hit, Hit-parade, Honours, Index, Indian, Interdiction, Inventory, Itemise, Lean, Leet, Line-up, Linked, Lloyds, Mailing, Manifest, Navy, Notitia, Official, Panel, Paradigm, Party, Prize, Register, Repertoire, Reserved, Roin, Roll, Roon, Roster, Rota, Rund, Schedule, Short, Sick, Slate, Slope, Strip, Syllabus (of Errors), Table, Tariff, Tick, Ticket, Tilt, Timetable, Tip, Transfer, Union, Waiting, Waybill, White, Wine, Wish

Listen(er) Attend, Auditor, Auscultate, Ear, Eavesdropper, Gobemouche, Hark, > **HEED**, Lithe, Lug, Monitor, Oyez, Sithee, Wire-tap, Yo-ho(-ho)

▷ **Listen to** *may indicate* a word sounding like another

Listless(ness) Abulia, Accidie, Acedia, Apathetic, Atony, Dawney, Draggy, Inanition, Indolent, Lackadaisical, Languor, Mooning, Mope, Mopus, Sloth, Thowless, Torpor, Waff

Lit Alight, Landed

▷ **Lit** *may indicate* an anagram

Litany Eirenicon

Literacy Emotional

Literal(ly), Literal sense Etymon, Misprint, Simply, Typo, Verbatim

Literary Academic, Bas bleu, Booksie, Erudite, Lettered

Literary girls Althea, Jenny, Maud, Pippa

Literature Belles lettres, Corpus, Fiction, Gongorism, Midrash, Page, Picaresque, Polite, Prose, Responsa, Splatterpunk, Wisdom

Lithe Flexible, Limber, Pliant, Souple, > **SUPPLE**, Svelte, Willowy

Lithium Li

Litigant Barrator, John-a-Nokes, John-a-Stiles, John Doe, Party, Richard Roe, Suer, Suitor

Litmus Indicator, Lacmus, Lichen

Litre L

Litter Bed, Brancard, Brood, Cacolet, Cubs, Debris, Doolie, Duff, Emu-bob, Farrow, Jampan, Kago, Kajawah, Kindle, Mahmal, Mor, Nest, Norimon, Palankeen, Palanquin, Palkee, Palki, Pup, > **REFUSE**, Scrap, Sedan, Stretcher, Sweepings, Team

Little Bagatelle, Billee, Brief, Chota, Curn, Dorrit, Drib, Drop, Fewtrils, Insect, Iota, John, Jot, Leet, Lilliputian, Limited, Lite, Lyte, Mini, Miniscule, Minnow, Minuscule, > **MINUTE**, Modicum, Morceau, Nell, Paltry, Paucity, Petite, Pink, Pitttance, Ronte, Runt, Scant, Scut, Shade, Shoestring, Shred, Shrimp, Slight, Sma', > **SMALL**, Smattering, Smidge(o)n, Smidgin, Some, Soupçon, Spot, Tad, Tich, Tine, Titch, Touch, Tyne, Vestige, Wee, Weedy, Whit, Women

Liturgical, Liturgy Doxology, Hallel, Rite, Versicle

Live(d), Livelihood, Living, Liveliness, Lively, Lives Active, Alert, Allegretto, Allegro, Am, Animated, Animation, Animato, AV, Awake, Be, Birkie, Bouncy, Breezy, Brio, Brisk, Cant(y), Capriccio(so), Cheery, Chipper, Chirpy, Cohabit, Con moto, Crouse, Durante vita, > **DWELL**, Ebullient, Entrain, Exist, Feisty, Frisky, Galliard, Gamy, Gay, Giocoso, Gracious, Grig, Hang-out, Hard, High jinks, Hijinks, Hot, Is, Jazz, Kedge, Lad, Lead, Mercurial, Merry, Outgo, Pacey, Peart, Pep, Piert, Quicksilver, Rackety, Racy, Reside, Rousing, Salt, Saut, Scherzo, Skittish, Spiritoso, Spirituel(le), Sprack, Spry, Spunky, Sustenance, Swinging, Vibrant, Vigoroso, Vital, Vitality, Vivace, Vive, Vivo, > **VOLATILE**, Vyvyan, Zappy, Zingy, Zippy, Zoe

▶ **Livelihood** *see* **LIVE(D)**

Liver(ish) Foie gras, Hepar, Hepatic(al), Porta, Puce, Resident, Tomalley

Liverpool, Liverpudlian Scouse

Liverwort Gemma-cup, Hepatica, Riccia

Livery(man) Ermine, Flunkeydom, Goldsmith, Skinner, Tiger, Uniform

Livid Blae, Bruised, Cross, > **FURIOUS**, Pale

Living Advowson, Benefice, Biont, Bread, Canonry, Crust, Glebe, Inquiline, Lodging, Quick, Resident, Simony, Subsistence, Symbiotic, Vicarage, Vital

Livingstone Doctor, Ken

Liza, Lizzie Bess, Betty, Flivver, Hexam, Tin

Lizard Abas, Agama, Amphisboena, Anguis, Anole, Basilisk, Bearded, Bearded-dragon, Blindworm, Blue-tongued, Brontosurus, Chameleon, Chuckwalla, Dinosaur, Draco, Eft, Evet, Fence, Flying, Frilled, Full-necked, Galliwasp, Gecko(ne), Gila, Gila monster, Glass snake, Goanna, Gotcha, Guana, Hatteria, Hellbender, Horned, Iguana, Jew, Kabaragoya, Komodo (dragon), Lacerta, Legua(a)n, Lounge, Mastigure, Menopome, Moloch, Monitor, Mosasaur(us), Mountain devil, Newt, Perentie, Perenty, Reptile, Sand, Sauria, Scincoid, Seps, Skink, Slow-worm, Snake, Stellio(n), Sungazer, Tegu(exin), Thorny devil, Tokay, Tuatara, Tuatera, Varan, Wall, Whiptail, Worm, Worral, Worrel, Zandoli, Zonure

Llama Alpaca, Alpaco, Guanaco, Huanaco, Paco, Vicuna

Load(ed), Loader, Loading, Loads Accommodation, Affluent, Ballast, Base, Boot-strap, Burden, Cargo, Charge, Cobblers, Dead weight, Disc, Dope, Drunk, Dummy, Fardel, Fother, Freight, Front-end, Fulham, Full, Gestant, Heap, Input, Jag, Lade, Lard, Last, Live, Onus, Pack, Packet, Pay, Peak, Power, Prime, Rich, Seam, Shipment, Some, Span, Super, Surcharge, > **TIGHT**, Tod, Traction, Ultimate, Useful, Wealthy, Weight, Wharfinger, Wing

Loaf(er), Loaves Baguette, Batch, Baton, Bloomer, Bludge, Brick, Bum, Bu(r)ster, Cad, Cob, Coburg, Cottage, Danish, Farmhouse, French stick, Hawm, Hoe-cake, Idle, > LAZE, Long tin, Lusk, Manchet, Miche, Mouch, Pan, Pan(h)agia, Plain, Quartern, Roll, Roti, Shewbread, Showbread, Slosh, Split tin, Square tin, Sugar, Tin, Vantage, Vienna, Yob

Loam Clay, Loess, Loss, Malm

Loan(s) Advance, Balloon, Benevolence, Bottomry, Bridging, Debenture, Droplock, Imprest, Lane, Mutuum, Omnium, Out, Prest, Respondentia, Roll-over, Soft, Start-up, Sub, Time, War

Loathe, Loathing, Loathsome Abhor(rent), Abominate, Carrion, Detest, Hate, Nauseate, Scunner, Ug(h)

Lob Loft, Sky, Underarm

Lobby Demo, Division, Entry, Foyer, Gun, Hall, Press, Urge

Lobe(d) Anisocercal, Fluke, Frontal, Insula, Jugum, Lacinia, Lap, Occipital, Optic, Palmate, Parietal, Pinnule, Runcinate, Segment, Temporal, Uvula, Vermis

Lobster Cock, Crawfish, Crayfish, Crustacean, Decapoda, Langouste, Newburg, Norway, Pot, Rock, Scampo, Spiny, Thermidor, Tomalley

Local(ity) Area, Endemic, Home, Inn, Insider, Landlord, Native, Near, Nearby, Neighbourhood, Number, Parochial, Pub, Regional, Resident, Swadishi, Tavern, Topical, Vicinal

▷ **Local** *may indicate* a dialect word

Locale Scene, Site

Locate Connect, Find, Fix, Lay, Pinpoint, Plant, Site, Spot

Location Address, Milieu, Node, Place, Recess, Site, Situation, Sofar, Ubiety, Website, Zone

Loch, Lough Allen, Ashie, Awe, Derg, Earn, Eil, Erne, Etive, Fine, Gare, Garten, Holy, Hourn, Katrine, > LAKE, Larne, Leven, Linnhe, Lomond, Long, Moidart, Morar, More, Nakeel, Neagh, Ness, Rannoch, Ryan, Shiel, Strangford, Tay, Torridon

Lock(ing), Locker, Locks, Lock up Bar, Bolt, Canal, Central, Chubb®, Clinch, Combination, Cowlick, Curlicue, Davy Jones, Deadbolt, Detent, Drop, Fastener, Fermentation, Foretop, Gate, Haffet, Haffit, Handcuff, Hasp, Hold, Intern, Key, Latch, Lazaretto, Man, Mortise, Percussion, Prison, Quiff, Ragbolt, Ringlet, Sasse, Scalp, Scissors, > SECURE, Sluice, Snap, Spring, Stock, Strand, Tag, Talon, Time, Trap, Tress, Tuft, Vapour, Villus, Ward, Wheel, Wrestle, Yale®

Locket Lucy

Lockjaw Tetanus, Trismus

Locksmith Garret-master, Hairdresser

Locomotive Banker, Bogie, Bul(l)gine, Engine, Iron horse, Mobile, Rocket, Steam, Steamer, Train

Locum Deputy, Relief, Stopgap

Locus Centrode, Horopter, Lemniscate, Place, Spot

Locust, Locust tree Anime, Carob, Cicada, Hopper, Nymph, Robinia, Seventeen-year, Voetganger

Lode Comstock, Lodge, Mother, Reef, Vein

Lodestone Magnes, Magnet

Lodge(r) Billet, Board(er), Box, Cosher, Deposit, Dig, Doss, Entertain, Freemason, Grange, Guest, Harbour, Host, Inmate, Layer, Lie, Masonic, Nest, Orange, Parasite, PG, Quarter, Rancho, Room(er), Roomie, Stay, Storehouse, Stow, Sweat, Tenant, Tepee, Wigwam

Lodging(s) Abode, B and B, Chummage, Dharms(h)ala, Digs, Dosshouse, Ferm,

Grange, Grove, Hostel, Inquiline, Kip, Minshuku, Pad, Padding-ken, Pension, Pied-à-terre, Quarters, Resiant, Rooms, Singleen, YHA

Loft(iness), Lofty Aerial, Airy, Arrogant, Attic, Celsitude, Chip, Choir, Garret, Grand, Haymow, High, Jube, Lordly, Magniloquent, Noble, Olympian, Pulpitum, Rarefied, Rigging, Rood, Roost, Tallat, Tallet, Tallot

Log Billet, Black box, Cabin, Chip, Chock, Diarise, Diary, Hack, Ln, Mantissa, Nap(i)erian, Neper, Patent, > **RECORD**, Stock, Yule

Logarithm Common, Lod, Mantissa, Nap(i)erian, Natural

Logic(al) Alethic, Aristotelian, Chop, Dialectic(s), Distributed, Doxastic, Epistemics, Formal, Fuzzy, Heuristics, Iff, Mathematical, Modal, Organon, Philosophical, Premise, Pusser's, Ramism, Rational(e), Reason, Sequacious, Sorites, Symbolic, Tense, Trivium

Logo Colophon

Loin(s) Flank, Inguinal, Lungie, Lunyie, Reins

Loincloth Dhoti, Lungi, Pareu, Waist-cloth

Loiter(ing) Dally, Dare, Dawdle, Dilatory, Dilly-dally, Idle, Lag, Lallygag, Leng, Lime, > **LINGER**, Mooch, Mouch, Potter, Saunter, Scamp, Suss, Tarry

Lola Dolores

Loll Hawm, Lounge, Sprawl

Lollipop, Lolly Ice pole, Lulibub

Lolly Money, Sweetmeat

London(er) 'Arry, Big Smoke, Cockaigne, Co(c)kayne, Cockney, East-ender, Flat-cap, Jack, Roseland, Smoke, Town, Troynovant, Wen

London pride None-so-pretty

Lone(r), Lonely Remote, Rogue, Secluded, Sole, Solitary, Unked, Unket, Unkid

Long(er), Longing, Longs Ache, Aitch, Ake, Appetent, Aspire, Brame, Covet, Desire, Die, Earn, Erne, Far, Greed, Green, Grein, > **HANKER**, Huey, Hunger, Inveterate, Island, Itch, L, Lanky, Large, Lengthy, Longa, Lust, Macron, Miss, More, > **NO LONGER**, Nostalgia, Option, Pant, Parsec, > **PINE**, Prolix, Sesquipedalian, Side, Sigh, Tall, Thirst, Trews, Weary, Wish, Wist, Yearn, Yen

Long-eared Spicate

Longitude Celestial, Ecliptic, Meridian

Long-lashed Mastigophora(n)

Long live(d) Banzai, Macrobian, Viva, Zindabad

Longshoreman Hobbler, Hoveller, Wharfinger

Long-suffering Job, Patient, Stoical

Long-tailed Macrural

Long-winded Prolix, Verbose, Wordy

Loo Ajax, Bog, Can, Chapel, Dike, Game, Gents, Jakes, John, Privy, Toilet

Look(s), Look at Air, Aspect, Behold, Belgard, Bonne-mine, Busk, Butcher's, Butcher's hook, Clock, Close-up, Crane, Daggers, Decko, Deek, Dekko, Ecce, Ecco, Expression, Eye, Face, Facies, Gander, Gawp, Gaze, Geek, Glance, Glare, Gledge, Glimpse, Glom, Goggle, Good, Grin, Hallo, Hangdog, Hey, Iliad, Inspect, Keek, La, Leer, Lo, Mien, New, Ogle, Peek, Peep, Prospect, Ray, Recce, Refer, > **REGARD**, Scan, Scrutinise, Search, See, Seek, Shade, Sheep's eyes, Shufti, Shufty, Spy, Squint, Squiz, Survey, Toot, V, Vista, Wet

Look-out (man) Cockatoo, Crow's nest, Dixie, Huer, Mirador, Sangar, Sentinel, Sentry, Sungar, Toot(er), Watch, Watchtower

▷ **Look silly** *may indicate* an anagram

Loom Beamer, Dobby, Emerge, Impend, Jacquard, Lathe, Menace, Picker, Temple, Threaten, Tower

Loon Diver

Loop(ed), Loophole, Loopy Articulatory, Becket, Bight, Billabong, Bouclé, Carriage, Chink, Closed, Coil, Eyelet, Eyesplice, Fake, Frog, Frontlet, Grom(m)et, Ground, Grummet, Hank, Henle's, Hysteresis, Infinite, Kink, Knop, Lasket, Lippes, Lug, Noose, Oillet, Parral, Parrel, Pearl(-edge), Picot, Prusik, Purl, Scrunchie, Staple, Stirrup, Tab, Terry, Toe, Twist

Loos Anita

Loose(n), Loose woman Absolve, Abstrict, Afloat, Anonyma, Baggage, Bail, Besom, Bike, Chippie, Chippy, Cocotte, Cutty, Demi-mondaine, Demirep, Demivierge, Desultory, Dissolute, Dissolve, Doxy, Draggletail, Dratchell, Drazel, Emit, Flirt-gill, Floosie, Floozie, Floozy, Floppy, Franion, Free, Gangling, Gay, Hussy, Insecure, Jade, Jezebel, Lax, Light-heeled, Loast, Mob, Mort, Naughty pack, Pinnace, Profligate, Quail, Ramp, > RELAX, Sandy, Scrubber, Skanky-ho, Slag, Slapper, Streel, Tart, Tramp, Trull, Ungyve, Unhasp, Unhitch, Unknit, Unknot, Unlace, Unpin, Unreined, Unscrew, Unthread, Untie, Vague, Waistcoateer, Wappend, Whore

Loot Boodle, Booty, Cragh, Creach, Foray, Haul, Mainour, Peel, Pluck, > PLUNDER, Ransack, Rape, Reave, Rieve, Rob, Sack, Smug, Spoils, Spoliate, Swag, Treasure, Waif

Lop Behead, Clop, Curtail, Detruncate, Droop, Shroud, Sned, Trash

Lope Stride

Loquacious Chatty, Gabby, Garrulous, Rambling

Lord(s), Lordship, Lordly Adonai, Arrogant, Boss, Byron, Cyril, Dieu, Domineer, Dominical, Duc, Earl, Elgin, Gad, God, Haw-haw, Herr, Imperious, Jim, Justice, Kami, Kitchener, Landgrave, Law, Ld, Liege, Lonsdale, Losh, Lud, Mesne, Misrule, Mynheer, Naik, Oda Nobunaga, Omrah, Ordinary, Ormazd, Ormuzd, Peer, Sea, Seigneur, Seignior, Shaftesbury, Sire, Spiritual, Taverner, Temporal, Tuan, Ullin

Lords and ladies Wake-robin

Lore Cab(b)ala, Edda, Lair, Lare, Riem, Upanis(h)ad

Lorelei Siren

Lorgnette Starers

Lorna Doone

Lorry Artic(ulated), Camion, Crummy, Drag, Flatbed, Juggernaut, Low-loader, Rig, Tipper, Tonner, > TRUCK, Wagon

Lose(r) Also-ran, Decrease, Drop, Elude, Forfeit, Hesitater, Leese, Misère, Mislay, Misplace, Nowhere, Tank, Throw, Tine(r), Tyne, Underdog, Unsuccessful, Waste, Weeper

Loss, Lost Anosmia, Aphesis, Aphonia, Apocope, Apraxia, Astray, Attainder, Boohai, Chord, Cost, Dead, Decrease, Depreciation, Detriment, Disadvantage, Elision, Extinction, Foredamned, Forfeited, Forgotten, Forlorn, Gone, Lore, Lorn, Lurch, Missing, Omission, Outage, Pentimento, Perdition, Perdu, Perished, Preoccupied, Privation, Psilosis, Reliance, Tine, Tinsel, Tint, Toll, Traik, Tribes, Tyne(d), Ullage, Unredeemed, Wastage, Wasted, Will, Write-off, Wull

Loss of memory Amnesia, Black-out, Fugue, Infonesia, Paramnesia

▷ **Lost** *may indicate* an anagram or an obsolete word

Lot(s) Abundant, Amount, Aret(t), Badly, Batch, Boatload, Caboodle, Cavel, Chance, Deal, Dole, Doom, Drove, Due, > FATE, Fortune, Group, Hantle, Hap, Heaps, Horde, Host, Item, Job, Kevel, Kismet, Lashings, Legion, Luck, Manifold, Many, Mass, Moh, Moira, Mony, Mort, Myriad, Oceans, Omnibus, Oodles, Pack, Parcel, Parking, Plenitude, Plenty, Portion, Power, Purim, Raft, Rich, Scads, Set, Sight, Slather, Slew, Slue, Sortilege, Sortition, Stack, Sum, Tall order, The works, Tons, Vole, Wagonload, Weird

Loth Averse, Circumspect, Sweer(t), Sweir(t)

Lothario Lady-killer, Libertine, Poodle-faker, Rake, Womaniser

Lotion After-shave, Blackwash, Calamine, Collyrium, Cream, Eye-wash, Humectant, Setting, Suntan, Unguent, Wash, Yellow wash

Lottery, Lotto Art union, Ballot, Bingo, Cavel, Draw, Gamble, National, Pakapoo, Pools, Postcode, Punchboard, Raffle, Rollover, Scratchcard, Sweepstake, Tattersall's, Tombola

Lotus (eater), Lotus land Asana, Djerba, Lotophagus, Padmasana

Loud(ness), Loudly Bel, Big, Blaring, Booming, Brassy, Decibel, F, FF, Flashy, Forte, Fracas, Full-mouthed, Garish, Gaudy, Glaring, Hammerklavier, High, Lumpkin, Noisy, Orotund, Plangent, Raucous, Roarie, Siren, Sone, Stentor(ian), Strident, Tarty, Vocal, Vociferous, Vulgar

Loudspeaker Action, Boanerges, Bullhorn, Hailer, Megaphone, Stentor, Subwoofer, Tannoy®, Tweeter, Woofer

▶ **Lough** see LOCH

Louis Baker, Roi

Louisianian Cajun

Lounge(r) Cocktail, Da(c)ker, Daiker, Departure, Hawm, Idle, Laze, Lizard, Loll, Lollop, Parlour, Paul's man, Sitkamer, Slouch, Sun, Transit

Louse (up), Lousy, Lice Acrawl, Argulus, Bolix, Bollocks, Chat, Cootie, Crab, Crummy, Fish, Head, Isopod(a), Kutu, Nit, Oniscus, Pedicular, Phthiriasis, Plant, Psocoptera, Psylla, Slater, Snot, Sowbug, Sucking, Vermin, Whale

Lout Clod(hopper), Coof, Cuif, Hallian, Hallion, Hallyon, Hick, Hob, Hobbledehoy, Hooligan, Hoon, Jack, Jake, Keelie, Lager, Larrikin, Litter, Lob(lolly), Loord, Lubber, Lumpkin, Oaf, Oik, Rube, Swad, Tout, Tripper, Yahoo, Yob(bo)

Love(r) Abelard, Adore, Adulator, Affection, Agape, Amant, Amateur, Ami(e), Amoret, Amoroso, Amour, Antony, Ardour, Ariadne, Aroha, Aucassin, Beau, Bidie-in, Blob, Calf, Care, Casanova, Chamberer, Cicisbeo, Concubine, Coquet, Court, Courtly, Cupboard, Cupid, Dona(h), Dotard, Dote, Doxy, Duck(s), Ducky, Dulcinea, Eloise, Eloper, Emotion, Enamorado, Eros, Fan, Fancy man, Flame, Frauendienst, Free, Goose-egg, Greek, Idolise, Inamorata, Inamorato, Isolde, Jo, Kama, Lad, Leman, Like, Lochinvar, Loe, Loo, Lurve, Nihility, Nil, Nothing, Nought, O, Pairs, Paramour, Pash, Passion, Philander, -phile, Platonic, Protestant, Psychodelic, Puppy, Revere, Romance, Romeo, Sapphism, Spooner, Stale, Storge, Suitor, Swain, Thisbe, Touch, Toyboy, Troilus, True, Turtle(-dove), Valentine, Venus, Virtu, Worship, Zeal, Zero

Love-apple Tomato, Wolf's-peach

Love-bite Hickey

Love-child By-blow, Come-by-chance

Love-in-a-mist Nigella

Love letter Capon

Lovely Adorable, Belle, Dishy, Dreamy, Exquisite, Nasty

Love-making > INTERCOURSE, Kama Sutra, Sex, Snog

Love-sick Smit(ten), Strephon

Loving(ly) Amoroso, Amorous, Fond, Tender

Low(est), Low-cut, Lower(ing) Abase, Abate, Abysmal, Amort, Area, Avail(e), Avale, B, Basal, Base(-born), Bass(o), Beneath, Caddish, Cartoonist, Cheap, Church, Condescend, Contralto, Cow, Croon, Crude, Darken, Debase, Décolleté, Deepmost, Degrade, Demean, Demit, Demote, Depress, Devalue, Dim, Dip, Dispirited, Doldrums, Drawdown, Drop, Early, Embase, Flat, Foot, Frown,

Gazunder, Glare, Guernsey, Gurly, Hedge, Humble, Ignoble, Imbase, Inferior, Jersey, Laigh, Lallan, Law, Light, Lite, Mass, Mean, Menial, Moo, Mopus, Morose, Nadir, Net, Nether, Nett, Ostinato, Paravail, Plebeianise, Profound, Prole, Relegate, Ribald, Rock-bottom, Sad, Scoundrel, Scowl, Settle, Shabby, Short, Soft, Stoop, Subordinate, Sudra, Undermost, Unnoble, Vail, Vulgar, Weak, Wretched

Lowbrow Philistine

Lowdown Gen, Info

▷ **Lower** *may refer to* cattle

Lowland(er) Carse, Gallovidian, Glen, Laigh, Lallans, Merse, Mudflat, Plain, Polder, Sassenach, Vlei

Low-lying Callow, Epigeous, Fens, Inferior, Sump

Low person Boor, Bunter, Cad, Caitiff, Cocktail, Demirep, Ratfink, Snot

Loyal(ty) Adherence, Allegiant, Brick, Dependable, Esprit de corps, Faithful, Fast, Fidelity, Gungho, Leal, Patriotic, Stalwart, Staunch, > TRUE, True blue, Trusty

Loyalist Hard core, Paisley, Patriot, Tory

Lozenge Cachou, Catechu, Fusil, Jujube, Mascle, Pastille, Pill, Rhomb, Rustre, Tablet, Troche

LSD Acid, Money

Lubber(ly), Lubbers Booby, Clod, Clumsy, Gawky, Hulk, Lob, Looby, Oaf, Slowback, Swab, Swads

Lubricant, Lubricate, Lubrication Carap-oil, Coolant, Derv, Fluid, Force-feed, Grease, Oil, Petrolatum, Sebum, Unguent, Vaseline®, Wool-oil

Luce Ged

Lucerne Alfalfa, Medick, Nonsuch

Lucia Mimi

Lucid Bright, Clear, Perspicuous, Sane

Lucifer Devil, Match, Proud

Luck(y) Amulet, Auspicious, Beginner's, Bonanza, Break, Caduac, Cess, Chance, Charmed, Chaunce, Daikoku, Dip, Fate, Fluke, > FORTUNE, Godsend, Hap, Heather, Hit, Jam(my), Joss, Lady, Lot, Mascot, Mozzle, Pot, Prosit, Providential, Pudding-bag, Purple patch, Seal, Seel, Sele, Serendipity, Sess, Sonsie, Sonsy, Star(s), Streak, Success, Talisman, Tinny, Tough, Turn-up, Windfall

Luckless Hapless, Wight

Lucre Money, Pelf, Tin

Lucy Locket

Lud Gad

Luddite Saboteur, Wrecker

Ludicrous Absurd, Bathetic, Bathos, Farcical, Inane, Irish, Jest, Laughable, Risible

Ludo Uckers

Luff Derrick

Lug Ear, Earflap, Sea-worm, Sowle, Tote, Tow

Luggage Bags, Carryon, Cases, Dunnage, Excess, Grip, Hand, Kit, Petara, Suiter, Traps, Trunk

Luggage-carrier Grid

Lugubrious Dismal, Drear

Luke-warm Laodicean, Lew, Tepid

Lull, Lullaby Berceuse, Calm, Cradlesong, Hushaby, Respite, Rock, Sitzkreig, Soothe, Sopite

Lulu Stunner

Lumber(ing) Clump, Galumph, Jumble, Pawn, Ponderous, Raffle, Saddle, Scamble, Timber

Lumberjack Bushwhacker, Feller, Logger

Luminance, Luminous, Luminosity, Luminescence Aglow, Arc, Foxfire, Glow, Ignis-fatuus, L, Light, Nit, Phosphorescent, Sea-dog, Wildfire, Will o' the wisp

Lumme Coo, Lor

Lump(y) Aggregate, Bubo, Bud, Bulge, Bur(r), Caruncle, Chuck, Chunk, Clat, Claut, Clod, Clot, Cob, Combine, Dallop, Da(u)d, Dollop, Enhydros, Epulis, Flocculate, Ganglion, Geode, Gnarl, Gob(bet), Goiter, Goitre, Grape, Hunch, Hunk, Inium, Knarl, Knob, Knub, Knur(r), Knurl, Lob, Lunch, Malleolus, Mass, Mote, Mott, Myxoma, Neuroma, Nibble, Nirl, Node, Nodule, Nodulus, Nub, Nubble, Nugget, Nur(r), Nurl, Osteophyte, Plook, Plouk, Quinsy, Raguly, Sarcoma, Scybalum, Sitfast, Slub, Strophiole, Tragus, Tuber(cle), Wart, Wodge

Lumpsucker Sea-owl

Lunacy, Lunatic Bedlam, Dementia, Demonomania, Folly, Insanity, Mad(ness), Psychosis

Lunar Evection, Mascon

▷ **Lunatic** *may indicate* an anagram

Lunch(time) Dejeune, Déjeuner, L, Nacket, Nocket, Nuncheon, Packed, Piece, Ploughman, Pm, Power, Tiff(in), Working

Lung(s) Bellows, Coalminer's, Farmer's, Green, Iron, Lights, Pulmo, Pulmonary, Soul

Lung disease Anthracosis, Byssinosis, Emphysema, Farmer's lung, Pneumoconiosis, Siderosis, Silicosis, Tuberculosis

Lunge Breenge, Breinge, Dive, Stab, Thrust, Venue

Lungfish Dipnoi(an)

Lupin Arsene

Lurch Reel, Stoit, Stumble, Swee

Lure Bait, Bribe, Carrot, Decoy, Devon minnow, Entice, Horn, Inveigle, Jig, Judas, Roper, Spinner, Spoonbait, Spoonhook, Stale, Temptation, Tice, Tole, Toll, Train, Trepan, Wormfly

Lurid Gruesome, Purple

Lurk(ing) Dare, Latitant, Skulk, Slink, Snoke, Snook, Snowk

Lusatia(n) Wend(ic), Wendish

Luscious Succulent

Lush Drunk, Fertile, Green, Juicy, Lydian, Sot, Tosspot, Verdant

Lust(ful), Lusty Cama, Concupiscence, Corflambo, Desire, Eros, Frack, Greed, Kama, Lech(ery), Lewd, Megalomania, Obidicut, Randy, Rank, Raunchy, Salacious, Venereous

Lustre, Lustrous Brilliance, Census, Galena, Gaum, Gilt, Gloss, Gorm, Inaurate, Lead-glance, Pentad, Reflet, Satiny, Schiller, > **SHEEN**, Water

Lute, Lutist Amphion, Chitarrone, Cither, Dichord, Orpharion, Pandora, Theorbo, Vielle

Lutetium Lu

Lutheran Adiaphorist, Calixtin(e), Pietist

Lux Lx

Luxemburg L

Luxuriant, Luxuriate, Luxurious, Luxury (lover) Bask, Clover, Cockaigne, Cockayne, Copious, Deluxe, Dolce vita, Extravagant, Fleshpots, Lavish, Lucullan, Lush, Mollitious, Ornate, Pie, Plush, Posh, Rank, > **RICH**, Ritzy, Sumptuous, Sybarite, Wallow

Lycanthropist Werewolf

Lydia Languish
Lye Buck
▶ **Lying** *see* LIE
Lymph Chyle
Lymphoma Burkett's
Lynch(ing) Dewitt, Hang, Necktie party
Lynx Bobcat, Caracal, Rooikat
Lyre Cithern, Harp, Psaltery, Testudo
Lyric(al), Lyricist, Lyrist Cavalier, Dit(t), Epode, Gilbert, Melic, Ode, Orphean, Paean, Pean, Poem, Rhapsodic, Song

Mm

M Married, Member, Metre, Mike, Mile, Thousand
Mac Mino, Scot, Waterproof
Macabre Gothic, Grotesque, Sick
Macaroni Beau, Blood, Cat, Dandy, Elbow, Exquisite, Fop, Jack-a-dandy, Olio, Pasta, Petitmaitre
Macaroon Biscuit, Signal
Macaulay Layman
Mace Club, Nutmeg, Sceptre, Spice
Mace-bearer Beadle, Bedel, Poker
Macedonian Philip, Stagirite, Stagyrite
Machine(ry) Apparat(us), Appliance, Automaton, Bathing, Bulldozer, Calender, Centrifuge, Cycle, > **DEVICE**, Dialyser, Dredge(r), Drum, Engine, Enginery, Facsimile, Fax, Fruit, Gin, Hawk-eye®, Heck, Hopper, Hot-press, Instrument, Jawbreaker, Lathe, Life-support, Loom, Milling, Moulinet, Mule, Nintendo®, Party, Planer, Plant, Press, Processor, Propaganda, Pulsator, Robot, Rowing, Sewing, Slicer, Slot, Spinning jenny, Tape, Tedder, Throstle, Time, Transfer, Turbine, Turing, Twin tub, Typewriter, Vending, Virtual, War, Washing, Weighing, Wimshurst, Wind(mill), Wringer
Macho Jock
Mackerel Albacore, Brack, Dory, Fish, Horse, Pacific, Pimp, Scad, Scomber, Sky, Spanish, Spotted, Trevally
Mackintosh Burberry®, Mac, Mino, Oilskin, Slicker, Waterproof
Macropus Euro, Wallaroo
Mad(den), Madman, Madness Angry, Balmy, Bananas, Barking, Barmy, Bedlam, Besotted, Bonkers, Crackbrained, Crackpot, Crazy, Cuckoo, Cupcake, Daffy, Delirious, Dement, Distract, Dotty, Enrage, Fay, Fey, Folie, Folly, Frantic, Frenetic(al), Fruitcake, Furioso, Fury, Gelt, Gyte, Harpic, Hatter, Idiotic, Incense, Insane, Insanie, Insanity, Into, Irritate, Kook, Loco, Lunatic, Lycanthropy, Madbrained, Maenad, Mania, Mattoid, Mental, Meshug(g)a, Midsummer, Motorway, Mullah, Psycho, Rabid, Rasputin, Raving, Redwood, Redwud, Scatty, Screwy, Short-witted, Starkers, Tonto, Touched, Troppo, Unhinged, Wacko, Wood, Wowf, Wrath, Wud, Xenomania, Yond, Zany
▷ **Mad(den)** *may indicate* an anagram
Madagascan, Madagascar Aye-aye, Hova, Indri, Lemur, Malagasy, RM
Madam(e) Baggage, Lady, Proprietress
Madcap Impulsive, Tearaway
Madder Alizari, Chay(a), Gardenia, Genipap, Rose, Rubia, Shaya
Made (it) Built, Did, Fec(it), Ff, Gart, Invented
Madge Pie
▷ **Madly** *may indicate* an anagram
Madonna Lady, Lily, Mary, Pietà, Sistine, Virgin
Madrigal Ballet, Fala, Song
Maelstrom Voraginous, Vortex, Whirlpool

Maenad Devotee, Fan
Maestro Artist, Toscanini, Virtuoso
Mafia Camorra, Capo, Cosa nostra, Godfather, Mob, Ndrangheta, Omerta, The Mob
Mag Mail
Magazine Arsenal, Clip, Colliers, Contact, Cornhill, Cosmopolitan, Digizine, Economist, Field, Girlie, Glossy, Granta, Jazz mag, Lady, Lancet, Listener, Magnet, Organ, Periodical, Pictorial, Playboy, Pulp, Punch, She, Skin, Slick, Spectator, Store, Strand, Tatler, Time, Vogue, Warehouse, Weekly, Yoof
Magdalene St. Mary
Maggie Rita
Maggot Bot, Flyblow, Gentiles, Gentle, Grub, Larva, Mawk, Myiasis, Whim, Worm
Magi Balthazar, Gaspar, Melchior
Magic(al), Magician, Magic square Archimage, Art, Baetyl, Black, Black art, Charm, Circle, Conjury, Diablerie, Diablery, Enchanting, Faust, Faustus, Genie, Goetic, Goety, Gramary(e), Grimoire, Hermetic, Houdini, Illusionist, Incantation, Math, Medea, Merlin, Mojo, Moly, Morgan le Fay, Myal, Nasik, Natural, Necromancer, Obeah, Pawaw, Powwow, Prospero, Reim-kenner, Rhombus, Shamanism, Sorcery, Sortilege, Spell, Speller, Supernatural, Sympathetic, Talisman, Thaumaturgics, Theurgy, Voodoo, White, Wizard, Zendik
Magistracy, Magistrate Aedile, Amman, Amtman, Archon, Avoyer, Bailie, Bailiff, Bailli(e), Burgess, Burgomaster, Cadi, Censor, Consul, Corregidor, Demiurge, Doge(ate), Draco, Edile, Effendi, Ephor, Field cornet, Finer, Foud, Gonfalonier, JP, Judiciary, Jurat, Kotwal, Landamman(n), Landdrost, Lord Provost, Maire, Mayor, Mittimus, Novus homo, Podesta, Portreeve, Pr(a)efect, Pr(a)etor, Prior, Proconsul, Propraetor, Provost, Qadi, Quaestor, Recorder, Reeve, Shereef, Sherif, Stad(t)holder, Stipendiary, Syndic, Tribune, Worship
Magnanimity, Magnanimous Big, Charitable, > GENEROUS, Largeness, Lofty, Noble
Magnate Baron, Bigwig, Industrialist, Mogul, Onassis, Randlord, Tycoon, Vanderbilt, VIP
Magnesia, Magnesium Humite, Kainite, Mg, Periclase
Magnet(ic), Magnetism Animal, Artificial, Attraction, Bar, Charisma, Field, Gauss, Horseshoe, It, Loadstone, Lodestone, Maxwell, Od, Oersted, Permanent, Personal, Polar, Pole, Pole piece, Poloidal, Pull, Remanence, Retentivity, Solenoid, Terrella, Terrestrial, Tesla, Tole
Magnificence, Magnificent Gorgeous, Grandeur, Imperial, Laurentian, Lordly, Noble, Pride, Regal, Royal, Splendid, Splendo(u)r, State, Superb
Magnifier, Magnify(ing) Aggrandise, Augment, Binocle, > ENLARGE, Exaggerate, Increase, Loupe, Megaphone, Microscope, Teinoscope, Telescope
Magniloquent Bombastic, Orotund
Magnitude Absolute, Abundance, Extent, Muchness, Photoelectric, Scalar, Size, Visual
Magnolia An(n)ona, Beaver-tree, Champac, Champak, Mississippi, Sweet bay, Umbrella-tree, Yulan
Magpie Bell, Bird, Chatterer, Madge, Mag, Margaret, Outer, Pica, Piet, Pyat, Pyet, Pyot
Magus Artist
Magyar Hungarian, Szekel(y), Szekler, Ugrian, Ugric
Mahogany Acajou, Carapa, Cedrela, Philippine, Wood

Mahommedan Dervish, Shiah

Maid(en) Abigail, Aia, Amah, Biddy, Bonibell, Bonne, Bonnibell, Chamber, Chloe, Clothes-horse, Damosel, Dell, Dey, Femme de chambre, First, Girl, Guillotine, Ignis-fatuus, Imago, Inaugural, Io, Iras, Iron, Lorelei, M, Marian, May, Miss, Nymph, Opening, Over, Parlour, Pucelle, Rhine, Skivvy, Soubrette, Suivante, Thestylis, Tirewoman, Tweeny, Valkyrie, Virgin, Walkyrie, Wench, Wicket

Maidenhair Fern, Ginkgo

Mail Air, >ARMOUR, Byrnie, Cataphract, Chain, Da(w)k, Direct, E(lectronic), Express, Fan, Habergeon, Hate, Hauberk, Helm, Junk, Letter, Metered, Panoply, Pony express, Post, Ring, Send, Snail, Spam, Surface, Tuille(tte), Voice

Mailboat Packet

Maim Cripple, Impair, Lame, Main, Mayhem, Mutilate, Vuln

Main(s) Atlantic, Brine, Briny, >CENTRAL, Chief, Cockfight, Conduit, Essential, Foremost, Gas, Generally, Grid, Gross, Head, >KEY, Lead(ing), Major, Pacific, Palmary, Predominant, Prime, Principal, Ring, >SEA, Sheer, Spanish, Staple, Water

Mainland Continent, Pomona

Mainstay Backbone, Bastion, Pillar, Support

Maintain, Maintenance Alimony, Allege, Ap(p)anage, Argue, Assert, Aver, Avouch, Avoure, Avow, Claim, Contend, Continue, Defend, Escot, Insist, Keep (up), Preserve, Run, Sustain, Upbear, Uphold, Upkeep

Maize Corn, Hominy, Indian, Indian corn, Mealie, Popcorn, Samp, Silk, Stamp, Zea

Majestic, Majesty August, Britannic, Dignity, Eagle, Grandeur, Imperial, Maestoso, Olympian, Regal, SM, Sovereign, Stately, Sublime, Tuanku

Major(domo) Barbara, Drum, >IMPORTANT, Pipe, PM, Seneschal, Senior, Sergeant, Star, Trumpet, Wig

Majority Absolute, Age, Body, Eighteen, Landslide, Latchkey, Maturity, Moral, Most, Preponderance, Relative, Silent, Working

Make(r), Make do, Making Amass, Brand, Build, Clear, Coerce, Coin, Compel, Compulse, Concoct, Creant, Create, Devise, Earn, Execute, Fabricate, Factive, Fashion, Faute de mieux, Fet(t), Forge, Form, Gar(re), God, Halfpenny, Mail(e), Manage, Marque, Prepare, Production, Reach, Render, Shape, Sort, Temporise, Wright

▷ **Make** *may indicate* an anagram

Make believe Fantasy, Fictitious, Pretend, Pseudo

Make good Abet, Compensate, Remedy, Succeed, Ulling

Make hay Ted

Make off Bolt, Leg it, Mosey, Run, Scarper

Makeshift Bandaid, Crude, Cutcha, Expedient, Jury-rigged, Kacha, Kludge, Kutcha, Lash-up, Mackle, Pis-aller, Rude, Stopgap, Timenoguy

Make up Ad lib, Compose, Concealer, Constitution, Cosmetics, Fucus, Gaud, Gawd, Gene, Greasepaint, Identikit®, Kohl, Liner, Lipstick, Maquillage, Mascara, Metabolism, Paint, Pancake, Powder, Reconcile, Rouge, Slap, Tidivate, Titivate, Toiletry, Visagiste, War paint, White-face

Maladroit Awkward, Clumsy, Graceless, Inelegant, Unperfect

Malady Disease, Illness

Malagas(e)y Hova, RM

Malaise Affluenza

Malapropism Catachresis, Slipslop

Malaria Ague, Marsh-fever, Paludism, Tap, Vivax

Malawi Nyasa

Malay(an), Malaysian Austronesian, Datuk, D(a)yak, Jawi, Madurese, Moro, Sakai, Tokay, Tuan

Male Arrhenotoky, Buck, Bull, Butch, Dog, Ephebe, Ephebus, Gent, Hob, John Doe, Macho, Mansize, Masculine, Ram, Rogue, Spear(side), Stag, Stamened, Telamon, Tom

Malediction Curse, Cuss, Oath, Slander

Malefactor Criminal, Felon, Villain

Malevolent, Malevolence Evil, Fell, Malign, Pernicious

Malformation Teratogenesis

Malfunction Glitch, Hiccup

Mali RMM

Malice, Malicious Bitchy, Catty, Cruel, Despiteous, Envy, Hatchet job, Malevolent, Malign, Narquois, Prepense, Schadenfreude, Serpent, Snide, Spite, Spleen, Venom, Virulent, Vitriol

Malign(ant), Malignity Asperse, Backbite, Baleful, Defame, Denigrate, Gall, Harm, Hate-rent, Hatred, Libel, Poor-mouth, Sinister, Slander, Spiteful, Swart(h)y, Toxin, Vicious, Vilify, Vilipend, Viperous, Virulent

Malinger(er) Dodge, Leadswinger, Scrimshank, Shirk, Skrimshank, Truant

Mall Parade

Mallard Duck, Sord

Malleable Clay, Ductile, Fictile, Pliable

▷ **Malleable** *may indicate* an anagram

Mallet Beetle, Club, Hammer, Mace, Maul, Serving, Stick

Mallow Abutilon, Dwarf, Musk, Sida, Urena

Malodorous Mephitic

Malpractice(s) Sculduggery, Skulduggery

Malt Brewer's grain, Diastase, Grains, Grist, Wort

Maltese (cross) Falcon, GC

Maltreat Abuse, Harm, Maul, Mishandle, Misuse

Mammal Animal, Armadillo, Artiodactyl, Binturong, Bobcat, Cacomistle, Cacomixle, Caracal, Cervid, Cetacean, Charronia, Chevrotain, Chiropteran, Ciscus, Colugo, Creodont, Dhole, Dinothere, Dolphin, Dugong, Eutheria, Fisher, Glires, Glutton, Grison, Guanaco, Hydrax, Hyrax, Indri, Jaguarondi, Jaguarundi, Kinkajou, Lagomorph, Leporid, Linsang, Loris, Lynx, Manatee, Margay, Marten, Meerkat, Mongoose, Monotreme, Musteline, Numbat, Olungo, Otter, Pachyderm, Pangolin, Peccary, Pekan, Perissodactyl, Pika, Pine marten, Pinniped, Platypus, Polecat, Porpoise, Primate, Pronghorn, Pudu, Raccoon, Rasse, Rhytina, Sable, Shrew, Sirenian, Skunk, Sloth, Solenodon, Springhaas, Taguan, Tahr, Takin, Tamandu(a), Tanrec, Tapir, Tayra, Teledu, Tenrec, Theria(n), Titanothere, Tylopod, Uintathere, Vicuna, Viverrid, Weasel, Whale, Wolverine, Zorilla

Mammon Money, Riches, Wealth

Mammoth Epic, Gigantic, Huge, Jumbo, Mastodon, Whopping, Woolly

Man(kind) Ask(r), Best, Betty, Bimana(l), Biped, Bloke, Bo, Boxgrove, Boy, Cad, Cairn, Calf, Castle, Cat, Chal, Chap, Checker, Chequer, Chiel, Cockey, Cod, Contact, Continuity, Crew, Cro-Magnon, Cuffin, Cully, Dog, Don, Draught, Dude, Emmanuel, Essex, Everyman, Family, Fancy, Fella, Feller, Fellow, Folsom, Friday, Front, G, Gayomart, Geezer, Gent, Grimaldi, Guy, He, Heidelberg, Himbo, Hombre, Hominid, Homme, Homo, Homo sapiens, Inner, IOM, Iron, Isle, Jack, Java, Joe (Bloggs), Joe Blow, Joe Sixpack, John(nie), John Doe, Josser, Limit, Lollipop, M, Male, Medicine, Microcosm, Mister,

Mon, Mondeo, Mr, Muffin, Mun, Neanderthal, Nutcracker, Oreopithecus, Organisation, Ou, Paleolithic, Party, Pawn, Peking, Person, Piece, Piltdown, Pin, Pithecanthropus, Property, Raff, Remittance, Renaissance, Resurrection, Rhodesian, Right-hand, Rook, Sandwich, Servant, Servitor, Ship, Sinanthropus, Sodor, Soldier, Solo, Spear, Staff, Stag, Straw, Third, Thursday, Trinil, Twelfth, Tyke, Type, Utility, Valet, Vir, White van, Wight

Man-about-town Boulevardier

Manacle Fetter, Handcuff, Iron, Shackle

Manage(r), Manageable, Management, Managing Adhocracy, Administer, Agent, Amildar, Attain, Aumil, Behave, Boss, Chief, Come by, Conduct, Contrive, Control, Cope, Darogha, Direct, Docile, Exec(utive), Fare, Fend, Find, Floor, Fund, Gerent, Get by, Govern, Grieve, Handle, Head bummer, Honcho, IC, Impresario, Intendant, Line, Logistical, MacReady, Maitre d('hotel), Manipulate, Manoeuvre, Middle, Nomenklatura, Organise, Proctor, Procurator, Regisseur, Rig, Roadie, > RUN, Scrape, Shift, Steward, Succeed, Suit, Superintend, Swing, Tawie, Top, Tractable, Transact, Treatment, Trustee, Wangle, Wield(y), Yare

Manatee Lamantum, Mermaid, Sea-ape

Manchu Fu

Mandarin Bureaucrat, Chinaman, Kuo-Yu, Nodding, Satsuma, Yamen

Mandate Authority, Decree, Fiat, Order

Mandrake Springwort

Mandrel Triblet

Mane(d), Manes Crest, Encolure, Jubate, Larva(e), Shades

Manege Horseplay, Train

Manganese Mn, Synadelphite, Wadd

Manger Cratch, Crib, Hack, Stall

Mangle Agrise, Butcher, Distort, Garble, Hack, Hackle, Haggle, Wring(er)

▷ **Mangle** *may indicate* an anagram

Mango Dika

Manhandle Frogmarch, Maul, Rough

Manhater Misanthrope

Manhattan Bowery

Mania Cacoethes, Craze, Frenzy, Passion, Rage

Manichaean Albi

Manifest(ation), Manifestly Attest, Avatar, Epiphany, Evident, Evince, Exhibit, Extravert, Extrovert, Feat, List, Marked, Mode, Notably, Obvious, Open, Show

Manifesto Plank, Platform, Policy, Pronunciamento

Manifold(ness) Many, Multeity, Multiple

Manila Abaca, Cheroot

Manioc Cassava

Maniple Fannel, Fanon

Manipulate, Manipulative, Manipulator, Manipulation Chiropractor, Cog, Control, Cook, Demagogic, Diddle, Fashion, Finagle, Gerrymander, Handle, Jerrymander, Juggle, Legerdemain, Logodaedalus, Masseuse, Osteopath, Play off, Ply, Rig, Tweeze, Use, Wangle, > WIELD

▷ **Manipulate** *may indicate* an anagram

Manna Alhagi, Food, Trehala, Turkish

Manner(ism), Mannerly, Manners Accent, A la, Appearance, Attitude, Bedside, Behaved, Behaviour, Bon ton, Breeding, Carriage, Conduct, Couth, Crew, Custom, Deportment, Ethos, Etiquette, Farand, Farrand, Farrant, Habit, How, Mien, Mister, Mode, Morality, Mores, Of, Ostent, Panache, Politesse,

Presentation, P's & Q's, Quirk, Rate, Sort, Style, Table, Thew(s), Thewe(s), Trick, Upsee, Upsey, Upsy, Urbanity, Way, Wise

Manoeuvre(s) Campaign, Castle, Christie, Christy, Engineer, Exercise, Faena, Fianchetto, Fork, Gambit, Half-board, Heimlich, Hot-dog, Jink(s), Jockey, Manipulate, Op(eration), Pendule, Pesade, Ploy, Renversement, Ruse, Skewer, Use, U-turn, Valsalva, Wear, Wheelie, Whipstall, Wile, Zigzag

▷ **Manoeuvre** *may indicate* an anagram

Man-of-war Armada, Bluebottle, Destroyer, Ironclad, Portuguese

Manor (house) Area, Demain, Demesne, Estate, Hall, Kelmscott, Vill(a), Waddesdon

Mansion Casa, Knole, Luton Hoo, Mentmore, Penshurst Place, Queen's House, Seat, Stourhead, Stowe

Mantle Asthenosphere, Authority, Burnous(e), Capote, Caracalla, Chlamydate, Dolman, Elijah, Gas, Pall, Pallium, Paludament, Pelisse, Rochet, Sima, Toga, Tunic, Veil

Mantuan Maro, Virgil

Manual Blue collar, Bradshaw, Cambist, Console, Enchiridion, Great (organ), Guide, Hand, Handbook, How-to, Portolan(o), Positif, Sign

Manufacture, Manufacturing Fabricate, Industrial, Kanban, Make, Produce

Manure Compost, Dressing, Dung, Fertiliser, Green, Guano, Hen-pen, Lime, Muck, Sha(i)rn, Tath

Manuscript(s) Book of Kells, Codex, Codicology, Folio, Hand, Holograph, Longhand, Miniscule, MS, Opisthograph, Palimpsest, Papyrus, Parchment, Script, Scroll, Scrowl(e), Vellum

Manx(man) Cat, IOM, Kelly, Kelt

▷ **Manx** *may indicate* a last letter missing

Many C, CD, Countless, D, Hantle, Herd, Horde, Host, L, Lot, M, Manifold, Mony, Multi(tude), Myriad, Scad, Sight, Stacks, Tons, Umpteen

▷ **Many** *may indicate* the use of a Roman numeral letter

Maoist Naxatile, Red Guard

Maori (house) Hauhau, Hori, Mallowpuff, Moa hunter, Tangata whenua, Te reo, Wahine, Whare

Map(ping) Atlas, Card, Cartogram, Chart, Chorography, Chromosome, Cognitive, Contour, Digital, Face, Genetic, Inset, Key, Loxodromic, Mappemond, Mental, Mosaic, Moving, Mud, OS, Perceptual, Plan, Plot, Relief, Road, Sea-card, Sea-chart, Strip, Topography, Weather

Maple Acer, Flowering, Manitoba, Mazer, Norway, Plane, Silver, Sugar, Sycamore, Syrup

Map-maker Cartographer, OS, Speed

Maquis Queach, Underground

Mar Blight, Denature, Dere, Impair, Soil, Spoil, Taint

Marabout Sofi, Sufi

Marathon Comrades, Huge, London, Race, Two Oceans

Marauder Amalekite, Attacker, Bandit, Pillager, Pirate, Predator, Prowler

Marble(s), Marbling Aeginetan, Agate, All(e)y, Arch, Arundelian, Bonce, Bonduc, Bool, Boondoggle, Bowl, Carrara, Chequer, Cipollino, Commoney, Devil's, Dump, Elgin, Humite, Hymettus, Knicker, Languedoc, Lucullite, Marl, Marmarosis, Marmoreal, Marver, Mottle, Nero-antico, Nickar, Nicker, Onychite, Onyx, Paragon, Parian, Pavonazzo, Pentelic(an), Petworth, Phigalian, Plonker, Plunker, Purbeck, Rance, Ringer, Ring-taw, Ruin, Sanity, Scagliola, Spangcockle, Taw, Variegate, Xanthian

Marcel Proust

March(ing) Abut, Adjoin, Advance, Anabasis, Border(er), Borderland, Dead, . Defile, Demo, Etape, File, Footslog, Forced, Freedom, Fringe, Galumph, Go, Goosestep, Hikoi, Hunger, Ides, Jarrow, Lide, Limes, Lockstep, Long, Meare, Music, > **PARADE**, Procession, Progress, Protest, Quick, Rogue's, Route, Slow time, Step, Strunt, Strut, Trio, Tromp, Wedding, Yomp

▷ **March** *may indicate* 'Little Women' character, Amy, Beth, Jo, Meg

Marco Il Milione, Polo

Mare Dam, Flanders, Horse, M, MacCurdle's, Shanks's, Spanish, Yaud

Margaret Anjou, Meg, Peg, Rita

Margarine Oleo

Marge, **Margin(al)** Annotate, Border, Brim, Brink, Curb, Edge, Fimbria, Hair's breadth, Kerb, Lean, Leeway, Limit, Lip, Littoral, Neck, Nose, Peristome, Profit, Rand, Repand, > **RIM**, Selvedge, Sideline, Tail, Term

Marginal note Apostil(le), K'ri

Margosa Melia, Nim

Maria(nne) France, Tia

Marie Dressler, Tempest

Marigold Calendula, Kingcup, Tagetes

Marijuana Alfalfa, Camberwell carrot, Dagga, Gage, Ganja, Grass, Greens, Gungeon, Ha-ha, Hay, Herb, Jive, Kaif, Kef, Kif, Leaf, Locoweed, Mary-Jane, Pot, Roach, Rope, Shit, Sinsemilla, Splay, Spliff, Tea, Toke, Weed

Marina Wharf

Marine (creature) Aquatic, Bootie, Bootneck, Cephalopod, Chaetognath, Cnidarian, Coelenterate, Comatulid, Ctenophora, Cunjevoi, Enteropneusta, Flustra, Foram(inifer), Galoot, Graptolite, Harumfrodite, Hemichorda, Holothurian, Horse, Hydrocoral, Hydroid, Hydromedusa, Jolly, Leatherneck, Lobster, Mercantile, Mere-swine, Mistress Roper, Oceanic, Physalia, Pollywag, Pollywog, Salpa, Sea-soldier, Seston, Thalassian, Ultra

Mariner AB, Ancient, MN, Noah, RM, Sailor, Salt, Seafarer, Spacecraft, Tar

Marionette(s) Fantoccini, Puppet

Marjoram Amaracus, Origan, Pot, Sweet, Wild, Winter-sweet

Mark(ing), **Marked**, **Marks** Accent, Antony, Apostrophe, Asterisk, Astrobleme, Badge, Banker, Bethumb, Birth, Blaze, Blot, Blotch, Brand, Bruise, Bull, Butt, Cachet, Caract, Caret, Caste, CE, Cedilla, Charter, Chequer, Cicatrix, Class, Clout, Colon, Comma, Coronis, Crease, Criss-cross-row, Dash, Denote, Dent, Diacritic, Diaeresis, Dieresis, Distinction, DM, Duckfoot quote, Ensign, Enstamp, Exclamation, Expression, Feer, Fleck, Glyph, Gospel, Grade, Guillemet, Hacek, Hair-line, Hash, Hatch, Heed, High water, Hyphen, Impress(ion), Indicium, Ink, Inscribe, Insignia, Interrogation, Keel, Kite, Kumkum, Lentigo, Line, Ling, Livedo, Logo, Lovebite, Low water, M, Macron, MB, Merk, Mottle, NB, Notal, Note, Notice, Obelisk, Observe, Oche, Paginate, Paraph, Period, Pilcrow, Pit, Plage, Pling, Point, Popinjay, Port wine, Post, Presa, Printer's, Proof, Punctuation, Question, Quotation, Record, Reference, Register, Regulo, Ripple, Roundel, Sanction, Scar, Score, Scratch, Section, See, Service, Shadow, Shilling, Sigil, Sign, Smit, Smut, Smutch, Speck, Splodge, Splotch, Stain, Stencil, Stigma(ta), Strawberry, Stress, Stretch, Sucker, Swan-upping, Symbol, Tag, Target, Tatow, Tattoo, Tee, Theta, Thread, Tick, Tika, Tikka, Tilak, Tilde, Tittle, Token, Touchmark, Trace, Track, Trout, Tug(h)ra, Twain, Umlaut, Ure, Victim, Wand, Warchalking, Watch, Weal, Welt

Marker Bollard, Buck, Cairn, Fanion, Flag, Ink, Inukshuk, Label, Scorer, Tie

Market(ing), **Market day**, **Market place** Agora, Alcaiceria, Baltic, Bazaar, Bear, Billingsgate, Black, Borgo, Bull, Buyer's, Capital, Captive, Cattle, Change,

Chowk, Common, Denet, Direct, Discount, Dragon, EC, Emerging, Emporium, Errand, Exchange, Fair, Feeing, Flea, Forum, Forward, Free, Grey, Growth, Internal, Kerb, Lloyds, Main, Mandi, Mart, Mercat, Money, Niche, Nundine, Open, Outlet, Piazza, Relationship, Sale, Sellers', Share, Shop, Single, Social, Sook, Souk, Spot, Stance, Staple, Stock, Stock Exchange, Tattersall's, Terminal, Test, Third, Tiger, Trade, Tron, Tryst, Vent, Viral, Wall Street

Marksman Sharpshooter, Shootist, Shot, Sniper, Tell

Marlborough Blenheim

Marlene Lilli

Marmalade Cat, Mammee-sapota, Preserve, Squish

Marmoset Jacchus, Mico, Midas, Monkey, Wistiti

Marmot Bobac, Bobak, Dassie, Groundhog, Hoary, Hyrax, Rodent, Whistler, Woodchuck

Maroon Brown, Castaway, Enisle, Firework, Inisle, Isolate, Strand

Marquee Pavilion, Tent, Top

Marquess, Marquis Granby, Lorne, Sade

Marquetry Boul(l)e, Buhl, Inlay

Marriage > ALLIANCE, Bed, Beenah, Bigamy, Bridal, Buckle-beggar, Civil, Coemption, Common law, Confarreation, Conjugal, Connubial, Coverture, Digamy, Endogamy, Espousal, Exogamy, Gandharva, Genial, Group, Hedge, Hetaerism, Hetairism, Hymen(eal), Jugal, Ketubah, Knot, Levirate, Match, Mating, Matrilocal, Matrimony, Mésalliance, Mixed, Monandry, Monogamy, Morganatic, Noose, Nuptial, Open, Pantagamy, Patrilocal, Punalua, Putative, Sacrament, Shidduch, Shotgun, Tie, Trial, > UNION, Wedding, Wedlock

Marriageable Marrow, Nubile, Parti

Marriage-broker Shadchan

Marrow Courgette, Friend, Gist, Medulla, Myeloid, Pith, Pumpkin, Squash, Vegetable

Marry, Married Ally, Amate, Buckle, Cleek(it), Confarreate, Couple, Coverture, Espouse, Feme covert, Forsooth, Goody, Hitch, Join, Knit, M, Mate, Matron, Memsahib, Pair, Pardie, Quotha, Splice, Tie, Troggs, Troth, Unite, W, Wed, Wive

Mars Areography, Ares, Red (planet)

Marsh(y) Bayou, Bog, Chott, Corcass, Emys, Everglades, Fen, Hackney, Maremma, Merse, Mire, Morass, Ngaio, Paludal, Plashy, Pontine, Pripet, Quagmire, Romney, Salina, Salt, Shott, Slade, Slough, Sog, Spew, Spue, Swale, Swamp, Taiga, Terai, Vlei, Wetlands

Marshal Arrange, Array, Commander, Earp, Foch, French, Hickok, MacMahon, Muster, Neil, Ney, Order, Pétain, Provost, Shepherd, Tedder, Usher, Yardman

Marshmallow Althaea, Mallowpuff

Marsupial Bandicoot, Bilby, Cuscus, Dasyure, Dibbler, Didelphia, Diprotodont, Dunnart, Honey mouse, Honey possum, Kangaroo, Koala, Macropod, Metatheria, Notoryctes, Nototherium, Numbat, Opossum, Pad(d)ymelon, Pademelon, Petaurist, Phalanger, Polyprodont, Possum, Potoroo, Pouched mouse, Pygmy glider, Quokka, Quoll, Roo, Tammar, Tasmanian devil, Theria, Thylacine, Tuan, Wallaby, Wambenger, Wombat, Yapo(c)k

Marten Fisher, Mustela, Pekan, Pine, Sable, Woodshock

Martha Vineyard

Martial (arts) Bellicose, Budo, Capoeira, Capuera, Chopsocky, Dojo, Iai-do, Judo, Ju-jitsu, Karate, Kick boxing, Kung Fu, Militant, Muay thai, Ninjutsu, Shintaido, Tae kwon do, T'ai chi (chuan), Warlike, Wushu

Martin Bird, Luther, Swallow

Martinet Captious, Ramrod, Stickler

Martini® Cocktail, Henry

Martyr(dom), Martyrs Alban, Alphege, Colosseum, Donatist, Justin, Latimer, Metric, MM, Passional, Persecute, Sebastian, Stephen, Suffer, Tolpuddle, Wishart

Marvel(lous) Bodacious, Bully, Epatant, Fab, Lulu, Magic, Marl, Miracle, Mirific, Phenomenon, Prodigious, Superb, Super-duper, Swell, Terrific, Wonder

Marx(ism), Marxist Aspheterism, Chico, Comintern, Commie, Groucho, Gummo, Harpo, Karl, Menshevik, Revisionism, Tanky, Tipamaro, Zeppo

Mary Bloody, Celeste, Madonna, Moll, Morison, Our Lady, Tum(my), Typhoid, Virgin

Marylebone Station

Marzipan Marchpane

Mascara Eye-black

Masculine, Masculinity He, He-man, Linga(m), M, Machismo, Macho, Male, Manly, Virile

Maser Laser

Mash(er) Beat, Beau, Beetle, Brew, Lady-killer, Pap, Pestle, Pound, Sour, Squash

Mask(ed) Bird cage, Camouflage, Cloak, Cokuloris, Death, Disguise, Dissemble, Domino, False face, Gas, Hide, Larvated, Life, Loo, Loup, Mascaron, Matte, Oxygen, Persona, Respirator, Screen, Semblance, Shadow, Stalking-horse, Stocking, Stop out, Template, Visor, Vizard

Mason(ry) Ashlar, Ashler, Brother, Builder, Cowan, Emplecton, Isodoma, Isodomon, Lodge, Moellon, Nogging, Opus, Perry, Random, Squinch, Stylobate

Masque(rade), Masquerader Comus, Domino, Guisard, Mum(m), Pose, Pretend

Mass(es) Aggregate, Agnus dei, Anniversary, Banket, Bezoar, Bike, Body, Bulk, Cake, Chaos, Clot, Congeries, Conglomeration, Consecration, Core, Crith, Critical, Crowd, Demos, Density, Flake, Flysch, Folk, Geepound, Gravitational, Great, Herd, High, Horde, Hulk, Inertial, Jud, Kermesse, Kermis, Kilo(gram), Kirmess, Low, Lump, M, Majority, Missa, Month's mind, Mop, Nest, Phalanx, Pile, Plumb, Pontifical, Populace, Proper, Raft, Requiem, Rest, Ruck, Salamon, Salmon, Scrum, Sea, Serac, Service, Shock, Sicilian, Size, Slub, Slug, Solar, Solemn, Solid, Stack, Stroma, Sursum corda, Te Igitur, Tektite, Trental, Vesper, Vigil, Volume, Wad, Weight, Welter

Massacre Amritsar, Blood-bath, Butcher, Carnage, Glencoe, Havock, Manchester, Peterloo, Pogrom, Purge, St Bartholomew's Day, Scullabogue, Scupper, September, Sicilian vespers, Slaughter, Slay, Wounded Knee

Massage, Masseur An mo, Chafer, Do-in, Effleurage, Hellerwork, > **KNEAD**, Malax, Palp, Petrissage, Physio, Rolf(ing), Rubber, Shampoo, Shiatsu, Stone, Stroke, Swedish, Tapotement, Thai, Tripsis, Tui na

Massive Big, Bull, Colossal, Gargantuan, Heavy, Herculean, Huge, Monumental, Strong, Titan

Mast(ed), Masthead Acorn, Banner, Captain's, Crosstree, Flag, Foretop, High top, Hounds, Jigger, Jury, M, Mizzen, Mooring, Pannage, Pole, Racahout, Royal, Ship-rigged, Spar, Top-gallant, Truck, Venetian

Master(ly) Artful, Baalebos, Baas, Beak, Beat, Boss, Buddha, Bwana, Careers, Checkmate, Conquer, Control, Dan, Dominate, Dominie, Employer, Enslave, Exarch, Expert, Gov, Grand, Harbour, Herr, Himself, International, Learn, Lord, MA, Maestro, Mas(s), Massa, Mes(s), Nkosi, Old, Ollamh, Ollav, Oner, Oppress, Original, Overcome, Overlord, Overpower, Overseer, Passed, Past, Pedant, Rabboni, Seigneur, Seignior, Signorino, Sir(e), Skipper, > **SUBDUE**, Subjugate,

Superate, Surmount, Swami, Tame, Task, Thakin, Towkay, Tuan, Usher, Vanquish, Virtuoso

Mastermind Brain, Conceive, Direct

Masterpiece Chef d'oeuvre, Creation

Master-stroke Coup, Triumph

Masturbate, Masturbation Abuse, Frig, Gratify, Jerk off, Jock, Onanism, Toss off, Wank, Whack off

Mat(ted), Matting Bast, Coaster, Doily, Dojo, Doyley, Felt, Inlace, Pad, Paunch, Place, Plat, Prayer, Rug, Table, Taggy, > TANGLE, Tat(ami), Tatty, Taut, Tawt, Tomentose, Welcome, Zarf

Matador Card, Espada, Ordonez, Theseus, Torero

Match(ed) Agree, Alliance, Amate, Balance, Besort, Bonspiel, Bout, Carousel, Compare, Congreve, Contest, Cope, Correlate, Correspond, Counterpane, Doubles, Emulate, Engagement, Equal(ise), Equate, Even, Exhibition, Fellow, Fit, Fixture, Four-ball, Friction, Friendly, Fusee, Fuzee, Game, Go, Greensome, International, Joust, Light, Locofoco, Love, Lucifer, Main, Marrow, Marry, Meet, Mouse, Needle, Pair(s), Paragon, Parti, Pit, Prizefight, Promethean, Reproduce, Return, Rival, Roland, Rubber, Safety, Shield, Singles, Slanging, Slow, Spunk, Striker, Suit, Sync, > TALLY, Team, Test, Tie, Twin, Union, Venue, Vesta, Vesuvian, Wedding

Matchbox label (collecting) Phillumeny

Match girl Bride

Match-holder Lin(t)stock

Matchless Non(e)such, Orinda

Matchmaker Blackfoot, Broker, Pairer, Promoter, Shadchan

Mate, Mating Achates, Adam, Amigo, Amplexus, Bedfellow, Bo, Breed, Buddy, Buffer, Butty, Check, Chess, China, Chum, Cobber, Cock, Comrade, Consort, Crony, Cully, Digger, Eve, Feare, Feer, Fellow, Fere, Fiere, First, Fool's, Husband, Ilex, Maik, Make, Marrow, Marry, Match, Mister, Nick, Oldster, Oppo, > PAIR, Pal, Panmixia, Panmixis, Paragon, Partner, Pheer(e), Pirrauru, Running, Scholar's, Second, Serve, Sex, Skaines, Smothered, Soul, > SPOUSE, Tea, Wack, Wacker, Wife, Wus(s)

Material Agalmatolite, Aggregate, Agitprop, Apt, Armure, Ballast, Blastema, Bole, Borsic, Byssus, Celluloid, Cellulose, Ceramic, Cermet, > CLOTH, Cob, Compo, Copy, Corfam®, Corporeal, Data, Documentation, Earthy, > FABRIC, Factual, Fallout, Fettling, Fibrefill, Fibreglass, Fines, Flong, Frit(t), Fuel, Gang(ue), Germane, Hylic, Illusion, Illuvium, Interfacing, Lambskin, Macintosh, Matter, Metal, Oilskin, Papier-maché, Pertinent, Physical, Pina-cloth, Plasterboard, Positive, Pug(ging), Raw, Relevant, Sackcloth, Sagathy, Skirting, Stuff, Substance, Swish, Tangible, Tape, Textile, Thingy, Towelling, Tusser, Wattle and daub

Materialise Appear, Apport, Click, Reify

Materialist(ic) Banausian, Hylist, Hyloist, Philistine, Somatist

Mathematician Apollonius, Archimedes, Archytas, Bernoulli, Bessel, Boole, Briggs, Cantor, Cocker, Descartes, Diophantus, Dunstable, Eratosthenes, Euclid, Euler, Fermat, Fibonacci, Fourier, Gauss, Godel, Goldbach, Gunter, Hawking, Laplace, Leibniz, Lie, Mercator, Napier, Newton, Optime, Pascal, Penrose, Playfair, Poisson, Ptolemy, Pythagoras, Pytheas, Riemann, Torricelli, Turing, Wrangler, Zeno

Mathematics, Mathematical, Maths Algebra, Applied, Arithmetic, Arsmetrick, Calculus, Geometry, Higher, Logarithms, Mechanics, New, Numbers, Porism, Pure, Topology, Trig, Trigonometry

Matilda Liar, Swag, Untruthful, Waltzing
Matinee Coat, Idol, Show
Mating Pangamy
Matins Nocturn
Matricide Orestes
Matrimony Bed, Conjugal, Marriage, Sacrament, Spousal, Wedlock
Matrix Active, Array, Boston, Hermitian, Jacobian, Mould, Orthogonal, Pattern, Scattering, Square, Uterus
Matron Dame, Hausfrau, Lucretia, Nurse, Warden
Matt(e) Dense, Dingy, Dull
Matter Alluvium, Bioblast, Biogen, Body, Concern, Consequence, Dark, Degenerate, Empyema, Epithelium, Gear, Gluon, Go, Grey, Hyle, Impost(h)ume, Issue, Mass, Material, Molecule, Phlegm, Pith, Point, Positron, Protoplasm, Pulp, Pus, Quark, Reck, Reke, Scum, Shebang, Signify, Solid, Subject, > SUBSTANCE, Thing, Topic, Tousle, Touzle, White, Ylem
Matthew Arnold
Mattress Bed(ding), Biscuit, Dutch, Featherbed, Foam, Futon, Lilo®, Pallet, Palliasse, Spring, Tick
Mature, Maturity Adult, Age, Blossom, Bold, Concoct, Develop, Mellow, Metaplasis, Old, Puberty, Ripe(n), Rounded, Seasoned, Upgrow(n)
Maudlin Fuddled, Mawkish, Sentimental, Sloppy, Too-too
Maul Hammer, Manhandle, Paw, Rough
Maundy Money, Nipter, Thursday
Mauretanian, Mauritania(n) Moor, RIM
Mausoleum Helicarnassus, Mole, Sepulchre, Taj Mahal, Tomb
Mauve Lilac, Mallow, Perkin's
Maverick Misfit, Nonconformist, Rogue
Mavis Throstle
Maw Crop, Gorge, Gull(et), Oesophagus
Mawkish Sickly
Maxim Adage, Aphorism, Apo(ph)thegm, Axiom, Byword, Gnome, Gorki, Gun, Hiram, Moral, Motto, Proverb, Restaurateur, > RULE, Saw, Saying, Sentence, Sentiment, Watchword
Maximum All-out, Full, Highest, Most, Peak, Utmost
May Blossom, Can, Hawthorn, Merry, Might, Month, Mote, Quickthorn, Shall, Whitethorn
Maybe Happen, Mebbe, Peradventure, Percase, Perchance, Perhaps, Possibly
▷ **May become** *may indicate* an anagram
May day Beltane, SOS
Mayfair WI
Mayfly Ephemera, Ephemeroptera, Green-drake, Sedge
Mayhem Chaos, Crime, Damage, Havoc, Pandemonium
Mayonnaise Aioli, Rémoulade
Mayor Alcaide, Burgomaster, Casterbridge, Councilman, Porteeve, Provost, Whittington
Maze Labyrinth, Meander, Warren, Wilderness
MC Compere, Host, Ringmaster
MD Doctor, Healer
ME Yuppie flu
Me I, Mi
Mead(ow) Flood, Grass, Haugh, Hydromel, Inch, Lea(se), Ley, Meath(e), Metheglin, > PASTURE, Runnymede, Saeter, Salting, Water

Meadowsweet Dropwort

Meagre Bare, Exiguous, Measly, Paltry, Pittance, Scant, Scrannel, Scranny, Skimpy, Skinny, Spare, Sparse, Stingy, Thin

Meal(s) Banquet, Barbecue, Barium, Beanfeast, Blow-out, Board, Breakfast, Brunch, Buffet, Cassava, Cereal, Cholent, Chota-hazri, Collation, Corn, Cornflour, Cottoncake, Cottonseed, Cou-cou, Cribble, Dejeune(r), Deskfast, Dinner, Drammock, Ervalenta, Fare, Farina, Feast, Flour, Food, Grits, Grout, Hangi, High tea, Iftar, Indian, Lock, Lunch, Mandioc, Mandioc(c)a, Mani(h)oc, Matzo, Melder, Meltith, Mensal, Mess, Mush, No-cake, Nosh, Nuncheon, Obento, Ordinary, Picnic, Piece, Plate, Poi, Polenta, Porridge, Prandial, Prix fixe, Rac(c)ahout, Refection, Repast, Revalenta, Rijst(t)afel, Salep, Scambling, Scoff, Seder, Smorgasborg, Snack, Spread, Square, Supper, Table d'hote, Takeaway, Tea, Thali, Tiffin, Tightener, Twalhours, Undern

Meal-ticket LV

Mean(ing), Meant Aim, Arithmetic(al), Average, Base, Betoken, Bowsie, Caitiff, Connotation, Curmudgeon, Definition, Denotate, Denote, Design, Dirty, Drift, Essence, Ettle, Feck, Footy, Foul, Geometric(al), Gist, Golden, Hang, Harmonic, Humble, Hunks, Ignoble, Illiberal, Imply, Import, Inferior, Insect, Intend, Intermediate, Lexical, Low, Mang(e)y, Marrow, Medium, Mesquin, Method, Mid, Miserly, Narrow, Near, Norm, Nothing, One-horse, Ornery, Paltry, Par, Penny-pinching, Petty, Piker, Pinch-penny, Pith, Point, Purport, > **PURPOSE**, Quadratic, Ratfink, Revenue, Roinish, Roynish, Scall, Scrub, Scurvy, Semanteme, Semantic(s), Sememe, Sense, Shabby, Signify, Slight, Small, Sneaky, Snoep, Snot, Sordid, Sparing, Spell, Stingy, Stink(ard), Stinty, Substance, Symbol, Thin, Threepenny, Tightwad, Two-bit, Value, Whoreson

Meander Fret, Ring, Sinuate, Stray, Wander, Weave, Wind

Meaningless Ducdame, Empty, Hollow, Hot air, Insignificant, Nonny, Rumbelow

Means Agency, Dint, Income, Media, Method, Mode, Opulence, Organ, Private, Resources, Staple, Substance, Tactics, Visible, Ways, Wherewithal

Meantime, Meanwhile Among, Emong, Greenwich, Interim

Measles Morbilli, Roseola, Rose-rash, Rubella, Rubeola

Measure(d), Measuring, Measurement By(e)law, Calibre, Circular, Crackdown, > **DANCE**, Demarche, > **DIMENSION**, Distance, Dose, Dry, Gavotte, Gross, Imperial, Limit, Linear, Moratorium, Of, Offset, Precaution, Prophylactic, Quickstep, Ration, Share, > **SIZE**, Standard, Statute, Step, Strike, Struck, Survey, Token, Wine

MEASURES

2 letters:		4 letters:	
As	Erg	Acre	Foot
Em	Fat	Aune	Gage
En	Hin	Bath	Gill
Mu	Lay	Boll	Hide
	Lea	Bolt	Inch
	Ley	Comb	Koss
3 letters:	Log	Cord	Last
Are	Lug	Coss	Line
Bel	Mil	Cran	Link
Cab	Rod	Dram	Maze
Cor	Tot	Epha	Mete
Ell	Wey		Mile

- Mole
- Mott
- Muid
- Nail
- Omer
- Pace
- Peck
- Pint
- Pole
- Pood
- Ream
- Reau
- Rood
- Rope
- Shot
- Span
- Tape
- Thou
- Unit
- Vara
- Volt
- Warp
- Yard

- **5 letters:**
- Anker
- Ardeb
- Barye
- Bekah
- Bigha
- Caneh
- Carat
- Chain
- Clove
- Combe
- Coomb
- Crore
- Cubit
- Cumec
- Cusec
- Depth
- Ephah
- Fermi
- Float
- Gauge
- Grain
- Groma
- Hanap
- Homer
- Joule
- Kaneh
- Lento

Liang
Ligne
Lippy
Loure
Mease
Meter
Metre
Optic®
Perch
Plumb
Quart
Romer
Ruler
Scale
Sound
Stade
Stere
Tesla
Therm
Toise
Verst
Wecht
Yojan

6 letters:
Albedo
Alnage
Arpent
Arshin
Barrel
Barren
Beegha
Bovate
Bushel
Chenix
Chopin
Cicero
Cubage
Denier
Double
Etalon
Fathom
Firkin
Firlot
Gallon
Height
Hemina
Jigger
Kelvin
Kilerg
League
Lippie

Liquid
Metage
Modius
Morgan
Noggin
Oxgang
Parsec
Pascal
Pottle
Radius
Runlet
Sazhen
Stadia
Tierce
Yojana

7 letters:
Aneroid
Arshine
Breadth
Burette
Caliper
Candela
Chalder
Choenix
Coulomb
Cyathus
Decibel
Drastic
Entropy
Furlong
Geodesy
Lambert
Leaguer
Pelorus
Quarter
Rundlet
Sleever
Spondee
Venturi
Virgate

8 letters:
Angstrom
Calliper
Carucate
Chaldron
Crannock
Desyatin
Diameter
Fistmele
Foot rule

Hogshead
Kilogray
Luxmeter
Mutchkin
Odometer
Oximeter
Parasang
Puncheon
Tape-line
Teraflop
Waywiser

9 letters:
Astrolabe
Bolometer
Cryometer
Decalitre
Decastere
Dosimeter
Ergometer
Eriometer
Kilometre
Lysimeter
Manometer
Mekometer
Nipperkin
Oenometer
Potometer
Steradian
Tappet-hen
Telemeter
Titration
Tonometer
Yardstick

10 letters:
Amphimacer
Anemometer
Barleycorn
Bathometer
Centimetre
Cyclometer
Densimeter
Dessiatine
Dessyatine
Drosometer
Eudiometer
Goniometer
Gravimeter
Humidistat
Hydrometer
Hygrometer

- Lactometer
- Micrometer
- Millimetre
- Opisometer
- Photometer
- Piezometer
- Resistance
- Touchstone
- Tromometer

Winchester

11 letters:
Actinometer
Auxanometer
Colorimeter
Dioptometer
Dynamometer
Intoximeter

Jacob's staff
Stereometer
Venturi tube
Weighbridge

12 letters:
Cathetometer
Densitometer
Electrometer

Electronvolt
Extensimeter
Extensometer
Galactometer
Nephelometer
Tellurometer
Viscosimeter

Meat(s) Aitchbone, Bacon, Bard, Beef, Biltong, Brawn, Brisket, Brown, Burger, Cabob, Carbonado, Carrion, Charcuterie, Chop, Collop, Confit, Croquette, Cut, Devon, Easy, Edgebone, Entrecote, Escalope, Essence, Fanny Adams, Fleishig, Fleishik, Flesh, Flitch, Force, Galantine, Gigot, Gobbet, Gosht, Griskin, Ham, Haslet, Jerky, Joint, Junk, Kabab, Kabob, Kebab, Kebob, Lamb, Loin, Luncheon, Mart, Mince, Mutton, Noisette, Offal, Olive, Pastrami, Pem(m)ican, Piccata, Pith, Pork, Processed, Rack, Red, Rillettes, Roast, Saddle, Sasatie, Satay, Scaloppino, Schnitzel, Scran, Scrapple, Sey, Shashlik, Shishkebab, Side, Sirloin, Sosatie, Spam®, Spare rib, Spatchcock, Spaul(d), Steak, Tenderloin, Tongue, Variety, Veal, Venison, Vifda, Virgate, Vivda, Weiner schnitzel, White, Wurst

Meatball(s) Cecils, Croquette, Faggot, Falafel, Felafel, Fricadel, Goujon, Knish, Kofta, Kromesky, Quenelle, Rissole

Meat extract Brawn, Gravy, Juice, Stock

Meatless Banian, Lent, Maigre, Vegetarian

Mecca Centre, Kaaba, Keblah, Kibla(h), Qibla

Mechanic(s) Apron-man, Artificer, Artisan, Banausic, Bottom, Engineer, Fitter, Fluid, Fundi, Grease monkey, Greaser, Hand, Journeyman, Kinematics, Kinetics, Newtonian, Operative, Quantum, Rock, Soil, Statics, Statistical, Technician, Wave

▷ **Mechanic(al)** *may indicate* characters from 'A Midsummer Night's Dream'

Mechanical, Mechanism Action, Apparatus, Auto, Banausic, Defence, Derailleur, Escape, Escapement, Gimmal, Instrument, Machinery, Movement, Organical, Pulley, Pushback, Servo, Synchromesh, Trippet, Works

Medal(lion)(s) Award, Bar, Bronze, Congressional, Decoration, Dickin, DSM, GC, George, Gold, Gong, Gorget, Military, MM, Numismatic, Pan(h)agia, Purple Heart, Putty, Roundel, Silver, Tony, Touchpiece, VC, Vernicle

Meddle(r), Meddlesome Busybody, Dabble, Finger, Hen-hussy, > **INTERFERE**, Interloper, Marplot, Mell, Monkey, Officious, Potter, Pragmatic, Pry, Snooper, Spoilsport, Tamper, Tinker, Trifle

Media Mass, Mixed, New, PR

Mediate, Mediator ACAS, Arbitrate, Intercede, Interpose, Intervene, Liaison, Muti, Referee, Thirdsman, Trouble-shooter

Medical, Medicament, Medication, Medicine (chest) Allopathy, Alternative, Andrology, Anodyne, Antacid, Antibiotic, Antidote, Antisepsis, Antiseptic, Arnica, Asafetida, Ayurveda, Bi, Bismuth, Brunonian, Buchu, Bucku, Calumba, Carminative, Charm, Chiropody, Chlorodyne, Chrysarobin, Clinician, Complementary, Cordial, Corpsman, Cubeb, Curative, Defensive, Diapente, Diascordium, Diatessaron, Dose, Draught, Drops, > **DRUG**, Dutch drops, Electuary, Elixir, Emmenagogue, Empirics, Enema, Epulotic, Excipient, Expectorant, Fall-trank, Febrifuge, Feldsher, Folk, Forensic, Fringe, Galen, Galenism, Genitourinary, Gutta, Herb, Herbal, Hesperidin, Holistic,

Hom(o)eopathy, Horse-drench, Iatric(al), Imhotep, Industrial, Inhalant, Inro, Internal, Iodine, Ipecac(uanha), Iron, Ko cycle, Lariam®, Laxative, Leechcraft, Legal, Loblolly, Lotion, Magnesia, Menthol, Mishmi, Mixture, Moxar, Muti, Nephritic, Nervine, Nostrum, Nuclear, Nux vomica, Officinal, Oporice, Orthopoedics, Osteopath, Palliative, Panacea, Paregoric, Patent, Pathology, Pharmacy, Physic, Physical, Pill, Placebo, Polychrest, Posology, Potion, Poultice, Preparation, Preventive, Proctology, Psionic, Psychiatry, Quinacrine, Quinine, Quin(quin)a, Radiology, Relaxative, > REMEDY, Salve, Sanative, Sanguinaria, Senna, Serology, Simple, Space, Specific, Sports, Steel, Stomachic, Stramonium, Stupe, Suppository, Synergast, Syrup, Tabasheer, Tabashir, Tablet, Tar-water, Tetracycline, Therapeutics, TIM, Tisane, Tonic, Totaquine, Trade, Traditional Chinese, Traumatology, Treatment, Troche, Valerian, Veronal, Veterinary, Virology

Medicine man Koradji

Medick Snail

Medieval Archaic, Feudal, Gothic, Med, Old, Trecento

Mediocre Fair, Indifferent, Middling, Ordinary, Pap, Respectable, So-So, Undistinguished

Meditate, Meditation, Meditator, Meditative Brood, Chew, Cogitate, Gymnosophy, Hesychast, Muse, Mystic, Pensive, Ponder, Reflect, Reverie, Revery, Ruminate, Thanatopsis, Transcendental, Vipassana, Weigh, Yoga, Zazen

Mediterranean Levant, Midi

Medium Agency, Average, Channel, Clairvoyant, Contrast, Culture, Dispersive, Element, Ether, Even, Happy, Home, Intermediary, Interstellar, M, Magilp, Mean, Megilp, Midsize, Midway, Milieu, Oils, Organ, Ouija, Planchette, Press, Radio, Regular, Shaman, Spiritist, Spiritualist, Television, Telly, TV, Vehicle

Medley Charivari, Collection, Gallimaufry, Jumble, Macedoine, Melange, Mix, Pastiche, Patchwork, Pi(e), Pot-pourri, Quodlibet, Ragbag, Salad, Salmagundi, Series, Tat

▷ **Medley** *may indicate* an anagram

Medusa Planoblast

Meek Docile, Griselda, Humble, Milquetoast, Patient, Tame

Meerschaum Sepiolite

Meet(ing), Meeting place Abide, Abutment, AGM, Appointment, Apropos, Assemble, Assembly, Assignation, Audience, Baraza, Bosberaad, Camporee, Caucus, Chapterhouse, Chautauqua, Clash, Conclave, Concourse, Concur, Confluence, Confrontation, Congress, Connivance, Consistory, Consulta, Contact, Conterminous, Convene, Convent(icle), Convention, Converge, Conversazione, Convocation, Correspond, Cybercafé, Defray, Demo, EGM, Encounter, Ends, Experience, Face, Find, Fit, For(e)gather, Forum, Fulfil, Gemot, Giron, Gorsedd, Guild, Gyeld, Gymkhana, Gyron, Howf(f), Hunt, Hustings, Imbizo, Indaba, Infall, Interface, Interview, Join, Junction, Kgotla, Korero, Lekgotla, Liaise, Marae, Moot, Obviate, Occlusion, Occur, Oppose, Overflow, Pay, Plenary, Plenum, Pnyx, Pow-wow, Prayer, Prosper, Quadrivial, Quaker, Quorate, Quorum, Race, Races, Rally, Rencontre, Rencounter, Rendezvous, Reunion, Sabbat(h), Satisfy, Seance, See, Seminar, Session, Sit, Social, Sports, Suitable, Summit, Symposium, Synastry, Synaxis, Synod, Tackle, Talkfest, Town, Track, Tryst, Venue, Vestry, Wapinshaw, Wardmote, Wharepuni, Workshop

Megalith(ic) Sarsen, Skara Brae, Stonehenge

Megalomaniac Monarcho

Megaphone Bull-horn
Megapode Mound-bird, Talegalla
Meiosis Understatement
Melancholy, Melancholic Adust, Allicholy, Allycholly, Anatomy, Atrabilious,
   Cafard, Despond(ency), Dreary, Dump(s), Gloom, Heart-sore, Hipped, Hump,
   Hyp, Hypochondria, Jaques, Lienal, Pensieroso, Pensive, Saturnine, Sombre,
   Spleen, Splenetic, Triste, Tristesse, Weltschmerz
Melanesian Kanak
Mêlée Brawl, Commotion, Fracas, Rally, Salmagundi, Scrum
Melia Margosa, Neem, Nim
Mellifluent, Mellifluous Cantabile, Melodic
Mellow Fruity, Genial, Mature, Ripe, Smooth
Melodrama(tic) Bathos, Histrionic, Sensation, Transpontine
Melody, Melodious Air, Arioso, Cabaletta, Cantabile, Cantilena, Canto (fermo),
   Cantus, Conductus, Counterpoint, Descant, Dulcet, Euphonic, Fading,
   Musical, Orphean, Plainsong, Ranz-des-vaches, Refrain, Songful, Strain,
   Theme, Tunable, > TUNE(S)
Melon(like) Cantaloup(e), Cas(s)aba, Gourd, Honeydew, Mango, Musk, Nar(r)as,
   Ogen, Pepo, Persian, Rock, Spanspek, Winter
Melt(ed), Melting Ablate, Colliquate, > DISSOLVE, Eutectic, Eutexia, Flux,
   Found, Fuse, Fusil(e), Liquescent, Liquid, Run, Smectic, Syntexis, Thaw, Touch
Member Adherent, Arm, Branch, Bro(ther), Chin, Confrère, Cornice, Coulisse,
   Crossbeam, Crypto, Direction, Felibre, Fellow, Forearm, Forelimb, Founder,
   Gremial, Insider, Keel, Leg, Limb, Lintel, Longeron, M, MBE, Montant, MP,
   Organ, Part, Partisan, Private, Rood-beam, Soroptomist, Stile, Stringer, Strut,
   Syndic, Toe
Membrane, Membranous Amnion, Arachnoid, Axilemma, Caul, Cell,
   Chorioallantois, Chorion, Choroid (plexus), Chromoplast, Conjunctiva,
   Cornea, Cyst, Decidua, Dissepiment, Dura (mater), Endocardium,
   Endometrium, Endosteum, Ependyma, Exine, Extine, Film, Fr(a)enum,
   Frenulum, Haw, Hyaloid, Hymen, Indusium, Intima, Intine, Involucre, Mater,
   Mediastinum, Meninx, Mesentery, Mucosa, Mucous, Nictitating, Patagium,
   Pellicle, Pericardium, Pericarp, Perichondrium, Pericranium, Periost(eum),
   Periton(a)eum, Pia mater, Pleura, Putamen, Retina, Rim, Sarcolemma,
   Scarious, Schneiderian, Sclera, Serosa, Serous, Skin, Synovial, Tectorial, Tela,
   Third eyelid, Tissue, Tonoplast, Trophoblast, Tympan(ic), Vacuolar, Velamen,
   Velum, Vitelline, Web, Yolk-sac
Memento, Memoir Keepsake, Locket, Relic, Remembrancer, Souvenir, Token,
   Trophy
Memo(randum) Bordereau, Cahier, Chit, IOU, Jot, Jurat, Minute, Note, Notepad,
   > REMINDER
Memoirist Casanova
Memorable, Memorise, Memory Bubble, Cache, Catchy, Collective, Con,
   Core, Echoic, Engram(ma), Extended, Flash (bulb), Folk, Get, Historic,
   Iconic, Immortal, Immunological, Learn, Living, Long-term, Main,
   Memoriter, Mind, Mneme, Mnemonic, Mnemosyne, Non-volatile, Notable,
   Pelmanism, Photographic, RAM, Recall, Recovered, > REMEMBER, Retention,
   Retrospection, Ro(a)te, ROM, Samskara, Screen, Semantic, Short-term,
   Souvenir, Sovenance, Static, Virtual, Volatile, Word, Working
Memorial Cenotaph, Cromlech, Ebenezer, Gravestone, Hatchment, Headstone,
   Marker, Monument, Mount Rushmore, Obelisk, Plaque, Relic, Statue, Tomb,
   Trophy, War

▶ **Memory loss** *see* LOSS OF MEMORY

Men(folk) Amadoda, Chaps, Chess, Cuffins, Male, Mortals, OR, Race, Troops

Menace, Menacing Danger, Endanger, Foreboding, Minatory, Peril, Pest, Threat(en)

Menagerie Ark, Circus, Zoo

Mend Beet, Bete, Bushel, Cobble, Correct, Darn, Fix, Heal, Improved, Patch, Piece, Recover, Remedy, > REPAIR, Set, Sew, Solder, Trouble-shoot

Mendelevium Md

Mendicant Beggar, Fakir, Franciscan, Servite

Menial Bottlewasher, Drudge, Drug, Eta, Fag, Flunkey, Lowly, Scullion, Servile, Toady, Underling

Meninx (D)jerba

Menopause Andropause

Menstruation Menarche, Menses

Mental (condition), Mental disorder Alienism, Doolally, Eject, Hallucinosis, Insane, Noetic, Paranoia, Psychic

▷ **Mental** *may indicate* the chin

Mention(ed) Allusion, Bename, Benempt, Broach, Bynempt, Citation, Hint, Name, Notice, Quote, Refer, Speech, State, Suggest, Touch

Mentor Rebbe, Tutor

Menu Agenda, Card, Carte, Carte du jour, Cascading, Drop-down, Fare, List, Table d'hôte, Tariff

Mercantile Commercial, Trade

Mercator Cartographer

Mercenary Arnaout, Condottiere, Freelance, Greedy, Hack, Hessian, Hireling, Landsknecht, Legionnaire, Pindaree, Pindari, Rutter, Sordid, Spoilsman, Venal, Wildgeese

Merchandise Cargo, Goods, Line, Produce, Ware(s)

Merchant(man) Abudah, Antonio, Broker, Bun(n)ia, Burgher, Chandler, Chap, Crare, Crayer, Dealer, Factor, Flota, Hoastman, Importer, Jobber, Law, Magnate, Marcantant, Mercer, Monger, Négociant, Pedlar, Polo, Retailer, Shipper, Speed, Stapler, Sutler, Trader, Vintner, Wholesaler

Mercia Offa

Merciful, Mercy Amnesty, Charity, Clement, Compassionate, Corporal, Grace, Humane, Kind, Kyrie, Lenient, Lenity, Miserere, Misericord(e), Pacable, Pity, Quarter, Ruth, Sparing, Spiritual

Merciless Cruel, Hard, Hard-hearted, Inclement, Pitiless

Mercurial, Mercuric sulphide, Mercury Azoth, Cyllenius, Fulminating, Herald, Hermes, Hg, Horn, Hydrargyrum, Messenger, Quicksilver, Red-man, Spurge, Tiemannite, Volatile

Mere(ly) Allenarly, Bare, Common, Lake, Pond, Pool, Pure, Sheer, Tarn, Very

Merge(r), Merging Amalgamate, Blend, Coalesce, Conflate, Consolidate, Die, Elide, Fusion, Incorporate, Interflow, Liquesce, Meld, Melt, Mingle, Syncretism, Synergy, Unify, Unite

Meridian Magnetic, Noonday, Prime

Meringue Pavlova

Merit(ed) CL, Condign, Deserve, Due, Earn, Found, Rate, Virtue, Worth(iness)

Mermaid Dugong, Halicore, Merrow, Siren, Tavern, Undine

Merriment, Merry Andrew, Bonny, Boon, Cant, Cherry, Chirpy, Crank, Elated, Full, Gaudy, Gay, Gean, Gleesome, Greek, Jocose, Jocular, Jocund, Jolly, Joyous, L'allegro, Lively, Nitid, On, Page, Riant, Sportive, Sunny, Vogie, Waggery, Wassail

Merry Andrew Clown, Jack-pudding, Pickle-herring
Merry-go-round Carousel, Whirligig
Merry-making Cakes and ale, Carnival, Festivity, Gaiety, Gaud, Gawd, Revel
Merrythought Clavicle, Collarbone, Wishbone
Mesh Cancellate, Chain, Entangle, Net, Reseau
Mess(y) Balls-up, Bedraggled, Boss, Botch, Canteen, Caudle, Chaos, Clamper, Clutter, Cock-up, Failure, Farrago, Fiasco, Flub, Garboil, G(l)oop, Glop, Gory, Guddle, Gunge, Gunk, Gun-room, Hash, Horlicks, Hotch-potch, Hugger-mugger, Imbroglio, Lash-up, Louse, Mash, Meal, Mismanage, Mix, Mixter-maxter, Modge, Muck, Muff, Muss, Mux, Pi(e), Piss-up, Plight, Pollute, Pottage, Screw-up, Scungy, Shambles, Shambolic, Shemozzle, Sight, Slaister, Smudge, Snafu, Soss, Sty, Sully, Untidy, Wardroom, Whoopsie, Yuck(y)
Message(s) Aerogram, Bull, Bulletin, Cable, Contraplex, Dépêche, Despatch, Dispatch, Email, Errand, Error, Flame, Missive, News, Note, Pager, Posting, Postscript, Radiogram, Rumour, Signal, Slogan, SOS, Stripagram, Strippergram, Subtext, Telegram, Telephone, Telex, Text, Tidings, Wire, >WORD
Messenger Angel, Apostle, Azrael, Caddie, Caddy, Chaprassi, Chuprassy, Courier, Culver, Despatch-rider, Emissary, Envoy, Forerunner, Gaga, Gillie-wetfoot, Gillie Whitefoot, Hatta, Herald, Hermes, Internuncio, Iris, Ladas, Mercury, Nuncio, Page, Peon, Post, Pursuivant, Runner, Send, Shellycoat, Valkyrie
Messiah Christ, Emmanuel, Immanuel, Mahdi, Mashiach, Saviour, Son of man
Met Old Bill, Weather
Metabolism Basal
Metal(s), **Metallic**, **Metalware** Ag, Aglet, Aiglet, Aiguillette, Al, Aluminium, Antimony, Babbitt, Base, Bell, Billon, Brassy, Britannia, Cadmium, Chrome, Chromium, Cobalt, Copper, Death, Dutch, Dysprosium, Er(bium), Europium, Expanded, Filler, Foil, Fusible, Gallium, Germanium, Gib, Heavy, Hot, Ingot, Invar®, Iridium, Iron, Jangling, Leaf, Magnolia, Manganese, Mineral, Misch, Mitis, Monel(l), Muntz, Natrium, Nickel, Noble, Nonferrous, Ore, Osmium, Parent, Perfect, Planchet, Platinum, Precious, Prince's, Protore, Regulus, Rhenium, Road, Ruthenium, Samarium, Scrap, Sheet(-iron), Slug, Sm, Sn, Sodium, Speculum, Speiss, Sprue, Steel, Strontium, Taggers, Tantalum, Terbic, Terbium, Terne, Thallium, Thorium, Thrash, Tin, Tole, Tramp, Transition, Tutania, Tutenag, Type, White, Wolfram, Yellow, Zinc
Metal-worker Founder, Lorimer, Smith, Spurrier, Tubal Cain
Metamorphose Transmogrify
▷ **Metamorphosing** *may indicate* an anagram
Metamphetamine Ice
Metaphor Conceit, Figure, Image, Kenning, Malonym, Mixed, Symbol, Trope, Tropical
Metaphysics Ontology
Mete Inflict
Meteor(ic), **Meteorite** Achondrite, Aerolite, Aerosiderite, Bolide, Chondrite, Comet, Drake, Falling star, Fireball, Germinid, Leonid, Perseid, Quantrantid, Siderite, Siderolite, Star(dust), Stony, Tektite
Meter Alidad(e), Electric, Exposure, Gas, Light, Orifice, Parking, Postage, Postal, Torque, Torsion, Water, White
Methane Alkane
Methedrine Speed
Method(ology), **Methodical** Art, Billings, Buteyko, Direct, Feldenkrais,

Formula, Gram's, Historical, Hi-tec(h), Kenny, Line, Manner, Mode, Modus, Modus operandi, Monte Carlo, Montessori, Neat, Orderly, Ovulation, Painstaking, Ploy, Procedure, Process, Q, Rhythm, Schafer's, Scientific, Socratic, Stanislavski, > **SYSTEM**, Tactics, Technique, Way

Methodism, **Methodist** Huntingdonian, Jumper, Methody, Primitive, Ranter, Scientism, Southcottian, Swaddler, Wesley

Methuselah Bottle, Macrobiote

Meticulous Careful, > **EXACT**, Finicky, Minute, Precise, Punctilious, Quiddler, Scrupulous, Thorough

Metier Line, Trade, Vocation

Metre Alexandrine, Amphibrach, Amphimacer, Anapaest, Antispast, Arsis, Ballad, Cadence, Choliamb, Choree, Choriamb, Common, Dipody, Galliambic, Iambic, Long, M, Prosody, Rhythm, Sapphic, Scansion, Scazon, Service, Short, Spondee, Strophe, Tripody, Trochee

Metric (system) MKS

Metroland Subtopia

Metropolitan Eparch

Mettle Ardour, Bravery, Courage, Ginger, Guts, Pith, > **PLUCK**, Pride, Smeddum, Spirit, Spunk, Steel

Mew Caterwaul, Miaou, Miaow, Pen, Purr, Seagull, Waul, Wrawl

Mews Meuse, Muse(t), Musit, Stables

Mexican (Indian) Atlalt, Aztec, Carib, Chicano, Chichibec, Diaz, Greaser, Gringo, Hairless, Hispanic, Maya, Mixe-Zoque, Mixtec, Montezuma, Nahuatl, Nortéño, Olmec, Otomi, Pachuco, Spic, Spik, Taino, Toltec, Wetback, Zapotec, Zuni

Mezzanine Entresol

Mezzo-soprano Tessa

Mica Biotite, Daze, Fuchsite, Glimmer, Lepidolite, Lepidomelane, Muscovite, Paragonite, Phlogopite, Rubellan, Sericite, Talc, Verdite, Vermiculite

Micawber Wilkins

Mick(ey) Greek, Mouse

Micro Mu

Microbe, **Microorganism** Germ, Lactobacillus, Organism

Microphone Bug, Carbon, Crystal, Lavaliere, Lip, Mike, Radio, Ribbon, Throat

Microscope Compound, Confocal, Dissecting, Electron, Engyscope, Lens, Optical, Phase-contrast, Proton, Reflecting, SEM, Simple, Solar, TEM, Ultraviolet

Mid(st) Amongst, Mongst

Midas Goldinger, Tamarin

Midday Meridian, N, Noon, Noon-tide, Noon-time

Middle, **Middling** Active, Basion, Centre, Core, Crown, Enteron, Excluded, Eye, Girth, Heart, Loins, Median, Mediocre, Meridian, Meseraic, Mesial, Mesne, Meso, Midriff, Moderate, Noon, Passive, Turn, Twixt, Wa(i)st

Middle age Menopause

Middle-cambrian Menevian

Middle class Bourgeois, Hova

Middle Eastern Arab, Iraqi, Omani

Middleman Broker, Comprador(e), Diaphragm, Interlocutor, Intermediary, Jobber, Median, Navel, Regrater, Regrator

Middlesex Hermaphrodite

Midge Gall, Gnat

Midget Dwarf, Homunculus, Lilliputian, Pygmy, Shrimp

Midianite Prowler
Midlands Mercia
Midnight G, O am
▶ **Midnight** *see* PAST MIDNIGHT
Midriff Phrenic, Skirt, Waist
Midshipman Brass-bounder, Easy, Middy, Oldster, Reefer, Snottie, Snotty
▶ **Midst** *see* MID
Midwife Accoucheur, Doula, Gran(nie), Granny, Howdie, Howdy, Lucina, Mab,
   Obstetric
Mien Air, Bearing, Demean, Manner
Might(iness), Mighty Force, Main, Mote, Nibs, Potence, > POWER, Prowess,
   Puissant, Should, Strength
Mignon(ette) Dyer's rocket, Fillet, Reseda, Weld
Migraine Megrim, Scotodinia, Teichopsia
Migrant Externe, Gastarbeiter, Lemming, Traveller
Migrate, Migration, Migratory Colonise, Diapedesis, Diaspora, Drift, Eelfare,
   Exodus, Fleet, Great Trek, Run, Tre(c)k, Volkwanderung
Mikado Emperor, Kami
Mike Bug, Stentorphone
Milanese Patarine
Mild(ly) Balmy, Benign, Bland, Clement, Euphemism, Genial, Gentle, Lenient,
   Litotes, Mansuete, Meek, > MODERATE, Pacific, Patient, Sarcenet, Sars(e)net,
   Temperate
Mildew Downy, Foxing, Fungus, Mould, Oidium, Powdery, Vine
Mile(s) Admiralty, Coss, Coverdale, Food, Geographical, Knot, Kos, Li, Milliary,
   Nautical, Passenger, Roman, Royal, Sea, Soldier, Square, Standish, Statute,
   Swedish, Train
Milesian Teague
Milestone Milliary, MS
Milfoil Yarrow
Militant, Military Activist, Aggressive, Battailous, Black Panther, Commando,
   Hawkish, Hezbollah, Hizbollah, Hizbullah, Hostile, Ireton, Landwehr,
   Mameluke, Martial, Presidio, Provisional, Provo, Soldatesque, West Point
Militia Fyrd, Guard, Haganah, Minuteman, Reserve, Tanzim, Trainband,
   Yeomanry
Milk(er), Milky Acidophilus, Beestings, Bland, Bleed, Bonny-clabber, Bristol,
   Casein, Colostrum, Condensed, Creamer, Crud, Curd, Emulge, Evaporated,
   Exploit, Galactic, Glacier, Goat's, Jib, Kefir, Kephir, K(o)umiss, Lactation,
   Lacteal, Latex, Madzoon, Magnesia, Malted, Matzoon, Mess, Opaline,
   Pasteurised, Pinta, Posset, Raw, Sap, Semi-skimmed, Shedder, Skim(med),
   Soya, Squeeze, Strippings, Stroke, Suckle, UHT, Whig, Whole, Yaourt,
   Yogh(o)urt
Milking-machine, Milking parlour Loan, Tapper
Milking-pail Leglan, Leglen, Leglin
Milkless Agalactic, Dry, Eild
Milkmaid, Milkman Chalker, Dey, Emulge, Kefir, Kephir, Radha, Rounder,
   Roundsman, Skimmed
Milksop Coward, Meacock, Namby-pamby, Nance, Pance, Weakling
Milk-vetch Loco
Milkweed Asclepias
Milkwort Senega
Milky Way Via Lactea

Mill(ing), Mills Aswarm, Barker's, Boxing, Coffee, Economist, Gang, Gastric, Grind(er), Hayley, Kibble, Knurl, Mano, Melder, Molar, Nurl, Paper, Pepper, Post, Powder, Press, Pug, Quern, Reave, Rob, Rolling, Satanic, Scutcher, Smock, Stamp, Stamping, Strip, Sugar, Surge, Thou, Tide, Tower, Tuck, Water, Wool(len), Works

Miller Dusty, Glen, Grinder, Jester, Joe, Molendinar, Multurer

Millet Bajra, Bajree, Bajrii, Couscous, Dari, Dhurra, Doura, Dur(r)a, Grain, Miliary, Negro-corn, Pearl, Proso, Ragee, Raggee, Ragi, Whisk

Millionaire Astor, Carnegie, Rockefeller, Rothschild, Vanderbilt

Millions, Millionth Crore, Femto-, Milliard, Muckle, Pico-

Millipede Songololo

Millstone Ligger, Rind, Rynd

Mim Perjink

Mime, Mimic(ry) Ape, Batesian, Copycat, Farce, Imitate, Impersonate, Lipsync, Mina, Mullerian, Mummer, Parody, Sturnine

Mimosa Cacoon, Saman

Mince Cecils, Chop, Dice, Grate, Grind, Prance, Rice

Mind(er) Aide, Beware, Brain, Genius, Handler, > HEED, Herd, Id, Intellect, Noology, Noosphere, One-track, Phrenic, Psyche, Psychogenic, Resent, Sensorium, Tabula rasa, Tend, Thinker, Wit, Woundwort

Mine, Mining Acoustic, Antenna, Bomb, Bonanza, Bottom, Bouquet, Burrow, Camouflet, Chemical, Claymore, Colliery, Contact, Creeping, Dane-hole, Data, Dig(gings), Drifting, Egg, Eldorado, Excavate, Explosive, Floating, Flooder, Fougade, Fougasse, Gallery, Gob, Golconda, Gold, Gopher, Grass, Homing, Land, Limpet, Magnetic, Naked-light, Nostromo, Open-cast, Open-cut, Ophir, Pit, Placer, Pressure, Prospect, Rising, Sap, Set(t), Show, Sonic, Stannary, Stope, Strike, Strip, Undercut, Wheal, Win, Workings

Mine-deflector Otter, Paravane

Mine-owner Operator

Miner, Mine-worker, Mine-working Butty-gang, Collier, Continuous, Cutter, Digger, Forty-niner, Geordie, Leaf, Molly Maguire, NUM, Oncost(man), Pitman, Shot-firer, Stall, Tributer, UDM

Mineral Accessory, Essential, Index

● MINERALS

3 letters:	Emery	Galena	Silica
YAG	Flint	Gangue	Sphene
	Fluor	Garnet	Spinel
4 letters:	Macle	Glance	Tincal
Gang	Mafic	Gypsum	Zircon
Mica	Nitre	Hauyne	
Sard	Prase	Illite	7 letters:
Spar	Topaz	Jargon	Alunite
Talc	Trona	Lithia	Anatase
Trap	Umber	Natron	Apatite
Urao		Nosean	Axinite
	6 letters:	Pinite	Azurite
5 letters:	Acmite	Pyrite	Barytes
Balas	Albite	Quartz	Biotite
Borax	Augite	Rutile	Bornite
Chert	Blende	Schorl	Brucite

Calcite	Andesine	Mimetite	Columbite
Calomel	Ankerite	Monazite	Covellite
Catseye	Antimony	Nephrite	Cystolith
Cuprite	Aphanite	Noselite	Dolomitic
Cyanite	Asbestos	Orpiment	Elaeolite
Diamond	Autunite	Petuntse	Endomorph
Dysodil	Blue john	Picotite	Enhydrite
Epidote	Boehmite	Prehnite	Enstatite
Euclase	Boracite	Pyroxene	Erythrite
Eucrite	Braunite	Resalgar	Fibrolite®
Fahlore	Bronzite	Rock-salt	Fluorspar
Felspar	Brookite	Sanidine	Gehlenite
Gahnite	Calamine	Saponite	Germanite
Göthite	Cerusite	Siderite	Geyserite
Gummite	Chlorite	Smectite	Gmelinite
Hessite	Chromite	Sodalite	Goslarite
Ice spar	Cinnabar	Stannite	Haematite
Jadeite	Cleveite	Stibnite	Harmotome
Jargoon	Corundum	Stilbite	Hercynite
Kainite	Crocoite	Taconite	Hiddenite
Kernite	Cryolite	Tenorite	Hornstone
Kyanite	Datolite	Titanite	Kaolinite
Leucite	Dendrite	Troilite	Kermesite
Mellite	Diallage	Xenotime	Kieserite
Mullite	Diaspore	Zaratite	Magnetite
Nacrite	Disthene		Malachite
Olivine	Dolomite	**9 letters:**	Manganite
Pennine	Dysodile	Alabaster	Marcasite
Peridot	Dysodyle	Allophane	Margarite
Pyrites	Epsomite	Amazonite	Marialite
Realgar	Erionite	Amphibole	Microlite
Rosaker	Euxenite	Anglesite	Microlith
Sylvine	Fayalite	Anhydrite	Millerite
Sylvite	Feldspar	Anorthite	Mispickel
Thorite	Flinkite	Aragonite	Mizzonite
Thulite	Fluorite	Argentite	Moonstone
Tripoli	Galinite	Atacamite	Muscovite
Turgite	Gibbsite	Blackjack	Natrolite
Ulexite	Goethite	Blacklead	Nepheline
Uralite	Gyrolite	Carnelian	Nephelite
Uranite	Hematite	Carnotite	Niccolite
Uranium	Idocrase	Celestine	Nitratine
Zeolite	Ilmenite	Celestite	Olivenite
Zincite	Iodyrite	Cerussite	Ottrelite
Zoisite	Jarosite	Chabazite	Paramorph
Zorgite	Lazulite	Chalybite	Pargasite
	Lazurite	Cheralite	Pectolite
8 letters:	Lewisite	Chondrule	Periclase
Adularia	Limonite	Cobaltine	Pericline
Allanite	Massicot	Cobaltite	Perimorph
Analcime	Meionite	Coccolite	Phenacite
Analcite	Melilite	Columbate	Pleonaste

- Polianite
- Pollucite
- Powellite
- Proustite
- Rhodonite
- Rubellite
- Scapolite
- Scheelite
- Scolecite
- Spodumene
- Sylvanite
- Tantalite
- Tremolite
- Troostite
- Tungstite
- Uraninite
- Uvarovite
- Variscite
- Vulpinite
- Wavellite
- Wernerite
- Willemite
- Witherite
- Wulfenite
- Zinkenite

10 letters:
- Actinolite
- Alabandine
- Alabandite
- Andalusite
- Bastnasite
- Calaverite
- Carnallite
- Chalcocite
- Chessylite
- Chrysolite

Colemanite
Cordierite
Crocoisite
Dyscrasite
Forsterite
Gadolinite
Garnierite
Glauconite
Halloysite
Heulandite
Honey-stone
Hornblende
Indicolite
Indigolite
Jamesonite
Laurdalite
Meerschaum
Microcline
Oligoclase
Orthoclase
Perovskite
Phosgenite
Polybasite
Polyhalite
Pyrolusite
Pyrrhotite
Redruthite
Riebeckite
Ripidolite
Samarskite
Sapphirine
Saussurite
Serpentine
Smaragdite
Sperrylite
Sphalerite
Staurolite

Tennantite
Thaumasite
Thenardite
Thorianite
Tiemannite
Torbernite
Tourmaline
Triphylite
Vanadinite
Wolframite

11 letters:
Alexandrite
Annabergite
Apophyllite
Baddeleyite
Bastnaesite
Cassiterite
Chiastolite
Chrysoberyl
Clinochlore
Crocidolite
Dendrachate
Franklinite
Greenockite
Hypersthene
Idiomorphic
Josephinite
Molybdenite
Pentlandite
Phosphorite
Piedmontite
Pitchblende
Plagioclase
Pseudomorph
Psilomelane
Pyrargyrite

Sillimanite
Smithsonite
Tetradymite
Vermiculite
Vesuvianite
Ythro-cerite

12 letters:
Adularescent
Arfvedsonite
Arsenopyrite
Babingtonite
Chalcanthite
Chalcopyrite
Cristobalite
Dumortierite
Feldspathoid
Fluorapatite
Hemimorphite
Pyromorphite
Pyrophyllite
Senarmontite
Skutterudite
Strontianite
Synadelphite
Tetrahedrite
Wollastonite

13 letters:
Cummingtonite
Rhodochrosite

15 letters:
Gooseberry-stone
Montmorillonite

Mineral water Apollinaris, Tonic
Minesweeper Oropesa, Unity
Mingle Blend, Circulate, Consort, Interfuse, Mell, > MIX, Participate, Socialise, Unite
Mini Cab, Car, Skirt, Teen(s)y
Miniature, Miniaturist Cosway, Microcosm, Midget, Model, Toy, Young
Minimise, Minimum (range) Bare, Downplay, Fewest, Least, Neap, Shoestring, Stime, Styme, Threshold, Undervalue
▷ **Minimum of** *may indicate* the first letter
Minion Flunkey, Lackey, Pet, Subordinate, Tool, Vassal
Minister Ambassador, Attend, Buckle-beggar, Cabinet, Chancellor, Chaplain, Cleric, Coarb, Commissar, Deacon, Dewan, Diplomat, Divine, D(i)wan, Dominee, Dominie, Envoy, First, Foreign, Holy Joe, Mas(s)john, Mes(s)john, Moderator, Nurse, Officiant, Padre, Parson, Pastor, Peshwa, Preacher,

Predikant, Presbyter, Prime, Rector, Secretary, Seraskier, > SERVE, Stickit, Subdeacon, Tend, Visier, Vizier, Wazir, Wizier

Ministry Defence, Department, Dept, DoE, MOD, MOT, Orders, Service

Mink Kolinsky, Mutation, Vison

Minnow Penk, Pink, Tiddler

Minoan Knossus

Minor(ity) Child, Comprimario, Ethnic, Faction, Few, Infant, Junior, Less, Minutia, Nonage, One-horse, Petty, Pupillage, Slight, Small-time, Trivial, Ward

Minotaur Bull-headed

Minstrel Allan-a-dale, Bard, Blondel, Bones, Busker, Cantabank, Christy, Cornerman, Gleeman, Hamfatter, Joculator, Jongleur, Minnesinger, Nigger, Pierrot, Scop, Singer, Taillefer

Mint Aim, Bugle-weed, Catnip, Coin, Ettle, Fortune, Herb, Horse, Humbug, Labiate, Monarda, Monetise, Nep, New, Penny-royal, Polo®, Poly, Royal, Selfheal, Stamp, Strike, Unused, Utter

Minute(s), Minutiae Acta, Alto, Degree, Detailed, Diatom, Entry, Infinitesimal, Little, Micron, Mo, Mu, Nano-, Pinpoint, Resume, Small, Teen(t)sy, Teeny, Tine, Tiny, Trivia, Tyne, Wee

Minx Hellion

Miracle, Miraculous Cana, Marvel, Merel(l), Meril, Morris, Mystery, Phenomenon, Supernatural, Thaumaturgic, Theurgy, Wirtschaftswunder, Wonder, Wonderwork

Mirage Fata morgana, Illusion, Loom, Northern lights

Mire Bog, Glaur, Lair(y), Latch, Lerna, Lerne, Loblolly, Marsh, Mud, Quag, Sludge, Soil

Mirky Dark, Dirk(e)

Mirror(ed) Alasnam, Busybody, Cambuscan, Catoptric, Cheval, Claude Lorraine glass, Coelostat, Conde, Dare, Enantiomorph, Glass, Image, Imitate, Lao, Magnetic, Merlin, One-way, Pierglass, Primary, Psyche, Rearview, > REFLECT, Reynard, Shisha, Siderostat, Sign, Specular, Speculum, Stone, Two-way, Vulcan, Wing

Mirror-image Perversion

Mirth(ful) Cheer, Dream, Festive, Hilarity, Joy, Laughter, Spleen

▷ **Misalliance** *may indicate* an anagram

Misanthrope Cynic, Timon

Misapplication Catachresis, Misuse

Misappropriate, Misappropriation Asport, Detinue, Purloin, Steal

Miscarry Abort, Backfire, Fail, Slink

Miscegenation Allocarpy

Miscellaneous, Miscellany Assortment, Chow, Collectanea, Diverse, Etceteras, Misc, Odds and ends, Odds and sods, Olio, Omnium-gatherum, Potpourri, Raft, Ragbag, Sundry, Varia, Variety, Various

Mischief(-maker), Mischievous Ate, Bale, Bane, Cantrip, Cloots, Devilment, Diablerie, Dido, Disservice, Gremlin, Harm, Hellery, Hellion, Hob, Imp, Injury, Jinks, Larrikin, Litherly, Malicho, Mallecho, Monkey-tricks, Nickum, Owl-spiegle, Pestilent, Pickle, Prank, Puckish, Rascal, Scally(wag), Scamp, Scapegrace, Shenanigans, Spriteful, Tricksy, Wag, Wicked, Widgie

Misconception Delusion, Idol(on), Idolum, Misunderstanding

Misconduct Impropriety, Malfeasance, Malversation

Miscreant Reprobate, Sinner

Misdeed Offence, Peccadillo, Trespass, Wrong

▷ **Misdelivered** *may indicate* an anagram

Misdemeanour Delict, Offence, Peccadillo, Tort, Wrongdoing

Miser(ly) Carl, Cheapskate, Cheese-parer, Close, Curmudgeon, Gare, Grasping, Harpagon, Hunks, Marner, Meanie, Mingy, Niggard, Nipcheese, Nipcurn, Nipfarthing, Pennyfather, Pinch-commons, Puckfist, Runt, Scrape-good, Scrape-penny, Screw, Scrimping, Scrooge, Skinflint, Snudge, Storer, Tightwad, Timon

Miserable, **Misery**, **Miserably** Abject, Angashore, Bale, Cat-lap, Crummy, Distress, Dole, Forlorn, Gloom, Grief, Hell, Joyless, Lousy, Perdition, Punk, Sad, Scungy, Sorry, Sourpuss, Tragic, Triste, > **UNHAPPY**, Woe(begone), Wretched

Misfire Dud

Misfit Drop-out, Geek, Loner, Maverick, Sad sack

Misfortune Accident, Affliction, Bale, Calamity, Curse, Disaster, Distress, Dole, Hex, Ill, Reverse, Rewth, Ruth, Wroath

Misgiving(s) Anxiety, Doubt, Dubiety, Qualms, Scruples

Misguide(d) Impolitic

▷ **Misguided** *may indicate* an anagram

Mishandle Abuse

Mishap Accident, Contretemps, Misaunter, Misfortune, Wroath

Mishit, **Misstroke** Crab, Draw, Edge, Fluff, Muff, Sclaff, Shank, Slice, Thin, Top

Misinterpret(ation) Mondegreen, Wrest

Mislay Leese, Lose

Mislead(ing) Blind, Bum steer, Cover-up, Deceive, Delude, Dupe, Equivocate, Fallacious, False, Gag, Red herring, Runaround, Smoke and mirrors

▷ **Misled** *may indicate* an anagram

Mismanage Blunder, Bungle, Muddle

Mismatch Kludge

Misplace(ment) Ectopia

Misplay Fluff, Whitechapel

Misprint Error, Literal, Slip, Typo

Mispronunciation Cacoepy, Lallation, Lambdacism

Misrepresent(ation) Abuse, Belie, Calumny, Caricature, Colour, Distort, Falsify, Garble, Lie, Slander, Subreption, Traduce

Miss(ing) Abord, Avoid, AWOL, Colleen, Desiderate, Dodge, Drib, Err(or), Fail, Forego, Gal, > **GIRL**, Kumari, Lack, Lass, Link, Lose, Mademoiselle, Maid, Maiden, Mile, Muff(et), Near, Neglect, Negligence, Omit, Otis, Overlook, Senorita, Shy, Skip, Spinster, Stoke, Unmeet, Wanting, Whiff

▷ **Miss** *may refer to* Missouri

Missal Breviary, Te igitur, Triodion

Misshapen Crooked, Deformed, Dysmelia, Gnarled

Missile Air-to-air, Ammo, Anti-ballistic, Arrow, Artillery, Atlas, Ball, Ballistic, Beam Rider, Blue streak, Bolas, Bolt, Bomb, Boomerang, Brickbat, Bullet, Condor, Cruise, Dart, Dingbat, Doodlebug, Dum-dum, Exocet®, Falcon, Fléchette, Genie, Grenade, Guided, HARM, Harpoon, Hawk, Hellfire, Hound Dog, ICBM, Interceptor, Jired, Kiley, Kyley, Kylie, Lance, Mace, MARV, Maverick, Minuteman, MIRV, Missive, Mx, Onion, Patriot, Pellet, Pershing, Phoenix, Polaris, Poseidon, Qual, Quarrel, Rocket, SAM, Scud, Sea Skimmer, Sergeant, Shell, Shillelagh, Shot, Shrike, Side-winder, Smart bomb, Snowball, Sparrow, Spartan, Spear, Sprint, SSM, Standard Arm, Standoff, Styx, Subroc, Surface to air, Surface to surface, Talos, Tartar, Terrier, Thor, Titan, Tomahawk, Torpedo, Tracer, Trident, UAM, Warhead

Mission(ary) Aidan, Alamo, Antioch, Apostle, Assignment, Augustine, Bethel,

Caravan, Charge, Delegation, Embassage, Embassy, Errand, Evangelist,
Foreign, Iona, Legation, Livingstone, LMS, Message, NASA, Ninian, Op, Paul,
Quest, Reclaimer, Redemptionist, Schweitzer, Task, Vocation, Xavier
Missis, Missus, Mrs Devi, Maam, Mrs, Wife
Missive Letter, Message, Note
Missouri Mo
▸ **Misstroke** *see* MISHIT
Mist(y) Blur, Brume, Cloud, Dew, Drow, Dry-ice, Film, Fog, Haar, Haze, Hoar,
Miasma, Moch, Nebular, Niflheim, Rack, Red, Roke, Scotch, Sea-fret, Sfumato,
Smir(r), Smog, Smur, Vapour
Mistake(n) Barry (Crocker), Bish, Bloomer, Blooper, Blunder, Boner, Boob,
Booboo, Boss, Botch, Clanger, Clinker, Confound, Deluded, Domino, Erratum,
Error, Fault, Floater, Flub, Fluff, Gaffe, Goof, Howler, Identity, Incorrect,
Lapse, Malapropism, Miss, Muff, Mutual, Nod, Off-beam, Oversight, Plonker,
Pratfall, Screw-up, > SLIP, Slip-up, Solecism, Stumer, Trip, Typo
▷ **Mistake(n)** *may indicate* an anagram
Mister Babu, Effendi, Mr, Sahib, Senor, Shri, Sir, Sri
Mistletoe Album, Missel, Parasite, Viscum
Mistreat Abuse, Attrite, Manhandle, Violate
Mistress Amie, Aspasia, Canary-bird, Chatelaine, Concubine, Courtesan,
Demimondaine, Devi, Doxy, Goodwife, Herself, Hussif, Inamorata,
Instructress, Lady, Leman, Maintenon, Martha, Montespan, Mrs, Natural,
Paramour, Stepney, Teacher, Wardrobe, Wife
Mistrust(ful) Askant, Doubt, Gaingiving, Suspect, Suspicion
Misunderstand(ing) Disagreement, Discord, Mistake
Misuse Abuse, Catachresis, Defalcate, Malappropriate, Malapropism, Maltreat,
Perversion, Torment
Mite Acaridian, Acarus, Bit, Cheese, Child, Flour, Forage, Fowl, Gall, Harvest,
Itch, Lepton, Little, (Red) spider, Rust, Sarcoptes, Speck, Sugar, Trombiculid,
Tyroglyphid, Varroa, Widow's
Mitigate, Mitigating Abate, Allay, Allieve, Ameliorate, Assuage, Extenuating,
Lenitive, Lessen, Mease, Palliate, Quell, Relief, Relieve
Mitosis Anaphase
Mitre Hat, Tiar(a)
Mitt(en), Mittens Fist, Glove, Hand, Paw, Pockies
Mix(ed), Mixer, Mixture, Mix-up Alloy, Amalgam, Associate, Assortment,
Attemper, Balderdash, Bigener, Bland, Blend, Blunge, Bordeaux, Brew,
Carburet, Card, Caudle, Chow, Cocktail, Co-meddle, Compo, Compound,
Conglomerate, Consort, Cross, Cut, Disperse, Dolly, Drammock, Embroil,
Emulsion, Entectic, Farrago, Fold-in, Freezing, Garble, Grill, Griqua,
Heather, Hobnob, Hotchpotch, Hybrid, Imbroglio, Interlace, Intermingle,
Isomorphous, Jumble, Lace, Lard, Lignin, Linctus, Load, Macedoine, Matissé,
Meddle, Medley, Melange, Mell, Meng(e), Ment, Mess, Mestizo, Metis,
Ming(le), Miscellaneous, Miscellany, Mishmash, Mong, Motley, Muddle,
Muss(e), Neapolitan, Octaroon, Octoroon, Olio, Olla, Pi(e), Potin, Pousowdie,
Powsowdy, Praiseach, Promiscuous, Raggle-taggle, Ragtag, Salad, Scramble,
Spatula, Stew, Stir, Temper, Through-other, Trail, Vision, Yblent
▷ **Mixed** *may indicate* an anagram
Mizzle Decamp, Scapa, Scarper
Mnemonic Quipo, Quipu, Reminder
Moab(ite) Balak, Ruth, Wash-pot
Moan(ing) Beef, Bleat, Complain, Groan, Hone, Keen, > LAMENT, Meane,

Plangent, Sough, Wail, W(h)inge

Moat Dike, Ditch, Foss(e)

Mob(ster) Army, Assail, Canaille, Crew, Crowd, Doggery, Faex populi, Gaggle, Gang, Herd, Hoi-polloi, Hoodlum, Lynch, Ochlocrat, Press, Rabble, Raft, Ragtag, Ribble-rabble, Riff-raff, Rout, Scar-face

Mobile, Mobilise, Mobility Donna, Downward, Fluid, Horizontal, Movable, Plastic, Rally, Thin, Upward(ly), Vagile, Vertical

Mob-rule Ochlocracy

Mocassin Larrigan, Shoe, Snake

Mock(ery), Mocking Ape, Banter, Chaff, Chyack, Cod, Cynical, Deride, Derisory, Dor, Ersatz, False, Farce, Fleer, Flout, Gab, Geck, Gibe, Gird, Guy, Imitation, Irony, Irrisory, Jape, > **JEER**, Jibe, Lampoon, Laugh, Mimic, Narquois, Parody, Paste, Pillorise, Rail(lery), Rally, Ridicule, Sacrilege, Sardonic, Satirise, Scout, Sham, Simulate, Slag, Travesty, Wry

Mocking-bird Mimus, Sage-thrasher

Mode Aeolian, Convention, Dorian, Ecclesiastical, Fashion, Form, Formal, Greek, Gregorian, Iastic, Ionian, Locrian, Lydian, Major, Manner, Material, Medieval, Minor, Mixolydian, Phrygian, Plagal, Rate, Real-time, Sleep, Step, Style, Ton

Model(ler), Modelling Archetype, Bozzeto, Cast, Copy, Demonstration, Diorama, Doll, Dummy, Ecorché, Effigy, Epitome, Example, Exemplar, Fictor, Figure, Figurine, Icon, Ideal, Image, Instar, Jig, Last, Lay-figure, Layman, Madame Tussaud, Manakin, Manikin, Mannequin, Maquette, Mark, Mock-up, > **MOULD**, Norm, Original, Orrery, Papier-mache, Parade, Paragon, Pattern, Phelloplastic, Pilot, Plasticine, Pose(r), Posture-maker, Prototype, Replica, Role, Scale, Sedulous, Sitter, Specimen, Standard, Superwaif, T, Template, Templet, Terrella, Toy, Trilby, Twiggy, Type, Typify, Waif, Waxwork, Working

▷ **Model(s)** *may indicate* an anagram

Modem Subset

Moderate(ly), Moderation Abate, Allay, Alleviate, Assuage, Average, Centre, Chasten, Continent, Diminish, Discretion, Ease, Gentle, Girondist, Ho, Lessen, Lukewarm, Measure, Mediocre, Medium, Menshevik, Mezzo, Middling, Mild, Mitigate, OK, Politique, Reason(able), Slake, So-so, Sumptuary, Temper(ate), Temperance, Tolerant, Tone, Via media, Wet

Modern(ise) AD, Aggiornamento, Contemporary, Fresh, Latter(-day), Neonomian, Neoterical, > **NEW**, Present-day, Progressive, Recent, Retrofit, Swinger, Update, Up-to-date

Modest(y) Aidos, Blaise, Chaste, Decent, Demure, Discreet, Humble, Ladylike, Maidenly, Mim, Mussorgsky, Propriety, Prudish, Pudency, Pure, Reserved, Shame, Shy, Unassuming, Unpretending, Unpretentious, Verecund

Modicum Dash

Modifiable, Modification, Modifier, Modify Adapt, Adverb, Alter, Backpedal, Change, Enhance, Extenuate, H, Leaven, Misplaced, Plastic, Qualify, Retrofit, Sandhi, Scumble, Soup, Streamline, Temper, Vary

Modulation, Module, Modulus Accent, Bulk, Cadence, Command, Frequency, Habitat, Inflexion, Lem, Lunar, Mitigate, Phase, Pulse, Service, Tune, Unit, Vary, Velocity, Young's

Mogul Bigwig, Magnate, Padishah, Plutocrat, Taipan, VIP

Mohair Moire

Mohammed, Mohammedan (era) Hadith, Hegira, Hejira, Hejra, Hijra, Islamite, Mahdi, Mahoun(d), Moslem, Muezzin, Mussulman, Prophet, Said, Shiite, Sunna(h)

Moist(en), Moisture Baste, Bedew, Damp, Dank, De(a)w, Humect, Latch, Love-in-a-mist, Madefy, Mesarch, Moil, Nigella, Oozy, Slake, Slocken, Sponge, Wet

▷ **Moither** *may indicate* an anagram

Molar Grinder, Mill-tooth, Secodont, Tooth, Wang

Molasses Blackstrap, Sorghum, Treacle

Mole(hill) Breakwater, Fen-cricket, Golden, Hydatidiform, Jetty, Marsupial, Miner, Mo(u)diewart, Moudi(e)wart, Mouldiwarp, Naeve, Notoryctes, Orology, Pier, Sea-wall, Shrew, Sleeper, Spot, Spy, Star-nose(d), Talpa, Want(hill), Want knap, Warp

Molecular, Molecule Acceptor, Atom, Buckyball, Carbene, Cavitand, Chiral, Chromophore, Closed chain, Cobalamin, Codon, Coenzyme, Cofactor, Dimer, DNA, Electrogen, Enantiomorph, Footballene, Fullerene, Gram, Hapten, Iota, Isomer, Kinin, Ligand, Long-chain, Metabolite, Metameric, Monomer, Peptide, Polymer, Polysaccharide, Quark, Replicon, Ribozyme, Semantide, Stereoisomer, Trimer, Uridine, Vector

Molendinar Mill

Molest(er) Annoy, Bother, Harass, Nonce, Scour

Moll(y), Mollie Bloom, Bonnie, Carousal, Cutpurse, Flanders, Girl, Maguire, Malone, May, Sissy

Mollify Appease, Fob, Mease, Mitigate, Pacify, Relax, Soften, Temper

Mollusc(s) Ammonite, Amphineura, Arca, Argonaut, Ark-shell, Belemnite, Bivalve, Bulla, Capiz, Cephalopod, Chiton, Clam, Cockle, Conch, Cone-shell, Cowrie, Cowry, Cuttle(fish), Dentalium, Doris, Gaper, Gast(e)ropod, Goniatite, Heart-cockler, Heart-shell, Helix, Horse mussel, Lamellibranch, Limpet, Malacology, Marine boxer, Money cowry, Murex, Mussel, Mya, Nautilus, Neopilina, Octopod, Octopus, Olive, Opisthobranch, Oyster, Pandora, Paper nautilus, Paper-sailor, Pearly nautilus, Pecten, Pelican's-foot, Pholas, Piddock, Pinna, Polyp, Poulpe, Pteropod, Quahaug, Quahog, Razor-clam, Razor-fish, Razorshell, Saxicava, Scallop, Scaphopoda, Sea-hare, Sea-lemon, Sea-slug, Sepia, > SHELLFISH, Shipworm, Slug, Snail, Solen, Spat, Spirula, Spoot, Squid, Strombus, Tectibranch, Tellen, Tellin, Teredo, Toheroa, Top-shell, Triton, Trochophore, Trochus, Trough-shell, Turbo, Tusk-shell, Unio, Univalve, Veliger, Venus, Venus shell, Vitrina, Wentletrap, Whelk, Wing-shell, Winkle

Mollycoddle Indulge, Nanny, Pamper

Moloch Thorn-devil

Molten Dissolved, Fusil, Melted

Molybdenum Mo

Moment(s), Momentous Bending, Bit, Dipole, Electromagnetic, Flash, Hogging, Import, Instant, Jiffy, Magnetic, > MINUTE, Mo, Nonce, Psychological, Pun(c)to, Sands, Sec, Shake, Stound, Stownd, Tick, Time, Trice, Twinkling, Weighty, Wink

Momentum Impetus, L, Speed, Thrust

Mona(s) I, IOM

Monaco Grimaldi

Mona Lisa La Gioconda

Monarch(y) Autocrat, Butterfly, Constitutional, Crown, Emperor, HM, K, Karling, King, Limited, Merry, Potentate, Q, Queen, R, Raine, Reign, Ruler, Tsar

Monarchist Cavalier

Monastery Abbey, Abthane, Charterhouse, Chartreuse, Cloister, Community, Gompa, Hospice, Lamaserai, Lamasery, La Trappe, Laura, Priory, Vihara, Wat

Monastic Abthane, Celibate, Holy, Monkish, Oblate, Secluded
Monday Black, Collop, Handsel, J'ouvert, Meal, Oatmeal, Plough, Whit
Mondrian Piet
Monetary, Money Ackers, Akkas, Allowance, Annat, Ante, Appearance, Assignat, Banco, Batta, Blood, Blunt, Boodle, Bottle, Brass, Bread, Bread and honey, Broad, Cabbage, Capital, Cash, Caution, Change, Chink, Cob, > **COIN**, Collateral, Conscience, Crackle, Cranborne, Crinkly, Currency, Danger, Dib(s), Dingbat, Dosh, Dust, Earnest, Easy, Even, Fat, Fee, Fiat, Float, Folding, Fonds, Fund, Funny, Gate, Gelt, Gilt, Gold, Grant, Gravy, Greens, Hard, Head, Hello, Hoot, Hot, Housekeeping, Hush, Idle, Ingots, Investment, Kale, Key, L, Lolly, Loot, Lucre, M, Mammon, Maundy, Mazuma, Means, Mint, Monopoly, Moola(h), Narrow, Necessary, Needful, Nest-egg, Note, Numismatic, Nummary, Oaker, Ochre, Offertory, Oof, Option, Outlay, P, Packet, Paper, Passage, Payroll, Peanuts, Pecuniary, Pelf, Pin, Pine-tree, Pittance, Plastic, Plum, Pocket, Posh, Press, Prize, Proceeds, Profit, Protection, Purse, Push, Ready, Rebate, Resources, Revenue, Rhino, Rogue, Rowdy, Salt(s), Scratch, Scrip, Seed, Shin-plaster, Ship, Short, Siller, Silly, Silver, Slush, Smart, Soap, Soft, Spondulicks, Stake, Sterling, Stipend, Stuff, Subsistence, Sugar, Sum, Table, Takings, Tender, Tin, Toea, Token, Tranche, Treaty, Tribute, Turnover, Viaticum, Wad, Wealth, Wonga
Money-box Penny-pig, Piggy bank
Moneylender Gombeen, Shylock, Usurer
Moneymaking Earner, Profitable, Quaestuary
Mongol(ian) Bashkir, Buriat, Buryat, Calmuck, Chuvash, Evenski, Golden Horde, Kalmuck, Kara-Kalpak, Kazak(h), Khalkha, Kubla(i) Khan, Kyrgyz, Lapp, Lepcha, Manchoo, Manchu, Mishmi, Mogul, Samoyed, Shan, Sherpa, Tamerlane, Tatar, Tungus(ic), Uig(h)ur, Ural-altaic, Uzbak
Mongoose Ichneumon, Mangouste, Meerkat, Suricate, Urva
Mongrel Bitser, Cross(bred), > **DOG**, Goorie, Goory, Hybrid, Kuri, Lurcher, Mutt, Quadroon, Tyke, Underbred, Zo
Monitor Detect, Goanna, Iguana, Lizard, Observe, Offer, Ofgas, Ofgem, Oflot, Ofsted, Oftel, Ofwat, Prefect, Record, Screen, Track, Warship, Watchdog, Whole-body, Worral, Worrel
Monk(s) Abbey-lubber, Abbot, Acoemeti, Angelico, Archimandrite, Arhat, Asser, Augustinian, Austin, Basilian, Bede, Beghard, Benedictine, Bernardine, Bethlehemite, Bhikhu, Black, Bonaventura, Bonze, Brother, Bruno, Caedmon, Caloyer, Carthusian, Celestine, Cellarist, Cenobite, Cistercian, Cluniac, Coenobite, Cowl, Culdee, Dan, Dervish, Dom, Dominican, Félibre, Feuillant, Fraticelli, Friar, General, Gyrovague, Hegumen, Hermit, Hesychast, Hildebrand, Ignorantine, Jacobin, Jacobite, Jerome, Lama, Maurist, Mechitharist, Mekhitarist, Mendel, Norbertine, Obedientiary, Oblate, Olivetan, Order, Pelagian, Prior, Rakehell, Rasputin, Recluse, Recollect, Religieux, Roshi, Salesian, Sangha, Savonarola, Simeon Stylites, Sub-prior, Talapoin, Theatine, Thelemite, Thelonius, Thomas à Kempis, Tironensian, Trappist, Votary
Monkey Anger, Ape, Aye-aye, Baboon, Bandar, Bobbejaan, Bonnet, Bushbaby, Capuchin, Catar(r)hine, Cebidae, Cebus, Chacma, Coaita, Colobus, Cynomolgus, Diana, Douc, Douroucouli, Drill, Durukuli, Entellus, Galago, Gelada, Gibbon, Gorilla, Grease, Green, Grison, Grivet, Guenon, Guereza, Hanuman, Hoolock, Howler, Hylobates, Indri, Jacchus, Jackey, Jocko, Kippage, Langur, Leaf, Lemur, Loris, Macaco, Macaque, Magot, Malmag, Mandrill, Mangabey, Marmoset, Meddle, Meerkat, Mico, Midas, Mona, Mycetes, Nala,

Nasalis, New World, Old World, Orang-utang, Ouakari, Ouistiti, Phalanger, Platyrrhine, Powder, Primate, Proboscis, Pug, Puzzle, Rage, Ram, Rhesus, Sago(u)in, Saguin, Sai(miri), Sajou, Saki, Sapajou, Satan, Semnopithecus, Siamang, Sifaka, Silen(us), Silverback, Simian, Simpai, Slender loris, Spider, Squirrel, Talapoin, Tamarin, Tamper, Tana, Tarsier, Tee-tee, Titi, Toque, Trip-hammer, Troop, Tup, Uakari, Vervet, Wanderoo, White-eyelid, Wistiti, Wou-wou, Wow-wow, Wrath, Zati

Monkey-nut Earth-pea

Monkey-puzzle Araucaria, Bunya-bunya

Monkshood Aconite

Monocle Eye-glass, Gig-lamp, Lorgnon, Quiz(zing-glass)

Monocot(yledon) Araceae, Endogen, Tradescantia

Monodon Narwhal

Monogram, Monograph Chi-rho, Cipher, Study, Treatise, Tug(h)ra

Monolith Ayers Rock, Cenotaph, Chambers Pillar, Uluru

Monologue Interior, Patter, Rap, Recitation, Soliloquy, Speech

Monopolise, Monopoly Appalto, Bloc, Bogart, Cartel, Corner, Engross, Octroi, Régie, Trust

Monotonous, Monotony Boring, Dull, > FLAT, Grey, Humdrum, Same(y), Sing-song, Tedious

Monsoon Hurricane, Typhoon, > WIND

▷ **Monsoon** *may indicate* weekend (Mon soon)

Monster, Monstrous Alecto, Apollyon, Asmodeus, Bandersnatch, Behemoth, Bunyip, Caliban, Cerberus, Cete, Chichevache, Chim(a)era, Cockatrice, Colossal, Cyclops, Dabbat, Deform, Dinoceras, Dismayd, Div, Dragon, Echidna, Enormous, Erebus, Erinys, Erl-king, Eten, Ettin, Evil-one, Fiend, Fire-drake, Frankenstein, Freak, Geryon, Ghost, Giant, Gila, Golem, Gorgon, Green-eyed, Grendel, Harpy, Hippocampus, Hippogriff, Huge, Hydra, Jabberwock, Kraken, Lamia, Leviathan, Lilith, Lusus naturae, Mastodon, Medusa, Minotaur, Misbegotten, Moloch, Mylodont, Nessie, Nicker, Nightmare, Ogopogo, Ogre, Ogr(e)ish, Opinicus, Orc, Outrageous, Pongo, Sarsquatch, Satyral, Scylla, Serra, Shadow, Simorg, Simurg(h), Siren, Skull, Snark, Spectre, Sphinx, Spook, Stegodon, Stegosaur, Succubus, Taniwha, Teras, Teratoid, Triceratops, Troll, Typhoeus, Typhon, Unnatural, Vampire, Vast, Wasserman, Wendego, Wendigo, Wer(e)wolf, Wyvern, Xiphopagus, Yowie, Ziffius

Month(ly) Ab, Abib, Adar, Anomalistic, April, Asadha, Asvina, August, Bhadrapada, Brumaire, Bul, Calendar, Cheshvan, Chislev, December, Dhu-al-Hijjah, Dhu-al-Qadah, Diaconic, Elul, February, Floreal, Frimaire, Fructidor, Germinal, Hes(h)van, Iy(y)ar, January, July, Jumada, June, Jysaitha, Kartuka, Kisleu, Kislev, Lide, Lunar, Lunation, Magha, March, Margasirsa, May, Messidor, Mo, Moharram, Moon, Muharram, Muharrem, Nisan, Nivose, Nodical, November, October, Periodical, Phalguna, Pluviose, Prairial, Rabia, Rajab, Ramadan, Ramazon, Rhamadhan, Safar, Saphar, September, Sha(a)ban, Shawwal, S(h)ebat, Sidereal, Sivan, Solar, Stellar, Synodic, Tammuz, Tebeth, Thermidor, Tisri, Tropical, Vaisakha, Veadar, Vendemiaire, Ventose

Monument Ancient, Arch, Archive, Cenotaph, Charminar, Column, Cromlech, Dolmen, Henge, Megalith, Memorial, Menhir, Monolith, National, Pantheon, Pyramid, Sacellum, Stele(ne), Stone, Stonehenge, Stupa, Talayot, Tombstone, Trilith, Trilithon, Urn

Mood(y) Active, Anger, Atmosphere, Attitude, Capricious, Conjunctive, Dudgeon, Enallage, Fettle, Fit, Glum, Grammar, Humour, Hump, Imperative,

Indicative, Mercurial, Morale, Optative, Passive, Peat, Pet, Revivalist, Sankey, Spleen, Subjunctive, Temper, Tid, Tone, Tune, Vein, Vinegar, Whim

Moon(light), Moony Aah, Alignak, Aningan, Apogee, Artemis, Astarte, Blue, Callisto, Calypso, Cheese, Cynthia, Diana, Epact, Eye, Flit, Full, Gander, Ganymede, Gibbous, Glimmer, Grimaldi, Harvest, Hecate, Hunter's, Hyperion, Inconstant, Juliet, Leda, Lucina, Luna(r), Mani, Mascon, McFarlane's Buat, Midsummer, Mock, Month, Mope, New, Nimbus, Nocturne, Octant, Oliver, Paddy's lantern, Paraselene, Paschal, Pasiphaë, Phoebe, Plenilune, Proteus, Raker, Satellite, Selene, Set, Shepherd, Shot, Sickle, Sideline, Silvery, Sonata, Stargaze, Stone, Syzygy, Thebe, Thoth, Titan, Triton, Umbriel, Wander

Moonraker Astrogeologist, Gothamite

Moonshine(r) Hootch, Poteen, Rot, Shebeener

Moor(ing), Moorish Berth, Culloden, Dock, Fen, Heath, Iago, Ilkley, Makefast, Marston, Moresque, Moroccan, Mudéjar, Othello, Palustrine, Roadstead, Ryepeck, Saracen, Tether, > **TIE**, Wold

Mop(ping) Dwile, Flibbertigibbet, Girn, Glib, Shag, Squeegee, Squilgee, Swab, Swob, Thatch, > **WIPE**

Mope Boody, Brood, Peak, Sulk

Mor Humus

Moral(ity), Morals Apologue, Austere, Deontic, Ethic(al), Ethos, Everyman, Fable, High-minded, Integrity, Precept, Principled, Puritanic, Righteous, Sittlichkeit, Tag, Upright, Virtuous, Well-thewed

Morale Ego, Mood, Spirit, Zeal

Moralise, Moralising Preach, Sententious

Moralist Prig, Prude, Puritan, Whitecap

Morass Bog, Fen, Flow, Marsh, Moss, Quagmire, Slough

Morbid(ity) Anasarca, Ascites, Cachaemia, Dropsy, Ectopia, Ghoul(ish), Gruesome, Pathological, Plethora, Prurient, Religiose, Sick, Sombre

Mordant Biting, Caustic, Critic(al), Sarcastic, Tooth

Mordent Inverted, Pralltriller, Upper

More Added, Additional, Else, Extra, Increase, Less, Mae, Merrier, Mo(e), > **NO MORE**, Over, Piu, Plus, Stump, Utopia

Moreover Also, Besides, Eft, Either, Eke, Further, Too, Yet

Morgan Buccaneer, Pirate

Moribund Dying, Stagnant, Withered

Mormon Danite, Latter-day Saint, Salt Lake City, Utah, Young

Morning Ack-emma, Am, Antemeridian, Dawn, Daybreak, Early, Forenoon, Matin(al), Morrow, Sparrowfart

Morning-glory Bindweed, Ipomoea, Turbith, Turpeth

Morning-star Morgenstern, Phosphor(us), Threshel, Venus

Moroccan, Morocco Agadir, French, Leather, Levant, MA, Mo(o)r, Persian, Riff, Tangerine, Venus

Moron Fool, Idiot, Schmuck, > **STUPID**

Morose Acid, Boody, Churlish, Crabby, Cynical, Disgruntled, Gloomy, Glum, Grum, Moody, Sour-eyed, Sullen, Surly

Morph Phase

Morris Car, Dance, Fivepenny, Merel(l), Meril, Nine Men's, Ninepenny

Morrow Future

Morse Code, Endeavour, Iddy-umpty, Walrus

Morsel Bit, Bite, Bouche, Canape, Crumb, Dainty, Morceau, Ort, Scrap, Sippet, Sop, Tidbit, Titbit

Mortal(ity) Averr(h)oism, Being, Deathly, > **FATAL**, Grave, Human, Lethal, Yama

Mortar, Mortar-board Bowl, Cannon, Cement, Co(e)horn, Compo, Grout, Gunite, Hawk, Life, Metate, Mine-thrower, Minnie, Moaning (Minnie), Parget, Plaster, Pot gun, Screed, Square, Squid, Toc emma, Trench(er)

Mortgage(e) Balloon, Bond, Cedula, Chattel, Debt, Dip, Encumbrance, Endowment, First, Hypothecator, Loan, Pension, Pledge, Wadset(t)

Mortification, Mortified, Mortify Abash, Ashame, Chagrin, Crucify, Crush, Gangrene, Humble, Humiliate, Infarct, Necrose, Penance, Sick, Sphacelus, Wormwood

Mosaic Buhl, Cosmati, Inlay, Intarsia, Musive, Opus musivum, Pietra dura, Screen, Tarsia, Terrazzo, Tessella(te), Tessera, Tobacco, Venetian

Moscow Dynamo

Moses Grandma

▶ **Moslem** *see* MUSLIM

Mosque Dome of the Rock, El Aqsa, Jami, Masjid, Medina

Mosquito Aedes, Anopheles, Culex, Culicine, Gnat, Parasite, Stegomyia

Moss(y) Acrogen, Agate, Bryology, Carrag(h)een, Ceylon, Club, Fog, Fontinalis, Hag(g), Hypnum, Iceland, Irish, Lecanoram, Lichen, Litmus, Liverwort, Long, Lycopod, Marsh, Musci, Muscoid, Parella, Peat, Polytrichum, Reindeer, Rose, Scale, Selaginella, Spanish, Sphagnum, Staghorn, Tree, Usnea, Wall, Wolf's claw

Most Largest, Major, Maxi(mum), Optimum

Mot Quip, Saying

Mote Atom, Particle, Speck

Moth(s) Abraxas, Antler, Arch, Arctiidae, Atlas, Bag, Bee, Bell, Bobowler, Bogong, Bombycid, Brown-tail, Buff-tip, Bugong, Burnet, Cabbage, Cactoblastus, Carpenter, Carpet, Cecropia, Cinnabar, Clearwing, Clifden nonpareil, Clothes, Codlin(g), Corn (-borer), Dagger, Dart-moth, Death's head, Diamondback, Drepanid, Drinker, Eggar, Egger, Emerald, Emperor, Ermine, Flour, Fox, Geometer, Geometrid, Ghost, Giant peacock, Gipsy, Goat, Goldtail, Gooseberry, Grass, Gypsy, Hawk, Herald, Honeycomb, Hook-tip, House, Hummingbird, Imago, Io, Kentish glory, Kitten, Lackey, Lappet, Large Emerald, Lasiocampidae, Leafroller, Leopard, Lepidoptera, Lichen, Lobster, Luna, Lymantriidae, Magpie, Meal, Mother of pearl, Mother Shipton, Muslin, Noctua, Noctuid, Notodonta, Nun, Oak-egger, Owl, Owlet, Peppered, Pine-beauty, Pine-carpet, Plane, Plume, Polyphemus, Privet hawk, Processionary, Prominent, Psyche, Pug-moth, Purple Emperor, Puss, Pyralidae, Red underwing, Sallow-kitten, Saturnia, Saturniid, Scavenger, Silkworm, Silver-Y, Sphingid, Sphinx, Swift, Tapestry, Thorn, Tiger, Tinea, Tineidae, Tortrix, Turnip, Tussock, Umber, Underwing, Unicorn, Vapourer, Veneer, Wainscot, Wave, Wax, Wheat, Winter, Woodborer, Yellow underwing, Y-moth, Zygaena

Mothball(s) Abeyance, Camphor, Naphtha, Preserver

Mother Bearer, Church, Cognate, Cosset, Courage, Dam(e), Dregs, Ean, Earth, Eve, Foster, Generatrix, Genetrix, Genitrix, Goose, Hubbard, Lees, Ma, Machree, Madre, Mam(a), Mamma, Mater, Maya, Minnie, Mom, Multipara, Mum, Native, Nature, Nourish, Nursing, Parity, Pourer, Primipara, Reverend, Shipton, Superior, Surrogate, Wit

▷ **Mother** *may indicate* a lepidopterist (moth-er)

Motherless Adam, Orphan

Motif Anthemion, Design, Gist, Idée, Theme

Motion Contrary, Diurnal, Early day, Fast, Gesture, Harmonic, Impulse, Kepler, Kinematics, Kinetic, Link, Move, Oblique, Offer, Parallactic, Peculiar,

Perpetual, PL, Proper, Proposal, Rack and pinion, Rider, Similar, Slow, Spasm, Wave

Motionless Doggo, Frozen, Immobile, Quiescent, Stagnant, Stasis, Still, Stock-still

Motive, Motivate, Motivation Actuate, Cause, Ideal, Impel, Incentive, Intention, Mainspring, Mobile, Object, > **PURPOSE**, Spur, Ulterior

Motley Jaspé, Medley, Piebald, Pied

Motor(boat) Auto, Car, Dynamo, Electric, Engine, Hot rod, Inboard, Induction, Jato, Linear, Outboard, Scooter, Stator, Synchronous, Thruster, Turbine, Universal, Water

Motorcycle, Motorcyclist Bikie, Chookchaser, Farm-bike, Hell's Angel, Moped, Pipsqueak, Scooter, Scramble, Trail bike, Yamaha®

Motorist(s) AA, Driver, Petrolhead, RAC

Motorman Austin, Benz, Ford, Morris

Motor race Rally, Scramble, TT

Motorway Autobahn, Autopista, Autoput, Autoroute, Autostrada, Expressway, M(1), Throughway, Thruway

Mottle(d) Brindled, Chiné, Jaspé, Marbled, Marly, Mirly, Pinto, Poikilitic, Tabby

Motto Device, Epigraph, Gnome, Impresa, Imprese, Impress(e), Legend, Maxim, Mot, Poesy, Posy, Saw

Mou(e) Grimace, Mim

Mould(ed), Mouldable, Moulding, Mouldy Accolade, Architrave, Archivolt, Astragal, Baguette, Balection, Beading, Bend, Black, Blow, Blue, Bolection, Bread, Briquet(te), Cabling, Casement, Cast(ing), Cavetto, Chessel, Chill, Cornice, Coving, Cyma, Cymatium, Dariole, Die, Die-cast, Dogtooth, Doucine, Dripstone, Ductile, Echinus, Egg and dart, Emboss, Flong, > **FORM**, Foughty, Fousty, Fungose, Fungus, Fusarol(e), Fust, Gadroon, Godroon, Green, Hood-mould, Hore, Humus, Injection, Iron, Jelly, Leaf, Machine, Matrix, Mildew, Model, Mool, Moulage, Mucid, Mucor, Must, Myxomycete, Nebule, Noble rot, Ogee, Ovolo, Palmette, Papier-mâché, Phycomycete, Picture, Pig, Plasm(a), Plastic, Plat, Platband, Plate, Prototype, Prunt, Quarter-round, Reeding, Reglet, Rhizopus, Rot, Rust, Sandbox, Scotia, Shape, Slime, Smut, Soil, Soot(y), Storiated, Stringcourse, Stucco, Surbase, Tailor, Talon, Template, Templet, Timbale, Tondino, Torus, Trochilus, Vinew, Water table

Moult(ing) Cast, Metecdysis, Mew, Shed

Mound Agger, Bank, Barp, Barrow, Berm, Cone, Dike, Dun, Embankment, Heap, Hog, Kurgan, Mogul, Molehill, Monticule, Mote, Motte, Orb, Pile, Pingo, Pome, Rampart, Rampire, Remblai, Tel(l), Teocalli, Teopan, Tuffet, Tumulus, Tussock

Mound-bird Megapode

Mount(ed), Mounting, Mountain (peak), Mountains > **ALPINE**, Aspiring, Back, Barp, Ben, Berg, Board, Breast, Butter, Chain, Charger, > **CLIMB**, Colt, Cordillera, Cradle, Dew, Display, Djebel, Dolly, Escalade, Frame, Hinge, Horse, Inselberg, Jebel, Massif, Monture, Mt, Nunatak, Orography, Orology, Passe-partout, Pike, Pile, Pin, Pownie, Quad, Ride, Saddlehorse, Scalado, Scale, Set, Soar, Stage, Stanley, > **STEED**, Stie, Strideways, Tel, Tier, Tor, Turret, Upgo, Volcano

● **MOUNTAINS**
●
●

2 letters:	**3 letters:**	Ore	Blue
K2	Apo		Bona
	Ida	**4 letters:**	Cook
	Kaf	Alai	Etna

Fuji
Harz
Hoss
Jaya
Jura
Meru
Nebo
Oeta
Ossa
Rigi
Ubac
Zeil

5 letters:
Abora
Adams
Aldan
Altai
Amara
Andes
Aneto
Athos
Atlas
Badon
Black
Blanc
Coast
Djaja
Eiger
Ellis
Ghats
Green
Guyot
Hekla
Horeb
Idris
Kamet
Kenya
Logan
Munro
Ozark
Rocky
Rydal
Sayan
Serra
Sinai
Siple
Smoky
Snowy
Table
Tabor
Tatra

Tyree
Tyrol
Uinta
Urals
Welsh
White

6 letters:
Ala Dag
Amhara
Anadyr
Arafat
Ararat
Averno
Balkan
Bogong
Carmel
Cho Oyu
Dragon
Egmont
Elbert
Elberz
Elbrus
Erebus
Gilead
Hermon
Hoggar
Hoosac
Katmai
Kazbek
Kunlun
Lhotse
Makalu
Mourne
Olives
Ortles
Pamirs
Pelion
Pindus
Pisgah
Pocono
Robson
Scopus
Sintra
Sorata
Steele
Tasman
Taunus
Taurus
Umbria
Vernon
Vosges

Zagros

7 letters:
Aetolia
Ala Dagh
Aorangi
Aragats
Arcadia
Bernina
Brocken
Buffalo
Calvary
Cariboo
Cascade
Chianti
Corbett
Dapsang
Everest
Helicon
Kennedy
Khingan
Kuenlun
Lebanon
Lucania
Manaslu
Markham
Nan Shan
Olympic
Olympus
Palomar
Perdido
Pilatus
Rainier
Rhodope
San Juan
Scafell
Selkirk
Skiddaw
Snowdon
Sperrin
Sudeten
Tibesti
Travers
Whitney
Wicklow

8 letters:
Ben Nevis
Cambrian
Carstenz
Catskill
Caucasus

Cevennes
Cumbrian
Demavend
Grampian
Hymettus
Illimani
Jungfrau
Kinabalu
King Peak
Leibnitz
McKinley
Mulhacen
Ngaliema
Pennines
Pyrenees
Rushmore
St Helen's
Taraniki
Tien Shan
Vesuvius
Victoria
Wrangell

9 letters:
Aconcagua
Allegheny
Annapurna
Apennines
Ben Lomond
Blue Ridge
Cairngorm
Catskills
Caucasian
Connemara
Demavrand
Dolomites
El Capitan
Grampians
Guadalupe
Helvellyn
Highlands
Himalayas
Hindu Kush
Jebel Musa
Karakoram
Lenin Peak
Longs Peak
Marmolada
Mont Blanc
Nanda Devi
Parnassus
Pikes Peak

Shivering
Sugarloaf
Tirich Mir
Tupungato
Vancouver
Venusberg
Voralberg
Weisshorn
Woodroffe
Yablonovy
Zugspitze

10 letters:
Arakan Yoma
Armageddon
Black Hills
Cantabrian
Carpathian
Delectable
Dhaulagiri
Equatorial
Erymanthus
Erzgebirge
Great Gable
Great Smoky
Harney Peak
Horselberg
Laurentian
Matterhorn
Monte Corno
Montserrat
Pentelikon
Puncak Jaya
Puy de Sancy
St Michael's

Tengri Khan
Teton Range
Waziristan
Wellington
Wetterhorn

11 letters:
Adirondacks
Alaska Range
Appalachian
Bartle Frere
Bimberi Peak
Brooks Range
Drakensberg
Fairweather
Gerlachovka
Kilimanjaro
Kirkpatrick
Kolyma Range
Nanga Parbat
Salmon River
Scafell Pike
Sierra Madre

12 letters:
Albert Edward
Cascade Range
Eastern Ghats
Godwin Austen
Gran Paradiso
Ingleborough
Kanchenjunga
Ruahine Range
Sierra Morena
Sierra Nevada

Slieve Donard
Tararua Range
Victoria Peak
Vindhya Range
Vinson Massif
Wasatch Range
Western Ghats

13 letters:
Carrantuohill
Croagh Patrick
Flinders Range
Grossglockner
Humphrey's Peak
Kangchenjunga
Massif Central
Petermann Peak
San Bernardino
Stanovoi Range
Tibesti Massif

14 letters:
Admiralty Range
Bohemian Forest
Carnarvon Range
Finsteraarhorn
Hamersley Range
Kaikoura Ranges
Kommunizma
  Peak
Liverpool Range
Musgrove Ranges
Ruwenzori Range
Stirling Ranges
Thadentsonyane

Wind River Range

15 letters:
New England
  Range
Teutoburger Wald

16 letters:
Emperor
  Seamounts
Macdonnell
  Ranges
Thabana-
  Ntlenyana

17 letters:
Continental
  Divide
Transylvanian
  Alps

18 letters:
Great Dividing
  Range

19 letters:
Macgillicuddy's
  Reeks

20 letters:
Salmon River
  Mountains

Mountain-building Orogenesis
Mountaineer(ing) Abseil, Alpinist, Arnaut, Climber, Hunt, Sherpa, Smythe, Upleader
Mountebank Antic(ke), Baladin(e), Charlatan, Jongleur, Quack, Saltimbanco
Mourn(er), Mournful, Mourning Adonia, Black, Dirge, Dole, Elegiac, Grieve, Grone, Half-mast, Hatchment, Jamie Duff, Keen, Lament, Niobe, Omer, Ovel, Plangent, Saulie, Shibah, Shivah, Shloshim, Sorrow, Tangi, Threnetic, Threnodial, Weeds, Weep, Willow
Mouse(like), Mousy Black eye, Deer, Dun(nart), Fat, Field, Flitter, Harvest, Honey, House, Icon, Jumping, Marsupial, Meadow, Muridae, Murine, Pocket, Pouched, Rodent, Shiner, Shrew, Vermin, Waltzer, White-footed
Mousse Styling
Moustache Boxcar, Burnside, Charley, Charlie, Chevron, Excrement, Fu Manchu, Handlebar, Hindenburg, Horseshoe, Kaiser, Mistletoe, Pencil, Pyramid, Regent, Roman T, Soupstrainer, Toothbrush, Walrus, Waxed, Wings, Zapata

Mouth(piece) Aboral, Bazoo, Bocca, Brag, Buccal, Cakehole, Chapper, Check, Crater, Debouchure, Delta, Embouchure, Estuary, Fipple, Gab, Gam, Geggie, Gills, Gob, Gum, Hard, Kisser, Labret, Lawyer, Lip, Manubrium, Maw, Neb, Orifex, Orifice, Os, Oscule, Ostium, Outfall, Outlet, Port, Potato trap, Rattle-trap, Speaker, Spokesman, Spout, Stoma, Swazzle, Swozzle, Teat, Trap, Trench, Uvula

Mouthful Bite, Gob, Morceau, Morsel, Sip, Sup, Taste

Mouthless Astomatous

Mouth-organ Harmonica, Harp, Palp, Sang

Move(d), Mover, Movable, Moving Act, Actuate, Affect, Andante, Astir, Budge, Carry, Catapult, Chattel, Coast, Counter-measure, Coup, Decant, Démarche, Displace, Disturb, Ease, Eddy, Edge, Evoke, False, Flit, Flounce, Fluctuate, Forge, Frogmarch, Gambit, Gee, Go, Gravitate, Haulier, Hustle, Inch, Instigate, Jee, Jink, Kedge, Kinetic, Knight's progress, Link, Mill, Mobile, Mosey, Motivate, Nip, Opening, Overcome, Pan, People, Poignant, Prime, Proceed, Progress, Prompt, Propel, Quicken, Qui(t)ch, Rearrange, Redeploy, Relocate, Remuage, Retrocede, Roll, Rouse, Roust, Sashay, Scoot, Scramble, Scroll, Scuttle, Sealed, Sell, Shift, Shog, Shoo, Shunt, Sidle, Skelp, Slide, Soulful, Spank, Steal, Steer, Step, Stir, Styre, Sway, Swish, Tack, Tactic, Taxi, Transfer, Translate, Translocate, Transplant, Transport, Travel, Troll, Trundle, Turn, Unstep, Up, Upsticks, Vacillate, Vagile, Veronica, Vire, Volt(e), Waft, Wag, Wapper, Whirry, Whish, Whisk, Whiz, Wuther, Yank, Zoom, Zwischenzug

Movement(s) Action, Advection, Aerotaxis, Al Fatah, Allegro, Allemande, Almain, Andantino, Antic, Azapo, Badinerie, Bandwagon, Brownian, Cadence, Capoeira, Cell, Charismatic, Chartism, Chemonasty, Constructivism, Course, Crusade, Dadaism, Diaspora, Diastole, Ecumenical, Enlightenment, Eoka, Eurhythmics, Expressionism, Faction, Feint, Fianchetto, Fris(ka), Gait, Gallicanism, Geneva, Gesture, Groundswell, Hip-hop, Honde, Imagism, Indraught, Inkatha, Intermezzo, Jhala, Jor, Kata, Keplarian, Kin(a)esthetic, Kinesis, Kinetic, Larghetto, Largo, Lassu, Ligne, Logistics, Manoeuvre, Mudra, Nastic, Naturalism, Naziism, New Wave, Nihilism, Official, Operation, Orchesis, Oxford, Pantalon, Parallax, Pase, Passade, Pedesis, Photokinesis, Photonasty, Piaffer, Pincer, Play, Populist, Poule, Poulette, Procession, Progress, Provisional, Punk, Puseyism, Reformation, REM, Renaissance, Resistance, Ribbonism, Risorgimento, Romantic, Rondo, Saccade, Scherzo, Seiche, Sinn Fein, Solifluction, Solifluxion, Spuddle, Stir(e), Sturm und Drang, Swadeshi, Swing, Symbolist, Tachism, Tamil Tigers, Tantrism, Taxis, Tectonic, Telekinesis, Tide, Tractarianism, Transhumance, Trend, Trenise, Ultramontanism, UNITA, Verismo, Veronica, Wheel, Women's, Zionism

Movie Bioscope, Buddy, Cine(ma), Disaster, Film, Flick, Nudie, Popcorn, Road, Slasher, Snuff, Splatter, Talkie

Mow(er), Mowing Aftermath, Cut, Grimace, Lattermath, Lawn, Math, Rawing, Rawn, Rowan, Rowen, Rowing, Scytheman, Shear, Sickle, Tass, Trim

MP Backbencher, Commoner, Gendarme, Member, Politico, Provost, Redcap, Retread, Snowdrop, Stannator, Statist, TD

▶ **Mr** *see* MISTER

▶ **Mrs** *see* MISSIS

Mrs Copperfield Agnes, Dora

Mrs Siddons Tragic muse

Much Abundant, Far, Glut, Great, Lots, Mickle, Scad, Sore, Viel

Mucilage Gum, > MUCUS, Putty, Resin

Muck (up), Mucky Bungle, Dirt, Dung, Island, Leep, Manure, Midden, Mire, Rot,

Sludge, Soil, Sordid, Spoil, Stercoral

Mucker Fall, Pal, Purler

Mucus Phlegm, Pituate, Pituita, Snivel, Snot, Sputum

Mud(dy) Adobe, Clabber, Clart, Clay, Cutcha, Dirt, Drilling, Dubs, Fango, Glaur, Glob, Gutter, Kacha, Lahar, Lairy, Limous, > MIRE, Moya, Ooze, Peloid, Pise, Riley, Roily, Salse, Slab, Slake, Sleech, Slime, Slob, Slough, Sludge, Slur(ry), Slush, Stulch, Tocky, Trouble, Turbid, Volcanic

Muddle Befog, Bemuse, Botch, Cock up, Confuse, Disorder, Embrangle, Fluster, Gump, Mash, Mêlée, Mess, Mix, Mull, Pickle, Puddle, Shemozzle, Snarl-up, Stupefy, Tangle

▷ **Muddled** *may indicate* an anagram

Mudfish Lepidosiren

Mudguard Splashboard, Wing

Mudlark Ragamuffin, Urchin

Muesli Granola

Muff Boob, Botch, Bungle, Drop, Snoskyn

Muffin Bun, Mule, Popover

Muffle(d), Muffler Damp, Envelop, Hollow, Mob(b)le, Mute, Scarf, Silencer, Sourdine, Stifle

Mug(ger), Muggy Assault, Attack, Bash, Beaker, Bock, Can, Club, Con, Croc(odile), Cup, Dial, Dupe, Enghalskrug, Face, Fool, Footpad, Gob, Humid, Idiot, Latron, Learn, Mou, Noggin, Pan, Pot, Puss, Rob, Roll, Sandbag, Sap, Sconce, Simpleton, Steamer, Stein, Sucker, Swot, Tankard, Tax, Thief, Thug(gee), Tinnie, Tinny, Toby, Trap, Ugly, Visage, Yap

Mulatto Griff(e)

Mulberry Artocarpus, Breadfruit, Cecropia, Contrayerva, Cow-tree, Jack, Morat, Morus, Murrey, Overlord, Sycamine

Mulch Compost

Mulct Fine

Mule Ass, Bab(o)uche, Barren, Donkey, Funnel, Hybrid, Mocassin, Moccasin, Moyl(e), Muffin, Muil, Pack, Rake, Shoe, Slipper, Spinning, Sumpter

Muleteer Arriero

Mull Brood, Chew, Kintyre, Ponder, Promontory, Study

Mullein Aaron's rod

Mullet Goatfish

Mullion Monial

Multi-coloured Scroddled

Multiform Allotropic, Diverse, Manifold

Multiple, Multiplication, Multiplied, Multiplier, Multiply Augment, Breed, Double, > INCREASE, Modulus, Populate, Product, Proliferate, Propagate, Scalar, Severalfold

Multi-purpose Polychrest

Multitude Army, Crowd, Hirsel, Horde, Host, Legion, Populace, Shoal, Sight, Throng, Zillion

Mum(my) Boutonné, Carton(n)age, Corpse, Egyptian, Embalm, Mamma, Mine, Mute, Quiet, Sh, Silent, Tacit, Whisht, Wordless

Mumble Grumble, Moop, Moup, Mouth, Mump, Mushmouth, Mutter, Royne, Slur

Mumbo jumbo Hocus pocus, Mammet, Maumet, Mawmet, Mommet

Mummer Actor, Mime, Scuddaler, Scudler, Skudler

Mumps Parotitis

Munch Champ, Chew, Chomp, Scranch

Mundane Banal, Common, Earthly, Nondescript, Ordinary, Prosaic, Quotidian, Secular, Subcelestial, Trite, Workaday, Worldly
Municipal Civic
Munificent Bounteous, Generous, Liberal, Profuse
Munition(s) Arms, Artillery, Matériel, Ordnance
Munro Saki
Mural(s) Fresco, Graffiti
Murder(er), Murderess, Murderous Aram, Assassin, Blue, Bluebeard, Bravo, Burke, Butcher, Butler, Cain, Cathedral, Crackhalter, Crippen, Cutthroat, Do in, Eliminate, Filicide, First degree, Fratricide, Genocide, Hare, Hit, Hitman, Homicide, Internecine, Judicial, > **KILL**, Liquidate, Locusta, Made man, Massacre, Matricide, Modo, Parricide, Patricide, Petty treason, Poison, Red, Regicide, Ripper, Ritual, Ritz, Second degree, Sikes, Slaughter, Slay, Strangle(r), Take out, Thagi, Throttle, Thug(gee), Whodun(n)it
Murk(y) Black, Dirk(e), Gloom, Obscure, Rookish, Stygian
Murmur(ing) Brool, Bruit, Bur(r), Burble, Coo, Croodle, Croon, Grudge, Heart, Hum, > **MUTTER**, Purr, Repine, Rhubarb, Rumble, Rumour, Souffle, Sowf(f), Sowth, Sturnoid, Undertone, Whisper
Murphy Chat, Potato, Pratie, Spud, Tater
Muscle, Muscular Abductor, Abs, Accelerator, Accessorius, Adductor, Anconeus, Aryepiglottic, Arytaenoid, Athletic, Attollens, Beef(y), Beefcake, Biceps, Bowr, Brachialus, Brawn, Buccinator, Ciliary, Clout, Complexus, Corrugator, Creature, Cremaster, Deltoid, Depressor, Diaphragm, Digastric, Dilat(at)or, Duvaricator, Effector, Elevator, Erecter, Erector, Evertor, Extensor, Eye-string, Flexor, Force, Gastrocnemius, Gemellus, Glut(a)eus, Gluteus maximus, Gracilis, Hamstring, Hiacus, Iliacus, Intrinsic, Involuntary, Kreatine, Lat, Latissimus dorsi, Laxator, Levator, Lumbricalis, Masseter, Mesomorph, Might, Motor, Mouse, Myalgia, Mylohyoid, Nasalis, Oblique, Occlusor, Omohyoid, Orbicularis, Pathos, Pec(s), Pectoral, Perforans, Perforatus, Peroneus, Plantaris, Platysma, Popliteus, > **POWER**, Pronator, Protractor, Psoas, Pylorus, Quad(riceps), Quadratus, Rambo, Rectus, Retractor, Rhomboid, Risorius, Rotator, Sarcolemma, Sarcous, Sartorius, Scalene, Scalenus, Serratus, Sinew, Smooth, Soleus, Sphincter, Spinalis, Splenial, Sthenic, Striated, Striped, Supinator, Temporal, Tenaculum, Tendon, Tensor, Teres, Thenar, Thew, Tibialis, Tonus, Trapezius, Triceps, Vastus, Voluntary, Zygomatic
Muscovite Mica, Talc
Muse(s), Muse's home, Musing Aglaia, Aonia(n), Attic, Calliope, Clio, Cogitate, Consider, Erato, Euphrosyne, Euterpe, Helicon, Inspiration, IX, Melpomene, Mull, Nine, Nonet, Pensée, Pierides, Poly(hy)mnia, Ponder, > **REFLECT**, Ruminate, Study, Teian, Terpsichore, Thalia, Tragic, Urania, Wonder
Museum Alte-Pinakothek, Ashmolean, BM, British, Fitzwilliam, Gallery, Getty, Guggenheim, Heritage centre, Hermitage, Hunterian, Louvre, Metropolitan, Parnassus, Prado, Repository, Rijksmuseum, Science, Smithsonian, Tate, Uffizi, VA, V and A, Waxworks
Mush Cree, Goo, Mess, Porridge, Puree, Schmaltz, Slop
Mushroom Agaric, Blewits, Boletus, Burgeon, Button, Cep, Champignon, Chanterelle, Darning, Enoki, Expand, Fly agaric, > **FUNGUS**, Gyromitra, Horse, Hypha(l), Ink-cap, Liberty cap, Magic, Matsutake, Meadow, Morel, Oyster, Parasol, Penny-bun, Pixy-stool, Porcino, Russula, Sacred, St George's, Scotch bonnet, Shaggymane, Shiitake, Sickener, Spread, Start-up, Straw, Truffle, Upstart, Velvet shank, Waxcap
Music Absolute, Light, Medieval, Minstrelsy, > **MUSICAL INSTRUMENTS**, Phase,

Piece, Pop(ular), Post-rock, Score

- **MUSIC**
-
- **3 letters:**
- Air
- AOR
- Art
- Dub
- Emo
- Gat
- Jor
- Pop
- Rag
- Rai
- Rap
- Rug
- Ska
- Son
-
- **4 letters:**
- Alap
- Duet
- Folk
- Funk
- Go-go
- Jazz
- Loco
- Meno
- Note
- Opus
- Prom
- Raga
- Riff
- Rock
- Romo
- Soca
- Soul
- Surf
- Tala
- Trad
- Trio
- Tune
- Zouk
-
- **5 letters:**
- Alaap
- Alapa
- Bebop
- Canon
- Chant
- Cliff

Cu-bop
Disco
Dream
Early
Fugue
Funky
House
Indie
Jhala
Kwela
Largo
March
Motet
Muzak®
Neume
Nonet
Outro
Piped
Ragga
Rondo
Roots
Rough
Salon
Salsa
Sheet
Sokah
Staff
Suite
Swing
Thema
Tonal
Truth
Vocal
World

6 letters:
Arioso
Bebung
Bouree
Decani
Doo-wop
Enigma
Equali
Facade
Fugato
Gagaku
Galant
Garage

Gospel
Gothic
Grunge
Hip-hop
Jungle
Khayal
Kwaito
Lydian
Mantra
Marabi
Mashup
Melody
Motown®
New Age
Pycnon
Ragini
Redowa
Reggae
Rhythm
Rootsy
Sextet
Sonata
Strain
Techno
Techno
Thrash
Trance
Verset
Zydeco

7 letters:
Allegro
Andante
Ars nova
Ballade
Baroque
Bhangra
Bluette
Bourree
Britpop
Cadenza
Calypso
Cantata
Ceilidh
Chamber
Chorale
Country
Dad rock

Euterpe
Fanfare
Gangsta
Hardbag
Introit
Klezmer
Landler
Marcato
Melisma
Messiah
Morceau
New Wave
Numbers
Organum
Orphean
Partita
Passion
Pecking
Pibroch
Prelude
Qawwali
Quartet
Quintet
Ragtime
Rastrum
Requiem
Reverse
Romanza
Rondeau
Rondino
Rosalia
Roulade
Sanctus
Scherzo
Setting
Skiffle
Soukous
Toccata
Trip hop
Ziganka

8 letters:
Acid rock
Aleatory
Berceuse
Chaconne
Cock rock
Concerto

- Concrete
- Coranach
- Coronach
- Entracte
- Fantasia
- Flamenco
- Folk rock
- Glam rock
- Hard core
- Hard rock
- High life
- In nomine
- Janizary
- Karnatak
- Lollipop
- Madrigal
- Maggiore
- Mariachi
- Mbaqanga
- Modality
- Nocturne
- Notation
- Old skool
- Oratorio
- Parlando
- Partitur
- Pastiche
- Postlude
- Psalmody
- Punk rock
- Rhapsody
- Ricercar
- Saraband

Serenade
Serenata
Symphony
Synth-pop

9 letters:
Acid-house
Allemande
Antiphony
Arabesque
Bagatelle
Bluegrass
Breakbeat
Cantilena
Capriccio
Dixieland
Drum'n'bass
Fioritura
Grandioso
Hillbilly
Honky-tonk
Interlude
Obbligato
Partitura
Pastorale
Plainsong
Polyphony
Prick-song
Quodlibet
Ricercare
Rock'n'roll
Septimole
Spiritual

Swingbeat
Tambourin
Technopop
Toccatina
Voluntary
Warehouse

10 letters:
Albumblatt
Anacrustic
Chopsticks
Coloratura
Desert rock
Electronic
Gangsta rap
Gothic rock
Heavy metal
Hindustani
Humoresque
Incidental
Intermezzo
Jam session
Martellato
New Country
Percussion
Polyhymnia
Ritornello
Rockabilly
Rocksteady
Seguidilla
Toccatella
Twelve-tone
Urban blues

11 letters:
Motor rhythm
Passacaglia
Psychobilly
Raggamuffin
Renaissance
Sinfonietta
Solmisation
Stadium rock
Third stream
Thrash metal

12 letters:
Boogie-woogie
Concertstuck
Contrapuntal
Divertimento
Electroclash
Nunc Dimittis
Pralltriller

13 letters:
Detroit techno
Progressional

14 letters:
Rhythm and blues

15 letters:
Musique concrete
Progressive rock

Musical Arcadian, Azione, Brigadoon, Cats, Chess, Euphonic, Evergreen, Evita, Gigi, Grease, Hair, Harmonious, Kabuki, Kismet, Lyric, Mame, Melodic, Oliver, Opera, Operetta, Orphean, Revue, Showboat
Musical box Juke-box, Polyphon(e)
Musical chairs Level-coil

MUSICAL INSTRUMENTS

2 letters:
Ax
Gu

3 letters:
Axe
Gue
Kit
Oud
Saz

Uke
Zel

4 letters:
Buva
Chyn
Crwd
Drum
Fife
Gong

Harp
Horn
Kora
Koto
Lure
Lute
Lyre
Moog®
Oboe
Pipa

Rate
Reed
Rote
Sang
Tuba
Vina
Viol
Zeze

5 letters:
- Aulos
- Banjo
- Cello
- Clave
- Cobza
- Corno
- Crowd
- Crwth
- Esraj
- Flute
- Gazog
- Guiro
- Gusla
- Gusle
- Gusli
- Kazoo
- Mbira
- Naker
- Nebel
- Organ
- Piano
- Quena
- Rebec
- Regal
- Sanko
- Sansa
- Sarod
- Shalm
- Shawm
- Sitar
- Stick
- Tabla
- Tabor
- Tibia
- Veena
- Viola
- Zanze
- Zinke

6 letters:
- Antara
- Bisser
- Bongos
- Citole
- Cornet
- Cymbal
- Euphon
- Flugel
- Guitar
- Kanoon
- Maraca

Poogye
Racket
Rebeck
Ribibe
Sancho
Santir
Santur
Shalme
Shofar
Sittar
Spinet
Syrinx
Tom-tom
Trigon
Vielle
Violin
Zither
Zufolo

7 letters:
Anklong
Bagpipe
Bandore
Bandura
Baryton
Bassoon
Bazooka
Celesta
Celeste
Cembalo
Chikara
Cithara
Cittern
Clarino
Clarion
Clavier
Console
Cornett
Dichord
Dulcian
Fagotto
Flutina
Gamelan
Gazogka
Gittern
Hautboy
Helicon
High-hat
Kalimba
Kantela
Kantele
Kithara

Klavier
Lyricon
Mandola
Marimba
Musette
Ocarina
Pandora
Pandore
Pandura
Pianola®
Piccolo
Poogyee
Posaune
Rackett
Sackbut
Sambuca
Samisen
Santour
Sarangi
Saxhorn
Saxtuba
Serpent
Tambour
Tambura
Theorbo
Timbrel
Timpano
Trumpet
Tympany
Ukelele
Vihuela
Violone
Zuffolo

8 letters:
Angklung
Archlute
Autoharp®
Barytone
Berimbau
Bouzouki
Calliope
Canorous
Carillon
Charango
Cimbalom
Clarinet
Clarsach
Clavecin
Cornetto
Cornpipe
Cromorna

Cromorne
Crumhorn
Dulcimer
Gemshorn
Guarneri
Guimbard
Handbell
Hautbois
Humstrum
Jew's harp
Key-bugle
Langspel
Lyra-viol
Mandolin
Manzello
Martenot
Melodeon
Melodica
Mirliton
Oliphant
Ottavino
Pan pipes
Phorminx
Polyphon
Psaltery
Recorder
Reco-reco
Slughorn
Spinette
Sticcado
Sticcato
Surbahar
Tamboura
Tamburin
Tenoroon
Theremin
Triangle
Trombone
Virginal
Vocalion
Zambomba
Zampogna

9 letters:
Accordion
Aerophone
Alpenhorn
Balalaika
Bandoneon
Bandurria
Banjulele
Bombardon

- Chalumeau
- Cornemuse
- Decachord
- Dulcitone®
- Euphonium
- Flageolet
- Flexatone
- Gittarone
- Gutbucket
- Harmonica
- Harmonium
- Idiophone
- Kent-bugle
- Krummhorn
- Langspiel
- Mandoline
- Monochord
- Mouth-harp
- Nose flute
- Orpharion
- Pantaleon
- Pastorale
- Polyphone
- Saxophone
- Seraphine
- Slughorne
- Snare-drum

Sopranino
Stockhorn
Trompette
Vibraharp
Washboard
Xylophone
Xylorimba

10 letters:
Bullroarer
Chitarrone
Clavichord
Colascione
Concertina
Cor anglais
Didgeridoo
Flugelhorn
French horn
Gramophone
Hurdy-gurdy
Kettledrum
Lagerphone
Mellophone
Nun's fiddle
Ophicleide
Orpheoreon
Pentachord

Shakuhachi
Squeeze-box
Stylophone®
Symphonium
Tambourine
Thumb piano
Vibraphone
Wokka board

11 letters:
Chordophone
Clairschach
Contrabasso
Harmoniphon
Harpsichord
Heckelphone
Nickelodeon
Orchestrina
Orchestrion
Phonofiddle
Straduarius
Synthesizer
Trump-marine
Violincello
Wobble-board

12 letters:
Chapman stick
Chinese block
Clavicembalo
Glockenspiel
Harmoniphone
Metallophone
Penny-whistle
Sarrusophone
Stock and horn
Stradivarius
Tromba-marina
Tubular bells

13 letters:
Contrabassoon
Ondes Martenot
Panharmonicon
Physharmonica

14 letters:
Glass harmonica
Jingling Johnny
Ondes musicales
Piano accordion

Music-hall Alhambra, Disco, Empire, Odeon
Musician(s), Musicologist Accompanist, Arion, Arist, Beiderbecke, Brain, Chanter, Clapton, Combo, > **COMPOSER**, Conductor, Crowder, Duet, Ensemble, Executant, Flautist, Gate, Grove, Guido d'Arezzo, Guslar, Handel, Jazzer, Jazzman, Joplin, Mahler, Mariachi, Menuhin, Minstrel, Muso, Noisenik, Nonet, Octet, Orphean, Pianist, Quartet, Quintet, Rapper, Reed(s)man, Répétiteur, Rubinstein, Septet, Session, Sextet, Sideman, Spohr, String, Techno, Tortelier, Troubador, Trouvère, Violinist, Wait
Musk Civet, Mimulus, Must
Musket Brown Bess, Caliver, Carabine, Eyas, Flintlock, Fusil, Hawk, Jezail, Nyas, Queen's-arm, Weapon
Musketeer Aramis, Athos, D'Artagnan, Fusilier, Ja(e)gar, Porthos, Rifleman, Sam
Muslim (ritual), Moslem Alaouite, Alawite, Ali, Almohad(e), Balochi, Baluchi, Berber, Black, Caliph, Dato, Dervish, Druse, Fatimid, Ghazi, Hadji, Hafiz, Hajji, He'zbolah, Iranian, Islamic, Ismaili, Karmathian, Khotbah, Khotbeh, Khutbah, Mahometan, Mogul, Mohammedan, Moor, Morisco, Moro, Mufti, Mus(s)ulman, Mutazilite, Nawab, Panislam, Paynim, Pomak, Said, Saracen, Say(y)id, Senus(s)i, Shafiite, Shia(h), Shiite, Sofi, Sonnite, Sufi, Sulu, Sunna, Sunni(te), Tajik, Turk, Ummah, Wahabee, Wahabi(te), Wahhabi
Muslin Butter, Cloth, Coteline, Gurrah, Jamdani, Leno, Mousseline, Mull, Nainsook, Organdie, Tarlatan, Tiffany
Musquash Ondatra
Mussel(s) Bearded, Bivalve, Clabby-doo, Clam, Clappy-doo, Deerhorn, Moules

marinières, Mytilus, Niggerhead, Pearl, Swan, Unio, Zebra
Mussorgsky Modest
Must(y) Amok, Essential, Foughty, Froughy, Frowsty, Frowy, Funky, Fust, Man,
Maun(na), Mote, Mould, Mucid, Mun, Need(s)-be, Shall, Should, Stum, Wine
▷ **Must** *may indicate* an anagram
Mustard Black, Charlock, Cress, English, Erysimum, French, Garlic, Nitrogen,
Praiseach, Quinacrine, Runch, Sauce-alone, Senvy, Treacle, Wall, White, Wild
Mustard plaster Sinapism
Muster Array, Assemble, Bangtail, Call up, Mass, Raise, Rally, Really, Recruit,
Round-up, Wappenshaw
Mutability Wheel
Mutate, Mutant, Mutation Auxotroph(ic), Change, Somatic, Sport, Suppressor,
Terata, Transform
▷ **Mutation** *may indicate* an anagram
Mute(d) Deaden, Dumb, Harpo, Noiseless, Silent, Sordino, Sordo, Sourdine,
Stifle
Mutilate(d), Mutilation Castrate, Concise, Deface, Dismember, Distort, Garble,
Hamble, Injure, Maim, Mangle, Mayhem, Obtruncate, Riglin, Tear
▷ **Mutilate(d)** *may indicate* an anagram
Mutineer, Mutiny Bounty, Caine, Christian, Curragh, Indian, Insurrection,
Meerut, Nore, Pandy, > REVOLT, Rising, Sepoy
Mutter(ing) Chunter, Fremescent, Grumble, Mumble, Mump, Murmur,
Mussitate, Rhubarb, Roin, Royne, Rumble, Whittie-whattie, Witter
Mutton Colonial goose, Em, Ewes, Fanny Adams, Gigot, Macon, Saddle, Sheep,
Theave, Traik
Mutual (aid) Common, Log-roll, Reciprocal, Symbiosis
Muzzle Decorticate, Gag, Jaw, Mouth, Restrain, Snout
My Coo, Gemini, Golly, Gosh, Ha, Lor, Lumme, Musha, Odso, Oh, Our, Tush
Mynah Stare, Starling
Mynheer Stadholder
Myopia, Myopic Hidebound, Mouse-sight, Narrow, Short-sighted, Thick-eyed
Myriad Host, Zillion
Myristic Nutmeg
Myrrh Stacte
Myrtle Callistemon, Crape, Crepe, Eucalyptus, Gale, Jambolana, Tasmanian,
Tooart, Tuart
Mysterious, Mystery Abdabs, Abdals, Acroamatic, Arcane, Arcanum, Cabbala,
Closed book, Craft, Creepy, Cryptic, Dark, Deep, Delphic, Eleusinian, Enigma,
Esoteric, Grocer, G(u)ild, Incarnation, Inscrutable, Miracle, Mystagogue,
Numinous, Occult, Original sin, Orphic, Penetralia, Riddle, > SECRET, Telestic,
Trinity, UFO, Uncanny, Whodunit
▷ **Mysterious(ly)** *may indicate* an anagram
Mystic (word), Mystical Abraxas, Agnostic, Cab(e)iri, Epopt, Fakir, Familist,
Hesychast, Mahatma, Occultist, Quietism, Rasputin, Secret, Seer, Sofi, Sufi,
Swami, Tantrist, Theosophy, Transcendental, Zohar
Mystify Baffle, Bamboozle, Bewilder, Metagrabolise, Metagrobolise, Puzzle
Myth(ology), Mythical (beast) Allegory, Behemoth, Bunyip, Centaur,
Cockatrice, Dragon, Euhemerism, Fable, Fantasy, Fictitious, Folklore, Garuda,
Geryon, Griffin, Hippocampus, Impundulu, Kelpie, Kylin, Legend, Leviathin,
Lore, Otnit, Pantheon, Pegasus, Phoenix, Sea horse, Selkie, Solar, Speewah,
Sphinx, Sun, Thunderbird, Tokoloshe, Unicorn, Urban, Wivern, Wyvern, Yale,
Yeti

Nn

N Name, Nitrogen, Noon, North, November
Nab Arrest, Capture, Collar, Grab, Seize
Nabob Deputy, Nawab, Wealthy
Nadir Bottom, Depths, Dregs, Minimum
Nag(ging) Badger, Bidet, Brimstone, Callet, Cap, Captious, Complain, Fret,
  Fuss, Harangue, Harp, Henpeck, Horse, Jade, Jaw, Keffel, Peck, Pester, Plague,
  Rosinante, Rouncy, > SCOLD, Tit, Xant(h)ippe, Yaff
Nail(ed) Brad, Brod, Catch, Clinker, Clout, Coffin, Fasten, Hob, Keratin, Onyx,
  Pin, Rivet, Screw, Secure, Shoe, Sisera, Sparable, Sparrow-bill, Spick, Spike,
  Sprig, Staple, Stub, Stud, Tack(et), Talon, Tenpenny, Tenterhook, Thumb,
  Tingle, Toe, Unguis, Wire
Naive(té) Artless, Green, Guileless, Gullible, Ingenuous, Innocence, Open,
  Pollyanna, Simpliste, Simplistic, Unsophisticated, Wide-eyed
Naked Adamical, Artless, Bare, Blunt, Buff, Clear, Cuerpo, Defenceless,
  Encuerpo, Exposed, Gymno-, Kaal gat, Nuddy, Nude, Querpo, Raw, Scud,
  Simple, Skyclad, Stark(ers), Uncovered
Namby-pamby Milksop, Nance, Sissy, Weak, Weakling, White-shoe
Name(d), **Names** Agnomen, Alias, Allonym, Anonym, Appellation, Appoint,
  Baptise, Behight, Byline, Call, Celeb(rity), Christen, Cite, Cleep, Clepe,
  Cognomen, Day, Designate, Dinges, Dingus, Dit, Domain, Dub, Epithet,
  Eponym, Exonym, Family, First, Generic, Given, Handle, Hete, Hight,
  Hypocorism, Identify, Identity, Label, Maiden, Marque, Masthead, Mention,
  Metronymic, Middle, Moni(c)ker, Mud, N, Nap, Nemn, Nom, Nomen(clature),
  Noun, Onomastics, Onymous, Patronymic, Pennant, Personage, Pet, Place,
  Proper, Proprietary, Pseudonym, Quote, Red(d), Repute, Scilicet, Sign,
  Signature, Sir, Specify, Stage, Street, Substantive, Tag, Teknonymy, Term,
  > TITLE, Titular, Titule, Toponymy, Trade, Trivial
Name-dropper Eponym
Nameless Anon, Unchrisom
Namely Ie, Scilicet, To-wit, Videlicet, Viz
Namesake Homonym
Name unknown Anon, A N Other, NU
Nancy Coddle, Effeminate, Milksop
Nanny Ayah, Foster, Goat, Nurse
Naos Cell(a)
Nap(py) Ale, Bonaparte, Diaper, Doze, Drowse, Fluff, Frieze(d), Fuzz, Happen,
  Hippin(g), Kip, Moze, Oose, Ooze, Oozy, Power, Put(t), Shag, Siesta, > SLEEP,
  Slumber, Snooze, Tease, Teasel, Teaze, Tipsy, Tuft
Nape Niddick, Noddle, Nucha, Scrag, Scruff, Scuff, Scuft
Napier Logarithm
Napkin Cloth, Diaper, Doily, Doyley, Linen, Muckender, Paper, Sanitary,
  Serviette, Table
Napless Threadbare

Napoleon Badinguet, Bonaparte, Boustrapa, Cognac, Coin, Consul, Corporal Violet, Corsican, December, Little Corporal, Nantz, Nap, Pig, Rantipole
Napper Bonce, Shearman
Narcissus Echo, Egocentric, Jonquil
Narcotic Ava, Benj, B(h)ang, Charas, Churrus, Coca, Codeine, Datura, Dope, > DRUG, Heroin, Hop, Kava, Laudanum, Mandrake, Marijuana, Meconium, Methadone, Morphia, Opiate, Pituri, Sedative, Tea, Trional
Nark Grass, Inform, Irritate, Nose, Pique, Roil, Squealer, Stag
Narrate, Narration, Narrative, Narrator Allegory, Anecdote, Cantata, Describe, Diegesis, Fable, History, Oblique, Periplus, Plot, Raconteur, Récit, Recite, Recount, Saga, Scheherazade, Splatterpunk, Story, Tell, Voice-over
Narrow(ing), Narrow-minded Alf, Bigoted, Borné, Constringe, Cramp, Ensiform, Grundy(ism), Hidebound, Illiberal, Insular, Kyle, Limited, Meagre, Nary, One-idead, Parochial, Phimosis, Pinch, Provincial, Prudish, Puritan, Scant, Sectarian, Shrink, Slender, Slit, Specialise, Squeak, Stenosed, Strait, Suburban, Verkramp, Waist
Narwhal Monodon
Nasal Adenoidal, Twang
Nash Beau
Nashville Bath
Nastiness, Nasty Disagreeable, Drevill, Filth, Fink, Ghastly, Lemon, Lo(a)th, Malign(ant), Noxious, Obscene, Odious, Offensive, Ribby, Sordid, Vile
Nat(haniel) Hawthorne, Winkle
Natal Inborn, Native, Patrial
Natant Afloat, Swimming
Nation(s), National(ist) Anthem, Baathist, Casement, Chetnik, Country, Cuban, Debt, Eta, Federal, Five, Folk, Grand, Indian, IRA, Israeli, Jingoist, Land, Mexican, Pamyat, Patriot, > PEOPLE, Plaid Cymr, Polonia, Race, Rainbow, Risorgimento, Scottish, Six, SNP, Subject, Swadeshi, United, Verkrampte, Vietminh, Wafd, Yemini, Young Ireland, Zionist
Native(s) Abo(rigin), Aborigine, African, Amerind, Annamese, Arab, Ascian, Australian, Autochthon, Aztec, Basuto, Belonging, Bengali, Boy, Bushman, Cairene, Carib, Carioca, Chaldean, Citizen, Colchester, Conch, Creole, Criollo, Domestic, Dyak, Edo, Enchorial, Eskimo, Fleming, Fuzzy-wuzzy, Genuine, Habitual, Home-bred, Inborn, Inca, Indigene, Indigenous, Inhabitant, Intuitive, John Chinaman, Kaffir, Libyan, Local, Malay, Maori, Micronesian, Moroccan, Norwegian, Oyster, Polack, Portuguese, Scythian, Son, Spaniard, Te(i)an, Thai, Tibetan, Uzbeg, Uzbek, Whitstable, Yugoslav
Nativity Birth, Jataka, Putz
Natron Urao
Natter Chat, Gossip, Jack, Prate
Natty Bumppo, Chic, Dapper, Leatherstocking, Smart, Spruce
Natural(ly), Naturalised, Naturalism Artless, Ass, Denizen, Easy, Genuine, Homely, Idiot, Illegitimate, Inborn, Inbred, Indigenous, Ingenerate, Inherent, Innate, Moron, Native, Nidget, Nitwit, Nude, Ordinary, Organic, Prat, Real, Simpleton, Simpliciter, Sincere, True, Undyed, Untaught, Verism
Naturalist Buffon, Darwin, Wallace, White
Nature Adam, Akin, Character, Disposition, Esse(nce), Ethos, Haecceity, Human, Inscape, Mould, Quiddity, Quintessence, Second, SN, Temperament
Naught Cypher, Failure, Nil, Nothing, Zero
Naughty Bad, Disobedient, Girly, Improper, Light, Marietta, Nonny, Rascal, Remiss, Spright, Sprite, Wayward

Nausea, Nauseous Disgust, Fulsome, Malaise, Queasy, Sickness, Squeamish, Wamble, Wambly

Nave Aisle, Apse, Centre, Hub, Nef

Navel Belly-button, Naff, Nave, Omphalos, Umbilicus

Navigate, Navigator Albuquerque, Bougainville, Cabot, Cartier, Columbus, Control, Da Gama, Dias, Direct, Franklin, Frobisher, Gilbert, Hartog, Haul, Henry, Hudson, Keel, Magellan, Navvy, Orienteer, Pilot, Sail, Star-read, > **STEER**, Tasman, Traverse, Vancouver, Vespucci

Navigation (aid, system) Asdic, Cabotage, Celestial, Decca, Dectra, Fido, Gee, Inland, Loran, Loxodromics, Navarho, Omnirange, Portolan(o), Portulan, Radar, Satnav, Shoran, Tacan, Teleran®, Vor

Navvy Workhorse

Navy, Naval AB, Armada, Blue, Fleet, French, Maritime, Merchant, N, Red, RN, Senior Service, Wren

Nawab Huzoor, Nabob, Viceroy

Nazi Brownshirt, Gauleiter, Hess, Hitler, Jackboot, SS, Stormtrooper, Wer(e)wolf

NB Niobium, Nota bene

NCO Bombardier, Corp(oral), Havildar, Noncom, Orderly, Sergeant, SM

Neanderthal Mousterian

Neap Low, Tide

Neapolitan Ice

Near(er), Nearest, Nearby, Nearly, Nearness About, Adjacent, All-but, Almost, Anigh, Approach, Approximate, Beside, By, Close, Cy pres, Degree, Even, Ewest, Feckly, Forby, Gain, Handy, Hither, Imminent, Inby(e), Mean, Miserly, Narre, Neist, Next, Nie, Niggardly, Nigh, Outby, Propinquity, Proximity, Short-range, Stingy, Thereabout(s), To, Upon, Warm, Well-nigh

Neat(ly) Bandbox, Cattle, Clean-cut, Clever, Dainty, Dapper, Deft, Dink(y), Doddy, Donsie, Elegant, Feat(e)ous, Featly, Featuous, Gayal, Genty, Gyal, Intact, Jemmy, Jimpy, Lower, Nett, Ninepence, Orderly, Ox(en), Preppy, Pretty, Rother, Shipshape, Short, Smug, Snod, Spruce, Straight, > **TIDY**, Trig, Trim, Unwatered

Neb Beak, Bill, Nose, Snout

Nebula, Nebulous Aeriform, Celestial, Cloudy, Gum, Hazy, Horsehead, Obscure, Planetary, Shadowy, Vague

Necessary, Necessarily Bog, Cash, De rigueur, > **ESSENTIAL**, Estovers, Important, Indispensable, Intrinsic, Money, Needful, Ought, Perforce, Prerequisite, Requisite, Vital, Wherewithal

Necessitate, Necessity Ananke, Compel, Constrain, Cost, Emergency, Entail, Exigent, Fate, Indigence, Logical, Mathematical, Must, Natural, Need, Need-be, Oblige, Perforce, Require, Requisite

Neck(ed) Bottle, Brass, Canoodle, Cervical, Cervix, Channel, Col, Crag, Craig, Crop, Cuff, Embrace, Ewe, Gall, Gorgerin, Halse, Hawse, Inarm, Inclip, Isthmus, Kiss, Mash, Nape, Pet, Polo, Rack, Rubber, Scoop, Scrag, Scruff, Smooch, Snog, Stiff, Strait, Surgical, Swan, Swire, Theorbo, Torticollis, Trachelate, Vee

▷ **Necking** *may indicate* one word around another

Necklace Anodyne, Brisingamen, Chain, Choker, Collar, Corals, Lava(l)lière, Lunula, Mangalsutra, Negligee, Pearls, Rope, Sautoir, String, Torc, Torque

Neckline Boat, Collar, Cowl, Crew, Décolletage, Lanyard, Palter, Plunging, Sweetheart, Turtle, Vee

Neckwear Ascot, Barcelona, Boa, Bow, Collar, Cravat, Fur, Rail, Steenkirk, Stock, Tie

Necromancer Goetic, Magician, Ormandine, Osmand, Witch, Wizard

Necrosis Infarct, Sphacelus
Nectar Ambrosia, Amrita, Honey, Mead
Ned(dy) Donkey, Kelly, Ludd
Need(ed), Needy Beggarly, Call, Demand, Desiderata, Egence, Egency, Exigency, Gap, Gerundive, Impecunious, Indigent, > LACK, Mister, Pressing, PRN, Require, Strait, Strapped, Want
Needle(s) Acerose, Acicular, Aciform, Between, Bodkin, Cleopatra's, Darning, Dip, Dry-point, Electric, Goad, Gramophone, Hagedorn, Hype, Hypodermic, Ice, Icicle, Inoculate, Leucotome, Magnetic, Miff, Monolith, Neeld, Neele, Netting, Obelisk, Pine, Pinnacle, Pique, Pointer, Prick, R(h)aphis, Sew, Sharp, Spanish, Spicule, Spike, Spine, Stylus, Tattoo, Tease, Thorn, Wire
Needlewoman Cleopatra, Seamstress
Needlework Baste, Crewel, Drawn(-thread), Embroidery, Fag(g)oting, Fancy work, Mola, Patchwork, Petit point, Plainwork, Rivière, Sampler, Smocking, Spanish, Tapestry, Tattoo, Woolwork, Worsted-work
Ne'er-do-well Badmash, Budmash, Bum, Good-for-nothing, Scullion, Shiftless, Skellum, Wastrel
Negation, Negative Ambrotype, Anion, Apophatic, Cathode, Denial, Double, Enantiosis, False, Ne, No, Non, Nope, Nullify, Pejorative, Photograph, Refusal, Resinous, Unresponsive, Veto, Yin
Neglect(ed), Neglectful, Negligence, Negligent Careless, Casual, Cinderella, Contributory, Cuff, Default, Dereliction, Disregard, Disuse, Failure, Forget, Forlorn, Heedless, Inadvertence, Inattention, Incivism, Laches, Malpractice, Misprision, Omission, Oversight, Pass, Pass-up, > REMISS, Shirk, Slight, Slipshod, Undone, Waif, Wanton
▷ **Neglected** *may indicate* an anagram
Negligee Déshabillé, Manteau, Mob, Nightgown, Peignoir, Robe
Negligible Fig, Minimal
Negotiate, Negotiator Arbitrate, Arrange, Bargain, Clear, Confer, Deal, Diplomat, Haggle, Intermediary, Liaise, Manoeuvre, Mediator, Parley, Trade, Transact, Treat(y), Weather
Negro(id) > AFRICAN, Baganda, Bambara, Barotse, Bemba, Bergdama, Bini, Black, Buck, Chewa, Creole, Cuffee, Cuffy, Damara, Dinge, Duala, Dyula, Ebon(y), Edo, Efik, Ethiop, Ewe, Fang, Ga, Ganda, Gullah, Hausa, Hottentot, Hutu, Ibibio, Ibo, Igorot, Jim Crow, Kikuyu, Kongo, Luba, Luganda, Malinke, Maninke, Mestee, Moke, Moor, Mossi, Mustee, Ndebele, Nilote, Nupe, Nyanja, Nyoro, Ovambo, Pondo, Quashee, Quashie, Sambo, Snowball, Spade, Susu, Temne, Thick-lips, Tiv, Tonga, Tsonga, Tswana, Twi, Uncle Tom, Vanda, Watu(t)si, Wolof, Xhosa, Yoruba, Zambo, Zulu
Negus Emperor, Rumfruction, Selassie
Nehru Pandit
Neigh Bray, Hinny, Nicker, Whicker, Whinny
Neighbour(ly), Neighbouring, Neighbours Abut(ter), Adjoin, Alongside, Amicable, Bor, Border, But, Friendly, Joneses, Nearby, Next-door, Vicinal
Neighbourhood Area, Community, District, Environs, Locality, Precinct, Vicinage, Vicinity
Neither Nor
Nell(ie), Nelly Bly, Dean, Trent
Nelson Columnist, Eddy, Horatio
Nemesis Alastor, Avenger, Deserts, Downfall, Fate, Retribution, Revenge
Neodymium Nd
Neolithic Avebury, Halafian, Stonehenge

Neon Ne
Nepalese Gurkha
Neper N
Nephrite Yu
Nepotism Kin, Partisan, Patronage
Neptune God, Planet, Poseidon
Neptunium Np
Nerd Anorak, Otaku
Nereid Cymodoce, Nymph, Panope
Nerve(s), Nervous(ness), Nervure, Nerve centre, Nervy Abdabs, Abducens, Accessory, Acoustic, Afferent, Aflutter, Afraid, Alveolar, Appestat, Auditory, Axon, Baroreceptor, Bottle, Bouton, Buccal, Chord, Chutzpah, Collywobbles, Column, Commissure, Cones, Courage, Cranial, Cyton, Depressor, Edgy, Effector, Efferent, Electrotonus, Epicritic, Excitor, Facial, Gall, Ganglion, Glossopharyngeal, Grit, Guts, Habdabs, Heart-string, High, Highly-strung, Hyp, Hypoglossal, Impudence, Jitters, Jittery, Median, Mid-rib, Motor, Myelon, Nappy, Neck, Nidus, Octulomotor, Olfactory, Optic, Pavid, Perikaryon, Proprioceptor, Rad, Radial, Receptor, Restiform, Restless, Sacral, Sangfroid, Sauce, Sciatic, Screaming abdabs, Screaming meemies, Sensory, Shaky, Shpilkes, Solar plexus, Splanchnic, Spunk, Squirrel(l)y, Steel, Strung-up, Synapse, Tense, Tizzy, Toey, Tongue-tied, Trembler, Tremulous, Trigeminal, Trochlear, Twitchy, Ulnar, Uptight, Vagus, Vapours, Vestibulocochlear, Wandering, Willies, Windy, Yips
Nervous disease, Nervous disorder Chorea, Epilepsy, Neuritis, Tetany
▷ **Nervously** *may indicate* an anagram
Ness Cape, Headland, Ras
Nessus Centaur
Nest Aerie, Aery, Aiery, Ayrie, Bike, Bink, Brood, Byke, Cabinet, Cage, Caliology, Clutch, Dray, Drey, Eyrie, Eyry, Lodge, Love, Nid, Nide, Nidify, Nidus, Norwegian, Sett, Termitarium, Wurley
Nestle Burrow, Coorie, Cose, Courie, Cuddle, Nuzzle, Snug(gle)
Nestor Counsellor, Kea, Sage
Net(ting), Nets, Network Anastomosis, Bamboo, BR, Bunt, Butterfly, Cast, Casting, Catch, Caul, Clap, Clathrate, Clear, Cobweb, Crinoline, Crossover, Drift, Earn, Eel-set, Enmesh, Equaliser, Ethernet, Fetch, Filet, Final, Fish, Flew, Flue, Fyke, Gill, > GRID, Hammock, Heliscoop, Internet, Intranet, JANET, Kiddle, Lace, LAN, Land, Landing, Lattice, Leap, Line, Linin, Mains, Malines, Maze, > MESH, Mosquito, Neural, Neuropic, Old boys', PCN, Plexus, Portal system, Pound, Pout, Purse-seine, Quadripole, Reseau, Rete, Retiary, Reticle, Reticulate, Reticulum, Ring, Safety, Sagene, Screen, Sean, Seine, Set(t), Shark, Snood, Sweep-seine, System, Tangle, Tela, Telex, Toil, Torpedo, Trammel, Trap, Trawl, Tulle, Tunnel, Usenet, WAN, Web, Wide-area, Wire
Netball Let
Nether Below, Inferior, Infernal, Lower, Under
Nettle(rash) Anger, Annoy, Day, Dead, Hemp, Hives, Horse, Irritate, Labiate, Nark, Pellitory, Pique, Ramee, Rami, Ramie, Rile, Roman, Ruffle, Sting, Urtica(ceae), Urticaria
Neuralgia, Neuritis Migraine, Sciatica, Tic
Neurosis Compulsion, Obsessive-compulsive, Shellshock
Neuter Castrate, Gib, Impartial, Neutral, Sexless, Spay
Neutral(ise) Alkalify, Angel gear, Buffer zone, Counteract, Grey, Impartial, Inactive, Schwa, Sheva, Shiva, Unbiased

Neutron(s) Fast, Nucleon, Thermal, Virgin

Never(more) Nary, Nathemo(re), No more, Nowise, St Tibb's Eve

Never-ending Age-long

Nevertheless Algate, Anyhow, But, Even, However, Quand même, Still, Tout de même, Yet

▷ **New** *may indicate* an anagram

New(s), News agency Bulletin, Copy, Coranto, Dope, Euphobia, Evangel, Flash, Forest, Fresh, Fudge, Gen, Green, Griff, Info, Innovation, Intelligence, Item, Kerygma, Latest, Mint, Modern, N, Novel, Oil(s), Original, PA, Paragraph, Pastures, Pristine, Propaganda, Recent, Report, Reuter, Scoop, Span, Split, Star Tass, Tass, Teletext®, Tidings, Ultramodern, Unco, Usenet, Wire service, Word

New boy Cyte

Newcomer Dog, Freshman, Griffin, Immigrant, Jackaroo, Jackeroo, Jillaroo, Johnny-come-lately, Novice, Parvenu, Pilgrim, Settler, Tenderfoot, Upstart

Newfoundland Dog, Nana, Vinland

Newgate Calendar

Newly wed Benedick, Benedict, Bride, Groom, Honeymooner, Neogamist

Newman Cardinal, Noggs

New moon Rosh Chodesh

Newsman, News-reader Announcer, Editor, Journalist, Press, Reporter, Sub, Sysop

Newsmonger, News-vendor Butcher, Gossip, Quidnunc

Newspaper Blat(t), Broadsheet, Courier, Daily, Express, Fanzine, Feuilleton, Freesheet, Gazette, Guardian, Herald, Journal, Jupiter, Le Monde, Mercury, National, Organ, Patent inside, Patent outside, Post, Pravda, Press, Print, Rag, Red-top, Scandal sheet, Sheet, Spoiler, Squeak, Sun, Tabloid, Today

Newsreel Actualities

Newt(s) Ask(er), Eft, Evet, Swift, Triton, Urodela

Newton N

New world USA

New year Hogmanay, Neer-day, Rosh Hashana(h), Tet

New York(er) Big apple, Gotham, Knickerbocker

New Zealand(er) Aotearoa, Enzed, Jafa, Kiwi, Maori, Mooloo, Moriori, Pakeha, Pig Island, Shagroon, Zelanian

Next Adjacent, Adjoining, After, Alongside, Beside, Following, Immediate, Later, Nearest, Neist, Proximate, Proximo, Sine, Subsequent, Syne

Nib J, Pen, Point, Tip

Nibble Bite, Brouse, Browse, Byte, Crop, Eat, Gnaw, Knap(ple), Moop, Moup, Munch, Nag, Nepit, Nosh, Peck, Pick, Snack

Nice(ty) Accurate, Amene, Appealing, Cool, Dainty, Fastidious, Fine, Finical, Genteel, Lepid, Mooi, Ninepence, Pat, Pleasant, Precise, Quaint, Rare, Refined, Subtil(e), Subtle, Sweet, T

Niche Alcove, Almehrahb, Almery, Ambry, Apse, Aumbry, Awmrie, Awmry, Columbarium, Cranny, Exedra, Fenestella, Mihrab, Recess, Slot

Nicholas Santa

Nick(ed) Appropriate, Arrest, Bin, Blag, Can, Chip, Cly, Colin, Copshop, Cut, Denay, Dent, Deny, > DEVIL, Erose, Groove, Hoosegow, Kitty, Knock, Nab, Nap, Nim, Nock, Notch, Pinch, Pook, Pouk, Prison, Scratch, > STEAL, Steek, Swan-upping, Swipe, Thieve, Whip, Wirricow, Worricow, Worrycow

Nickel (silver) Coin, Garnierite, Jitney, Millerite, Ni, Packfong, Paktong, Zaratite

Nicker Bonduc, Neigh, Whinny

Nickname Alias, Byname, Byword, Cognomen, So(u)briquet, To-name

Nicotine Tobacco, Weed
Nifty Smart, Stylish
Nigeria(n) Biafran, Efik, Hausa, Ibibio, Ibo, Igbo, Nupe, WAN, Yoruba
Niggard(ly) Dry-fist, Illiberal, Mean, Miser, Near-(be)gaun, Nippy, Nirlit,
Parsimonious, Pinchcommons, Pinchgut, Pinchpenny, Scrunt, Skinflint,
Tightwad
Niggle Carp, Gripe, Nag, Trifle
Night(s), Nightfall Acronychal, Arabian, Darkmans, First, Gaudy, Guest, Guy
Fawkes, Hen, Leila, Nacht, Nicka-nan, Nutcrack, Nyx, School, Stag, Twelfth,
Twilight, Walpurgis, Watch, White
Night-blindness Day-sight, Nyctalopia
Night-cap Biggin, Cocoa, Kilmarnock cowl, Nip, Pirnie, Sundowner
Nightclub Clip joint, Dive, Honkytonk
Night-dew Serein, Serene
Nightdress Wylie-coat
Nightingale Bulbul, Florence, Jugger, Lind, Philomel, Scutari, Swedish, Watch
Nightjar Evejar, Fern-owl, Goatsucker, Poorwill, Potoo
Night-light Moonbeam
Nightmare, Nightmarish Cacod(a)emon, Ephialtes, Incubus, Kafkaesque,
Oneirodynia, Phantasmagoria
Night-rider Revere
Nightshade Belladonna, Bittersweet, Black, Circaea, Deadly, Dwale,
Enchanter's, Henbane, Morel, Solanum, Woody
Nightwatchman Charley, Charlie, Rug-gown
Nightwork Lucubrate
Nihilist Anarchist, Red, Sceptic
Nil Nothing, Nought, Zero
Nile Albert, Blue, Luvironza, Victoria, White
Nimble, Nimbly Active, > AGILE, Alert, Deft, Deliver, Fleet, Light, Light-footed,
Lissom(e), Lithe, Quiver, Sciolto, Springe, Spry, Supple, Swack, Wan(d)le,
Wannel, Wight, Ya(u)ld
Nimbus Aura, Aureole, Cloud, Gloriole, Halo
Nimrod Hunter
Nincompoop Ass, Imbecile, Ninny, Stupid
Nine, Ninth Choral, Ennead, Muses, Nonary, Nonet, Novenary, Pins, Sancho,
Skittles, Tailors, Worthies
Nine hundred Sampi
Nine of Diamonds Curse of Scotland
Nineteen(th) Bar, Decennoval
Ninetieth, Ninety N, Nonagesimal
Ninevite Assyrian
Ninny (hammer) Fool, Goose, Idiot, Stupid, Tony
Ninon Nan
Niobium Nb
Nip(per) Bite, Check, Chela, Chill, Claw, Dram, Fang, Gook, Jap, Lad, Lop, Nep,
Nirl, Peck, Pincers, Pinch, Pook, Pop, Scotch, Sneap, Susan, Taste, Tot, Tweak,
Urchin, Vice, Vise
Nipa At(t)ap, Palm
Nipple Dug, Grease, Jogger's, Mastoid, Pap, Teat
Nis Brownie, Goblin, Kobold, Sprite
Nit Egg, Insect, Louse
Nitre Saltpetre

Nitric, Nitrogen Azote, Azotic, Gas, N, Quinoline
Nitroglycerine Glonoin
Nitwit Ass, Flat, Fool, Simpleton, > STUPID
No Aikona, Denial, Na(e), Nah, Negative, Nix, Nope, Nyet, O, Refusal
Noah Arkite, Beery, Utnapishtim
Nob(by) Grandee, Parage, Prince, Swell, Toff
Nobble Dope, Hilch, Injure, Interfere
▷ **Nobbled** *may indicate* an anagram
Nobelium No
Noble(man), Noblewoman, Nobility Adeline, Aristocrat, Atheling, Baron(et),
 Bart, Boyar, Brave, Bt, Burgrave, Childe, Count, County, Daimio, Dom, Don,
 Doucepere, Douzeper(s), Duc, Duke, Duniwassal, Earl, Empress, Eorl, Ethel,
 Eupatrid, Fine, Gent, Glorious, Graf, Grandee, Grandeur, Great, Heroic,
 Hidalgo, Highborn, Infant, Jarl, Junker, King, Landgrave, Lord, Magnate,
 Magnifico, Manly, Margrave, Marquis, Nair, Nayar, Palatine, Patrician, Peer,
 Rank, Seigneur, Seignior, Sheik(h), Stately, Sublime, Thane, Thegn, Titled,
 Toiseach, Toisech, Vavasour, Vicomte, Vidame, Viscount
Nobody Gnatling, Jack-straw, Nebbish, Nemo, None, Nonentity, Nyaff, Pooter,
 Quat, Schlepp, Scoot, Shlep
Nocturnal (creature) Bat, Galago, Moth, Night, Owl
Nod(ding) Agree, Assent, Beck(on), Bob, Browse, Catnap, Cernuous, Doze,
 Headbang, Mandarin, Nutant, Somnolent
Node, Nodular, Nodule Ascending, Boss, Descending, Enhydros, Geode, Knot,
 Lump, Lymph, Milium, Pea-iron, Ranvier, Root, Swelling, Thorn, Tubercle
No doubt Iwis, Ywis
Noel Christmas, Coward, Yule
Nog(gin) Ale, Cup, > DRINK, Peg
No good Dud, NG, Ropy
No-hoper Gone goose
Noise, Noisy Ambient, Babel, Bedlam, Big, Blare, Bleep, Blip, Bobbery,
 Boing, Boink, Bruit, Cangle, Charm, Chellup, Clamant, Clamour, Clangour,
 Clash, Clatter, Clitter, Clutter, Coil, Crackle, Creak, Deen, Din, Dirdum,
 Euphonia, Euphony, F, Flicker, Fuss, Hewgh, Hubbub, Hue, Hullabaloo, Hum,
 Hurly-burly, Knocking, Loud, Mush, Obstreperous, Ping, Pink, Plangent,
 Quonk, Racket, Report, Roar, Robustious, Rorie, Rort, Rory, Row(dow-dow),
 Rowdedow, Rowdy(dow)(dy), Rucous, Schottky, Scream, Screech, Shindig,
 Shindy, Shot, Shreek, Shreik, Shriech, Shriek, Solar, Sone, Sonorous, Sound,
 Strepent, Strepitation, Strepitoso, Stridor, Surface, Thermal, Thunder,
 Tinnitus, Top, Tumult, > UPROAR, VIP, Vociferous, White, Zoom
Noisome Fetid, Invidious, Noxious, Offensive, Rank
No longer Ex, Past
Nomad(ic) Amalekite, Ammonites, Bedawin, Bed(o)uin, Bedu, Berber, Chal,
 Edom(ite), Fula(h), Gypsy, Hottentot, Hun, Hunter-gatherer, Itinerant, Kurd,
 Kyrgyz, Rom, Rootless, Rover, Saracen, Sarmatian, Strayer, Tsigane, Tsigany,
 Tuareg, Turk(o)man, Unsettled, Vagabond, Vagrant, Zigan
Noman Ta(r)tar
Nome Province
Nominal Formal, Onomastic, Titular, Trifling
Nominate, Nomination Appoint, Baptism, Designate, Elect, Present,
 > PROPOSE, Slate, Specify, Term
Nomogram Abac
No more Gone, Napoo

Nomothete Enactor, Legislator
Non-attender Absentee, Recusant
Non-believer Atheist, Cynic, Infidel, Sceptic
Non-catalyst Zymogen
Nonchalance, Nonchalant Blasé, Casual, Cool, Debonair, Insouciant, Jaunty, Poco
Noncommittal Trimmer
Non-communist West
Non-conformist, Non-conformity Beatnik, Bohemian, Chapel, Deviant, Dissent(er), Dissident, Ebenezer, Heresiarch, Heretic, Maverick, Odd-ball, Outlaw, Pantile, Patarine, Rebel, Recusant, Renegade, Renegate, Sectarian, Wesleyan
Nondescript Dull, Grey, Insipid, Neutral, Nyaff
None Nada, Nary, Nil, Nought, Zero
Nonentity Cipher, Nebbich, Nebbish(er), Nebish, Nobody, Pipsqueak, Quat
Non-essential Adiaphoron, Extrinsic, Incidental
Nonesuch Model, Nonpareil, Paradigm, Paragon, Rarity
Nonetheless Mind you
▷ **Nonetheless** *may Indicate* an 'o' to be omitted
Non-finite Verbid
Non-gypsy Gajo, Gorgio
Non-interference Laissez faire
Non-Jewish Goy, Shi(c)ksa, Shkitzim, Sho(y)getz
Non-juror Usager
Non-Maori Tangata tiriti, Tauiwi
Non-Muslim Raia, Rayah
No-nonsense Hardball
Nonpareil Nonesuch, Pearl, Peerless, Type, Unequal, Unique
Nonplus(sed) Baffle, Bewilder, Blank, Perplex, Stump
Non-professional Amateur, Laic
Non-radiative Auger
Non-resident Extern, Outlier
Non-runner Scratched, Solid
Nonsense Absurdity, Amphigon, Amphigory, Balderdash, Baloney, Bilge, Bizzo, Blague, Blah, Blarney, Blat(her), Blether, Bollocks, Boloney, Bora(c)k, Borax, Bosh, Bull, Bulldust, Bullshit, Bull's wool, Buncombe, Bunkum, Clamjamfr(a)y, Clamjamphrie, Claptrap, Cobblers, Cock, Cockamamie, Cod, Codswallop, Crap, Crapola, Drivel, Dust, Eyewash, Faddle, Falderal, Fandangle, Fiddlededee, Fiddle-faddle, Fiddlesticks, Flannel, Flapdoodle, Flim-flam, Folderol, Footling, Fudge, Gaff, Galimatias, Gammon, Get away, Gibberish, Guff, Gum, Hanky-panky, Haver, Hogwash, Hokum, Hooey, Horsefeathers, Humbug, Jabberwocky, Kibosh, Kidstakes, Malark(e)y, Moonshine, Mouthwash, My eye, Niaiserie, Phooey, Piffle, Pishogue, Pshaw, Pulp, Ratbaggery, Rats, Rhubarb, Rigmarole, Rot, Rubbish, Scat, Shenanigans, Shit(e), Squit, Stuff, Tom(foolery), Tommy-rot, Tosh, Trash, Tripe, Tush, Twaddle, Unreason, Waffle
Non-sequitur Anacoluthia, Irrelevant
Non-stick Tusche
Non-stop Through
Non-U Naff
Non-violence Ahimsa, Pacificism, Satyagraha
Non-white Coloured, Yolk

Noodle(s) Capellini, Crispy, Daw, Fool, Head, Laksa, Lokshen, Manicotti, Mee, Moony, Pasta, Sammy, Simpleton, Soba, Udon

Nook Alcove, Angle, Corner, Cranny, Niche, Recess, Rookery

Noon Am end, M, Midday, N, Narrowdale

No one Nemo, None

Noose Fank, Halter, Lanyard, Loop, Necktie, Rope, Rope's end, Snare, Twitch

▶ **Nor** *see* NOT

Nordic, Norse(man) Icelander, Norn, Scandinavian, Viking

▶ **Nordic** *see* NORWAY, NORWEGIAN

Norm Canon, Criterion, Rule, Standard

Normal Average, Conventional, Customary, Everyday, General, Natural, Norm, Ordinary, Orthodox, Par, Perpendicular, Regular, Standard, Unexceptional, Usu(al)

Normal eyes Emmetropia

Norman French, Rufus

▶ **Norse** *see* NORWAY, NORWEGIAN

North(ern), Northerner Arctic, Boreal, Cispontine, Copperhead, Doughface, Eskimo, Geographic, Hyperborean, Magnetic, N, Norland, Runic, Septentrion, True, Up

North American (Indian) Ab(e)naki, Algonki(a)n, Algonqui(a)n, Apache, Arapaho, Assiniboine, Basket Maker, Blackfoot, Brave, Caddoan, Cajun, Cayuga, Cherokee, Cheyenne, Chibcha, Chickasaw, Chinook, Chipewyan, Choctaw, Comanche, Copperskin, Creek, Crow, Delaware, Dene, Erie, Fox, Galibi, Geronimo, Haida, Hiawatha, Hopi, Huron, Injun, Iroquois, Kiowa Apache, Kootenai, Kootenay, Kutenai, Kwakiuti, Lakota, Mahican, Malecite, Mandan, Manhattan, Massachuset(ts), Melungeon, Menominee, Mescalero, Micmac, Mikasuki, Miniconjou, Minneconjou, Mission, Mogollon, Mohave, Mohawk, Mohegan, Mohican, Montagnais, Montagnard, Mound Builder, Mugwump, Muskogee, Narraganset, Natchez, Navaho, Nez Percé, Nootka, Northern P(a)iute, Oglala, Ojibwa(y), Okanagon, Okinagan, Omaha, Oneida, Onondaga, Osage, P(a)iute, Palouse, Papago, Papoose, Pawnee, Pequot, Pima, Plains, Pocahontas, Pomo, Ponca, Pontiac, Potawatom, Pueblo, Quapaw, Red(skin), Sachem, Sagamore, Sahaptan, Sahapti(a)n, Salish, Sannup, Sauk, Scalper, Seminole, Senecan, Serrano, Shawnee, Shoshone, Sioux, Sitting Bull, Siwash, Southern P(a)iute, Status, Suquamash, Susquehannock, Tahitan, Taino, Tarahumara, Teton, Tewa, Tiwa, Tlingit, Tribe, Tsimshian, Tuscarora, Ute, Wampanoag, Wichita, Winnebago, Wyandot(te), Yalkama, Yanqui, Yuman, Zuni

Northwestern Aeolis

Norway, Norwegian Bokmal, Fortinbras, Landsma(a)l, N, Nordic, Norweyan, Nynorsk, Rollo

Nose, Nosy A(d)jutage, Aquiline, Beak, Bergerac, Boko, Bouquet, Catarrhine, Conk, Cromwell, Curious, Desman, Droop, Fink, Flair, Gnomon, Grass, Grecian, Greek, Grog-blossom, Honker, Hooter, Index, Informer, Leptorrhine, Meddle, Muffle, Muzzle, Nark, Neb, Nozzle, Nuzzle, Parker, Platyrrhine, Proboscis, Prying, Pug, Rhinal, Roman, Schnozzle, Shove, Smelly, Sneb, Sniff, Snoot, Snout, Snub, Squeal, Stag, Stickybeak, Toffee

Noseband Barnacle, Cavesson, Musrol

Nose-bleed Epistaxis

Nosh Eat, Food, Nibble, Snack

Nostalgia Longing, Retrophilia, Yearning

Nostril(s) Blowhole, Cere, Choana, Nare

Nostrum Elixir, Medicine, Remede, Remedy

Not, Nor Dis-, Na(e), Ne, Neither, Never, No, Pas, Polled, Taint

Notable, Notability Conspicuous, Distinguished, Eminent, Especial, Landmark, Large, Lion, Memorable, Signal, Striking, Unco, VIP, Worthy

Not allowed NL

▷ **Not allowed** *may indicate* a word to be omitted

Notary Escribano, Scrivener

Notation(al) Benesh, Cantillation, Descriptive, Entry, Hexadecimal, Memo, Octal, Polish, Positional, Romic, Staff, Tablature

Notch(ed) Crena(l), Crenel, Cut, Dent, Erode, Erose, Gain, Gap, Gimp, Indent, Jag, Kerf, Nick, Nock, Raffle, Score, Sinus, Snick, Tally, Vandyke

Not clear Blocked, NL, Obscure, Opaque, Pearl

Note(s), Notebook A, Acciaccatura, Accidental, Adversaria, Advice, Agogic, Apostil(le), Apparatus, Appoggiatura, Arpeggio, Auxiliary, B, Bill(et), Bradbury, Breve, C, Cedula, Chit(ty), Chord, Cob, Comment, Conceit, Continental, Cover, Credit, Crotchet, Currency, D, Debit, Delivery, Demand, Dig, Dominant, E, E-la, F, Fa(h), Fame, Fiver, Flat, Flim, G, Gamut, Gloss(ary), Gold, Grace, Greenback, Heed, Hemiole, Identic, Index rerum, IOU, Item(ise), Jot(tings), Jug(-jug), Key, Kudos, La, Large, Leading, Lichanos, Line, Log, Long, Longa, Marginalia, Masora(h), Me, Melisma, Melody, Memo(randum), Mese, Mi, Minim, Minute, > **MONEY**, Mordent, Nachschlag, Natural, NB, Nete, Neum(e), Oblong, Observe, Octave, Oncer, Ostmark, Outline, Parhypate, Passing, Post-it®, Pound, Promissory, Prompt, Prosiambanomenos, Protocol, PS, Quarter, Quaver, Rag-money, Re, Record, Remark, Renown, Request, Root, Scholion, Scholium, Semibreve, Semiquaver, Semitone, Sextolet, Sharp, Shinplaster, Shoulder, Si, Sick, Smacker, Sol, Stem, Strike, Subdominant, Submediant, Subtonic, Supertonic, Te, Ten(ner), Third, Tierce, Tonic, Treasury, Treble, Undecimole, Ut, Variorum, Verbal, Wad, Warison, Whole

Note-case Pochette, Purse, Wallet

▷ **Notes** *may indicate* the use of letters A-G

Noteworthy Eminent, Extraordinary, Memorable, Particular, Signal, Special

Nothing, Nought Cipher, Devoid, Diddlysquat, Emptiness, FA, Gratis, Nada, Napoo, Naught, Nihil, Niks-nie, Nil, Nix(-nie), Noumenon, Nowt, Nuffin, Nullity, O, Rap, Rien, Sweet FA, Void, Zero, Zilch, Zip(po)

Notice(able) Ad(vertisement), Advice, Affiche, Apprise, Attention, Avis(o), Banns, Bill, Blurb, Caveat, Circular, Cognisance, Crit, D, Descry, Discern, Dismissal, Enforcement, Gaum, Get, Gorm, Handbill, > **HEED**, Intimation, Marked, Mensh, Mention, NB, No(t)chel, Obit, Observe, Oyez, Placard, Plaque, Playbill, Poster, Press, Proclamation, Prominent, > **REMARK**, Review, See, Short, Si quis, Spot, Spy, Sticker, Tent, Whip

Notify Acquaint, Advise, Apprise, Awarn, Inform, > **TELL**, Warn

Notion(al) Academic, Conceit, > **CONCEPT**, Crotchet, Fancy, Hunch, Idea, Idee, Idolum, Inkling, Opinion, Reverie, Vapour, Whim

Notoriety, Notorious Arrant, Byword, Crying, Egregious, Esclandre, Fame, Flagrant, Infamous, Infamy, Notour, Proverbial, Reclame, > **RENOWN**, Repute

No trump Laical, Lay, NT

Notwithstanding Although, Despite, Even, For, Howbeit, However, Nath(e)less, Natheless(e), Naythles, Nevertheless, Spite

Nougat Montelimar, Sundae

▶ **Nought** *see* **NOTHING**

Noughts and crosses Tic(k)-tac(k)-to(e)

Noun Abstract, Agent, Aptote, Collective, Common, Count, Gerund, Mass, N,

Proper, Substantive, Tetraptote, Verbal

Nourish(ing), Nourishment Aliment, Battill, Cherish, Cultivate, Feed, Ingesta, Meat, Nurse, Nurture, Nutrient, Promote, Replenish, Sustenance, Trophic

Nous Intellect, Intelligence, Reason

Nova Scotia(n) Acadia, Blue-nose

Novel(ty) Aga-saga, Bildungsroman, Bonkbuster, Book, Campus, Change, Different, Dime, Dissimilar, Emma, Epistolary, Fad, Fiction, Fresh, Gimmick, Gothic, Graphic, Historical, Horror, Idiot, Innovation, Ivanhoe, Kenilworth, Kidnapped, Kim, Middlemarch, > NEW, Newfangled, Original, Outside, Page-turner, Pamela, Paperback, Pendennis, Penny dreadful, Persuasion, Picaresque, Pot-boiler, Primeur, Pulp, Rebecca, Roman-à-clef, Romance, Roman fleuve, Sex and shopping, Shilling-dreadful, Shilling-shocker, Ulysses, Unusual, Whodun(n)it, Yellowback

▷ **Novel** *may indicate* an anagram

▶ **Novelist** *see* WRITER

Novice Acolyte, Apprentice, Beginner, Cadet, Chela, Colt, Cub, Greenhorn, Griffin, Jackaroo, Jillaroo, Johnny-raw, Kyu, L, Learner, Neophyte, Patzer, Postulant, Prentice, Rookie, Tenderfoot, Tyro(ne), Unweaned

Now(adays) AD, Alate, Anymore, Current, Here, Immediate, Instanter, Interim, Nonce, Nunc, Present, Pro tem, This

Nowhere Limbo

Nowt Cattle, Cows, Ky(e), Neat, Nothing

Noxious Harmful, Offensive, Poisonous, Venomous

Nozzle A(d)jutage, Fishtail, Nose, Nose-piece, Rose, Spout, Stroup, Syringe, Tewel, Tuyere, Tweer, Twier, Twire, Twyer(e)

Nuance Gradation, Nicety, Overtone, Shade

Nub Crux, Gist, Knob, Lump, Point

Nubile Beddable, Marriageable, Parti

Nuclear, Nucl(e)ide, Nucleus Cadre, Calandria, Centre, Core, Crux, Daughter, Deuteron, Eukaryon, Euratom, Even-even, Even-odd, Heartlet, Hub, Isomer, Isotone, Karyon, Kernel, Linin, Mushroom, Nuke, Pith, Prokaryon, Synkaryon, Triton

▷ **Nucleus** *may indicate* the heart of a word

Nude, Nudism, Nudist, Nudity Adamite, Altogether, Aphylly, Bare, Buff, Eve, Exposed, Full-frontal, Gymnosophy, > NAKED, Nuddy, Scud, Stark, Stripped, Undress

Nudge Dunch, Dunsh, Elbow, Jostle, Poke, Prod

Nudibranch Sea-slug

Nugget Chunk, Cob, Gold, Lump

Nuisance Bore, Bot, Bugbear, Chiz(z), Drag, Impediment, Inconvenience, Mischief, Pest, Plague, Public, Terror, Trial

Null(ification), Nullify Abate, Cancel, Counteract, Defeasance, Destroy, Diriment, Disarm, Invalid(ate), Negate, Neutralise, Recant, Terminate, Undo, Veto, Void

Numb(ness) Asleep, Blunt, Dead(en), Stun, Stupor, Torpefy, Torpescent, Torpid, Unfeeling

Number(s) Abscissa, Abundant, Accession, Air, Aleph-null, Aleph-zero, Algebraic, Algorithm, Aliquant, Aliquot, Amicable, Anaesthetic, Antilog, Apocalyptic, Apostrophus, Army, Atomic, Augend, Avogadro, Babylonian, Binary, Box, Brinell, Calculate, Cardinal, Cetane, Chromosome, Class, Cocaine, Coefficient, Cofactor, Complex, Composite, Concrete, Constant, Coordination, Count, Cyclic, Decillion, Deficient, Deficit, Diapason, Digit, Drove, E, Edition,

Epidural, Ether, Eucaine, Ex-directory, F, Feck, Frost(bite), Froude, Gas, Gobar,
Golden, Googol, Handful, Hantle, Hash(mark), Hemlock, Host, Imaginary,
Include, Index, Infimum, Integer, Irrational, Isospin, Item, Lac, Lakh,
Legion(s), Lepton, Livraison, Local, Mach, Magazine, Magic, Mass, Melodic,
Milliard, Minuend, Minyan, Mixed, Mort, Muckle, Multiple, Multiplex,
Multiplicity, Multitude, Myriadth, Nasik, Natural, Neutron, No(s), Nonillion,
Nth, Nucleon, Num, Numerator, Numerical, Octane, Octillion, Opiate,
Opium, Opposite, Opus, Ordinal, OT, Paginate, Par, Paucal, Peck, Perfect,
Pile, PIN, Plural, Prime, Proton, Quantum, Quarternion, Quorum, Quotient,
Radix, Raft, Random, Rational, Real, Reckon, Registration, Regulo®, Repunit,
Reynolds, Sampi, Scads, Serial, Sight, Slew, Slue, Some, Square, Strangeness,
Strength, Subtrahend, Summand, Surd, T, Tale, Telephone, Tell, Thr(e)ave,
Totient, Totitive, Transcendental, Transfinite, Troop, Turn-out, Umpteen,
Umpty, Urethane, Verse, Wave, Whole, Wrong, Zeroth
▷ **Number** *may indicate* a drug
Numeral(s) Arabic, Chapter, Figure, Ghubar, Gobar, Integer, Number, Roman
Numerous(ness) Divers, Galore, Legion, Lots, Many, Multeity, Myriad
Numskull Blockhead, Booby, Dunce, Stupid
Nun Beguine, Bhikkhuni, Clare, Cluniac, Conceptionist, Dame, Minim,
Minoress, Mother Superior, Pigeon, Poor Clare, Prioress, Religeuse, Sister, Top,
Ursuline, Vestal, Vowess, Zelator, Zelatrice, Zelatrix
▷ **Nun** *may indicate* a biblical character, father of Joshua
Nuptial (chamber) Bridal, Marital, Marriage, Thalamus
Nurse(ry) Aia, Alice, Amah, Ayah, Bonne, Caledonia, Care(r), Cavell, Charge,
Cherish, Crèche, Day, Deborah, District, Dry, EN, Flo(rence), Foster, Gamp,
Glumdalclitch, Harbour, Karitane, Mammy, Midwife, Minister, Mother, Mrs
Gamp, Nan(n)a, Nanny, Night, Nightingale, Nourice, Nourish, Parabolanus,
Phytotron, Playroom, Playschool, Plunket, Probationer, RN, Seminary, SEN,
Sister, Staff, Suckle, Tend, VAD, Visiting, Wet
Nursery(man) Conservatory, Crèche, Garden, Hothouse, Rhyme, Seedsman,
Slope
▷ **Nursing** *may indicate* one word within another
Nurture Cultivate, Educate, Feed, Foster, Suckle, Tend
Nut(s), Nutcase, Nutshell, Nut tree, Nutty Acajou, Acorn, Almond, Amygdalus,
Anacardium, Aphorism, Arachis, Areca, Arnut, Babassu, Barcelona, Barking,
Barmy, Bats, Beech-mast, Bertholletia, Betel, Brazil, Briefly, Buffalo, Butterfly,
Butternut, Cashew, Cob, Coffee, Cola, Coquilla, Coquina, Core, Cranium,
Cuckoo, Dukka(h), En, Filberd, Filbert, Gelt, Gilbert, Gland, Glans, Goober,
Gum, Hazel, Head, Hickory, Illipe, Ivory, Kernel, Kola, Lichee, Li(t)chi, Litchi,
Loaf, Lug, Lunatic, Lychee, Macadamia, Macahuba, Macaw-palm, Macoya,
Manic, Marking, Mast, Mockernut, Monkey, Noisette, Noodle, Nucule,
Palmyra, Para, Pate, Pecan, Philippina, Philippine, Philopoena, Physic, Pili,
Pine, Pistachio, Praline, Prawlin, Quandang, Quantong, Queensland, Rhus,
Sapucaia, Sassafras, Shell, Skull, Slack, Sleeve, Stuffing, Supari, Thumb, Tiger,
Walnut, Weirdo, Wing, Zany, Zealot
▷ **Nut** *may indicate* Egyptian god, father of Osiris
▶ **Nutcase, Nutshell** *see* **NUT**
Nutmeg Connecticut, CT, Mace, Myristica
Nutrient, Nutriment, Nutrition Eutrophy, Food, Ingesta, Protein, Sustenance,
Trace element, Trophic
▷ **Nuts** *may indicate* an anagram
Nuzzle Snoozle

Nyasaland Malawi

Nymph(et) Aegina, Aegle, Amalthea, Arethusa, Callisto, Calypso, Camenae, Carme, Clytie, Constant, Cymodoce, Daphne, Doris, Dryad, Echo, Egeria, Eurydice, Galatea, Hamadryad, Hesperides, Houri, Hyades, Ida, Insect, Larva, Liberty, Lolita, Maelid, Maia, Maiden, Mermaid, Naiad, Nereid, Oceanid, Oenone, Oread, Pupa, Rusalka, Sabrina, Scylla, Siren, Sylph, Syrinx, Tessa, Tethys, Thetis, Water, Wood

Oo

O Blob, Duck, Nought, Omega, Omicron, Oscar, Oxygen, Spangle, Tan, Zero

Oaf Auf, Changeling, Dolt, Fool, Ocker, Stupid, Twit

Oak(s) Bog, Bur, Cerris, Classic, Cork, Desert, Dumbarton, Durmast, Flittern, Fumed, Gabriel, Herne, Holly, Holm, Honour, Ilex, Jerusalem, Kermes, Live, Major, Parliament, Pedunculate, Philemon, Poison, Quercus, Red, Roble, Royal, Sessile, Silky, Swamp, Swilcar, > TREE, Turkey, Watch, White

Oakley Annie

Oar(s), Oarsmen Blade, Ctene, Eight, Leander, Organ, Paddle, Palm, Propel, Rower, Scull, Spoon, Stroke, Sweep

Oasis Buraimi, Haven, Hotan, Refuge, Spring, Tafilalet, Tafilelt

Oat(meal), Oats Ait, Athole brose, Avena, Brome-grass, Fodder, Grain, Grits, Groats, Gruel, Haver, Loblolly, Parritch, Pilcorn, Pipe, Porridge, Quaker®, Rolled, Wild

Oatcake Bannock, Clapbread, Farle, Flapjack, Jannock

Oath Affidavit, Begorrah, Curse, Dang, Demme, Doggone, Drat, Ecod, Egad, Expletive, God-so, Gospel, Halidom, Hippocratic, Igad, Imprecation, Jabers, Lumme, Lummy, Nouns, Oons, Promise, Sacrament, Sal(a)mon, Sapperment, Saucer, Sdeath, Sfoot, Sheart, 'slid, Strewth, Stygian, Swear, Tarnation, Tennis-court, Voir dire, Vow, Zbud, Zounds

Obdurate Adamant, Cruel, Hard, Intransigent, Stony, Stubborn, Tenacious

Obedient, Obedience, Obey Bent, Bridlewise, Canonical, Comply, Dutiful, Follow, Hear, Mindful, Obsequious, Observe, Obtemper, Passive, Perform, Pliant, Servant, Yielding

Obeisance > BOW, Salaam

Obelisk, Obelus Aguilla, Column, Dagger, Monument, Needle, Pillar

Oberon King, Merle

Obese, Obesity Bariatrics, Corpulent, Fat, Stout

Object(s), Objection(able), Objective(ness), Objector Ah, Aim, Ambition, Argue, Article, Bar, Beef, Case, Cavil, Challenge, Clinical, Complain(t), Conchy, Conscientious, Cow, Demur, Direct, End, Exception, Fuss, > GOAL, Her, Him, Impersonal, Improper, Indifferent, Indirect, Intensional, Intention, It, Item, Jib, Loathe, Mind, Moral, Niggle, Non-ego, Noumenon, Obnoxious, Offensive, Oppose, Outness, Plan, Plot, Point, Protest, Question, Quibble, Quiddity, Rebarbative, Recuse, Refuse, Resist, Retained, Sake, Scruple, Sex, Subject, Sublime, Target, Thing, Transitive, Tut, Ultimate, Unbiased, Virtu, Wart

▷ **Object** *may indicate* a grammatical variant

Objectless Intransitive

Oblate, Oblation Gift, Monk, Offering, Sacrifice

Oblige, Obliging, Obligation, Obligatory Accommodate, Affable, Behold, Binding, Burden, Charge, Compel, Complaisant, Compliant, Contract, Corvée, Debt, De rigueur, Duty, Easy, Encumbent, Force, Giri, Gratify, Impel, Incumbent, IOU, Mandatory, Must, Necessitate, Obruk, Promise, Recognisance, Sonties, Synallagmatic, Tie, Wattle

Oblique(ly) Askance, Askew, Asklent, Asquint, Athwart, Awry, Cross, Diagonal, Indirect, Perverse, Plagio-, Separatrix, Sidelong, Skew, Slanting, Solidus, Squint, Virgule
▷ **Oblique** *may indicate* an anagram
Obliterate(d) Annul, Blot, Dele(te), Efface, Expunge, Exterminate, Rase, Rast, Raze, Wipe
Oblivion, Oblivious Forgetful, Lethe, Limbo, Nirvana, Obscurity
Oblong Rectangular
Obnoxious Foul, Horrid, Offensive, Pestilent, Repugnant, Septic, Sod
Obscene(ly), Obscenity Bawdy, Blue, Fescennine, Gross, Hard-core, Indecent, Lewd, Lubricious, Paw(paw), Porn(o), Salacious, Smut, Vulgar
Obscure, Obscurity Abstruse, Anheires, Becloud, Befog, Blend, Blot out, Cloud, Cobweb, Conceal, Cover, Cryptic, Darken, Deep, Dim, Disguise, Eclipse, Encrypt, Envelop, Esoteric, Filmy, Fog, Hermetic, Hide, Indistinct, Mantle, Mist, Murk, Nebular, Night, Nubecula, Obfuscate, Obnubilate, Opaque, Oracular, Overcloud, Overshade, Overshadow, Recherché, Recondite, Shadowy, Tenebrific, Twilit, Unclear, > VAGUE, Veil, Vele, Wrap
▷ **Obscure(d)** *may indicate* an anagram
Obsequious Bootlicker, Brown nose, Creeping Jesus, Fawn, Fulsome, Grovelling, Menial, Parasitic, Pig, Servile, Sleeveen, Slimy, Subservient, Suck-hole, Sycophantic, Tantony, Toady
Observance, Observant, Observation Adherence, Alert, Attention, Comment, Custom, Empirical, Espial, Eyeful, Holy, Honour, Lectisternium, Mass, > NOTICE, Obiter dicta, Percipient, Recce, Remark, Right, Rite, Ritual, Vising
Observatory Arecibo, Atalaya, Greenwich, Herstmonceux, Hurstmonceux, Jodrell Bank, Lookout, Mount Palomar, Tower
Observe(d), Observer Behold, Bystander, Celebrate, Commentator, Detect, Espy, Eye, Fly-on-the-wall, Heed, Keep, Mark, NB, Note, Notice, Obey, Onlooker, Optic, Regard(er), Remark, Rite, Scry, See, Sight, Spectator, Spial, Spot, Spy, Study, Take, Twig, View, Voyeur, Witness
Obsess(ed), Obsession, Obsessive Besot, Bug, Bugbear, Craze, Dominate, Fetish, Fixation, Hang-up, Haunt, Hobbyhorse, Hooked, Idée fixe, Infatuation, Mania, Monomania, Necrophilia, Neurotic, One-track, Preoccupy, Thing
Obsolete, Obsolescence, Obsolescent Abandoned, Antique, Archaic, Dated, Dead, Defunct, Disused, Extinct, Latescent, Obs, Outdated, Outworn, Passé, Planned
Obstacle Barrage, Barrier, Boyg, Cheval de frise, Chicane, Dam, Drag, Dragon's teeth, Drawback, Gate, Handicap, Hindrance, Hitch, Hurdle, Node, Oxer, Remora, Rock, Sandbank, Snag, Stimie, Stumbling-block, Stymie, Tank-trap
Obstetrics Gynaecology, Midwifery, Tocology, Tokology
Obstinacy, Obstinate Asinine, Buckie, Bullish, Contumacious, Cussed, Die-hard, Dour, Entêté, Froward, Headstrong, Inflexible, Intractable, Intransigent, Mule, Persistent, Perverse, Pervicacious, Pig-headed, Recalcitrant, Refractory, Restive, Rusty, Self-will, Stiff(-necked), Stubborn, Thraward, Thrawart, Wilful
Obstreperous Noisy, Truculent, Unruly
Obstruct(ion) Bar, Block, Bottleneck, Chicane, Clog, Crab, Cross, Cumber, Dam, Embolus, Fil(l)ibuster, Gridlock, Hamper, Hedge, Hinder, Hurdle, Ileus, Impede, Let, Obstacle, Occlude, Sab(otage), Snooker, Stall, Stap, Stonewall, Stop, Stymie, Sudd, Thwart, Trammel, Trump
Obtain Achieve, Acquire, Cop, Exist, Gain, Get, Land, Pan, Prevail, Procure, Realise, Secure, Succeed, Wangle, Win

Obtrude, **Obtrusive** Expel, Impose, Loud, Prominent, Push, Sorn, Thrust

Obtuse Blunt, Dense, Dull, Purblind, Stupid, Thick

Obverse Complement, Cross, Face, Front, Head

Obviate Forestall, Preclude, Prevent

Obvious Apparent, Axiom, Blatant, Brobdingnag, Clear, Distinct, Evident, Flagrant, Frank, Inescapable, Kenspeck(le), Manifest, Marked, Open(ness), Open and shut, Overt, Palpable, Patent, Pikestaff, Plain, Pronounced, Salient, Self-evident, Stark, Transparent, Truism, Visible

Occasion Call, Cause, Ceremony, Encheason, Event, Fete, Field day, Nonce, > OPPORTUNITY, Reason, Ride, Sometime, Tide, Time

Occasional(ly) Casual, Chance, Daimen, Intermittent, Irregular, Motive, Orra, Periodic, Sometimes, Sporadic, While

Occident(al) West, Western(er)

Occlude, **Occlusion** Absorb, Clog, Coronary, Embolism, Obstruct

Occult(ist) Angekkok, Arcane, Art, Esoteric, I-ching, Magic, Mysterious

Occupant, **Occupation**, **Occupy(ing)** Absorb, Activity, Avocation, Beset, Business, Busy, Denizen, Embusy, Employ, Engage, Engross, Fill, Hold, In, Incumbent, Indwell, Inhabitant, Inmate, Involve, Line, Metier, People, Profession, Pursuit, Reserved, Resident, Runrig, Sideline, Squat, Stay, Tenancy, Tenant, Tenure, Thrift, Trade, Upon, Use, Vocation, Walk of life

Occur(rence) Arise, Be, Betide, Betime, Case, Contingency, Crop up, Event, Fall, Happen, Incident, Instance, Outbreak, Outcrop, Pass, Phenomenon

Ocean(ic), **Oceania** Abundance, Abyssal, Antarctic, Arctic, Atlantic, Blue, Deep, German, Hadal, Herring-pond, Indian, Melanesia, Micronesia, Pacific, Panthalassa, Pelagic, Polynesia, Sea(way), Southern, Thalassic, Waves, Western

Och aye Troggs

Ochre Keel, Ruddle, Sienna

Octave Diapason, Diminished, Eight, Great, Ottava, Perfect, Small, Utas

Octopus Blue-ringed, Cephalopod, Cuero, Devilfish, Paper nautilus, Polyp, Poulp(e), Scuttle, Squid

Octoroon Mestee, Mestizo, Mustee

Od Energy, Force

Odd (person), **Oddity** Abnormal, Anomaly, Bizarre, Card, Cure, Curio, Droll, Eccentric, Eery, Erratic, Gink, Impair, Imparity, Jimjam, Offbeat, Original, Orra, Outré, Paradox, Parity, Peculiar, Queer, Quiz, Random, Rare, Remote, Rum, Screwball, Singular, > STRANGE, Unequal, Uneven, Unmatched, Unusual, Weird, Whims(e)y

▷ **Odd(s)** *may indicate* an anagram or the odd letters in words

Odd job man Joey, Orraman, Rouster, Smoot, Thronner

Odds, **Oddments** Bits, Carpet, Chance, Gubbins, Handicap, Line, Long, Price, Short, SP, Tails, Variance

Ode Awdl, Dit, Epicede, Epicedium, Epinicion, Epinikion, Genethliacon, Horatian, Hymn, Lay, Lyric, Monody, Paeon, Pindaric, Poem, Sapphic, Song, Stasimon, Strophe, Threnody, Verse

Odin One-eyed, Woden

Odium, **Odious** Comparison, Disestimation, Disgrace, Foul, Hatred, Heinous, Invidious, Ponce, Repugnant, Stigma

Odorous, **Odour** Air, Bad, BO, Flavour, Funk, Good, Hum, Opopanax, Perfume, Quality, Redolence, Sanctity, Scent, Smell, Whiff

Odourless Silent

Odyssey Epic, Journey, Wandering

Oedipus Complex, Parricide

Oeillade Glance, Leer, Ogle, Wink

Oesophagus Crop

Oestrogen, Oestrus Frenzy, Heat, Mestranol, Must, Rut, Stilb(o)estrol

Of (me) About, Among, Aus, By, De, From, My, Re

▷ **Of** *may indicate* an anagram

Of course Certainly, Natch, Yes

Off Absent, Agee, Ajee, Away, Discount, Distance, Far, From, High, Inexact, Licence, Odd, Reasty, Reesty, Relache, Start

▷ **Off** *may indicate* an anagram

Offal Cagmag, Carrion, Chitterling, Entrails, Fry, Gralloch, Gurry, Haggis, Ha(r)slet, Heart, Innards, Kidney, Lamb's fry, Lights, Liver, Numbles, Sweetbread, Tripe, Variety meat

Off-beat Zoppo

Off-colour Pale, Seedy, Wan

▷ **Off-colour** *may indicate* an anagram

Offence Attack, Crime, Delict, Delinquency, Distaste, Fault, Huff, Hurt, Lapse, Miff, Misdemeanour, Misprision, Outrage, Peccadillo, Pip, Pique, Piracy, Regrate, Sedition, > SIN, Summary, Trespass, Umbrage, Violation

Offend(ed), Offender Affront, Anger, Annoy, Boobhead, Bridles, Culprit, Default, Disoblige, Displease, Distaste, Hip, Huff, Hurt, Hyp, Infringe, Inveigh, Miffy, Miscreant, Nettle, Nonce, Nuisance, Peeve, Provoke, Sin(ner), Stray, Transgress, Twoccer, Violate, Wrongdoer

Offensive Affront, Aggressive, Alien, Attack, Bombardment, Campaign, Cruel, Embracery, Execrable, Eyesore, Foul, Hedgehog, Hedgepig, Indelicate, Miasmic, Nasty, Noisome, Obnoxious, Obscene, Peccant, Personal, Push, Putrid, Rank, Repugnant, > RUDE, Scandalous, Scurrilous, Sortie, Storm, Ugly, Unbecoming

Offer(ing) Alms, Altarage, Anaphora, Bargain, Bid, Bode, Bouchée, Cadeau, Corban, Deodate, Dolly, Epanophora, Extend, Ex voto, Gift, Godfather, Hold, Inferiae, Invitation, Oblation, Overture, Peddle, Plead, Potla(t)ch, Present, Propine, > PROPOSAL, Propose, Propound, Sacrifice, Shewbread, Shore, S(h)raddha, Special, Stamp, Stand, Submit, Tender, Utter, Volunteer, Votive, Wave, Xenium

Offhand Airy, Banana, Brusque, Casual, Cavalier, Curt, Extempore, Impromptu, Indifferent, Snappy

Office(s) Agency, Bedelship, Box, Branch, Broo, Bucket shop, Bureau, Buroo, Caliphate, Chair, Colonial, Complin(e), Consulate, Crown, Daftar, Dataria, Dead-letter, Deanery, Den, Divine, Employment, Evensong, Foreign, Function, Holy, Home, Job, Land, Last, Left luggage, Lieutenancy, Little, Mayoralty, Met(eorological), Ministry, Missa, Mistery, Mudiria, Mutessarifat, Mystery, Nocturn, Nones, Obit, Oval, Palatinate, Papacy, Patent, Personnel, Pipe, Place, Plum, Portfolio, Position, Post, Prelacy, Press, Prime, Printing, Provosty, Record, Regency, Register, Registry, Rite, See, Seraskierate, Shogunate, Sinecure, Situation, Stationery, Tariff, Tenebrae, Terce, Ticket, Tierce, Tol(l)booth, Tribunate, Vespers, War, Yamen

Officer(s) Acater, Adjutant, Admiral, Ag(h)a, Agistor, Aide, Apparitor, Bailiff, Beatty, Bimbashi, Black Rod, Blimp, Blue Rod, Bombardier, Bos(u)n, Brass-hat, Brigadier, Bumbailiff, Capt(ain), Catchpole, Catchpoll, Cater, Centurion, Chamberlain, Chancellor, CIGS, Colonel, Commander, Commissioner, Commodore, Compliance, Constable, Cop(per), Co-pilot, Cornet, Coroner, Counter-round, Cursitor, Darogha, Datary, Deacon, Decurion, Duty, Earl

Marshal, Ensign, Equerry, Exciseman, Executive, Exon, Field Marshal, Filacer, Filazer, First, Flag, Flying, Gallant, Gazetted, Gen(eral), GOC, Group, Gunner, Havildar, Hayward, Hetman, Ima(u)m, Incumbent, Infirmarian, Intendant, Jamadar, Janty, Jauntie, Jaunty, Jemadar, Jemidar, Jonty, Jurat, Justiciar, Lance-sergeant, Liaison, Lictor, Lord High Steward, Lt, Marshal, Mate, Moderator, NCO, Number one, Nursing, Official Solicitor, Orderly, Oxon, Petty, Pilot, Pipe major, PO, Posse, Prefect, Prison, Probation, Proctor, Provost, Provost-marshal, Purser, Pursuivant, Quartermaster, Relieving, Remembrancer, Returning, Rodent, Rupert, Samurai, Sbirro, Schout, Sea Lord, Second mate, Select-man, Serang, Sergeant-major, Sewer, Sexton, Sheriff, Silver-stick, Skipper, SL, SM, Speaker, Staff, Striper, Sub(altern), Suba(h)dar, Subchanter, Sublieutenant, Supercargo, Superintendent, Tahsildar, Tidewaiter, Tindal, Tipstaff, Treasurer, Tribune, Usher, Varlet, Waldgrave, Warden, Wardroom, Warrant, Watch, Yeoman

Official(s), Officiate, Officious Aga, Agent, Amban, Amtman, Atabeg, Atabek, Attaché, Authorised, Beadle, Bossy, Bureaucrat, Catchpole, Censor, Chamberlain, Chancellor, Chinovnik, Claviger, Commissar, Commissioner, Consul, Count, Dean, Diplomat, Dogberry, Ealdorman, Ephor, Equerry, Escheater, Eurocrat, Executive, Fonctionnaire, > FORMAL, Functionary, Gauleiter, Gymnasiarch, Hayward, Incumbent, Inspector, Intendant, Jack-in-office, Jobsworth, Keeper, Landdrost, Lictor, Linesman, Mandarin, Marplot, Marshal, Mayor, MC, Meddlesome, Mirza, Mueddin, Mukhtar, Nazir, Notary, Ombudsman, Omlah, Overbusy, Palatine, Paymaster, Pleaseman, Plenipotentiary, Polemarch, Pontificate, Poohbah, Postmaster, Pragmatic, Prefect, Proctor, Procurator, Prog, Proveditor, Reeve, Regisseur, Registrar, Remembrancer, Shammash, Shammes, Sherpa, Silentiary, Souldan, Staff, Steward, Suffete, Suit, Syndic, Timekeeper, Tipstaff, Tribune, Trier, Trior, Turncock, Valid, Valuer General, Veep, Verderer, Verger, Vizier, Walla(h), Whiffler, Whip, Woodward, Yamen, Yeoman

Offprint Separate

Off-putting Dehortative, Discouraging, Manana, Negative, Procrastination, Rebarbative, Repellent, Yips

Offset Balance, Cancel, Compensate, Counter(act), Counterbalance

Offshoot Bough, Branch, Limb, Lye, Member, Outgrowth, Plant, Scion, Sien, Swarm

Offspring Boy, Burd, Chick, Children, Daughter, Descendant, Family, Fry, Get, Girl, Heir, Procreation, Product, Progeny, Seed, Sient, Son, Spawn

Offstage Wings

Often Frequent, Habitual, Repeated

▷ **Often** *may indicate* 'of ten'

Ogee Cyma, Moulding, Talon

Ogle Drake, Eliad, Eye, Glance, Leer, Oeillade, Wodewose

Ogre(ss) Baba yaga, Boyg, Brute, Eten, Etten, Fiend, Giant, Monster, Orc

Ohio Buckeye

Oil(y), Oil producer Aj(o)wan, Aleuritis, Anele, Anoint, Apiezon®, Argan, Attar, Balm, Balsam, Banana, Bath, Beech-mast, Ben, Benne, Benni, Bergamot, Bittern, Bone, BP, Bribe, Brilliantine, Butter, Cajeput, Cajuput, Camphire, Camphor, Camphorated, Canola, Carapa, Carron, Carvacrol, Castor, Chaulmoogra, Chaulmugra, Chinese wood, Chrism, Citronella grass, Clove, Coal, Coconut, Cod-liver, Cohune, Colza, Copra, Corn, Cotton-seed, Creasote, Creosote, Croton, Crude, Derv, Diesel, Dittany, Drying, Elaeis, El(a)eoptene, Essence, Essential, Ethereal, Eucalyptus, Eugenol, Evening primrose,

Extra virgin, Fatty, Fish, Fixed, Fuel, Fusel, Gas, Gingelli, Gingelly, Gingili, Golomynka, Good, Grapeseed, Grass, Groundnut, Guttiferae, Hazelnut, Heavy, Jojoba, Kerosene, Kerosine, Lamp, Lavender, Linalo(o)l, Linseed, Lipid, Long, Lubricant, Lumbang, Macassar, Magilp, Megilp, Menthol, Midnight, Mineral, Mirbane, Moringa, Multigrade, Musk, Mustard, Myrbane, Myrrhol, Naphtha, Neat's-foot, Neem, Neroli, Niger, Nim, Nimb, Nut, Oint, Oiticica, Oleo, Olive, Ottar, Otto, Palm, Paraffin, Parathion, Patchouli, Peanut, Pellitory, Petroleum, Picamar, Pomade, Poon, Poppy, Pristane, Pulza, Pyrrole, Ramtil, Rape, Rapeseed, Retinol, Ricinus, Rock, Rose, Rosin, Rusa, Safrole, Sandalwood, Sassafras, Savin(e), Sebum, Seed, Semsem, Sesame, Shale, Short, Sleek, Slick, Slum, Smalmy, Smarmy, Smeary, Snake, Spearmint, Sperm, Spike(nard), Spindle, Stand, Star-anise, Sunflower, Sweet, Tall(ow), Tolu, Train, Tung, Turpentine, Ulyie, Ulzie, Unction, Vanaspati, Vegetable, Verbena, Virgin, Vitriol, Volatile, Wallaba, Walnut, Whale, Wintergreen, Wood, Wool, Ylang-ylang, Yolk

Oilcake Poonac

Oilcan Pourie

Oilcloth American, Lino

Oilman Driller, Prospector, Rigger, Texan

Oil painting Master, Titian

Ointment Balm, Basilicon, Boracic, Boric, Cerate, Cream, Nard, Pomade, Pomatum, Salve, Spikenard, Theriac, Unguent, Vaseline®, Zinc

OK Agree(d), Approve, Authorise, Clearance, Copacetic, Copesettic, Go-head, Green light, Hunky-dory, Initial, Kosher, Right(o), Sanction, Sound, U, Vet

Okra Bhindi, Lady's fingers

Old(er), Oldie Ae(t), Aged, Aine(e), Ancient, Antique, Auld, Bean, Decrepit, Dutch, Fogram, Former, Gaffer, Geriatric, Glory, Golden, Gray, Grey, Hills, Hoary, Immemorial, Major, Methusaleh, Moore, Nestor, Nick, O, OAP, Obsolete, Off, Ogygian, One-time, Outworn, Palae-, Passé, Primeval, Ripe, Rugose, Sen(escent), Senile, Senior, Shot, Signeur, Stale, Trite, Venerable, Veteran, Victorian(a), Worn

Old boy, Old girl Alumnae, Alumnus, Fossil, OB

Old days Once, Past, Yore

Old English OE

Old-fashioned Aging, Ancient, Antediluvian, Antwackie, Arch(aic), Arriere, Bygone, Corn(y), Dated, Dowdy, Fuddy-duddy, Medieval, Museum piece, Neanderthal, No tech, Obsolete, Ogygian, Oldfangled, Outdated, Outmoded, Passé, Primeval, Quaint, Relic, Retro, Rinky-dink, Schmaltzy, Shot, Square, Square-toes, Steam, Stick-in-the-mud, Traditional, Uncool, Vieux jeu, Worm-eaten

Old hat Clichéd

Old maid Biddy, Spinster

Old man, Old woman Anile, Aunty, Bodach, Burd, Cailleach, Crow, Faggot, Fantad, Fantod, Fogey, Fogramite, Fogy, Fussy, Gammer, Geezer, Grandam, Grannam, Greybeard, Greyhen, Husband, Kangaroo, Luckie, Lucky, Methuselah, Mort, Mzee, OAP, Oom, Presbyte, Rudas, Trot, Trout, Wife, Wight, Woopie, Wrinkly

Old-timer Hourglass, Sundial, Veteran

Olid Fetid, Foul, High, Rancid, Rank

Olio Hash, Medley, Mess, Potpourri, Stew

Olive (grove), Olivine Calamata, Cerulein, Drupe, Dunite, Gethsemane, Kalamata, Olea(ster), Peridot, Queen

Oliver Bath, Cromwell, Goldsmith, Hardy, Noll, Protector, Twist

Olympian, Olympus Asgard, Athlete, Celestial, Elis, Pantheon, Quadrennium, Zeus

Omelette Crepe, Foo yong, Foo yung, Frittata, Fu yung, Pancake, Spanish, Tortilla

Omen Abodement, Absit, Augury, Auspice, Foreboding, Forewarning, Freet, Freit, Portent, Presage, Prodrome, Sign, Token, Warning

Omentum Caul, Epiploon

Ominous Alarming, Baleful, Bodeful, Dire, Dour, Forbidding, Grim, Inauspicious, Oracular, Sinister, Threatening

Omission, Omit Aph(a)eresis, Apocope, Apospory, Apostrophe, Asyndeton, Caret, Disregard, Drop, Elide, Elision, Ellipse, Ellipsis, Failure, Haplography, Haplology, Lipography, Loophole, Miss, Neglect, Nonfeasance, Oversight, Paral(e)ipomenon, Senza, Skip

Omnibus Anthology, Coach, Collection

Omniscient Encyclopedia

Omnivorous Pantophagous

On (it) Aboard, About, Agreed, An, An't, At, Atop, By, Game, In, Leg, O', Of, Oiled, Over, Pon, Re, Tipsy, Up(on)

▷ **On** *may indicate* an anagram

On account of Over

▷ **On board** *may indicate* chess, draughts, or 'SS' around another word

Once(r) Ance, > **AT ONCE**, Bradbury, Earst, Erst(while), Ever, Ex, Fore, Former, Jadis, Oner, Onst, Secular, Sole, Sometime, Whilom

One(self) A, Ace, Ae, Alike, An(e), Any, Body, Chosen, Eeny, Ego, Ein, Formula, Individual, Integer, Me, Monad, Per se, Single(ton), Singular, Solo, Tane, Un, Unit(y), Unitary, United, Us, Yin, You

One-act-er Playlet

One-eared Monaural

One-eyed Arimasp(ian), Cyclops

One-man band Moke

One o'clock 1 am, NNE

One-off Ad hoc

One-rayed Monact

Onerous Arduous, Exacting, Taxing, Tedious, Weighty

Onion(s) Bengi, Bonce, Bulb, Chibol, Chive, Cibol, Cive, Eschalot, Green, Head, Ingan, Jibbons, Leek, Lyonnaise, Moly, Pearl, Ramp, Ramson, Rocambole, Ropes, Scallion, Scilla, Shal(l)ot, Soubise, Spanish, Spring, Squill, Sybo(e), Sybow, Tree, Welsh

Onlooker Bystander, Kibitzer, Rubberneck, Spectator, Witness

Only Allenarly, Anerly, But, Except, Just, Meer, Merely, Nobbut, Seul, Singly, Sole

Onset Affret, Attack, Beginning, Charge, Dash, Ending, Rush, > **START**, Thrust

Onslaught Attack, Dead-set, Onset, Raid, Spreagh, Storm

On time Pat, Prompt, Punctual

Onus Burden, Charge, > **DUTY**, Responsibility

Onward Advance, Ahead, Away, Forth, Forward, Progress

Oodles Heaps, Lashings, Lots, Slather

Oolite Pisolite, Roestone

Oomph Energy, It, SA, Verve

Ooze Drip, Exhale, Exude, Gleet, Mud, Percolate, Pteropod(a), Seep, Sew, Sipe, Slime, Slob, Spew, Spue, Sweat, Sype, Transude

Opal(escent) Cymophanous, Fire, Gem, Girasol, Girosol, Hyalite, Hydrophane,

Liver, Menilite, Noble, Potch, Wood

Opaque, Opacity Dense, Dull, Intense, Leucoma, Obscure, Obtuse, Onycha, Roil, Thick

Open(er), Opening, Openness Adit, Ajar, Antithesis, Anus, Apert(ure), Apparent, Apse, Autopsy, Bald, Bare, Bat, Bay, Bole, Breach, Break, Broach, Buttonhole, Candid, Cardia, Cavity, Champaign, Chance, Chasm, Chink, Circumscissile, Clear, Crevasse, Dehisce, Deploy, Dispark, Door, Dup, Embrasure, Exordium, Expansive, Eyelet, Fair, Fenestra, Fissure, Fistula, Flue, Fontanel(le), Foramen, Frank, Free, Gambit, Gap, Gaping, Gat, Gate, Give, Glasnost, Glottis, Guichet, Gullwing, Hagioscope, Hatch, Hatchback, Hiatus, Hilus, > HOLE, Inaugural, Intake, Interstice, Intro, Key, Lacy, Lance, Lead, Loid, Loophole, Loose, Machicolation, Manhole, Meatus, Micropyle, Mofette, Moongate, Mouth, Oillet, Orifice, Oscule, Osculum, Ostiole, Ostium, Overture, Patent, Peephole, Pert, Pervious, Pick(lock), Placket, Plughole, Pore, Port(age), Porta, Porthole, Preliminary, Premiere, Prise, Pro-am, Public, Pylorus, Receptive, Rent, Riva, Room, Scuttle, Scye, Sesame, Sicilian, Sincere, Slit, Spare, Spirant, Squint, Start, Stenopaic, Stoma, Syrinx, Thereout, Touchhole, Trapdoor, Trema, Trou, Truthful, Unbar, Unbolt, Unbutton, Uncork, Undo, Unfurl, Unhasp, Unlatch, Unscrew, Unsubtle, Untie, Unzip, Vent, Vulnerable, Window

Open air Alfresco, Sub divo, Sub Jove

Opera Aida, Ariadne, Ballad, Bouffe, Buffo, Burletta, Carmen, Comic, Comique, Dramma giocoso, Electra, ENO, Ernani, Falstaff, Faust, Fedora, Fidelio, Glyndebourne, Grand, Hansel and Gretel, Horse, Idomineo, Iolanthe, Light, Lohengrin, Lulu, Macbeth, Met, Musical, Nabucco, Norma, Oater, Oberon, Onegin, Open Wingrave, Orfeo, Otello, Parsifal, Pastorale, Patience, Pinafore, Rienzi, Rigoletto, Ruddigore, Savoy, Scala, Seria, Singspiel, Soap, Space, Tell, The Met, Threepenny, Tosca, Turandot, Verismo, Werther, Work, Zarzuela

Opera-glasses Jumelle

Opera-lover Wagnerite

Opera-singer Baritone, Bass, Contralto, Diva, Savoyard, Soprano

Operate, Operation(s), Operative Act(ion), Activate, Actuate, Agent, Artisan, Attuition, Barbarossa, Caesarean, Campaign, Conduct, Couching, Current, Desert Storm, Detective, Exercise, Function, Game, Hobday, Holding, Keystroke, Liposuction, Logical, Manipulate, Mechanic, Mules, Overlord, Practice, Run, Sealion, Shirodkar's, Sortie, Strabotomy, Ure, Valid, Wertheim, Work

Operator Agent, Conductor, Dealer, Laplace, Manipulator, Nabla, Sparks, Surgeon

Opiate, Opium Dope, Drug, Hop, Laudanum, Meconin, Meconium, Narcotic, Religion, Soporific, Thebaine

Opinion, Opinionative Attitude, Belief, Bet, Consensus, Cri, Dictum, Dogma, Doxy, Entêté, Esteem, Feeling, Groundswell, Guess, Judgement, Mind, Parti pris, Private, Public, Pulse, Say, Second, Sense, Sentence, Sentiment, Tenet, Utterance, View, Viewpoint, Voice, Vox pop, Vox populi

Opossum Lie, Marmose, Phalanger, Tarsipes, Vulpine, Yapo(c)k

Oppidan Cit, Townsman, Urban

Opponent(s) Adversary, Antagonist, Anti, E-N, Enemy, E-S, Foe, Gainsayer, N-E, N-W, S-E, S-W, W-N, W-S

Opportune, Opportunist, Opportunity Appropriate, Apropos, Break, Carpetbagger, > CHANCE, Day, Equal, Facility, Favourable, Ganef, Ganev, Ganof, Godsend, Go-go, Golden, Gonif, Gonof, Heaven-sent, Occasion, Opening, Pat,

Photo, Room, Seal, Seel, Sele, Snatcher, Tide, Timely, Timous, Well-timed, Window

Oppose(d), Opposer, Opposing, Opposite, Opposition Against, Agin, Anti, Antipathy, Antipodes, Antiscian, Antithesis, Antithetic, Antonym, Argue, At, Au contraire, Averse, Battle, Black, Breast, Colluctation, Combat, Confront, Contradict, Contrary, Converse, Counter, Diametric, Dis(en)courage, Disfavour, Dissent, Distance, E contrario, Face, Foreanent, Fornen(s)t, Hinder, Hostile, Impugn, Inimical, Inverse, Militate, Mugwump, Noes, Object, Overthwart, Polar, Reaction, Reluct, Repugn, Resist, Retroact, Reverse, Rival, Shadow, Subtend, Syzygy, Teeth, Terr, Thereagainst, Thwart, Toto caelo, Traverse, V, Versus, Vis-a-vis, Withstand

Oppress(ion), Oppressive Airless, Bind, Burden, Close, Crush, Despotic, Incubus, Jackboot, Onerous, Overpower, Persecute, Ride, Stifling, Sultry, Tyrannise

Opprobrium Disgrace, Envy, Odium, Scandal

Oppugn Attack, Criticise

Opt, Option(al) Alternative, > CHOICE, Choose, Crown-jewel, Default, Elect, Facultative, Fine, Leipzig, Local, Menu, Pick, Plump, Select, Share, Soft, Trade(d), Traditional, Voluntary, Votive, Wale, Zero(-zero)

Optic(al), Optics Active, Adaptive, Electron, Fibre, Fire, Lens, Prism, Reticle, Visual

Optimism, Optimist(ic) Bull, Chiliast, Expectant, Feelgood, Hopeful, Morale, Pangloss, Pollyanna, Rosy, Sanguine, Upbeat, Utopiast, Yea-sayer

Opulent Abundant, Affluent, Moneyed, Rich, Wealthy

Opus Piece, Study, Work

Or Au, Either, Ere, Gold, Ossia, Otherwise, Sol

Oracle(s), Oracular Delphi, Dodonian, Mirror, Prophet, Pythian, Pythoness, Sage, Seer, Sibyl(line), Thummim, Urim, Vatic

Oral Acroamatic, Sonant, Spoken, Verbal, Viva, Viva voce, Vocal

Orange An(n)atta, Annatto, Arnotto, Aurora, Bergamot, Bigarade, Bilirubin, Bitter, Blood, Blossom, Calamondin, Chica, Claybank, Clockwork, Croceate, Flame, Flamingo, Fulvous, Jaffa, Kamala, Kamela, Kamila, Karaka, Kumquat, Mandarin, Mock, Naartje, Nacarat, Nartjie, Navel, Osage, Pig, Roucou, Ruta, Satsuma, Seville, Shaddock, Sour, Sweet, Tangerine, Tenné, Ugli, Ulsterman

Orang-utan Ape, Monkey, Satyr

Orate, Oration Address, Declaim, Eloge, Elogium, Elogy, Eulogy, Harangue, Panegyric, Philippics, Speech

Oratorio, Orator(y) Boanerges, Brompton, Brougham, Cantata, Cicero, Creation, Demosthenes, Diction, Elijah, Hwyl, Isocrates, Lectern, Morin, Nestor, Prevaricator, Proseucha, Proseuche, Rhetor, Samson, Spellbinder, Stump, Tub-thumper, Windbag, Yarra-banker

Orb Ball, Eyeball, Firmament, Globe, Mound, Pome, Sphere

Orbit Apse, Apsis, Circuit, Dump, Eccentric, Ellipse, Eye, Graveyard, Osculating, Parking, Path, Periastron, Perigee, Perihelion, Perilune, Periselenium, Polar, Revolution, Stationary, Synchronous

Orcadian Hoy

Orchard Arbour, Grove, Holt

Orchestra(te), Orchestration Chamber, Charanga, Concertgebouw, Concerto, ECO, Ensemble, Gamelan, Hallé, LPO, LSO, Palm-court, Pit, Ripieno, Score, SNO, String, Symphony

Orchid Adam and Eve, Adder's mouth, Arethusa, Bake-in-a-cradle, Bee, Bee-orchis, Bird's nest, Bog, Burnt-tip, Butterfly, Calanthe, Calypso, Cattleya,

Cooktown, Coralroot, Cymbidium, Cypripedium, Disa, Epidendrum, Fly, Fly orchis, Fragrant, Fringed orchis, Frog, Helleborine, Lady, Lady's slipper, Lady's tresses, Lizard, Man, Marsh, Military, Moccasin-flower, Monkey, Musk, Naked lady, Odontoglossum, Oncidium, Pogonia, Purple-fringed, Puttyroot, Pyramidal, Rattlesnake plantain, Salep, Scented, Slipper, Snakemouth, Soldier, Spider, Spotted, Swamp pink, Twayblade, Vanda, Vanilla

Ord Beginning, Point

Ordain Arrange, Command, Decree, Destine, Enact, Induct, Japan, Priest

Ordeal Corsned, Disaster, Preeve, Test, > TRIAL, Via Dolorosa

Order(ed), Orderly, Orders Acoemeti, Adjust, Affiliation, Alphabetical, Anton Piller, Apollonian, Apple-pie, Arrange, Array, Attendant, Attention, Attic, Avast, Bade, Banker's, Bankruptcy, Bath, Batman, Battalia, Bed, Behest, Benedictine, Bespoke, Bid, Book, Call, Camaldolite, Canon, Category, Caveat, CB, Chaprassi, Charter, Cheque, Chit, Chuprassy, Class, Coherent, Command(ment), Committal, Compensation, Composite, Corinthian, Cosmos, Court, Decorum, Decree, Demand, Dictate, Diktat, Direct(ion), Directive, Dispone, Distringas, Dominican, Doric, DSO, Edict, Embargo, Enclosed, Enjoin, En règle, Establishment, Eutaxy, Eviction, Exclusion, Feldsher, Fiat, Firing, Firman, Form(ation), Franciscan, Fraternity, Freemason, Garnishee, Garter, Gilbertine, Ginkgo, Grade, Habeas corpus, Heast(e), Hecht, Hest, Holy, Indent, Injunction, Interdict, Ionic, Irade, Khalsa, Kilter, Kosmos, Language, Lexical, Loose, Mail, Mandamus, Mandate, Marching, Market, Marshal, Masonic, Medjidie, Merit, Methodical, Minor, Mittimus, Monastic, Monitor, Natural, Neatness, Nunnery, OBE, Oddfellows, Official, OM, Open, Orange, Ord, Ordain, Organic, Pecking, Possession, Postal, Precedence, Precept, Premonstrant, Prescribe, Preservation, Provisional, Pyragyrite, Rank, Receiving, Reception, Règle, Regular, Religious, Restraining, Return, Right, Rule, Ruly, Sailing, Sealed, Search, Series, Settle, Shipshape, Short, Side, Standing, State, Statutory, Stop(-loss), Straight, Subpoena, Summons, Supersedere, Supervision, System, Tabulate, Tall, Taxis, Tell, Templar, Third, Thistle, Tidy, Trim, Tuscan, Ukase, Uniformity, Warison, Warrant, Word, Writ

▷ **Ordering** *may indicate* an anagram

Ordinal Book, Number, Second, Sequence

Ordinance Byelaw, Decree, Edict, Law, Prescript, Rescript, Rite, Statute

Ordinary Average, Banal, Bog standard, Canton, Chevron, Comely, Common (or garden), Commonplace, Cot(t)ise, Everyday, Fess(e), Flanch, Flange, Folksy, Grassroots, Hackneyed, Mediocre, Middling, Mundane, > NORMAL, O, OR, Plain, Prosy, Pub, Rank and file, Run-of-the-mill, Saltier, Saltire, Simple, Tressure, Trivial, Unexceptional, Uninspired, Usual, Workaday, Your

Ordnance Artillery, Cannon, Guns, Supply

Ordure Cess, Dung, Fertiliser, Manure

Ore Alga, Babingtonite, Bauxite, Bornite, Breunnerite, Calamine, Calaverite, Cerusite, Chalcocite, Chalcopyrite, Coffinite, Coin, Coltan, Copper, Crocoite, Element, Galenite, Glance, Haematite, Hedyphane, Horseflesh, Ilmenite, Iridosmine, Ironstone, Kidney, Limonite, Mat, Melaconite, Middlings, Millhead, Milling grade, Mineral, Minestone, Niobite, Oligist, Peacock, Phacolite, Pipe, Pitchblende, Proustite, Psilomelane, Pyrargyrite, Pyromorphite, Realgar, Red-lead, Schlich, Seaweed, Siderite, Sinoptite, Slime, Slug, Smaltite, Speiss, Sphalerite, Stephanite, Stilpnosiderite, Stream-tin, Tenorite, Tetrahedrite, Tin, Wad(d), White-lead, Yellow cake

Organ(s), Organic Adnexa, Anlage, Apollonicon, Appendix, Archegonium, Barrel, Biogenic, Calliope, Carpel, Chair, Chamber, Chemoreceptor, Chord,

Claspers, Clave, Conch(a), Console, Corti's, Cribellum, Ctene, Ear, Echo, Electric, Electronic, Electroreceptor, End, Essential, Exteroceptor, Feeler, Fin, Flabellum, Fundus, Gametangium, Gill, Glairin, Gonad, Hammond®, Hand, Hapteron, Harmonica, Harmonium, House, Hydraulos, Imine, Isomere, Kerogen, Kidney, Lien, Light, Liver, Lung-book, Means, Mechanoreceptor, Media, Medulla, Melodion, Ministry, Nasal, Natural, Nectary, Nephridium, Newspaper, Oogonia, Ovipositor, Palp, Pancreas, Parapodium, Part, Pedal, Photophore, Photoreceptor, Physharmonics, Pipe, Pipeless, Placenta, Plastid, Portative, Positive, Prothallus, Pulmones, Purtenance, Pyrophone, Radula, Receptor, Recit, Reed, Regal, Relict, Sang, Saprobe, Scent, Sense, Sensillum, Serra, Siphon, Spinneret, Spleen, Sporangium, Sporophore, Stamen, Steam, Stratocyst, Swell, Syrinx, Tentacle, Textual, Theatre, Theca, Thymus, Tongue, Tonsil, Tool, Tympanum, Uterus, Vegetative, Velum, Viscera, Viscus, Vitals, Voice, Voluntary, Womb, Wurlitzer®

Organise(d), Organisation, Organiser Activate, Anatomy, > ARRANGE, Association, Brigade, Caucus, Collect, Comecon, Company, Constitution, Coordinate, Design, Embody, Entrepreneur, Fascio, Firm, Impresario, Infrastructure, Jaycee, Ku Klux Klan, Logistics, Machine, Mafia, Marshal, Mobilise, Octopus, Orchestrate, Outfit, Personal, Quango, Rally, Regiment, Resistance, Rosicrucian, Run, Setup, Social, Soroptimist, Sort, Stage, Steward, System, Tidy, Together, UN

▷ **Organise(d)** *may indicate* an anagram

Organism Aerobe, Agamic, Being, Biont, Biotic, Cell, Chimeric, Chlamydia, Ciliate, Clade, Coral, Diplont, Ecad, Endogenous, Entity, Epizoite, Epizoon, Eucaryote, Euglena, Eukaryote, Germ, Halobiont, Halophile, Haplont, Holophyte, Holoplankton, Homeotherm, Incross, Infauna, Infusoria(n), Lichen, Macrobiote, Medusa, Meroplankton, Microbe, Moneron, Morphology, Nekton, Neuston, Paramecium, Pathogen, Phenetics, Plankter, Plankton, Protist, Protozoan, Radiolarian, Saprobe, Streptococcus, Symbion(t), Torula, Virino, Volvox

Organ-part, Organ-stop Bourdon, Clarabella, Diapason, Gamba, Montre, Nasard, Principal, Pyramidon, Quint, Salicet

Organ-tuner Reed-knife

Orgy Bacchanalia(n), Binge, Blinder, Bust, Carousal, Dionysian, Feast, Revel, Saturnalia, Spree, Wassail

Orient(al) Adjust, Annamite, Chinoiserie, Dawn, Dayak, E, East(ern), Fu Manchu, Hindu, Levant, Leyton, Malay, Mongolian, Pareoean, Shan, Sunrise, Tatar, Thai, Tibetan, Turk(o)man

Orifice Aperture, Blastosphere, Gap, Hole, Micropyle, Nare, Opening, Pore, Spiracle, Trema, Vent

Origen's work Tetrapla

Origin(al), Originate, Originating Abo, Adam, Arise, Beginning, Birth, Come, Cradle, Creation, Derive, Editio princeps, Elemental, Emanate, Epicentre, Etymon, Extraction, First, Firsthand, Focus, Found, Generic, Genesis, Genetical, Germ, Grow, Hatch, Incunabula, Initial, Innovate, Invent, Master, Mother, Nascence, Natality, New, Novel, Ord, Primal, Primary, Primigenial, Primordial, Pristine, Prototype, Provenance, Rise, Root, Seminal, Source, Spring, Start, Ur, Ylem, Zoism

Oriole Firebird, Hangbird

Orison Blessing, Prayer

Ormer Abalone, Haliotis

Ornament(al), Ornamentation Acroter(ia), Adorn, Anaglyph, Antefix,

Anthemion, Aplustre, Arabesque, Bahuti, Ball-flower, Barbola, Baroque, Barrette, Bead, Bedeck, Bez(z)ant, Billet, Blister, Boss, Bracelet, Breloque, Broider, Bugle, Bulla, Cartouche, Chase, Clock, Cockade, Corbeil(le), Cornice, Crocket, Cross-quarters, Curin, Curlicue, Decorate, Decoration, Diamanté, Die-work, Diglyph, Dog's-tooth, Doodad, Embellish, Emblem(a), Enrich, Epaulet(te), Epergne, Fallal, Fandangle, Fiddlehead, Figuration, Figurine, Filagree, Filigrain, Filigree, Fleuret, Fleurette, Fleuron, Florid, Fret, Fretwork, Frill, Frounce, Furbelow, Furnish, Gadroon, Gaud, Gingerbread, Gorget, Griff(e), Guilloche, Gutta, Headwork, Heitiki, Helix, Illustrate, Inlay, Knotwork, Labret, Lambrequin, Leglet, Macrome, Mantling, Mense, Millefleurs, Mordent, Moresque, Motif, Nail-head, Netsuke, Nicknackery, Niello, O, Okimono, Ovolo, Palmette, Parure, Paternoster, Paua, Pawa, Pectoral, Pendant, Picot, Pipe, Pompom, Pompo(o)n, Pounce, Pralltriller, Prettify, Prunt, Purfle, Quatrefoil, Rel(l)ish, Rocaille, Rococo, Spangle, Tassel, Tettix, Tiki, Tool, Torque, Torsade, Tracery, Trappings, Trill, Trimming, Trinket, Triquetra, Turn, Wally, Water-leaf, Whigmaleerie, Whigmaleery
Ornate Baroque, Churrigueresque, Dressy, Elaborate, Fancy, Florid, Flowery
▷ **Ornate** *may indicate* an anagram
Ornithologist Audubon, Birdman
Orotund Bombastic, Grandiose, Pompous, Rhetorical, Sonant
Orphan Annie, Foundling, Topsy, Ward
Orpiment Arsenic, Zarnich
Orpington Buff, Hen
Ort Bit, Crumb, Morsel, Remnant
Orthodox Cocker, Conventional, Hardshell, Proper, Sound, Standard
Orthorhombic Enstatite
Ortolan Bird, Bunting, Rail
Oscar Award, O, Wilde
Oscillate, Oscillation, Oscillator Dynatron, Excitor, Fluctuate, Librate, Parasitic, Rock, Seiche, Squeg, Swing, Vibrate, Waver
Osier Red, Reed, Sallow, Willow
Osmium Os
Osmosis Reverse
Osprey Fish-hawk, Ossifrage, Pandion
Osseous Bony, Hard, Skeletal, Spiny
Ostensibly Apparent, External, Seeming
Ostentation, Ostentatious Camp, Display, Dog, Eclat, Epideictical, Extravagant, Fantoosh, Flamboyant, Flash(y), Flaunt, Florid, Flourish, Garish, Gaudy, Highfalutin(g), Parade, Pomp, Ponc(e)y, Pretence, Puff, > SHOW(ING), Side, Splash, Swank, Tacky, Tulip
Ostracise, Ostracism Banish, Blackball, Boycott, Cut, Exclude, Exile, Petalism, Potsherd, Snub, Taboo, Tabu
Ostrich Em(e)u, Estrich, Estridge, Nandoo, Nandu, Ratite, Rhea, Struthio(nes), Titanis
Othello Moor, Morisco
Other(wise), Others Additional, Aka, Alia, Alias, Allo-, Alternative, Besides, Different, Distinct, Else, Et al, Etc, Excluding, Former, Further, Rest, Significant
Other things Alia
▷ **Otherwise** *may indicate* an anagram
Otiose Idle, Indolent, Ineffective, Lazy, Needless, Superfluous
Otis Bustard

Otter Edal, Paravane, Tarka
Otto Attar, Chypre, Mahratta
Ottoman Osmanli, Porte, Rumelia, Turk
Oubliette Dungeon, Pit, Prison
Ouch Brooch, Ornament, Ow
Ought All, Should
Ouida Ramee
Ounce Cat, Fluid, Liang, Oz, Panther, Tael, Uncial
Our(selves) Us, We
▶ **Ousel** *see* OUZEL
Oust Depose, Dislodge, Eject, Evict, Expel, Fire, Supplant, Unnest
Out Absent, Aglee, Agley, Asleep, Aus, Begone, Bowl, Dated, En ville, Exposed, External, Forth, Haro, Harrow, Hors, Oust, Skittle, Striking, Stump, Taboo, Uit, Unfashionable, Up, York
▷ **Out** *may indicate* an anagram
Out and out Absolute, Arrant, Rank, Sheer, Stark, Teetotal, Thorough, Totally, Utter
Outback Backblocks, Bundu, The mulga
Outbreak Epidemic, Eruption, Explosion, Flare-up, Plague, Putsch, Rash, Recrudescence
Outburst Access, Blurt, Bluster, Boutade, Evoe, Explosion, Fit, Flaw, Furore, Fusillade, Gush, Gust, Paroxysm, Passion, Philippic, Salvo, Storm, Tantrum, Tumult, Volley
Outcast Cagot, Discard, Eta, Exile, Exul, Ishmael, Leper, Mesel, Pariah, Rogue
Outcome Aftermath, Consequence, Dénouement, Effect, Emergence, End, Event, > RESULT, Sequel, Upshot
Outcrop Basset, Blossom, Crag, Creston, Inlier, Mesa, Spur, Tarpit
Outcry Alew, Bray, > CLAMOUR, Halloo, Howl, Hue, Protest, Racket, Shright, Steven, Uproar, Utas
Outdated Archaic, Dinosaur, Effete, Feudal, Fossil, Obsolete, Outmoded, Passé, Square
Outdo Beat, Cap, Picnic, Surpass, Top, Trump, Worst
Outdoor(s) Alfresco, External, Garden, Open air, Plein-air
Outer External, Extrogenous, Magpie, Superficial, Top
Outfit(ter) Accoutrement, Catsuit, Ensemble, Equipage, Fitout, Furnish, Get-up, Haberdasher, Habit, Kit, Rig, Samfoo, Samfu, Strip, Suit, Team, Trousseau, Weed(s)
Outflow Anticyclone, Discharge, Effluence, Eruption, Surge
Outgoing Egression, Exiting, Extrovert, Open, Retiring
Outgrowth Ala(te), Aril, Bud, Enation, Epiphenomenon, Exostosis, Offshoot, Root-hair, Sequel, Trichome
Outhouse Lean to, Privy, Shed, Skilling, Skillion, Skipper, Stable
Outing Excursion, Jaunt, Junket, Picnic, Sortie, Spin, Spree, Treat, Trip, Wayzgoose
Outlandish Barbarous, Bizarre, Exotic, Foreign, Peregrine, Rum
Outlaw Allan-a-Dale, Attaint, Badman, Ban, Bandit(ti), Banish, Exile, Fugitive, Hereward, Horn, Proscribe, Robin Hood, Rob Roy, Ronin, Tory, Waive
Outlay Cost, Expense, Mise
Outlet Débouché, Egress, Escape, Estuary, Exit, Femerall, Market, Opening, Outfall, Overflow, Sluice, Socket, Spout, Tuyere, Tweer, Twier, Twire, Twyer(e), Vent
Outline Adumbration, Aperçu, Circumscribe, Configuration, Contorno,

Contour, Delineate, Digest, > **DRAFT**, Esquisse, Footprint, Layout, Note, Perimeter, Plan, Profile, Prospectus, Relief, Scenario, Schematic, Shape, Silhouette, Skeletal, Skeleton, Sketch, Summary, Syllabus, Synopsis, T(h)alweg, Trace

Outlook Casement, Perspective, Prospect, View, Vista, Weltanschauung

Outmoded Wasm

▷ **Out of** *may indicate* an anagram

Out of date Corny, Obs, Passé, Scrap, Square, Worn

Out of form Amorphous, Awry

Out of order Fritz

Out of sorts Cachectic, Nohow, Peevish, Poorly

▷ **Out of sorts** *may indicate* an anagram

Out of tune Discordant, Flat, Scordato, Scordatura

Outpost Colony, Picquet

Outpour(ing) Effuse, Flood, Flow, Gush, Libation, Stream, Torrent

Output Data, Get, Produce, Production, Turnout, Yield

▷ **Output** *may indicate* an anagram

Outrage(ous) Affront, Appal, Atrocity, Desecrate, Disgust, Egregious, Enorm(ity), Flagrant, Insult, OTT, Rich, Sacrilege, Scandal, Shocking, Ungodly, Violate

▷ **Outrageously** *may indicate* an anagram

Outright Clean, Complete, Entire, Point-blank, Utter

Outset Beginning, Start

Outshine Eclipse, Excel, Overshadow, Surpass

Outside Ab extra, Crust, Exterior, External, Front, Furth, Hors, Periphery, Rim, Rind, Rine, Surface

Outsider Alien, Bolter, Bounder, Cad, Extern, Extremist, Foreigner, Incomer, Oustiti, Palagi, Pariah, Ring-in, Stranger, Stumer, Unseeded, Upstart

Outsize Capacious, Giant, Gigantic, Huge, OS

Outskirts Edge, Fringe, Periphery, Purlieu

Outspoken Bluff, Blunt, Broad, Candid, Explicit, Forthright, Frank, Plain, Rabelaisian, Round, Vocal

Outstanding Ace, Beaut(y), Belter, Billowing, Bulge, Chief, Egregious, Eminent, Especial, Exceptional, Extant, First, Fugleman, Highlight, Humdinger, Impasto, Jut, Lulu, Marked, Matchless, Oner, Owing, Paragon, Phenomenal, Pièce de résistance, Prince, Prize, Prominent, Promontory, Prosilient, Proud, Purler, Relief, Relievo, Salient, Signal, Special, Squarrose, Star, Stellar, Strout, Superb, Tour de force, Unpaid, Unsettled

Outstrip Best, Cap, Cote, Distance, Exceed, Overtake

Outward Efferent, Extern(e), External, Extrinsic, Extrorse, Extrovert, Posticous, Postliminary, Superficial

Outweigh Preponderate

Outwit Baffle, Best, Circumvent, Dish, Euchre, Fox, Over-reach, > **THWART**, Trick

Outwork Demilune, Jetty, Moon, Tenail(le), Tenaillon

Outworn Decrepit, Obsolete, Used

Ouzel Ring, Water

Oval(s) Cartouche, Cassini, Ellipse, Henge, Navette, Obovate, Ooidal

Ovary Oophoron

Ovation Applause, Cheer, Standing

Oven(-like) Aga®, Calcar, Camp, Convection, Cul-de-four, Dutch, Electric, Furnace, Gas, Haybox, Horn(it)o, Kiln, Lear, Leer, Lehr, Lime kiln, Maori, Microwave, Muffle, Norwegian, Oast, Oon, Stove

Over Above, Across, Again, Atop, C, Clear, Done, Finished, Hexad, Left, Maiden, Of, On, Ore, Ort, Owre, Sopra, Spare, Superior, Surplus, Uber, Yon
Overact Burlesque, Emote, Ham, Hell, Hoke
Overactive Hyper
Overall(s) Boiler suit, Denims, Dungarees, Dust-coat, Fatigues, Smicket, Smock, Tablier
Overbearing Arrogant, Dogmatic, Domineering, High-muck-a-muck, Imperious, Insolent, Lordly
Overbid Gazump
Overcast Cloudy, Lowering, Sew, Sombre
Overcharge Clip, Extort, Fleece, Gyp, OC, Rack-rent, Rook, Rush, Soak, Sting
Overcoat Benjamin, Benny, British warm, > COAT, Crombie, Dolman, Grego, Inverness, Joseph, Paletot, Petersham, Pos(h)teen, Prince Albert, Raglan, Redingote, Spencer, Surtout, Tabard, Taglioni, Ulster, Warm, Wooden, Wrap-rascal
Overcome Beat, Bested, Conquer, Convince, Defeat, Hit for six, Kill, Master, Mither, Prevail, Quell, Speechless, Subdue, Subjugate, Superate, Surmount, Vanquish, Win
Overcrowd Congest, Jam, Pack
Overdo(ne) Exceed, Ham, Hokey, Hokum, OTT, Percoct, Tire
Overdose OD
Overdraft Red
▷ **Overdrawn** *may indicate* 'red' outside another word
Overdress(ing) Dudism, Flossy, Overall
Overdue Behindhand, Belated, Excessive, Late
Overeat(ing) Binge, Gorge, Hypertrophy, Satiate
Overemphasize Rub in, Stress
Overfeed Gorge, Sate, Stuff
Overflow Lip, Nappe, Ooze, Ream, Redound, Spillage, Surfeit, Teem
Overfull Brimming, Hept
Overgrow(n) Ivy'd, Jungle, Ramp(ant), Rank, Rhinophyma
Overhang(ing) Beetle, Bulge, Cornice, > JUT, Project, Shelvy
Overhaul Bump, Catch, Overtake, Recondition, Revision, Service, Strip
Overhead(s) Above, Aloft, Ceiling, Cost, Exes, Hair(s), Headgear, Oncost, Rafter, Upkeep, Zenith
Overhear Catch, Eavesdrop, Tap
Overindulge(nt) Crapulent, Crass, Pig
Overjoy Elate, Thrill
Overland Portage
Overlap(ping) Correspond, Equitant, Imbricate, Incubous, Kern(e), Limbous, Obvolute, Stretto, Tace, Tasse
Overlay Ceil, Smother, Stucco, Superimpose, Veneer
Overlearned Pedantic
Overload Burden, Plaster, Strain, Surcharge, Tax
Overlook Condone, Disregard, Excuse, Forget, Miss, Pretermit, Superintend, Waive
Overlord Excess, Invasion
Overlying Incumbent, Jessant, Pressing
Overmuch Excessive, Surplus, Too, Undue
Overplay Ham, Hoke
Overpower(ing) Crush, Evince, Mighty, Onerous, Oppress, Overwhelm, Subdue, Surmount, Swelter, Whelm

Overpraise Adulate
Over-refined Dainty, Nice, Pernickety, Precious
Overrule Abrogate, Disallow, Veto
Overrun Exceed, Extra, Infest, Inundate, Invade, Swarm, Teem
Overseas Abroad, Colonial, Outremer
Oversee(r) Baas, Boss, Captain, Care, Deputy, Direct, Eyebrow, Foreman,
  Forewoman, Grieve, Handle, Induna, Moderator, Periscope, Steward,
  Supercargo, Survey(or)
Oversentimental Byronic, Slushy
Overshadow Cloud, Dominate, Eclipse, Obscure, Outclass
Overshoe Arctic, Galosh, Sandal, Snowboot
Oversight Blunder, Care, Error, Gaffe, Lapse, Neglect, Parablepsis
Overstate(ment) Embroider, Exaggerate, Hyperbole
Overstrained Epitonic
Overt Manifest, Patent, Plain, Public
Overtake Catch, For(e)hent, Lap, Leapfrog, Overget, Overhaul, > **PASS**,
  Supersede, Usurp
Overthrow Dash, Defeat, Demolish, Depose, Down, Labefact(at)ion, Ruin,
  Smite, Stonker, Subvert, Supplant, Topple, Unhorse, Usurp, Vanquish,
  Whemmle, Whommle, Whummle, Worst
Overture Advance, Carnival, Concert, Egmont, French, Hebrides, Intro, Italian,
  Leonora, Offer, > **OPENING**, Prelude, Propose, Sinfonia, Toccata, Toccatella,
  Toccatina
Overturn(ing) Catastrophe, Quash, Reverse, Tip, Topple, Up(set), Upend,
  Whemmle
Overvalue Exaggerate, Salt
Overweening Bashaw, Cocky, Excessive, Imperious, Presumptuous
Overweight Sunk
Overwhelm(ed), Overwhelming Accablé, Assail, > **CRUSH**, Defeat, Foudroyant,
  Inundate, KO, Mind-boggling, Oppress, Overcome, Scupper, Smother,
  Submerge, Swamp, Whup
Overwork(ed) Fag, Hackneyed, Ornament, Slog, Stale, Supererogation, Tax,
  Tire, Toil
Overwrought Frantic, Hysterical, Ore-rested, Ornate, Rococo
Ovid Naso
Ovum Egg, Oosphere, Seed
Owe(d), Owing Attribute, Due, OD
Owen Glendower
Owl(s) African, Barn, Barred, Blinker, Boobook, Brown, Bubo, Bunter, Chinese,
  Eagle, Elegant, English, Fish, Glimmergowk, Hawk, Hoo(ter), Horned, Howlet,
  Jenny, Little, Long-eared, Longhorn, Madge, Moper, Mopoke, Mopus, Night,
  Ogle, Parliament, Ruru, Saw-whet, Scops, Screech, Sea, Snowy, Strich, Striges,
  Strigiformes, Tawny, Wood
Own(er), Owning, Ownership Admit, Agnise, Confess, Domain, Dominium,
  Fess, Have, Hold, Mortmain, Nain, Of, Possess, Proper, Proprietor, Recognise,
  Reputed, Title, Use
Ox(en) Anoa, Aquinas, Aurochs, Banteng, Banting, Bison, Bonas(s)us, Buffalo,
  Bugle, Bullock, Cat(t)alo, Fee, Gaur, Gayal, Gyal, Kouprey, Mart, Musk, Neat,
  Ovibos, Rother, Sapi-utan, S(e)ladang, Steare, Steer, Stirk, Taurus, Ure, Urus,
  Water, Yak, Yoke, Zebu, Z(h)o
Oxford (group) Buchmanism, OU, Puseyism, Shoe
Oxhead Aleph

Oxidation, Oxide Alumina, Anatase, Ceria, Erbium, Eremacausis, Gothite, Gummite, Holmia, Kernite, Lithia, Magnesia, Nitrous, Psilomelane, Quicklime, Red lead, Rutile, Samarskite, Strontia, Thoria, Zaffer, Zaffre

▷ **Oxtail** *may indicate 'x'*

Oxygen (and lack of) Anoxia, Epoxy, Liquid, Lox, Loxygen, O, Vital air

Oyer Hearing, Trial

Oyster (bed), Oyster disease, Oyster-eater Avicula, Bivalve, Bonamia, Bush, Cul(t)ch, Kentish, Lay, Mollusc, Native, Ostrea, Ostreophage, Pandore, Pearl, Plant, Prairie, Salsify, Scalp, Scaup, Seed(ling), Spat, Spondyl, Vegetable

Oyster-catcher Sea-pie

Oyster-plant Gromwell, Salsify

Oz Amos, Australia

Ozone Air, Atmosphere, Oxygen

Pp

P Papa, Parking, Penny, Piano, Prince
PA Aide
Pabulum Aliment, Cheer, Food, Fuel, Nourishment
Pace, Pacemaker Canter, Clip, Cracking, Dog-trot, Easter, Gait, Geometruc, Jog-trot, Lope, Measure, Military, Pari passu, Pioneer, > **RATE**, Roman, Scout's, Snail's, Spank, Speed, Stride, Stroll, Tempo, Tramp, Tread, Trot
Pachyderm Armadillo, Elephant, Hippo, Mastodon, Rhino
Pacific, Pacify Appease, Bromide, Conciliate, Dove, Ease, Irenic, Lull, Mild, Moderate, Ocean, Placate, Placid, Quiet, Serene, Soothe, Subdue, Sweeten, Tranquil
Pacifist CO, Conciliator, D(o)ukhobor, Dove
Pack(age), Packed, Packing Bale, Blister, Bobbery, Box, Bubble, Bundle, Cards, Cold, Compress, Congest, Cram, Crate, Crowd, Cry, Deck, Dense, Dunnage, Embox, Entity, Everest, Excelsior, Face, Fardel, Floe, Gasket, Gaskin, Glut, Hamper, Hunt, Ice, Jam, Kennel, Knapsack, Load, Matilda, Pair, > **PARCEL**, Pikau, Power, Pun, Rout, Rucksack, Set, Shiralee, Shrink-wrap, Steeve, Stow, Suits, Tamp, Tread, Troop, Truss, Wad, Wet, Wolf, Wrap
Packet Boat, Bundle, Deck, Liner, Mailboat, Mint, Parcel, Pay, Red, Roll, Sachet, Steam, Steamboat, Wage
Pack-horse Sumpter
Packman Chapman, Hawker, Hiker, Pedlar, Tinker
Pact Agreement, Alliance, Bargain, Bilateral, Cartel, Contract, Covenant, Locarno, Munich, Suicide, > **TREATY**, Warsaw
Pad(ding) Batting, Bombast, Brake, Bustle, Compress, Crash, Cushion, Dabber, Damper, Dossil, Enswathe, Expand, Falsies, Filler, Flat, Frog, Gumshield, Hard, Hassock, Horse, Ink, Launch, Leg-guard, Lily, Nag, Note, Numnah, Patch, Paw, Ped, Pillow, Pincushion, Plastron, Pledget, Plumper, Pouf(fe), Protract, Pudding, Pulvillus, Scratch, Shoulder, Stamp, Stuff, Sunk, Tablet, Thief, Touch, Tournure, Tylopod, Tympan, Velour(s), Velure, Wad, Wase, Writing
Paddington Bear, Station
Paddle, Paddle boat, Paddle-foot Canoe, Dabble, Doggy, Oar, Pinniped, Seal, Side-wheel, Spank, Splash, Stern-wheeler, Wade
Paddock Field, Frog, Holding, Meadow, Park, Sacrifice
Paddy, Paddy field Fury, Ire, Irishman, Mick, Pat(rick), Pet, Rag, Rage, Sawah, Tantrum, Temper, Wax
Padre Chaplain, Cleric, Father, Monk, Priest
Paean Hymn, Ode, Praise, Psalm
Paedophile Nonce
Pagan Animist, Atheist, Gentile, Gentoo, Godless, Heathen, Idolater, Infidel, Odinist, Paynim, Saracen
Page(s), Pageboy Back, Bellboy, Bellhop, Bleep, Boy, Buttons, Callboy, Centrefold, Flyleaf, Folio, Foolscap, Front, Gate-fold, Groom, Haircut, Home, Hornbook, Leaf, Messenger, Moth, Octavo, Op-ed, P, Pane, PP, Problem, Quarto,

Ream, Recto, Ro, Servant, Sheet, Side, Squire, Tear sheet, Tiger, Title, Varlet, Verso, Web, Yellow

Pageant Cavalcade, Pomp, Spectacle, Tattoo, Triumph

Pagoda Temple, To

Pah Pish, Tush, Umph

▸ **Paid** *see* PAY

Pail Bucket, Kettle, Leglan, Leglen, Leglin, Piggin

Pain(ful), Pains Ache, Aggrieve, Agony, Ake, Algesis, Angina, Anguish, Arthralgia, Bad, Bale, Bedsore, Bitter, Bore, Bot(t), Bother, Burn, Colic, Cramp, Crick, Distress, Dole, Doleur, Dolour, Dool(e), Dysmenorhoea, Dysury, Eina, Excruciating, Fibrositis, Gip, Grief, Gripe, Growing, Gyp, Harrow, Heartburn, Hemialgia, > HURT, Ill, Kink, Laborious, Mal, Mastalgia, Mastodynia, Metralgia, Migraine, Misery, Mulligrubs, Myalgia, Neuralgia, Nociceptive, Pang, Persuant, Pest, Pleurodynia, Prick, Pungent, Rack, Raw, Referred, Sair, Sciatica, Smart, Sore, Sorrow, Splitting, Sten(d), Sting, Stitch, Strangury, Stung, Teen(e), Tene, Throe, Topalgia, Torment, Tormina, Torture, Twinge, Wrench, Wring

▷ **Pain** *may indicate* bread (French)

Painkiller Aminobutene, Analgesic, Bute, Cocaine, Distalgesic, Enkephalin, Jadeite, Meperidine, Metopon, Morphine, Number, Pethidine

Painlessness Analgesia

Painstaking Assiduous, Careful, Diligent, Elaborate, Exacting, Meticulous, Sedulous, Studious, Thorough

Paint(ed), Painting Abstract, Acrylic, Action, Airbrush, Alla prima, Aquarelle, Arcimboldo, Art autre, Art deco, Artificial, Art nouveau, Ash Can School, Barbizon, Bice, Blottesque, Camaieu, Canvas, Cellulose, Chiaroscuro, Clair-obscure, Clobber, Coat, Colour, Cubism, Dadaism, Daub, Dayglo, Decorate, Depict, Diptych, Distemper, Duco, Eggshell, Emulsion, Enamel, Encaustic, Fard, Fauvism, Finery, Finger, Flemish, Fore-edge, Fresco, Fucus, Genre, Gild, Gloss, Gouache, Grease, Grisaille, Hard-edge, Historical, Impasto, Impressionism, Intimism(e), Intonaco, Intumescent, Lead, Limn, Luminous, Magilp, Matt, Megilp, Mehndi, Miniate, Miniature, Modello, Mona Lisa, Monotint, Mural, Naive, Neo-Impressionism, Nightpiece, Nihonga, Nocturne, Non-drip, Oaker, Ochre, Oil, Old Master, Oleo(graph), Op art, Orphism, Paysage, Pentimento, Pict, Picture, Pigment, Pinxit, Plein air, Pointillism(e), Portray, Poster, Post-Impressionism, Predella, Primitive, Quadratura, Raddle, Rosemaling, Roughstuff, Sand, Scenography, Scumble, Secco, Sfumato, Sien(n)ese, Skyscape, Spray, Stencil, Stereochrome, Still life, Stipple, Suprematism, Tablature, Tachism(e), Tall-oil, Tanka, Tempera, Tenebrism, Thangka, Tondo, Ukiyo-e, Umber, Umbrian, Vanitas, Veduta, Vorticism, War, Wax

Painted woman Courtesan, Harlot, Pict, Tart

Painter > ARTIST, Blaue Reiter, Colourist, Cubist, Decorator, Gilder, Illusionist, Impressionist, Limner, Miniaturist, Paysagist, Plein-airist, Pre-Raphaelite, Primitive, Sien(n)ese, Soutine, Sunday, Yeats

Pair(ing) Brace, Cooper, Couple(t), Duad, Duo, Dyad(ic), Exciton, Fellows, Geminate, Item, Jugate, Link, Match, Mate, Minimal, Ocrea, Pigeon, Pr, Span, Synapsis, Syndyasmian, Syzygy, Tandem, Thummim, Twa(e), Tway, Two, Urim, Yoke

Paisley Orange, Shawl

Pakistan(i) Pathan

Pal Ally, Amigo, Bud(dy), China, Chum, Comrade, Crony, Cully, Mate

Palace Alhambra, Basilica, Blenheim, Buckingham, Court, Crystal, Edo, Elysee, Escorial, Escurial, Fontainebleau, Forbidden City, Fulham, Gin, Holyrood, Holyroodhouse, Hotel, Istana, Lambeth, Lateran, Linlithgow, Louvre, Mansion, Nonsuch, Palatine, Picture, Pitti, Quirinal, St James's, Sans Souci, Schloss, Seraglio, Serail, Shushan, Topkapi, Trianon, Tuileries, Valhalla, Vatican, Versailles

Paladin Champion, Charlemagne, Defender, Douzeper, Fièrabras, Ganelon, >KNIGHT, Ogier, Oliver, Orlando, Rinaldo, Roland

Palanquin Doolie, Litter, Palkee, Palki, Sedan

Palatable, Palatalized, Palate Cleft, Dainty, Hard, Moulle, Relish, Roof, Sapid, Savoury, Soft, Taste, Toothsome, Uranic, Uraniscus, Uvula, Velum

Palatial Ornate, Splendid

Palatinate, Palatine Officer, Pfalz

Palaver Chatter, Debate, Parley, Powwow, >TALK

Pale, Paling Ashen, Blanch, Bleach, Cere, Dim, English, Etiolate(d), Fade, >FAINT, Fence, Ghostly, Haggard, Insipid, Jewish, Lily (white), Livid, Mealy, Ox-fence, Pallescent, Pastel, Peelie-wally, Picket, Sallow, Shilpit, Stang, Verge, Wan, Whey-faced, White, Wishy-washy

Paleography Diplomatics

Pal(a)eolithic Acheulean, Acheulian, Chellean, Gravettian, Levallois(ian), Lower, Madelenian, Magdalenian, Middle, Perigordian, Solutrean, Strepyan, Upper

Paleozoic Silurian

Palestine, Palestinian Amorite, Gadarene, Intifada, Israel, Pal, Per(a)ea, PLO, Samaria

Palette Board, Cokuloris

Palindrome, Palindromic Cancrine, Sotadic

Palisade Barrier, Fence, Fraise, Stacket, Stockade

Pall Bore, Cloy, Damper, Glut, Mantle, Mortcloth, Satiate, Shroud

Palladium Defence, Pd, Safeguard

Pallas Athene

Pallet Bed, Cot, Couch, Mattress, Tick

Palliate, Palliative Alleviate, Anetic, Ease, Extenuate, Lessen, Mitigate, Reduce, Relieve, Sedative

Pallid Anaemic, Ashen, Insipid, Pale, Wan, Waxy

Palm Accolade, Areca, Assai, Atap, Babassu, Bangalow, Betel, Buriti, Burrawang, Bussu, Cabbage, Calamus, Carna(h)uba, Carnauba, Chamaerops, Chiqui-chiqui, Coco, Cohune, Conceal, Coquito, Corozo, Corypha, Cycad, Date (tree), Doom, Doum, Elaeis, Euterpe, Fan, Feather, Fob, Foist, Gomuti, Gomuto, Groo-groo, Gru-gru, Hand, Ita, Itching, Ivory, Jip(p)i-Jap(p)a, Jipyapa, Jupati, Kentia, Kittul, Laurels, Loof, Looves, Macahuba, Macaw, Macoya, Moriche, Nikau, Nipa, Oil, Palmyra, Paxiuba, Peach, Pupunha, Raffia, Raphia, Rat(t)an, Royal, Sabal, Sago, Sugar, Talipat, Talipot, Thenar, Toddy, Triumph, Troelie, Troolie, Trooly, Trophy, Vola, Washingtonia, Wax, Wine, Zatia

Palmer Lilli, Pilgrim

Palmerston Pam

Palmistry Ch(e)irognomy

Palm-leaf Frond

Palpable Evident, Gross, Manifest, Patent, Plain, Tangible

Palpitate Flutter, Pulsate, Throb, Twitter, Vibrate

Palsy Bell's, Cerebral, Paralysis, Shakes

Paltry Bald, Cheap, Exiguous, Mean, Measly, Peanuts, Pelting, Petty, Poor, Puny,

Scald, Scalled, Sorry, Tin(-pot), Tinny, Trashy, Trifling, Two-bit, Vile, Waff, Whiffet

Pamper(ed) Cocker, Coddle, Cosher, Cosset, Cuiter, Feather-bed, Gratify, High-fed, > INDULGE, Mollycoddle, Overfeed, Pet, Spoon-fed

Pamphlet Brochure, Catalogue, Chapbook, Leaflet, Notice, Sheet, Tract

Pan Agree, Auld Hornie, Bainmarie, Balit, Basin, Betel(-pepper), Braincase, Chafer, Dent, Dial, Drip, Dripping, Goat-god, Goblet, God, Hard, Ice-floe, Iron, Karahi, Ladle, Lavatory, Muffin, Nature-god, Pancheon, Panchion, Patella, Patina, Peter, Poacher, Preserving, Prospect, Roast, Salt, Search, Skid, Skillet, Slag, Slate, Spider, Vessel, Warming, Wo(c)k, Work

Panacea All-heal, Azoth, Catholicon, Cure(-all), Elixir, Ginseng, Parkleaves, Remedy, Tutsan

Panache Bravura, Crest, Dash, Flair, Paz(z)azz, Piz(z)azz, Plume, Pzazz, Show, Talent

Pancake Blin(i), Blintz(e), Burrito, Crêpe (suzette), Drop(ped)-scone, Flam(m), Flapjack, Flaune, Flawn, Fraise, Fritter, Froise, Pikelet, Poppadum, Quesadilla, Scotch, Slapjack, Spring roll, Suzette, Taco, Tortilla, Tostada, Waffle

Pancreas Sweetbread

Panda Bear-cat, Chi-chi, Chitwah, Common, Giant, Lesser, Red

Pandarus Go-between

Pandemonium Inferno

Pander Broker, Indulge, Pimp, Procurer, Toady

Pane Glass, Light, Panel, Quarrel, Quarry, Sheet

Panegyric Eulogy, Laudation, Praise, Tribute

Panel(ling) Adoption, Board, Cartouche, Children's, Dashboard, Fa(s)cia, Gore, Hatchment, Inset, Instrument, Jury, Lacunar, Mandorla, Mimic, Orb, Patch(board), People's, Rocker, Screen, Skreen, Solar, Stile, Stomacher, Tablet, Valance, Volet, Wainscot

Pang Achage, Ache, Crick, Qualm, Spasm, Stab, Stound, Twinge, Wrench

Pangloss Optimist

Pangolin Ant-eater, Manis

Panhandle(r) Beggar, W. Virginia

Panic Alar(u)m, Amaze, Consternation, Fear, Flap, Flat-spin, Fright, Funk, Guinea-grass, Lather, Millet, Raggee, Raggy, Ragi, Sauve qui peut, > SCARE, Scarre, Stampede, Stampedo, Stew, Tailspin, > TERROR

Panicle Thyrse

Panjandrum Bashaw

Pannier Basket, Cacolet, Corbeil, Dosser, Saddlebag, Skip, Whisket

Panoply Armour, Array, Pomp

Panorama, Panoramic Range, Scenery, Veduta, View, Vista

Pansy Gay, Heart's-ease, Herb-trinity, Kiss-me-quick, Nance, Powder-puff, Queer, Viola

Pant(s) Bags, Breeches, Capri, Cargo, Chaps, Chinos, Culottes, Deck, Dhoti, Drawers, Fatigues, Flaff, Gasp, Gaucho, Harem, Hot, Long johns, Longs, Parachute, Pech, Pedal-pushers, Pegh, Puff, Ski, Slacks, Smalls, Stovepipe, Sweat, Throb, Toreador, Training, Trews, Trousers, Wheeze, Yearn

Pantaloon Columbine, Dupe, Pants

Pantheism Idolatry, Immanency

Panther Bagheera, Black, Cat, Cougar, Grey, Jaguar, Leopard, Pink

Panties Briefs, Knickers, Scanties, Step-ins, Undies

Pantomime, Pantomime character Aladdin, Charade, Cheironomy, Dumb-show, Farce, Galanty, Harlequinade, Pierrot, Play

Pantry Buttery, Closet, Larder, Spence, Stillroom
Pap Dug, Mealie, Mush, Nipple, Teat, Udder
Papal, Papist Catholic, Clementine, Concordat, Guelf, Guelph, Pontifical, RC, Roman, Vatican
Paper(s), Paperwork, Papery Allonge, Art, Atlas, Ballot, Baryta, Bible, Blotting, Bond, Broadsheet, Broadside, Bromide, Brown, Building, Bumf, Bumph, Carbon, Cartridge, Cellophane®, Chad, Chinese, Chiyogami, Cigarette, Colombier, Command, Commercial, Confetti, Corrugated, Cream-laid, Cream-wove, Credentials, Crepe, Crown, Cutch, Daily, Decorate, Demy, Document, Dossier, Elephant, Emery, Emperor, Essay, Exam, File, Filter, Final, Flock, Folio, Foolscap, Fourdrinier, FT, Galley, Garnet, Gem, Glass(ine), Glumaceous, Grand Jesus, Graph, Greaseproof, Green, Guardian, Hieratica, India, Jesus, Journal, Kent cap, Kraft, Kutch, Lace, Laid, Lavatory, Legal cap, Linen, Litmus, Manifold, Manil(l)a, Marble, Mercantile, Mirror, MS, Munimenti, Music(-demy), News(print), Note, Oil, Onion-skin, Order, Packing, Pad, Page, Papillote, Papyrus, Parchment, Pickwick, Plotting, Position, Post, Pot(t), Pravda, Press, Print, Quair, Quarto, Quire, Rag, Ramee, Rami(e), Ream, Retree, Rhea, Rice, Rolled, Rolling, Royal, Satin, Saxe, Scent, Scotsman, Scrip, Scroll, Scrowl, Sheaf, Sheet, Silver, Slipsheet, Spoilt, Stamp, State, Sugar, Sun, Tabloid, Taffeta, Tap(p)a, Tar, TES, Test, Thesis, Thread, Tiger, Tissue, Today, Toilet, Torchon, Touch, Tracing, Trade, Transfer, Treatise, Treeware, Turmeric, Vellum, Velvet, Voucher, Walking, Waste, Watch, Wax(ed), Web, Whatman®, White, Willesden, Wood(chip), Worksheet, Wove, Wrapping, Writing, Zine
Paperback Limp(back)
Paper-cutting, Paper-folding Decoupage, Kirigami, Origami, Psaligraphy
Papier-mâché Carton-pierre, Flong
Par Average, Equate, Equivalent, > **NORMAL**, Scratch
Parable Allegory, Fable, Proverb
Parabola Arc, Curve, Hyperbola
Parachute, Parachutist Aigrette, Brake, Drag, Drogue, Extraction, Float, Golden, Jump, Para, Parabrake, Red Devil, Ribbon, Silk, Sky-diving, Skyman, Thistledown, Umbrella
Parade (ground) Air, Arcade, Cavalcade, Church, Concours d'elegance, Display, Dress, Drill, Easter, Emu, Flaunt, Gala, Hit, Identification. Procession, Identity, Maidan, March-past, Monkey-run, Pageantry, Passing-out, Pomp, Prom(enade), Sashay, Show, Sick, Ticker tape, Troop
Paradise Arcadia, Avalon, Bliss, Eden, Elysium, Fool's, Garden, Heaven, Lost, Malaguetta, Nirvana, Park, Regained, Shangri-la, Svarga, Swarga, Swerga, > **UTOPIA**
Paradox(ical) Absurdity, Cantor's, Contradiction, Dilemma, Electra, French, Gilbertian, Hydrostatic, Koan, Liar, Olber's, Puzzle, Russell's, Sorites, Twin, Zeno's
Paraffin Earthwax, Kerosene, Kerosine, Liquid, Ozocerite, Ozokerite, Photogen(e), Propane
Paragon Model, Non(e)such, Pattern, Pearl, Phoenix, Rose
Paragraph (mark) Balaam, Note, Passage, Piece, Pilcrow
Parakeet Parrot, Popinjay, Rosella
Parallax Annual, Daily, Diurnal, Geocentric, Heliocentric
Parallel Analog, Collimate, Corresponding, Equal, Even, Forty-ninth, Like
Parallelogram Rhomb
Paralysis, Paralyse Apoplexy, Cataplexy, Cramp, Curarise, Cycloplegia,

Diplegia, Halt, Hemiplegia, Infantile, Lithyrism, Monoplegia, Numbness, Palsy, Paraplegia, Paresis, Polio, Quadriplegia, Radial, Scram, Shock, Shut, Spastic, Spina bifida, Stun

Paramedic Ambulance-man

Paramilitary Phalangist, SAS, Sena

Paramount Chief, Dominant, Greatest, Overall, Premier, > **SUPREME**, Topless, Utmost

Paramour Franion, Gallant, Leman, Lover, Mistress, Thais

Paranormal Clairvoyant, ESP, Spiritual, Telekinesis

Parapet (space) Barbette, Bartisan, Bartizan, Battlement, Brisure, Bulwark, Crenel, Flèche, Machicolation, Merlon, Rampart, Redan, Surtout, Terreplein, Top, Wall

Paraphernalia Belongings, Equipment, Gear, Trappings

Parasite, Parasitic Ascarid, Autoecious, Babesiasis, Bilharzia, Biogenous, Biotroph, Bladder-worm, Bloodsucker, Bonamia, Bot, Candida, Coccus, Conk, Copepod, Crab-louse, Cryptosporidium, Cryptozoite, Dodder, Ectophyte, Endamoeba, Endophyte, Entophyte, Entozoon, Epiphyte, Epizoon, Facultative, Filarium, Flatworm, Flea, Gapeworm, Giardia, Gregarinida, Haematozoon, Hair-eel, Heartworm, Heteroecious, Hook-worm, Ichneumon, Inquiline, Isopod, Kade, Ked, Lackey, Lamprey, Leech, Leishmania, Licktrencher, Liverfluke, Louse, Lungworm, Macdonald, Mallophagous, Mistletoe, Monogenean, Necrotroph, Nematode, Nit, Obligate, Orobanche, Pinworm, Plasmodium, Puccinia, Pulix, Rafflesia, Redia, Rhipidoptera, Rickettsia, Roundworm, Schistosoma, Scrounger, Shark, Smut-fungus, Sponge(r), Sporozoa(n), Strepsiptera, Strongyle, Strongyloid, Stylops, Sucker, Symphile, Tapeworm, Tick, Toady, Toxoplasma, Trematode, Trencher-friend, Trencher-knight, Trichina, Trichomonad, Tryp(anosoma), Vampire, Viscum, Wheatworm, Worms

Parasol Awning, Brolly, En tout cas, Sunshade, Umbrella

Paratrooper Skyman

Parcel Allocate, Allot, Aret, Bale, Bundle, Holding, Lot, Package, Packet, Sort, Wrap

Parch(ed) Arid, Bake, Dry, Graddan, Roast, Scorched, Sere, Thirsty, Toast, Torrid

Parchment Diploma, Forel, Mezuzah, Panel, Papyrus, Pell, Pergameneous, Roll, Roule, Scroll, Sheepskin, Vegetable, Vellum, Virgin

Pard Leopard, Pal, Partner

Pardon(able), Pardoner Absolve, Amnesty, Anan, Assoil, Clear, Condone, Eh, Excuse, > **FORGIVE**, Grace, Mercy, Quaestionary, Qu(a)estor, Release, Remission, Remit, Reprieve, Venial, What

Pare Flaught, Flay, Peel, Shave, Skive, Sliver, Strip, Whittle

Parent(al) Ancestral, Father, Forebear, Genitor, Maternal, Mother, Paternal, Single, Storge

Parenthesis Aside, Brackets, Innuendo

Parhelion Sun-dog

Pariah Ishmael, Leper, Outcast, Pi(e)dog, Pyedog

Paris(ian), Parisienne Abductor, Athene, Elle, Gai, Gay, Grisette, Lutetia (Parisiorum), Lutetian, Maillotin, Midinette, Trojan

Parish Charge, District, Flock, Kirkto(w)n, Parischan(e), Parishen, Parochin(e), Peculiar, Province, Title

Parity Smithsonian

Park(ing) Algonquin, Amusement, Battery, Brecon Beacons, Business, Common, Country, Daintree, Dales, Dartmoor, Death Valley, Enclosure,

Etosha, Everglades, Exmoor, Fiordland, Forest, Fun, Game, Garage, Gardens, Grand Canyon, Green, Green lung, Grounds, Hwange, Hyde, Jasper, Jasper National, Jurassic, Kakadu, Kalahari Gemsbok, Katmai, Kejionkujik, Kobuk Valley, Kruger, Lake District, Lamington, Lung, Mammoth Cave, Mansfield, Mesa Verde, Motor, Mount Aspiring, Mount McKinley, Mount Rainier, Mungo, Nahanni National, Nairobi, National, Northumberland, Osterley, P, Paradise, Peak District, Phoenix, Pitch, Pittie-ward, Prater, Preserve, Rec, Regent's, Riding Mountain, Safari, Sanctuary, Sandown, Science, Sequoia, Sequoia National, Serengeti, Shenandoah, Shenandoah National, Siding, Snowdonia, Stand, Stop, Theme, Trailer, Tsavo, Valet, Wildlife, Wind, Wood Buffalo, Yard, Yellowstone, Yosemite

Parker Dorothy, Nos(e)y

Parkleaves Tutsan

Parley Confer, Discourse, Palaver, Speak, Tret

Parliament Addled, Althing, Barebones, Black, Boule, Bundestag, Commons, Congress, Cortes, Council, Cross-bench, Dail, Diet, D(o)uma, Drunken, Eduskunta, European, Folketing, House, Imperial, Knesset, Lack-learning, Lagt(h)ing, Landst(h)ing, Lawless, Legislature, Lok Sabha, Long, Lords, Majlis, Merciless, Mongrel, Odelst(h)ing, Political, Rajya Sabha, Reichsrat, Reichstag, Riksdag, Rump, St Stephens, Sanhedrin, Seanad, Seanad Eireann, Sejm, Short, Stannary, States-general, Stirthing, Stormont, Stort(h)ing, Thing, Tynwald, Tynwald (Court), Unicameral, Unlearned, Useless, Vidhan Sabha, Volkskammer, Volksraad, Westminster

Parliamentarian Cabinet, Fairfax, Ireton, Leveller, Member, MP, Roundhead, Whip

Parlour Beauty, Funeral, Lounge, Massage, Milking, Salon, Snug

Parnassus Museum, Verse

Parody Burlesque, Cod, Lampoon, Mock, Piss-take, Satire, Sendup, Skit, Spoof, Travesty

Parole Pledge, Promise, Trust, Word

Paronychia Agnail, Felon, Whitlow

Paroxysm Fit, Frenzy, Rapture, Spasm, Subintrant, Throe

Parricide Cenci

Parrot Amazon, Cockatoo, Conure, Copy, Flint, Green leek, Grey, Imitate, Kaka(po), Kea, Lorikeet, Lory, Lovebird, Macaw, Mimic, Nestor, Owl, Parakeet, Paroquet, Poll(y), Popinjay, Psittacine, Quarrion, Repeat, Rosella, Rote, Stri(n)gops, T(o)uraco

Parrot-bill Glory-pea

Parry Block, Counter, Defend, Dodge, Forestall, Parade, Riposte, Sixte, Tac-au-tac, Thwart, Ward

Parsee Zoroastrian

Parsimonious, Parsimony Cheese-paring, Mean, Narrow, Near(ness), Niggardly, Stingy, Tight

Parsley Apiol, Cicely, Dog, Kecks, Kex, Persillade, Pot-herb

Parsnip Buttered, Buttery, Dill, Masterwort, Sium, Skirret

Parson Clergyman, Cleric, Minister, Non juror, Pastor, Priest, Rector, Rev, Sky-pilot, Soul-curer, Yorick

Part(s), Parting Accession, Aliquot, Antimere, Area, Aught, Bulk, Bye, Cameo, Character, Chunk, Cog, Component, Constituent, Crack, Cue, Dislink, Diverge, Dole, Element, Episode, Escapement, Farewell, Fascicle, Fork, Fraction, Goodbye, Half, Instalment, Into, Lathe, Lead, Leave, Leg, Lill, Lilt, Lines, List, Livraison, Member, Meronym, Parcel, Passus, > PIECE, Portion, Primo,

Principal, Private, Proportion, Pt, Quota, Rape, Ratio, Region, Rive, Role, Scena, Scene, Secondo, Section, Sector, Segment, Separate, Serial, Sever, Shade, Share, Shed, Sleave, Sle(i)ded, > **SOME**, Spare, Split, Stator, Sunder, Synthon, Tithe, Unit, Vaunt, Voice, Walk on, Wrench

Partake(r) Allottee, Eat, Participate, Share

Parthenogenesis Deuterotoky, Thelytoky

Partial(ity), Partially Biased, Ex-parte, Fan, Favour, Halflins, Imbalance, Incomplete, One-sided, Predilection, Slightly, Unequal, Weakness

Participate Engage, Join, Partake, Share

Participle Dangling, Misrelated, Past, Perfect, Present

Particle(s) Alpha, Anion, Antineutron, Antiproton, Atom, Baryon, Beta, Bit, Boson, Corpuscle, Curn, Dander, Delta, Deuteron, Effluvium, Elementary, Fermion, Fleck, Fragment, Fundamental, Gauge boson, Gemmule, Globule, Gluon, Grain, Granule, Graviton, Hadron, Heavy, Higgs, Hyperon, Ion, J, Jot, J/psi, Kaon, Lambda, Lemail, Lemel, Lepton, Meson, Micelle, Microsome, Mite, Molecule, Mote, Muon, Neutrino, Neutron, Nibs, Nobiliary, Omega-minus, Parton, Photon, Pion, Plasmagene, Platelet, Positron, Prion, Proton, Psi(on), Quark, Radioactivity, Shower, Sigma, Sinter, Smithereen, Spark, Speck, Strange, Subatom, Tachyon, Tardyon, Tau neutrino, Tauon, Thermion, Tittle, Virion, W, Whit, WIMP, X-hyperon, Z

Parti-coloured Fancy, Motley, Piebald, Pied, Variegated

Particular Choosy, Dainty, > **DETAIL**, Endemic, Especial, Essential, Express, Fiky, Fog, Fussy, Item, Itself, London fog, Nice, Niffy-naffy, Own, Pea-souper, Peculiar, Pernickety, Pet, Point, Prim, Proper, > **RESPECT**, Special, Specific, Stickler, Strict, Stripe

Partisan Adherent, Axe, Biased, Carlist, Champion, Devotee, Factional, Fan, Irregular, Partial, Provo, Sider, Spear, Supporter, Yorkist

Partition(ed) Abjoint, Bail, Barrier, Brattice, Bretasche, Bulkhead, Cloison, Cubicle, Diaphragm, Dissepiment, Division, Hallan, Mediastinum, Parpane, Parpen(d), Parpent, Parpoint, Perpend, Perpent, Replum, > **SCREEN**, Scriene, Septum, Tabula, Wall, With

Partlet Hen, Overlaid

Partner(ship) Accomplice, Ally, Associate, Bidie-in, Butty, Cahoot(s), Coachfellow, Cohab(itee), Cohabitor, Colleague, Comrade, Confederate, Consort, Copemate, Couple, Dutch, Escort, E-W, Firm, Gigolo, Mate, N-S, Oppo, Pal, Pard, Sidekick, Silent, Sleeping, Sparring, Spouse, Stablemate, Stand, Symbiosis

▷ **Part of** *may indicate* a hidden word

Partridge Bird, Chik(h)or, Chukar, Chukor, Covey, Quail, Red-legged, Tinamou, Ynambu

Party Acid house, Alliance, Apparat, Assembly, At-home, Ba'ath, Ball, Band, Barbecue, Bash, Beano, Bee, Bloc, Blowout, Body, Bottle, Bunfight, Bust, Caboodle, Camp, Carousal, Carouse, Caucus, Celebration, Clambake, Cocktail, Commando, Communist, Concert, Congress, Conservative, Contingent, Cookie-shine, Cooperative, Coterie, Cult, Democratic, Detail, Ding, Discotheque, Do, Drum, Faction, Falange, Federalist, Fest, Fête champêtre, Fête Galante, Fianna Fáil, Fine Gael, Firing, Funfest, Gala, Gang, Garden, Green, Greenback, Grumbletonian, Guelf, Guelph, Guilty, Hen, High heels, Hoedown, Hooley, Hoot(a)nannie, Hoot(a)nanny, Hootenannie, Hootenanny, House, Housewarming, Hurricane, Irredentist, Jol(lities), Junket, Junto, Kettledrum, Kitchen tea, Klat(s)ch, Knees-up, Kuomintang, L, Labour, Launch, Lib, Liberal, Love-in, Low heels, Luau, Mallemaroking, Mollie, Musicale,

National, Neck-tie, Octobrist, Opposition, Orgy, People's, Person, Petting, Plaid, Progressive, Prohibition, Pyjama, Rage, Rave, Rave-up, Razzle(-dazzle), Reception, Republican, Revel, Ridotto, Rocking, Rort, Rout, SDP, Search, Sect, Set, Shindig, Shine, Shivoo, Shower, Shower tea, Side, Slumber, Smoker, SNP, Soc(ialist), Social, Social credit, Social Democratic, Soiree, Spree, Squad(rone), Squadrone volante, Stag, Symposium, Tailgate, Tea, Teafight, Third, Thrash, Tory, Treat, Ultramontane, Unionist, United, Wafd, Warehouse, Whig, Whoop-de-do(o), Wine, Wingding, Working
Partygoer Raver, Reveller, Socialite
Party-piece Solo
Parvenu Arriviste, Upstart
Pascal Blaise, Pa, Pressure
Pash Crush, Devotion
Pasha Achmed, Dey, Emir, Ismet
Pass(ed), Passing, Pass on, Past Ago, Agon, Annie Oakley, Aorist, Approve, Arise, Arlberg, Before, Behind, Bernina, Beyond, Bolan, Botte, Brenner, Brief, By, Bygone, Caudine Forks, Cerro Vordo, Chal(l)an, Chilkoot, Chine, Chit(ty), Clear, Col, Cote, Cross, Cursory, Death, Defile, Delate, Demise, Diadron, Die, Disappear, Double, Elapse, Emit, Enact, End, Ensue, Ephemeral, Exceed, Exeat, Faena, Foist, Forby, Forgone, Former, Forward, Gap, Gate, Gha(u)t, Glencoe, Glide, Go, Great St Bernard, Gulch, Halse, Hand, Happen, Hause, Hospital, Impart, Impermanent, In transit, Jark, Khyber, Killiecrankie, Kloof, La Cumbre, Lap, Late, Lead, Long syne, Mesmerism, Migrate, Moravian Gate, Mount Cenis, Nek, Notch, Nutmeg, Nye, Occur, Oer, OK, Okay, Oke, Omit, One-time, Overhaul, Overshoot, Overslaugh, Overtake, Pa, Palm, Participle, Perish, Permeate, Permit, Perpetuate, Poll, Poort, Predicament, Preterit(e), Pretty, Proceed, Propagate, Pun(c)to, Qualify, Railcard, Reach, Reeve, Refer, Relay, Retroactive, Retrospect, Reverse, Roncesvalles, Safe conduct, St Bernard, St Gotthard, San Bernardino, Sanitation, Scissors, Senile, Serve, Shipka, Simplon, Since, Skim, Skip, Skirt, Slap, Sling, Snap, Spend, Stab, State, Thermopylae, Thread, Through, Ticket, Tip, Transient, Transilient, Transitory, Transmit, Transude, Travel, Triptyque, Troop, Uspallata, Veronica, Vet, Visa, Visé, Wall, Wayleave, Weather, While, Wrynose, Yesterday, Yesteryear, Ygoe
Passable Adequate, Fair, Navigable, Tolerable
Passage Adit, Airway, Aisle, Alley(way), Alure, Apostrophe, Arcade, Archway, Areaway, Arterial, Atresia, Breezeway, Bylane, Cadenza, Caponier(e), Career, Channel, Chute, Citation, Clause, Close, Coda, Conduit, Corridor, Creep, Crossing, Crush, Cundy, Dead-end, Deambulatory, Defile, Drake, Drift, Duct, Eel-fare, Episode, Excerpt, Extract, Fare, Fat, Fistula, Flat, Flight, Flue, Gallery, Gangway, Gap, Gat, Gate, Ginnel, Gut, Hall, Head, Inlet, Journey, Kyle, Lane, Lapse, Larynx, Loan, Lobby, Locus, Meatus, Melisma, Middle, Mona, Movement, Northeast, Northwest, Para(graph), Path, Pend, Pericope, Phrase, Pore, Portion, Prelude, Prose, Purple, Ride, Ripieno, Rite, Ritornell(o), Rough, Route, Sailing, Screed, Shaft, Shunt, Slap, Slype, Snicket, Sprue, Strait, Street, Stretta, Stretto, Subway, Sump, Text, Thirl, Thorough(fare), Throat, Tour, Trachea, Trance, Transe, Transit(ion), Travel, Tunnel, Tutti, Undercast, Unseen, Ureter, Voyage, Way, Windpipe
▷ **Passage of arms** *may indicate* 'sleeve'
Passé Corny, Dated, Ex, Obsolete
Passenger(s) Cad, Commuter, Fare, Payload, Pillion, Rider, Slacker, Steerage, Straphanger, Transit, Traveller, Voyager, Way, Wayfarer
Passion(ate), Passionately Anger, Appetite, Ardour, Con fuoco, Fervour, Fire,

Flame, Frampold, Fury, Gust, Gutsy, Hate, Heat, Hot, Hunger, Hwyl, Ileac, Iliac, Intense, Ire, Irish, Kama, Love, Lust, Mania, Obsession, Oestrus, Rage, Reverent, Stormy, Sultry, Torrid, Violent, Warm, Wax, Wrath, Yen, Zeal

Passion-fruit Water-lemon

Passion play Oberammergau

Passive (stage) Apathetic, Dormant, Inert, Pathic, Patient, Pupa, Supine, Yielding

Pass out Faint, Graduate, Swarf, Swarve, Swoon

Passover Agadah, Haggada, Omer, Pesach

Passport Access, Clearance, Congé(e), ID, Key, Laissez-passer, Nansen, Navicert, Sea-letter, Visa, Visitor's

Password Code, Countersign, Logon, Nayword, Parole, Sesame, Shibboleth, Sign, Tessera, Watchword

▶ **Past** *see* PASS

Pasta Agnolotti, Cannelloni, Capelletti, Cellentani, Conchiglie, Durum, Farfal, Farfel, Fedelini, Fettuc(c)ine, Fusilli, Gnocch(ett)i, Lasagna, Lasagne, Linguini, Macaroni, Manicotti, Noodles, Orzo, Penne, Perciatelli, Ravioli, Rigatoni, Ruote, Spaghetti, Spaghettina, Tagliarini, Tagliatelle, Tortelli(ni), Vermicelli, Ziti

Paste, Pasty Ashen, Batter, Beat, Berbere, Botargo, Boule, Bridie, Cerate, Clobber, Cornish, Dentifrice, Dough, Electuary, Fake, Filler, Fondant, Frangipane, Glue, Guarana, Hard, Harissa, Knish, Lute, Magma, Marzipan, Masala, Mastic, Miso, Mountant, Pale, Pallid, Pâté, Patty, Pearl-essence, Pie, Piroshki, Pirozhki, Poonac, Punch, Putty, Rhinestone, Rout, Slip, Slurry, Soft, Spread, Strass, Tahina, Tahini, Tapenade, Taramasalata, Wan

Pastern Hobble, Knee, Tether

Pastiche Cento, Collage, Medley, Patchwork, Potpourri

Pastille Jujube, Lozenge

Pastime Diversion, Game, Hobby, Recreation, Seesaw, Sport

Past master Champion, Expert, Historian, Pro

Past midnight 1 am

Pastor(al) Arcadia, Bucolic, Curé, Eclogue, Endymion, Idyl(l), Minister, Priest, Rector, Rural, Shepherd, Simple

Pastry Apfelstrudel, Baclava, Bakemeat, Baklava, Beignet, Bouchée, Brik, Calzone, Chausson, Choux, Clafoutis, Coquile, Creamhorn, Cream puff, Croustade, Cruller, Crust, Danish, Dariole, Dough, Eclair, Empanada, Feuilleté, Filo, Flaky, Flan, Frangipane, French, Gougère, Hamantasch, Millefeuille, Phyllo, Pie, Pie-crust, Pirog, Piroshki, Pirozhki, Profiterole, Puff, Quiche, Rough-puff, Rug(g)elach, Samosa, Shortcrust, Strudel, Tart, Turnover, Vol-au-vent

Pasture Alp, Eadish, Eddish, Feed, Fell, Fodder, Grassland, Graze, Herbage, Kar(r)oo, Lair, Lare, Lea, Lease, Leasow(e), Leaze, Ley, Machair, Mead(ow), Pannage, Potrero, Raik, Rake, Soum, Sowm, Tie, Transhume, Tye

▶ **Pasty** *see* PASTE

Pat Apt, Bog-trotter, Butter, Chuck, Clap, Dab, Glib, Lump, Print, Prompt, Rap, Slap, Tap

Patch(y) Bed, Bit, Cabbage, Clout, Coalsack, Cobble, Cooper, Court plaster, Cover, Friar, Fudge, > MEND, Mosaic, Nicotine, Pasty, Piebald, Piece, Plage, Plaque, Plaster, Pot, Purple, Shinplaster, Shoulder, Solder, Tingle, Tinker, Vamp, Variegated

Patchwork Cento, Miscellany, Mosaic, Piecing

Pate, Pâté Crown, Paste, Rillettes, Taramasalata, Terrine

Patent(ed) Breveté, Copyright, Evident, Letters, Licence, License, Obvious, Overt, Plain, Rolls
Pater(nity) Father, Filiation, Walter
Paterfamilias Coarb, Master
Path(way) Aisle, Allée, Alley, Arc, Berm, Berme, Boreen, Borstal(l), Bridle, Byroad, Causeway, Causey, Clickstream, Course, Eclipse, Embden-Meyerhof, Flare, Flight, Garden, Gate, Gennel, Ginnel, Glide, Lane, Ley, Locus, Mean-free, Metabolic, Orbit, Pad, Parabola, Primrose, Ride, Ridgeway, Route, Run, Runway, Sidewalk, Spurway, Stie, Sty(e), Swath(e), Tow, Track, Trail, Trajectory, Trod, Walkway, > WAY, Xystus
Pathan Pakhto, Pakhtu, Pashto, Pashtu, Pushto(o), Pushtu
Pathetic(ally) Doloroso, Drip, Forlorn, Piss-poor, Piteous, Poignant, Sad, Schnook, Touching
Pathfinder Compass, Explorer, Guide, Pioneer, Scout
Pathological Diseased, Gangrene, Morbid, Septic
Pathos Bathos, Pity, Sadness, Sob-stuff
Patience Calm, Endurance, Forbearance, Fortitude, Indulgence, Longanimity, Monument, Operetta, Solitaire, Stoicism, Virtue
Patient(s) Calm, Case, Clinic, Forbearing, Grisel(da), Grisilda, Invalid, Job, Long-suffering, Passive, Private, Resigned, Stoic, Subject, Ward
Patois Argot, Cant, Dialect, Gumbo, Jargon, Jive, Lingo, Scouse
Patriarch Aaron, Abraham, Abuna, Catholicos, Ecumenical, Elder, Enoch, Isaac, Levi, Maron, Methuselah, Nestor, Noah, Pope, Simeon, Venerable
Patrician Aristocrat, Noble, Senator
Patrick Mick, Paddy, Pat, Spens
Patrimony Ancestry, Estate, Heritage
Patriot(ic), Patriotism Cavour, Chauvinist, DAR, Emmet, Flag-waving, Flamingant, Garibaldi, Hereward, Irredentist, Jingoism, Loyalist, Maquis, Nationalist, Revere, Tell
Patrol Armilla, Guard, Outguard, Picket, Piquet, Prowl-car, Reconnaissance, Scout, Sentinel, Sentry-go, Shark, Shore, Turm
Patron(age), Patronise(d), Patronising Advowson, Aegis, Auspices, Benefactor, Business, Champion, Client, Customer, Donator, Egis, Fautor, Maecenas, Nepotic, Protector, Protégé, Provider, Shopper, > SPONSOR, Stoop, Stoup
Patsy Dupe, Hendren, Scapegoat, Stooge
Patter Backchat, Cant, Jargon, Lingo, Mag, Pitch, Rap, S(c)htick, Schtik, Spiel
Pattern(ed) Argyle, Bird's eye, Blueprint, Branchwork, Broché, Check, Chequer, Chladni figure, Clock, Design, Dévoré, Diaper, Diffraction, Dog's tooth, Draft, Egg and dart, Epitome, Example, Exemplar, Fiddle, Figuration, Format, Fractal, Fret, Gestalt, Grain, Grammadion, Greek key, Herringbone, Holding, Hound's tooth, Intarsia, Intonation, Koru, Matel(l)asse, Matrix, Meander, > MODEL, Moire, Mosaic, Norm, Paisley, Paradigm, Paragon, Pinstripe, Plan, Polka-dot, Pompadour, Precedent, Prototype, Queenstitch, Quincunx, Radiation, Raster, Shawl, Stencil, Symmetry, Syndrome, Tala, Tangram, Tattersall, Template, Tessella, Tessera, Tracery, Traffic, Tread, Type, Willow
Patty Bouchée, Pie
Paul Jones, Oom, Pry, Revere, Robeson, S, St
Pauline Day-boy, Perils
Paunch Belly, Corporation, Gut, Kite, Kyte, Pod, Rumen, Tripe, Tum
Pauper Bankrupt, Beggar, Have-not, Mendicant, Penniless
Pause Break, Breakpoint, Breather, Caesura, Cessation, Cesura, Comma, Desist, Er, Fermata, Hesitate, Interkinesis, Interregnum, Interval, Limma, Lull,

Pitstop, > **RESPITE**, Rest, Selah, Stop, Tacet, Time out

Pave(ment), Paving Causeway, Clint, Corsey, Crazy, Diaper, Granolith, Limestone, Path, Roadside, Set(t), Sidewalk, Tessellate, Travolator, Trottoir

Pavilion Ear, Gazebo, Jingling Johnny, Kiosk, Marquee, Tent

Paw Kangaroo, Maul, Mitt, Pad, Pat, Pud, Pug

Pawky Dry, Humorous, Shrewd, Sly

Pawn(shop) Agent, Betel, Chessman, Counter, Derby, Dip, Gage, Gallery, Hanging, Hock, Hostage, Isolated, Leaving-shop, Lumber, Monte-de-piété, Monti di pieta, Pan, Passed, Peacock, Piece, Pignerate, Pignorate, Pledge, Pop, Security, Siri, Spout, Tiddleywink, Tool, Wadset, Weed

Pawnbroker, Pawnee Hockshop, Lumberer, Moneylender, Nunky, Pledgee, Sheeny, Uncle, Usurer

Pax Peace, Truce

Pay(master), Payment, Paid, Pay off, Pay out Advertise, Agterskot, Amortise, Annat, Annuity, Ante, Arles, Atone, Basic, Batta, Blench, Bonus, Bukshee, Bukshi, Cain, Cashier, Cens, Cheque, COD, Commute, Compensate, Consideration, Damage, Defray, Disburse, Discharge, Dividend, Down, Dub, Emolument, Endow, Equalisation, Eric, Escot, Farm, Fee, Feu-duty, Finance, Foot, Fork out, Fund, Gale, Gate, Give, Grassum, Grave, Greenmail, Han(d)sel, Hazard, Hire, Hoot(oo), HP, Imburse, Kain, Kickback, Leads and lags, Lobola, Lobolo, Mail, Meet, Merchet, Metayage, Mise, Modus, Overtime, Payola, Pension, Pittance, Pony, Posho, Prebendal, Premium, Primage, Pro, Pro forma, Progress, Purser, Quarterage, Quit(-rent), Ransom, Redundancy, Refund, Remittance, Remuneration, Rent, Requite, Residual, Respects, Royalty, Salary, Satisfaction, Scot, Screw, Scutage, Settle, Severance, Shell, Shell out, Sick, Sink, Sold(e), Soul-scat, Soul-scot, > **SPEND**, Square, Stipend, Strike, Stump, Sub, Subscribe, Sweetener, Table, Take-home, Tar, Tender, Token, Tommy, Transfer, Treasure, Treat, Tribute, Truck, Unpurse, Usance, Veer, Wage, Wardcorn, X-factor

Pea(s) Carling, Chaparral, Chickling, Desert, D(h)al, Dholl, Egyptian, Garbanzo, Goober, Hastings, Legume, Mangetout, Marrow, Marrowfat, Passiform, Petit pois, Pigeon, Pulse, Rounceval, Split, String, Sturt's desert, Sugar

Peace(ful), Peace-keeper, Peace organisation, Peace symbol Ahimsa, Ataraxy, Calm, Ease, Frith, Halcyon, Interceder, Irenic(on), King's, Lee, Lull, Nirvana, Olive, Order, Pacific, Pax, Pbuh, Queen's, Quiet, Repose, Rest, Salem, Serene, Sh, Shalom, Siesta, Silence, Still, Tranquil, Truce, UN

Peacemaker ACAS, Arbitrator, Conciliator, Mediator, Trouble-shooter

Peach Blab, Cling, Clingstone, Dish, Dob, Freestone, Inform, Laetrile, Malakatoone, Melba, Melocoto(o)n, Nectarine, Oner, Quandang, Shop, Sneak, Split, Squeak, Stunner, Tattle, Tell, Victorine

Peachum Polly

Peacock Coxcomb, Dandy, Fop, Junonian, Muster, Paiock(e), Pajock(e), Pavo(ne), Pawn, Payock(e), Pown, Sashay

Peak(y) Acme, Aiguille, Alp, Apex, Ben, Cap, Climax, Comble, Communism, Crag, Crest, Darien, Drawn, Eiger, Gable, Gannett, Horn, Matterhorn, Mons, > **MOUNTAIN**, Nevis, Nib, Nunatak, Optimum, Pale, Petermann, Pikes, Pin, Pinnacle, Piton, Pyramidal, Rainier, Sallow, Snowdon, Spire, Stalin, Sukarno, Top, Tor, Visor, Widow's, Zenith

Peal Carillon, Chime, Clap, Toll, Triple

Peanut(s) Arnut, Chickenfeed, Goober, Groundnut, Monkey-nut, Pittance

Pear Aguacate, Alligator, Anchovy, Anjou, Asian, Avocado, Bartlett, Bergamot, Beurré, Blanquet, Carmelite, Catherine, Colmar, Conference, Cuisse-madame,

Jargonelle, Muscadel, Muscatel, Musk, Nashi, Neli(e)s, Nelis, Perry, Poperin, Poppering, Poprin, Prickly, Pyrus, Queez-maddam, Seckel, Seckle, Taylor's Gold, Warden, William

Pearl(s), Pearly Barocco, Barock, Baroque, Cultured, False, Gem, Imitated, Jewel, Mabe, Margaret, Margaric, Nacrous, Olivet, Orient, Prize, Rope, Seed, Simulated, String, Sulphur, Unio(n)

Pear-shaped Obconic, Pyriform

Peasant Bonhomme, Boor, Bumpkin, Chouan, Churl, Clodhopper, Contadino, Cossack, Cottar, Cotter, Cott(i)er, Fellah(s), Fellahin, Hick, Jungli, Kern(e), Kisan, Kulak, M(o)ujik, Muzhik, Quashi(e), Raiyat, Roturier, Rustic, Ryot, Swain, Tyrolean, Volost, Whiteboy, Yokel

Pea-shaped Pisiform

Peat(y) Moss-litter, Sod, Turbary, Turbinacious, Turf, Yarfa, Yarpha

Pebble(s), Pebbly Banket, Bibble, Calculus, Cobblestone, Dornick, Dreikanter, Gallet, Gooley, Gravel, Psephism, Pumie, Pumy, Scree, Shingle, Ventifact

Peccadillo Mischief, Misdemeanour, Offence

Peccary Mexican hog

Peck Bill, Bushel, Dab, Forpet, Forpit, Gregory, Kiss, Lip, Lippie, Nibble, Pickle, Tap

Pecksniff Charity

Peculiar(ity) Appropriate, Characteristic, Distinct, Eccentric, Especial, Exclusive, Ferly, Funny, Idiosyncratic, Kink, Kooky, Odd, Own, Proper, Queer, Quirk, Singular, > SPECIAL, Specific, Strange, Unusual

▷ **Peculiar** *may indicate* an anagram

Pedagogue Academic, B.Ed, Teacher

Pedal Bike, Chorus, Cycle, Damper, Lever, P, Rat-trap, Soft, Sostenuto, Sustaining, Treadle, Treddle

Pedal-coupler Tirasse

Pedant(ic) Casaubon, Chop logic, Dogmatic, Dryasdust, Elucubrate, Inkhorn, Intellectual, Jobsworth, Lucubrate, Pedagogue, Pernickety, Pompous, Precisian, Quibbler, Scholastic, Sesquipedalian

Peddle, Pedlar Bodger, Boxwallah, Camelot, Chapman, Cheapjack, Colporteur, Drummer, Duffer, Hawk, Huckster, Jagger, Packman, Pedder, Pether, Sell, Smouch, Smouse(r), Sutler, Tallyman, Tink(er), Yagger

▷ **Peddling** *may indicate* an anagram

Pedestal Acroter(ion), Dado, Footstool, Pillar, Support

Pedestrian Banal, Commonplace, Dull, Earth-bound, Ganger, Hack, Hike, Itinerant, Jaywalker, Laborious, Mundane, Trite, Voetganger, Walker

Pedigree(s) Ancestry, Blood, Breeding, Descent, Genealogy, House, Lineage, Phylogeny, Stemma(ta), Stirps, Studbook, Thoroughbred, Whakapapa

Pediment Fronton

Peduncle Scape, Stalk

Peek Eye, Glance, Glimpse, Peep

Peel(er) Bark, Bobby, Candied, Decorticate, Desquamate, Exfoliate, Flype, Orange, Pare, PC, Pill, Rind, Rine, Scale, Shell, Skin, > STRIP, Tirr, Zest

▷ **Peeled** *may indicate* outside letter(s) to be removed from a word

Peep(er), Peephole Cheep, Cook, Crow, Glance, Gledge, Judas, Keek, Kook, Lamp, Nose, Peek, Pink, Pry, Spy, Squeak, Squint, Stime, Styme, Voyeur

Peer(age), Peers Archduke, Aristocrat, Backwoodsman, Baron(et), Burke, Coeval, Daimio, Doucepere, Douzeper(s), Duke, Earl, Egal, Elevation, Equal, Eyeball, Gynt, Life, Lord, Match, Noble, Paladin, Peregal, Pink, Rank, Representative, Scry, Spiritual, Squint, Stare, Stime, Styme, Temporal, Toot,

Tweer, Twire

Peerless Matchless, Nonpareil, Supreme

Peevish(ness) Capernoited, Captious, Crabby, Cross, Doddy, Frabbit, Frampal, Frampold, Franzy, Fretful, Lienal, Meldrew, Moody, Nattered, Petulant, Pindling, Protervity, Querulous, Shirty, Sour, Spleen, Teachie, Testy, Te(t)chy

Peewit Lapwing, Peewee

Peg Cheville, Cleat, Cotter-pin, Crawling, Die, Fix, Freeze, Knag, Leg, Margaret, Nail, Nog, Pin, Piton, Snort, Spigot, Spile, Square, Stengah, Stinger, Support, Tap, Tee, Thole, Tholepin, Thowel, Toggle, Tot, Tuning, Vent, Woffington

Pegboard Solitaire

Pelagic Deep-sea, Marine, Oceanic

Pelf Lucre, Mammon, Money, Notes, Riches

Pelican Alcatras, Bird, Crossing, Golden Hind, LA, Louisiana, Steganopode

Pellagra Maidism

Pellet Birdshot, Bolus, Buckshot, Bullet, Pill, Pithball, Prill, Slug

Pelt Assail, Clod, Fleece, Fur, Hail, Hide, Hie, Lam, Pepper, Random, Sealskin, Shower, Skin, Squail, Stone

Peltast Soldier, Targeteer

Pelvis Ilium, Pubis, Renal

Pen Ballpoint, Bamboo, Bic®, Biro®, Cage, Calamus, Cartridge, Catching, Confine, Coop, Corral, Crawl, Crow-quill, Cru(i)ve, Cub, Cyclostyle, Dabber, Data, Enclosure, Fank, Farm, Felt(-tipped), Fold, Fountain, Gaol, Gladius, Hen, Highlighter, Hoosegow, J, > JAIL, Keddah, Kraal, Lair, Light, Marker, Mew, Mure, Music, Piggery, Poison, Pound, Quill, Ree, Reed, Ring, Rollerball, Scribe, Stell, Stie, Stir, Sty(e), Stylet, Stylo, Stylograph, Stylus, Submarine, Swan, Tank, Write

▷ **Pen** *may indicate* a writer

Penal(ize) Cost, Fine, Gate, Handicap, Huff, Mulct, Punitive, Servitude

Penalty Abye, Amende, Cost, Death, Eric, Fine, Fixed, Forfeit, Han(d)sel, Huff, Keltie, Kelty, Pain, Price, Punishment, Sanction, Wide

Penance Atonement, Shrift

Penates Lares

Pence D, P, Peter's

Penchant Predilection

Pencil Beam, Ca(l)m, Caum, Charcoal, Chinagraph®, Crayon, Draft, Draw, Eyebrow, Fusain, Grease, Harmonic, Ink, Keelivine, Keelyvine, Lead, Outline, Propelling, Slate, Stump, Styptic

Pendant Albert, Chandelier, Drop, Girandole, Laval(l)ière, Necklace, Poffle, Stalactite

Pending Imminent, In fieri, Unresolved, Until

Pendragon Uther

Pendulous, Pendulum Compensation, Dewlap, Foucault's, Metronome, Noddy, One-way, Swing, Wavering

Penetrate, Penetrating, Penetration Acumen, Acuminate, Bite, Bore, Bridgehead, Cut, Enpierce, Enter, Imbue, Impale, Incisive, Indent, Indepth, Infiltrate, Insight, Into, Intrant, Lance, Permeate, Pierce, Probe, Sagacious, Shear, Thrust, Touch, X-ray

Penguin Aeroplane, Anana, Auk, Blue, Emperor, Fairy, Gentoo, King, Korora, Little, Macaroni, Rock-hopper

Penicillin Fleming

Peninsula Alaska, Alte, Antarctic, Arabian, Ards, Arm, Avalon, Baja California, Balkan, Banks, Bataan, Black Isle, Boothia, Cape, Cape Cod, Cape Verde,

Chalcidice, Chersonese, Chukchi, Coromandel, Crimea, Deccan, Delmarva, East Cape, Eyre, Florida, Freycinet, Gallipoli, Galloway, Gaspé, Gower, Iberia(n), Indo-China, Istria, Jutland, Kamchatka, Kathiawar, Kintyre, Kola, Kowloon, Labrador, Leizhou, Liaodong, Liaotung, Lleyn, Luichow, Malay, Melville, Neck, Northland, Nova Scotia, Olympic, Otago, Palmer, Peloponnese, Portland, Promontory, Quiberon, Scandinavian, Seward, Sinai, Spit, Spur, Taimyr, Talmyr, Tasman, Taymar, The Lizard, Upper, Wilson's Promontory, Wirral, Yorke, Yucatan

Penis Archie, Cor(e)y, Dick, Dildo(e), Dipstick, Dong, Ferret, Giggle(stick), Horn, Jack, John Thomas, Knob, Membrum virile, Mojo, Pecker, Peezle, Percy, Phallus, Pillicock, Pintle, Pisser, Pizzle, Plonker, Prick, Rod, Roger, Schlong, Shaft, Stiffy, Tockley, Tonk, Tool, W(h)ang, Willie, Willy, Winkle, Yard, Zeppelin

Penitent(iary) Calaboose, Clink, Contrite, Gaol, Jail, Jug, Prison, Repenter, Rosary, Stir

Pennant, Pennon Banner, Broad, Bunting, Fane, Flag, Guidon, Streamer

Penniless Bankrupt, Boracic, Broke, Bust, Impecunious, Poor, Skint, Strapped

Penny Bean, Cartwheel, Cent, Copper, D, Dreadful, Gild, Honest, P, Pretty, Sen, Sou, Sterling, Stiver, Win(n), Wing

Penny-farthing Bicycle, Ordinary

Pension(er) Allowance, Ann(at), Annuitant, Board, Chelsea, Cod, Cor(r)ody, Gratuity, Guest-house, Half-board, Occupational, Payment, Personal, Retire, Serps, Stakeholder, Stipend, Superannuation

Pensive Dreamy, Moody, Musing, Thoughtful, Triste, Wistful

Pentateuch T(h)orah

Pentecost Whit(sun)

Penthouse Cat, Lean-to, Roof

Peon Peasant, Serf, Slave, Ticca

Peony Moutan

People Bods, Body, Chosen, Commonalty, Commons, Demos, Ecology, Enchorial, Flower, Folk, Fraim, Gens, Guild, Human, Inca, Inhabit, Janata, Kin, Land, Lapith, Lay, Man(kind), Men, Mob, Nair, Nation(s), Nayar, One, Peculiar, Personalities, Phalange, Populace, Proletariat(e), Public, Punters, Quorum, Race, Settle, Society, Souls, They, Tribe, Volk

Pep Buck, Dash, Enliven, Gism, Go, Jism, Jissom, Stamina, Verve, Vim

Pepper Alligator, All-spice, Ava, Betel, Bird, Black, Capsicum, Cayenne, Chilli, Condiment, Cubeb, Devil, Dittander, Dittany, Ethiopian, Green, Guinea, Jalapeno, Jamaica, Kava, Long, Malaguetta, Matico, Negro, Paprika, Pelt, Pim(i)ento, Piper, Red, Riddle, Sambal, Spice, Sprinkle, Sweet, Szechwan, Tabasco®, Wall, White, Yaqona, Yellow

Peppercorn Nominal

Peppermint Bull's Eye, Humbug, Pandrop

Per By, Each, Through

Perambulate, Perambulator Buggy, Expatiate, Pedestrian, Pram, Stroller, Wagon, Walker

Perceive, Perception, Perceptive Acumen, Alert, Anschauung, Apprehend, Astute, Clairvoyance, Clear-eyed, Cryptaesthetic, Descry, Dianoia, Discern, Divine, ESP, Extrasensory, Feel, Insight, Intelligence, Intuit(ion), Kinaesthesia, Notice, Observe, Pan(a)esthesia, Remark, > **SEE**, Sense, Sensitive, Sentience, Shrewd, Subliminal, Tact, Taste, Tel(a)esthesia, Telegnosis, Understanding

Percentage Agio, Commission, Contango, Cut, Mark-up, Proportion, Royalty,

Scalage, Share, Vigorish
Perch(ing) Aerie, Alight, Anabis, Bass, Comber, Eyrie, Fish, Fogash, Gaper, Insessorial, Lug, Perca, Pole, Roost, Ruff(e), Seat, Serranid, > SIT, Wall-eye, Zingel
Percolate, **Percolation** Filter, Infiltrate, Leach, Lixiviate, Ooze, Osmosis, Permeate, Seep, Sipe, Soak, Strain, Sype
Percussion (cap) Amorce, Chinese temple block, Idiophone, Impact, Knee, Knock, Thump, Timbrel
Percy Hotspur, Shelley
Perdition Ades, Hades
Peremptory Absolute, Decisive, Haughty, Imperative, Imperious
Perennial Continual, Enduring, Flower, Livelong, Perpetual, Recurrent
Perfect(ly), **Perfection(ist)** Absolute, Accomplish, Accurate, Acme, Apple-pie, Bloom, Complete, Consummation, Cross-question, Dead, Develop, Fare-thee-well, Finish, Flawless, Fulfil, Full, Holy, Ideal(ist), Impeccable, Intact, It, Mint, Par, Paragon, Past, Pat, Peace, Pedant, Point-device, Practice, Present, Pure, Quintessential, Refine, Siddha, Soma, Sound, Spot-on, Stainless, Sublime, The nines, Thorough, Three-pricker, Unblemished, Unqualified, Utopian, Utter, Whole, Witeless
Perfidy Betrayal, Falsehood, Treachery, Treason
Perforate(d), **Perforation**, **Perforator** Cribrate, Cribrose, Drill, Eyelet, Hole, > PIERCE, Prick, Punch, Puncture, Riddle, Trephine, Trocar
Perforce Necessarily, Needs
Perform(ed), **Performer**, **Performing** Achieve, Act(or), Appear, Artist(e), Basoche, Busk, Chansonnier, Discharge, Do, Enact, Entertainer, Execute, Exert, Exhibit, Fancy Dan, Fire-eater, Fulfil, Function, Geek, Hand, Headliner, Hersall, Implement, Interlocutor, Majorette, Make, Moke, On, Perpetrate, Player, Praxis, Recite, Render, Ripieno, Strongarm, Supererogate, Sword-swallower, Throw, Vaudevillian, Virtuoso
Performance Accomplishment, Achievement, Act, Auto, Bravura, Broadcast, Command, Concert, Dare, Deed, Demonstration, Discharge, Entracte, Execution, Gas, Gig, Hierurgy, Holdover, Hootenanny, Masterstroke, Matinee, One-night stand, Operation, Perpetration, Practice, Première, Production, Recital, Rehearsal, Rendering, Rendition, Repeat, Repertoire, Rigmarole, Scene, Show, Sneak preview, Solo, Specific, Spectacle, Stunt, Turn
Perfume (box) Aroma, Attar, Bergamot, Cassolette, Chypre, Civet, Cologne, C(o)umarin, Enfleurage, Fragrance, Frangipani, Incense, Ionone, Lavender (water), Linalool, Millefleurs, Muscone, Muskone, Myrrh, Opopanax, Orris, Orrisroot, Patchouli, Patchouly, Pomander, Potpourri, Redolence, > SCENT, Terpineol
Perfunctory Apathetic, Careless, Cursory, Indifferent, Token
Perhaps A(i)blins, Belike, Haply, Happen, May(be), Peradventure, Percase, Perchance, Possibly, Relative, Say, Yibbles
▷ **Perhaps** *may indicate* an anagram
Perigee Apsis, Epigeum
Peril(ous) > DANGER, Hazard, Jeopardy, Precarious, Risk, Threat, Yellow
Perimeter Boundary, Circuit, Circumference, Limits
Period(ic) Abbevillian, Acheulian, AD, Age, Alcher(ing)a, Annual, Aurignacian, Azilian, Cambrian, Carboniferous, Chalcolithic, Chukka, Chukker, Climacteric, Cooling off, Cretaceous, Critical, Curse, Cycle, Day, Devonian, Diapause, Dot, Dreamtime, > DURATION, Eocene, Epoch, Excerpt, Floruit, Full-stop, Glacial, Grace, Hercynian, Holocene, Horal, Incubation, Innings,

Periodic(al) | 504

Interregnum, Jurassic, Kalpa, Latency, Latent, Lesson, Liassic, Limit, Meantime, Meanwhile, Mesolithic, Mesozoic, Middle Kingdom, Miocene, Monthly, Neocomian, Neolithic, Neozoic, Octave, Olde-worlde, Oligocene, Ordovician, Paleolithic, Permian, Phanerozoic, Phase, Phoenix, Pleistocene, Pliocene, Pre-Cambrian, Protohistory, Quarter, Quarternary, Reformation, Refractory, Regency, Rent, Riss, Romantic, Safe, Season, Session, Sidereal, Silurian, Span, Spell, Stage, Stop, Stretch, Synodic, Term, Tertiary, Trecento, Triassic, Trimester, Usance, Window

Periodic(al) Catamenia, Comic, Digest, Economist, Etesian, Journal, Liassic, Listener, Mag, New Yorker, Organ, Paper, Phase, Publication, Punch, Rambler, Regency, Review, Solutrean, Solutrian, Spectator, Strand, Stretch, Tatter, Tract

Peripatetic Gadabout, Itinerant, Promenader, Travelling

Periphery Ambit, Bounds, Fringe, Outskirts, Surface

Periscope Eye(-stalk)

Perish(able), Perished, Perishing Brittle, > DIE, End, Ephemeral, Expire, Fade, Forfair, Fungibles, Icy, Tine, Tint, Transitory, Tyne, Vanish

Periwinkle Apocynum, Blue, Myrtle

Perjure(d) Forswear, Lie, Mansworn

Perk(s), Perky Brighten, Chipper, Freshen, Jaunty, LV, Perquisite

Perm(anent) Abiding, Durable, Enduring, Eternal, Everlasting, Fixed, For keeps, Full-time, Indelible, > LASTING, Marcel, Stable, Standing, Stative, Wave

Permeability, Permeate Infiltrate, Leaven, Magnetic, Osmosis, Penetrate, Pervade, Seep

Permission, Permit(ted) Allow, Authorise, Carnet, Chop, Clearance, Congé(e), Consent, Copyright, Enable, Grant, Lacet, Laisser-passer, Latitude, Leave, Legal, Let, Liberty, Licence, License, Lief, Luit, Nihil obstat, Ok(e), Pace, Pass, Placet, Planning, Power, Pratique, Privilege, Sanction, Stamp-note, Suffer, Ticket, Triptyque, Visa, Vouchsafe, Way-leave, Wear

Pernicious Evil, Harmful, Lethal, Noisome, Pestilent, Wicked

Pernickety Fikish, Niggly

Peroration Pirlicue, Purlicue

Peroxide Bleach, Blonde, Colcothar

Perpendicular Aplomb, Apothem, Atrip, Cathetus, Erect, Normal, Orthogonal, Plumb, Sheer, Sine, > UPRIGHT, Vertical

Perpetrate Commit, Effect, Execute

Perpetual Constant, Eternal, Incessant, Sempiternal

Perplex(ed), Perplexity Anan, Baffle, Bamboozle, Beset, Bewilder, Bother, Buffalo, Bumbaze, Cap, Confound, Confuse, Embarrass, Feague, Floor, Flummox, Knotty, Meander, Mystify, Nonplus, Out, Puzzle, Quizzical, Stump, Tangle, Tickle, Tostication

Perquisite Ap(p)anage, Emolument, Extra, Gratuity, > PERK, Tip

Perrier Stoner

Perry Mason

Persecute, Persecution Afflict, Annoy, Badger, Crucify, Dragon(n)ades, Harass, Haze, Intolerant, Oppress, Pogrom, Ride, Torment, Torture, Witch hunt

Persevere, Perseverance Assiduity, Continue, Fortitude, Insist, Patience, Persist, Plug, Stamina, Steadfastness, Stick, Stickability, Tenacity

Persia(n) Babee, Babi, Bahai, Cyrus, Farsi, Iran(ian), Mazdean, Mede, Middle, Pahlavi, Parasang, Parsee, Pehlevi, Pushtu, Samanid, Sassanid, Sohrab, Xerxes, Zoroaster

Persimmon Kaki, Sharon fruit

Persist(ence), Persistent Adhere, Assiduity, Chronic, Continual, Diligent,

Doggedness, Endure, Importunate, Labour, Longeval, Lusting, Nag, Persevere, Press, Sedulous, Sneaking, Stick, Tenacity, Urgent

Person(s), Personal(ly) Alter, Being, Bird, Bod(y), Chai, Chal, Character, Chi, Cookie, Displaced, Entity, Everymen, Figure, First, Fish, Flesh, Head, Human, Individual, In propria persona, One, Own, Party, Passer-by, Pod, Private, Quidam, Second, Selfhood, Skate, Sod, Soul, Specimen, Tales, Third, Walla(h)

Personage, Personality Anima, Celeb(rity), Character, Charisma, Dignitary, Ego, Grandee, Identity, Jekyll and Hyde, Multiple, Noble, Notability, Panjandrum, Presence, Psychopath, Sama, Schizoid, Seity, Sel, Self, Sell, Split, Star, Tycoon, Viscerotonia

Personified, Personification, Personify Embody, Incarnate, Prosopop(o)eia, Represent

Personnel Employees, Hands, Liveware, Manpower, Staff

Perspective Attitude, Distance, Linear, Point of view, Proportion, Slant, View, Vista

Perspicacious Astute, Clear-sighted, Discerning, Keen, Shrewd

Perspiration, Perspire, Perspiring Aglow, Forswatt, Glow, Hidrosis, Sudor, Suint, Sweat, Swelter

Persuade(d), Persuasion, Persuasive Cajole, Coax, Cogent, Conviction, Convince, Disarm, Eloquent, Faith, Feel, Forcible, Geed, Get, Induce, Inveigle, Lead on, Move, Plausible, > PREVAIL, Religion, Soft sell, Suborn, Truckled, Wheedle, Winning

Pert(ness) Bold, Brisk, Cocky, Dicacity, Flippant, Forward, Fresh, Impertinent, Insolent, Jackanapes, Minx, Saucy, Tossy

Pertain Belong, Concern, Relate, Touch

Pertinacious Dogged, Obstinate, Persistent, Stickler, Stubborn

Pertinent Apropos, Apt, Fit, Germane, Relevant, Timely

Perturb(ation) Aerate, Confuse, Dismay, Disturb, Dither, State, Trouble, Upset, Worry

Peru(vian) Inca, PE, Quechua(n), Quichua(n)

Peruse, Perusal Examine, Inspect, Read, Scan, Scrutiny, > STUDY

Pervade, Pervasion, Pervasive(ness) Diffuse, Drench, Immanence, Permeate, Saturate

Perverse, Perversion, Pervert(ed) Aberrant, Abnormal, Algolagnia, Awry, Cam(stairy), Camsteary, Camsteerie, Cantankerous, > CONTRARY, Corrupt, Cussed, Deviate, Distort, Donsie, False, Gee, Kam(me), Kinky, Licentious, Misuse, Nonce, Paraphilia, Refractory, Sadist, Sicko, Stubborn, Thrawn, Traduce, Unnatural, Untoward, Uranism, Warp(ed), Wayward, Wilful, Wrest, Wry

▷ **Perverted** *may indicate* an anagram

Pessimism, Pessimist(ic) Alarmist, Bear, Crapehanger, Crepehanger, Cynic, Defeatist, Doomwatch, Doomy, Doubter, Downbeat, Fatalist, Glumbum, Jeremiah, Killjoy, Negative

Pest(er) Badger, Bedbug, Blight, Bot, > BOTHER, Brat, Breese, Bug, Dim, Disagreeable, Earbash, Fly, Fowl, Harass, Irritate, Mither, Mouse, Nag, Nudnik, Nuisance, Nun, Pize, Plague, Rotter, Scourge, Tease, Terror, Thysanoptera, Vermin, Weevil

Pesticide DDT, Derris, Heplachlor, Mouser, Permethrin, Synergist, Warfarin

Pestilence, Pestilent Curse, Epidemic, Evil, Lues, Murrain, Noxious, Outbreak, Pernicious, Plague

Pet Aversion, Cade, Canoodle, Caress, Chou, Coax, Coddle, Cosset, Dandle, Daut(ie), Dawt(ie), Dod, Dort, Ducky, Favourite, Fondle, Glumps, Hamster,

Huff, Hump, Ire, Jarta, Jo, Lallygag, Lapdog, Miff, Mouse, Neck, Pique, Rabbit, Smooch, Snog, Spat, Strum, Sulk(s), Tantrum, Teacher's, Tiff, Tout, Towt, Umbrage, Virtual, Yarta

Petal Ala, Keels, Labellum, Leaf, Standard, Vexillum

Petard Firework, Squib

Peter Aumbry, Bell, Dwindle, Grimes, Pan, Principle, Quince, Quint, Rabbit, Safe, Saint, Sellers, Simon, Simple, Wane, Weaken

Petite Dainty, Mignon, Small

Petition(er) Appeal, Beg, Boon, Crave, Entreaty, Millenary, Orison, Plaintiff, Postulant, Prayer, Representation, Request, Round robin, Solicit, Sue, Suit(or), Suppli(c)ant, Vesper

Pet-name Hypocorisma, Nickname, So(u)briquet

Petrel Bird, Mother Carey's chickens, Nelly, Prion, Procellaria, Stormbird, Stormy, Wilton's

Petrify(ing) Fossilise, Frighten, Lapidescent, Niobe, Numb, Ossify, Scare, Terrify

Petrol(eum) Cetane, Cutting, Diesel, Esso®, Ethyl, Fuel, Gas, High-octane, High-test, Ligroin, Maz(o)ut, Octane, Oilstone, Olein, Rock-tar, Unleaded, Vaseline

Petticoat Balmoral, Basquine, Crinoline, Female, Filabeg, Fil(l)ibeg, Jupon, Kilt, Kirtle, Phil(l)abeg, Phil(l)ibeg, Placket, Sarong, Shift, Underskirt, Wylie-coat

Pettifogger Lawmonger

Petty, Pettiness Baubling, Bumbledom, Childish, Little, Mean, Minor, Narrow, Niggling, Nyaff, One-horse, Parvanimity, Picayunish, Pimping, Puisne, Shoestring, Small, Small-minded, Stingy, Tin, Trivial, Two-bit

Petulance, Petulant Fretful, Huff, Moody, Peevish, Perverse, Procacity, Querulous, Sullen, Toutie, Waspish

Pew Box, Carrel, Chair, Seat, Stall

Pewter Trifle, Tutenag

Phalanger Cus-cus, Honey-mouse, Opossum, Petaurist, Possum, Sugar glider, Tait, Tarsipes, Tuan, Wambenger

Phalanx Cohort, Coterie, Legion

Phalarope Lobe-foot

Phallus Linga(m), Penis, Priapus

Phantasist, Phantasm Apparition, Chimera, Spectre, Werewolf

Phantom Apparition, Bogey, Bugbear, Eidolon, Idol, Incubus, Maya, Pepper's ghost, Shade, Spectre, Tut, Wraith

Pharaoh Amenhotep, Cheops, Egyptian, Rameses, Thutmose, Tut, Tutankhamen, Tutankhamun, Tyrant

Pharisee Formalist, Humbug, Hypocrite, Nicodemus

Pharmacist > CHEMIST, Dispenser, MPS, Preparator

Phase Colourm, Cycle, Form, Period, Post-boost, Quarter, REM, Stage, State, Synchronise, Transition

Pheasant Argus, Bird, Fireback, Junglefowl, Mona(u)l, Nide, Nye, Peacock, Ring-necked, Tragopan

Phenol Orcine, Orcinol, Resorcin, Xylenol

Phenomenon Autokinetic, Blip, Effect, Event, Figure ground, Flying saucer, Flysch, Heterography, Marvel, Miracle, Mirage, Paranormal, Psi, Reynaud's, Synergy

Phial Bologna, Bottle, Flask

Phil, Philip Fluter, Macedonia, Pip

Philander(er) Flirt, Lothario, Playboy, Toyer, > TRIFLE, Wolf, Womaniser
Philanthropist, Philanthropy Altruist, Benefactor, Carnegie, Charity, Coram,
 Donor, Humanist, Humanitarian, Nobel, Rockefeller, Samaritan, Shaftesbury,
 Tate, Wilberforce
Philately Timbromania
Phileas Fogg
▶ **Philip** *see* PHIL
Philippic Diatribe, Invective, Tirade
Philippine(s) Bisayan, Igorot, Moro, PI, RP, Tagalog, Visayan
Philistine, Philistinism Artless, Ashdod, Barbarian, Foe, Gath, Gaza, Gigman,
 Goliath, Goth, Lowbrow, Podsnappery, Vandal
Philology Linguistics, Semantics, Speechcraft
Philosopher, Philosophy Activism, Ahimsa, Analytical, Animism,
 Anthrosophy, Antinomianism, Attitude, Averr(h)oism, Comtism,
 Conceptualism, Cracker-barrel, Deontology, Empiricism, Enlightenment,
 Epistemology, Ethics, Existentialism, Fatalism, Hedonism, Hobbism,
 Humanism, Idealism, Ideology, -ism, Linguistic, Logical atomism, Logos,
 Marxism, Materialism, Metempiricism, Monism, Moral(ist), Natural,
 Neoplatonism, Nihilism, Nominalism, Opinion, Peripatetic, Phenomenology,
 Populism, Positivism, Rationalism, Realism, Scientology, Shankara(-charya),
 Stoic, Synthetic, Taoism, Theism, Theosophy, Transcendentalism, Ultraism,
 Utilitarianism, Utopianism, Voluntarism, Yoga

PHILOSOPHERS

4 letters:
Aver
Ayer
Hume
Kant
Mach
Mill
Ryle
Sage
Weil
Wolf
Yogi
Zeno

5 letters:
Amiel
Bacon
Comte
Croce
Cynic
Dewey
Hegel
Locke
Paine
Plato
Quine
Renan

Smith
Sorel
Taine

6 letters:
Cicero
Engels
Godwin
Herder
Hobbes
Holist
I Ching
Kaizen
Ortega
Pascal
Popper
Pyrrho
Sartre
Scotus
Seneca
Thales

7 letters:
Abelard
Aquinas
Atomist
Bentham

Bergson
Casuist
Diderot
Eleatic
Emerson
Erasmus
Erigena
Herbart
Hypatia
Leibniz
Malthus
Marcuse
Mencius
Meng-tse
Russell
Sankhya
Sceptic
Schlick
Sensist
Sheffer
Sophist
Spencer
Spinoza
Steiner
Thomist
Vedanta

8 letters:
Avicenna
Berkeley
Boethius
Cyreniac
Diogenes
Eclectic
Epicurus
Foucault
Harrison
Megarian
Menippus
Neoteric
Occamist
Old Moore
Plotinus
Plutarch
Rousseau
Socrates
Xenophon

9 letters:
Academist
Aristotle
Bosanquet
Cartesian
Cleanthes

- Confucius
- Descartes
- Euhemerus
- Heidegger
- Leucippus
- Lucretius
- Nietzsche
- Ockhamist
- Rosminian
- Santayana
- Schelling
- Schoolman
- Whitehead

10 letters:
Anacharsis
Anaxagoras
Anaximenes
Antiochene
Antiochian
Apemanthus
Apollonius
Aristippus
Campanella
Chrysippus
Democritus
Empedocles
Heraclitus

Nominalist
Paracelsus
Parmenides
Protagoras
Pythagoras
Saint Simon
Swedenborg
Xenocrates
Xenophanes

11 letters:
Anaximander
Antisthenes
Kierkegaard

Montesquieu
Occam's razor

12 letters:
Callisthenes
Gymnosophist
Schopenhauer
Wittgenstein

13 letters:
Deipnosophist
Metaphysician

Philosophic(al) Rational, Resigned, Thoughtful, Tranquil

Philtre Aphrodisiac, Charm, Drug, Hippomanes, Potion

Phlegm(atic) Calm, Composed, Pituita(ry), Pituite, Stolid, Unperturbed, Unruffled

Phloem Leptome, Liber

Phobia Aversion, Dread, Fear, Thing

Phoebe, Phoebus Apollo, Artemis, Day-star, Deaconess, Moon, Selene, Sol, Sun

Phoenician Tripolitania

Phoenix Fum, Fung, Paragon, Self-begotten

Phone Bell, Blower, Call, Cellular, Dial, Intercom, Mobile, Moby, Pay, Ring, Smart, > TELEPHONE

Phonetic(s) Acoustic, Articulatory, Mouille, Oral, Palaeotype, Palatal, Plosion, Spoken, Symbol, Synaeresis

▷ **Phonetically** *may indicate* a word sounding like another

Phon(e)y Bogus, Charlatan, Counterfeit, Fake, Hokey, Impostor, Poseur, > SHAM, Specious, Spurious

▷ **Phony** *may indicate* an anagram

Phosphate Monazite, Torbernite, Vivianite, Wavellite, Xenotime

Phosphor(escent), Phosphorescence, Phosphorus Briming, Foxfire, Friar's lantern, Ignis fatuus, Jack o'lantern, Luminescent, Noctilucent, P, Pyrosome, Sarin, Tabun, Will o' the wisp

Photo(copy), Photograph(y), Photographic, Photo finish Ambrotype, Angiogram, Beefcake, Calotype, Clog, Close-up, Composite, Contre-jour, Daguerrotype, Diazo, Duplicate, Enprint, Exposure, Ferroprint, Ferrotype, Film, Flash, Headshot, Heliochrome®, Heliotype, Hologram, Infra-red, Kallitype, Kirlian, Kodak®, Microdot, Microfilm, Microgram, Micrograph, Monochrome, Mugshot, Negative, Opaline, Panel, Picture, Pinhole, Platinotype, Positive, Print, Resorcin, Rotograph, Rotogravure, Schlieren, Sepia, Shoot, Shot, Shutterbug, Snap, Spirit, Still, Take, Talbotype, Time-lapse, Tintype, Tomography, Topo, Trimetrogon, Vignette, Wire, Woodburytype, Xerography, X-ray

Photographer Beaton, Brandt, Cameraman, Cameron, Cartier-Bresson, Daguerre, Fox Talbot, Paparazzo, Schlierin, Shutterbug

Phrase Asyndeton, Buzzword, Catch(word), Cliché, Comma, Expression, Heroic, Hook, Laconism, Leitmotiv, Locution, Mantra, Noun, Phr, Refrain, Riff, Slogan, Tag, Term

Phrygian Midas

Phthisis Decay, TB
Phylactery Amulet, Talisman, Tefillin, Tephillin
Phyllopod Brine-shrimp
Physic(s) Cryogenics, Culver's, Cure, Dose, Geostatics, Health, Kinematics,
   Medicine, Nuclear, Nucleonics, Particle, Photometry, Purge, Remedy,
   Rheology, Science, Solid-state, Thermodynamics, Ultrasonics
Physical Bodily, Carnal, Corpor(e)al, Material, Natural, Tangible
Physician Allopath, Doctor, Galen, Hakim, Harvey, Hippocrates, Internist,
   Leech, Linacre, Lister, Medic(o), Mesmer, Mindererus, Paean, Paracelsus,
   Practitioner, Preceptor, Quack, Roget, Sézary, Stahl, Therapist, Time
Physicist Alfren, Ampere, Angstrom, Appleton, Archimedes, Avogadro,
   Becquerel, Bohr, Born, Bose, Bragg, Brewster, Carnot, Cockcroft, Coulomb,
   Crookes, Curie, Dalton, Davisson, Debye, Dirac, Einstein, Faraday, Fermi,
   Galileo, Gauss, Geiger, Giorgi, Hahn, Hawking, Heaviside, Heisenberg,
   Henry, Hertz, Hooke, Huygens, Joliot-Curie, Josephson, Joule, Kerv, Kirchhoff,
   Landau, Lawe, Lodge, Lorentz, Mach, Marconi, Newton, Oersted, Ohm,
   Oppenheimer, Pauli, Pic(c)ard, Planck, Popov, Rayleigh, Reaumur, Ro(e)ntgen,
   Rutherford, Schottky, Scientist, Sievert, Stark, Torricelli, Tyndall, Van Allen,
   Van der Waals, Volta, Watson-Watt, Weber, Wheeler, Young
Physiognomist, **Physiognomy** Face, Features, Lavater
Physiologist Pavlov
Physiotherapist Masseur
Physique Body, Build, Figure, Pyknic
PI, **Pious** Craw-thumper, Devotional, Devout, Fraud, Gallio, God-fearing, Godly,
   Holy, Holy Willie, Mid-Victorian, Religiose, Sanctimonious, Savoury, Smug,
   Wise, Zaddik
Piaffe Spanish-walk
Pianist Anda, Arrau, Hambourg, Hess, Hofmann, Liszt, Mingus, Morton,
   Pachmann, Padarewski, Répétiteur, Tatum, Vamper, Virtuoso
Piano Baby grand, Bechstein, Boudoir grand, Celesta, Celeste, Concert grand,
   Cottage, Flugel, Forte, Grand, Honkytonk, Keyboard, Overstrung, P, Player,
   Prepared, Semi-grand, Softly, Steinway, Stride, Thumb, Upright
Piano-maker Erard
Picaroon Brigand, Corsair, Pirate, Rogue
Piccadilly Whist
Piccolo Ottavino
Pick(er), **Pickaxe**, **Picking**, **Pick up** Break, Choice, > CHOOSE, Cream, Cull, Elite,
   Flower, Gather, Glean, Gurlet, Hack, Hopper, Mattock, Nap, Nibble, Oakum,
   Plectrum, Pluck, Plum, Select, Single, Sort, Steal, Strum, Tong, Wale
▷ **Picked** *may indicate* an anagram
Picket Demonstrate, Flying, Pale, Palisade, Protester, Stake, Tether, Tie
Pickings Harvest, Profits, Scrounging, Spoils
Pickle(r) Achar, Brine, Cabbage, Caper, Chow-chow, Chutney, Corn, Cure,
   Dilemma, Dill, Eisel, Esile, Gherkin, Girkin, Jam, Kimchi, Marinade, Marinate,
   Mess, Mull, Olive, Onion, Peculate, Peregrine, Piccalilli, > PLIGHT, Samp(h)ire,
   Scrape, Souse, Vinegar, Wolly
Picklock Oustiti, Peterman
Pick-me-up Bracer, Drink, Restorer, Reviver, Tonic
Pickpocket(s) Adept, Bung, Cly-faker, Cutpurse, Dip, Diver, Fagin, File, Nipper,
   Swell mob, Wire
Pick-up Arrest, Light o'love, Truck, Ute
Picnic Alfresco, Braaivleis, Burgoo, Clambake, Fun, Outing, Push-over, Spread,

Wase-goose, Wayzgoose

Picture(s) Anaglyph, Arpillera, Art, Bambocciades, Bitmap, Canvas, Collage, Cyclorama, Decoupage, Depict, Describe, Diptych, Drawing, Drypoint, Emblem, Epitome, Etching, Film, Flick, Fresco, Gouache, Graphic, Histogram, Icon, Identikit®, Imagery, Inset, Kakemono, Landscape, Likeness, Lithograph, Montage, Motion, Movie, Moving, Movy, Mugshot, Myriorama, Oil, Photo, Photofit, Photogram, Photomosaic, Photomural, Pin-up, Pix, Plate, Polyptych, Portrait, Predella, Prent, Presentment, Print, Retraitt, Retrate, Scene, Shadowgraph, Shot, Slide, Snapshot, Stereochrome, Stereogram, Stereograph, Stevengraph, Still-life, Table(au), Talkie, Thermogram, Tone, Topo, Transfer, Transparency, Vanitas, Veetograph, Vision, Votive, Vraisemblance, Word, Zincograph

Picturesque Idyllic, Scenic

Pidgin Chinook jargon, Creole, Fanagalo, Fanakalo, Japlish, New Guinea, Police Motu, Solomon Islands, Tok Pisin

Pie(s) Anna, Banoffee, Battalia, Bridie, Camp, Chewet, Cobbler, Cottage, Curry puff, Custard, Deep-dish, Easy, Flan, Hash, Humble, Madge, Mess, Mince, Mud, Mystery bag, Pandowdy, Pastry, Pasty, Patty, Périgord, Pica, Piet, Pirog, Pizza, Pyat, Pyet, Pyot, Quiche, Rappe, Resurrection, Shepherd's, Shoofly, Spoil, Squab, Stargaz(e)y, Star(ry)-gazy, Sugar, Tart, Tarte tatin, Torte, Tourtiere, Turnover, Tyropitta, Umble, Vol-au-vent, Warden

▷ **Pie** *may indicate* an anagram

Piebald Calico, Dappled, Motley, Pied, Pinto, Skewbald

Piece(s) Add, Bishop, Bit, Blot, Cameo, Cannon, Cent, Charm, > CHESSMAN, Chip, Chunk, Coin, Companion, Component, Concerto, Conversation, Crumb, Domino, End, Extract, Flitters, Fragment, Frust, Gat, Goring, > GUN, Haet, Hait, Hunk, Item, Join, Mammock, Medaillons, Mite, Money, Morceau, Morsel, Museum, Nip, Novelette, Oddment, Off-cut, Ort, Part, Party, Patch, Pawn, Period, Peso, Pistareen, Pole, > PORTION, Recital, Scliff, Scrap, Section, Set, Shard, Sherd, Skliff, Slice, Sliver, Sou, Speck, String, Stub, Swatch, Tait, Tate, Tile, Toccata, Truncheon, Wedge

Pièce de résistance Star-turn

Piecemeal, Piecework Gradually, Intermittent, Jigsaw, Serial, Tut

Pie-crust Coffin, Lid, Pastry

Pied-à-terre Nest, Pad

Pieman Shepherd

Pier(s) Anta, Groyne, Jetty, Jutty, Landing, Mole, Plowman, Quay, Slipway, Swiss roll, Wharf

Pierce(d), Piercer, Piercing Accloy, Awl, Broach, Cleave, Cribrose, Dart, Drill, Endart, Fenestrate(d), Gimlet, Gore, Gride, Gryde, Hull, Impale, Jag, Keen, Lance, Lancinate, Lobe, Move, Needle, Penetrate, Perforate, Pike, Poignant, Punch, Puncture, Riddle, Rive, Shrill, Skewer, Slap, Sleeper, Spear, Spike, Spit, Stab, Steek, Stiletto, Sting, Thirl, Thrill(ant)

Piety Devotion, Purity, Sanctity

Piffle Bilge, Codswallop, Hogwash, Tommy-rot, Twaddle

Pig(s), Piggy, Pigskin Anthony, Babe, Babirusa, Baconer, Barrow, Bartholomew, Bessemer, Bland, Boar, Bonham, British lop, Bush, Captain Cooker, Doll, Duroc, Elt, Farrow, Fastback, Football, Gadarene, Gilt, Gloucester, Glutton, Gride, Grumphie, Guffie, Guinea, Gus, Ham, Hog, Ingot, Iron, Javelina, Kentledge, Kintledge, Lacombe, Landrace, Lard, Large black, Large white, Lingot, Long, Middle white, Napoleon, Old Spot, Peccary, Policeman, Pork(er), Razorback, Rosser, Runt, Saddleback, Shoat, Shot(e), Shott, Slip, Snowball,

Sounder, Sow, Squealer, Sucking, Suid(ae), Tamworth, Tayassuid, Tithe, Toe, Tootsie, Vietnamese pot-bellied, Warthog, Welsh, Yelt

Pig-disease Bullnose

Pigeon Archangel, Barb, Bird, Cape, Capuchin, Carrier, Clay, Cropper, Culver, Cumulet, Dove, Fairy swallow, Fantail, Goura, Gull, Homer, Homing, Horseman, Jacobin, Kuku, Manumea, Nun, Owl, Passenger, Peristeronic, Pouter, Ringdove, Rock(er), Roller, Ront(e), Ruff, Runt, Scandaroon, Solitaire, Spot, Squab, Squealer, Stock-dove, Stool, Talkie-talkee, Tippler, Tooth-billed, Tumbler, Turbit, Wonga-wonga, Zoozoo

Pigeonhole Classify, Compartment, File, Postpone, Shelve, Slot, Stereotype

Pigeon-house Columbary, Cote, Dovecot(e)

Pig-food Mast, Swill

Pig-iron Kentledge, Kintledge

Pigment(ation) Anthoclore, Anthocyan(in), Argyria, Betacyanin, Bilirubin, Biliverdin, Bister, Bistre, Bronzing, Cappagh-brown, Carmine, Carotene, Carotenoid, Carotin, Carotinoid, Chloasma, Chlorophyll, Chrome, Chromogen, Cobalt, Colcothar, Colour, Crocus, Dye, Etiolin, Flake-white, Flavin(e), Fucoxanthin, Gamboge, Gossypol, Haem, H(a)ematin, H(a)emocyanin, H(a)emoglobin, Hem(e), Iodopsin, Lamp-black, Lithopone, Liverspot, Lutein, Luteolin, Madder, Melanin, Monastral®, Naevus, Nigrosine, Ochre, Opsin, Orpiment, Paris-green, Phthalocyanine, Phycobilin, Phycoerythrin, Phycophaein, Phycoxanthin, Phytochrome, Porphyrin, Pterin, Quercetin, Realgar, Red lead, Respiratory, Retinene, Rhiboflavin, Rhodopsin, Scheele's green, Sepia, Sienna, Sinopia, Smalt, Tapetum, Tempera, Terre-verte, Tincture, Toner, Ultramarine, Umber, Urobilin, Urochrome, Verditer, Viridian, Whitewash, Xanthophyll, Xanthopterin(e), Zinc white

Pigtail Braid, Cue, Plait, Queue

Pi jaw Cant

Pike Assegai, Crag, Dory, Fogash, Gar(fish), Ged, Gisarme, Glaive, Hie, Holostei, Javelin, Lance, Luce, Partisan, Pickerel, Ravensbill, Scafell, Snock, Spear, Speed, Spontoon, Vouge, Walleyed

▶ **Pilaster** *see* PILLAR

Pile(d), Piles, Piling Agger, Amass, Atomic, Bing, Bomb, Camp-sheathing, Camp-shedding, Camp-sheeting, Camp-shot, Clamp, Cock, Column, Crowd, Deal, Down, Emerods, Farmers, Fender, Fig, Floccus, Fortune, Galvanic, Hair, Haycock, Heap, Hept, Historic, Hoard, Load, Lot, Marleys, Mass, Nap, Post, Pyre, Raft, Reactor, Ream(s), Rouleau, Screw, Shag, Sheet, > STACK, Starling, Stilt, Trichome, Upheap, Voltaic, Wealth, Windrow, Wodge

Pile-driver Tup

Pilfer(ing) Crib, Filch, Finger, Maraud, Miche, Nick, Peculate, Pickery, Pickle, Pinch, Plagiarise, Plunder, Purloin, Snitch, > STEAL

Pilgrim(age) Aske, Childe Harold, Expedition, Fatima, Hadj(i), Haji, Hajj(i), Karbala, Kerbela, Loreto, Lourdes, Mecca, Palmer, Pardoner, Reeve, Scallop-shell, Shrine, Voyage, Yatra

Pill(s) Abortion, Ball, Beverley, Bitter, Bolus, Caplet, Capsule, Dex, Doll, Dose, Globule, Lob, Medication, Medicine, Number nine, Peel, Pellet, Pep, Pilula, Pilule, Placebo, Poison, Protoplasmal, Radio, Sleeping, Spansule, Tablet, Troche, Trochisk, Upper

Pillage Booty, Devastate, Plunder, Ransack, Rapine, Ravage, Razzia, Robbery, Sack, Spoil

Pillar(ed), Pillars Anta, Apostle, Atlantes, Baluster, Balustrade, Boaz, Canton, Caryatides, Cippus, Columel, Column, Earth, Eustyle, Gendarme, Hercules,

Herm, Impost, Islam, Jachin, Lat, Man, Modiolus, Monolith, Newel, Nilometer, Obelisk, Pedestal, Peristyle, Pier, Post, Respond, Stalactite, Stalagmite, Stoop, Telamon, Tetrastyle, Trumeau

Pill-box Hat, Inro

Pillion Cushion, Pad, Rear

Pillory Cang(ue), Cippus, Crucify, Jougs, Little-ease, Pelt, Satirise, Slam

Pillow(case) Bear, Beer, Bere, Bolster, Cod, Cow, Cushion, Headrest, Hop, Lace, Pad, Pulvinar

Pilot Ace, Airman, Auto(matic), Aviator, Captain, > **CONDUCT**, Experimental, George, Govern, Guide, Hobbler, Lead, Lodesman, Lodestar, Palinure, Palinurus, Pitt, Prune, Shipman, Steer, Test, Tiphys, Trial, Usher, Wingman

Pimento Allspice

Pimp Apple-squire, Bludger, Fancyman, Fleshmonger, Hoon, Mack, Pandarus, Pander, Ponce, Procurer, Solicit, Souteneur

Pimpernel Bastard, Bog, Scarlet, Water, Wincopipe, Wink-a-peep, Yellow

Pimple, **Pimply** Blackhead, Botch, Bubukle, Button, Gooseflesh, Grog-blossom, Hickey, Horripilation, Papula, Plook, Plouk, Pock, Pustule, Quat, Rumblossom, Rum-bud, Spot, Tetter, Uredinial, Wen, Whelk, Whitehead, Zit

Pin Bayonet, Belaying, Bolt, Brooch, Cotter, Curling, Dowel, Drawing, Drift, End, Fasten, Fid, Firing, Fix, Gam, Gudgeon, Hair, Hairgrip, Hob, Joggle, Kevel, King, Nail, Needle, Nog, Panel, Peg, Pintle, Pivot, Preen, Rivet, Rolling, Safety, Scarf, SCART, Scatter, Shear, Skewer, Skittle, Skiver, Spike, Spindle, Split, Staple, Stick, Stump, Swivel, Taper, Thole, Thumbtack, Tre(e)nail, U-bolt, Woolder, Wrest, Wrist

Pinafore Apron, Brat, HMS, Overall, Pinny, Save-all, Tire

Pince-nez Nose-nippers

Pincers Chela, Claw, Forceps, Forfex, Nipper, Tweezers

Pinch(ed) Arrest, Bit, Bone, Chack, Constrict, Cramp, Crimp, Crisis, Emergency, Gaunt, Misappropriate, Nab, Nick, Nim, Nip, Peculate, Peel, Pilfer, Pocket, Pook(it), Prig, Pugil, Raft, Rob, Scrimp, Scrounge, Skimp, Smatch, Snabble, Snaffle, Sneak, Sneap, Sneeshing, Snuff, Squeeze, > **STEAL**, Swipe, Tate, Tweak, Twinge

Pine(s), **Pining** Arolla, Bristlecone, Celery, Cembra, Chile, Cluster, Cone, Conifer, Cypress, Droop, Dwine, Earn, Erne, Fret, Ground, Hone, Hoop, Huon, Jack, Japanese umbrella, Jeffrey, Kauri, Languish, Languor, Loblolly, Lodgepole, Long, Longleaf, Monkey-puzzle, Moon, Norfolk Island, Norway, Nut, Oregon, Parana, Picea, Pitch, Radiata, Red, Scotch, Scots, Screw, Softwood, Spruce, Starve, Stone, Sugar, Tree, Umbrella, Urman, Waste, White, Yearn

Pineapple Anana, Bomb, Bromelia, Grenade, Pina, Poll, Sorosis, Tillandsia

Ping Knock, Whir(r)

Pinguin Anana(s)

Pinion Fetter, Penne, Pinnoed, Secure, Shackle, Wing

Pink Blush, Carolina, Castory, Clove, Colour, Coral, Dianthus, Dutch, Emperce, FT, Fuchsia, Gillyflower, Knock, Lake, Lychnis, Moss, Mushroom, Oyster, Peach-blow, Peak, Perce, Pierce, Pompadour, Pounce, Rose(ate), Ruddy, Salmon, Scallop, Shell, Shocking, Shrimp, Spigelia, Spit, Stab, Tiny

Pinnacle Acme, Apex, Crest, Crown, Height, Needle, Pinnet, Summit

Pinniped Seal

Pin-point Focus, Highlight, Identify, Isolate, Localise

Pint(s) Cab, Jar, Log, Reputed

Pintail Duck, Smeath, Smee(th)

Pin-up Cheesecake, Dish, Star

Pioneer Baird, Bandeirante, Blaze, Boone, Colonist, Emigrant, Explore, Fargo, Fleming, Frontiersman, Harbinger, Innovator, Lead, Marconi, Oecist, Pathfinder, Planter, Rochdale, Sandgroper, Settler, Spearhead, Trail-blazer, Trekker, Voortrekker, Waymaker, Wells

▸ **Pious** *see* PI

Pip Ace, Acinus, Blackball, Bleep, Hip, Hump, Phil, Pyrene, Seed, Star

Pipe(s), Piper, Pipeline, Piping Antara, Aorta, Aulos, Balance, Barrel, Blub, Boatswain's, Bong, Briar, Broseley, Bubble, Calabash, Call, Calumet, Chanter, Cheep, Cherrywood, Chibouk, Chibouque, Chillum, Churchwarden, Clay, Cob, Conduit, Corncob, Crane, Cutty, Down, Downcomer, Drain, Drill, Dry riser, Duct, Dudeen, Dudheen, Ell, Escape, Exhaust, Faucet, Feed, Fistula, Flue, Flute, Gage, Gedact, Gedeckt, Hawse, Hod, Hogger, Hooka(h), Hose, Hubble-bubble, Hydrant, Indian, Irish, Jet, Kalian, Kelly, Mains, Manifold, Marsyas, Meerschaum, Mirliton, Montre, Narghile, Narg(h)il(l)y, Nargile(h), Oat(en), Oboe, Organ, Ottavino, Pan, Peace, Pepper, Pibroch, Piccolo, Pied, Pifferaro, Pitch, Poverty, Pule, Qanat, Quill, Rainwater, Recorder, Ree(d), Rise, Riser, Sack-doudling, Salicional, Sennit, Serpent, Service, Sewer, Shalm, Shawm, Shrike, Siphon, Skirl, Sluice, Soil, Squeak, Stack, Standpipe, Stopcock, Stummel, Syrinx, Tail, Throttle, Tibia, Tootle, Trachea, Tremie, Tube, Tubule, Tweet, U-bend, Uillean(n), Union, Uptake, U-tube, Vent, Volcanic, Waste, Water(-spout), Weasand, Whistle, Woodnote

Pipefish Sea-adder

Pipe-laying Graft

Pipit Bird, Skylark, Titlark

Pippin Apple, Orange, Ribston

Pipsqueak Nobody

Piquancy, Piquant Pungent, Racy, Relish, Salt, Sharp, Spicy, Tangy

Pique Dod, Huff, Resentment, Titillate

Piracy, Pirate, Piratical Algerine, Barbarossa, Blackbeard, Boarder, Bootleg, Brigand, Buccaneer, Buccanier, Cateran, Condottier, Conrad, Corsair, Crib, Dampier, Fil(l)ibuster, Flint, Hijack, Hook, Kidd, Lift, Loot, Morgan, Picaro(on), Pickaroon, Plagiarise, Plunder, Rakish, Rover, Sallee-man, Sallee-rover, Sea-king, Sea-rat, Sea-robber, Silver, Skull and crossbones, Smee, Steal, Teach, Thief, Viking, Water-rat, Water-thief

Piranha Caribe, Characinoid, Piraya

Pistillate Female

Pistol Air, Ancient, Automatic, Barker, Barking-iron, Colt®, Dag, Derringer, Gat, > GUN, Hackbut, Horse, Luger®, Pepperbox, Petronel, Puffer, Revolver, Rod, Saloon, Shooter, Starter, Starting, Very, Water, Weapon

Piston Four-stroke, Plunger, Ram, Trunk

Pit(ted) Abyss, Alveolus, Antrum, Bottomless, Catch, Cave, Cesspool, Chasm, Cloaca, Colliery, Crater, Den, Depression, Depth, Dungmere, Ensile, Fossa, Fovea, Foxhole, Hangi, Heapstead, Hell, Hole, Hollow, Inferno, Inspection, Khud, Lacunose, Lime, Mark, Match, Measure, > MINE, Mosh, Orchestra, Parterre, Pip, Play, Pock, Pock-mark, Potato, Punctate, Putamen, Pyrene, Ravine, Scrobicule, Silo, Soakaway, Solar plexus, Stone, Sump, Tar, Tear, Trap, Trou-de-loup

Pitch(ed) Absolute, Asphalt, Atilt, Attune, Bitumen, Burgundy, Coal-tar, Concert, Crease, Diamond, Dive, Ela, Elect, Encamp, Erect, Establish, Fever, Fling, Fork, Ground, International, Intonation, Key, Labour, Length, Level, Lurch, Maltha, Mineral, Nets, Neume, Patter, Peck, Perfect, Philosophical, Piceous, Pight, Pin, Plong(e), Plunge, Pop, Resin, Rock, Ruff(e), Sales, Scend,

Seel, Send, Shape, Sling, Slope, Soprarino, Spiel, Stoit, Tar, Tessitura, Tilt, Tone, Tonemic, Tonus, Tremolo, Tune, Vibrato, Wicket, Wood
Pitchblende Cleveite
Pitcher(-shaped) Aryt(a)enoid, Ascidium, Bowler, Cruse, Ewer, Jug, Steen, Urceolus
Pitchfork Hurl, Toss
Pitfall Danger, Hazard, Trap
Pith(y) Ambatch, Aphorism, Apo(ph)thegm, Core, Down, Essence, Gnomic, Hat-plant, Heart, Marrow, Medulla, Moxa, Nucleus, Rag, Succinct, Terse
Pithead Broo, Brow, Minehead
Pithless Thowless
Pitiless Flint-hearted, Hard, Ruthless
Piton Rurp
Pitt Chatham
Pity, Piteous, Pitiful Ah, Alack, Alas, Commiseration, > COMPASSION, Mercy, Pathos, Rue, Ruth(ful), Seely, Shame, Sin, Sympathy
Pivot(al) Ax(i)le, Central, Focal, Fulcrum, Gooseneck, Gudgeon, Kingbolt, Revolve, Rotate, Slue, > SWIVEL, Trunnion, Turn, Wheel
Pixie Brownie, Elf, Fairy, Gremlin, Sprite
Pizza Calzone, Pepperoni
Placard Affiche, Bill, Playbill, Poster
Placate Appease, Conciliate, Pacify, Propitiate, Soothe
Place Ad loc, Aim, Allocate, Berth, Bro, Decimal, Deploy, Deposit, Fix, Habitat, Hither, Howf, Identify, Impose, > IN PLACE OF, Install, Job, Joint, Juxtapose, Lay, Lieu, Locality, Locate, Locus, Pitch, Plat, Plaza, Point, Posit, > POSITION, Put, Realm, Region, Resting, Scene, Second, Set, Site, Situate, Situation, Spot, Stead, Sted(e), Stedd(e), Stratify, Town, Vendome
Placid Cool, Easy, Easy-osy, Quiet, Tame, Tranquil
Plagiarise, Plagiarist Copy, Crib, Lift, Pirate, Steal
Plague (spot) Annoy, Bane, Bedevil, Black death, Boil, Bubonic, Burden, Cattle, Curse, Dog, Dun, Goodyear, Goujeers, Harry, Infestation, Locusts, Lues, Murrain, Murran, Murrin, Murrion, Pest, Pester, Pox, Press, Scourge, Tease, Token, Torture, Try, Vex
Plaid Maud, Roon, Shepherd's, Tartan, Wales
Plain(s) Abraham, Archimedes, Artless, Ascetic, Au naturel, Bald, Banat, Bare, Blatant, Broad, Campagna, Campo, Candid, Carse, Ceará, Chryse, Clavius, Clear, Cook, Dowdy, Downright, Dry, Esdraelon, Evident, Explicit, Flat, Flood, Girondist, Gran Chaco, Great, Homely, Homespun, Inornate, Kar(r)oo, Lande, Langrenus, Llano, Lombardy, Lowland, Maidan, Manifest, Marathon, Mare, Monochrome, Nullarbor, Obvious, Ocean of storms, Oceanus Procellarum, Olympia, > ORDINARY, Outspoken, Overt, Packstaff, Pampa(s), Paramo, Patent, Pikestaff, Playa, Polje, Prairie, Prose, Ptolemaeus, Purbach, Sabkha(h), Sabkha(t), Sailing, Salisbury, Savanna(h), Secco, Serengeti, Sharon, Simple, Sodom, Spoken, Staked, Steppe, Tableland, Thessaly, Tundra, Vega, Veldt, Visible, Walled
Plainsman Llanero
Plainsong Ambrosian, Chant
Plaint(ive) Complaint, Dirge, Lagrimoso, Lament, Melancholy, Sad, Whiny
Plaintiff Doe, Impeacher, Litigant, Suer
Plait Braid, Crimp, Cue, Frounce, Furbelow, Goffer, Intertwine, Pigtail, Plica, Plight, Queue, Ruche, Sennit, Sinnet, Splice
Plan(ned), Planner, Planning Aim, American, Angle, Architect, Arrange,

Axonometric, Blueprint, Brew, Budget, Care, Chart, Commission, Complot, Contingency, Contrive, Dalton, Dart, Deliberate, Delors, Design, Desyne, Device, Devise, Diagram, Draft, Drawing, Elevation, Engineer, European, Family, Five-Year, Floor, Format, Galveston, Game, Ground, Hang, Ichnography, Idea, Idee, Instal(l)ment, Intent, Lay(out), Leicester, Map, Marshall, Master, Mastermind, Mean, Outline, Pattern, Pipe-dream, Plat, Plot, Ploy, Policy, Premeditate, Prepense, Procedure, Programme, Project, Projet, Proposal, Protraction, Rapacki, Scenario, Schedule, Scheme, Schlieffen, Spec(ification), Stratagem, Strategy, Subterfuge, System, Tactician, Town, Wheeze

Plane Aero(dyne), Air, > **AIRCRAFT**, Airliner, Airship, Bandit, Block, Boeing, Bomber, Bus, Camel, Canard, Cartesian, Chenar, Chinar, Comet, Concorde, Crate, Dakota, Datum, Delta-wing, Even, Facet, Fault, Fillester, Fillister, Flat, Focal, Galactic, Glider, Gotha, Homaloid, Hurricane, Icosahedron, Icosohedra, Inclined, Jack, Jet, Jointer, Jumbo, Level, Main, MIG, Mirage, Mosquito, Moth, Octagon, Perspective, Platanus, Polygon, Pursuit, Rocket, Router, Shackleton, Shave, Smooth, Sole, Spitfire, Spokeshave, Spy, Stealth (bomber), STOL, Surface, Sycamore, Tail, Taube, Thrust, Tow, Trainer, Tree, Trident, Trying, Viscount

Plane figure Endecagon, Hendecagon

Planet(s), Planetary Alphonsine, Ariel, Asteroid, Body, Cabiri, Ceres, Chiron, Constellation, Earth, Eros, Extrasolar, Georgian, Giant, Hyleg, Inferior, Inner, Jovian, Jupiter, Major, Mars, Mercury, Minor, Moon, Neptune, Pluto, Primary, Psyche, Quartile, Red, Satellitium, Saturn, Sphere, Starry, Sun, Superior, Terrestrial, Uranus, Venus, Vista, Vulcan, World

Plangent Mournful

Plank Board, Chess, Deal, Duckboard, Garboard, Plonk, Sarking, Slab, Spirketting, Straik, Strake, Stringer, Weatherboard, Wood, Wrest

Plankton Neuston, Pelagic, Red tide, Seston, Spatfall

Plant(s), Plant part Acrogen, Annual, Anther, Bed, Biennial, Diota, CAM, Cotyledon, Cultigen, Cultivar, Dibble, Ecad, Embed, Endogen, Enrace, Epiphyte, Establish, Factory, Fix, Forb, Growth, G(u)ild, Halophyte, Herbarium, House, Insert, Instil, Inter, Labiate, Land, Lathe, Machinery, Ornamental, Phloem, Pilot, Power, Sensitive, Sere, Shrub, Simple, Sow, Succulent, Therophyte, Tree, Vegetal, Vegetation, Works

PLANTS

3 letters:	Aloe	Sego	Aroid
Dal	Anil	Sola	Benni
Kex	Arum	Sunn	Blite
Meu	Deme	Taro	Boree
Pia	Fern	Thea	Buchu
Rue	Grex	Vine	Bucku
Set	Herb	Weld	Bugle
Til	Ixia	Wort	Calla
Udo	Kali	Yarr	Canna
Urd	Loco		Chufa
Yam	More	5 letters:	Clary
	Nard	Ajwan	Clote
4 letters:	Ombu	Anise	Cress
Alga	Rhus	Anona	Fouat

Fouet
Gemma
Glaux
Gorse
Guaco
Hosta
Inula
Jalap
Kenaf
Kudzu
Lotus
Lurgi
Medic
Morel
Murva
Musci
Orpin
Orris
Oshac
Panax
Sedge
Sedum
Spink
Tetra
Timbo
Urena

6 letters:
Acacia
Acorus
Ajowan
Alisma
Alpine
Annona
Arnica
Bablah
Betony
Burnet
Cactus
Cassia
Catnep
Cnicus
Cosmea
Cosmos
Cowpea
Croton
Datura
Derris
Dodder
Exacum
Exogen
Fat hen

Gnetum
Hyssop
Iberis
Knawel
Madder
Mallow
Manioc
Medick
Mimosa
Moorva
Nerium
Nettle
Nuphar
Orchis
Orpine
Pachak
Protea
Rattle
Reseda
Retama
Rubber
Sesame
Silene
Smilax
Spider
Spurge
Spurry
Squill
Styrax
Teasel
Thrift
Tulipa
Tutsan
Yarrow
Zinnia

7 letters:
Alkanet
All-good
Allseed
Alyssum
Brinjal
Burdock
Caltrop
Cardoon
Carduus
Carline
Cat's ear
Chervil
Dasheen
Dioecia
Dittany

Dogbane
Ephedra
Felwort
Filaree
Fly-trap
Freesia
Frogbit
Gentian
Gerbera
Haemony
Henbane
Ipomoea
Isoetes
Lantana
Lucerne
Lychnis
Madwort
Mahonia
Manihot
Melilot
Mercury
Mullein
Nemesia
Nigella
Nonsuch
Opuntia
Palmiet
Pareira
Petunia
Puccoon
Ragwort
Rhodora
Ruellia
Saffron
Salfern
Salsola
Sampire
Sanicle
Scandix
Setwall
Skirret
Spignel
Spiraea
Spurrey
Stapela
Statice
Syringa
Tagetes
Thallus
Triffid
Tritoma
Vanilla

Vervain
Weigela
Zedoary

8 letters:
Acanthus
Agrimony
Angelica
Arenaria
Asphodel
Bindi-eye
Buckbean
Buplever
Camomile
Canaigre
Centaury
Costmary
Cyclamen
Diandria
Dielytra
Dogberry
Dumbcane
Feverfew
Fluellin
Foxglove
Fumitory
Geophyte
Gesnaria
Gnetales
Gromwell
Hag-taper
Henequen
Hepatica
Hibiscus
Larkspur
Lavender
Mandrake
Mariposa
Monstera
Oleander
Opopanax
Plumbago
Psilotum
Putchock
Ratsbane
Roly-poly
Samphire
Scammony
Sea-blite
Self-heal
Silphium
Sparaxis

- Spergula
- Stapelia
- Staragen
- Starwort
- Tamarisk
- Tritonia
- Tuberose
- Tuckahoe
- Wait-a-bit
- Wormseed

9 letters:
- Adderwort
- Andromeda
- Arrowhead
- Arrowroot
- Artemisia
- Artillery
- Aubrietia
- Bald-money
- Brooklime
- Broom-rape
- Butterbur
- Celandine
- Colocasia
- Coltsfoot
- Cordaites
- Coreopsis
- Coriander
- Dittander
- Erythrina
- Euphorbia
- Eyebright
- Fenugreek
- Germander

Groundsel
Herb-paris
Hoarhound
Horehound
Horse-tail
Liver-wort
Lousewort
Mare's-tail
Moneywort
Moschatel
Ouviranda
Patchouli
Pearlwort
Penstemon
Pimpernel
Portulaca
Rafflesia
Rocambole
Santoline
Screwpine
Spearmint
Spearwort
Spikenard
Stone-crop
Sweet-gale
Tomatillo
Tormentil
Wake-robin
Wincopipe
Wolf's bane
Woundwort

10 letters:
Alexanders
Ampelopsis

Angiosperm
Aspidistra
Astralagus
Dyer's-broom
Earth-smoke
Five-finger
Fraxinella
Fritillary
Goat-sallow
Goat's-thorn
Goat-willow
Goldilocks
Icosandria
Immortelle
Maidenhair
Mignonette
Parkleaves
Pentstemon
Rest-harrow
Salicornia
Touch-me-not
Tropophyte
Yellowroot

11 letters:
Acidanthera
Bear's-breech
Bristle-fern
Callitriche
Convolvulus
Dusty-miller
Hurtleberry
Incarvillea
Loosestrife
Meadowsweet

Nancy-pretty
Pelargonium
Schizophyte
Sempervivum
Swiss cheese
Thallophyte
Thimbleweed
Tous-les-mois
Wintergreen

12 letters:
Adam's flannel
Epacridaceae
Midsummermen
Morning glory
Parsley-piert
Pasqueflower
Phytobenthos
Resurrection
Southernwood
Venus flytrap
Wandering jew
Water-soldier

13 letters:
Townhall clock
Traveller's joy

14 letters:
Chincherinchee
Lords and ladies
Shepherd's purse

Plantagenet Angevin, Broom
Plantain Mato(o)ke, Ribwort, Waybread
Plantation Arboretum, Bosket, Bosquet, Estate, Grove, Hacienda, Pen, Pinetum, Ranch, Tara, Vineyard
Plant disease Anthracnose, Bunt, Club-root, Curlytop, Frogeye, Psillid yellows, Rosette, Smut, Sooty mould
Planted In, Under
Planter Dibber, Farmer, Settler, Trowel
Plaque Calculus, Dental, Plateau, Scale
Plasma Dextran, Sigmond
Plaster(ed) Bandage, Blister, Blotto, Butterfly clip, Cake, Cataplasm, Clam, Clatch, Compo, Court, Daub, Diachylon, Diachylum, Drunk, Emplastrum, Fresco, Gesso, Grout, Gypsum, Intonaco, Leep, Lit, Mud, Mustard, Oiled, Parge(t), Porous, Poultice, Render, Roughcast, Scratch-coat, Screed, Secco, Shellac, Sinapism, Smalm, Smarm, Smear, Sowsed, Staff, Sticking, Stookie, Stucco, Teer

Plastic Bakelite®, Cel(luloid), Cling film, Ductile, Fablon®, Fictile, Fluon, Formica®, Ionomer, Laminate, Loid, Lucite®, Melamine, Perspex®, Plexiglass®, Pliant, Polyethylene, Polystyrene, Polythene, Polyvinyl, PVC, Reinforced, Styrene, Styrofoam®, Teflon®, Urea-formaldehyde, Vinyl, Wet-look, Yielding

▷ **Plastic** *may indicate* an anagram

Plastic surgeon McIndoe

Plastic surgery Neoplasty, Otoplasty, Rhinoplasty

Plate(s), Plated, Platelet, Plating Acierage, Ailette, Angle, Anode, Armadillo, Armour, Ashet, Baffle, Bakestone, Baleen, Batten, Brass, Butt, Chamfrain, Chape, Charger, Chrome, Coat, Coccolith, Communion, Copper, Cramper, Cribellum, Ctene, Dasypus, Deadman, Denture, Diaphragm, Disc, Dish, Echo, Electro, Electrotype, Elytron, Elytrum, Enamel, Entoplastron, Escutcheon, Face, Fashion, Fine, Fish, Flatware, Foil, Frog, Frons, Futtock, Glacis, Gold, Graal, Ground, Gula, Half, Home, Horseshoe, Hot, Illustration, L, Lame, Lamella, Lamina, Lanx, Latten, Licence, Mascle, Mazarine, Nail, Nef, Neural, Nickel, Notum, Number, Ortho, Osteoderm, Paten, Patina, Patine, Pauldron, Peba, Petri, Phototype, Planometer, Plaque, Plastron, Platter, Pleximeter, Poitrel, Prescutum, Print, Quarter, Race, Registration, Riza, Rove, Salamander, Scale, Screw, Scrim, Scutcheon, Scute, Scutum, Seg, Selling, Sheffield, Shield, Sieve, Silver, Slab, Soup, Spacer, Spoiler, Squama, Steel, Stencil, Stereo(type), Sternite, Strake, Surface, Swash, T, Tablet, Tace, Tasse(l), Tectonic, Tergite, Terne, Theoretical, Tin(ware), Torsel, Touch, Trade, Trencher, Trophy, Tsuba, Tuill(ett)e, Tymp, Urostegite, Vane, Vanity, Vassail, Vessail, Vessel, Wall, Water, Web, Wet, Whirtle, Whole, Wortle, Wrap(a)round, Zincograph

Plateau Altiplano, Deccan, Eifel, Field, Fjeld, Had(h)ramaut, Highland, Highveld, Horst, Kalahari, Kar(r)oo, La Mancha, Langres, Laurentian, Mat(t)o Grosso, Mesa Verde, Meseta, Nilgiris, Ozark, Paramo, Piedmont, Puna, Shan, Shillong, Tableland, The Kimberleys, Ustyurt

Platform Accommodation, Almemar, Bandstand, Barbette, Base, Bema, Bier, Catafalque, Catwalk, Crane, Crow's nest, Dais, Deck, Dolly, Drilling, Emplacement, Entablement, Estrade, Exedra, Exhedra, Flake, Footpace, Footplate, Foretop, Gangplank, Gantry, Gauntree, Gauntry, Gravity, Hustings, Kang, Landing stage, Machan, Oil, Pad, Paint-bridge, Pallet, Perron, Plank, Podium, Predella, Production, Programme, Pulpit, Raft, Rig, Rostrum, Round-top, Scaffold, Shoe, Skidway, Soapbox, Space, Sponson, > **STAGE**, Stand, Stereobate, Stoep, Stylobate, Tee, Terminal, Thrall, Ticket, Top, Traverser, Tribunal, Tribune, Turntable, Wharf

Platinum Pt, Ruthenium, Sperrylite

Platitude Bromide, Cliché, Truism

Platocephalus Flat-headed

Platonic, Platonist Academician, Ideal, Spiritual

Platoon Company, Squad, Team

Platter Dish, EP, Graal, Grail, Lanx, LP, Plate, Record, Salver, Trencher

Platypus Duckbill, Duck-mole, Water mole

Plausible, Plausibility Cogent, Credible, Fair, Glib, Oil, Probable, Proball, Sleek, Smooth, Specious

Play(ing) Accompany, Active, Amusement, Antic, Antigone, Brand, Bust, Candida, Caper, Charm, Chronicle, Clearance, Crucible, Curtain-raiser, Daff, Dandle, Docudrama, Drama, Echo, Endgame, Equus, Escapade, Everyman, Extended, Fair, Finesse, Foul, Frisk, Frolic, Fun, Gamble, Gambol, Game, Ghosts, Hamlet, Harp, Holiday, Inside, Interlude, Jam, Jape, Jest, Jeu, Kinderspiel, Kitchen-sink, Laik, Lake, Latitude, Lear, Leeway, Licence, Lilt,

Long, Loot, Macbeth, Mask, Masque, Match, Medal, Melodrama, Miracle, Monodrama, Morality, Mousetrap, Mummers, Mysteries, Nativity, Nurse, Oberammergau, One-acter, Orestaia, Othello, Parallel, Passion, Perform, Personate, Portray, Prank, Pretend, Recreation, Represent, Riff, Role, Rollick, Romp, Room, Rope, RUR, Satyr, Saw, Shadow, Shoot, Sketch, Sport, Stage, Straight, Strain, Strike up, Stroke, Strum, Tolerance, Tonguing, Toy, Tragedy, Tragicomedy, Trifle, Tweedle, Twiddle, Two-hander, Vamp, Vent, Whitechapel, Word

▷ **Play** *may indicate* an anagram

Playback Echo, Repeat, Replay

Playboy Hedonist, Rake, Roué

Player(s) Actor, Athlete, Back, Black, Brass, Bugler, Busker, Cast, CD, Centre, Colt, Contestant, Defenceman, DVD, E, East, ENSA, Equity, Fiddle, Flanker, Fullback, Gary, Ghetto-blaster, Goalie, Half, Half-back, Half-forward, Harlequin, Hooker, Infielder, It, Juke-box, Kest, Linebacker, Lineman, Lion, Lock, Longstop, Lutanist, Lutenist, Man, Midfield, Mid-on, Mime, Musician, Musician(er), N, Nero, North, Ombre, Onside, Orpheus, Pagliacci, Participant, Pianola®, Pitcher, Pocket, Pone, Pro, Prop, Quarterback, Record, Rover, S, Scrape, Scratch, Scrum half, Seagull, Secondo, Seed, Shamateur, Shortstop, Side, South, Split end, Stand-off, Stand-off half, Stereo, Striker, Strings, Strolling, Super, Sweeper, Team, Thespian, Tight end, Troubador, Troupe, Upright, Utility, Virtuosi, W, Walkman®, West, White, Wing, Winger, Wingman

Playfair Code

Playfellow Actor, Chum, Companion

Playful Arch, Coy, Frisky, Humorous, Kittenish, Ludic, Merry, Piacevole, Scherzo, Skittish, Sportive

Playgirl Actress, Electra

Playgoer Groundling

Playground Close, Garden, Park, Rec(reational), Rectangle, Theatre, Tot lot, Yard

Playhouse Amphitheatre, Cinema, Theatre, Wendy

Playsuit Rompers

Playwright Aeschylus, Albee, Anouilh, Arden, Ayckbourn, Barrie, Barry, Beaumarchais, Beaumont, Beckett, Behan, Bellow, Bennett, Besier, Bolt, Brecht, Chekhov, Congreve, Corneille, Coward, Dekker, Delaney, > **DRAMATIST**, Dramaturge, Dramaturgist, Drinkwater, Dryden, Euripides, Feydeau, Fletcher, Frayn, Fry, Gems, Genet, Goldoni, Gorky, Harwood, Hay, Ibsen, Jonson, Marlowe, Massinger, Menander, Miller, Molière, Mortimer, O'Casey, Odets, O'Neill, Orton, Osborne, Pinero, Pinter, Pirandello, Priestley, Racine, Rattigan, Rostard, Scriptwriter, Shaw, Sheridan, Sherry, Simpson, Sophocles, Stoppard, Storey, Strindberg, Synge, Tate, Terence, Thespis, Travers, Vanbrugh, Webster, Wesker, Wilde

Plea Appeal, Claim, Defence, Entreaty, Excuse, Exoration, Non contendere, Orison, Placitum, Prayer, Rebuttal, Rebutter, Rogation, Suit

Plead(er) Answer, Argue, Beg, Entreat, > **IMPLORE**, Intercede, Litigate, Moot, Vakeel, Vakil

Please(d), Pleasant, Pleasing, Pleasure(-seeker) Aggrate, Agreeable, Alcina, Algolagnia, Amene, Amuse, Arride, Benign, Bitte, Braw, Cheerful, Chuffed, Comely, Comfort, Content, Cute, Delectation, Delice, Delight, Do, Euphonic, Fair, Felicitous, Fit, Flatter, Fun, Genial, Glad, Gladness, Gratify, Hedonism, Jammy, Joy, Kama, Kindly, Lepid, List, Oblige, Piacevole, Primrose path,

Prithee, Prythee, Queme, Satisfy, Suit, Tasty, Tickle, Tickle pink, Treat, Vanity, Voluptuary, Wally, Will, Winsome, Wrapped, Xanadu List

Pleasure-garden, Pleasure-ground Lung, Oasis, Park, Policy, Ranelagh, Tivoli

Pleat Accordion, Box, Crimp, Fold, French, Frill, Goffer, Gusset, Inverted, Kick, Knife, Plait, Pranck(e), Prank, Sunburst, Sunray

Pleb(eian) Common, Essex man, Homely, Laic, Ordinary, Roturier

Pledge Affidavit, Arles, Band, Betroth, Bond, Borrow, Bottomry, Dedicate, Deposit, Earnest(-penny), Engage, Fine, Gage, Guarantee, Hock, Hypothecate, Impignorate, Mortgage, Oath, Pass, Pawn, Pignerate, Pignorate, Plight, Promise, Propine, Sacrament, Security, Stake, Surety, Teetotal, Toast, Troth, Undertake, Vow, Wad, Wed

Pleiades Alcyone, Celaeno, Electra, Maia, Merope, Sterope, Taygete

Plenitude Stouth and routh

Plentiful, Plenty Abounding, Abundance, Abundant, Ample, Bags, Copious, Copy, Easy, Excess, Foison, Fouth, Ful(l)ness, Fushion, Galore, Goshen, Lashings, Lots, Oodles, Pleroma, Profusion, Quantity, Riches, Rife, Routh, Rowth, Scouth, Scowth, Slue, Sonce, Sonse, Umpteen

Plenum Spaceless

Pliable, Pliant Amenable, Flexible, Limber, Limp, Lithe, Malleable, Plastic, Sequacious, Supple, Swack, Swank

▸ **Pliers** *see* PLY

Plight Betrothal, Case, Misdight, Peril, Pickle, Pledge, State, Troth

Plimsoll(s) Dap, Gutty, Gym-shoe, Line, Mutton-dummies, Sandshoe, Tacky

Plinth Acroter, Base, Block, Socle, Stand, Zocco

Plod(der) Drudge, Ploughman, Traipse, Tramp, Trog, Trudge

Plonk Rotgut, Wine

Plop Cloop, Drop, Fall, Plap, Plump

Plot(s) Allotment, Babington, Bed, Brew, Carpet, Chart, Cliché, Connive, Conspiracy, Conspire, Covin, Covyne, Engineer, Erf, Erven, Frame-up, Graden, Graph, Gunpowder, Imbroglio, Intrigue, Locus, Lot, Machination, Map, Meal-tub, Odograph, Pack, Patch, Plan, Plat, Popish, Rye-house, Scenario, > **SCHEME**, Sect(ion), Seedbed, Shot, Site, Story, Taluk, Terf, Turf, Web

Plotter Artist, Cabal, Camarilla, Catesby, Conspirator, Engineer, Oates, Schemer

Plough(man), Ploughed, Ploughing Arable, Ard, Arval, Big Dipper, Breaker, Bull tongue, Chamfer, Charles's wain, Contour, Dipper, Disc, Drail, Drill, Ear, Earth-board, Ere, Fail, Fallow, Farmer, Feer, Flunk, Gadsman, Gang, Great bear, Harrow, Lister, Middlebreaker, Middlebuster, Mouldboard, Piers, Pip, Push, Rafter, Rib, Ridger, Rive, Rotary, Rove, Sand, Scooter, Septentrion(e)s, Sill, Sow, Stump-jump, Swing, Till(er), Trench, Triones, Wheel

Plough-cleaner Pattle, Pettle

Ploughshare Co(u)lter, Sock

Ploughwise Boustrophedon

Plover Bud, Lapwing, Pretincole, Prostitute, Stand, Tewit, Wing

Plowman Piers

Ploy Brinkmanship, Dodge, M(a)cGuffin, Manoeuvre, Stratagem, Strike, Tactic, Wile

Pluck(ing), Plucky Avulse, Bare, Carphology, Cock, Courage, Deplume, Epilate, Evulse, Floccillation, Gallus, Game, > **GRIT**, Guts, Loot, Mettle, Pick, Pinch, Pip, Pizzicato, Plectron, Plectrum, Ploat, Plot, Plunk, Pook(it), Pouk(it), Pull, Race, Scrappy, Snatch, Spin, Spirit, Spunk, Summon, Tug, Twang, Tweak, Tweeze, Yank

Plug Ad, Banana, Block, Bung, Caulk, Chew, Commercial, Dam, DIN, Dook,

Dossil, Dottle, Douk, Fipple, Fother, Gang, Glow, Go-devil, Hype, Jack, Lam, Operculum, Pessary, Phono, Prod, Promote, Publicity, Ram, Rawlplug®, Recommendation, Safety, Spark(ing), Spile, Spiling, Stop(per), Stopple, Strobili, Suppository, Tampion, Tap, Tent, Tompion, Vent, Wage, Wander, Wedge

Plum Bullace, Cherry, Choice, Damask, Damson, Gage, Greengage, Ground, Japanese, Kaki, Mammee-sapota, Marmalade, Maroon, Mirabelle, Mussel, Myrobalan, Naseberry, Persimmon, Proin(e), Pruin(e), Prune, Quetsch, Raisin, Sapodilla, Sebesten, Victoria

Plumage, Plume Aigrette, Crest, Eclipse, Egret, Feather, Hackle, Mantle, Panache, Preen, Ptilosis, Quill

Plumb(er) Bullet, Dredge, Fathom, Lead(sman), Perpendicular, Plummet, Sheer, Sound, Test, True, Vertical

Plumbago Graphite, Wad(d), Wadt

Plummet Dive, Drop, Lead, > **PLUNGE**

Plump(er) Bold, Bonnie, Bonny, Buxom, Choose, Chubbed, Chubby, Cubby, Dumpy, Embonpoint, Endomorph, Fat, Fleshy, Flop, Fubsy, Full, Lie, Matronly, Opt, Plank, Plonk, Plop, Podgy, Portly, Roll-about, Rolypoly, Rotund, Round, Rubenesque, Sonsie, Sonsy, Soss, Souse, Squab, Squat, Stout, Swap, Swop, Tidy, Well-fed

Plunder(er) Berob, Booty, Depredate, Despoil, Devastate, Escheat, Fleece, Forage, Freebooter, Gut, Harry, Haul, Herriment, Herryment, Hership, Loot, Maraud, Peel, Pill(age), Privateer, > **RANSACK**, Rape, Rapparee, Raven, Ravin, Ravine, Reave, Reif, Reive, Rieve, Rifle, Rob, Sack, Scoff, Shave, Skoff, Spoil(s), Spoliate, Sprechery, Spuilzie, Spuly(i)e, Spulzie, Swag

Plunge(r) Dasher, Demerge, Dive, Douse, Dowse, Duck, Enew, Immerge, Immerse, La(u)nch, Nose-dive, Plummet, Plump, Raker, Send, Sink, Souse, Swoop, Thrust

Plural Multiply, Pl

Plus Addition, And, Gain, More, Positive

Plush(ed) Die, Luxurious, Smart, Tint, Velour, Velvet

Pluto(crat), Plutonic Abyssal, Dis, Hades, Hypogene, Nob, Pipeline, Underground

Plutonium Pu

Ply, Plier(s) Bend, Birl, Cab, Exercise, Exert, Gondoliers, Importune, Layer, Practise, Run, Trade, Wield

▷ **Plying** *may indicate* an anagram

PM Addington, Afternoon, Arvo, Asquith, Attlee, Autopsy, Bute, Cabinet-maker, Chatham, De Valera, Disraeli, Gladstone, Major, Melbourne, Peel, Pitt, Portland, Premier, > **PRIME MINISTER**, Salisbury, Taoiseach

Pneumonia Visna

Poach Cook, Encroach, Filch, Lag, Steal, Trespass

Pochard Duck, Scaup

Pocket Air, Appropriate, Bag, Bin, Cavity, Cly, Cup, Enclave, Fob, Glom, Hideaway, Hip, Jenny, Misappropriate, Patch, Placket, Plaid-neuk, Pot, Pouch, Purloin, Purse, Sac, Sky, Slash, Sling, Slit, Steal, Take, Watch

Pod(s) Babul, Bean, Belly, Carob, Chilli, Dividivi, Engine, Gumbo, Lablab, Lomentum, Neb-neb, Okra, Pipi, Pregnant, Siliqua, Tamarind, Vanilla

Podgy Roly-poly

Poem(s), Poetry Acmeism, Acrostic, Aeneid, Alcaic, Anthology, Awdl, Ballad(e), Beowulf, Bestiary, Byliny, Caccia, Canzone, Cargoes, Cento, Choliamb, Choriamb, Cicada, Cinquain, Complaint, Concrete, Decastich, Dit(t),

Dithyramb, Divan, Dizain, Doggerel, Duan, Dunciad, Eclogue, Elegy, Elene, Epic(ede), Epigram, Epilogue, Epithalamium, Epode, Epopee, Epopoeia, Epos, Epyllion, Erotic, Fifteener, Finlandia, Gauchesco, Georgic, Ghazal, Graveyard, Haikai, Haiku, Heptastich, Heroic, Hexastich, Hokku, Hull, Hypermeter, Idyll, If, Iliad, Imagism, Jazz, Lay, Limerick, Logaoedic, London, Mahabharata(m), Mahabharatum, Melic, Metaphysical, Metre, Mock-heroic, Monostich, Nostos, Ode, Palinode, Paracrostic, Parnassus, Pastoral, Penill(ion), Pentastich, Poesy, Prelude, Prose, Prothalamion, Punk, Purana, Qasida, Quatorzain, Quatrain, Quire, Ramayama, Rat-rhyme, Renga, Rhapsody, Rig-Veda, Rime, Rondeau, Rondel, Rubai(yat), Rune, Scazon (iambus), Senryu, Sestina, Sijo, Sirvente, Song, Sonnet, Spondee, Stanza, Stornello, Symphonic, Tanka, Telestich, Temora, Tercet, Tetrastich, Title, Tone, Triolet, Tristich, Verse, Versicle, Villanelle, Voluspa, Voluspe, Waka

Poet(s) Bard(ling), Cavalier, Cumberland, Cyclic, Elegist, Georgian, Iambist, Imagist, Lake, Laureate, Layman, Lyrist, Maker, Meistersinger, Metaphysical, Metrist, Minnesinger, Minstrel, Mistral, Monodist, Odist, Parnassian, Performance, PL, Pleiade, Poetaster, Rhymer, Rhymester, Rhymist, Rymer, Scald, Scop, Skald, Smart, Sonneteer, Spasmodic, Thespis, Tragic, Trench, Troubadour, Trouvère, Trouveur, Vers librist(e), Water

● **POETS**
●
● **2 letters:**
● AE
●
●
● **3 letters:**
● Gay
● Poe
●
●
● **4 letters:**
● Abse
● Blok
● Cory
● Dyer
● Gray
● Gunn
● Hogg
● Hood
● Hugo
● Hunt
● Lang
● Omar
● Ovid
● Owen
● Pope
● Rowe
● Rumi
● Tate
● Vega
●
● **5 letters:**
● Arion

Auden	Moore	George
Blair	Nashe	Glycon
Blake	Noyes	Goethe
Burns	Plath	Graves
Byron	Pound	Hesiod
Cadou	Prior	Horace
Carew	Rilke	Hughes
Cinna	Rishi	Landor
Clare	Sachs	Larkin
Dante	Tasso	Lawman
Donne	Theon	Lowell
Eliot	Yeats	Milton
Frost	Young	Morris
Gower		Motion
Griot	**6 letters:**	Ossian
Heine	Arnold	Pindar
Hesse	Austin	Racine
Homer	Barham	Sappho
Horne	Barnes	Seaman
Hulme	Belloc	Shanks
Iqbal	Brecht	Sidney
Keats	Brooke	Tagore
Keyes	Butler	Thomas
Lewis	Clough	Villon
Logue	Cowper	Virgil
Lorca	Crabbe	Waller
Lucan	Dowson	
Makar	Dryden	**7 letters:**
Marot	Dunbar	Addison
Meyer	Ennius	Alcaeus

Aretino	Shelley	Macaulay	Stevenson
Ariosto	Sitwell	Mallarmé	Swinburne
Beddoes	Skelton	Menander	
Belleau	Sotades	Petrarch	**10 letters:**
Bridges	Southey	Rossetti	Baudelaire
Caedmon	Spender	Schiller	Chatterton
Campion	Spenser	Shadwell	Drinkwater
Chapman	Statius	Stephens	Fitzgerald
Chaucer	Terence	Suckling	Longfellow
Collins	Thomson	Taliesin	Propertius
Corinna	Vaughan	Tennyson	Tannhauser
Cynwulf	Whitman	Thompson	Theocritus
Emerson		Traherne	Wordsworth
Flaccus	**8 letters:**	Tyrtaeus	
Flecker	Anacreon	Verlaine	**11 letters:**
Heredia	Betjeman	Whittier	Apollinaire
Herrick	Brentano		Archilochus
Hopkins	Browning	**9 letters:**	Asclepiades
Housman	Campbell	Aeschylus	Maeterlinck
Juvenal	Catullus	Bunthorne	Pherecrates
Layamon	Cummings	Coleridge	
Martial	Cynewulf	Euripides	**12 letters:**
Marvell	Davenant	Goldsmith	Archilochian
Montale	Day Lewis	Lamartine	Aristophanes
Newbolt	De la Mare	Lucretius	
Orpheus	Hamilton	Marinetti	**14 letters:**
Pushkin	Kynewulf	Masefield	Dante Alighieri
Ronsard	Laforgue	Quasimodo	
Russell	Langland	Shenstone	**15 letters:**
Sassoon	Leopardi	Simonides	Ettrick Shepherd
Service	Lovelace	Sophocles	

Poetaster Della-Cruscan
Poetess Ingelow, Orinda
Poet laureate Motion, PL
▶ **Poetry** *see* POEM
Poignant Acute, Biting, Haunting, Keen, Pungent, Stirring, Touching
Point(ed), Pointer, Points Accumulation, Ace, Acerose, Acro-, Aculeate, Aim,
  Ainode, Antinode, Antler, Apex, Aphelion, Apogee, Appui, Apse, Apsis, Bar,
  Barb, Barrow, Bisque, Boiling, Break(ing), Brownie, Calk, Cape, Cardinal,
  Cash, Centre, Choke, Clou, Clue, Colon, Comma, Compass, Compensation,
  Cone, Conic, Corner, Cover, Crisis, Critical, Crux, Culmination, Cultrate, Curie,
  Cursor, Cusp, Cuss, Cutting, Decimal, Degree, Detail, Dew, Diamond, Direct,
  Dot, Dry, E, Ear, End, Entry, Epanodos, Epee, Equant, Equinoctial, Eutectic,
  Exclamation, Fang, Fastigiate, Feature, Fesse, Fielder, Firing, Fitch(e), Five,
  Fixed, Flash, Focal, Focus, Foreland, Fourteen, Freezing, Fulcrum, Gallinas,
  Game, Germane, Gist, Gnomon, Gold, Hastate, Head, High, Hinge, Hint,
  Home-thrust, Ideal, Index, Indicate, Indicator, Intercept, Ippon, Isoelectric,
  Jester, Keblah, Kiblah, Kip(p), Knub, Lace, Lagrangian, Lance, Lead, Limit,
  Lizard, Locate, Locus, Low, Mandelbrot set, Mark, Match, Melting, Metacentre,
  Microdot, Moot, Mucro, N, Nail, Nasion, Near, Neb, Needle, Neel, Ness, Nib,
  Nocking, Node, Nodus, Nombril, Now, Nub, Obelion, Obelisk, Objective,

Opinion, Ord, Particle, Peak, Pedal, Penalty, Perigee, Perihelion, Perilune, Pin, Pinch, Pinnacle, Place, Power, Pressure, Promontory, Prong, Prow, Punctilio, Punctual, Punctum, Purpose, Radix, Rallying, Ras, Reef, Respect, Rhumb, Rhumbline, S, Sample, Saturation, Scribe, Seg(h)ol, Set, Shaft, Sheva, Show, Shy, Silly, Socket, Sore, Spearhead, Spicate, Spick, Spike, Spinode, Spinulose, Stage, Stagnation, Starting, Stationary, Steam, Sticking, Stigme, Stiletto, Sting, Stipule, Strong, Sum, Suspension, Synapse, Tacnode, Talking, Taper, Tax, Technicality, Tine, > TIP, Tongue, Train, Transition, Trig, Trigger, Triple, Turning, Urde(e), Urdy, Use, Vane, Vanishing, Vantage, Verge, Verse, Vertex, Vowel, Voxel, W, Weak, Yad, Yield, Yuko

Pointless Blunt, Curtana, Flat, Futile, Inane, Inutile, Muticous, Otiose, Stupid, Vain

Point of honour Pundonor

Poise Aplomb, Balance, Composure, P, Serenity

Poison(er), Poisoning, Poisonous Abron, Aconite, Acrolein, Adamsite, Aflatoxin, Aldrin, Amanita, Antiar, Apocynum, Aqua-tofana, Arsenic, Aspic, Atropia, Atropin(e), Bane, Barbasco, Belladonna, Boletus, Borgia, Botulism, Brom(in)ism, Brucine, Bufotalin, Cacodyl, Cadaverine, Calabar-bean, Cannabin, Cicuta, Colchicine, Coniine, Contact, Cowbane, Coyotillo, Curare, Curari, Cyanide, Cyanuret, Datura, Daturine, Deadly nightshade, Digitalin, Dioxin, Dumbcane, Durban, Echidnine, Embolism, Emetin(e), Envenom, Ergotise, Fluorosis, Flybane, Flypaper, Food, Formaldehyde, Gelsemin(in)e, Gila, Gossypol, Hebenon, Hebona, Hemlock, Henbane, Hydragyrism, Hydrastine, Hyoscyamine, Iodism, Lead, Lewisite, Limberneck, Lindane, Lobeline, Locoweed, Malevolent, Manchineal, Mandragora, Mephitic, Mezereon, Miasma, Mineral, Monkshood, Muscarine, Mycotoxin, Nerve gas, Neurine, Neurotoxin, Neutron, Nicotine, Noogoora burr, Noxious, Obeism, Ouabain, Ourali, Ourari, Paraquat®, Paris green, Phallin, Phalloidin, Phosphorism, Picrotoxin, Pilocarpine, Plumbism, Ptomaine, Py(a)emia, Raphania, Ratsbane, Rot, Safrole, Salicylism, Samnitis, Santonin, Sapraemia, Sarin, Sassy wood, Saturnism, Saxitoxin, Septic(aemia), Solanine, Solpuga, Soman, Stibine, Stibium, Stonefish, Strophanthus, Strychnine, Sugar of lead, Surinam, Systemic, Tanghin, Tanghinin, Tetro(do)toxin, Thebaine, Thorn-apple, Timbo, Toxaphene, Toxic, Toxicology, Toxicosis, Toxin, Toxoid, Trembles, Tropine, Tutu, Upas, Urali, Uroshiol, Venefic, Venin, Venom(ous), Veratridine, Veratrin(e), Viperous, Virose, Virous, Virulent, Wabain, Warfarin, Wolfsbane, Woorali, Woorara, Wourali, Yohimbine

Poke, Poky Bonnet, Broddle, Chook, Garget, Itchweed, Jab, Jook, Meddle, Mock, Nousle, Nudge, Nuzzle, Ombu, Peg, Pick, Pote, Pouch, Powter, > PRISON, > PROD, Prog, Proke, Punch, Root(le), Rout, Rowt, Sporan, Stab, Thrust

Poker (work) Bugbear, Curate, Draw, Game, High-low, Mistigris, Penny ante, Pyrography, Red-hot, Salamander, Strip, Stud(-horse), Tickler, Tine

Poland PL, Sarmatia

Polar, Pole(s), Poler Anode, Antarctic, Arctic, Boom, Bowsprit, Bum(p)kin, Caber, Celestial, Copernicus, Cowl-staff, Cracovian, Crossbar, Extremity, Fishgig, Fizgy, Flagstaff, Flagstick, Galactic, Gas, Geomagnetic, Janker, Kent, Liberty, Lug, Magnetic, Mast, May, N, Nadir, Negative, Nib, North, Periscian, Po, Polack, Positive, Punt, Quant, Quarterstaff, Racovian, Range, Ricker, Ripeck, Rood, Ry(e)peck, S, Shaft, Slav, South, Spar, Sprit, Staff, Stang, Starosta, Stilt, Sting, Stobie, Telegraph, Terrestrial, Thyrsos, Thyrsus, Topmast, Totem, Vegetal, Zenith

▷ **Polar** *may indicate* with a pole

Polaris Rhodanic, Rocket, Star
Polecat Ferret, Fitch, Fitchet, Foulmart, Foumart, Weasel
Polemic(al) Argument, Controversy, Debate, Eristic(al)
Police(man), Policewoman Babylon, Bear, Beast, Bizzy, Black and Tans, Blue,
  Bluebottle, Bobby, Bog(e)y, Bull, Busy, Carabinero, Carabiniere, Catchpole,
  Centenier, Cheka, Chekist, CID, Constable, Cop(per), Cotwal, Crusher,
  Detective, Dibble, Druzhinnik, Europol, Filth, Flatfoot, Flattie, Flic, Flying
  Squad, Force, Fuzz, Garda, Gendarme, Gestapo, Gill, G-man, Guard, Gumshoe,
  Harmanbeck, Heat, Hermandad, Inspector, Interpol, Jamadar, Jemadar,
  John Hop, Keystone, Kitchen, Kotwal, Limb, Mata-mata, Met(ropolitan),
  Military, Morse, Mountie, MP, Mulligan, Nabman, Nark, Ochrana, Officer,
  OGPU, Ovra, Patrolman, PC, Peeler, Peon, Pig, Polis, Polizei, Porn squad, Posse
  (comitatus), Prefect, Provincial, Puppy-walker, Ranger, Redbreast, Redcap,
  Regulate, RIC, Riot, Robert, Rosser, Rozzer, RUC, Sbirro, SC, Secret, Securitate,
  Securocrat, Sepoy, Shamus, Sleeping, Slop, Smokey, Sowar(ry), Special, Stasi,
  State trooper, Super, Sureté, Sweeney, Texas Rangers, T(h)anadar, The Bill, The
  Law, Thirdborough, Thought, Trap, Vice squad, Vigilante, Walloper, Wolly,
  Woodentop, Zabtieh, Zaptiah, Zaptieh, Zomo
Police car Black Maria, Panda, Patrol, Prowl
Police station Copshop, Lock-up, Tana, Tanna(h), Thana(h), Thanna(h),
  Watchhouse
Policy Assurance, Ballon d'essai, CAP, Comprehensive, Course, Demesne,
  Endowment, Expedience, Floating, Good neighbour, Insurance, Knock for
  knock, Laisser-faire, Lend-lease, Line, Method, Open(-sky), Plank, Platform,
  Pork-barrel, Practice, Programme, Reaganism, Revanchism, Scorched earth,
  Stop-go, Tack, Tactics, Ticket, Traditional, Valued
Polish(ed), Polisher Beeswax, Black, Blacklead, Bob, Bruter, Buff, Bull,
  Burnish, Chamois, Complaisant, Edit, Elaborate, Elegant, Emery, Enamel,
  Finish, French, Furbish, Gentlemanly, Glass, Gloss, Heelball, Hone, Inland,
  Lap, Lustre, Nail, Perfect, Planish, Polite, Pumice, Refinement, Refurbish,
  Rottenstone, Rub, Sand, Sandblast, Sandpaper, Sejm, Sheen, Shellac, Shine,
  Slick, Slickenside, Supercalender, Tutty, Urbane, Veneer, Wax
Polite Civil, Courteous, Genteel, Grandisonian, Mannered, Suave, Urbane,
  Well-bred
Politic(al), Politics Apparat, Body, Chartism, Civic, Diplomacy, Discreet,
  Expedient, Falange, Fascism, Gesture, Leftism, Party, Poujadism, Power,
  Practical, Public, Radicalism, Rightism, State, Statecraft, Tactful, Wise
Politician(s) Bright, Carpet-bagger, Catiline, Chesterfield, Congressman,
  Demagogue, Demo(crat), Diehard, Disraeli, Eden, Evita, Green, Incumbent,
  Independent, Ins, Isolationist, Laski, Left, Legislator, Liberal, Log-roller, MEP,
  Minister, Moderate, MP, Parliamentarian, Parnell, Politico, Polly, Puppet, Rad,
  Rep, Senator, Socialist, Statesman, Statist, Tadpole, Taper, TD, Tory, Trotsky,
  Unionist, Veep, Warhorse, Whig, Wilberforce
Poll(ing) Ballot, Bean, Canvass, Count, Cut, Deed, Dod, Election, Exit, Gallup,
  Head, Humlie, Hummel, Lory, MORI, Nestor, Not(t), Opinion, Parrot,
  Pineapple, Pow, Push, Scrutiny, Straw, Votes
▷ **Poll** *may indicate* a first letter
Pollack Fish, Lob, Lythe
Pollard Doddered
Pollen, Pollinate(d), Pollination Anemophilous, Beebread, Dust, Errhine,
  Farina, Fertilised, My(i)ophily, Witch-meal, Xenia
Pollenbrush Scopa

Pollex Thumb
Pollster Psephologist
Pollute(d), Pollutant, Pollution Adulterate, Contaminate, Defile, Dirty, File, Foul, Impure, Infect, Miasma, Noise, Nox, Oil slick, Rainout, Soil, Soilure, Stain, Sully, Taint, Violate, Waldsterben
Polly Flinders, Parrot, Peachum
Polo Chukka, Marco, Mint, Navigator
Polonium Po
Poltergeist Apport, Ghost, Spirit, Trouble-house
Poltroon Coward, Craven, Dastard, Scald, Scaramouch
Polyandry Nair
Polygraph Lie-detector
Polymath Knowall, Toynbee
Polymer Elastomer, Isotactic, Lignin, Oligomer, Resin, Silicone, Tetramer, Trimer
Polymorphic Multiform, Proteus, Variform
Polynesian Moriori, Tahitian, Tongan
Polyp(s) Alcyonaria, Hydra, Hydranth, Nematophore, Obelia, Sea-anemone, Tumour
Polyphony Counterpoint
Polystyrene Expanded
Polyzoan Sea-mat
Pom Choom
Pomander Pounce(t)-box
Pomegranate Punica, Punic apple
Pommel Beat, Knob, Pound, Pummel
Pomp(ous) Big, Bombastic, Budge, Ceremonial, Display, Dogberry, Euphuistic, Fustian, Grandiloquent, Grandiose, Heavy, Highfalutin(g), High-flown, High-muck-a-muck, High-sounding, Hogen-mogen, Inflated, Orotund, Ostentatious, Pageantry, Parade, Pretentious, Solemn, Splendour, Starchy, State, Stilted, Stuffy, Turgid
Pom-pom Ball, Tassel
Ponce Pander, Solicit, Souteneur
Poncho Ruana
Pond(s) Dew, Dub, Hampstead, Lakelet, Lentic, Mill, Pool, Pound, Puddle, Settling, Slough, Stank, Stew, Tank, Turlough, Vivarium, Viver
Ponder(ous) Brood, Cogitate, Contemplate, Deliberate, Heavy, Laboured, Mull, Muse, Perpend, Poise, Pore, Reflect, Ruminate, > THINK, Vise, Volve, Weight(y), Wonder
Poniard Bodkin, > DAGGER, Dirk, Stiletto
Pontiff, Pontifical, Pontificate Aaron, Aaronic, Antipope, Dogmatise, Papal
Pontoon Blackjack, Bridge, Caisson, Chess, Game, Twenty one, Vingt-et-un
Pony Canuck, Cayuse, Cow, Dales, Dartmoor, Eriskay, Exmoor, Fell, Garran, Garron, Gen(n)et, GG, Griffin, Griffon, Gryfon, Gryphon, Jennet, Jerusalem, Mustang, New Forest, One-trick, Pit, Polo, Pownie, Sable Island, Shanks', Sheltie, Shetland, Show, Tangun, Tat(too), Timor, Welsh, Welsh mountain, Western Isles
Poodle Barbet, Swan
Pooh Bah, Bear, Pugh, Winnie, Yah
Pool Backwater, Bank, Bethesda, Billabong, Birthing, Bogey hole, Cenote, Cess, Collect, Combine, Dub, Dump, Flash, Flow, Gene, Jackpot, Jacuzzi®, Kitty, Lido, Lin(n), Meer, Mere, Mickery, Mikvah, Mikveh, Millpond, Moon, Natatorium,

Piscina, Piscine, Plash, Plesh, Plunge, > **POND**, Reserve, Share, Siloam, Snooker, Spa, Stank, Sump, Tank, Tarn, Water(ing) hole, Wave

Poor(ly) Bad, Bare, Base, Bijwoner, Breadline, Buckeen, Bywoner, Catchpenny, Cheapo, Churchmouse, Conch, Cronk, Destitute, Gritty, Hard-up, Have-nots, Hopeless, Humble, Hungry, Ill(-off), Impecunious, Indigent, Lazarus, Lean, Low, Low-downer, Meagre, Mean, Needy, Obolary, Pauper, Peaky, Poxy, Roinish, Rop(e)y, Roynish, Sad, Scrub, Shabby, Shitty, Sober, Sorry, Sub, Thin, Third-rate, Trashy, Undeserving, Unwell, Wattle, Wishy-washy

▷ **Poor** *may indicate* an anagram

Poorhouse Union, Workhouse

Pooter Nobody, Nonentity

Pop (off), **Popper**, **Popping** Bang, Brit, Burst, Cloop, Crease, Die, Father, Fr, Gingerbeer, Hip-hop, Hock, Insert, Lumber, Mineral, Nip, Pater, Pawn, Pledge, Population, Press-stud, Punk, Sherbet, Soda, Splutter, Weasel

▷ **Pop** *may indicate* an anagram

Pope(s) Adrian, Alexander, Atticus, Benedict, Black, Boniface, Clement, Dunciad, Eminence, Fish, Great Schism, Gregory, Hildebrand, Holiness, Innocent, Joan, Leo, Papa, Pius, Pontiff, Ruff(e), Schism, Sixtius, Theocrat, Tiara, Urban, Vatican, Vicar of Christ

Pop-gun Bourtree-gun

Popinjay Barbermonger, Coxcomb, Dandy, Fop, Macaroni, Prig, Skipjack

Poplar Abele, Aspen, Balsam, Cottonwood, Lombardy, Trembling, White

Poppet Valve

Poppy Argemone, Bloodroot, Blue, California, Chicalote, Coquelicot, Corn, Diacodin, Eschscholtzia, Field, Flanders, Horned, Iceland, Matilija, Mawseed, Opium, Papaver, Plume, Ponceau, Prickly, Puccoon, Rhoeadales, Shirley, Tall, Welsh

Poppycock Bosh, Nonsense, Rubbish

Popular(ity) Common, Cult, Demotic, Enchorial, General, Grass roots, Heyday, Hit, In, Laic, Lay, Mass, Plebeian, Prevalent, Public, Successful, Tipped, Trendy, Vogue

Population, **Populace** Catchment, Census, Demography, Inhabitants, Malthusian, Mass, Mob, > **PEOPLE**, Public, Universe

Porcelain Arita, Artificial, Bamboo, Belleek®, Blanc-de-chine, Celadon, Chelsea, China, Coalport, Crackle(ware), Crown Derby, Dresden, Eggshell, Famille, Famille jaune, Famille noir, Famille rose, Famille verte, Goss, Hard-paste, Hizen, Imari, Jasper, Jasper(ware), Limoges, Lithophane, Meissen, Minton, Parian, Sèvres, Softpaste, Spode, Sung

Porch Galilee, Lanai, Stoa, Stoep, Veranda(h)

Porcupine Hedgehog, Urson

Pore Browse, Hole, Hydrathode, Lenticel, Muse, Ostium, Outlet, Ponder, Stoma, Study

Porgy Braise, Scup(paug)

Pork Bacon, Boar, Brawn, Chap, Crackling, Flitch, Griskin, Ham, Pancetta, Salt, Scrapple, Scruncheon, Scrunchion, Spare-rib, Tenderloin

Porn(ography), **Pornographic** Curiosa, Erotica, Hard, Hard-core, Jazz mag, Rhyparography, Soft, Soft-core

Porous Cellular, Permeable, Pumice, Sponge

Porpoise Bucker, Dolphin, Mereswine, Pellach, Pellack, Pellock, Phocaena, Sea pig, Sea swine

Porridge Berry, Bird, Brochan, Brose, Burgoo, Busera, Crowdie, Drammach, Drammock, Gaol, Grits, Grouts, Gruel, Hominy, Kasha, Mabela, Mahewu,

Mealie pap, Oaten, Oatmeal, Parritch, Pease-brose, Polenta, Pottage, Praiseach, Sadza, Samp, Sentence, Skilly, Stirabout, Stretch, Sup(p)awn, Time, Ugali
Porridge stick Thible, Thivel
Port(s) Beeswing, Carry, Cinque, Container (terminal), Entrepot, Free, Gate, Geropiga, > **HARBOUR**, Haven, Hithe, Hythe, Induction, Larboard, Left, Manner, Mien, Parallel, Tawny, Treaty, Wine

● **PORTS**
●
● **3 letters:**
● Abo
● Ayr
● Gao
● Hué
● Rio
● Rye
● **4 letters:**
● Acre
● Aden
● Akko
● Amoy
● Apia
● Baku
● Bari
● Boma
● Cobh
● Cork
● Deal
● Dill
● Elat
● Faro
● Gary
● Hilo
● Hull
● Icel
● I-pin
● Kiel
● Kobe
● Kure
● Lima
● Linz
● Naha
● Oban
● Omsk
● Oran
● Oslo
● Oulu
● Perm
● Pori
● Pula

Puri
Ruse
Safi
Said
Sfax
Suez
Susa
Suva
Tema
Tyre
Vigo
Wick
Wuhu

5 letters:
Akaba
Anzio
Aqaba
Arhus
Arica
Aulis
Bahia
Barry
Basra
Batum
Belem
Bharu
Blyth
Brest
Cadiz
Cairo
Canea
Colon
Dakar
Davao
Derry
Dilli
Dover
Duala
Dubai
Eilat
Elath

Emden
Gabes
Galle
Gavie
Genoa
Ghent
Gijon
Goole
Haifa
Hania
Izmir
Jaffa
Jambi
Jedda
Jidda
Kerch
Kochi
Larne
Leith
Lulea
Mainz
Malmo
Masan
Merca
Miami
Mocha
Mokpu
Narva
Newry
Omaha
Osaka
Ostia
Palos
Ponce
Poole
Pusan
Pylos
Rabat
Rouen
Saida
Sakai
Salto

Selby
Sidon
Skien
Split
Surat
Susah
Tampa
Tanga
Tunis
Turku
Vaasa
Varna
Visby
Vlore
Volos
Yalta
Yeisk
Yeysk
Yibin

6 letters:
Aarhus
Abadan
Agadir
Albany
Alborg
Ancona
Andong
Annaba
Balbao
Bastia
Batumi
Bergen
Bilbao
Blanca
Bombay
Bootle
Boston
Bremen
Burgas
Cairns
Calais

Callao	Napier	**7 letters:**	Kolding
Candia	Naples	Aalborg	Kowloon
Cannes	Narvik	Abidjan	Kuching
Canton	Nassau	Ajaccio	La Plata
Cavite	Nelson	Almeria	Latakia
Chania	Ningbo	Antalya	Legaspi
Cochin	Ningpo	Antibes	Le Havre
Cuiaba	Nizhni	Antwerp	Lepanto
Cuyaba	Odense	Aracaju	Livorno
Da Nang	Odessa	Astoria	Lorient
Danzig	Oporto	Augusta	Makurdi
Darwin	Ostend	Averiro	Marsala
Dieppe	Padang	Bayonne	Massaua
Djambo	Patras	Berbera	Massawa
Douala	Peoria	Bristol	Maulman
Dunbar	Pesaro	Buffalo	Memphis
Dundee	Quincy	Calabar	Messina
Durban	Rabaul	Cam Ranh	Milazzo
Durres	Ragusa	Canopus	Mombasa
Elblag	Recife	Catania	Moulman
Galata	Rijeka	Changde	Munster
Galati	Rimini	Chilung	Nanning
Gdansk	Rostov	Cologne	Neusatz
Gdynia	Samara	Colombo	Newport
Harbin	Samsun	Conakry	Niigata
Havana	Santos	Corinth	Niteroi
Hobart	Sasebo	Corunna	Novi Sad
Ichang	Savona	Cotonou	Oakland
Iloilo	Skikda	Dunedin	Okayama
Inchon	Smyrna	Dunkirk	Onitsha
Jaffna	Sousse	El Minya	Otranto
Jarrow	Speyer	Ephesus	Pahsien
Juneau	St John	Esbjerg	Palermo
Kalmar	St Malo	Foochow	Pelotas
Kisumu	St Paul	Funchal	Phocaea
Lepaya	Suakin	Geelong	Piraeus
Lobito	Sydney	Grimsby	Qingdao
Lubeck	Tacoma	Halifax	Randers
Mackay	Timaru	Hamburg	Rangoon
Madras	Tobruk	Harwich	Rapallo
Malaga	Toulon	Heysham	Rosario
Manaos	Tromso	Hodeida	Rostock
Manaus	Tyumen	Horsens	Runcorn
Manila	Velsen	Houston	Salerno
Matadi	Venice	Incheon	Sao Luis
Menado	Vyborg	Iquique	Seattle
Mersin	Weihai	Iquitos	Sekondi
Mobile	Whitby	Kaolack	Setubal
Mumbai	Wismar	Karachi	Seville
Muscat	Wonsan	Kavalta	Shantou
Namibe	Yantai	Kherson	Shantow
Nantes		Kinsale	Sinuiji

Stettin
St John's
St Louis
Sukhumi
Swansea
Tampico
Tangier
Taranto
Trabzon
Trapani
Trieste
Tripoli
Ushuaia
Wanxian
Wenchow
Wenzhou
Whyalla
Yakutsk
Yichang

8 letters:
Aberdeen
Acapulco
Alicante
Arbroath
Auckland
Badalona
Barletta
Batangas
Benghazi
Benguela
Bordeaux
Boulogne
Brindisi
Brisbane
Caesaria
Cagliari
Calcutta
Changsha
Cheribou
Chimbote
Chingtao
Chongjun
Cuxhaven
Drogheda
Dunleary
El Ferrol
Elsinore
Falmouth
Flushing
Freetown
Gisborne

Gonaives
Goteborg
Greenock
Haiphong
Hakodate
Hamilton
Hangzhou
Harfleur
Hartford
Hastings
Helsinki
Holyhead
Honolulu
Iraklion
Istanbul
Jayapura
Jinjiang
Kanazawa
Kawasaki
Keflavik
Kingston
Klaipeda
La Coruna
La Guaira
La Guyara
La Spezia
Les Cayes
Limassol
Mariupol
Matanzas
Mayaguez
Monrovia
Montreal
Murmansk
Mytilene
Nagasaki
Nan-ching
Newhaven
Nha Trang
Novgorod
Nykøbing
Pago Pago
Paramibo
Pavlodar
Paysandu
Penzance
Pevensey
Plymouth
Pnom Penh
Pozzuoli
Qui Nhong
Ramsgate

Salvador
Samarang
Sandakan
San Diego
Sandwich
Santarem
Savannah
Schiedam
Semarang
Shanghai
Sorrento
Stockton
Syracuse
Szczecin
Taganrog
Takoradi
Tarshish
Tauranga
Teresina
Tjirebon
Tsingtao
Valdivia
Valencia
Veracruz
Victoria
Wanganui
Weymouth
Yarmouth
Yokohama
Yokosuka
Zaanstad

9 letters:
Anchorage
Angostura
Annapolis
Antserana
Archangel
Baltimore
Barcelona
Bhavnagar
Carnarvon
Cartagena
Cherbourg
Chisimaio
Cleveland
Constanta
Dartmouth
Den Helder
Dordrecht
Dubrovnik
Ellesmere

Esperance
Europoort
Famagusta
Fishguard
Fleetwood
Flensburg
Fortaleza
Fremantle
Gallipoli
Gateshead
Gravesend
Guataquil
Hangchoio
Helsinger
Hiroshima
Immingham
Inhambane
Jasselton
Kagoshima
Kirkcaldy
Kozhikode
Kronstadt
Las Palmas
Lowestoft
Magdeburg
Mahajanga
Mangalore
Maracaibo
Mariehamn
Marseille
Matamoros
Matsuyama
Melbourne
Milwaukee
Morecambe
Newcastle
Nuku'alofa
Palembang
Phnom Penh
Pontianak
Port Louis
Port Sudan
Rotterdam
Santa Cruz
Santander
Schleswig
Sheerness
Singapore
Stavanger
St George's
St Nazaire
Stornoway

Stralsund
Stranraer
Takamatsu
Taomasina
Tarragona
Trebizond
Trondheim
Tynemouth
Volgograd
Weihaiwei
Whangerei
Zamboanga
Zeebrugge

10 letters:
Alexandria
Belize City
Birkenhead
Bratislava
Bridgeport
Bridgetown
Caernarvon
Casablanca
Charleston
Cheboksary
Chittagong
Cienfuegos
Copenhagen
Corrientes
East London
Felixstowe
Folkestone
Fray Bentos
Georgetown
Gothenburg
Hammerfest
Hartlepool
Herakleion

Joao Pessoa
Karlskrona
Khabarovsk
Khota Bharu
Kitakyushu
La Rochelle
Launceston
Los Angelos
Louisville
Matozinhos
Montevideo
Mostaganem
New Bedford
New Orleans
Norrkoping
Paramaribo
Pittsburgh
Pontevedra
Port Gentil
Portobello
Portsmouth
Port Talbot
Providence
Queenstown
Sacramento
Santa Marta
Sebastopol
Sevastopol
Sunderland
Talcahuano
Thunder Bay
Townsville
Valparaiso
Willemsted

11 letters:
Baranquilla
Bremerhaven

Cheng-chiang
Dares Salaam
Grangemouth
Helsingborg
Hermonpolis
Kaliningrad
Makhachkala
New Plymouth
Newport News
Nuevo Laredo
Pointe-Noire
Porto Alegre
Punta Arenas
Rockhampton
San Fernando
Scarborough
Shimonoseki
Southampton
Telukketong
Trincomalee
Vlaardingen
Vladivostok

12 letters:
Angtofagasta
Bandjarmasin
Bandjermasin
Barranquilla
Buenaventura
Chandemagore
Ciudad Bolwar
Dun Laoghaire
Jacksonville
Kota Kinabalu
Kristiansand
Milford Haven
Philadelphia
Pointe-a-Pitre

Ponta Delgada
Port Adelaide
Port Harcourt
Prince Rupert
Rio de Janeiro
San Francisco
San Sebastian
Santo Domingo
South Shields
St Petersburg
Tanjungpriok
Thessaloniki
Ujung Pandang
Usti nad Labem

13 letters:
Charlottetown
Corpus Christi
Florianopolis
Great Yarmouth
Ho Chi Minh City
Port Elizabeth
Tandjungpriok
Trois Rivieres
Wilhelmshaven

14 letters:
Mina Hassen Tani
Santiago de Cuba

15 letters:
Alexandroupolis
Sault Saint Marie

16 letters:
Reggio di Calibria

Portable Lapheld, Laptop, Palmtop
Portend, Portent(ous) Augur, Awesome, Bode, Dire, Omen, Phenomenon, Presage, > **WARN(ING)**
Porter Ale, Bearer, Bellboy, Bellhop, Bummaree, Caddie, Caddy, Cole, Concierge, Coolie, Door-keeper, Doorman, Dvornik, Entire, Hamaul, Ham(m)al, Humper, Janitor, October, Ostiary, Red-cap, Stout
Portfolio Holding
Portico Colonnade, Decastyle, Distyle, Dodecastyle, Exedra, Loggia, Narthex, Parvis(e), Porch, Propylaeum, Prostyle, Stoa, Veranda(h), Xystus
Portion Aliquot, Ann(at), Bit, Deal, Distribute, Dole, Dose, Dotation, Fraction, Fragment, Helping, Heritage, Hunk, Instalment, Jointure, Lot, Measure, Mess, Modicum, Nutlet, Ounce, > **PART**, Piece, Ratio, Scantle, Scantling, Section, Segment, Serving, Share, Size, Slice, Something, Spoonful, Tait, Taste, Tate,

Tittle, Tranche, Wodge
Portland Bill, Cement, Stone
Portly Ample, Corpulent, Gaucie, Gaucy, Gawcy, Gawsy, Stout
Portmanteau Bag, Combination, Holdall, Valise
Portrait(ist) Carte de visite, Depiction, Drawing, Eikon, Icon, Identikit, Ikon, Image, Kit-cat, Lely, Likeness, Painting, Retraitt, Retrate, Sketch, Vignette
Portray(al) Caricature, Depict, Describe, Feature, Image, Limn, Paint, Render, Represent, > SHOW
Portsmouth Pompey
Portugal, Portuguese Lusitania(n), Luso-, Macanese, Senhor
Pose(r), Poseur Aesthete, Affect(ation), Arabesque, Asana, Ask, Contrapposto, Drape, Lotus, Mannequin, Man(n)ikin, Masquerade, Model, Place, Plastique, Posture, Pretend, Problem, Propound, Pseud, Sit, Stance, Sticker, Tickler
Poseidon Earthshaker
Posh Classy, Grand, Lah-di-dah, Ornate, Ritzy, Swanky, Swish, U
Position Asana, Attitude, Bearing(s), Close, Codille, Delta, Emplacement, Enfilade, False, Fixure, F(o)etal, Foothold, Fowler's, Grade, Instal, Lay, Lie, Location, Locus, Lodg(e)ment, Lotus, Missionary, Mudra, Office, Open, Pass, Peak, Place, Plant, Point, Pole, Post, Put, Recumbent, Root, Seat, Set(ting), Sextile, Sims, Site, Situ, Situs, Stance, Standing, Standpoint, Station, Status, Strategic, Syzygy, Tagmeme, Thesis, Tierce, Trendelenburg's, Viewpoint
Positive, Positivist Absolute, Anode, Assertive, Categorical, > CERTAIN, Comte, Definite, Emphatic, False, Plus, Print, Sure, Thetic, Upbeat, Yang, Yes
Posse Band, Mob, Vigilantes
Possess(ed), Possession(s), Possessive Adverse, Apostrophe, Asset, Aver, Bedevil, Belonging(s), Demonic, Driven, Energumen, Estate, Have, Haveour, Haviour, Heirloom, His, Hogging, Know, Lares (et) penates, Mad, Obsessed, Occupation, > OWN, Sasine, Seisin, Sprechery, Substance, Tenancy, Usucap(t)ion, Vacant, Worth
Possible, Possibility, Possibly Able, Contingency, Feasible, Likely, Maybe, Mayhap, Off-chance, Peradventure, Perchance, Perhaps, Posse, Potential, Prospect, Resort, Viable, Will
▷ **Possibly** *may indicate* an anagram
Possum Burramys, Cataplexy, Opossum, Ringtail, Sugar glider, Sugar squirrel, Tait
Post(s), Postage Affix, After, Assign, Bitt, Bollard, Carrick bitt, Command, Correspondence, Dak, Dawk, Delivery, Dragon's teeth, Emily, Excess, Finger, First, Flagpole, Graded, Gradient, Guardhose, Hitching, Hurter, Jamb, Joggle, King, Last, Listening, Log, Mail, Mast, Newel, Observation, Outstation, Pale, Paling, Parcel, Pendant, Penny, Picket, Pile, Piling, Piquet, Placard, Place, Plant, Plum, Pole, Position, Presidio, Puncheon, Pylon, Queen, Quintain, Quoin, Registered, Remit, Residency, RM, Seat, Send, Snubbing, Spile, Staff, Staging, Stake, Starting, Station, Stell, Stoop, Stoup, Studdle, Term(inal), Tom, Tool, Trading, Upright, Vacancy, Waymark, Winning
Postcard(s) Deltiology
Poster Advertisement, Affiche, Bill, Broadsheet, Placard, Playbill, Sender
Posterior Behind, Bottom, Jacksie, Jacksy, Later, Lumbar, Pygal, Rear, Tail
Post-free Franco
Postman, Postmaster, Postwoman Carrier, Courier, Emily, Hill, Messenger, Nasby, Pat, Portionist, Sorter
Postmark Frank
Post mortem Autopsy, Enquiry, Necropsy

Postpone(ment) Adjourn, Contango, Defer, Delay, Frist, Hold over, Long-finger, Moratorium, Mothball, Pigeon-hole, Postdate, Prorogue, Reprieve, Respite, Shelve, Stay, Suspend, Withhold

Postulant Candidate, Noumenon, Novice

Postulate Assert, Assume, Claim, Propound

Posture(r), Posturing Affectation, Asana, Attitude, Birkie, Camp, Carriage, Decubitus, Deportment, Mudra, Pose, Pretence, Site, Stance, Vorlage

Posy Bouquet, Buttonhole, Corsage, Nosegay, Tussiemussie, Tuzzi-muzzy

Pot(s), Potting, Potty Abridge, Aludel, Bankroll, Basil, Belly, Cafetière, Cannabis, Casserole, Ca(u)ldron, Ceramic, Chamber, Chanty, Chatti, Chatty, Chimney, Cocotte, Crewe, Crock(ery), Crucible, Cruse(t), Cupel, Delf(t), Dixie, Ewer, Flesh, Gage, Gallipot, Ganja, Gazunder, Grass, Hash(ish), Helmet, Hemp, In off, Inurn, Jardinière, Jordan, Kettle, Kitty, Livery, Lobster, Lota(h), Maiolica, Majolica, Marijuana, Marmite, Melting, Ming, Olla, Olpe, Pan, Papper, Pat, Pint, Pipkin, Planter, Po, Pocket, Poot, Posnet, > POTTERY, Pounce, Pout, Prize, Quart, Samovar, Shoot, Skeet, Skillet, Steamer, Stomach, Tajine, Tea, Test, Throw, Togine, Trivet, Tureen, Urn, Vial, Ware, Wash, Wok

Potash Kalinite, Polverine, Sylvine, Sylvite

Potassium K, Kalium, Pearl ash, Saleratus, Saltpetre

Potation Dram, Drink

Potato(es) Batata, Chat, Couch, Datura, Duchesse, Early, Fluke, Hashbrowns, Hog, Hole, Hot, Irish, Jersey, Kidney, Kumara, Lyonnaise, Mash, Murphy, Parmentier, Peel-and-eat, Pratie, Praty, Roesti, Rumbledethump(s), Seed, Solanum, Stovies, Sweet, Tatie, Tattie, Teddy, Tuber, Ware, White, Yam

Pot-bearer Trivet

Pot-bellied Kedge, Kedgy, Kidge, Paunchy, Portly, Stout

Potboiler Hob

Pot-boy Basil, Ganymede, Scullion

Potent(ate) Dynamic, Emeer, Emir, Emperor, Huzoor, Influential, Kinglet, Mogul, Nawab, Panjandrum, Powerful, Ras, Ruler, Satrap, Squirearch, Sultan

Potential(ly) Action, Capacity, Electric, Electrode, In posse, Ionization, Making(s), Manqué, Possible, Promise, Resting, Scope, Viable

▷ **Potentially** *may indicate* an anagram

Pothole(r) Giant's kettle, Spelunker

Pot-house Shebeen, Tavern

Potion Dose, Draught, Drink, Dwale, Love, Mixture, Philtre, Tincture

Pot-pourri Hotchpotch, Medley, Pasticcio, Salmi

Potsherd Ostracon, Ostrakon

Pottage Berry

Potter Cue, Dabbity, Dabble, Dacker, Daidle, Daiker, Dibble, Dilly-dally, Dodder, Etruscan, Fettle, Fiddle, Footer, Footle, Fouter, Gamesmanship, Harry, Idle, Mess, Minton, Muck, Niggle, One-upmanship, Plouter, Plowter, Spode, Thrower, Tiddle, Tink(er), Troke, Truck, Wedgewood, Wedgwood

▷ **Potter** *may indicate* a snooker-player

Pottery Agatewear, Bank, Basalt, Bisque, Celadon, Ceramet, Ceramic, China, Creamware, Crock, Crouch-ware, Dabbity, Delf(t), Earthenware, Encaustic, Etruria, Faience, Flatback, Gombroon, Granitewear, Hollowware, Jomon, Lustreware, Maiolica, Majolica, Ming, Pebbleware, Raku, Red-figured, Satsuma, Scroddled, Sgraffito, Slab, Slipware, Smalto, Spode, Spongeware, Stoneware, Studio, Sung, Terra sigillata, Ware, Wedgwood®, Wemyss, Whieldon

Pouch(ed) Bag, Brood, Bum-bag, Bursa, Caecum, Cheek, Cisterna, Codpiece,

Diverticulum, Fanny pack, Gill, Jockstrap, Marsupial, Poke, Purse, Sac, Scrip, Scrotum, Spleuchan, Sporran, Tobacco

Poultice Application, Cataplasm, Embrocation, Epithem(a), Lenient, Plaster

Poultry Dorking, Fowl, Gallinaceous, Poot, Pout, Welsummer

Poultry disease Keel, Scaly-leg, Vent gleet

Pounce Claw, Jump, Lunge, Powder, Sere, Souse, Sprinkle, Swoop, Talon

Pound(er) Ache, As, Bar, Bash, Batter, Beat, Bombard, Bradbury, Bray, Broadpiece, Bruise, Catty, Contund, Coop, Drub, Embale, Enclosure, Ezra, Fold, Green, Hammer, Hatter, Imagist, Intern, Iron man, Jail, Kiddle, Kidel, Kin, Knevell, L, Lam, Lb, Lock, Mash, Nevel, Nicker, Oncer, One-er, Oner, Pale, Pen, Penfold, Pestle, Pin, Pindar, Pinfold, Powder, Pulverise, Pun, Quid, Quop, Rint, Smacker, Sov(ereign), Squid, Stamp, Strum, Tenderise, Thump, Tower, Weight

Pour Be mother, Birl(e), Bucket, Cascade, Circumfuse, Decant, Diffuse, Flood, Flow, Jaw, Jirble, Libate, Rain, Seil, Shed, Sile, Skink, Spew, Stream, Teem, Turn, Vent, Weep, Well

Pout Bib, Blain, Brassy, Eel, Fish, Horn(ed), Mope, Mou(e), Scowl, Sulk, Tout, Towt, Whiting

Poverty Beggary, Dearth, Deprivation, Illth, Indigence, > LACK, Locust years, Need, Penury, Poortith, Puirtith, Squalor, Want

Powder(ed), Powdery Alumina, Amberite, Araroba, Baking, Ballistite, Boracic, Calamine, Chalk, Cosmetic, Crocus, Culm, Curry, Custard, Cuttlefish, Dentifrice, Dover's, Dust, Dusting, Explosive, Face, Floury, Fulminating, Giant, Glaucous, Goa, Gregory, Grind, Gun, Hair, Kohl, Levigate, Lithia, Litmus, Lupulin, Meal, Mould-facing, Moust, Mu(i)st, Pemoline, Percussion, Persian, Plate, Pollen, Pounce, Priming, Prismatic, Projecting, Pruinose, Pulver, Pulvil, Putty, Rachel, Rochelle, Rottenstone, Rouge, Saleratus, Seidlitz, Seme(e), Sherbet, Silver iodide, Sitosterol, Smeddum, Smokeless, Snuff, Spode, Spodium, Talc(um), Thimerosal, Toner, Tooth, Triturate, Tutty, Washing, Zein

Power(ful), Powers Ability, Able, Aeon, Aggrandisement, Almighty, Amandla, Arm, Attorney, Autarchy, Authority, Axis, Big, Chakra, Cham, Charisma, Clairvoyance, Clout, Cogency, Command, Corridor, Cube, Danger, Despotic, Diadem, Dioptre, Dominion, Effective, Eminence, Eminence grise, Empathy, Empery, Energy, Eon, Exponent, Facility, Faculty, Fire, Flower, Force, Force majeure, Geothermal, Grey, Hefty, Hegemony, High, Hildebrandic, Horse, Hot, Hp, Hydroelectric, Imperium, Influence, Kami, Kilowatt, Log, Logarithm, Lusty, Mana, Mastery, Megalomania, Might, Mogul, Motive, Motor, Movers and shakers, Muscle, Nature, Nth, Nuclear, Od-force, Omnificent, Omnipotent, Option, P, Panjandrum, People, Pester, Plenipotency, Posse, Potency, Prepollence, Prepotent, Puissant, Punch, Regime, Resolving, Siddhi, Sinew, Solar, Soup, Stamina, Staying, Steam, Stiff, Stopping, Strength, > STRONG, Supercharge, Supreme, Suzerain, Teeth, Telling, Throne, Tidal, Tycoon, Tyrone, Valency, Vertu(e), Vigour, Vis, Volt, Vroom, Water, Watt, Wattage, Wave, Weight, Wind, World

Powerless Diriment, Downa-do, Freewheel, Hamstrung, Helpless, Impotent, Impuissant, Incapable, Unable, Unarmed, Weak

Powwow Confab, Conference, Council, Meeting

Pox Orf, Pize

Practical, Practicable Active, Brass tacks, Doable, Easy-care, Hard-boiled, Joker, No-nonsense, Nuts and bolts, On, Pragmatic, Realist(ic), Realpolitik, Rule of thumb, Sensible, Shrewd, Useful, Utilitarian, Viable, Virtual

Practice, Practise, Practitioner, Practised Abuse, Adept, Custom, Distributed, Do, Drill, Enure, Exercise, General, Group, Habit, Inure, Ism, Keep, Knock-up,

Massed, Meme, Nets, Operate, Order, Ply, Policy, Praxis, Private, Prosecution, Pursuit, Rehearsal, Rehearse, Restrictive, Rite, Rut, Sadhana, Sharp, Target, Teaching, Test-run, Trade, Tradition, Train, Trial, Ure, Usage, Use

Pragmatic, Pragmatist Ad hoc, Busy, Dogmatic, Humanist, Meddling, Officious, Realist

Prairie IL, Illinois, Llano, Plain, Savanna, Steppe, Tundra, Veldt

Prairie dog Whippoorwill, Wishtonwish

Praise(worthy) Acclaim, Adulation, Alleluia, Allow, Anthem, Applause, Belaud, Bless, Blurb, Bouquet, Butter, Carol, Citation, CL, Commend(ation), Compliment, Dulia, Encomium, Envy, Eulogise, Eulogium, Eulogy, Exalt, Extol, Gloria, Glory, Hero-worship, Herry, Hery(e), Hosanna, Hymn, Hype, Incense, Kudos, Laud, Lip service, Lo(o)s, Meritorious, Panegyric, Puff(ery), Rap, Roose, Tribute

Pram Carriage, Cart, Scow

Prance Brank, Canary, Caper, Cavort, Galumph, Gambol, Jaunce, Jaunse, Prank(le), Swagger, Tittup, Trounce

Prang Accident, Crash, Smash, Whale

Prank(s) Attrap, Bedeck, Bedizen, Caper, Dido, Escapade, Fredaine, Frolic, Gaud, Jape, Lark, Mischief, Rag, Reak, Reik, Rex, Rig, Spoof, Trick, Vagary

Praseodymium Pr

Prat Bottom, > **STUPID PERSON**

Prate Babble, Boast, Haver, Talk

Prattle Babble, Blat(her), Chatter, Gab(nash), Gas, Gibber, Gossip, Gup, Lalage, Patter, Smatter, Yap

Prawn Banana, Dublin Bay, Scampi, School, Shrimp

Pray(ing) Appeal, Beg, Beseech, Daven, > **ENTREAT**, Impetrate, Intone, Invoke, Kneel, Mantis, Solicit, Wrestle

Prayer (book), Prayers Acoemeti, Act, Amidah, Angelus, Ardas, Ave (Maria), Bead, Beadswoman, Bede, Bene, Bidding, Breviary, Collect, Common, Confiteor, Cry, Cursus, Daven, Deus det, Devotion, Eleison, Embolism, Entreaty, Epiclesis, Euchologion, Evensong, Geullah, Grace, Hail Mary, Hallan-shaker, Imam, Intercession, Invocation, Kaddish, Khotbah, Khotbeh, Khutbah, Kol Nidre, Kyrie, Kyrie eleison, Lauds, Litany, Lord's, Lychnapsia, Ma(c)hzor, Mantis, Mat(t)ins, Mincha(h), Missal, Musaf, Novena, Orant, Orarium, Orison, Our Father, Paternoster, Patter, Petition, Phylactery, Placebo, Plea, Proseucha, Proseuche, Puja, Requiem, Requiescat, Rogation, Rosary, Salat, Secret, Shema, Siddur, State, Stations of the Cross, Suffrage, Te igitur, Tenebrae, Triduum, Venite, Yajur-Veda, Yizkov

▷ **Prayer** *may indicate* one who begs

Preach(er) Ainger, Boanerges, Devil-dodger, Dominican, Donne, Ecclesiastes, Evangelist, Exhort, Gospeller, Graham, Holy Roller, Itinerant, Knox, Lecture, Mar-text, Minister, Moody, > **MORALISE**, Patercove, Pontificate, Postillate, Predicant, Predicate, Predikant, Priest, Prophet, Pulpiteer, Rant, Spintext, Spurgeon, Teach

Preamble Introduction, Preface, Proem, Prologue

Precarious Dangerous, Parlous, Perilous, Risky, Touch and go, Trickle, Uncertain, Unsteady

Precaution Care, Fail-safe, Guard, In case, Prophylaxis, Safeguard

Precede(nce), Precedent Antedate, Example, Forego, Forerun, Head, Herald, Pas, Predate, Preface, Priority, Protocol

Precept Adage, Canon, Commandment, Maxim, Motto, Saw

Precession Larmor

Precinct(s) Ambit, Area, Banlieue, Close, Courtyard, District, Environs, Pedestrian, Peribolos, Region, Shopping, Temenos, Verge, Vihara

Precious Adored, Chary, Chichi, Costly, Dear, Dearbought, Ewe-lamb, La-di-da, Murr(h)a, Owre, Precise, Rare, Valuable

Precipice Bluff, Cliff, Crag, Krans, Kran(t)z, Sheer

Precipitate, Precipitation, Precipitous Abrupt, Accelerate, Cause, Deposit, Hailstone, Headlong, Impetuous, Launch, Lees, Pellmell, Pitchfork, Rash, Sca(u)r, Sheer, Shoot, Sleet, Snowflake, Start, > STEEP, White

Precis Abstract, Aperçu, Epitome, Résumé, Summary

Precise(ly), Precisian, Precision Absolute, Accurate, Dry, Exact, Explicit, Fine-drawn, Literal, Minute, Nice(ty), Particular, Perfect, Plumb, Point-device, Prig, Prim, Punctilious, Spang, Specific, Starchy, Stringent, Succinct, Surgical, Tight, Very

Preclude Bar, Debar, Estop, Foreclose, Hinder, Impede, Prevent

Precocious Advanced, Bratpack, Forward, Premature

Preconception Ideating

Precursor Avant-courier, Forerunner, Harbinger

Predator(y) Carnivore, Eagle, Fox, Glede, Harpy-eagle, Jackal, Kestrel, Kite, Lycosa, Marauder, Predacious, Puma, Tanrec, Tarantula, Tenrec

Pre-dawn Antelucan, Ante lucem

Predecessor Ancestor, Forebear, Foregoer

Predestined Doomed, Fated, Tramway

Predicament Box, Dilemma, Embarrassment, Embroglio, Hobble, Hole, Jam, Pass, Peril, Pickle, Plight, Quandary, Scrape, Spot

Predict(ion), Predictable, Predictor Augur, Belomancy, Bet, Damn, Divination, Forecast, Foreordain, Foresay, Foreshadow, Foreshow, Forespeak, Foretell, Forsay, Horoscope, Nap, Necromancy, Portend, Presage, Previse, Prognosis, Prophecy, Prophesy, Regular, Second-guess, Soothsayer

Predilection Fancy, Liking, Prejudice, Taste, Tendency

Predisposition Aptitude, Inclination, Parti-pris, Tendency

Predominate Abound, Govern, Overshadow, Prevail, Reign

Pre-eminence, Pre-eminent Arch, Foremost, Palm, Paramount, Primacy, Supreme, Topnotch, Unique

Pre-empt Enter

Preen Perk, Primp, Prink, Prune

Prefab(ricated) Quonset

Preface Foreword, Herald, Intro, Preamble, Precede, Proem, Prolegomenon, Usher

Prefect Pr(a)eposter, Prepositor

Prefer(ence), Preferred Advance, Choose, Discriminate, Elect, Faard, Faurd, Favour, Imperial, Incline, Lean, Liquidity, Predilect(ion), Prefard, Priority, Proclivity, Promote, Sooner, Stocks, Taste, Will

Prefix Eka, Introduce, Name

Pregnancy, Pregnant Big, Clucky, Cyesis, Ectopic, Enceinte, Fertile, Gestation, Gravid(a), Great, Heavy, Knocked-up, Phantom, Pseudocyesis, Pudding-club, Stomack, With child

Prehistoric Ancient, Azilian, Beakerfolk, Brontosaurus, Cambrian, Clovis, Cro-magnon, Eocene, Folsom, Mound Builder, Ogygian, Primeval, Primitive, Pteranodon, Pterodactyl(e), Pterosaur, Saurian, Sinanthropus, Stonehenge, Titanosaurus, Trilith(on)

Prejudice(d) Bias, Bigotry, Derry, Discrimination, Down, Illiberal, Impede, Injure, Insular, Intolerance, Partiality, Parti pris, Preoccupy, Prepossession,

Racism

Prelate Archiepiscopal, Cardinal, Churchman, Exarch, Monsignor, Odo, Priest

Preliminary Draft, Exploration, Heat, Initial, Introductory, Precursory, Previous, Prodrome, Prolusion, Rough, Title-sheet

Prelude Entree, Forerunner, Intrada, Overture, Proem(ial), Ritornell(e), Ritornello

Premature Early, Precocious, Pre(e)mie, Premy, Previous, Slink, Untimely, Untimeous

Premedication Atropia

Premeditate Anticipate, Foresee, Plan

Premier Chief, Leader, Main, PM, > PRIME MINISTER, Tojo

Premise(s) Assumption, Datum, Epicheirema, Ground, Hypothesis, Inference, Lemma, Postulate, Property, Proposition, Reason

Premium Ap, Bond, Bonus, Discount, Grassum, Pm, Reward, Scarce, Share

Premonition Hunch, Omen, Presentiment, Prodromal, Warning

Preoccupation, Preoccupied, Preoccupy Absorb, Abstracted, Distrait, Engross, Hang-up, Intent, Obsess, Thing

Prepaid Pro-forma, Sae

Prepare(d), Preparation Address, A la, Arrange, Attire, Boun, Bowne, Busk, Calver, Cock, Concoct, Cooper, Countdown, Decoct, Did, Do, Dress, Edit, Forearm, Game, Groom, Ground, Inspan, Key, Lay, Legwork, Lotion, Measure, Mobilise, Parasceve, Prime, Procinct, Prothesis, Provide, Psych, > READY, Rehearsal, Ripe, Rustle up, Set, Spadework, Stand-to, Suborn, Train, Truss, Warm-up, Whip up, Yare

▷ **Prepare(d)** *may indicate* an anagram

Preponderance, Preponderant, Preponderate Important, Majority, Outweigh, Paramount, Prevalence, Sway

Preposition Premise

Prepossessing, Prepossession Attractive, Fetching, Predilection, Winsome

Preposterous Absurd, Chimeric, Foolish, Grotesque, Unreasonable

▷ **Preposterous** *may indicate* a word reversed

Pre-Raphaelite Rossetti, Waterhouse

Prerequisite Condition, Essential, Necessity, Sine qua non

Prerogative Faculty, Franchise, Liberty, Privilege, Right

Presage Abode, Foresight, Omen, Portend, Presentiment, Prophesy

Presbyter(ian) Berean, Blue, Cameronian, Covenanter, Elder, Knox, Macmillanite, Moderator, Sacrarium, Whig(gamore)

Prescient Clairvoyant, Fly

Prescribe Appoint, Assign, Dictate, Enjoin, Impose, Ordain, Rule, Set

Prescription Cipher, Decree, Direction, Formula, Medicine, R, Rec, Receipt, Ritual, Specific

Presence Aspect, Bearing, Closeness, Company, Debut, Hereness, Real, Shechinah, Shekinah, Spirit

Present(ation), Presented, Presenter, Presently Ad sum, Anchorman, Anon, Assists, Autocutie, Award, Bestow, Bonsela, Boon, Bounty, Box, Breech, By, Cadeau, Congiary, Coram, Current, Debut, Dee-jay, Deodate, DJ, Donate, Dotal, Douceur, Dower, Emcee, Endew, Endow, Endue, Enow, Etrenne, Existent, Fairing, Feature, Front-man, Gie, > GIFT, Give, Going, Grant, Gratuity, Hand, Here, Hodiernal, Inst, Introduce, Largess(e), Linkman, MC, Mod, Nonce, Now, Nuzzer, On hand, Porrect, Potlach, Pr, Prevailing, Produce, Proffer, Pro-tem, Put, Render, Show, Slice, Tip, Today, Vee-jay, Xenium, Yeven

Preserve(d), Preservative, Preserver Bottle, Burnettize, Can, Chill, Confect,

Confiture, Corn, Creosote, Cure, Dehydrate, Dry, Eisel, Embalm, Fixative, Formaldehyde, Formalin, Freeze, Guard, Hain, Hesperides, Jam, Jerk, Keep, Kinin, Kipper, Konfyt, Kyanise, Life, > **MAINTAIN**, Marmalade, Mummify, Pectin, Peculiar, Piccalilli, Pickle, Pot, Powellise, Salt, Salve, Saut, Souse, Store, Stratify, Stuff, Tanalith, Tanalized, Tar, Tin, Vinegar, Waterglass

Preside(nt) Abe, Adams, Banda, Carter, Chair, Childers, Cleveland, Coolidge, Coty, Dean, De Gaulle, Director, Eisenhower, Ford, Garfield, Grant, Harding, Harrison, Hoover, Ike, Johnson, Kennedy, Kruger, Lead, Lincoln, Madison, Moderator, Nixon, Old Hickory, P, Peron, Polk, Pompidou, Pr(a)eses, Prexy, Roosevelt, Sa(a)dat, Speaker, Superintendent, Supervisor, Taft, Tito, Truman, Tyler, Veep, Washington, Wilson

Press(ed), **Pressing**, **Pressure** Acute, Aldine, Armoire, Atmospheric, Bar, Bench, Blackmail, Blood, Bramah, Button, Cabinet, Chivvy, Clarendon, Closet, Clothes, Coerce, Cram, Crease, Crimp, Critical, Crowd, Crush, Cupboard, Cylinder, Dragoon, Drill, Dun, Durable, Duress, Duresse, Enforcement, Enslave, Exigent, Filter, Fluid, Fly, Force, Fourth estate, Goad, Greenmail, Gutter, Hasten, Head, Heat, Herd, Hie, Hug, Hustle, Hydraulic, Impact, Important, Importune, Inarm, Iron, Isobar, Jam, Jostle, Knead, Leverage, Lie, Lobby, Mangle, Megabar, Microbar, Mill, Minerva, Newspapers, Obligate, Onus, Osmotic, PA, Partial, Pascal, Peer, Permanent, Persist, Piezo-, Ply, Prease, Printing, Private, Psi, Pump, > **PUSH**, Racket, Ram, Ratpack, Record, Recruit, Reporter, Ridge, Roll, Rotary, Rounce, Rush, Samizdat, Screw, Scrooge, Scrouge, Scrowdge, Scrum, Serr(e), Sit, Speed, Spur, Squash, Squeeze, Stop, Strain(t), Straint, Stress, Tension, Thlipsis, Threap, Threep, Throng, Throttle, Thrutch, Torr, Tourniquet, Turgor, > **URGE**, Urgence, Urgency, Vanity, Vapour, Vice, Waid(e), Wardrobe, Weight, Wine, Wring, Yellow

Press agent Flack, Spin doctor

Press-gang Force, Impress, Shanghai

Pressman Ed, PRO, Reporter, Twicer

Prestidigitate(r) Conjure, Juggle, Legerdemain, Magician, Palm

Prestige, **Prestigious** Cachet, Credit, Distinguished, Fame, Influence, Kudos, Notable, Status

Presume, **Presumably**, **Presumption**, **Presumptuous** Allege, Arrogant, Audacity, Believe, Bold, Brass, Cocksure, Cocky, Doubtless, > **EXPECT**, Familiar, Forward, Gall, Impertinent, Insolent, Liberty, Outrecuidance, Pert, Probably, Suppose, Uppish, Whipper-snapper

Pretence, **Pretend(er)**, **Pretext** Act, Affect(ation), Afflict, Assume, Blind, Bluff, Charade, Charlatan, Claim, Claimant, Cover, Cram, Dissemble, Dissimulate, Excuse, False, Feign, Feint, Gondolier, Hokum, Humbug, Hypocrisy, Impostor, Jactitation, Kid(stakes), Lambert Simnel, Let-on, Make-believe, Malinger, Masquerade, Obreption, Old, Parolles, Perkin Warbeck, Pose, Profess, Pseud(o), Quack, Sham, Simulate, Stale, Stalking-horse, Subterfuge, Suppose, Warbeck, Young

Pretension, **Pretentious(ness)** Arty, Bombast, Chi-chi, Fantoosh, Fustian, Gaudy, Grandiose, High-falutin(g), Kitsch, La-di-da, Orotund, Ostentatious, Overblown, Paraf(f)le, Pompous, Pseud(o), Sciolism, Showy, Snobbish, Squirt, Tat, Tattie-peelin, Tinhorn, Toffee-nosed, Uppity, Wanky, Whippersnapper

Pretty Attractive, Becoming, Chocolate-box, Comely, Cute, Dear, Decorate, Dish, Elegant, Fair(ish), Fairway, Inconie, Incony, Keepsaky, Looker, Moderately, Pass, Peach, Picturesque, Primp, Quite, Sweet, Twee, Winsome

Prevail(ing) Dominate, Endure, Go, Induce, Persist, Persuade, Predominant, Preponderate, Reign, Ring, Triumph, Victor, Win

Prevalent Catholic, Common, Dominant, Endemic, Epidemic, Obtaining, Rife, Widespread

Prevaricate, Prevarication Equivocate, Hedge, Lie, Runaround, Stall, Whittie-whattie

Prevent(ive) Avert, Bar, Debar, Deter, Disenable, Embar, Estop, Foreclose, Forfend, Help, Impound, Inhibit, Keep, Let, Obstruct, Obviate, Preclude, Prophylactic, Stop, Theriac, Trammel

Preview Sneak, Trailer, Vernissage

Previous(ly) Afore, Already, Before, Earlier, Ere(-now), Fore, Foreran, Former, Hitherto, Once, Prior

Prey Booty, Feed, Kill, Pelt, Plunder, Predate, Proul, Prowl, Quarry, Raven, Ravin(e), Soyle, Spreagh, Victim

Price(d), Pricing, Price-raising Appraise, Assess, Charge, Consequence, Contango, > COST, Dearth, Due, Evens, Exercise, Expense, Fee, Fiars, Hammer, Hire, Intervention, Issue, Limit, List, Loco, Market, Offer, Packet, Perverse, Predatory, Prestige, Quotation, Quote, Rate, Regrate, Reserve, Shadow, Song, Spot, Starting, Street value, Striking, Trade, Unit, Upset, Value, Vincent, Weregild, Wergeld, Wergild, Worth, Yardage

Prick(ed), Prickle, Prickly Acanaceous, Accloy, Argemone, Arrect, Bearded, Brakier, Bramble, Brog, Bunya, Cactus, Cloy, Cnicus, Echinate, Goad, Gore, Hedgehog, Hedgepig, Impel, Inject, Jab, Jook, Juk, Kali, Penis, Perse, Pierce, Prod, Puncture, Rowel, Rubus, Ruellia, Seta, Setose, Smart, Spicula, Spinate, Stab, Star-thistle, Stimulus, Sting, Tattoo, Tatu, Teasel, Thistle, Thorn, Tingle, Urge

Prickly heat Miliaria

Prickly-pear Opuntia, Tuna

Pride Bombast, Brag, Conceit, Elation, Esprit de corps, Glory, Hauteur, Hubris, Inordinate, Lions, London, Machismo, Plume, Preen, Purge, Triumphalism, Vainglory, Vanity

Priest(ess), Priests Aaron, Abaris, Abbess, Abbot, Ananias, Annas, Archimandrite, Bacchae, Bacchantes, Baptes, Becket, Bonze, Brahmin, Cardinal, Clergyman, Cleric, Cohen, Concelebrant, Corybant(es), Curé, Dalai Lama, Druid, Eli, Elisha, Father, Fetial, Flamen, Fr, Habacuc, Habakkuk, Hero, Hieratic, Hierophant, High, H(o)ungan, Io, Jethro, Lack-Latin, Lama, Laocoon, Levite, Lucumo, Mage, Magus, Mallet, Mambo, Marabout, Metropolitan, Minister, Missionary, Monsignor, Mufti, Norma, Oratorian, Padre, Papa, Parson, Pastor, Patercove, Patrico, Pawaw, Père, Pontifex, Pontiff, Pope, Pope's knight, Powwow, Pr, Preacher, Prelate, Presbyter, Prior(ess), Pythia, Rabbi, Rebbe, Rector, Rev, Sacerdotal, Salian, Savonarola, Seminarian, Shaman, Shaveling, Sky pilot, Spoiled, Tohunga, Vicar, Vivaldi, Worker, Zadok

Prig Dandy, Fop, Humbug, Nimmer, Pilfer, Prude, Puritan

Prim Demure, Mun, Neat, Old-maidish, Perjink, Preceese, Precise, Proper, Starchy

Primacy, Primate Ape, Aye-aye, Bandar, Bigfoot, Biped, Bishop, Bush baby, Cardinal, Ebor, Gibbon, Hanuman, Hominid, Jackanapes, King-kong, Loris, Macaque, Magot, Mammal, Marmoset, > MONKEY, Orang, Pongid, Potto, Prosimian, Protohuman, Quadruman, Ramapithecus, Rhesus, Sifaka, Tarsier

Prima donna Diva, Patti, Star

Prim(a)eval Ancient, Prehistoric, Primitive

Prime(r), Primary, Priming Arm, Basic, Bloom, Cardinal, Charging, Chief, Choice, Claircolle, Clearcole, Clerecole, Closed, Detonator, Direct, Donat, Donet, Election, Enarm, First, Flower, Heyday, Mature, Open, Original,

Paramount, Peak, Radical, Remex, Sell-by-date, Supreme, Thirteen, Tip-top, Totient, Totitive, Valuable, Windac, Windas, Ylem

Prime Minister Asquith, Attlee, Baldwin, Balfour, Begin, Bute, Canning, Chamberlain, Chatham, Dewan, Disraeli, Diwan, Eden, Grand Vizier, Grey, Home, Leaderene, North, Number Ten, Peel, Pitt, PM, Premier, Shastri, Tanaiste, Taoiseach, Thatcher, Walpole

Primitive Aborigine, Amoeba, Antediluvian, Arabic, Archaic, Atavistic, Barbaric, Caveman, Crude, Early, Evolué, Fundamental, Naive, Neanderthal, Neolithic, Old, Persian, Primordial, Pro, Prothyl(e), Protomorphic, Protyl(e), Radical, Rudimentary, Savage, Subman, Turkish, Uncivilised, Ur

Primordial Blastema, Fundamental, Original

Primrose, Primula Evening, League, Oenothera, Onagra, Ox-lip, Pa(i)gle, Rosebery, Vicar, Yellow

Prince(ly) Ahmed, Albert, Ameer, Amir, Amphitryon, Anchises, Arjuna, Atheling, Barnmecide, Black, Cadmus, Caliph, Chagan, Charming, Crown, Czarevich, Elector, Equerry, Eugene, Florizel, Fortinbras, Gaekwar, Gospodar, Guicowar, Hal, Highness, Hospodar, Huzoor, Igor, Inca, Infante, Khan, Ksar, Lavish, Lucumo, Maharaja, Margrave, Meleager, Merchant, Mir, Mirza, Nawab, Nizam, Noble, Otto, P, Pantagruel, Pendragon, Pirithous, Porphyrogenite, Potentate, Rainier, Rajah, Rana, Ras, Rasselas, Ratoo, Ratu, Regal, RH, Rudolph, Rupert, Serene, Sharif, Shereef, Sherif, Siegfried, Student, Tengku, Tereus, Tsar(evich), Tunku, Upper Roger

Princess Andromache, Andromeda, Anne, Ariadne, Begum, Creusa, Czarevna, Czarista, Danae, Di(ana), Electra, Electress, Eudocia, Europa, Hermione, Hesione, Ida, Imogen, Infanta, Iseult, Isolde, Jezebel, Maharanee, Maharani, Pocahontas, Procne, Rani, Regan, Tou Wan, Tsarevna, Tsarista, Turandot

Principal Arch, Capital, Central, > **CHIEF**, Decuman, Especial, First, Foremost, Head, Leading, Main(stay), Major, Mass, Protagonist, Ringleader, Staple, Star

Principality Andorra, Lichtenstein, Moldavia, Monaco, Muscovy, Wales, Wal(l)achia

Principle(s), Principled Animistic, Anthropic, Archimedes, Axiom, Basis, Bernouilli, Brocard, Canon, Carnot, Code, Cosmological, Criterion, Cui bono, Cy pres, D'Alembert's, Doctrine, Dogma, Element, Entelechy, Essential, Exclusion, Fermat's, First, Fourier, Gause's, Generale, Germ, Ground rule, Guideline, Heisenberg, Honourable, Huygen's, Key, Law, Least time, Le Chatelier's, Logos, Methodology, Organon, Ormazd, Ormuzd, Pauli-exclusion, Peter, Plank, Platform, Pleasure, Precept, Prescript, Rationale, Reality, Reason, Reciprocity, Relativity, Remonstrance, Rudiment, Rule, Sakti, Seed, Shakti, Spirit, Summum bonum, Tenet, Theorem, Ticket, Uncertainty, Verification, Vital, Yang, Yin

Prink Beautify, Bedeck, Dress

Print(er), Printing Baskerville, Batik, Benday, Bromide, Calotype, Caveman, Caxton, Chapel, Chromo, Cibachrome, Cicero, Collotype, Contact, Copperplate, Dab, Dot matrix, Electrothermal, Elzevir, Engrave, Etching, Ferrotype, Fine, Flexography, Font, Gravure, Gurmukhi, Gutenberg, Half-tone, Hectograph, Heliotype, Image, Impact, Impress, Incunabula, India, Ink-jet, Intaglio, Italic, Jobbing, Laser, Letterpress, Letterset, Line, Line-engraving, Lino-cut, Lithograph, Logotype, Lower-case, Matrix, Mimeograph®, Monotype®, Moon, Non-impact, Off-line, Offset, Old-face, Oleo, Oleograph, Opaline, Phototype, Plate, Platinotype, Positive, Press, Publish, Remarque, Report, Reproduction, Retroussage, Rotogravure, Samizdat, Screen, Serigraph, Ship, Silk-screen, Small, Smoot, Splash, Spore, Stamp, Stenochrome, Stonehand,

Strike, Thermal, Three-colour, Trichromatic, Typesetter, Typothetae, Whorl, Woodburytype, Woodcut, Xerography, Xylograph, Zincograph

Printing-press Rounce

Prior(ity) Abbot, Afore, Antecedent, Anterior, Aperture, Earlier, Former, Hitherto, Monk, Overslaugh, Pre-, Precedence, Prefard, Preference, Previous, Privilege, Shutter, Triage

▸ **Prise** *see* PRIZE

Prism(s), Prismatic Catadioptric, Iriscope, Nicol, Periaktos, Rhombohedron, Spectrum, Teinoscope, Wollaston

Prison Albany, Alcatraz, Bagnio, Barracoon, Bastille, Bin, Bird, Boob, Bridewell, Brig, Brixton, Bullpen, Cage, Can, Cell, Chillon, Chok(e)y, Clink, Club, College, Confine, Cooler, Coop, Counter, Dartmoor, Dispersal, Dungeon, Durance, Fleet, Fotheringhay, Gaol, Glass-house, Guardhouse, Guardroom, Gulag, Hokey, Holloway, Hoos(e)gow, Hulk(s), Internment, > JAIL, Jug, Kitty, Limbo, Lob's pound, Lock-up, Logs, Lumber, Marshalsea, Massymore, Mattamore, Maze, Newgate, Nick, Oflag, Open, Panopticon, Pen, Penitentiary, Pentonville, Pit, Poke(y), Porridge, Pound, Princetown, Quad, Quod, Rasp-house, Reformatory, Roundhouse, Scrubs, Shop, Sing-sing, Slammer, Spandau, Stalag, State, Stir, Strangeways, The Leads, Tol(l)booth, Tower, Tronk, Wandsworth, Wormwood Scrubs

Prisoner Canary-bird, Captive, Collegian, Collegiate, Con(vict), Detainee, Detenu, Hostage, Inmate, Internee, Jailbird, Lag, Lifer, Political, POW, Trustee, Trusty, Yardbird, Zek

Pristine Fire-new, Fresh, New, Original, Unmarked, Unspoiled

Private(ly) Ain, Aside, Atkins, Auricular, Buccaneer, Byroom, Clandestine, Close, Closet, Conclave, Confidential, Enisle(d), Esoteric, Homefelt, Hush-hush, In camera, Individual, Inner, Intimate, Non-com, Own, Personal, Piou-piou, Poilu, Proprietary, Pte, Rank(er), Retired, Sanction, Sapper, Secret, Several, > SOLDIER, Squaddie, Sub rosa, Tommy

Privateer(s) Buccaneer, Corsair, Freebooter, Marque(s), Pirate

Privation Hardship, Penury, Want

Privileg(ed) Birthright, Blest, Charter, Curule, Enviable, Exempt, Favour, Franchise, Freedom, Indulgence, Insider, Liberty, Mozarab, Nomenklatura, Octroi, Parliamentary, Patent, Prerogative, Pryse, Regale, Regalia, Right, Sac

Privy Apprised, Can, Closet, Intimate, Jakes, John, Loo, Necessary, Reredorter, Secret, Sedge, Siege

Prize(s), Prizewinner, Prized Acquest, Apple, Archibald, Assess, Award, Best, Booby, Booker, Bravie, Capture, Champion, Consolation, Creach, Cup, Dux, Efforce, > ESTEEM, Force, Garland, Goncourt, Grice, Honour, Jackpot, Jemmy, Lever, Lot, Money, Nobel, Palm, Pearl, Pewter, Pie, Plum, Plunder, Pot, Pulitzer, Purse, Ram, Reprisal, > REWARD, Scalp, Ship, Spreaghery, Sprechery, Stakes, Taonga, Tern, Treasure, Trophy, Turner, Value

Pro Aye, Coach, For, Harlot, Moll, Paid, Tramp, Yea, Yes

▸ **Pro** *see* PROSTITUTE

Probable, Probability Apparent, Belike, Conditional, Ergodic, Feasible, Likely, Marginal, Mathematical, Possible, Posterior, Verisimilar

Probation(er) Novice, Novitiate, Stibbler, Test, Trainee, Trial

Probe Antenna, Bore, Bougie, Canopus, Cassini, Corot, Delve, Dredge, Explore, Fathom, Feeler, Fossick, Galileo, Giotto, Inquire, Investigate, Magellan, Mariner, Mars Surveyor, Pelican, Pioneer, Poke, Pump, > SEARCH, Seeker, Sonde, Sound, Space, Stardust, Stylet, Tent, Thrust, Tracer, Venera

Probity Honour, Integrity, Justice

Problem(s) Acrostic, BO, Boyg, Brainteaser, Crisis, Crux, Dilemma, Egma, Enigma, Facer, Glitch, Handful, Hang-up, Headache, Hitch, Hurdle, Indaba, Knot(ty), Koan, Miniature, Musive, Net, Nuisance, Obstacle, Pons asinorum, Poser, Quandary, Question, Re, Rebus, Riddle, Rider, Snag, Sorites, Sum, Teaser, Thing, Tickler, Toughie, Trouble, Tsuris, Yips

Problem-solving Synectics

Proboscis Haustellum, Promuscis, Snout, Trunk

Proceed(s), Proceeding, Procedure Acta, Afoot, Algorithm, Continue, Course, Do, Drill, Emanate, Fand, Flow, Fond, Goes, Haul, Issue, Machinery, March, Mechanics, Method, Mine, MO, Modal, Move, On, Pass, Practice, Praxis, Process, Profit, Protocol, Punctilio, Pursue, Put, Rake, Return, Rite, Ritual, Routine, Sap, Steps, System, Take, Use, Yead(s), Yede, Yeed

Process(ing), Procession, Processor Acromion, Action, Additive, Ala, Ambarvalia, Axon, Ben Day, Bessemer, Bosch, Castner, Catalysis, Cavalcade, Cortège, Cyanide, Demo, Diagonal, Front-end, Haber, Handle, Managing, Markov, Method, Moharram, Mond, Motorcade, Muharram, Odontoid, Open hearth, -osis, Pageant, Parade, Parallel, Paseo, Photosynthesis, Pipeline, Planar, Pomp, Primary, Recycle, Screen, Secondary, Series, Silkscreen, Skimmington, Solvay, Speciation, Sterygoid, String, Subtractive, Thermite, Thought, Torchlight, Train, Treat, Trial, Turn(a)round, Unit, Xiphoid, Zygomatic

Proclaim, Proclamation Announce, Annunciate, Ban, Blaze, Blazon, Boast, Broadsheet, Cry, Edict, Enounce, Enunciate, Herald, Indiction, Kerygma, Oyez, Preconise, Predicate, Profess, Publish, Ring, Shout, Trumpet, Ukase

Procrastinate, Procrastinating Defer, Delay, Dilatory, Dilly-dally, Linger, Pettifog, Postpone, Shelve, Temporise, Vacillate

Procreate Beget, Engender, Generate, Initiate

Procrustean Conformity

Proctor Agent, King's, Monitor, Prog, Proxy, Queen's

Procurator, Procure(r) Achieve, Aunt, Crimp, Earn, Get, Induce, Naunt, Obtain, Pander, Pilate, Pimp, Sort, Suborn

Prod Cattle, Egg, Goad, Impel, Jab, Job, Jog, Nudge, Poke, Pote

Prodigal Costly, Lavish, Profligate, Spendall, Unthrift, Wanton, Wasteful, Waster

Prodigious, Prodigy Abnormal, Amazing, Huge, Immense, Infant, Monster, Monument, Mozart, Phenomenal, Portentous, Tremendous, Wonder, Wonderwork, Wunderkind

Produce(r), Producing Afford, Breed, Cause, Create, Crop, Ean, Edit, Effect, Engender, Evoke, Exhibit, Extend, Fruit, Generate, Get, Grow, Home-grown, Impresario, Issue, Kind, Make, Offspring, Onstream, Originate, Output, Propage, Propound, Raise, Son, Spawn, Stage, Supply, Teem, Throw, Wares, Whelp, Yield

▷ **Produces** *may indicate* an anagram

Product(ion), Productive(ness), Productivity Actualities, Apport, Artefact, Ashtareth, Ashtaroth, Astarte, Bore, Coefficient, Commodity, Drama, End, Factorial, Fecund, Fertile, Fruit, Genesis, Global, Handiwork, Harvest, Net domestic, Net national, Output, Outturn, Pair, Partial, Profilic, Result, Rich, Scalar, Show, Speiss, Uberous, Uberty, Vector, Waste, Work, Yield

▷ **Production** *may indicate* an anagram

Proem Foreword, Overture, Pre, Preface

Profane, Profanation, Profanity Coarse, Coprolalia, Desecrate, Impious, Irreverent, Sacrilege, Unholy, Violate

Profess(ed), Professor Absent-minded, Academic, Adjoint, Admit, Asset, Avow, Challenger, Claim, Declare, Disney, Emeritus, Higgins, Hodja, Kho(d)ja, Know-all, Ostensible, Own, Practise, Pundit, Regent, Regius, RP, STP, Visiting

Profession(al) Admission, Assurance, Buppy, Business, Career, Creed, Expert, Métier, Practitioner, Pretence, Pursuit, Regular, Salaried, Skilled, Trade, Vocation, Yuppie

Proffer Give, Present, Proposition, Tender

Proficiency, Proficient Able, Adept, Alert, Dan, Expert, Forte, Past master, Practised, Skill, Technique

Profile Analysis, Contour, Cross, Half-face, Long, Loral, Low, Outline, Silhouette, Sketch, Statant, T(h)alweg, Vignette

Profit(able), Profiteer, Profits Advantage, Arbitrage, Asset, Avail, Benefit, Boot, Bunce, Cere, Clear, Divi(dend), Economic, Edge, Emblements, Emoluments, Exploit, Fat, Gain, Graft, Gravy, Grist, Gross, Income, Increment, Issue, Jobbery, Juicy, Leech, Lucrative, Makings, Margin, Melon, Milch cow, Mileage, Moneymaker, Net, Pay(ing), Perk, Pickings, Preacquisition, Rake-off, Return, Reward, Royalty, Spoils, Use, Usufruct, Utile, Utility, Vail

Profligate Corinthian, Corrupt, Degenerate, Dissolute, Extravagant, Lecher, Libertine, Lorel, Losel(l), Oatmeal, Rakehell, Reprobate, Roué, Spend-all, Wastrel

Profound Altum, Bottomless, Complete, Deep, Intense, Recondite

Profuse, Profusion Abundant, Copious, Excess, Free, Galore, Lavish, Liberal, Lush, Quantity, Rank, Rich, Two-a-penny

Progenitor, Progenitrix Ancestor, Ma, Predecessor, Sire, Stock

Progeny Children, Descendants, Fruit, Issue, Offspring, Seed

Prognosis Forecast, Prediction

Prognosticate, Prognostication Augur, Foretell, Omen, Predict, Presage, Prophesy

Program(ming), Programming language, Programmer Ada, Algol, Applet, Basic, BIOS, Bloatware, Boot, Bot, Cancelbot, Chatbot, Cobol, Coder, Columbus, CU See Me, Debugger, Dictionary, Est, Executive, Firmware, Fortran, Freeware, Inputter, Java®, Linear, Linker, LISP, Loader, Logic, LOGO, Object, Package, Parser, Pascal, PROLOG, PROM, Router, Screensaver, Search engine, Shell, Small-talk, SNOBOL, Software, Source, Spellchecker, Spreadsheet, SQL, Sustaining, Systems, Telnet, Translator, Utility, Web browser, Web crawler, Worm

Programme Agenda, Broadcast, Card, Chat show, Code, Documentary, Docusoap, Dramedy, Est, Event, Faction, Fly-on-the-wall, Infotainment, Linear, Mockumentary, PDL, Phone-in, Plan, Playbill, Prank, Regimen, Report, Schedule, Scheme, Sepmag, Show, Sitcom, Sked, Soap, Software, Syllabus, System, Telecast, Telethon, Timetable

Progress(ive), Progression > ADVANCE, Afoot, Arithmetic, Avant garde, Course, Fabian, Flow, Forge, Forward, Forward-looking, Gain, Geometric, Go, Growth, Harmonic, Headway, Incede, Liberal, Move, Onwards, Paraphonia, Pilgrim's, Prosper, Rack, Rake's, Reformer, Roll, Run, Sequence, Series, Step, Vaunce, Way, Yead, Yede, Yeed

Prohibit(ed), Prohibition(ist) Ban, Block, Debar, Dry, Embargo, Estop, Forbid, Hinder, Index, Injunct, Interdict, Noli-me-tangere, Off-limits, Prevent, Pussyfoot, Rahui, Suppress, Taboo, Tabu, Verboten, Veto

Project(ile), Projecting, Projection, Projector Aim, Ammo, Assignment, Astral, Astrut, Ball, Ballistic, Beetle, Bullet, Butt, Buttress, Cam, Cast, Catapult, Channel, Cinerama®, Cog, Conceive, Condyle, Conic, Console,

Corbel, Coving, Crossette, Cutwater, Denticle, Diascope, Discus, Eaves, Echinus, Elance, Enterprise, Episcope, Excrescence, Exsert, Extrapolate, Fet(ter)lock, Flange, Gair, Gore, Guess, Hangover, Helicity, Hoe, Homolosine, Hurtle, Inion, Jut, Kern, Knob, Ledge, Lobe, Lug, Magic lantern, Malleolus, Manhattan, Mercator, Mitraille, Mollweide, Mucro, Mutule, Nab, Nose, Nunatak(er), Olecranon, Opaque, Orillion, Orthogonal, Orthographic, Outcrop, Outjet, Outjut, Outshot, Overhang, Overhead, Oversail, Peter's, Pitch, Planetarium, Planisphere, Polyconic, Pork barrel, Prickle, Promontory, > **PROTRUDE**, Proud(er), Quillon, Raguly, Roach, Rocket, Sail, Salient, Sally, Sanson-Flamsteed, Scaw, Scheme, Screen, Shelf, Shrapnel, Sinusoidal, Skaw, Snag, Snout, Spline, Sponson, Sprocket, Spur, Squarrose, Stand out, Stereopticon, Stick out, Tang, Tappet, Tenon, Throw, Toe, Tracer, Trimetric, Trippet, Trunnion, Turnkey, Turtleback, Tusk, Umbo, Undertaking, Villus, Vitascope, Zenithal

Prolapse Procidence

Proletarian, Proletariat People, Plebeian, Popular

Proliferate Expand, Increase, Multiply, Propagate, Snowball

Prolific Abounding, Fecund, Fertile, Fruitful, Profuse, Teeming

Prolix(ity) Lengthy, Prosaic, Rambling, Rigmarole, Verbose, Wire-draw, Wordy

Prologue Introduce, Preface

Prolong(ed) Extend, Lengthen, Protract, Sostenuto, Spin, Sustain

Prom(enade) Alameda, Boulevard, Cakewalk, Catwalk, Crush-room, Esplanade, Front, Mall, Parade, Paseo, Pier, Sea-front, Stroll, > **WALK**

Prometheus Fire

Promethium Pm

Prominence, Prominent Antitragus, Blatant, Bold, Colliculus, Condyle, Conspicuous, Egregious, Emphasis, Featured, Gonion, High profile, Important, Insistent, Luminary, Manifest, Marked, Obtrusive, Outstanding, Salient, Signal, Teat, Toot, Tragus

Promiscuous, Promiscuity Casual, Fast, Free, Indiscriminate, Light, Mixed, Motley, Pell-mell, Slapper, Trollop, Whoredom

Promise, Promising Accept, Assure, Augur, Auspicious, Avoure, Behest, Behight, Behote, Bode, Coming, Compact, Covenant, Engagement, Foretaste, Guarantee, Hecht, Hest, Hete, Hight, IOU, Likely, Manifest, Parole, Pledge, Plight, Pollicitation, Potential, Recognisance, Recognizance, Rosy, Sign, Sponsor, Swear, Tile, Undertake, Vow, Warranty, Word

Promised land Beulah, Canaan, Israel

Promissory note IOU, PN

Promontory Bill, Cape Sable, Cliff, Flamborough Head, Foreland, Giant's Causeway, Hatteras, Headland, Hoe, Hogh, Mull, Naze, Ness, Nose, Peak, Pillars of Hercules, Spit, The Lizard, Tintagel Head

Promote(r), Promotion Adman, Advance, > **ADVERTISE**, Advocate, Aggrandise, Aid, Assist, Blurb, Boost, Campaign, Dog and pony show, Elevate, Encourage, Exponent, Foment, Foster, Further, Help, Hype, Increase, Make, Pracharak, Prefer, Prelation, Promulgate, Provoke, Queen, Rear, Remove, Run, Salutary, Sell, Sponsor, Spruik, Stage, Step, Subserve, Tendencious, Tendentious, Upgrade, Uplead, Uprate

Prompt(er), Promptly, Promptness Actuate, Alacrity, Autocue®, Believe, Celerity, Chop-chop, Cue, Egg, Expeditious, Frack, Idiot-board, Immediate, Incite, Inspire, Instigate, Move, On-the-nail, Opposite, Pernicious, Premove, Punctual, Quick, Ready, Speed(y), Spur, Stimulate, Sudden, Tight, Tit(e), Titely, Tyte, Urgent

Promulgate Preach, Proclaim, Publish, Spread

Prone Apt, Groof, Grouf, Grovel, Liable, Lying, Prostrate, Recumbent, Subject, Susceptible

Prong Fang, Fork, Grain, Peg, Tang, Tine

Pronghorn Cabrie, Cabrit

Pronoun Personal, Reciprocal, Relative

Pronounce(d), Pronouncement Adjudicate, Affirm, Articulate, Assert, Asseveration, Clear, Conspicuous, Declare, Definite, Dictum, Emphatic, Enunciate, Fiat, Indefinite, Marked, Opinion, Palatalise, Pontificate, Recite, Utter, Velarise, Vocal, Voice, Vote

Pronto PDQ

Pronunciation Betacism, Cacoepy, Delivery, Diction, Etacism, Itacism, Lallation, Orthoepy, Phonetics, Plateasm, Proclitic, Received, Rhotacism, Sound, Tense

Proof Apagoge, Argument, Bona fides, Confirmation, Direct, Evidence, Firm, Foundry, Galley, Godel's, Indirect, Positive, Preif(e), Probate, Pull, Quality, Refutation, Remarque, Reproduction, Resistant, Revision, Secure, Slip, Strength, Test, Tight, Token, Trial, Upmake, Validity

Prop Airscrew, Bolster, Buttress, Clothes, Crutch, Dog-shore, Fulcrum, Leg, Loosehead, Misericord(e), Pit, Point d'appui, Punch(eon), Rance, Rest, Shore, Sprag, Spur, Staff, Stay, Stempel, Stemple, Stilt, Stoop, Stoup, Studdle, Stull, > SUPPORT, Tighthead, Trig, Underpin

Propaganda, Propagandist Agitprop, Ballyhoo, Black, Brainwashing, Chevalier, Doctrine, Exponent, Goebbels, Grey, Promotion, Psyop, Psywar, Publicity, Slogan, Spin doctor, White

Propagate, Propagator Breed, Dispread, Generate, Graft, Hatch, Increase, Produce, Promulgate, Provine, Spread, Tan-bed

Propel(ler) Airscrew, Ca', Drive, Fin, Frogmarch, Launch, Leg, Lox, > MOVE, Oar, Paddle, Pedal, Project, Push, Rotor, Row, Screw, Throw

Propensity Aptness, Bent, Inclination, Penchant, Tendency

Proper(ly) Ain, Convenance, Correct, Decent, Decorous, Due, Eigen, En règle, Ethical, > FIT, Genteel, Governessy, Kosher, Noun, Ought, Own, Pakka, Pathan, Prim, Pucka, Pukka, Puritanic, Real, Seemly, Suitable, Tao, Trew, True, Veritable, Well

Property Assets, Attribute, Aver, Belongings, Chattel, Chose, Contenement, Dead-hand, Demesne, Des res, Dowry, Effects, Enclave, Escheat, Escrow, Estate, Fee, Feu, Flavour, Fonds, Freehold, Goods, Hereditament, Hot, Hotchpot, Immoveable, Inertia, Intellectual, Jointure, Leasehold, Living, Means, Mortmann, Paraphernalia, Peculium, Personal, Personalty, Premises, Private, Public, Quale, Quality, Real, Stock, Stolen, Theft, Time-share, Timocracy, Trait, Usucapion, Usucaption

Prophesy, Prophet(ess), Prophetic Amos, Augur, Bab, Balaam, Calchas, Cassandra, Daniel, Deborah, Divine, Druid, Elias, Elijah, Elisha, Ezekiel, Ezra, Fatal, Fatidical, Forecast, Foretell, Former, Geomancer, Habakkuk, Haggai, Hosea, Is, Isa, Is(a)iah, Jeremiah, Joel, Jonah, Latter, Mahdi, Mahound, Major, Malachi, Mani, Mantic, Micah, Minor, Mohammed, Mopsus, Mormon, Moses, Nahum, Nathan, Nostradamus, Obadiah, Old Mother Shipton, Ominous, Oracle, Portend, Predictor, Prognosticate, Pythoness, Seer, Sibyl, Tipster, Tiresias, Vatic, Vaticinate, Voluspa, Zachariah, Zarathistra, Zechariah, Zephaniah, Zoroaster, Zwickau

Prophylactic, Prophylaxis Inoculation, Preventive, Serum, Vaccine, Variolation

Propitiate Appease, Atone, Pacify, Reconcile, Sop

Propitious Benign, Favourable, Lucky
Proponent Advocate, Backer, Partisan
Proportion(ate) Commensurable, Dimension, Inverse, Portion, Pro rata, Quantity, Quota, Ratio, Reason, Regulate, Relation, Sine, Size, Soum, Sowm
Proposal, Propose Advance, Bid, Bill, Canvass, Eirenicon, Feeler, Irenicon, Mean, Motion, Move, Nominate, Offer, Overture, Plan, Pop, Proffer, Propound, Recommend, Resolution, Scheme, Slate, Submission, > SUGGEST, Table, Tender, Volunteer, Woot, Would
Proposition Asses' bridge, Axiom, Convertend, Corollary, Deal, Disjunction, Ergo, Hypothesis, Identical, Lemma, Overture, Pons asinorum, Porism, Premise, Premiss, Rider, Sorites, Spec, Superaltern, Theorem, Thesis
Propound Advocate, Purpose, State
Proprietor, Propriety Correctitude, Decorum, Etiquette, Grundy, Keeper, Lord, Master, Owner, Patron, Rectitude
Prosaic Common, Drab, Flat, Humdrum, Tedious, Workaday
Proscenium Forestage
Proscribe Exile, Outlaw
Prose, Prosy Euphuism, Haikai, Polyphonic, Purple, Saga, Stich, Verbose, Version, Writing
Prosecute, Prosecutor, Prosecution Allege, Avvogadore, Charge, Crown, Fiscal, Furtherance, Impeach, Indict, Practise, Public, Sue, Wage
Proselytise(r), Proselytism Indoctrination, Propagandism, Souper
Prospect(or) Bellevue, Explore, Forty-niner, Fossick, Look-out, Mine, Opportunity, > OUTLOOK, Panorama, Perspective, Pleases, Possibility, Reefer, Scenery, Search, Sourdough, View, Vista, Visto, Wildcatter
Prospectus Menu, Pathfinder
Prosper(ity), Prosperous Blessed, Blossom, Boom, Fair, Fat cat, Flourish, Get ahead, Heyday, Mérimée, Palmy, > SUCCEED, Thee, Thrift, Thrive, Up, Warison, Wealth, Welfare, Well-heeled, Well-to-do
Prostitute, Prostitution Brass, Bulker, Callet, Catamite, Chippie, Cockatrice, Cocotte, Debase, Dell, Demi-mondaine, Dolly-mop, Doxy, Fancy woman, Fille de joie, Harlot, Hetaera, Hetaira, Hierodule, Ho, Hooker, Jailbait, Loose-fish, Loose woman, Madam, Magdalen(e), Moll, Mutton, Night-walker, Plover, Pole-cat, Pro, Punk, Quail, Quiff, Rent-boy, Road, Rough trade, Scrubber, Shippie, Slap, Social evil, Stew, Streetwalker, Strumpet, Tart, Trull, Venture, Wench, Whore
Prostrate, Prostration Collapse, Exhausted, Fell, Flat, Flatling, Ko(w)tow, Laid, Obeisance, Overcome, Procumbent, Prone, Repent, Throw
Protactinium Pa
Protean Amoebic, Fusible, Variable
Protect(ed), Protection, Protector Adonise, Aegis, Alexin, Arm, Armour, Asylum, Auspice, Bastion, Bestride, Bield, Buckler, Chaffron, Chain mail, Chamfrain, Chamfron, Charm, Cherish, Cloche, Coat, Cocoon, Coleor(r)hiza, Conserve, Cover, Covert, Cromwell, Cushion, Danegeld, Data, Defend, Defilade, Degauss, Egis, Enamel, Entrenchment, Escort, Estacade, Faun, Flank, Gobo, Groundsheet, Guard(ian), Gumshield, Hedge, House, Hurter, Immune, Inalienable, Indemnify, Insure, Keckle, Keep, Kickback, Lee, Mac(k)intosh, Mail, Male, Mollycoddle, Mother, Mouthpiece, Mudguard, Muniment, Noll, Nosey, Oliver, Orillion, Overall, Parados, Patent, Patron, Police, Pomander, Preserve, Rabbit's foot, Redome, Revetment, Ride shotgun, Safeguard, Sandbag, Save, Schanse, Schan(t)ze, Screen, Scug, Shadow, Sheathing, Sheeting, Shelter, > SHIELD, Skug, Splashback, Splashboard, Splasher,

Starling, Sunscreen, Talisman, Tribute, Tutelar, Umbrella, Underseal, Vaccine, Ward(ship), Warhead, Warrant, Weatherboard, Weatherstrip, Windbreaker, Windshield, Wing, Write

Protégé Pupil, Tutee, Ward

Protein Abrin, Actin, Actomyosin, Adipsin, Alanine, Albumen, Albumin, Aleuron(e), Allergen, Amandine, Analogon, Angiotensin, Antibody, Aquaporin, Avidin, Bradykinin, Calmodulin, Capsid, Capsomere, Caseinogen, Ceruloplasmin, Collagen, Complement, Conchiolin, Conjugated, Cytokine, Dystrophin, Elastin, Enzyme, Factor VIII, Ferritin, Fibrin, Fibrinogen, Fibroin, Flagellin, Gelatin, Gliadin(e), Glob(ul)in, Glutelin, Gluten, Haemoglobin, Haptoglobin, Histone, Hordein, Immunoglobulin, Incaparina, Interferon, Interleukin, Lactalbumin, Lectin, Legumin, Leptin, Leucin(e), Lewy bodies, Luciferin, Lymphokine, Lysin, Meat, Mucin, Myogen, Myoglobin, Myosin, Opsin, Opsonin, Ossein, Ovalbumin, Pepsin(e), Peptide, Phaseolin, Prion, Prolamin(e), Properdin, Protamine, Proteose, Prothrombin, Quorn®, Renin, Repressor, Ribosome, Sclerotin, Sericin, Serum albumin, Serum globulin, Single-cell, Soya, Spectrin, Spongin, Tempeh, Thrombogen, Toxalbumin, Transferrin, Tropomyosin, Troponin, TSP, Tubulin, Vitellin, Zein

Protest(er) Andolan, Aver, Avouch, Black Bloc(k), Clamour, Come, Démarche, Demo, Demonstrate, Demur, Deprecate, Dharna, Dissent, Expostulate, Gherao, Go-slow, Hartal, Inveigh, Lock-out, Luddite, March, Moonlighter, Nimby, Object, Outcry, Picket, Plea, Refus(e)nik, Remonstrate, Sit-in, Squawk, Squeak, Squeal, Suffragette, Work-to-rule

Protestant Amish, Anabaptist, Anglo, Calvin, Congregationalism, Covenanter, Cranmer, Dissenter, Evangelic, Gospeller, Huguenot, Independent, Lady, Loyalist, Lutheran, Mennonite, Methodist, Moravian, Neo-orthodoxy, Nonconformist, Oak-boy, Orangeman, Peep o' day Boys, Pentecostal, Pietism, Prod, Puritan, Religioner, Sacramentarian, Stundist, Swaddler, Wasp, Wesleyan

Protocol Agreement, Code, Convention, Etiquette, Genevan, Point to Point

Proton Nucleon, Quark

Protoplasm(ic) Coenocyte, Coenosarc, Cytode, Sarcode

Prototype Blueprint, Exemplar, Model, Original, Pattern

Protozoa(n) Am(o)eba, Foraminifer, Giardia, Globigerina, Gregarine, Heliozoan, Infusoria, Leishmania, Mastigophoran, Moner(a), Moneron, Paramecium, Peritricha, Radiolaria, Rhizopod, Thrichomonad, Trophozoite, Trypanosome, Volvox, Vorticella

Protract(ed) Delay, > EXTEND, Lengthen, Livelong, Prolong

Protrude, Protrusion Bulge, Eventration, Exsert, Jut, Pop, Pout, Project, Pseudopodium, Rectocele, Strout, Tel

Protuberance, Protuberant Apophysis, Bulge, Bump, Burl, Condyle, Crankle, Gibbous, Hump, Knap, Knob, Malleolus, Node, Papillose, Papule, Spadix, Swelling, Tragus, Tuber, Tubersity, Venter

Proud Arrogant, Boaster, Cocky, Conceited, Dic(k)ty, Elated, Flush, Haughty, Haut, Level, Lordly, Orgulous, Protruding, Superb, Vain

Prove(d), Proving Apod(e)ictic, Argue, Ascertain, Assay, Attest, Authenticate, Aver, Confirm, Convince, Deictic, Evince, Justify, > PROOF, Quote, > SHOW, Substantiate, Test

Proverb Adage, Axiom, Byword, Gnome, Maxim, Paroemia, Saw

▷ **Proverbial** *may refer to* the biblical Proverbs

Provide(d), Provident(ial) Afford, Allow, Arrange, Besee, Bring, Cater, Compare, Conditional, Endow, Equip, Far-seeing, Fend, Find, Furnish, Generate, Give,

Grubstake, Heaven sent, If, Lay on, Maintain, Proviso, Purvey, Serve, So, Sobeit, > **SUPPLY**, Suttle

Province, Provincial(ism) Acadia, Alberta, Anjou, Antwerp, Aquitaine, Area, Chinghai, Connacht, Dauphine, District, Drenthe, Eparchy, Eritrea, Exclave, Eyalet, Forte, Friesland, Gamsu, Gascony, Gaul, Gauteng, Gelderland, Groningen, Guangdong, Guelderland, Guienne, Guyenne, Hainau(l)t, Hebel, Helvetia, Henan, Hesse-Nassau, Hubei, Hunan, Ifni, Illyriaim, Insular, Jehol, Jiangsu, Jiangxi, Jiazhou, Jilin, Kaliningrad, Kansu, Kiangsu, Kiaochow, Kirin, Kosovo, Kwazulu, Land, Languedoc, Leinster, Liaoning, Liege, Limousin, Limpopo, Livonia, Lorraine, Lusitania, Lyonnais, Manitoba, Marche, Maritime, Mofussil, Mpumalanga, Munster, Namur, Narrow, Natal, New Brunswick, Ning(h)sia, Nivernais, Nome, Normandy, North Brabant, North West (frontier), Oblast, Ontario, Orange Free State, Orleanais, Otago, Overijssel, Palatinate, Pale, Paphlagonia, Patavinity, Petrographic, Picardy, Poitou, Prairie, Provence, Punjab, Qinghai, Quebec, Realm, Regional, R(h)aetia, Roussillon, Rural, Sanjak, Santa Cruz, Saskatchewan, Satrapy, Shaanx, Shandong, Shansi, Shantung, Shanxi, Shensi, Shoa, Sichuan, Sikang, Sind, Sircar, South Holland, Subah, Suburban, Syrophoenicia, Szechwan, Territory, Tirol, Touraine, Transvaal, Tsinghai, Tyrol, Ulster, Utrecht, Vilayet, Western, West Prussia, Yunnan, Zeeland, Zhejiang

Provision(s), Provisional Acates, A(p)panage, Board, Fodder, Insolvency, Jointure, Larder, Makeshift, Proggins, Scran, Skran, Stock, Supply, Suttle, Viands, Viaticum, Victuals

Proviso, Provisional Caution, Caveat, Clause, Condition, Interim, IRA, On trial, Reservation, Salvo, Stipulation, Temporary, Tentative

Provocation, Provocative, Provoke Agacant, Alluring, Egg, Elicit, Erotic, Exacerbate, Excite, Flirty, Harass, Incense, Induce, Inflame, Instigate, Irk, Irritate, Needle, Nettle, Occasion, Pique, Prompt, Raise, Red rag, Sedition, Spark, Stimulate, Tar, Tease, Urge, Vex, Wind up

Provost Dean, Keeper, Marshal, Warden

Prow Bow, Cutwater, Fore, Nose, Prore, Stem

Pro-war Hawk

Prowess Ability, Bravery, Forte, Fortitude

Prowl(er) Hunt, Lurch, Lurk, Mooch, Prole, Rache, Ramble, Ratch, Roam, Rove, Snoke, Snook, Snowk, Tenebrio, Tom

Proxime accessit Next best

Proximity Handiness

Proxy Agent, Attorn, Deputy, PP, Regent, Sub, Surrogate, Vicar, Vice

Prude(nce), Prudent, Prudery Bluenose, Canny, Caution, Circumspect, Comstocker, Conservative, Discreet, Discretion, Foresight, Frugal, Grundyism, Judicious, Metis, Mrs Grundy, Politic, Prig, Prissy, Provident, Sage, Sensible, Sparing, Strait-laced, Strait-lacer, Thrifty, Tight-laced, Vice-nelly, Victorian, Ware, Wary, Well-advised, Wise

Prune(r) Bill-hook, Dehorn, Lop, Plum, Proign, Proin(e), Reduce, Reform, Secateur, Shred, Sned, Thin, Trim

Prunella Hedge-sparrow, Self-heal

Prurient Avaricious, Itchy, Lewd, Obscene

Prussia(n) Blue, Junker, Pruce, Spruce, Westphalian

Pry Ferret, Force, Lever, Meddle, Nose, Paul, Peep, Question, Search, Snoop, Stickyback, Toot

Psalm Anthem, Cantate, Chant, Chorale, Hallel, Hymn, Introit, Jubilate, Metrical, Miserere, Neck-verse, Paean, Penitential, Proper, Ps, Song, Tone,

Tract, Venite

Pseud(o) Bogus, Mock, Posy, Sham, Spurious

Pseudonym Aka, Alias, Allonym, Anonym, Pen-name, Stage-name

Pshaw Chut, Pooh, Tilley-valley, Tilly-fally, Tilly-vally

Psyche Ego, Self, Soul, Spirit, Superego

Psychiatrist, Psychologist Adler, Alienist, Clare, Coué, Ellis, Freud, Headshrinker, Jung, Laing, Rat-tamer, Reich, Shrink, Trick-cyclist

Psychic, Psychosis ESP, Korsakoff's, Lodge, Medium, Seer, Telekinesis, Telepathic

Psychological, Psychology, Psychologist Analytical, Behaviourism, Clinical, Depth, Dynamic, Educational, Experimental, Eysenck, Gestalt, Hedonics, Humanistic, Industrial, Latah, Occupational, Organisational, Piaget, Social, Structural

Psychosis, Psychotic Korsakoff's, Manic-depressive, Organic

Ptarmigan Rype

Ptomaine Neurine

Pub Bar, Beerhall, Beverage room, Boozer, Chequers, Free-house, Gin-palace, Houf(f), House, Howf(f), Inn, Jerry-shop, Joint, Local, Mughouse, Pothouse, Potshop, Rubbidy, Rubbity, Shanty, Tavern, Tiddlywink

Puberty Adolescence, Hebetic, Teens

Pubescence Tomentum

Public Apert, Bar, Civil, Common, Demos, General, Inn, Lay, Limelight, National, Open, Out, Overt, Populace, State, Vulgar, World

Publican Ale-keeper, Bung, Host, Landlord, Licensee, Tapster, Taverner

Publication Announcement, Bluebook, Broadsheet, Edition, Ephemera, Exposé, Festschrift, Issue, > JOURNAL, Lady, Mag, Organ, Pictorial, Samizdat, Tabloid, Tatler, Tract, Tribune, Yearbook

Publicist, Publicity Ad(vert), Airing, Ballyhoo, Coverage, Exposure, Flack, Glare, Headline, Hype, Leakage, Limelight, Notoriety, Plug, PRO, Promotion, Propaganda, Réclame, Spin-doctor, Splash

Publish(er), Published, Publishing, Publicise Air, Blaze, Cape, Delator, Desktop, Disclose, Edit, Electronic, Evulgate, Gollancz, Issue, Noise, OUP, Out, Pirate, Plug, Post, Print(er), Proclaim, Propagate, Put about, Release, Run, Vanity, Vent, Ventilate

Puck Disc, Elf, Lob, Sprite, Squid

Pucker(ed) Cockle, Contract, Gather, Plissé, Purse, Ruck, Shir(r), Wrinkle

Pud Fin, Paw

Pudding Afters, Baked Alaska, Bakewell, Black, Blancmange, Blood, Brown Betty, Cabinet, Charlotte, Christmas, Clootie dumpling, College, Custard, Dessert, Drisheen, Duff, Dumpling, Eve's, Flummery, Fritter, Fromenty, Frumenty, Furme(n)ty, Furmity, Haggis, Hasty, Hodge, Hog's, Kugel, Mealie, Milk, Nesselrode, Panada, Pandowdy, Parfait, Pease, Plum, Popover, Rice, Roly-poly, Sago, Semolina, Sowens, Sponge, Spotted dick, Stickjaw, Stodge, Suet, Summer, Sundae, Sweet, Tansy, Tapioca, Umbles, White hass, White hause, White hawse, Yorkshire, Zabaglione

Puddle Collect, Dub, Flush, Pant, Plash, Plouter, Plowter, Pool, Sop

Puff(ed), Puffer, Puffy Advertise, Blouse, Blow, Blowfish, Blurb, Bouffant, Breath, Chuff, Chug, Drag, Encomist, Eulogy, Exsufflicate, Fag, Flaff, Flatus, Fluffy, Fuff, Globe-fish, Grampus, Gust, Hype, Lunt, Pech, Pegh, Pluffy, Plug, Powder, Recommend, Skiff, Slogan, Steam, Swell, Toke, Waff, Waft, Waif, Whiff, Whiffle

Puffin Fratercula, Rockbird, Sea-parrot, Tammie Norie, Tam Noddy

Pug(ilist) Belcher, Boxer, Bruiser, Carlin, Fancy, Fistic, Monkey
Pugnacious Aggressive, Belligerent, Combative
Puke Retch, Sick, Vomit
Pukka Authentic, Genuine, Real, True
Pulchritude Beauty, Cheese-cake, Grace
Pull (up) Adduce, Attraction, Crane, Drag, Draw, Earn, Force, Haul, Heave, Heeze, Hook, > INFLUENCE, Lug, Mousle, Pluck, Rein, Ring, Rove, Rug, Saccade, Sally, Sole, Sool(e), Sowl(e), Stop, Tit, Tow, Trice, Tug, Undertow, Wrest, Yank
Pulley Block, Capstan, Idle(r), Jack-block, Swig, Trice, Trochlea, Truckle
Pullover Jersey, Jumper, Sweater, Sweatshirt, Tank-top, Windcheater
Pullulate Teem
▶ **Pull up** *see* PULL
Pulp Cellulose, Chyme, Chymify, Crush, Flong, Gloop, Kenaf, Marrow, Mash, Mush, Pap, Paste, Pomace, Pound, Puree, Rot, Rubbish, Squeeze, Squidge, Wood
Pulpit(e) Ambo(nes), Lectern, Mimbar, Minbar, Pew, Rostrum, Tent, Tub, Wood
Pulsate Beat, Palpitate, Quiver, Throb, Vibrate
Pulse Alfalfa, > BEAN, Beat, Calavance, Caravance, Chickpea, D(h)al, Dholl, Dicrotic, Flageolet, Garbanzo, Gram, Groundnut, Ictus, Lentil, Lucerne, Pea, Rhythm, Sain(t)foin, Soy beans, Sphygmus, Sync, Systaltic, Systole, Throb
Pulverise Calcine, Comminute, Contriturate, Demolish, Grind, > POUND, Powder
Puma Catamount, Cougar, Mountain lion, Panther
Pummel(ling) Beat, Drub, Fib, Knead, Nevel, Pound, Tapotement, Thump
▷ **Pummelled** *may indicate* an anagram
Pump Bellows, Bowser, Centrifugal, Chain, Compressor, Cross-question, Donkey, Drive, Electromagnetic, Elicit, Feed, Filter, Force, Grease-gun, Grill, Heart, Heat, Hydropult, Inflate, Knee-swell, Lift, Mud, Nodding-donkey, Parish, Petrol, Piston, Pulsometer, Question, Rotary, Scavenge, Shoe, Stirrup, Stomach, Suction, Turbine, Vacuum, Water, Wind
Pumphandle Sweep
Pumpkin Butternut, Cashaw, Gourd, Pampoen, Quash, Queensland blue
Pun Calembour, Clinch, Equivoque, Paragram, Paronomasia, Quibble, Ram, Wordplay
Punch(ed) Antic, Biff, Blow, Boff, Bolo, Box, Bradawl, Bumbo, Card, Centre, Chad, Check, Chop, Clip, Cobbler's, Dry-beat, Fib, Fid, Fist(ic), Gang, Glogg, Haymaker, Hit, Hook, Horse, Jab, Key, Kidney, Knobble, Knubble, KO, Lander, Mat, Milk, Nail set, Nubble, One-er, Overhand, Perforate, Pertuse, Planter's, Plug, Poke, Polt, Pommel, Pounce, Prod, Pummel, Rabbit, Roundhouse, Rum, Rumbo, Slosh, Sock, Sting(o), Stoush, Sucker, Suffolk, Sunday, Swop, Upper-cut, Wap, Wind, Zest
Punctilious Exact, Formal, Nice, Particular, Picked, Precise, Prim, Stickler
Punctual(ity) Politesse, Prompt, Regular
Punctuate, Punctuation (mark) Apostrophe, Bracket, Close, Colon, Comma, Duckfoot quote, Emphasize, Guillemet, Interabang, Interrobang, Interrupt, Mark, Semicolon
Puncture(d) Bore, Centesis, Criblé, Cribrate, Deflate, Drill, Flat, Hole, Lumbar, Perforate, Pierce, Prick, Scarify
Pundit Egghead, Expert, Guru, Maven, Oracle, Sage, Savant, Swami, Teacher
Pungency, Pungent Acid, Acrid, Acrolein, Alum, Ammonia, Bite, Bitter, Caustic, Hot, Mordant, Nidorous, Piquant, Poignant, Point, Racy, Sair, Salt, Spice, Sting, Tangy, Witty

Punish(ed), Punishing, Punishment Amerce, Attainder, Baffle, Bastinado, Beat, Birch, Brasero, Cane, Capital, Cart, Castigate, Chasten, Chastise, Come-uppance, Commination, Corporal, Correct, Cucking-stool, Dam(nation), Defrock, Desert(s), Detention, > DISCIPLINE, Fatigue, Fine, Flog, Gantlope, Gate, Gauntlet, Gruel, Hellfire, Hiding, Horsing, Hot seat, Imposition, Impot, Interdict, Jankers, Jougs, Keelhaul, Knout, Laldie, Laldy, Lambast(e), Lines, Log, Marmalise, Necklace, Nemesis, Pack-drill, Pandy, Penalise, Penance, Penology, Perdition, Picket, Pillory, Pine, Rap, Reprisal, Retribution, Ruler, Scaffold, Scath, Scourge, Sentence, Six of the best, Smack, Smite, Spank, Spif(f)licate, Stocks, Strafe, Straff, Strap, Strappado, Swinge(ing), Talion, Tar and feather, Toco, Toko, Tophet, Treadmill, Trim, Tron, Trounce, Tumbrel, Tumbril, Visit, War(r)ison, What for, Whip, Ywrake, Ywroke
▷ **Punish** *may indicate* an anagram
Punk Goop, Inferior, Neer-do-well, Nobody, Touchwood, Worthless
Punnet Basket, Thug
Punt(er), Punting Antepost, Back, Bet, Gamble, Kent, Kick, Pound, Quant, Turfite, Wager
Puny Frail, Inferior, Petty, Reckling, Runtish, Scram, Shilpit, Sickly, Small, Weak
Pup(py) Cub, Whelp
Pupa Chrysalis, Exarate, Neanic, Nymph, Obtect
Pupil Abiturient, Apple, Apprentice, Boarder, Cadet, Catechumen, Dayboy, Disciple, Etonian, Exit, Eyeball, Follower, Gyte, Junior, L, Monitor, Prefect, Preppy, Protégé(e), Scholar, Senior, Student, Tutee, Ward
▷ **Pupil** *may refer to* an eye
Puppet(eer) Bunraku, Creature, Doll, Dummy, Faineant, Fantoccini, Glove, Guignol, Jack-a-lent, Judy, Mammet, Marionette, Mawmet, Mommet, Motion(-man), Pageant, Pawn, Pinocchio, Promotion, Punch(inello), Quisling, Rod, Tool
Purchase(r), Purchasing Acquisition, Bargain, Buy, Coff, Compulsory, Earn, Emption, Gadsden, Get, Grip, Halliard, Halyard, Hold, Layaway, > LEVERAGE, Louisiana, Parbuckle, Perquisitor, Secure, Shop, Toehold
Pure, Purity Absolute, Cando(u)r, Cathy, Chaste, Chiarezza, Clean(ly), Cosher, Fine, Good, Holy, Immaculate, Incorrupt, Innocent, Intemerate, Inviolate, Kathy, Kosher, Lily, Lilywhite, Maidenhood, Me(a)re, Net(t), Pristine, Quintessence, Sanctity, Sheer, Simon, Simple, Sincere, Snow-white, Stainless, True, Unalloyed, Vertue, Virgin, Virtue, White
Puree Coulis, Fool
Purgative, Purge Aloes, Aloetic, Araroba, Cacoon, Calomel, Cascara, Cassia, Castor-oil, Catharsis, Cholagogue, Colquintida, Croton, Delete, Diacatholicon, Diarrh(o)ea, Drastic, Elaterin, Elaterium, Eliminate, Eluant, Emetic, Enos®, Erase, Evacuant, Exonerate, Expiate, Flux, Gleichschaltung, Hiera-picra, Hydragogue, Ipecacuanha, Ipomoea, Jalap, Jalop, Laxative, McCarthyism, Physic, Picra, Pride's, Relaxant, Scour, Scur, Senna, Soil, Turbith, Turpeth, Wahoo
Purification, Purifier, Purify(ing) Absolve, Bowdlerise, Catharsis, Clay, Clean(se), Depurate, Despumate, Dialysis, Distil, Edulcorate, Elution, Exalt, Expurgate, Filter, Fine, Gas-lime, Green vitriol, Lustre, Lustrum, Niyama, Refine, Retort, Samskara, Sanctify, Scorify, Scrub, Try
Puritan(ical) Bible belt, Bluenose, Digger(s), Ireton, Ironsides, Pi, Pilgrim, Plymouth Colony, Precisian, Prude, Prynne, Roundhead, Seeker, Strait-laced, Traskite, Waldenses, Wowser, Zealot

Purl(er) Cropper, Eddy, Fall, Knit, Ripple, Stream

Purloin Abstract, Annex, Appropriate, Lift, Nab, Pilfer, Snaffle, Sneak, Steal

Purple Amarantin(e), Amethyst, Assai, Aubergine, Burgundy, Cassius, Chlamys, Claret, Corkir, Cudbear, Dubonnet, Eminence, Golp(e), Heather, Heliotrope, Hyacinthine, Imperial, Indigo, Korkir, Lavender, Lilac, Magenta, Mallow, Mauvin(e), Mulberry, Murrey, Orcein, Orcin(e), Orcinol, Pance, Pansy, Plum, Pompadour, Pontiff, Porporate, Proin(e), Puce, Puke, Punic, Purpurin, Rhodopsin, Royal, Solferino, Tyrian, Violet, Visual

Purport Bear, Claim, Drift, Feck, Mean, Tenor

Purpose Advertent, Aim, Avail, Cautel, Design, Ettle, Goal, Here-to, > INTENT, Mean(ing), Meant, Mint, Motive, Object, Plan, Point, Raison d'être, > REASON, Resolution, Resolve, Sake, Telic, Telos, Tenor, Use

Purposeless Dysteleology, Otiose

Purr Curr, Rumble

Purse Ad crumenam, Bag, Bung, Caba, Clutch, Crease, Crumenal, Fisc, Fisk, Long Melford, Mermaid's, Pocket, Prim, Privy, Prize, Public, Pucker, Spleuchan, Sporran, Wallet, Whistle

▷ **Pursed** *may indicate* one word within another

Pursue(r), **Pursuit** Alecto, Business, Chase, Chivvy, Course, Dog, Follow, Follow up, Hobby, Hot-trod, Hound, Hunt, Line, Practice, Practise, Proceed, Prosecute, Quest, Scouring, Stalk, Trivial

Purulent Mattery

Purvey(or) Cater, Provide, Provisor, Sell, Supply

Pus Empyema, Matter, Purulence, Quitter, Quittor

Push(er), **Push in** Airscrew, Barge, Birr, Boost, Bunt, Butt, Detrude, Drive, Edge, Effort, Elbow, Fire, Horn, Hustle, Impulse, Invaginate, Jostle, Motivation, Nose, Nudge, Nurdle, Obtrude, Pitchfork, Plod, Ply, Press, Promote, Propel, Railroad, Ram, Sell, > SHOVE, Snoozle, Subtrude, Thrust, Urge

Pushchair Baby buggy®, Buggy, Stroller, Trundler

Pushover Doddle, Soda

Pusillanimous Coward, Timid, Weak, Weak-kneed, Yellow

Puss(y) Amentum, > CAT, Catkins, Face, Galore, Hare, Malkin, Mouth, Rabbit, Septic

Pussyfoot Dry, Equivocate, Inch, Paw, Steal, TT

Pustule Blotch, Pimple

Put (off; on; out; up) Accommodate, Add, Bet, Cup, Daff, Defer, Dish, Do, Don, Douse, Implant, Impose, Incommode, Inn, Lade, Lodge, Lump, Oust, Pit, Place, Plonk, Set, Smore, Snuff, Station, Stow

Put away Sheathe, Store, Stow

Put down Abase, Degrade, Demean, Disparage, Floor, Humiliate, Land, Snuff, Write

▷ **Put off** *may indicate* an anagram

Putrefaction, **Putrefy(ing)**, **Putrid** Addle, Bitter, Corrupt, Decay, Fester, Olid, Rot, Sepsis, Septic

Putt(ing) Gimme, Gobble, Green, Hash, Pigeon, Sink, > STUPID PERSON

Putter Chug, Club

Put together Assemble, Compile, Synthesize

Puzzle(r) Acrostic, Baffle, Bemuse, Bewilder, Brainteaser, Chinese, Confuse, Conundrum, Crossword, Crux, Egma, Elude, Enigma, Fox, Glaik, Gravel, Intrigue, Jigsaw, Kittle, Logogriph, Magic pyramid, Mind-bender, Monkey, Mystify, Nonplus, Perplex, Ponder, Pose(r), Rebus, Riddle, Rubik's cube®, Sorites, Sphinx, Stick(l)er, Stump, Tangram, Tickler, Wordsearch, Wordsquare

Pygmy Atomy, Dwarf, Negrillo, Negrito, Pyknic, Thumbling
Pyjamas Baby-doll, Churidars, Jimjams
Pyramid Cheops, Chephren, Frustum, Population, Stack, Teocalli
Pyre Bale(-fire), Bonfire, Brasero, Darga, Gha(u)t
Pyrenean Basque
Pyrites Fool's gold, Iron, Mispickel, Mundic, White
Pyrotechnics Arson, Fireworks
Pyroxene Aegirine, Aegirite, Diopside
Pyrus Service-tree
Pythagoras Samian
Pythian (seat) Delphic, Tripod
Python Anaconda, Diamond, Kaa, > SNAKE, Zombi(e)

Qq

Q Koppa, Quebec, Question
QC Silk
Qua As
Quack Charlatan, Crocus, Dulcamara, Empiric, Fake, Homeopath, > IMPOSTOR, Katerfelto, Mountebank, Pretender, Saltimbanco
Quad(rangle) Close, Complete, Compluvium, Court, Em, En, Horse, Pane
Quadrilateral Lambeth, Tetragon, Trapezium, Trapezoid
Quadrille Dance, Lancers, Matador(e), Pantalon
Quaff Carouse, Drink, Imbibe
Quagmire Bog, Fen, Imbroglio, Marsh, Morass, Swamp, Wagmoire
Quail Asteria, Bevy, Bird, Blench, Bob-white, Button, Caille, Colin, Flinch, Harlot, Hen, Quake, Shrink, Tremble
Quaint Cute, Naive, Odd, Old-world, Picturesque, Strange, Twee, Wham, Whim(sy)
Quake(r), Quaking Aminadab, Broad-brim, Dither, Dodder, Fox, Friend, Fry, Hicksite, Obadiah, Penn, Quail, Seism, Shake(r), Shiver, > TREMBLE, Tremor, Trepid
Qualification, Qualified, Qualify Able, Adapt, Adverb, Capacitate, Caveat, Competent, Condition, Degree, Diplomatic, Entitle, Fit, Graduate, Habilitate, Meet, Pass, Proviso, Restrict, Temper, Versed
Quality Aroma, Attribute, Body, Calibre, Cast, Charisma, Essence, Fabric, Fame, First water, Five-star, Flavour, Grade, Inscape, It, Kite-mark, Long suit, Mystique, Pitch, Premium, Primary, Property, Q, Quale, Reception, Sort, Standard, Stature, Style, Substance, Suchness, Thew, Thisness, Timbre, Tone, Up-market, Vinosity, Virgin, Virtu(e), Water, Worth
Qualm Compunction, Misgiving, Scruple
Quandary Dilemma, Fix, Predicament, Trilemma
Quantity > AMOUNT, Analog(ue), Batch, Bundle, Capacity, Deal, Dose, Feck, Fother, Hundredweight, Idempotent, Intake, Jag, Lock, Lot, Mass, Measure, Melder, Myriad, Nonillion, Number, Ocean(s), Operand, Parameter, Parcel, Peck, Plenty, Posology, Pottle, Qs, Qt, Quire, Quota, Quotient, Ream, Scalar, Slather, Slew, Slue, Sum, Surd, Tret, Unknown, Vector, Warp, Whips
Quantum Graviton, Phonon, Photon
Quarantine Isolate, Lazarette
Quark Flavo(u)r, Strange
Quarrel(some) Affray, Aggress, Altercate, Arrow, Barney, Barratry, Barretry, Bate, Bicker, Brabble, Brattle, Brawl, Breach, Breeze, Broil, Brulyie, Brulzie, Bust-up, Cagmag, Cantankerous, Carraptious, Cat and dog, Caterwaul, Chance-medley, Chide, Clash, Combative, Contretemps, Difference, Disagree, Dispute, Dust-up, Eristic, Estrangement, Exchange, Fall out, Feisty, Fracas, Fractious, Fratch(et)y, Fray, Hassle, Issue, Jar, Loggerheads, Outcast, Outfall, Pugnacious, Ragbolt, Row, Spat, Squabble, Tiff, Tink, Vendetta, Wap, Whid, Wrangle

Quarry, Quarry face Chalkpit, Chase, Game, Heuch, Mine, Pit, Prey, Scabble, Scent, Stone pit, Victim

Quart Winchester

Quarter(ing), Quarters Airt, Barrio, Billet, Canton(ment), Casern(e), Chinatown, Clemency, Close, Coshery, District, Dorm, E, Empty, Enclave, Fardel, Farl, First, Focsle, Forecastle, Forpet, Forpit, Fourth, Ghetto, Ham(s), Harbour, Haunch, Last, Latin, Medina, > MERCY, N, Note, Oda, Pity, Point, Principium, Quadrant, Region, S, Season, Sector, Tail, Trimester, W, Wardroom, Warp, Winter

Quarter-day LD

▷ **Quarterdeck** *may indicate* a suit of cards

Quartet Foursome, Mess, Tetrad

Quartz Agate, Amethyst, Bristol diamond, Buhrstone, Cacholong, Cairngorm, Chalcedony, Chert, Citrine, Flint, Granophyre, Jasp(er), Morion, Onyx, Plasma, Prase, Rainbow, Rose, Rubasse, Sapphire, Silex, Silica, Smoky, Stishovite, Tiger-eye, Tonalite, Whin Sill

Quash Abrogate, Annul, Quell, Recant, Scotch, Subdue, Suppress, Terminate, Void

Quaver(ing) Shake, Tremulous, Trill, Vibrate, Warble

Quay Bund, Levee, Wharf

Queasy Delicate, Nauseous, Squeamish

Quebec Q

Queen(ly) Adelaide, African, Alcestis, Alexandra, Anna, Anne, Artemesia, Atossa, Balkis, Beauty, Bee, Begum, Bess, Boadicea, Boudicca, Brunhild(e), Camilla, Candace, Card, Caroline, Cleopatra, Closet, Clytemnestra, Coatcard, Dido, Drag, Drama, Eleanor(a), Ellery, Ena, ER, Esther, FD, Gertrude, Guinevere, Hatshepset, Hatshepsut, Hecuba, Helen, Hera, Here, Hermione, Hippolyta, HM, Isabel, Isabella, Ishtar, Isolde, Jocasta, Juno, King, Leda, Maam, Mab, Maeve, Marie Antoinette, Mary, Matilda, May, Medb, Mobled, Monarch, Nance, Nefertiti, Omphale, Pance, Pansy, Parr, Paunce, Pawnce, Pearly, Penelope, Persephone, Phaedram, Prince, Proserpina, Qu, R, Ranee, Rani, Regal, Regina(l), Sara, Semiramis, Sheba, Sultana, Titania, Victoria, Virgin, Warrior

Queen Anne Mrs Morley

Queer(ness) Abnormal, Berdash, Bizarre, Crazy, Cure, Curious, Fey, Fie, Fifish, Gay, Nance, Nancy, > ODD, Outlandish, Peculiar, Pervert, Poorly, Quaint, Rum, Spoil, Uranism, Vert

Quell Alegge, Allay, Calm, Quiet, Repress, Subdue, Suppress

Quench Assuage, Cool, Extinguish, Satisfy, Slake, Slo(c)ken, Sta(u)nch, Yslake

▸ **Query** *see* QUESTION

Quest Goal, Graal, Grail, Hunt, Pursuit, Venture

Question(ing), Questionnaire Appose, Ask, Bi-lateral, Burning, Catechise, Chin, Contest, Conundrum, Cross-examine, Debrief, Dichotomous, Direct, Dispute, Dorothy Dixer, Doubt, Erotema, Eroteme, Erotesis, Examine, Fiscal, Good, Grill, Heckle, Impeach, Impugn, Indirect, Information, Innit, Interpellation, Interrogate, Interview, Koan, Leading, Loaded, Maieutic, Matter, Open, Oppugn, Pop, Pose, Previous, Probe, Problem, Pump, Q, Qu, Quaere, Quiz, Rapid-fire, Refute, Rhetorical, Riddle, Speer, Speir, Survey, Suspect, Tag, Teaser, Tickler, Vexed, West Lothian, WH, What, Worksheet

Questionable Ambiguous, Dubious, Fishy, Socratic

Question-master Interrogator, Socrates, Torquemada, Ximenes

Queue Braid, Breadline, Cercus, Crocodile, Cue, Dog, File, Kale, > LINE, Pigtail,

Plait, Plat, Stack, Tail(back), Track

Quibble(r), Quibbling Balk, Carp, Carriwitchet, Casuist, Cavil, Chicaner, Dodge, Elenchus, Equivocate, Hairsplitting, Nitpick, Pedantry, Pettifoggery, Prevaricate, Pun, Quiddity, Quillet, Quirk, Sophist

Quiche Flan, Tart

Quick(en), Quickening, Quicker, Quickly, Quickness Accelerate, Acumen, Adroit, Agile, Alive, Allegr(ett)o, Animate, Apace, Breakneck, Breathing, Brisk, Celerity, Chop-chop, Citigrade, Cito, Con moto, Core, Cracking, Cuticle, Dapper, Deft, Enliven, Existent, Expeditious, Express, Fastness, Festination, Foothot, Gleg, Hasten, Hie, High-speed, Hotfoot, Impulsive, Jiffy, Keen, Lickety-split, Living, Mercurial, Mistress, Mosso, Nailbed, Nimble, Nippy, Pdq, Piercing, Piu mosso, Post-haste, Prestissimo, Presto, Prompt, Pronto, Rapid, Rath(e), Ready, Rough and ready, Schnell, Sharp, Skin, Slippy, Smart, Snappy, Snort, Sodain(e), Soon, Spry, Streamline, Sudden, Swift, Swith, Tout de suite, Trice, Up tempo, Veloce, Vital, Vite, Vivify, Wikiwiki, Yare

Quicksand Flow, Syrtis

Quicksilver Mercury

Quid Chaw, Chew, L, Nicker, Oner, Plug, Pound, Quo, Sov, Tertium, Tobacco

Quid pro quo Mutuum, Tit-for-tat

Quiescence, Quiescent Calm, Di(o)estrus, Inactive, Inert, Latent, Still

Quiet(en), Quietly Accoy, Allay, Appease, Barnacle, Calm, Compose, Conticent, Doggo, Ease, Easeful, Easy, Encalm, Entame, Gag, Grave, Kail, Laconic, Loun(d), Low, Lown(d), Low-profile, Lull, Meek, Mp, Muffle, Mute, P, Pacify, Pauciloquent, Pause, Peace, Piano, Pipe down, QT, Reserved, Reticent, Sedate, Settle, Sh, Shtoom, Silence, Sitzkrieg, Sly, Sober, Soothe, Sotto voce, Still, Stum(m), Subact, Subdued, Tace, Taciturn, Tranquil, Wheesht, Whish, Whisht, Whist

Quill Calamus, Feather, Float, Plectre, Plectron, Plectrum, Plume, Remex

Quillwort Isoetes

Quilt(ed), Quilting Comfort(er), Continental, Counterpane, Cover, Crazy, Doona®, Duvet, Echo, Eiderdown, Futon, Kantha, Matel(l)asse, Patchwork, Trapunto

Quince Bael, Bel, Bengal, Bhel, Flowering, Japanese, Japonica

Quinine China, Crown-bark, Kina, Quina, Tonic

Quinsy Angina, Cynanche, Garget, Squinancy

Quintessence Heart, Pith

Quintet Pentad, Trout

Quip Carriwitchet, Crack, Epigram, Gibe, Jest, Jibe, Joke, Taunt, Zinger

Quirk Concert, Foible, Idiosyncrasy, Irony, Kink, Twist

Quisling Collaborator, Traitor

Quit(s) Abandon, Absolve, Ap(p)ay, Cease, Desert, Even(s), Go, Leave, Meet, Resign, > STOP

Quite Actually, All, Ap(p)ay, Clean, Dead, Enough, Enow, Fairly, Fully, Precisely, Real, Right, Sheer, Very

Quiver(ing) Aspen, Quake, Shake, Sheath, The yips, Tremble, Tremolo, Tremor, Tremulate, Trepid, Vibrant, Vibrate

Qui vive Go-go

Quixote, Quixotic Don, Errant, Impractical

Quiz Bandalore, Bee, Catechism, Examine, Interrogate, I-spy, Mastermind, Oddity, Probe, Pump, Question, Smoke, Trail, Yo-yo

Quizzical Curious, Derisive, Odd, Queer, Socratic

Quod Can, Clink, Jail, Prison

Quoit Disc(us), Disk, Ring
Quondam Once, Sometime, Whilom
Quorum Minyan
Quota Numerus clausus, Proportion, Ration, Share
Quotation, Quote(d), Quote Adduce, Citation, Cite, Co(a)te, Duckfoot, Epigraph, Evens, Extract, Forward, Instance, Name, Price, Recite, Reference, Say, Scare, Soundbite, Tag, Verbatim, Wordbite
Quoth Co, Said
Quotient Achievement, Intelligence, Kerma, Quaternion, Ratio, Respiratory

Rr

R Arithmetic, King, Queen, Reading, Recipe, Right, Romeo, Run, Writing

Rabbi Dayan, Mashgiah, Rav, Rebbe

Rabbit Angora, Astrex, Brer, British lop, Buck, Bun(ny), Chat, Con(e)y, Cottontail, Daman, Dassie, Doe, Earbash, Harp, Haver, Hyrax, Jabber, Jack, Klipdas, Long white, Lop-eared, Marmot, Muff, Nest, Novice, Oarlap, Palaver, Patzer, Prate, Rattle, Rex, Rock, Snowshoe, Tapeti, Terricole, Waffle, Welsh, White, Witter, Yak, Yap, Yatter

Rabble Canaille, Clamjamphrie, Clanjamfray, Colluvies, Crowd, Doggery, Galere, Herd, Hoi-polloi, Horde, Legge, Mob, Raffle, Rag-tag, Rascaille, Rascal, Riff-raff, Rout, Scaff-raff, Shower, Tag, Tagrag

Rabelaisian Pantagruel, Panurge

Rabid, Rabies Extreme, Frenzied, Hydrophobia, Lyssa, Mad, Raging, Virulent

Raccoon Coati, Panda, Procyon

Race(course), Racing, Race meeting Aintree, Ancestry, Arms, Ascot, Autocross, Belt, Boat, Boskop, Breed, Broose, Brouze, Bumping, Career, Catadrome, Caucus, Cesarewitch, Chantilly, Chase, Claiming, Classic, Cone, Contest, Corso, Country, Course, Current, Cursus, Cyclo-cross, Dash, Derby, Doggett's Coat and Badge, Dogs, Doncaster, Drag, Dromos, Egg and spoon, Enduro, Epsom, Event, Fastnet, Flapping, Flat, Flow, Fun-run, Generation, Ginger, Goodwood, Grand National, Grand Prix, Handicap, Hare and hounds, Harness, Herrenvolk, Hialeah, Hippodrome, Human(kind), Hurry, Inca, Indy, Indy Car, Kermesse, Kind, Lampadedromy, Lampadephoria, Leat, Leet, Leger, Le Mans, Lick, Lignage, Line(age), Longchamps, Madison, Man, Marathon, Master, Meets, Mile, Motocross, > **NATIONAL**, Newmarket, Nursery, Nursery stakes, Oaks, Obstacle, One-horse, Paceway, Palio, Paper chase, Pattern, Picnic, Plate, Pluck, Point-to-point, Potato, Pursuit, Rallycross, Rallying, Rapids, Rat, Redcar, Regatta, Relay, Rill, Rod, Ronne, Roost, Sack, St Leger, Scramble, Scratch, Scud, Scurry, Seed, Selling, Shan, Slalom, Slipstream, Sloot, Slot-car, Sluit, Speedway, Sprint, Stakes, Steeplechase, Stem, Stirp(s), Stirpes, Stock, Strain, Streak, Strene, Sweepstake, Tail, Taste, Tear, Thousand Guineas, Three-legged, Tide, Torch, Torpids, Towcester, Tribe, Trotting, TT, Turf, Two-horse, Two Thousand Guineas, Velodrome, Volsungs, Walking, Walk-over, Waterway, Wetherby, Wetter, Whid, White, Wincanton

Racehorse, Racer Eclipse, Filly, Go-kart, Hare, Maiden, Novice, Plater, Red Rum, Steeplechaser, Trotter

Raceme Corymb, Panicle

Racial (area) Apartheid, Colour, Ethnic, Ghetto, Quarter

Rack Agonise, Bin, Cloud, Cratch, Drier, Flake, Frame, Hack, Hake, Plate, Pulley, Roof, Stretcher, Toast, Torment, Torture

Racket(eer) Bassoon, > **BAT**, Battledore, Bloop, Brattle, Caterwaul, Chirm, Clamour, Crime, Deen, Din, Discord, Earner, > **FIDDLE**, Gyp, Hubbub, Hustle, > **NOISE**, Noisiness, Protection, Ramp, Rort, Sokaiya, Stridor, Swindle, Tumult, Uproar, Utis

Racy Ethnic, Piquant, Pungent, Ribald, Salty, Spicy, Spirited
Rad Rem
Radar Angel, AWACS, Beacon, DEW line, Doppler, Gadget, Gee, Gull, Lidar, Loran, Monopulse, Navar, Rebecca-eureka, Shoran, Surveillance, Teleran®, Tracking
Raddle Hurdle, Ochre, Red
Radial Quadrant, Rotula, Spoke
Radiance, **Radiant** Actinic, Aglow, Aureola, Beamish, Brilliant, Gleam(y), Glory, Glow, Happy, Lustre, Refulgent, Shechina, Sheen, Shekinah
Radiate, **Radiating**, **Radiation**, **Radiator** Actinal, Adaptive, Air-colour, Beam, Bremsstrahlung, C(h)erenkov, Disseminate, Dosimetry, Effuse, Emanate, Emit, Exitance, Fluorescence, Gamma, Glow, Hawking, Heater, Infrared, Ionizing, Isohel, Laser, Millirem, Pentact, Photon, Pulsar, Quasar, Rem(s), Rep, Roentgen, > SHINE, Sievert, Spherics, Spoke, Stellate, Stray, SU, Sun, Synchroton, Terrestrial, Ultra violet, UVA, UVB, Van Allen, Visible
Radical Allyl, Amide, Amyl, Aryl, Benzil, Benzoyl, Bolshevist, Bolshie, Butyl, Calumba, Carbene, Cetyl, Dyad, Ester, Extreme, Fundamental, Gauchist, Genre-busting, Glyceryl, Glycosyl, Hydroxy, Innate, Isopropyl, Leftist, Leveller, Ligand, Maximalist, Methyl, Montagnard, Nitryl, Oxonium, Parsnip, Phenyl, Phosphonium, Pink, Propyl, Red, Revolutionary, Rhizocaul, Root, Rudiment, Sulfone, Sulphone, Trot(sky), Uranyl, Vinyl, Whig, Xylyl
Radio Boom-box, Cat's whisker, CB, Cellular, Citizen's band, Crystal set, Digital, Ether, Gee, Ghetto-blaster, Local, Loudspeaker, Marconigraph, Receiver, Reflex, Set, Simplex, Sound, Steam, Talkback, Tranny, Transceiver, Transistor, Transmitter, Transponder, Walkie-talkie, Walkman®, Walky-talky, Wireless
Radioactive, **Radioactivity** Actinide, Americium, Astatine, Bohrium, Cobalt 60, Emanation, Fall-out, Hot, Nucleonics, Plutonium, Radon, Steam, Thorium, Uranite
Radiogram Cable, Telegram, Wire
Radish Charlock, Mooli, Runch
Radium Ra
Radius Long, Schwarzschild, Short
Radon Rn
Raffia Rabanna
Raffle(s) Burglar, Draw, Lottery, Sweepstake
Raft(ing) Balsa, Catamaran, Float, Kontiki, Life, Pontoon, Whitewater
Rafter Barge-couple, Beam, Chevron, Jack, Joist, Ridge, Spar, Timber
Rag(ged), **Rags** Bait, Bate, Clout, Coral, Daily, Deckle, Dud(s), Duddery, Duddie, Duster, Fent, Figleaf, Glad, Guyed, Haze, Kid, Lap(pie), Lapje, Mop, Nose, Paper, Red, Remnant, Revel, Rivlins, Roast, Rot, S(c)hmatte, Scold, Scrap, > SHRED, Slate, Slut, Splore, Tack, Tat(t), Tatter(demalion), Tatty, Taunt, > TEASE, Tiger, Tongue, Uneven
▷ **Rag(ged)** *may indicate* an anagram
Rage, **Raging** > ANGER, Ardour, Bait, Bate, Bayt, Chafe, Conniption, Explode, Fashion, Fierce, Fit, Fiz(z), Fume, Furibund, Furore, Fury, Gibber, Go, Ire, Mode, Monkey, Paddy(-whack), Passion, Pelt, Pet, Pique, Rabid, Rail, Ramp, Rant, Road, Snit, Storm, Tear, Temper, Ton, Trolley, Utis, Wax, Wrath
Raglan Sleeve
Ragout Compot, Goulash, Haricot, Stew
Rag-picker Bunter
Raid(er) Assault, Attack, Baedeker, Bodrag, Bust, Camisado, Chappow, Commando, Corporate, Dawn, Do, For(r)ay, Imburst, Incursion, Inroad, Inrush,

Invade, Jameson, Maraud, March-treason, Mosstrooper, Pict, Pillage, Plunder, Ram, Ransel, Razzia, Reive, Sack, Scrump, Skrimp, Skrump, Smash-and-grab, Sortie, Spreagh, Storm, Viking

Rail(er), Railing Abuse, Amtrack, Arm, Arris, Balustrade, Ban, Banister, > **BAR**, Barre, Barrier, Bird, Bullhead, Cloak, Conductor, Coot, Corncrake, Crake, Criticise, Dado, Fender, Fiddle, Fife, Flanged, Flat-bottomed, Flow, Gush, Insult, Inveigh, Light, Live, Metal, Neckerchief, Notornis, Parclose, Picture, Pin, Plate, Post, Pulpit, Rag, Rate, Rave, Rung, Scold, Slang-whang, Slate, Slip, Snash, Sneer, Sora, Soree, Spar, T, Taffrail, Takahe, Taunt, Thersites, Third, Towel, Train, Vituperation, Weka

Raillery Badinage, Banter, Chaff, Persiflage, Sport

Railroad, Railway Amtrak, BR, Bulldoze, Cable, Cash, Coerce, Cog, Cremaillère, Dragoon, El, Elevated, Funicular, GWR, Inclined, L, Light, Lines, LMS, LNER, Loop-line, Maglev, Marine, Metro, Monorail, Mountain, Narrow-gauge, Rack, Rack and pinion, Rly, Road, Rollercoaster, Ropeway, ROSCO, Ry, Scenic, SR, Stockton-Darlington, Switchback, Telpher-line, Track, Train, Tramline, Tramway, Trans-Siberian, Tube, Underground

Railwayman Driver, Guard, NUR, Stephenson, Stoker

Raiment Apparel, Clothes, Garb, Ihram

Rain(y) Acid, Brash, Deluge, Drizzle, Hyad(e)s, Hyetal, Mistle, Mizzle, Oncome, Onding, Onfall, Pelt, Pluviose, Pluvious, Pour, Precipitation, Right, Roke, Scat, Seil, Serein, Serene, Shell, Shower, Sile, Silver thaw, Skiffle, Skit, Smir(r), Smur, Soft, Spat, Spet, Spit, Storm, Thunder-plump, Virga, Weep, Wet, Yellow

Rainbow(-maker) Arc, Bifrost, Bruise, Dew-bow, Indescence, Iris, Moon-bow, Spectroscope, Sunbow, Sundog, Water-gall, Weather-gall, White

Raincoat Burberry®, Gaberdine, Mac, Mino, Oils(kins), Slicker, Waterproof

Raingauge Ombrometer, Udometer

Rain-maker Indra

Rain tree Saman

Raise(d), Raising Advance, Aggrade, Attollent, Boost, Build, Cat, Coaming, Cock, Collect, Elate, > **ELEVATE**, Emboss, Enhance, Ennoble, Erect, Escalate, Exalt, Extol, Fledge, Grow, Heave, Heezie, Heft, High, Hike, Hoist, Increase, Jack, Key, Leaven, Lift, Mention, Overcall, Perk, Rear, Regrate, Repoussé, Revie, Rouse, Saleratus, Siege, Sky, Snarl, Step-up, Sublimate, Upgrade, Weigh

Rake, Raker, Rakish Casanova, Comb, Corinthian, Croupier, Dapper, Dissolute, Enfilade, Jaunty, Lecher, Libertine, Lothario, Raff, Reprobate, Rip, Roué, Scan, Scour, Scowerer, Scratch, Strafe, Stubble, Swash-buckler, Swinge-buckler, Wagons

Rale Crepitus, Rattle

Rally, Rallying-point Autocross, Autopoint, Badinage, Banter, Demo, Gather, Jamboree, Meeting, Mobilise, Monte Carlo, Muster, Oriflamme, Persiflage, Recover, Rely, Rest, Risorgimento, Roast, Rouse, Scramble

Ralph Imp, Nader, Rackstraw

Ram Aries, Battering, Buck, Bunt, Butter, Corvus, Crash, Drive, Hidder, Hydraulic, Mendes, Pun, Sheep, Stem, Tamp, Tup, Wether

Ramble(r), Rambling Aberrant, Aimless, Digress, Incoherent, Liana, Liane, Rigmarole, Roam, Rose, Rove, Skimble-skamble, Sprawl, Stray, Stroll, Vagabond, Wander

Rameses Pharaoh

Ramp Bank, Gradient, Helicline, Incline, Slipway, Slope

Rampage Fury, Spree, Storm, Warpath

Rampant Lionel, Predominant, Profuse, Rearing, Rife

▷ **Rampant** *may indicate* an anagram or a reversed word
Rampart Abat(t)is, Brisure, Butt, Defence, Fortification, Parapet, Terreplein, Vallum, Wall
Ramrod Gunstick
Ramshackle Decrepit, Heath Robinson, Rickety, Rickle
Ranch Bowery, Corral, Dude, Farm, Hacienda, Spread
Rancid Frowy, Reast(y), Reest(y), Sour, Turned
Rancour Gall, Hate, Malice, Resentment, Spite
Rand Border, R, Roon
Random Accidental, Aleatoric, Arbitrary, > **AT RANDOM**, Blind, Casual, Desultory, Fitful, > **HAPHAZARD**, Harvest, Hit-or-miss, Hobnob, Indiscriminate, Scattershot, Sporadic, Stochastic
▷ **Random(ly)** *may indicate* an anagram
Range(r), Rangy Align, Ambit, Andes, Atlas, AZ, Ballpark, Band, Bowshot, Bushwhack, Capsule, Carry, Cheviot, Compass, Cotswolds, Course, Darling, Diapason, Dispace, Dolomites, Dynamic, Err, > **EXTENT**, Eye-shot, Flinders, Forest, Gamut, Glasgow, Gunshot, Hamersley, Harmonic, Helicon, Himalayas, Interquartile, Ken(ning), Kolyma, Ladakh, Leggy, Limit, Line, Long, Massif, Middleback, > **MOUNT**, Orbit, Oven, Owen Stanley, Palette, Point-blank, Prairie, Purview, Rake, Reach, Register, Repertoire, Rifle, Roam, Rocket, Scale, Scope, Sc(o)ur, Selection, Short, Sierra, Sloane, Spectrum, Sphere, Stove, Strzelecki, Tape, Tessitura, Teton, Texas, Tier, Urals, Waldgrave, Wasatch, Waveband, Woomera
Rank(s) Arrant, Ayatollah, Begum, Brevet, Caste, Category, Cense, Classify, Cornet, Curule, Degree, Dignity, Downright, Earldom, Estate, Etat(s), Flight sergeant, Grade, Graveolent, Gross, High, Hojatoleslam, Hojatolislam, Majority, Olid, Parage, Percentile, Place, Range, Rate, Rooty, Row, Seed, Seigniorage, Sergeant, Serried, Shoulder-strap, Sort, Standing, > **STATION**, Status, Substantive, Taxi, Tier, > **TITLE**, Titule, Utter, Viscount
Rankle Chafe, Gall, Irritate, Nag
Ransack Fish, Loot, Pillage, Plunder, Rifle, Ripe, Rob, Rummage
Ransom King's, Redeem, Release, Rescue
Rant(er), Ranting Bombast, Declaim, Fustian, Ham, Harangue, Rail, Rodomontade, Scold, Spout, Spruik, Stump, Thunder, Tub-thump
Rap(ped) Blame, Censure, Chat, Clour, Gangsta, Halfpenny, Knock, Ratatat, Shand, Strike, Swapt, Tack, Tap
Rapacious Accipitrine, Esurient, Exorbitant, Greedy, Harpy, Kite, Predatory, Ravenous, Ravine
Rape Abuse, Assault, Belinda, Cole-seed, Colza, Creach, Creagh, Date, Deflower, Despoil, Gangbang, Hundred, Lock, Lucretia, Navew, Oilseed, Plunder, Statutory, Stuprate, Thack, Tow, Violate
Rapid(ity), Rapidly Chute, Dalle, Double-quick, Express, Fast, Meteoric, Mosso, Presto, Pronto, Quick-fire, Riffle, Sault, Shoot, Skyrocket, Speedy, Stickle, Swift, Tantivy, Veloce, Wildfire
Rapier Sword, Tuck
Rappel Abseil
Rapport Accord, Affinity, Agreement, Harmony
Rapprochement Detente, Reconciliation
Rapt Riveted
Raptor Eagle, Kestrel, Osprey, Standgale, Staniel, Stannel, Stanyel, Stooper
Rapture, Rapturous Bliss, > **DELIGHT**, Ecstasy, Elation, Joy, Trance
Rare, Rarity Blue moon, Curio, Earth, Geason, Infrequent, Intemerate, One-off,

Rear, Recherché, Scarce, Seeld, Seld(om), Singular, > **UNCOMMON**, Uncooked, Underdone, Unusual

Rarefied Thin

Rascal(ly) Arrant, Bad hat, Cad, Cullion, Cur, Deer, Devil, Gamin, Hallian, Hallion, Hallyon, > **KNAVE**, Limner, Loon, Losel, Low, Nointer, Rip, Rogue, Scallywag, Scamp, Scapegrace, Schelm, Skeesicks, Skellum, Skelm, Smaik, Spalpeen, Tinker, Toe-rag, Varlet, Varmint, Villain

Rash(er) Acne, Bacon, Barber's, Brash, Collop, Daredevil, Eruption, Erysipelas, Exanthem(a), Fast, Foolhardy, Harum-scarum, > **HASTY**, Headlong, Hives, Hotspur, Ill-advised, Impetigo, Impetuous, Imprudent, Impulsive, Lardo(o)n, Lichen, Madbrain, Madcap, Miliaria, Morphew, Nappy, Nettle, Outbreak, Overhasty, Precipitate, Purpura, Reckless, Roseola, Rubella, Sapego, Scarlatina, Serpigo, Spots, Tetter, Thoughtless, Unheeding, Unthinking, Urticaria

Rasp(er) File, Grate, Odontophore, Risp, Rub, Scrape, Scroop, Xyster

Raspberry Berate, Black(cap), Boo, Bronx-cheer, Etaerio, Hindberry, Razz

Rastafarian Dread

Rat(s), Ratty Agouta, Bandicoot, Blackleg, Blackneb, Boodie, Brown, Bug-out, Camass, Cane, Cur, Defect, Desert, Fink, Footra, Foutra, Geomyoid, Gym, Heck, Hydromys, Informer, Kangaroo, Mall, Maori, Mole, Moon, Norway, Pack, Poppycock, Potoroo, Pshaw, Pup(py), Renegade, Renegate, Rice, Rink, Rodent, Roland, Rot(ten), Scab, Sewer, Shirty, Squeal, Stinker, Turncoat, Vole, Water, Wharf, Whiskers, White, Wood

Rat-catcher Cat, Ichneumon, Mongoose, Pied Piper

Rate(s), Rating A, Able, Apgar, Appreciate, Assess, Base, Basic, Bit, Carpet, Castigate, Cess, Classify, Cost, Count, Credit, Deserve, Erk, Estimate, Evaluate, Exchange, Grade, Headline, Hearty, Hurdle, Incidence, ISO, Lapse, Leading, Mate's, Mortality, Mortgage, MPH, Octane, Ordinary, OS, Pace, Penalty, Percentage, PG, Piece, Poor, Prime (lending), Rag, Rebuke, Red, Refresh, Reproof, Rocket, Row, Sailor, Scold, > **SET**, Slew, > **SPEED**, Standing, Starting, Surtax, TAM, Tax, Tempo, Tog, U, Upbraid, Value, Water, Wig, World-scale, X

Rather Degree, Fairly, Gey, Instead, Lief, Liever, Loor, More, Prefer, Pretty, Some(what), Sooner, Yes

Ratify Amen, Approve, Confirm, Pass, Sanction, Validate

Ratio Advance, Albedo, Aspect, Bypass, Cash, Compression, Cosine, Distinctiveness, Duplicate, Focal, Fraction, Golden, Gyromagnetic, Inverse, Liquidity, Loss, Mass, Neper, PE, Pi, Pogson, Poisson's, Position, Proportion, Protection, Quotient, Reserve, Savings, Signal-to-noise, Sin(e), Slip, Tensor, Trigonometric

Ration(s) Allocate, Apportion, Compo, Dole, Etape, Iron, K, Quota, Restrict, Scran, Share, Short commons, Size

Rational(isation) A posteriori, Dianoetic, Level-headed, Logical, Lucid, Matter-of-fact, Sane, Sensible, Sine, Sober, Tenable

Rationale Motive

Rattle (box), Rattling Chatter, Clack, Clank, Clap, Clatter, Clitter, Conductor, Crescelle, Crotalaria, Death, Demoralise, Disconcert, Gas-bag, Hurtle, Jabber, Jangle, Jar, Maraca, Natter, Nonplus, Rale, Rap, Red, Reel, Rhonchus, Ruckle, Sabre, Shake, Sistrum, Sunn, Tirl, Upset, Yellow

Raucous Guttural, Hoarse, Loud, Strident

Ravage Depredation, Desecrate, Despoil, Havoc, Pillage, Prey, Ruin, Sack, Waste

Rave, Raving Boil, Enthuse, Praise, Redwood, Redwud, Storm, Ta(i)ver, Tear

Ravel Disentangle, Explain, Involve, Snarl, Tangle

Raven(ous) Black, Corbel, Corbie, Corvine, Croaker, Daw, Grip, Hugin, Munin, Unkindness

Ravine Arroyo, Barranca, Barranco, Canada, Chasm, Chine, Clough, Coulee, Couloir, Dip, Flume, Ghyll, Gorge, Grike, Gulch, Gully, Kedron, Khor, Khud, Kidron, Kloof, Lin(n), Nal(l)a, Nallah, Nulla(h), Pit

Ravish Constuprate, Debauch, Defile, Devour, Rape, Stuprate, Transport, Violate

Raw Brut, Chill, Coarse, Crude, Crudy, Damp, Fresh, Greenhorn, Natural, Recruit, Rude, Uncooked, Wersh

Raw-boned Gaunt, Lanky, Lean, Randle-tree

Ray(s), Rayed Actinic, Alpha, Beam, Beta, Canal, Cathode, Cosmic, Death, Delta, Diactine, Dun-cow, Eagle, Electric, Extraordinary, Fish, Gamma, Grenz, Guitarfish, Homelyn, Manta, Medullary, Monactine, Numbfish, Ordinary, Polyact, Positive, R, Radius, Re, Roentgen, Roker, Röntgen, Sawfish, Sea-devil, Sephen, Shaft, Skate, Starburst, Stick, Sting, Stingaree, Tetract, Thornback, Torpedo, Vascular

Rayon Acetate, Faille, Viscose

Raze Annihilate, Bulldoze, Demolish, Destroy, Level

Razor(-maker) Cut-throat, Occam, Safety

Razorbill Murre

Razor-fish Solen

Razz Raspberry

RE Sappers

Re About, Rhenium, Touching

Reach(ed) Ar(rive), Attain, Boak, Boke, Carry, Come, Get out, Hent, Hit, Key-bugle, Lode, Octave, Peak, Raught, Rax, Retch, Ryke, Seize, Stretch, Touch, Win

Reach-me-downs Slop-clothing

React(or), Reaction(ary) Allergy, Anaphylaxis, Answer, Backlash, Backwash, Behave, Blimp, Blowback, Bourbon, Breeder, Bristle, Bummer, CANDU, Catalysis, Chain, Chemical, Converter, Convertor, Core, Counterblast, Dark, Dibasic, Diehard, Diels-Adler, Dinosaur, Double-take, Falange, Fast(-breeder), Feedback, Fission, Flareback, Furnace, Fusion, Gas-cooled, Graphite, Gut, Hydrolysis, Imine, Insulin, Interplay, Junker, Kickback, Knee-jerk, Light, Magnox, Neanderthal, Nuclear, Outcry, Oxidation, Photolysis, Pile, Poujade, Reciprocate, Recoil, Redox, Repercussion, Respond, Reversible, Rigid, Sensitive, Solvolysis, Spallation, Sprocket, Swing-back, Thermal, Thermonuclear, Tokamak, Vaccinia, Wassermann, Water

▷ **Reactionary** *may indicate* reversed or an anagram

Read(ing) Bearing, Browse, Decipher, Decode, Exegesis, First, Grind, Grounden, Haftarah, Haphtarah, Interpret, Learn, Lection, Lesson, Lu, Maftir, Maw, Pericope, Peruse, Pore, Rad, Rennet-bag, Scan, Second, See, Solve, Speed, Stomach, > STUDY, Third, Vell, Ycond

Reader(s) ABC, Alidad(e), Bookworm, Document, Editor, Epistoler, Homeridae, Lay, Lector, Primer, Silas Wegg, Tape, Taster

Readiest, Readily, Readiness, Ready Alacrity, Alamain, Alert, Amber, Apt, Atrip, Available, Boun, Bound, Brass, Cash, Conditional, Dough, Eager, Early, Eftest, Fettle, Fit, Forward, Game, Geared-up, Gelt, Go, Keyed, Latent, Lolly, Masterman, Money, On, Predy, Prepared, Present, Prest, Primed, Prompt, Reckoner, Ripe, Set, Soon, Spot, Turnkey, Usable, Wherewithal, Willing, Yare, Yark

Readjust Mend, Regulate, Retrue

Readymade Bought, Precast, Prepared, Prêt-à-porter, Slops, Stock, Store

Reagent Analytical, Grignard, Ninhydrin, Reactor, Schiff's, Titrant

Real, Reality, Realities, Really Actual, Bona-fide, Coin, Deed, De facto, Dinkum, Dinky-di(e), Earnest, Echt, Ens, Entia, Entity, Essence, > **GENUINE**, Honest, Indeed, Mackay, McCoy, McKoy, Naive, Ontic, Quite, Royal, Simon Pure, Sooth, Sterling, Substantial, Tangible, Tennis, Thingliness, True, Verismo, Verity, Very, Virtual

Realgar Rosaker, Zarnec, Zarnich

Realise, Realisation, Realism, Realistic Achieve, Attain, Attuite, Cash, Dirty, Down-to-earth, Embody, Encash, Fetch, Fruition, Fulfil, Learn, Magic, Naive, Practical, Sell, Sense, Suss, Understand

▸ **Realities, Reality** *see* **REAL**

Realm Domain, Dominion, Field, Kingdom, Land, Region, Special(i)ty, UK

Ream Bore, Foam, Froth, Paper, Printer's, Rime, Screed

Reap(er) Binder, Crop, Death, Earn, Gather, Glean, Harvest, Scythe, Shear, Sickleman, Solitary, Stibbler

Reappear(ance) Emersion, Materialise, Recrudesce

Rear(ing) Aft, Back(side), Background, Baft, Behind, Breeches, Bring-up, Bunt, Cabré, Catastrophe, Derrière, Foster, Haunch, Hind, Hindquarters, Loo, Natch, Nousell, Nurture, Prat, > **RAISE**, Serafile, Serrefile, Tonneau

Rearmament Moral

Rearrange(ment) Adjust, Anagram, Ectopia, Reorder

Reason(able), Reasoning A fortiori, Analytical, Apagoge, A priori, Argue, Argument, Basis, Call, Cause, Colour, Consideration, Deduce, Expostulate, Fair, Ground(s), Hypophora, Ijtihad, Inductive, Intelligent, Justification, Logic, Logical, Logistics, Logos, Mind, Moderate, Motive, Noesis, Petitio principii, Plausible, Point, Practical, Pretext, Pro, Proof, Pure, Purpose, Ratiocinate, Rational(e), Sanity, Sense, Sensible, Settler, Syllogism, Synthesis, Temperate, Think, Why, Wit

Reave Despoil, Reif, Rob, Spoil

Rebate Diminish, Lessen, Refund, Repayment

Rebecca Sharp

Rebel(lion), Rebellious Aginner, Apostate, Arian, Beatnik, Bolshy, Boxer, Cade, Contra, Croppy, Danton, Diehard, Disobedient, Emeute, Fifteen, Forty-five, Frondeur, Glendower, Hampden, Hereward the Wake, Iconoclast, Insurgent, Insurrection, IRA, Jacobite, Jacquerie, Kick, Luddite, Mutine(er), Mutiny, Oates, Putsch, Rebecca, Recalcitrant, Recusant, Reluct, Resist, Revolt, Rise, Rum, Scofflaw, Sedition, Sepoy, Spartacus, Steelboy, Straw, Tai-ping, Ted, Titanism, Tyler, Venner, Warbeck, Whiteboy, Zealot

▷ **Rebellious** *may indicate* a word reversed

Rebirth Palingenesis, Renaissance, Revival, Samsara

Rebound Backfire, Bounce, Cannon, Elastic, Recoil, Repercussion, Ricochet, Snapback

Rebuff Check, Cold-shoulder, Noser, Quelch, Repulse, Retort, Rubber, Sneb, Snib, Snub

Rebuke Admonish, Berate, Check, Chide, Earful, Lecture, Neb, Objurgate, Rap, Rate, Razz, Reprimand, Reproof, Reprove, Rollick, Scold, Score, Slap, Slate, Snib, Snub, Strop, Threap, Threep, Tick off, Trim, Tut, Upbraid, Wig

Rebut Disprove, Refute, Repulse, Retreat

Recalcitrant Mulish, Obstinate, Unruly, Wilful

Recall(ing) Annul, Eidetic, Encore, Evocative, Partial, Reclaim, Recollect, Redolent, Remember, Remind, Reminisce, Repeal, Retrace, Revoke, Total,

Unsay, Withdraw

Recant(ation) Disclaim, Palinode, Retract, Revoke

Recap(itulate), Recapitulation Epanodos, Summarise

Recapture Rescue

▷ **Recast** *may indicate* an anagram

▶ **Recce** *see* RECONNAISSANCE

Recede Decline, Ebb, Lessen, Regress, Shrink, Withdraw

Receipt(s) Acknowledge, Chit, Docket, Recipe, Revenue, Take, Voucher

Receive(d), Receiver Accept, Accoil, Admit, Aerial, Antenna, Assignee, Bailee, Dipole, Dish, Donee, Ear, Fence, Get, Grantee, Greet, Hydrophone, Inherit, Intercom, Official, Pernancy, Phone, Pocket, Radio, Reset, Responser, Responsor, Roger, Set, Take, Tap, Transistor, Wide

Recent(ly) Alate, Current, Fresh, Hot, Just, Late, Modern, New, Yesterday, Yestereve, Yesterweek

Receptacle Ash-tray, Basket, Bin, Bowl, Box, Ciborium, Container, Cyst, Hell-box, Locket, Loom, Monstrance, Receiver, Reliquary, Relique, Reservatory, Sacculus, Spermatheca, Tank, Thalamus, Tidy, Tore, Torus, Trash can

Reception, Receptive Accoil, At home, Bel-accoyle, Couchée, Court, Durbar, Entertainment, Greeting, Helpdesk, Infare, Kursaal, Levée, Open, Ovation, Pervious, Ruelle, Saloon, Sensory, Soirée, Teleasthetic, Welcome

Recess(ion) Alcove, Antrum, Apse, Apsidal, Apsis, Bay, Bole, Bower, Break, Closet, Columbarium, Corrie, Cove, Croze, Dinette, Ebb, Embrasure, Exedra, Fireplace, Grotto, Hitch, Inglenook, Interval, Loculus, Mortise, > NICHE, Nook, Oriel, Outshot, Rabbet, Rebate, Respite, Rest, Slump, Withdrawal

▷ **Recess** *may indicate* 'reversed'

Rechabite TT

Réchauffé Hachis, Hash, Salmi

Recidivist Relapser

▷ **Recidivist** *may indicate* 'reversed'

Recipe Dish, Formula, Prescription, R, Receipt, Take

Recipient Assignee, Beneficiary, Disponee, Grantee, Heir, Legatee, Receiver

Reciprocal, Reciprocate Corresponding, Elastance, Exchange, Inter(act), Mutual, Repay, Return

Recital, Recitation(ist), Recite(r) Ave, Concert, Declaim, Diseuse, Enumerate, Incantation, Litany, Monologue, Parlando, Quote, Reading, Reel, Relate, Rhapsode, Say, Sing, Tell

Reckless(ness) Blindfold, Careless, Catiline, Desperado, Desperate, Devil-may-care, Gadarene, Harum-scarum, Hasty, Headfirst, Headlong, Hell-bent, Irresponsible, Madcap, Perdu(e), Ramstam, Rantipole, > RASH, Slapdash, Temerity, Ton-up, Wanton, Wildcat

▷ **Reckless** *may indicate* an anagram

Reckon(ing) Assess, Bet, Calculate, Cast, Census, Computer, Consider, Count, Date, Doomsday, Estimate, Fancy, Figure, Guess, Number, Rate, Settlement, Shot, Tab

Reclaim(ed), Reclamation Assart, Empolder, Impolder, Innings, Novalia, Polder, Recover, Redeem, Restore, Swidden, Tame, Thwaite

Recline Lean, Lie, Lounge, Rest

Recluse Anchor(et), Anchorite, Ancress, Eremite, Hermit, Solitaire

Recognise(d), Recognition Accept, Acknow(ledge), Admit, Anagnorisis, Appreciate, Ascetic, Cit(ation), Exequatur, Identify, Isolated, Ken, > KNOW, Nod, Oust, Own, Reward, Salute, Scent, Standard, Voice, Wat, Weet

Recoil Backlash, Bounce, Kick(back), Quail, Rebound, Redound, Repercussion,

Resile, Reverberate, Shrink, Shy, Spring, Start

Recollect(ion) Anamnesis, Memory, Pelmanism, Recall, > REMEMBER, Reminisce

▷ **Recollection** *may indicate* an anagram

Recommend(ation) Advise, Advocate, Counsel, Direct, Endorse, Exhort, Nap, Promote, Rider, Suggest, Testimonial, Tip, Tout

Recompense Cognisance, Deodand, Deserts, Expiate, Guerdon, Pay, Remunerate, Repayment, Requite, Restitution, Reward

Reconcile(d) Adapt, Adjust, Affrended, Atone, Harmonise, Henotic, Make up, Mend

Recondite Difficult, Esoteric, Mystic, Obscure, Occult, Profound

Reconnaissance, Reconnoitre Case, Investigate, Recce, Scout, Survey

Reconstitute, Reconstitution Diagenesis

Reconstruction Perestroika

Record(er), Record company, Recording Album, Ampex, Analogue, Annal(ist), Archive, Archivist, Audit trail, Aulos, Bench-mark, Black box, Blue Riband, Book, Campbell-Stokes, Can, Cartulary, Casebook, CD, Chart, Chronicle, Clickstream, Clog-almanac, Coat(e), Daybook, Diary, Dictaphone®, Dictograph®, Digital, Disc, Document, Dossier, Eloge, Elpee, EMI, Endorsement, English flute, Enter, Entry, EP, Ephemeris, Estreat, Ever, Filater, File, Film, Flight, Flute, Form, Forty-five, Gram, Hansard, Helical scan, Hierogrammat, History, Incremental, Indie, Journal, Lap-chart, Ledger, List, Log, Logbook, LP, Mark, Maxi-single, Memento, Memo(randum), Memorial, Memorise, Meter, Mind, Minute, Mono, Noctuary, Notate, Notch, Note, Odometer, Pass book, Platter, Playback, Pressing, Previous, Protocol, Public, Quipo, Quipu, Quote, Rapsheet, Rec, Regest, Register, Release, Roll, Score(board), Seven-inch, Seventy-eight, Shellac, Single, Spectogram, Sphygmogram, Stenotype®, Tachograph, Tally, Tallyman, Tape, Thirty-three, Toast, Trace, Track, Transcript, Travelog, Trip, Twelve-inch, VERA, Vid(eo), Videotape, Vote, Wax, Wire, Wisden, Worksheet, Write

Record-holder Champion, Sleeve

Record-player DJ, Stereo

Recount Describe, Enumerate, > NARRATE, Relate, Tell

Recourse Access, Resort

Recover(y) Amend, Clawback, Comeback, Common, Convalescence, Cure, Dead cat bounce, Get over, Lysis, Over, Perk, Pull through, Rally, Reclaim, Recoup, Redeem, Regain, Repaint, Replevin, Replevy, Repo(ssess), Rescript, Rescue, Resile, > RETRIEVE, Revanche, Salvage, Salve, Second-wind, Spontaneous, Upswing

Recreate, Recreation Diversion, Hobby, Palingenesia, Pastime, Play, Revive, Sport

Recriminate, Recrimination Ruction

Recruit(s) Attestor, Bezonian, Choco, Conscript, Crimp, Draft, Employ, Engage, Enlist, Enrol, Headhunt, Intake, Muster, Nignog, Nozzer, Press, Rookie, Sprog, Volunteer, Wart, Yobbo

Rectangle, Rectangular Golden, Matrix, Oblong, Quad, Square

Rectifier, Rectify Adjust, Amend, Dephlegmate, Redress, Regulate, > REMEDY, Right, Silicon

Recto Ro

Rector R

Rectum Tewel

Recuperate Convalesce, Rally, Recover

Recur(rent), Recurring Chronic, Quartan, Quintan, Recrudesce, Repeated, Repetend, Return

▷ **Recurrent** *may indicate* 'reversed'

Red(den), Redness Admiral, Alizarin, Angry, Archil, Ashamed, Auburn, Beet, Bilirubin, Blush, Bolshevik, Brick, Burgundy, C, Carmine, Carroty, Castory, Cent, Cerise, Cherry, Chica, Chinese, Choy-root, Chrome, Cinnabar, Claret, Coccineous, Commo, Communist, Congo, Copper, Coquelicot, Coral, Corallin(e), Corkir, Cramesy, Cremosin, Crimson, Crocoite, Cuprite, Cyanin, Damask, Debit, Duster, Embarrassed, Eosin, Eric, Erik, Erythema, Flame, Flaming, Florid, Flush, Foxy, Garnet, Geranium, Ginger, Gory, Grog-blossom, Gu(les), Guly, Hat, Henna, Herring, Incarnadine, Indian, Inflamed, Infra, Inner, Intertrigo, Jacqueminot, Keel, Kermes, Korkir, Lac-lake, Lake, Lateritious, Left(y), Lenin, Letter, Magenta, Maoist, Maroon, Marxist, Menshevik, Miniate, Minium, Modena, Murrey, Neaten, Orchel, Orchilla-weed, Orseille, Oxblood, Phenol, Pillar-box, Plethoric, Plum, Pompeian, Ponceau, Poppy, Pyrrhous, Raddle, Radical, Raspberry, Raw, Realgar, Rhodamine, Rhodopsin, Ridinghood, Roan, Rosaker, Rose, Rot, Rouge, Roy, Rubefy, Rubella, Rubescent, Rubicund, Rubric, Ruby, Ruddle, Ruddy, Rufescent, Russ(e), Russet, Russian, Rust(y), Rutilant, Sang-de-boeuf, Sanguine, Santalin, Sard, Scarlet, Sericon, Setter, Solferino, Stammel, Tape, Tidy, Tile, Titian, Trot, Trotsky, Turacin, Turkey, Tyrian, Venetian, Vermeil, Vermilion, Vermily, Vinaceous, Wallflower, Wine

▷ **Red** *may indicate* an anagram

Redcoat Rust, Soldier

Redeem(er), Redemption Cross, Liberate, Mathurin, Messiah, Ransom, Retrieve, Salvation, Save

Red-faced Coaita, Florid, Flushed

Red-head Auburn, Blue(y), Carroty, Commissar, Mao, Rufus

Red herring Soldier

Redirect Sublimate

▷ **Rediscovered** *may indicate* an anagram

Redolent Aromatic, Fragrant, Reeking, Suggestive

Redoubtable Stalwart

Redress Amends, Offset, Recompense, Rectify, Remedy, Right

Redshank Gambet, Totanus

Redskin Indian, Tomato

Red spot Tika

Reduce(r), Reduced, Reduction Abatement, Allay, Alleviate, Amortize, Attenuate, Beggar, Beneficiate, Clip, Commute, Condense, Contract, Cut, Cutback, Damping, Debase, Decimate, Decrease, Decrement, Demote, Deoxidate, Deplete, Depreciation, Detract, Devalue, Diminish, Diminuendo, Discount, Downsize, Draw-down, Epitomise, Foreshorten, Grind, Jeff, Kinone, > **LESSEN**, Lite, Markdown, Mitigate, Moderate, Palliate, Pot, Pulp, Put, Quinol, Razee, Remission, Retrench, Rundown, Scant, Shade, Shorten, Shrinkage, Slash, Strain, Taper, Telescope, Thin, Weaken, Write-off

Redundancy, Redundant Frill, Futile, Needless, Otiose, Pleonasm, Superfluous, Surplus

Redwood Amboyna, Mahogany, Sanders, Wellingtonia

Reed Arundinaceous, Broken, Calamus, Free, Oboe, Papyrus, Pipe, Quill, Raupo, Rush, Sedge, Seg, Sley, Spear, Sudd, Syrinx, Thatch, Twill, Whistle

Reef Atoll, Barrier, Bioherm, Bombora, Cay, Coral, Fringing, Great Barrier, Key, Knot, Lido, Motu, Saddle, Sca(u)r, Skerry, Witwatersrand

Reefer Cigarette, Jacket, Joint
Reek Emit, Exude, Stink
Reel Bobbin, Dance, Eightsome, Hoolachan, Hoolican, News, Pirn, Spin, Spool, Stagger, Strathspey, Sway, Swift, Swim, Totter, Virgina, Wheel, Whirl, Wintle
Refectory Frater
Refer Advert, Allude, Assign, Cite, Direct, Mention, Pertain, Relate, Remit, Renvoi, Renvoy, See, Submit, Touch, Trade
Referee Arbiter, Commissaire, Mediate, Oddsman, Official, Ref, Umpire, Voucher, Whistler, Zebra
Reference Allusion, Apropos, Character, Coat, Grid, Index, Innuendo, Mention, Passion, Quote, Regard, Renvoi, Respect, Retrospect, Testimonial, Vide
Referendum Mandate, Plebiscite, Vox populi
Refill Replenish
Refine(d), Refinement, Refiner(y) Alembicate, Attic, Catcracker, Couth, Cultivate, Culture, Distinction, Elaborate, Elegance, Exility, Exquisite, Genteel, Grace, Nice, Nicety, Polish(ed), Polite, Précieuse, Pure, Rare(fy), Recherché, Saltern, Sieve, Sift, Smelt, Sophisticated, Spirituel, Sublimate, Subtilise, Tasteful, Try, U, Urbane, Veneer
Reflect(ing), Reflection, Reflective, Reflector Albedo, Blame, Catoptric, Cat's eye®, Cats-eye, Chaff, Chew, Cogitate, > **CONSIDER**, Echo, Glass, Glint, Image, Meditate, Mirror, Muse, Nonspecular, Ponder, Ricochet, Ruminate, Spectacular, Speculum, Symmetrical, Tapetum, Thought
Reflex Achilles, Babinski, Bent, Cancrizans, Knee-jerk, Patellar, Pavlovian, Re-entrant, Single-lens, Tic
Reform(er) Amend, Apostle, Beveridge, Bloomer, Calvin, Chartism, Chastise, Correct, Enrage, Fry, Ghandi, Gradualism, Howard, Hussite, Improve, Knox, Land, Lollard, Luther, Meiji, Melanchthon, Mend, Mucker, New Deal, Owenite, PR, Progressionist, Protestant, Proudhon, Puritan, Rad(ical), Really, Recast, Reclaim, Reconstruction, Rectify, Regenerate, Resipiscence, Ruskin, Satyagraha, Savonarola, Syncretise, Tariff, Transmute, Tyndale, Wycliffe, Young Turk, Zwingli
▷ **Reform(ed)** *may indicate* an anagram
Reformatory Borstal, Magdalen(e)
Refract(ion), Refractive, Refractor(y) Anaclastic, Double, Firestone, Obstinate, Perverse, Prism, Recalcitrant, Refringe, Restive, Stubborn, Sullen, Wayward
Refrain Abstain, Alay, Avoid, Bob, Burden, Chorus, Desist, Epistrophe, Fa-la, Forbear, Hemistich, Mantra, O(v)erword, Repetend, Ritornello, Rumbelow, Rum(p)ti-iddity, Rum-ti-tum, Spare, Tag, Tirra-lirra, Tirra-lyra, Turn again, Undersong, Wheel
Refresh(ment), Refresher Air, Bait, Be(a)vers, Buffet, Cheer, Elevenses, Enliven, Food, Four-hours, Nap, New, Nourishment, Purvey, Refection, Reflect, Refocillate, Reinvigorate, Renew, Repast, Restore, Revive, Seltzer, Shire, Slake, Water
Refrigerator Chill, Chiller, Cooler, Deep freeze, Esky®, Freezer, Freon, Fridge, Ice-box, Minibar, Reefer
Refuge Abri, Ark, Asylum, Bolthole, Burrow, Dive, Fastness, Funkhole, Girth, Grith, Harbour, Haven, Hideaway, Hole, Holt, Home, Hospice, Oasis, Port, Reefer, Resort, Retreat, Sheet-anchor, > **SHELTER**, Soil, Stronghold, Women's
Refugee DP, Economic, Escapist, Fugitive, Grenzganger, Huguenot, Reffo
Refund Clawback, Repayment
▷ **Refurbished** *may indicate* an anagram
Refusal, Refuse Attle, Bagasse, Ba(u)lk, Bilge, Bin, Black, Blackball, Boycott,

Bran, Brash, Breeze, Brock, Bull, Bunkum, Cane-trash, Chaff, Clap-trap, Crane, Crap, Cul(t)ch, Debris, Decline, Denay, Deny, Disown, Draff, Drivel, Dross, Dunder, Dung, Eighty-six, Fag-end, Fenks, Fiddlesticks, Finks, First, Flock, Frass, Garbage, Gob, Guff, Hards, Hogwash, Hold-out, Hurds, Husk, Interdict, Jib, Junk, Knickknackery, Knub, Lay-stall, Leavings, Litter, Lumber, Mahmal, Marc, Megass(e), Midden, Mullock, Mush, Nay(-say), Nill, No, Noser, Nould, Nub, Offal, Off-scum, Orts, Pellet, Pigwash, Pot all, Punk, Radwaste, Raffle, Rape(cake), Rat(s), Rebuff, Recrement, Recusance, Red(d), Redargue, Reest, Regret, Reneg(u)e, Renig, Rot, > **RUBBISH**, Ruderal, Scaff, Scrap, Scree, Scum, Sewage, Shant, Shell heap, Slag, Sordes, Spurn, Sullage, Sweepings, Swill, Tinpot, Tip, Toom, Tosh, Trade, Trash, Tripe, Trock, Troke, Trumpery, Turndown, Twaddle, Unsay, Utter, Wash, Waste, Wastrel

▷ **Re-fused** *may indicate* an anagram

Refutation, Refute Deny, Disprove, Elench(us), Rebut, Redargue, Refel

Regain Recover, Revanche

▶ **Regal** *see* **ROYAL**

Regalia > **CIGAR**, Mound, Orb, Sceptre

Regard(ing) As to, Attention, Care, Consider, > **ESTEEM**, Eye, Gaum, Look, Observe, Odour, Pace, Rate, Re, Respect, Revere, Sake, Steem, Value, Vis-à-vis

Regardless Despite, Heedless, Irrespective, Notwithstanding, Rash, Uncaring, Unmindful, Willy-nilly

Regatta Head of the river, Henley

Regenerate Restore

Regent Interrex, Ruler, Viceroy

Regent's Park Zoo

Reggae Ska

Regicide Ireton, Macbeth

Regime(n) Administration, Control, Diet(etics), Method, Reich

Regiment Black Watch, Buffs, Colour(s), Discipline, Greys, Ironsides, Lifeguard, Monstrous, Nutcrackers, Organise, RA, RE, REME, Rifle, Royals, Tercio, Tertia

▷ **Regiment** *may indicate* an anagram

Region Arctogaea, > **AREA**, Asir, Belt, Brittany, Bundu, Camargue, Chiasma, Climate, Clime, Critical, D, District, E, End, F, Hinterland, Holarctic, Hundred, Lothian, Lusitania, Lycia, Lydia, Macao, Macedonia, Maghreb, Manchuria, Masuria, Matabeleland, Mauretania, Mecklenburg, Mesopotamia, Midi, Molise, Murcia, Mysia, Namaqualand, Negeb, Negev, Nejd, New Castile, New Quebec, Nubia, Nuristan, Offing, Ogaden, Old Castile, Opher, Oriental, Ossetia, Oudh, Pannonia, Pargana, Part, Pergunnah, Piedmont, Province, Quart(er), Realm, Refugium, Ruthenia, Sector, Sogdiana, Stannery, Strathclyde, Subtopia, Tagma, Territory, Tetrarchate, Thule, Tract, Tundra, Ultima Thule, Umbria, Variable, Vaud, Weald, Zone

Register(ing), Registration, Registry Actuarial, Almanac, Annal, Cadastral, Cadastre, Calendar, Cartulary, Cash, Census, Check-in, Diptych, Enlist, Enrol, Enter, Gross, Handicap, Index, Indicate, Inscribe, Inventory, Land, Ledger, List, Lloyd's, Log, Matricula, Menology, NAI, Net, Note, Notitia, Parish, Park, Patent, Read, Record, Reg(g)o, Rent-roll, Roll, Roule, Score, Ship's, Soprano, Terrier, Voice

Registrar Actuary, Greffier, Protocolist, Recorder, Specialist

Regress(ion) Backslide, Recidivism, Revert

Regret(ful), Regrettable Alack, Alas, Apologise, Deplore, Deprecate, Ewhow, Forthwink, Ichabod, Lackaday, Lament, Mourn, Otis, Pity, Remorse, Repentance, Repine, > **RUE**, Ruth, Sorrow, Tragic

Regular(ity), Regularly Clockwork, Constant, Custom, Episodic, Even, Giusto, Goer, Habitual, Habitué, Hourly, Insider, Methodic, Nine-to-five, Normal, Often, Orderly, Orthodox, Patron, Peloria, Periodic, Rhythmic, Routine, Set, Smooth, > STANDARD, Stated, Statutory, Steady, Strict, Symmetric, Uniform, Usual, Yearly

Regulate, Regulation, Regulator Adjust, Appestat, Bye-law, Code, Control, Correction, Curfew, Customary, Direct, Gibberellin, Governor, Guide, King's, Logistics, Metrostyle, Order, Ordinance, Police, Queen's, Rule, Snail, Square, Standard, Statute, Stickle, Stopcock, Sumptuary, Thermostat, Valve

Regulus Matte

Regurgitation Trophallaxis

Rehabilitate, Rehabilitation Cure, Orthotics, Physio(therapy), Repone

Rehearsal, Rehearse Band-call, Dress, Drill, Dry-block, Dry-run, Dummy-run, Practice, Practise, Preview, Recite, Repeat, Trial

Reichenbach Falls, Od

Reign Era, Govern, Meiji, Prevail, Raine, Realm, Restoration, > RULE

Reimburse(ment) Indemnity, Recoup, Redress, Repay

Rein(s) Bearing, Check, Control, Curb, Free, Gag, Leading strings, Lumbar, Restrain

Reindeer Blitzen, Caribou, Comet, Cupid, Dancer, Dasher, Donner, Moss, Prancer, Rudolf, Tarand, Vixen

Reinforce(ment) Aid, Augment, Bolster, Boost, Brace, Buttress, Cleat, Line, Negative, Partial, Plash, Pleach, Recruit, Reserve, > STRENGTHEN, Support, Tetrapod, Underline

Reinstate Repone

Reinvigorate Recruit

Reiterate(d), Reiteration Battology, Emphasize, Ostinato, Plug, > REPEAT

Reject(ion) Abhor, Abjure, Athetise, Bin, Blackball, Brush off, Cast, Cast off, Deny, Dice, Discard, Disclaim, Discount, Disdain, Diss, Elbow, Export, Flout, Frass, Iconoclasm, Jilt, Kest, Kill, Knock-back, Ostracise, Oust, Outcast, Outtake, Pip, Plough, Rebuff, Recuse, Refuse, Reny, Repel, Reprobate, Repudiate, Repulse, Scout, Scrub, Spet, Spin, Spit, > SPURN, Sputum, Thumbs-down, Turndown, Veto

Rejoice, Rejoicing Celebrate, Exult, Festivity, Gaude, Glory, Joy, Maffick, Sing

Rejoin(der), Rejoined Answer, Counter, Relide, Reply, Response, Retort, Reunite

Rejuvenation Shunamitism

Relapse Backslide, Deteriorate, Recidivism, Regress, Revert, Sink

Relate(d), Relation(ship), Relative Account, Affair, Affine, Affinity, Agnate, Akin, Allied, Antibiosis, Appertain, Associate, Blood, Brer, Brisure, Cognate, Commensal, Concern, Connection, Connexion, Consanguinity, Coosen, Cousin, Coz, Deixis, Dispersion, Eme, Enate, False, Formula, German(e), Granny, Heterogeneous, Homologous, Impart, Industrial, Item, Kin, Kinsman, Labour, Liaison, Link, Love-hate, Mater, Material, Matrix, Mutualism, Narrative, One-to-one, Osculant, Pertain, Phratry, Pi, Plutonic, Poor, Privity, > PROPORTION, Proxemics, Public, Race, Rapport, Rapprochement, Ratio, Reciprocity, Recite, Recount, Rede, Refer(ence), Relevant, Respect(s), Sib(b), Sibbe, Sibling, Sine, Sybbe, Symbiosis, Syntax, Tale, Tell, Who

Relating to Of

Relax(ation), Relaxant, Relaxed Abate, Atony, Autogenics, Calm, Chalone, Chill out, Com(m)odo, Contrapposto, Degage, Detente, Diversion, Downbeat, Ease, Easy-going, Flaccid, Gallamine, Icebreaker, Laid-back, Leisured, Lesh states, Lighten, > **LOOSEN**, Mellow out, Mitigate, Peace, Relent, Relief, Remit, Rest, Slacken, Sleep, Toneless, Unbend, Unknit, Unrein, Untie, Unwind, Veg out

▷ **Relaxed** *may indicate* an anagram

Relay(er) Convey, Medley, Race, Shift, Tell, Telstar, Torch-race

▷ **Relay(ing)** *may indicate* an anagram

Release Abreact, Announcement, Bail, Catharsis, Clear, Day, Death, Deliver(y), Desorb, Disburden, Discharge, Disclose, Disengage, Disimprison, Dismiss, Disorb, Emancipate, Enfree, Excuse, Exeem, Exeme, Extricate, Exude, Free, Handout, Happy, > **LIBERATE**, Manumit, Merciful, Moksa, Parole, Press, Quietus, Quittance, Relinquish, Ripcord, Soft, Spring, Tre corde, Unconfine, Uncouple, Undo, Unhand, Unleash, Unloose, Unpen, Unshackle, Unteam, Untie

Relegate Banish, Consign, Demote, Exile, Sideline, Stellenbosch

Relent Bend, Mollify, Soften, Yield

Relentless Cruel, Hard, Hardface, Inexorable, Pitiless, Rigorous, Stern

Relevance, **Relevant** Ad rem, Applicable, Apposite, Apropos, Apt, Bearing, Germane, Material, Pertinent, Point, Valid

▸ **Reliable**, **Reliance** *see* **RELY**

Relic Antique, Ark, Artefact, Fly-in-amber, Fossil, Leftover, Memento, Neolith, Remains, Sangraal, Sangrail, Sangreal, Souvenir, Survival

Relict Survivor, Widow

Relief, **Relieve(d)** Aid, Air-lift, Allay, Allegeance, Alleviate, Alms, Anaglyph, Anastatic, Anodyne, Assistance, Assuage, Bas, Beet, Beste(a)d, Bete, Cameo, Cavo-relievo, Comfort, Cure, Détente, Ease(ment), Emboss, Emollient, Free, Grisaille, High, Indoor, Let-up, Lighten, Low, Lucknow, Mafeking, On the parish, Outdoor, Palliate, Phew, Photo, Pog(e)y, Reassure, Redress, Remedy, Replacement, Repoussé, Reprieve, > **RESCUE**, Respite, Retirement, Rid, Spare, Spell, Stand-in, Stiacciato, Succour, Taper, Tax, Tondo, Toreutics, Wheugh, Whew, Woodcut

Religion, **Religious (sect)** Animism, Baha'i, Biblist, Bogomil, Buddhism, Camaldolite, Cargo cult, Carthusian, Celestine, Christadelphian, Christianity, Cistercian, Coenobite, Confucianism, Congregant, Creed, Culdee, Denomination, Devout, Din, Doctrine, Druse, Druz(e), Faith, Falun Gong, Familist, Gilbertine, Gnosticism, God-squad, Gueber, Guebre, Hadith, Hare Krishna, Has(s)id, Hieratic, Hospital(l)er, Ignorantine, Islam, Ismaili, Jain(a), Jansenism, Jehovah's Witness, Jesuit, Jewry, Judaism, Lamaism, Loyola, Lutheran, Macumba, Mahatma, Manichee, Maoism, Mazdaism, Mazdeism, Missionary, Missioner, Mithraism, Moony, Mormonism, New Light, Nun, Opium, Orphism, Pagan, Pantheist, Parseeism, Parsism, Pi, Piarist, Pietà, Postulant, Premonstratensian, Progressive, Rastafarian, Reformation, Resurrectionist, Revealed, Revivalism, Sabbatarian, Sabian, Sacramentarian, Santeria, Scientology®, Serious, Shaker, Shamanism, Shango, Shiism, Shinto(ism), Sikhism, Sodality, Solifidian, Sons of Freedom, Spike, Sunna, Swedenborgian, Taoism, Theatine, Theology, Tractarianism, Tsabian, Utraquist, Voodooism, Whore, Wicca, Zabian, Zarathustric, Zealous, Zend-avesta, Zoroaster, Zwinglian

Religious book Bible, Koran, Missal, NT, OT, Sefer, Tantra, Targum, T(h)orah

Relinquish Abdicate, Cede, Demit, Discard, Drop, Forlend, Remise, Waive(r), Yield

Reliquary Chef, Encolpion, Encolpium, Simonious, Tope

Relish(ing) Botargo, Catsup, Chakalaka, Chow-chow, Condiment, Enjoy,

Flavour, Gentleman's, Gout, Gust(o), Ketchup, Lap(-up), Lust, Opsonium, Palate, Pickle, Sapid, Sar, Sauce, Savour, Seasoning, Tang, Tooth, Worcester sauce, Zest

Reluctant Averse, Backward, Chary, Circumspect, Grudging, Half-hearted, Laith, Loth, Nolition, Renitent, Shy, Unwilling

Rely, Reliance, Reliant, Reliable Addiction, Authentic, Bank, Confidence, Constant, > **COUNT**, Dependent, Found, Hope, Jeeves, Lean, Loyal, Mensch, Presume, Pukka, Rest, Safe, Secure, Solid, Sound, Sponge, Stand-by, Staunch, Trustworthy, Trusty, Unfailing

Remain(der), Remaining, Remains Abide, Ash(es), Balance, Bide, Continue, Corse, Dreg(s), Dwell, Embers, Estate, Exuviae, Fag-end, Kreng, Last, Late, Lave, Left, Lie, Locorestive, Manet, Nose, Oddment, Orts, Other, Outstand, Persist, Relic(ts), Reliquae, > **REMNANT**, Residue, Rest, Ruins, Scourings, Scraps, Stay, Stick, Stub, Surplus, Survive, Tag-end, Talon, Tarry, Wait, Wreck(age)

Remark Aside, Barb, Bromide, Comment(ary), Descry, Dig, Epigram, Generalise, Mention, Noise, > **NOTE**, Notice, Obiter dictum, Observe, Platitude, Pleasantry, Reason, Sally, Shot, State

Remarkable, Remarkably Amazing, Arresting, Beauty, Bodacious, Conspicuous, Dilly, Egregious, Extraordinary, Heliozoan, Legendary, Lulu, Mirable, Notendum, Noteworthy, Phenomenal, Rattling, > **SIGNAL**, Singular, Some, Striking, Tall, Unco, Uncommon, Visible

Remedial, Remedy Aid, An mo, Antacid, Antibiotic, Antidote, Antiodontalgic, Antispasmodic, Arcanum, Arnica, Azoth, Bach, Bach flower, Basilicon, Calomel, Catholicon, Corrective, Cortisone, > **CURE**, Dinic, Drug, Elixir, Femiter, Feverfew, Fumitory, Ginseng, Heal, Ipecac, Leechdom, Medicate, Medicine, Moxa, Nosode, Nostrum, Palliative, Panacea, Panpharmacon, Paregoric, Poultice, Provisional, Rectify, Redress, Repair, Rescue, Salutory, Salve, Simillimum, Simple, Specific, Taraxacum, Therapeutic, Tonga, Treatment, Tutsan

Remember(ing), Remembrance Bethink, Commemorate, Con, Mem, Memorial, Memorise, Mention, Mneme, Recall, Recollect, Remind, Reminisce, Retain, Rosemary, Souvenir

▷ **Remember** *may indicate* RE-member, viz. Sapper

Remind(er) Aftertaste, Aide-memoire, Bookmark, Evocatory, Evoke, Jog, Keepsake, Mark, Memento, Memo, Mnemonic, Mnemotechnic, Monition, Nudge, Phylactery, Prod, Prompt, Souvenir, Token

Reminiscence(s), Reminiscent Ana, Evocative, Memory, Recall, Recollect, Remember, Retrospect

Remiss Careless, Derelict, Lax, Lazy, Negligent, Tardy

Remission Abatement, Absolution, Acceptilation, Indulgence, Pardon, Pause, Spontaneous

Remit Excuse, Forward, Pardon, Postpone

Remnant Butt, End, Fent, Heeltap, Left-over, Odd-come-short, Offcut, Relic, > **REMAINDER**, Rump, Trace, Vestige

Remonstrate Argue, Complain, Expostulate, Protest, Reproach

Remorse Angst, Ayenbite, Breast-beating, Compunction, Contrition, Had-i-wist, Pity, > **REGRET**, Rue, Ruing, Ruth, Sorrow

Remote Aloof, Aphelion, Back blocks, Backveld, Backwater, Backwood, Bullamakanka, Bundu, > **DISTANT**, Far flung, Forane, Inapproachable, Insular, Irrelevant, Jericho, Long(inquity), Out(part), Outback, Scrub, Secluded, Shut-out, Slightest, Surrealistic, Unlikely, Withdrawn, Woop woop

Remount(s) Remuda

Removal, Remove(d) Abduct, Ablation, Abstract, Apocope, Asport, Banish, Blot, Circumcision, Clear, Couch, Declassify, Dele(te), Depilate, Depose, Deracinate, Detach, Detract, Dishelm, Dislodge, Disloign, Dispel, Doff, Efface, Eject, Eloi(g)n, Emend, Eradicate, Erase, Esloyne, Estrange, Evacuate, Evict, Exalt, Excise, Extirpate, Extradite, Extricate, Far, Flit, Huff, Nick, Razee, Redline, Remble, Rid, Scratch, Sequester, Shift, Spirit, Sublate, Subtract, Supplant, Transfer, Transport, Unperson, Unseat, Uproot

Remuneration Pay, Return, Reward, Salary, Solde

Remus Uncle

Renaissance Awakening, Cinquecento, High, Quattrocento, Revival

Rend Cleave, Harrow, Lacerate, Rip, Rive, Rupture, Tear

Render(ing) Construe, Deliver, Do, Gie, Give, Interpretation, Make, Melt, Pebble-dash, Plaster, Provide, Recite, Represent, Restore, Setting, Tallow, Try, Yeve

Rendezvous Date, Meeting, Philippi, Tryst, Venue

Rendition Account, Delivery, Interpretation, Translation

Rene Descartes

Renegade, Renege Apostate, Default, Defector, Deserter, Rat(ton), Traitor, Turncoat

▷ **Renegade** *may indicate* a word reversal

Renew(al) Instauration, Neogenesis, Palingenesis, Refresh, Replace, Resumption, Retrace, Revival, Urban

Rennet Steep, Vell

Renounce, Renunciation Abandon, Abdicate, Abjure, Abnegate, Disclaim, Disown, For(e)go, For(e)say, Forfeit, Forisfamiliate, Forsake, Forswear, Kenosis, Outclaim, Quitclaim, Recede, Relinquish, Renay, Retract, Sacrifice

Renovate(d), Renovation Duff, Face-lift, Instauration, Makeover, Refurbish, Renew, Repair, Restore, Revamp

Renown(ed) Fame, Glory, Illustrious, Kudos, Lustre, Notoriety, Prestige, Stardom

Rent(er), Renting Broken, Charge, Cornage, Cost, Crack, Cranny, Cuddeehih, Cuddy, Division, Economic, Fair, Farm, Fee, Fissure, Gale, Gavel, Ground, > HIRE, Lease, Let, List, Mail, Market, Occupy, Peppercorn, Quit-rent, Rack, Rip, Rived, Riven, Screed, Seat, Slit, Split, Stallage, Subtenant, Tare, Tenant, Tithe, Tore, Torn, Tythe, White

Reorganise Rationalise

▷ **Reorganised** *may indicate* an anagram

Reorientate Rabat

Repair(s), Repairer, Reparation Amend(s), Anaplasty, Assythement, Botch, Cobble, Damages, Darn, Doctor, Excision, Fettle, Fitter, Go, Haro, Harrow, Jury rig, > MEND, Overhaul, Patch, Piece, Recompense, Redress, Refit, Reheel, Remedy, Renew, Renovate, Repoint, Resort, Restore, Retouch, Revamp, Running, Satisfaction, Stitch, Ulling, Vamp, Volery

Repartee Backchat, Badinage, Banter, Persiflage, Rejoinder, Retort, Riposte, Wit

Repast Bever, Collection, Food, Meal, Tea, Treat

Repay(ment) Avenge, Compensate, Quit, Refund, Requite, Retaliate, Reward, Satisfaction

Repeal Abrogate, Annul, Cancel, Rescind, Revoke

Repeat(edly), Repetition, Repetitive Again, Alliteration, Anadiplosis, Anaphora, Ancora, Battology, Belch, Bis, Burden, Burp, Copy, Ditto(graphy), Duplicate, > ECHO, Echolalia, Encore, Epanalepsis, Epistrophe, Epizuexis,

Eruct, Facsimile, Habitual, Harp, Image, Imitate, Ingeminate, Iterate, Iterum, Leit-motiv, Merism, Ostinato, Palillogy, Parrot, Passion, Perpetuate, Playback, Polysyndeton, Recite(r), Redo, Refrain, Regurgitate, Reiterate, Renew, Rep, Repetend, Reprise, Rerun, Retail, Rondo, Rosalia, Rote, Same(y), Screed, Segno, Symploce, Tautology, Tautophony, Thrum, Verbigerate

Repel(lent) Estrange, Harsh, Offensive, Rebarbative, Reject, Repulse, Revolt, Squalid, Turn-off, Ug(h), Ward

Repent(ant), Repentance Metanoia, Penitent, Regret, Rue, Sackcloth, Yamim Nora'im

Repercussion Backlash, Backwash, Effect, Impact, Recoil

Repertoire, Repertory Company, Depot, Rep, Store

▸ **Repetition** *see* REPEAT

Replace(ment), Replaceable, Replacing Change, Deputise, Diadochy, For, Pre-empt, Prosthesis, Raincheck, Refill, Replenish, Restore, Stand-in, Substitute, Supersede, Supplant, Surrogate, Taxis, Transform, Transliterate, Understudy

Replay Action, Instant, Iso(lated), Segno

Replenish Refill, Refresh, Revictual, Stock, Supply, Top

Replete, Repletion Awash, Full, Gorged, Plenitude, Plethora, Sated, Satiation

Replica Clone, Copy, Duplicate, Facsimile, Image, Repetition, Spit

Reply Accept, Answer, Churlish, Duply, Over, Rejoinder, Rescript, Response, Retort, Roger, Surrebut, Surrebutter, Surrejoin, Triply

Report(er) Account, Announce, Auricular, Bang, Blacksmith, Bruit, Bulletin, Cahier, Clap, Columnist, Comment, Commentator, Correspondent, Court, Cover, Crack, Crump, Cub, Debrief, Disclose, Dispatch, Dissertation, Explosion, Fame, Fireman, Grapevine, Hansard, Hearsay, Jenkins, Journalist, Legman, Libel, News, Newshawk, Newshound, Newsman, Noise, Pop, Pressman, Protocol, Relate, Relay, Representation, Repute, Return, Roorback, Rumour, Sitrep, Sound(bite), Staffer, State(ment), Stringer, Tale, > TELL, Thesis, Transcribe, Tripehound, Troop, Update, Weather, Whang, Wolfenden, Write up

▹ **Reported** *may indicate* the sound of a letter or word

Repose Ease, Kaif, Kef, Kif, Lie, Lig, Peace, Relax, > REST, Serenity

Repository Ark, Cabinet, Container, Genizah, Reservoir, Sepulchre, Vault

Reprehend Blame, Censure, Criticise, Rebuke, Warn

Represent(ation), Representative, Represented Agent, Ambassador, Anaconic, Caricature, Client, Commercial, Cross-section, Delegate, Depict, Deputation, Describe, Display, Drawing, Drummer, Effigy, Elchee, Eltchi, Emblem, Embody, Emissary, Example, Figurative, Image, John Bull, Legate, Lobby, Map, Mimesis, Mouthpiece, MP, Personate, Personify, Portray, Proportional, Quintessence, Rep, Resemble, Salesman, Senator, Shop steward, Simulacrum, Spokesman, Stand-in, Steward, Symbolic, Syndic, Tableau, Tiki, Transcription, Typical, Vakeel, Vakil, Vehicle

▹ **Represented** *may indicate* an anagram

Repress(ed) Check, Curb, Pent, Quell, Sneap, Stifle, Stultify, Subjugate, Withhold

Reprieve Delay, Postpone, Relief, Respite

Reprimand Admonish, Bounce, Carpet, > CENSURE, Chew out, Chide, Dressing-down, Earful, Jobe, Lace, Lambast, Lecture, Rark up, Rating, Rebuke, Reproof, Rocket, Rollicking, Slate, Strafe, Targe, Tick off, Tongue-lashing, Wig

Reprint Copy, Paperback, Replica

Reprisal(s) Marque, Retaliation, Revenge

Reproach Blame, Braid, Byword, Chide, Discredit, Dispraise, Exprobate, Gib, Mispraise, Odium, Opprobrium, Rebuke, Ronyon, Runnion, Scold, Shend, Sloan, Stigma, Taunt, Truant, Upbraid, Upcast, Yshend

Reprobate Cur, Lost soul, Outcast, Rascal, Scallywag, Scamp

Reprocess Re-make

Reproduce(r), Reproduction, Reproductive (organ) Amphimixis, Ape, Apomixis, Archegonium, Carpel, Clone, Copy, Counterfeit, Depict, Ectype, Edition, Etch, Eugenics, Gamogenesis, Gemmate, Homogenesis, Isospory, Megaspore, Meristematic, Mono, Multiply, Oogamy, Ozalid®, Parthogenesis, Phon(e)y, Playback, Proliferate, Propagate, Pullulation, Refer, Replica, Roneo®, Schizogony, Seminal, S(h)akti, Simulate, Spermatia, Stereo, Strobilation, Syngamy, Syngenesis

▷ **Reproduce** *may indicate* an anagram

Reproof, Reprove Admonish, Berate, Chide, Correction, Corruption, Lecture, Rate, Rebuff, Rebuke, Scold, Sloan, Tut, Upbraid

Reptile, Reptilian Agamid, Alligarta, Alligator, Base, Basilisk, Caiman, Cayman, Chameleon, Chelonian, Creeper, Crocodile, Diapsid, Dicynodont, Dinosaur, Galliwasp, Goanna, Herpetology, Lacertine, Lizard, Mamba, Pteranodon, Pterodactyl, Rhynchocephalian, Sauroid, > SNAKE, Squamata, Synapsid, Tegu(exin), Thecodont, Therapsid, Theriodontia, Tortoise, Tuatara, Tuatera, Turtle, Worm

Republic Banana, Federal, Fifth, First, Fourth, People's, State, Third

REPUBLICS

1 letter:	Congo	Bharat	**7 letters:**
R	Czech	Brazil	Adharca
	Egypt	Bukavu	Albania
3 letters:	Gabon	Buryat	Algeria
RMM	Ghana	France	Andorra
UAR	Haiti	Gambia	Armenia
	India	Greece	Bashkir
4 letters:	Italy	Guinea	Belarus
Chad	Kenya	Guyana	Bolivia
Cuba	Khmer	Ingush	Burundi
Eire	Libya	Israel	Chechen
Fiji	Malta	Kalmyk	Chuvash
Iran	Nauru	Latvia	Comoros
Iraq	Niger	Malawi	Croatia
Komi	Palau	Mexico	Ecuador
Laos	Sakha	Myanma	Estonia
Mali	Sudan	Panama	Finland
Peru	Syria	Poland	Georgia
Togo	Tatar	Rwanda	Germany
Tuva	Yakut	Second	Hungary
	Yemen	Serbia	Iceland
5 letters:	Zaire	Turkey	Ireland
Adhar		Udmurt	Jibouti
Altai	**6 letters:**	Uganda	Kalmuck
Belau	Adygai	Weimar	Khakass
Benin	Adygei	Zambia	Lebanon
Chile	Angola		Liberia

- Moldova
- Myanmar
- Namibia
- Nigeria
- Romania
- Senegal
- Somalia
- Surinam
- Tunisia
- Ukraine
- Uruguay
- Vanuatu
- Vietnam

8 letters:
- Botswana
- Bulgaria
- Cambodia
- Cameroon
- Chechnya
- Colombia
- Dagestan
- Djibouti
- Dominica
- Esthonia
- Honduras
- Karelian
- Kiribati
- Malagasy
- Maldives

Mongolia
Pakistan
Paraguay
Portugal
Roumania
Sinn Fein
Slovakia
Slovenia
Sri Lanka
Tanzania
Zimbabwe

9 letters:
Argentina
Badakshan
Cape Verde
Costa Rica
Dominican
Guatemala
Indonesia
Kazakstan
Lithuania
Macedonia
Mauritius
Nicaragua
San Marino
Singapore
Venezuela

10 letters:
Azerbaijan
Bangladesh
Belorussia
El Salvador
Gorno-Altai
Kara-Kalpak
Kazakhstan
Kyrgyzstan
Madagascar
Mauritania
Montenegro
Mordvinian
Mozambique
North Korea
North Yemen
South Korea
Tajikistan
Ubang-Shari
Uzbekistan
Yugoslavia

11 letters:
Afghanistan
Burkino-Faso
Byelorussia
Cote d'Ivoire
Philippines
Sierra Leone
South Africa

Switzerland
West Germany

12 letters:
Guinea-Bissau
Turkmenistan

13 letters:
Bashkortostan
North Ossetian

15 letters:
Kabardino-Balkar
United Provinces

16 letters:
Congo-Brazzaville
Karachai-
  Cherkess

17 letters:
Bosnia-
  Herzegovina
Mari El-
  Nakhichevan
Sao Tomele
  Principe
Trinidad and
  Tobago

Republican Antimonarchist, Democrat, Fenian, Fianna Fail, Girondist, IRA, Iraqi, Leveller, Montagnard, Mugwump, Plato, Red, Sansculotte, Sansculottic, Sinn Fein, Whig

Repudiate Abjure, Deny, Discard, Disclaim, Disown, Ignore, Recant, Reject, Renounce, Repel, Retract

Repugnance, Repugnant Abhorrent, Alien, Disgust, Distaste, Fulsome, Horror, Loathing, Revulsion

Repulse, Repulsive Grooly, Lo(a)th, Off-putting, Rebuff, Rebut, Refel, Refuse, Repel, Repugnant, Slimy, Squalid, Ugly, Vile

Reputable, Reputation, Repute(d) Bubble, Dit, Estimate, Fame, Good, Izzat, Loos, Los, Name, Note, Notoriety, Odour, Opinion, Prestige, Putative, Regard, Renown, Said, Sar, > **STANDING**, Stink, Trustworthy

Request Adjure, Appeal, Apply, Ask, Beg, Desire, Entreaty, Invite, Petition, Plea, Prayer, Solicit, Supplication

Requiem Agnus dei, Mass

Require(d), Requirement Charge, Crave, De rigueur, Desire, Enjoin, Entail, Exact, Expect, Incumbent, Lack, Necessity, Need, Prerequisite

Requisite, Requisition Commandeer, Due, Embargo, Essential, Indent, Necessary, Needful, Order, Press, Simplement

Rescind Abrogate, Annul, Recant, Remove, Repeal

Rescue Aid, Air-sea, Deliver, Free, Liberate, Ransom, Recover, Recower, Redeem,

Regain, Relieve, Reprieve, Retrieve, Salvage, Salvation, > **SAVE**

Research(er) Boffin, Delve, Dig, Enquiry, Explore, Fieldwork, Investigate, Legwork, Market, Motivation(al), Operational, Pioneer, Sus(s), Think-tank

Resell Scalp

Resemblance, Resemble, Resembling Affinity, Apatetic, Approach, Assonant, Dead ringer, Likeness, -oid, -opsis, Replica, Similitude, Simulate

Resent(ful), Resentment Anger, Bridle, Chippy, Choler, Cross, Derry, Dudgeon, Grudge, Indignation, Ire, Jaundiced, Malign, Miff, Pique, Rankle, Smart, Spite, Umbrage

Reservation, Reserve(d), Reservist(s) Aloof, Arrière-pensée, Backlog, Bashful, Book, By, Caveat, Central, Cold, Demiss, Detachment, Distant, Earmark, Engage, Ersatz, Except, Fall-back, Fort Knox, Gold, Hold, Husband, Ice, Indian, Introvert, Landwehr, Layby, Locum, Mental, Militiaman, Nature, Nest-egg, Nineteenth man, Proviso, Qualification, Reddendum, Res, Rest, Restraint, Retain, Reticence, Retiring, Rez, Salvo, Sanctuary, Save, Scenic, Scruple, Set aside, Special, Stand-by, Stand-offishness, Starch, Stash, Stock(pile), TA(men), Uncommunicate, Understudy, Warren, Waves, Withhold

Reservoir Basin, Cistern, G(h)ilgai, Gilgie, Header tank, Repository, Rybinsk, Service, Stock, Sump, Tank, Water tower

Reset Taxis

Reside(nce), Resident(s) Abode, Address, Amban, Chequers, Commorant, Consulate, Denizen, Dwell, Embassy, Establishment, Expatriate, Exurbanite, Gremial, Guest, Home, In, Indweller, Inholder, Inmate, Intern, Ledger, Lei(d)ger, Lieger, Liveyer(e), Lodger, Metic, Occupant, Pad, Parietal, Permanent, Resiant, Settle, Sojourn, Stay, Tenant, Up, Vicinage, Villager, Yamen

Residual, Residue Ash, Astatki, Boneblack, Calx, Caput, Chaff, Cinders, Coke, Crud, Dottle, Draff, Dregs, Expellers, Greaves, Leavings, Mazout, Mortuum, Remainder, Remanent, Remnant, Slag, Slurry, Snuff, Vinasse

Resign(ed), Resignation Abandon, Abdicate, Demit, Fatalism, Heigh-ho, Leave, Meek, > **QUIT**, Reconcile, Stoic, Submit

Resilience, Resilient Bounce, Buoyant, Elastic, Flexible, Recoil, Springy

Resin Acaroid, Acrylic, Agila, Alkyd, Amber, Amine, Amino, Anime, Arar, Asaf(o)etida, Bakelite®, Balsam, Bal(sa)m of Gilead, Benjamin, Benzoin, Bursera, Cannabin, Cannabis, Caranna, Carauna, Charas, Cholestyramine, Churrus, Colophony, Conima, Copai(ba), Copaiva, Copal(m), Coumarone, Courbaril, Cymene, Dam(m)ar, Dammer, Dragon's blood, Elaterite, Elemi, Epoxy, Frankincense, Galbanum, Galipot, Gambi(e)r, Gamboge, Glyptal, Guaiacum, Gum, Hasheesh, Hashish, Hing, Jalapin, Kino, Labdanum, Lac, Ladanum, Lignaloes, Mastic, Melamine, Methacrylate, Myrrh, Olibanum, Opopanax, Perspex®, Phenolic, Phenoxy, Plastisol, Podophyllin, Polycarbonate, Polyester, Polymer, Polysterene, Polyvinyl, Propolis, Retinite, Roset, Rosin, Rosit, Rozet, Rozit, Sagapenum, Sandarac(h), Saran®, Scammony, Shellac, Storax, Styrax, Synthetic, Takamaka, Taxin, Urea, Vinyl, Xylenol

Resist Bristle, Buck, Combat, Contest, Defy, Face, Fend, Gainstrive, Impede, Oppose, Redound, Reluct, Stand (pat), Toughen, > **WITHSTAND**

Resistance, Resistant, Resistor Barretter, Bleeder, Ceramal, Cermet, Chetnik, Coccidiostat, Combat, Drag, Element, Friction, Hostile, Immunity, Impediment, Internal, Invar, Klendusic, Klepht, Maquis, Maraging, Megohm, Microhm, Negative, Obstacle, Ohm, Passive, Pat, Pull, R, Radiation, Reluctance, Renitent, Resilient, Rheostat, Sales, Satyagraha, Soul-force, Specific, Stability, Stand, Stonde, Stubborn, Tough

Resolute, Resolution Analysis, Bold, Cast-iron, Casuistry, Courage, Decided, Decision, Denouement, Determined, Doughty, > **FIRM**, Fortitude, Granite, Grim, Grit, Hardiness, Insist, Joint, Pertinacity, Promotion, Rede, Resolve, Stable, Stalwart, Staunch, Stout, Strength, Sturdy, Telic, Tenacity, Unbending, Valiant, Willpower

Resolve(d), Resolver Analyse, Calculate, Decide, Declare, > **DETERMINE**, Deux et machina, Factorise, Fix, Hellbent, Intent, Nerve, > **PURPOSE**, Settle, Steadfast, Tenacity, Vow, Will

▷ **Resolved** *may indicate* an anagram

Resonance, Resonant Canorous, Electromer, Morphic, Orotund, Parallel, Ringing, Sonorous, Timbre, Vibrant

Resort Centre, Dive, Etaples, Expedient, Frame, Frequent, Haunt, Hove, Hydro, Invoke, Lair, Last, Las Vegas, Lowestoft, Morecambe, Nassau, Paignton, Pau, Pis aller, Rapallo, Recourse, Repair, Riviera, Southend, Spa(w), Stand by, Use, Watering place, Zermatt

▷ **Resort(ing)** *may indicate* an anagram

Resound(ing) Echo, Plangent, Reboant, Reboation, Reverberate, Ring

Resource(s), Resourceful Assets, Beans, Bottom, Chevisance, Clever, Enterprise, Faculty, Funds, Gumption, Human, Ingenious, Input, Inventive, Means, Natural, Sharp, Stock-in-trade, > **VERSATILE**, Wealth

Respect(ed), Respectable, Respectful Admire, Ahimsa, Aspect, Behalf, Consider, Decent, Deference, Devoir, Duty, Esteem, Gigman, Homage, > **HONOUR**, Intent, Kempt, Latria, Obeisant, Officious, Pace, Particular, Preppy, Prestige, Proper, Reference, Regard, Relation, Reputable, Revere, Sir, S(t)irrah, U, Venerate, Wellborn, Well-thought-of, Wise, Worthy

Respirator, Respire, Respiration Artificial, Blow, Breathe, Exhale, Gasmask, Inhale, Iron lung, Pant, Snorkel

Respite Break, Breather, Frist, Interval, Leisure, Let up, Pause, Reprieve, Rest, Stay, Truce

Respond, Response, Responsive Amenable, Answer, Antiphon, Comeback, Conditioned, Echo, Feedback, Flechman, Grunt, Immune, Kneejerk, Kyrie, Litany, Nastic, Pavlovian, Photonasty, React(ion), Reflex, Reply, Repost, Retort, Rheotaxis, Rheotropism, Rise, Synapte, Syntonic, Tender, Thigmotropic, Tic, Tropism, Unconditioned, Voice, Warm

Responsibility, Responsible Anchor, Answerable, Baby, Blame, Buck, Charge, Culpable, Dependable, Diminished, Duty, Frankpledge, Hot seat, Incumbent, Instrumental, Liable, Mea culpa, Onus, Pigeon, Sane, Solid, Stayman, Trust

Rest (day) Alt, Anchor, Avocation, Balance, Bed, Beulah, Break, Breather, Calm, Catnap, Cetera, Comma, Depend, Dwell, Ease, Easel, Etc, Fermata, Feutre, Fewter, Gite, Half-time, Halt, Inaction, Jigger, Lave, Lean, Lie, Lie-in, Light, Lodge, Loll, Lound, Lyte, Nap, Nooning, Others, Overlie, Pause, Quiescence, Quiet, Relache, Relax, Rely, Remainder, Repose, Requiem, Residue, Respite, Sabbath, Siesta, > **SLEEP**, Slide, Sloom, Slumber, Spell, Spider, Stopover, Support, Surplus, Time out, Y-level

Re-start Da capo

Restaurant, Restaurateur Automat, Beanery, Bistro, Brasserie, British, Cabaret, Cafe, Canteen, Chew'n'spew, Chip-shop, Chophouse, Commissary, Cook shop, Creperie, Diner, Eatery, Eating-house, Estaminet, Greasy spoon, Grill, Grillroom, Grub shop, Luncheonette, Maxim's, Noshery, Padrone, Rathskeller, Ratskeller, Roadhouse, Rotisserie, Slap-bang, Steakhouse, Takeaway, Taqueria, Taverna, Teahouse, Tearoom, Teashop, Trattoria

Rest-home Aggie, Hospice

Resting-place Bed, Couch, Dharmsala, Gite, Grave, Inn, Khan, Serai, She'ol, Stage

Restitute, Restitution Amends, Apocatastasis, Reparation, Restore, Return

Restive, Restless(ness) Chafing, Chorea, Fikish, Free-arm, Itchy, Jactitation, Toey, Unsettled

▷ **Restless** *may indicate* an anagram

Restoration, Restorative, Restore(d) Cure, Descramble, Heal, Mend, Pentimento, Pick-me-up, Postliminy, Rally, Recondition, Redeem, Redintegrate, Redux, Refurbish, Regenerate, Rehabilitate, Rejuvenate, Remedial, Renew, Renovate, Repone, Restitute, Resuscitate, Retouch, Revamp, Revive, Stet, Tonic

Restrain(ed), Restraint Abstinence, Ban, Bate, Bit, Bottle, Branks, Bridle, Cage, Chain, Chasten, > CHECK, Cohibit, Compesce, Confinement, Contain, Control, Cramp, Curb, Dam, Decorum, Detent, Dry, Duress, Embargo, Enfetter, Estoppel, Freeze, Halt, Hamshackle, Handcuffs, Harness, Heft, Hinder, Hopple, Impound, Inhibit, Jess, Lid, Low-key, Manacle, Measure, Mince, Moderation, Muzzle, Quiet, Rein, Repress, Restrict, Ritenuto, Shackle, Sober, Sobriety, Squeeze, Stay, Stent, Stint, Straitjacket, Temper, Tether, Tie, Trash

Restrict(ed), Restriction Band, Bar, Bind, Bit, Burden, Cage, Catch, Censorship, Chain, Circumscribe, Closet, Condition, Cord, Corset, Cramp, Curb, DORA, Fence, Fold, Gate, Ground, Guard, Hamper, Hidebound, Hobble, Inhibit, Intern, Kennel, Let, > LIMIT, Lock, Mere, Narrow, Net, Nick, Pale, Parochial, Pen, Pent, Pier, Pin, Pot-bound, Private, Proscribed, Qualify, Regulate, Rein, Rope, Safety belt, Scant, Seal, Section, Selected, Shackle, Snare, Squeeze, Stenopaic, Stent, Stint, Stop, Straiten, Stunt, Tether, Tie

Restructure, Restructuring Perestroika

Result(s) Aftermath, Ans(wer), Bring, Causal, Consequence, Effect, Emanate, End, Ensue, Entail, Event, Eventuate, Finding, Fruict, Fruits, Issue, Karmic, Knock-on, Lattermath, > OUTCOME, Outturn, Pan, Proceeds, Quotient, Sequel, Side-effect, Sum, Upshot, Wale

Resume, Résumé Continue, Pirlicue, Purlicue, Summary

Resurrect(ion) Anabiosis, Rebirth, Revive, Zomb(ie)

Resuscitate(d), Resuscitation Mouth-to-mouth, Quicken, Redivivus, Restore, Revive

Retail(er) Chandler, Dealer, > NARRATE, Sell, Shopkeeper, Tell

Retain(er), Retains Brief, Contain, Deposit, Fee, Hold, Hold-all, Keep, Panter, Pantler, Reserve, Retinue, Servant

Retaliate, Retaliation Avenge, Counter, Lex talionis, Quid pro quo, Quit(e), Redress, Repay, Reprisal, Requite, Retort, Talion

Retard(ed) Arrest, Brake, Cretin, Encumber, Hinder, Slow

Retch Boak, Bock, Boke, Cowk, Gap, Heave, Keck, Reach, Vomit

Reticence, Reticent Clam, Coy, Dark, Reserve, Restraint, Secretive, Shy, Taciturn

Reticule, Reticulum Bag, Carryall, Dragnet, Lattice, Net

Retina Detached, Fovea, Macula lutea

Retinue Company, Cortège, Equipage, Following, Meiney, Meinie, Meiny, Sowarry, Suite

Retire(d), Retiree, Retirement, Retiring Abed, Aloof, Baccare, Backare, Backpedal, Blate, Bowler-hat, Cede, Coy, Depart, Ebb, Emeritus, Essene, Former, Leave, Lonely, Modest, Mothball, Nun, Outgoing, Pension, Perfing, Private, Quit, Recede, Recluse, Reserved, Resign, Retract, Retread, Retreat, Retrocedent, Roost, Rusticate, Scratch, Shy, Superannuate, Unassertive,

Withdraw

▷ **Retirement** *may indicate* 'bed' around another word, or word reversed

Retort Alembic, Comeback, Courteous, Quip, Repartee, > REPLY, Retaliate, Riposte, Still, Tu quoque

Retract(ion) Backpedal, Backtrack, Disavow, Epanorthosis, Palinode, Recall, Recant, Renounce, Revoke

Retreat Abbey, Arbour, Ashram(a), Asylum, Backpedal, Backwater, Bower, Bug, Camp David, Cell, Cloister, Convent, Crawfish, Dacha, Departure, Donjon, Girth, Grith, Hermitage, Hideaway, Hide-out, Hole, Interstadial, Ivory-tower, Katabasis, Lair, Lama(sery), Mew, Monastery, Nest, Neuk, Nook, Recede, Recoil, Recu(i)le, Redoubt, Reduit, Refuge, Retire, Retraite, Right-about, Rout, Shelter, Skedaddle, Stronghold, Withdraw

Retribution Come-uppance, Deserts, Nemesis, Revenge, Reward, Utu, Vengeance

Retrieve(r), Retrieval Access, Bird-dog, Field, Gundog, Labrador, Read-out, Recall, Recoup, Recover, Redeem, Rescue, Salvage

Retroflex Cacuminal

Retrograde Backward, Deasi(u)l, Deasoil, Decadent, Decline, Hindward, Rearward, Regrede

Retrospect(ive) Contemplative, Ex post facto, Hindsight, Regardant

Return(s) Agen, Bricole, Census, Comeback, Day, Diminishing, Dividend, Elect, Er, Extradite, Gain, Pay, Proceeds, Profit, Rebate, Rebound, Recur, Redound, Regress, Reject, Render, Rent, Repay, Replace, Reply, Requital, Respond, Restitution, Restore, Retour, Revenue, Reverse, Revert, Riposte, Takings, Tax, Traffic, > YIELD

Rev Gun, Minister

Reveal(ing), Revelation Advertise, Air, Apocalyptic, Bare, Betray, Bewray, Confess, Descry, Disclose, Discover, Discure, > DIVULGE, Epiphany, Exhibit, Explain, Expose, Giveaway, Hierophantic, Impart, Indicate, Ingo, Kythe, Leak, Let on, Manifest, Open, Satori, > SHOW, Spill, Tell-tale, Unclose, Uncover, Unfold, Unheal, Unmask, Unveil

Revel(ling), Revelry Ariot, Bacchanalia, Bend, Carnival, Carouse, Comus, Dionysian, Feast, Gloat, Glory, Joy, Merriment, Orgy, Rant, Rejoice, Riot, Roister, Rollicks, Rout, Saturnalia, Splore, Swig, Upsee, Ups(e)y, Wallow, Wassail, Whoopee

Reveller Bacchant, Birler, Corybant, Guisard, Guiser, Maenad, Merrymaker, Orgiast, Silenus

Revenant Fetch, Ghost, Spectre

Revenge(ful) Aftergame, Avenge, Commination, Goel, Grenville, Montezuma's, Reprise, Requite, Retaliation, Revanche, Ultion, Utu, Vindictive

Revenue Capital, Finance, Fisc(al), Fisk, Income, Inland, Internal, Jag(h)ir, Jaghire, Prebend, Primitiae, Rent, Taille, Tax, Turnover, Zamindar, Zemindar

Reverberate Echo, Recoil, Reflect, Repercuss, Resound

Revere(nce) Admire, Awe, Bostonian, Dread, Dulia, Esteem, Hallow, Hery, Homage, > HONOUR, Hyperdulia, Latria, Obeisance, Paul, Respect, Venerate

Reverie Daydream, Dream(iness), Fantasy, Memento

Revers Lap(p)el

Reversal, Reverse, Reversing, Reversion Antithesis, Antonym, Arsy-versy, Atavism, Back(slide), Change-over, Chiasmus, Commutate, Counter(mand), Escheat, Evaginate, Exergue, Flip, Inversion, Misfortune, > OPPOSITE, Overturn, Palindrome, Pile, Regress, Revoke, Rheotropic, Switchback, Tails, Throwback, Transit, Turn, Un-, Undo, U-turn, Verso, Vice versa, Volte-face

Revert Annul, Backslide, Regress, Relapse, Resort, Retrogress, Return
Review(er) Appeal, Censor, Critic, Critique, Editor, Encomium, Feuilleton, Footlights, Inspect, Judicial, Magazine, March-past, Notice, Pan, Recapitulate, Repeat, Revise, Rundown, Spithead, Summary, Survey, Write-up
▷ **Review** *may indicate* an anagram or a reversed word
Revile, Reviling Abuse, Execrate, Inveigh, Rail, Rayle, Vilify, Vituperate
Revise(r), Revision Alter, Amend, Correct, Diaskeuast, Edit, Peruse, Reappraise, Reassess, Recense, Reform, Rev, Update
▷ **Revise(d)** *may indicate* an anagram
Revival, Revive, Revivify, Reviving Araise, Enliven, Gothic, Greek, Rake up, Rally, Reanimate, Reawake(n), Rebirth, Redintegrate, Refresh, Rekindle, Renaissance, Renascent, Renew, Renovate, Restore, Resurrect, Resuscitate, Risorgimento, Romantic, Rouse, Wake
Revoke Abrogate, Cancel, Countermand, Negate, > **RECALL**, Repeal, Rescind
Revolt(ing), Revolution(ary) Agitator, Agitprop, American, Anarchist, Apostasy, Appal, Bloodless, Bolivar, Bolshevik, Bolshevist, Boxer, Bulldog, Cade, Castro, Chartist, Che, Chinese, Circle, Commune, Coup d'etat, Cultural, Cycle, Danton, Dervish, Disgust, Emeute, Emmet, Engels, Enrage, February, Fenian, Foul, French, Girondin, Girondist, Glorious, Green, Grody, Guevara, Gyration, Industrial, Inqilab, > **IN REVOLT**, Insurgent, Insurrection, Intifada, IRA, Jacobin, Jacquerie, Komitaji, Lap, Lenin, Marat, Marx, Maximalist, Maypole, Minimalist, Montagnard, Mountain, Mutiny, Nauseating, Nihilist, Orbit, Outbreak, Palace, Paris commune, Peasants, Poujadist, Putsch, Radical, > **REBEL(LION)**, Red, Red Shirt, Reformation, Riot, Rise, Robespierre, Roll, Rotation, Round, Run, Russian, Sandinista, Sansculotte(rie), Sedition, Sicilian vespers, Spartacus, Syndicalism, Thermidor, Trot(sky), Twist, Up(rise), > **UPRISING**, Velvet, Villa, Wat Tyler, Weatherman, Whirl, Wolfe Tone, Young Turk, Zapata
▷ **Revolutionary** *may indicate* 'reversed'
Revolve(r), Revolving Carrier, Catherine wheel, Centrifuge, Colt®, Gat, Girandole, Grindstone, > **GUN**, Gyrate, Iron, Klinostat, Lathe, Maelstrom, Peristrephic, Pistol, Pivot, Roller, Rotate, Rotifer, Rotor, Roundabout, Run, Six-shooter, Tone, Turn(stile), Turntable, Turret, Wheel, Whirl(igig), Whirlpool
Revue Follies
Reward Albricias, Bonus, Bounty, Compensate, Consideration, Desert, Emolument, Fee, Guerdon, Head money, Medal, Meed, Payment, Premium, Price, Prize, Profit, Purse, Recompense, Reguerdon, Remuneration, Requital, Requite, S, Shilling, Tribute, Wage, War(r)ison
Reword Edit, Paraphrase
Reworking Rifacimento
Rex Priam, R
Reynolds Joshua, PRA
Rhapsodic, Rhapsody Ecstasy, Epic, Music, Unconnected
Rhea Em(e)u, Nandoo, Nandu, Ostrich
Rhenium Re
Rhesus Bandar, Macaque, Monkey
Rhetoric(al) Anaphora, Apophasis, Aureate, Bombast, Chiasmus, Ecbole, Eloquence, Enantiosis, Epistrophe, Erotema, Eroteme, Erotesis, Euphemism, Hendiadys, Hypallage, Hyperbole, Oratory, Paral(e)ipsis, Peroration, Platform, Pleonasm, Syllepsis, Synoeciosis, Trivium
Rhino Blunt, Bread, Cash, Lolly, Loot, > **MONEY**, Tin
Rhinoceros Baluchitherium, Keitloa, Square-lipped, White

Rhodes, Rhodesia(n) Cecil, Colossus, Ridgeback, Scholar, Zimbabwe
Rhodium Rh
Rhubarb Pie-plant, Rhapontic, Rheum, Rot, Spat
Rhyme(s), Rhymer, Rhyming Assonance, Clerihew, Closed couplet, Couplet, Crambo, Cynghanedd, Doggerel, Eye, Feminine, Head, Identical, Internal, Male, Masculine, Measure, Near, Nursery, Pararhyme, Perfect, Poetry, Rich, Riding, Rime riche, Rondel, Royal, Runic, Sight, Slang, Slant, Tail(ed), Tercet, Terza-rima, Thomas, Triple, > VERSE, Virelay, Vowel
Rhythm(ic) Agoge, Alpha, Asynartete, Backbeat, Beat, Beta, Bo Diddley beat, Breakbeat, Cadence, Circadian, Duple, Hemiol(i)a, In-step, Meter, Movement, Oompah, Pulse, Pyrrhic, Rove-over, Rubato, Scotch catch, Scotch snap, Sdrucciola, Singsong, Sprung, Swing, Syncopation, Tala, Talea, > TEMPO, Time, Voltinism
Rib(bed), Ribbing, Rib-joint Bar, Chaff, Chiack, Chip, Chyack, Cod, Costa, Cross-springer, Dutch, Eve, False, Fin, Floating, Futtock, Groin, Intercostal, Lierne, Nervate, Nervular, Nervure, Ogive, Persiflage, Rack, Rag, Rally, Short, Spare, Springer, Subcosta, Taunt, Tease, Tierceron, Tracery, True, Wife
Ribald(ry) Balderdash, Bawdy, Coarse, Scurrilous, Smut, Sotadic, Vulgar
Ribbon Band, Bandeau, Blue, Bow, Braid, Caddis, Caddyss, Cordon, Fattrels, Ferret, Fillet, Grosgrain, Hatband, Infula, Multistrike, Pad, Petersham, Radina, Rein, Soutache, Taenia, Tape, Teniate, Tie, Torsade, Yellow
Ribless Ecostate
Rice Arborio, Basmati, Bir(i)yani, Brown, Canada, Carnaroti, Elmer, Entertainer, Indian, Kedgeree, Miracle, Paddy, Patna, Pilaf, Pilau, Pilaw, Pillau, Reis, Risotto, Spanish, Sushi, Twigs, Water, Wild
Rich(es) Abounding, Abundant, Affluent, Amusing, Bonanza, Comic, Copious, Croesus, Dives, Edmund, Edwin, Fat, Feast, Fertile, Flush, Fruity, Full, Golconda, Haves, Heeled, High, Larney, Loaded, Lush, Luxurious, Mammon, Moneybags, Moneyed, Nabob, Oberous, > OPULENT, Plenteous, Plush, Plutocrat, Resonant, Rolling, Sumptuous, Toff, Vulgarian, > WEALTHY, Well-heeled, Well-to-do
Richard Angevin, Burbage, Dick(y), Lionheart, Rick, Roe
Richthofen Red Baron
Rick (burning) Goaf, Sprain, Swingism, Wrench
Rickets, Rickety Dilapidated, Rachitis, Ramshackle, Shaky, Unsound
▷ **Rickety** *may indicate* an anagram
Rickshaw Pedicab, Tuktuk
Ricochet Boomerang, Glance, Rebound
Rid Clear, Deliver, Ditch, Eliminate, Eradicate, Expunge, Free, Obviate, Offload, Purge, Scrub, Shot
Riddle Boulter, Charade, Colander, Dilemma, Enigma, Koan, Logogriph, Pepper, Perforate, Permeate, Puzzle, Screen, Searce, Search, Sieve, Sift, Siler, Sorites, Strain, Tems(e), Trommel
Ride, Riding Annoy, Aquaplane, Bareback, Bestride, Big dipper, Bruise, Canter, Coast, Crog(gy), Cycle, District, Division, Drive, Equitation, Field, Hack, Harass, Haute école, Hitchhike, Merry-go-round, Mount, Pick(-a-)back, Pickpack, Piggyback, Postil(l)ion, Rape, Revere's, Roadstead, Rollercoaster, Sit, Spin, Stang, Switchback, Third, Trot, Weather, Welter, Wheelie, Whip, White-knuckle
Rider(s) Addendum, Adjunct, Appendage, Attachment, Boundary, Cavalier, Charioteer, Circuit, Codicil, Condition, Corollary, Dispatch, Equestrian, Eventer, Freedom, Gaucho, Godiva, Guidon, Haggard, Horseman, Jockey,

Lochinvar, Messenger, Peloton, Postil(l)ion, Proviso, PS, Revere, Spurrer, Walkyrie

Ridge Alveolar, Anthelix, Antihelix, Arete, Arris, As(ar), Balk, Bank, Baulk, Berm, Bur(r), Carina, Chine, Clint, Costa, Crease, Crest, Crista, Cuesta, Darling Range, Drill, Drum(lin), Dune, Esker, Fret, Gonys, Gyrus, Hammock, Hoe, Hogback, Horst, Hummock, Interfluve, Keel, Knur(l), Ledge, Linch, Lynchet, Mid-Atlantic, Mid-ocean, Missionary, Nek, Nut, Oceanic, Pressure, Promontory, Ramp, Rand, Raphe, Razor-back, Reef, Rib, Rig, Rim, Sastruga, Screw-thread, Serac, Serpentine, Shoulder, Sowback, Torus, Varix, Verumontanum, Vimy, Wale, Weal, Whelp, Whorl, Windrow, Withers, Wrinkle, Yardang, Zastruga

Ridicule, **Ridiculous** Absurd, Badinage, Bathos, Chaff, Cockamamie, Deride, Derisory, Egregous, Foolish, Gibbet, Gibe, Gird, Guy, Haze, Jibe, Josh, Laughable, Ludicrous, Mimic, Mock, Paradox, Pasquin, Pillory, Pish, Pooh-pooh, Raillery, Rich, Roast, Satire, Scoff, Scout, Screwy, Sight, Silly, Skimmington, Taunt, Travesty

Ridinghood Nithsdale, Red

Riding-master RM

Riding-school Manège

Rife Abundant, Manifest, Numerous, Prevalent

Riffle Rapid

Riff-raff Canaille, Hoi polloi, Mob, Populace, Rag-tag, Scaff, Scum, Trash

Rifle Air, Armalite®, Bone, Browning, Bundook, Burgle, Calic, Carbine, Chassepot, Enfield, Enfield musket, Express, Garand, > **GUN**, Kalashnikov, Lee Enfield, Loot, Martini®, Martini-Henry, Mauser®, MI, Minié, Pea, Petronel, Pilfer, Ransack, Remington, Repeater, Rob, Ruger, Shiloh, Springfield, Winchester®

Rift Altercation, Chasm, Crevasse, Fault, Fissure, Gap, Gulf, Split

Rig(ging) Accoutre, Attire, Bermuda, Drilling, Equip, Feer, Gaff, Get-up, Gunter, Hoax, Jack-up, Mainbrace, Manipulate, Marconi, Martingale, Oil, Outfit, Panoply, Ratline, Ropes, Schooner, Semisubmersible, Slant, Sport, Stack, Standing, Strip, Swindle, Tackle, Trull, Wanton

▷ **Rigged** *may indicate* an anagram

Right(en), **Rightness**, **Rights** Accurate, Advowson, Ancient lights, Angary, Appropriate, Appurtenance, Befit, Blue-pencil, BNP, Bote, Cabotage, Champart, Civil, Claim, Competence, Conjugal, Conservative, Copyhold, > **CORRECT**, Cor(r)ody, Coshery, Cure, Curtesy, Customer, De jure, Dexter, Direct, Divine, Doctor, Droit, Due, Easement, Eminent domain, Emphyteusis, Equity, Esnecy, Estover, Ethical, Exactly, Faldage, Farren, Fascist, Feu, Fire-bote, Fitting, Forestage, Franchise, Free-bench, Freedom, Gay, Germane, Gunter, Haybote, Hedge-bote, Human, Infangthief, Interest, Isonomy, Iure, Junior, Jural, Jus, Leet, Legit, Letters patent, Liberty, Lien, Maritage, Meet, Miner's, Moral, Naam, New, Ninepence, Off, Offhand, Offside, OK, Okay, Oke, Okey-dokey, Option, Ortho-, Oughtness, Paine, Passant, Pat, Patent, Performing, Ploughbote, Pose, Postliminy, Prerogative, Primogeniture, Priority, Prisage, Privilege, Proper, Property, Pukka, R, Rain, Reason, Recourse, Rectify, Rectitude, Redress, Remainder, Remedy, Repair, Rt, Sac, Sake, Side, So, Soc, Squatter's, Stage, Starboard, Stillicide, Tao, Tenants', Terce, Ticket, Title, Trivet, True, Turbary, User, Usucap(t)ion, Usufruct, Venville, Vert, Warren, Womens'

Right-angle(d) Orthogonal

Righteous(ness) Devout, Good, Just, Moral, Pharisee, Prig, Rectitude,

Sanctimonious, Tzaddik, Virtuous

Right-hand Dexter, E, Far, Recto, RH, Ro

Right-winger Falangist, Neo-fascist

Rigid(ity) Acierated, Catalepsy, Craton, Extreme, Fixed, Formal, Hard and fast, Hard-set, Hard-shell, Hidebound, Inflexible, Renitent, Rigor, Set, Slavish, Starch(y), Stern, Stiff, Stretchless, Strict, Stringent, Tense, Turgor

Rigmarole Nonsense, Palaver, Paraphernalia, Protocol, Ragman, Ragment, Riddlemeree, Screed

Rigorous, Rigour Accurate, Austere, Cruel, Exact, Firm, Hard, Inclement, Iron-bound, Stern, Strait, Strict, Stringent

Rile Anger, Annoy, Harry, Irritate, > **NETTLE**, Vex

▷ **Rile(y)** *may indicate* an anagram

Rill Purl, Sike

Rim Atlantic, Border, Chimb, Chime, Edge, Felloe, Felly, Flange, Kelyphitic, > **LIP**, Margin, Pacific, Strake, Verge

Rime Crust, Frost, Hoar, Rhyme, Rhythm

Rind Bark, Peel, Skin

Ring(ed), Ringer, Ringing, Rings Anchor, Angelus, Annual, Annulus, Anthelion, Arcus, Arena, Band, Bangle, Bell, Broch, Brogh, Call, Cambridge, Carabiner, Cartel, Cartouche, Change, Chime, Circinate, Circle, Circlet, Circlip, Circus, Claddagh, Clam, Clang, Clink, Coil, Collet, Cordon, Corona, Corral, Corrida, Crawl, Cricoid, Cringle, Cromlech, Cycle, Cyclic, Dead, Death's head, Dial, Dicyclic, Ding, Disc, Dohyo, Dong, D(o)uar, Draupnir, Echo, Encircle, Encompass, Engagement, Enhalo, Enlace, Environ, Enzone, Eternity, Extension, Eyelet, Fainne, Fairlead(er), Fairy, Ferrule, Fisherman, Fistic(uffs), Gas, Gimmal, Gird(le), Girr, Gloriole, Groin, Grom(m)et, Growth, Grummet, Guard, Gyges, Gymmal, Gyre, Halo, Hob, > **HOOP**, Hoop-la, Hula-hoop, Ideal, Inner, Inorb, Involucre, Jougs, Jow, Karabiner, Kartell, Keeper, Key, Knell, Knock-out, Kraal, Lifebelt, Link, Loop, Luned, Lute, Magpie, Manacle, Manilla, Marquise, Mourning, Napkin, Newton's, Nibelung, Nose, O, Orb, Outer, Pappus, Peal, Pele, Pen, Phone, Ping, Piston, Potato, Price, Prize, Puteal, Quoit, Resonant, Resound, Retaining, Round, Rove, Rundle, Runner, Scarf, Scrunchy, Seal, Signet, Slinger, Slip, Snap-link, Solomon, Sound, Spell, Split, Stemma, Stemme, Stonehenge, Surround, Swivel, Syndicate, Tang, Tattersall, Teething, Terret, Territ, Thimble, Timbre, Ting, Tingle, Tink, Tinnitius, Tintinnabulate, Toe, Token, Toll, Toplady, Tore, Torquate, Torques, Torret, Torus, Travelling, Tree, Trochus, Turret, Tweed, Varvel, Vervel, Vice, Vortex, Wagnerian, Washer, Wedding, Welkin, Withe, Woggle, Zero

Ring-dance Carol

Ring-leader Bell-wether, Fugleman, Instigator

Ringlet Curl(icue), Lock, Tendril, Tress

Ringmaster Wagner

Ringworm Serpigo, Tinea

Rinse Bathe, Blue, Cleanse, Douche, Sind, Sine, Swill, Synd, Syne, Tint, Wash

Riot(er), Riotous(ly), Riots Anarchy, Brawl, Clamour, Demo, Deray, Gordon, Hilarious, Hubbub, Luddite, Medley, Melee, Nicker, Orgy, Pandemonium, Peterloo, Petroleur, Porteous, Profusion, Quorum, Race, Rag, Rebecca, Rebel, Roaring, Roister, Rout, Rowdy, Ruction, Ruffianly, Scream, Swing, Tumult

▷ **Rioters, Riotous** *may indicate* an anagram

Rip(ping) Basket, Buller, Cur, Grand, Handful, Horse, Lacerate, Rent, Rep, Splendid, Tear, Tide, Topnotch, To-rend, Unseam

Ripe, Ripen(ing) Auspicious, Full, Mature, Mellow, Rathe, Ready

Riposte Repartee, Retaliate, Retort

Ripple Bradyseism, Fret, Overlap, Popple, Purl, Undulation, Wave, Wavelet, Wrinkle

▷ **Rippling** *may indicate* an anagram

Rise(r), Rising Advance, Appreciate, Ascend, Assurgent, Bull, Butte, Cause, Dutch, Easter, Eger, Elevation, Emerge, Emeute, Eminence, Erect, Escalate, Hance, Hauriant, Haurient, Heave, Heliacal, Hike, Hill, Hummock, Hunt's up, Improve, Increase, Insurgent, Intumesce, Jibe, Knap, Knoll, Lark, Levee, Levitate, Lift, Mount, Mutiny, Orient, Peripety, Prove, Putsch, Rear, Resurgent, Resurrection, > **REVOLT**, Saleratus, Scarp, Sklim, Soar, Stand, Stie, Sty, Surface, Surge, The Fifteen, Tor, Tower, Transcend, Up, Upbrast, Upburst, Upgo, Uprest, Upsurge, Upswarm, Upturn, Well

Risk(y) Actuarial, Adventure, Back, Calculated, Chance, Compromise, > **DANGER**, Daring, Dice, Dicy, Emprise, Endanger, Fear, Gamble, Game, Hairy, Hazard, Imperil, Jeopardy, Liability, Peril, Precarious, Security, Shoot the works, Spec, Touch and go, Touchy, Unsafe, Venture

Risorgimento Renaissance

Risqué Blue, Racy, Salty, Scabrous, Spicy

Rissole(s) Cecils, Croquette, Faggot, Quennelle, Veggieburger

Rite(s) Asperges, Bora, Ceremony, Exequies, Initiation, Liturgy, Nagmaal, Obsequies, Powwow, Ritual, Sacrament, Sarum use, Superstition, York

Ritual Agadah, Arti, Ceremony, Chanoyu, Customary, Formality, Haggada, Lavabo, Liturgy, Mumbo-jumbo, Puja, Rite, Sacring, Seder, Social, Use

Rival(ry), Rivals Absolute, Acres, Aemule, Binocular, Compete, Emulate, Emule, Envy, Fo(n)e, > **MATCH**, Needle, Opponent, Retinal, Touch, Vie

River Ea, Estuary, Flood, Flower, Fluvial, Potamic, R, Riverain, Runner, Stream, Tributary, Waterway

● **RIVERS**

2 letters:	Lot	Aras	Huon
Ob	Lys	Arno	Idle
Po	Nar	Aude	Isar
Xi	Ord	Avon	Iser
	Red	Back	Isis
3 letters:	San	Beni	Juba
Aar	Tay	Bomu	Kama
Aln	Tet	Dart	Kill
Axe	Ure	Deva	Kura
Ayr	Usk	Doon	Kwai
Bug	Wye	Dove	Lahn
Cam		Earn	Lech
Dee	**4 letters:**	Ebbw	Lena
Don	Abus	Ebro	Liao
Ems	Abzu	Eden	Lune
Esk	Acis	Eder	Maas
Exe	Adur	Elbe	Main
Fal	Aire	Erne	Meta
Fly	Alma	Esla	Milk
Han	Alph	Eure	Mino
Inn	Amur	Gila	Mole
Lee	Aran	Gota	Nene

Neva	Congo	Rhone	Crouch
Nile	Cross	Rogue	Cydnus
Nith	Dasht	Saône	Dalles
Oder	Desna	Seine	Danube
Ohio	Douro	Shari	Dawson
Oise	Drava	Shire	Donets
Ouse	Drave	Siret	Duddon
Oxus	Duero	Skien	Durack
Prut	Dvina	Slave	Finlay
Ruhr	Eblis	Snake	Fraser
Saar	Firth	Snowy	Gambia
Sava	Fleet	Somme	Ganges
Soar	Forth	Spree	Glomma
Spey	Gogra	Staff	Granta
Styx	Green	Stour	Hodder
Swan	Havel	Swale	Hudson
Swat	Indre	Tagus	Humber
Taff	Indus	Tamar	Iguacu
Tana	Isere	Tapti	Irtish
Tarn	James	Tarim	Irwell
Tees	Jumna	Teign	Itchen
Teme	Juruá	Terek	Japura
Test	Kasai	Tiber	Javari
Tyne	Kenga	Tisza	Javary
Uele	Kuban	Tobol	Jhelum
Ural	Lethe	Trent	Jordan
Vaal	Liard	Tweed	Kagera
Waal	Loire	Volga	Kennet
Wear	Marne	Volta	Kistna
Xero	Mbomu	Warta	Kolyma
Yalu	Meuse	Weser	Komati
Yare	Minho	Xiang	Liffey
Yate	Mosel	Xingu	Mamoré
Yser	Mulla	Yaqui	Medway
Yuan	Mures	Yarra	Mekong
Yuen	Namoi	Yssel	Mersey
	Negro	Yukon	Mohawk
5 letters:	Neman		Molopo
Abana	Niger	**6 letters:**	Morava
Acton	Ogowe	Amazon	Murray
Adige	Onega	Angara	Neckar
Afton	Oreti	Arzina	Neisse
Agate	Peace	Atbara	Nyeman
Aisne	Pearl	Barcoo	Ogooue
Aldan	Pecos	Barrow	Orange
Apure	Pelly	Bio-bio	Orwell
Argun	Piave	Calder	Ottawa
Avoca	Pison	Canton	Pahang
Boyne	Plate	Chenab	Parana
Cauca	Purus	Clutha	Peneus
Chari	Rance	Colima	Platte
Clyde	Rhine	Croton	Pripet

- Rakaia
- Ribble
- Riffle
- Rother
- Sabine
- Salado
- Sambre
- Santee
- Severn
- Struma
- Sutley
- Swanee
- Tanana
- Tarsus
- Teviot
- Thames
- Ticino
- Tigris
- Tugela
- Tyburn
- Ubangi
- Ussuri
- Vardar
- Vitava
- Wabash
- Wairau
- Wensum
- Wharfe
- Wupper
- Yarrow
- Yellow

7 letters:
- Acheron
- Aruwimi
- Berezua
- Bermejo
- Caqueta
- Cauvery
- Chagres
- Cocytus
- Damodar
- Darling
- Derwent
- Detroit
- Dnieper
- Dubglas
- Durance
- Ettrick
- Fitzroy
- Garonne
- Genesee

Gironde
Guapore
Helmand
Hooghly
Huang He
Hwangho
Iguassu
Irawadi
Kanawha
Krishna
Lachlan
Limpopo
Lualaba
Madeira
Manning
Maranon
Maritsa
Mataura
Meander
Moselle
Narbada
Narmada
Niagara
Orinoco
Orontes
Pechora
Pharpar
Potomac
Red Deer
Rubicon
Sabrina
Salinas
Salween
Salzach
Sanders
Scheldt
Senegal
Shannon
Songhua
St Croix
Swannee
Tapajos
Thomson
Ucayali
Uruguay
Vistula
Waikato
Washita
Welland
Yangtse
Yenisey
Zambesi

8 letters:
Amu Darya
Anderson
Apurimac
Araguaia
Araguaya
Blue Nile
Canadian
Cherwell
Chindwin
Clarence
Columbia
Daintree
Demerara
Dneister
Dordogne
Flinders
Franklin
Gascoyne
Godavari
Granicus
Guadiana
Klondike
Kootenay
Maeander
Mahanadi
Menderes
Missouri
Mitchell
Okanagan
Okavango
Okovango
Ouachita
Pactolus
Paraguay
Parnaiba
Putamayo
Rio Negro
Safid Rud
Saguenay
Suwannee
Syr Darya
Tonle Sap
Torridge
Toulouse
Tunguska
Victoria
Volturno
Wanganui
Windrush
Zhu Jiang

9 letters:
Ashburton
Billabong
Churchill
Crocodile
Euphrates
Irrawaddy
Kuskokwim
Mackenzie
Magdalena
Murchison
Parnahiba
Pilcomayo
Porcupine
Qu'Appelle
Rangitata
Richelieu
Rio Branco
Rio Grande
Salambria
Santa Cruz
White Nile
Wisconsin

10 letters:
Black Volta
Blackwater
Chao Phraya
Courantyne
Great Slave
Housatonic
Kizil Irmak
Phlegethon
Rangitaiki
Rangitikei
St Lawrence
White Volta
Yesil Irmak

11 letters:
Aegospotami
Assiniboine
Brahmaputra
Cooper Creek
Lesser Slave
Madre de Dios
Mississippi
Monongahela
Shatt-el-Arab
Susquehanna
Yellowstone

- **12 letters:** Sao Francisco **13 letters:** **17 letters:**
- Guadalquivir Saskatchewan Little Bighorn North
- Murrumbidgee Saskatchewan

River-bank, Riverside Brim, Carse, Riparian
River-bed Thalweg
River-mouth Firth, Frith
Rivet Bolt, Clinch, Clink, Concentrate, Explosive, Fasten, Fix, Pean, Peen, Stud, Transfix
Rivulet Beck, Brook, Burn, Gill, Rill, Runnel, Strand
RNA > DNA, Messenger, Riboromal, Ribosome, Ribozyme, Transcribe, Transfer, Uracil
Roach Fish, Red-eye
Road(s), Roadside, Road surface A, A1, Access, Anchorage, Arterial, Asphalt, Autobahn, Autopista, Autostrada, Ave(nue), B, Beltway, Boulevard, Burma, Carriageway, Causeway, Cloverleaf, Coach, Concession, Corduroy, Corniche, Course, Cul-de-sac, Dirt, Driveway, Escape, Exit, Expressway, Fairway, Feeder, Fly-over, Fly-under, Foss(e) Way, Freeway, Grid, Hampton, Highway, Horseway, Kerb, Lane, Loan, Loke, Mall, Metal, M1, Motorway, Orbital, Overpass, Parkway, Path, Pike, Post, Private, Rd, Relief, Ride, Ridgeway, Ring, > ROUTE, Royal, Service, Shoulder, Shunpike, Skid, Slip, Speedway, Spur(way), St(reet), Switchback, Tarmac, Tar-seal, Thoroughfare, Tobacco, Toby, Track(way), Trunk, Turning, Turnpike, Underpass, Unmade, Verge, Via, Way
Road-block Barrier, Cone, Jam, Toll
Road-keeper Way-warden
Road-maker Drunkard, Macadam, Navigator, Telford, Wade
Roam Extravagate, Peregrinate, Rake, Ramble, Rove, Stray, Wander, Wheel
Roan Barbary, Bay, Horse, Leather, Schimmel, Strawberry
Roar(ing) Bawl, Bell(ow), Bluster, Boom, Boys, Cry, Forties, Guffaw, Laugh, Roin, Rote, Rout, Royne, Thunder, Tumult, Vroom, Wuther, Zoom
Roast Bake, Barbecue, Baste, Birsle, Brent, Cabob, Cook, Crab, Crown, Decrepitate, Grill, Kabob, Pan, Ridicule, Scald, Scathe, Sear, Slate, Tan, Torrefy
Rob(bed), Robber(y) Abduct, Bandalero, Bandit, Barabbas, Bereave, Blag, Brigand, Burgle, Bust, Cabbage, Cacus, Cateran, Clyde, Dacoit, Dakoit, Daylight, Depredation, Despoil, Do, Drawlatch, Fake, Filch, Fleece, Flimp, Footpad, Gilderoy, Heist, Hership, Highjack, High toby, Highwayman, Hijack, Hold-up, Hustle, Job, Ladrone, Land-pirate, Larceny, Latrocinium, Latron, Loot, Mill, Mosstrooper, Pad, Pandoor, Pandour, Pillage, Pinch, Piracy, Pluck, Plunder, Procrustes, Rapine, Reave, Reft, Reive, Rieve, Rifle, Roberdsman, Robertsman, Roll, Rover, Roy, Rubbet, Rustler, Sack, Sciron, Screw, Short change, Sinis, Skinner, Smash and grab, Snaphaunch, Spoliation, > STEAL, Steaming, Stick-up, Sting, Swindle, Thief, Toby, Turn-over, Turpin
Robe(s) Alb, Amice, Amis, Attrap, Camis, Camus, Cassock, Chimer, Chrisom(-cloth), Christom, Dalmatic, Dolman, > DRESS, Gown, Ihram, Jilbab, Kanzu, Khalat, Khilat, Kill(a)ut, Kimono, Mantle, Parament, Parliament, Pedro, Peplos, Pontificals, Regalia, Rochet, Saccos, Sanbenito, Soutane, Sticharion, Stola, Stole, Talar, Tire, Vestment, Yukata
Robert Bob(by), Bridges, Browning, Burns, Cop, Flic, Peel, Rab, Rob
Robin Adair, American, Bird, Cock, Day, Goodfellow, Hob, Hood, Puck(-hairy), Ragged, Redbreast, Reliant, Round, Ruddock, Starveling, Wake
Robot Android, Automaton, Cyborg, Dalek, Golem, Nanobot, Puppet, RUR, Telechir

Robust Hale, Hardy, Healthy, Hearty, Iron, Lusty, Muscular, Sound, Stalwart, Sthenic, Stout, Strapping, Sturdy, Vigorous

Roc Bird, Ruc, Rukh

Rock(s), **Rocker**, **Rocking**, **Rocky** Acid, Ages, Agitate, Astound, Cap, Cock, Country, Cradle, Dogger, Edinburgh, Erathem, Erratic, Garage, Gib(raltar), Heavy metal, Hybrid, Mantle, Marciano, Matrix, Native, Nunatak(kr), Permafrost, Petrology, Platform, Plymouth, Punk, Quake, Reel, Reggae, Reservoir, Rip-rap, Rudaceous, Sally, Sedimentary, > SHAKE, Shoogle, Showd, Soft, Stonehenge, Stun, Sway, Swee, Swing, Ted, Teeter, Totter, Unstable, Unsteady, Wall, Weeping, Wind, Windsor

ROCKS

2 letters:	Krans	Oolith	Needles
Aa	Loess	Ophite	Olivine
	Magma	Pelite	Ophites
3 letters:	Nappe	Pluton	Outcrop
Gem	Scalp	Pumice	Outlier
Jow	Scree	Rognon	Peridot
Tor	Shale	Sarsen	Picrite
	Slate	Schist	Remanie
4 letters:	Solid	Sinter	Rhaetic
Bell	Stone	Skerry	Sinking
Crag	Trass	Sklate	Spilite
Gang	Uluru	S. Peter	Syenite
Glam	Wacke	Stonen	Thulite
Jura		Synroc	Tripoli
Lava	6 letters:	Tephra	Wenlock
Lías	Albite		
Noup	Aplite	7 letters:	8 letters:
Reef	Arkose	Aquifer	Adularia
Sill	Banket	Archean	Aegirine
Sima	Basalt	Arenite	Andesite
Trap	Dacite	Boulder	Aphanite
Tufa	Diapir	Breccia	Archaean
Tuff	Dunite	Clastic	Asbestos
Zoic	Flaser	Cuprite	Basanite
	Flysch	Cyanean	Brockram
5 letters:	Fossil	Diamond	Burstone
Ayers	Gabbro	Diorite	Calcrete
Brash	Gangue	Eucrite	Calc-tufa
Calpe	Garnet	Fastnet	Calc-tuff
Chair	Gibber	Felsite	Ciminite
Chalk	Gneiss	Geofact	Diabasic
Chert	Gossan	Granite	Dolerite
Cliff	Gozzan	Greisen	Dolomite
Craig	Inlier	Lignite	Eclogite
Elvan	Kingle	Lorelei	Eklogite
Emery	Marble	Marlite	Elvanite
Flint	Masada	Minette	Eutaxite
Geode	Norite	Molasse	Fahlband
Glass	Oolite	Moraine	Footwall

Ganister
Hepatite
Hornfels
Idocrase
Inchcape
Isocline
Laterite
Lenticle
Lopolith
Mesolite
Mudstone
Mylonite
Obsidian
Peperino
Petuntse
Phyllite
Pisolite
Plutonic
Porphyry
Psammite
Psephite
Ragstone
Regolith
Rhyolite
Rocaille
Roe-stone
Saxatile
Saxonite
Scorpion
Sunstone
Taconite
Tarpeian
Tephrite
The Olgas
Tonalite
Trachyte
Trappean
Volcanic
Xenolith

9 letters:
Anticline
Argillite
Batholite
Batholith
Bentonite

Bluestone
Buhrstone
Claystone
Cockhorse
Colluvium
Cornstone
Dalradian
Diatomite
Dolostone
Eddystone
Evaporite
Firestone
Flagstone
Flowstone
Gannister
Goslarite
Granulite
Greensand
Greystone
Greywacke
Hornstone
Impactite
Intrusion
Ironstone
Laccolite
Laccolith
Limestone
Meteorite
Mica-slate
Migmatite
Monadnock
Monocline
Monzonite
Mortstone
Mugearite
Natrolite
Neocomian
Ophiolite
Ottrelite
Pegmatite
Phonolite
Phosphate
Pleonaste
Propylite
Protogine
Quartzite

Sandstone
Saprolite
Scablands
Schistose
Siltstone
Soapstone
Tachylyte
Theralite
Tinguaite
Toadstone
Travertin
Underclay
Variolite
Ventifact
Vulcanite
Whinstone
Whunstane
Zechstein

10 letters:
Ailsa Craig
Amygdaloid
Camptonite
Epidiorite
Foundation
Granophyre
Greenstone
Grey-wether
Hypabyssal
Ignimbrite
Kersantite
Kimberlite
Lherzolite
Limburgite
Mica-schist
Novaculite
Orthophyre
Palagonite
Peridotite
Phenocryst
Pitchstone
Pyroxenite
Rupestrian
Schalstein
Serpentine
Sparagmite

Stinkstone
Stonebrash
Syntagmata
Teschenite
Touchstone
Travertine
Troctolite

11 letters:
Agglomerate
Amphibolite
Annabergite
Anorthosite
Carbonatite
Geanticline
Halleflinta
Lamprophyre
Monchiquite
Napoleonite
Nephelinite
Phillipsite
Pyroclastic
Symplegades

12 letters:
Babingtonite
Baltic Shield
Granodiorite
Grossularite
Slickenslide
Stromatolite
Syntagmatite
Thunderstone

13 letters:
Hypersthenite

14 letters:
Roche moutonnée

18 letters:
Scandinavian
  Shield

Rock-boring Pholas
Rock-cress Arabis
Rocket Arugula, Booster, Capsule, Carpet, Congreve, Dame's, Delta, Drake,
  Dressing down, Dyer's, Engine, Eruca, Flare, Ion, Jato, London, Multistage,
  Onion, Posigrade, Reprimand, Reproof, Retro, Rockoon, Salad, SAM, Sea,

Skylark, Soar, Sonde, Sounding, Step, Stephenson, Take-off, Thruster, Tourbillion, Ullage, Upshoot, V1, Vernier, Von Braun, Wall, Warhead, Weld, Yellow, Zero stage

Rock-living Rupicoline, Saxatile, Saxicoline, Saxicolous

Rock-pipit Sea-lark

▷ **Rocky** *may indicate* an anagram

Rococo Baroque, Fancy, Ornate, Quaint

Rod(-shaped), Rodlike, Rods Aaron's, Baculiform, Bar, Barbel(l), Barre, Birch, Caduceus, Caim, Came, Can, Cane, Centre, Connecting, Control, Cue, Cuisenaire, Dipstick, Divining, Dowser, Drain, Ellwand, Fasces, Filler, Fin-ray, Firearm, Fisher, Fishing, Fly, Fuel, Gun, Handspike, Jacob's staff, Kame, King, Laver, Lightning, Linchpin, Lug, Moses, Napier's bones, Nervure, Newel, Notochord, Perch, Pin, Pistol, Piston, Pitman, Pointer, Pole, Pontie, Pontil, Ponty, Probang, Puntee, Punty, Raddle, Regulating, Rhabdoid, Rhabdus, Rood, Scollop, Shaft, Sounding, Spindle, Spit, Stadia, Stair, Stanchion, Staple, Stave, Stay-bolt, Stick, Strickle, Switch, Tension, Tie, Track, Triblet, Tringle, Trocar, Twig, Urochord, Ventifact, Verge, Virgate, Virgulate, Wand, Welding, Withe

Rod-bearer Lictor

Rode Raid

Rodent Acouchi, Acouchy, Ag(o)uti, Bandicoot, Bangsring, Banxring, Beaver, Biscacha, Bizcacha, Bobac, Bobak, Boomer, Capybara, Cavy, Chickaree, Chincha, Chinchilla, Chipmunk, Civet, Coypu, Cricetus, Dassie, Deer-mouse, Delundung, Dormouse, Fieldmouse, Gerbil(le), Glires, Glutton, Gnawer, Gopher, Groundhog, Guinea pig, Ham(p)ster, Hedgehog, Hog-rat, Hutia, Hyrax, Jerboa, Jird, Lemming, Marmot, Mole rat, Mouse, Murid, Mus, Musk-rat, Musquash, Ochotona, Ondatra, Paca, Porcupine, Potoroo, Rat, Ratel, Ratton, Renegade, Runagate, Sciurine, Sewellel, Shrew, S(o)uslik, Spermophile, Springhaas, Springhase, Squirrel, Taguan, Taira, Tuco-tuco, Tucu-tuco, Vermin, Viscacha, Vole, Woodchuck, Woodmouse

Roderick Random, Usher

Rodomontade Bluster, Boast, Bombast, Brag, Gas

Roe Avruga, Caviar(e), Coral, Fry, Melt, Milt(z), Pea, Raun, Rawn

Roger Ascham, Bacon, Jolly, OK, Rights

Rogue, Roguish(ness) Arch, Bounder, Charlatan, Chiseller, Drole, Dummerer, Elephant, Espiegle(rie), Ganef, Ganev, Ganof, Gonif, Gonof, Greek, Gypsy, Hedge-creeper, Hempy, Herries, Imp, Knave, Latin, Limmer, Monkey, Panurge, Picaresque, Picaroon, Pollard, Poniard, Rapparee, Ra(p)scal(l)ion, Riderhood, Savage, Scamp, Schellum, Schelm, Skellum, Sleeveen, Slip-string, Sly, Swindler, Varlet, Villain, Wrong'un

Roil Agitate, Annoy, Churn, Provoke, Vex

Roister(er) Blister, Carouse, Ephesian, Revel, Rollick, Scourer, Scowrer, Swashbuckler, Swinge-buckler

Role Bit, Cameo, Capacity, Function, Metier, > **PART**, Prima-donna, Stead, Title, Travesty

Roll(ed), Roller, Roll-call, Rolling, Rolls Absence, Bagel, Bap, Barrel, Beigel, Billow, Bolt, Bridge, Brioche, Butterie, Calender, Cambridge, Chamade, Comber, Convolv(ut)e, Cop, Couch, Court, Croissant, Cylinder, Dandy, Drum, Dutch, Electoral, Enswathe, Eskimo, Even, Fardel, Fardle, Flatten, Forward, Furl, Go, Hotdog, Inker, Involute, Labour, List, Loaded, Lurch, Makimono, Mangle, Mano, Matricula, Motmot, Moving, Music, Muster, Notitia, Opulent, Paradiddle, Patent, Paupiette, Pay, Petit-pain, Piano, Pigeon, Pipe, Platen, Rafale, Ragman, Record, Reef, Reel, Register, Ren, Rent, Revolute, Revolve,

Rhotacism, Ring, Road, Rob, Rolag, Roster, Rota, Rotate, Rotifer, Roulade, Rouleau, RR, Rub-a-dub, Rumble, Run, Sausage, Schnecke(n), Skin up, Snap, Somersault, Spool, Spring, Sway, Swell, Swiss, Table, Tandem, Taxi, Temple, Tent, Terrier, Toilet, Tommy, Trill, Trindle, Trundle, Victory, Volume, Volutation, Wad, Wallow, Wamble, Waul, Wave, Wawl, Web, Welter, Western, Wince, Wrap

Rollick(ing) Frolic, Gambol, Romp, Sport

▷ **Rollicking** *may indicate* an anagram

Roly-poly Chubby

Roman Agricola, Agrippa, Calpurnia, Candle, Catholic, Cato, Consul, CR, Crassus, Decemviri, Decurion, Empire, Flavian, Galba, Holiday, Italian, Jebusite, Latin, Maecenas, Papist, Patrician, PR, Quirites, Raetic, RC, Retarius, Rhaetia, Road, Scipio, Seneca, Sulla, Tarquin, Tiberius, Type, Uriconian, Volsci

Romance, Romantic (talk) Affair, Amorous, Byronic, Casanova, Catalan, Dreamy, Fancy, Fantasise, Fib, Fiction, Gest(e), Gothic, Historical, Invention, Ladin(o), Ladinity, Langue d'oc(ian), Langue d'oil, Langue d'oui, Lie, Neo-Latin, Novelette, Poetic, Quixotic, R(o)uman, Stardust, Tale

▸ **Romanian** *see* RO(U)MANIAN

Romanov Nicholas

▸ **Romany** *see* GYPSY

Romeo Casanova, Montagu, Swain

Romp(ing) Carouse, Escapade, Fisgig, Fizgig, Frisk, Frolic, Hoyden, Randy, Rig, Sport, Spree

Ron Glum, Moody

Rondo Rota

Rontgen R, X-ray

Roo Joey

Roof (edge), Roofing Belfast, Bell, Ceil, Cl(e)ithral, Cover, Curb, Divot, Dome, Drip, Eaves, French, Gable, Gambrel, Hardtop, Hip(ped), Home, Imperial, Jerkin-head, Leads, Mansard, Monopitch, Palate, Pavilion, Pent, Pitched, Pop-top, Porte-cochère, Rigging, Saddle, Saddleback, Shingle, Skillion, Skirt, Span, Sun(shine), Tectiform, Tectum, Tegula, Thatch, Thetch, Tiling, Top, Uraniscus

Roof-climber Stegopholist

Roofless Hypaethral, Upaithric

Rook Bird, Castle, Cheat, Crow, Fleece, Fool, Overcharge, R, Swindle

Rookie Beginner, Colt, Galoot, Greenhorn, Nignog, Novice, Recruit, Tyro

Room(s), Roomy Antechamber, Anteroom, Apadana, Apartment, Assembly, Attic, Ben, Berth, Bibby, Boardroom, Boiler, Boudoir, Bower, But, Cabin(et), Camarilla, Camera, Capacity, Casemate, CC, Ceiling, Cell, Cellar, Cenacle, Chamber, Changing, Chat, Chaumer, Closet, Cockloft, Commodious, Compartment, Conclave, Consulting, Control, Cubicle, Cuddy, Cutting, Dark, Day, Delivery, Digs, Dissecting, Divan, Dojo, Drawing, Dressing, Durbar, Elbow, End, Engine, Ex(h)edra, Extension, Foyer, Gap, Garret, Genizah, Green, Grill, Gun, Herbarium, Incident, Kiva, Kursaal, Lab, Latitude, Laura, Lavra, Lebensraum, Leeway, Library, Living, Locker, Lodge, Loft, Loo, Lounge, Margin, Megaron, Misericord(e), Mould-loft, Music, Oda, Operations, Orderly, Oriel, Pad, Palm Court, Panic, Parlour, Parvis, Penetralia, Pentice, Pentise, Powder, Priesthole, Private, Projection, Property, Public, Pump, Reception, Recitation, Recovery, Recreation, Rest, Rm, Robing, Rumpus, Sacristy, Salle, Salon, Sanctum, Scope, Scriptorium, Scullery, Serdab, Servery, Shebang, Single, Single-end, Sitkamer, Smoking, Snug, Solar, Solarium, ﹥ SPACE, Spacious,

Spare, Spence, Spheristerion, Staff, Standing, Steam, Still, Stock, Stowage, Street, Strong, Studio, Study, Suite, Sun, Tap, Tea, Tiring, Tool, Twin, Ullage, Utility, Vestiary, Vestry, Voorkamer, Waiting, Ward, Wash, Wiggle, Work, Zeta

Roost(er) Cock, Perch, Siskin, Sit

Root(ing), Roots Beet, Buttress, Calumba, Cassava, Cheer, Contrayerva, Costus, Cube, Culver's, Dasheen, Delve, Deracinate, Derris, Dig, Eddo, Elacampane, Eradicate, Eringo, Eryngo, Etymic, Extirpate, Fibrous, Foundation, Gelseminine, Ginseng, Grass, Grout, Grub, Heritage, Horseradish, Hurrah, Implant, Irradicate, Jalap, Jicama, Lateral, Licorice, Mallee, Mandrake, Mangold, Mishmee, Mishmi, Mooli, More, Myall, Nousle, Nuzzle, Origins, Orris, Pachak, Pneumatophore, Poke, Prop, Pry, Putchock, Putchuk, Race, Radical, Radish, Radix, Repent, Rhatany, Rhizic, Rhizoid, Rhizome, Scorzonera, Senega, Sessile, Setwall, Snuzzle, Source, Square, Stock, Tap, Taro, Tuber, Tuberous, Tulip, Turbith, Turnip, Turpeth, Vetiver, Yam, Zedoary

Rootless Psilotum

Rope(s) Abaca, Backstay, Ba(u)lk, Becket, Bind, Bobstay, Boltrope, Brail, Breeching, Bunt-line, Cable, Cablet, Colt, Cord, Cordage, Cordon, Cringle, Downhaul, Drag, Earing, Fake, Fall, Flemish coil, Fore-brace, Foresheet, Forestay, Funicular, Futtock-shroud, Gantline, Grist, Guest, Guide, Guy, Halliard, Halser, Halter, Halyard, Hawser, Hawser-laid, Headfast, Inhaul, Jack-stay, Jeff, Jump, Kernmantel, Knittle, Ladder, Lanyard, Lasher, Lashing, Lasso, Line, Longe, Lunge, Mainbrace, Mainsheet, Manil(l)a, Marlin(e), Messenger, Monkey, Mooring, Nettle, Nip, Noose, Oakum, Outhaul, Painter, Parbuckle, Pastern, Prolonge, Prusik, Rawhide, Reef point, Riata, Roband, Robbin, Rode, Runner, Sally, Seal, Selvagee, Sennit, Sheet, Shroud, Sinnet, Span, Spancel, Spun-yarn, Stay, Sternfast, Stirrup, String, Sugan, Swifter, Tackle, Tail, Tether, Tie, Timenoguy, Tippet, Tow(line), Trace, Trail, Triatic, Triatic stay, Vang, Wanty, Warp, Widdy, Wire

Rosalind Ganymede

Rosary Beads, Mala, Paternoster

Rose(-red), Rosie, Rosy Albertine, Amelanchier, Aurorean, Avens, Bear's-foot, Blooming, Bourbon, Breare, Briar, Brier, Cabbage, Canker, Ceiling, Cherokee, China, Christmas, Compass, Corn, Damask, Dog, Eglantine, Eglatère, England, Floribunda, Geum, Golden, G(u)elder, Hellebore, Hybrid, Jack, Jacque, Jacqueminot, Lal(age), Lancaster, Lee, Moss, Multiflora, Musk, Noisette, Opulus, Peace, Petra, Pink, Potentilla, Promising, Provence, Province, Provincial, Provine, Pyrus, Quillaia, Quillaja, Rambler, Red(dish), Remontant, Rhodo-, Rock, Rugosa, Snowball, Sprinkler, Standard, Sweetbrier, Tea, Tokyo, Tudor, White, Whitethorn, York

Rose-apple Jamboo, Jambu

Rose-bay Oleander

Rosette Buttonhole, Chou, Cockade, Favour, Patera, Rosula

Rosin Colophony, Resin, Roset, Rosit, Rozet, Rozit

Rosinante Jade

Roster List, Register, Scroll, Table

Rostrum Ambo, Bema, Lectern, Podium, Pulpit, Tribune

Rot(ten), Rotting Addle, Baloney, Boo, Bosh, Botrytis, Bull, Caries, Carious, Corrode, Corrupt, Crown, Daddock, Decadent, > DECAY, Decompose, Decrepitude, Degradable, Dotage, Dry, Eat, Erode, Fester, Foot, Foul, Kibosh, Manky, Mildew, Noble, Nonsense, Poppycock, Poxy, Punk, Putid, Putrefy, Putrid, Rail, Rancid, Rank, Rat, Ret, Ring, Rust, Sapropel, Septic, Soft, Sour, Squish, Twaddle, Wet

Rotate, Rotating, Rotation, Rotator Feather, Gyrate, Lay-farming, Optical, Pivot, Pronate, Rabat(te), Reamer, Revolve, Roll, Selsyn, Trundle, Turn, Turntable, Twiddle, Vorticose, Wheel, Windmill

Rote Heart, Memory, Recite, Routine

Rotor Auxiliary, Flywheel, Impeller

▸ **Rotten** *see* **ROT**

▷ **Rotten** *may indicate* an anagram

Rotter Cad, Knave, Stinker, Swine

Rotund Chubby, Corpulent, Plump, Round, Stout

Rotunda Pantheon

Roué Debauchee, Decadent, Libertine, Profligate, Rake(-shame), Rip

Rouge Blush, Gild, Jeweller's, Raddle, Redden, Reddle, Ruddy

Rough(en), Roughly, Roughness About, Approximate, Asper(ate), Burr, C, Ca, Choppy, Circa, Coarse, Craggy, Crude, Exasperate, Frampler, Grained, Gross, Gruff, Gurly, Gusty, Hard, Harsh, Hispid, Hoodlum, Hooligan, Impolite, Imprecise, Incondite, Inexact, Irregular, Jagged, Karst, Keelie, Kokobeh, Muricate, Push, Ragged, Ramgunshoch, Raspy, Raucle, Rip, Risp, Robust, Row, Rude, Rugged, Rusticate, Rusty, Sandblast, Scabrid, Sea, Shaggy, Sketchy, Some, Spray, Spreathe, Squarrose, Stab, Strong-arm, Swab, Tartar, Tearaway, Ted, Textured, Uncut, Violent, Yahoo

Roughage Ballast, Bran, Fodder

Rough breathing Asper, Rale, Wheeze

Roughcast Harl

▷ **Roughly** *may indicate* an anagram

Roulette Russian

Ro(u)manian, Rumanian Ro, R(o)uman, Vlach, Wal(l)achian

Round(ness) About, Ammo, Ball, Beat, Bombe, Bout, Cartridge, Catch, Circle, Complete, Cycle, Dome, Doorstep, Figure, Full, Global, Globate, Hand, Jump-off, Lap, Leg, Milk, O, Oblate, Orb, Orbicular, Orbit, Ought, Patrol, Peri-, Pirouette, Plump, Qualifying, Quarter, Quarter-final, Rev, Ring, Robin, Roly-poly, Ronde, Rondure, Rota, Rotund, Route, Routine, Rundle, Rung, Salvo, Sandwich, Sarnie, Sellinger's, Semi-final, Shot, Skirt, Slice, Sphaer, Sphere, Spherical, Spiral, Step, Table, Tour, Tubby, U-turn

▷ **Round** *may indicate* a word reversed

Roundabout Ambages, Approximately, Bypass, Carousel, Circle, Circuit, Circumambient, Circumbendibus, Circus, Devious, Eddy, > **INDIRECT**, Merry-go-round, Peripheral, Rotary, Tortuous, Turntable, Waltzer, Whirligig

Round building Tholos, Tholus

Rounders Patball

Round-mouth Hag

Round-up Bang-tail muster, Collate, Corner, Corral, Gather, Herd, Rodeo, Spiral

Roup Auction, Croak, Pip, Roop

Rouse, Rousing Abrade, Abraid, Abray, Amo(o)ve, Animate, Beat, Bestir, Emotive, Enkindle, Firk, Flush, Hearten, Heat, Innate, Kindle, Rear, Send, Stimulate, Suscitate, Unbed, Waken, Whip

Rousseau Emile

Rout Clamour, Debacle, Defeat, Drub, Fleme, Flight, Hubbub, Hurricane, Rabble, Retreat, Rhonchal, Snore, Thiasus, Upsee, Upsey, Upsy, Vanquish, Whoobub

Route Avenue, Byroad, Causeway, Course, Direction, Itinerary, Line, Ling, Path, Red, Road, Stock, Track, Trade, Via, Way

Routine Automatic, Day-to-day, Drill, Everyday, Grind, Groove, Habitual,

Ho-hum, Jogtrot, Pattern, Perfunctory, Pipe-clay, Red tape, Rota, Rote, Round, Rut, S(c)htick, Schtik, Treadmill, Workaday

Rove(r), Roving Car, Discursive, Enrange, Errant, Gad, Globetrotter, Marauder, Nomad, Proler, Prowl, Ralph, Range, > ROAM, Slub(b), Stray, Vagabond, Varangarian, Viking, Wander

Row(er) Align, Altercation, Arew, Argue, Argument, Bank, Barney, Bedlam, Bobbery, Bow, Brattle, Cannery, Colonnade, Death, Debate, Deen, Din, Dispute, Dust-up, Feud, File, Fireworks, Food, Fyle, Hullabaloo, Line(-up), Noise, Note, Oar, Paddle, Parade, Peripteral, Pull, Quarrel, Rammy, Range, Rank, Raunge, Remigate Tone, Rew, Rhubarb, Rotten, Ruction, Rumpus, Scene, Scull, Series, Set, Shindig, Shindy, Shine, Skid, Spat, Splore, Stern, Street, Stridor, Stroke, Stushie, Sweep, Terrace, Tier, Tiff, Torpid, Wetbob, Wherryman

Rowan Ash, Quicken

Rowdy, Rowdiness Cougan, Hooligan, Loud, Noisy, Rorty, Rough, Roughhouse, Ruffian, Scourer, Scozza, Skinhead, Stroppy, Unruly, Uproarious

Roy Rob

Royal(ty), Royalist Academy, Angevin, Basilical, Battle, Bourbon, Emigré, Exchange, Fee, Hanoverian, Imperial, Imposing, Inca, Kingly, King's man, Majestic, Malignant, Palatine, Payment, Pharaoh, Plantagenet, Prince, Princess, Purple, Queenly, Regal, Regis, Regius, Regnal, Sail, Sceptred, Society

Rub(bing), Rubber(y), Rub out Abrade, Attrition, Balata, Buff, Buna®, Bungie, Bungy, Bunje(e), Bunjie, Bunjy, Butyl, Calk, Calque, Camelback, Caoutchouc, Chafe, Cold, Condom, Corrade, Corrode, Cow gum®, Crepe, Cul(t)ch, Destroy, Dunlop®, Ebonite, Efface, Elastic, Elastomer, Embrocate, Emery, Erase, Factice, Fawn, Foam, Fray, Fret, Friction, Fridge, Frottage, Fudge, Funtumia, Gall, Galoch, Goodyear®, Grate, Graze, Grind, Guayule, Gum elastic, Gutta-percha, Hale, Hard, Hevea, India, Inunction, Irritate, Isoprene, Jelutong, Lagos, Latex, Leather, Masseur, Negrohead, Neoprene, Nuzzle, Obstacle, Para, Polish, Pontianac, Pontianak, Root, Safe, Sandpaper, Scour, Scrub, Scuff, Seringa, Silastic®, Smoked, Sorbo®, Sponge, Stroke, Synthetic, Towel, Trace, Ule, Vulcanite, Wild, Wipe, Xerotripsis

▷ **Rubbed** *may indicate* an anagram

Rubbish Balls, Brack, Bull, Bunkum, Clap-trap, Cobblers, Debris, Dre(c)k, Drivel, Fiddlesticks, Garbage, Grot, Grunge, Hogwash, Kak, Landfill, Leavings, Litter, Mullock, Nonsense, Phooey, Raff, Raffle, > REFUSE, Stuff, Tinpot, Tip, Tom(fool), Tosh, Trade, Tripe, Trouch, Twaddle

Rubbish heap Dump, Lay-stall, Sweepings, Toom

Rubble Brash, Debris, Detritus, Moellon, Random, Remains, Riprap, Talus

Rubidium Rb

Ruby Agate, Balas, Brazilian, Colorado, Cuprite, Oriental, Pigeon's blood, Port, Red, Star

Ruck Furrow, Scrum, Wrinkle

Rucksack Backpack, Bergen, Pikau

Ruction Ado, Fuss, Quarrel

Rudder Budget, Helm, Steerer

Ruddle Lemnian

Ruddy Bally, Bloody, Flashy, Florid, Red, Roseate, Rubicund, Sanguine

Rude Abusive, Barbaric, Bestial, Bumpkin, Callow, Churlish, Coarse, Discourteous, Elemental, Goustrous, Green, Ill-bred, Impolite, Indecorous, Inficete, Ingram, Ingrum, Insolent, Ocker, Offensive, Peasant, Raw, Risque, Rough, Simple, Surly, Unbred, Uncomplimentary, Uncourtly, Unlettered, Unmannered, Vulgar

Rudiment(ary), Rudiments ABC, Absey, Anlage, Beginning, Element, Embryo, Foundation, Germ(en), Germinal, Inchoate, Seminal, Vestige

Rudolph Hess, Reindeer

Rue(ful) Boulevard, Dittany, Harmala, Harmel, Herb of grace, Mourn, Regret, Repent, Ruta, Sorry

Ruff Collar, Crest, Fraise, Frill, Partlet, Pope, Rabato, Rebato, Ree, Trump

Ruffian Apache, Bashi-bazouk, Brute, Bully, Cut-throat, Desperado, Goon(da), Highbinder, Hoodlum, Hooligan, Keelie, Larrikin, Lout, Miscreant, Mohock, Myrmidon, Phansigar, Plug-ugly, Raff, Rowdy, Skinhead, Sweater, Tearaway, Thug, Toe-ragger, Trailbaston, Tumbler

Ruffle(d) Bait, Dishevel, Falbala, Flounce, Fluster, Fret, > FRILL, Gather, Irritate, Jabot, Peplum, Rouse, Ruche, Rumple, Shirty, Tousle

▷ **Ruffle** *may indicate* an anagram

Rug Afghan, Bearskin, Carpet, Drugget, Ensi, Flokati, Gabbeh, Hearth, Herez, Heriz, Kelim, K(h)ilim, Kirman, Lap robe, Mat, Maud, Numdah, Oriental, Prayer, Runner, Rya, Scatter, Travelling

Rugby (player) Back, Fifteen, Forward, Harlequin, Lion, Pack, Quin, RU, Scrum, Sevens, Threequarter, Wing

Rugged Craggy, Harsh, Knaggy, Rough, Strong

Ruin(ed), Ruins Annihilate, Blast, Blight, Blue, Carcase, Collapse, Corrupt, Crash, Crock, Damn, Decay, Defeat, Demolish, Despoil, Destroy, Devastate, Disfigure, Dish, Disrepair, Dogs, Doom, Downcome, Downfall, End, Fordo, Hamstring, Heap, Hell, Insolvent, Inure, Kaput(t), Kibosh, Loss, Mar, Mocers, Mother's, Overthrow, Petra, Pot, Puckerood, Ravage, Reck, Relic, Scotch, Scupper, Scuttle, Shatter, Sink, Smash, Spill, > SPOIL, Stramash, Subvert, Undo, Unmade, Ur, Violate, Whelm, Woe, Wrack

▷ **Ruined** *may indicate* an anagram

Rule(r), Rules, Ruling Abbasid, Alexander, Algorithm, Align, Ameer, Amir, Archduke, Ardri(gh), Aristocrat, Arret, Article, Atabeg, Atabek, Autocrat, Bajayet, Bajazet, Ban, Bey, Bismarck, Bodicea, Bosman, Boudicca, Bretwalda, Britannia, Burgrave, Bylaw, Caesar, Caligula, Caliph, Calliper, Canon, Caractacus, Castro, Catapan, Caudillo, Chagan, Chain, Cham, Chandragupta, Charlemagne, Cheops, Chogyal, Cleopatra, Club-law, Code, Condominium, Constitution, Control, Cosmocrat, Criterion, Cromwell, Czar, Decree, Dergue, Despot, Dewan, Dey, Dictator, Diwan, Doge, Domineer, Dominion, Duce, Dynast, Elector, Emir, Emperor, Empire, Establishment, Estoppel, Ethnarch, Etiquette, Exarch, Fatwa, Feint, Fetwa, Fleming's, Formation, Formula, Franco, Fuhrer, Gaekwar, Gag, Gaikwar, Genghis Khan, Gerent, Global, Golden, Govern, Govern-all, Ground, Haile Selassie, Heptarch, Herod, Hespodar, Hierarch, Hitler, Home, Hoyle, Hyleg, Imam, Inca, Jackboot, Jamshid, Jamshyd, Judges, K, Kabaka, Kaiser, Khan, Khedive, King, Law, Leibniz's, Lesbian, Lex, Lindley, Liner, Maharaja, Majority, Mameluke, Manchu, Matriarchy, Maxim, McNa(u)ghten, Mede, Meteyard, Method, Mikado, Ministrate, Mir, Miranda, Mistress, Mogul, Monarch, Montezuma, Motto, Mpret, Mudir, Naismith's, Napoleon, Nawab, Negus, Nero, Netiquette, Nizam, Norm(a), Oba, Ochlocrat, Oligarch, Omayyad, Oppress, Ordinal, Overlord, Padishah, Parallel, Parallelogram, Pasha, Pendragon, Pericles, Peshwa, Pharaoh, Phase, Phrase-structure, Pie, Plantocrat, Plumb, Plutocrat, Podesta, Pope, Potentate, Precedent, Precept, Prescript, President, Prester John, Prevail, Prince, Principate, Principle, Protocol, Pye, Queen, Queensberry, R, Rafferty's, Raine, Raj(ah), Rajpramukh, Rana, Realm, Rector, Regal, Regent, Regula, Reign, Rewrite, Rex, Ring, Rubric, Sachem, Sagamore, Saladin, Sassanid,

Satrap, Scammozzi's, Serkali, Setting, Shah, Shaka, Sheik, Sherif, Shogun, Sirdar, Slide, Sophi, Sophy, Souldan, Sovereign, Squier, Squire, Stadtholder, Stalin, Standard, Statute, Stratocrat, Suleiman, Sultan, Sutra, Suzerain, Swaraj, Sway, Synarchy, Tamerlane, Ten-minute, Tenno, Ten-yard, Tetrarch, Thearchy, Three, Thumb, Toparch, Transformation(al), Trapezoid, Tsar, T-square, Tutankhamun, Tycoon, Tyrant, Umayyad, Vali, Viceroy, Wali, Wield, Zamorin

Rule-book Code, Pie, Pye

Rum(mer) Abnormal, Bacardi, Bay, Cachaca, Daiquiri, Demerara, Eerie, Eery, Glass, Grog, Island, Jamaica, Odd(er), Peculiar, Quaint, Queer, Screech, Strange, Tafia, Weird

▸ **Rumanian** see RO(U)MANIAN

Rumble, Rumbling Borborygmus, Brool, Curmurring, Drum-roll, Groan, Growl, Guess, Lumber, Mutter, Rumour, Thunder, Tonneau, Twig

Ruminant, Ruminate Antelope, Cabrie, Camel, Cavicornia, Champ, Chew, Contemplate, Cow, Gemsbok, Gnu, Goat, Meditate, Merycism, Nyala, Okapi, Pecora

Rummage Delve, Fish, Foray, Jumble, Powter, Ransack, Root, Rootle, Scavenge, Search, Tot

Rummy Canasta, Cooncan, Game, Gin, Queer

Rumour Breeze, Bruit, Buzz, Canard, Cry, Fame, Furphy, > GOSSIP, Grapevine, Hearsay, Kite, Kite-flying, Mail, Noise, On-dit, Pig's-whisper, Report, Repute, Say-so, Smear, Tale, Talk, Underbreath, Unfounded, Vine, Voice, Whisper, Word

Rump Arse, Bottom, Buttocks, Croup(e), Croupon, Crupper, Curpel, Derriere, Parliament, Podex, Pygal, Steak, Uropygium

Rumple Corrugate, Crease, Mess, Tousle, Wrinkle

Rumpus Commotion, Riot, Row, Ruction, Shindig, Shindy, Shine, Stushie, Tirrivee, Uproar

Run(ning), Run away, Run into, Run off, Runny, Runs Admin(ister), Arpeggio, Bleed, Bolt, Break, Bunk, Bye, Career, Chase, Coop, Corso, Course, Cresta, Cross-country, Current, Cursive, Cut, Dash, Decamp, Direct, Double, Drive, Dry, Dummy, Escape, Extra, Fartlek, Flee, Flit, Flow, Fly, Follow, Fun, Fuse, Gad, Gallop, Gauntlet, Go, Green, Ground, Hare, Haste(n), Hennery, Hie, · Home, Idle, Jog, Jump bail, Ladder, Lauf, Leg, Leg bye, Lienteric, Lope, Manage, Marathon, Melt, Milk, Mizzle, Mole, Molt, Neume, Now, On, On-line, Operate, Pace, Paper chase, Pelt, Ply, Pour, Print, Purulent, R, Race, Range, Red, Renne, Rin, Romp, Roulade, Rounder, Ruck, Scamper, Scapa, Scarper, Schuss, Scud, Scutter, Scuttle, See, Sequence, Shoot, Single, Skate, Skedaddle, Ski, Skid, Skirr, Skitter, Slalom, Slide, Smuggle, Spew, Split, Spread, Sprint, Sprue, Squitters, Stampede, Straight, Streak, Stream, Taxi, Tear, Tenor, Tie-breaker, Trial, Trickle, Trill, Trot

Runaway Drain, Easy, Escapee, Fugitive, Fugue, Refugee

Run down Asperse, Belie, Belittle, Calumniate, Denigrate, Derelict, Dilapidated, Infame, Knock, Low, Obsolesce(nt), Poorly, Rack, Résumé, Scud, Tirade, Traduce

Rune, Runic Ash, Futhark, Futhorc, Futhork, Kri, Ogham, Spell, Thorn, Wen, Wyn(n)

Rung Crossbar, Roundel, Rundle, Stave, Step, Tolled, Tread

Runner(s) Atalanta, Bean, Blade, Bow Street, Carpet, Coe, Courser, Deserter, Emu, Field, Geat, Gentleman, Gillie-wetfoot, Harrier, Hatta, Hencourt, Internuncio, Lampadist, Leg bye, Legman, Messenger, Miler, Milk, Mohr,

Mousetrap, Nurmi, Owler, Rug, > **RUN(NING)**, Sarmentum, Scarlet, Series, Slipe, Smuggler, Stolon, Stream, Trial

▷ **Running, Runny** *may indicate* an anagram

Runt Dilling, Oobit, Oubit, Reckling, Scalawag, Scrog, Smallest, Titman, Woobut, Woubit

Run through Impale, Pierce, Rehearsal

Runway Airstrip, Drive, Slipway, Strip, Tarmac®

Run wild Lamp, Rampage

Rupee(s) Lac, Lakh, Re

Rupert Bear

Rupture Breach, Burst, Crack, Hernia, Rend, Rhexis, Rift, Split

Rural Agrarian, Agrestic, Boo(h)ai, Boondocks, Bucolic, Country, Cracker-barrel, Forane, Georgic, Hick, Mofussil, Platteland, Praedial, Predial, Redneck, Rustic, Sticks, The Shires, Wops-wops

Ruse Artifice, Decoy, Dodge, Engine, Hoax, Pawk, Stratagem, > **TRICK**

Rush(ed) Accelerate, Barge, Bolt, Bustle, Career, Charge, Dart, Dash, Eriocaulon, Expedite, Faze, Feese, Feeze, Feze, Fly, Frail, Friar, Gad, Gold, Gust, Hare, Hasten, High-tail, > **HURRY**, Hurtle, Jet, Juncus, Lance, Lash, Leap, Luzula, Moses, Onset, Palmiet, Pellmell, Phase, Pheese, Pheeze, Phese, Plunge, Precipitate, Railroad, Rampa(u)ge, Rash, Rayle, Reed, Rip, Scamp(er), Scirpus, Scour, Scud, Scurry, Sedge, Spate, Speed, Stampede, Star(r), Streak, Streek, Surge, Swoop, Swoosh, Tear, Thrash, Thresh, Tilt, Torrent, Tule, Viretot, Zap, Zoom

Rusk Zwieback

Russell AE, Bertrand, Jack

Russet Rutile

Russia(n), Russian headman, Russian villagers Apparatchik, Ataman, Belorussian, Beria, Bolshevik, Boris, Boyar, Byelorussian, Chukchee, Chukchi, Circassian, Cossack, D(o)ukhobor, Dressing, Esth, Igor, Ingush, Ivan, Kabardian, Kalmuk, Kalmyck, Leather, Lett, Mari, Menshevik, Mingrel(ian), Minimalist, Mir, Muscovy, Octobrist, Osset(e), Red, Romanov, Rus, Russ(niak), Russki, Ruthene, Salad, Serge, Slav, Stakhanovite, SU, Thistle, Udmurt, Uzbeg, Uzbek, Vladimir, Vogul, White, Yakut, Yuri, Zyrian

Rust(y) Aeci(di)um, Blister, Brown, Corrode, Cor(ro)sive, Erode, Etch, Ferrugo, Iron oxide, Iron-stick, Maderise, Oxidise, Puccinia, Rubiginous, Soare, Stem, Teleutospore, Telium, Uredine, Uredo, Verdigris, Yellow

Rust-fungus Aecidiospore

Rustic Arcady, Bacon, Bor(r)el(l), Bucolic, Bumpkin, Chawbacon, Churl, Clodhopper, Clown, Corydon, Cracker-barrel, Culchie, Damon, Doric, Forest, Georgic, Hayseed, Hick, Hillbilly, Hind, Hob, Hobbinoll, Hodge, Homespun, Idyl(l), Pastorale, Peasant, Pr(a)edial, Put(t), Rube, Rural, Strephon, Swain, Sylvan, Villager, Villatic, Yokel

▷ **Rustic** *may indicate* an anagram

Rusticate Banish, Seclude

Rustle(r), Rustling Abactor, Crinkle, Duff, Fissle, Frou-frou, Gully-raker, Poach, Speagh(ery), Sprechery, Steal, Stir, Susurration, Swish, Thief, Whig

Rust-proof Zinced

Rut Channel, Furrow, Groove, Heat, Routine, Sulcus, Track

Ruth Babe, Compassion, Mercy, Pity, Remorse

Ruthenium Ru

Rutherfordium Rf

Ruthless Brutal, Cruel, Dog eat dog, Fell, Hard, Hardball, Hard-bitten

Rwanda(n) Tutsi
Rye Gentleman, Grain, Grass, Spelt, Whisky

Ss

S Ogee, Saint, Second, Sierra, Society, South, Square

SA It, Lure

Sabbatarian Wee Free

Sabbath Juma, Lord's Day, Rest-day, Shabbat, Sunday, Witches

Sabbatical Leave

Sabine Horace, Women

Sable American, Black, Jet, Negro, Pean, Zibel(l)ine

Sabotage, Saboteur Destroy, Frame-breaker, Ratten, Spoil, Treachery, Undermine, Vandalise, Wrecker

Sabre, Sabre rattler Jingo, Sword, Tulwar

Sabrina Severn

Sac Air, Allantois, Amnion, Aneurism, Aneurysm, Bag, Bladder, Bursa, Caecum, Cisterna, Cyst, Embryo, Follicla, Pericardium, Peritoneum, Pod, Scrotum, Spermatheca, Tylose, Tylosis, Vesica, Vocal, Yolk

Saccharine Dulcite, Dulcose

Sack(cloth), Sacking Bag, Bed, Boot, Bounce, Budget, Burlap, Can, Cashier, Chasse, Chop, Congé, Congee, Dash, Depredate, Despoil, Discharge, Doss, Fire, Gunny, Havoc, Hop-pocket, Jute, Knap, Lay waste, Loot, Mailbag, Maraud, Mitten, Pillage, Plunder, Poke, Push, Rapine, Reave, Replace, Road, Rob, Sanbenito, Sherris, Sherry, Spoliate, Vandalise

▷ **Sacks** *may indicate* an anagram

Sacrament Baptism, Communion, Confirmation, Eucharist, Extreme unction, Housel, Lord's supper, Matrimony, Nagmaal, Orders, Penance, Promise, Reconciliation, Ritual, Unction, Viaticum

Sacred, Sacred place Adytum, Churinga, Hallowed, Heart, Hierurgy, Holy, Ineffable, Nine, Omphalos, Padma, Pietà, Sacrosanct, Sanctum, Taboo, Tapu, Temenos

Sacrifice Alcestic, Cenote, Forego, Gambit, Hecatomb, Holocaust, Immolate, Iphigenia, Isaac, Lay down, Molech, Moloch, Oblation, > **OFFERING**, Peace offering, Relinquish, Sati, Suovetaurilia, Supreme, Surrender, Suttee, Taurobolium, Tophet, Vicarious, Victim

Sacrilege, Sacrilegious Blaspheme, Impiety, Profane, Violation

Sacristan, Sacristy Diaconicon, Sceuophylax, Sexton

Sacrosanct Inviolable

Sad(den), Sadly, Sadness Alas, Attrist, Blue, Con dolore, Dejected, Desolate, Disconsolate, Dismal, Doleful, Dolour, Downcast, Drear, Dull, Dumpy, Heartache, Lovelorn, Low, Lugubrious, Mesto, Oh, Plangent, Sorrowful, Sorry, Tabanca, Tearful, Tear-jerker, Threnody, Tragic, Triste, Tristesse, Unhappy, Wan, Wo(e)begone

Saddle (bag, cloth, girth, pad) Alforja, Aparejo, Arson, Burden, Cantle, Cinch, Col, Crupper, Demipique, Lumber, Numnah, Oppress, Pack, Pad, Panel, Pigskin, Pilch, Pillion, Seat, Sell(e), Shabrack, Shabracque, Side, Stock, Tree, Western

Saddle-bow Arson
Saddler Whittaw(er)
Sadie Thompson
Sadism, Sadistic Algolagnia, Cruel
▷ **Sadly** *may indicate* an anagram
Safari Expedition, Hunt
Safe(ty) Active, Allright, Almery, Ambry, Coolgardie, Copper-bottomed,
Delouse, Deposit, GRAS, Harmless, Immunity, Impunity, Inviolate, Keister,
Night, Passive, Peter, Reliable, Roadworthy, Sanctuary, Secure, Sound,
Strong-box, Strongroom, Sure, Whole-skinned, Worthy
Safeguard Bulwark, Caution, Ensure, Fail-safe, Frithborh, Fuse, Hedge,
Palladium, Protection, Register, Ward
Saffron Crocus, Yellow
Sag(gy) Decline, Dip, Droop, Hang, Hogged, Lop, Slump, Swayback, Wilt
Saga Aga, Chronicle, Edda, Epic, Icelandic, Laxdale, Legend, Odyssey, Volsunga
Sagacity Commonsense, Depth, Elephant, Judgement, Sapience, Wisdom
Sage(s) Abaris, Aquinian, Bactrian, Bias, Carlyle, Cheronian, Chilo(n), Clary,
Cleobulus, Confucius, Counsellor, Greybeard, Hakam, Herb, Imhotep,
Jerusalem, Maharishi, Mahatma, Malmesbury, Manu, Mirza, Orval, Pandit,
Periander, Philosopher, Pittacus, Rishi, Salvia, Savant, Seer, Seven, Solon,
Tagore, Thales, Wiseacre, Wood
Sage-brush Nevada
Sahib Pukka
Said Co, Emir, Port, Quo(th), Related, Reputed, Spoken, Stated
▷ **Said** *may indicate* 'sounding like'
Sail(s), Sailing Bunt, Canvas, Circumnavigate, Cloth, Coast, Course, Cross-jack,
Cruise, Drag, Drift, Fan, Fore(course), Fore-and-aft, Full, Gaff(-topsail), Genoa,
Goose-wing, Head, Jib, Jigger, Jut, Lateen, Leech, Luff, Lug, Moon, Moonraker,
Muslin, Navigate, Parachute spinnaker, Peak, Plain, Plane, Ply, Rag, Reef,
Rig, Ring-tail, Royal, Sheet, Spanker, Spencer, Spinnaker, Spritsail, Square,
Staysail, Steer, Studding, Stun, Suit, Top(-gallant), Top-hamper, Van, Vela,
Wardrobe, Water, Yard
Sailor(s) AB, Admiral, Anson, Argonaut, Blue-jacket, Boatman, Boatswain,
Bosun, Budd, Commodore, Crew, Deckhand, Drake, Evans, Freshwater,
Galiongee, Gob, Greenhand, Grommet, Hat, Hearties, Helmsman, Hornblower,
Hydronaut, Jack, Janty, Jauntie, Jaunty, Jonty, Khalasi, Killick, Killock,
Kroo(boy), Krooman, Kru(boy), Kruman, Lascar, Leadsman, Limey, Loblolly
boy, Lt, Lubber, Mariner, Matelot, Matlo(w), Middy, MN, Nelson, Noah, NUS,
Oceaner, OS, Polliwog, Pollywog, Popeye, Powder monkey, Privateer, Rating,
RN, Salt, Seabee, Seacunny, Sea-dog, Sea-lord, > SEAMAN, Serang, Shellback,
Sin(d)bad, Stowaway, Submariner, Tar, Tarp(aulin), Tarry-breeks, Tindal,
Triton, Waister, Wandering, Water-dog, Yachtsman
Saint(ly), Saints Agatha, Agnes, Aidan, Alban, Alexis, Alvis, Ambrose,
Andrew, Anselm, Anthony, Asaph, Audrey, Augustine, Barbara, Barnabas,
Bartholomew, Basil, Bees, Benedict, Bernard, Boniface, Brandan, Brendan,
Bridget, Brigid, Canonise, Canonize, Catharine, Cecilia, Chad, Christopher,
Clement, Columba(n), Crispian, Crispin(ian), Cuthbert, Cyr, David, Denis,
Denys, Diego, Dominic, Dorothea, Dunstan, Dymphna, Elmo, Eloi, Elvis,
Eulalie, Francis, Genevieve, George, Gertrude, Giles, Hagiology, Hallowed,
Helena, Hilary, Hilda, Hugh, Ignatius, James, Jerome, John, Joseph, Jude,
Just, Kentigern, Kevin, Kilda, Latterday, Lawrence, Leger, Leonard, Linus,
Loyola, Lucy, Luke, Malo, Margaret, Mark, Martha, Martin, Matthew, Michael,

Monica, Mungo, Nicholas, Ninian, Odyl, Olaf, Oswald, Pancras, Patrick, Patron, Paul(inus), Peter, Pi, Pillar, Plaster, Polycarp, Quentin, Regulus, Ride, Rishi, Roch, Ronan, Roque, Rosalie, Rule, S, Sebastian, Severus, Simeon, Simon, SS, St, Stanislaus, Stephen, Sunday, Swithin, Templar, Teresa, Thecia, Theresa, Thomas, Tobias, Ursula, Valentine, Veronica, Vincent, Vitus, Walstan, Wilfred, William, Winifred

St Anthony's Fire Ergotism, Erysipelas

St Elmo's Fire Corona discharge, Corposant

St James Scallop-shell

St Jerome Hieronymic

St John's bread Carob

St Lucia WL

St Paul's Wren-ch

St Vincent WV

Sake Account, Behalf, Cause, Drink

Sal Volatile

Salacious, Salacity Lewd, Lust, Obscene, Scabrous

Salad Burnet, Caesar, Calaloo, Calalu, Chef's, Chicon, Corn, Cos, Cress, Cucumber, Days, Endive, Escarole, Fennel, Finnochio, Finoc(c)hio, Frisée, Fruit, Greek, Guacamole, Lactuca, Lamb's lettuce, Lettuce, Lovage, Mesclum, Mesclun, Mixture, Niçoise, Purslane, Radicchio, Radish, Rampion, Rocket, Rojak, Roquette, Russian, Salmagundi, Salmagundy, Slaw, Tabbouleh, Tabbouli, Tomato, Waldorf, Word

▷ **Salad** *may indicate* an anagram

Salamander Axolotl, Congo eel, Ewt, Hellbender, Lizard, Menopome, Mole, Mudpuppy, Olm, Proteus, Siren, Snake, Spring-keeper

Salami, Salami technique Fraud, Peperoni

Salary Emolument, Fee, Hire, Pay, Prebend, Screw, Stipend, > **WAGE**

Sale(s) Auction, Cant, Car-boot, Clearance, Farm-gate, Fire, Garage, Jumble, Market, Outroop, Outrope, Raffle, Retail, Roup, Rummage, Subhastation, Trade, Turnover, Venal, Vend, Vendue, Vent, Voetstoets, Voetstoots, Warrant, Wash, White, Wholesale

Saleroom Pantechnicon

Salesman Agent, Assistant, Bagman, Broker, Buccaneer, Bummaree, Counterhand, Drummer, Huckster, Loman, Pedlar, Rep, Retailer, Tallyman, Tout, Traveller

Salient Coign, Jut, Projection, Prominent, Redan, Spur

Saliva Drool, Parotid, Ptyalism, Sial(oid), Slobber, Spawl, Spit(tle), Sputum

Sallow Adust, Pallid, Pasty, Sale, Sauch, Wan

Sally Aunt, Boutade, Charge, Dash, Escape, Excursion, Flight, Foray, Issue, Jest, Mot, Pleasantry, Quip, Sarah, Sortie, Witticism

Salmagundi Mess

Salmon Alevin, Atlantic, Australian, Baggit, Blueback, Blue-cap, Boaz, Burnett, Chinook, Chum, Cock, Coho(e), Dog, Dorado, Grav(ad)lax, Grilse, Humpback, Kelt, Keta, King, Kipper, Kokanee, Lax, Ligger, Lox, Masu, Mort, Nerka, Oncorhynchus, Ouananiche, Par(r), Peal, Pink, Quinnat, Red, Redfish, Rock, Samlet, Shedder, Skegger, Slat, Smelt, Smolt, Smout, Smowt, Sockeye, Sparling, Spirling, Sprod

Salon, Saloon Barrel-house, Car, Hall, Honkytonk, Last chance, Lounge, Pullman, Sedan, Shebang, Tavern

Salt(s), Salty AB, Acid, Alginate, Aluminate, Andalusite, Aspartite, Attic, Aurate, Azide, Base, Bath, Bicarbonate, Bichromate, Borate, Borax, Brackish,

Brine, Bromate, Bromide, Capr(o)ate, Caprylate, Carbamate, Carbonate, Carboxylate, Cerusite, Chlorate, Chlorite, Chromate, Citrate, Complex, Corn, Cure(d), Cyanate, Cyclamate, Datolite, Deer lick, Diazonium, Dichromate, Dioptase, Dithionate, Double, Enos, Epsom, Ferricyanide, Formate, Glauber, Glutamate, Halite, Halo-, Health, Hydrochloride, Hygroscopic, Iodide, Ioduret, Isocyanide, Lactate, Lake-basin, Lithate, Liver, Magnesium, Malate, Malonate, Manganate, Matelot, Microcosmic, Monohydrate, Mucate, Muriate, NaCl, Nitrate, Nitrite, Oleate, Osm(i)ate, Oxalate, Palmitate, Pandermite, Perchlorate, Periodate, Phosphate, Phosphite, Phthalate, Picrate, Piquancy, Plumbate, Plumbite, Potassium, Powder, Propionate, Pyruvate, Rating, Resinate, Rochelle, Rock, Rosinate, Sailor, Sal ammoniac, Salify, Sal volatile, Saut, Sea-dog, Seafarer, Seasoned, Sebate, Selenate, Smelling, Soap, Sodium, Solar, Stannate, Stearate, Suberate, Succinate, Sulfite, Sulphate, Sulphite, Sulphonate, Table, Tannate, Tantalate, Tartrate, Tellurate, Thiocyanate, Thiosulphate, Titanate, Tungstate, Uranin, Urao, Urate, Vanadate, Volatile, Water-dog, White, Wit(ty), Xanthate

Salt meat Mart
Saltpetre Caliche, Chile, Cubic, Nitre, Norway
Salt-water Sea
Salubrious Healthy, Sanitary, Wholesome
Salutary Beneficial, Good, Wholesome
Salutation, Salute Address, Ave, Banzai, Barcoo, Bid, Cap, Cheer, Command, Coupé(e), Curtsey, Embrace, Feu de joie, Fly-past, Genuflect, Greet, Hail, Hallo, Halse, Homage, Honour, Jambo, Kiss, Present, Salaam, Salvo, Sieg Heil, Toast, Tribute, Wassail
Salvador Dali
Salvage Dredge, Lagan, Ligan, Reclaim, Recover, Recycle, Rescue, Retrieve, Tot
Salvation(ist) Booth, Redemption, Rescue, Soterial, Yeo
Salve Anele, Anoint, Assuage, Ave, Lanolin(e), Lotion, Ointment, Remedy, Saw, Tolu, Unguent, Weapon
Salver Tray, Waiter
Salvo Fusillade, Salute, Volley
Sal volatile Hartshorn
Sam Browse, Soapy, Uncle, Weller
Samara Ash-key
Samaritan Good
Samarium Sm
Same(ness) Ae, Agnatic, Contemporaneous, Do, Egal, Ejusd(en), Equal, Ib(id), Ibidem, Id, Idem, Identical, Identity, Ilk, Iq, Like, One, Thick(y), Thilk, Uniform, Ylke
Samovar Urn
Samoyed Dog, Uralian, Uralic
Sample, Sampling Biopsy, Blad, Browse, Example, Fare, Foretaste, Handout, Matched, Muster, Pattern, Pree, Prospect, Quadrat, Quota, Scantling, Specimen, Spread, Stratified, Swatch, Switch, > TASTE, Transect, Try
Samuel Pepys, Smiles
Samurai Ronin
▷ **Sam Weller** *may indicate* the use of 'v' for 'w' or vice versa
Sanctify Consecrate, Purify, Saint
Sanctimonious Banbury, Creeping Jesus, Devout, Goody-goody, Pi, Religiose, Righteous, Saintly
Sanction Allow, Appro, Approbate, Approof, Approve, Authorise, Bar,

Countenance, Endorse, Imprimatur, Mandate, OK, Pass, Pragmatic, Ratify, Sustain

Sanctities, Sanctity Halidom, Holiness, Hollidam, Sonties

Sanctuary, Sanctum Adytum, Asylum, By-room, Cella, Ch, Church, Frithsoken, Frithstool, Girth, Grith, Holy, Kaaba, Lair, Naos, Oracle, Penetralia, Preserve, Refuge, Sacellum, Sacrarium, > **SHELTER**, Shrine, Tabernacle, Temple

Sand(bank), Sandbar, Sands, Sandy Alec, Alex, Areg, Arena(ceous), Arenose, Arkose, As, Atoll, Bar, Barchan(e), Bark(h)an, Beach, Caliche, Dene, Desert, Dogger Bank, Down, Dudevant, Dune, Dupin, Eremic, Erg, Esker, Foundry, Gat, George, Ginger, Goodwin, Grain, Granulose, Hazard, Light, Loess, Machair, Nore, Oil, Overslaugh, Podsol, Podzol, Portlandian, Psammite, Ridge, Sabulous, Sawney, Seif, Shelf, Shoal, Shore, Singing, Tar, Tee, Time, Tombolo

Sandal(s) Alpargata, Buskin, Calceamentum, Chappal, Espadrille, Flip-flop, Ganymede, Geta, Huarache, Jelly, Patten, Pump, Talaria, Thong, Zori

Sandalwood Algum, Almug, Chypre, Pride, Santal

Sandarac Arar

Sander Pike-perch

Sandhurst RMA

Sand-loving Ammophilous, Psammophil

Sandpiper Bird, Dunlin, Knot, Oxbird, Ree, Ruff, Sandpeep, Stint, Terek

Sandstone Arkose, Dogger, Fa(i)kes, Flysch, Grit, Hassock, Itacolumite, Kingle, Molasse, New Red, Old Red, Quartzite, Red

Sandstorm Haboob, Tebbad

Sandwich Bruschetta, Butty, Club, Croque-monsieur, Cuban, Doorstep, Earl, Hamburger, Island, Jeely piece, Open, Piece, Roti, Round, Sarney, Sarnie, Smorbrod, Smorgasbord, Smorrebrod, Stottie, Sub, Submarine, Thumber, Toastie, Triple-decker, Twitcher, Victoria, Wad

▷ **Sandwich(es)** *may indicate* a hidden word

Sane, Sanity Compos mentis, Formal, Healthy, Judgement, Rational, Reason, Sensible, Wice

Sangfroid Aplomb, Cool, Poise

Sanguine Confident, Hopeful, Optimistic, Roseate, Ruddy

Sanitary Hygienic, Salubrious, Sterile

Sanskrit Purana, Ramayana, Sutra, Upanishad, Vedic

Santa Claus Abonde, Kriss Kringle

Sap Benzoin, Bleed, Cremor, Drain, Enervate, Entrench, Ichor, Juice, Laser, Latex, Lymph, Mine, Mug, Pulque, Ratten, Resin, Roset, Rosin, Rozet, Rozit, Secretion, Soma, Sura, Swot, Undermine, Weaken

Sapid Flavoursome, Savoury, Tasty

Sapience, Sapient Discernment, Sage, Wisdom

Sapling Ash-plant, Ground-ash, Plant, Tellar, Teller, Tiller, Youth

Sapper(s) Miner, RE

Sapphire Star, White

Sappho Lesbian

Sapwood Alburnum

Sarah Battle, Gamp, Sal

Sarcasm, Sarcastic Antiphrasis, Biting, Cutting, Cynical, Derision, Irony, Mordacious, Mordant, Pungent, Quip, Quotha, Sarky, Satire, Sharp, Smartmouth, Snide, Sting, Wisecrack

Sardine Fish, Sard

Sardonic Cutting, Cynical, Ironical, Scornful, Wry

Sargasso Ore, Sea(weed)

Sark Chemist, CI, Shirt
Sarong Sulu
SAS Red Devils
Sash Baldric(k), Band, Belt, Burdash, Cummerbund, Obi, Scarf, Window
Sassaby Tsessebe
Sassenach English, Lowlander, Pock-pudding
Satan Adversary, Apollyon, Arch-enemy, Cram, > DEVIL, Eblis, Evil One, Lucifer, Shaitan, Tempter
Satchel Bag, Scrip
Sate(d), **Satiate** Cloy, Glut, Replete, Sad, Surfeit
Satellite Adrastea, Ananke, Ariel, Artificial, Astra, Atlas, Attendant, Aussat, Belinda, Bianca, Bird, Callisto, Calypso, Camenae, Carme, Charon, Communications, Comsat®, Cordelia, Cosmic, Cressida, Deimos, Desdemona, Despina, Dione, Disciple, Early bird, Earth, Echo, Elara, Enceladus, Europa, Explorer, Fixed, Follower, Galatea, Galilean, Ganymede, Geostationary, Helene, Henchman, Himalia, Hipparchus, Hyperion, Iapetus, Intelsat, Io, Janus, Lackey, Larissa, Leda, Lysithea, Meteorological, Metis, Mimas, Miranda, Moon, Mouse, Nereid, Oberon, Ophelia, Orbiter, Pan, Pandora, Pasiphae, Phobos, Phoebe, Portia, Prometheus, Puck, Rhea, Rosalind, Sinope, Sputnik, Syncom, Telesto, Telstar, Tethys, Thalassa, Thebe, Tiros, Titan, Titania, Triton, Umbriel, Weather
▶ **Satin** *see* SILK
Satire, **Satirical**, **Satirist** Arbuthnot, Archilochus, Burlesque, Butler, Candide, Chaldee, Dryden, Horace, Iambographer, Juvenal, Lampoon, Lash, Lucian, Menippean, Mockery, Pantagruel, Parody, Pasquil, Pasquin(ade), Pope, Raillery, Sarky, Sotadic, Spoof, Squib, Swift, Travesty
Satisfaction, **Satisfactory**, **Satisfy(ing)**, **Satisfactorily** Agree, Ah, Ap(p)ay, Appease, Assuage, Atone, Change, Compensation, Complacent, > CONTENT, Defrayment, Enough, Feed, Fill, Fulfil, Glut, Gratify, Indulge, Jake, Job, Liking, Meet, OK, Pacation, Palatable, Pay, Please, Propitiate, Qualify, Redress, Repay, Replete, Sate, Satiate, Serve, Settlement, Slake, Square, Suffice, Tickety-boo, Well
Saturate(d) Drench, Glut, Imbue, Impregnate, Infuse, Permeate, > SOAK, Sodden, Steep, Waterlog
Saturday Holy
Saturn God, Kronos, Lead, Planet, Rocket
Satyr Faun, Leshy, Lesiy, Libertine, Marsyas, Pan, Silen(us), Woodhouse, Woodwose
Sauce, **Saucy** Alfredo, Allemanse, Apple, Arch, Baggage, Barbecue, Béarnaise, Béchamel, Bigarade, Bold(-faced), Bolognese, Bordelaise, Bourguignonne, Bread, Brown, Caper, Carbonara, Catchup, Catsup, Chasseur, Chaudfroid, Cheek, Chilli, Condiment, Coulis, Cranberry, Cream, Cumberland, Custard, Dapper, Dip, Dressing, Enchilada, Espagnole, Fenberry, Fondue, Fu yong, Fu yung, Gall, Garum, Gravy, Hard, Hoisin, Hollandaise, Horseradish, HP®, Impudence, Jus, Ketchup, Lip, Malapert, Marinade, Marinara, Matelote, Mayonnaise, Melba, Meunière, Mint, Mirepoix, Mole, Mornay, Mousseline, Nam pia, Nerve, Newburg, Nuoc mam, Oxymal, Oyster, Panada, Parsley, Passata, Peart, Pert, Pesto, Piri-piri, Pistou, Ravigote, Relish, Remoulade, Rouille, Roux, Sabayon, Sal, Salpicon, Salsa, Salsa verde, Sambal, Sass, Satay, Shoyu, Soja, Soubise, Soy, Soya, Stroganoff, Sue, Supreme, Sweet and sour, Tabasco®, Tamari, Tartar(e), Tomato, Topping, Tossy, Velouté, Vinaigrette, White, Wine, Worcester, Worcestershire

Sauceboat-shaped Scaphocephalate

Saucepan Chafer, Goblet, Skillet, Stockpot

Saucer Ashtray, Discobolus, UFO

Sauna Bath, Sudatorium, Sudorific

Saunter Amble, Dander, Lag, Mosey, Promenade, Roam, Shool, Stroll, Toddle

Sausage(s) Andouillette, Banger, Black pudding, Blood, Boerewors, Bologna, Boudin, Bratwurst, Cervelat, Cheerio, Chipolata, Chorizo, Cumberland, Devon, Drisheen, Frankfurter, Hot dog, Kishke, Knackwurst, Knockwurst, Liver(wurst), Mortadella, Mystery bag, Pep(p)eroni, Polony, Salami, Sav(eloy), Snag(s), String, White pudding, Wiener(wurst), Wienie, Wurst, Zampone

Sausage-shaped Allantoid

Savage Ape, Barbarian, Boor, Brute, Cannibal, Cruel, Feral, Fierce, Grim, Gubbins, Immane, Inhuman, Maul, Noble, Sadistic, Truculent, Vitriolic, Wild

Savanna Plain, Sahel

Savant Expert, Mahatma, Sage, Scholar

Save, Saving(s) Bank, Bar, Besides, But, Capital, Conserve, Deposit, Economy, Except, Hain, Hoard, Husband, ISA, Keep, Layby, National, Nest egg, Nirlie, Nirly, PEPS, Preserve, Put by, Reclaim, Redeem, Relieve, Reprieve, > **RESCUE**, Reskew, Sa', Salt, Salvage, Scrape, Scrimp, Shortcut, Slate club, Spare, Stokvel, Succour, TESSA, Unless

Saviour Deliverer, Jesu(s), Messiah, Redeemer

Savour(ed), Savoury Aigrette, Bouchée, Canapé, Devils-on-horseback, Essence, Fag(g)ot, Flavour, Olent, Ramekin, Relish, Resent, Sair, Sapid, Sar, Smack, Starter, Tang, > **TASTE**, Vol au vent

Savoy Cabbage, Opera

Saw Adage, Aphorism, Apothegm, Azebiki, Back, Band, Beheld, Bucksaw, Buzz, Chain, Circular, Cliché, Compass, Coping, Cross-cut, Crown, Cut, Dictum, Dovetail, Dozuki, Flooring, Frame, Fret, Gang, Glimpsed, Gnome, Grooving, Hack, Hand, Jig, Keyhole, Legend, Log, Maxim, Met, Motto, Pad, Panel, Paroemia, Pitsaw, Proverb, Pruning, Quarter, Rabbeting, Rack, Ribbon, Rip, Ryoba, Sash, Saying, Scroll, Serra, Skil®, Skip-tooth, Slogan, Span, Spied, Stadda, Stone, Sweep, Tenon, Trepan, Trephine, Whip, Witnessed

Sawbones Surgeon

Saw-toothed Runcinate

Saxifrage Burnet, Golden, Heuchera, London Pride, St Patrick's cabbage

Saxon Cedric, Hengist, Wend

Say, Saying(s) Adage, Agrapha, Allege, Aphorism, Apophthegm, Apostrophise, Articulate, Axiom, Beatitude, Bon mot, Bromide, Byword, Cant, Catchphrase, Cliché, Declare, Dict(um), Eg, Enunciate, Epigram, Express, Fadaise, Gnome, Impute, Logia, Logion, > **MAXIM**, Mean, Mot, Mouth, Observe, Predicate, Pronounce, Proverb, Put, Quip, Recite, Rede, Relate, Remark, Report, Saine, Saw, Sc, Sententia, > **SPEAK**, Suppose, Sutra, Utter, Voice, Word

▷ **Say, Saying(s)** *may indicate* a word sounding like another

Scab(by) Blackleg, Crust, Eschar, Leggism, Leprose, Mangy, Rat, Scald, Scall, Sore, Strike-breaker

Scabbard Frog, Pitcher, Sheath, Tsuba

Scabies Itch, Psora, Scotch fiddle

Scabrous Harsh, Rough, Thersites

Scaffold(ing), Scaffolder Gallows, Gantry, Hoarding, Putlock, Putlog, Rig, Spiderman, Stage

Scald Blanch, Burn, Leep, Ploat, Plot

Scale, Scaly Analemma, API gravity, Ascend, Balance, Baumé, Beaufort,

Binet- Simon, Bismar, Brix, Bud, Burnham, Celsius, Centigrade, Ceterach, Chromatic, > **CLIMB**, Desquamate, Diagonal, Diatonic, Douglas, Elo, Escalade, Fahrenheit, Flake, Full, Furfur, Gamme, Gamut, Ganoid, Gapped, Gauge, Gravity, Gunter's, Hexachord, Humidex, Indusium, Interval, Kelvin, Ladder, Lamina, Layer, Leaf, Lepid, Lepidote, Leprose, Libra, Ligule, Likert, Lodicule, Loricate, Magnitude, Major, Mercalli, Mesel, Minor, Mohs, Munsell, Natural, Nominal, Octad, Ordinal, Palea, Palet, Patagium, Peel, Pentatonic, Pholidosis, Placoid, Plate, Platform, Ramentum, > **RANGE**, Rankine, Ratio, Réaumur, Regulo, Richter, Scan, Scarious, Scent, Scincoid, Scurf, Scutellate, Shin, Skink, Sliding, Speel, Squama, Squame(lla), Submediant, Tegmentum, Tegula, Tonal, Tridymite, Tron(e), Vernier, Wage, Wentworth, Wind

Scallop(ed) Bivalve, Clam, Coquille, Crenate, Escalop, Frill, Gimp, Mush, Pecten, Vandyke

Scallywag Rascal, Scamp, Skeesicks

Scalp Cut, Scrape, Skin, Trophy

Scalpel Bistoury, Knife

Scam Ramp

Scamp Fripon, Imp, Limb, Lorel, Lorrell, Losel, Lozell, Neglect, > **RASCAL**, Reprobate, Rip, Rogue, Scallywag, Skeesicks

Scamper Gambol, Lamp, Run, Scurry, Skedaddle, Skelter, Skitter

Scan(ning), Scanner CAT, CT, Examine, Helical, Interlaced, OCR, Optical, Peruse, PET, Rake, Raster, Scrutinise, Sector, SEM, Sequential, SPET, Survey, Tomography, Ultrasound, Vertical, Vet

Scandal(ous), Scandalise Belie, Canard, Commesse, Disgrace, Exposé, Gamy, Hearsay, Muck-raking, Opprobrium, Outrage, Shame, Slander, Stigma, Stink, Watergate

Scandinavian Dane, Finn, Laplander, Lapp, Nordic, Norseland, Northman, Olaf, Runic, Squarehead, Swede, Varangian, Viking

Scandium Sc

Scant(y) Bare, Brief, Exiguous, Ihram, Jejune, Jimp, Poor, Scrimpy, Short, Shy, Skimpy, Slender, Spare, Sparse, Stingy

Scapegoat Butt, Fall-guy, Hazazel, Joe Soap, Patsy, Stooge, Target, Victim, Whipping-boy

Scapula Blade, Omoplate

Scar(face) Al, Blemish, Cheloid, Cicatrix, Cliff, Craig, Epulotic, Hilum, Keloid, Leucoma, Leukoma, Mark, Pockmark, Stigma, Ulosis, Wipe

Scarab Beetle, Gem

Scarce(ly), Scarcity Barely, Dear, Dearth, Famine, Few, Hardly, Ill, Lack, Rare, Scanty, Seldom, Short, Strap, Uncommon, Want

Scare(mongering), Scaring Alarmist, Alert, Amaze, Fleg, Fright, Gally, Gliff, Hairy, Panic, Skeer, Spook, Startle

Scarecrow Bogle, Bugaboo, Dudder, Dudsman, Gallibagger, Gallibeggar, Gallicrow, Gallybagger, Gallybeggar, Gallycrow, Malkin, Mawkin, Potato-bogle, Ragman, S(h)ewel, Tattie-bogle

Scarf Babushka, Belcher, Cataract, Comforter, Cravat, Curch, Doek, Dupatta, Fichu, Hai(c)k, Haique, Headsquare, Hyke, Lambrequin, Madras, Mantilla, Muffettee, Muffler, Neckatee, Nightingale, Orarium, Pagri, Palatine, Pashmina, Pugg(a)ree, Rail, Rebozo, Sash, Screen, Stole, Tallith, Tippet, Trot-cosy, Trot-cozy, Vexillum

Scarifier Scuffler

Scarlet Cinnabar, Cochineal, Crimson, Pimpernel, Pink, Ponceau, Red, Vermilion

Scarper Bunk, Run, Shoo, Welsh
Scat Aroint, Dropping
Scathe, Scathing Mordant, Sarcastic, Savage, Severe, Vitriolic
Scatter(ed), Scattering Bestrew, Broadcast, Diaspora, Disject, Dispel,
  > DISPERSE, Dissipate, Flurr, Interspace, Litter, Rout, Scail, Skail, Sow, Sparge,
  Splutter, Sporadic, Spread, Sprinkle, Squander, Straw, Strew
Scatterbrain(ed) Dippy, Ditsy
Scavenge(r) Dieb, Forage, Hunt, Hy(a)ena, Jackal, Rake, Ratton, Rotten, Scaffie,
  Sweeper, Totter
Scenario Outline, Plot, Script
Scene(ry) Arena, Boscage, Coulisse, Decor, Flat(s), Landscape, Locale, Prop,
  Prospect, Set, Set piece, Sight, Site, Sketch, Stage, Tableau, Tormenter,
  Tormentor, Transformation, Venue, View
Scent Aroma, Attar, Chypre, Cologne, Eau de cologne, Essence, Fragrance,
  Frangipani, Fumet(te), Gale, Moschatel, Nose, Odour, Orris, Ottar, Otto,
  Perfume, Sachet, Smell, Spoor, Vent, Waft, Wind
Scentless Anosmia
Sceptic(al), Scepticism Agnostic, Cynic, Doubter, Incredulous, Infidel,
  Jaundiced, Nihilistic, Pyrrho(nic), Sadducee, Solipsism
Schedule Agenda, Calendar, Itinerary, Prioritise, Programme, Register, Slot,
  Table, Timescale, Timetable
Scheme(r), Scheming Colour, Concoct, Conspire, Crafty, Cunning, Dare, Darien,
  Dart, Decoct, Devisal, Diagram, Dodge, Draft, Gin, Honeytrap, Intrigue,
  Jezebel, Machiavellian, Machinate, Manoeuvre, Nostrum, Pilot, > PLAN, Plat,
  Plot, Project, Proposition, Purpose, Put-up job, Racket, Ruse, Stratagem,
  System, Table, Wangle, Wheeze
Schism(atic) Disunion, Division, Eastern, Great, Greek, Heterodox, Rent, Split,
  Western
Schizo(phrenia) Catatonic, Dementia praecox, Hebephreni
Schmaltz Goo, Slush
Schmieder S
Schmuck Gunsel
Schnapps Enzian
Scholar, Scholast Abelard, Academic, Alumni, Atticus, BA, Bookman, Boursier,
  Catachumen, Clergy, Clerisy, Clerk, Commoner, Demy, Disciple, Erasmus,
  Erudite, Etonian, Exhibitioner, Extern(e), Externat, Goliard, Graduate,
  Grecian, Hafiz, Inkhorn, Jowett, Literate, Littérateur, MA, Mal(l)am, Masorete,
  Noter, Occam Ulama, Pauline, Plutarch, Polymath, Pupil, Rhodes, Sap, Savant,
  Schoolboy, Sizar, Soph, > STUDENT, Tabardar, Taberdar, Taberder, Tom Brown
Scholarship Bursary, Education, Erudition, Exhibition, Grant, Learning, Lore,
  Mass, Rhodes
School Academy, Ampleforth, Approved, Ashlan, Barbizon, Bauhaus,
  Beacon, Benenden, Bluecoat, Board, Boarding, Charm, Charterhouse,
  Chartreux, Chautauqua, Cheder, Choir, Church, Classical, Coed, Community,
  Composite, Comprehensive, Conservative, Conservatoire, Conservatory, Cool,
  Correspondence, Council, Crammer, Cult, Dada, Dame, Day, Direct grant,
  Dojo, Downside, Drama, Drill, Driving, Dual, Educate, Elementary, Essenes,
  Eton, Exercise, External, Faith, Fettes, Finishing, First, Flemish, Frankfurt,
  Free, Gam, Giggleswick, Gordonstoun, Grade, Grammar, Grant-aided,
  Grant-maintained, Group, Gymnasien, Gymnasium, Harrow, Heder, Hedge,
  High, Historical, Honour, Hospital, Hostel, Hypermodern, Independent,
  Industrial, Infant, Institute, Integrated, Intermediate, Ionic, Jim Crow,

Junior, Kailyard, Kaleyard, Kant, Kindergarten, Lake, Lancing, Language, Life, List D, Loretto, Lower, LSE, Lycée, Madrassah, Magnet, Mahayana, Maintained, Maintaining, Manchester, Mannheim, Marlborough, Middle, National, Night, Normal, Nursery, Oundle, Palaestra, Parnassian, Parochial, Pensionnat, Perse, Piano, Play, Pod, Poly, Porpoises, Prep, Preparatory, Primary, Private, Progymnasium, Provided, Public, RADA, Ragged, RAM, Ramean, Real, Reformatory, Repton, Residential, Rhodian, Roedean, Rossall, Rydal, Sabbath, Sadducee, Satanic, Scandalous, Sciences, Scul, Scull(e), Secondary(-modern), Sect, Seminary, Separate, Shoal, Single-sex, Ski, Slade, Song, Spasmodic, Special, State, Stonyhurst, Stowe, Style, Summer, Sunday, Teach, Tonbridge, Trade, > TRAIN, Tutor, Upper, Voluntary(-aided), Voluntary-controlled, Wellington, Whales, Winchester, Yeshiva

Schoolboy, Schoolgirl Carthusian, Coed, Colleger, East, Etonian, Fag, Gait, Geit, Gyte, Miss, Monitor, Oppidan, Petty, Stalky, Wykehamist

School-leaver Abiturient

Schoolmaam, Schoolman, Schoolmaster, Schoolmistress Beak, Dominie, Duns, Holofernes, Miss, Occam, Orbilius, Pedagogue, Pedant, Sir, Squeers, Teacher, Ursuline

Schooner Glass, Hesperus, Prairie, Ship, Tern

Sciatica Hip-gout

Science Anatomy, Anthropology, Art, Astrodynamics, Astrophysics, Atmology, Axiology, Biology, Botany, Chemistry, Cognitive, Computer, Dismal, Domestic, Earth, Electrodynamics, Eth(n)ology, Euphenics, Exact, Geology, Information, Life, Mechanics, Natural, Noble, Nomology, Ology, Ontology, Optics, Pedagogy, Physical, Physics, Policy, Political, Rocket, Rural, Skill, Social, Soft, Soil, Sonics, Stinks, Stylistics, Tactics, Technics, Technology

Science fiction Cyberpunk

Scientist Alchemist, Anatomist, Archimedes, Aston, Astronomer, Atomist, Boffin, BSc, Cavendish, Climatologist, Copernicus, Curie, Dalton, Davy, Dopper, Einstein, Expert, Faraday, Fourier, FRS, Galileo, Geodesist, Harvey, Heaviside, Kennelly, Lodge, Lovell, Newton, Oersted, Pascal, Pasteur, Pauli, Piccard, Potamologist, Reaumur, Researcher, Volta

Scimitar Acinaciform, Sword

Scintillate Dazzle, Emicate, Gleam, Glitter, > SPARKLE

Scion Graft, Imp, Offspring, Sprig, Sprout

Scissors Clippers, Criss-cross, Cutters, Forfex, Nail, Probe, Shears

Scoff Belittle, Boo, Chaff, Deride, Dor, Eat, Feast, Flout, Food, Gall, Gibe, Gird, Gobble, > JEER, Mock, Rail, Rib, Ridicule, Roast, Scaff, Scorn, Sneer, Taunt

Scold(ing) Admonish, Berate, Callet, Catamaran, Chastise, Chide, Clapperclaw, Cotquean, Do, Earful, Flite, Flyte, Fuss, Jaw(bation), Jobation, Lecture, Nag, Objurgate, Philippic, Rant, Rate, > REBUKE, Reprimand, Reprove, Revile, Rouse on, Row, Sas(s)arara, Sis(s)erary, Slang, Slate, Termagant, Threap, Threep, Through-going, Tick-off, Tongue-lash, Trimmer, Upbraid, Virago, Wig, Xant(h)ippe, Yaff, Yankie, Yap

Sconce Candlestick, Crown, Forfeit, Head, Ice, Nole

Scone Drop, Girdle

Scoop Bale, Dipper, Exclusive, Gouge, Grab, Hollow, Ladle, Lap, Pale, Shovel, Trowel

Scope Ambit, Diapason, Domain, Elbow-room, Extent, Freedom, Gamut, Ken, Latitude, Leeway, Play, Purview, Range, Remit, Room, Rope, Scouth, Scowth, Size, Sphere

Scorch(er) Adust, Blister, Brasero, > BURN, Char, Destroy, Frizzle, Fry, Parch,

Scouther, Scowder, Scowther, Sear, Singe, Soar, Speed, Swale, Swayl, Sweal, Sweel, Torrefy, Torrid, Wither

Score Apgar, Behind, Bill, Birdie, Bradford, Bye, Capot, Chase, Conversion, Count, Crena, Debt, Eagle, Etch, Full, Groove, Hail, Honours, Ingroove, Ippon, Law, Magpie, Make, Music, Net, Nick, Notation, Notch, Partitur(a), Peg, Pique, Point, Record, Repique, Rit(t), Rouge, Run, Rut, Scotch, Scratch, Scribe, Scrive, Set, Single, Spare, Stria, String, Sum, Tablature, > TALLY, Twenty, Vocal, Waza-ari, Win

Score-board, Score-sheet Card, Telegraph

▷ **Scoring** *may indicate* an anagram

Scorn(ful) Arrogant, Bah, Contempt, Contumely, Deride, Despise, Dis(s), Disdain, Dislike, Flout, Geck, Haughty, Insult, Meprise, Mock, Opprobrium, Putdown, Rebuff, Ridicule, Sarcastic, Sardonic, Sarky, Scoff, Scout, Sdaine, Sdeigne, Sneer, Spurn, Wither

Scorpion Book, Chelifer, False, Father-lasher, Pedipalp(us), Vinegarroon, Water, Whip

Scot(sman), Scots(woman), Scottish Angus, Antenati, Berean, Blue-bonnet, Bluecap, Caledonian, Celt, Clansman, Covenanter, Duni(e)wassal, Dunniewassal, Erse, Fingal, Gael, Highland, Ian, Jock, Kelt, Kiltie, Kitty, Knox, Laird, Lallan(s), Lot, Lowland, Luckie, Lucky, Mac, Mon, Peght, Pict, Ross, Sandy, Sawn(e)y, Shetlander, Stuart, Tartan, Tax, Teuchter, Torridonian

Scotch(man) Censor, Dish, Distiller, Glenlivet®, Notch, Score, Scratch, Thwart, Usquebaugh, Whisky

Scot-free Wreakless

Scotland Alban(y), Albion, Caledonia, Gaeltacht, Gaidhealtachd, Lallans, Lothian, NB, Norland, Scotia

Scoundrel Cur, Fink, Knave, Reprobate, Scab, Smaik, Varlet, > VILLAIN

Scour Beat, Depurate, Full, Holystone, Purge, Quarter, Scrub

▷ **Scour** *may indicate* an anagram

Scourge Bible-thumper, Cat, Discipline, Flagellate, Knout, Lash, Pest, > PLAGUE, Scorpion, Whip, Wire

Scout Akela, Beaver, Bedmaker, Colony, Disdain, Explorer, Flout, Guide, King's, Outrider, Pathfinder, Pickeer, Pioneer, Queen's, Reconnoitre, Rover, Runner, Scoff, Scorn, Scourer, Scurrier, Scurriour, Sea, Sixer, Spial, Spyal, Talent, Tenderfoot, Tonto, Track, Vedette, Venture

Scowl(ing) Frown, Glower, Gnar, Lour, Lower, Sullen

Scrabble Paw

Scrag(gy) Bony, Dewitt, Ewe-necked, Neck, Scrawny

Scram Begone, Hence, Scat, Shoo

Scramble Addle, Clamber, Encode, Grubble, Hurry, Mêlée, Mix, Motocross, Muss(e), Scamble, Sprattle, Sprawl, Swerve

Scrap(s), Scrappy Abandon, Abrogate, > BIT, Cancel, Conflict, Cutting, Discard, Dump, > FIGHT, Fisticuffs, Fragment, Fray, Iota, Jot, Mêlée, Mellay, Morceau, Morsel, Odd, Off-cut, Ort, Ounce, Papier colle, Patch, Piece, Pig's-wash, Rag, Rase, Raze, Remnant, Scarmoge, Scissel, Scissil, Scrub, Set-to, Shard, Sherd, Shred, Skerrick, Skirmish, Snap, Snippet, Spall, Tait, Tate, Tatter, Titbit, Trash, Truculent, Whit

Scrap book Album, Grangerism

Scrap box Tidy

Scrape(r) Abrade, Agar, Bark, Clat, Claw, Comb, Curette, D and C, Erase, Escapade, Grate, Graze, Harl, Hoe, Hole, Jar, Kowtow, Lesion, Lute, Predicament, Racloir, Rake, Rasorial, Rasp, Rasure, Raze, Razure, Saw,

Scalp, Scart, Scrat(ch), Scroop, Scuff, Shave, Skimp, Skive, Squeegee, Strake, Stridulate, Strigil, Xyster

Scraping noise Curr, Scroop

Scrap merchant Didakai, Didakei, Diddicoi, Diddicoy, Didicoi, Didicoy, Gold-end-man, Totter

Scratch(es), Scratched Annul, Cancel, Cla(u)t, Claw, Cracked heels, Curry, Devil, Efface, Eradicate, Erase, Grabble, Graze, Nick, Par, Periwig, Quit, Race, Rase, Rasp, Rast, Root, Satan, Scarify, Scart, Score, Scrab(ble), Scram(b), Scrape, Scrattle, Scrawm, Scrawp, Scrooch, Scrorp, Scrub, Spag, Streak, Striation, Tease, Teaze, Wig

▷ **Scratch(ed)** *may indicate* an anagram

Scrawl Doodle, Scribble, Squiggle

Scream(er) Bellow, Cariama, Caterwaul, Comedian, Comic, Cry, Eek, Headline, Hern, Kamichi, Laugh, Priceless, Primal, Riot, Scare-line, Screech, Seriema, Shriek, Skirl, Squall, Sutch, Yell

Scree Bahada, Bajada, Eluvium, Talus

Screech(ing) Cry, Screak, Screich, Screigh, Scriech, Scritch, Skreigh, Skriech, Skriegh, Ululant, Whoot

Screed Megillah, Ms, Plastered, Tirade

Screen(s) Abat-jour, Arras, Backstop, Blind(age), Block, Blue, Boss, Brise-soleil, Camouflage, Chancel, Check, Chick, Cinerama®, Cloak, Cornea, Coromandel, Cover, Cribble, Curtain, Divider, Dodger, Eyelid, Festoon-blind, Fire, Fluorescent, Glib, Gobo, Grille, Hallan, Help, Hide, Hoard, Hoarding, Iconostas(is), Intensifying, Jube, Lattice, Mantelet, Mask, Nintendo, Nonny, Obscure, Organ, Over-cover, Parclose, Partition, Part-off, Pella, Purdah, Radar, Retable, Riddle, Rood, Scog, Sconce, Scope, > **SHADE**, Shelter, Shield, Shoji, Show, Sift, Sight, Silver, Skug, Small, Smoke, Split, Sunblock, Televise, Tems, Touch, Transenna, Traverse, Umbrella, VDU, Vet, Wide, Windbreak, Window, Windshield, Winnow

Screw Adam, Allen, Archimedes, Butterfly, Cap, Coach, Countersunk, Double-threaded, Dungeoner, Extort, Female, Grub, Ice, Interrupted, Jailer, Jailor, Lag, Lead, Levelling, Lug, Machine, Male, Micrometer, Miser, Monkey-wrench, Niggard, Perpetual, Phillips®, Prop(ellor), Robertson, Salary, Skinflint, Spiral, Thumb(i)kins, Twin, Twist, Vice, Worm

Screwdriver Pozidriv®, Ratchet, Stubby, Tweaker

Scribble Doodle, Pen, Scrawl

Scribe Clerk, Ezra, Mallam, Scrivener, Sopherim, Tabellion, Writer, WS

Scrimmage Bully, Maul, Mêlée, Rouge, Scrap, Skirmish, Struggle

Scrimp Economise, Pinch, Save, Scrape, Skrimp

Script Book, Calligraphy, Gurmukhi, Hand, Hiragana, Italic, Jawi, Kana, Libretto, Linear A, Linear B, Lines, Lombardic, Miniscule, Nagari, Nastalik, Nastaliq, Ogam, Ronde, Scenario, Screenplay, Shooting, Writing

Scripture(s), Scriptural version Adi Granth, Agadah, Antilegomena, Avesta, Bible, Gemara, Gematria, Gospel, Granth (Sahib), Guru Granth, Haggada(h), Hermeneutics, Hexapla, Holy book, Holy writ, Koran, K'thibh, Lesson, Lotus Sutra, Mishna(h), OT, Rig-veda, Smriti, Tantra, Targum, Testament, Upanishad, Veda, Vedic, Verse, Vulgate

Scrofula Crewels, Cruel(l)s, King's evil, Struma

Scroll(-work) Cartouche, Dead Sea, Gohonzon, Makimono, Megillah, Mezuza(h), Parchment, Pell, Roll, Roul(e), Scrow, Sefer Torah, Torah, Turbinate, Vitruvian, Volume, Volute

Scrooge Blagueur, Miser

Scrounge(r) Blag, Bludge(r), Borrow, Bot, Cadge, Forage, Freeload, Layabout, Ligger, Scunge, Sponge

Scrub(ber) Cancel, Chaparral, Cleanse, Dele(te), Gar(r)igue, Hog, Holystone, Loofa(h), Luffa, Mallee, Masseur, Negate, Pro, Rub, Scour, Tart

▷ **Scrub** *may indicate* 'delete'

Scruff(y) Dog-eared, Grubby, Nape, Raddled, Tatty, Uncombed, Untidy

Scrum Maul, Mob, Rouge, Ruck

Scrummy, Scrumptious Delectable, Delicious, Toothy, Yum-yum

Scrunt Carl

Scruple(s), Scrupulous Compunction, Conscience, Doubt, Meticulous, Nicety, Precise, Punctilious, Qualm, Queasy, Righteous, Stickle

Scrutinise, Scrutiny Check, Docimasy, Examine, Inspect, Observe, Peruse, Pore, Pry, > SCAN, Study

Scud East, Scoot, Spark, Spindrift, Spoom, Spoon, Spray

Scuff Brush, Shuffle

Scuffle Bagarre, Brawl, Scarmage, Skirmish, Struggle, Tussle

▷ **Scuffle** *may indicate* an anagram

Scull Oar, Row

Sculpt(ure) Acrolith, Aeginetan, Bas-relief, Boast, Bronze, Calvary, Canephor(a), Canephore, Canephorus, Carve, Chryselephantine, Della-robbia, Figure, Kore, Kouros, Mobile, Nude, Pergamene, Pieta, Relief, Relievo, Sc, Scabble, Scapple, Shape, Stabile, > STATUARY, Topiary

Sculptor Arp, Artist, Bartholdi, Bernini, Brancusi, Canova, Cellini, Daedalus, Della Robbia, Donatello, Giacometti, Gibbons, Gill, Hepworth, Klippel, Landseer, Michelangelo, Myron, Nollekens, Paclozzi, Phidias, Pisano, Praxiteles, Pygmalion, Rodin, Scopas, Stevens, Wheeler

Scum Confervoid, Dregs, Dross, Epistasis, Glass-gall, Kish, Legge, Mantle, Mother, Rabble, Sandiver, Scorious, Slag, Slime, Spume, Sullage

Scupper Drain, Ruin, Scuttle, Sink

Scurf, Scurvy Dander, Dandriff, Dandruff, Furfur, Horson, Lepidote, Leprose, Scabrous, Scall, Scorbutic, Whoreson, Yaw(e)y, Yaws

Scurrilous Fescennine, Profane, Ribald, Sotadic, Thersites, Vulgar

Scurry Beetle, Hurry, Scamper, Scutter, Skedaddle, Skelter

Scut Fud, Tail

Scute Plate

Scuttle Abandon, Dan, Hod, Purdonium, Scoop, Scrattle, Scupper, Sink, Wreck

Scythe Bushwhacker, Cut, Hook, Sickle, Sieth, Snath(e), Snead, Sneath, Sned

Sea(s) Adriatic, Aegean, Amundsen, Andaman, Arabian, Arafura, Aral, Azov, Baltic, Banda, Barents, Beam, Beaufort, Bellingshausen, Benthos, Bering, Billow, Biscay, Bismarck, Black, Blue, Bosp(h)orus, Brine, Briny, Caribbean, Caspian, Celebes, Celtic, Ceram, Channel, China, Chukchi, Coral, Dead, Ditch, Drink, Euphotic, Euripus, Euxine, Flores, Galilee, Great, Greenland, Head, Herring-pond, High, Hudson Bay, Icarian, Inland, Ionian, Irish, Japan, Java, Kara, Kattegat, Labrador, Laptev, Ler, Ligurian, Main, Mare, Marmara, Marmora, Med, Mediterranean, Narrow, Nordenskjold, North, Norwegian, > OCEAN, Offing, Offshore, Oggin, Okhotsk, Pelagic, Philippine, Polynya, Quantity, Red, Ross, Sargasso, Seven, Skagerrak, South, South China, Spanish main, Strand, Sulu, Tasman, Tethys, Thalassic, Tiberias, Tide, Tide-rip, Timor, Tyrrhenian, Waddenzee, Water, Weddell, White, Yellow, Zee

Sea-anemone Actinia, Zoantharia

Sea-bear Fur-seal, Otary, Seal, Seecatchie

Sea-beast Ellops, Manatee

Sea-bream Carp, Fish, Porgie, Porgy, Tai

Sea-cow Dugong, Lamantin, Manatee, Rhytina, Sirenian

Sea-cucumber Bêche-de-mer, Trepang

Sea-dog Salt, Tar

Sea-ear Abalone, Paua

Sea-fight Naumachy

Seafood Crab, Crevette, > FISH, Lobster, Prawn, Shrimp, Zooplankton

Sea-front, Seaside Beach, Coast(line), Esplanade, Littoral, Orarian, Prom(enade)

Sea-god Neptune, Nereus, Triton

Sea-green Glaucous, Incorruptible, Robespierre

Sea-horse Hippocampus, Hippodame, Lophobranchiate, Morse, Pipefish, Tangie

Seal(s), Seal box Airtight, Appose, Bachelor, Bladdernose, Bull(a), Cachet, Cap, Caulk, Chesterfield, Chop, Clinch, Close, Cocket, Common, Consign, Crab-eater, Cylinder, Eared, Earless, Elephant, Emblem, Fob, Fur, Gasket, Great, Greenland, Hair, Harbour, Harp, Hermetic, Hooded, Hudson, Impress, Jark, Lute, Monk, Obsign, O-ring, Otary, Phoca, Pinnipedia, Pintadera, Pod, Privy, Proof, Quarter, Ribbon, Ringed, Rookery, Saddleback, Sea-bear, Sealch, Sea-leopard, Sealgh, Seecatch(ie), Selkie, Sigil, Signet, Silkie, Silky, Size, Skippet, Solomon's, Sphragistic, Stamp, Tar, Wafer, Washer, Water, Weddell, Whitecoat, Womb, Zalophus

Sea-legs Balance, Pleons

Sea-level Geoid

Sea-lily Crinoid, Palmatozoa

Seam Channel, Commissure, Fell, French, Furrow, Join, Layer, Middle-stitching, Monk's, Sew, Suture, Welt

Seaman, Seamen AB, Crew, Jack, Lascar, Lubber, Mariner, OD, Ordinary, PO, RN, > SAILOR, Salt, Swabby, Tar

Sea-mat Flustra, Hornwrack

Sea-matiness Gam

Sea-monster Kraken, Merman, Wasserman

Sea-mouse Bristle-worm

Séance Communication, Session, Sitting

Sea-parrot Puffin

Sear Brand, Burn, Catch, Cauterise, Frizzle, Parch, Scath(e), Scorch, Singe, Wither

Search(ing) Beat, Comb, Dragnet, Examine, Ferret, Fingertip, > FORAGE, Fossick, Frisk, Global, Grope, Home, Hunt, Indagate, Inquire, Jerk, Jerque, Kemb, Manhunt, Perquisition, Perscrutation, Probe, Proll, Prospect, Proul, Prowl, Quest, Rake, Rancel, Ransack, Ransel, Ranzel, Ravel, Ripe, Root, Rootle, Rummage, Scan, Scour, Scur, Sker, Skirr, Snoop, Strip, Thumb, Trace, Zotetic

Sea-rover Norseman, Viking

Sea-serpent, Sea-snake Ellops, Hydrophidae, Phoca

▶ **Seaside** *see* SEA-FRONT

Sea-slug Bêche-de-mer, Trepang

Sea-snail Neritidae

Season(able), Seasonal, Seasoned, Seasoning Accustom, Age, Aggrace, Autumn, Betimes, Christmas, Close, Condiment, Devil, Dress, Duxelles, Easter, Enure, Etesian, Fall, Fennel, Festive, Flavour, Garlic, G(h)omasco, Growing, Hiems, High, In, Inure, Lent, Marjoram, Master, Mature, Nutmeg, Open, Paprika, Pepper, Powellise, Practised, Ripen, Salt, Sar, Seal, Seel, Seil,

Sele, Silly, Solstice, Spice, Spring, Summer(y), Tahini, Ticket, Tide, Time, Whit, Winter, Xmas

Sea-squirt Ascidian, Cunjevoi

Seat Backside, Banc, Banquette, Bench, Bleachers, Booster, Borne, Bosun's chair, Bottom, Box, Bucket, Bum, Bunker, Buttocks, Canapé, Centre, Chair, Chaise longue, Coit, Couch, Creepie, Croup(e), Croupon, Cushion, Davenport, Deckchair, Derriere, Dick(e)y, Dicky, Divan, Ejector, Epicentre, Faldistory, Faldstool, Foundation, Fud, Fundament, Gradin, Hall, Home, Hot, Houdah, Howdah, Humpty, Hurdies, Jump, Knifeboard, Love, Marginal, Marquise, Mercy, Misericord, Natch, Nates, Ottoman, Palanquin, Palfrey, Perch, Pew, Pillion, Pit, Pouffe, Ringside, Rumble, Rumble-tumble, Rump, Saddle, Safe, Sagbag, Sedes, Sedile, Sedilium, See, Sell, Settee, Settle, Siege, Siege Perilous, Sliding, Sofa, Squab, Stool, Strapontin, Subsellium, Sunk(ie), Sunlounger, Synthronus, Throne, Tonneau, Window, Woolsack

Sea-urchin Asteria, Echinus, Pluteus, Whore's egg

Sea-vampire Manta

Sea-wall Bulwark, Dyke, Groyne

Sea-weed Agar, Alga(e), Arame, Badderlock, Bladderwort, Bladderwrack, Carrag(h)een, Ceylon moss, Chondrus, Conferva, Coralline, Cystocarp, Desmid, Diatom, Driftweed, Dulse, Enteromorpha, Fucus, Gulfweed, Heterocontae, Hornwrack, Kelp, Kilp, Kombu, Konbu, Laminaria, Laver, Lemon-weed, Nori, Nullipore, Oarweed, Ore, Peacock's tail, Phyco-, Porphyra, Redware, Rockweed, Sargasso, Seabottle, Sea-furbelow, Sea-lace, Sea-lettuce, Sea-mat, Sea-moss, Sea-tangle, Seaware, Sea-whistle, Sea-wrack, Tang, Tetraspore, Ulva, Varec(h), Vraic, Wakame, Wakane, Ware, Wrack

Sea-wolf Pirate

Sea-worm Palolo, Spunculid

Sebastian Coe

Secede, Secession(ist) Adullamite, Antiburgher, Defy, Desert, Dissident, Flamingant, Sever, Splinter

Seclude, Seclusion Cloister, Incommunicado, Isolate, Maroon, Nook, Privacy, Purdah, Quarantine, Retiracy, Retreat, Secret, Sequester, Shyness, Solitude

Second(s), Secondary Abet, Alternative, Another (guess), Appurtenance, Assist, Back(er), Beta, Coming, Comprimario, Deuteragonist, Ephemeris, Flash, Friend, Imperfect, Indirect, Inferior, Instant, Jiffy, Latter, Leap, Lesser, Minor, Mo(ment), Nature, Other, Pig's-whisper, Redwood, Runner-up, Sec, Shake, Share, Side(r), Sight, Silver, Split, Subsidiary, Support, Tick, Trice, Twinkling, Wind

Second-best Worsted

▶ **Second-class** *see* SECOND-RATE

Second coming Parousia

Second earth Antichthon

Second-hand Hand-me-down, Hearsay, Preloved, Reach-me-down, Re-paint, Tralatitious, Used, Vicarious

Second-rate, Second-class B, Inferior, Mediocre

Second-sight Deuteroscopy, Divination, Tais(c)h

Second tine Bay, Bez

Second-year student Semi(e)(-bajan), Sophomore

Secrecy, Secret(s), Secretive Apocrypha, Arcana, Arcane, Arcanum, Backstairs, Cabbalistic, Cagey, Clam, Clandestine, Closet, Code, Conventicle, Covert, Cryptadia, Cryptic, Crypto, Dark, Dearn, Deep, Deep-laid, Dern, Devious, Esoteric, Hidden, Hidling, Hidlin(g)s, Hole and corner, Hugger-mugger,

Hush-hush, Hushy, Inly, Inmost, Latent, Mysterious, Mystical, Mystique, Open, Oyster, Password, Penetralia, Petto, > PRIVATE, Privity, Privy, QT, Rune, Scytale, Shelta, Silent, Sly, State, Stealth, Sub rosa, Tight-lipped, Top, Trade, Unbeknown, Undercover, Underhand, Undescried, Unknown, Unre(a)d, Unrevealed, Untold

Secretary Aide, Amanuensis, Chancellor, Chronicler, CIS, Desk, Desse, Famulus, Home, Minuteman, Moonshee, Munshi, Notary, Parliamentary, Permanent, Private, Scrive, Social, Steno(grapher), Stenotyper, Temp

Secretary-bird Messenger, Serpent-eater

Secrete, Secretion Aequorin, Allomone, Apocrine, Autacoid, Cache, Castor, Chalone, Cuckoo-spit, Discharge, Emanation, Exude, Hide, Hormone, Juice, Lac, Lerp, Melatonin, Mucus, Musk, Osmidrosis, Pruina, Renin, Resin, Rheum, Saliva, Sebum, Secern, Smegma, Spit(tle), Trypsin

▶ **Secret society** *see* SECT

Sect(arian), Secret society Abelite, Adamite, Ahmadiy(y)ah, Albigenses, Amish, Anabaptist, Assassin, Babee, Babi, Bahai, Bigendian, Brahmin, Cabal, Cainite, Calixtine, Camorra, Cathar, Clan, Clapham, Covenantes, Crypto, Cult, Cynic, Danite, Darbyite, Dissenter, Docate(s), Donatist, Druse, Druze, Dunkard, Dunker, Ebionite, Encratite, Essene, Familist, Gheber, Ghebre, Giaour, Gnostic, Group, Gueber, Guebre, Gymnosophist, Harmonist, Harmonite, Hassid, Hauhau, Hemerobaptist, Hesychast, Hillmen, Illuminati, Ismaili, Jacobite, Jansenist, Karaite, Karmathian, Little-endian, Lollard, Macedonian, Macmillanite, Mandaean, Marcionite, Maronite, Monothelite, Montanist, Moonie, Mormon, Mucker, Muggletonian, Nazarine, Ophites, Order, Partisan, Patripassian, Paulician, Perfectionist, Pharisee, Philadelphian, Phrygian, Picard, Pietist, Plymouth Brethren, Plymouthite, Porch, Pure Land, Rappist, Ribbonism, Sabbatian, Sabian, Sadducee, Sandeman, School, Schwenkfelder, Seekers, Senus(s)i, Seventh Day Adventist, Sex, S(h)aiva, Shaker, Shembe, Shia(h), Soka Gakkai, Sons of Freedom, Therapeutae, Tunker, Ultraquist, Unitarian, Valdenses, Vaudois, Wahabee, Wahabi(i)te, Waldenses, Yezdi, Yezidee, Yezidi, Zealot, Zen, Zezidee

Section, Sector Caesarian, Chapter, Classify, Conic, Cross, Cut, Division, Ellipse, Eyalet, Gan, Golden, Gore, Hyperbola, Lith, Lune, Meridian, Metamere, Mortice, Movement, Octant, Outlier, Panel, Passus, > PIECE, Platoon, Private, Public, Quarter, Rhythm, Rib, Segment, Severy, Slice, Stage, Ungula, Unit, Warm, Zenith, Zone

Secular Earthly, Laic, Non-CE, Profane, Temporal, Worldly

Secure, Security Anchor, Assurance, Bag, Bail, Band, Bar, Batten, Belay, Bellwether, Bolt, Bond, Bottomry, Buck Rogers, Calm, Catch, Cement, Chain, Cheka, Cinch, Clamp, Clasp, Clench, Clinch, Close, Cocoon, Collateral, Collective, Consols, Cushy, Debenture, Dunnage, Engage, Ensure, Equity, Establishment, Fasten, Fastness, Fortify, Frap, Fungibles, Gilt, Grith, Guarantee, Guy, Hypothec, Immune, Indemnity, Invest(ment), Knot, Lace, Land, Lash, Latch, Lien, Listed, Lock, Lockaway, Long-dated, Longs, Medium-dated, Mortgage, Nail, National, Obtain, Patte, Pin, Pledge, Pot, Pre-empt, Preference, Protect, Quad, Rope, Rug, > SAFE, Safety, Settle, Snell, Snug, Social, Sound, Stable, Stanchion, Staple, Staylace, Stock, Strap, Sure(ty), Tack, Take, Tie, Tight, Trap, Trice, Warrant, Watertight, Wedge, Win

Sedan Battle, Brougham, Chair, Jampan(i), Jampanee, Litter, Palanquin, Palkee, Palki, Saloon

Sedate Calm, Cool, Decorous, Dope, Douce, Drug, Sad, Serene, Sober(sides), Staid, Stand

Sedative Amytal®, Anodyne, Aspirin, Barbitone, Bromide, Chloral, Depressant, Hypnic, Laurel water, Lenitive, Lupulin, Meprobamate, Metopryl, Miltown, Narcotic, Nembutal®, Opiate, Paraldehyde, Pethidine, Phenobarbitone, Premed(ication), Scopolamine, Seconal®, Soothing, Thridace, Valerian, Veronal

Sedentary Inactive, Sessile, Stationary

Sedge Carex, Chufa, Grey, Seg, Xyris

Sediment Alluvium, Chalk, Deposit, Dregs, F(a)eces, Fecula, Foots, Grounds, Grouts, Lees, Molasse, Placer, Residue, Salt, Sapropel, Silt, Sludge, Terrigenous, Till, Turbidite, Varve, Warp

Sedition, Seditious Incitement, Insurrection, Revolt, Riot, Treason

Seduce(r), Seductive Allure, Betray, Bewitch, Bribe, Cuckold-maker, Debauch, Dishonour, Entice, Honeyed, Honied, Jape, Lothario, Luring, Mislead, Pull, Siren, Slinky, Tempt, Trepan, Undo, Wrong

▷ **Seduce** *may indicate* one word inside another

See(ing) Acknow, Apostolic, Barchester, Behold, Bishopric, C, Consider, Deek, Descry, Diocesan, Discern, Durham, Ecce, Ely, Episcopal, Eye, Glimpse, Holy, La, Lo, Meet, Norwich, Notice, Observe, Papal, Perceive, Realise, Remark, Ripon, Rumble, Since, Sodor and Man, Spae, Spot, Spy, Truro, Twig, Understand, V, Vatican, Vid(e), View, Vision, Visit, Voila, Witness, York

Seed(s), Seedy Achene, Argan, Arilli, Arillode, Ash-key, Bean, Ben, Best, Bonduc, Cacoon, Caraway, Carvy, Cebadilla, Cevadilla, Chickpea, Cocoa, Colza, Coriander, Corn, Crabstone, Cum(m)in, Dragon's teeth, Embryo, Endosperm, Ergot, Favourite, Fern, Germ, Grain, Gritty, Issue, Ivory-nut, Kernel, Lima, Lomentum, Mangy, Miliary, Niger, Nucellous, Nut, Offspring, Ovule, Pea, Pinon, Pip, Poorly, Poppy, Sabadilla, Scuzz, Semen, Seminal, Sesame, Shabby, Shea-nut, Silique, Sorus, Sow, Sperm, Spore, Terminator, Zoosperm

Seed-case Aril, Bur(r), Endopleura, Husk, Pea(s)cod, Pod, Testa, Theca

Seed-leaf Cotyledon

Seedsman Driller, Nurseryman, Sower

Seek(er) Ask, Beg, Busk, Chase, Court, Endeavour, Ferret out, Pursue, Quest, Scur, Search, Skirr, Solicit, Suitor

Seem(ingly) Appear, Look, Ostensible, Purport, Quasi, Think

Seemly Comely, Decent, Decorous, Fit, Suitable

Seep Dribble, Exude, Leak, Ooze, Osmose, Percolate

Seer Augur, Auspex, Eye, Melampus, Nahum, Observer, Oculiform, Onlooker, Prescience, Prophet, Sage, Sibyl, Soothsayer, T(e)iresias, Witness, Zoroaster

Seesaw Bascule, Teeter(-totter), Tilt, Vacillate, Wild mare

Seethe(d) Boil, Bubble, Churn, Ferment, Simmer, Smoulder, Sod

Segment Antimere, Arthromere, Cut, Division, Gironny, Gyronny, Intron, Lacinate, Lobe, Merome, Merosome, Metamere, Part, Pig, Propodeon, Prothorax, Scliff, Share, Shie, Skliff, Somite, Split, Sternite, Syllable, Tagma, Telson, Trochanter, Urite, Uromere

Segregate, Segregation Apartheid, Exile, Insulate, Intern, > **ISOLATE**, Jim Crow, Seclude, Separate

Seidlitz Powder, Rochelle

Seismic Terremotive

Seismograph Tromometer

Seize, Seizure Angary, Apprehend, Areach, Arrest, Assume, Attach(ment), Bag, Bone, Capture, Claw, Cleek, Cly, Collar, Commandeer, Confiscate, Distrain, Distress, Extent, For(e)hent, > **GRAB**, Grip, Hend, Impound, Impress, Maverick, Na(a)m, Nab, Nap, Nim, Poind, Possess, Pot, Raid, Replevy, Rifle, Sequestrate,

Smug, Tackle, Trover, Usurp, Wingding

Seldom Infrequent, Rare, Unoften

Select(ion), **Selecting**, **Selector** Assortment, Bla(u)d, Cap, Casting, Choice, Choose, Classy, Cull, Darwinism, Discriminate, Draft, Draw, Eclectic, Edit, Elite, Excerpt, Exclusive, Extract, Favour, Garble, Inside, K, Kin, Nap, Natural, Pericope, > PICK, Pot-pourri, Prefer, Recherché, Sample, Seed, Sex, Single, Sort, Stream, Tipster, Triage, UCCA

Selenium Se, Zorgite

Self Atman, Auto, Character, Ego, Person, Psyche, Seity, Sel, Soul

Self-confidence Aplomb, Ego

Self-contained Absolute, Reticent, SC, Taciturn

Self-contradictory Absurd, Irish

Self-control, **Self-discipline** Ascesis, Encraty, Modesty, Patience, Restraint, Temper(ance)

▶ **Self-defence** *see* MARTIAL (ARTS)

Self-esteem Amour-propre, Conceit, Confidence, Egoism, Pride

Self-evident Axiom, Manifest, Obvious, Patent, Truism, Truth

Self-existence Solipsism

Self-fertilisation, **Self-origination** Aseity, Autogamy

Self-governing Autonomy, Idior(r)hythmic, Kabele, Kebel, Puritanism, Swaraj

Self-help Smiles

Self-important, **Self-indulgent**, **Self-interested** Aristippus, Arrogant, Chesty, Cocky, Conceited, Immoderate, Jack-in-office, Licentious, Narcissistic, Pompous, Pragmatic, Profligate, Solipsist, Sybarite

Selfish(ness) Avaricious, Egoist, Grabby, Greedy, Hedonist, Mean, Solipsism

Selfless(ness) Non-ego, Tuism

Self-limiting Kenotic

▶ **Self-origination** *see* SELF-FERTILISATION

Self-pollinating Cl(e)istogamic

Self-possession Aplomb, Composure, Cool, Nonchalant

Self-satisfied, **Self-satisfaction** Complacent, Narcissism, Smug, Tranquil

Self-service Automat, Buffet, Cafeteria, Supermarket

Self-sufficiency Absolute, Autarky, Complete

Self-taught Autodidact

Sell(er), **Selling** Apprize, Auction, Barter, Bear, Betray, Catch, Chant, Chaunt, Cope, Costermonger, Direct, Dispose, Do, Fancier, Flog, Go, Hard, Have, Hawk, Hustle, Inertia, Knock down, Market, Marketeer, Menage, Merchant, Missionary, Oligopoly, Pardoner, Peddle, Peddler, Pick-your-own, Purvey, Push, Pyramid, Rabbito(h), Realise, Rep, Retail, Ruse, Simony, Soft, Stall-man, Sugging, Switch, > TRADE, Vend

Selvage Border, Edge, Roon

Semantics General, Generative, Interpretive, Notional, Onomasiology

Semaphore Signal, Tic-tac, Wigwag

Semblance Aspect, Likeness, Sign, Verisimilitude

Semen Jis(so)m, Milt, Spunk

Semi-conductor Germanium, LED, Thryristor

Seminar(y) Class, Colloquium, Group, Theologate, Tutorial, Workshop

Semiotics Syntactics

Semi-paralysis Dyaesthesia

Semitic Accadian, Akkadian, Ammonite, Amorite, Arab, Aramaic, Canaanite, Chaldean, Geez, Jewish, Phoenician

Semitone Pycnon

Senate Council, Curia, Seanad (Eireann)
Senator Antiani, Cicero, Elder, Legislator, Solon
Send, Sent Consign, > DESPATCH, Disperse, Emit, Entrance, Issue, Launch, Mail, Order, Post, Rapt, Ship, Transmit, Transport
Send back Refer, Remand, Remit, Return
Send down Lower, Rusticate
Send up Chal(l)an, Lampoon, Promote
Senegal SN
Senescence Age
Senile, Senility Caducity, Dementia, Disoriented, Doddery, Doitit, Dotage, Eild, Eld, Gaga, Nostology, Twichild
Senior Aîné, Doyen, Elder, Father, Grecian, Mayor, Père, Primus, Superior, Upper
Senna Bladder
Senor(a) Caballero, Don(a), Hidalga, Hidalgo
Sensation(al) Acolouthite, Anoesis, Aura, Blood, Commotion, Emotion, Empfindung, Feeling, Gas, Impression, Lurid, Melodrama, Par(a)esthesia, Pyrotechnic, Shocker, Shock-horror, Showstopper, Splash, Stir, Styre, Synaesthesia, Thrill, Tingle, Vibes, Wow, Yellow
Sense, Sensual, Sensing Acumen, Aura, Carnal, Coherence, Common, Dress, ESP, Faculty, Feel, Gross, Gumption, Gustation, Hearing, Horse, Idea, Import, Instinct, Intelligence, Intuition, Lewd, Meaning, Nous, Olfactory, Palate, Perceptual, Rational, Receptor, Remote, Rumble-gumption, Rumgumption, Rum(m)el-gumption, Rum(m)le-gumption, Sight, Sixth, Slinky, Smell, Sybarite, Synesis, Taste, Touch, Voluptuary, Voluptuous, Wisdom, Wit
Senseless Absurd, Anosmia, Illogical, Inane, Mad, Numb, Stupid, Stupor, Unconscious, Unwise
Sensible Aware, Dianoetic, Down to earth, Prudent, Raisonné, Rational, Sane, Solid, Well-balanced
Sensitive, Sensitivity Algesia, Alive, Allergic, Atopy, Dainty, Delicate, Erethism, Erogenous, Hypaesthesia, Keen, Nesh, Nociceptive, Orthochromatic, Passible, Sympathetic, Tactful, Tender, Thermaesthesia, Thin-skinned, Ticklish, Touchy(-feely), Vulnerable
Sensor Detector, Palpi, Remote
Sentence(s) Assize, Bird, Carpet, Clause, Closed, Commit, Complex, Compound, Condemn, Custodial, Death, Decree(t), Deferred, Doom, Fatwah, Indeterminate, Judgement, Life, Matrix, Open, Pangram, Paragraph, Period(ic), Porridge, Predicate, Rap, Rheme, Rune, Simple, Stretch, Suspended, Swy, Tagmene, Time, Topic, Verdict, Versicle, Weigh off
Sententious Concise, Gnomic, Laconic, Pithy, Pompous, Terse
Sentiment(al), Sentimentality Byronism, Corn, Cornball, Drip, Feeling, Goo, Govey, Gucky, Gush, Hokey, Icky, Maudlin, Mawkish, Mind, Mush, Namby-pamby, Nostalgia, Opinion, Romantic, Rose-pink, Rosewater, Saccharin, Schmaltzy, Sloppy, Smoochy, Soppy, Spoony, Sugary, Tear-jerker, Traveller, Treacly, Twee, View, Weepy, Yucky
Sentry Custodian, Guard, Jaga, Picket, Sentinel, Vedette, Vidette, Watch
Separate(d), Separation, Separately Abstract, Asunder, Atmolysis, Avulsion, Comma, Compartmentalise, Cull, Cut, Decollate, Decompose, Decouple, Deduct, Deglutinate, Demarcate, Demerge, Detach, Dialyse, Diastasis, Diazeuxis, Diremption, Disally, Discerp, Disconnect, Discrete, Disjunction, Dissociate, Distance, Distinct, Disunite, Divide, Division, Divorce, Eloi(g)n, Elute, Elutriate, Esloin, Estrange, Filter, Grade, Heckle, Hive, Hyphenate, Insulate, Intervene, Isolate, Judicial, Laminate, Lease, Legal, Monosy, Part,

Particle, Peel off, Piece, Prescind, Ramify, Red(d), Rift, Scatter, Schism, Screen, Scutch, Secern, Segregate, Sequester, Sever, Several, Shed, Shore, Shorn, Sift, Sleave, Sle(i)ded, Solitary, Sort, > **SPLIT**, Steam-trap, Stream, Sunder, Sundry, Tems(e), Tmesis, Try, Twin(e), Unclasp, Unravel, Winnow, Wrench, Yandy

Sepia Cuttle, Ink

Seppuku Hara-kiri, Hari-kari

Septic Poisonous, Rotting

Septimus Small

Septum Mediastinum

Sepulchral, Sepulchre Bier, Cenotaph, Charnel, Crypt, Funeral, Monument, Pyramid, Tomb, Vault, Whited

Sequel After-clap, Consequence, Effect, Outcome, Suite

Sequence Agoge, Algorithm, Byte, Chronological, Continuity, Continuum, Escape, Fibonacci, Intervening, Intron, Line, Main, Order, Peptide, Polar, Program(me), Routine, Run, Seriatim, Series, Signal, Succession, Suit, Suite, Train, Vector

Sequester, Sequestrate Confiscate, Esloin, Esloyne, Impound, Isolate, Retire, Seclude, Separate

Sequin Paillette, Zecchino

Sequoia Redwood

Seraph Abdiel, > **ANGEL**

Serb(ian) Chetnik

Sere Arid, > **DRY**, Scorch, Wither

Serenade(r) Aubade, Charivari, Horning, Love song, Minstrel, Nocturne, Shivaree, Sing-song, Wait, Wake

Serene, Serenity Calm, Composed, Impassive, Placid, Repose, Sangfroid, Sedate, Smooth, > **TRANQUIL**

Serf(dom) Adscript, Bondman, Ceorl, Churl, Helot, Manred, > **SLAVE**, Thete, Thrall, Vassal, Velle(i)nage

Serge Russian, Say

Sergeant Buztuz, Colour, Cuff, Drill, Havildar, Kite, Lance, > **NCO**, Platoon, RSM, Sarge, SL, SM, Staff, Technical, Troy

Serial Episode, Feuilleton, Heft, Livraison

Series Actinide, Actinium, Balmer, Catena, Chain, Concatenation, Continuum, Course, Cycle, Cyclus, Electromotive, Enfilade, Engrenage, En suite, Episode, Ethylene, Fibonacci, Fourier, Geometric, Gradation, Harmonic, Homologous, Lanthanide, Line, Links, Loop, Maclaurin's, Methane, Neptunium, Partwork, Power, > **PROGRESSION**, Radioactive, Rest, Routine, Rubber, Run, Sequence, Ser, Sitcom, String, Succession, Suit, Taylor's, Thorium, Time, Tone, Train, Uranium, World

Serious(ly) Critical, Earnest, Grave, Gravitas, Heavy, Important, Major, Momentous, Pensive, Sad, Serpentine, Sober, Solemn, Sombre, Staid, Straight(-faced), Very

Sermon Address, Discourse, Gatha, Homily, Lecture, Preachment, Spital

Serow Goral, Thar

Serpent(ine) Adder, Amphisbaena, Anguine, Apepi, Apophis, Asp, Aspic(k), Basilisk, Boa, Caduceus, Cockatrice, Dipsas, Firedrake, Midgard, Nagas, Ophiolite, Ouroboros, Peridotite, Retinalite, Sea-snake, Shesha, > **SNAKE**, Traitor, Uraeus, Viper, Wyvern

Serrate(d) Diprionidian, Saw, Scallop, Serried

Serum Antilymphocyte, Antitoxin, ATS, Fluid, Humoral, Opsonin, Senega

Serval Bush-cat

Servant, Serve(r) Attendant, Ayah, Batman, Bearer, Bedder, Bedmaker, Between-maid, Boot-catcher, Boots, Boy, Butler, Caddie, Chaprassi, Chuprassy, Civil, Columbine, Cook, Daily, Domestic, Dromio, Drudge, Employee, Factotum, Famulus, File, Flunkey, Footboy, Footman, Friday, Gehazi, G(h)illie, Gip, Gully, Gyp, Haiduk, Handmaid, Helot, Henchman, Heyduck, Hireling, Iras, Jack, Jack-slave, Jeames, Khansama(h), Khidmutgar, Khitmutgar, Kitchen-knave, Lackey, Lady's maid, Lazy Susan, Maid, Major-domo, Man, Man Friday, Menial, Minion, Myrmidon, Nethinim, Obedient, Page, Pantler, Person, Postman, Public, Retainer, Retinue, Scout, Scrub, Scullion, Servitor, Sewer, Skip, Slavey, Soubrette, Steward, Tapsman, Tendance, Theow, Thete, Tiger, Tweeny, Underling, Vails, Vales, Valet, Valkyrie, Varlet, Vassal, Waiter, Wash-rag, Weller

Serve, Service(s) Ace, Act, Active, Amenity, Answer, Arriage, Asperges, Assist, ATS, Attendance, Avail, Benediction, Breakfast, Candlemas, Cannonball, Ceefax®, China, Civil, Communion, Community, Complin(e), Corvée, Credo, Devotional, Dinnerset, Diplomatic, Dish, Divine, Do, Dow, Drumhead, Duty, Ecosystem, Employ, Evensong, Facility, Fault, Fee, Feudal, Fish, Foreign, Forensic, Forward, > **FUNCTION**, Further, Go, Help, Helpline, Hour, Ka(e), Kol Nidre, Let, Line, Ling, Lip, Litany, Liturgy, Mass, Mat(t)ins, Memorial, Mincha, Minister, Ministry, Missa, National, Nocturn, Nones, Oblige, Office, Oracle, Overarm, Overhaul, Pass, Pay, Personal, Pit stop, Possum, Pottery, Prime, Proper, Public, RAF, Requiem, Rite, RN, Room, Sacrament, Secret, Selective, Senior, Sext, Shacharis, Shaharith, Shuttle, Silver, Social, Sorb, Stead, Sted, Sue, Tableware, Tea, Tenebrae, Trental, Uncork, Under-arm, Use, Utility, Vespers, Wait, Waiterage, Watch-night, Worship, Yeoman('s)

Service-book Hymnal, Hymnary, Missal, Triodion

▷ **Serviceman** *may indicate* a churchman

Servile, Servility Abasement, Base, Crawling, Knee, Lickspittle, Menial, Obsequious, Slavish, Slimy, Suck-hole, Sycophantic, Truckle

Serving Helping, Heuristic, Portion

Servitude Bondage, Domination, Peonism, Slavery, Thrall, Vassalry, Yoke

Sesame Gingelly, Gingili, Grapple-plant, Jinjilli, Semsem, Tahini, Til

Session(s) Bout, Executive, Galah, Jam, Kirk, Meeting, Nightshift, Petty, Poster, Quarter, Rap, Round, Séance, Sederunt, Settle, Sitting, Term

Set(ting) (down; in; off; out; up) Activate, Adjust, Appoint, Arrange, Batch, Bent, Bezel, Boun, Brooch, Cabal, Cake, Case, Cast, Chaton, Class, Claw, Clique, Cliveden, Closed, Coagulate, Cock, Cockshy, Collection, Collet, Comp(ositor), Companion, Compose, Congeal, Context, Coterie, Couvert, Crew, Crystal, Cyclorama, Data, Dead, Decline, Decor, Detonate, Diorama, Dispose, Earnest, Earth, Environment, Establish, Explode, Film, Fit, Flagstone, Flash, Flat(s), Found, Garniture, Geal, Gel, Genome, Group, Harden, Ilk, Incut, Infinite, Jee, Jeel, Jell(y), Jet, Kit, Laid, Land, Lay, Leg, Locale, Locate, Lot, Mandelbrot, Milieu, Mise en scène, Monture, Mournival, Nest, Occident, Open, Ordered, Ordinate, Ouch, Parure, Permanent, Physique, Pitch, Place(ment), Plant, Plaste, Ply, Posed, Posit, Power, Put, Radio, Ready, Receiver, Relay, Rigid, Rooted, Rubber, Saw, Scenery, Series, Showcase, Sink, Smart, Solidify, Squad, Stand, Stationed, Stede, Stell, Stick, Stiffen, Still, Stream, Subscriber, Suit, Suite, Surround, Synchronize, Tar, Tea, Team, Teeth, Televisor, Telly, Tiffany, Till, Toilet, Trigger, Truth, Tube, Venn (diagram), Weather, Wide-screen, Yplast

Setback Bodyblow, Checkmate, Hiccup, Jolt, Relapse, Retard, Retreat, Reversal, Scarcement, Sickener, Tes, Vicissitude

Setter Cement, Comp, Dog, English, Gordon, Gundog, Irish, Pectin, Red, Smoot,

Sphinx, Trend

Settle(d), Settler, Settlement Adjust, Agree, Alight, Appoint, Arrange,
Ascertain, Ausgleich, Avenge, Balance, Bandobast, Bed, Bench, Boer,
Borghetto, Bundobust, Bustee, Camp, Clear, Clench, Clinch, Colonial,
Colonise, Colony, Compose, Compound, Compromise, Crannog, Decide, Defray,
Determine, Diktat, Discharge, Dispose, Dorp, Dowry, Ekistics, Encamp, Endow,
Ensconce, Entail, Establish, Expat, Faze, Feeze, Fix, Foot, Foreclose, Gravitate,
Gridironer, Guilder, Habitant, Illegitimate, Informal, Jointure, Kibbutz,
Land, Ledge, Light, Lyte, Manyat(t)a, Merino, Mission, Moshav, Nahal, Nest,
Nestle, Oecist, Oikist, Opt, Outpost, Over, Pa(h), Pakka, Pale, Patroon, Pay,
Peise, Penal, Perch, Pheazar, Pheese, Pheeze, Phese, Pilgrim, Pioneer, Placate,
Planter, Populate, Port Arthur, Port Nicholson, Presidio, Pucka, Pueblo, Pukka,
Rancheria, Rancherie, Readjust, Reduction, Reimburse, Remit, Reside,
Resolve, Rest, Sate, Satisfaction, Secure, Sedimentary, Set fair, Shagroon,
Silt, Smoot, Sofa, Soldier, Solve, Soweto, Square, State, Still, Straits, Subside,
Taurus, Township, Ujamaa, Utu, Vest(ed), Viatical, Voortrekker
▷ **Settlement** *may indicate* an anagram
▷ **Settler** *may indicate* a coin
Set upon Assail, Attack, Sick
Seven(th) Ages, Days, Dials, Great Bear, Hebdomad, Hepta-, Hills, Magnificent,
Nones, Pleiad(es), S, Sages, Seas, Septenary, Septimal, Sins, Sisters, Sleepers,
Stars, Wonders, Zeta
Seventy S
Sever Amputate, Cut, Detach, Divide, Sunder
Several Divers, Many, Multiple, Some, Sundry
Severe(ly), Severity Acute, Bad, Caustic, Chronic, Cruel, Dour, Draconian,
Drastic, Eager, Extreme, Grave, Grievous, Gruel(ling), Hard, > **HARSH**, Ill,
Inclement, Morose, Penal, Rhadamanthine, Rigo(u)r, Roaring, Roundly,
Serious, Sharp, Snell(y), Sore, Spartan, Stern, Strict, Swingeing
Sew(ing), Sew up Baste, Clinch, Cope, Embroider, Fell, Machine, Mitre,
Overcast, Overlock, Run, Seam, Seel, Stitch, Tack, Whip
Sewage, Sewer Cesspool, Cloaca, Culvert, Dorcas, > **DRAIN**, Effluence, Jaw-box,
Jaw-hole, Mimi, Needle, Privy, Shore, Soil, Sough, Soughing-tile, Waste
Sex(y) Bed-hopping, Coupling, Cunnilingus, Erotic, Fair, Favours, Fellatio,
Female, Foreplay, Fornication, French, Gam(ic), Gamahuche, Gamaruche,
Gender, Hanky-panky, Hump, Incest, Intercourse, Kind, Libidinous, Libido,
Lingam, Lumber, Male, Mate, Nookie, Oomph, Opposite, Oral, Paedophilia,
Pederasty, Phat, Priapean, Race, Randy, Raunchy, Rut(ish), Safe, Salacious,
Screw, Sect, Steamy, Sultry, Teledildonics, Troilism, Unprotected, Venereal,
Venery, VI, Voluptuous, Weaker
Sex appeal It, Oomph, SA
Sexcentenarian Shem
Sexless Agamogenetic, Atoke, N, Neuter
Sextet Over, Six
Sexton Blake, Fossor, Sacristan, Shammes, Warden
Seychelles SY
Sh P, Quiet
Shabby Base, Buckeen, Dog-eared, Down-at-heel, Fusc(ous), Grotty, Mangy,
Mean, Moth-eaten, Oobit, Oorie, Oubit, Ourie, Outworn, Owrie, Raunch,
Scaly, Scruffy, Seedy, Shoddy, Squalid, Tacky, Tatty, Worn, Woubit
Shack Heap, Hideout, Hovel, Hut
Shackle(s) Bilboes, Bind, Bracelet, Chain, Entrammel, Fetter(lock), Gyve,

Hamper, Irons, Manacle, Restrict, Tie, Trammel, Yoke
Shad Allice, Allis, Fish, Twait(e)
Shaddock Grapefruit, Pomelo
Shade(d), **Shades**, **Shading**, **Shadow**, **Shady** Adumbrate, Arbour, Arcade, Awning, Blend, Blind, Bongrace, Bowery, Brise-soleil, Brocken spectre, Buff, Cast, Chiaroscuro, Chroma, Cloche, Cloud, Cross-hatch, Degree, Dis, Dog, Dubious, Eclipse, Eye, Five o'clock, Galanty, Gamp, Ghost, Gradate, Gray, Hachure, Hell, Herbar, Hint, Hue, Inumbrate, Larva, Lee, Melt, Mezzotint, Nuance, Opaque, Overtone, Parasol, Phantom, Presence, Rain, Ray-Bans®, Satellite, Screen, Shroud, Sienna, Silhouette, Silvan, Skia-, Soften, Spectre, Spirit, Stag, Sunglasses, Swale, Swaly, Tail, Tinge, Tint, Tone, Ugly, Umbra(tile), Umbrage(ous), Underhand, Velamen, Velar(ium), Velum, Visor
Shadowless Ascian
Shaft(ed), **Shafting** Arbor, Arrow, Axle tree, Barb, Barrow-train, Beam, Capstan, Cardan, Chimney, Column, Crank, Cue, Diaphysis, Disselboom, Dolly, Drive, Fil(l), Fust, Idler, Incline, Journal, Lamphole, Limber, Loom, Mandrel, Mandril, Manhole, Moon pool, Moulin, Parthian, Passage, Pile, Pit, Pitch, Pole, Propeller, Quill (drive), Ray, Scape, Scapus, Shank, Snead, Spindle, Staff, Stairwell, Stale, Steal(e), Steel, Stele, Stem, Stulm, Sunbeam, Thill, Tige, Trave, Upcast, Well, Winning, Winze
Shag Cronet, Hair, Intercourse, Nap, Pile, Scart(h), Skart(h), Tire, Tobacco
Shaggy Ainu, Comate, Hairy, Hearie, Hirsute, Horrid, Horror, Nappy, Rough, Rugged, Shock, Shough, Tatty, Untidy
Shah Ruler, Sophi, Sophy
Shake(n), **Shakes**, **Shaky** Ague(-fit), Astonish, Brandish, Coggle, Concuss, Dabble, Dick(e)y, Didder, Dither, Dodder, > **DT's**, Feeble, Groggy, Hod, Hotch, Jar, Jiggle, Joggle, Jolt, Jounce, Judder, Jumble, Milk, Mo, Nid-nod, Press flesh, Quake, Quiver, Quooke, Rattle, Rickety, Rickle, > **ROCK**, Rouse, Shimmer, Shiver, Shock, Shog, Shoogle, Shudder, Succuss(ation), Sweat, Tremble, Tremolo, Tremor, Tremulous, Trill(o), Tumbledown, Undulate, Vibrate, Vibrato, Wag, Waggle, Wind, Wobble, Wonky
▷ **Shake** *may indicate* an anagram
Shakedown Blackmail, Chantage, Pallet
Shakespeare Bard, Will, WS
Shale Blaes, Fa(i)kes, Kerogen, Rock, Till, Torbanite
Shall Sal
Shallot C(h)ibol, Onion, Scallion, Sybo(e), Sybow
Shallow(s) Ebb, Flat, Fleet, Flew, Flue, Justice, Neritic, Shoal, Slight, Superficial
Sham Apocryphal, Bluff, Bogus, Braide, Charade, Counterfeit, Deceit, Fake, > **FALSE**, Hoax, Idol, Impostor, Mimic, Mock, Phony, Pinchbeck, Postiche, Potemkin, Pretence, Pseudo, Repro, Simulated, Snide, Spurious
Shamble(s) Abattoir, Bauchle, Butchery, Mess, Shuffle, Totter, Tripple
Shame(ful), **Shame-faced** Abash, Aidos, Chagrin, Contempt, Crying, Degrade, Discredit, Disgrace, Dishonour, Embarrass, Fi donc, Fie, Gross, Hangdog, Honi, Humiliate, Ignominy, Infamy, Inglorious, Modesty, Mortify, Pity, Pudency, Pudor, Pugh, Shend, Sin, Slander, Stain, Stigma, Yshend
Shameless Audacious, Brash, Immodest, Ithyphallic
Shampoo(ing) Massage, Tripsis, Wash
Shandy Drink, Sterne, Tristram
Shanghai Abduct, Kidnap, Trick
Shank Leg, Shaft, Steal(e), Steel, Steil, Stele, Strike
Shanty, **Shanty town** Boatsong, Bothy, Bustee, Cabin, Dog-hole, Favela,

Forebitter, Hutment, Lean-to, Pondok, Sea, Shack, Song

Shape(d), Shapely, Shaping Blancmange, Boast, Bruting, Cast, Contour, Face, Fashion, Figure, Form, Format, Geoid, Gnomon, Headquarters, Hew, Holohedron, Jello, Model, Morph, > MOULD, Net, Pendentive, Ream, Rhomb(us), Scabble, Sculpt, Spile, Tromino, Turn, Whittle, Wrought, Zaftig, Zoftig

Shapeless Amorphous, Chaos, Dumpy, Indigest, Vague

Shard Fragment, Sliver, Splinter

Share(d), Shares, Sharing Allocation, Allotment, Apportion, Blue-chip, Bovate, Cahoots, Chop, Co, Cohabit, Coho(e), Common, Communal, Contango, Culter, Cut, Deferred, Divi(dend), Divide, Divvy, Dole, Dutch, Equity, Finger, Golden, Impart, Interest, Job, Kaffer, Kaf(f)ir, Kangaroo, Lion's, Market, Moiety, Odd lot, Ordinary, Oxgang, Oxgate, Oxland, Parcener, > PART, Partake, Participate, Penny, PIBS, Plough, Plough-iron, Portion, Prebend, Pref(erred), Preference, Pro rata, Prorate, Quarter, Quota, Rake off, Ration, Rug, Rundale, Scrip, Security, Shr, Slice, Snack, Snap, Sock, Split, Stock, Taurus, Teene, Time, Tranche, Two-way, Whack

Shareholder Stag

Shark Angel, Basking, Beagle, Blue, Bluepointer, Bonnethead, Bronze-whaler, Carpet, Cestracion, Cow, Demoiselle, Dog(fish), Flake, Fox, Gummy, Hammerhead, Houndfish, Huss, Lemonfish, Loan, Mackerel, Mako, Miller's dog, Monkfish, Noah, Nurse, Penny-dog, Plagiostomi, Porbeagle, Requiem, Rhin(e)odon, Rigg, Sail-fish, Saw, School, Sea-ape, Sea-lawyer, Sharp, Shovelhead, Smoothhound, Soupfin, Squaloid, Swindler, Thrasher, Thresher, Tiger, Tope, Usurer, Whale, Wobbegong, Zygaena

Sharkskin Shagreen

Sharp(er), Sharpen(er), Sharpness Abrupt, Accidental, Acerose, Acidulous, Acrid, Aculeus, Acumen, Acuminate, Acute, Alert, Angular, Arris, Bateless, Becky, Benchstone, Bitter, Brisk, Cacuminous, Cheat, Clear, Coticular, Cutting, Dital, Edge(r), Fine, Fly, Gleg, Grind, Hone, Hot, Keen, Kurtosis, Massé, Oilstone, Penetrant, Peracute, Piquant, Poignant, Pronto, Pungent, Razor, Rogue, Rook, Set, Shrewd, Snap, Snell, Sour, Spicate, Strop, Swindler, Tart, Testy, Tomium, Twenty-twenty, Vivid, Volable, Whet

Sharpshooter Bersaglier, Franc-tireur, Sniper, Tirailleur, Voltigeur

Shatter(ing) Astone, Break, Brisance, Craze, Dash, Explode, Shiver, Smash, Smithereen, Splinter, Unnerve

Shave(r), Shaving(s) Barb(er), Excelsior, Filings, Flake, Grain, Moslings, Pare, Plane, Pogonotomy, Poll, Raze, Scrape, Skive, Sliver, Splinter, Swarf, Todd, Tonsure, Whittle

Shaw Artie, Green, Spinn(e)y, Wood

Shawl Afghan, Buibui, Cashmere, Chuddah, Chuddar, Dopatta, Dupatta, Fichu, India, Kaffiyeh, Kashmir, Mantilla, Maud, Paisley, Partlet, Prayer, Serape, Stole, Tallis, Tallit(ot), Tallith, Tonnag, Tozie, Tribon, Whittle, Wrap(per), Zephyr

She A, Hoo

Sheaf Aplustre, Bundle, Folder, Gait, Garb(e), Gerbe, Mow, Shock, Thr(e)ave

Shear(s), Shearer Clip, Cut, Fleece, Greasy, Pinking, Poll, Ring(er), Shave, Snips, Trim, Wind

Sheath Axolemma, Capsule, Case, Cocoon, Coleorhiza, Condom, Cover, Extine, Fingerstall, Glume, Medullary, Myelin, Neurilemma, Neurolemma, Oc(h)rea, Perineurium, Periosteum, Quiver, Rhinotheca, Root, Scabbard, Spathe, Thecal, Thumbstall, Vagina, Volva, Wing

Sheave Bee, Clevis

Shed(ding), Shedder Autotomy, Barn, Cast, Cho(u)ltry, Coducity, Depot, Discard, Doff, Drop, Ecdysis, Effuse, Emit, Exuviate, Hangar, Hovel, Hut, Infuse, Lair, Lean-to, Linhay, Linny, Mew, Milking, Moult, Outhouse, Pent, Potting, Salmon, Shearing, Shippen, Shippon, Shuck, Skeo, Skillion, Skio, Slough, Sow, Spend, Spent, Spill, Tilt, Tool

Sheen Glaze, Gloss, Luminance, Lustre, Patina, Schiller, Shine

Sheep(ish) Ammon, Ancon(es), Aoudad, Argali, Barbary, Bell(wether), Bharal, Bident, Bighorn, Black, Blackface, Blate, Border Leicester, Broadtail, Burhel, Burrel(l), Caracul, Cheviots, Coopworth, Corriedale, Cotswold, Coy, Crone, Dinmont, Dorset Down, Dorset Horn, Down, Drysdale, Embarrassed, Ewe, Exmoor, Fank, Fat-tailed, Flock, Fold, Hair, Hampshire, Hampshire Down, Hangdog, Herdwick, Hidder, Hirsel, Hog(g), Hogget, Jacob, Jemmy, Jumbuck, Karakul, Kent, Kerry Hill, Lamb, Lanigerous, Leicester, Lincoln, Lo(a)ghtan, Loghtyn, Lonk, Marco Polo, Masham, Merino, Mor(t)ling, Mouf(f)lon, Mountain, Muflon, Mug, Mus(i)mon, Mutton, Oorial, Ovine, Oxford Down, Perendale, Portland, Ram, Rambouillet, Romeldale, Romney Marsh, Rosella, Ryeland, Scottish Blackface, Shearling, Shorthorn, > SHY, Soay, Southdown, Spanish, Stone('s), Suffolk, Sumph, Swaledale, Teeswater, Teg(g), Texel, Theave, Trip, Tup, Two-tooth, Udad, Urial, Vegetable, Welsh Mountain, Wensleydale, Wether, Wiltshire Horn, Woollyback, Yow(e), Yowie

Sheep disease Blue tongue, Braxy, Dunt, Gid, Hoove, Louping-ill, Orf, Rubbers, Scrapie, Sturdy, Swayback, Variola, Water-brain, Wildfire, Wind

Sheepdog Collie, Huntaway, Maremma

Sheepfold Fank, Pen

Sheepskin Basan, Caracul, Karakul, Mouton, Roan, Wool

Sheeptrack Terracette

Sheer Absolute, Clear, Main, Mere, Peekaboo, Plumb, Precipitous, Pure, Simple, Stark, Steep, Swerve, Thin, Utter

Sheet(s), Sheeting Balance, Cellophane, Cere-cloth, Cerement, Charge, Chart, Clean, Crime, Cutch, Dope, Expanse, Film, Flow, Fly, Folio, Foolscap, Heft, Ice, Inset, Leaf, Membrane, Nappe, Out-hauler, Page, Pot(t), Pour, Proof, Prospectus, Ream, Rope, Sail, Scandal, Scratch, Shroud, Stern, Stratus, Taggers, Tarpaulin(g), Tear, Tentorium, Terne, Thunder, Time, Title, Web, White, Winding

Sheet-anchor Letter-weight, Paperweight

Sheet-iron Taggers, Terne(plate)

Sheikdom Bahrein, Dubai

Shekel Mina, Sickle

Sheldrake Bergander

Shelf, Shelve(s) Bank, Bar, Bracket, Continental, Counter, Credence, Delay, Dresser, Étagère, Hob, Ice, Ledge, Leeboard, Mantle, Overmantel, Postpone, Rack, Retable, Ross Ice, Shunt, Sidetrack, Sill, Spinsterhood, Whatnot, Windowsill

Shell(ed), Shellfish Abalone, Acorn-shell, Admiral, Ambulacrum, Ammo, Argonaut, Balamnite, Balanus, Balmain bug, Bivalve, Blitz, Boat, Bombard, Buckie, Camera, Capiz, Capsid, Carapace, Cartridge, Casing, Chank, Chelonia, Chitin, Clam, Clio, Coat-of-mail, Cochlea, Cockle, Cohog, Conch, Cone, Copepoda, Cover, Cowrie, Cowry, Crab, Crustacea, Cuttlefish, Dariole, Deerhorn, Dentalium, Dop, Drill, Electron, Escallop, Eugarie, Foraminifer, Framework, Frustule, Globigerina, Haliotis, Hull, Husk, Hyoplastron, Isopoda, Lamp, Langouste, Limacel, Limpet, Lobster, Lorica, Lyre, Malacostraca,

Midas's ear, Mollusc, Monocoque, Moreton Bay bug, Mother-of-pearl, Murex, Music, Mussel, Nacre, Nautilus, Ormer, Ostracod, Ostrea, Otter, Oyster, Paua, Pawa, Peag, Peak, Pea(s)cod, Pecten, Pereia, Periostracum, Periwinkle, Pipi, Pipsqueak, Plastron, Pod, Prawn, Projectile, Purple, Putamen, Quahog, Razor, Sal, Scalarium, Scallop, Scollop, Sea-ear, Sea-pen, Shale, Shard, Sheal, Sheel, Shiel, Shill, Shock, Shot, Shrapnel, Shrimp, Shuck, Sial, Smoke-ball, Spend, Spindle, Star, Stomatopod, Stonk, Straddle, Strafe, Stromb(us), Swan-mussel, Tear, Test(a), Thermidor, Toheroa, Tooth, Top, Torpedo, Trivalve, Turbo, Turritella, Tusk, Univalve, Valency, Venus, Wakiki, Wampum, Whelk, Whiz(z)bang, Winkle, Xenophya, Yabbie, Yabby, Zimbi

Shelled Cracked, Kernel

▷ **Shelled** *may indicate* an anagram

Shell money Wakiki, Wampum, Zimbi

Shelter Abri, Anderson, Asylum, Awn, Awning, Belee, Bender, Bield, Billet, Blind, Blockhouse, Booth, Bunker, Burladero, Butt, Cab, Carport, Casemate, Cot(e), Cove, Covert, Coverture, Defence, Dodger, Donga, Dripstone, Dug-out, Fall-out, Garage, Gunyah, Harbour, Haven, Hithe, Hospice, Hostel, House, Hovel, Humpy, Hut, Hutchie, Kipsie, Lee, Lee-gage, Loun, Lound, Lown, Lownd, Mai mai, Mission, Morrison, Nodehouse, > REFUGE, Retreat, Roof, Sanctuary, Scog, Sconce, Scoog, Scoug, Screen, Scug, Shed, Shiel(ing), Shroud, Skug, Snowshed, Stell, Storm-cellar, Succah, Sukkah, Summerhouse, Tax, Tent, Testudo, Tortoise, Tupik, Twigloo, Umbrage, Weather, Wheelhouse, Wi(c)kiup, Wickyup, Wil(t)ja, Windbreak

Shemozzle Debacle

Shenanigan Antic

Shepherd(ess) Abel, Acis, Amaryllis, Amos, Bergère, Bo-peep, Chloe, Clorin, Conduct, Corin, Corydon, Cuddy, Daphnis, Dorcas, Drover, Endymion, Escort, Ettrick, German, Good, Grubbinol, Gyges, Herdsman, Hobbinol, Lindor, Marshal, Menalcas, Padre, Pastor(al), Pastorella, Phebe, Sheepo, Strephon, Tar-box, Thenot, Thyrsis, Tityrus

Sheriff Bailiff, Deputy, Earp, Grieve, Land-dros(t), Lawman, Process-server, Shireman, Shirra, Shrievalty, Viscount

Sherry Amoroso, Bristol milk, Cobbler, Cyprus, Doctor, Fino, Gladstone, Jerez, Manzanilla, Oloroso, Palo cortado, Sack, Solera, Whitewash, Xeres

Sherwood Anderson, Forest

Shibboleth Password

Shield(s), **Shield-shaped** Ablator, Achievement, Aegis, Ancile, Armour, Arms, Baltic, Biological, Bodyguard, Box, Buckler, Canadian, Cartouche, Clypeus, Defend, Dress, Escutcheon, Fence, Gobo, Guard, Gyron, Hatchment, Heat, Hielaman, Insulate, Laurentian, Lozenge, Mant(e)let, Mask, Pavis(e), Pelta, Protect, Ranfurly, Riot, Rondache, Scandinavian, Screen, Scute, Scutum, Sheffield, Sternite, Targe(t), Thyroid, Vair, Visor

Shift(er), **Shifty** Amove, Astatic, Back, Blue, Budge, Change, Chemise, Core, Cymar, Day, Devious, Displace, Dogwatch, Doppler, Einstein, Evasive, Expedient, Fend, Function, Graveyard, Great Vowel, Hedging, Lamb, Landslide, Linen, Louche, Move, Night, Nighty, Paradigm, Red, Relay, Remove, Rota, Ruse, Scorch, Sell, Shirt, Shovel, Shunt, Simar(re), Slicker, Slip(pery), Sound, Spell, Split, Stagehand, Stick, Stint, Swing, Tour, Transfer, Tunic, Turn, Vary, Veer, Warp

▷ **Shift(ing)** *may indicate* an anagram

Shilling Bob, Deaner, Falkiner, Hog, King's, Queen's, S, Teston

Shilly-shally Whittie-whattie

Shimmer(ing) Chatoyant, Glint, Glitter, Iridescence, Shine
▷ **Shimmering** *may indicate* an anagram
Shin Clamber, Climb, Cnemial, Leg, Shank, Skink, Swarm
Shindig, Shindy Bobbery, Row, Rumpus, Shivoo, Uproar
Shine(r), Shining, Shiny Aglow, Beam, Bright, Buff, Burnish, Deneb, Effulge, Excel, Flash, Gleam, Glimmer, Glisten, Glitzy, Gloss, > **GLOW**, Irradiant, Japan, > **LAMP**, Leam, Leme, Lucent, Luminous, Lustre, Mouse, Nitid, Phosphoresce, Polish, Radiator, Refulgent, Relucent, Resplend, Rutilant, Skyre, Sleek, Twinkle, Varnish
Shingle(s), Shingly Beach, Chesil, Cut, Dartre, Dartrous, Gravel, Herpes, Herpetic, Shake, Shale, Stone, Zona, Zoster
Shinpad Greave
Shinty Caman, Camanachd
▷ **Shiny** *may indicate* a star
Ship(ping) Boat, Container, Convoy, Cruiser, > **DISPATCH**, Embark, Export, Flagship, Flatboat, Her, Hulk, Jolly, Keel, Man, Marine, MV, Post, Privateer, Prize, Prow, Raft, Ram, Sail, Saique, She, Smack, SS, Tall, Transport, Tub, Vessel, Victualling, Weather

● **SHIPS**
●
●

1 letter:	Long	Laker	**6 letters:**
Q	Nina	Liner	Argosy
	Pink	Moses	Banker
2 letters:	Pont	Oiler	Barque
PT	Pram	Pinky	Bateau
	Prau	Pinto	Bawley
3 letters:	Proa	Plate	Beagle
Ark	Ro-ro	Praam	Bethel
Cat	Saic	Prore	Bireme
Cog	Scow	Pucan	Borley
Dow	Snow	Razee	Bounty
Fly	Tern	Rover	Caique
Hoy	Trow	Sabot	Carack
Kit	Yawl	Scoot	Carvel
Red	Zulu	Screw	Castle
		Scull	Coaler
4 letters:	**5 letters:**	Shell	Cobble
Argo	Aviso	Skiff	Codder
Bark	Barge	Slave	Cooper
Brig	Broke	Sloop	Crayer
Buss	Camel	Tramp	Curagh
Cock	Canoe	Troop	Cutter
Cott	Coble	U-boat	Decker
Dhow	Coper	Umiak	Dingey
Dory	Crare	Wager	Dinghy
Duck	Dandy	Whiff	Dogger
Fire	Dingy	Xebec	Droger
Flat	Drake	Yacht	Dromon
Grab	Ferry	Zabra	Drover
Isis	Funny	Zebec	Dugout
Koff	Ketch		Flying

Frigot	Catboat	Tugboat	Lapstreak
Galiot	Clipper	Vedette	Leviathan
Galley	Coaster	Victory	Lightship
Gay-you	Collier	Vidette	Mayflower
Goldie	Coracle		Minelayer
Hooker	Counter	**8 letters:**	Monoxylon
Howker	Currach	Acapulco	Multihull
Jigger	Curragh	Bilander	Outrigger
Launch	Dredger	Billyboy	Peter-boat
Lorcha	Drifter	Cabotage	Shear-hulk
Lugger	Drogher	Corocore	Sheer-hulk
Masula	Dromond	Corocoro	Steamboat
Monkey	Factory	Corvette	Submarine
Mother	Felucca	Dahabieh	Vaporetto
Nuggar	Flattop	Faldboat	Whale-back
Packet	Flyboat	Foldboat	Whaleboat
Pedalo	Frigate	Galleass	
Pequod	Gabbard	Galliass	**10 letters:**
Pinkie	Gabbart	Gallivat	Brigantine
Pirate	Galleon	Hoveller	Golden Hind
Pitpan	Galliot	Indiaman	Hydroplane
Pulwar	Galloon	Ironclad	Icebreaker
Puteli	Geordie	Longboat	Knockabout
Randan	Gondola	Longship	Mine-hunter
Sampan	Gunboat	Mackinaw	Paddleboat
Sandal	Jetfoil	Mary Rose	Quadrireme
School	Kontiki	Masoolah	Santa Maria
Schuit	Liberty	Merchant	Trekschuit
Schuyt	Lymphad	Monohull	Triaconter
Settee	Masoola	Mosquito	Windjammer
Slaver	Mistico	Pinafore	
Tanker	Monitor	Savannah	**11 letters:**
Tartan	Mudscow	Schooner	Barquentine
Tender	Oomiack	Shanghai	Bellerophon
Tonner	Patamar	Showboat	Berthon-boat
Torpid	Pelican	Training	Cockleshell
Trader	Pinnace		Dreadnought
Trek-ox	Piragua	**9 letters:**	Merchantman
Turret	Pirogue	Bucentaur	Minesweeper
Whaler	Polacca	Catamaran	Penteconter
Wherry	Polacre	Cutty Sark	Quinquereme
Zebeck	Pontoon	Dahabeeah	Side-wheeler
	Revenge	Dahabiyah	Skidbladnir
7 letters:	Sculler	Dahabiyeh	Submersible
Belfast	Shallop	Dromedary	Supertanker
Bidarka	Sharpie	First-rate	Three-decker
Bumboat	Steamer	Freighter	Three-master
Capital	Stew-can	Frigatoon	Torpedo boat
Caravel	Tartane	Hydrofoil	
Carrack	Titanic	Klondiker	**12 letters:**
Carract	Trawler	Klondyker	East Indiaman
Carrect	Trireme	Lapstrake	Fore-and-after

- Great Eastern
- Marie Celeste

Stern-wheeler
Tangle-netter

13 letters:
Paddle steamer

14 letters:
Ocean greyhound

Shipmate Crew, Hearty, Sailor
Shipping line P and O
Ship's biscuit Dandyfunk, Dunderfunk
Shipshape Apple-pie, Neat, Orderly, Tidy, Trim
Shipwreck Split
Shire County
Shirk(er) Cuthbert, Dodge, Embusqué, Evade, Funk, Malinger, Mike, Pike, Poler, Scrimshank, Skive, Skrimshank, Slack, Soldier
Shirt Black, Boiled, Brown, Bush, Calypso, Camese, Camise, Chemise, Choli, Cilice, Dasheki, Dashiki, Dick(e)y, Dress, Fiesta, Garibaldi, Grandad, Hair, Hawaiian, Hoodie, Jacky Howe, Kaftan, Kaross, K(h)urta, Nessus, Non-iron, Parka, Partlet, Polo, Red, Safari, Sark, Serk, Shift, Smock, Sports, Stuffed, Subucula, Swan(n)dri®, Sweat, T
Shiva Destroyer
Shiver(ing), **Shivers**, **Shivery** Aguish, Break, Chitter, Crumble, Dash, Dither, Fragile, Frisson, Grew, Grue, Malaria, Nither, Oorie, Ourie, Owrie, Quake, Quiver, > SHAKE, Shatter, Shrug, Shudder, Smash, Smither, Smithereens, Splinter, Timbers, Tremble
▷ **Shiver(ed)** *may indicate* an anagram
Shoal Bar, Fish, Quantity, Reef, Run, School, Shallows, Shelf, Tail
Shock(ed), **Shocker**, **Shocking** Acoustic, Aghast, Agitate, Anaphylactic, Appal, Astound, Astun, Awhape, Bombshell, Brunt, Bunch, Consternate, Culture, Defibrillate, Disgust, Dorlach, Dreadful, Drop, Earthquake, ECT, Egregious, Electric, Epatant, Epiphenomenon, Fleg, Floccus, Forelock, Gait, Galvanism, Gobsmack, Hair, Horrify, Impact, Infamous, Insulin, Jar, Jolt, Live, Mane, Mop, Outrage, Poleaxe, Putrid, Recoil, Return, Revolt, Rick(er), Scandal(ise), Seismic, Shaghaired, Shake, Sheaf, Shell, Shilling, Shook, Stagger, Start(le), Stitch, Stook, Stound, Stun, Thermal, Trauma, Turn
Shock-absorber Buffer, Oleo, Snubber
▷ **Shocked** *may indicate* an anagram
Shod Calced
Shoddy Cagmag, Catchpenny, Cheap, Cheapjack, Cheapo, Cloth, Cowboy, Drecky, Gimcrack, Imitation, Oorie, Ourie, Owrie, Rag-wool, Ropy, Schlock, > SHABBY, Tatty, Tawdry, Tinny
Shoe(s) Accessory, Arctic, Athletic, Ballet, Balmoral, Bauchle, Blocked, Boat, Boot, Brake, Brogan, Brogue, Brothel creepers, Buskin, Calceate, Calk(er), Calkin, Casuals, Caulker, Cawker, Charlier, Chaussures, Chopin(e), Clodhopper, Clog, Co-respondent, Court, Creeper, Dap, Deck, Espadrille, Flattie, Galoche, Galosh, Gatty, Geta, Ghillie, Golosh, Gumshoe, Gym, High-low, High tops, Hot, Hush-puppies®, Jandal®, Jellies, Kletterschue, Kurdaitcha, Launch(ing), Loafer, Mary-Janes®, Mocassin, Moccasin, Muil, Mule, Open-toe, Oxford, Oxonian, Panton, Patten, Peeptoe, Pennyloafer, Pile, Plate, Plimsole, Plimsoll, Poulaine, Pump, Rivlin, Rope-soled, Rubbers, Rullion, Sabaton, Sabot, Saddle, Safety, Sandal, Sandshoe, Sannie, Scarpetto, Shauchle, Skid, Skimmer, Slingback, Slip-on, Slipper, Slip-slop, Sneaker, Snow, Sock, Soft, Solleret, Spike, Stoga, Stogy, Suede, Tackies, Takkies, Tennis, Tie, Topboot, Track, Trainer, Upper, Vamp(er), Veld-schoen, Veldskoen, Velskoen, Vibram®, Vibs, Wagon lock, Wedgie, Welt, Winkle-picker, Zori
Shoeless Barefoot, Discalced

Shoemaker Blacksmith, Clogger, Cobbler, Cordiner, Cordwainer, Cosier, Cozier, Crispi(a)n, Farrier, Gentle craft, Leprechaun, Sachs, Smith, Snob, Soutar, Souter, Sowter, Sutor

Shoe-string Cheap, Lace, Pittance

Shoe-toe Poulaine

Shoo Away, Begone, Hoosh, Off, Scat(ter), Voetsek

Shoot(er), Shooting Ack-ack, Airgun, Arrow, Bine, Bostryx, Braird, Breer, Bud, Bulbil, Catapult, Chit, Cyme, Dart(le), Delope, Discharge, Drib, Elance, Enate, Eradiate, Film, Fire, Flagellum, Germ, Germain(e), Germen, Germin(ate), Glorious twelfth, > GUN, Gunsel, Head-reach, Hurl, Imp, Layer, Limb, Loose, Offset, Photocall, Photograph, Pluff, Plug, Poot, Pop, Pot, Pout, Ramulus, Rapids, Ratoon, Riddle, Rod, Rove, Runner, Septembriser, Skeet, Snap, Snipe, Spire, Spirt, Spout, Spray, Sprout, Spurt, Spyre, Start, Stole, Stolon, Strafe, Sucker, Tellar, Teller, Tendril, Tiller, Trap, Turion, Twelfth, Twig, Udo, Vimen, Wand, Weapon, Wildfowler, Zap

Shop(s), Shopper Agency, Arcade, Atelier, Betray, Boutique, Bucket, Buy, Chain, Charity, Chippy, Closed, Coffee, Commissary, Co-op, Cop, Corner, Cut-price, Dairy, Delicatessen, Denounce, Dolly, Duddery, Duka, Duty-free, Emporium, Factory, Galleria, Gift, Grass, In bond, Inform, Luckenbooth, Machine, Mall, Mall-rat, Market, Megastore, Muffler, Off-licence, Open, Opportunity, Outlet, Parlour, Patisserie, Personal, Precinct, Print, PX, Retail, RMA, Salon, Sex, Shambles, Share, Shebang, Spaza, Squat, > STORE, Studio, Sundry, Superette, Supermarket, Superstore, Swap, Tally, Tea, Thrift, Tommy, Tuck, Union, Vintry, Warehouse, Works

Shopkeeper British, Butcher, Chemist, Clothier, Gombeen-man, Greengrocer, Grocer, Haberdasher, Hosier, Ironmonger, Merchant, Newsagent, Provisioner, Retailer, Stationer, Tradesman

Shoplift(er) Boost, Heist

Shore Bank, Beach, Buttress, Coast, Coastline, Coste, Eustatic, Foreside, Landfall, Littoral, Offing, Prop, Rance, Rivage, Saxon, Seaboard, Strand, Strandline, Support

Short(en), Shortly Abbreviate, Abridge, Abrupt, Anon, Apocope, Brief, Brusque, Commons, Compendious, Concise, Contract, Crisp, Cross, Curt, Curtail, Curtal, Diminish, Drink, Eftsoons, Epitomise, Ere-long, Fubsy, Fuse, Inadequate, Lacking, Laconical, Light, Limited, Low, Mini, Near, Nip, Nutshell, Pudsey, Punch, Pyknic, Reduce, Reef, Retrench, Scanty, Scarce, Shrift, Shy, Soon, Sparse, Spirit, Squab, Squat, Squat(ty), Staccato, Stint, Stocky, Strapped, Stubby, Succinct, Syncopate, Systole, Taciturn, Teen(s)y, Temporaneous, Terse, Tight, Tot, Towards, Transient, Wee

Shortage Dearth, Deficit, Drought, Famine, Lack, Need, Paucity, Scarcity, Sparsity, Wantage

Short circuit Varistor

Shortcoming Weakness

Shorthand Gregg, Outline, Phonographic, Pitman, Speedwriting®, Stenotypy, Tachygraphy, Tironian, Tironian notes, Triphone, Weblish

Short-headed Brachycephal

Short-lived Ephemeral, Fragile, Meson, Transitory

Shorts Bermuda, Board, Boxer, Briefs, Culottes, Cycling, Hot pants, Kaccha, Lederhosen, Plus-fours, Stubbies®, Trunks

Short-sight Myopia, Myosis

Short-winded Breathless, Concise, Puffed, Purfled, Pursy, Succinct

Shot(s) Aim, All-in, Ammo, Approach, Attempt, Backhand, Ball, Barrage,

Bisque, Blank, Blast, Bricole, Bull, Bullet, Burl, Canna, Cannonball, Cartridge, Case, Chain, Chatoyant, Chip, Cover, Crab, Crack, Daisy cutter, Dink, Dolly, Dram, Draw, Drop, Dunk, Exhausted, Forehand, Gesse, Glance, Go, Grape, Guess, Gun-stone, Hook, Jump, Langrage, Langrel, Langridge, Longjenny, Magpie, Marksman, Massé, Matte, Money, Mulligan, Multi-coloured, Noddy, Parthian, Parting, Passing, Pelican, Pellet, Penalty, Phiff, Photo, Plant, Pop, Pot, Puff, Rid, Round, Safety, Salvo, Scratch, Shy, Sighter, Silk, Six, Slam-dunk, Slap, Slice, Slug, Slung, Sped, Spell, Spent, Square cut, Stab, Still, Throw, Tonic, Tracking, Trial, Try, Turn, Volley, Warning, Wrist

Should Ought

Shoulder(-blade) Carry, Cold, Crossette, Epaule, Frozen, Hard, Hump, Omohyoid, Omoplate, Pick-a-back, Roadside, Scapula, Shouther, Soft, Spald, Spall, Spaul(d), Speal, Spule, Tote, Withers

Shout(er), Shouting Barrack, Bawl, Bellock, Bellow, Boanerges, Call, Claim, Clamour, Cry, Din, Exclaim, Geronimo, Heckle, Hey, Hoi(cks), Holla, Holla-ho(a), Holler, Hollo, Holloa, Hooch, Hosanna, Howzat, Hue, Parnell, Rah, Rant, Root, Round, Sa sa, Treat, Trumpet, Vociferate, Whoop, Yell(och), Yippee, Yoohoo, Yorp

Shove Barge, Birr, Elbow, Jostle, Push, Ram, Spoon, Thrust

Shovel Backhoe, Dustpan, Hat, Main, Peel, Power, Scoop, Shool, Spade, Steam, Trowel, Van

Show(ing), Shown, Showy Anonyma, Appearance, Aquacade, Bench, Betray, Branky, Broadcast, Brummagem, Burlesque, Cabaret, Chat, Circus, Come, Con, Cruft's, Demo(nstrate), Depict, Diorama, Display, Do, Dressy, Dumb, Effeir, Effere, Endeictic, Entertainment, Epideictic, Establish, Evince, > **EXHIBIT**, Expo, Extravaganza, Exude, Facade, Fair, Fangled, Farce, Flamboyant, Flash, Flaunt, Floor, Galanty, Game, Garish, Gaudy, Gay, Give, Glitz(y), Gloss, Horse, Indicate, Jazzy, Kismet, Light, Loud, Manifest, Matinée, Meritricious, Minstrel, Musical, Naumachy, Ostensible, Ostentatious, Pageant, Panel game, Pantomime, Parade, Patience, Performance, Phen(o), Point, Pomp, Portray, Pretence, Pride, Procession, Prog(ramme), Project, Prominence, Prove, Pseudery, Puff, Puppet, Quiz, Raree, Razzmatazz, Reality, Represent, Reveal, Revue, Road, Roll-out, Rushes, Screen, Shaw, Sight, Sitcom, Slang, Soap, Son et lumière, Specious, Spectacle, Splash, Splay, Stage, Stunt, Talk, Tamasha, Tattoo, Tawdry, Telethon, Theatrical, Three-man, Tinhorn, Unbare, Uncover, Usher, Vain, Variety, Vaudeville, Veneer, Wear, Wild west, Zarzuela

Showdown Confrontation, Crunch

Shower Douche, Exhibitor, Flurry, Hail, Indicant, Indicator, Kitchen tea, Meteor, Party, Pelt, Pepper, Precipitation, Rain, Scat, Scouther, Scowther, Skatt, Skit, Snow, Spat, Spet, Spit, Splatter, Spray, Sprinkle, Ticker tape

▷ **Showers** *may indicate* an anagram

Showgirl Evita, Nanette

▷ **Showing, Shown in** *may indicate* a hidden word

Showman Bailey, Barnum, Entertainer, Goon, Impresario, Lord Mayor, MC, Ringmaster

Show-off Exhibitionist, Extrovert, Jack the lad, Peacock, Poseur, Sport, Swagger, Swank

Showpiece Flagship

Show-place Exhibition, Olympia, Pavilion, Theatre

Shrapnel Fragment, Shell, Splinter

Shred Clout, Filament, Grate, Julienne, Mammock, Mince, Mummock, Rag, Screed, Swarf, Tag, Ta(i)ver, Tatter, Thread, To-tear, Wisp

Shrew Bangsring, Banxring, Callet, Catamaran, Elephant, Fury, Hellcat, Kate, Marabunta, Nag, Otter, Pygmy, Show, Solenodon, Sondeli, Sorex, Spitfire, Squirrel, Tana, Termagant, Tree, Trull, Tupaia, Virago, Vixen, Xant(h)ippe, Yankie, Yenta

Shrewd Acute, Arch, Argute, Artful, Astucious, Astute, Callid, Canny, Clued-up, Cute, File, Gnostic, Gumptious, Hard-nosed, Judicious, Knowing, Pawky, Politic, Sagacious, Sapient(al), Wily, Wise

Shriek Cry, Scream, Scrike, Shright, Shrike, Shrill, Shritch, Skirl, Yell

Shrift Attention, Penance, Short

Shrike Bird, Butcher-bird

Shrill Argute, High, Keen, Piping, Reedy, Screech, Sharp, Skirl, Treble

Shrimp(s) Fairy, Freshwater, Krill, Mantis, Midge, Opossum, Potted, Prawn, Runt, Sand, Skeleton, Small, Spectre, Squill(a), Stomatopod

Shrine Adytum, Altar, Dagoba, Dargah, Delphi, Fatima, Feretory, Harem, Holy, Joss house, Kaaba, Marabout, Martyry, Naos, Pagoda, Reliquary, Scrine, Scryne, Stupa, Tabernacle, Temple, Tope, Vimana, Walsingham

Shrink(age), Shrinking, Shrunk Alienist, Analyst, Blanch, Blench, Boggle, Cling, Compress, Constringe, Contract, Cour, Cower, Creep, Crine, Cringe, Dare, Decrew, Depreciate, Dread, Dwindle, Flinch, Funk, Gizzen, Less, Nirl, > **PSYCHIATRIST**, Pycnosis, Quail, Recoil, Reduce, Sanforised, Shrivel, Shrug, Shy, Sphacelate, Timid, Violet, Wane, Wince, Wizened

Shrivel(led) Cling, Crine, Desiccate, Dry, Nirl, Parch, Scorch, Scrump, Sear, Shrink, Skrimp, Skrump, Tabid, Welk, Wither, Wizened, Writhled

Shropshire Salop

Shroud(s) Chadri, Chuddah, Chuddar, Cloak, Cloud, Conceal, Cover, Futtock, Grave-cloth, Pall, Rigging, Screen, Sheet, Sindon, Turin, Veil, Winding-sheet, Wrap

Shrub(bery) Aalii, Acacia, Alhagi, Andromeda, Aphelandra, Arboret, Arbutus, Aucuba, Azalea, Barberry, Beautybrush, Bosky, Bottlebrush, Brere, Brush, Buaze, Buazi, Buckthorn, Buddleia, Bullace, > **BUSH**, Camellia, Caper, Cascara, Clianthus, Cola, Coprosma, Coyotillo, Crossandra, Cytisus, Daphne, Dead-finish, Deutzia, Dogwood, Epacris, Eriostemon, Fatsia, Feijoa, Firethorn, Frangipani, Frutex, Fynbos, Gardenia, Garrya, Gorse, Guayule, Hakea, Hardhack, Hebe, Henna, Hibiscus, Hop-tree, Horizontal, Inkberry, Jaborandi, Jasmine, Jessamine, Jetbread, Jojoba, Joshua tree, Juniper, Kat, Krameria, Lantana, Laurustine, Lavender, Ledum, Lignum, Manoao, Maqui(s), Matico, Melaleuca, Mesquit, Mimosa, Mistletoe, Monte, Myrica, Myrtle, Nabk, Ninebark, Ocotillo, Olea(cea), P(a)eony, Parkleaves, Patchouli, Pittosporum, Pituri, Plant, Poinsettia, Privet, Protea, Pyracantha, Pyxie, Qat, Rhatany, Rhododendron, Rhus, Rock rose, Romneya, Rue, Ruta, Salal, Savanna(h), Savin(e), Schefflera, Senna, Shadbush, Shallon, Skimmia, Smilax, Southernwood, Spekboom, Spicebush, Steeplebush, Sumach, Supplejack, Sweetsop, Tamarisk, Tea-tree, Thyme, Titi, Toyon, Tutsan, Tutu, Undergrowth, Wahoo, Waratah, Ya(u)pon, Yupon, Zamia

Shrug Discard, Toss

Shudder(ing) Abhor, Ashake, Frisson, Grew, Grise, Grue, Horror, Jerk, Quake, Shake, Spasm, Tremble

Shuffle(d) Dodge, Drag, Hedge, Make, Mix, Palter, Permute, Redeployment, Riffle, Scuff, Shamble, Shauchle, Stack

▷ **Shuffle(d)** *may indicate* an anagram

Shun Attention, Avoid, Eschew, Evade, Forbear, Ignore, Ostracise, Secede, > **SPURN**

Shunt Move, Shelve, Shuttle, Side-track
Shut(s), Shut (down; in; out; up) Bar, Close, Confined, Coop, Debar, Embar, Emure, Fasten, Fend, Impale, Impound, Latch, Lay-off, Lock, Rid, Scram, Seal, Shet, Slam, Spar, Steek, Telescope, Tine, To
Shutter(s) Blind, Dead-lights, Douser, Jalousie, Louvre, Persiennes, Shade
Shuttle Alternate, Commute, Drawer, Flute, Go-between, Orbiter, Shoot, Shunt, Space, Tat(t), Weave
Shy Bashful, Blate, Blench, Cast, Catapult, Chary, Coy, Deficient, Demure, Farouche, Flinch, Funk, Heave, Jerk, Jib, Laithfu', Leery, Lob, Mim, Mims(e)y, Rear, Recoil, Reserved, Reticent, Retiring, Sheepish, Shrinking, Skeigh, Start, Thraw, Throw, Timid, Tongue-tied, Toss, Try, Verecund, Violet, Willyard, Willyart, Withdrawn
Siamese, Simaese twins Chang, Eng, Seal-point, T(h)ai
Siberian Chukchi, Ostiak, Ostyak, Samo(y)ed, Tungus, Vogul, Yakut
Sibilant Hissing, Whistling
Sibling Brother, German, Kin, Sister
Sibyl Oracle, Prophetess, Seer, Soothsayer, Witch
Sicilian Sicanian, Trinacrian
Sick(en), Sickening, Sickliness, Sickly, Sickness Aegrotat, Affection, Ague, Ail, Bad, Bends, Cat, Chalky, Chunder, Colic, Crapulence, Crook, Decompression, Delicate, Disorder, Donsie, Gag, Hangover, Icky, Ill, Infection, Leisure, Maid-pale, Mal, Mawkish, Morbid, Morning, Motion, Mountain, Nauseous, Pale, Peaky, Pestilent, Pindling, Plague, Puly, Puna, Queachy, Queasy, Queechy, Radiation, Regorge, Repulsive, Retch, Serum, Shilpit, Sleeping, Soroche, Space, Spue, Squeamish, Sweating, Travel, Twee, Uncle Dick, Valetudinarian, Virus, Vomit, Wamble-cropped, Wan
Sick bay San
Sickle(-shaped) Falcate, Falx, Hook, Scythe
Side Abeam, Airs, Ally, Beam, Blind, Border, Branch, Camp, Cis-, Distaff, Edge, Effect, Eleven, English, Epistle, Ex intraque parte, Facet, Flank, Flip, Gospel, Gunnel, Hand, Hypotenuse, Iliac, Lateral, Lee(ward), Left, Off, On, OP, Pane, Part, Partisan, Party, Port, Pretension, Profile, Prompt, Rave, Reveal, Right, Rink, Silver, Slip, Spear, Starboard, Swank, > **TEAM**, Weak, Wind, Windward, Wing, XI
Sideboard(s) Beauf(f)et, Buffet, Cellaret, Commode, Credence, Credenza, Dresser, Whiskers
Side-effect, Side-issue Fall-out, Logograph, Logogriph, Offshoot, Secondary, Spin-off
Side-line Hobby, Lye, Siding, Spur
Side-step Crab, Dodge, Evade, Hedge, Maori, Volt
Side-track Distract, Divert, Shunt
Sidewalk Crab, Footpath, Pavement
Sideways Askance, Indirect, Laterally, Laterigrade, Oblique
Siding Alliance, Byway, Lie, Lye, Spur
Sidle Edge, Passage
Siege (work) Alamo, Beleaguer, Beset, Blockade, Gherao, Investment, Ladysmith, Leaguer, Mafeking, Obsidional, Perilous, Poliorcetic, Ravelin, Surround
Siesta Nap, Noonday, Nooning
Sieve, Sift(ing) Analyse, Bolt(er), Boult(er), Bunting, Colander, Coliform, Cribble, Cribrate, Cribrose, Cullender, Eratosthenes, Ethmoid, Filter, Molecular, Riddle, Screen, Searce, Search, Separate, Siler, Strain, Sye, Tamis,

Tammy, Tems(e), Trommel, Try, Winnow

Sigh Exhale, Heave, Lackaday, Long, Moan, Sough, Suspire, Welladay

Sight(ed) Aim, Barleycorn, Bead, Conspectuity, Eye(ful), Eyesore, Glimpse, Ken, Long, Oculated, Panoramic, Peep, Prospect, Range, Rear, Riflescope, Scene, Scotopia, Second, See, Short, Spectacle, Taish, Vane, > VIEW, Visie, Vision, Vista

Sight-screen Eyelid

Sightseer, Sightseeing Lionise, Observer, Rubberneck, Tourist, Tripper, Viewer

Sign(s), Signing, Signpost Accidental, Ache, Addition, Ale-stake, Ampassy, Ampersand, Aquarius, Archer, Aries, Arrow, Auspice, Autograph, Badge, Balance, Beck, Beckon, Board, Brand, Bull, Bush, Call, Cancer, Capricorn, Caract, Caret, Chevron, Clue, Coronis, Crab, Cross, Cue, Dactylology, Diacritic, Di(a)eresis, Diphone, Division, DS, Earmark, Emblem, Endeixis, Endorse, Endoss, Enlist, Evidence, Exit, Fascia, Fish, Gemini, Gesture, Goat, Grammalogue, Hallmark, Hamza(h), Harbinger, Hex, Hieroglyphic, Hint, Ideogram, Indian, Indicate, Indication, Indicium, Initial, Inscribe, Ivy-bush, Leo, Lexigram, Libra, Local, Logogram, Minus, Multiplication, Negative, Neume, Nod, Notice, Obelisk, Obelus, Omen, Peace, Phraseogram, Pisces, Plus, Positive, Presa, Presage, Prodromus, Radical, Ram, Rest, Rune, Sacrament, Sagittarius, Sain, Scorpio, Segno, Semeion, Shingle, Show, Sigil, Sigla, Signal, Star, Subscribe, Subtraction, Superscribe, Symbol, Symptom, Syndrome, Tag, Taurus, Tic(k)tac(k), Tilde, Titulus, Token, Trace, Triphone, Twins, Umlaut, V, Vestige, Virgo, Vital, Warning, Waymark, Word, Zodiac

Signal(ler) Alarm, Aldis lamp, Alert, Amber, Assemble, Baud, Beacon, Bell, Bleep, Bugle, Buzz, Chamade, Code, Compander, Compandor, Cone, Cue, Detonator, Diaphone, Distress, Earcon, Flag, Flagman, Flare, Flash, Fog, Gantry, Gesticulate, Gong, Griffin, Gun, Harmonic, Heliograph, Heliostat, Herald, Hooter, Horse and hattock, Icon, Important, Interrupt, Interval, Luminance, Mark, Mase, Megafog, Message, Modem, Morse, Navar, NICAM, Notation, Noted, Output, Password, Peter, Pinger, Pip, Pulsar, Radio, Renowned, Reveille, Robot, Salient, Semaphore, Semiology, Singular, Smoke, Sonogram, SOS, Spoiler, Squawk, Taps, Target, Tchick, Telegraph, Teles(e)me, Thumb, Tic(k)-tac(k), Time, Traffic, Troop, Very, Video, V-sign, Waff, Waft, Wave, Wave-off, Wigwag

Signature Alla breve, Autograph, By-line, Digital, Hand, John Hancock, John Henry, Key, Mark, Onomastic, Specimen, Subscription, Time

Signet Ring, Seal, Sigil, Sphragistics

Significance, Significant Cardinal, Consequence, Emblem, Great, Impact, Important, Indicative, Key, Magnitude, Material, Matter, Meaningful, Milestone, Moment(ous), Noted, Noteworthy, Other, Paramount, Pith, Pregnant, Salient, Special, Telling

Signify Bemean, Denote, Imply, Indicate, Intimate, Matter, > MEAN, Represent

Sign language Ameslan, Semaphore, Tic(k)tac(k)

Sikh(ism) Granth, Kaccha, Kangha, Kara, Kesh, Khalsa, Kirpan, Mazhbi, Mechanised, Nanak, (Ranjit) Singh

Silas Uncle, Wegg

Silence(r), Silent Amyclaean, Choke-pear, Clam, Clamour, Conticent, Creepmouse, Dumbstruck, Earplug, Gag, Hesychastic, Hist, Hush, Hushkit, Mim(budget), Muffler, Mum(p), Mumchance, Mute, Obmutescent, Omertà, Quench, Quiesce, > QUIET, Reticence, Shtoom, Shush, Speechless, Still, Sulky, Tace(t), Tacit(urn), Throttle, Tight-lipped, Wheesh(t), Whis(h)t

Silhouette Contour, Outline, Planform, Profile, Shadow figure, Shadowgraph, Shape, Skyline

Silica(te) Albite, Analcite, Andalusite, Chabazite, Chert, Cristobalite, Datolite, Diopside, Dioptase, Float-stone, Harmotome, Hiddenite, Humite, Iolite, Kieselguhr, Kyanite, Monticellite, Montmorillonite, Olivine, Opal, Penninite, Pinite, Rhodonite, Riebeckite, Saponite, Scapolite, Silex, Staurolite, Tridymite, Tripoli, Ultrabasic, Vermiculite, Vitreous, Zeolite

Silicon Chip, Si

Silk(y), Silk screen Alamode, Atlas, Barathea, Brocade, Bur(r), Charmeuse®, Chenille, Chiffon, Cocoon, Corn, Crape, Crepe, Duchesse, Dupion, Faille, Fibroin, Filature, Filoselle, Florence, Florentine, Flosh, Floss, Flox, Foulard, Gazar, Gazzatum, Georgette, Gimp, Glossy, KC, Kincob, Lustrine, Lustring, Lutestring, Makimono, Malines, Marabou(t), Matelasse, Mercery, Moiré, Ninon, Oiled, Organza, Ottoman, Paduasoy, Parachute, Peau de soie, Pongee, Prunella, Prunelle, Prunello, Pulu, Raw, Samite, Sars(e)net, Satin, Schappe, Seal(ch), Sendal, Seric, Sericeous, Sericite, Serigraph, Shalli, Shantung, Sien-tsan, Sleave, Sleek, Sle(i)ded, Slipper satin, Smooth, Spun, Surah, Tabaret, Tabby, Taffeta, Tasar, Thistledown, Tiffany, Tram, Tulle, Tussah, Tusseh, Tusser, Tussore, Vegetable, Velvet, Wild

Silkworm (eggs), Silkworm disease Bombyx, Eria, Graine, Multivoltine, Muscardine, Sericulture, Tussore

Sill Ledge, Straining, Threshold

Silly, Silliness Absurd, Anserine, Brainless, Buffer, Crass, Cuckoo, Daft, Dandy, Ditsy, Divvy, Dumb, Fatuous, Folly, Fool, Footling, Frivolous, Goopy, Goosey, Gormless, Hen-witted, Idiotic, Imbecile, Inane, Inept, Infield(er), Liminal, Mid-off, Mid-on, Mopoke, Puerile, Season, Simple, Soft(y), Spoony, > STUPID, Tripe, Wacky

▷ **Silly** *may indicate* relating to a sill

Silt Alluvium, Deposit, Dregs, Land, Lees, Residue, Sullage, Varve

Silver(skin) Ag, Albata, Alpac(c)a, Arg(ent), Argyria, Cardecue, Cerargyrite, Diana's tree, Free, Fulminating, German, Grey, Horn, Luna, Nickel, One-legged, Pakt(h)ong, Parcel-gilt, Pegleg, Piastre, Plate, Plateresque, Ruby, Stephanite, Sterling, Sycee, Thaler

▷ **Silver** *may indicate* a coin

Silversmith Demetrius, Lamerie, Plater

Simian Apelike, Catar(r)hine

Similar(ity) Analog(ue), Analogical, Corresponding, Equivalent, Etc, Homoeoneric, Homogeneous, Homologous, Homonym, Kindred, > LIKE, Parallel, Patristic, Resemblance, Samey, Suchlike

Similitude Parable

Simmer Bubble, Poach, Seethe, Stew

Simon Bolivar, Cellarer, Magus, Peter, Pure, Simple

Simper Bridle, Giggle, Smirk

Simple(r), Simplicity, Simplify, Simply Aefa(u)ld, Afa(w)ld, Arcadian, Artless, Austere, Bald, Bare, Basic, Crude, Doddle, Doric, > EASY, Eath(e), Elegant, ESN, Ethe, Facile, Fee, Folksy, Gomeral, Gotham, Green, Herb(alist), Herborist, Homespun, Idyllic, Incomposite, Inornate, Jaap, Japie, Mere, Moner(on), Naive(té), Naked, Niaiserie, Noddy, One-fold, Open and shut, Ordinary, Paraphrase, Pastoral, Peter, Plain, Pleon, Provincial, Pure, Reduce, Rustic, Saikless, Sapid, Semplice, Sheer, Silly, Simon, Spartan, Stupid, Tout court, Woollen

Simpleton Abderite, Airhead, Cokes, Cuckoo, Duffer, Flat, Fool, Gaby, Gomeral, Gomeril, Greenhorn, Juggins, Spoon, > STUPID PERSON, Wiseacre, Zany

Simulate, Simulating Affect, Anti, Feign, Pretend

Simultaneous Coinstantaneous, Contemporaneous, Synchronous, Together
Sin(ful) Aberrant, Accidie, Acedia, Actual, Anger, Avarice, Besetting, Bigamy,
Covetousness, Crime, Deadly, Debt, Depravity, Envy, Err, Evil, Folly, Gluttony,
Hamartiology, Harm, Hate, Impious, Lapse, Lust, Misdeed, Misdoing, Mortal,
> OFFENCE, Original, Peccadillo, Piacular, Pride, Scape, Scarlet, Shirk, Sine,
Sloth, Transgress, Trespass, Unrighteous, Venial, Vice, Wicked, Wrath, Wrong
Sinai Horeb, Mount
Since Ago, As, Meantime, Seeing, Sens, Sinsyne, Sith(en), Whereas
Sincere(ly), Sincerity Bona-fide, Candour, Earnest, Entire, Frank, Genuine,
Heartfelt, Honest, Open, Real(ly), True, Verity, Whole-hearted
Sinclair Lewis, Upton
Sine Versed
Sinecure Bludge, Commendam
Sinew(y) Fibre, Ligament, Nerve, String, Tendinous, Tendon
▶ **Sinful** *see* SIN
Sing(ing) Barbershop, Bel canto, Bhajan, Carol, Chant, Cheep, Chorus,
Coloratura, Community, Cough, Croon, Crow, Diaphony, Diddle, Doo-wop,
Glee club, Gorgia, Hum, Inform, Intone, Karaoke, Kirtan, La-la, Lilt, Melic,
Parlando, Peach, Pen(n)illion, Pipe, Plainchant, Rand, Rant, Rap, Record,
Render, Scat, Second(o), Solmization, Sprechgesang, Sprechstimme, Squeal,
Tell, Thrum, Trill, Troll, Vocalise, Warble, Yodel
Singe Burn, Char, Scorch
Singer Alto, Balladeer, Bard, Baritone, Bass, Bing, Bird, Blondel, Callas, Canary,
Cantabank, Cantatrice, Cantor, Car, Carreras, Caruso, Castrato, Chaliapin,
Chanteuse, Chantor, Chazan, Cher, Chorister, Coloratura, Comprimario,
Crooner, Dawson, Diva, Dylan, Ella, Falsetto, Folk, Gleemaiden, Gleeman,
Grass, Haz(z)an, Heldentenor, Isaac, Kettle, Lark, Lauder, Lead, Lind, Lorelei,
Lulu, Mathis, Melba, Minstrel, Oscine, Patti, Pitti, Precentor, Prima donna,
Qawwal, Robeson, Session, Sinatra, Siren, Snitch, Songstress, Soprano,
Soubrette, Stoolie, Succentor, Swan, Tatiana, Tenor, Torch, Treble, Troubador,
Vocalist, Voice, Wait, Warbler
Single, Singly Ace, Aefa(u)ld, Aefawld, Alone, Azygous, Bachelor, Celibate,
Discriminate, EP, Exclusive, Feme sole, Matchless, Monact, Mono, Odd,
One-off, Only, Pick, Run, Sole, Solitary, Spinster, Unattached, Uncoupled,
Unique, Unwed, Versal, Yin
Single-cell Protista
Single-chambered Monothalamous
Singlestick Sword
Singlet Tunic, Vest
Singular(ity) Curious, Especial, Exceptional, Extraordinary, Ferly, Naked, Odd,
Once, One, Peculiar, Queer(er), Rare, > UNIQUE, Unusual
Singultus Hiccup
Sinister Bend, Dark, Dirke, Evil, L, Left, Lh, Louche, > OMINOUS
Sink(ing), Sunken Basin, Bog, Cadence, Carbon, Cower, Delapse, Depress,
Descend, Devall, Dip, Down, Drain, Draught-house, Drink, Drop, Drown, Ebb,
Flag, Founder, Gravitate, Heat, Hole, Immerse, Invest, Jawbox, Kitchen, Lagan,
Laigh, Lapse, Ligan, Merger, Pad, Pot, Prolapse, Put(t), Relapse, Sag, Scupper,
Scuttle, Set, Settle, Shipwreck, Slump, Steep-to, Sty, Submerge, Subside, Swag,
Swamp
Sinner Evildoer, Malefactor, Offender, Reprobate, Trespasser
Sinuous Curvy, Ogee, Slinky, Snaky, Wavy, Winding
Sinus Cavity, Recess

Sip(ping) Delibate, Haporth, Libant, Sample, Sowp, Sup, Taste, Tiff(ing)
Siphon Draw, Rack, Soda, Suck, Transfer
Sir Dan, Dom, K, Knight, Kt, Lord(ing), Sahib, Signor, Sirrah, Stir, Stirra(h), Towkay, Tuan
Sire Beget, Father, Get
Siren Alarm, Alert, Diaphone, Enchanter, Femme fatale, Hooter, Houri, Leucosia, Ligea, Lorelei, Mermaid, Oceanides, Parthenope, Salamander, Teaser, Temptress, Vamp
Sirenian Dugong, Lamantin, Manatee, Manati, Sea-cow
Sirloin Backsey
Sirree Bo
Sisal Agave
Siskin Aberdevine, Bird, Finch
Sister(s) Anne, Beguine, Lay, Minim, > NUN, Nurse, Out, Religeuse, Sib, Sibling, Sis, Sob, Soul, Swallow, Theatre, Titty, Ursuline, Verse, Weird
Sisyphean Uphill
Sit(ter), Sitting Bestride, Clutch, Dharna, Duck, Gaper, Lit de justice, Model, MP, Perch, Pose, Reign, Represent, Roost, Séance, Sejeant, Session, Squat
Site, Siting Area, Brownfield, Building, Camp, Feng shui, Greenfield, Home-page, Location, Lot, Pad, Place, Plot, Rogue, Sacred, Silo, Spot, Stance
Situation Ballpark, Berth, Cart, Case, Catch, Catch-22, Cliff-hanger, Contretemps, Cow, Dilemma, Galère, Hole, Job, Lie, Location, Lurch, Matrix, Niche, No-win, Office, Plight, Position, Post, Scenario, Schmear, Schmeer, Set-up, Shebang, Showdown, Status quo, Sticky wicket, Strait, Where, Worst case
Six(th) Digamma, French, German, Half(-a)dozen, Hexad, Italian, Neapolitan, Prime, Senary, Sestette, Sextet, Sice, Size, Vau, VI
Six counties NI
Six days Hexa(e)meron
Six feet Fathom
Sixpence Bender, Kick, Slipper, Tanner, Tester(n), Testril(l), Tizzy, VID, VIP, Zack
Sixteen Sweet
Sixty Degree, Threescore
Size(able) Amplitude, Area, Bulk, Calibre, Countess, Demy, Displacement, > EXTENT, Format, Girth, Glair, Glue, Gum, Imperial, Measure, Physique, Plus, Pot(t), Princess, Proportion, Tempera, Tidy, Trim
Sizzle Fry, Hiss, Scorch
Skate(r), Skateboarder, Skating Blade, Bob, Cheap, Choctaw, Cousins, Curry, Dean, Figure, Fish, Free, Grommet, In-line, Maid, Mohawk, Rock(er), Roller, Rollerblade®, Runner, Speed
Skedaddle Shoo, Vamoose
Skein Hank, Hasp
Skeleton, Skeletal Anatomy, Atomy, Axial, Bones, Cadaverous, Cadre, Cage, Coenosteum, Corallite, Corallum, Family, Framework, Key, Ossify, Outline, Scenario, Sclere, Tentorium
Sketch(y) Cameo, Character, Charade, Croquis, Delineate, Diagram, Doodle, Draft, > DRAW, Ebauche, Esquisse, Illustration, Limn, Line, Maquette, Modello, Outline, Pencilling, Playlet, Pochade, Précis, Profile, Skit, Summary, Tenuous, Thumbnail, Trick, Vignette, Visual
Skew Agee, Ajee, Oblique, Sheer, Squint, Swerve, Veer
Skewer Brochette, En brochette, Prong, Spit, Transfix
Ski(ing) Aquaplane, Glide, Glissade, Hot-dog, Langlauf, Mogul, Nordic, Schuss,

Super G, Telemark, Vorlage, Wedeln
Skid Aquaplane, Drift, Jackknife, Side-slip, Slew, Slide, Slip, Slither, Spinout
▷ **Skidding** *may indicate* an anagram
Skiff Canoe, Dinghy, Outrigger
Skill(ed), Skilful Ability, Able, Ace, Address, Adept, Adroit, Art, Bravura, Canny, Chic, Competence, Craft, Deacon, Deft, Dextrous, Enoch, Expertise, Facility, Feat, Finesse, Flair, Gleg, Habile, Hand, Handicraft, Handy, Hend, Hot, Ingenious, Knack, Know-how, Knowing, Lear(e), Leir, Lere, Masterly, Masterpiece, Mean, Mistery, Mystery, Mystique, Practised, Proficient, Prowess, Quant, Resource, Savvy, Science, Skeely, Sleight, Soft, Speciality, Tactics, Talent, Technic, Technique, Touch, Trade, Trick, Versed, Virtuoso
Skim Cream, Despumate, Flit, Glide, Graze, Plane, Ream, Scan, Scud, Scum, Skiff, Skitter
Skimp Restrict, Scamp, Scrimp, Stint
Skin(s) Agnail, Armour, Bark, Basan, Basil, Box-calf, Calf, Callus, Case, Cere, Chevrette, Coat, Corium, Cortex, Crackling, Cutaneous, Cuticle, Cutis, Deacon, Deer, Derm(a), Dermatome, Dermis, Dewlap, Disbark, Ectoderm, Enderon, Epicanthus, Epicarp, Epidermis, Eschar, Excoriate, Exterior, Fell, Film, Flaught, Flay, Flench, Flense, Flinch, Forel, Fourchette, Goldbeater's, Hangnail, Hide, Jacket, Kip, Kirbeh, Leather, Membrane, Muktuk, Nebris, Pachyderm, Parfleche, Peau, Peel, Pell, Pellicle, Pelt, Perinychium, Plew, Plu(e), Prepuce, Pteryla, Rack, Rape, Rind, Scalp, Scarskin, Serosa, Shell, Shoder, Spetch, Strip, Tegument, Tulchan, Veneer, Water-bouget, Wattle, Woolfell
Skin disease, Skin trouble Boba, Boil, Buba, Causalgia, Chloasma, Chloracne, Cowpox, Cradle cap, Cyanosis, Dartre, Dermatitis, Dermatosis, Dyschroa, EB, Ecthyma, Erysipelas, Exanthem(a), Favus, Flay, Framboesia, Gum rash, Herpes, Hives, Ichthyosis, Impetigo, Leishmaniasis, Lichen, Livedo, Lupus vulgaris, Mal del pinto, Mange, Miliaria, Morphew, Morula, Patagium, Pemphigus, Pinta, Pityriasis, Prurigo, Psoriasis, Pyoderma, Rash, Red-gum, Ringworm, Rosacea, Rose-rash, St Anthony's Fire, Sapego, Scabies, Sclerodermia, Scurvy, Seborrhoea, Serpigo, Strophulus, Telangiectasis, Tetter, Tinea, Vaccinia, Verruca, Verruga, Vitiligo, Xanthoma, Xerodermia, Yaws, Yawy
Skinflint Dryfist, Miser, Niggard, Pinch-gut, Scrooge, Tightwad
Skinful Drunk, Sausage
Skinhead Not, Punk, Scalp
Skink Seps
Skinny Barebone, Bony, Dermal, Emaciate, Lean, Scraggy, Thin, Weed
Skint Broke, Ghat, Penniless, Stony
Skip(ped), Skipper Boss, Caper, Captain, Cavort, Drakestone, Dumpster, Elater, Frisk, Hesperian, Jump, Jumping-mouse, Lamb, Luppen, Miss, Omit, Patroon, Ricochet, Saury, Scombresox, Spring, Tittup, Trounce(r)
Skirl Humdudgeon, Pibroch, Pipe, Screigh
Skirmish(er) Brush, Dispute, Escarmouche, Fray, Pickeer, Spar, Tirailleur, Velitation
Skirt(ing) Bases, Bell, Border, Bouffant, Cheongsam, Circle, Coat, Crinoline, Culotte(s), Dado, Dirndl, Edge, Fil(l)ibeg, Fringe, Fustanella, Fustanelle, Girl, Gore, Grass, Harem, Hobble, Hoop, Hug, Hula, Kilt, Lamboys, Lava-lava, Marge, Mini, Mopboard, Pareo, Pareu, Pencil, Peplum, Petticoat, Philibeg, Pinafore, Piu-piu, Plinth, Puffball, Ra-ra, Rim, Sarong, Sidestep, Stringboard, Tace, Tail, Taslet, Tasse(t), Tonlet, Tutu, Wrap(a)round, Wrapover
Skit Lampoon, Parody, Sketch

Skittish Coy, Curvetting, Frisky, Restless
Skittle(s) Bayle, Bowl, Kail(s), Kayle, Kingpin, Ninepin, Pin, Spare
Skive(r) Absentee, Scrimshank, Shirk
Skivvy Drudge, Slave
Skrimshank Bludge, Skive
Skulk Lurk, Mooch, Shool
Skull Bregma(ta), Calvaria, Cranium, Fontanel, Head, Malar, Maz(z)ard, Obelion, Occiput, Pannikell, Phrenology, Scalp, Sinciput
Skullcap Ya(r)mulka, Yarmulke, Zucchetto
Skunk Atoc, Atok, Hognosed, Polecat, Teledu, Zoril(lo)
Sky(-high) Air, Azure, Blue, Canopy, Carry, E-layer, Element, Empyrean, Ether, Firmament, Heaven, Lift, Loft, Mackerel, Occident, Octa, Uranus, Welkin
Sky-diver Para
Skylark Aerobatics, Bird
Skylight Abat-jour, Aurora, Comet, Lunette, Star
Skyline Horizon, Rooftops
Sky-pilot Chaplain, Vicar
Slab Briquette, Bunk, Bunk(er), Cake, Chunk, Dalle, Hawk, Ledger, Marver, Metope, Mihrab, Mud, Paving-stone, Planch, Plank, Sclate, Sheave, Slate, Slice, Stela, Stelene, Tab, Tile
Slack(en), Slackness Abate, Careless, Crank, Dilatory, Dross, Ease, Easy-going, Glen, Idle, Lax(ity), Let-up, Loose, Malinger, Nerveless, Relax, Release, Remiss, Shirk, Skive, Slow, Surge, Unscrew, Veer
Slag Basic, Calx, Cinder, Dross, Scoria, Scum, Sinter, Tart
Slake Abate, Cool, Quench, Refresh, Satisfy
Slalom Super-G
Slam Crash, Criticise, Dad, Grand, Little, Pan(dy), Small, Sock, Swap, Swop, Vole, Wap
Slander(ous) Asperse, Backbite, Calumny, Defame, Derogatory, Detraction, Disparage, Libel, Malediction, Malign, Missay, Mud, Obloquy, Sclaunder, Smear, Traduce, Vilify, Vilipend
Slang Abuse, Argot, Back, Berate, Cant, Colloquial, Ebonics, Flash, Jargon, Lingo, Nadsat, Parlyaree, Polari, Rhyming, Slate, Tsotsitaal, Velan, Zowie
Slant(ed), Slanting Angle, Asklent, Atilt, Bevel, Bias, Brae, Cant, Careen, Chamfer, Clinamen, Diagonal, Escarp, Oblique, Prejudice, Slew, > **SLOPE**, Splay, Squint, Talus, Tilt, Virgule
Slap Clatch, Clout, Cuff, Make-up, Pandy, Piston, Sclaff, Scud, Skelp, Smack, Spat, Tape, Twank
Slapdash Careless, Hurried, Random
Slash(ed) Chive, Cut, Gash, Hack, Jag, Lacerate, Laciniate, Leak, Oblique, Rash, Rast, Reduce, Scorch, Scotch, Separatrix, Slit, Solidus, Wee
Slat(s) Fish, Jalousie, Louvre
Slate, Slaty Cam, Countess, Credit, Criticise, Decry, Double, Duchess, Duchy, Enter, Griseous, Imperial, Killas, Knotenschiefer, Lady, Marchioness, Ottrelite, Pan, Peggy, Polishing, Princess, Queen, Rag(g), Roof, Schalstein, Shingle, Slat, Small, Tomahawk, Viscountess
Slater Hellier, Insect
Slattern Bag, Besom, Drab, Drazel, Frump, Mopsy, Sloven, Slummock, Sozzle, Traipse, Trapes, Trollop
Slaughter(house), Slaughterer Abattoir, Behead, Bleed, Bloodshed, Butcher, Carnage, Decimate, Hal(l)al, Holocaust, Jhatka, Kill, Mactation, > **MASSACRE**, S(c)hechita(h), Scupper, Shambles, Shechita(h), Shochet, Smite

Slav Bohunk, Croat, Czech, Kulak, Polabian, Serb, Sorb, Wend(ic)

Slave(ry), Slaves Addict, Aesop, Aida, Androcles, Barracoon, Blackbird, Bond, Bond(s)man, Bondwoman, Bordar, Boy, Caliban, Coffle, Contraband, Dogsbody, Drudge, Drug, Dulocracy, Dulosis, Esne, Galley, Gibeonite, Helot, Hierodule, Mameluke, Mamluk, Marmaluke, Maroon, Minion, Odalisk, Odali(s)que, Peasant, Pr(a)edial, Rhodope, Serf, Servitude, Spartacus, Terence, Theow, Thersites, Thete, Thrall, Topsy, Vassal, Villein, Wage, White, Yoke

Slave-driver, Slave-owner Assam, Task-master

Slaver Bespit, Dribble, Drivel, Drool, Slobber, Spawl

Slay(er), Slaying Destroy, Execute, Ghazi, > KILL, Mactation, Murder, Quell, Saul, Slaughter

Sleazy Flimsy, Scuzzy, Seamy, Sordid, Squalid, Thin

Sled(ge), Sleigh(-ride) Bob, Dray, Hurdle, Hurly-hacket, Kibitka, Komatik, Lauf, Luge, Mud-boat, Polack, Pulk(h)(a), Pung, Skidoo®, Slipe, Stoneboat, Tarboggin, Toboggan, Train, Travois

Sleek Bright, Shine, Silky, Smarm, Smooth, Smug

Sleep, Sleeper(s), Sleepiness, Sleeping, Sleepy Beauty, Bed, Bivouac, Blet, Car, Catnap, Coma, Couchette, Crash, Cross-sill, Cross-tie, Dormant, Dormient, Doss, Doze, Drowse, Earring, Endymion, Epimenides, Gum, Hibernate, Hypnology, Hypnos, Kip, Lethargic, Lie, Morpheus, Nap, Narcolepsy, Nod, Over, Paradoxical, Petal, Psychopannychism, REM, Repast, Repose, Rest, Rip Van Winkle, Rough, Sandman, Seven, Shuteye, Skipper, Sloom, Slumber, Snooz(l)e, Somnolent, Sopor(ose), Sownd, Swone, Tie, Torpid, Twilight, Wink, Zizz

Sleeping place Bed, Cot, Dormitory, Kang

Sleepless Wake-rife, Wauk-rife

Sleep-walking Noctambulation

Sleet Graupel, Hail

Sleeve (opening) Arm(hole), Batwing, Bishop's, Bush, Collet, Cover, Dolman, Gatefold, Gigot, Gland, Leg-o'-mutton, Liner, Magyar, Manche, Pagoda, Pudding, Querpo, Raglan, Sabot, Scye, Slashed, Trunk, Turnbuckle, Wind

▶ **Sleigh** *see* SLED

Sleight Artifice, Conjury, Cunning, Dodge, Legerdemain, Trick

Slender(ness) Asthenic, Ectomorph, Elongate, Exiguity, Exility, Fine, Flagelliform, Flimsy, Gracile, Jimp, Leptosome, Loris, Narrow, Skinny, Slight, Slim, Small, Spindly, Stalky, Styloid, Svelte, Sylph, Tenuous, Trim, Waif

Sleuth Bloodhound, Detective, Dick, Eye, Lime-hound, Lyam(-hound), Lyme(-hound)

Slew Number, Skid, Slide, Twist

Slice Cantle, Chip, Collop, Cut, Doorstep, Fade, Frustrum, Piece, Rasure, Round, Sector, Segment, Share, Sheave, Shive, Slab, Sliver, Tranche, Wafer, Whang

▷ **Slice of** *may indicate* a hidden word

Slick Adroit, Glim, Oil, Smooth, Suave

Slide Chute, Cursor, Diapositive, Drift, Ease, Glissando, Hair, Hirsle, Ice-run, Illapse, Lantern, Mount, Pulka, Schuss, Skid, Skite, Slip, Slippery dip, Slither, Snowboard, Transparency

Slight(ly) Affront, Belittle, Cold shoulder, Cut, Detract, Disparage, Disregard, Facer, Flimsy, Halfway, Insult, Misprise, Neglect, Nominal, Pet, Petty, Rebuff, Remote, > SLENDER, Slim, Slimsy, Slur, Small, Smattering, Sneaking, Snub, Subtle, Superficial, Sylphine, Tenuous, Thin, Tiny, Wee, Wispy

Slim Bant, Jimp, Macerate, Reduce, Slender, Slight, Sylph, Tenuous, Thin

Slime, Slimy Glair, Glit, Guck, Gunk, Mother, Muc(o)us, Myxomycete, Oily, Ooze, Sapropel, Slake, Sludge, Uliginous

Sling Balista, Catapult, Drink, Fling, Hang, Parbuckle, Prusik, Support, Toss, Trebuchet

Slink Lurk, Skulk, Slope

Slip(ped), Slipping, Slips Boner, Cover, Cutting, Disc, Docket, Drift, EE, Elapse, Elt, Engobe, Error, Faux pas, Fielder, Form, Freudian, Glide, Glissade, Infielder, Label, Landslide, Lapse, Lapsus linguae, Lath, Lauwine, Mistake, Muff, Nod, Oversight, Parapraxis, Petticoat, Pink, Prolapse, Ptosis, Quickset, Rejection, Relapse, Run, Scape, Sc(h)edule, Scoot, Set, Shim, Sin, Ski, Skid, Skin, Skite, Slade, Slidder, Slide, Slither, Slive, Spillican, Stumble, Surge, Ticket, Trip, Tunicle, Underskirt, Unleash, Wage(s)

Slipper(s) Baboosh, Babouche, Babuche, Baffies, Calceolate, Carpet, Eel, Japanese, Mocassin, Moccasin, Moyl, Mule, Pabouche, Pampootie, Pantable, Pantof(f)le, Panton, Pantoufle, Pump, Rullion, Runner, Ski, Sledge, Sneaker, Sock

Slippery Foxy, Glid, Icy, Lubric, Shady, Shifty, Skidpan, Slick

Slipshod Careless, Hurried, Jerry, Lax, Slapdash, Slatternly, Sloppy, Slovenly, Toboggan

▷ **Slipshod** *may indicate* an anagram

Slit Buttonhole, Cranny, Cut, Fent, Fissure, Fitchet, Gash, Gill, Loop, Pertus(at)e, Placket, Placket-hole, Race, Rit, Scissure, Spare, Speld(er), Vent

Slithy Tove

Sliver Flake, Fragment, Moslings, Rove, Shaving, Slice, Splinter, Trace

Slob(ber) Drool, Lout, Slaver, Smarm, Wet

Sloe Blackthorn, Slae

Slog(ger) Drag, Strike, Swink, Swot, Traipse, Tramp, Trape, Trudge, Yacker, Yakka, Yakker

Slogan Amandla, Byword, Catchword, Jai Hind, Mot(to), Phrase, Rallying-cry, Slughorn(e), Tapline, Warcry, Watchword

Sloop Cutter, Hoy, Ship

Slop(s) Cop(per), Gardyloo, Jordeloo, Muck, Policeman, Rossers, Rozzers, Schmaltz, Sop, Spill, Swill

Slope(s), Sloping Acclivity, Angle, Anticline, Bahada, Bajada, Bank, Batter, Bevel, Borrow, Borstal(l), Brae, Breast, Chamfer, Cuesta, Declivity, Delve, Diagonal, Dry, Escarp, Fla(u)nch, Geanticline, Glacis, Grade, Gradient, Heel, Hill, Incline, Kant, Lean, Natural, Nursery, Oblique, Pent, Periclinal, Pitch, Rake, Ramp, Rollway, Scarp, Schuss, Scrae, Scree, Shelve, Sideling, Skewback, Slant, Slippery, Slipway, Splay, Steep, Stoss, Talus, Tilt, Verge, Versant, Weather

Sloppily, Sloppy Lagrimoso, Lowse, Madid, Mushy, Remiss, Schmaltzy, Slapdash, Slipshod, Sloven, Slushy, Untidy

▷ **Sloppy** *may indicate* an anagram

Slosh(y) Dowse, Fist, Splash, Wet

Slot(ted) Expansion, Graveyard, Groove, Hasp, Hesp, Hole, Key, Keyway, Mortice, Mortise, Seat, Slit, Swanmark, Time

Sloth(ful) Accidie, Acedia, Ai, Bradypus, Edentate, Ground, Idle, Inaction, Indolent, Inertia, Lazy, Lie-abed, Megatherium, Mylodon, Slugabed, Sweer(t), Sweered, Sweir(t), Three-toed, Unau

Slot machine One-armed bandit, Pokey, Pokie

Slouch Mooch, Mope, Slump

Slough(ing) Cast, Despond, Ecdysis, Eschar, Exuviae, Lerna, Marish, Marsh, Morass, Paludine, Shed, Shuck, Swamp

Sloven(ly) Careless, Dag(gy), D(r)aggle-tail, Frowsy, Grobian, Jack-hasty, Rag-doll, Ratbag, Slaister, Slammakin, Slammerkin, Slattern, Sleazy, Slipshod,

Slubberdegullion, Slubberingly, Slummock, Streel, Untidy

Slow(ing), Slower, Slowly Adagio, Allargando, Andante, Brady, Brake, Broad, Calando, Crawl, Dawdle, Deliberate, Dilatory, Dull, Dumka, ESN, Flag, Gradual, Inchmeal, Lag, Langram, Larghetto, Largo, Lash, Lassu, Late, Lean-witted, Leisurely, Lentando, Lento, Lifeless, Loiter, Meno mosso, Obtuse, Pedetentous, Rall(entando), Rein, Reluctant, Retard, Ribattuta, Ritardando, Ritenuto, Slack, Slug, Sluggish, Snaily, Solid, Stem, Tardigrade, Tardive, Tardy

Slow-match Portfire

Sludge Activated, Gunge, Mire, Muck, Sapropel

Slug(s) Ammo, Bêche-de-mer, Blow, Bullet, Cosh, Drink, Limaces, Limax, Linotype®, Mollusc, Nerita, Pellet, Shot, Snail, Trepang

Sluggard Drone, Lazy, Lie-abed, Lusk, Unau

Sluggish Dilatory, Drumble, Idler, Inactive, Inert, Jacent, Lacklustre, Laesie, Languid, Lazy, Lentor, Lethargic, Lug, Phlegmatic, Saturnine, Sleepy, > **SLOW**, Stagnant, Tardy, Torpid, Unalive

Sluice Aboideau, Aboiteau, Drain, Gutter, Koker, Penstock, Rinse, Sasse

Slum Basti, Bustee, Busti, Cabbagetown, Ghetto, Pavela, Rookery, Shanty, Slurb, Warren

Slumber Doze, Drowse, Nap, Nod, Sleep, Sloom, Snooze

Slump Decrease, Depression, Deteriorate, Dip, Flop, Recession, Sink, Slouch

Slur(ring) Defame, Drawl, Innuendo, Libel, Opprobrium, Slight, Smear, Synaeresis, Tie

Slush Bathos, Boodle, Bribe, Drip, Money, Mush, Pap, Slop, Sposh, Swash

Slut Candle, Dollymop, Draggle-tail, Dratchell, Drazel, Floosie, Harlot, Slattern, Sow, Tart, Traipse, Trapes, Trollop

Sly Christopher, Clandestine, Coon, Covert, Cunning, Foxy, Furtive, Leery, Peery, Reynard, Shifty, Sleekit, Sleeveen, Slicker, Stealthy, Subtle, Tinker, Tod, Tricky, Weasel, Wily

▷ **Slyly** *may indicate an anagram*

Smack(er) Buss, Cuff, Flavour, Foretaste, Fragrance, Hooker, Kiss, Lander, Lips, Pra(h)u, Relish, Salt, Saut, Skelp, Slap, Slat, Smatch, Smouch, Soupçon, Spank, Spice, Splat, Tack, > **TANG**, Taste, Thwack, Tincture, Trace, X, Yawl

Small (thing) Ateleiosis, Atom, Bantam, Beer, Bijou, Bittie, Bitty, Centesimal, Curn, Denier, Diminutive, Dinky, Drib, Elfin, Few, Fry, Grain, Haet, Ha'it, Half-pint, Handful, Holding, Insect, Ion, Leet, Lilliputian, Limited, Lite, > **LITTLE**, Lock, Low, Meagre, Measly, Midget, Mignon, Miniature, Minikin, Minute, Mite, Modest, Modicum, Peerie, Peewee, Petit(e), Petty, Pigmean, Pigmy, Pink(ie), Pinky, Pint-size, Pittance, Pocket, Poky, Poujadist, Rap, Reduction, Runt, S, Santilla, Scattering, Scrump, Scrunt, Scut, Shrimp, Single, Skerrick, Slight, Slim, Smattering, Smidge(o)n, Smidgin, Smithereen, Smout, Soupçon, Sprinkling, Spud, Stim, Stunted, Tad, Thin, Tidd(l)y, Tiny, Titch(y), Tittle, Tot(tie), Totty, Trace, Trivial, Unheroic, Wee, Weedy, Whit

Smallest Least, Minimal, Runt

Smallholder, Smallholding Croft, Nursery, Rundale, Share-cropper, Stead

Small-minded(ness) Parvanimity, Petty

Smallness Exiguity, Exility, Paucity

Smallpox Alastrim, Variola

Smarm(y) Oil, Smoothie, Unctuous

Smart(en), Smartest Ache, Acute, Alec, Astute, Best, Bite, Chic, Classy, Clever, Cute, Dandy, Dapper, Dressy, Elegant, Flash, Flip, Fly, Groom, Gussy up, Kookie, Kooky, Natty, Neat, Nifty, Nip, Nobby, Pac(e)y, Pacy, Posh, Preen, Primp, Prink, Pusser, Raffish, Rattling, Ritzy, Saucy, Slick, Sly, Smoke, Smug, Snappy,

Soigné(e), Spiff, Sprauncy, Sprightly, Spruce, Sprush, Spry, Sting, Swagger, Sweat, Swish, Tiddley, Tippy, Titivate, Toff, U, Well-groomed, Wiseacre

Smash(ed), Smasher, Smashing Atom, Bingle, Brain, Break, Crush, Demolish, Devastate, Dish, Forearm, High, Jarp, Jaup, Kaput, Kill, Lulu, Shatter, Shiver, Slam, Squabash, Stave, Super, Terrific, Tight, To-brake, > **WRECK**

Smash(ed) *may indicate* an anagram

Smear Assoil, Bedaub, Besmirch, Blur, Borm, Cervical, Clam, Daub, Defile, Denigrate, Discredit, Drabble, Enarm, Gaum, Gild, Gorm, Lick, Oil, Pap(anicolaou), Pay, Plaster, Slairg, Slaister, Slake, Slather, Slime, Slubber, Slur, Smalm, Smarm, Smudge, Sully, Teer, Traduce, Wax

Smell(ing), Smelly Aroma, Asafoetida, BO, Caproate, Effluvium, Empyreuma, Fetor, F(o)etid, Fug, Gale, Gamy, Graveolent, Guff, Hing, Honk, Hum, Mephitis, Miasm(a), Musk, Nidor, Niff, Nose, Odour, Olent, Olfact(ory), Osmatic, Perfume, Pong, Ponk, Pooh, Rank, Redolent, Reech, Reek, Sar, Savour, > **SCENT**, Sniff, Snifty, Snook, Snuff, Steam, Stench, Stifle, Stink, Tang, Whiff

Smelling salts Sal volatile

Smelt(ing) Atherinidae, Melt, Salmon, Scoria, Sparling, Speiss, Spirling

Smile(s), Smiling Agrin, Beam, Cheese, Favour, Gioconda, Grin, Rictus, Samuel, Self-help, Simper, Smirk

Smirk Grimace, Simper

Smite, Smitten Assail, Enamoured, Hit, Strike, Strook

Smith Adam, Farrier, FE, Forger, Hammerman, Mighty, Stan, Vulcan, Wayland

Smithy Forge, Smiddy, Stithy

Smock Blouse, Chemise, Drabbet, Gather, Shift, Slop, Smicket

Smoke(r), Smoking, Smoky Blast, Bloat, Censer, Chain, Chillum, > **CIGAR(ETTE)**, Cure, Fog, Fuliginous, Fume, Funk, Gasper, Hemp, Incense, Indian hemp, Inhale, Kipper, Latakia, Lum, Lunt, Mainstream, Manil(l)a, Nicotian, Passive, Peat reek, Pother, Pudder, Puff, Reech, Reek, Reest, Roke, Smeech, Smeek, Smoor, Smoulder, Smudge, Snout, Toke, Vapour, Viper, Water, Whiff, Wreath

Smoke-hating Misocapnic

Smoking-room Divan

Smollett Tobias

▸ **Smooch** *see* SMOUCH

Smooth(e), Smoother, Smoothly Bland, Brent, Buff, Chamfer, Clean, Clockwork, Dress, Dub, Easy, Even, Fettle, File, Flat, Fluent, Glabrous, Glare, Glassy, Glib, Goose, Iron, Legato, Level, Levigate, Linish, Mealy-mouthed, Mellifluous, Oil, Plane, Plaster, Rake, Roll, Rub, Sand(er), Satiny, Scrape, Sleek, Slick, Slickenslide, Slur, Smug, Snod, Sostenuto, Streamlined, Suave, Swimmingly, Terete, Terse, Trim, Urbane

Smooth-haired Lissotrichous

Smother Burke, Choke, Muffle, Oppress, Overlie, Smoor, Smore, Smoulder, Stifle, Suppress

Smouch Cheat, Kiss, Lallygag, Lollygag, Neck

Smoulder Burn, Seethe

Smudge Blur, Dab, Offset, Slur, Smear, Smooch, Stain

Smug Complacent, Conceited, Goody-two-shoes, Neat, Oily, Pi, Sanctimonious, Self-satisfied, Trim

Smuggle(d), Smuggler, Smuggling Body-packer, Bootleg, Contraband, Contrabandist, Donkey, Fair trade, Gunrunning, Moonshine, Mule, Owler, Rum-runner, Run, Secrete, Steal, Traffic

Smut(ty) Bawdy, Blight, Blue, Brand, Burnt-ear, Coom, Filth, Grime, Racy, Soot, Speck, Stinking

Smut-fungus Basidia, Ustilago

Snack Bever, Bhelpuri, Bite, Blintz, Breadstick, Brunch, Butty, Canapé, Chack, Crudités, Elevenses, Entremets, Four-by-two, Gorp, Meze, Nacket, Nibble, Nocket, Nooning, Nuncheon, Pdkos, Pie, Popcorn, Rarebit, Refreshment, Samo(o)sa, Sandwich, Sarnie, Savoury, Tapa, Taste, Toast(y), Vada, Voidee, Wada, Zakuska

Snaffle Bit, Bridoon, Grab, Purloin

Snag Catch, Contretemps, Drawback, Hindrance, Hitch, Impediment, Knob, Nog, Obstacle, Remora, Rub, Snubbe, Stub, Tear

Snail Brian, Cowrie, Cowry, Dew, Dodman, Escargot, Garden, Gasteropod, Giant African, Helix, Hodmandod, Limnaea, Lymnaea, Nautilus, Nerite, Planorbis, Pond, Ramshorn, Roman, Slow, Slug, Strombus, Unicorn-shell, Univalve, Wallfish, Whelk, Wing

Snake Adder, Aesculapian, Amphisbaena, Anaconda, Anguine, Anguis, Apod(e), Asp, Bandy-bandy, Berg-adder, Blacksnake, Blind, Blue-racer, Boa, Boma, Boomslang, Brown, Bull, Bush-master, Camoodi, Carpet, Cerastes, Clotho, Coachwhip, Cobra, Coluber, Congo, Constrictor, Copperhead, Coral, Corn, Cottonmouth, Cribo, Crotalidae, Daboia, Death-adder, Dendrophis, Diamond(-back), Dipsas, Dugite, Elaps, Ellops, Fer-de-lance, Garter, Glass, Grass, Habu, Hamadryad, Hognose, Homorelaps, Hoop, Horned viper, Horsewhip, Hydra, Indigo, Jararaca, Jararaka, Joe Blake, Kaa, K(a)rait, King (cobra), Lachesis, Langaha, Mamba, Massasauga, Meander, Milk, Mocassin, Moccasin, Mulga, Naga, Naia, Naja, Ophidian, Pipe, Pit-viper, Plumber's, Puff-adder, Python, Racer, Rat, Rattler, Reptile, Ribbon, Ringhals, Ringneck, Rinkhals, River jack, Rock, Sand viper, Seps, > SERPENT, Sidewinder, Slowworm, Smooth, Spitting, Squamata, Sucuruju, Surucucu, Taipan, Takshaka, Thirst, Thread, Tiger, Timber rattlesnake, Tree, Uraeus, Vasuki, Viper, Water (moccasin), Whip, Wind, Worm

Snake-charmer Lamia

Snake-in-the-grass Peacher, Rat, Traitor

Snake-root Senega

Snap(per), Snappy, Snap up Autolycus, Bite, Break, Brittle, Camera, Click, Cold, Crack, Cross, Curt, Edgy, Fillip, Girnie, Glom, Gnash, Hanch, Knacker, Knap, Livery, Mugshot, Photo, Photogene, Scotch, Snack, Snatch, Spell, Still, Tetchy, Vigour

Snare Bait, Benet, Engine, Enmesh, Entrap, Gin, Grin, Hook, Illaqueate, Inveigle, Net, Noose, Rat-trap, Springe, Springle, Toil, > TRAP, Trapen, Trepan, Web, Weel, Wire

Snarl(ing) Chide, Complicate, Cynic, Enmesh, Girn, Gnar(l), Gnarr, Growl, Grumble, Knar, Knot, Snap, Tangle, Yirr

Snatch Claucht, Claught, Excerpt, Fragment, Glom, Grab, Kidnap, Nip, Pluck, Race, Rap, Rase, Raunch, Refrain, Snippet, Song, Spell, Strain, Take, Tweak, Wrap, Wrest

▷ **Snatch** *may indicate* the first letter of a word

Snazzy Cat

Snead Snath

Sneak(y) Area, Carry-tale, Clipe, Clype, Inform, Lurk, Mumblenews, Nim, Peak, Scunge, Skulk, Slink, Slip, Slyboots, Snitch, Snoop, Split, Steal, Stoolie, Surreptitious, Tell(-tale), Underhand

Sneer(ing) Barb, Critic, Cynical, Fleer, Gibe, Jeer, Scoff, Smirk, Snide

Sneeze (at), Sneezing Atishoo, Neese, Neeze, Ptarmic, Scorn, Sternutation

Snick Click, Cut, Edge, Glance

Snicker Snigger, Titter, Whinny

Snide Bitchy, Shand

Sniff Inhale, Nose, Nursle, Nuzzle, Scent, Smell, Snivel, Snort, Snuffle, Vent, Whiff

Snigger Giggle, Laugh, Snicker, Snirtle, Titter, Whicker

Snip(pet) Bargain, Cert, Clip, Cut, Doddle, Piece, Sartor, Snatch, Snick, Tailor

Snipe(r) Bird, Bushwhacker, Criticise, Franc-tireur, Gutter, Heather-bleat(er), Heather-bluiter, Heather-blutter, Pick off, Scape, Shoot, Walk, Wisp

Snitch Conk, Konk, Nose

Snivel Blubber, Snotter, Snuffle, Weep, Whine

Snob(bery), Snobbish Cobbler, Crispin, High-hat, Inverted, Scab, Side, Snooty, Soutar, Souter, Sowter, Toffee-nose, Vain, Vamp

Snooker Pool, Stimie, Stimy, Stym(i)e

Snoop(er) Meddle, Nose, Pry, Tec

Snooty Bashaw, Snob(bish)

Snooze Calk, Caulk, Dove, Doze, Nap, Nod, Siesta, Sleep

Snore, Snoring Rhonchus, Rout, Snort, Stertorous, Zz

Snort(er) Drink, Grunt, Nare, Nasal, Roncador, Snore, Toot

Snot(ty) Mucoid

Snout Bill, Boko, Cigar, Gasper, Gruntie, Informer, Muzzle, Nose, Nozzle, Proboscis, Schnozzle, Tinker, Tobacco, Wall

Snow(y), Snowstorm Brig, Buran, Cocaine, Coke, Corn, Cornice, Crud, Firn, Flake, Flurry, Graupel, Half-pipe, Heroin, Marine, Mogul, Neve, Nival, Niveous, Oncome, Onding, Powder, Red, Sastruga, Spotless, Stall, Virga, White-out, Wintry, Wreath, Yellow, Zastruga

Snowball Accelerate, Cramp-bark, Cumulative, Guelder-rose, Increase, Magnify, Opulus, Pelt, Rose

Snowdrop Avalanche

Snowflake Leucojum, St Agnes' flower

Snow-goose Wav(e)y

Snowman Abominable, Eskimo, Junkie, Sherpa, Yeti

Snowmobile Sno-cat

Snowshoe Bear paw, Racket, Racquet

Snub Cut, Diss, Go-by, Lop, Pug, Put-down, Quelch, Rebuff, Reproof, Retroussé, Set-down, Short, Slap, Slight, Sloan, Sneap, Snool, Wither

Snuff(le) Asarabacca, Dout, Errhine, Extinguish, Maccabaw, Maccaboy, Maccoboy, Ptarmic, Pulvil, Rappee, Smother, Snaste, Sneesh(an), Sniff, Snift, Snush, Tobacco, Vent

Snuffbox Anatomical, Mill, Mull

Snug(gle) Burrow, Cose, > COSY, Couthie, Couthy, Croodle, Cubby, Cuddle, Embrace, Lion, Neat, Nestle, Nuzzle, Rug, Snod, Tight, Trim

So Argal, Ergo, Forthy, Hence, Sae, Sic(h), Sol, Therefore, This, Thus, True, Very, Yes

Soak Bate, Bath(e), Beath, Bewet, Bloat, Blot, Buck, Cree, Deluge, Drench, Drink, Drook, Drouk, Drown, Drunk, Duck, Dunk, Embay, Embrue, Fleece, Grog, Imbrue, Infuse, Lush, Macerate, Marinate, Mop, Oncome, Permeate, Rait, Rate, Ret(t), Rinse, Sipe, Sog, Sop, Souce, Souse, Sows(s)e, Steep, Sype, Thwaite, Toper, Wet

Soap(y), Soap opera Cake, Carbolic, Castile, Eluate, Flake, Flannel, Flattery, Green, Joe, Lather, Marine, Metallic, Moody, Mountain, Pears®, Pinguid, Saddle, Saponaceous, Saponin, Sawder, Slime, Soft, Spanish, Suds, Sudser, Sugar, Syndet, Tablet, Tall-oil, Toheroa, Toilet, Washball, Windsor, Yellow

Soapstone French chalk, Steatite, Talc

Soar(ing) Ascend, Essorant, Fly, Glide, Hilum, Rise, Tower, Zoom

Sob (stuff) Blub(ber), Boohoo, Goo, Gulp, Lament, Singult, Singultus, Snotter, Wail, Weep, Yoop

Sober(sides) Abstemious, Calm, Demure, Pensive, Sedate, Staid, Steady, TT

Sobriquet Byname, Cognomen, Nickname, To-name

So-called Alleged, Nominal, Soi-disant

Sociable, Sociability Affable, Cameraderie, Chummy, Cosy, Extravert, Extrovert, Folksy, Friendly, Genial, Gregarious

Social(ise) Convivial, Hobnob, Hui, Mingle, Mix, Musicale, Phatic, Tea-dance, Yancha

Socialism, Socialist Ba'(a)th, Champagne, Chartist, Dergue, Engels, Fabian, Fourierism, Guild, ILP, International, Lansbury, Left(y), Marxism, Menchevik, Menchevist, National, Nihilism, Owen(ist), Owenite, Pinko, Red, Revisionist, St Simonist, Sandinista, Spartacist, Utopian, Webb

Socialite Deb

Society Affluent, Association, Beau monde, Benefit, Body, Broederbond, Building, Camorra, Carbonari, Class, Club, College, Company, Conger, Co-op, Cooperative, Culture, Danite, Defenders, Dorcas, Eleutheri, Elite, Elks, Fabian, Fashion, Foresters, Freemans, Freemasons, Friendly, Friends, Glee club, Grotian, Group, Guilds, Haut monde, Hetairia, High, Humane, Illuminati, Institute, Invincibles, John Birch, Ku-klux-klan, Kyrle, Law, Linnean, Lodge, Mafia, Malone, Masonic, Mau-mau, Menage, Molly Maguire, National, Oddfellows, Oral, Orangemen, Oratory, Order, Permissive, Phi Beta Kappa, Plunket, Plural, Pop, Provident, Repertory, Ribbonism, Rosicrucian, Rotary, Royal, S, School, Secret, Soc, Soroptomist, Sorority, Stakeholder, Tammany, Theosophical, Toc H, Ton, Tong, Triad, U, Whiteboy, World

Sociologist Weber

Sock(s) Argyle, Argyll, Biff, Bobby, Bootee, Digital, Hose(n), Punch, Rock, Slipper, Slosh, Strike, Tabi, Walk, Wind

Socket Acetabulum, Alveole, Budget, Gudgeon, Hollow, Hosel, Hot shoe, Jack, Nave, Ouch, Pod, Point, Port, Power-point, Shoe, Strike, Torulus, Whip

Sock-eye Nerka, Salmon

Socrates, Socratic Ironist, Maieutics, Sage

Sod Clump, Delf, Delph, Divot, Gazo(o)n, Mool, Mould, Mouls, Scraw, Sward, Turf

Soda, Sodium Acmite, Arfvedsonite, Baking, Barilla, Bicarb, Caustic, Club, Cream, La(u)rvikite, Na, Natrium, Natron, Reh, Saleratus, Splash, Trona, Washing

Sofa Canapé, Chesterfield, Couch, Daybed, Divan, Dos-à-dos, Dosi-do, Ottoman, Settee, Squab, Tête-à-tête

So far As, As yet, Until, Yonder

Soft(en), Softener, Softening, Softly Amalgam, Anneal, B, BB, Blet, Boodle, Calm, Casefy, Cedilla, Cree, Dim, Dolcemente, Doughy, Ease, Emolliate, Emollient, Flabby, Gentle, Hooly, Humanise, Intenerate, Lash, Lax, Lenient, Lenition, Limp, Low, Macerate, Malacia, Malax(ate), Malleable, Mardarse, Mardie, Mease, Mellow, Melt, Mild, Milksop, Mitigate, Modulate, Mollify, Mollities, Morendo, Mulch, Mush(y), Mute, Neale, Nesh, Option, P, Palliate, Pastel, Piano, Plushy, Porous, Propitiate, Rait, Rate, Relent, Scumble, Sentimental, Silly, Slack, Squashy, Squidgy, Squishy, Sumph, Talcose, Temper, > **TENDER**, Tone, Velvet, Weak

Softness Lenity

Software Firewall, Firmware, Groupware, Middleware, Parser, Payware, Shareware, Spreadsheet, Stiffware, Vaccine, Windows

Sog(gy) Sodden

Soil(ed), Soily Acid, Adscript, Agrology, Agronomy, Alkali(ne), Alluvium, Azonal, Bedraggle, Chemozem, Clay, Cohesive, Defile, Desecrate, Desert, Dinge, Dirt(y), Discolour, Earth, Edaphic, Frictional, Gault, Glebe, Grey, Grimy, Ground, Gumbo, Hotbed, Humus, Illuvium, Intrazonal, Lair, Land, Latosol, Lithosol, Loam, Loess, Lome, Loss, Mire, Mool, Mo(u)ld, Mud, Mulch, Mull, Night, Peat, Ped, Pedalfer, Pedocal, Pedology, Phreatic, Planosol, Podsol, Podzol, Prairie, Pure, Regar, Regolith, Regosol, Regur, Rendzina, Rhizosphere, Root-ball, Sal, Sedentary, Smudge, Smut, Solonchak, Solonetz, Solum, Soot, Stain, Stonebrash, Sub, Sully, Tarnish, Tash, Terrain, Terricolous, Tilth, Top, Tschernosem, Udal, Umber, Virgin, Yarfa, Yarpha, Zonal

Soirée Drum, Levee, Musicale

Sojourn Abide, Respite, Stay, Tarry

Sol G, Soh, Sun

Solace Cheer, Comfort

Solar(ium) Heliacal, Tannery

Sold Had

Solder Blaze, Join, Spelter, Tin, Weld

Soldier(s) Achilles, Alpini, Amazon, Ant, Anzac, Army, Arna(o)ut, Askari, Atkins, ATS, Banner, Bashi-Bazouk, Battalion, Bersaglier(e), Bluff, Bod, Bombardier, Borderer, Botha, Brave, Brigade, Buff-coat, Buff-jerkin, Butter-nut, Cadet, Caimac(am), Campaigner, Cannon-fodder, Car(a)bineer, Car(a)binier, Cataphract, Centinel(l), Centonel(l), Centurion, Chasseur, Chindit, Chocko, Choco, Chocolate, Cohort, Colonel, Colours, Commando, Confederate, Contingent, Cornet, Corp(s), Cossack, Crusader, Cuirassier, Ded, Desert rat, Detail, Dog-face, Doughboy, Draftee, Dragoon, Dugout, Emmet, Engineer, Enomoty, Evzone, Fag(g)ot, Federal, Fencibles, Fighter, Flanker, Foederatus, Foot, Forlorn-hope, Fugleman, Fusilier, Fuzzy-wuzzy, Fyrd, Gallo(w)glass, Galoot, General, GI, Gippo, Goorkha, Grenadier, Grim dig, Grunt, Guardee, Guardsman, Guerilla, Gurkha, Gyppo, Hackbuteer, Hobbler, Hoplite, Hussar, Immortal, Impi, Inf(antry), Iron Duke, Ironside, Irregular, Jackman, Janissary, Janizary, Jawan, Joe, Johnny Reb(el), Kaimakam, Kern(e), Kitchener, Knight, Lancer, Landsknecht, Lansquenet, Lashkar, Leatherneck, Legionary, Legionnaire, Levy, Line, Linesman, Lobster, Maniple, Martinet, Men-at-arms, Miles (gloriosus), Militiaman, Miner, Minuteman, Musketeer, Nahal, Naik, Nasute, Nizam, Non-com, Old moustache, OR, Orderly, Palatine, Palikar, Pandoor, Pandour, Paratroop, Partisan, Peltast, Peon, Perdu(e), Persevere, Phalanx, Pikeman, Piou-piou, Pistoleer, Platoon, Poilu, Point man, Pongo, Post, POW, Private, Rajput, Ranger, Rank(er), Rank and file, Rapparree, Rat-tail, Reb, Redcoat, Reformado, Regiment, Regular, Reiter, Reservist, Retread, Rifleman, Rutter, Sabre, Saddler, Sammy, Samurai, SAS, Sebundy, Sentinel, Sepoy, Serviceman, Signaller, Silladar, Snarler, So(d)ger, Soldado, Sowar(ee), Sowarry, Spearman, Squaddie, Squaddy, Stalhelm(er), Stormtrooper, Strelitz, Subaltern, Swad(dy), Sweat, Targeteer, Tarheel, Templar, Terrier, Territorial, Timariot, Tin, Tommy, Toy, Train-band, Trencher, Trooper, Troops, Turco(pole), Uhlan, Unknown, Velites, Vet(eran), Voltigeur, Volunteer, Wagon, Warhorse, Warmonger, Warrior, Whitecoat, Yardbird, Yeoman, Zouave

▷ **Soldiers** *may indicate* bread for boiled eggs

Sole, Solitaire, Solitary Alone, Anchoret, Anchorite, Clump, Convex,

Dover, Dropped, Fish, Incommunicado, Lemon, Lonesome, Megrim, Merl, Meunière, Monastical, Monkish, Only, Pad, Palm, Patience, Pelma, Planta(r), Plantigrade, Platform, Recluse, Scaldfish, Single(ton), Skate, Slip, Smear-dab, Tap, Thenar, Tread, Unique, Vibram®, Vola

Solemn Agelast, Austere, Devout, Earnest, Grave, Gravitas, Impressive, Majestic, Owlish, Po-faced, Sacred, Sedate, Serious, Sober, Sobersides

Solent Lee

Solicit Accost, Approach, Ask, Attract, Bash, > BEG, Canvass, Commission, Cottage, Importun(at)e, Plead, Ply, Proposition, Speer, Speir, Tout, Woo

Solicitor(s) Advocate, Attorney, Avoué, Beggar, Canvasser, Hallanshaker, Law-agent, Lawyer, Notary, Side-bar, SL, Tout, Trull, Writer to the Signet, WS

Solid(arity), Solidify Cake, Chunky, Clot, Clunky, Compact, Comradeship, Concrete, Cone, Congeal, Consolidate, Cube, Cylinder, Dense, Enneahedron, Firm, Foursquare, Freeze, Frustrum, Fuchsin(e), Gel, Hard, Holosteric, Impervious, Masakhane, Merbromin, Octahedron, Pakka, Petrarchan, Platonic, Polyhedron, Prism, Pucka, Pukka, Robust, Set, Skatole, Stilbene, Sublimate, Substantial, Tetrahedron, Thick, Unanimous

Solipsism Egotism, Panegoism

Solitude Privacy, Seclusion

Solo Aria, Cadenza, Cavatine, Concertante, Lone, Monodrama, Monody, Ombre, One-man, Scena, Variation

Solon Sage

So long Cheerio, Ciao, Goodbye, Tata

Solstice Summer, Tropic, Winter

Soluble Alkaline, Surfactant

Solution Acetone, Alkali, Ammonia, Amrit, > ANSWER, Austenite, Benedict's, Collodion, Colloidal, Dakin's, Dobell's, Eclairassement, Electrolyte, Elixir, Emulsion, Eusol, Fehling's, Final, Key, Leachate, Limewater, Lixivium, Lye, Oleoresin, Rationale, Reducer, Ringer's, Rinse, Saline, Solid, Solvent, Soup, Standard, Suspensoid, Tincture, Titrate, Viscose

▷ **Solution** *may indicate* an anagram

Solve(d), Solver Assoil, Casuist, Clear, Crack, Decode, Holmes, Loast, Loose, Read(er), Suss out, Troubleshoot, Unclew, Undo, Unriddle

Solvent Acetaldehyde, Acetone, Afloat, Alcahest, Aldol, Alkahest, Anisole, Aqua-regia, Banana oil, Cleanser, Cyclohexane, Cyclopentane, Decalin, Diluent, Dioxan(e), Eleunt, Eluant, Ether, Funded, Furan, Hexane, Ligroin, Megilp, Menstruum, Methanol, Methylal, Naphtha, Paraldehyde, Picoline, Protomic, Pyridine, Sound, Stripper, Terebene, Terpineol, Tetrachloromethane, Thinner, Thiophen, Toluene, Toluol, Trike, Trilene, Turpentine

Sombre Dark, Drab, Drear, Dull, Gloomy, Grave, Morne, Subfusc, Subfusk, Sullen, Triste

Some Any, Arrow, Ary, Certain, Divers, Few, One, Part, Portion, Quota, These, They, Wheen

▷ **Some** *may indicate* a hidden word

Somebody Dignitary, Name, Notable, One, Person, Quidam, Someone, > VIP

Somehow Somegate

▷ **Somehow** *may indicate* an anagram

Somersault Barani, Deltcher, Flip(-flap), Flip-flop, Handspring, Pitchpole, Pitchpoll

Something Aliquid, Chattel, Matter, Object, Summat, What, Whatnot

Sometime(s) Erstwhile, Ex, Former, Occasional, Off and on, Quondam

Somewhat Bit, -ish, Mite, Partly, Quasi, Quite, Rather
Somewhere Somegate
Son Boy, Descendant, Disciple, Epigon(e), Fils, Fitz, Lad, Lewis, M(a)c, Offspring, Prodigal, Progeny, Scion
Song Air, Amoret, Anthem, Antistrophe, Aria, Art, Aubade, Ayre, Ballad, Ballant, Ballata, Barcarol(l)e, Belter, Berceuse, Bhajan, Blues, Brindisi, Burden, Burthen, Cabaletta, Calypso, Cancionero, Canticle, Cantilena, Canzona, Canzone, Canzonet(ta), Carmagnole, Carol, Catch, Cavatina, Chanson, Cha(u)nt, Come-all-ye, Conductus, Corn-kister, Cycle, Descant, Dirge, Dithyramb, Ditty, Epithalamion, Epithalamium, Fado, Fit, Flamenco, Folk, Forebitter, Glee, Gorgia, Gradual, Hillbilly, Hum, Hymeneal, Hymn, Internationale, Jug(-jug), Lament, Lay, Lied(er), Lilt, Lullaby, Lyric, Madrigal, Magnificat, Marseillaise, Matin, Melic, Melisma, Melody, Mento, Negro spiritual, Noel, Number, Nunc dimittis, Oat, Paean, Pane, Part, Patter, Pennillion, Plain, Plaint, Plantation, Prick, Prothalamion, Prothalamium, Psalm, Qawwali, Rap, Recitativo, Relish, Rhapsody, Rispetto, Roulade, Roundelay, Rune, Scat, Sea-shanty, Secular, Serenade, Shanty, Siren, Sirvente, Skolion, Sososholoza, Spiritual, Stave, Strain, Strophe, Swan, Taps, Tenebrae, Theme, Torch, Trill, Tune, Villanella, Volkslied, Warble, Wassail, Waulking, Yodel, Yodle
Songbook Cancionero, Hymnal, Kommersbuch, Libretto, Psalter
Songsmith, **Songwriter** Dowland, Espla, Foster, Kern, Minot, Zappa
Sonnet Amoret, Elizabethan, English, Italian, Miltonic, Petrarch(i)an, Shakespearean, Shakespearian, Spenserian
Sonometer Monochord
Soon(er) Anon, Directly, Erelong, Lief, OK, Oklahoma, Presently, Shortly, Tight, Timely, Tit(ely), Tite, Tyte
Soot(y) Colly, Coom, Crock, Fuliginous, Gas black, Grime, Lampblack, Smut, Speck
Soothe, **Soothing** Accoy, Allay, Anetic, Anodyne, Appease, Assuage, Bucku, Calm, Compose, Demulcent, Dulcet, Emollient, Irenic, Lenitive, Lull, Mellifluous, Mollify, Pacific, Paregoric, Poultice, Quell, Rock
Soothsayer Astrologer, Augur, Calchas, Chaldee, Divine, Forecaster, Haruspex, Melampus, Oracle, Picus, Prophet, Pythoness, > **SEER**, Shipton, Tiresias
Sop Appease, Berry, Douceur, Rait, Ret, Sponge
Sophist(ic) Casuist, Elenchic, Quibbler
Sophisticate(d) Blasé, Boulevardier, City slicker, Civilised, Cosmopolitan, Couth, Doctor, High-end, Patrician, Polished, Sative, Slicker, Svelte, Urbane, Worldly
▷ **Sophoclean** *may indicate* Greek (alphabet, etc)
Sophomore Semie
Soporific Barbiturate, Bromide, Drowsy, Halothane, Hypnotic, Lullaby, Narcotic, Opiate, Sedative, Tedious
Soppiness, **Soppy** Maudlin, Schwarmerei, Sloppy, Slushy
Soprano Castrato, Crespin, Descant, Lind, Patti, Treble
Sorb Wend
Sorcerer, **Sorceress**, **Sorcery** Angakok, Ashipu, Circe, Conjury, Diablerie, Hoodoo, Kadaitcha, Kurdaitcha, Lamia, Mage, Magian, Magic(ian), Magus, Medea, Merlin, Morgan le Fay, Mother Shipton, Necromancer, Obi, Pishogue, Shaman, Sortilege, Venefic(ious), Voodoo, Warlock, Witch, Wizard
Sordid Base, Low-life, Scungy, Seamy, Sleazy, Squalid, Vile
Sore(ly), **Sores** Abrasion, Anthrax, Bitter, Blain, Boil, Canker, Chancre, Chap,

Chilblain, Cold, Dearnly, Felon, Gall, Impost(h)ume, Ireful, Kibe, Quitter, Quittor, Raw, Running, Rupia(s), Saddle, Sair, Shiver, Sitfast, Surbate, Ulcer(s), Whitlow, Wound

Sore throat Garget, Prunella, Quinsy, Tonsillitis

Sorghum Milo

Sorrel Common, French, Hetty, Mountain, Oca, Roman, Sheep, Soar(e), Sore, Sourock

Sorrow(ful) Affliction, Distress, Dole, Dolente, Dolour, Emotion, Fee-grief, > GRIEF, Lament, Misery, Nepenthe, Penance, Pietà, Remorse, Rue, Triste, Wae, Waugh, Wirra, Woe, Yoop

Sorry Ashamed, Contrite, Miserable, Oops, Penitent, Pitiful, Poor, Regretful, Relent, Wretched

▷ **Sorry** *may indicate* an anagram

Sort(ing) Arrange, Brand, Breed, Category, Character, Classify, Collate, Drive, Grade, > KIND, Nature, Pranck(e), Prank, Sift, Species, Stamp, Tidy, Triage, Type, Variety

Sortie Attack, Foray, Mission, Outfall, Raid, Sally

▸ **Sorts** *see* OUT OF SORTS

So-so Average, Indifferent, Mediocre, Middling

So to speak Quasi

▷ **So to speak** *may indicate* 'sound of'

Sotto voce Murmur, Whisper

▸ **Soubriquet** *see* SOBRIQUET

Sough Rustle, Sigh

Soul(ful) Alma, Ame, Anima, Animist, Atman, Ba, Bardo, Brevity, Deep, Entelechy, Eschatology, Expressive, Heart, Inscape, Larvae, Lost, Manes, Object, Person, Pneuma, Psyche, Saul, Shade, Spirit, Universal

Sound(ed), Soundness, Sound system Accurate, Ach-laut, Acoustic, Affricate, Albemarle, Alveolar, Amphoric, Audio, Bay, Bleep, Blow, Boing, Bong, Cacophony, Chime, Chirr(e), Chord, Chug, Clam, Clang, Clink, Clop, Clunk, Continuant, Dah, Dental, Dit, Dive, Dolby®, Echo, Euphony, Fast, Fathom, Fere, Fettle, Fit, Good, Hale, Harmonics, Healthy, Hearty, Hi-fi, Ich-laut, Inlet, Knell, Kyle, Labiodental, Lo-fi, Long Island, Lucid, Mach, Madrilene, McMurdo, Mersey, Milford, Mouillé, Music, Narrow, > NOISE, Onomatopaeia, Oompah, Optical, Orthodox, Palatal, Palato-alveolar, Pamlico, Paragog(u)e, Peal, Pectoriloquy, Phone(me), Phonetic, Phonic, Phonology, Pitter(-patter), Plap, Plink, Plonk, Plop, Plosion, Plumb, Plummet, Plunk, Probe, Puget, Put-put, Quadraphonic(s), Quadrophonic(s), Rale, Rational, Real, Reliable, Ring, Roach, Robust, Rong, Rumble, Rustle, Sabin, Safe, Sandhi, Sane, S(c)hwa, Scoresby, Sensurround®, Skirl, Solid, Sonance, Sone, Souffle, Sough, Sowne, Splat, Stereo, Stereophony, Strait, Surround, Swish, Tamber, Tannoy®, Thorough, Timbre, Ting, Tone, Toneme, Trig, Triphthong, Trumpet, Twang, Ultrasonic(s), Unharmed, Uvular, Valid, Voice, Vowel, Wah-wah, Watertight, Well, Whistle, Whole(some), Whump, Wolf

Sounder Echo, Lead

Soundproof Deaden

Sound-track Dubbing, Stripe

Soup Alphabet, Avgolemono, Bird's nest, Bisk, Bisque, Borsch, Bouillabaisse, Bouillon, Brewis, Broth, Burgoo, Chowder, Cock-a-leekie, Consommé, Duck, Garbure, Gazpacho, Gomb(r)o, Gruel, Gumbo, Harira, Hoosh, Julienne, Kail, Kale, Madrilene, Marmite, Mess, Minestrone, Mock turtle, Mulligatawny, Oxtail, Palestine, Pea(se), Pot-au-feu, Pot(t)age, Primordial, Puree, Ramen,

Rubaboo, Sancoche, Shchi, Shtchi, Skilligalee, Skilligolee, Skilly, Skink, Stock, Tattie-claw, Toheroa, Turtle, Vichyssoise

▷ **Soup** *may indicate* an anagram

Soupçon Thought, Touch

Sour(puss) Acerb, Acescent, Acid, Acidulate, Alegar, Bitter, Citric, Crab, Esile, Ferment, Moody, Stingy, Subacid, > TART, Turn, Verjuice, Vinegarish

Source Authority, Basis, Bottom, Centre, Database, Derivation, Egg, Fons, Font, Fount, Fountain-head, Germ, Head-stream, Literary, Mine, Mother, Origin, Parent, Pi, Pion, Point, Provenance, Quarry, Reference, Rise, Riverhead, Root, Seat, Seed, Spring, Springhead, Urn, Well, Wellhead, Wellspring, Widow's cruse, Ylem

Sour milk Curds, Smetana, Whey, Whig, Yogh(o)urt

Souse Beath, Duck, Immerse, Pickle, Plunge, Soak, Spree, Steep

South(ern), Southerner Austral, Dago, Decanal, Decani, Deep, Dixieland, Meridian, Meridional, S

South Africa(n) Azania, Bantu, Caper, Ciskei, Grikwa, Griqua, Hottentot, Kaf(f)ir, Qwaqwa, SA, Springbok, Swahili, Xhosa, ZA, Zulu

South American Araucanian, Arawak, Argentino, Aymara, Bolivian, Carib, Chibcha, Chilean, Galibi, Guarani, Inca, Jivaro, Kechua, Llanero, Mam, Mapuchi, Mochica, Quechua, SA, Tapuyan, Tupi

Southwark Boro'

Souvenir Keepsake, Memento, Relic, Remembrance, Scalp, Token, Trophy

Sovereign(ty), Sovereign remedy Anne, Autocrat, Bar, Condominium, Couter, Dominant, ER, Goblin, Haemony, Harlequin, Imperial, Imperium, James, King, L, Liege, Nizam, Pound, Quid, Royalty, Ruler, Shiner, Supreme, Swaraj, Synarchy, Thick'un, Thin'un

Soviet Circassian, Council, Estonian, Russian, Supreme, Volost

Sow(ing) Catchcrop, Elt, Foment, Gilt, Inseminate, Plant, Scatter, Seed, Sprue, Strew, Yelt

Soya Tempe(h)

Spa Baden, Baden-Baden, Bath, Buxton, Evian, Godesberg, Harrogate, Hydro, Kurhaus, Kursaal, Leamington, Vichy

Space(d), Spacing, Spacious, Space man Abyss, Acre, Area, Areola, Bay, Bracket, Breathing, Cellule, Cishinar, Clearing, C(o)elom, Compluvium, Concourse, Contline, Crookes, Cubbyhole, Deep, Diastema, Distal, Distance, Elbow-room, Esplanade, Ether, Exergue, Expanse, Extent, Footprint, Forecourt, Freeband, Gap, Glade, Glenn, Goaf, Gob, Gutter, Hair, Hash(mark), Headroom, Homaloid, Indention, Inner, Intergalactic, Interplanetary, Interstellar, Interstice, Invader, Kerning, Killogie, Kneehole, Lacuna, Lair, Lebensraum, Legroom, Life, Logie, Lumen, Lunar, Lung, Machicolation, Maidan, Metope, Mihrab, Muset, Musit, Orbit, Outer, Peridrome, Personal, Plenum, Pomoerium, Priest hole, Proportional, Quad, Retrochoir, > ROOM, Ruelle, Sample, Sheets, Shelf room, Slot, Spandrel, Spandril, Step, Storage, Third, Topological, Tympanum, Ullage, Uncluttered, Vacuole, Vacuum, Vast, Vector, Void

Spacecraft, Space agency, Space object, Spaceship, Space station Apollo, Capsule, Columbia, Deep Space, Explorer, Galileo, Genesis, Giotto, Lander, LEM, Luna, Lunik, Mariner, MIR, Module, NASA, Orbiter, Pioneer, Probe, Quasar, Ranger, Salyut, Shuttle, Skylab, Soyuz, Sputnik, Starship, Tardis, Viking, Vostok, Voyager, Zond

Space walk EVA

Spade Breastplough, Caschrom, Cas crom, Castrato, Detective, Flaughter, Graft, Loy, Negro, Paddle, Pattle, Pettle, Pick, S, Shovel, Slane, Spit, Suit, Turf,

Tus(h)kar, Tus(h)ker, Twiscar

Spain E, Hesperia, Iberia

Spalpeen Sinner

Span Age, Arch, Attention, Bestride, Bridge, Chip, Ctesiphon, Extent, Life, Memory, Range

Spangle(d) Avanturine, Aventurine, Glitter, Instar, O, Paillette, Sequin

Spaniard, Spanish Alguacil, Alguazil, Andalusian, Barrio, Basque, Cab, Caballero, Carlist, Castilian, Catalan, Chicano, Dago, Don, Fly, Grandee, Hidalgo, Hispanic, Jose, Main, Mestizo, Mozarab, Pablo, Papiamento, Señor, Spic(k), Spik

Spaniel Blenheim, Cavalier, Clumber, Cocker, Crawler, Creep, Dog, Fawner, Field, Irish (water), King Charles, Maltese, Papillon, Placebo, Skip-kennel, Springer, Sussex, Tibetan, Toad-eater, Toady, Toy, Water, Welsh springer

Spank(ing) Cob, Paddywhack, Rapid, Scud, Slap, Slipper, Sprack

Spanner Arc, Box, Bridge, Clapper, Key, Ring, Shifter, Socket, Torque, Wrench

Spar Barytes, Blue John, Boom, Bowsprit, Box, Cauk, Cawk, Fight, Gaff, Iceland, Jib-boom, Mainyard, Manganese, Martingale, Mast, Nail-head, Outrigger, Rafter, Rail, Ricker, Schiller, Shearleg, Sheerleg, Snotter, Spathic, Sprit, Steeve, Stile, Tabular, Triatic, Whiskerboom, Whiskerpole, Yard

Spare, Sparing Angular, Cast-off, Dup(licate), Economical, Free, Frugal, Gash, Gaunt, Hain, Lean, Lenten, Other, Pardon, Reserve, Rib, Save, Scant, Skimp, Slender, Stint, Subsecive, Thin

Spark Animate, Arc, Beau, Blade, Bluette, Dandy, Flash, Flaught, Funk, Ignescent, Kindle, Life, Muriel, Scintilla, Smoulder, Spunk, Trigger, Vital, Zest

Sparkle(r), Sparkling Aerated, Aventurine, Coruscate, Diamanté, Effervesce, Elan, Emicate, Fire, Fizz, Flicker, Frizzante, Glamour, Glint, Glisten, Glitter, Life, Pétillant, Scintillate, Seltzer, Seltzogene, Spangle, Spritzig, Spumante, Twinkle, Verve, Witty, Zap

Sparrow Bird, Cape, Isaac, Java, Junco, Mah-jong(g), Mossie, Passerine, Piaf, Prunella, Spadger, Speug, Sprug, Sprug(gy), Titling

Sparrow-grass Asparagus, Sprue

Sparse Meagre, Rare, Scant, Thin

Spartan(s) Austere, Basic, Enomoty, Hardy, Helot, Heraclid, Lacedaemonian, Laconian, Lysander, Menelaus, Severe, Valiant

Spasm(odic) Blepharism, Chorea, Clonus, Cramp, Crick, Fit(ful), Hiccup, Hippus, Hyperkinesis, Intermittent, Irregular, > **JERK**, Kink, Laryngismus, Nystagmus, Paroxysm, Periodical, Start, Tetany, Throe, Tonic, Tonus, Trismus, Twinge, Twitch, Writer's cramp

▷ **Spasmodic** *may indicate* an anagram

Spastic Athetoid, Clonic, Jerky

Spat(s) Bicker, Brattle, Gaiters, Legging, Quarrel, Shower, Tiff

Spate Flood, Sluice, Torrent

Spatter Disject, Ja(u)p, Scatter, Splash, Splosh, Spot, Sprinkle

▷ **Spattered** *may indicate* an anagram

Spawn(ing), Spawning place Anadromous, Blot, Fry, Progeny, Propagate, Redd, Roud, Seed, Spat, Spet, Spit

Speak(er), Speaking Address, Articulate, Broach, Chat, Cicero, Collocuter, Communicate, Converse, Coo, Declaim, Dilate, Discourse, Diseur, Dwell, Effable, Elocution, Eloquent, Expatiate, Express, Extemporise, Filibuster, Intercom, Intone, Inveigh, Jabber, Jaw, Lip, Loq, Mang, Mention, Mike, Mina, Mouth, Mouthpiece, Nark, Open, Orate, Orator, Palaver, Parlance, Parley, Pontificate, Prate, Preach, Prelector, Rhetor, > **SAY**, Sayne, Spout, Spruik,

Squawk box, Stump, Talk, Tannoy®, Tongue, Trap, Tub-thumper, Tweeter, Utter, Voice, Waffle, Witter, Word

Speakeasy Fluent, Shebeen

Spear Ash, Asparagus, Assagai, Assegai, Dart, Gad, Gavelock, Gig, Gungnir, Hastate, Impale, Javelin, Lance(gay), Launcegaye, Leister, Morris-pike, Partisan, Pierce, Pike, Pilum, Skewer, Spike, Trident, Trisul(a), Waster

Spear-rest Feutre, Fewter

Special Ad hoc, Constable, Designer, Distinctive, Extra, Important, Notable, Notanda, Particular, Peculiar, S, Specific

Specialise, Specialist(s) Authority, Concentrate, Connoisseur, Consultant, ENT, Expert, Illuminati, Maestro, Major, Quant, Recondite, Technician

Species Class, Genre, Genus, Kind, Pioneer, Strain, Taxa

Specific(ally), Specified, Specify As, Ascribe, Assign, Concretize, Cure, Define, Detail, Explicit, Full-blown, Itemise, Medicine, Namely, Precise, Remedy, Sp, Special, State, Stipulate, The, Trivial

Specimen(s) Example, Exempla, Imago, Model, Sample, Slide, Swab, Topotype, Type

Specious False, Glib, Hollow, Pageant, Plausible, Spurious

Speck(led) Atom, Bit, Dot, Fleck, Floater, Freckle, Gay, Muscae volitantes, Particle, Peep(e), Pip, Spot, Spreckle, Stud

Spectacle(d), Spectacles, Spectacular Arresting, Barnacles, Bifocals, Blazers, Blinks, Bossers, Cheaters, Colourful, Epic, Escolar, Giglamps, > **GLASSES**, Goggles, Horn-rims, Nose-nippers, Oo, Optical, Outspeckle, Pageant, Pince-nez, Pomp, Preserves, Raree-show, Scene, Show, Sight, Son et lumière, Sunglasses, Tamasha, Tattoo, Trifocal, Varifocals

Spectator(s) Bystander, Dedans, Etagère, Eyer, Gallery, Gate, Groundling, Kibitzer, Observer, Onlooker, Standerby, Witness

Spectograph Aston

Spectral, Spectre Apparition, Boggle, Bogy, Brocken, Eidolon, Empusa, Ghost, Idola, Iridal, Malmag, Phantasm, Phantom, Phasma, Spirit, Spook, Tarsier, Walking-straw, Wraith

Spectrum Absorption, Band, Continuous, Emission, Iris, Optical, Rainbow, Sunbow, Sundog, Visible, X-ray

Speculate, Speculative, Speculator, Speculation Agiotage, Arbitrage, Bear, Better, Bull, Conjecture, Flier, Flyer, Gamble, Guess, Ideology, If, Imagine, Meditate, Notional, Operate, Pinhooker, Shark, Stag, Theoretical, Theorise, Theory, Thought, Trade, Wonder

Speech, Speech element Accents, Address, Argot, Articulation, Bunkum, Burr, Curtain, Delivery, Dialect, Diatribe, Diction, Direct, Discourse, Dithyramb, Drawl, Eloge, English, Eulogy, Filibuster, Free, Gab, Glossolalia, Harangue, Idiolect, Idiom, Inaugural, Indirect, Jargon, Keynote, King's, Lallation, > **LANGUAGE**, Lingua franca, Litany, Maiden, Monologue, Morph(eme), Motherese, Musar, Oblique, Oral, Oration, Parabasis, Parle, Peroration, Phasis, Philippic, Phonetics, Prolocution, Prolog(ue), Queen's, Reported, Rhetoric, Sandhi, Scanning, Screed, Sermon, Side, Slang, Soliloquy, Stemwinder, Stump, Tagmeme, Talk, Taxeme, Tirade, Tongue, Vach, Visible, Voice, Wawa, Whistle-stop

Speech defect, Speech disease Dysarthria, Dysphasia, Dysphoria, Echolalia, Idioglossia, Lisp, Palilalia, Paralalia, Paraphasia, Pararthria, Psellism, Stammer, Stutter

Speechless Alogia, Dumb, Dumbstruck, Inarticulate, Mute, Silent, Tongue-tied

Speed(ily), Speedy Accelerate, Alacrity, Amain, Amphetamine, Apace, Average,

Bat, Belive, Belt, Breakneck, Burn, Celerity, Clip, Dart, Despatch, DIN, Dispatch, Expedite, Fangy, Fast, Film, Fleet, Further, Gait, Gallop, Goer, Group, Gun, Haste, Hie, Hotfoot, Hypersonic, Induce, Instantaneous, Knot, Landing, Lick, Mach, Merchant, MPH, > PACE, Phase, Pike, Post-haste, Pronto, Race, Rapidity, Rate, RPS, Rush, Scorch, Scud, Scurr, Skirr, Soon, Spank, Split, Stringendo, Supersonic, Swift, Tach, Tear, Tempo, Ton up, V, Velocity, Vroom, Wave, Whid, Wing

Speedwell Brooklime, Fluellin, Germander, Veronica

Spelaean Troglodyte

Spelk Skelf, Splinter

Spell(ing) Abracadabra, Bewitch, Bout, Cantrip, Charm, Conjuration, Do, Elf-shoot, Enchantment, Entrance, Fit, Go, Gri(s)-gri(s), Hex, Incantation, Innings, Jettatura, Juju, Knur, > MAGIC, Need-fire, Nomic, Open sesame, Orthography, Period, Philter, Philtre, Phonetic, Pinyin, Relieve, Ride, Romaji, Run, Rune, Scat, Shot, Signify, Snap, Snatch, Sorcery, Sp, Span, Spasm, Splinter, Stint, Stretch, Tack, Tour, Trick, Turn, Weird, Whammy, Witchcraft

Spelling-book ABC, Grimoire

Spencer Topcoat, Tracy, Vest

Spend(er), Spending Anticipate, Birl, Blue, Boondoggling, Consume, Deplete, Disburse, Exhaust, Fritter, Lash out, Live, Outlay, Pass, Pay, Shopaholic, Splash, Splash out, Splurge, Ware

Spendthrift Essex man, High-roller, Prodigal, Profligate, Profuser, Scattergood, Wastrel

Spent Consumed, Dead, Done, Expended, Stale, Tired, Used, Weak, Weary

Sperm Seed, Semen

Spew Eject, Emit, Gush, Spit, Vomit

Sphagnum Moss, Peat

Sphere, Spherical Armillary, Celestial, Discipline, Element, Field, Firmament, Globe, Mound, Orb(it), Planet, Prolate, Province, Realm, Schwarzschild, Theatre, Wheel

Sphinx Hawk-moth, Oracle, Riddler

Spice, Spicy Amomum, Anise, Aniseed, Aryl, Cardamom, Cardamon, Cardamum, Cassareep, Cassaripe, Cinnamon, Clove, Clow, Coriander, Cubeb, Cum(m)in, Dash, Devil, Garam masala, Ginger, Mace, Malaguetta, Marjoram, Masala, Myrrh, Nutmeg, Oregano, Paprika, Peppercorn, Pimento, Piperic, Piquant, Salsa verde, Season, Stacte, Staragen, Tamal(e), Tamara, Tansy, Tarragon, Taste, Turmeric, Vanilla, Variety

Spick Dink, Neat, Spike, Tidy

Spicule Sclere, Tetract

Spider(s) Anancy, Ananse, Arachnid, Aranea, Araneida, Arthrapodal, Attercop, Bird, Black widow, Bobbejaan, Cardinal, Cheesemite, Chelicerate, Citigrade, Diadem, Epeira, Epeirid, Ethercap, Ettercap, Funnel-web, Harvester, Harvestman, House, Hunting, Huntsman, Jumping, Katipo, Lycosa, Mite, Money, Mygale, Orb-weaver, Pan, Phalangid, Podogona, Pycnogonid, Red, Redback, Rest, Ricinulei, Saltigrade, Scorpion, Solifugae, Solpuga, Spinner, Strap, Tarantula, Telary, Trapdoor, Violin, Water, Wolf, Zebra

Spiderwort Tradescantia

Spiel Spruik

Spignel Baldmoney, Meu

Spigot Bung, Plug, Tap

Spike(d) Barb, Brod, Calk, Calt(h)rop, Chape, Cloy, Crampon, Ear, Fid, Foil, Gad, Goad, Grama, Herissé, Icicle, Impale, Lace, Locusta, Marlin(e), Nail, > PIERCE,

Point, Pricket, Prong, Puseyite, Rod, Sharp, Shod, Skewer, Spadix, Spear, Spicate, Spicule, Spire, Strobiloid, Tang, Thorn, Tine

Spill(age) Divulge, Drop, Fidibus, Jackstraw, Lamplighter, Leakage, Let, Overflow, Overset, Reveal, Scail, Scale, Shed, Skail, Slop, Stillicide, Taper, Tumble

Spin(ner), **Spinning** Aeroplane, Arabian, Arachne, Bielmann, Birl, Camel, Centrifuge, Cribellum, Cut, Day trip, Dextrorse, DJ, Flat, Flip, Gimp, Googly, Gymp, Gyrate, Gyre, Gyroscope, Hurl, Isobaric, Lachesis, Mole, Nun, Peg-top, Pirouette, Pivot, PR, Precess, Prolong, Purl, Rev(olve), Ride, Rotate, Royal, Screw, Side, Sinistrorse, Slide, Spider, Stator, Strobic, Swirl, Swivel, Throstle, Tirl, Toss, Trill, Twirl, Twist, Wheel, Whirl, Work

Spinach Florentine, Orach(e), Popeye

Spinal (chord), **Spine**, **Spiny** Acromion, Aculeus, Areole, Backbone, Barb, Chine, Coccyx, Column, Doorn, Dorsal, Epidural, Muricate, Myelon, Notochord, Ocotillo, Prickle, Quill, Rachial, Ray, R(h)achis, Thorn, Tragacanth

Spindle(-shanks), **Spindly** Arbor, Bobbin, Capstan, Fusee, Fusiform, Fusil, Mandrel, Pin, Scrag, Staff, Triblet

▶ **Spine** *see* **SPINAL**

Spinel Balas, Picotite

Spineless Muticous, Timid, Weak

Spinn(e)y Coppice, Shaw, Thicket

Spinning-wheel Chark(h)a

Spinster Discovert, Feme sole, Old maid, Tabby

Spiral Archimedes, Cochlea, Coil, Dexiotropic, Dextrorse, Ekman, Gyrate, Helical, Helix, Hyperbolic, Inflationary, Logarithmic, Loxodromical, Screw, Scroll, Sinistrorse, Spin, Tailspin, Turbinate, Volute, Whorl, Wind

Spire(-shaped) Broach, Flèche, Peak, Shaft, Steeple, Thyrsoid

Spirit(s), **Spirited** Ahriman, Akvavit, Alcohol, Ammonia, Angel, Animal, Animation, Applejack, Apsaral, Aquavit, Aqua vitae, Arak, Arch(a)eus, Ardent, Ariel, Arrack, Asmoday, Astral, Bitters, Blithe, Boggart, Bogle, Brandy, Bravura, Brio, Brollachan, Buggan(e), Buggin, Cant, Cherub, Courage, Creature, Crouse, Daemon, Dash, Deev, Deva, Distillation, Div, Djinn(i), Domdaniel, > **DRINK**, Dryad, Duende, Duppy, Dybbuk, Eblis, Eidolon, Elan, Element(al), Emit, Empusa, Entrain, Erdgeist, Esprit, Essence, Ethos, Eudemon, Fachan, Faints, Familiar, Feints, Feisty, Feni, Fenny, Fetich(e), Fetish, Fettle, Fight, Firewater, Fuath, Gamy, Geist, Geneva, Genie, Genius, > **GHOST**, Ghoul, Ginger, Ginn, Gism, Glastig, Glendoveer, Go, Grappa, Gremlin, Grit, Grog, Gumption, Gytrash, Hartshorn, Heart, Hollands, Holy, Huaca, Imp, Incubus, Indwelt, Jann, Jinn(i), Jinnee, Jism, Ka, Kachina, Kelpie, Kindred, Kirsch, Kobold, Larva, Lemur(e), > **LIQUOR**, Lively, Loki, Manes, Manito(u), Manitu, Mare, Marid, Metal, Meths, Methyl(ated), Mettle, Mindererus, Mobbie, Mobby, Morale, Nain rouge, Neutral, Nis, Nix, Nobody, Numen, Ondine, Orenda, Panache, Paraclete, Party, Pecker, Pep, Peri, Pernod®, Petrol, Phantom, Pluck(y), Pneuma, Poltergeist, Pooka, Potato, Poteen, Presence, Proof, Psyche, Puck, Python, Racy, Rakee, Raki, Rakshas(a), Rectified, Rosicrucian, Ruin, Rum(bullion), Rye, Salt, Samshoo, Samshu, Saul, Schnapps, Seraph, Shade, Shadow, Shaitan, She'ol, Short, Smeddum, Soul, Spectre, Spright, Sprite, Spunk, Steam, Strunt, Surgical, Sylph, Tafia, Tangie, Taniwha, Team, Tequila, Tokoloshe, Ton, Turpentine, Turps, Undine, Verve, Vigour, Vim, Vodka, Voodoo, Water horse, Weltgeist, White, Wili, Wine, Witblits, Wood, Wraith, Zeitgeist, Zephon, Zing, Zombie

Spiritless Craven, Dowf, Insipid, Languid, Meek, Milksop, Poor, Tame, Vapid

Spirit-level Vial

Spiritual(ism), Spiritualist Aerie, Aery, Coon-song, Ecclesiastic, Ethereous, Eyrie, Eyry, Incorporeal, Negro, Planchette, Platonic, Psychic, Table-rapping, Table-turning

Spirt Gush, Jet, Rush

Spit(ting), Spittle Barbecue, Broach, Chersonese, Dead ringer, Dribble, Drool, Emptysis, Eructate, Expectorate, Fuff, Gob, Golly, Gooby, Goss, Grill, Hawk, Hockle, Impale, Jack, Lookalike, Peninsula, Ras, Ringer, Rotisserie, Saliva, Skewer, Slag, Spade(ful), Spawl, Spear, Sputter, Sputum, Tombolo, Yesk, Yex

Spite(ful) Backbite, Bitchy, Catty, Grimalkin, Harridan, Irrespective, Malevolent, Malgrado, Malice, Mau(l)gre, Mean, Petty, Pique, Rancour, Spleen, Venom, Waspish

Spitfire Cacafogo, Cacafuego, Wildcat

Spittoon Cuspidor(e)

Spiv Lair, Rorter

Splash Blash, Blue, Dabble, Dash, Dog, Drip, Feature, Flouse, Fl(o)ush, Gardyloo, Jabble, Ja(u)p, Jirble, Paddle, Plap, Plop, Plowter, Sket, Slosh, Slush, Soda, Sozzle, Spairge, Spat(ter), Spectacle, Splat(ch), Splatter, Splodge, Splosh, Splotch, Spray, Spree, Squatter, Swash, Swatter, Water, Wet

Splay(ed) Flew, Flue, Patte(e), Spread

Spleen Acrimony, Bite, Lien, Melt, Milt(z), Pip, Stomach, Vitriol, Wrath

Splendid, Splendour Ah, Braw, Brilliant, Bully, Capital, Champion, Clinker, Dandy, Eclat, Effulgent, Excellent, Fine, Finery, Fulgor, Gallant, Garish, Glitterand, Glittering, Glorious, Glory, Gorgeous, Grand(eur), Grandiose, Ha, Heroic, Lustrous, Majestic, Mooi, Noble, Palatial, Panache, Pomp, Proud, Radiant, Rich, Ripping, Royal, Stunning, Super(b), Wally

Splice(d) Braid, Eye, Join, Knit, Mainbrace, Wed

▷ **Spliced** *may indicate* an anagram

Splint Airplane, Banjo, Brace, Cal(l)iper, Splenial, T

Splinter(s) Bone-setter, Breakaway, Flinder, Fragment, Matchwood, Shatter, Shiver, Skelf, Sliver, Spale, Spall, Speel, Spelk, Spell, Spicula, Spill

Split Axe, Banana, Bifid, Bifurcate, Bisect, Break, Burst, Chasm, Chine, Chop, Clint, Clove(n), Crack, Crevasse, Cut, Departmentalise, Disjoin, Distrix, > **DIVIDE**, Division, Divorce, End, Fissile, Fissure, Flake, Fork(ed), Fragment, Grass, Lacerate, Partition, Red(d), Rift(e), Rip, Rive, Russian, Ryve, Schism, Scissor, Segregate, Separate, Septemfid, Sever, Share, Skive, Slit, Sliver, Spall, Spalt, Speld, Tattle, Tmesis, Told, To-rend, To-tear, Wedge

▷ **Split** *may indicate* a word to become two; one word inside another; or a connection with Yugoslavia

Splodge, Splotch Blot, Drop, Splash

Splurge Binge, Indulge, Lavish, Spend, Splash, Spree

Splutter Chug, Expectorate, Fizz, Gutter, Spray, Stammer

Spoil(s), Spoilt Addle, Agrise, Agrize, Agryze, Blight, Blunk, Booty, Botch, Bribe, Coddle, Corrupt, Crool, > **DAMAGE**, Dampen, Deface, Defect, Deform, Dish, Foul, Hames, Harm, Impair(ed), Indulge, Loot, Maderise, Maltreat, Mar, Mardy, Muck, Mutilate, Mux, Pamper, Pet, Pickings, Pie, Plunder, Prize, Queer, Rait, Rate, Ravage, Ret, Rot, Ruin, Scupper, Spuly(i)e, Swag, Taint, Tarnish, Vitiate, Wanton, Winnings

▷ **Spoil(ed), Spoilt** *may indicate* an anagram

Spoilsport Damper, Killjoy, Party pooper, Wet blanket, Wowser

Spoke(s) Concentric, Radius, Ray, Rung, Said, Sed, Strut

▷ **Spoken** *may indicate* the sound of a word or letter

Spokesman Foreman, Mouthpiece, Orator, Prophet, Representative

Spoliation, Spoliative Devastation, Pillage, Plunder, Predatory, Reif

Sponge(r), Spongy Alcoholic, Ambatch, Argentine, Battenburg, Bum, Cadge, Cake, Cleanse, Diact, Diploe, Fozy, Free-loader, Glass-rope, Hexact, Hyalonema, Leech, Lig, Lithistid(a), Loofa(h), Madeira, Madeleine, Mermaid's glove, Mooch, Mop, Mouch, Mump, Parasite, Parazoa, Pentact, Poachy, Porifera(n), Quandong, Rhabdus, Sarcenchyme, Scambler, Schnorrer, Scrounge, Shark, Shool, Siphonophora, Smell-feast, Sooner, Sop, Sucker, Swab, Sycophant, Tetract, Tiramisu, Tylote, Vegetable, Velamen, Venus's flowerbasket, Wangle, Wipe, Zimocca, Zoophyte

Spongewood Sola

Sponsor(ship) Aegis, Angel, Auspice, Backer, Egis, Finance, Godfather, Godparent, Gossip, Guarantor, Lyceum, Patron, Surety

Spontaneous Aleatoric, Autonomic, Gratuitous, Immediate, Impromptu, Impulsive, Instant, Intuitive, Natural, Ultroneus, Unasked, Unpremeditated, Unprompted

Spoof Chouse, Cozenage, Deception, Delusion, Fallacy, > **HOAX**, Imposture, Ramp, Swindle, Trick

Spook(s), Spooky CIA, Eerie, Fantom, Frightening, Ghost, Phantom, Shade

Spool Bobbin, Capstan, Pirn, Reel, Trundle

Spoon(ful), Spoon-shaped Apostle, Canoodle, Cochlear, Deflagrating, Dollop, Dose, Gibby, Greasy, Labis, Ladle, Mote, Neck, Rat-tail, Runcible, Scoop, Scud, Server, Snuff, Spatula, Sucket, Trolling, Woo, Wooden

Spoonerism Marrowsky, Metathesis

Spoor Trace, Track, Trail

Sporadic Fitful, Isolated, Occasional, Patchy

Spore (case) Conidium, Ex(t)ine, Fungus, Glomerule, Lenticel, Seed, Sorus, Telium, Uredinium

Sporran Pock

Sport(s), Sporting, Sportive Aikido, Amusement, Angling, Aquatics, Autocross, Basho, Blood, Bonspiel, Breakaway, Brick, Bungee-jumping, By-form, Contact, Curling, Cyclo-cross, Daff, Dalliance, Dally, Deviant, Drag-racing, Extreme, Field, Freak, Frisky, Frolic, Fun, > **GAME**, Gent, Gig, Hang-gliding, In, Joke, Karate, Kickboxing, Korfball, Laik, Lake, Langlauf, Lark, Merimake, Merry, Morph, Mutagen, Octopush, Orienteering, Pal, Pancratium, Paragliding, Parakiting, Parapenting, Parasailing, Parascending, Paraskiing, Polo, Rallycross, Recreate, Rogue, RU, Rules, Shinny, Shinty, Skijoring, Snowboarding, Softball, Spectator, Speedball, Speed-skating, Speedway, Squash, Steeplechase, Sumo, Tailing, Tournament, Tourney, Toy, Trampolining, Trapshooting, Wakeboarding, Water polo, Wear, Weightlifting, Windsurfing, Winter, Wrestling

▷ **Sport(s)** *may indicate* an anagram

Sportsman, Sportsmen All-rounder, Athlete, Blue, Corinthian, Hunter, Nimrod, Pentathlete, Pitcher, Shamateur, Shikaree, Shikari

Spot(s), Spotted, Spotting, Spotty Ace, Acne, Area, Areola, Areole, Baily's beads, Bausond, Bead, Beauty, Befoul, Blackhead, Blain, Blemish, Blind, Blip, Blob, Blot, Blotch(ed), Blur, Brind(l)ed, Carbuncle, Caruncle, Cash, Check, Cloud, Colon, Comedo, Corner, Curn, Cyst, Dance, Dapple(-bay), Dick, Discern, Discover, Dot, Drop, Eruption, Espy, Eye, Facula, Flat, Fleck, Floater, Fogdog, Foxed, Freak, Freckle, Furuncle, G, Gay, Gräfenberg, Gricer, Guttate, High, Hot, Jam, Leaf, Lentago, Location, Loran, Mackle, Macle, Macul(at)e, Mail, Meal, Measly, Microdot, Milium, Moil, Mole, Morbilli, Mote, Motty, Muscae volitantes, Naevoid, Note, Notice, Ocellar, Ocellus, Paca, Papule, Paraselene, Pardal, Parhelion, Patch, Peep(e), Penalty, Petechia, Pied, Pimple, Pin, Pip, Place, Plook, Plot, Plouk, Pock, Punctuate, Pupil, Pustule, Quat, Radar, Rash, Recognise, Red, Rose-drop, Scotoma, Situation, Skewbald, Smut, Soft, Speck(le), Speculum, Splodge, Spy, Stigma, Sully, Sun, Taint, Tar, Tight, Touch, Trouble, Weak, Whelk, Whitehead, X, Yellow, Zit

Spotless Clean, Immaculate, Virginal

Spotlight Ace, Baby, Bon-bon, Brute, Maxi-brute

Spot on To a t

Spouse Companion, Consort, F(i)ere, Hubby, Husband, Mate, Oppo, Partner, Pheer, Pirrauru, Significant other, Wife, Xant(h)ippe

Spout(er) Adjutage, Erupt, Gargoyle, Geyser, Grampus, Gush, Impawn, Jet, Mouth, Nozzle, Orate, Pawn, Pourer, Raile, Rote, Spurt, Stream, Stroup, Talk, Tap, Vent

Sprain(ed) Crick, Rax, Reckan, Rick, Stave, Strain, Wrench, Wrick

Sprat Brit, Fish, Garvie, Garvock

Sprawl Loll, Scramble, Sprangle, Spread, Stretch, Urban

Spray Aerosol, Aigrette, Atomiser, Buttonhole, Corsage, Cyme, Egret, Fly, Hair, Mace®, Nasal, Posy, Rose, Rosula, Shower, Sparge, Spindrift, Splash, Spoondrift, Sprent, Sprig, Sprinkle, Spritz, Strinkle, Syringe, Twig

▷ **Spray** *may indicate* an anagram

Spread(ing), Spreader Air, Apply, Banquet, Bestrew, Beurre, Blow-out, Branch, Bush, Butter, Carpet, Centre, Contagious, Couch, Coverlet, Coverlid, Deploy, Diffract, Diffuse, Dilate, Disperse, Dissemination, Distribute, Divulge, Double, Drape, Dripping, Elongate, Emanate, Expand, Extend, Fan, Feast, Flare, Guac(h)amole, Honeycomb, Jam, Lay, Marge, Marmite®, Metastasis, Multiply, Nutter, Oleo, Open, Overgrow, Paste, Pâté, Patent, Patulous, Perfuse, Pervade, Picnic, Propagate, Radiate, Ran, Run, Scale, Set, Sheet, Slather, Smear, Smorgasbord, Sow, Span, Speld, Spelder, Spillover, Splay, Sprawl, Spray, Straddle, Straw, Stretch, Strew, Strow, Suffuse, Systemic, Tath, Teer, Unfold, Unguent, Vegemite®, Widen, Wildfire

▷ **Spread** *may indicate* an anagram

Spree Bat, Beano, Bender, Binge, Bum, Bust, Carousal, Frolic, Jag, Jamboree, Juncate, Junket, Lark, Loose, Randan, Rantan, Razzle(-dazzle), Revel, Rouse, Splore, Tear, Ups(e)y

Sprig Brad, Branch, Cyme, Nail, Sien, Spray, Syen, Twig, Youth

Sprightly Agile, Airy, Chipper, Jaunty, Mercurial

Spring(s), Springtime, Springy Aganippe, Alice, Arise, Bolt, Bounce, Bound, Box, Bunt, Cabriole, Caper, Capriole, Castalian, Cavort, Cee, Coil, Dance, Elastic, Eye, Fount(ain), Gambado, Germinate, Geyser, Grass, Hair, Helix, Hippocrene, Hop, Hot, Jump, Leaf, Leap, Lent, Lep, Litt, Low-water, May, Mineral, Originate, Persephone, Pierian, Pounce, Prance, Primavera, Prime, Resilient, Ribbon, Rise, Saddle, Season, Skip, Snap, Spa, Spang, Spaw, Stem, Stot, Submarine, Sulphur, Thermae, Thermal, Trampoline, Valve, Vault, Vaute, Vawte, Vernal, Voar, Ware, Watch, Waterhole, Weeping, Well(-head), Whip, Winterbourne

▷ **Spring(y)** *may indicate* an anagram

Springbok Amabokoboko

Springless Telega

Springtail Apterygota

Sprinkle(r), Sprinkling Asperge, Aspergill(um), Bedash, Bedrop, Bescatter, Caster, Dredge, Dust, Hyssop, Lard, Poucet, Powder, Rose, Scatter,

Scouthering, Shower, Sow, Spa(i)rge, Spatter, Splash, Spray, Spritz, Strinkle

Sprint(er) Burst, Dash, Race, Rash, Run, Rush, Wells

Sprite Apsaras, Croquemitaine, Echo, Elf, Fairy, Fiend, Genie, Goblin, Gremlin, Hobgoblin, Icon, Ondine, Puck, Spirit, Troll, Trow, Umbriel, Undine

Sprout Braird, Breer, Brussels, Bud, Burgeon, Chit, Crop, Eye, Germ(inate), Grow, Pullulate, Shoot, Spire, Tendron, Vegetate

Spruce Dapper, Engelmann, Natty, Neat, Norway, Picea, Pitch-tree, Prink, Shipshape, Sitka, Smart, Spiff, Tidy, Tree, Trim, Tsuga, White

Spry Active, Agile, Constance, Dapper, Nimble, Volable

Spud Murphy, Potato, Spade, Tater, Tatie

Spume Eject, Foam, Froth, Lather, Spet, Spit

Spunk Courage, Grit, Pluck, Tinder

Spur Accourage, Activate, Calcar(ate), Encourage, Fame, Fire, Galvanise, Goad, Heel, Incite, Limb, Lye, Needle, Offset, Prick, Rippon, Rowel, Shoot, Spica, Stimulus, Strut, Stud, Tar, Urge

Spurge (tree) Candelilla, Croton, Euphorbia, Kamala, Poinsettia, Ricinus

Spurious Adulterine, Apocryphal, Bogus, Counterfeit, Dog, False, Phoney, Pseudo, Sciolism

▷ **Spurious** *may indicate* an anagram

Spurn Despise, Disdain, Ignore, Jilt, Reject, > **SCORN**, Shun

Spurt Burst, Forge, Geyser, Jet, Outburst, Pump, Spout

Sputter Fizzle, Spit, Splutter, Stutter

Spy(ing), Spies Agent, Beagle, Caleb, CIA, Cicero, Curtain-twitcher, Descry, Dicker, Emissary, Espionage, Fink, Fuchs, Informer, Keeker, Mata Hari, MI, Mole, Mouchard, Nark, Nose, Operative, Pimp, Plant, Pry, Recce, Scout, See, Setter, Shadow, Sinon, Sleeper, Spetsnaz, Spook, Tout, Wait

Spyhole Eyelet, Judas-hole, Oillet, Peephole

Squab Chubby, Cushion, Obese

Squabble Argue, Bicker, Brabble, Quarrel, Rhubarb, Row, Scrap

Squad(ron) Band, Blue, Company, Crew, Death, Drugs, Escadrille, Fifteen, Firing, Flying, Fraud, Hit, Nahal, Platoon, Red, Snatch, Vice, White, Wing

Squalid, Squalor Abject, Colluvies, Dickensian, Dinge, Dingy, Filth, Frowsy, Grungy, Poverty, Scuzzy, Seedy, Sleazy, Slum(my), Slurb, Sordid

Squall Blast, Blow, Chubasco, Commotion, Cry, Drow, Flaw, Flurry, Gust, Line, Sumatra, Wail, White, Yell, Yowl

Squander Blow, Blue, Fritter, Frivol, Lash, Mucker, Slather, Splash, Splurge, Ware, > **WASTE**

Square(d), Squares Agree, Anta, Ashlar, Ashler, Bang, Barrack, Belgrave, Berkeley, Block, Bribe, Chequer, Compone, Compony, Corny, Deal, Dinkum, Even(s), Fair, Fog(e)y, Forty-nine, Fossil, Four, Gobony, Grey, Grosvenor, Latin, Least, Leicester, Level, Magic, Market, Meal, Mitre, Nasik, Neandert(h)aler, Nine, Norma, Old-fashioned, Palm, Passé, Pay, Perfect, Piazza, Place, Platz, Plaza, Quad(rangle), Quadrate, Quarry, Quits, Red, Rood, S, Set(t), Sloane, Solid, Squier, Squire, Straight, T, Tee, Times, Traditionalist, Trafalgar, Try, Unhip

Squash(y) Adpress, Butternut, Conglomerate, Crush, Gourd, Kia-ora, Knead, Marrow, Mash, Obcompress, Oblate, Pattypan, Press, Pulp, Shoehorn, Silence, Slay, Slew, Slue, Soft, Squeeze, Squidge, Squidgy, Suppress, Torpedo

Squat(ter) Bywoner, Crouch, Croup(e), Dumpy, Fubby, Fubsy, Hunker, Pudsey, Pyknic, Rook, Ruck, Sit, Spud, Stubby, Stumpy, Swatter, Usucaption

Squaw Kloo(t)chman

Squawk Cackle, Complain, Cry, Scrauch, Scraugh

Squeak(er) Cheep, Creak, Narrow, Peep, Pip, Scroop, Shoat, Squeal
Squeal(er) Blow, Eek, Howl, Inform, Pig, Screech, Sing, Sneak, Tell, Wee, Yelp
Squeamish(ness) Delicate, Disgust, Missish, Nervous, Prudish, Queasy, Reluctant
Squeeze Bleed, Chirt, Coll, Compress, Concertina, Constrict, Cram, Credit, Crowd, Crush, Dispunge, Exact, Express, Extort, Hug, Jam, Mangle, Milk, Preace, Press, Sandwich, Sap, Scrooge, Scrouge, Scrowdge, Scruze, Shoehorn, Squash, Squish, Sweat, Thrutch, Thumbscrew, Wring
Squelch Gurgle, Squash, Squish, Subdue
Squib Banger, Damp, Firework, Lampoon
Squid Calamari, Calamary, Cephalopod, Ink-fish, Loligo, Mortar, Nautilus, Octopus, Sleeve fish
Squiffy Drunk, Tiddley
▷ **Squiggle** *may indicate* an anagram
Squint(ing) Boss-eyed, Cast, Cock-eye, Cross-eye, Glance, Gledge, Glee, Gley, Hagioscope, Heterophoria, Louche, Proptosis, Skellie, Skelly, Sken, Squin(n)y, Strabism, Swivel-eye, Vergence, Wall-eye
Squire Armiger(o), Beau, Donzel, Escort, Hardcastle, Headlong, Land-owner, Scutiger, Swain, Western, White
Squirm(ing) Fidget, Reptation, Twist, Worm, Wriggle, Writhe
Squirrel, Squirrel's nest Aye-aye, Boomer, Bun, Cage, Chickaree, Chipmuck, Chipmunk, Dray, Drey, Flickertail, Flying, Fox, Gopher, Grey, Ground, Hackee, Hoard(er), Meerkat, Petaurist, Phalanger, Red, Sciuroid, Sewellel, Skug, S(o)uslik, Spermophile, Taguan, Vair, Zizel
Squirt(er) Chirt, Cockalorum, Douche, Jet, Scoosh, Scoot, Skoosh, Spirt, Spout, Spritz, Urochorda, Wet, Whiffet, Whippersnapper
Sri Lanka(n) Ceylon, Cingalese, CL, Serendip, Sinhalese, Vedda
St Saint, Street
Stab Bayonet, Crease, Creese, Dag, Effort, Go, Gore, Guess, Jab, Knife, Kreese, Kris, Lancinate, Pang, Pierce, Pink, Poniard, Prick, Prong, Stick, Stiletto, Wound
Stabilise(r), Stability Aileron, Balance, Emulsifier, Even, Maintain, Pax Romana, Peg, Permanence, Plateau, Poise, Steady, Tail panel
Stable(s) Augean, Balanced, Barn, Byre, Certain, Constant, Durable, Equerry, Equilibrium, Firm, Livery, Loose box, Manger, Mews, Poise, Secure, Solid, Sound, Stall, Static(al), Steadfast, Steady, Stud, Sure
Stableman Groom, Lad, Ostler
Stachys Betony
Stack(s) Accumulate, A gogo, Chimney, Clamp, Cock, End, Funnel, Heap, Lum, > PILE, Rick, Shock, Staddle
Stadium Arena, Ballpark, Bowl, Circus, Circus Maximus, Coliseum, Hippodrome, Speedway, Velodrome
Staff Alpenstock, Ash-plant, Bato(o)n, Bourdon, Burden, Caduceus, Cane, Crook, Crosier, Cross(e), Crozier, Crutch, Cudgel, Entourage, Equerry, Etat-major, Faculty, Ferula, Ferule, Flagpole, General, Linstock, Lituus, Mace, Omlah, Pastoral, Personnel, Pike, Pole, Rod, Runic, Sceptre, Seniority, Skeleton, Stave, Stick, Taiaha, Tapsmen, Tau, Thyrsus, Truncheon, Verge, Wand, Workers, Workforce
Stag Actaeon, Brocket, Buck, Deer, For men, Imperial, Line, Male, Party, Royal, Rutter, Ten-pointer, Wapiti
Stage Act, Anaphase, Apron, Arena, Bardo, Bema, Boards, Catasta, Centre, Chrysalis, Committee, Diligence, Dog-leg, Estrade, Fare, Fargo, Fit-up, Grade,

Juncture, Key, Landing, Leg, Level, Metaphase, Milestone, Moment, Mount,
Oidium, Phase, Phasis, Pier, Pin, Platform, Point, Prophase, Proscenium, PS,
Puberty, Report, Rostrum, Scene, Sensorimeter, Sound, Stadium, Step, Stor(e)y,
Subimago, Theatre, Thrust, Transition, Trek, Yuga
Stage-coach Diligence, Thoroughbrace
Stagecraft Pinafore
Stagehand Flyman, Grip
Stagger(ed) Alternate, Amaze, Astichous, Awhape, Daidle, Falter, Floor,
Lurch, Recoil, Reel, Rock, Shock, Stoiter, Stot(ter), Stumble, Sway, Teeter,
Thunderstricken, Thunderstruck, Titubate, Tolter, Totter, Wamble, Wintle
▷ **Staggered** *may indicate* an anagram
Stagirite, Stagyrite Aristotle
Stagnant, Stagnation Foul, Inert, Scummy, Stasis, Static
Staid Decorous, Demure, Formal, Grave, Matronly, Prim, Sad, Sober,
Stick-in-the-mud
Stain(er) Aniline, Bedye, Besmirch, Blemish, Blob, Blot, Blotch, Discolour,
Dishonour, Dye, Embrue, Ensanguine, Eosin, Fox, Gram's, Grime, Imbrue,
Iodophile, Keel, Maculate, Mail, Meal, Mote, Portwine, Slur, Smirch, Smit, Soil,
Splodge, Splotch, Stigma, Sully, Taint, Tarnish, Tinge, Tint, Vital, Woad
Stair(case), Stairs Apples, Apples and pears, Caracol(e), Cochlea,
Companionway, Escalator, Flight, Perron, Rung, Spiral, Step, Tread, Turnpike,
Vice, Wapping, Winding
Stake(s) Ante, Bet, Claim, Gage, Holding, Impale, Impone, Interest, Lay, Loggat,
Mark, Mise, Paal, Pale, Paliform, Paling, Palisade, Peel, Peg, Pele, Picket, Pile,
Play, Post, Pot, Punt, Put, Rest, Revie, Risk, Septleva, Spike, Spile, Stang, Stob,
Straddle, Sweep, Tether, Vie, Wager, Welter
Stalactite Dripstone, Dropstone, Helictite, Lansfordite, Soda straw
Stale Aged, Banal, Flat, Fozy, Frowsty, Fusty, Hackneyed, Handle, Hoary, Mouldy,
Musty, Old, Pretext, Rancid, Urine, Worn
▷ **Stale** *may indicate* an obsolete word
Stalemate Deadlock, Dilemma, Hindrance, Impasse, Mexican standoff,
Saw-off, Standoff, Tie, Zugswang
Stalk(s) Anthophore, Bun, Cane, Caulicle, Follow, Funicle, Garb(e), Gynophore,
Ha(u)lm, Keck(s), Kecksey, Keksye, Kex, Ommatophore, Pedicel, Pedicle,
Peduncle, Petiole, Petiolule, Phyllode, Pursue, Rush, Scape, Seta, Shaw, Spear,
Spire, Stem, Sterigma, Stipe(s), Stride, Strig, Strut, Stubble, Stump, Trail, Yolk
Stalking-horse Stale
Stall(s) Arrest, Bay, Booth, Box, Bulk, Crib, > DELAY, Floor, Flypitch, Hedge,
Kiosk, Loose-box, Orchestra, Pen, Pew, Prebendal, Seat, Shamble, Sideshow,
Stand, Starting, Stasidion, Temporise, Trap, Traverse, Travis, Trevis(s), Whip
Stallion Cooser, Cuisser, Cusser, Entire, > HORSE, Stag, Staig, Stonehorse, Stud
Stalwart Anchor-man, Buirdly, Firm, Manful, Robust, Sturdy, Trusty, Valiant
Stamen(ed) Androecium, Octandria, Polyandria
Stamina Endurance, Fibre, Fortitude, Guts, Last, Stamen, Stay, Steel
Stammer(ing) Balbutient, Er, Hesitate, Hum, Psellism, Sputter, Stumble,
> STUTTER, Waffle
Stamp(s), Stamped Appel, Cast, Character, Date(r), Die, Enface, Frank,
Imperforate, Impress, Imprint, Incuse, Label, Matchmark, Mint, Pane, Penny
black, Perfin, Philately, Pintadera, Postage, Press(ion), Rubber, Seal, Seebeck,
Se-tenant, Signet, Spif, Strike, Swage, Tête-bêche, Touch, Touchmark, Trading,
Trample, Tread, Tromp, Type
Stamp-collecting Philately, Timbrology, Timbrophily

Stampede Debacle, Flight, Panic, Rampage, > RUSH
Stance Attitude, Pose, Position, Posture
Stand(ing), Stand for, Stand up Apron, Arraign, Attitude, Base, Be, Bear, Bide, Binnacle, Bipod, Bristle, Brook, Canterbury, Caste, Confrontation, Cradle, Crease, Dais, Degree, Desk, Dock, Dree, Dumb-waiter, Easel, Etagère, Face, Foothold, Freeze, Gantry, Gueridon, Hard, Hob, Insulator, Klinostat, Last, Lazy Susan, Lectern, Leg, Music, Nef, Odour, One-night, Ovation, Pedestal, Place, Plant, Podium, Pose, Position, Pou sto, Prestige, Promenade, Protest, Qua, Rack, Rank, Regent, Remain, Represent, Repute, Rise, Stall, Statant, Station, > STATUS, Stay, Stillage, Stock, Stool, Straddle, Straphang, Stroddle, Strut, Table, Tantalus, Taxi, Teapoy, Terrace, > TREAT, Tree, Tripod, Trivet, Umbrella, Upright, Whatnot
Standard(s) Banner, Base, Baseline, Basic, Benchmark, Bogey, British, Canon, CAT, Classic(al), Cocker, Colour(s), Criterion, Double, Eagle, English, Ethics, Examplar, Example, Exemplar, Flag, Ga(u)ge, Gold, Gonfalon, Guidon, Ideal, Labarum, Level, Living, Model, Norm(a), Normal, Numeraire, Old Glory, Oriflamme, Par, Parker Morris, Pennon, Principle, Rate, Regular, Rod, Rose, Routine, Royal, > RULE, Silver, Spec(ification), Staple, Sterling, Stock, Time, Touchstone, Tricolour, Troy, Two-power, Usual, Valuta, Vexillum, Yardstick
Standard-bearer Alferez, Cornet, Ensign, Vexillary
Stand-by Adminicle, Reserve, Substitute, Support, Understudy
Stand-in Double, Locum, Stunt man, Sub(stitute), Surrogate, Temp, Understudy
Standish Miles
Stand-off(ish) Aloof, Remote, Reserved, Stalemate, Upstage
Standpoint Angle
Standstill Deadset, Halt, Jam
Stanley Baldwin, Knife, Rupert
Stannic Tin
Stanza Ballad, Elegiac, Envoi, Envoy, Heroic, Ottava, Poem, Sixaine, Spenserian, Staff, Stave, Tetrastich, Verse
Staple Basic, Bread, Chief, Maize, Pin, Wool
Star(s) Aster(isk), Body, Celebrity, Constant, Constellation, Cynosure, Double, Exploding, Falling, Feather, Feature, Film, Fixed, Flare, Giant, Headline, Hero, Hexagram, Idol, Lead, Lion, Mogen David, Movie, Multiple, Pentacle, Personality, Pip, Pointer, Principal, Pulsating, Shell, Shine, Shooting, Sidereal, Solomon's seal, Spangle, Starn(ie), Stellar, Stern, Swart, (The) Pointers, Top-liner, Ultraviolet, Variable, Vedette

● **STARS**
●
●
● **3 letters:** | Nova | Alpha | Mensa
● Dog | Pavo | Ceres | Merak
● Sol | Pole | Comet | Mizar
● | Ursa | Delta | Norma
● **4 letters:** | Vega | Deneb | North
● Argo | Vela | Draco | Polar
● Beta | Zeta | Dubhe | Radio
● Dark | | Dwarf | Rigel
● Grus | **5 letters:** | Gamma | Rigil
● Lode | Acrux | Hyads | Spica
● Lyra | Agena | Indus | Theta
● Mira | Algol | Lupus | Venus

Virgo
Wagon
Whale

6 letters:
Alioth
Alkaid
Altair
Aquila
Auriga
Binary
Bootes
Carbon
Carina
Castor
Cygnus
Dorado
Esther
Etoile
Fornax
Galaxy
Hyades
Lizard
Megrez
Merope
Meteor
Mullet
Octans
Phecda
Plough
Pollux
Psyche
Pulsar

Puppis
Quasar
Saturn
Sirius
Sothis
Uranus
Vesper
Volans

7 letters:
Antares
Calaeno
Canopus
Capella
Cepheus
Chamber
Columba
Dolphin
Epsilon
Estoile
Evening
Gemingo
Lucifer
Morning
Neutron
Perseus
Phoenix
Polaris
Procyon
Proximo
Regulus
Sabaism
Serpens

Sterope
Triones
Wagoner

8 letters:
Achernar
Arcturus
Barnard's
Circinus
Denebola
Equuleus
Hesperus
Magnetar
Mira Ceti
Pegasean
Phosphor
Pleiades
Praesepe
Red dwarf
Red giant
Scorpius
Synastry
Waggoner

9 letters:
Aldebaran
Andromeda
Bellatrix
Big Dipper
Black hole
Centaurus
Collapsar
Delphinus

Fire-drake
Fomalhaut
Meteorite
Ophiuchus
Pentagram
Rigil-Kent
Supernova
Wolf-Rayet

10 letters:
Betacrucis
Betelgeuse
Betelgeuze
Brown dwarf
Cassiopeia
Orion's belt
Phosphorus
Supergiant
White dwarf

11 letters:
Circumpolar

12 letters:
Little Dipper

13 letters:
Southern Cross

14 letters:
Proxima centaur

Starboard Right

Starch(y), **Starch producer** Amyloid, Arrowroot, Cassava, Ceremony, Congee, Conjee, Coontie, Coonty, Cycad, Farina, Fecula, Formal, Glycogen, Manioc, Maranta, Pentosan, Stamina, Statolith, Tapioca, Tous-les-mois

Stare Eyeball, Fisheye, Gape, Gapeseed, Gawp, Gaze, Geek, Goggle, Gorp, Look, Outface, Peer, Rubberneck

Starfish Asterid, Asteroid(ea), Bipinnaria, Brittlestar, Ophiurid, Radiata

Star-gaze(r), **Star-gazing** Astrodome, Astronomy, Copernicus

Stark Apparent, Austere, Bald, Bare, Gaunt, Harsh, Naked, Nude, Sheer, Stiff, Utterly

Starling Bird, Murmuration, Pastor, Stare

Star of Bethlehem Chincherinchee, Chinkerinchee

Start(ed), **Starter** Ab ovo, Abrade, Abraid, Abray, Activate, Actuate, Begin, Boggle, Bot, Broach, Bug, Bump, Chance, Commence, Crank, Create, Crudites, Dart, Ean, Embryo, Face-off, False, Fire, Flinch, Float, Flush, Flying, Found, Gambit, Gan, Genesis, Getaway, Gun, Handicap, Head, Hot-wire, Impetus, Imprimis, Incept(ion), Initiate, Instigate, Institute, Intro, Jerk, Jump, Jump-off, Kick-off, L, Lag, Launch, Lead, Off, Offset, Onset, Ope(n), Ord, Origin, Outset,

Preliminary, Prelude, Proband, Put-up, Reboot, Resume, Roll, Rouse, Scare, Set off, Shy, Slip, Snail, Spring, Spud, String, Tee-off, Wince

▷ **Start** *may indicate* an anagram or first letter(s)

Startle, Startling Alarm, Bewilder, Disturb, Eye-opener, Flush, Frighten, Magical, Rock, Scare

Starvation, Starve(d), Starving Anorexia, Anoxic, Bant, Clem, Cold, Deprive, Diet, Famish, Inanition, Macerate, Perish, Pine, Undernourished

▷ **Starving** *may indicate* an 'o' in the middle of a word

State(s) Affirm, Alabama, Alaska, Alle(d)ge, Andorra, Aread, Arizona, Ark(ansas), Arrede, Assert, Assever, Attest, Aver, Avow, Bahar, Balkan, Belize, Benin, Brunei, Buffer, California, Carolina, Case, Chad, Cite, Client, Colorado, Commonwealth, Condition, Confederate, Conn(ecticut), Country, Critical, Cutch, Dakota, Declare, Del(aware), Dependency, Dixie, Dubai, Durango, Emirate, Empire, Etat, Ethiopia, Federal, Fettle, Fla, Flap, Florida, Free, Ga, Gabon, Georgia, Ghana, Guatemala, Gulf, Habitus, Hawaii, Hesse, Honduras, Humour, Ia, Idaho, Illinois, Indiana, Iowa, Jalisco, Jamahiriya, Jharkand, Jigawa, Johore, Jumhouriya, Kalat, Kano, Kansas, Karnataka, Kashmir, Kedah, Kelantan, Kentucky, Kerala, Khelat, Kingdom, Kogi, Kutch, Kuwait, Kwara, Land, Lesh, Louisiana, Madras, Maine, Malawi, Malay, Manipur, Maranhao, Maryland, Mass(achusetts), Md, Me, Meghalaya, Mess, Mewar, Mi(chigan), Michoacán, Minas Gerais, Minnesota, Mississippi, Missouri, Mizovam, Montana, Morelos, Mysore, Nagaland, Name, Nanny, Nation, Native, Nayarit, NC, Nebraska, Negri Sembilan, Nevada, New Hampshire, New Jersey, New Mexico, New South Wales, New York, Nirvana, Nuevo Léon, NY, Oaxaca, Ogun, Ohio, Oklahoma, Oman, Ondo, Orange Free, Oregon, Orissa, Osun, Oyo, Pa, Pahang, Palatinate, Papal, Para, Paraiba, Parana, Penang, Pennsylvania, Perak, Perlis, Pernambucio, Piaui, Plateau, Plight, Police, Pradesh, Predicament, Predicate, Premise, Pronounce, Protectorate, Prussia, Puebla, Punjab, Puppet, Qatar, Quantum, Queensland, Queretaro, Quintana Roo, Rajasthan, Realm, Reich, Republic, RI, Rivers, Rogue, Rondonia, Roraima, Saarland, Sabah, St Kitts and Nevis, St Vincent, Samoa, San Luis Potosi, Santa Catarina, Sao Paulo, Sarawak, Satellite, Saxony(-Anholt), Say, Schleswig-Holstein, Selangor, Sergipe, Sikkim, Slave, Sokoto, Sonora, Sorry, South Australia, South Carolina, South Dakota, Sparta, Standing, Steady, Styria, Succession, Swat, Tabasco, Tamaulipas, Tamil Nadu, Tanganyika, Tasmania, Tennessee, T(e)rengganu, Texas, Threeness, Thuringia, Tiaxcala, Tocantina, Togo, Ton(g)kin(g), Travancore, Tripura, Trucial, Udaipur, UK, Uncle Sam, Union, United, US, Ut, Utah, Uttaranchai, Utter Pradesh, Va, Vatican City, Venezuela, Veracruz, Vermont, Victoria, Virginia, Washington, Welfare, West Virginia, Wis(consin), Wyoming, Yucatan, Zacatecas

▷ **Stated** *may indicate* a similar sounding word

Stately, Stately home August, Dome, Grand, Imposing, Majestic, Mansion, Noble, Regal

Statement Account, Affidavit, Aphorism, Assertion, Attestation, Avowal, Bill, Bulletin, Communiqué, Deposition, Dictum, Diktat, Encyclical, Evidence, Expose, Factoid, Generalisation, Indictment, Invoice, Jurat, Manifesto, Mission, Outline, Paraphrase, Pleading, Press release, Profession, Pronouncement, Proposition, Protocol, Quotation, Release, Remonstrance, Report, Sentence, Soundbite, Sweeping, Testimony, Truism, Utterance, Verb

Stateroom Bibby, Cabin

Statesman American, Attlee, Botha, Briand, Bright, Canning, Cato, Clarendon, Diplomat, Disraeli, Draco, Elder, Flaminius, Franklin, Genro, Georgian,

Gladstone, Gracchi, Grotius, Guy, Kissinger, Kruger, Lafayette, Lie, North, Politician, Politico, Seneca, Smuts, Stein, Talleyrand, Tasmanian, Thiers, Walpole, Wealsman, Yankee

Static Atmospherics, Becalmed, Electricity, Inert, Maginot-minded, Motionless, Sferics, Stationary

Station(s) Action, Base, Berth, Birth, Camp, Caste, CCS, Comfort, Crewe, Deploy, Depot, Dressing, Euston, Filling, Fire, Garrison, Gas, Halt, Head, Hill, Hilversum, Ice, Lay, Location, Marylebone, Outpost, Panic, Petrol, Pitch, Place, Plant, Point, Police, Polling, Post, Power, Quarter, Radio, Rank, Relay, Rowme, Seat, Service, Sheep, Sit, Space, Stance, Stand, Status, Stond, Subscriber, Tana, Tanna(h), Terminus, Testing, Thana(h), Thanna(h), Tracking, Triangulation, Victoria, Waterloo, Waverley, Way, Weather, Work

Stationary Fasten, Fixed, Immobile, Parked, Sessile, Stable, Static

Stationer(y), Stationery-case Continuous, Papeterie

Statistic(ian), Statistics Actuary, Descriptive, Fermi-Dirac, Figure, Gradgrind, Graph, Lod, Number, Parametric, Percentage, Quantum, Sampling, Student's t, Vital

Statuary, Statue(tte) Acrolith, Bronze, Bust, Colossus (of Rhodes), Discobolus, Effigy, Figure, Figurine, Galatea, Idol, Image, Kore, Kouros, Liberty, Memnon, Monument, Oscar, Palladium, Pietà, Sculpture, Sphinx, Stonework, Tanagra, Torso, Xoanon

Stature Growth, Height, Inches, Rank

Status Beacon, Caste, Class, Political, > **POSITION**, Prestige, Quo, Rank, Standing

Statute Act, Capitular, Chapter 7, Chapter 11, Decree, Edict, Law, Novels

Staunch Amadou, Leal, Resolute, Steady, Stem, Stout, Styptic, Watertight

Stave Break, Dali, Forestall, Lag, Slat, Stanza, Ward

Stay(s) Alt, Avast, Bide, Board, Bolster, Cohab(it), Corselet, Corset, Embar, Endure, Fulcrum, Gest, Guy, Hawser, Indwell, Jump, Lie, Lig, Linger, Lodge, Manet, Moratorium, Piers, Prop, > **REMAIN**, Reprieve, Restrain, Settle, Sist, Sleepover, Sojourn, Stem, Stop off, Stop-over, Strut, Sustain, Tarry, Triatic, Villeggiatura

Stay-at-home Indoor, Tortoise

STD Aids, Herpes, Telephone, VD

Steadfast Changeless, Constant, Firm, Implacable, Resolute, Sad, Stable

Steady Andantino, Ballast, Beau, Boyfriend, Changeless, Composer, Constant, Even, Faithful, Firm, Girlfriend, Measured, Regular, Rock, Stabilise, Stable, Unswerving

Steak Carpet-bag, Chateaubriand, Chuck, Fillet, Flitch, Garni, Mignon, Minute, Pope's eye, Porterhouse, Rump, Slice, Tartare, T-bone, Tenderloin, Tournedos, Vienna

Steal(ing) Abstract, Bag, Bandicoot, Bone, Boost, Cabbage, Cly, Condiddle, Convey, Creep, Crib, Duff, Embezzle, Filch, Glom, Grab, Half-inch, Heist, Hotting, Joyride, Kidnap, Knap, Lag, Liberate, Lift, Loot, Mag(g), Mahu, Mill, Naam, Nam, Nap, Nick, Nim, Nip, Nym, Peculate, Pilfer, Pillage, Pinch, Piracy, Plagiarise, Plunder, Poach, Prig, Proll, Purloin, Ram-raid, Remove, Rifle, Rob, Rustle, Scrump, Skrimp, Smug, Snaffle, Snatch, Sneak, Snitch, Souvenir, Swipe, Take, Theft, Thieve, Tiptoe, TWOC, Whip

Stealth(y) Art, Catlike, Covert, Cunning, Furtive, Obreption, Surreptitious, Tiptoe

Steam(ed), Steamy Boil, Condensation, Cushion, Dry, Fume, Gaseous, Het, Humid, Live, Mist, Porn, Radio, Roke, Sauna, Spout, Vapor, Vapour, Wet

Steamer, Steamboat Kettle, Showboat, Side-wheeler, SS, Str, Tramp, Turbine

Steam-hammer Ram

Steed Charger, Horse, Mount

Steel(y) Acierate, Adamant, Bethlehem, Blade, Blister, Bloom, Brace, Carbon, Cast, Chrome, Chromium, Cold, Concrete, Crucible, Damascus, Damask, High-carbon, High-speed, Magnet, Manganese, Maraging, Martensite, Metal, Mild, Nickel, Pearlite, Ripon, Rolled, Sorbite, Spray, Stainless, Structural, Sword, Toledo, Tool, Tungsten, Vanadium, Wootz

Steelyard Bismar

Steep Abrupt, Arduous, Brent, Costly, Embay, Expensive, High-pitched, Hilly, Krans, Krantz, Kranz, Macerate, Marinade, Marinate, Mask, Precipice, Precipitous, Rait, Rapid, Rate, Ret, Saturate, Scarp, > SHEER, Soak, Sog, Souse, Stey, Stickle, Tan

Steeple(jack) Spiderman, Spire, Turret

Steer(er), Steering Ackerman, Airt, Buffalo, Bullock, Cann, Castor, Con(n), Cox, Direct, > GUIDE, Helm, Navaid, Navigate, Ox, Pilot, Ply, Power, Rudder, Stot, Whipstaff, Zebu

Stem Alexanders, Arrow, Axial, Biller, Bine, Bole, Caudex, Caulicle, Caulome, Check, Cladode, Cladophyll, Confront, Corm, Culm, Dam, Epicotyl, Floricane, Ha(u)lm, Kex, Pedicle, Peduncle, Pin, Pseudaxis, Rachis, R(h)achilla, Rhachis, Rhizome, Rise, Rod, Sarment, Scapus, Seta, Shaft, Shank, Sobole(s), Spring, Stalk, Staunch, Stipe, Stolon, Stopple, Straw, Sympodium, Tail

Stench F(o)etor, Funk, Miasma, Odour, Smell, Stink, Whiff

Stencil Copy, Duplicate, Mimeograph®, Pochoir

Stenographer, Stenography Amanuensis, Secretary, Shorthand, Typist

Step(s) Act, Balancé, Chassé, Choctaw, Corbie, Curtail, Dance, Démarche, Echelon, Escalate, False, Flight, Fouetté, Gain, Gait, Glissade, Goose, Grecian, Greece, Grees(e), Greesing, Grese, Gressing, Griece, Grise, Grize, Halfpace, Lavolt, Lock, Measure, Move, Notch, Pace, Pas, Pas de souris, Phase, Pigeon's wing, Quantal, Raiser, Ratlin(e), Rattlin(e), Rattling, Roundel, Roundle, Rung, Shuffle, Slip, Stage, Stair, Stalk, Stile, Stope, Stride, Toddle, Trap, Tread, Trip, Unison, Waddle, Walk, Whole, Winder

Stephen Martyr, Stainless

Stepmother Novercal

Stepney Spare

Steppe Kyrgyz, Llano, Plain

Stereo Personal

Stereotype(d) Hackney, Ritual

Sterile, Sterilise(r), Sterility Acarpous, Aseptic, Atocia, Autoclave, Barren, Dead, Fruitless, Impotent, Infertile, Neuter, Pasteurise, Spay

Sterling Excellent, Genuine, Pound, Silver, Sound

Stern Aft, Austere, Counter, Dour, Flinty, Grim, Hard, Implacable, Iron, Isaac, Nates, Poop, Rear, Relentless, Rugged, Stark, Strict, Tailpiece, Transom

Steroid Anabolic, Androsterone, Calciferol, Cortisone, Dexamethasone, Ergosterol, Fusidic, Lumisterol, Mifepristone, Nandrolone, Predniso(lo)ne, Spironolactone, Testosterone

Sterol Stigmasterol

Stertorous Snore

Stet Restore

Stevedore Docker, Dockhand, Longshoreman, Stower, Wharfinger

Stevenson RLS, Tusitala

Stew(ed), Stews Bagnio, Bath, Blanquette, Boil, Bordel(lo), Bouillabaisse, Bouilli, Braise, Bredie, Brothel, Burgoo, Carbonade, Carbonnade, Casserole,

Cassoulet, Cholent, Chowder, Coddle, Colcannon, Compot(e), Daube, Flap, Fuss, Goulash, Haricot, Hash, Hell, Hot(ch)pot(ch), Irish, Jug, Lather, Lobscouse, Maconochie, Matapan, Matelote, Mulligan, Navarin, Olla podrida, Osso bucco, Paddy, Paella, Pepperpot, Pot-au-feu, Pot-pourri, Ragout, Ratatouille, Rubaboo, Salmi, Sass, Scouse, Seethe, Simmer, Slumgullion, Squiffy, Stie, Stove, Stovies, Sty, Succotash, Sweat, Swelter, Tajine, Tatahas, Tzimmes, Zamzawed, Zarzuela

Steward Butler, Cellarer, Chamberlain, Chiltern Hundreds, Dewan, Factor, Hind, Malvolio, Manciple, Maormor, Mormaor, Official, Oswald, Panter, Purser, Reeve, Seneschal, Sewer, Shop, Smallboy, Sommelier, Waiter

▷ **Stewed** *may indicate* an anagram

Stibnite Antimony, Kohl

Stick(ing) (out), **Sticks**, **Sticky**, **Stuck** Adhere, Affix, Agglutinant, Aground, Ash, Ashplant, Atlatl, Attach, Bamboo, Bastinado, Bat, Baton, Bauble, Bayonet, Bludgeon, Bond, Boondocks, Caman, Cambrel, Cammock, Cane, Celery, Cement, Chalk, Chapman, Clag, Clam(my), Clarty, Clave, Cleave, Cling, Clog, Club, Cocktail, Cohere, Coinhere, Composing, Control, Crab, Crosier, Cross(e), Crotch, Crozier, Crummack, Crummock, Cue, Distaff, Divining-rod, Dog, Dure, Endure, Fag(g)ot, Firewood, Flak, Founder, Fuse, Gad(e), Gaid, Gambrel, Gelatine, Glair, Gliadin, Glit, Glue, Goad, Gold, Goo, Gore, Ground-ash, Gum, Gunge, Gunk, Harpoon, Hob, Hurley, Immobile, Impale, Inhere, Isinglass, Jab, Jam, Jut, Kebbie, Kid, Kierie, Kindling, Kip, Kiri, Knitch, Knobkerrie, Ko, Lance, Lath(i), Lathee, Lentisk, Limy, Lug, Message, Minder, Molinet, Orange, Parasitic, Paste, Penang-lawyer, Persist, Phasmid, Piceous, Pierce, Piolet, Plaster, Pogo, Pole, Posser, Protrude, Protuberant, Pugol, Quarterstaff, Rash, Ratten, Rhubarb, Rhythm, Rod, Ropy, Scouring, Seat, Shillela(g)h, Shooting, Size, Ski, Smudge, Spanish windlass, Spear, Spurtle, Squail(er), Staff, Stand, Stang, Stob, Stodgy, Supplejack, Swagger, Switch, Swizzle, Swordstick, Tacamahac, Tack(y), Tally, Tar, Thick, Throwing, Toddy, Truncheon, Trunnion, Twig, Vare, Viscid, Viscous, Waddy, Wait, Walking, Wand, White, Woolder, Woomera(ng)

Sticker Araldite®, Barnacle, Bur, Glue, Label, Limpet, Partisan, Poster, Slogan

Stickler Pedant, Poser, Problem, Purist, Rigid, Rigorist, Tapist

Stiff, **Stiffen(er)**, **Stiffening**, **Stiffness** Anchylosis, Angular, Ankylosis, Baleen, Bandoline, Brace, Buckram, Budge, Corpse, Corpus, Dear, Defunct, Expensive, Formal, Frore(n), Frorn(e), Gammy, Goner, Grommet, Gut, Hard, Lignin, Mort, Myotonia, Petrify, Pokerish, Prim, Ramrod, Rigid, Rigor, Rigor mortis, Sad, Set, Shank-iron, Size, Solid, Starch, Stark, Stay, Steeve, Stieve, Stilted, Stoor, Stour, Stowre, Sture, Trubenize®, Unbending, Whalebone, Wigan, Wooden

Stifle Crush, Dampen, Funk, Muffle, Scomfish, Smore, Smother, Stive, Strangle

Stigma(tise) Blemish, Brand, Carpel, Discredit, Note, Slur, Smear, Spot, > **STAIN**, Wound

Stile Gate, Steps, Sty

Stiletto Bodkin, Heel, Knife

Still Accoy, Airless, Alembic, Assuage, Becalm, Calm, Check, Current, Doggo, Ene, Even(ness), Freeze-frame, Higher, Howbe, However, Hush, Illicit, Inactive, Inanimate, Inert, Kill, Languid, Limbec(k), Lull, Motionless, Nevertheless, Patent, Peaceful, Photograph, Placate, Placid, Posé, Pot, Quiescent, Quiet, Resting, Silent, Snapshot, Soothe, Stagnant, Static, Stationary, Though, Yet

Stilt Avocet, Bird, Poaka, Prop, Scatch

Stilted Formal, Pedantic, Stiff, Unruffled, Wooden

Stimulant, Stimulate, Stimulus Activate, Adrenaline, Antigen, Arak, Arouse, Auxin, Benny, Caffeine, Cinder, Clomiphene, Coca, Conditioned, Coramine, Cue, Dart, Digitalin, Digoxin, Egg, Energise, Evoke, Excitant, Fillip, Fuel, Galvanize, Ginger, Goad, Hormone, Incite, Innerve, Inspire, Irritate, Jog, Key, K(h)at, Kick, L-dopa, Mneme, Motivate, Nikethamide, Oestrus, Oxytocin, Paraphilia, Pemoline, Pep, Philtre, Pick-me-up, Piquant, Pituitrin, Prod, Promote, Provoke, Psych, Qat, Rim, Roborant, > ROUSE, Rowel, Rub, Sassafras, Sensuous, Spur, Sting, Stir, Tannin, Tar, Theine, Tickle, Titillate, Tone, Tonic, Unconditioned, Upper, Whet(stone), Wintergreen, Winter's bark

Sting(ing) Aculeate, Barb, Bite, Cheat, Cnida, Goad, Nematocyst, Nettle(tree), Overcharge, Perceant, Piercer, Poignant, Prick, Pungent, Rile, Scorpion, Sephen, Smart, Spice, Stang, Stimulus, Surcharge, Tang, Trichocyst, Urent, Urtica

Sting-ray Sephen, Trygon

Stingy Cheeseparing, Chintzy, Close, Costive, Hard, Illiberal, Mean, Miserly, Narrow, Near, Niggardly, Nippy, Parsimonious, Skimpy, Snippy, Snudge, Tight(wad), Tight-arse

▷ **Stingy** *may indicate* something that stings

Stink(er), Stinking, Stinks Abroma, Atoc, Atok, Brock, Cacodyl, Crepitate, Desman, Fetor, Foumart, Guff, Heel, Hellebore, Malodour, Mephitis, Miasma, Ming, Niff, Noisome, Rasse, Reek, Rich, Science, > SMELL, Sondeli, Stench, Teledu

Stinkbird Hoa(c)tzin

Stint Chore, Economise, Limit, Scamp, Scantle, Scrimp, Share, Skimp

Stipend Ann(at), Annexure, Pay, Prebend, Remuneration, Salary, Wages

Stipulate, Stipulation Clause, Condition, Covenant, Insist, Provision, Proviso, Rider, Specify

Stipule Ocrea

Stir(red), Stirring Accite, Admix, Ado, Afoot, Agitate, Amo(o)ve, Animate, Annoy, Bird, Bother, Bustle, Buzz, Can, Churn, Cooler, Excite, Foment, Furore, Fuss, Gaol, Hectic, Impassion, Incense, Incite, Inflame, Instigate, Insurrection, Intermix, Jee, Jog, Kitty, Limbo, Live, > MIX, Move, Noy, Paddle, Penitentiary, Poss, Pother, > PRISON, Prod, Provoke, Quad, Quatch, Quetch, Quinche, Qui(t)ch, Quod, Rabble, Rear, Roil, Rouse, Roust, Rummage, Rustle, Sod, Steer, Styre, Swizzle, To-do, Upstart, Wake

▷ **Stir(red), Stirring** *may indicate* an anagram

Stirrup (guard) Bone, Footrest, Footstall, Iron, Stapes, Tapadera, Tapadero

Stitch (up) Bargello, Basket, Baste, Blanket, Blind, Box, Buttonhole, Cable, Chain, Couching, Crewel, Crochet, Cross, Daisy, Embroider, Feather, Fell, Flemish, Florentine, Garter, Gathering, Grospoint, Hem, Herringbone, Honeycomb, Insertion, Kettle, Knit, Lazy daisy, Lock, Monk's seam, Moss, Needle, Open, Overcast, Overlock, Pearl, Petit point, Pinwork, Plain, Purl, Queen, Rag, Railway, Rib, Rope, Running, Saddle, Satin, Screw, Sew, Slip, Spider, Stab, Stay, Steek, Stem, Stockinette, Stocking, Straight, Sutile, Suture, Tack, Tailor's tack, Tent, Topstitch, Vandyke, Whip, Whole

Stock(ed), Stocks, Stocky Aerie, Aery, Ambulance, Amplosome, Barometer, Blue-chip, Bouillon, Bree, Breech, Brompton, Buffer, But(t), Capital, Carry, Cattle, Choker, Cippus, Congee, Conjee, Court-bouillon, Cravat, Dashi, Debenture, Delta, Die, Endomorph, Equip, Fumet, Fund, Gamma, Gear(e), Government, Graft, Gun, Handpiece, He(a)rd, Hilt, Hoosh, Industrial, Intervention, Inventory, Joint, Just-in-time, Kin, Larder, Laughing, Line, Little-ease, Locuplete, Omnium, Pigeonhole, Preferred, Pycnic, Race, Ranch,

Recovery, Rep(ertory), Replenish, Reserve, Rolling, Root, Scrip, Seed, Shorts, Soup, Squat, Staple, Steale, Steelbow, Stirp(e)s, > **STORE**, Strain, Stubby, Supply, Surplus, Talon, Tap, Team, Tie, Utility, Virginia

Stockade Barrier, Eureka, Zare(e)ba, Zereba, Zeriba

Stocking(s) Bas, Boot-hose, Fishnet, Hogger, Hose, Leather, Legwarmer, Moggan, Netherlings, Nylons, Seamless, Sheer, Sock, Spattee, Support, Tights

Stockman, Stockbroker Broker, Jobber, Neatherd

Stodge, Stodgy Dull, Filling, Heavy

Stoic(al) Impassive, Job, Logos, Patient, Philosophical, Plato, Porch, Seneca(n), Spartan, Stolid, Zeno

Stoke(r), Stokes Bram, Coal-trimmer, Fire(man), Fuel, S, Shovel

Stole(n) Bent, Epitrachelion, Hot, Maino(u)r, Manner, Manor, Nam, Orarion, Orarium, Reft, Scarf, Staw, Tippet, Tweedle

Stolid Deadpan, Dull, Impassive, Phlegmatic, Po(-faced), Thickset, Wooden

Stomach(ic) Abdomen, Abomasum, Accept, Appetite, Belly, Bible, Bingy, Bonnet, Bread-basket, Brook, C(o)eliac, Corporation, Epigastrium, Epiploon, Fardel-bag, Gaster, Gizzard, Gut, Heart, Jejunum, King's-hood, Kite, Kyte, Little Mary, Manyplies, Mary, Maw, Mesaraic, Midriff, Omasum, Paunch, Potbelly, Propodon, Proventriculus, Psalterium, Pylorus, Read, Rennet, Reticulum, Rumen, Stick, Swagbelly, > **SWALLOW**, Tripe, Tum, Tun-belly, Urite, Vell, Venter, Wame, Washboard, Wem, Zingiber

Stomach-ache Colic, Colitis, Collywobbles, Giardiasis, Gripe, Gutrot, Mulligrubs

Stone(d), Stone age, Stones, Stony Blotto, Drunk, Henge, Imposing, Ink, Inukshuk, Lucky, Lydian, Mort, Niobe(an), Pelt, Precious, Rolling, Sermon, Standing, Step(ping), Through, Touch

STONES

2 letters:	Lode	Flint	Sneck
St	Onyx	Gooly	Stela
	Opal	Grape	Stele
3 letters:	Plum	Jewel	Topaz
Gem	Ragg	Kenne	Wacke
Hog	Sard	Lapis	Wyman
Pit	Skew	Logan	
Rag	Slab	Menah	**6 letters:**
Tin	Soap	Metal	Amazon
	Tile	Mocha	Ashlar
4 letters:	Trap	Paste	Ashler
Bath		Prase	Baetyl
Blue	**5 letters:**	Pumie	Bezoar
Celt	Agate	Quern	Brinny
Door	Amber	Quoin	Chesil
Flag	Balas	Quoit	Chisel
Hone	Beryl	Rubin	Cobble
Horn	Black	Rufus	Coping
Iron	Chalk	Rybat	Cultch
Jasp	Chert	Satin	Dolmen
Kerb	Coade	Scone	Flusch
Lias	Culch	Scree	Fossil
Lime	Drupe	Slate	Gibber

Gooley
Goolie
Gravel
Humite
Jargon
Jasper
Kidney
Kingle
Ligure
Lithic
Menhir
Metate
Mosaic
Muller
Nutlet
Oamaru
Paving
Pebble
Pot-lid
Pumice
Pyrene
Rip-rap
Samian
Sarsen
Scarab
Summer
Tanist
Yonnie

7 letters:
Asteria
Avebury
Blarney
Bologna
Boulder
Breccia
Callais
Cat's eye
Chuckie
Curling
Girasol

Granite
Hyacine
Hyalite
Jargoon
Lia-fail
Lithoid
Moabite
Olivine
Parpane
Parpend
Parpent
Pennant
Peridot
Perpend
Perpent
Petrous
Pudding
Purbeck
Putamen
Rocking
Rosetta
Sardine
Sardius
Sarsden
Scaglia
Schanse
Schanze
Smaragd
Staddle
Tektite
Telamon
Thunder
Tripoli
Urolith

8 letters:
Aerolite
Aerolith
Amethyst
Asteroid
Baguette

Cabochon
Calculus
Cinnamon
Cromlech
Cryolite
Ebenezer
Elf-arrow
Endocarp
Essonite
Ganister
Girasole
Lapidate
Megalith
Menamber
Monolith
Nephrite
Omphalos
Onychite
Parpoint
Peastone
Petrosal
Phengite
Pisolite
Portland
Rollrich
Sapphire
Sardonyx
Scalpins
Schantze
Specular
Tonalite
Voussoir

9 letters:
Alabaster
Asparagus
Cairngorm
Carnelian
Cholelith
Chondrite
Cornelian

Crossette
Dichroite
Firestone
Gannister
Greensand
Hessonite
Hoarstone
Lithiasis
Meteorite
Paleolith
Pipestone
Rubicelle
Scagliola
Trilithon
Turquoise
Ventifact

10 letters:
Adamantine
Alectorian
Aragonites
Chalcedony
Draconites
Enhydritic
Foundation
Gastrolith
Grey-wether
Kimberlite
Lherzolite
Lithophyte
Pearlstone
Rhinestone

11 letters:
Peristalith

12 letters:
Carton-pierre
Philosopher's

Stone-crop Orpin(e), Sedum, Succulent
Stone-pusher Sisyphus
Stone-thrower Bal(lista), Catapult, David, Mangonel, Onager, Perrier, Sling,
   Trebuchet
Stone-wall(er) Block, Mule, Revet
Stone-worker Jeweller, Knapper, Sculptor
Stooge Butt, Cat's-paw, Feed, Straight man
Stook(s) Sheaf, Stack, Thr(e)ave
Stool Buffet, Coppy, Cracket, Creepie, Cricket, Cucking, Curule, Cutty,
   Ducking, Faeces, Hassock, Milking, Music, Piano, Pouf(fe), Repentance, Seat,

Sir-reverence, Step, Stercoral, Sunkie, Taboret, Tripod, Tripos, Turd

Stoop Bend, Condescend, C(o)urb, Daine, Deign, Incline, Porch, Slouch

Stop(page), Stopcock, Stopper, Stopping Abort, An(n)icut, Arrest, Avast, Bait, Ba(u)lk, Bide, Blin, Block, Brake, Buffer, Bung, Canting-coin, > CEASE, Cessation, Chapter, Check, Checkpoint, Cheese, Cholestasis, Clarabella, Clarino, Clarion, Clog, Close, Colon, Comfort, Comma, Conclude, Cork, Coupler, Cremo(r)na, Cremorne, Cromorna, Cut, Deactivate, Debar, Demurral, Desist, Deter, Devall, Diapason, Diaphone, Discontinue, Discourage, Dit, Dolce, Dot, Dulciana, Echo, Embargo, End, Field, Fifteenth, Flag, Flue, Flute, Foreclose, Foundation, Fr(a)enum, Freeze, Full, Gag, Gamba, Gemshorn, Glottal, Gong, Halt, Hamza(h), Hartal, Hinder, Hitch, Ho, Hold, Hoy, Intermit, Ischuria, Jam, Kibosh, Let-up, Lill, Lin, Lute, Media, Mutation, Nasard, Oboe, Obturate, Occlude, Oppilate, Organ, Outspan, Pause, Period, Piccolo, Pit, Plug, Point, Poop, Preclude, Prevent, Principal, Prorogue, Pull-in, Pull over, Pull-up, Punctuate, Quash, Quint, Quit, Racket, Red, Reed, Refrain, Register, Rein, Remain, Request, Rest, Salicet, Scotch, Screw-top, Semi-colon, Sese, Sesquialtera, Sext, Sist, Snub, Solo, Spigot, Stall, Stanch, Standstill, Stash, Stasis, Station, Staunch, Stay, Stive, Strike, Subbase, Subbass, Suction, Supersede, Suppress, Suspend, Tab, Tamp(ion), Tap, Tenuis, Terminate, Toby, Toho, Truck, Voix celeste, Vox angelica, Vox humana, Waldflute, Waldhorn, Waypoint, When, Whistle, Whoa

Stopgap Caretaker, Gasket, Gaskin, Interim, Makeshift, Temporary

Storage, Store(house), Store Accumulate, Arsenal, Backing, Barn, Bin, Bottle, Bottom drawer, Boxroom, Bunker, Buttery, Cache, Cell, Cellar, Chain, Clamp, Clipboard, Convenience, Co-op(erative), Co-operative, Cootch, Core, Cupboard, Cutch, Database, Deli, Dene-hole, Dépanneur, Department(al), Depository, Depot, Dime, Discount, Dolia, Dolly-shop, Elevator, Emporium, Ensile, Entrepot, Etape, Fund, Garner, Genizah, Girnal, Glory hole, Go-down, Granary, Groceteria, > HOARD, Hold, Hope chest, House, Humidor, Husband, Hypermarket, Imbarn, Larder, Lastage, Lazaretto, Liquor, Lumber room, Magazine, Main, Mart, Mattamore, Memory, Mine, Morgue, Mothball, Mow, Multiple, Nest-egg, Off-licence, Package, Pantechnicon, Pantry, Pithos, Provision, Pumped, Rack(ing), RAM, Repertory, Reposit, ROM, Sector, > SHOP, Silage, Silo, Spence, Spooling, Springhouse, Squirrel, Stack, Stash, Stock, Stockroom, Stow, Superbaza(a)r, Superette, Supermarket, Supply, Tack-room, Tank, Thesaurus, Tithe-barn, Tommy-shop, Virtual, Volutin, Warehouse, Woodshed, Woodyard, Wool (shed)

▶ **Storey** see STORY

Stork Adjutant, Antigone, Argala, Bird, Jabiru, Marabou(t), Marg, Saddlebill, Wader, Wood, Wood ibis

Stork's bill Erodium

Storm(y) Ablow, Adad, Assail, Attack, Baguio, Blizzard, Bluster, Bourasque, Brouhaha, Buran, Calima, Charge, Cyclone, Devil, Dirty, Dust, Electric, Enlil, Expugn, Furore, Gale, Gusty, Haboob, Hurricane, Ice, Magnetic, Monsoon, Onset, Oragious, Rage(ful), Raid, Rain, Rampage, Rant, Rave, Red spot, Rugged, Rush, Shaitan, Snorter, Squall, Sumatra, Tea-cup, Tebbad, Tempest, Tornade, Tornado, Tropical, Unruly, Violent, Weather, Willy-willy, Wroth, Zu

▷ **Stormy** may indicate an anagram

Story, Storyline, Storey, Stories Account, Allegory, Anecdote, Apocrypha, Arthuriana, Attic, Bar, Basement, Baur, Bawr, Biog, Blood and thunder, Chestnut, Clearstory, Clerestory, Cock and bull, Conte, Cover, Decameron, Edda, Epic, Episode, Etage, Exclusive, Exemplum, Fable, Fabliau, Fib, Fiction,

Flat, Floor, Folk-tale, Gag, Geste, Ghost, Hard-luck, Heptameron, Hitopadesa, Horror, Idyll, Iliad, Jataka, Lee, Legend, Lie, Mabinogion, Marchen, Mezzanine, Myth(os), Mythus, Narrative, Nouvelle, Novel(la), Oratorio, Parable, Passus, Pentameron, Plot, Rede, Report, Romance, Rumour, Saga, Scoop, Script, Serial, SF, Shaggy dog, Shocker, Short, Smoke-room, Sob, Spiel, Spine-chiller, Splash, Stage, Success, Tale, Tall, Thread, Thriller, Tier, Triforium, Upper, Version, Yarn

Story-teller Aesop, Fibber, Griot, Liar, Munchausen, Narrator, Raconteur, Shannachie, Tusitala

Stoup Benitier, Bucket, Vessel

Stout(ness) Ale, Beer, Black velvet, Burly, Chopping, Chubby, Embonpoint, Endomorph, Entire, Fat, Fubsy, Hardy, Humpty-dumpty, Lusty, Manful, Milk, Obese, Overweight, Porter, Portly, Potbelly, Robust, Stalwart, Stalworth, Sta(u)nch, Strong, Stuggy, Sturdy, Substantial, Tall, Velvet

Stove Baseburner, Break, Calefactor, Cockle, Cooker, Furnace, Gasfire, Oven, Potbelly, Primus®, Range, Salamander

Stow Cram, Flemish (down), Load, Pack, Rummage, Stack, Stash, Steeve

Strabismus Squint

Straddle Bestride, Strodle

Strafe Bombard, Shell, Shoot

Straggle(r), Straggly Estray, Gad, Meander, Ramble, Rat-tail, Spidery, Sprawl, Stray, Wander

Straight(en), Straightness Align, Bald, Beeline, Correct, Die, Direct, Downright, Dress, Frank, Gain, Het(ero), Home, Honest, Lank, Legit, Level, Neat, Normal, Orthotropous, Rectilineal, Rectitude, Righten, Sheer, Slap, Tidy, True, Unbowed, Uncurl, Unlay, Upright, Veracious, Virgate

Straight edge Lute, Ruler

Straightforward Candid, Direct, Easy, Even, Forthright, Honest, Jannock, Level, Plain sailing, Pointblank, Simple

Straight-haired Leiotrichous

Strain(ed), Strainer, Straining Agonistic, Ancestry, Aria, Breed, Carol, Clarify, Colander, Distend, Drawn, Effort, Exert, Filter, Filtrate, Fit, Fitt(e), Force, Fray, Fytt(e), Intense, Kind, Melody, Milsey, Molimen, Music, Note, Overtask, Passus, Percolate, Plus, Pressure, Pull, Purebred, Rack, Raring, Reck(an), Retch, Rick, Seep, Seil(e), Set, Shear, Sieve, Sift, Sile, Stape, Start, Stock, Streak, Stress, Stretch, Sye, Tamis, Tammy, Tax, Tenesmus, Tense, Tension, Threnody, Try, Tune, Unease, Vein, Vice, Work, Wrick

Strait(s) Bab el Mandeb, Basilan, Bass, Bering, Bosp(h)orus, Canso, Channel, Condition, Cook, Crisis, Cut, Dardanelles, Davis, Denmark, Desperate, Drake Passage, Euripus, Formosa, Foveaux, Gat, Gibraltar, Golden Gate, Gut, Hormuz, Hudson, Johor, Juan de Fuca, Kattegat, Kerch, Korea, Kyle, Little Belt, Lombok, Mackinac, Magellan, Malacca, Menai, Messina, Mona Passage, Narrow, North Channel, Otranto, Palk, Predicament, Soenda, Solent, Sound, St, Sumba, Sunda, Taiwan, Tatar, Tiran, Torres, Tsugaru, Windward Passage

Straiten(ed) Impecunious, Impoverish, Poor, Restrict

Strait-laced Blue-nosed, Narrow, Primsie, Puritan, Stuffy

Strand(ed) Abandon, Aground, Bank, Beach, Desert, Fibre, Haugh, Hexarch, Isolate, Lock, Maroon, Neaped, Ply, Rice, Rope, Shore, Sliver, Thread, Three-ply, Tress, Wisp

Strange(ness), Stranger Alien, Aloof, Amphitryon, Curious, Eerie, Exotic, Foreign, Fraim, Frem(d), Fremit, Frenne, Funny, Guest, Malihini, New, Novel, Odd(ball), Outlandish, Outsider, Quare, Queer, Rum, S, Screwy, Selcouth, Singular, Tea-leaf, Uncanny, Unco, Uncommon, Unked, Unket, Unkid, Unused,

Unusual, Wacky, Weird, Wondrous
▷ **Strange** *may indicate* an anagram
Strangle(r) Choke, Garotte, Jugulate, Suppress, Throttle, Thug(gee)
Strap(ping) Able-bodied, Band, Barber, Beat, Bowyangs, Brail, Braw, Breeching, Browband, Crupper, Cuir-bouilli, Curb, Deckle, Girth, Halter, Harness, Holdback, Jess, Jock(ey), Larrup, Lash, Ligule, Lorate, Lore, Manly, Martingale, Nicky-tam, Octopus, Pandy, Rand, Rein, Robust, Shoulder, Sling, Spider, Strop, Surcingle, Suspender, T, Tab, Taws(e), T-bar, Thong, Throatlash, Throatlatch, Trace, Tump-line, Wallop, Watch
Stratagem, Strategist, Strategy Artifice, Clausewitz, Coup, Deceit, Device, Dodge, Exit, Fetch, Finesse, Fraud, Heresthetic, Kaupapa, Masterstroke, Maximum, Minimax, Plan, Rope-a-dope, > **RUSE**, Scheme, Scorched earth, Sleight, Subterfuge, Tactic(s), Tactician, Trick, Wile
Stratum, Strata Bed, Coal Measures, Kar(r)oo, Layer, Neogene, Permian, Schlieren, Seam, Syncline
Straw(s), Strawy Balibuntal, Boater, Buntal, Chaff, Cheese, Halm, Hat, Haulm, Hay, Insubstantial, Last, Leghorn, Monkey-pump, Nugae, Oaten, Panama, Parabuntal, Pea(se), Pedal, Short, Sipper, Stalk, Stramineous, Strammel, Strummel, Stubble, Trifles, Wisp, Ye(a)lm
Strawberry Barren, Birthmark, Fragaria, Garden, Hautbois, Hautboy, Potentilla, Wild
Stray Abandoned, Chance, Depart, Deviate, Digress, Err, Forwander, Foundling, Gamin, Maverick, Meander, Misgo, Pye-dog, Ramble, Roam, Sin, Straggle, Streel, Traik, Unowned, Waff, Waif, Wander
Streak(ed), Streaker, Streaky Archimedes, Bended, Blue, Brindle, Comet, Flaser, Flash, Fleck, Freak, Hawked, Highlights, Lace, Layer, Leonid, Lowlight, Mark, Merle, Mottle, Primitive, Race, Run, Schlieren, Seam, Shot, Striate, Striga, Strip(e), Vein, Venose, Vibex, Waif, Wake, Wale, Yellow
Stream Acheron, Anabranch, Arroyo, Beam, Beck, Bogan, Bourne, Burn, Consequent, Course, Current, Driblet, Fast, Flow, Flower, Freshet, Gulf, Gush, Headwater, Influent, Jet, Kill, Lade, Lane, Leet, Logan, Meteor, Nala, Obsequent, Pokelogan, Pour, Pow, Riffle, Rill, River, Rivulet, Rubicon, Run, Runnel, Sike, Slough, Spruit, Star, Streel, Subsequent, Syke, The Fleet, Thrutch, Tide-race, Torrent, Tributary, Trickle, Trout, Watercourse, Water-splash, Winterbourne
Streamer Banderol(e), Bandrol, Banner(all), Bannerol, Pennon, Pinnet, Ribbon, Tape, Vane
Streamline(d), Streamliner Clean, Fair, Fairing, Simplify, Sleek, Slim
Street Alley, Ave(nue), Bowery, Broad, Carey, Carnaby, Cato, Causey, Champs Elysées, Cheapside, Civvy, Close, Corso, Court, Crescent, Downing, Drive, Easy, Fleet, Gate, Grub, Harley, High(way), Kármán vortex, Lane, Lombard, Main, Meuse, Mews, One-way, Parade, Paseo, Queer, Road, Sesame, Side, Sinister, St, Strand, Terrace, Thoroughfare, Threadneedle, Throgmorton, Two-way, Vortex, Wall, Wardour, Watling, Way, Whitehall
Street arab Mudlark
Streetcar Desire, Tram
Strength(en), Strengthening Afforce, Ausforming, Bant, Beef, Brace, Brawn, Build, Confirm, Consolidate, Enable, Energy, Field, Foison, Force, Forte, Fortify, Freshen, Grit, Heart, Herculean, Horn, Intensity, Iron, Line, Main, Man, Might, Munite, Muscle, Nerve, > **POWER**, Prepotence, Pre-stress, Proof, Reinforce, Roborant, Sinew, Spike, Stamina, Steel, Sthenia, Stoutness, > **STRONG**, Tensile, Thews, Titration, Ultimate, Unity, Vim, Yield

Strenuous Arduous, Effort, Exhausting, Hard, Laborious, Vehement
Strephon Rustic, Wooer
Stress(ed) Accent, Arsis, Birr, Brunt, Emphasis, Ictus, Impress, Italicise, Marcato, Orthotonesis, Oxytone, Paroxytone, Post-traumatic, Primary, Proof, PTSD, Rack, Ram, Rhythm, RSI, Sentence, Sforzando, Shear, Strain, Taut, Tense, > TENSION, Try, Underline, Underscore, Urge, Wind shear, Word, Yield (point)
Stretch(able), **Stretched**, **Stretcher**, **Stretching** Belt, Brick, Crane, Distend, Draw, Ectasis, Eke, Elastic, Elongate, Expanse, Extend, Extensile, Farthingale, Fib, Frame, Give, Gurney, Lengthen, Litter, Narrows, Outreach, Pallet, Pandiculation, Porrect, Procrustes, Prolong, Protend, Pull, Rack, Rax, > REACH, Sentence, Shiner, Span, Spell, Spread, Spreadeagle, Strain, Taut, Tend, Tense, Tensile, Tenter, Term, Time, Tract, Tractile, Tree, Trolley
Striate Lineolate, Vein
Stricken Beset, Hurt, Overcome, Shattered
Strict Dour, Harsh, Literal, Medic, Narrow, Orthodox, Penal, Proper, Puritanical, Rigid, Rigorous, Severe, Spartan, Stern, Strait(-laced), Stringent
Stride Gal(l)umph, Leg, Lope, March, Pace, Piano, Stalk, Sten, Straddle, Stroam, Strut, Stump
Strident Brassy, Grinding, Harsh, Raucous, Screech
Strife Bargain, Barrat, Colluctation, Conflict, Conteck, Contest, Discord, Disharmony, Dissension, Feud, Food, Friction, Ignoble, Scrap(ping), Sturt
Strike(r), **Striking**, **Strike out** Affrap, Air, Alight, Annul, Appulse, Arresting, Attitude, Backhander, Baff, Band, Bandh, Bang, Bash, Bat, Baton, Batsman, Batter, Beat, Belabour, Better, Biff, Black, Bla(u)d, Bonanza, Bop, Buff, Buffet, Bund(h), Butt, Cane, Catch, Chime, Chip, Clap, Clash, Clatch, Clip, Clock, Clout, Club, Cob, Collide, Constitutional, Coup, Cue, Cuff, Dad, Dent, Dev(v)el, Ding, Dint, Dismantle, Distingué, Douse, Dowse, Dramatic, Drive, Dush, Eclat, Evenement, Fet(ch), Fillip, Firk, Fist, Flail, Flog, Frap, General, Get, Go-slow, Gowf, Hail, Hartal, Head-butt, > HIT, Horn, Hour, Hunger, Ictus, Illision, Impact, Impinge, Impress, Jarp, Jaup, Jole, Joll, Joule, Jowl, Knock, Lam, Lambast, Laser, Lay(-off), Lightning, Match, Middle, Notable, Noticeable, Official, Out, Pash, Pat(ter), Pat, Pean, Peen, Pein, Pene, Percuss, Picket, Pize, Plectrum, Pronounced, Pummel, Punch, Ram, Rap, Remarkable, Rolling, Roquet, Salient, Scrub, Scutch, Shank, Sideswipe, Sitdown, Sit-in, Slam, Slap, Slat, Slog, Slosh, Smack, Smash, Smite, Sock, Souse, Sowce, Sowse, Spank, Stayaway, Stop(page), Stub, Swap, Swat, Swinge, Swipe, Swop, Sympathy, Tan, Tapotement, Tat, Thump, Tip, Token, Tonk, Tripper, Unconstitutional, Unofficial, Walk-out, Wallop, Wap, Whack, Whang, Whap, Wherrit, Who does what, Whomp, Whop, Wick, Wildcat, Wipe, Wondrous, Zap
Strike-breaker Blackleg, Fink, Rat, Scab
String(s), **Stringy** Band, Beads, Bootlace, Bow, Bowyang, Cello, Chalaza, Chanterelle, Cord, Cosmic, Creance, Cremaster, Drill, Enfilade, Fiddle, Fillis, First, G, Glass, Gut, Henequin, Heniquin, Hypate, Idiot, Injection, Keyed, Lace, Lag, Lichanos, Macramé, Mese, Necklace, Nete, Nicky-tam, Paramese, Pledget, Production, Proviso, Purse, Quint, Ripcord, Rope, Second, Series, Shoe(-tie), Sinewy, Snare, Straggle, Strand, Sympathetic, Team, Tendon, Thairm, Tie, Tough, Train, Trite, Viola, Violin, Wreathed
String-course Moulding, Table
Stringent Extreme, Rigid, Severe, Strict, Urgent
Strip(ped), **Stripper**, **Striptease** Airfield, Armband, Band, Bare, Bark, Batten, Belt, Bereave, Blowtorch, Casparian, Chippendale, Comic, Cote, Defoliate,

Denude, Deprive, Derobe, Despoil, Devest, Disbark, Dismantle, Dismask, Disrobe, Divest, Drag, Ecdysiast, Ecdysis, Ecorché, Fannel(l), Fiche, Film, Flashing, Flaught, Flay, Fleece, Flench, Flense, Flight, Flinch, Flounce, Flype, Furring, Gaza, Goujon, Hatband, Infula, Jib, Label, Landing, Lap-dancer, Lardon, Lath, Ledge, Linter, List, Littoral, Loading, Maniple, Median, Mobius, Panhandle, Parting, Peel, Pillage, Pluck, Pull, Puttee, Puttie, Rand, Raunch, Raw, Ribbon, Ring-bark, Roon, Royne, Rumble, Rund, Runway, Screed, Scrow, Shear, Shed, Shim, Shuck, Skin, Slat, Slit, Sliver, Spellican, Spilikin, Spill(ikin), Splat, Splent, Spline, Splint, Splinter, Spoil, Straik, Strake, Strap, Streak, Strop, Sugar soap, Swath, Sweatband, Tack, Tee, Thong, Tirl, Tirr, Uncase, Undeck, Undress, Unfrock, Unrig, Unrip, Unvaile, Valance, Weather, Widow, Zone

Stripe(d) Band, Bausond, Candy, Chevron, Cingulum, Cove, Endorse, Lance-jack, Laticlave, Line, List, Magnetic, > **NCO**, Ombré, Pale, Paly, Pin, Pirnie, Pirnit, Slash, Snip, Straik, Strake, Streak, Stroke, Tabaret, Tabby, Tiger, Tragelaph(us), Vitta, Weal

Strive, Striving Aim, Aspire, > **ATTEMPT**, Contend, Endeavour, Enter, Kemp, Labour, Nisus, Pingle, Press, Strain, Struggle, Toil, Try, Vie

Stroke Apoplex(y), Backhander, Bat, Bisque, Blow, Boast, Breast, Butterfly, Caress, Carom, Chip, Chop, Counterbuff, Coup, Coy, Crawl, Dash, Dint, Dog(gy)-paddle, Down-bow, Drear(e), Drere, Dropshot, Effleurage, Estrarnazone, Exhaust, Feat, Flick, Fondle, Foozle, Forehand, Glance, Ground, Hairline, Hand(er), Ictus, Inwick, Jenny, Jole, Joll, Joule, Jowl, Knell, Knock, Lash, Lightning, Like, Line, Loft, Long jenny, Loser, Massé, Oarsman, Oblique, Odd, Off-drive, Outlash, Palp, Paw, Pot-hook, Pull, Punto reverso, Put(t), Reverso, Ridding straik, Roquet, Rub, Scart, Scavenge, Sclaff, Scoop, Seizure, Sheffer's, Short jenny, Sider, Sixte, Slash, Smooth, Solidus, Spot, Strike, Stripe, Sweep, Swipe, Tact, Tittle, Touch, Touk, Trait, Trudgen, Trudgeon, Tuck, Upbow, Virgule, Wale, Whang

Stroll(er), Strolling Ambulate, Bummel, Dander, Daun(d)er, Dawner, Flanerie, Flaneur, Idle, Lounge, Ramble, Saunter, Stravaig, Stray, Toddle, Walk, Walkabout, Wander

Strong(est) Able, Brawny, Cast-iron, Doughty, Durable, F, Firm, Fit, Forceful, Forcible, Forte, Full-blown, Hale, Heady, Hercules, Humming, Husky, Intense, Mighty, Nappy, Pithy, Pollent, Potent, Powerful, Pungent, Racy, Rank, Robust, Samson, Solid, Stalwart, Stark, Steely, Sthenic, Stiff, Stout, Str, Strapping, > **STRENGTH**, Sturdy, Substantial, Suit, Tarzan, Tenable, Thesis, Thickset, Trusty, Vegete, Vehement, Vigorous, Violent, Virile, Well-built, Well-set, Ya(u)ld

Stronghold Acropolis, Aerie, Bastion, Castle, Citadel, Eyrie, Eyry, Fastness, Fortress, Keep, Kremlin, Redoubt, Tower

Strontium Sr

Strop Leather, Sharpen, Strap

Struck Aghast, Raught, Smitten

Structural, Structure Allotrope, Analysis, Anatomy, Armature, Building, Catafalque, Cold frame, Compage(s), Data, Deep, Edifice, Erection, Fabric, Fairing, Format(ion), Formwork, Frame, Galea, Heterarchy, Hyperbolic, Hyperfine, Ice-apron, Kekulé, Lantern, Macrocosm, Mole, Organic, Palmation, Pediment, Pergola, Phloem, Physique, Pod, Power, Protein, Retinaculum, Set-up, Shape, Skeleton, Sponson, Sporocarp, Squinch, Starling, Stylobate, Surface, Syntax, System, Tectonic, Telomere, Texas, Texture, Trochlea, Undercarriage

Struggle Agon(ise), Agonistes, Buckle, Camp, Chore, Class, Conflict, Contend,

Contest, Cope, Debatement, Effort, Endeavour, Fight, Flounder, Grabble, Grapple, Kampf, Labour, Luctation, Mill, Pingle, Rat-race, Reluct, Scrape, Scrimmage, Scrum, Scrummage, Scuffle, Slugfest, Sprangle, > STRIVE, Toil, Tug, Tussle, Uphill, Vie, War(sle), Wrestle

▷ **Struggle** *may indicate* an anagram

Strum Thrum, Tweedle, Vamp

Strumpet Cocotte, Harlot, Hiren, Lorette, Paramour, Succubus, Wench

Strut(ter), Strutting Bracket, Brank, Bridging, Cock, Dolphin striker, Flounce, Haught(y), Jet, Kingrod, Longeron, Martingale boom, Member, Nervure, Peacock, Pown, Prance, Prop, Scotch, Shore, Spur, Stalk, Stretcher, Strunt, Swagger, Swank, Tail-boom, Tie-beam

Stuart Anne, James, Pretender

Stub(by) Butt, Counterfoil, Dout, Dowt, Dumpy, Squat, Stob, Stocky

Stubble Ar(r)ish, Bristle, Designer, Hair, Ill-shaven, Stump

Stubborn(ness) Adamant, Bigoted, Contumacious, Cussed, Diehard, Dogged, Entêté, Hard(-nosed), Hidebound, Intransigent, Inveterate, Moyl(e), Mulish, Mumpsimus, Obdurate, Obstinate, Opinionated, Ornery, Ortus, Pertinacious, Perverse, Recalcitrant, Reesty, Refractory, Rigwiddie, Rigwoodie, Self-willed, Stiff, Stout, Tenacious, Thrawn, Wrong-headed

Stuck Fast, Glued, Jammed, Set, Stopped, Wedged

Stuck-up Chesty, Highty-tighty, Hoity-toity, La(h)-di-da(h), Proud, Sealed, Vain

Stud(ded) Boss, Cooser, Cripple, Cu(i)sser, Farm, Frost, He-man, Knob, Nail, Press, Race, Rivet, Seg, Set, Shear, Sire, Stop

Student(s) Alphabetarian, Alumnus, Apprentice, Bajan, Bejant, Bursar, Bursch(en), Cadet, Catachumen, Class, Coed, Commoner, Dan, Dig, Disciple, Dresser, Dux, Exchange, Exhibitioner, Extensionist, External, Form, Fresher, Freshman, Gownsman, Graduand, Green welly, Gyte, Ikey, Internal, Junior, Kommers, Kyu, > LEARNER, Magistrand, Matie, Mature, Medical, Nomologist, NUS, Opsimath, Ordinand, Oxonian, Peking duck, Pennal, Plebe, Poll, Postgraduate, Preppy, Pupil, Reader, Sap, > SCHOLAR, Self-taught, Semi, Seminar, Seminarian, Shark, Sizar, Sizer, Smug, Softa, Soph(omore), Sophister, Subsizar, Swot, Templar, Tiro, Tosher, Trainee, Tuft, Tukkie, Tutee, Wedge, Wonk, Wooden wedge, Wrangler, Year

Studio(s) Atelier, Bottega, Elstree, Gallery, Pinewood, Workshop

Study, Studied, Studies, Studious Analyse, Bone, Brown, Carol, Case, Classics, Con(ne), Conscious, Consider, Course, Cram, Den, Dig, Etude, Feasibility, Field, Gen up, Learn, Liberal, Lucubrate, Media, Motion, Mug, Mull, Muse, Nature, Perusal, Peruse, Pilot, Pore, Post-doctoral, Probe, Read, Recce, Reconnoitre, Research, Reverie, Revise, Sanctum, Sap, Scan, Scrutinise, Specialize, Stew, Swot, Take, Time and motion, Trade-off, Tutorial, Typto, Voulu, Work

Stuff(iness), Stuffing, Stuffy Airless, Bombast, Canvas, Close, Cloth, Codswallop, Cram, Crap, Dimity, Farce, Feast, Fiddlesticks, Fill, Force, Forcemeat, Frows(t)y, Frowzy, Fug, Gear, Gobble, Gorge, Guff, Havers, Hooey, Horsehair, Hot, Lard, Line, Linen, > MATERIAL, Matter, Musty, No-meaning, Nonsense, Overeat, Pad, Pang, Panne, Pompous, Ram, Replete, Rot, Salpicon, Sate, Satiate, Scrap, Sob, Stap, Steeve, Stew, Stifling, Taxidermy, Trig, Upholster, Wad, Youth

Stultify Repress, Ridicule, Smother

Stumble Blunder, Bobble, Err, Falter, Flounder, Founder, Lurch, Peck, Snapper, Stoit, Titubate, Trip

Stump(ed), Stumps, Stumpy Black, Butt, Clump, Fag-end, Floor, More, Nog, Nonplus, Orate, Runt, Scrag, Snag, Snooker, Squab, St, Staddle, Stob, Stock,

Stool, Stub(ble), Stud, Tortillon, Tramp, Truncate, Wicket

Stun(ning), Stunned Astonish, Astound, Awhape, Bludgeon, Concuss, Cosh, Daze, Dazzle, Deafen, Donnard, Donnert, Dove, Drop-dead, Glam, KO, Shell-shocked, Shock, Stoun, Stupefy, Taser®

Stunner Belle, Bobby-dazzler, Cheese, Cosh, Doozy, KO, Peach, Taser®

Stunt(ed) Aerobatics, Confine, Droichy, Dwarf, Escapade, Feat, Gimmick, Hot-dog, Hype, Jehad, Jihad, Loop, Nirl, Puny, Ront(e), Runt, Ruse, Scroggy, Scrub(by), Scrunt(y), Stub, Trick, Wanthriven, Wheelie

Stupefaction, Stupefy(ing) Amaze(ment), Assot, Benumb, Dozen, Dumbfound, Etherise, Fuddle, Hocus, Narcoses, Numb, Stonne, Stun

Stupid, Stupid person Dense, Dull(ard), Fatuous, Foolish, Gormless, Gross, Inane, Insensate, Mindless, Natural, Obtuse, Silly, Thick, Torpid, Vacuous

STUPID PERSON

3 letters:
Ass
Auf
Bob
Cod
Daw
Dim
Div
Fon
Git
Jay
Lob
Log
Nit
Oaf
Owl
Put
Sap
Sot
Twp
Yap

4 letters:
Berk
Bete
Bobb
Bozo
Burk
Cake
Calf
Clod
Clot
Cony
Coof
Coot
Daft
Dill

Dite
Doat
Does
Dolt
Dorb
Dork
Dote
Dozy
Flat
Fogy
Fool
Fozy
Gaby
Gaga
Geck
Gelt
Goat
Goof
Goon
Goop
Gouk
Gowk
Gull
Gump
Hash
Jerk
Lown
Meff
Mome
Mong
Mook
Mutt
Nana
Nerd
Nerk
Nong
Nurd

Ouph
Poon
Poop
Prat
Putt
Putz
Rook
Simp
Stot
Tony
Twit
Warb
Yo-yo
Zany

5 letters:
Blent
Bobby
Booby
Brute
Bumbo
Chick
Chump
Clunk
Cokes
Crass
Cuddy
Cully
Dicky
Divvy
Dorba
Dubbo
Dumbo
Dummy
Dunce
Dweeb
Eejit

Fogey
Galah
Golem
Goofy
Goose
Hoser
Idiot
Kerky
Klutz
Looby
Loony
Lowne
Moron
Neddy
Ninny
Noddy
Ocker
Ouphe
Patch
Prune
Quo-he
Schmo
Simon
Snipe
Spoon
Stock
Stupe
Sumph
Taver
Twerp
Waldo
Wally
Yampy

6 letters:
Bampot
Boodle

Buffer
Cretin
Cuckoo
Cuddie
Dawney
Dickey
Dimwit
Dodkin
Donkey
Doofus
Dottle
Drongo
Gaupus
Gunsel
Ignaro
Ingram
Ingrum
Josser
Lummox
Lurden
Nidget
Nig-nog
Nincum
Nitwit
Noodle
Nudnik
Numpty
Oxhead
Schlep
Schmoe
Scogan
Sucker
Taiver
Thicko
Tosser
Tumphy
Turkey
Turnip
Wommit
Wooden
Zombie

7 letters:
Airhead
Asinico
Asinine

Barmpot
Becasse
Buffoon
Charlie
Damfool
Dawbake
Dim bulb
Dizzard
Donnard
Donnart
Donnerd
Donnert
Gomeral
Gomeril
Gubbins
Half-wit
Haverel
Insulse
Jackass
Juggins
Jughead
Lurdane
Mafflin
Mampara
Muggins
Palooka
Pillock
Pinhead
Plonker
Pot-head
Saphead
Schmock
Schmuck
Schnook
Scoggin
Thickie
Tosspot
Want-wit
Wazzock

8 letters:
Abderian
Abderite
Anserine
Baeotian
Besotted

Blockish
Boeotian
Bonehead
Boofhead
Clodpole
Clodpoll
Crackpot
Deadhead
Dickhead
Dipstick
Dodipoll
Donnered
Dotterel
Dottrell
Dumbbell
Flathead
Gobshite
Goofball
Goose-cap
Imbecile
Knobhead
Liripipe
Liripoop
Lunkhead
Maffling
Meathead
Moon-calf
Omadhaun
Pea-brain
Shot-clog
Softhead
Tom-noddy
Wiseacre
Woodcock

9 letters:
Beccaccia
Blockhead
Braindead
Capocchia
Chipochia
Clarthead
Desipient
Doddipoll
Doddypoll
Dottipoll

Dumb-cluck
Gothamite
Half-baked
Ignoramus
Insipient
Jobernowl
Lamebrain
Malt-horse
Schlemiel
Schlemihl
Simpleton
Thickhead
Woodentop

10 letters:
Analphabet
Changeling
Dummelhead
Dunderhead
Dunderpate
Headbanger
Loggerhead
Muttonhead
Nincompoop
Sheepshead
Thimblewit
Touchstone
Woodenhead

11 letters:
Chowderhead
Featherhead
Hare-brained
Knucklehead
Leather-head
Ninny-hammer
Simple Simon
Thick-witted
Van der Merwe

12 letters:
Featherbrain
Hammerheaded
Shatterbrain

Stupidity Goosery, Hebetude, Thickness, Torpor
Stupor Catatony, Coma, Daze, Dwa(u)m, Fog, Lethargy, Narcosis, Trance
Sturdy Burly, Dunt, Gid, Hardy, Hefty, Lubbard, Lubber, Lusty, Stalwart, Staunch, Steeve, Stieve, Strapping, Strong, Stuffy, Thickset, Turnsick, Vigorous
Sturgeon Beluga, Ellops, Fish, Huso, Osseter, Sevruga, Sterlet

Stutter Hesitate, Stammer
Sty Frank, Hovel, Pen
Stye Eyesore, Hordeolum
Style(s), Stylish, Stylist Adam, A la, A-line, Band, Barocco, Barock, Baroque,
Biedermeier, Blow-dry, Burin, Call, Cantilena, Carry-on, Chic, Chinoiserie,
Chippendale, Class, Cultism, Cut, Dapper, Dash, Decor, Decorated, Demotic,
Diction, Directoire, Dub, Elan, Elegance, Empire, Entitle, Euphuism,
Execution, Face, Farand, > FASHION, Finesse, Flamboyant, Flossy, Form(at),
Genre, Gnomon, Gongorism, Gothic, Grace, Gr(a)ecism, Grand, Groovy,
Hair-do, Hand, Hepplewhite, Hip, Homeric, House, International (Gothic),
Intitule, Katharev(o)usa, Lapidary, Manner, Marivaudage, Mod(e), Modish,
Natty, New, Nib, Nifty, Old, Panache, Pattern, Pen, Perm, Perpendicular,
Personal, Phrase, Pistil, Pointel, Port, Post-modernism, Preponderant, Probe,
Queen Anne, Rakish, Rank, Regency, Rococo, Romanesque, Sheraton, Silk,
Snazzy, Spiffy, Sporty, Street, Swish, Taste, Term, Title, Ton, Tone, Touch,
Traditional, Tuscan, Uncial, Vogue, Way
Stymie Thwart
Styptic Alum, Amadou, Matico, Sta(u)nch
Suave Bland, Debonair, Oily, Smooth, Unctuous, Urbane
Sub Advance, Due, Submarine, Subordinate, U-boat, Under
Sub-atomic Mesic
Subconscious Inner, Instinctive, Not-I, Subliminal, Suppressed
Sub-continent India
Subdivision Arm, Branch, Oblast, Sanjak, Senonian, Wapentake
Subdominant Fah
Subdue(d) Abate, Adaw, Allay, Chasten, Conquer, Cow, Crush, Dant(on),
Daunt(on), Dominate, Entame, Lick, Low-key, Master, Mate, Mute, Overpower,
> QUELL, Quieten, Reduce, Refrain, Slow, Sober, Subact, Suppress, Tame, Under
Subfusc, Subfusk Dim, Dressy, Dusky, Evening, Sombre
Subhuman Apeman, Bestial
Subject(s), Subjection, Subject to Amenable, Art, Bethrall, Caitive, Case,
Citizen, Contingent, Core, Cow, Donne(e), Enthrall, Foundation, Gist, Hobby,
Hobby-horse, Inflict, Liable, Liege(man), Matter, National, On, Overpower,
PE, People, Poser, Rayah, RE, RI, Serf, Servient, Servitude, Sitter, Slavery, Snool,
Submit, Suit, > THEME, Thirl, Thrall, Topic, Under, Vassal
Subjugate Enslave, Master, Oppress, Overcome, Reduce, Repress, Suppress
Sublieutenant Cornet
Sublimate(r) Aludel, Cleanse, Suppress, Transfer
Sublime August, Empyreal, Grand, Great, Lofty, Majestic, Outstanding, Perfect,
Porte, Splendid
Submarine Diver, Innerspace, Nautilus, Pig-boat, Polaris, Sub, U-boat,
Undersea, X-craft
▷ **Submarine** *may indicate* a fish
Submerge(d) Dip, Dive, Drown, Embathe, Engulf, Imbathe, Lemuria,
Overwhelm, Ria, Sink, Take, Whelm
Submissive, Submit Acquiesce, Bow, Capitulate, Comply, Defer, Docile, File,
Knuckle, Meek, Obedient, Obtemperate, Passive, Pathetic, Refer, Render,
Resign, Snool, Stoop, Succumb, Truckle, > YIELD
Subordinate Adjunct, Dependent, Flunky, Inferior, Junior, Minion, Myrmidon,
Offsider, Postpone, Secondary, Second banana, Servient, Stooge, Subject,
Subservient, Subsidiary, Surrender, Under(ling), Underman, Under-strapper,
Vassal

Subscribe(r), Subscription Abonnement, Approve, Assent, Conform, Due, Pay, Sign(atory), Signature, Undersign, Underwrite

Subsequent(ly) Anon, Consequential, Future, Later, Next, Postliminary, Since, Then, Ulterior

Subservient Kneel, Obedient, Obsequious

Subside, Subsidence, Subsidy Abate, Adaw, Aid, Assuage, Bonus, Diminish, Ebb, Grant, Sink, Sit, Swag

Subsidiary, Subsidise Auxiliar(y), By(e), Feather-bed, Junior, Secondary, Side, Spin-off, Succursal

Subsist(ence) Batta, Bread-line, Dole, Keep, Live, Maintain, Rely, Survive

Substance, Substantial Ambergris, Anethole, Antithrombin, Antitoxin, Blocky, Body, Calyx, Cermet, Chalone, Chemzyne, Chitin, Chromatin, Colloid, Considerable, Content, Cosmin(e), Ectocrine, Ectoplasm, Elemi, Essential, Excipient, Extender, Exudate, Fabric, Fixative, Getter, Gist, Gluten, Gossypol, Gravamen, Growth, Guanazolo, Hearty, Hefty, Indol, Inhibitor, Iodoform, Iodophor, Isatin(e), Isomer, Lecithin, Leucotriene, Linin, Luciferin, Material, Matter, Meaning, Meat(y), Metol, Mineral, Mole, Morphogen, Mucigen, Murr(h)ine, Mutagen, Naloxone, Neurotoxin, Orgone, Papier mâché, Phlogiston, Polymer, Protyl(e), Purin(e), Queen (bee), Quid, Reality, Resin, Sense, Solid, Stuff, Sum, Surfactant, Sympathin, Tabasheer, Tabashir, Tangible, Tusche, Viricide, Volutin

Substandard Infra dig, Off, Poor, Schlo(c)k, Second, Small

▸ **Substantial** *see* SUBSTANCE

Substantiate Confirm, Flesh, Prove, Strengthen, Support

Substantive Direct, Noun

Substitute, Substitution Acting, Carborundum®, Change, Changeling, Commute, Creamer, Deputy, Dextran, Double, Dub, Emergency, Ersatz, -ette, Euphemism, Eusystolism, Exchange, Fill-in, Improvise, Instead, Lieu(tenant), Locum, Makeshift, Metonymy, Pinch-hit, Proxy, Regent, Relieve, Replace, Represent, Reserve, Resolution, Ringer, Seth, Simulacrum, Stand-in, Stead, Stopgap, Subrogate, Succedaneum, Surrogate, Switch, Swop, Synthetic, Understudy, Vicar(ial), Vicarious

Substructure Base, Foundation, Keelson, Platform, Podium

Subterfuge Artifice, Chicane, Evasion, Hole, Manoeuvre, Off-come, Ruse, Strategy, Trick

Subterranean Concealed, Mattamore, Sunken, Underground, Weem

Subtle(ty) Abstruse, Alchemist, Crafty, Fine(spun), Finesse, Ingenious, Nice, Nice(ty), Refinement, Sly, Thin, Wily

Subtle difference Nuance

Subtract(ion) Commission, Deduct, Discount, Sum, Take, Tithe, Withdraw

Suburb Banlieue, Environs, Exurbia, Faubourg, Garden, Outskirts, Purlieu, Subtopia

Subversion, Subvert Fifth column, Overthrow, Reverse, Sabotage, Sedition, Treasonous, Undermine, Upset

Subway Metro, Passage, Tube, Underground

Succeed, Success(ful), Success(ful) Accomplish, Achieve, Arrive, Blockbuster, Boffo, Breakthrough, Chartbuster, Contrive, Coup, Eclat, Effective, Efficacious, Fadge, Felicity, Flourish, Follow, Fortune, Gangbuster, Get, Go, Hit, Hotshot, Inherit, Killing, Landslide, Luck, Made, Manage, Masterstroke, Mega, Midas touch, Offcome, Pass, Prevail, Procure, Prosper, Purple patch, Reach, Replace, Riot, Score, Seal, Seel, Sele, Sell out, Soaraway, Socko, Speed, Stardom, Superstar, Sure thing, Tanistry, Triumph, Up, Up and coming, Upstart, Vault,

Weather, W(h)iz(z)kid, Win, Wow, Wunderkind

Succession Apostolic, Chain, Cognate, Dead men's shoes, Line, Order, Reversion, Sequence, Seriatim, Series, Suite

Successor Co(m)arb, Deluge, Descendant, Ensuite, Epigon(e), Heir, Incomer, Inheritor, Khalifa, Next, Syen

Succinct Brief, Cereus, Compact, Concise, Houseleek, Laconic, Pithy, Short

Succour Aid, Assist, Help, Minister, Relieve, Rescue, Sustain

Succulent Agave, Cactus, Echeveria, Juicy, Lush, Rich, Saguaro, Sappy, Spekboom, Tender, Toothy

Succumb Capitulate, Fall, Go under, Surrender, Yield

Such Like, Sae, Sike, Similar, That

Suck(er), Sucking Absorb, Acetabular, Acetabulum, Amphistomous, Antlia, Aphis, Aspirator, Ass, Bull's eye, Culicidae, Dracula, Drink, Dupe, Fawn, Fellatio, Gnat, Graff, Graft, Gull, Haustellum, Haustorium, Hoove, Lamia, Lamprey, Leech, Liquorice, Mammal, Monotremata, Mouth, Mug, Muggins, Osculum, Patsy, Plunger, Remora, Rook, Shoot, Siphon, Slurp, Smarm, Spire, Spyre, Straw, Surculus, Swig, Sycophant, Tellar, Teller, Tick, Tiller, Toad-eater, Turion, Vampire

Suckle Feed, Mother, Nourish, Nurse, Nurture

Suction Adhere, Pump, Siphon

Sud(s) Foam, Sapples

Sudanese Mahdi, Nuba

Sudden(ly) Abrupt, Astart, Astert, Extempore, Ferly, Fleeting, Foudroyant, Fulminant, Hasty, Headlong, Impulsive, Overnight, Rapid, Slap, Sodain, Subitaneous, Subito, Swap, Swop, Unexpected

Sue Ask, Beseech, Dun, Entreat, Implead, Implore, Litigate, Petition, Pray, Process, Prosecute, Woo

Suede Split

Suffer(er), Suffering Abide, Aby(e), Ache, Affliction, Agonise, Auto, Be, > **BEAR**, Brook, Calvary, Cop, Die, Distress, Dree, Dukkha, Endurance, Endure, Feel, Gethsemane, Golgotha, Grief, Hardship, Have, Incur, Let, Luit, Martyr, Pain, Passible, Passion, Passive, Patible, Patience, Pellagrin, Permit, Pine, Plague, Purgatory, Stand, Stomach, Sustain, Thole, Tolerate, Toll, Torment, Trial, Tribulation, Undergo, Use, Victim

Suffering remnant Macmillanite

Suffice, Sufficient Adequate, Ample, Basta, Do, Due, Enough, Enow, Experimental, Run to, Satisfy, Serve

Suffix Enclitic

Suffocate Asphyxiate, Choke, Smoor, Smore, Smother, Stifle, Strangle, Throttle

Suffrage(tte) Ballot, Feminist, Franchise, Manhood, Vote

Suffuse Colour, Glow, Imbue, Saturate, Spread

Sugar(y), Sugar cane Aldohexose, Aldose, Amygdalin, Arabinose, Barley, Beet, Blood, Brown, Candy, Cane, Caramel, Carn(e), Cassonade, Caster, Cellobiose, Cellose, Chaptalise, Confectioner's, Daddy, Demerara, Deoxyribose, Dextrose, Disaccharide, Flattery, Fructose, Fucose, Furanose, Galactose, Gallise, Glucose, Glucosoric, Goo(r), Granulated, Grape, Gur, Heroin, Hexose, Honeydew, Hundreds and thousands, Iced, Icing, Inulin, Invert, Jaggary, Jaggery, Jagghery, Lactose, Laevulose, Loaf, Lump, Maltose, Manna, Mannose, Maple, Money, Monosaccharide, Muscovado, Nectar, Palm, Panocha, Pentose, Penuche, Raffinose, Rhamnose, Ribose, Saccharine, Saccharoid, Simple, Sis, Sorbose, Sorg(h)o, Sorghum, Sparrow, Spun, Sweet, Trehala(se), Triose, White, Wood, Xylose

Sugar-daddy Lyle, Tate

Suggest(ion), Suggestive Advance, Advice, Advise, Connote, Counter-proposal, Cue, Hint, Idea, Imply, Innuendo, Insinuate, Intimate, Mention, Modicum, Moot, Posit, Prompt, Proposal, Propound, Provocative, Racy, Raise, Recommend, Redolent, Reminiscent, Risqué, Smacks, Soft core, Suspicion, Touch, Trace, Undertone, Wind, Wrinkle

Suicide Felo-de-se, Hara-kiri, Hari-kari, Kamikaze, Lemming, Lethal, Sati, Seppuku, Shinju, Suttee

Suit Action, Adapt, Adjust, Agree, Answer, Apply, Appropriate, Become, Befit, Beho(o)ve, Bequest, Beseem, Birthday, Boiler, Cards, Case, Cat, Clubs, Conform, Courtship, Demob, Diamonds, Dittos, Diving, Do, Drapes, Dress, Effeir, Effere, Etons, Fadge, Fashion, Fit, G, Garb, Gee, Gree, Hearts, Hit, Jump, Lis pendens, Long, Lounge, Major, Mao, Match, Minor, Monkey, NBC, Noddy, Orison, Outcome, Paternity, Petition, Plaint, Play, Plea, Please, Point, Prayer, Pressure, Process, Pyjama, Quarterdeck, Queme, Romper(s), Safari, Sailor, Salopettes, Samfoo, Samfu, Satisfy, Serve, Shell, Siren, Skeleton, Slack, Space, Spades, Strong, Sun, Sunday, Supplicat, Sweat, Swim, Tailleur, Three-piece, Track, Trouser, Trumps, Tsotsi, Twin, Two-piece, Uniform, Union, Wet, Zoot

Suitable Apposite, Appropriate, Apropos, Apt, Becoming, Capable, Congenial, Consonant, Convenance, Convenient, Due, Expedient, > FIT, Giusto, Keeping, Meet, Opportune, Relevant, Seasonal, Seemly, Very, Worthy

Suite Allemande, Apartment, Chambers, Ensemble, Entourage, Hospitality, Lounge, Nutcracker, Partita, Retinue, Rooms, Serenade, Set, Skybox, Tail, Three-piece, Train, Two-piece

Suitor Beau, Gallant, John Doe, Lover, Petitioner, Pretender, Suppli(c)ant, Swain, Wooer

Sulk(y), Sulkiness B(r)oody, Dod, Dort, Gee, Glout(s), Glower, Glum, Grouchy, Grouty, Grumps, Huff, Hump, Jinker, Mardy, Maungy, Mope, Mulligrubs, Mump, Pet, Pique, Pout, Spider, Strunt, Stuffy, Stunkard, Sullen, Tout(ie), Towt, Umbrage

Sullen Dorty, Dour, Farouche, Glum(pish), Grim, Moody, Peevish, Stunkard, Sulky, Surly, Truculent

Sully Assoil, Bedye, Besmirch, Blot, Defile, Glaur(y), Smear, Smirch, Smutch, Soil, Tarnish, Tar-wash

Sulphate, Sulphide Alum, Alunite, Blende, Bluestone, Bornite, Copperas, Coquimbite, Glance, Melanterite, Pyrites, Zarnec, Zarnich

Sulphur Baregine, Brimstone, Hepar, Oleum, S, Stannite, Thionic

Sultan(a), Sultanate Brunei, Caliph, Emir, Grand Seignoir, Grand Turk, Hen, Kalif, Oman, Osman, Padishah, Roxane, Saladin, Soldan, Suleiman, Tippoo, Tipu, Wadai

Sultry Humid, Sexy, Smouldering, Steamy, Tropical

Sum(s), Sum up Add(end), Aggregate, All, Amount, Arsmetric, Bomb, Connumerate, Encapsulate, Foot, Logical, Lump, Number, Perorate, Plumule, > QUANTITY, Re-cap, Refund, Remittance, Reversion, Solidum, Total, Vector

Summarize, Summary Abridge, Abstract, Aperçu, Bird's eye, Brief, Compendium, Condense, Conspectus, Digest, Docket, Epitome, Gist, Instant, Memo, Minute, Offhand, Outline, Overview, Precis, Recap, Resume, Résumé, Round-up, Syllabus, Synopsis, Tabloid, Tabulate, Tabulation, Wrap-up

Summer(time) Aestival, August, BST, Computer, Estival, Indian, Lintel, Luke, Prime, St Luke's, St Martin's, Season, Solstice, Totter

Summerhouse Belvedere, Chalet, Conservatory, Folly, Gazebo

Summit Acme, Acri-, Apex, Braeheid, Brow, Climax, Conference, > CREST,

Crown, Height, Hillcrest, Jole, Peak, Pike, Pinnacle, Spire, Vertex, Vertical, Yalta

Summon(s) Accite, Arrière-ban, Azan, Beck(on), Call, Cist, Cital, Citation, Command, Conjure, Convene, Convent, Drum, Evoke, Garnishment, Gong, Hail, Invocation, Muster, Order, Page, Post, Preconise, Rechate, Recheat, Reveille, Signal, Sist, Ticket, Warn, Warrant, Whoop, Writ

Sumo Makunouchi

Sump Bilge, Drain, Pool, Sink

Sumpter Led horse, Pack-horse

Sumptuous Expensive, Lavish, Palatial, Rich(ly), Superb

Sun(-god), Sunlight, Sunny, Sunshine Albedo, Amen-Ra, Amon-Ra, Apollo, Ashine, Aten, Bright, Cheer, Combust, Daily, Day(star), Dry, Earthshine, Glory, Heater, Helio(s), Helius, Horus, Mean, Midnight, New Mexico, Paranthelion, Parhelion, Pet-day, Phoebean, Photosphere, Ra, Radiant, Rays, Re, Rising, Shamash, Sol(ar), Soleil, Sonne, Surya, Svastika, Swastika, Tabloid, Tan, Titan, UV

Sunbathe Apricate, Bask, Brown, Tan

Sunbeam Car, Ray

Sunburn Bronze, Combust, Peeling, Tan

Sunday Advent, Best, Cantate, Care, Carle, Carling, Dominical, Easter, Fig, Jubilate, Judica, Laetare, Lord's Day, Lost, Low, Mid-Lent, Mothering, Orthodox, Palm, Passion, Quadragesima, Quasimodo, Quinquagesima, Refection, Refreshment, Remembrance, Rogation, Rose, Rush-bearing, S, Septuagesima, Sexagesima, Stir-up, Tap-up, Trinity, Whit

Sunday school SS

Sunder Divide, Divorce, Part, Separate, Sever, Split

Sundew Drosera, Eyebright

Sundial Analemma, Gnomon, Solarium

Sundry Divers, Several, Various

Sunflower Kansas, KS

Sunglasses Shades

▸ **Sun-god** *see* SUN

▸ **Sunken** *see* SINK

Sunrise, Sun-up Aurora, Cosmical, Dawn, East

Sunset Acronical, Evening

Sunshade Awning, Brise-soleil, Canopy, Chi(c)k, Cloud, Parasol, Umbrella

Sunspot Facula, Freckle, Macula

Sunstroke Heliosis, Siriasis

Sunwise Deasi(u)l, Deasoil, Deis(h)eal, Eutropic

Sun-worshipper Heliolater

Sup Dine, Eat, Feast, Sample, Sip, Swallow

Super A1, Arch, Extra, Fab(ulous), Great, Grouse, Ideal, Lulu, Paramount, Superb, Terrific, Tip-top, Tops, Walker-on, Wizard

Superadded Advene

Superb A1, Concours, Fine, Grand, Great, Majestic, Peerless, Phat, Splendid, Top-notch

Supercilious Aloof, Arrogant, Bashaw, Cavalier, Haughty, Lordly, Snide, Sniffy, Snooty, Snotty, Snouty, Superior, Toffee-nosed, Upstage

Superficial Cosmetic, Cursenary, Cursory, Dilettante, Exterior, Facile, Glib, Outside, Outward, Overlying, Perfunctory, Shallow, Sketchy, Skindeep, Smattering, Veneer

▷ **Superficial(ly)** *may indicate* a word outside another

Superfluous, Superfluity Cheville, De trop, Extra, Lake, Mountain, Needless, Otiose, Pleonastic, Plethora, Redundant, Spare, Unnecessary

Superhuman Bionic, Herculean, Heroic, Supernatural

Superintend(ent) Boss, Director, Foreman, Guide, Janitor, Oversee(r), Preside, Sewer, Supercargo, Surveillant, Warden, Zanjero

Superior(ity) Abbess, Abeigh, Above, Advantage, Aloof, Atop, Better, Brahmin, Choice, Condescending, Custos, De luxe, Dinger, Eminent, Excellent, Exceptional, Finer, Herrenvolk, High-grade, Lake, Liege, Mastery, Morgue, Mother, Nob, Outstanding, Over, Paramount, Predominance, Prestige, Pretentious, Prior, Superordinate, Supremacy, Swell, Top(-loftical), Transcendent(al), U, Udal, Upper(most), Uppish, Upstage

Superlative Best, Exaggerated, Peerless, Smasheroo, Supreme, Utmost

Superman Batman, Bionic, Titan, Ubermensch

Supermarket Co-op, Fund, GUM, Self service, Store

Supernatural Divine, Eerie, Fey, Fie, Fly, Gothic, Kachina, Mana, Metaphysical, Paranormal, Sharp, Siddhi, Uncanny, Unearthly, Wight

Supernova Plerion

Supernumerary Additional, Corollary, Extra, Mute, Orra

Supersede Replace, Stellenbosch, Supplant

Superstition Aberglaube, Abessa, Fable, Folk-lore, Freet, Myth, Uncertainty

Superstructure Mastaba(h)

Supertonic Ray

Supervise(d), Supervision, Supervisor Administer, Chaperone, Check, Direct, Engineer, Floorwalker, Foreman, Grieve, Handle, Honcho, Invigilate, Manager, Officiate, Overman, Oversee(r), Probation, Shopwalker, Stage-manage, Targe, Under, Walla(h)

Supine Inactive, Inert, Lying, Protract

Supper Dinner, > DRINK(ER), Hawkey, Hockey, Horkey, Last, Meal, Nagmaal, Repast, Soirée

Supplant Displace, Exchange, Oust, Replace, Substitute, Supersede

Supple Compliant, Leish, Limber, Lissom(e), > LITHE, Loose, Loose-limbed, Pliable, Souple, Wan(d)le, Wannel, Whippy

Supplement(ary) Addend(um), Addition, And, Annex(e), Appendix, Augment, Auxiliary, Codicil, Colour, Eche, Eke, Extra, Incaparina, Paralipomena, Postscript, Relay, Ripienist, Ripieno, Weighting

Supplicant, Supplicate Beg, Entreat, Importune, Invoke, Petition, Plead, Request, Schnorr, Sue

Supplier, Supplies, Supply Accommodate, Advance, Afford, Cache, Cater, Commissariat, Contribute, Crop, Endue, Equip, Excess, Exempt, Feed, Fill, Find, Fit, Foison, Fund, Furnish, Give, Grist, Grubstake, Heel, Holp(en), Indue, Issue, Lend, Lithely, Mains, Materiel, Pipeline, Plenish, Ply, > PROVIDE, Provision, Purvey, RASC, Retailer, Serve, Source, Stake, Stock, > STORE, Viands, Vintner, Water, Widow's cruse, Yield

Support(er), Supporting Abacus, Abet, Abutment, Adherent, Adminicle, Advocate, Affirm, Aficionado, Aid, Aidance, Aliment(ative), Ally, Ammunition, Anchor, Ancillary, Andiron, Anta, Appui, Arch, Arm, Assistant, Axle, Back(bone), Back-up, Baculum, Baluster, Banister, Bankroll, Barrack, Barre, Base, Batten, Beam, Bear, Befriend, Belt, Bibb, Bier, Bolster, Boom, Bouclée, Bra, Brace, Bracket, Brassiere, Breadwinner, Breast-summer, Bridge, Bridgeboard, Buttress, C(ee)-spring, Chair, Champion, Chaptrel, Clientele, Column, Confirm, Console, Corbel, Corbel-table, Cornerstone, Countenance, Cradle, Cross-beam, Crutch, Dado, Diagrid, Dog-shore, Doula,

Easel, Encourage, Endorse, Endow, Engager, Espouse, Family, Fan, Favour, Fid, Finance, Flying buttress, Fly-rail, Footrest, Footstool, For, Gamb, Gantry, Garter, Girder, Glia, Grass roots, Groundswell, Harpin(g)s, Headrest, Help, Henchman, Horse, Hound, Idealogue, Impost, Income, Instantiate, Ite, Jack, Jockstrap, Joist, Keep, Kingpost, Knee, Knighthead, Lectern, Leg, Lierne, Lifebelt, Lifebuoy, Lobby, Loper, Loyalist, Mahlstick, Mainstay, Maintain, Makefast, Miserere, Misericord(e), Monial, Moral, Mortsafe, Nervure, Neuroglia, -nik, Nourish, Paranymph, Parawalker, Partisan, Partizan, Partners, Patronage, Pedestal, Pessary, Pier, Pillar, Pin, Plinth, Poppet, Post, Potent, Price, Prop, Proponent, Prop-root, PTA, Pull-for, Purlin(e), Purlins, Pylon, Raft, Rally round, Reinforce, Relieve, Respond, Rest, Rind, Rod, Roof-plate, Root, Royalist, Rynd, Samaritan, Sanction, Sawhorse, Second, Shore, Skeg, Skeleton, Skewput, Skid, Sleeper, Sling, Snotter, Socle, Solidarity, Splat, Splint, Sponson, Sprag, Spud, Staddle, Staddlestone, Staff, Staging, Stake, Stalwart, Stanchion, Stand(-by), Stay, Steady, Stem(pel), Step, Stick, Stirrup, Stool, Stringer, Strut, Stylobate, Subscribe, Subsidy, Succour, Suffragist, Summer, Suppedaneum, Suspender, Sustain, Tailskid, Tee, Telamon, Tendril, Third, Tie, Tige, Torsel, Trabecula, Tress(el), Trestle, Tripod, Trivet, Truss, Underlay, Underpin, Understand, Unipod, Uphold, Upkeep, Viva, Waterwings, Y-level, Zealot

Suppose(d), Supposition An, Assume, Believe, Expect, Guess, Hypothetical, Idea, If, Imagine, Imply, Opine, Presume, Putative, Said, Sepad, Theory

Suppress(ion) Abolish, Adaw, Burke, Cancel, Censor, Clampdown, Crush, Cushion, Ecthlipsis, Elide, Elision, Gleichschaltung, Hush-up, Mob(b)le, Quash, Quell, Quench, Restrain, Silence, Smother, Squash, Stifle, Submerge, Subreption, Throttle

Suppurate, Suppuration Diapyesis, Discharge, Exude, Fester, Maturate, Ooze, Pus, Pyorrhoea, Rankle

Supreme, Supremacy, Supremo Apical, Baaskap, Caudillo, Consummate, Kronos, Leader, Napoleon, Overlord, Paramount, Peerless, Regnant, Sovereign, Sublime, Sudder, Superlative, Top, Utmost, White

Surcharge Addition, Extra, Tax

Surd Voiceless

Sure(ly) Assured, Ay, Bound, Cert(ain), Confident, Definite, Doubtless, Firm, Infallible, Know, Pardi(e), Pardy, Perdie, Positive, Poz, Safe, Secure, Shoo-in, Sicker, Syker, Uh-huh, Yep, Yes

Surety Bail, Frithborth, Guarantee, Mainprise, Security, Sponsional

Surf(er) Breach, Breaker, Grommet, Rollers, Rote, Sea, Waxhead

Surface Aerofoil, Appear, Area, Arise, Camber, Control, Day, Dermal, Dermis, Emerge, Epigene, Exterior, External, Face, Facet, Flock, Macadam, Meniscus, Outcrop, Outward, Paintwork, Patina, Pave, Plane, Reveal, Rise, Salband, Side, Skin, Soffit, Spandrel, Superficial, Superficies, Tarmac®, Tar-seal, Texture, Top, Toroid, Worktop

Surf-boat Masoola(h), Masula

Surfeit(ed) Blasé, Cloy, Excess, Glut, Overcloy, Plethora, Satiate, Stall, Staw

▷ **Surfer** *may indicate* programming

Surge Billow, Boom, Drive, Gush, Onrush, S(c)end, Seethe, Storm, Sway, Swell

Surgeon Abernethy, BCh, BS, CHB, CM, Doctor, House, Lister, Medic, Operator, Orthopod, Plastic, Sawbones, Staff, Tang, Vet(erinary)

Surgery Anaplasty, Cosmetic, Facelift, Keyhole, Knife, Laparotomy, Laser, Medicine, Nip and tuck, Nose job, Op, Open-heart, Osteoplasty, Plastic, Prosthetics, Reconstructive, Repair, Spare-part, Ta(g)liacotian, Zolatrics

Surly Bluff, Cantankerous, Chough, Chuffy, Churl(ish), Crabby, Crusty, Cynic, Glum, Gruff, Grum, Grumpy, Rough, Sullen, Truculent

Surmise Extrapolate, Guess, Imagine, Infer, Presume, Suppose

Surmount Beat, Climb, Conquer, Crest, Master, Overcome, Scan, Superate, Tide, Transcend

Surname Cognomen, Patronymic

Surpass Bang, Beat, Best, Cap, Cote, Ding, Eclipse, Efface, Exceed, Excel, Outdo, Outgun, Out-Herod, Outreach, Outshine, Outstrip, Overtop, Transcend

Surplice Cotta, Ephod, Rochet, Sark, Serk, Vakass

Surplus Excess, Extra, Glut, Lake, Mountain, Out-over, Over, Overage, Overcome, Remainder, Rest, Spare, Surfeit

Surprise(d), Surprising Alert, Amaze, Ambush, Arrah, Astonish, Bewilder, Blimey, Boilover, Bombshell, By Jove, Caramba, Catch, Confound, Coo, Cor, Crick(e)y, Crikey, Criminé, Cripes, Criv(v)ens, Dear, Eye-opener, Gadso, Gee, Geewhiz, Gemini, Geminy, Gemony, Gobsmacked, Golly, Good-lack, Gorblimey, Gordon Bennett, Gosh, Ha, Hah, Hallo, Heavens, Heck, Heh, Hello, Hey, Ho, Jeepers, Jeez(e), Law, Lawks, Lor, Lordy, Lummy, Marry, Musha, My, Obreption, Och, Odso, Omigod, Oops, Open-mouthed, Overtake, Phew, Pop-eyed, Really, Sheesh, Shock, Singular, Spot, Stagger, Startle, Strewth, Struth, Stun, Sudden, Treat, Turn-up, Uh, Whew, Whoops, Wonderment, Wow, Wrongfoot, Yikes, Yow, Zinger, Zowie

Surrealist Bizarre, Dali, Ernst, Grotesque, Magritte, Man Ray, Miro

Surrender Capitulate, Cave-in, Cession, Enfeoff, Extradite, Fall, Forego, Forfeit, Handover, Hulled, Kamerad, Naam, Recreant, Release, Relinquish, Remise, Rendition, Submit, Succumb, Waive, > **YIELD**

Surreptitious Clandestine, Covert, Fly, Furtive, Secret, Sly, Stealthy, Underhand

Surrey Carriage, Sy

Surrogate Agent, Depute, Deputy, Locum, Proxy

Surround(ed), Surrounding(s) Ambient, Amongst, Architrave, Background, Bathe, Bego, Beset, Bundwall, Circumvallate, Circumvent, Compass, Doughnutting, Ecology, Emball, Encase, > **ENCIRCLE**, Enclave, Enclose, Encompass, Enfold, Envelop, Environ, Enwrap, Fence, Gherao, Gird, Hedge, Hem in, Impale, Invest, Mid, Orb, Orle, Outflank, Outside, Perimeter, Setting, Wall

Surtees Jorrocks, Sponge

Surveillance, Survey(ing), Surveyor Behold, Cadastre, Case, Conspectus, Dialler, Domesday, Doomwatch, Espial, Examination, Eye, Geodesy, Groma, Look-see, Once-over, Ordnance, Patrol, Poll, Quantity, Recce, Reconnaissance, Regard, Review, Scan, Scrutiny, Stakeout, Straw poll, Supervision, Terrier, Theodolite, Triangulate, Trilateration, Vigil, Watch

Survival, Survive, Surviving, Survivor Cope, Die hard, Endure, Extant, Finalist, Hibakusha, Last, Leftover, Outdure, Outlast, Outlive, Outwear, Overlive, Persist, Relic(t), Ride, Street-wise, Viability, Warhorse, Weather

Susan Lazy

Susceptible, Susceptibility Anaphylaxis, Impressionable, Liable, Receptive, Vulnerable

Suspect, Suspicion, Suspicious Askance, Breath, Dodgy, Doubt, Dubious, Fishy, Grain, Guess, Hint, Hunch, Jalouse, Jealous, Leery, Misdeem, Misdoubt, Misgiving, Mislippen, Mistrust, Modicum, Notion, Paranoia, Queer, Scent, Smatch, Soupçon, Thought, Tinge, Whiff

▷ **Suspect, Suspicious** *may indicate* an anagram

Suspend(ed), Suspense, Suspension Abate, Abeyance, Adjourn, Anabiosis,

Anti-shock, Cliffhanger, Colloid, Dangle, Defer, Delay, Dormant, Freeze, Ground, > HANG, Hydraulic, Independent, Intermit, Mist, Moratorium, Nailbiter, Pensile, Poise, Prorogue, Put on ice, Reprieve, Respite, Rub out, Rusticate, Sideline, Sol, Stand off, Swing, Tenterhooks, Truce, Withhold

▷ **Suspended** *may indicate* 'ice' (on ice) at the end of a down light

Sussex Rape

Sustain(ed), **Sustaining**, **Sustenance** Abide, Afford, Aliment, Bear, Constant, Depend, Endure, Food, Keep, Last, Maintain, Nutrient, Nutriment, Pedal, Prolong, Sostenuto, Succour, Support, Tenuto, Upbear

Sutler Vivandière

Suture Button, Catgut, Cobbler, Lambda, Pterion, Purse-string, Stitch

Suzanne, **Suzie** Lenglen, Wong

Svelte Lithe, Slender, Slim

Swab Dossil, Dry, Mop, Pledget, Scour, Sponge, Squeegee, Stupe, Tampon, Tompon, Wipe

Swaddle, **Swaddling** Bind, Envelop, Incunabula, Swathe, Wrap

Swag Booty, Encarpus, Festoon, Haul, Loot, Maino(u)r, Manner, Matilda, Shiralee, Toran(a)

Swagger(er), **Swaggering** Birkie, Bluster, Boast, Brag, Bragadisme, Bravado, Bucko, Cock, Crow, Jaunty, Matamore, Nounce, Panache, Pra(u)nce, Roist, Roll, Rollick, Roul, Royster, Ruffle, Side, Strive, Swank, Swash(-buckler), Tigerism

Swain Amoretti, Beau, Churl, Corin, Damon, Hind, Lover, Rustic, Shepherd, Strephon, Wooer

Swallow(able), **Swallowing** Aerophagia, Ariel, Barn, Bird, Bolt, Cliff, Consume, Deglutition, Devour, Down, Drink, Eat, Endue, Englut, Engulf, Engulph, Esculent, Glug, Gobble, Gula, Gulp, Hirundine, Incept, Ingest, Ingulf, Ingurgitate, Itys, Lap, Martin, Martlet, Progne, Quaff, Shift, Sister, Slug, Stomach, Swig, Take, Take off

Swamp(y) Bog, Bunyip, Cowal, Cypress, Deluge, Dismal, Drown, Engulf, Everglade, Flood, Great Dismal, Inundate, Lentic, Lerna, Lerne, Loblolly, Mar(i)sh, Morass, Muskeg, Okavango, Okefenokee, Overrun, Overwhelm, Paludal, Quagmire, Slash, Slough, Sudd, Uliginous, Urman, Vlei, Vly, Wetland

Swan(s) Avon, Bewick's, Bird, Black, Cob, Cygnet, Cygnus, Game, Leda, Lindor, Mute, Pen, Seven, Seward, Song, Stroll, Trumpeter, Whistling, Whooper, Whooping

Swank(y) Boast, Lugs, Pretentious, Side, Style

Swan-song Finale, Last air

Swap, **Swop** > BARTER, Chop, Commute, Exchange, Scorse, Switch, Trade, Truck

▷ **Swap(ped)** *may indicate* an anagram

Sward Grass, Green, Lawn, Sod, Turf

Swarm(ing) Abound, Alive, Bike, Bink, Byke, Cast, Cloud, Crowd, Flood, Geminid, Hoatching, Host, Hotter, Infest, Meteor, Overrun, Pullulate, Rife, Shin, Shoal, Throng

Swarthy Dark, Dusky, Melanotic

Swash Swig, Swill

Swash-buckler Adventurer, Boaster, Braggart, Gascon, Swordsman

Swastika Filfot, Fylfot, Gamma(dion), Hakenkreuz

▶ **Swat** *see* SWOT

Swathe Bind, Enfold, Enroll, Swaddle, Wrap

Sway(ing) Careen, Carry, Command, Diadrom, Domain, Dominion, Flap, Fluctuate, Govern, Hegemony, Influence, Lilt, Oscillate, Prevail, Reel, Reign, Rock, Roll, Rule, Shog, Shoogle, Swag, Swale, Swee, Swing(e), Teeter, Titter,

Totter, Vacillate

Swear(ing), **Swear word** Attest, Avow, Coprolalia, Curse, Cuss, Depose, Execrate, Expletive, Invective, Jurant, Juratory, Oath, Pledge, Plight, Rail, Sessa, Tarnal, Tarnation, Verify, Vow

Sweat(ing), **Sweaty** Apocrine, Beads, Clammy, Cold, Diaphoresis, Excrete, Exude, Flop, Forswatt, Glow, Hidrosis, Lather, Ooze, Osmidrosis, > **PERSPIRE**, Secretion, Slave, Stew, Sudament, Sudamina, Sudate, Swelter

Sweater Aran, Argyle, Circassian, Circassienne, Cowichan, Fair Isle, Gansey, Guernsey, Indian, Jersey, Polo, Pullover, Roll-neck, Siwash, Skivvy, Slip-on, Slop-pouch, Sloppy Joe, Turtleneck, Woolly

Swede Nordic, Rutabaga, Scandinavian, Turnip

Sweeney Police, Todd

Sweep(er), **Sweeping(s)** Besom, Broad, Broom, Brush, Chimney, Chummy, Clean, Curve, Debris, Detritus, Expanse, Extensive, Lash, Libero, Lottery, Net, Oars, Pan, Phasing, Police-manure, Range, Scavenger, Scud, Sling, Snowball, Soop, Sooterkin, Street, Stroke, Surge, Swathe, Vacuum, Waft, Well, Wide

Sweepstake Draw, Gamble, Lottery, Raffle, Tattersall's, Tombola

Sweet(s), **Sweetener**, **Sweetmeat**, **Sweetness** Adeline, Afters, Alcorza, Aldose, Amabile, Aspartame, Barley sugar, Bombe, Bonbon, Bonus, Brandyball, Bribe, Bull's eye, Burnt-almonds, Butterscotch, Candy, Candyfloss, Caramel, Chaptalise, Charity, Charming, Cherubic, Choc(olate), Choccy, Cloying, Coconut ice, Comfit, Confect(ion), Confetti, Confiserie, Confit, Conserve, Crème, Cute, Cyclamate, > **DESSERT**, Dolce, Dolly, Dolly mixture, Douce(t), Dowset, Dragée, Dulcet, Dulcitude, Elecampane, Flummery, Fondant, Fool, Fragrant, Fresh, Fudge, Glucose, Glycerin, Gob-stopper, Goody, Gum(drop), Gundy, Hal(a)vah, Halva, Honey(ed), Humbug, Hundreds and thousands, Ice, Icky, Indican, Jelly baby, Jelly bean, Jube, Jujube, Kiss, Lavender, Lemon drop, Licorice, Liquorice, Lollipop, Lolly, Lozenge, Luscious, Marchpane, Marshmallow, Marzipan, Melodious, Mint, Mousse, Muscavado, Nectared, Noisette, Nonpareil, Nougat, Pandrop, Pastille, Pea, Peardrop, Pet, Pick'n'mix, Pie, Praline, Pud(ding), Redolent, Rock, Romic, Saccharin(e), Scroggin, Seventeen, Sillabub, Sixteen, Solanine, Soot(e), Sop, Sorbet, Spice, Split, Stickjaw, Sucker, Sucrose, Sugar, Sugarplum, Syllabub, Syrupy, Tablet, Taffy, Tart, Thaumatin, Toffee, Torte, Trifle, Truffle, Turkish delight, Twee, Uses, William, Winsome, Xylitol, Zabaglione

Sweetbread Bur(r), Inchpin, Pancreas

Sweetheart Amoret, Amour, Beau, Dona(h), Dowsabel(l), Doxy, Dulcinea, Flame, Follower, Honey(bunch), Honeybun, Jarta, Jo(e), Lass, Leman, Lover, Masher, Neaera, Peat, Romeo, Steady, Toots(y), True-love, Valentine, Yarta, Yarto

Sweet-seller Butcher, Confectioner

Swell(ing) Adenomata, Ague-cake, Anasarca, Aneurysm, Apophysis, Bag, Bellying, Berry, Billow, Blab, Blister, Bloat, Blow, Boil, Boll, Bolster, Botch, Braw, Bubo, Bulb, Bulge, Bump, Bunion, Capellet, Carnosity, Cat, Chancre, Chilblain, Clour, Cratches, Curb, Cyst, Dandy, Desmoid, Diapason, Dilate, > **DISTEND**, Dom, Don, Eche, Ectasia, Eger, Elephantiasis, Enhance, Entasis, Epulis, Excellent, Farcy-bud, Frog, Gall, Gathering, Gent, Goiter, Goitre, Gout, Grandee, Ground, H(a)ematoma, Heave, Heighten, Hove, Hydrocele, Hydroma, Hygroma, Increase, Inflate, Intumesce, Kibe, L, Lampas(se), Lampers, Louden, Lump, Macaroni, Mouse, Nodule, Odontoma, Oedema, OK, Onco-, Ox-warble, Parotitis, Plim, Plump, Protrude, Protuberance, Proud, Pulvinus, Rise, Roil, Scirrhus, Scleriasis, Sea, Shinsplints, Splenomegaly, Strout, Struma, Stye,

Surge, Teratoma, Toff, Torose, Torulose, Tragus, Tuber(cle), Tumescence,
Tumour, Tympany, Upsurge, Varicocele, Venter, Wallow, Warble, Wen, Whelk,
Windgall, Xanthoma

▷ **Swelling** *may indicate* a word reversed

Swelter(ing) Perspire, Stew, Sweat, Tropical

Swerve, Swerving Bias, Broach, Careen, Deflect, Deviate, Lean, Sheer, Shy,
Stray, Swee, Swing, Warp, Wheel

Swift(ly) Apace, Bird, Dean, Dromond, Fleet, Flock, Hasty, Martlet, Newt,
Nimble, Presto, Prompt, Pronto, Quick, > **RAPID**, Reel, Slick, Spanking,
Velocipede, Wight

Swig Drink, Gulp, Nip, Scour, Swill, Tighten

Swill Guzzle, Leavings, Rubbish, Slosh, Swash

▷ **Swilling** *may indicate* an anagram

Swim(ming) Bathe, Bogey, Bogie, Crawl, Dip, Float, Naiant, Natatorial, Paddle,
Reel, Run, Skinny-dip, Soom, Synchro(nized), Trudgen, Whirl

▷ **Swim** *may indicate* an anagram

Swimmer Bather, Cichlid, Duckbill, Duckmole, Dugong, Frogman, Leander,
Pad(d)le, Paidle, Planula, Pleopod, Pobble, Terrapin, Trudgen, Webb

▷ **Swimmer** *may indicate* a fish

Swimming costume Bathers, Bikini, Cossie, Maillot, Monokini, One-piece,
Tanga, Tankini, Tog, Trunks

Swindle(r) Beat, Bite, Bucket-shop, Bunco, Bunkosteerer, Cajole, Champerty,
> **CHEAT**, Chouse, Con, Crimp, Defraud, Diddle, Do, Escroc, Fiddle, Finagle,
Fineer, Fleece, Fraud, Gazump, Gip, Goose-trap, Graft, Grifter, Gyp, Hocus,
Hoser, Hustler, Leg, Leger, Long-firm, Magsman, Mountebank, Mulct, Nobble,
Peter Funk, Plant, Racket, Ramp, Rig, Rogue, Scam, Sell, Shark, Sharper,
Shicer, Shyster, Skelder, Skin, Skin game, Sting, Stitch-up, Stumer, Suck,
Swiz(z), Trick, Twist, Two-time

Swine(herd) Boar, Brute, Cad, Eumaeus, Gadarene, Heel, Hog, Peccary, Pig,
Porcine, Pork, Rotter, Sounder, Sow, Sybotic

Swing(er), Swinging Colt, Dangle, Flail, Hang, Hep, Kip(p), Lilt, Metronome,
Mod, Music, Oscillate, Pendulate, Pendulum, Rock, Rope, Shoogie, Shuggy,
Slew, Swale, Sway, Swee, Swerve, Swey, Swipe, Trapeze, Vibratile, Voop, Wave,
Wheel, Whirl, Yaw

Swipe(s) Backhander, Beer, Haymaker, Steal, Strike, Tap-lash

Swirl Eddy, Purl, Swoosh, Tourbill(i)on, Twist, Whirl

▷ **Swirling** *may indicate* an anagram

Swish Cane, Frou-frou, Rustle, Smart, Whir, Whisper

Swiss Genevese, Ladin, Roll, Tell, Vaudois

Switch(ed), Switches, Switching Birch, Change, Convert, Crossbar, Cryotron,
Dimmer, Dip, Exchange, Gang, Hairpiece, Knife, Legerdemain, Mercury,
Message, Pear, Replace, Retama, Rocker, Rod, Scutch, Thyristor, Time, Toggle,
Trip, Tumbler, Twig, Wave, Zap

▷ **Switched** *may indicate* an anagram

Switzerland CH, Helvetia

Swivel Caster, Pivot, Root, Rotate, Spin, Terret, Territ, Torret, Turret, Wedein

Swiz Chiz(z)

Swollen Blown, Bollen, Bombe, Bulbous, Full, Gourdy, Gouty, Incrassate,
Nodose, Puffy, Tumid, Turgescent, Turgid, Varicose, Ventricose, Vesiculate

Swoon Blackout, Collapse, Deliquium, Dover, Dwa(l)m, Dwaum, Faint

Swoop Descend, Dive, Glide, Plummet, Souse

▸ **Swop** *see* **SWAP**

Sword(-like), **Swordplay** Andrew Ferrara, Anelace, Angurvadel, Anlace, Arondight, Assegai, Balisarda, Balmung, Bilbo, Blade, Brand, Brandiron, Broad(sword), Brondyron, Caliburn, Cemitare, Claymore, Colada, Court, Curtal-ax, Curtana, Curtax, Cutlass, Daisho, Damascene, Damaskin, Damocles, Dance, Dirk, Duranda(l), Durindana, Ensate, Ensiform, Epée, Espada, Estoc, Excalibur, Falchion, Faulchi(o)n, Firangi, Foil, Forte, Fox, Gladius, Glaive, Gleave, Glorious, Hanger, Iai-do, Jacob's staff, Joyeuse, Katana, Kendo, Khanda, Kirpan, Kreese, Kris, Kukri, Kusanagi, Machete, Mandau, Merveilleuse, Mimming, Montanto, Morglay, Nothung, Parang, Philippan, Rapier, Rosse, Sabre, Samurai, Schiavone, Schlager, Scimitar, Semita(u)r, Shabble, Shamshir, Sharp, Sigh, Simi, Skene-dhu, Smallsword, Spadroon, Spirtle, Spit, Spurtle(blade), Steel, Toasting-iron, Toledo, Tuck, Tulwar, Two-edged, Waster, Whinger, Whiniard, Whinyard, White-arm, Xiphoid, Yatag(h)an

Sword-bearer, **Swordsman**, **Swordswoman** Aramis, Athos, Blade, Brenda(n), D'Artagnon, Fencer, Frog, Gladiator, Matador, Porthos, Selictar, Spadassin, Spadroon, Spartacus, Swashbuckler, Zorro

Sword-dancer Matachin

Swordfish Espada, Istiophorus, Xiphias

Sword-swallower Samite

Swot Dig, Grind, Kill, Mug, Read up, Smug, Stew, Strike, Swat

Sybarite Aristippus, Epicure, Hedonist, Voluptuary

Sycamore Acer, Maple, Plane, Tree

Sycophant(ic) Apple polisher, Brown-nose, Claqueur, Crawler, Creeper, Damocles, Fawner, Gnathonic, Lickspittle, Parasite, Pickthank, Placebo, Toad-eater, Toady, Yesman

Syllabary Hiragana, Kana, Katakana

Syllable(s) Acatalectic, Anacrusis, Aretinian, Nonsense, Om, Tonic

Syllabus Program(me), Prospectus, Résumé, Summary, Table

Syllogism Argument, Conclusion, Deduction, Enthymeme, Epicheirema

Sylph Ariel, Nymph

Symbol(ic), **Symbols**, **Symbolism**, **Symbolist** Acrophony, Agma, Algebra, Allegory, Ampersand, Aniconic, Ankh, Apostrophus, Aramanth, Asterisk, Badge, Cachet, Caret, Cedilla, Character, Chord, Choropleth, Cipher, Clef, Colon, Crest, Daffodil, Decadent, Del, Descriptor, Diesis, Dingbat, Double-axe, Eagle, Emblem, Emoticon, Eng, Equal, Fertility, Grammalogue, Grapheme, Hash, Heitiki, Hieroglyph, Hierogram, Hiragana, Ichthus, Icon, Iconography, Ideogram, Index, Kalachakra, Kanji, Length mark, Lexigram, Logo(gram), Logograph, Mandala, Mark, Menorah, Metaphor, Mezuzah, Minus, Mogen David, Moral, Motif, Mystical, Nabla, Neum(e), Nominal, Notation, Obelus, Om, One, Ouroborus, Paragraph, Pentacle, Phonetic, Phonogram, Phraseogram, Pi, Pictograph, Plus, Presa, Redon, Rose, Rune, Segno, Semicolon, Semiotic, Shamrock, Sigla, Sign, Slur, Smiley, Star of David, Status, Svastika, Swastika, Syllabary, Syllabogram, Synthetism, Tag, Talisman, Thistle, Tiki, Tilde, Token, Totem, Trademark, Triskele, Triskelion, Type, Uraeus, Wild card, Yoni

Symmetric(al), **Symmetry** Balance, Digonal, Diphycercal, Even, Harmony, Isobilateral, Mirror, Pseudocubic, Radial, Regular, Skew

Sympathetic, **Sympathise(r)**, **Sympathy** Approval, Commiserate, Commiseration, Compassion, Condole(nce), Condone, Congenial, Crypto, Empathy, Fellow-traveller, Humane, Par, Pity, Rapport, Ruth, Side, Vicarious

Symphony Concert, Eroica, Fifth, Jupiter, Manfred, Music, New World, Opus,

Pastoral, Sinfonia, Sinfonietta, Unfinished

Symposium Assembly, Conference, Synod

Symptom(s) Epiphenomenon, Feature, Indicia, Merycism, Mimesis, Prodrome, Semiotic, Sign, Syndrome, Token, Trait, Withdrawal

Synagogue Beit Knesset, Beth Knesseth, Shul, Temple

Synchronise(r) Coincide, Genlock, Tune

Syncopated, Syncopation, Syncope Abridged, Breakbeat, Revamp, Vasovagal, Zoppa, Zoppo

Syndicate Associate, Cartel, Combine, Mafioso, Pool, Ring, Stokvel

Syndrome Adams-Stokes, Asperger's, Carpal tunnel, Cerebellar, Characteristic, China, Chronic fatigue, Compartment, Cri du chat, Crush, Cushing's, Down's, Empty nest, Fetal alcohol, Fragile X, Goldenhar's, Gorlin, Guillain-Barré, Gulf War, Hutchinson-Gilford, Jerusalem, Klinefelter's, Korsakoff's, Locked-in, Marfan, ME, Menières, Munch(h)ausen's, Nonne's, Overuse, Pattern, POS, Postviral, Prader-Willi, Premenstrual, Proteus, Reiter's, Reye's, SARS, Sezary, Sick building, Sjogren's, Stevens-Johnson, Stockholm, Stokes-Adams, Sturge-Weber, Tall-poppy, Temperomandibular, TMJ, Tourette's, Toxic shock, Turner's, Wag the Dog, Wernicke-Korsakoff, Wobbler, XYY

Synod Assembly, Conference, Convocation, Whitby

Synonym(ous) Comparison, Reciprocal

Synopsis Abstract, Blurb, Conspectus, Digest, Outline, Résumé, Schema,
> SUMMARY

Syntax Grammar

Synthesis Amalgam, Aperture, Fusion, Merger

Synthesizer Moog®, Vocoder, Wind

Synthetic Empirical, Ersatz, Fake, False, Mock, Plastic, Polyamide, Silicone, Spencerian

Syphilis Chancre, Lues, Pip

Syrian Aramaean, Aramaic, Druse, Druz(e), Hittite, Hurrian, Levantine, Phoenician

Syringe(s) Douche, Flutes, Harpoon, Hypo, Hypodermic, Needle, Reeds, Spray, Squirt, Wash, Works

Syrphid Hoverfly

Syrup Capillaire, Cassis, Cocky's joy, Corn, Diacodion, Diacodium, Flattery, Golden, Grenadine, Linctus, Maple, Molasses, Moskonfyt, Orgeat, Quiddany, Rob, Sorghum, Sugar, Treacle

System(s), Systematic ABO, An mo, Bertillon, Binary, Braille, Code, Compander, Continental, Copernican, Cosmos, Course, Crystal, Decimal, Delsarte, Dewey (Decimal), Distributed, Early warning, Economy, Eocene, Ergodic, Establishment, Expert, Feudal, Formal, Giorgi, Grading, Harvard, HLA, Iastic, Immune, Imprest, Imputation, Inertial, Kalamazoo, Life-support, Limbic, Linear, Loop, Lymphatic, Madras, Merit, > METHOD, Metric, Microcosm, Midi, Miocene, Nervous, Network, Nicam, Notation, Octal, Operating, Order, Organon, Panel, Periodic, Permian, Pleiocene, Plenum, Points, Process, Ptolemaic, Purchase, Quota, Realtime, Regime, Regular, Respiratory, Root, Scheme, Scientific, Servo, SI, Sofar, Solar, Sonar, Sound, Spoils, Sprinkler, Squish lip, Stack(ing), Staff, Stanislavski, Star, Structure, Studio, Tally, Ternary, Theory, Tommy, Touch, Trias(sic), Truck, Turnkey, Tutorial, Two-party, Universe, Vestibular, Warehousing, Water, Weapon

Tt

T Bone, Junction, Potence, Tango, Tau-cross, Tee, Time, Toc(k)
Tab Bill, Check, > **LABEL**, Ring-pull, Stay-on, Tally, Trim
Tabby Blabbermouth, Brindled, > **CAT**, Gossip, Mottled, Spinster, Striped, Trout
Tabitha Gazelle
Table(-like) Alphonsine, Altar, Board, Bradshaw, Breakfast, Calendar, > **CHART**,
   Coffee, Console, Contingency, Counter, Credence, Credenza, Decision, Desk,
   Diagram, Dinner, Dolmen, Draw-leaf, Draw-top, Dressing, Drop-leaf, Drum,
   Ephemeris, Experience, Food, Gateleg, Glacier, Graph, Green-cloth, Gueridon,
   High, Imposing, Index, Key, League, Life, Light, > **LIST**, Lord's, Mahogany,
   Matrix, Mensa(l), Mesa, Monopode, Mortality, Multiplication, Occasional,
   Operating, Pembroke, Periodic, Piecrust, Pier, Plane, Platen, Pool, Prothesis,
   Pythagoras, Reckoner, Refectory, Roll, Round, Rudolphine, Sand, Schedule,
   Scheme, Slab, Sofa, Spoon, Stall, Statistical, Stone, Taboret, Tabular, Tea,
   Te(a)poy, Tide, Times, Toilet, Trestle, Trolley, Truth, Twelve, Washstand, Water,
   Whirling, Wool, Workbench, Writing
Tableau Semantic
Tablecloth Damask, Linen
Table-land Barkly, Kar(r)oo, Mesa, Plateau, Puna
Table-list Memo, Menu
Tablet Abacus, Album, Aspirin, Caplet, Eugebine, Graphics, Hatch, Medallion,
   Opisthograph, Osculatory, Ostracon, Ostrakon, > **PAD**, > **PILL**, Pilule, Plaque,
   Slate, Stele, Stone, Tombstone, Torah, Triglyph, Triptych, Troche, Trochisk,
   Ugarit, Votive
Table-talker Deipnosophist
Table-turner Tartar
Table-ware China, Cutlery, Silver
Taboo, Tabu Ban(ned), Bar, Blackball, Forbidden, Incest, Non dit, No-no,
   Unclean
Tacit, Taciturn(ity) Implicit, Laconic, Mumps, Oyster, Silent, Understood
Tack(y) Baste, Beat, Brass, Cheesy, Cinch, Clubhaul, Cobble, Gybe, Leg,
   Martingale, Nail, Saddlery, Salt-horse, > **SEW**, Sprig, Stirrup, Tailor's, Veer,
   Wear, White-seam, Yaw, Zigzag
Tackle Accost, Approach, Attempt, Beard, Bobstay, Burton, Claucht, Claught,
   Clevis, Clew-garnet, Collar, Dead-eye, Fishing, Garnet, Gear, Haliard, Halyard,
   Harness, Jury-rig, Rig, Rigging, Scrag, Straight-arm, Topping-lift
Tact, Tactful Delicacy, Diplomacy, Diplomatic, Discreet, Discretion, Politic,
   Savoir-faire
Tactic(s) Audible, Finesse, Hardball, Manoeuvre, Masterstroke, Plan, Ploy,
   Ruse, Salami, Shock, > **STRATEGY**, Strong-arm, Zwischenzug
Tactless(ness) Blundering, Brash, Crass, Gaffe, Gauche, Indelicate, Maladroit
Tadpole Ascidian, Polliwig, Polliwog, Pollywig, Pollywog, Porwiggle
Taffy Thief, Toffee, Welshman
Tag Aglet, Aiguillette, Cliché, Dog, Electronic, End, Epithet, > **FOLLOW**, Kabaddi,

Kimball, Label, Price, Question, Quote, Remnant, Tab, > TICKET, Treasury

Tail, Tailpiece Apocopate, > APPENDAGE, Bob, Brush, Caudal, Cercal, Cercus, Coda, Codetta, Colophon, Cue, Dock, Empennage, Fan, Fee, Flag, Floccus, > FOLLOW, Fud, Liripoop, Parson's nose, Pole, Pope's nose, PS, Queue, Rumple-bane, Scut, Seat, Stag, Stern, Telson, > TIP, Train, Uro(some), Uropygium, Women

Tailless Acaudal, An(o)urous, Fee-simple

Tail-lobes Anisocercal

Tailor(ed) Adapt, Bespoke, Bushel, Cabbager, Couturier, Cutter, Darzi, Durzi, Epicene, Feeble, Flint, Merchant, Nine, Outfitter, Pick-the-louse, Pricklouse, Sartor, Seamster, Snip, Starveling, Style, Whipcat, Whipstitch

▷ **Tailor** *may indicate* an anagram

Taint(ed) Besmirch, Blemish, Fly-blown, High, Infect, Leper, Off, Poison, > SPOIL, Stain, Stigma, Tinge, Trace, Unwholesome

Taiwan RC

Take(n), Take in, Taking(s), Take over Absorb, > ACCEPT, Adopt, Assume, Attract, Bag, Beg, Bite, Bone, Borrow, Bottle, > CAPTURE, Catch, Claim, Cop, Coup, Detract, Dishy, Distrain, Entr(y)ism, Exact, Expropriate, Get, Grab, Handle, Haul, Hent, House, Howe, Huff, Incept, Ingest, Mess, Misappropriate, Nick, Occupy, Pocket, Quote, R, Rec, Receipt, Receive, Recipe, Reverse, Rob, Seise, Sequester, Ship, Smitten, Snatch, Sneak, > STEAL, Stomach, Subsume, Swallow, Sweet, Swipe, Toll, Trump, Turnover, Usher, Usurp, Wan, Winsome, Wrest

Take away, Take off Aph(a)eresis, Asport, Carry-out, Deduct, Dock, Doff, Esloin, Exenterate, Expropriate, Jato, Parody, Parrot, Press-gang, Shanghai, Skit, Subtract, Vertical, VTO(L)

Take care Guard, See, Tend, Watch

▷ **Taken up** *may indicate* reversed

Take part Act, Engage, Side

Talbot House Toc H

Talc Potstone, Rensselaerite, Soapstone, Steatite, Venice

Tale(s) Allegory, Blood, Boccaccio, Conte, Decameron, Edda, Fable, Fabliau, Fairy, Fairy story, Fiction, Folk, Gag, Geste, Hadith, Iliad, Jataka, Jeremiad, Legend, Lie, Mabinogion, Maise, Ma(i)ze, Marchen, Mease, Milesian, Narrative, Odyssey, Old wives', Pentameron, Rede, Saga, Sandabar, Score, Sinbad, Sind(a)bad, Sob-story, Spiel, > STORY, Tradition, Traveller's, Weird

Tale-bearer, Tale-teller Gossip, Grass, Informer, Sneak, Tattler, Tusitala

Talent(ed) Ability, Accomplishment, Aptitude, Bent, Dower, Faculty, Flair, Forte, Genius, Gift, Ingenium, Knack, Long suit, Nous, Prodigy, Schtick, Strong point, Versatile, Virtuoso, W(h)iz(z), Whiz-kid

Talion Reprisal

Talisman Amulet, Charm, Saladin, Sampo, Scarab, Telesm

Talk(ing), Talking point, Talker, Talks Ana, Articulate, Babble, Bibble-babble, Blab, Blague, Blat, Blather, Blether-skate, Cant, Chalk, Chat, Chinwag, Chirp, Circumlocution, Colloquy, Commune, Confabulate, Confer, Converse, Coo, Cross, Descant, Dialog(ue), Diatribe, Dilate, Discourse, Diseur, Dissert, Double, Earbash, Earful, Express, Fast, Filibuster, Froth, Gab, Gabble, Gabnash, Gas, Gibber, Gossip, Grandiloquence, Guff, Harp, Imparl, Jabber, Jargon, Jaw, Jazz, Korero, Lip, Logorrhoea, Macrology, Mang, Maunder, Mince, Monologue, Motormouth, Nashgab, Natter, Noise, Omniana, Palabra, Palaver, Parlance, Parley, Patter, Pawaw, Pep, Perorate, Phraser, Pidgin, Pillow, Pitch, Potter, Powwow, Prate, Prattle, Presentation, Prose, Proximity, Ramble, Rap, Rigmarole, Rote, SALT, Shop, Slang(-whang), Small, Soliloquy, > SPEAK, Spiel,

Spout, Straight, Sweet, Table, Tachylogia, Topic, Turkey, Twaddle, Twitter, Unbosom, Up(s), Utter, Vocal, Waffle, Witter, Wongi, Wrangle, Yabber, Yack, Yak, Yalta, Yammer, Yap, Yatter

Talkative Chatty, Fluent, Gabby, Garrulous, Gash, Glib, Loquacious, Vocular, Voluble

Tall Etiolated, Exaggerated, Hie, High, Hye, Lanky, Lathy, Leggy, Lofty, Long, Procerity, Randle-tree, Rantle-tree, Tangle, Taunt, Tower, Towery

Tallboy Chest, Dresser

Tallow Greaves, Hatchettite, Lead-arming, Mineral, Vegetable, Wax

Tally >AGREE, Census, Correspond, Count, Match, Nickstick, Notch, Record, >SCORE, Stick, Stock, Tab, Tag

Talmud Gemara, Mishna

Talon Claw, Ogee, Single

Talus Scree

Tamarind Assam

Tamasha Fuss, To-do

Tame Amenage, Break, Docile, Domesticate, Lapdog, Mansuete, Meek, Mild, Safe, Snool, Subdue

Tammany Hall, Sachem

Tamp, Tampon Plug

Tamper(ing) Bishop, Cook, Doctor, Fake, Fiddle, Meddle, Medicate, Monkey, Nobble, Phreaking

Tam-tam Gong

Tan(ned), Tanned skin, Tanning Adust, Bablah, Babul, Bark, Basil, Beige, Bisque, Boarding, Bronze, >BROWN, Canaigre, Catechu, Furan, Furfuran(e), Insolate, Lambast, Leather, Neb-neb, Paste, Pipi, Puer, Pure, Spank, Sun, Sunbathe, Tenné, Umber, Val(l)onia, Valonea, Ybet

Tandem Duo, Randem

Tang Relish, Smack, Taste

Tangent Ratio, Slope, Touching

Tangible Concrete, Palpable, Plain, Solid, Tactual

Tangle Alga, Badderlock, Burble, Dulse, Embroil, Entwine, Fank, Fankle, Heap, Implication, Ket, >KNOT, Labyrinth, Laminaria, Lutin, Mat, Mix, Nest, Oarweed, Ore, Perplex, Pleach, >RAVEL, Sea-girdle, Seaweed, Skean, Skein, Snarl, Taigle, Taut(it), Tawt, Thicket, Varec

▷ **Tangled** *may indicate* an anagram

Tank Abrams, Alligator, Amphibian, Aquarium, Belly, Casspir, Centurion, Cesspool, Challenger, Chieftain, Cistern, Drop, Feedhead, Float, Flotation, Gasholder, Header, Keir, Kier, Mouse, Panzer, Pod, Quiescent, >RESERVOIR, Ripple, Sedimentation, Septic, Sherman, Shield pond, Sponson, Sump, Surge, Think, Tiger, Valentine, Vat, Ventral, Vivarium, Whippet

Tankard Blackjack, Peg, Pewter, Pot, Stein, Tappit-hen

Tanker Bowser, Lorry, Oiler

Tanner(y) Bender, Currier, Kick, Solarium, Sunbather, Sunshine, Tawery, Tester(n), 'VId', Zack

Tannin Catechu

Tantalise Entice, Tease, Tempt, Torture

Tantalum Ta

Tantivy Alew, Halloo

Tantrum Hissyfit, Paddy, Pet, Rage, Scene, Tirrivee, Tirrivie

Tanzania EAT

Tap(ping), Taps Accolade, Bibcock, Blip, Broach, Bug, Cock, Col legno, Drum,

Faucet, Flick, Hack, Mag, Milk, Mixer, Monitor, Paracentesis, Pat, Patter, Percuss, Petcock, > **RAP**, Spigot, Spinal, Stopcock, Stroup, Tack, Tat, Tit, Touk, Tuck, Water

Tape Chrome, DAT, > **DRINK**, Duct, Ferret, Finish, Gaffer, Grip, Idiot, Incle, Inkle, Insulating, Magnetic, Masking, Measure, Metal, Narrowcast, Paper, Passe-partout, Perforated, Punched, Record, Red, Scotch, Sellotape®, Shape, Sticky, Ticker, Video, Welding

Taper(ed), Tapering Diminish, Fastigiate, Featheredge, Fusiform, Lanceolate, Morse, Narrow, Nose, Subulate, Tail

Tapestry Alentous, Arras(ene), Aubusson, Bayeux, Bergamot, Crewel-work, Dosser, Gobelin, Hanging, Oudenarde, Petit point, Tapet

Tapeworm Echinococcus, Hydatid, Measle, Scolex, Taenia, Teniasis

Tapioca Cassava, Pearl, Yuca, Yucca

Tapir Anta, S(e)ladang

Tar, Tar product AB, Bitumen, Coal, Creosote, Egg, Gladwellise, Gob, Indene, Maltha, Matelot, Matlo, Mineral, Naphtha, Needle, OS, Parcel, Pay, Picamar, Picene, Pine, Pitch, Rating, Retene, Sailor, Salt, Uintahite, Uintaite, Wood, Xylol

Tardy Behindhand, Dilatory, Late, > **SLOW**

Tare Tine, Vetch

Target > **AIM**, Blank, Butt, Clout, Cockshy, Dart, Drogue, End, Hit, Home, Hub, Inner, Magpie, Mark, Motty, > **OBJECT**, Outer, Pelta, Pin, Prey, Prick, Quintain, Sitter, Sitting, Tee, Victim, Wand

Tariff List, Preferential, Protective, Rate, Revenue, Zabeta

Tarnish Defile, Discolour, Soil, Stain, Sully, Taint

Taro Arum, Coc(c)o, Dasheen, Eddo

Tarot Arcana

Tarpaulin Weathercloth

Tarragon Staragen

Tarry Bide, Dally, Leng, > **LINGER**, Stay, Sticky

Tarsier Malmag

Tarsus Saul

Tart Acetic, Acid, Bakewell, Broad, Charlotte, Cocotte, Croquante, Cupid, Custard, Dariole, Doxy, Duff, Flam(m), Flan, Flawn, Frock, Harlot, Hussy, Jade, Lemony, Mirliton, Moll, Mort, Nana, > **PIE**, Pinnace, Piquant, Pro, Quean, Quiche, Quine, > **SHARP**, Slapper, Slut, Snappy, Sour, Stew, Strumpet, Tatin, Tramp, Treacle, Trull, Unsweet

Tartan Argyle, Argyll, Maud, Plaid, Set(t), Trews

Tartar Argal, Argol, Beeswing, Calculus, Crust, Hell, Plaque, Rough, Scale, Tam(b)erlane, Zenocrate

Tashkent Uzbek

Task Assignment, Aufgabe, > **CHORE**, Duty, Errand, Exercise, Fag, Imposition, Mission, Ordeal, Pensum, Stint, Thankless, Vulgus

Tasmania Apple Isle, Van Diemen's Land

Tassel Pompom, Toorie, Tourie, Tsutsith, Tuft

Taste(ful), Taster, Tasty Acquired, Aesthetic, Appetite, Degust, Delibate, Delicious, Discrimination, > **EAT**, Fashion, Flavour, Form, Gout, Gust, Gustatory, Hint, Lekker, Lick, Palate, Penchant, Pica, Pree, Refinement, Relish, > **SAMPLE**, Sapor, Sar, Savour, S(c)hme(c)k, Sip, Smack, Smatch, Snack, Soupçon, Stomach, Succulent, Tang, Titbit, Toothsome, > **TRY**, Vertu, Virtu, Wine

Tasteless Appal, Brassy, Fade, Flat, Insipid, Stale, Tacky, Vapid, Vulgar, Watery,

Wearish, Wersh

Tat, **Tatter**, **Tatty** Rag, Ribbon, Roon, Scrap, Shred, Tag, Tan, Untidy

Tattie-bogle Scarecrow

Tattle(r) Blab, Chatter, Gash, > **GOSSIP**, Prate, Rumour, Sneak, Snitch, Totanus, Willet

Tattoo Devil's, Drum, Edinburgh, Moko, Rataplan, Row-dow, Tat

Tatum Art

Taught Up

Taunt Dig, Fling, Gibe, Gird, > **JEER**, Rag, Ridicule, Twight, Twit

Taut Stiff, Tense

Tavern Bar, Bodega, Bousing-ken, Bush, Fonda, > **INN**, Kiddleywink, Kneipe, Mermaid, Mitre, Mughouse, Pothouse, Shebeen, Taphouse

Taw Alley, Ally, Marble

Tawdry Catchpenny, > **CHEAP**, Flashy, Gaudy, Raffish, Sleazy, Tatty, Tinsey

Tawny Brindle, Dusky, Fawn, Fulvous, Mulatto, Port, Tan

Tawse Cat, Lash, Thong, Whip

Tax(ing), **Taxation** ACT, Agist, Aid, Alms-fee, Assess, Capitation, Carbon, Carucage, Cense, Cess, > **CHARGE**, Corporation, Council, Custom, Danegeld, Direct, Duty, Energy, EPT, Escot, Escuage, Exact, Excise, Exercise, EZT, Gabelle, Geld, Gift, Head, Hidage, Impose, Imposition, Impost, Impute, Indirect, Inheritance, IR, Jaghir(e), Jagir, Land, Levy, Likin, Lot, Murage, Negative, Octroi, Operose, Overwork, Pavage, PAYE, Peter-pence, Poll, Poundage, Primage, Property, Proportional, PT, Punish, Purchase, Rate, Regressive, Road, Rome-pence, Sales, Scat(t), Scot (and lot), Scutage, Sess, SET, Sin, Single, Skat, Stealth, Stent, Streetage, Stumpage, Super, Taille, Tallage, Talliate, Tariff, Task, Teind, Tithe, Tobin, Toilsome, Toll, Tonnage, Tribute, Try, Turnover, Unitary, Value-added, VAT, Wattle, Wealth, Weary, White rent, Windfall, Window, Withholding, Zakat

Tax area Tahsil, Talooka, Taluk(a)

Tax-collector, **Taxman** Amildar, Cheater, Exciseman, Farmer, Gabeller, Inspector, IR(S), Publican, Stento(u)r, Tithe-proctor, Tollman, Undertaker, Zemindar

Taxi Cab, Hackney, Samlor, Zola Budd

Taxidermist Venus

▸ **Taxman** *see* **TAX-COLLECTOR**

TB Scrofula

TE Lawrence, Ross, Shaw

Tea Afternoon, Assam, Beef, Black, Bohea, Brew, Brick, Bush, Cambric, Camomile, Caper, Ceylon, Cha, Chamomile, Chanoyu, China, Chirping-cup, Congo(u), Cream, Cuppa, Darjeeling, Earl Grey, Grass, Green, Gunfire, Gunpowder, Herb(al), High, Hyson, Indian, Jasmine, K(h)at, Kitchen, Labrador, Lapsang, Lapsang Souchong, Leaves, Ledum, Lemon, Malt, Manuka, Marijuana, Maté, Mexican, Mint, Morning, New Jersey, Oolong, Orange pekoe, Oulong, Paraguay, Pekoe, Post and rail, Pot, Qat, Red-root, Rooibos, Rosie Lee, Russian, Senna, Souchong, Stroupach, Stroupan, Switchel, Tay, Thea, Theophylline, Twankay, Yerba (de Maté)

Teach(er), **Teaching (material)**, **Teachings** Acharya, Adjoint, Agrege, AMMA, Apostle, Barbe, Beale, BEd, Bhagwan, Buss, Catechist, Chalkface, > **COACH**, Con(ne), Didactic, Didascalic, Docent, Doctrine, Dogma, Dominie, Dressage, Edify, > **EDUCATE**, Educationalist, Edutainment, EIS, ELT, Explain, Faculty, Froebel, Gerund-grinder, Gooroo, Gospel, Governess, Guru, Head, Heuristic, Hodja, Inculcate, Indoctrinate, Inform, Instil, Instruct, Ism, Kho(d)ja, Kumon

(Method), Lair, Lancasterian, Larn, Lear(e), Lecturer, Leir, Lere, Maam, Maggid, Magister, Maharishi, Mahavira, Mallam, Marker, Marm, Master, Maulvi, Mentor, Miss, Mistress, Molla(h), Monitor, Montessorian, Moola(h), Moolvi(e), Mufti, Mullah, Munshi, Mystagogue, Nuffield, Paedotribe, Pedagogue, Pedant, Pr(a)efect, Preceptor, Privat-docent, Proctor, Prof, Prog, PT, Pupil, Rabbi, Realia, Rebbe, Remedial, Rhetor, Scholastic, Schoolman, Scribe, Sensei, Show, Sir, Smriti, Socrates, Sophist, Staff, Starets, Staretz, Sunna, Supply, Swami, Tantra, Team, Train(er), Tutelage, Tutor, Usher

Teach-in Seminar

Teahouse Sukiya

Teak African, Bastard, White

Team Bafana bafana, Colts, Crew, Dream, Ecurie, Eleven, Equipe, Farm, Fifteen, Outfit, Oxen, Panel, Possibles, Probables, Relay, Scrub, > SIDE, Span, Special, Squad, Squadron, Staff, Tiger, Troupe, Turnout, Unicorn, United, XI

Tea-party Boston, Bunfight, Cookie-shine, Drum, Kettledrum, Shine

Teapot Billycan, Cadogan, Samovar

Tear(s), Tearable, Tearful, Tearing Beano, Claw, Crocodile, Divulsion, Drop, Eye-drop, Eye-water, Greeting, Hurry, Lacerate, Laniary, Pelt, Ranch, Rash, Reave, > REND, Rheum, Rip, Rive, Rume, Scag, Screed, Shred, Snag, Split, Spree, Tire, Waterworks, Wet, Worry, Wrench, Wrest

Tearaway Get, Hothead, Ned

Tear-jerker Onion

Tear-pit Crumen, Larmier

Tease, Teasing Arch, Backcomb, Badinage, Bait, Banter, Card, Chaff, Chap, Chiack, Chip, Chyack, Cod, Grig, Guy, Hank, Imp, Ironic, Itch, Josh, Kemb, Kid, Mag, Mamaguy, Nark, Persiflage, > RAG, Raillery, Rally, Razz, Rib, Rot, Strip, > TANTALISE, Toaze, Torment(or), Twilly, Twit, Worrit

Teasel Dipsacus, Valerian

Teat Dug, Dummy, Mamilla, Mastoid, Nipple, Pap, Soother, Tit

Tea-time Chat

Teaze Gig, Moze

Technetium Tc

Technical, Technician, Technique Adept, Alexander, Artisan, Brushwork, College, Delphi, Execution, Foley artist, Footsteps editor, Kiwi, Know-how, Manner, > METHOD, Operative, Salami, Sandwich, Science, Toe and heel

Technology, Technological High, State of the art, Stealth

Ted(dy) Bodgie, Dexter, Ducktail, Moult, Widgie, Yob

Tedium, Tedious Boring, Chore, Deadly, Doldrums, Drag, Dreich, Dull, Ennui, Heaviness, Long, Longspun, Longueur, Monotony, Operose, Prosy, Soul-destroying, > TIRING, Twaddle, Wearisome, Yawn

Tee Hub, Umbrella

Teem(ing) Abound, Bustling, Empty, Great, Pullulate, Swarm

Teenager Adolescent, Bobbysoxer, Junior, Juvenile, Minor, Mod, Rocker, Sharpie, Skinhead, Youth

▶ **Teeth** *see* TOOTH

Teething ring Coral

Teetotal(ler) Abdar, Blue Ribbon, Nephalist, Rechabite, Temperate, TT, Water-drinker, Wowser

Tegument Seed coat

Telecommunications Cellnet®, Vodafone®

Telegram, Telegraph Bush, Cable, Ems, Grapevine, Greetings, International, Message, Moccasin, Mulga wire, Singing, Telex, Wire

Telepathy, Telepathic Clairvoyance, ESP, Seer

Telephone Ameche, ATLAS, Bell, Blower, BT, Call, Cellphone, Centrex, Cordless, Dial, Dog and bone, GRACE, Handset, Horn, Intercom, Line, Lo-call®, Mercury, Mobile, Pay-station, Pdq, > **PHONE**, POTS, Ring, Squawk box, STD, Textphone, Touch-tone, Vodafone®, Wire

Teleprinter Creed

Telescope Altazimuth, Binocle, Cassegrain(ian), Collimator, Coudé, Electron, Finder, Galilean, Gemini, Glass, Gregorian, Heliometer, Hubble, Intussuscept, Meniscus, Newtonian, Night-glass, Optical, Palomar, Perspective, Radio, Reflector, Refractor, Schmidt, Shorten, Snooperscope, Spyglass, Stadia, Terrestrial, Tube, X-ray, Zenith

Teletext® Ceefax®, Oracle®

Television, Telly Box, Cable, Digital, Diorama, Event, Goggle box, Image orthicon, ITV, MAC, PAL, Pay, Plumbicon®, Projection, RTE, Satellite, SECAM, Set, Small screen, Subscription, Tree and branch, Tube, > **TV**, Video

Tell Acquaint, Announce, Apprise, Archer, Beads, Blab, Break, Clipe, Clype, Compt, Direct, > **DISCLOSE**, Divulge, Grass, Impart, Inform, > **NARRATE**, Noise, Notify, Number, Recite, Recount, Relate, Report, Retail, Rumour, Sneak, Snitch, Spin, Teach, William

Tellurium Te

Temerity Cheek, Gall, Impertinence, Imprudence, Impudence, Incaution, Rashness, Recklessness

Temper, Temperate Abstemious, Abstinent, Allay, Anneal, Assuage, Attune, Balmy, Bile, Blood, Calm, Choler, Comeddle, Continent, Dander, Delay, Ease, Fireworks, Flaky, Irish, Leaven, > **MILD**, Mitigate, Moderate, Modify, > **MOOD**, Neal, Paddy, Paddywhack, Pet, Radge, Rage, Season, Short fuse, Snit, Sober, Soften, Spitfire, Spleen, Strop, Swage, Tantrum, Techy, Teen, Teetotal, Tetchy, Tiff, Tone, Trim, Tune

Temperament(al) Bent, Blood, Choleric, Crasis, Disposition, Equal, Just, Kidney, Mean-tome, Melancholy, Mettle, Moody, > **NATURE**, Neel, Over-sensitive, Phlegmatic, Prima donna, Sanguine, Unstable, Viscerotonia

Temperance Moderation, Pledge, Rechabite

Temperature Absolute, Celsius, Centigrade, Chambré, Colour, Critical, Curie, Dew point, Fahrenheit, Fever, Flashpoint, Heat, Heterothermal, Hyperthermia, Kelvin, Regulo, Restrictive, Room, T, Thermodynamic, Weed, Weid

Tempest(uous) Bourasque, Euraquilo, Euroclydon, Gale, High, Marie, > **STORM(Y)**

Temple, Temple gate Adytum, Amphiprostyle, Artemis, Capitol, Cella, Chapel, Church, Delphi, Delubrum, Ephesus, Fane, Gompa, Gurdwara, Haffet, Haffit, Heroon, Inner, Mandir(a), Masjid, Middle, Monopteron, Monopteros, Mosque, Museum, Naos, Nymphaeum, Pagod(a), Pantheon, Parthenon, > **SHRINE**, Shul(n), Teocalli, Teopan, Torii, Vihara, Wat

Tempo Agoge, Rate, > **RHYTHM**, Rubato

Temporary Acting, Caretaker, Cutcha, Ephemeral, Hobjob, Interim, Kutcha, Locum, Makeshift, Pro tem, Provisional, Short-term, Stopgap, Temp, Transient, Transitional

Temporise(r) Politique

Tempt(ation), Tempting, Tempter, Temptress Allure, Apple, Bait, Beguile, Beset, Circe, Dalilah, Decoy, Delilah, > **ENTICE**, Eve, Groundbait, Impulse, Lure, Providence, Satan, Seduce, Siren, Snare, Tantalise, Test, Tice, Trial

Ten Commandments, Decad, Dectet, Decury, Denary, Googol, 10, Iota, Tera-,

Tribes, X

Tenacious, Tenacity Clayey, Determined, Dogged, Fast, Guts, Hold, Intransigent, Persevering, Persistent, Resolute, Retentive, Sticky

Tenancy, Tenant(s) Censuarius, Cosherer, Cottar, Cotter, Cottier, Dreng, Feuar, Feudatory, Gravelman, Homage, Ingo, Inhabit, Leaseholder, Lessee, > **LODGER**, Metayer, Occupier, Periodic, Rentaller, Renter, Secure, Shorthold, Sitting, Socager, Socman, Sokeman, Suckener, Tacksman, Valvassor, Vassal, Vavasour, Visit

Tend Care, Dress, Herd, Incline, Lean, Liable, Nurse, Prone, Run, Shepherd, Verge

Tendency Apt, Bent, Bias, Central, Conatus, Drift, Genius, Idiosyncrasy, Import, Militant, Penchant, Proclivity, Propensity, Trend

Tender(iser), Tenderly, Tenderness Affettuoso, Amoroso, Bid, Bill, Coin, Con amore, Crank, Dingey, Ding(h)y, Fond, Frail, Gentle, Green, Humane, Jolly-boat, Legal, Nesh, Nurse, > **OFFER**, Painful, Papain, Pinnace, Prefer, Present, Proffer, Proposal, Quotation, Red Cross, Sair, Shepherd, > **SOFT**, Sore, SRN, Submit, Sympathy, Tendre

Tenderfoot Babe, Chechacho, Chechako, Cub, Greenhorn, Innocent

Tenderloin Psoas, Undercut

Tendon Achilles, Aponeurosis, Hamstring, Kangaroo, Leader, Paxwax, Sinew, String, Vinculum, Whitleather

Tendril(led) Capreolate, Cirrose, Cirrus, Tentacle

Tenement(s) Dominant, Land, Rook, Tack

Tenet Adiaphoron, Creed, > **DOCTRINE**, Dogma

Tenfold Decuple

Tennis Close, Court, Deck, Lawn, LTA, Real, Royal, Set, Sphairistike, Squash, Table, Wimbledon

Tenon Cog, Dovetail, Lewis

Tenor Course, Domingo, > **DRIFT**, Effect, Ferreras, Gigli, Gist, Heroic, Pavarotti, Purport, Singer, T, Tide, Timbre, Trial, Vein

Tense Aor, Aorist, Case, Clench, Drawn, Edgy, Electric, Essive, Imperfect, Keyed up, Mood(y), Nervy, Overstrung, Past, Perfect, Pluperfect, Preterit, Preterite, Rigid, Simple, Stiff, Strained, Stressed(-out), Strict, T, > **TAUT**, Uptight

Tensing Sherpa

Tension Creative, High, Isometrics, Isotonic, Meniscus, Nerviness, Premenstrual, > **STRAIN**, Stress, Stretch, Surface, Tone, Tonicity, Tonus, Yips

Tent Bell, Bivvy, Cabana, Douar, Dowar, Duar, Kedar, Kibitka, Marquee, Oxygen, Pavilion, Probe, Pup, Red wine, Ridge, Shamiana(h), Shamiyanah, Shelter, Tabernacle, Teepee, Tepee, Tilt, Tipi, Top, Topek, Trailer, Tupek, Tupik, Wigwam, Wine, Y(o)urt

Tentacle Actinal, Cirrate, Feeler, Hectocotylus, Horn, Lophophore

Tentative Empirical, Experimental, Gingerly, Peirastic

Tent-dweller, Tent-maker Camper, Indian, Kedar, Omar, St Paul

Tenth Disme, Teind, Tithe

Ten Thousand Toman

Tenuous Frail, Slender, Slight, Thin, Vague

Tenure Blench, Burgage, Copyhold, Cottier(ism), Drengage, Fee-farm, Feu, Frankalmoi(g)n(e), Frank-fee, Gavelkind, Leasehold, Manorial, Occupation, Raiyatwari, Rundale, Runrig, Ryotwari, Socage, > **TERM**, Vavasory, Venville, Zemindar

Tepid Laodicean, Lukewarm

Terbium Tb

Terete Centric(al)

Term(s), Terminal, Termly Air, Anode, Buffer, Cathode, Coast, Coste, Designate, Desinant, Distal, Distributed, > EPITHET, Euphemism, Expression, Final, Gnomon, Goal, Half, Hilary, Inkhorn, Intelligent, Law, Lent, Major, Michaelmas, Middle, Minor, > PERIOD, Rail(head), Real, Removal, Sabbatical, Semester, Session, Stint, Stretch, Trimester, Trimestrial, Trinity, Ultimatum, Waterloo, > WORD, Work station, Zeroth

Termagant Jade, Shrew, Shrow, Spitfire, Vixen

Terminate, Termination, Terminus Abort, Axe, Conclude, Depot, Desinent, Earth, > END, Expiry, > FINISH, Goal, Liquidate, Naricorn, Railhead, Suffix

Termite Duck-ant

Tern Egg-bird, Scray, Three

Terrace Barbette, Beach, Bench, Linch, Lynchet, Offset, Perron, Shelf, Stoep, Tarras, Undercliff, Veranda(h)

Terra-cotta Tanagra

Terrain Area, Landscape, Scablands, Tract

Terrapin Diamondback, Emydes, Emys, Slider, Turtle

Terrible, Terribly Appalling, Awful, Deadly, Fell, Frightful, Ghastly, Horrible, Much, Odious, Very

Terrible person Humgruffi(a)n, Ivan, Ogre

Terrier Aberdeen, Airedale, Apsos, Australian, Bedlington, Black and tan, Border, Boston, Bull, Catalogue, Cesky, Dandie Dinmont, Fox, Griffon, Irish, Jack Russell, Kerry blue, Lakeland, Maltese, Manchester, Norfolk, Norwich, Pinscher, Pit bull, Ratter, Register, Scotch, Scottie, Scottish, Sealyham, Silky, Skye, Soft-coated wheaten, Staffordshire bull, Sydney silky, TA, Tibetan, Welsh, West Highland, West Highland white, Westie, Wire-haired, Yorkshire

Terrific, Terrified, Terrify(ing) Affright, Aghast, Agrise, Agrize, Agryze, Appal, Awe, Blood-curdling, Enorm, Fear, Fine, Fley, Gast, Helluva, Huge, Overawe, > PETRIFY, Scare, Superb, Unman, Yippee

Territory Abthane, Ap(p)anage, Colony, Domain, Dominion, Duchy, Emirate, Enclave, Exclave, Goa, Indian, Latium, Lebensraum, Manor, Margravate, No-man's-land, Northern, Northwest, Nunavut, Palatinate, Panhandle, Papua, Petsamo, Principate, Protectorate, Province, Realm, > REGION, Scheduled, Sphere, Sultanate, Ter(r), Trust, Union, Yukon

Terror(s) Blue funk, Bugaboo, Bugbear, Eek, > FEAR, Fright, Holy, Imp, Night, Panic, Skrik

Terrorist Alarmist, Al Fatah, Anarchist, Bogeyman, Bomber, Bully, Cagoulard, Desperado, Dynamitard, Eta, Grapo, Hijacker, Ku Klux Klan, Mau-mau, Maximalist, Mountain, Nightrider, Nihilist, Pirate, PLO, Provo, Red Brigade, Robespierre, Ustashi

Terry Ellen, Towel

Terse Abrupt, Brusque, Curt, Laconic, Pithy, Precise, Succinct

Tertiary Cainozoic, Eocene, Miocene, Oligocene, Palaeogene, Pliocene

Tessellation Mosaic

Test(er), Testing Achievement, Acid, Alpha, Ames, Amniocentesis, Apgar, Appro, Aptitude, Assay, Audition, Barany, Bench, Bender, Benedict, Beta, Blood, Breath, Breathalyser®, Brinell, Candle, Canopy, Check, Chi-square, Cis-trans, Cloze, Conn(er), Coomb's, Crash, Criterion, Crucial, Crucible, Crunch, Dick, Docimastic, Driving, Dummy-run, Eprouvette, Examine, Exercise, Experiment, Field, Flame, Frog, Ink-blot, Intelligence, International, Litmus, Mann-Whitney, Mantoux, Mazzin, Means, Medical, MOT, Mug, Neckverse, Needs, Objective, Oral, Ordalian, > ORDEAL, Pale, Pap,

Papanicolaou, Paraffin, Patch, Paternity, Performance, Personality, PH, Pilot,
Pons asinorum, Pree, Preeve, Preif, Preve, Probe, Projective, Proof, Prove,
Proving-ground, Pyx, Q-sort, Qualification, Quiz, Rally, Reagent, Road,
Rorschach, SAT, Scalogram, Schick's, Schilling, Schutz-Charlton, Scratch,
Screen, Shadow, Shibboleth, Showdown, Shroff, Sign, Significance, Sixpence,
Skin, Slump, Smear, Smoke, Snellen, Sound, Spinal, Stanford-Binet, Stress,
Tempt, Tensile, Touch, Touchstone, Trial, Trier, Trior, Try, Turing, Ultrasonic,
Viva, Wassermann's, Wilcoxon, Zack

Testament Bible, Covenant, Hagographa, Heptateuch, Hexateuch,
Hornolog(o)umena, Midrash, New, Old, Pentateuch, Scripture, Septuagint,
Tanach, Targum, Will

Testicle(s) Ballocks, Balls, Bollix, Bollocks, Cobblers, Cojones, Gool(e)y, Goolie,
Knackers, Monkey-gland, Monorchid, Nads, Nuts, Ridgel, Ridgil, Rig(gald),
Rocks, Stone

Testify, Testimonial, Testimony Character, Chit, Declare, Depone, Deposition,
> EVIDENCE, Rap, Scroll, Tribute, Viva voce, Witness

Testy, Tetchy Cross, Narky, Peevish, Ratty

Tetanus Lockjaw

Tête-a-tête Collogue, Confab, Hobnob, Twosome

Tether Cord, Endurance, Hitch, Noose, Picket, Seal, Stringhalt, > TIE

Tetrahedrite Fahlerz, Fahlore

Tetrarchy Iturea

Tetrasyllabic Paeon

Tetrode Resnatron

Teuton(ic) Erl-king, German, Goth, Herren, Vandal

Texas Ranger

Text(s), Textbook ABC, Body, Brahmana, Church, Codex, Donat, Ennage,
Greeked, Harmony, Libretto, Mandaean, Mantra, Mezuzah, Octapla, Op-cit,
Philology, Plain, Pyramid, Quran, Responsa, Rubric, Script, S(h)astra, Shema,
> SUBJECT, Sura, Sutra, Tefillin, Tephillin, Tetrapla, Thesis, Topic, Tripitaka,
Typography, Upanis(h)ad, Variorium, Vulgate, Zohar

Textile Cloth, Fabric, Mercy

Texture Constitution, Feel, Fiber, Fibre, Grain, Open, Wale, Weave, Woof

Thai(land) Karen, Lao(s), Mon, Shan, Siam

Thalamus Optic

Thallium Tl

Thames Father, Tamesis

Than And

Thane Banquo, Ross

Thank(s), Thankful, Thanksgiving Appreciate, Collins, Deo gratias, Gloria,
Grace, Gramercy, Grateful, Gratitude, Kaddish, Mercy, Roofer

Thankless Ingrate, Vain

That (is), That one As, Cestui, Das heisst, Dh, Exists, How, Ie, Ille, Namely, Que,
Sc, Such, Thence, Thon(der), What, Which, Yon, Yt

Thatch(er), Thatching At(t)ap, Daych, Hair, Heard, Hear(i)e, Hele, Hell, Mane,
PM, Reed, Straw, Thack, Theek, Wig

Thaw Debacle, Defreeze, Defrost, > MELT, Melt-water, Relax

▷ **Thaw** *may indicate* 'ice' to be removed from a word

The Der, Die, El, Il, La, Le, Los, T', Ye, Ze

Theatre(s), Theatrical(ity) Abbey, Adelphi, Balcony, Broadway, Camp, Cinema,
Circle, Coliseum, Criterion, Crucible, Drama, Event, Everyman, Field, Fringe,
Gaff, Gaiety, Globe, Grand Guignol, Great White Way, Hall, Haymarket,

Hippodrome, Histrionic, House, Kabuki, La Scala, Legitimate, Little, Lyceum, Melodramatic, Mermaid, Music-hall, National, News, Nickelodeon, Noh, Odeon, Odeum, Operating, OUDS, Palladium, Panache, Pennygaff, Pit, Playhouse, Political, Rep(ertory), Sadler's Wells, Shaftesbury, Sheldonian, Shop, Stage, Stalls, Stoll, Straw-hat, Street, Summer stock, Total, Touring, Vic, Windmill, Zarzuela

Theatregoer Circle, Gallery, Gods, Pit, Stalls

Theft, **Thieving** Appropriation, Burglary, Heist, Identity, Kinchinlay, Larceny, Maino(u)r, Manner, Petty larceny, Pilfery, Plagiarism, Plunder, Pugging, Ram-raid, Robbery, Stealth, Stouth(rief), > **THIEF**, Touch, TWOC

Their Her

Theist Believer, Unitarian

Them 'Em, Hem, Tho

Theme Burden, Crab canon, Donnée, Fugue, Idea, Leitmotiv, Lemma, Lemmata, > **MELODY**, Motif, Peg, Question, > **SUBJECT**, Text, Topic, Topos

Then(ce) Away, Next, Since, So, Syne, Thereupon, Tho

▷ **The northern** *may indicate* t'

Theodolite Diopter, Dioptre, Groma, Tacheometer, Tachymeter, Transit

Theologian, **Theologist**, **Theology** Abelard, Aquinas, Barth, Calvin, Christology, Colet, DD, Divine, Erastus, Eschatology, Eusebius, Exegetics, Genevan, Hase, Infralapsarian, Irenics, Jansen, Kierkegaard, Knox, Liberation, Moral, Mullah, Natural, Newman, Niebuhr, Origen, Paley, Pectoral, Pelagius, Pusey, Rabbi, Religious, Sacramentarian, Schoolman, Scotus, Softa, STP, Supralapsarian, Tertullian, Ulema, Universalist

Theorem, **Theoretical**, **Theorist**, **Theory** Academic, Atomic, Automata, Bayes(ian), Bernouilli's, Big bang, Binomial, Bohr, Boo-hurrah, Catastrophe, Chaos, Conspiracy, Corpuscular, Darwinian, Decision, Deduction, Dependency, Dictum, Domino, Dow, Einstein, Empiricism, Epigenesist, Exponential, Fermat's (last), Galois, Game, Gauge, Germ, Gödel's, Grotian, Guess, Holism, Hypothesis, Ideal, Identity, Ideology, Information, Ism(y), James-Lange, Kinetic, Laingian, Lamarckism, Lemma, MAD, Model, Monism, Mythical, Nernst heat, Notion, Number, Object relations, Perturbation, Poynting, Probability, Proof, Pure, Pythagoras, Quantity, Quantum, Relativity, Satisfaction, Set, Speculative, Steady state, String, System, Tachyon, TOE, Tychism, Vulcanist, Wasm, Wave, Wholism, Wolfian

Therapeutic, **Therapy** Aura-Soma, Aversion, Behaviour, Bowen, Cellular, Chavuttithirumal, Chelation, Cognitive, Cognitive-behavioural, Colour, Combination, Craniosacral, Crystal (healing), Curative, Curietherapy, Deep, Dianetics, Electric shock, Electroconvulsive, Family, Faradism, Fever, Flotation, Gemstone, Gene, Gestalt, Group, Hellerwork, HRT, Hypnosis, Implosive, Insight, Larval, Light, Live cell, Logop(a)edics, Looyenwork, Magnetic, Metamorphic technique, MLD, Movement, Music, Narco, Natal, Natural, Non directive, Occupational, ORT, Osteopathy, Past life, Pattern, Physical, Polarity, Pressure, Primal, Primal (scream), Psychodrama, Radiation, Radio, Radium, Rainbow, Reflexology, Regression, Reichian, Reiki, Relaxation, Retail, Rogerian, Rolfing, Root-canal, Sanatory, Scientology®, Scream, Sex, SHEN, Shiatsu, Shiatzu, Shock, Sound, Speech, Speleotherapy, Supportive, Thalassotherapy, Theriacal, Thermotherapy, Touch, > **TREATMENT**, Water cure, X-ray, Zone

There(after), **Thereby**, **Thereupon** Holla, Ipso facto, Present, Thither, Thon, Upon, Y, Yonder

Therefore Argal, Ergo, Forthy, Hence, So, Why

Thermometer Aethrioscope, Centesimal, Clinical, Gas, Glass, Maximum and minimum, Psychrometer, Pyrometer, Resistance, Thermograph, Water, Wet and dry bulb, Wet bulb

Thermoplastic Cel(luloid), Resin

Thesaurus Dictionary, Lexicon, Roget, Treasury

These Thir

Theseus Champion

Thesis Argument, Dissertation, Doctorial, Theme

Thespian > ACTOR, Ham, Performer

Thessalonian Lapith

They A

Thick(en), Thickening, Thickener, Thickness, Thickset Abundant, Algin, Burly, Bushy, Callosity, Callus, Clavate, Cloddy, Cruddle, Curdle, Dense, Dextrin(e), Dumose, Engross, Grist, Grouty, Grume, Guar, Gum, Hyperostosis, Incrassate, Inspissate, Kuzu, Liaison, Lush, Nuggety, Panada, Roux, Sclerosis, > SOLID, Soupy, Squat, Stumpy, > STUPID, Thieves, This, Thixotropic, Waulk, Wooden, Xantham

Thick-coated Atheromatous

Thicket Bosk, Brake, Brush, Cane-brake, Chamisal, Chapparal, Coppice, Copse, Dead-finish, Greve, Grove, Macchie, Maquis, Queach, Reedrand, Reedrond, Salicetum, Shola

Thick-lipped Labrose

Thick-skinned Armadillo, Callous, Pachyderm, Tough

Thief, Thieves, Thievish Abactor, Autolycus, Blood, Chummy, Coon, Corsair, Cutpurse, Dismas, Dysmas, Filcher, Flood, Footpad, Freebooter, Furacious, Ganef, Gestas, Heist, Hotter, Huaquero, Ice-man, Jackdaw, Kiddy, Kondo, Larcener, Light-fingered, Limmer, Looter, Mag, Montith, Nip(per), Nuthook, Pad, Peculator, Pilferer, Pirate, Plagiarist, Poacher, Poddy-dodger, Prig, Raffles, River-rat, > ROBBER, Rustler, St Nicholas's clerks, Shark, Shop-lifter, Sneak, Sticky fingers, Taffy, Taker, Tea-leaf, Thick

Thigh Femoral, Gaskin, Ham, Haunch, Hock, Meros

Thin(ner) Acetone, Attenuate, Bald, Bony, Cull, Dilute, Ectomorph, Emaciated, Enseam, Fine, Fine-drawn, Flimsy, Gaunt, Hairline, Hair('s-)breadth, Inseem, Lanky, Lean, Matchstick, Mawger, Puny, Rackabones, Rangy, Rare, Rarefied, Reedy, Scant, Scraggy, Scrannel, Scrawny, Sheer, Sieve, Skeletal, Skimpy, Skinking, Slender, Slim, Slimline, Slink, > SPARE, Sparse, Spindly, Stilty, Stringy, Subtle, Taper, Tenuous, Turps, Wafer, Washy, Waste, Watch, Water(y), > WEAK, Weedy, Whirtle, Wiry, Wispy, Wortle, Wraith

Thing(s) Alia, Article, Chattel, Chose, Doodah, Doofer, Entia, Fetish, Fixation, It, Item, Jingbang, Job, Last, Material, Matter, Noumenon, > OBJECT, Obsession, Paraphernalia, Phobia, Res, Tool, Vision, Whatnot

Thingummy Dingbat, Dinges, Doodah, Doofer, Doohickey, Gubbins, Whatsit, Yoke

Think(er), Thinking Associate, Believe, Brain, Brood, Casuistry, Cogitate, Conjecture, Consider, Contemplant, > CONTEMPLATE, Deem, Deliberate, Descartes, Dianoetic, Divergent, Esteem, Fancy, Fear, Feel, Fogramite, Ghesse, Gnostic, Guess, Hegel, Hold, > IMAGINE, Judge, Lateral, Meditate, Mentation, Mindset, Mull, Muse, Opine, Pensive, Philosopher, Phrontistery, Ponder, Pore, Presume, Ratiocinate, Rational, Reckon, Reflect, Reminisce, Ruminate, Synectics, Trow, Vertical, Ween, Wishful

Thin-skinned Sensitive

Third, Third rate Bronze, C, Eroica, Gamma, Gooseberry, Interval, Mediant,

Picardy, Quartan, Tertiary, Tertius, Tierce, Trisect

Third man Abel, Lime

Thirst(y) Adry, > CRAVE, Dives, Drought, Drouth, Dry, Hydropic, Nadors, Pant, Polydipsia, Thrist

Thirteen Baker's dozen, Devil's dozen, Long dozen, Riddle, Triskaidekaphobia, Unlucky

Thirty Lambda

Thirty nine books All-OT, OT

This Hic, Hoc, The, Thick, Thilk, Thir

Thistle Canada, Carduus, Carline, Cnicus, Dayshell, Echinops, Milk, Musk, Russian, Safflower, Scotch, Sow, Spear, Star, Thrissel, Thristle

This year Ha

Thomas Aquinas, Arnold, Christadelphian, De Quincey, Didymus, Doubting, Dylan, Erastus, Hardy, Loco, Parr, Rhymer, Tompion, True, Turbulent

Thong Babiche, Jandal®, Lash, Latchet, Leather, Lore, Riem, Shoe-latchet, > STRAP, Taws(e), Whang, Whip

Thor Thunderer

Thorax Chest, Peraeon, Pereion, Scutellum, Throat

Thorium Th

Thorn(y) Acantha, Bael, Bel, Bhel, Bramble, Briar, Coyotillo, Doom, Edh, Eth, Irritation, Jerusalem, Mahonia, Mayflower, Nabk, Nebbuk, Nebe(c)k, > NEEDLE, Pricker, Prickle, Slae, Spine, Spinescent, Spinulate, Trial, Wagn'bietjie, Y, Ye, Zare(e)ba, Zariba, Zeriba

Thorn-apple Jimpson-weed

Thornless Inerm

Thorough(ly) A fond, Complete, Deep, Even-down, Firm, Fully, Ingrained, Inly, Out, Out and out, Painstaking, Pakka, Pucka, Pukka, Ripe, Root and branch, Searching, Sound, Strict, Total, Tout à fait, Up

Thoroughbred Arab, Bloodstock, Pedigree

Thoroughfare Avenue, Broadway, Causeway, Freeway, Highway, Parkway, > ROAD, Street

Those Thaim, Them, Tho, Yon

Thou M, Mil

Though Albe, Albeit, All-be, Ever, Tho, Whenas

Thought(s), **Thoughtful(ness)** Avisandum, Broody, Censed, Cerebration, Cogitation, Concept, Considerate, Contemplation, Dianoetic, Felt, Idea, Innate, Kind, Maieutic, Mind, Musing, Notion, Opinion, Pensée, Pensive, Philosophy, Reflection, Rumination, Second

Thoughtless Blindfold, Careless, Heedless, Improvident, Incogitant, Inconsiderate, Pillock, > RASH, Reckless, Remiss, Scatter-brained, Vacant, Vain

Thousand(s) Chiliad, Gorilla, K, Lac, Lakh, M, Millenary, Millennium, Myriad, Plum, Toman

Thracian Spartacus

Thrall Captive, Esne, Serf, Slave

Thrash(ing) > BEAT, Belabour, Belt, Bepelt, Binge, Bless, Cane, Dress, Drub, Flail, Flog, Jole, Joll, Joule, Jowl, Lace, Laidie, Laidy, Lambast, Larrup, Lather, Leather, Lick, Marmelise, Paste, Ploat, Quilt, Slog, Smoke, Strap-oil, Swat, Tank, Targe, Thraiping, Towel, Trim, Trounce, Wallop, Whale, Whap, Writhe

Thread, **Threadlike** Acme screw, Ariadne, Bar, Bottom, Bride, Buttress, Chalaza, Chromatid, Chromatin, Chromosome, Clew, Clue, Cop(pin), Cord, Coventry blue, Eel-worm, End, Fibre, Filament, File, Filiform, Filose, Filoselle, Float, Flourishing, Gold, Gossamer, Heddle, Ixtle, Lace, Lap, Lingel, Lingle, Link,

Lisle, Lurex®, Meander, Mycellum, Nematode, Nematoid, Organzine, Pack, Pearlin(g), Pick, Plasmodesm, Ravel, Reeve, Sacred, Screw, Sellers screw, Seton, Silver, Single, > **STRAND**, Stroma, Suture, Tassel, Tendril, Theme, Thrid, Thrum, Trace, Tram, Trundle, Tussore, Twine, Warp, Watap, Wax(ed), Weft, Whitworth, Whitworth screw, Wick, > **WIND**, Wisp, Worm

Threadbare Hackneyed, Napless, Shabby, Worn

Threadworm Nemathelminth, Strongyl, Vinegar-eel

Threat(en), Threatened, Threatening Baleful, Blackmail, Bluster, Coerce, Comminate, Face, Fatwa, Fraught, Greenmail, Greymail, Hazard, Impend, Imperil, Loom, > **MENACE**, Minacious, Minatory, Mint, Omen, Overcast, Overhang, Parlous, Peril, Portent, Ramp, Sabre-rattling, Shore, Strongarm, Ugly, Veiled, Warning

Three, Threefold, Three-wheeler, Thrice Graces, Har, Harpies, Jafenhar, Leash, Muses, Musketeers, Pairial, Pair-royal, Prial, Ter, Tern, Terzetta, Thrice, Thridi, Tid, T.i.d, Tierce, Tray, Trey, Triad, Tricar, Triennial, Trifid, Trigon, Trilogy, Trinal, Trine, Trinity, Trio, Triple, Triptote, Troika

Three-D(imensional) Lenticular, Stereopsis

Three-day Triduan, Triduum

Threehalfpence Dandiprat, Dandyprat

Three-handed Cutthroat

Three-headed Cerberus, Geryon

Three hundred B, Carpet

Three-legged IOM, Triskele, Triskelion

Threepence, Threepenny bit Tickey, Tray, Trey, Treybit

Three-year old Staggard

Threnody Dirge, Epicede, > **LAMENT**

Thresh Beat, Flail, Separate

Threshold Absolute, Brink, Cill, Difference, Doorstep, Limen, Liminal, Sill, Tax, Verge

▶ **Thrice** see **THREE**

Thrift(y) Economy, Frugal, Husbandry, Oeconomy, Sea-grass, Sea-pink, Virtue

Thrill(er), Thrilling Atingle, Buzz, Delight, Dindle, Dinnle, Dirl, Dread, Dynamite, Emotive, > **ENCHANT**, Excite, Film noir, Frisson, Gas, Jag, Kick, Page-turner, Perceant, Plangent, Pulsate, Pulse, Quiver, Sensation, Thirl, Tinglish, Tremor, Vibrant, Whodunit

Thrive Batten, Blossom, Boom, Do, Fl, > **FLOURISH**, Flower, Grow, Mushroom, > **PROSPER**, Succeed, Thee

Throat(y) Craw, Crop, Deep, Dewlap, Fauces, Gorge, Gular, Gullet, Guttural, Hot coppers, Jugular, Maw, Pereion, Pharynx, Prunella, Quailpipe, Red lane, Roopit, Roopy, Strep, Swallet, Thrapple, Thropple, Throttle, Weasand, Wesand, Whistle, Windpipe

Throb(bing) Beat, Palpitate, Pant, Pit-a-pat, Pulsate, Quop, Stang, Tingle, Vibrato

▷ **Throbbing** *may indicate* an anagram

Throe(s) Agony, Pang, Paroxysm

Thrombosis Deep-vein

Throne Bed-of-justice, Cathedra, Episcopal, Gadi, Mercy-seat, Peacock, Rule, Seat, See, Siege, Tribune

Throng(ing) Crowd, Flock, Host, Press, Resort, Swarm

Throttle > **CHOKE**, Gar(r)otte, Gun, Mug, Regulator, Scrag, Silence, Stifle, Strangle, Strangulate, Thrapple, We(a)sand

Through, Throughout Along, Ana, By, Dia-, During, Everywhere, Over, Passim,

Per, Pr, Sempre, Sic passim, To, Trans, Via, Yont

▸ **Throw(n)** *see* TOSS

Throwback Atavism, Echo

Throw (up), Thrower, Throw-out Bin, Cast-off, Chunder, Discobolus, Egesta, Emesis, Jettison, Puke, Spew, Squirt, Squit

Thrush Ant, Aphtha, Bird, Chat, Fieldfare, Hermit, Homescreetch, Mavis, Missel, Mistle, Pitta, Prunella, Redwing, Sprue, Turdine, Veery

Thrust, Thruster Aventre, Bear, Boost, Botte, Burn, Detrude, Dig, Drive, Elbow, Exert, Extrude, Flanconade, Foin, > FORCE, Gist, Hay, Imbroc(c)ata, Impulse, Job, Lunge, Montant(o), Obtrude, Oust, Pass, Passado, Peg, Perk, Pitchfork, Poke, Potch(e), Pote, Probe, Propel, Pun, Punto, > PUSH, Put, Remise, Repost, Run, Shoulder, Shove, Single-stock, Sock, Sorn, Squat, Stap, Stick, Stoccado, Stoccata, Stock, Stuck, Thrutch, Tilt, Tuck

Thud Drum, Dump, Flump, Phut, Plod, Thump

Thug(s) Goon(da), Gorilla, Gurrier, Hoodlum, Loord, Ninja, Ockers, Phansigar, Plug-ugly, Roughneck, SS, Strangler, Ted, Tityre-tu, Tsotsi

Thule Ultima

Thulium Tm

Thumb Bally, Green, Hitch, Midget, Ovolo, Pollex, Scan, Tom

Thump(ing) Blow, Bonk, Clobber, Cob, Crump, Da(u)d, Drub, Dub, Hammer, Knevell, Knock, Nevel, Oner, Paik, > POUND, Pummel, Slam, Slosh, Souse, Swat, Swingeing, Thud, Trounce, Tund, Whud

Thunder(ing), Thunderstorm Bolt, Boom, Clap, Coup de foudre, Donnerwetter, Foudroyant, Foulder, Fulminate, Intonate, Lei-king, Pil(l)an, Raiden, > ROAR, Rumble, Summanus, Tempest, Thor, Tonant

Thursday Chare, Holy, Maundy, Sheer, Shere

Thus Ergo, Sic, So, Therefore

Thwart Baffle, Balk, > CROSS, Dash, Dish, Foil, Frustrate, Hamstring, Hogtie, Obstruct, Outwit, Pip, Prevent, Scotch, Snooker, Spike, Spite, Stonker, Stymie, Transverse

Thy Yourn

Thyme Basil, Lemon, Water

Thyroid Goitre, Myxodema

Tiara Cidaris, Crownet

Tiberius Gracchus

Tibetan Lamaist, Naga, Sherpa, Sitsang

Tic Vocal

Tick, Tick off Acarida, Acarus, Beat, Bloodsucker, Check, > CHIDE, Click, Cr, > CREDIT, Deer, HP, Idle, Instant, Jar, Ked, Mattress, Mile, Mo, Moment, Ricinulei, Second, Strap, Worm

Ticket(s) Billet, Bone, Brief, Carnet, Commutation, Complimentary, Coupon, Day, Docket, Dream, Excursion, Kangaroo, Label, Meal, One-day, One-way, Parking, Pass, Pass-out, Pawn, Platform, Raffle, Raincheck, Return, Scratchcard, Season, Single, Soup, Split, Straight, Stub, Supersaver, > TAG, Tempest, Tessera(l), Through, Tix, Transfer, Tyburn, Unity, Voucher, Walking, Zone

Ticket-seller Scalper

Tickle, Ticklish Amuse, Delicate, Divert, Excite, Gratify, Gump, > ITCH, Kittle, Queasy, Thrill, Titillate

Tiddler Brit, Tom

Tide, Tidal Current, Drift, Eagre, Easter, Eger, Estuary, Flood, High, High water, Lee, Low, Marigram, Neap, Red, Rising, Roost, Sea, Seiche, Slack water, Spring,

Surge, Trend, Wave

Tide-gate Aboideau, Aboiteau, Weir

Tidings Gospel, > **NEWS**, Rumour, Word

Tidy Comb, Considerable, Curry, Do, Fair, Fettle, Groom, Kempt, Large, Neat, > **ORDER**, Pachyderm, Predy, Preen, Primp, Red(d), Slick, Snug, Sort, Spruce, Trim, Valet

Tie, Tying Ascot, Attach, Barcelona, Berth, Bind, Black, > **BOND**, Bootlace, Bow, Bowyang, Cable, Cope, Cravat, Cup, Dead-heat, Drag, Draw, Four-in-head, Frap, Halter, Handicap, Harness, Holdfast, Kipper, > **KNOT**, Lash, Level, Ligament, Ligate, Ligature, Link, Marry, Match, Moor, Neck and neck, Oblige, Obstriction, Old School, Oop, Oup, Overlay, Raffia, Restrain, Rod, Scarf, School, Score draw, Semifinal, Shackle, Shoelace, Shoestring, Sleeper, Slur, Solitaire, Soubise, Splice, Stake, Strap, String, Tawdry-lace, Tether, Trice, Truss, Unite, White, Windsor

Tier Apron, Bank, Gradin(e), Knotter, Layer, Rank, Stage, Storey

Tierce Leash, Tc

Tiff Bicker, Contretemps, Difference, Dispute, Feed, Feud, Huff, Miff, Skirmish, Spat, Squabble

Tiffany Gauze

Tiger Bengal, > **CAT**, Clemenceau, Demoiselle, Lily, Machairodont, Machairodus, Margay, Paper, Sabre-tooth, Smilodon, Tamil, Tasmanian, Woods

Tight(en), Tightness, Tights Boozy, Bosky, Brace, Cinch, Close(-hauled), Constriction, Cote-hardie, > **DRUNK**, Fishnet, Fleshings, High, Hose, Jam, Leggings, Leotards, Lit, Loaded, Maillot, Mean, Merry, Niggardly, Oiled, Pang, Pantihose, Phimosis, Pickled, Pinch(penny), Plastered, Prompt, Proof, Rigour, Snug, Squiffy, Stenosis, > **STINGY**, Stinko, Strict, Stringent, Swift, Swig, Taut, Tense, Tipsy, Trig, Woozy

Tightrope(-walker) Aerialist, Blondin, Equilibrist, Funambulist, Petauriste

Tightwad Cheapskate, > **MISER**, Scrooge

Tile(d), Tiles Antefix, Arris, Azulejo, Carpet, Chapeau, Dalle, Derby, Dutch, Encaustic, Field, > **HAT**, Imbrex, Imbricate, Lid, Lino, Ostracon, Ostrakon, Peever, Quarrel, Quarry, Rag(g), Rooftop, Sclate, Shingle, Slat, > **SLATE**, Tegula, Tessella, Tessera, Titfer, Topper, Wall, Wally

Till Cashbox, Checkout, Coffer, Ear, Eulenspiegel, Farm, Hasta, Hoe, Husband, Lob, Peter, > **PLOUGH**, Set, Unto

Tiller Gardener, Helm, Ploughman, Rotavator, Wheel

Tilt Awning, Bank, Camber, Cant, Cock, Dip, Heel, Hut, Joust, Just, > **LIST**, Quintain, Rock, Tip, Unbalance

Timber Apron, Balk, Batten, Beam, Bond, Bridging, Cant-rail, Carapa, Chess, Clapboard, Compass, Coulisse, Cross-tree, Cruck, Dwang, Elmwood, Flitch, Four-by-two, Futchel, Futtock, Greenheart, Hardwood, Harewood, Intertie, Iroko, Ironwood, Joist, Knee, Knighthead, Lauan, Ligger, Lintel, Log, Lumber, Nogging, Nothofagus, Plank-sheer, Purlin(e), Putlock, Putlog, Pyengadu, Radiata, Ramin, Rib, Ridgepole, Roundwood, Rung, Sandalwood, Sapele, Sapodilla, Satinwood, Scantling, Shook, Shorts, Sissoo, Skeg, Sneezewood, Softwood, Souari, Stemson, Stere, Sternpost, Sternson, Straddle, Stull, Stumpage, Summer, Swing-stock, Towing-butts, Transom, Trestletree, Two-by-four, Wale, Wallplate, Weatherboard, Whitewood, > **WOOD**, Yang

Timbre Clang, Klang(farbe), Register, > **TENOR**, Tone

Time(s), Timer Access, Agoge, Apparent, Assymetric, Astronomical, Autumn, Awhile, Bird, BST, Central, Chronic, Chronometer, Chronon, Clock, Closing, Common, Compound, Connect, Core, Counter, Date, Day, Dead, Decade,

Dimension, Double, Duple, Duration, Early, Eastern, Eastern Standard, Egg-glass, Enemy, Eon, Ephemeris, Epoch, Equinox, Era, European, Eve(ning), Extra, Father, Flexitime, Forelock, Free, Full, Gest, Glide, Half, Healer, High, Horologe, Hour, Hourglass, Hr, Idle, Imprisonment, Injury, Innings, Instant, Interlude, Jiff, Juncture, Kalpa, Latent, Lay-day, Lead, Lean, Leisure, Life, Lighting-up, Lilac, Local, Mean, Menopause, Metronome, Mountain standard, Multiple, Needle, Nonce, Nones, Occasion, Oft, > **ON TIME**, Opening, Pacific, Paralysis, Part, Period, Phanerozoic, Pinger, Porridge, Post, Prelapsarian, Prime, Proper, Quadruple, Quality, Question, Quick, Reaction, Real, Reaper, Recovery, Response, Reverberation, Rhythm, Sandglass, Seal, > **SEASON**, Seel, Seil, Semeion, Serial, Session, Shelf-life, Sidereal, Sight, Simple, Sith(e), Slow, Solar, Solstice, Space, Span, Spare, Spell, Spin, Split, Spring, Standard, Stoppage, Stopwatch, Stound, Stownd, Stretch, Summer, Sundial, Sundown, Sythe, T, Tem, Tempo, Tempore, Tense, Thief, Three-four, Thunderer, Tick, Tid, Tide, Trice, Triple, Turnaround, Two-four, Universal, Usance, While, Winter, X, Yonks, Zero

Timebomb Demographic

Time-keeper, Timepiece Ben, Chronometer, Clock, Hourglass, Ref, Sand-glass, Sundial, Ticker, Tompion, Watch

Timeless Eternal, Nd, Undying

Timely Appropriate, Apropos, Happy, Opportune, Pat, Prompt

Timescale Geological

Time-server Prisoner, Trimmer

Timetable Bradshaw, > **CHART**, Schedule

Timid, Timorous Afraid, Aspen, Bashful, Blate, Chicken, Cowardly, Eerie, Eery, Faint-hearted, Fearful, Hare, Hen-hearted, Milquetoast, Mouse, Mous(e)y, Pavid, Pigeon-hearted, Pusillanimous, Quaking, Schnok, Shrinking, > **SHY**, Skeary, Sook, Yellow

Timothy Cat's-tail, Grass, Phleum

Tin(ned), Tinfoil, Tinny Argentine, Block, Britannia metal, Can, Cash, Debe, Dixie, Maconochie, Mess, > **MONEY**, Moola(h), Ochre, Plate, Rhino, Sn, Stannary, Stannic, Stream, Tain, Tole

Tincture Arnica, Bufo, Chroma, Elixir, Fur, Infusion, Laudanum, Metal, Or, Sericon, Sol, Spice, Taint, Tenné, Vert

Tinder Amadou, Faggot, Fuel, Funk, Punk, Spark, Spunk, Touchwood

Tine Antler, Bay, Cusp, Grain, Prong, Snag, Surroyal, Trey

Tinge(d) Dye, Eye, Flavour, Gild, > **HUE**, Infuscate, Taint, Tincture, Tone, Touch

Tingle, Tingling Dinnle, Dirl, Paraesthesia, Prickle, Thrill, Throb, Tinkle

Tinker Bell, Caird, Coster, Didakai, Didakei, Diddicoy, Didicoy, Didikoi, > **FIDDLE**, Gypsy, Mender, Pedlar, Potter, Prig, Putter, Repair, Sly, Snout, Tamper, Tramp, Traveller

Tinkle Pink

Tinsel(ly) Clinquant, Gaudy, Glitter, O, Spangle, Turkey

Tint Colour, Henna, Hue, Pigment, > **STAIN**, Tinct, Tinge, Woad

Tiny Atto-, Baby, Diddy, Dwarf, Ha'it, Infinitesimal, Itsy-bitsy, Lilliputian, Minikin, Minim, Mite, Negligible, Petite, Small, Smidgeon, Teeny, Tiddl(e)y, Tiddy, Tim, Tine, Tottie, Totty, Toy, Wee

Tip, Tipping Apex, Arrowhead, Ash-heap, Asparagus, Backshish, Baksheesh, Batta, Beer-money, Bonsel(l)a, Bonus, B(u)onamono, Cant, Cert, Chape, Counsel, Coup, Cowp, Crown, Cue, Cumshaw, Douceur, Dump, Extremity, Fee, Felt, Ferrule, Filter, Forecast, Glans, Gratillity, Gratuity, Heel, > **HINT**, Hunch, Inkle, Iridise, Lagniappe, Largess(e), List, Mess, Middenstead, Nap, Noop,

Ord, Perk, Perquisite, Point, Pointer, Pour, Pourboire, Previse, Prong, Straight, Suggestion, Summit, Tag, Tail, Tilt, Toom, Touch, Tronc, Vail, Vales, Whisper, Wink, Wrinkle
Tippet Cape, Fur, Scarf
Tipple Bib, Booze, > DRINK, Paint, Pot, Poteen
Tipster Prophet, Tout
Tipsy Bleary, Boozy, Bosky, > DRUNK, Elevated, Moony, Nappy, Oiled, On, Rocky, Screwed, Slewed, Slued, Squiffy, Wet
▷ **Tipsy** *may indicate* an anagram
Tiptoe Digitigrade
Tirade Diatribe, Invective, Jobation, Laisse, Philippic, Rand, Rant, Screed, Slang
Tire(d), Tiredness, Tiring All-in, Beat, Bore, Bushed, Caparison, Deadbeat, Dress, Drowsy, > EXHAUST, Fag, Fagged out, Fatigue, Flag, Fordid, Fordod, Forjeskit, Frazzle, Gruel, Irk, Jade, Lassitude, Limp, ME, Overspent, Pall, Poop, Puggled, > ROBE, Rubber, Sap, Shagged, Sicken, Sleepry, Sleepy, Spent, Swinkt, Tax, Tedious, Wabbit, Wappend, Weary, Wrecked
Tiresome Boring, Exhausting, Humdrum, Pill, Tedious, Vexing
Tirl Rattle, Risp, Strip, Turn
▶ **Tiro** *see* TYRO
Tissue Adenoid, Adhesion, Adipose, Aerenchyma, Aponeurosis, Archesporium, Callus, Carbon, Cartilage, Cementum, Chalaza, Cheloid, Chlorenchyma, Coenosarc, Collagen, Collenchyma, Commissure, Conducting, Connective, Cortex, Dentine, Diploe, Epimysium, Epineurium, Epithelium, Eschar, Evocator, Fabric, Fascia, Flesh, Gamgee, Gauze, Gleba, Glia, Granulation, Gum, Heteroplasia, Histogen, Histoid, Infarct, Keloid, Kleenex®, Lamina, Lies, Ligament, Luteal, Lymphoid, Macroglia, Marrow, Matrix, Mechanical, Medulla, > MEMBRANE, Meristem, Mesophyll, Mestom(e), Mole, Myelin(e), Myocardium, Neuroglia, Nucellus, Olivary, Pack, Palisade, Pannus, Paper, Papilla, Parenchyma, Periblem, Perichylous, Peridesmium, Perimysium, Perinephrium, Perineurium, Perisperm, Phellogen, Phloem, Pith, Placenta, Plerome, Polyarch, Pons, Primordium, Prosenchyma, Prothallis, Pterygium, Pulp, Radula, Sarcenet, Sars(e)net, Scar, Sclerenchyma, Sequestrum, Sinew, Soft, Somatopleure, Stereome, Stroma, Submucosa, Suet, Tarsus, Tela, Tendon, Tonsil, Tunica, Vascular, Velum, Web, Wound, Xylem, Zoograft
Tit, Tit-bit(s) Analecta, Canape, Crested, Currie, Curry, Delicacy, Dug, Nag, Nipple, Nun, Pap, Quarry, Sample, Scrap, Snack, Teat, Tug, Twitch, Willow, Wren, Zakuska
Titan(ic), Titaness Atlas, Colossus, Cronos, Cronus, Drone, Enormous, Giant, Huge, Hyperion, Kronos, Leviathan, Liner, Oceanus, Phoebe, Prometheus, Rhea, Themis, Vast
Titanium, Titanite Sagenite, Sphene, Ti
Tit for tat Deserts, Revenge, Talion
Tithe Disme, Dyzemas, Frankpledge, Teind, Tenth
Titian Abram, Auburn
Titillate Delight, Excite, Tickle
Titivate Primp
Title Abbe, > ADDRESS, Ag(h)a, Antonomasia, Appellative, Bahadur, Baroness, Baronet, Bart, Bhai, Bretwalda, Calif, Caliph, Caption, Charta, Chogyal, Claim, Conveyance, Count(ess), Courtesy, Credit, Dan, Datin, Datuk, Dauphin, Dayan, Deeds, Devi, Dom, Don, Don(n)a, Dowager, Dub, Duchess, Duke, Earl, Effendi, Eminence, Epithet, Esquire, Excellency, Fra, Frau(lein), Gospodin, Gyani, Hafiz, Handle, Header, Heading, Headline, Hojatoleslam, Hon,

Honour, Imperator, Interest, Kalif, Kaliph, Kaur, King, Lady, Lala, Lemma,
> **LIEN**, Lord, Mal(l)am, Marchesa, Marchese, Marquess, Marquis, Master,
Masthead, Maulana, Memsahib, Meneer, Mevrou, Miladi, Milady, Milord,
Mirza, Mr(s), Name, Nizam, Nomen, Padishah, Peerage, Pir, Polemarch, Prefix,
Prince(ss), Queen, > **RANK**, Reb, Reverence, Reverend, > **RIGHT**, Rubric, Sahib,
Sama, San, Sardar, Sayid, Senhor(a), Señor(a), Shri, Singh, Sir, Sirdar, Son,
Sowbhagyawati, Sri, Stratum, Tannie, Tenno, Torrens, Tycoon, V, Worship
Title-holder Cartouche, Champion, Landlord, Noble
Titmouse Bird, Hickymal, Mag, Reedling, Tit
Titter Giggle, Snigger, Tehee
Tittle Jot
Titus Oates
Tizz(y) Pother, Spin, Tanner, Testril, VId
TNT Explosive, Trotyl
To(wards) At, Beside, Inby, Onto, Prone, Shet, Shut, Till
Toad(y) Bootlicker, Bufo, Bumsucker, Cane, Clawback, Cocksucker, Crapaud,
Crawler, Fawn, Frog, Horned, Jackal, Jenkins, Knot, Lackey, Lick-platter,
Lickspittle, Midwife, Minion, Natterjack, Nototrema, Paddock, Parasite,
Pick-thank, Pipa, Placebo, Platanna, Puddock, Queensland cane, Sook,
Spade-foot, Surinam, Sycophant, Tree, Tuft-hunter, Walking, Xenopus,
Yesman
Toadstool Amanita, Death-cap, Death-cup, Destroying angel, Fly agaric,
> **FUNGUS**, Grisette, Horsehair, Paddock-stool, Parrot, Sulphur tuft, Verdigris,
Wax cap
Toast(er) Bacchus, Bell, Birsle, Brindisi, > **BROWN**, Bruschetta, Bumper, Cheers,
Chin-chin, Crostini, Crouton, French, Gesundheit, Grace-cup, Grill, Health,
Iechyd da, Kiaora, L'chaim, Lechayim, Loyal, Melba, Pledge, Pop up, Propose,
Prosit, Round, Scouther, Scowder, Scowther, Sentiment, Sippet, Skoal, Slainte,
Slainte mha(i)th, Soldier, Sunbathe, Wassail, Zwieback
Toastmaster MC, Symposiarch
Tobacco, Tobacco-field Alfalfa, Bacchi, Baccy, Bird's eye, Broadleaf, Burley,
Canaster, Capa, Caporal, Cavendish, Chew, Dottle, Filler, Honeydew,
Killikinnick, Kinnikinick, Latakia, Mundungus, Nailrod, Navy-cut,
Negro-head, Nicotian, Nicotine, Niggerhead, Perique, Pigtail, Plug, Quid,
Rapper, Régie, Returns, Shag, Sneesh, Snout, Snuff, Straight cut, Stripleaf,
Turkish, Twist, Vega, Virginia, Weed
Toboggan Sled(ge), Sleigh
Toby Dog, Highwayman, Jug
Tocsin Alarm, Siren
Today Hodiernal, Now, Present
Toddle(r) Baim, Gangrel, Mite, Tot, Totter, Trot, Waddle
Toddy Arrack, > **DRINK**, Sura, Whisky
To-do Sensation, Stir
Toe(s) Dactyl, Digit, Fissiped, Hallux, Hammer, Piggy, Pinky, Pointe, Poulaine,
Prehallux, Tootsie
Toff Nob, Nut, Swell
Toffee Banket, Butterscotch, Caramel, Cracknel, Gundy, Hard-bake,
Hokey-pokey, Humbug, Tom-trot
Toga Palla
Together Among, At-one, Atone, Attone, En bloc, En masse, Gathered, Infere,
> **JOINT**, Pari-passu, Sam, Unison, Wed, Y, Yfere, Ysame
Toggle Fastener, Netsuke

Togs Clothes, Gear, Rig, Strip

Toil(s) Drudge, Fag, Industry, > **LABOUR**, Mesh, Net, Seine, Sisyphus, Sweat, Swink, Tela, Tew, Trap, Trauchle, Travail, Tug, Web, > **WORK**, Wrest, Yacker, Yakka, Yakker

Toilet Can, Chemical, Coiffure, John, Lat(rine), > **LAVATORY**, Loo, Necessary house, Necessary place, Pot, Powder room, WC

Token Buck, Check, Counter, Coupon, Disc, Double-axe, Emblem, Gift, Indication, > **MEMENTO**, Nominal, Portend, Seal, Sign, Signal, Symbol, Symptom, Tessera, Valentine

Tolerable Acceptable, Bearable, Mediocre, Passable, So-so

Tolerance, Tolerant, Tolerate(d) Abear, Abide, > **ALLOW**, Bear, Broadminded, Brook, Endure, Enlightened, Hack, Had, Immunological, Latitude, > **LENIENT**, Lump, Mercy, Permit, Stand, Stick, Stomach, Studden, Suffer, Support, Thole, Wear, Zero

Toll Chime, Customs, Due, Duty, Excise, Joll, Joule, Jowl, Light-dues, Octroi, Pierage, Pike, Pontage, Rates, > **RING**, Scavage, Streetage, Tariff, Tax

Tom(my) Atkins, Bell, Bowling, Bread, Brown, > **CAT**, Collins, Edgar, Gib, Grub, Gun, He-cat, Jerry, Jones, Mog(gy), Nosh, Peeping, Private, Pte, Puss, Ram-cat, Sawyer, Snout, Soldier, Stout, Thos, Thumb, Tiddler, Tucker

Tomato Beef(steak), Cherry, Gooseberry, Husk, Love-apple, Plum, Portuguese, Strawberry, Tamarillo, Tree, Wolf's peach

Tomb(stone) Burial, Catacomb, Catafalque, Cenotaph, Cist, Coffin, Dargah, Durgah, Grave, Hypogeum, Kistvaen, Marmoreal, Mastaba, Mausoleum, Megalithic, Monument, Pyramid, > **SEPULCHRE**, Sepulture, Serdab, Shrine, Speos, Tell el Amarna, Tholos, Tholus, Through-stone, Treasury, Vault

Tombola Draw, Lottery, Raffle

Tomboy Gamine, Gilpey, Gilpy, Hoyden, Ladette, Ramp, Romp

Tome > **BOOK**, Volume

Tomfoolery Caper, Fandangle, Shenanigan

Tomorrow Future, Manana, Morrow

Tompion Watchman

Tom Snout Tinker

Ton(age) C, Chic, Displacement, Freight, Gross, Hundred, Long, Measurement, Metric, Register, Shipping, Short, T

Tone, Tonality Brace, Dialling, Engaged, Fifth, Harmonic, Hum, Inflection, Key, Klang, Ninth, Partial, Qualify, Quarter, Resultant, Ringing, Side, > **SOUND**, Strain, Temper, Tenor, Timbre, Touch, Trite, Whole

Tong(s) Curling, Lazy, Wafer

Tongue Brogue, Burr, Chape, Clack, Clapper, Doab, Double, Final, Forked, Glossa, Glossolalia, Jinglet, > **LANGUAGE**, Languet(te), Lap, Ligula, Lill, Lingo, Lingulate, Mother, Organ, Radula, Ranine, Rasp, Red rag, Single, Spit, Tab, Triple, Voice, Vulgar

Tongue-tied Mush-mouthed

Tongue-twister Jaw-breaker, Shibboleth

Tonic Bracer, C(h)amomile, Doh, Key, Mease, Medicinal, Mishmee, Mishmi, Myrica, Oporice, Pareira brava, Pick-me-up, Quassia, Refresher, Roborant, Sage tea, Sarsaparilla, Solfa

▷ **Tonic** *may indicate* a musical note

Tonsil, Tonsillitis Amygdala, Antiaditis, Pharyngeal, Quinsy

Tonsure(d) Epilate, Haircut, Peel, Pield

Tony Bête, Chic, Fool, Smart

Too Als(o), As well, Besides, Eke, Excessive, Item, Likewise, Moreover, Oer, Over,

Overly, Plus, Troppo

Took Naam, Nam, Set, Stole, Wan, Won

Tool Adze, Aiguille, Auger, Awl, Ax(e), Beetle, Bevel, Billhook, Bit, Broach, Brog, Bur(r), Burin, Calipers, Catspaw, Chaser, Chisel, Chopper, Clippers, Croze, Dibber, Dibble, Die, Dolly, Drawknife, Drawshave, Drift(pin), Eatche, Edge, Elsin, Eolith, Facer, Fid, File, Firmer, Float, Float-stone, Former, Fraise, Froe, Frow, Fuller, Gad, Gimlet, Go-devil, Gouger, Grapnel, Grattoir, Graver, Hammer, Hardy, Hob, Hoe, Husker, > IMPLEMENT, Insculp, > INSTRUMENT, Iron, Jackhammer, Jemmy, Jim Crow, Jointer, Laster, Loggerhead, Loom, Lute, Machine, Mallet, Marlin(e)spike, Microlith, Mitre square, Moon-knife, Muller, Nippers, Oustiti, Outsiders, Palaeolith, Pattle, Pawn, Penis, Percussion, Pestle, Pick, Picklock, Pitchfork, Piton, Plane, Pliers, Plunger, Power, Pricker, Property, Prunt, Punch, Puncheon, Rabble, Rasp, Reamer, Ripple, Roll(er), Rounder, Router, Sander, Saw, Scalpel, Scauper, Scissors, Scorper, Scraper, Screwdriver, Scriber, Scutch, Scythe, Seamset, Secateurs, Shoder, Sickle, Slater, Sleeker, Snake, Spanner, Spirit-level, Spitsticker, Spokeshave, Strickle, Strike, Strimmer®, Swage, Swingle, Swipple, Tint, Tjanting, Triblet, Trowel, Try square, Tweezers, Twibill, Upright, Vibrator, Vice, Wimble, Wrench

Toot(er) Blow, Horn, Parp, Trumpet

Tooth(ed), Toothy, Teeth Bicuspid, Bit, Buck, Bunodont, Canine, Carnassial, Chactodon, Cheek tooth, Cog, Cott's, Crena(te), Ctenoid, Cusp, Denticle, Dentin(e), Dentures, Egg, Eye, False, Fang, Gam, Gat, Gnashers, Grinder, Heterodont, Impacted, Incisor, Ivory, Joggle, Laniary, Milk, Mill, Molar, Nipper, Odontoid, Orthodontics, Overbite, Pawl, Pearly gates, Pectinate, Peristome, Permanent, Phang, Plate, Pre-molar, Prong, Ratch, Scissor, Secodont, Sectorial, Serration, Set, Snaggle, Sprocket, Store, Sweet, Trophi, Tush, Tusk, Uncinus, Upper, Wallies, Wang, Wiper, Wisdom, Wolf, Zalambdodont

Toothache, Tooth troubles Caries, Odontalgia

Toothless Edentate, Gummy, Pangolin

Toothpaste Dentifrice

Top (drawer; hole; line; notcher), Topmost, Topper Ace, Acme, A1, Altissimo, Apex, Apical, Behead, Best, Better, Big, Blouse, Blouson, Boob tube, Brow, Bustier, Cacumen, Cap, Capstone, Ceiling, Coma, Cop, Coping, Corking, Cream, > CREST, Crista, Crop, Crown, Culmen, De capo, Decollate, Diabolo, Dog, Dome, Double, Drawer, Dreid(e)l, Elite, Execute, Fighting, Finial, Flip, Gentry, Gyroscope, Halterneck, Hard, Hat, > HEAD, Height, Hummer, Humming, Imperial, Jumper, Lid, Nun, One-er, Optimate, Orb, Parish, > PEAK, Peerie, Peery, Peg, Peplos, Peplus, Pinnacle, Pitch, Replenish, Ridge, Roof, Sawyer, Screw, Secret, Shaw, Shirt, Skim, Slay, Soft, Spinning, Star, Summit, Superate, Superb, Supernal, Supreme, Supremo, Surface, Sweater, Tambour, Targa, Teetotum, Texas, Tile, Trash, T-shirt, Turbinate, Up(most), Uppermost, V, Vertex, Whipping, Whirligig

▷ **Top** *may indicate* first letter

Topaz Citrine, Colorado, Occidental, Oriental, Pycnite, Rose, Scottish, Spanish

Topcoat Finish, Overcoat, Ulster

Tope(r) Boozer, Bouser, Dagaba, Dagoba, > DRUNK, Sot, Tosspot

Topic(al) Head, Hobbyhorse, Item, Motion, Shop, Subject, Text, > THEME

Top-knot Tuft

Topping Grand, Icing, Meringue, Pepperoni, Piecrust, Streusel

Topple Oust, Overbalance, Overturn, Tip, Upend, > UPSET

Topsy Parentless

Topsy-turvy Careen, Cockeyed, Inverted, Summerset, Tapsalteerie, Tapsleteerie

Torch Brand, Cresset, Flambeau, Hards, Hurds, Lamp, Lampad, Link, Olympic, Plasma, Roughie, Tead(e), Wisp

Torch-bearer Usherette

Toreador Escamillo, Matador, Picador, Torero

Torment(ed), Tormentor Agony, Anguish, Bait, Ballyrag, Bedevil, Butt, Cruciate, Crucify, Curse, Distress, Excruciate, Frab, Gehenna, Grill, Harass, Hell, Martyrdom, Molest, Nag, Nettle, Pang, Pine, Plague, > **RACK**, Sadist, Tantalise, Tease

Tornado Cyclone, Twister, Waterspout

Toronto Hogtown

Torpedo Bangalore, Bomb, Fish, Ray, Subroc, Tin fish, Weapon

Torpedo-guard Crinoline

Torpid, Torpor Accidie, Acedia, Comatose, Dormant, Inertia, Languid, Lethargic, Sluggish, Slumbering

Torrent Flood, Spate

Torrid Amphiscian, Hot, Sultry, Tropical

Torsk Cusk

Tortilla Pancake, Taco

Tortoise Chelonia, Emydes, Emys, Galapagos, Giant, Hic(c)atee, Kurma, Pancake, Snapping-turtle, Terrapin, Testudo, Timothy, Turtle, Water

Tortoiseshell Epiplastra, Hawksbill, Testudo

Tortuous Ambagious, Twisty, Winding

▷ **Tortuous** *may indicate* an anagram

Torture, Torture chamber, Torture instrument Agonise, Auto-da-fé, Bastinade, Bastinado, Boot, Bootikin, Catasta, Chinese burn, Chinese water, Crucify, Engine, Excruciate, Flageolet, Fry, Gadge, Gauntlet, Gyp, Iron maiden, Knee-cap, Naraka, Persecute, Pilliwinks, Pine, Pinniewinkle, Pinnywinkle, > **RACK**, Sadism, Scaphism, Scarpines, Scavenger, Scavenger's daughter, Scourge, Strappado, Tantalise, Third degree, Thumbscrew, Tumbrel, Tumbril, Water, Wheel, Wrack

▷ **Tortured** *may indicate* an anagram

Torturer Torquemada

Torus Disc, Stellarator

Tory Abhorrer, Blimp, Blue, C, Opposition, Right, Tantivy, Unionist

Toss(ing), Throw(n) Abject, Bandy, Bounce, Buck, Bung, Buttock, Cant, Canvass, Cast, Catapult, > **CHUCK**, Cottabus, Crabs, Cross-buttock, Dad, Daud, Deal, Disconcert, Elance, Estrapade, Falcade, > **FLING**, Flip, Flump, Flutter, Flying (head)-mare, Free, Full, Gollum, Haunch, Heave, Hipt, Hoy, > **HURL**, Jack, Jact(it)ation, Jaculation, Jeff, Juggle, Jump, Lance, Lob, Loft, Pash, Pitch, Purl, Put(t), Round-arm, Seamer, Shy, Slat, Sling, Unhorse, Unseat, Upcast

Toss-up Cross and pile, Heads or tails

Tot Add, Babe, Bairn, > **CHILD**, Dop, Dram, Infant, Mite, Nightcap, Nip(per), Nipperkin, Slug, Snifter, Snort, Tad

Total, Toto Absolute, Aggregate, All(-out), Amount, Balance, Be-all, > **COMPLETE**, Entire, Gross, Lot, Sum, Tale, Tally, Unqualified, Utter, Whole

Totalitarian Autocrat, Despot, Etatiste, Fascist

Tote Bear, > **CARRY**, Yomp

Totem Fetish, Icon, Image, Pole

Tottenham Hotspur

Totter Abacus, Daddle, Daidle, Didakai, Didakei, Did(d)icoy, Didicoi, Halt, Ragman, Rock, > **STAGGER**, Swag, Sway, Topple, Waver

Touch(ed), Touching, Touchy Accolade, Adjoin, Affect, Anent, Badass, Barmy,

Cadge, Captious, Carambole, Caress, Carom, Common, Concern, Connivent, Contact, Contiguous, Emove, > **FEEL**, Finger, Finishing, Flick, Fondle, Haptic, Huffy, > **IN TOUCH**, Iracund, Irascible, J'adoube, Liaison, Libant, Loan, Loco, Midas, Miffy, Near, Nie, Nigh, Nudge, Palp, Pathetic, Paw, Potty, Re, Sense, Shade, Skiff, Soft, Sore, Spice, > **SPOT**, Tactile, Tactual, Tag, Tangible, Tap, Taste, Tat, Tickle, Tig, Tinderbox, Tinge, Titivate, Trace, Trait, Tuck, Vestige
Touchline Tangent
Touchstone Basanite, Criterion, Norm, Standard
Touchwood Absit omen, Monk, Punk, Spunk, Tinder
Tough(en) Adamantine, Anneal, Apache, Arduous, Ballsy, Burly, > **HARD**, Hard-boiled, Hard-nosed, Hardy, Heavy duty, He-man, Hood, Hoodlum, Husky, Indurate, Knotty, Leathern, Leathery, Nut, Pesky, Rambo, Rigwiddie, Rigwoodie, Roughneck, Sinewy, Spartan, Steely, Stiff, String, Sturdy, Teuch, Thewed, Tityre-tu, Virile
Toupee Hairpiece, Rug, Tour, > **WIG**
Tour(er), Tourist Barnstorm, Circuit, Cook's, Emmet, Excursion, Grand, Grockle, GT, Holiday-maker, Itinerate, > **JOURNEY**, Lionise, Mystery, Outing, Parra, Posting, Roadie, Rubberneck, Safari, Swing, Tiki, > **TRAVEL**, Trip(per), Viator, Whistle-stop
Tourmaline Schorl, Zeuxite
Tournament American, Basho, Bonspiel, Carousel, Drive, Event, Jereed, Jerid, Joust, Just, Ladder, Plate, Pro-am, Round robin, Royal, Super Twelve, Swiss, Tilt, Tourney, Wimbledon
Tourniquet Garrot, Throttle, Torcular
Tousle Dishevel, Rumple
Tout Barker, Laud, Ply, Praise, Runner, Solicit, Toot
Tow(ing) Aquaplane, Button, Fibre, > **HAUL**, Pull, > **ROPE**, Ski, Skijoring, Stupe, Track
▸ **Towards** *see* **TO**
Towel Dry, Jack, Nappy, Roller, Rub, Sanitary, Tea, Terry, Turkish
Tower Aspire, Atalaya, Babel, Barbican, Bastille, Bastion, Belfry, Bell, Bloody, Brattice, Brettice, Brogh, Campanile, Conning, Control, Cooling, Donjon, Dungeon, Edifice, Eiffel, Fly, Fortress, Gantry, Garret, Gate, Giralda, Gopura(m), Guérite, Horologium, Ivory, Keep, Leaning, Loom, Maiden, Martello, Minar(et), Monument, Mooring, Mouse, Nuraghe, Nurhag, Overtop, Peel, Pinnacle, Pound, Pylon, Rear, Rise, Rolandseck, Rood, Round, Sail, Sears, Shot, Sikhara, Silo, Ski-lift, Space Needle, Specula, Spire, Stealth, Steeple, Tête-de-pont, Texas, Tractor, Tugboat, > **TURRET**, Victoria, Watch, Water, Yagura, Ziggurat, Zikkurat
Town, Township Boom, Borgo, Borough, Bourg, Burg(h), City, Conurbation, County, Deme, Dormitory, Dorp, Favella, Garrison, Ghost, Ham(let), Intraurban, Market, Municipal, Nasik, One-horse, Podunk, Pueblo, Satellite, Shanty, Staple, Tinsel, Tp, Twin, Urban, Wick
Townee, Townsman Cad, Cit(izen), Dude, Freeman, Oppidan, Philister, Resident
Town hall Prytaneum
Toxaemia Eclampsia
Toxic(ity), Toxin Abrin, Antigen, Botulin, Cadaverine, Coumarin, Curare, Deadly, Dioxan, Eclampsia, Fluorin(e), Lethal, Muscarine, Phalloidin, Phenol, Phenothiazine, Psoralen, Ricin, Sepsis, Serology, Venin, Venomous, Virulence, Zootoxin
Toy Bauble, Bull-roarer, Cockhorse, Cyberpet, Dally, Dandle, Doll, Executive,

Faddle, Finger, Flirt, Frisbee®, Gewgaw, Golly, Gonk, Jack-in-the-box, Jumping-jack, Kaleidoscope, Kickshaw, Knack, Lego®, Noah's ark, Novelty, Paddle, Pantine, Peashooter, Plaything, Praxinoscope, Rattle, Scooter, Shoofly, Skipjack, Taste, Teddy, Thaumatrope, > **TRIFLE**, Trinket, Tu(r)ndun, Whirligig, Yoyo, Zoetrope

Trace Atom, Cast, Derive, Describe, Draft, Draw, Dreg, Echo, Footprint, Ghost, > **HINT**, Leaf, Limn, Mark, Memory, Outline, Relic, Relict, Remnant, Scintilla, Semblance, Sign, Smack, Soupçon, Strap, > **TOUCH**, Track, Vestige, Whiff, Whit

Tracery Filigree

Track(s), Tracker, Tracking, Trackman Aintree, Band, B-road, Caterpillar®, Cinder, Circuit, Course, Dog, DOVAP, Drift, Ecliptic, El, Fast, Fettler, Footing, Gaudy dancer, Hunt, Ichnite, Ichnolite, Inside, Lane, Ley, Line, Loipe, Loopline, Mommy, Monitor, Monza, > **PATH**, Persue, Piste, Pug, Pursue, Race, Raceway, Rail, Railway, Rake, Ridgeway, Route, Run, Rut, Siding, Sign, Skidway, Sleuth, Slot, Sonar, Speedway, Spoor, Tan, Tan-ride, Taxi, Tenure, Tideway, > **TRAIL**, Trajectory, Tram, Tramline, Tramroad, Tramway, Tread, Trode, Tug(boat), Twin, Wake, Wallaby, Way, Y

Tract(able), Tracts Area, Belt, Bench, Clime, Colporteur, Common, Dene, Enclave, Flysheet, Lande, Leaflet, Monte, Moor, Olfactory, > **PAMPHLET**, Prairie, Province, Purlieu, Pusey, Region, Screed, Taluk, Tawie, Terrain, Wold

Tractarian(ism) Newman, Oxford movement, Pusey(ism)

Tractor Bulldozer, Cat, Caterpillar®, Fendalton, Pedrail, Remuera, Skidder, Tower

Trade(r), Tradesman, Trading Arb(itrageur), Banian, Banyan, Bargain, Barter, Bricks and clicks, Bun(n)ia, Burgher, Business, Cabotage, Calling, Carriage, Chaffer, Chandler, Chapman, Cheapjack, Coaster, Comanchero, > **COMMERCE**, Coster, Costermonger, Crare, Crayer, Deal(er), Easterling, Errand, Exchange, Factor, Fair, Floor, Free, Handle, Horse, Hosier, Hot, Importer, Indiaman, Industry, Insider, Ironmonger, Jobber, Legrolling, Line, Merchant, Métier, Middleman, Mister, Monger, Mystery, Outfitter, Paralleling, Pitchman, Ply, Rag, Retailer, Roundtripping, Scalp, Screen, Sell, Simony, Slave, Stallenger, Stallinger, Stationer, Sutler, Suttle, > **SWAP**, Traffic, Transit, Trant, Truck, Union, Vaisya, Vend, Wholesaler, Wind

Trademark Brand, Chop, Idiograph, Label, Logo, Tm

Trade Union ASLEF, COHSE, Local, Solidarity, Syndicalism, UNISON, USDAW

Trading money, Trading post Cabotage, Fort, Wampum

Tradition(s), Traditional(ist) Ancestral, Classical, Convention, Custom(ary), Eastern, Folkway, Hadith, Heritage, Legend, Lore, Mahayana, Misoneist, Old guard, Old-school, Orthodox, Pharisee, Pompier, Practice, Purist, Suburban, Time-honoured, Trad, Tralaticious, Tralatitious

Traduce Abuse, Asperse, Defame, Impugn, Malign, Smear, Vilify

Traffic, Traffic pattern Barter, Broke, Cabotage, Clover-leaf, Commerce, Contraflow, Deal, Negotiate, Passage, Run, Smuggle, Through, Trade, Truck, Vehicular

Tragedian, Tragedy, Tragic Aeschylus, Buskin, Calamity, Cenci, Corneille, Dire, > **DRAMA**, Euripides, Macready, Melpomene, Oedipean, Oresteia, Otway, Pathetic, Seneca, Sophoclean, Thespian, Thespis

Trail(er), Trailing Abature, Audit, Bedraggle, Caravan, Condensation, Creep, Drag, Draggle, Follow, Ipomaea, Lag, Liana, Liane, Nature, Oregon, Path, Persue, Preview, Promo(tion), Pursue, Repent, Runway, Santa Fe, Scent, Shadow, Sign, Sleuth, Slot, Spoor, Stream, Streel, Tag, Trace, > **TRACK**, Trade, Traipse, Trape, Trauchle, Trayne, Troad, Vapour, Vine, Virga, Wake

Train(er), Training Advanced, APT, BR, Breed, Caravan, Cat, Cavalcade, Circuit, Coach, Commuter, Condition, Cortège, Diesel, Direct, Discipline, Dog, Dressage, Drill, Drive, Educate, Entourage, Enure, Epicyclic, Eurostar®, Exercise, Express, Fartlek, Field, Flier, Flight simulator, Freightliner®, Fuse, Gear, Ghan, Ghost, Gravy, Grounding, GWR, Handle(r), Instruct, Intercity®, Interval, Jerkwater, Journey, Liner, Link, LMS, LNER, Loco, Longe, Lunge, Maglev, Mailcar, Manège, Manrider, Mein(e)y, Meinie, Mentor, Milk, Nopo, Nurture, Nuzzle, Omnibus, Orient Express, Owl, Pack, Paddy, PE, Pendolino, Potty, Practise, > **PREPARE**, Procession, PT, Puffer, Puff-puff, Push-pull, Q, Queue, Rattler, Rehearse, Retinue, Road, Roadwork, Rocket, Ry, Sack, > **SCHOOL**, Series, Shoe, Shuttle service, Siege, Sinkansen, Skill centre, Sloid, Sloyd, Sowarree, Sowarry, Special, SR, Steer, String, Suite, Tail, Tame, > **TEACH**, Through, Tire, Tirocinium, Track shoe, Trail, Tube, Wage, Wagon, Wave, Way
▷ **Train(ed)** *may indicate* an anagram
Trainee > **APPRENTICE**, Cadet, Cub, Learner, Ordinand, Rookie, Rooky
Train-spotter Gricer
Trait Characteristic, Feature, Knack, Ph(a)enotype, Strain, Thew, Trick
Traitor Benedict Arnold, Betrayer, Casement, Dobber-in, Joyce, Judas, Judas Maccabaeus, Nid(d)ering, Nid(d)erling, Nithing, Proditor, Quisling, Renegade, Reptile, Tarpeian, Traditor, Treachetour, Turncoat, Viper, Wallydraigle, Weasel
Trajectory Parabola, Track
▷ **Trammel** *may indicate* an anagram
Tramp, Trample Bog-trotter, Bum, Caird, Clochard, Clump, Crush, Derelict, Dero, Dingbat, Dosser, Estragon, Footslog, Freighter, Gadling, Gook, Hike, Hobo, Knight of the road, Meff, Override, Overrun, Pad, Piker, Plod, Poach, Potch(e), Rover, Scorn, Ship, Splodge, Sundowner, Swagman, > **TINKER**, Toe-rag(ger), Track, Traipse, Tread, Trek, Trog, Tromp, Truant, Trudge, Tub, Vagabond, Vagrant, Weary Willie
Trampoline Trampet(te)
Trance Catalepsy, Cataplexy, Goa, Narcolepsy
Tranche Gold, Reserve
Tranquil(lity) Ataraxy, Calm, Composure, Easy, Halcyon, Lee, Quietude, Sedate, > **SERENE**
Tranquillise(r) Appease, Ataractic, Ataraxic, > **CALM**, Diazepam, Downer, Hypnone, Hypnotic, Librium®, Nervine, Nitrazepam, Oxazepam, Placate, Satisfy, Soothe, Still, Valium®
Transaction(s) Affair, Agio, Brokerage, Deal, Escrow, Fasti, Leaseback, Tr
Transcend(ent), Transcendental(ist) Excel, Mystic, Overtop, Surpass, Thoreau
Transcribe, Transcript Copy, Rescore, Tenor, > **TRANSLATE**, Transume
Transfer Alien, Alienate, > **ASSIGN**, Attorn, Calk, Cede, Communize, Consign, Convey(ance), Credit, Crosstalk, Decal, Demise, Devolve, Download, Exchange, Explant, Hive off, Make over, Mancipation, Metathesis, Mortmain, Nuclear, On-lend, Pass, Photomechanical, Provection, Reassign, Redeploy, Remit, Remove, Repot, Second, Settlement, Transduction, Transfection, Uproot, Virement
▷ **Transferred** *may indicate* an anagram
Transfix Impale, Rivet, > **SKEWER**, Spear, Spit
Transform(ation), Transformer Alter, Apotheosis, Balun, Change, Fourier, Lorentz, Metamorphism, Metamorphose, Metamorphosis, Metaplasia, Metastasis, Morphing, Permute, Rectifier, Sea change, Tinct, Toupee, Transmogrify, Wig
▷ **Transform(ed)** *may indicate* an anagram

Transfusion Apheresis

Transgress(ion) Encroach, Err, Infringe, Offend, Overstep, Peccancy, > **SIN**, Violate

Transient, Transit(ion), Transitory Brief, Ephemeral, Fleeting, Fly-by-night, Forbidden, Fugacious, Hobo, Metabasis, Passage, Passing, Provisional, Seque, T, Temporary

Transistor Drift, Epitaxial, Field-effect, Junction

Translate, Translation, Translator Calque, Construe, Convert, Coverdale, Crib, Explain, Free, Horse, Interpret, In vitro, Jerome, Key, Linguist, Loan, Machine, Metaphrase, Paraphrase, Pinyin, Polyglot, Pony, Reduce, Render, Rendition, Rhemist, Simultaneous, Targum, Tr, Transcribe, Transform, Trot, Unseen, Version(al), Vulgate, Wycliffe

▷ **Translate(d)** *may indicate* an anagram

Transmigrate, Transmigration Exodus, Metempsychosis, Passage, Trek

Transmit(ter), Transmitted, Transmission Air, Allele, Automatic, Band, Beacon, Broadband, > **BROADCAST**, Cable, Carry, CB, Communicate, Conduct, Consign, Contagion, Convection, Convey, Facsimile, Filler, Forward, Gearbox, Gene, Heredity, Impart, Intelsat, Manual, Microphone, Modem, Nicol, Permittivity, Propagate, Racon, Radiate, Radio, Receiver, Simplex, Simulcast, Sonabuoy, Synchronous, Tappet, Telecast, Telegony, Telemetry, Teleprinter, Televise, Telex, Tiros, Traduce, Traject, Tralaticious, Tralatitious, UART, Uplink, Upload, Walkie-talkie

Transom Reverse, Traverse

Transparent, Transparency Adularia, Clear, Crystal(line), Diaphanous, Dioptric, Glassy, Glazed, Hyaloid, Iolite, Leno, Limpid, Lucid, Luminous, Patent, Pellucid, Sheer, Slide, Tiffany

Transpire Happen, Occur

Transplant Allograft, Anaplasty, Graft, Repot, Reset, Shift

Transport(ed), Transporter, Transportation Active, Argo, Bear, Bike, Broomstick, BRS, Bus, Cargo, Carract, > **CARRY**, Cart, Charm, Convey, Delight, Ecstasy, Electron, Eloin, Enrapt, Enravish, Entrain, Esloin, Estro, Freight, Haul(age), Helicopter, Jerrican, Joy, Kurvey, Lug, Maglev, Mambrane, Monorail, Palanquin, Pantechnicon, Public, Put, Rape, Rapine, Rapture, Roadster, Ship, Shuttle, Sidecar, Sledge, Supersonic, Tanker, Tote, Trap, Tuktuk, Waft, Wheels, Wireway

Transpose, Transposition Anagram, Commute, Convert, Invert, Metathesis, Shift, Spoonerism, Switch, Tr

▷ **Transposed** *may indicate* an anagram

Transsexual Invert

Transubstantiate, Transubstantiation Capernaite

Transverse Across, Crosscut, Diagonal, Obliquid, Thwart

Transvest(it)ism, Transvestite Berdache, Berdash, Cross-dressing, Eonist

Tranter Dolly

Trap(s), Trapdoor, Trapped, Trappings Ambush, > **BAGGAGE**, Bags, Belongings, Booby, Buckboard, Bunker, Carriage, Catch, Catch-pit, Clapnet, Corner, Cru(i)ve, Deadfall, Death, Decoy, Dogcart, Downfall, Eelset, Emergent, Ensnare, Entrain, Fall, Fit-up, Fly, Flypaper, Frame-up, Fyke, Gig, Gin, Gob, Grin, Hatch, Ice-bound, Jinri(c)ksha(w), Keddah, Kettle, Kheda, Kiddle, Kidel, Kipe, Kisser, Knur(r), Light, Lime, > **LUGGAGE**, Lure, Mesh, Mouth, Net, Nur(r), Paraphernalia, Pitfall, Plant, Police, Pot, Poverty, Putcheon, Putcher, Quicksand, Radar, Regalia, Sand, Scruto, > **SNARE**, Speed, Spell, Spider, Springe, Stake-net, Star, Steam, Stench, Sting, Stink, Sun, Tangle, Tank,

Teagle, Toil, Tonga, Trou-de-loup, Two-wheeler, U, U-bend, Vampire, Web, Weel, Weir, Wire

Trapezist Leotard

Trapper Carson, Voyageur

Trash(y) Bosh, Deface, Dre(c)k, Garbage, Junk, Kitsch, Pulp, > **RUBBISH**, Schlock, Scum, Tinpot, Vandalise, White, Worthless

Trauma Insult, Shock

Travel(ler), Travelling Backpack, Bagman, Bushwhacker, Commercial, Commute, Crustie, Crusty, Drive, Drummer, Fare, Fellow, Fly, Fogg, Gipsen, Gipsy, Gitano, Globe-trotter, Go, Gulliver, Gypsy, Hike, Interrail, Itinerant, Journey, Long-haul, Marco Polo, Meve, Migrant, Motor, Move, Mush, New Age, Nomad, Passenger, Passepartout, Peregrination, Peripatetic, Pilgrim, Ply, Polo, Pootle, Range, Rep, Ride, Rom(any), Rove, Safari, Sail, Salesman, Samaritan, Space, > **TOUR**, Trek, Tripper, Tsigane, Viator, Voyage, Wanderjahr, Wayfarer, Wend, Wildfire, Zigan

Traverse Cross, Girdle, Measure, Quest, Trace

Travesty Burlesque, Charade, Distortion, Parody, Show, Skit

Trawl Drag-net, Hose-net, Net

Tray Antler, Bottle-slide, Carrier, Case, Charger, Coaster, Gallery, Joe, Lazy Susan, Plateau, > **SALVER**, Shower, Tea, Trencher, Voider, Waiter

Treacherous, Treachery Deceit, Delilah, Fickle, Ganelon, Guile, Insidious, Judas-kiss, Knife, Mala fide, Medism, Perfidious, Punic, Quicksands, Serpentine, Sleeky, Snaky, Trahison, Traitor, > **TREASON**, Two-faced, Viper

Treacle Black(jack), Butter, Molasses, Venice

Tread Clamp, Clump, Dance, Pad, Step, Stramp, Track, Trample

Treason Betrayal, High, Insurrection, Lèse-majesté, Lese-majesty, Perduellion, Petty, Sedition, > **TREACHERY**

Treasure(r), Treasury Banker, Bursar, Cache, Camerlengo, Camerlingo, Cherish, Chest, Cimelia, Coffer, Ewe-lamb, Exchequer, Fisc(al), Fisk, Godolphin, Golden, Heritage, Hoard, Montana, Palgrave, Pork barrel, > **PRIZE**, Procurator, Purser, Relic, Riches, Steward, Taonga, Thesaurus, Trove

Treat, Treatment Action, Acupuncture, Allopathy, Antidote, Archilowe, Arenation, Aromatherapy, Balneotherapy, Beano, Besee, Capitulate, Care, Chemotherapy, Chiropractic, Condition, Course, Cryotherapy, Cupping, Cure, Deal, Detox(ification), Dialysis, Do, > **DOCTOR**, Dose, Dress, Dutch, Enantiopathy, Entertain, Est, Facial, Faith-healing, Fango, Figuration, Foment, Frawzery, Handle, Holistic, Homeopathy, HRT, Hydrotherapy, Hypnotherapy, Immunotherapy, Intermediate, Jin shin do, Kenny, Laser, Manage, Medicate, Moxibustion, Naturopathy, Negotiate, Opotherapy, Osteopathy, > **OUTING**, Pasteur, Pedicure, Pelotherapy, Physic, Physiotherapy, Pie, Probiotics, Process, Prophylaxis, Psychoanalysis, Psychotherapy, Radiotherapy, Regale, Rehab(ilitation), Rest cure, Root, Secretage, Serotherapy, Shout, Shrift, Smile, > **STAND**, Tablet, Tebilise®, Thalassotherapy, Themotherapy, Therapy, Titbit, Traction, Twelve-step, Usance, Use, Vet

▷ **Treated** *may indicate* an anagram

Treatise Almagest, Commentary, Didache, Discourse, Dissertation, Essay, Monograph, Pandect, Prodrome, Summa, Tract(ate), Upanishad, Vedanta

Treaty Agreement, Alliance, Assiento, Concordat, Covenant, Entente, Jay's, Lateran, Maastricht, North Atlantic, > **PACT**, Private, Protocol, Rijswijk, Utrecht, Verdun, Versailles, Yorktown

Treble Castrato, Choirboy, Chorist(er), Pairial, Soprano, > **TRIPLE**, Triune, Voice

Tree(s) Actor, > **ANCESTRY**, Axle, Beam, Boom, Bosk, Bottle, Clump, Conifer,

Coppice, Corner, Deciduous, Decision, Dendrology, Descent, Family, Fault, Fringe, Gallows, Genealogical, Grove, Hang, Hardwood, Jesse, Nurse, Pedigree, Pole, Rood, Roof, Sawyer, Shoe, Softwood, Staddle, Stemma, Summer, Timber, Tyburn, Vista, > WOOD

- **TREES**

2 letters:	Eugh	**5 letters:**	Kauri
Bo	Gean	Abele	Khaya
Ti	Hule	Abies	Kiaat
	Jack	Ackee	Kokum
3 letters:	Kaki	Afara	Larch
Ash	Kiri	Agila	Lemon
Asp	Kola	Alamo	Lilac
Bay	Lime	Alder	Lotus
Bel	Lote	Alnus	Mahoe
Ben	Mako	Anona	Mahua
Box	Meal	Areca	Mahwa
Cow	Milk	Argan	Mamey
Elm	Ming	Aspen	Maple
Fir	Mott	Banak	Matai
Gum	Mowa	Beech	Melia
Ita	Nipa	Belah	Motte
Jak	Olea	Birch	Mugga
Koa	Ombu	Bodhi	Mulga
Mot	Palm	Boree	Mvule
Nim	Pine	Butea	Myall
Oak	Pipe	Cacao	Ngaio
Oil	Pith	Carap	Nikau
Sal	Plum	Cedar	Nyssa
Tea	Poon	Ceiba	Opepe
Til	Rain	China	Osier
Ule	Rata	Cocoa	Palas
Wax	Rhus	Cocus	Palay
Yew	Rimu	Coral	Panax
	Sack	Ebony	Pecan
4 letters:	Shea	Elder	Pinon
Acer	Silk	Fagus	Pipal
Aloe	Sloe	Fever	Pipul
Amla	Soap	Flame	Pitch
Arar	Sorb	Fruit	Plane
Atap	Tawa	Grass	Quina
Bael	Teak	Guava	Ramin
Bhel	Teil	Hakea	Roble
Bito	Titi	Hazel	Rowan
Cade	Toon	Hevea	Sabal
Coco	Tung	Holly	Saman
Cola	Tutu	Iroko	Sassy
Dali	Upas	Jambu	Scrog
Dhak	Yang	Jarul	Silva
Dika		Judas	Smoke
Dita		Karri	Sumac

Taxus	Damson	Obeche	Zamang
Thorn	Deodar	Orange	
Thuja	Diana's	Padauk	**7 letters:**
Thuya	Dragon	Padouk	Ailanto
Tilia	Durian	Pagoda	Amboina
Tsuga	Durion	Papaya	Arbutus
Tuart	Emblic	Pawpaw	Avodire
Tulip	Feijoa	Peepul	Bebeeru
Vitex	Fustet	Pepper	Bilimbi
Wahoo	Fustic	Platan	Bilsted
Wilga	Gallus	Pomelo	Bubinga
Withy	Garjan	Poplar	Buck-eye
Xylem	Gidgee	Popple	Bursera
Yacca	Gidjee	Protea	Cajeput
Yulan	Gingko	Puriri	Cajuput
Zaman	Ginkgo	Quince	Calamus
Zamia	Glinap	Red-bud	Camphor
	Gnetum	Ricker	Camwood
6 letters:	Gopher	Roucou	Canella
Abroma	Guango	Rubber	Carbeen
Acacia	Gurjun	Sabicu	Cassava
Alerce	Gympie	Sallow	Catalpa
Angico	Illipe	Samaan	Champac
Annona	Illipi	Sapele	Champak
Antiar	Jarool	Sapium	Chayote
Arbute	Jarrah	Sapota	Coquito
Arolla	Joshua	Saxaul	Corylus
Babaco	Jujube	She-oak	Corypha
Balsam	Kamala	Sinder	Cumquat
Banyan	Kamela	Sorrel	Daddock
Baobab	Karaka	Souari	Dagwood
Billan	Karite	Spruce	Dogwood
Bombax	Kowhai	Styrax	Dryades
Bonsai	Laurel	Sumach	Durmast
Bo-tree	Lebbek	Sunder	Geebung
Buriti	Linden	Sundra	Genipap
Cadaga	Locust	Sundri	Gluinap
Cadagi	Longan	Tallow	Gumtree
Carapa	Loquat	Tamanu	Hickory
Carica	Lucuma	Tewart	Hog-plum
Cashew	Lungah	Titoki	Holm-oak
Cembra	Macoya	Tooart	Jipyapa
Cerris	Mallee	Totara	Kumquat
Chaste	Manuka	Tupelo	Lacquer
Chenar	Mastic	Waboom	Lagetto
Cherry	Mazard	Wandoo	Lentisk
Chinar	Mimosa	Wicken	Logwood
Citron	Missel	Wicopy	Lumbang
Coffee	Mopane	Willet	Madrono
Cordon	Mopani	Willow	Mahaleb
Cornel	Myrtle	Witgat	Manjack
Cornus	Nutmeg	Yarran	Marasca

- Margosa
- Mazzard
- Mesquit
- Moringa
- Morrell
- Pereira
- Pimento
- Platane
- Pollard
- Populus
- Quassia
- Quicken
- Quillai
- Quinain
- Radiata
- Rampick
- Rampike
- Redwood
- Rock elm
- Saksaul
- Sandbox
- Saouari
- Sapling
- Sausage
- Sequoia
- Seringa
- Service
- Shittah
- Sourgum
- Soursop
- Spindle
- Sundari
- Trumpet
- Varnish
- Wallaba
- Wirilda
- Witchen
- Wych-elm
- Xylopia
- Zelkova

8 letters:
- Aguacate
- Algaroba
- Aquillia
- Bangalay
- Bangalow
- Basswood
- Benjamin
- Bergamot
- Berrigan
- Blackboy

Blimbing
Bountree
Bourtree
Breadnut
Brigalow
Calabash
Cinchona
Cinnamon
Cocoplum
Coolabah
Coolibah
Corkwood
Crabwood
Cudgerie
Dendroid
Dracaena
Espalier
Flittern
Fraxinus
Garcinia
Ghost-gum
Gnetales
Guaiacum
Hagberry
Hornbeam
Huon-pine
Igdrasil
Ironbark
Ironwood
Jelutong
Kingwood
Laburnum
Lacebark
Lecythis
Loblolly
Magnolia
Mahogany
Makomako
Mangrove
Manna-ash
Mesquite
Mulberry
Ocotillo
Oiticica
Oleaceae
Oleaster
Palmetto
Pandanus
Pichurim
Pinaster
Pithtree
Pyinkado

Quandang
Quandong
Quantong
Quillaia
Quillaja
Raintree
Rambutan
Rangiora
Rewa-rewa
Sago-palm
Sandarac
Santalum
Sapindus
Sapucaia
Sea grape
Shagbark
Simaruba
Snowball
Snowdrop
Soapbark
Sourwood
Standard
Stinging
Sweet gum
Sweetsop
Sycamine
Sycamore
Sycomore
Tamarack
Tamarind
Tamarisk
Taxodium
Umbrella
Whitegum
Wine-palm
Ygdrasil

9 letters:
Agila-wood
Ailantous
Albespine
Angophora
Azedarach
Bilimbing
Bitternut
Blackbutt
Blackwood
Bloodwood
Bolletrie
Boobialla
Bully-tree
Bulwaddee

Burrawary
Butternut
Caliatour
Caliature
Candlenut
Canoewood
Carambola
Casuarina
Chempaduk
Cherimoya
Chincapin
Chinkapin
Coachwood
Cordyline
Courbaril
Cupressus
Eaglewood
Evergreen
Firewheel
Flame-leaf
Greenwood
Grevillea
Hackberry
Ivory palm
Jacaranda
Kahikatea
Krummholz
Kurrajong
Lancewood
Lemonwood
Macadamia
Marmalade
Mirabelle
Mockernut
Monkeypot
Naseberry
Nux vomica
Paloverde
Paperbark
Paulownia
Persimmon
Pistachio
Pitch-pine
Poinciana
Ponderosa
Pontianac
Quebracho
Rauwolfia
Rose-apple
Sapodilla
Sassafras
Satinwood

Shellbark
Simarouba
Star-anise
Star-apple
Stinkwood
Tacamahac
Terebinth
Toothache
Torchwood
Wagenboom
Wayfaring
Whitebeam
Whitewood
Wych-hazel
Yggdrasil
Zebrawood

10 letters:
Arbor Vitae
Blackbully
Breadfruit
Bulletwood
Buttonball
Calamondin
Calliature
Candle-wood
Cannonball
Chamaerops

Chaulmugra
Cheesewood
Chinaberry
Chinquapin
Cottonwood
Cowrie-pine
Eucalyptus
Fiddlewood
Flamboyant
Flindersia
Frangipani
Green-heart
Hackmatack
Ilang-ilang
Jaboticaba
Jippi-jappa
Letter-wood
Lilly-pilly
Macrocarpa
Manchineel
Mangabeira
Mangosteen
Marblewood
Nithofagus
Palisander
Paper birch
Pohutukawa
Quercitron

Ribbonwood
Sandalwood
Sappanwood
Silk-cotton
Silverbell
Sneezewood
Spotted gum
Strawberry
Traveller's
Turpentine
Witch-hazel
Witgatboom
Woollybutt
Yellowwood
Ylang-ylang

11 letters:
Appleringie
Cabbage-palm
Chaulmougra
Chokecherry
Cryptomeria
Dipterocarp
Eriodendron
Flamboyante
Fothergilla
Gingerbread
Honey locust

Jesuit's bark
Leatherwood
Lignum vitae
Liquidambar
Maceranduba
Metasequoia
Pomegranate
Purpleheart
Shittimwood
Sitka spruce
Stringybark

12 letters:
Hercules' club
Liriodendron
Mammee-sapota
Masseranduba
Monkey-puzzle
Washingtonia
Wellingtonia

13 letters:
Paper-mulberry

14 letters:
Western hemlock

Tree-climber, Tree-dweller Monkey, Opossum, Sciurus, Squirrel, Unau
Tree disease Dutch elm, Waldsterben
Tree-man Ent
Tree-moss Usnea
Tree-paeony Moutan
Tree-pecker Picus
Tree-shrew Tana
Trefoil Bird's foot, Clover, Hop, Lotos, Lotus
Trek Hike, Journey, Leg, Odyssey, Safari, Yomp
Trellis Espalier, Lattice, Pergola, Treillage, Treille
Tremble, Trembling, Tremor Aftershock, Ashake, Butterfly, Dither, Dodder, Foreshock, Hotter, Intention, Judder, Moonquake, Palpitate, Quail, Quake, Quaver, Quiver, Seismal, > SHAKE, Shiver, Shock, Shudder, Stound, Temblor, Trepid, Twitchy, Vibrant, Vibrate, Vibration, Vibratiuncle, Vibrato, Wobble, Wuther, Yips
Tremendous Big, Enormous, Howling, Immense, Marvellous
Tremolo Bebung, Trillo
▶ **Tremor** *see* TREMBLE
Tremulous Dithering, Hirrient, Quaking, Shaky, Timorous
Trench(er) Boyau, Cunette, Cuvette, Delf, Delph, Dike(r), > DITCH, Dyke(r), Encroach, Fleet, Foss(e), Foxhole, Fur(r), Furrow, Grip, Gullet, Gutter, Leat, Line, Mariana, Moat, Oceanic, Outwork, Rill, Rille, Ring-dyke, Robber, Salient, Sap, Shott, Slit, Sod, Sondage

Trenchant Acid, Cutting

Trend(y) Bent, Bias, Chic, Climate, Drift, Fashion, Hep, In, Mainstream, New Age(r), Newfangled, Pop, Posey, Rage, Right-on, Style, Swim, Tendency, Tendenz, Tenor, Tide, Tonnish

Trespass(ing) Aggravated, Encroach, Errant, Hack, Impinge, Infringe, Offend, Peccancy, Sin, Trench, Wrong

Tress(es) Curl, Lock, Ringlet, Switch, Tallent

Trestle Sawhorse

Triad Chord

Trial Adversity, Affliction, Appro, Approbation, Approval, Assize, Attempt, Bane, Bernoulli, Bout, Clinical, Corsned, Court-martial, Cow, Cross, Dock, Essay, > **EXPERIMENT**, Field, Fitting, Hearing, Nuremberg, Ordeal, Pilot, Pree, Probation, Proof, Rehearsal, Scramble, Sheepdog, Show, Taste, Time

Triangle(d), Triangular Acute, Bermuda, Circular, Cosec, Deltoid, Equilateral, Eternal, Gair, Golden, Gore, Gyronny, Isosceles, Obtuse, Pascal's, Pedimental, Pendentive, Pyramid, Rack, Right-angled, Scalene, Similar, Spherical, Trigon, Tromino, Warning

Trias(sic) Bunter, Keuper, Muschelkalk, Rhaetic

Tribe(s), Tribal, Tribesmen Amalekite, Ammonites, Ashanti, Asher, Benjamin, Celt, Cherokee, Clan(nish), Creek, Dan, Dinka, Dynasty, Edomites, Ephraim, Family, Gad, Gens, Gentes, Gentilic, Gond, Goth, Hapu, Helvetii, Hittite, Horde, Hottentot, Ibo, Iceni, Israelite, Issachar, Jat, Judah, Kaffir, Kenite, Kurd, Lashkar, Levi, Lost, Manasseh, Masai, Moabite, Mongol, Moro, Naga, Naphtali, Nation, Nervii, Ngati, Ostrogoths, Pathan, Phyle, > **RACE**, Reuben, Riff, Rod, Sakai, Salian, Schedule, Senones, Senussi, Sept, Shawnee, Silures, Simeon, Standloper, Tasaday, Teuton, Trinobantes, Vandals, Wolof, Wyandot(te), X(h)osa, Zebulun

Tribune, Tribunal Aeropagus, Bema, Bench, > **COURT**, Divan, Employment, Forum, Hague, Industrial, Leader, Platform, Rienzi, Rota, Star-chamber, Waitangi

Tributary Affluent, Bogan, Branch, Creek, Fork

Tribute Cain, Capelline, Citation, Commemoration, Compliment, Dedication, Deodate, > **DUE**, Epitaph, Festschrift, Gavel, Heriot, Homage, Kain, Memento, Ode, Panegyric, Peter's pence, > **PRAISE**, Rome-penny, Scat(t), Tax, Toast, Wreath, Wroth

Trice Flash, Instant

Trichosanthin Q

Trick(ed), Trickery, Tricks(ter), Tricky Antic, Art, Artifice, Attrap, Awkward, Bamboozle, Begunk, Book, Bunco, Bunko, Cantrip, Capot, Catch, Cheat, Chicane(ry), Chouse, Claptrap, Cod(-act), Cog, Confidence, Coyote, Crook, Davenport, Deception, Deck, Delicate, Delude, Device, Dirty, > **DO**, > **DODGE**, Dupe, Elf, Elfin, Elvan, Fard, Feat, Fetch, Fiddle, Finesse, Flam, Flim-flam, Fob, Fox, Fraud, Fun, Game, Gaud, Gleek, Glike, Guile, Had, Hey presto, Hoax, Hocus(-pocus), Hoodwink, Hornswoggle, Hum, Illude, Illusion, Illywhacker, Jadery, Jockey, John, Kittle, Knack, Lark, Magsman, Mislead, Monkey, Monkey-shine, Nap, Nasruddin, Palter, Parlour, Pass, Pawk, Pleasantry, Pliskie, Prank, Prestige, Put-on, Quick, Ramp, Raven, Reak, Reik, Rex, Rig, Ropery, Roughie, Ruse, Scam, Sell, Set-up, Shanghai, Shavie, Shenanigan, Shifty, Shill, Skin-game, Skite, Skul(l)duggery, Skylark, Slam, Sleight, Slight, Slinter, Spoof, Stall, Stint, Subterfuge, Sug, Swiftie, Thimble-rig, Three-card, Ticklish, Trap, Tregetour, Trump, Turn, Tweedler, Undercraft, Underplot, Vole, Wangle, Wheeze, Wile, Wrinkle

▷ **Trick** *may indicate* an anagram

Trickle Drib(ble), Driblet, Dropple, Leak, Rill, Seep

Trickless Misère

Triclinic Anorthic

Trident Fork, Plane, Trisul(a)

Trifle(s), Trifling Bagatelle, Banal, Baubee, Bauble, Bibelot, Birdseed, Bit, Cent, Chickenfeed, Coquette, Dabble, Dalliance, > **DALLY**, Denier, Desipient, Do, Doit, Faddle, Falderal, Fallal, Fattrell, Feather, Fewtril, Fiddle, Fig, Fingle-fangle, Flamfew, Fleabite, Flirt, Folderol, Fool, Footle, Fribble, Frippery, Fritter, Frivol, Gewgaw, Idle, Iota, Kickshaw, Knick-knack, Luck-penny, Mite, Nick-nacket, Niff-naff, Nothing, Nugae, Nugatory, Nyaff, Palter, Paltry, Peanuts, Peddle, Peppercorn, Petty, Philander, Picayune, Piddle, Piffle, Pin, Pingle, Pittance, Play, Potty, Quelquechose, Quiddity, Quiddle, Slight, Small beer, Smatter, Song, Sport, Stiver, Strae, Straw, Sundry, Sweet Fanny Adams, Tiddle, Toy, Trinket, Trivia, Whifflery, Whim-wham, Whit

Trig(onometry) Neat, Sech, Spherical, Tosh, Trim

Trigger Activate, Detent, Hair, Instigate, Kryton, Pawl, Precipitate, Schmitt, Start, Touch off

Trill(ed), Triller, Trilling Burr, Churr, Hirrient, Quaver, Ribattuta, Roll, Staphyle, Trim, Twitter, Warble

Trilobite Olenellus, Olenus, Paradoxide

Trim(med), Trimmer, Trimming Ballast, Bleed, Braid, Bray, Chipper, Clip, Dapper, Dinky, Dress, Ermine, Face, Falbala, Fettle, File, Froufrou, Garni, Garnish, Garniture, Gimp, Guimpe, Macramé, Macrami, Marabou, Neat, Net(t), Ornament, Pare, Passament, Passement(erie), Pipe, Plight, Posh, Preen, Proign, Proyn(e), Pruin(e), Prune, Robin, Ruche, Sax, Sett, Shipshape, Smirk, Smug, Sned, Snod, > **SPRUCE**, Straddle, Stroddle, Strodle, Stylist, Svelte, Tiddley, > **TIDY**, Time-server, Torsade, Trick, Whippersnipper, Wig

Trinidadian Carib

Trinitarian, Trinity Mathurin(e), Triad, Trimurti, Triune, Word

Trinket(s) Bauble, Bibelot, Bijou(terie), Charm, Fallal, Nicknack, Toy, Trankum, Trumpery

Trio Catch, Graces, Skat, Terzetto

Trip(per) Awayday, Cruise, Dance, Day, Ego, Errand, > **FALL**, Field, Flight, Flip, Guilt, Head, High, Jolly, Journey, Junket, Kilt, Link, Outing, Pleasure, Power, Ride, Round, Run, Sail, Sashay, Spin, Spurn, > **STUMBLE**, Tour, Trek, Trial, Voyage

▷ **Trip** *may indicate* an anagram

Tripe Abracadabra, Bosh, Caen, Entrails, Offal, Rot

Triple, Triplet Codon, Hemiol(i)a, Sdrucciola, Ternal, Tiercet, Treble, Trifecta, Trilling, Trin(e), Tripling

Tripod Cat, Cortina, Highhat, Oracle, Triangle, Trippet, Trivet

Triptych Volet

Trishaw Cycle

Trite Banal, Boilerplate, Cornball, Corny, Hackneyed, Hoary, Laughable, Novelettish, Platitude, Rinky-dink, Stale, Stock, Time-worn

Triton Eft, Evet, Ewt, Trumpet-shell

Triumph(ant) Cock-a-hoop, Codille, Cowabunga, Crow, Eureka, Exult, Glory, Impostor, Killing, Oho, Olé, Ovation, Palm, Victorious, > **WIN**

Triumvir Caesar, Crassus, Pompey

Trivet Tripod, Trippet

Trivia(l), Triviality Adiaphoron, Bagatelle, Balaam, Bald, > **BANAL**, Footling,

Frippery, Frothy, Futile, Idle, Inconsequential, Light, Minutiae, Nitpicking, Nothingism, Paltry, Pap, Peppercorn, Pettifoggery, Petty, Picayune, Piddling, Piffling, Shallow, Small, Small beer, Small fry, Snippety, Squirt, Squit, Toy(s), Vegie

Trochee Choree

Troglodyte Ape, Caveman, Hermit, Spelean, Wren

Trojan Aeneas, Agamemnon, Dardan, Iliac, Priam, Teucrian, Troic

Troll > FISH, Gnome, Rove, Spoon, Trawl, Warble

Trolley Brute, Cart, Dolly, Gurney, Hostess, Shopping, Tea, Traymobile, Truck, Trundler

▶ **Trollop** *see* LOOSE WOMAN

Trombone Posaune

Troop(s), Trooper Alpini, Band, BEF, Brigade, Company, Depot, Detachment, Guard, Horde, Household, Logistics, Midianite, Militia, Pultan, Pulton, Pultoon, Pultun, SAS, School, Shock, Sowar, State, Storm, Subsidiary, Tp, Turm(e)

Troopship Transport

Trophy Adward, Ashes, > AWARD, Belt, Cup, Emmy, Memento, Palm, > PRIZE, Scalp, Schneider, Spoils, Tourist, TT

Tropic(al) Cancer, Capricorn, Derris, Jungle, Neogaea, Sultry

Trot(ter), Trot out Air, Crib, Crubeen, Job, Jog, Passage, Pettitoes, Piaffe, Pony, Ranke, Red(-shirt), Rising, Tootsie

Troth Perfay, Troggs

Trotsky(ist) Entr(y)ism, Leon, Militant Tendency

Troubador Blondel, Griot, Manrico, Minstrel, Singer, Sordello

Trouble(s), Troublemaker, Troublesome Ache, Ado, Affliction, Aggro, Agitate, Ail, Alarm, Annoy, Bale, Barrat, Beset, > BOTHER, Bovver, Brickle, Burden, Care, Coil, Concern, Debate, Disaster, Disquiet, Distress, Disturb, Dog, Dolour, Eat, Esclandre, Exercise, Fash, Fashious, Finger, Firebrand, Fossick, Gram(e), Grief, Hag-ride, Harass, Harry, Hassle, Hatter, Heat, Heist, Hellion, Hot water, Howdyedo, Hydra, Inconvenience, Infest, > IN TROUBLE, Jam, Kiaugh, Mess, Mixer, Moil, Molest, Noy, Perturb, Pester, Plague, Poke, Reck, Rub, Scrape, Shake, Shtuck, Soup, Spiny, Stir, Storm, Sturt, Tartar, Teen, Teething, Thorny, Tine, Toil, Trial, Tsouris, Tsuris, Turn-up, Tyne, Unsettle, Vex, > WORRY

Trouble-free Gallio

Trouble-shooter Ombudsman

▷ **Troublesome** *may indicate* an anagram

Trough Back, Bed, Bucket, Buddle, Channel, Chute, Culvert, Graben, Hod, Hutch, Langmuir, Launder, Leachtub, Manger, Pneumatic, Puerto Rico, Stock, Straik, Strake, Syncline, Troffer, Tundish, Tye, Watering

Trounce > BEAT, Hammer, Thump

Trouser(s) Bags, Bell-bottoms, Bloomers, Breeches, Capri pants, Churidars, Clam-diggers, Continuations, Cords, Corduroys, Cossacks, Culottes, Daks, Denims, Drainpipe, Drawers, Ducks, Dungarees, Eel-skins, Flannels, Flares, Galligaskins, Gaskins, Gauchos, Hip-huggers, Hipsters, Inexpressibles, Innominables, Jeans, Jodhpurs, Kaccha, Ke(c)ks, Knee cords, Lederhosen, Longs, Loons, Moleskins, Overalls, Oxford bags, Palazzo (pants), Palazzos, Pantaloons, Pants, Pedal pushers, Pegtops, Plus-fours, Plus-twos, Reach-me-downs, Salopettes, Shalwar, Ski pants, Slacks, Stovepipes, Strides, Strossers, Sweatpants, Trews, Trouse, Unmentionables, Unutterables, Utterless

Trout Aurora, Brook, Brown, Bull, Coral, Finnac(k), Finnock, Fish, Gillaroo,

Hag(fish), Herling, Hirling, Kamloops, Peal, Peel, Phinnock, Pogies, Quintet, Rainbow, Salmon, Sewen, Sewin, Speckled, Splake, Steelhead, Togue, Whitling

Trow Faith, Meseems

Trowel Float

Troy Ilium, Sergeant, T, Weight

Truant Absentee, AWOL, Dodge, Hooky, Kip, Mich(e), Mitch, Mooch, Mouch, Wag

Truce Armistice, Barley, Ceasefire, Fainites, Fains, Interlude, Pax, Stillstand, Treague, Treaty

Truck Bakkie, Bogie, Breakdown, Business, Cattle, Cocopan, Dealings, Dolly, Dumper, Flatbed, Forklift, Haul, Hopper, Journey, > **LORRY**, Low-loader, Pallet, Panel, Pick-up, Semi, Sound, Stacking, Tipper, Tow(ie), Traffic, Trolley, Trundle, Ute, Utility, Van, Wrecker

Trudge Footslog, Jog, Lumber, Pad, Plod, Stodge, Stramp, Taigle, Traipse, Trash, Trauchle, Trog, Vamp

True Accurate, Actual, Apodictic, Candid, Constant, Correct, Exact, Factual, Faithful, Genuine, Honest, Indubitable, Leal, Literal, Loyal, Platitude, Plumb, Pure, Real, Realistic, Richr, Right, Sooth, Very

Truffle Tuber, Tuberaceae

Trug Basket, Wisket

Truly Certainly, Certes, Fegs, Forsooth, Honestly, Indeed, Surely, Verily, Yea

Trump(s), Trumpet(er) Agami, Alchemy, Alchymy, Armstrong, Bach, Blare, Blast, Bray, Buccina, Bugle(r), Call, Card, Clarion, Conch, Cornet, Corona, Crow, Daffodil, Ear, Elephant, Fanfare, Hallali, Honours, > **HORN**, Invent, Jew's, Last, Lituus, Long ten, Lur(e), Lurist, Manille, Marine, Megaphone, > **NO TRUMP**, Proclaim, Ram's-horn, Rant, Resurrect, Ruff, Salpingian, Salpinx, Satchmo, Sennet, Shofar, Shophar, Slug-horn, Speaking, Surpass, Tantara, Tantarara, Tar(at)antara, Theodomas, Tiddy, Triton, Triumph

Trumpery Fattrels, Jimcrack, Paltry, Trashy

Truncate(d) Abrupt, Cut, Dock, Shorten

Truncheon Billie, Billy, Blackjack, Cosh, Night-stick, Warder

Trundle Hump, Trill, Troll

Trunk(s) Aorta(l), A-road, Body, Bole, Box, Bulk, Bus, But(t), Cabin, Carcase, Chest, Coffer, Hose, Imperial, Log, Peduncle, Pollard, Portmanteau, Portmantle, Proboscis, Ricker, Road, Saratoga, Shorts, STD, Stock, Stud, Synangium, Torso, Valise, Wardrobe

Truss > **BIND**, Ligate, Oop, Oup, Sheaf, Tie, Upbind

Trust(y), Trusting, Trustworthy Active, Affy, Authentic, Belief, Care, Cartel, Charge, Charitable, Combine, Confide, Credit, Dependable, Discretionary, > **FAITH**, Fiduciary, Gullible, Honest, Hope, Investment, Leal, Lippen, Loyal, National, NT, Reliable, Reliance, Rely, Repose, Reputable, Sound, Special, Split, Staunch, Tick, Trojan, Trow, True, Trump, Unit

Trustee Agent, Executor, Fiduciary, Pensioneer, Tr

Truth(ful), Truism Accuracy, Alethic, Axiom, Bromide, Cliché, Cold turkey, Dharma, Dialectic, > **FACT**, Facticity, Forsooth, Gospel, Home, Honesty, Idea(l), Logical, Maxim, Naked, Pravda, Reality, Sooth, Soothfast, Troggs, Veraity, Veridical, Verisimilitude, Verity, Vraisemblance

Try(ing) Aim, Approof, Assay, Attempt, Audition, Bash, Bid, Birl, Burden, Burl, Conative, Contend, Crack, Effort, Empiric(utic), > **ENDEAVOUR**, Essay, Examine, Experiment, Fand, Fish, Fling, Foretaste, Go, Harass, Hard, Hear, Impeach, Importunate, Irk, Offer, Ordalium, Practise, Pree, Prieve, Push-over, > **SAMPLE**, Seek, Shot, Sip, Stab, Strain, Strive, Taste, Tax, Tempt, Test, Touchdown, Whirl

Tryst Date, Rendezvous
Tsar(ist) Alexis, Emperor, Godunov, Octobrist, Ruler
TT Rechabite
Tub(by), Tubbiness, Tub-thumper Ash-leach, Back, Bath, Boanerges, Bran,
Corf, Cowl, Dan, Diogenes, Dolly, Endomorph, Firkin, Keeve, Kid, Kieve, Kit,
Luckydip, Mashing, Meat, Pin, Podge, Pot-bellied, Pudge, Pulpit, Stand, Swill,
Tun, Twin, Vat, Wash
Tuba Bombardon, Euphonium
Tube, Tubing, Tubular Acorn, Arteriole, Artery, Barrel, Blowpipe, Bronchus,
Burette, Calamus, Camera, Canaliculus, Cannula, Capillary, Casing, Catheter,
Cathode-ray, Cave, Conduit, Crookes, Digitron, Diode, Discharge, Drain, Drift,
Dropper, Duct, Electron, Endiometer, Epididymis, Eustachian, Extension,
Fallopian, Fistula, Fulgurite, Geissler, Germ, Grommet, Hose, Iconoscope,
Image(orthicon), Inner, Kinescope, Klystron, Macaroni, Malpighian, Matrass,
Metro, Neural, Nixie, Orthicon, Oval, Oviduct, Pentode, Picture, Pilot-static,
> **PIPE**, Pipette, Pitot, Pitot-static, Pneumatic, Pollen, Promethean, Salpinx,
Saticon®, Saucisse, Saucisson, Schnorkel, Shadow-mask, Shock, Sieve,
Siphon, Siphonet, Siphonostele, Siphuncle, Skelp, Skiatron, Sleeve, Snorkel,
Spaghetti, Speaking, Spout, Staple, Static, Stent, Storage, Straw, Strobotron,
Subway, Sucker, Swallet, Telescope, Teletron, Television, Terete, Test, Tetrode,
Thyratron, Tile, Torpedo, Torricellian, Trachea, Triniscope, Trocar, Trochotron,
Trunk, Tunnel, Tuppenny, U, Underground, Ureter, Urethra, Vacuum, Vas,
VDU, Vein, Vena, Venturi, Video, Vidicon®, Worm, X-ray
Tuber(s) Arnut, Arracacha, Bulb, Chufa, Coc(c)o, Dahlia, Dasheen, Earth-nut,
Eddoes, Mashua, Oca, Potato, Salep, Taproot, Taro, Yam
Tuberculosis Consumption, Crewels, Cruel(l)s, Decline, King's evil, Lupus,
Phthisis, Scrofula, White plague
Tuck Dart, Friar, Gather, Grub, Kilt, Pin, Pleat, Scran, Truss, Tummy
Tuesday Hock, Pancake, Shrove, Super
Tuft(ed) Amentum, Beard, C(a)espitose, Candlewick, Catkin, Cluster, Coma,
Comb, Cowlick, Crest, Dollop, Flaught, Floccus, Flock, Goatee, Hassock, Knop,
Lock, Pappus, Penicillate, Quiff, Scopate, Shola, Tait, Tassel, Tate, Toorie,
Toupee, Tourie, Tussock, Tuzz, Whisk
Tug Drag, Haul, Jerk, Lug, Pug, > **PULL**, Rive, Saccade, Ship, Sole, Soole, Sowl(e),
Tit, Tow, Towboat, Yank
Tui Poebird
Tuition Masterclass, Seminal
Tully Cicero
Tumble, Tumbler Acrobat, Cartwheel, Drier, Fall, > **GLASS**, Header, Pitch, Popple,
Purl, Realise, Spill, Stumble, Tailer, Topple, Trip, Twig, Voltigeur, Welter
▷ **Tumble** *may indicate* an anagram
Tumbledown Decrepit, Dilapidated, Ramshackle, Rickle, Ruinous
Tumbril Caisson
Tummy Belly, Colon, Mary, Paunch, Pod
Tummy-ache Colic, Gripe, Tormina
Tumour Adenoma, Anbury, Angioma, Angiosarcoma, Astroblastoma,
Astrocytoma, Burkitt('s) lymphoma, Cancer, Carcinoid, Carcinoma,
Carcinosarcoma, Chondroma, Condyloma, Crab(-yaws), Dermoid, Encanthis,
Encephaloma, Enchondroma, Endothelioma, Epulis, Exostosis, Fibroid,
Fibroma, Ganglion, Germinoma, Gioblastoma, Glioma, Granuloma, Grape,
> **GROWTH**, Gumma, Haemangioma, Haematoma, Hepatoma, Lipoma,
Lymphoma, Medullablastoma, Melanoma, Meningioma, Mesothelioma,

Metastasis, Mole, Myeloma, Myoma, Myxoma, Neoplasm, Nephroblastoma, Neuroblastoma, Neuroma, Odontoma, -oma, Oncology, Osteoclastoma, Osteoma, Osteosarcoma, Papilloma, Polypus, Retinoblastoma, Rhabdomyoma, Sarcoma, Scirrhous, Secondary, Seminoma, Steatoma, Struma, Syphiloma, Talpa, Teratoma, Thymoma, Wart, Warthin's, Wen, Wilm's, Windgall, Wolf, Xanthoma, Yaw

Tumult Brattle, Brawl, Coil, Deray, Ferment, Fracas, Hirdy-girdy, Hubbub, Hurly-burly, Reird, Riot, > ROAR, Romage, Rore, Stoor, Stour, Stowre, Stramash, Tew, > UPROAR

Tumulus Barrow, Mote, Motte

Tun Cask, Keg

Tundra Barren Grounds, Barren Lands

Tune(s), Tuneful, Tuner, Tuning Adjust, Air, Aria, Canorous, Carillon, Catch, Choral, Dump, Earworm, Etude, Fine, Fork, Harmony, Hornpipe, Jingle, Key, Maggot, Measure, Melisma, > MELODY, Old Hundred, > OUT OF TUNE, Peg, Port, Potpourri, Raga, Rant, Ranz-des-vaches, Signature, Snatch, Song, Spring, Strain, Sweet, Syntonise, Temper, Temperament, Theme, Tone, Tweak

Tungstate, Tungsten Scheelite, W, Wolfram

Tunic Ao dai, Caftan, Chiton, Choroid, Cote-hardie, Dalmatic, Dashiki, Gymslip, Hauberk, Kabaya, Kaftan, Kameez, K(h)urta, Salwar kameez, > SINGLET, Surcoat, Tabard, Toga

Tunicate Salpa

Tunnel(ler) Blackwall, Bore, Channel, Chunnel, Condie, Countermine, Culvert, Cundy, Earthworm, Euro, Gallery, Head, Mine, Qanat, Rotherhithe, Simplon, Smoke, Stope, Subway, Syrinx, Tube, Underpass, Water, Wind, Wormhole

Tunny Bonito, Tuna

Turban Bandanna, Hat, Mitral, Pagri, Puggaree, Puggery, Puggree, Sash, Scarf, Tulipant

Turbid Cloudy, Dense, Drumly, Roily

Turbine Francis, Gas, Impulse, Ram air, Reaction, Steam, Wind

Turbulence, Turbulent Becket, Bellicose, Buller, Factious, Fierce, Rapids, Stormy, Unruly

▷ **Turbulent** *may indicate* an anagram

Turf Caespitose, Clod, Divot, Earth, Fail, Feal, Flaught, > GRASS, Greensward, Peat, Screw, > SOD, Sward

Turk(ish) Anatolian, Bashaw, Bashkir, Bey, Bimbashi, Bostangi, Byzantine, Caimac(am), Crescent, Effendi, Golden Horde, Grand, Gregory, Horse(tail), Irade, Kaimakam, Kazak(h), Kurd, Mameluke, Mutessarif(at), Omar, Osman(li), Ottamite, Ottoman, Ottomite, Rayah, Scanderbeg, Selim, Seljuk(ian), Seraskier, Spahi, Tartar, Tatar, Timariot, Usak, Uzbeg, Uzbek, Yakut, Young

Turkey, Turkey-like Anatolia, Brush, Bubbly(-jock), Cold, Curassow, Eyalet, Flop, Gobbler, Norfolk, Plain, Scrub, Sultanate, Talegalla, Talk, TR, Trabzon, Vulturn

Turmeric Curcumine

Turmoil Chaos, Din, Ferment, Stoor, Stour, Tornado, Tracasserie, Tumult, > UPROAR, Welter

▷ **Turn(ing)** *may indicate* an anagram

Turn(ing), Turned away, Turned up, Turns Acescent, Act, Addle, Advert, Antrorse, Apostrophe, Apotropaic, Avert, Bad, Bank, Become, Bend, Buggins, Bump, Canceleer, Cancelier, Caracol(e), Careen, Cartwheel, Cast, Chainé, Chandelle, Change, Char(e), Chore, Christiana, Christie, Christy, Churn, Cock,

Coil, Crank(le), Cuff, Curd(le), Curve, Defect, Deflect, Demi-volt(e), Detour, Deviate, Dig, Digress, Divert, Ear, Earn, Elbow, Evert, Fadge, Flip, Forfend, Go, Good, Gruppetto, Hairpin, Handbrake, Head-off, Hie, High, Hinge, Hup, Immelmann, Influence, Innings, Intussuscept, Invert, Jar, Jink, Keel, Kick, Laeotropic, Lodging, Lot, Luff, Mohawk, Number, Obvert, Parallel, Parry, Penchant, Pivot, Plough, Pronate, Prove, PTO, Quarter, Quersprung, Rebut, Refer, Refract, Remuage, Retroflex, Retroussé, Retrovert, Rev, Revolt, Ride, Riffle, Rocker, Roll, Root, > **ROTATE**, Rote, Roulade, Rout, Routine, Screw, Secund, Sheer, > **SHOT**, Shout, Sicken, Skit, Slew, Slue, Solstice, Sour, > **SPELL**, Spin, Spot, Sprain, Star, Start, Stem, Step, Swash, Swing, Swivel, Telemark, Three-point, Throw, Tiptilt, Tirl, Torque, Transpose, Trend, Trick, Trie, Trochilic, Turtle, Twiddle, Twist, U, Uey, Up, Veer, Versed, Version, Vertigo, Volta, Volte-face, Volutation, Wap, Warp, Wedein, Wend, Went, > **WHEEL**, Whelm, Whirl, Whorl, Wimple, Wind, Wrest, Wriggle, Zigzag
Turn-coat Apostate, Cato, Defector, Quisling, Rat, Renegade, Tergiversate, Traitor
Turner Axle, Lana, Lathe, Painter, Pivot, Rose-engine, Spanner, Worm, Wrench
Turning point Crisis, Crossroads, Landmark, Watershed
Turnip(-shaped) Baggy, Bagie, Hunter, Jicama, Napiform, Navew, Neep, Prairie, Rutabaga, > **STUPID PERSON**, Swede, Tumshie
Turnkey Gaoler, Jailer
Turn-out Eventuate, Gathering, Product, Rig, Splay, Style
Turn over Capsize, Careen, Flip, Inversion, Production, PTO, Somersault, TO, Up-end
Turnpike Highway, Toll
Turnstile Tourniquet
Turntable Rota, Rotator
Turpentine Galipot, Rosin, Thinner, Turps, Venice
Turquoise Bone, Fossil, Ligure, Occidental, Odontolite, Turkey stone
Turret(ed) Barmkin, Bartisan, Garret, Louver, Louvre, Pepperbox, Sponson, > **TOWER**, Turriculate
Turtle, Turtle head Bale, Calipash, Calipee, Chelone, Diamondback, Emys, Floor, Green, Hawk(s)bill, Inverted, Leatherback, Loggerhead, Matamata, Mossback, Mud, Musk, Ridley, Screen, Snapper, Snapping, Soft-shelled, Stinkpot, Terrapin, Thalassian
Tusk Gam, Horn, Ivory, Tooth, Tush
Tusker Dicynodont, Elephant, Mastodon
Tussle Giust, Joust, Mêlée, Scrimmage, Scrum, Scuffle, Skirmish, Touse, Touze, Towse, Towze, Tuilyie, Wrestle
Tussock Hassock, Niggerhead, Tuft
Tut(-tut) Och, Pooh
Tutelary Guardian, Protector
Tutor Abbé, Aristotle, Ascham, Bear, > **COACH**, Crammer, Don, Instruct, Leader, Mentor, Preceptor, Répétiteur, Supervisor, Teacher
Tuxedo DJ
TV Baird, Box, Cable, Digital, Idiot-box, Lime Grove, Monitor, PAL, Pay, Reality, SECAM, Sky, Tele, > **TELEVISION**, Telly, Tube, Video
Twaddle Blether, Drivel, Rot, Slipslop, Tripe
Twang Nasal, Pluck, Plunk, Rhinolalia
Tweak Pluck, Twiddle, Twist, Twitch
Tweed(y) Donegal, Harris®, Homespun, Lovat, Raploch
Tweet Chirrup

Twelfth, Twelve Apostles, Dozen, Epiphany, Glorious, Grouse, Midday, Midnight, N, Night, Noon, Ternion, Twal

Twenty, Twenty-sided Icosahedron, Score, Vicenary, Vicennial, Vicesimal, Vigesimal

Twenty-five Pony, Quartern

Twenty-four Thr(e)ave

Twerp Pipsqueak

▸ **Twice** *see* TWO

Twice-yearly Biennial, Equinox

Twiddle Fidget, Twirl

Twig(s) Besom, Birch, Cotton, Cow, Dig, Grasp, Kow, Osier, Realise, Reis, Rice, Rumble, Sarment, See, Sprig, Sticklac, Switch, Understand, Walking, Wand, Wattle, Wicker, Withe

Twilight Astronomical, Civil, Cockshut, Crepuscular, Demi-jour, Dusk, Gloam(ing), Gotterdämmerung, Nautical, Summerdim

Twill Cavalry, Chino

Twin(s) Asvins, Castor, Coetaneous, Conjoined, Didymous, Dioscuri, Ditokous, Dizygotic, Double, Fraternal, Gemel, Hemitrope, Identical, Isogeny, Kindred, Macle, Monozygotic, Pigeon-pair, Pollux, Siamese, Tweedledee, Tweedledum

Twine Braid, Coil, Cord, Inosculate, Packthread, Sisal, Snake, String, Twist, Wreathe

Twinge Pang, Scruple, Stab

Twinkle, Twinkling Glimmer, Glint, Mo(ment), > SPARKLE, Starnie, Trice

Twirl Spin, Swivel, Tirl, Tirlie-wirlie, Trill, Twiddle, Twizzle, Whirl

▷ **Twirling** *may indicate* an anagram

Twist(ed), Twister, Twisting, Twisty Anfractuous, Askant, Askew, Baccy, Becurl, Bought, Braid, Card-sharper, Chisel, Coil, Contort, Convolution, Crinkle, Crinkum-crankum, Crisp, Cue, Curl(icue), Cyclone, Deform, Detort, Distort, > DODGE, Entwine, Garrot, Helix, Imposture, Kink, Mangulate, Mat, Möbius strip, Oliver, Pandanaceous, Plait, Quirk, Raddle, Ravel, Rick, Rogue, Rotate, Rove, Serpent, Skew, Slew, Slub(b), Slue, Snake, Snarl, Spin, Spiral, Sprain, Squiggle, Squirm, Swivel, Tendril, Thrawn, Torc, Tornado, Torque, Torsade, Torsion, Torticollis, Tortile, Turn, Tweak, Twiddle, Twine, Twirl, Typhoon, Valgus, Volvulus, Wamble, Warp, Welkt, Wigwag, Wind, Wound-wrap, Wrast, Wreathe, Wrench, Wrest, Wrethe, Wrick, Wriggle, Wring, Writhe, Wry, Zigzag

▷ **Twisted, Twisting** *may indicate* an anagram

Twit, Twitter Chaff, Cherup, Chirrup, Dotterel, Gear(e), Giber, > JEER, Stupid, Taunt, Tweet, Warble

Twitch(ing), Twitchy Athetosis, Clonic, Grass, Jerk, Life-blood, Start, Subsultive, Tic, Tig, Tit, Tweak, Twinge, Vellicate, Yips

Two(some), Twice Bice, Bis, Bisp, Both, Brace, Couple(t), Deuce, Double, Duad, Dual, Duet, Duo, Dyad, > PAIR, Swy, Tête-à-tête, Twain, Twins, Twister

Two-edged Ancipitous

Two-faced Dihedral, Dorsiventral, Hypocritical, Janus, Redan

Two-gallon Peck

Two-headed Amphisbaenic, Dicephalous, Orthos

Two hundred H

Two hundred and fifty E, K

Two-master Brig

Two-rayed Diactinal

Two-sided Bilateral, Equivocatory

Two thousand Z

Two-up Kip, Swy

Two-wheeler Bicycle, Scooter

Tycoon Baron, Empire-builder, Magnate, Mogul, Plutocrat, Shogun

Type(s), Typing A, Agate, Aldine, Antimony, Antique, B, Balaam, Baskerville, Bastard, Bembo, Black-letter, Blood, Bodoni, Body, Bold face, Bourgeois, Braille, Brand, Brevier, Brilliant, Canon, Caslon, Category, Character, Chase, Cicero, Clarendon, Class, Columbian, Condensed, Cut, Egyptian, Elite, Elzevir, Em, Emblem, Emerald, English, Face, Font, Form(e), Founder's, Fount, Fraktur, Fudge, Garamond, Gem, Genre, Gent, Gothic, Great primer, Gutenberg, Hair, Ilk, Image, Kern(e), Key, Kidney, Kind, Late-star, Ligature, Light-faced, Longprimer, Ludlow, Minion, Modern, Moon, Mould, Non-pareil, Norm, Old English, Old-face, Old Style, Paragon, Pattern, Pearl, Peculiar, Personality, Pi, Pica, Pie, Plantin, Point, Primer, Print, Quad(rat), Roman, Ronde, Ruby, Sanserif, Secretary, Semibold, Serif, Serological, > **SORT**, Sp, Species, Spectral, Stanhope, Style, Times, Tissue, Touch, Version

▷ **Type of** *may indicate* an anagram

Typewriter Golfball, Portable, Stenograph, Stenotype®, Varityper®

Typhoid, Typhus Camp-fever, Tick-borne

Typhoon Cyclone, Hurricane, Monsoon, Tornado, Wind

Typical Average, Characteristic, Classic, Echt, Normal, Representative, Standard, Symbolic, True-bred, Usual

Typist Audio, Printer, Temp

Tyrannise(d) Domineer, Lord, Under

Tyrant, Tyranny, Tyrannical Absolutism, Autocrat, Caligula, Despot, Dictator, Drawcansir, Gelon, Herod, Lordly, Nero, Oppressor, Pharaoh, Sardanapalus, Satrap, Stalin, Totalitarian, Tsar, Yoke

Tyre Balloon, Cross-ply, Cushion, Michelin, Pericles, Pneumatic, Radial, Radial(-ply), Recap, Remould, Retread, Shoe, Sidewall, Slick, Snow, Spare, Tread, Tubeless, Whitewall

Tyro Beginner, Ham, > **NOVICE**, Rabbit, Rookie, Rooky, Starter

Tyrolese R(h)aetian

Uu

U, U-type Gent, Unicorn, Universal, Uranium
Ubiquitous Everywhere, Omnipresent
Udder Bag, Dug
Ugandan Obote
Ugly Cow, Customer, Eyesore, Foul, Gorgon, Gruesome, Hideous, Homely, Huckery, Loth, Mean, Ominous, Plain
Ugrian Ostiak, Ostyak, Samo(y)ed, Vogul
UK GB
Ukase Decree
Ukraine Ruthene, UR
Ulcer(ous) Abscess, Aphtha, Bedsore, Canker, Chancroid, Decubitus, Duodenal, Gastric, Helcoid, Noli-me-tangere, Noma, Peptic, Phagedaena, Rodent, Rupia, Sore, Varicose, Wolf
Ulster NI, Overcoat, Raincoat, Ulad
Ulterior External, Hidden
Ultimate Absolute, Basic, Deterrent, Eventual, Final, Furthest, Last, Maximum, So, Supreme, Thule
Ultra Drastic, Extreme, Radical
Ultra-modern Space age
Ultra-republican Leveller
Ulysses Bloom, Grant, Odysseus
Umbellifer(ous) Angelica, Arnut, Car(r)away, Dill, Honewort, Narthex, Pig-nut, Seseli
Umber Burnt, Mottled, Raw, Waved
Umbrage Offence, Pique, Resentment, Shade
Umbrella(-shaped) Bubble, Bumbershoot, Chatta, Gamp, Gingham, Gloria, Mush(room), Nuclear, Parasol, Sunshade, Tee
Umbria Eugubine, Iguvine
Umpire Arb(iter), Byrlawman, Daysman, Decider, Judge, Oddjobman, Odd(s)man, Overseer, Oversman, Referee, Rule, Stickler, Thirdsman
Unabashed Bare-faced, Brazen, Shameless
Unable Can't, Incapable
Unaccented Atonic, Proclitic
Unacceptable Non-U, Not on, Out, Stigmatic
Unaccompanied A cappella, Alone, High-lone, Secco, Single, Solo, Solus
Unaccustomed Desuetude, New
Unadorned Bald
Unadulterated Sincere
Unaffected Artless, Genuine, Homely, Natural, Plain, Sincere, Unattached
Unaided Single-handed, Solo
Unaltered Constant, Same
Unambiguous Univocal
Unanimous Accord, Nem con

Unanswerable Erotema, Irrefragable, Irrefutable
Unarguable Erotema
Unarmed Inerm, Naked, Vulnerable
Unashamed Blatant, Brazen, Open
Unassigned Adespota, Anonymous
Unassuming Lowly
Unattached Freelance, Loose
Unattractive Drac(k), Lemon, Minger, Plain, Plug-ugly, Rebarbative, Seamy, Ugly
Unattributable Anon
Unauthentic Plagal
▷ **Unauthentic** *may indicate* an anagram
Unavail(able), Unavailing Bootless, Futile, Ineluctable, Lost, No use, Off, Useless, Vain
Unavoidable Inevitable, Necessary, Perforce
Unaware Heedless, Ignorant, Incognisant, Innocent, Oblivious
Unbalanced Asymmetric, Deranged, Doolalli, Doolally, Loco, Lopsided, Uneven
Unbearable Bassington, Intolerable
Unbeaten All-time
Unbecoming, Unbefitting Improper, Infra dig, Shabby, Unfitting, Unseemly, Unsuitable, Unworthy
Unbelievable, Unbeliever Agnostic, Atheist, Cassandra, Doubter, Giaour, Heathen, Incredible, Infidel, Pagan, Painim, Paynim, Sceptic, Tall, Zendik
Unbent Relaxed
Unbiased Fair, Impartial, Just, Neutral, Objective, Unattainted
Unblemished Spotless, Vestal
Unblinking Alert, Astare, Fearless
Unborn Future, Unbred
Unbowed In-kneed, Resolute
Unbreakable Infrangible, Inviolate
Unbridled Fancy free, Footloose, Lawless, Uncurbed, Unrestricted, Unshackled, Untramelled
Unburden Confide, Offload, Relieve, Unload
Uncanny Eerie, Eldritch, Extraordinary, Geason, Rum, Spooky, Weird
Uncastrated Stone
Uncertain(ty) Blate, Broken, Chancy, Chary, Contingent, Delicate, Dicey, Dither, Doubtful, Dubiety, Grey, Heisenberg, Hesitant, Iffy, Indeterminate, Indistinct, Irresolute, Peradventure, Queasy, Risky, Slippery, Tentative, Vor
▷ **Uncertain** *may indicate* an anagram
Unchallengeable, Unchallenge(d) Irrecusable, Sackless
Unchangeable, Unchanged, Unchanging As is, Enduring, Eternal, Idempotent, Immutable, Monotonous, Pristine, Stable, Standpat
Uncharacteristic Atypical
Uncharged Neutral, Neutron
Unchaste Corrupt, Immodest, Immoral, Impure, Lewd, Wanton
Unchecked Rampant
Uncivil(ised) Barbaric, Benighted, Boondocks, Discourteous, Disrespectful, Giant-rude, Goth, Heathen, Impolite, Military, Rude, Rudesby
Uncle Abbas, Afrikaner, Arly, Bob, Dutch, Eme, Nunky, Oom, Pawnbroker, Pop-shop, Remus, Sam, Tio, Tom, Usurer, Vanya
Unclean Defiled, Dirty, Impure, Obscene, Ordure, Squalid, Tabu, T(e)refa(h)
Unclear Ambitty, Hazy, Nebulous, Obscure

Unclothed Bald, Nude
Uncloven Soliped
Uncommitted Laodicean
Uncommon Rare, Strange, Unusual
▷ **Uncommon(ly)** *may indicate* an anagram
Uncommunicative Reserved, Tight-lipped
Uncompanionable Threesome
Uncomplimentary Blunt
Uncomprehending Anan, Ignorant
Uncompromising Cutthroat, Hardline, Hardshell, Intransigent, Rigid, Strict, Ultra
Unconcealed Open, Pert
Unconcerned Bland, Careless, Casual, Cold, Indifferent, Insouciant, Nonchalant, Strange
Unconditional Absolute, Free, Pure
Unconnected Asyndetic, Detached, Disjointed, Off-line
Unconscious(ness) Asleep, Catalepsy, Cold, Comatose, Instinctive, Non-ego, Not-I, Subliminal, Trance, Under
Unconsidered Impetuous, Rash
Uncontrolled Atactic, Free, Incontinent, Loose, Loose cannon, Wild
Unconventional Beatnik, Bohemian, Drop-out, Eccentric, Gonzo, Heretic, Heterodox, Informal, Irregular, Offbeat, Original, Outlandish, Outré, Raffish, Unorthodox
▷ **Unconventional** *may indicate* an anagram
Unconverted Neat
Unconvincing Farfet(ched), Lame, Thin
Uncoordinated Asynergia, Ataxic, Awkward, Clumsy
Uncorrect Stet
Uncouth(ness) Backwoodsman, Bear, Crude, Gothic, Inelegant, Rough, Rube, Rude, Rugged, Uncivil
Uncover(ed) Bare, Disclose, Dismask, Expose, Inoperculate, Open, Overt, Peel, Reveal, Shave, Shill, Shuck, Uncap, Unveil
Unction, Unctuous(ness) Anele, Balm, Chrism, Extreme, Oil(y), Ointment, Oleaginous, Ooze, Smarm, Soapy
Uncultivated, Uncultured Artless, Bundu, Fallow, Ignorant, Philistine, Rude, Tramontane, Wild
Undamaged Intact, Sound, Whole
Undated Sine die
Undecided Doubtful, Moot, Non-committal, Open-ended, Pending, Pendulous, Uncertain, Wavering
Undefiled Chaste, Clean, Pure, Virgin
Undeniable Fact, Incontestable, Irrefutable
Under Aneath, Below, Beneath, Hypnotized, Sotto, Sub-, Unconscious
Underarm Axilla, Lob
Underburnt Samel
Under-butler Bread-chipper
Undercarriage Bogie, Chassis
Undercoat Base, Primer
Undercooked Rare, Raw, Samel
Undercover Espionage, Secret, Veiled
Undercurrent Acheron, Undertone, Undertow
Underdevelopment Ateleiosis

Underdog Cerberus, Loser, Victim

▸ **Undergarment** *see* **UNDERWEAR**

Undergo Bear, Dree, Endure, Solvate, Sustain

Undergraduate Fresher, L, Pup, Sizar, Sophomore, Student, Subsizar, Tuft

Underground (group) Basement, Catacomb, Cellar, Hell, Hypogaeous, Irgun, Kiva, Macchie, Maquis, Mattamore, Metro, Phreatic, Pict, Plutonia, Pothole, Secret, Souterrain, Subsoil, Subterranean, Subway, Tube

Undergrowth Brush, Chaparral, Firth, Frith, Scrub

Underhand Dirty, Haunch, Insidious, Lob, Oblique, Secret, Sinister, Sly, Sneaky, Surreptitious

Underlease Subtack

Underline Emphasise, Insist

Underling Bottle-washer, Cog, Inferior, Jack, Menial, Munchkin, Subordinate

Underlying Subjacent

Undermine Erode, Fossick, Sap, Subvert, Tunnel, Weaken

Undernourished Puny, Starveling

Underpass Simplon, Subway

Underside Bed, Soffit

Understand(able), **Understanding** Accept, Acumen, Agreement, Apprehend, Capeesh, Clear, Cognisable, Comprehend, Conceive, Concept, Cotton-on, Deal, Dig, Enlighten, Entente, Exoteric, Fathom, Follow, Gather, Gauge, Gaum, Geddit, Gorm, Grasp, Have, Head, Heels, Insight, Ken, Kind, Knowhow, Learn, Light, Omniscient, Pact, Plumb, Rapport, Rapprochement, Realise, Savey, Savvy, See, Sense, Sole, Substance, Tolerance, Treaty, Tumble, Twig, Uptak(e), Wisdom, Wit

Understate(d), **Understatement** Litotes, M(e)iosis, Subtle

Understood Implicit, OK, Perspicuous, Roger, Tacit, Unspoken

Understudy Deputy, Double, Stand-in, Sub

Undertake, **Undertaking** Attempt, Contract, Covenant, Enterprise, Feat, Guarantee, Pledge, Promise, Scheme, Shoulder, Venture, Warranty

Undertaker Entrepreneur, Mortician, Obligor, Sponsor, Upholder

Under-ten Unit, Yarborough

Undertone Murmur, Rhubarb, Sotto voce

Underwater Demersal

Underwear Balbriggan, Bloomers, Bodice, Body, Body stocking, Body suit, Bra(ssiere), Briefs, Broekies, Camiknickers, Camisole, Chemise, Chemisette, Chuddies, Combinations, Combs, Corset, Dainties, Drawers, (French) knickers, Frillies, Girdle, Innerwear, Jump, Linen, Lingerie, Linings, Long Johns, Pantalets, Pantaloons, Panties, Pantihose, Panty girdle, Petticoat, Scanties, Semmit, Shift, Shorts, Singlet, Skivvy, Slip, Smalls, Stays, Step-ins, Subucula, Suspenders, Tanga, Teddy, Thermal, Underdaks, Undergarments, Underpants, Undershirt, Underthings, Undies, Unmentionables, Vest, Wyliecoat, Y-fronts®

Underworld Chthonic, Criminal, Hades, Hell, Lowlife, Mafia, Shades, Tartar(e), Tartarus, Tartary

Underwrite, **Underwritten** Assure, Endorse, Guarantee, Insure, Lloyds, PS

Undeserving Immeritous

Undesirable Kibitzer

Undeveloped Backward, Depauperate, Green, Inchoate, Latent, Nubbin, Ridgel, Ridgil, Ridgling, Rig, Riggald, Riglin(g), Rudimentary, Seminal

Undifferentiated Thalliform, Thallus

Undigested Crude

Undignified (end) Disaster, Foot, Improper, Infra dig, Unseemly

Undiluted Neat, Pure, Sheer, Straight
Undiminished Entire, Intact, Whole
Undiplomatic Brusque, Tactless
Undisciplined Hothead, Rule-less, Rulesse, Sloppy, Unruly, Wanton
Undisclosed Hidden, In petto
Undisguised Apert, Clear, Plain
Undistinguished Plebeian
Undivided Aseptate, Complete, Entire, Indiscrete, One
Undo(ing) Annul, Defeat, Destroy, Disconnect, Downfall, Dup, Poop, Poupe, Release, Ruin, Unravel
Undoctored Neat
Undone Arrears, Left, Postponed, Ran, Ruined
Undoubtedly Certes, Ipso facto, Positively, Sure
Undress(ed) Bare, Disarray, Disrobe, En cuerpo, Expose, Négligé, Nude, Nue, Peel, Querpo, Raw, Rough, Self-faced, Spar, Strip, Unapparelled
Undulate, Undulating Billow, Nebule, Ripple, Roll, Wave
▷ **Unduly** *may indicate* an anagram
Undyed Greige
Undying Amaranthine, Eternal
Unearth(ly) Astral, Dig, Discover, Disentomb, Exhumate, Indagate
Unease, Uneasiness, Uneasy Angst, Anxious, Creeps, Disquiet, Inquietude, Itchy, Malaise, Restive, Shy, Tense, The willies, Uptight, Windy, Womble-cropped
Unedifying Idle
Unembarrassed Blasé, Dégagé
Unemotional Bland, Cool, Iceberg, Matter-of-fact, Sober, Stolid
Unemployed, Unemployment Drone, Idle, Latent, Lay-off, Redundant, Residual, Stalko, Surfie
Unending Chronic, Eternal, Lasting, Sempiternal
Unenlightened Ignorant, Nighted
Unenthusiastic Damp, Tepid
Unenveloped Achlamydeous
Unequal(led) Aniso-, Disparate, Non(e)such, Scalene, Unjust
Unerring Dead, Exact, Precise
Unestablished Free
Unethical Amoral, Corrupt, Immoral
Uneven(ness) Accident, Blotchy, Bumpy, Erose, Irregular, Jaggy, Patchy, Ragged, Scratchy
▷ **Unevenly** *may indicate* an anagram
Unexceptional Ordinary, Workaday
Unexpected(ly) Abrupt, Accidental, Adventitious, Fortuitous, Inopinate, Snap, Sodain(e), Sudden, Turn-up, Unawares, Unwary
Unexperienced Strange
Unexplained Obscure
Unfading Evergreen, Immarcescible
Unfailing Sure
Unfair Bias(s)ed, Crook, Dirty, Inclement, Invidious, Mean, Partial
Unfaithful Disloyal, Godless, Infidel, Traitor, Two-timing
Unfamiliar New, Quaint, Strange
Unfashionable Cube, Dowdy, Out(moded), Out-of-date, Passe, Square
▷ **Unfashionable** *may indicate* 'in' to be removed
Unfavourable Adverse, Ill, Inimical, Poor, Untoward

Unfeeling Adamant, Callous, Cold, Cruel, Dead, Hard, Inhuman(e), Insensate, Robotic

Unfinished Crude, Inchoate, Raw, Scabble, Scapple, Stickit

Unfit(ting) Cronk, Disabled, Faulty, Ill, Impair, Inept, Outré, Trefa, Tre(i)f, Unable

▷ **Unfit** *may indicate* an anagram

Unfixed Isotropic, Loose

Unfledged Gull

Unflinching Fast, Staunch

Unfold Deploy, Display, Divulge, Evolve, Interpret, Open, Relate, Spread

Unforced Voluntary

Unforeseen Accident, Sudden

Unfortunate(ly) Accursed, Alack, Alas, Hapless, Ill-starred, Luckless, Shameless, Sorry, Unlucky

Unfounded Groundless

Unfriendly Aloof, Antagonistic, Asocial, Chill(y), Cold, Fraim, Fremd, Fremit, Hostile, Icy, Remote, Surly

Unfruitful Abortive, Barren, Sterile

Unfulfilled Manqué

Ungainly Awkward, Gawkish, Uncouth, Weedy

Ungenerous Small

Ungodliness, Ungodly Impiety, Pagan, Perfidious, Profane

Ungracious Cold, Offhand, Rough, Rude

Ungrammatical Anacoluthia

Ungrateful Ingrate, Snaky

Unguent Nard, Pomade, Salve

Ungulate Antelope, Dinoceras, Eland, Equidae, Hoofed, Moose, Rhino, Ruminantia, Takin, Tapir, Tylopoda

Unhappily, Unhappy, Unhappiness Blue, Depressed, Disconsolate, Dismal, Distress, Doleful, Downcast, Down-hearted, Dysphoria, Glumpish, Love-lorn, Lovesick, Miserable, Sad, Sore, Tearful, Unlief, Upset

▷ **Unhappily** *may indicate* an anagram

Unharmed Safe, Scatheless

Unharness Outspan

Unhealthy Bad, Clinic, Diseased, Epinosic, Insalubrious, Morbid, Noxious, Peaky, Prurient, Sickly

Unholy Profane, Wicked

Unhurried Patient

Uniat Maronite, Melchite

Unicorn Ch'i-lin, Coin, Monoceros, Moth, Myth, Narwhal

Unidentified Anon, Anonym(ous), Incognito, Ligure

Unification, Unify(ing) Henotic, Integrate, Risorgimento, Unite

Uniform Abolla, Battledress, Consistent, Dress, Equable, Equal, Even, Flat, Forage-cap, Homogeneous, Homomorphic, Identical, Khaki, Kit, Livery, Regimentals, Regular, Rig, Robe, Same, Sole, Standard, Steady, Strip, Unvaried

Unimaginative Banausic, Literalistic, Pedestrian, Pooter

Unimpaired Entire, Intact, Sound

Unimportant Cog, Expendable, Fiddling, Footling, Frivolous, Idle, Immaterial, Inconsequent, Inconsiderable, Insignificant, MacGuffin, Makeweight, Minnow, Minutiae, Negligible, Nugatory, Peripheral, Petty, Small-time, Trifling, Trivia(l)

Unimpressible Cynical

Uninformed Ingram
Uninhabited Bundu, Deserted, Lonely
Uninhibited Bold, Raunchy
Uninspired Humdrum, Pedestrian, Pompier, Tame
Unintelligent Dumb, Obtuse, Stupid
Unintelligible Arcane, Code, Greek
Unintentional Inadvertent
Uninterested, Uninteresting Apathetic, Bland, Dreary, Dry, Dull, Grey, Incurious, Nondescript
Uninterrupted Constant, Continuous, Incessant, Running, Steady
Uninvited Gatecrasher, Interloper, Intruder, Sorner, Trespasser, Umbra
Union(ist) Affiance, Allegiance, Alliance, Anschluss, Art, Association, Bed, Benelux, Bond, Close, Combination, Company, Concert, Confederacy, Covalency, Craft, Credit, Customs, Diphthong, Economic, Enosis, Ensemble, Equity, EU, European, Fasciation, Federal, Federation, French, Frithgild, Fusion, Group, Guild, Heterogamy, Horizontal, Impanation, Industrial, Knight of labour, Liaison, Liberal, Link-up, Management, Marriage, Match, Merger, NUM, Nuptials, NUR, NUS, NUT, Pan-American, Parabiosis, Pearl, RU, Rugby, Samiti, Sex, Sherman, Solidarity, Soviet, Splice, Sponsal, Student, Symphysis, Syngamy, Synizesis, Synostosis, Synthesis, Syssarcosis, Teamsters, > TRADE UNION, TU, U, UNISON, USDAW, Uxorial, Verein, Vertical, Vienna, Wedding, Wedlock, Wield, Zollverein, Zygosis
Unique(ness) Alone, A-per-se, Hacceity, Inimitable, Irreplaceable, Lone, Matchless, Nonesuch, Nonpareil, Nonsuch, One-off, Only, Peerless, Rare, Singular, Sole, Sui generis
Unisex(ual) Epicene, Hermaphrodite
Unison Chorus, Harmony, One, Sync
Unit Abampere, Absolute, Ace, Amp, Angstrom, Archine, Archiphoneme, Bar, Bargaining, Barn, Base, Baud, Becquerel, Bioblast, Biogen, Biophor(e), Bit, Brigade, Byte, Cadre, Candela, Cell, Centimorgan, Centipoise, Chaldron, Chronon, Codon, Congius, Corps, Coulomb, Crith, Cusec, Dalton, Daraf, Darcy, Debye, Degree, Denier, Derived, Dessiatine, Detachment, DIN, Dioptre, Division, Dobson, Dol, Dyne, Echelon, Ecosystem, Electromagnetic, Electron, Electrostatic, Element, Em, EMU, En, Energid, Ensuite, Episome, Erg, Erlang, Farad, Feedlot, Fermi, Field, Flight, Foot-candle, Foot-lambert, Foot-pound, Foot-ton, Fresnel, Fundamental, Gal, Gauss, Gestalt, GeV, Gigabit, Gigaflop, Gigahertz, Gigawatt, Gilbert, Glosseme, Gram, Grav, Gray, Hartree, Henry, Hertz, Hide, Hogshead, Holon, Ion, Item, Jansky, Joule, K, Kelvin, Kilderkin, Kilerg, Kilowatt, Lambert, Langley, Last, League, Lexeme, Lumen, Lux, Maceral, Magneton, Man-hour, Maxwell, Measure, Megabyte, Megahertz, Megaton, Megawatt, Megohm, Message, Metre, Mho, Micella, Micelle, Microcurie, Microinch, Micron, Mil, Module, Mole, Monad, Monetary, Mongo(e), Morgen, Morpheme, Mutchkin, Neper, Nepit, Nest, Newton, Nit, Octa, Oersted, Ohm, Okta, Organ, Panzer, Parasang, Pascal, Ped, Pennyweight, Peripheral, Phoneme, Phot, Phyton, Pixel, Ploughgate, Point, Poise, Poundal, Power, Practical, Probit, Protoplast, RA, Radian, Rem, Remen, Rep, Ro(e)ntgen, Rutherford, Sabin, Sealed, Second, Secure, Semeion, Sememe, Shed, SI, Siemens, Sievert, Singleton, Sink, Slug, Sone, Steradian, Stere, Stilb, Stock, Stoke(s), Strontium, Syllable, Syntagm(a), TA, Tagmeme, Terabyte, Terminal, Tesla, Tetrapody, Tex, Therblig, Therm, Tog, Token, Torr, Vanitory, Vanity, Var, Vara, Volt, Wall, Watt, Weber, Wing, X, Yrneh
Unitarian Arian, Paulian, Racovian, Socinian

Unite(d) Accrete, Bind, Coalesce, Combine, Concordant, Connate, Connect, Consolidate, Consubstantiate, Covalent, Fay, Federal, Federalise, Federate, Fuse, Gene, Injoint, Inosculate, Join, Kingdom, Knit, Lap, Link, Marry, Meint, Meng, Ment, Merge, Meynt, Ming, Nations, Oop, Oup, Siamese, Solid, States, Tie, > WED, Weld, Yoke

United Ireland Fine Gael

United Kingdom Old Dart, UK

Unity Harmony, One, Solidarity, Sympathy, Togetherness

Univalent Monatomic

Universal, Universe All, Catholic, Cosmos, Creation, Ecumenic(al), Emma, Expanding, General, Global, Infinite, Inflationary, Island, Macrocosm, Mandala, Microcosm, Sphere, U, Via Lactea, World(wide)

University Academe, Academy, Alma mater, Aston, Berkeley, Bonn, Brown, Campus, Civic, College, Columbia, Cornell, Exeter, Gown, Harvard, Ivy League, Open, OU, Oxbridge, Pennsylvania, Princeton, Reading, Redbrick, St Andrews, Sorbonne, Varsity, Whare wangea, Yale

Unjust(ified) Groundless, Inequity, Iniquitous, Invalid, Tyrannical

Unkempt Dishevelled, Greebo, Mal soigné, Raddled, Raggle-taggle, Scody, Scuzzy, Shaggy

Unknown Agnostic, Anon, A.N.Other, Hidden, Ign, Incog(nito), N, Nobody, Noumenon, Occult, Quantity, Secret, Soldier, Strange, Symbolic, Tertium quid, Warrior, X, Y

Unleavened Azymous

Unless Nisi, Save, Without

Unliable Exempt

Unlicensed Illicit

Unlike(ly) Difform, Disparate, Dubious, Far-fetched, Improbable, Inauspicious, Long shot, Outsider, Remote, Tall, Unlich

Unlimited Almighty, Boundless, Indefinite, Measureless, Nth, Universal, Vast

Unlisted Ex-directory

Unload Disburden, Discharge, Drop, Dump, Jettison, Land, Strip

Unlock(ed) Bald

Unlucky Donsie, Hapless, Ill(-starred), Inauspicious, Infaust, Jonah, Misadventure, Misfallen, S(c)hlimazel, Stiff, Thirteen, Untoward, Wanchancie, Wanchancy

Unman Castrate

Unmannerly Crude, Discourteous, Impolite, Low bred, Rude

Unmarried Bachelor, Common-law, Single, Spinster

Unmask Expose, Rumble

Unmatched Bye, Champion, Orra, Unique

Unmentionable(s) Bra, Foul, Secret, > UNDERWEAR, Undies

Unmindful Heedless, Oblivious

Unmistakable Clear, Manifest, Plain

Unmitigated Absolute, Arrant, Sheer, Ultra

Unmixed Me(a)re, Neat, Nett, Pure, Raw, Straight

Unmoved, Unmoving Adamant, Doggo, Firm, Serene, Static, Stolid

Unnamed Anon

Unnatural Abnormal, Affected, Cataphysical, Contrived, Eerie, Flat, Geep, Irregular, Strange

▷ **Unnaturally** *may indicate* an anagram

Unnecessary De trop, Extra, Gash, Gratuitous, Needless, Otiose, Redundant, Superfluous

Unnerve, Unnerving Discouraging, Eerie, Rattle
Unobserved Backstage, Sly, Unseen
Unobtrusive Low profile
Unoccupied Empty, Idle, Vacant, Void
Unofficial Fringe, Wildcat
Unoriginal Banal, Copy, Derivative, Imitation, Plagiarised, Slavish
Unorthodox Heretic, Heterodox, Maverick, Off-the-wall, Unconventional
▷ **Unorthodox** *may indicate* an anagram
Unpaid Amateur, Brevet, Hon(orary), Outstanding, Voluntary
Unpaired Azygous, Bye
Unpalatable Acid, Bitter, Unsavoury
Unparalleled Supreme, Unique
Unpartitioned Aseptate
Unperturbed Bland, Calm, Serene
Unplanned Impromptu, Improvised, Spontaneous
Unpleasant, Unpleasant person Cow, Creep, Fink, God-awful, Grim, Grotty, Harsh, Horrible, Icky, Invidious, Nasty, Obnoxious, Odious, Offensive, Painful, Pejorative, Rank, Rebarbative, Shady, Shitty, Shocker, Snarky, Sticky, Toerag, Wart
Unploughed Lea-rig
Unpolluted Sterile
Unpopular Hat(e)able
Unpractical Futile, Orra
Unpredictable Aleatory, Dicy, Erratic, Maverick, Wild card
Unprepared Ad lib, Extempore, Impromptu, Last minute, Unready
Unpretentious Quiet
Unprincipled Amoral, Dishonest, Irregular, Reprobate, Unscrupulous
Unproductive Arid, Atokal, Atokous, Barren, Dead-head, Eild, Fallow, Futile, Lean, Poor, Shy, Sterile, Yeld, Yell
Unprofitable Bootless, Fruitless, Lean, Thankless
Unprogressive Inert, Square
Unprotected Exposed, Nude, Vulnerable
Unpublished Inedited
Unpunctual Tardy
Unqualified Absolute, Entire, Outright, Perfect, Profound, Pure, Quack, Sheer, Straight, Thorough, Total, Utter
Unquestionably, Unquestioning Absolute, Certain, Doubtless, Implicit
Unravel Construe, Disentangle, Feaze, Fray, Solve
Unready Unripe
Unreal(istic) Eidetic, En l'air, Escapist, Fake, Fancied, Illusory, Insubstantial, Mirage, Oneiric, Phantom, Phon(e)y, Planet Zog, Pseudo, Romantic, Sham, Spurious
Unreasonable, Unreasoning Absurd, Bigot, Extreme, Illogical, Irrational, Misguided, Perverse, Rabid, Steep
Unrecognised Incognito, Inconnu, Invalid, Thankless, Unsung
Unrefined Coarse, Common, Crude, Earthy, Gur, Impure, Rude, Vul(g), Vulgar
Unrehearsed Extempore, Impromptu
Unrelenting Implacable, Remorseless, Severe, Stern
Unreliable Dodgy, Dubious, Erratic, Fair-weather, Fickle, Flighty, Fly-by-night, Shonky, Unstable, Wankle, Wonky
Unremarkable Nondescript
Unremitting Dogged, Intensive

Unresponsive Cold, Frigid, Nastic, Rigor
Unrest Discontent, Ferment
Unrestrained Effusive, Extravagant, Free, Hearty, Homeric, Immoderate, Incontinent, Lax, Lowsit, Rampant, Wanton, Wild
Unreturnable Ace
Unrighteousness Adharma
Unrivalled Nonesuch
Unromantic Classic(al), Mundane
Unruffled Calm, Placid, Serene, Smooth, Tranquil
Unruly Anarchic, Bodgie, Buckie, Camstairy, Camsteary, Camsteerie, Coltish, Exception, Fractious, Lawless, Obstreperous, Ragd(e), Raged, Ragged, Rambunctious, Rampageous, Rattlebag, Riotous, Tartar, Turbulent, Turk, Wanton, Wayward, Zoo
▷ **Unruly** *may indicate* an anagram
Unsafe Deathtrap, Fishy, Insecure, Perilous, Precarious, Vulnerable
Unsatisfactory, **Unsatisfying** Bad, Lame, Lousy, Meagre, Rocky, Thin, Wanting
Unsavoury Epinosic
Unscramble Decode, Decrypt
Unscripted Ad lib
Unscrupulous Rascally, Slippery
Unseasonable, **Unseasoned** Green, Murken, Raw, Untimely
Unseat Depose, Dethrone, Oust, Overset, Overthrow, Throw
Unseemly Coarse, Improper, Incivil, Indecent, Indign, Seedy, Untoward
Unselfish Altruist, Generous
Unsent Square
Unsettle(d) Faze, Homeless, Hunky, Indecisive, Nervous, Outstanding, Queasy, Restive, Troublous
▷ **Unsettled** *may indicate* an anagram
Unsexy N, Neuter
Unsheltered Bleak, Exposed, Homeless
Unsight(ed), **Unsightly** Eyeless, Hideous, Repulsive, Ugly
Unsinning Impeccable, Pure
Unskilled Awkward, Dilutee, Gauche, Green, Inexpert, Rude
Unsmiling Agelastic
Unsociable Anchoretic, Grouchy, Solitary, Stay-at-home
Unsophisticated Alf, Boondocks, Boonies, Bushie, Cornball, Corny, Cracker-barrel, Direct, Down-home, Faux-naif, Hillbilly, Homebred, Homespun, Inurbane, Jaap, Jay, Naive, Provincial, Rube, Verdant
Unsound Barmy, Infirm, Invalid, Shaky, Wildcat, Wonky
▷ **Unsound** *may indicate* an anagram
Unsparing Severe
Unspeakable Dreadful, Ineffable, Nefandous
Unspecific General, Generic, Vague
Unspoiled, **Unspoilt** Innocent, Natural, Perfect, Pristine, Pure
Unspoken Silent, Tacit
Unstable, **Unsteady** Anomic, Astatic, Bockedy, Casual, Crank, Crank(y), Dicky, Erratic, Flexuose, Flexuous, Fluidal, Giddy, Groggy, Infirm, Insecure, Labile, Rickety, Shaky, Shifty, Slippy, Tickle, Tottery, Totty, Variable, Volatile, Walty, Wambling, Wankle, Warby, Wobbly
Unstated Concordat, Tacit, Unknown
▶ **Unsteady** *see* UNSTABLE
Unstressed Enclitic

▷ **Unstuck** *may indicate* an anagram
Unsubstantial Aeriform, Airy, Flimsy, Paltry, Shadowy, Slight, Thin, Yeasty
Unsuccessful Abortive, Futile, Manqué, Vain
Unsuitable Impair, Improper, Inapt, Incongruous, Inexpedient, Malapropos, Unbecoming, Unfit
Unsupported Astylar, Floating, Unfounded
Unsure Hesitant, Tentative
Unsurpassed All-time, Best, Supreme
Unsuspecting Credulous, Innocent, Naive
Unsweetened Brut, Natural
Unsymmetrical Heterauxesis(m), Irregular, Lopsided
Unsympathetic Short shrift
Unthinking Mechanical
Untidy Daggy, Dowd(y), Frowzy, Litterbug, Ragged, Raunchy, Scruff(y), Slipshod, Slovenly, Tatty
▷ **Untidy** *may indicate* an anagram
Untie Free, Undo, Unlace
Until Hasta
Untilled Fallow
Untiring Assiduous
Untold Secret, Umpteen, Unread, Unred, Vast
Untouchable Burakumin, Dalit, Harijan, Immune, Sancrosanct, Sealed
Untouched Intact, Inviolate, Pristine, Virgin
▷ **Untrained** *may indicate* 'BR' to be removed
Untried New, Virgin
Untrue, Untruth Apocryphal, Eccentric, Fabrication, Faithless, False(hood), Lie, Prefabrication, Unleal
Untrustworthy Dishonest, Fickle, Fly-by-night, Mamzer, Momzer, Shifty, Sleeky, Tricky
Untypical Anomalous, Isolated, Unusual
Unused, Unusable Impracticable, New, Over, Wasted
Unusual(ly) Abnormal, Atypical, Exceptional, Extra(ordinary), Freak, New, Novel, Odd, Out-of-the-way, Outre, Particular, Rare, Remarkable, Singular, Special, > STRANGE, Unco, Unique, Untypical, Unwonted
▷ **Unusual** *may indicate* an anagram
Unutterable Ineffable
Unvarying Constant, Eternal, Stable, Static, Uniform
Unveil Expose, Honour
Unvoiced Surd
Unwanted De trop, Exile, Gooseberry, Nimby, Outcast, Sorn
Unwavering Steadfast
Unwed Celibate, Single
Unwelcome, Unwelcoming Frosty, Icy, Lulu, Obtrusive, (Persona) Non grata
Unwell Ailing, Crook, Dicky, Ill, Impure, Poorly, Quazzy, Queasy, Seedy, Shouse, Toxic
Unwholesome Miasmous, Morbid, Noxious
Unwieldy Cumbersome, Elephantine
Unwilling(ness) Averse, Disinclined, Intestate, Loth, Nolition, Nolo, Obdurate, Perforce, Reluctant
Unwind Relax, Straighten, Unreave, Unreeve
▷ **Unwind** *may indicate* an anagram
Unwinnable Catch 22

Unwise Foolish, Ill-advised, Impolitic, Imprudent, Inexpedient, Injudicious, Rash

Unwitting Accidental, Nescient

Unwonted Inusitate

Unworkable Impossible, Inoperable

Unworried Carefree

Unworthy Below, Beneath, Indign, Inferior

Unwritten Verbal

Unyielding Adamant, Eild, Firm, Hardline, Inexorable, Inextensible, Intransigent, Obdurate, Rigid, Steely, Stubborn, Tough, Unalterable

Unyoke Outspan

Up(on), Upturned, Upper, Uppish A, Acockbill, Afoot, Antidepressant, Arrogant, Astir, Astray, Astride, Cloud-kissing, Euphoric, Heavenward, Hep, Horsed, Incitant, Off, On, Primo, Range, Ride, Riding, Risen, Skyward, Speed, > UPPER CLASS, Vamp, Ventral

Up-anchor Atrip, Weigh

Upbeat Anacrusis, Arsis

Upbraid Abuse, Rebuke, Reproach, Reprove, Scold, Storm, Twit

Upcountry Anabasis, Inland

Update Brief, Renew, Report

Upheaval Cataclysm, Chaos, Eruption, Rummage, Seismic, Stir

▷ **Upheld** *may indicate* 'up' in another word

Uphill Arduous, Borstal, Sisyphean

Uphold Assert, Defend, Maintain

Upholstery Lampas, Moquette, Trim

Upkeep Support

Upland(s) Alps, Downs, Hilly, Wold

Uplift Boost, Edify, Elate, Elevation, Exalt, Hoist, Levitation, Sky

Upper class, Upper crust Aristocrat, County, Crachach, Nobility, Patrician, Posh, Sial, Top-hat, Tweedy, U

Upright(s), Uprightness Aclinic, Anend, Apeak, Apeek, Aplomb, Arrect, Atrip, Erect, Goalpost, Honest, Incorrupt, Jamb, Joanna, Merlon, Moral, Mullion, Orthograde, Perpendicular, Piano, Pilaster(s), Post, Rectitude, Roman, Splat, Stanchion, Stares, Stile, Stud, Vertical, Virtuous

Uprising Incline, Intifada, Rebellion, Revolt, Tumulus

Uproar(ious) Ballyhoo, Bedlam, Blatancy, Brouhaha, Charivari, Clamour, Clangour, Collieshangie, Commotion, Cry, Din, Dirdam, Dirdum, Durdum, Emeute, Ferment, Flaw, Fracas, Furore, Garboil, Hell, Hoopla, Hubbub(oo), Hullabaloo, Hurly(-burly), Katzenjammer, Madhouse, Noise, Noyes, Outcry, Pandemonium, Racket, Raird, Reird, Riotous, Roister, Romage, Rowdedow, Rowdydow(dy), Ruckus, Ruction, Rumpus, Stramash, Turmoil, Whoobub

Uproot Deracinate, Eradicate, Evict, Outweed, Supplant, Weed

Upset(ting) Aggrieve, Alarm, Bother, Capsize, Catastrophe, Choked, Coup, Cowp, Crank, Derange, Dip, Discomboberate, Discombobulate, Discomfit, Discomfort, Discommode, Disconcert, Dismay, Disquiet, Distraught, Disturb, Dod, Eat, Fuss, Inversion, Keel, Miff, Nauseative, Offend, Overthrow, Overturn, Perturb, Pip, Pother, Purl, Rattle, Rile, Ruffle, Rumple, Sad, Seel, Shake, Sore, Spill, Tapsalteerie, Tip, Topple, Trauma, Undo, Unsettled

▷ **Upset** *may indicate* an anagram; a word upside down; or 'tes'

Upshot Outcome, Result, Sequel

Upside down Inverted, Resupinate, Tapsie-teerie, Topsy-turvy

Upstart Buckeen, Jumped-up, Mushroom, Parvenu, Vulgarian

▷ **Upstart** *may indicate* 'u'
Upstream Thermal
Upsurge Thrust, Waste
Uptake Shrewdness, Understanding, Wit
Up to Till, Until
Up-to-date Abreast, Contemporary, Current, Mod, New-fashioned, Right-on, State-of-the-art, Swinging, Topical, Trendy
Upwards Acclivious, Aloft, Antrorse, Cabré
Uranium Pitchblende, U, Yellowcake
Urban Civic, Megalopolis, Municipal, Town
Urbane Civil, Debonair, Refined, Townly
Urchin Arab, Brat, Crinoid, Crossfish, Cystoid, Echinoderm, Echinoidea, Echinus, Gamin, Guttersnipe, Gutty, Heart, Mudlark, Nipper, Pluteus, Ragamuffin, Sand-dollar, Sea, Sea-egg, Spatangoidea, Spatangus, Street-arab, Townskip
Urge, Urgent Admonish, Ca, Coax, Constrain, Crying, Dire, Drive, Egg, Enjoin, Exhort, Exigent, Goad, Hard, Hie, Hoick, Hunger, Hurry, Id, Immediate, Impel, Impulse, Incense, Incite, Insist(ent), Instance, Instigate, Itch, Kick, Libido, Nag, Peremptory, Persuade, Press(ing), Prod, Push, Set on, Spur, Strong, Threapit, Threepit, Wanderlust, Whig, Yen
▷ **Urgent** *may indicate* 'Ur-gent', viz. Iraqi
Uriah Hittite, Humble, Umble
Urinal Bog, John, Jordan, > LAVATORY, Loo, Pissoir
Urinate, Urine Chamber-lye, Emiction, Enuresis, Lant, Leak, Micturition, Oliguria, Pee, Piddle, Piss, Planuria, Relieve, Slash, Stale, Strangury, Tiddle, Werris (Creek), Widdle
Urn(s), Urn-shaped Cinerarium, Ewer, Grecian, Olla, Ossuary, Samovar, Storied, Tea, Urceolate, Vase
Us 's, UK, Uns, We
Usage, Use(r), Used, Utilise Application, Apply, Avail, Boot, Consume, Custom, Deploy, Dow, > EMPLOY, End, Ex, Exercise, Exert, Expend, Exploit, Flesh, Habit, Hand-me-down, Inured, Manner, Ply, Practice, Sarum, Spare, Spent, Sport, Take, Tradition, Treat, Ure, Wield, With, Wont
Useful Asset, Availing, Commodity, Dow, Expedient, Invaluable
Useless Base, Bung, Cumber, Dead-wood, Dud, Empty, Futile, Gewgaw, Grotty, Idle, Inane, Ineffective, Lame, Lemon, Nonstarter, Otiose, Plug, Sculpin, Sterile, Swap, US, Vain, Void, Wet
Usher Black Rod, Chobdar, Commissionaire, Conduct(or), Doorman, Escort, Guide, Herald, Huissier, Macer, Rod, Show, Steward
Usual Common, Customary, Habit(ual), Natural, Normal, Ordinary, Routine, Rule, Solito, Stock, Typical, Wont
Usurer, Usury Gombeen, Loanshark, Moneylender, Note-shaver, Shark, Uncle
Usurp(er) Abator, Arrogate, Encroach, Invade
Ut As, Doh, Utah
Utah Ut
Utensil(s) Batterie, Battery, Chopsticks, Colander, Cookware, Corer, Fish-kettle, Fork, Funnel, Gadget, Grater, Gridiron, Implement, Instrument, Knife, Mandolin(e), Ricer, Scoop, Skillet, Spatula, Spoon, Things, Tool, Zester
▶ **Utilise** *see* USE
Utilitarian Benthamite, Mill, Practical, Useful
Utility Elec(tricity), Expected, Gas, Public, Water
Utmost Best, Extreme, Farthest, Maximum, Nth

Utopia(n) Adland, Cloud-cuckoo-land, Ideal, Pantisocracy, Paradise, Perfect, Shangri-la

Utter(ance), Uttered, Utterly Absolute, Accent, Agrapha, Agraphon, Aread, Arrant, Cry, Dead, Deliver, Dictum, Dog, Downright, Ejaculate, Emit, Enunciate, Express, Extreme, Glossolalia, Issue, Judgement, Lenes, Lenis, Mint, Most, Oracle, Pass, Phonate, Pronounce, Pure, Quo(th), Rank, Rap, Rattle, Remark, Saw, > SAY, Sheer, Stark, State, Syllable, Tell, Vend, Vent, Very, Voice

Uvula Staphyle

Vv

V Anti, Bomb, Del, Five, Nabla, See, Sign, Verb, Verse, Versus, Victor(y), Volt, Volume

Vacancy, Vacant Blank, Empty, Glassy, Hole, Hollow, Inane, Place, Space, Vacuum

Vacation Holiday, Leave, Non-term, Outing, Recess, Trip, Voidance

Vaccination, Vaccine Antigen, Bacterin, Cure, HIB, Jenner, MMR, Sabin, Salk, Serum, Subunit

Vacillate, Vacillating Dither, Feeble, Hesitate, Shilly-shally, Trimmer, Wabble, Wave(r)

Vacuous Blank, Empty, Toom, Vacant

Vacuum Blank, Cleaner, Dewar, Emptiness, Magnetron, Nothing, Plenum, Thermos®, Torricellian, Ultra-high, Void

Vade-mecum Ench(e)iridion, Notebook

Vagabond Bergie, Gadling, > GYPSY, Hobo, Landlo(u)per, Rapparee, Romany, Rover, Runabout, Runagate, Tramp

Vagrant Beachcomber, Bum, Bummer, Caird, Crusty, Derro, Dosser, Drifter, Gangrel, Gang-there-out, Goliard, Gypsy, Hobo, Landlo(u)per, Lazzarone, Nomad, Patercove, Rinthereout, Rogue, Romany, Scatterling, Strag, Straggle, Stroller, Swagman, Tinker, > TRAMP, Truant, Walker

Vague(ness) Amorphous, Bleary, Blur, Confused, Dim, Equivocal, Hazy, Ill-defined, Ill-headed, Indeterminate, Indistinct, Loose, Mist, Nebulous, Shadowy, Woolly-minded

▷ **Vaguely** *may indicate* an anagram

Vain Bootless, Coxcomb, Coxcomical, Egoistic, Empty, Fruitless, > FUTILE, Hollow, Idle, Peacock, Profitless, Proud, Strutting, Useless, Vogie

Vainglory Panache

Valance Pand, Pelmet

Vale Addio, Adieu, Cheerio, Coomb, Dean, Dedham, Dene, Ebbw, Enna, Glen, Ta-ta, Tempé, Valley

Valediction, Valedictory Apopemptic, Cheerio, Farewell

Valentine Card, Sweetheart

Valerian All-heal, Cetywall, Greek, Red, Setuale, Setwale, Setwall, Spur

Valet Aid, Andrew, Gentleman's gentleman, Jeames, Jeeves, Man, Passepartout, Quint, Servant, Skip-kennel

Valetudinarian Hypochondriac, Invalid

Valiant Brave, Doughty, Heroic, Resolute, Stalwart, Stouthearted, Wight

Valid(ate) Confirm, Establish, Just, Legal, Rational, Sound

Valise Bag, Case, Dorlach, Satchel

Valkyrie Brynhild

Valley Ajalon, Aosta, Baca, Barossa, Bekaa, Bolson, Clough, Comb(e), Coomb, Cwm, Dale, Dargle, Dean, Death, Defile, Dell, Den, Dene, Dingle, Dip, Drowned, Dry, Gehenna, Ghyll, Glen, Graben, Great Glen, Great Rift, Grindelwald, Hanging, Haugh, Heuch, Hollow, Hope, Humiliation, Hutt,

Ladin, Lagan, Lallan, Nemean, Olympia, Ravine, Rhondda, Ria, Rift, San Fernando, Silicon, Slack, Slade, Strath(spey), Tempe, Tophet, Trossachs, Umbria, Valdarno, Vale, Vallambrosa, Water

Valour Bravery, Courage, Heroism, Merit, Prowess

Valuable, Valuation, Value Absolute, Acid, Appraise, Appreciate, Apprize, Assess(ment), Asset, Bargain, Calibrate, Carbon, Checksum, Cherish, CIF, Cop, Cost, Crossover, Denomination, Equity, Esteem, Estimate, Expected, Face, Feck, Hagberg, Intrinsic, Limit, Market, Modulus, Net present, Net realizable, Nominal, Nuisance, Omnium, Par, pH, Place, Precious, Present, Price, Prize, Prys, Quartile, Rarity, Rate, Rateable, Rating, Regard, Residual, Respect, Rogue, Salt, Sentimental, Set, Steem, Stent, Store, Street, Surrender, Taonga, Time, Treasure, Valuta, > **WORTH**

Valueless Bum, Fig, Mare's nest, Orra, Useless, Worthless

Valve Acorn, Air, Aortic, Ball, Bicuspid, Bleed, Butterfly, Check, Clack, Cock, Drawgate, Dynatron, Escape, Exhaust, Flip-flop, Foot, Gate, Induction, Magnetron, Mitral, Mixing, Needle, Non-return, Pallet, Pentode, Petcock, Piston, Poppet, Pulmonary, Puppet, Radio, Resnatron, Safety, Seacock, Semilunar, Shut-off, Sleeve, Slide, Sluice, Sluicegate, Snifter, Snifting, Stopcock, Suction, Tap, Tetrode, Thermionic, Throttle, Thyratron, Triode, Turncock, Vacuum, Ventil, Vibroton

Vamoose Abscond, Decamp, Scat, Scram

Vamp Adlib, Charm, Rehash, Seduce, Siren, Strum, Twiddle

Vampire Bat, Dracula, False, Ghoul, Lamia, Lilith, Pontianak, Stringes

Van(guard) Advance, Box-car, Brake, Camper, Cart, Delivery, Dormobile®, Forefront, Foremost, Front, Furniture, Guard's, Head, Kombi®, Lead, Leader(s), Lorry, Loudspeaker, Luggage, Meat wagon, Panel, Panel-truck, Pantechnicon, Patrol-wagon, Prison, Removal, Spearhead, Truck, Ute, Wagon

Vanadium V

Vandal(ise), Vandalism Desecrate, Hooligan, Hun, Loot, Pillage, Ravage, Rough, Sab(oteur), Sack, Saracen, Skinhead, Slash, Trash

Vandyke Beard, Painter

Vane(s) Dog, Fan, Guide, Rudder, Telltale, Vexillum, Weather(cock), Web, Wind (tee), Wing

Vanessa Butterfly

Vanilla Pinole

Vanish(ed) Cease, Disappear, Disperse, Dissolve, Evanesce(nt), Evaporate, Extinct, Faint(ed), Mizzle, Slope, Unbe

Vanity Amour-propre, Arrogance, Ego, Esteem, Futility, Pomp, Pretension, Pride, Self-conceit, Self-esteem

Vanquish Beat, Conquer, Floor, Master, Overcome

Vantage (point) Ascendancy, Coign(e), Height

Vaporise, Vapour Boil, Cloud, Effluent, Fog, Fume, Halitus, Iodine, Miasma, Mist, Reek, Roke, > **STEAM**, Steme, Water

▸ **Variable, Variance, Variant, Variation** *see* VARY

Varicose Haemorrhoids

▸ **Varied, Variety** *see* VARY

▷ **Varied** *may indicate* an anagram

Variegate(d) Calico, Dappled, Flecked, Fretted, Motley, Mottle, Pied, Rainbow, Skewbald, Tissue

▷ **Variety of** *may indicate* an anagram

Various Divers(e), Manifold, Multifarious, Separate, Several, Sundry

Various years Vy

Varlet Cad, Knave

Varnish(ing) Arar, Bee-glue, Copal, Cowdie-gum, Dam(m)ar, Desert, Dope, Dragon's-blood, Glair, Japan, Lacquer, Lentisk, Nail, Nibs, Oil, Resin, Sandarac, Shellac, Spirit, Tung-oil, Tung-tree, Vernis martin, Vernissage

Vary(ing), Variable, Variance, Variant, Variation, Varied, Variety Ablaut, Aelotropy, Alter, Amphoteric, Assortment, Breed, Brew, Cepheid, Change, Chequered, Colour, Contrapuntal, Counterpoint, Daedal(e), Dedal, Dependent, Differ, Discrepancy, Diverse, Diversity, Dummy, Eclectic, Enigma, Farraginous, Fickle, Fluctuating, Form, Grid, Iid, Inconsistent, Inconstant, Independent, Isochor, Isopleth, Line, Medley, Mix, Morph, Morphosis, Multifarious, Multiplicity, Mutable, Nuance, Olio, Omniform, Orthogenesis, Parametric, Partita, Protean, Random, Remedy, Response, Smorgasbord, Sort, Species, Spice, Sport, Stirps, Stochastic, Strain, Timeserver, Tolerance, Twistor, Var, Versatile, Versiform, Version, Vicissitude, Vl, Wane, Wax, X, Y, Z

Vase Bronteum, Canopus, Cornucopia, Diota, Hydria, Jardiniere, Kalpis, Lecythus, Lekythos, Moon flask, Murr(h)a, Portland, Pot, Potiche, Stamnos, Urn, Vessel

Vassal Client, Daimio, Feoffee, Lackey, Liege, Man, Manred, Servant, Vavaso(u)r

Vast(ness) Big, Cosmic, Cyclopic, Enormous, Epic, Extensive, Huge(ous), Immense, Mighty, Monumental, Ocean, Prodigious

Vat Back, Barrel, Blunger, Chessel, Copper, Cowl, Cuvee, Fat, Girnel, Keir, Kier, Pressfat, Stand, Tank, Tan-pit, Tub, Tun, Winefat

Vatican Rome, V

Vaudeville Zarzuela

Vaughan Silurist

Vault(ed), Vaulting Arch, Barrel, Cavern, Cellar, Chamber, Clear, Cross, Crypt, Cul-de-four, Cupola, Dome, Dungeon, Fan, Firmament, Fornicate, Groin, Hypogeum, Jump, Kiva, Leap(frog), Lierne, Ossuary, Palm, Pend, Pendentive, Pole, Rib, Safe, Sepulchre, Severy, Shade, Souterrain, Tholus, Tomb, Tunnel, Underpitch, Wagon, Weem, Wine

▷ **Vault** *may indicate* an anagram

Vaunt Boast, Brag, Crow

Veal Escalope, Fricandeau, Galantine, Scallop, Schnitzel, Wiener schnitzel

Vector, Vector operator Dyad, Nabla, Phasor, Polar, Radius

Veer Bag, Boxhaul, Broach, Deviate, Draw, Gybe, Splay, Swerve, Tack, Turn, Wear, Yaw

Vegetable(s) Alexanders, Allium, Artichoke, Asparagus, Aubergine, Beans, Beet(root), Borecole, Brassica, Broccoli, Cabbage, Calabrese, Calaloo, Calalu, Cardoon, Carrot, Castock, Cauliflower, Celeriac, Celery, Chard, Chicory, Chiffonade, Chive, Choko, Chufa, Cocoyam, Colcannon, Cole, Collard, Corn-on-the-cob, Coulis, Courgette, Crout, Cucumber, Custock, Daikon, Endive, Escarole, Eschalot, Fennel, Finocchio, Flora, Gherkin, Greens, Guar, Hastings, Inert, Ingan, Jerusalem artichoke, Jicama, Kale, Kohlrabi, Kumara, Kumera, Lablab, Leek, Legume(n), Lettuce, Macedoine, Mangel(-wurzel), Mangetout, Mangold, Marrow(-squash), Mirepoix, Mooli, Navew, Neep, Oca, Okra, Okro, Olitory, Onion, Orach(e), Parsnip, Pea(se), Pepper, Pimento, Plant, Potato, Pottage, Pratie, Primavera, Pulse, Pumpkin, Quinoa, Radicchio, Radish, Rapini, Ratatouille, Rocambole, Root, Rutabaga, Sabji, Salad, Salsify, Samphire, Sauce, Sauerkraut, Savoy, Scorzonera, Shallot, Sibol, Sium, Skirret, Sorrel, Spinach(-beet), Spinage, Sprouts, Spud, Squash, Succotash, Swede, Sweet corn, Sweet potato, Taro, Tomato, Tonka-bean, Triffid, Turnip, Udo, Wort, Yam, Zucchini

Vegetable extract Solanine

Vegetarian Herbivore, Maigre, Meatless, Parev(e), Parve, Pythagorean, Vegan, Veggie

Vegetate, Vegetator, Vegetation Alga, Brush, Cover, Flora, Gar(r)igue, Greenery, Herb, Maquis, Quadrat, Scrub, Stagnate, Sudd, Transect

Vehemence, Vehement(ly) Amain, Ardent, Fervid, Forcible, Frenzy, Heat, Hot, Intense, Violent

Vehicle Ambulance, Amtrack, Artic, Articulated, ATV, Autocycle, Autorickshaw, Brake, Brancard, Buckboard, Buggy, Bus, Cab, Camper, Car, Caravan, Carry-all, Cart, Channel, Chariot, Commercial, Conveyance, Crate, Curricle, Cycle, Dennet, Dog-cart, Dormobile®, Dray, Duck, Dune buggy, Estate car, Fiacre, Float, Fly, Four-by-four, Four-seater, Gharri, Gharry, Gladstone, Go-cart, Go-kart, Go-Ped®, Gritter, Growler, Half-track, Hansom, Hatchback, Hearse, Hovercraft, Jeep®, Jeepney, Jet-Ski, Jingle, Jinker, Jitney, Juggernaut, Kago, Kart, Koneke, Landau, Land Rover, Launch, LEM, Limber, Litter, Lorry, Machine, Means, Medium, Micro-scooter, Minibus, Minicab, Minivan, Motor, Multipurpose, Norimon, Offroad, Paddock-basher, Pantechnicon, Pedicab, Penny-farthing, People carrier, People-mover, Perambulator, Personnel carrier, Phaeton, Pick-up, Quad, Recreational, Re-entry, Ricksha(w), Runabout, Samlor, Sand-yacht, Scow, Shay, Shuttle, Sidecar, Skibob, Skidoo®, Sled(ge), Sleigh, Sno-Cat®, Snowmobile, Snowplough, Soyuz, Spider, Stanhope, Station wagon, Steam-car, Sulky, Surrey, Tarantas(s), Taxi, Tempera, Three-wheeler, Tipcart, Tip-up, Tonga, Tracked, Tractor, Trailer, Tram, Transporter, Trap, Tricar, Tricycle, Trishaw, Troika, Trolley, Trolleybus, Truck, Tuk tuk, Tumble-car(t), Tumbril, Turbo, Two-seater, Two-wheeler, Unicycle, Ute, Utility, Vahana, Velocipede, Vespa, Volante, Wagon, Wheelbarrow, Wrecker

Veil Burk(h)a, Calyptra, Chad(d)ar, Chador, Chuddah, Chuddar, Cover, Curtain, Envelop, Hejab, Hijab, Humeral, Kalyptra, Kiss-me, Lambrequin, Mantilla, Mist, Obscure, Purdah, Sacramental, Scene, Veale, Volet, Weeper, Wimple, Yashmak

Vein Artery, Azygas, Basilic, Coronary, Costa, Diploic, Epithermal, Fahlband, Gate, Hemiazygous, Innominate, Jugular, Ledge, Lode, Mainline, Media, Midrib, Mood, Nervure, Organic, Percurrent, Portal, Postcava, Precava, Pulmonary, Rake, Rib, Saphena, Sectorial, Spur, Stockwork, Stringer, Style, Thread, Varicose, Varix, Vena, Venule, Vorticose

Vellum Cutch, Kutch, Parchment

Velocity Angular, Escape, Mustard, Muzzle, Orbital, Radial, Rate, Speed, Terminal, V

Velvet Bagheera, Chenille, National, Panné, Pile, Three-pile, Velour, Velure

Venal Corruptible, Mercenary, Sale

Vend(or) Hawk, Pedlar, Rep, Sammy, Sell, Sutler

Vendetta Feud

Veneer Facade, Gloss, Varnish

Venerable Aged, August, Bede, Guru, Hoary, Sacred, Sage, Vintage

Venerate, Veneration Adore, Awe, Douleia, Dulia, Hallow, Homage, Idolise, Latria, Revere, Worship

Venereal NSU, VD

Venery Chase

Venetian Blind, Doge, Gobbo, Polo

Vengeance, Vengeful Commination, Erinyes, Reprisal, Ultion, Vindictive, Wannion, Wrack, Wreak

Venison Cervena, Deer
Venom(ous) Gall, Gila, Jamestown-weed, Jim(p)son-weed, Poison, Rancour, Solpuga, Spite, Toxic, Virus
Vent Airway, Aperture, Belch, Chimney, Emit, Express, Fumarole, Issue, Ostiole, Outlet, Smoker, Solfatara, Spiracle, Undercast, Wreak
Venter Uterus
Ventilate, Ventilator Air, Air-brick, Air-hole, Discuss, Express, Louvre, Plenum, Shaft, Voice, Windsail, Windway, Winze
Venture(d) Ante, Chance, Dare, Daur, Durst, Flutter, Foray, Handsel, Hazard, Jump, Opine, Presume, Promotion, Risk, Spec, Throw
Venue Bout, Locale, Place, Showground, Stadium, Tryst, Visne
Venus Cohog, Cytherean, Hesper(us), Love, Lucifer, Morning-star, Phosphorus, Primavera, Quahog, Rokeby, Vesper
Venus fly-trap Dionaea
Veracity, Veracious Accurate, Factual, Sincere, Truth(ful)
Veranda(h) Balcony, Gallery, Lanai, Patio, Piazza, Porch, Sleep-out, Stoep, Stoop, Terrace
Verb(al), Verbs Active, Argy-bargy, Auxiliary, Causative, Conative, Copula, Ergative, Infinitive, Intransitive, Irregular, Modal, Passive, Phrasal, Preterite, Stative, Transitive, Vb, Word-of-mouth
Verbascum Mullein
Verbatim Literally
Verbena Vervain
Verbose, Verbosity Padding, Prolix, Talkative, Wordy
Verdant Lush
Verdict Decision, Formal, Judg(e)ment, Majority, Open, Opinion, Pronouncement, Resolution, Ruling, Special
Verdigris Aeruginous, Patina
Verge Border, Brink, > EDGE, Hard shoulder, Incline, Long paddock, Rim
Verger Beadle, Pew-opener
Verify Affirm, Ascertain, Check, Confirm, Crosscheck, Prove, Validate
Verily Yea
Verisimilitude Artistic, Authenticity, Credibility
Verity Fact, Sooth, Truth
Vermifuge Cow(h)age, Cowitch
Vermilion Cinnabar, Minium, Red
Vermin(ous) Carrion, Catawampus, Lice, Mice, Ratty, > RODENT, Scum
Vermouth Absinthiated, French, It(alian), Martini®
Vernacular Common, Dialect, Idiom, Jargon, Lingo, Native, Patois
Veronica Hebe, Hen-bit, Speedwell
Verruca Wart
Versatile Adaptable, All-rounder, Flexible, Handy, Protean, Resourceful
Verse(s), Versed Dactyl, Free, Linked, Logaoedic, Passus, Poetry, Political, Reported, > RHYME

VERSES

1 letter:	4 letters:	Epos	Sijo
V	Awdl	Hymn	Song
	Blad	Neck	Vers
3 letters:	Duan	Poem	
Fit	Epic	Rime	

5 letters:
- Blank
- Blaud
- Canto
- Comus
- Epode
- Gazal
- Haiku
- Hokku
- Ionic
- Lyric
- Meter
- Poesy
- Renga
- Rubai
- Spasm
- Stave
- Tanka
- Tract
- Triad

Miurus
Octave
Pantun
Rondel
Scazon
Stanza
Strain
Tercet

6 letters:
- Adonic
- Ballad
- Burden
- Ghazal
- Ghazel
- Gnomic
- Haikai
- Heroic
- Jingle
- Laisse

7 letters:
Alcaics
Couplet
Dimeter
Elegiac
Epigram
Fabliau
Huitain
Leonine
Pantoum
Pennill
Prosody
Pythian
Rondeau
Sapphic
Sestina
Sestine
Sixaine
Stiches
Strophe
Tiercet
Triolet
Tripody

8 letters:
Cinquain
Clerihew
Doggerel
Glyconic
Kyrielle
Madrigal
Nonsense
Pindaric
Quatrain
Rhopalic
Rove-over
Rubaiyat
Scansion
Senarius
Sirvente
Terzetta
Trimeter
Tristich
Versicle

9 letters:
Amphigory
Asclepiad
Beatitude
Dithyramb
Ditrochee
Goliardic
Hexameter
Macaronic
Monometer
Octameter

Octastich
Saturnian
Stornello
Terza rima
Vers libre

10 letters:
Asynartete
Catalectic
Cynghanedd
Fescennine
Mock-heroic
Ottava rima
Pennillion
Pentameter
Rhyme-royal
Serpentine
Tetrameter
Villanelle

11 letters:
Acatalectic
Alexandrine
Hudibrastic
Riding-rhyme
Septenarius

12 letters:
Archilochian
Hudibrastics

Versed sine Sagitta
Versifier Lyricist, Poetaster, Rhymer, Rhymester
Version Account, Adaptation, Authorised, Cover, Edition, Form, Paraphrase, Rede, Rendering, Rendition, Revision, Translation
Vertebra(e), **Vertebrate** Agnathan, Amniote, Amphioxus, Ascidian, Atlas, Axis, Bone, Centrum, Cervical, Chordae, Cyclostome, Dorsal, Gnathostome, Ichthyopsida, Lamprey, Lumbar, Placoderm, Reptile, Sauropsida, Spondyl, Tetrapod, Tunicata, Vermis
Vertex Apex, Crest, Crown, Summit, Zenith
Vertical Apeak, Apeek, Atrip, Erect, Lapse, Montant, Ordinate, Perpendicular, Plumb, Prime, Sheer, Standing, Stemmed, Stile, Upright
Vertigo Dinic, Dizziness, Fainting, Giddiness, Megrim, Nausea, Staggers, Whirling
Verve Dash, Energy, Go, Panache, Vigour
Very (good, well) A1, Ae, Assai, Awfully, Boffo, Bonzer, Boshta, Boshter, Dashed, Def, Ever, Extreme(ly), Fell, Frightfully, Gey, Grouse, Heap, Hellova, Helluva, Highly, Jolly, Light, Mighty, Molto, Much, OK, Opt, Precious, Precise, Purler, Real, Right, Self same, So, Sore, Stinking, Très, Utter, V, VG, Way
Vesicle Ampul, Bladder

Vespers Evensong, Lychnic, Placebo, Sicilian
Vessel > BOAT, Capillary, Container, Craft, Dish, Pressure, Receptacle, Seed,
  > SHIP, Utensil, Vascular

● **VESSELS**

3 letters:
Bin
Cog
Cup
Dow
Fat
Obo
Pan
Pig
Pyx
Tub
Urn
Vas
Vat

4 letters:
Bowl
Buss
Cask
Cowl
Dhow
Etna
Font
Grab
Horn
Lota
Olpe
Skin
Snow
Vase
Vein
Vena
Vial
Zulu

5 letters:
Aorta
Blood
Cogue
Crare
Crewe
Crock
Cruet
Cupel
Dandy
Dixie
Gourd
Ketch
Laver
Lotah
Mazer
Oiler
Pokal
Quart
Round
Scoop
Shell
Stean
Steen
Stoop
Stoup
Tazza
Varix
Xebec
Zabra

6 letters:
Aludel
Argyle
Argyll
Artery
Beaker
Bicker
Bouget
Bucket
Carafe
Carboy
Chatty
Copper
Crayer
Dinghy
Dogger
Dolium
Elutor
Flagon
Frigot
Galiot
Galley
Goblet
Goglet
Guglet
Humpen

Kettle
Lorcha
Mortar
Noggin
Retort
Rumkin
Sampan
Sconce
Shippo
Situla
Steane
Tassie
Trough
Tureen
Venule
Wherry

7 letters:
Amphora
Ampulla
Canteen
Chalice
Cistern
Costrel
Creamer
Cresset
Cuvette
Cyathus
Dredger
Drifter
Felucca
Frigate
Galleon
Galliot
Gurglet
Jugular
Mudscow
Patamar
Pinnace
Pitcher
Polacca
Precava
Steamer
Tankard
Terreen
Washpot

8 letters:
Calabash
Cauldron
Ciborium
Colander
Coolamon
Crucible
Cucurbit
Decanter
Figuline
Galleass
Galliass
Gallipot
Gallivat
Jerrican
Longboat
Monteith
Pancheon
Panchion
Pannikin
Sinusoid

9 letters:
Alcarraza
Autoclave
Bucentaur
Calandria
Casserole
Cullender
Destroyer
Hydrofoil
Tappit-hen

10 letters:
Bathyscaph
Deep-sinker
Jardinière
Triaconter

11 letters:
Aspersorium
Bathyscaphe

12 letters:
Lachrymatory

Vest Beset, Confer, Gilet, Modesty, Semmit, Singlet, Skivvy, Spencer, Sticharion, String, Undercoat, Undershirt, Waistcoat

Vestibule Anteroom, Atrium, Entry, Exedra, Foyer, Hall, Lobby, Narthex, Oeil-de-boeuf, Porch, Portico, Pronaos, Tambour

Vestige Hint, Mark, Mention, Shadow, Sign, Trace

Vestment Alb, Canonicals, Chasuble, Chimar, Chimer(e), Cotta, Dalmatic, Ephod, Fannel, Fanon, Garb, > GARMENT, Maniple, Mantelletta, Omophorion, Pallium, Parament, Ph(a)elonian, Pontificals, Raiment, Rational, Rochet, Rocquet, Sakkos, Sticharion, Stole, Surplice, Tunic(le)

Vestry Common, Sacristy, Select

Vet(ting), Veterinary, Vets Check, Doc(tor), Examine, Ex-serviceman, Inspect, OK, Screen, Veteran, Zoiatria, Zootherapy

Vetch Bitter, Ers, Fitch, Kidney, Locoweed, Milk, Tare, Tine

Veteran BL, Expert, GAR, Master, Oldster, Old sweat, Old-timer, Old 'un, Retread, Seasoned, Soldier, Stager, Stalwart, Stalworth, Vet, War-horse

▷ **Veteran** *may indicate* 'obsolete'

Veto Ban, Bar, Debar, Item, Local, Negative, Pocket, Reject, Taboo, Tabu

Vex(ing), Vexed Anger, Annoy, Bother, Chagrin, Debate, Fret, Gall, Grieve, Harass, Irritate, Madden, Mortify, Pester, Rankle, Rile, Sore, Spite, Tease, Torment, Trouble, Worrisome

Vexation(s) Barrator, Chagrin, Drat, Grief, Nuisance, Pique, Spite, Trouble

Vexatious Trying

Vexillum Web

Via By, Per, Through

Viable Economic, Going, Healthy, Possible

Vial Spirit-level

Viand Cate

Vibrant, Vibration Chatter, Energetic, Harmonogram, Plangent, Resonant, Rumble, Uvular

Vibrate, Vibration(s) Atmosphere, Diadrom, Dinnle, Dirl, Flutter, Fremitus, Hotter, Jar, Judder, Oscillate, Pulse, Quake, Resonance, Seiche, Shimmy, Shudder, Thrill, Throb, Tingle, Tremble, Tremor, Trill, Twinkle, Wag, Whir(r)

Viburnum Opulus

Vicar Apostolic, Bray, Choral, Elton, Forane, General, Incumbent, Lay, Pastoral, Plenarty, Primrose, Rector, Rev(erend), Trimmer

Vice Clamp, Crime, Deputy, Eale, Evil, Greed, Iniquity, Instead, Jaws, Regent, Second (in command), > SIN

Vice-president Croupier, Veep

Viceroy Khedive, Nawab, Provost, Satrap, Willingdon

Vichy water Eau

Vicinity Area, Environs, Hereabouts, Locality, Neighbourhood, Region

Vicious Flagitious, Hotbed

Victim Abel, Angel, Butt, Casualty, Dupe, Fashion, Frame, Host, Lay-down, Mark, Martyr, Nebbich, Neb(b)ish, Pathic, Patsy, Pigeon, Prey, Quarry, Sacrifice, Scapegoat

Victor(y) Banzai, Beater, Cadmean, Captor, Champ(ion), Conqueror, Conquest, Epinicion, Epinikion, Flagship, Fool's mate, Gree, Gris, Hallelujah, Hugo, Jai, Kobe, Landslide, Lepanto, Ludorum, Mature, Moral, Nike, Palm, Philippi, Pyrrhic, Runaway, Scalp, Signal, Triumph, VE (day), Vee, Vic, Walk-away, Walkover, Win(ner)

Victoria(n) Aussie, Plum, Prig, Station

Victualler Caterer, Grocer, Licensed, Purveyor, Supplier, Vivandiere

Video Digital, Interactive, Laser vision, Minitel, Pixelation, Promo, Reverse, Scratch, Still, Vera

Vie Compete, Contend, Emulate, Strive

Vienna Wien

Vietnamese Cham

View(er) Aim, Angle, Aspect, Belief, Bird's eye, Cineaste, Consensus, Consider, Cosmorama, Dekko, Dogma, Doxy, Endoscope, Exploded, Eye, Facet, Gander, Glimpse, Grandstand, Helicopter, Idea, Introspect, Kaleidoscope, Landscape, Line, Notion, Opinion, Optic®, Outlook, Pan, Panorama, Point, Private, Profile, > **PROSPECT**, Scan, Scape, Scene(ry), See, Sight, Skyscape, Slant, Specular, Standpoint, Stereoscope, Strain, Synop(sis), Tenet, Terrain, Thanatopsis, Theory, Vantage-point, Veduta, Vista, Visto, Watch, Witness, Worm's eye

Viewpoint Attitude, Belvedere, Grandstand, Perspective, Sight

Vigil, Vigilant(e) Awake, Aware, Deathwatch, Eve, Guardian angel, Hawk-eyed, Lyke-wake, Pernoctate, Wake, Wake-rife, Wary, Watch, Whitecap

Vignette Print, Profile, Sketch

Vigorous(ly), Vigour Athletic, Bant, Billy-o, Billy-oh, Birr, Blooming, Brisk, Con brio, Drastic, Elan, Emphatic, Energetic, Flame, Forceful, Furioso, Go, Green, Heart(y), Heterosis, Hybrid, Lush, Lustihood, Lusty, P, Pep, Pith, Potency, Punchy, Pzazz, Racy, Rank, Robust, Round, Rude, Spirit, Sprack, Sprag, Steam, Sthenic, Stingo, Strength, Strong, Thews, Tireless, Tone, Tooth and nail, Trenchant, Vegete, Vim, Vitality, Vivid, Voema, Zip

▷ **Vigorously** *may indicate* an anagram

Viking Dane, Norseman, Rollo, R(y)urik, Varangian

Vile Base, Corrupt, Depraved, Dregs, Durance, Earthly, Mean, Offensive, Scurvy, Vicious

Vilify Smear

Villa Bastide, Chalet, Dacha, House

Village Aldea, Auburn, Burg, Clachan, Corporate, Dorp, Endship, Global, Gram, Greenwich, Hamlet, Kaik, Kainga, Kampong, Kraal, Manyat(t)a, Mir, Pueblo, Rancheria, Rancherie, Shtetl, Skara Brae, Thorp(e), Ujamaa, Vill, Wick

Villain(y) Baddy, Bluebeard, Bravo, Crim(inal), Crime, Dastard, Dog, Heavy, Iago, Knave, Macaire, Miscreant, Mohock, Nefarious, Ogre, Reprobate, Rogue, Scab, Scelerat, Scoundrel, Skelm, Tearaway, Traitor

Villein Bordar, Churl, Serf

Vim Go, Vigour, Vitality, Zing

Vincent Van Gogh

Vindicate, Vindication Absolve, Acquit, Apologia, Avenge, Clear, Compurgation, Darraign(e), Darrain(e), Darrayn, Defend, Deraign, Justify

Vindictive Hostile, Malevolent, Repay(ing), Spiteful, Vengeful

Vine(yard) Ampelopsis, Ayahuasco, Balloon, Balsam apple, Bine, Bush rope, Chateau, Clinging, Clos, Colocynth, Cru, Cubeb, Cypress, Dodder, Domaine, Grapery, Hop, Idaean, Kangaroo, Kudzu, Lawyer, Liana, Martha's, Matrimony, Muskmelon, Naboth's, Quinta, Russian, Sarsaparilla, Stephanotis, Supplejack, Swallowwort, Trumpet, Turpeth, Vitis, Wonga-wonga, Yam, Yquem

Vinegar Acetic, Acetum, Alegar, Balsam, Eisel(l), Esile, Malt, Oxymel, Tarragon, Wine, Wood

Vintage Classic, Crack, Cru, Old, Quality

Viola, Violet African, Alto, Amethyst, Archil, Crystal, Dame's, Dog, Dog's tooth, Gamba, Garden, Gentian, Gridelin, Hesperis, Ianthine, Indole, Ionone, Kiss-me, Mauve, Methyl, Neapolitan, Orchil, Pansy, Parma, Prater,

Saintpaulia, Shrinking, Sweet, Tenor, Visual, Water

Violate, Violating, Violation Abuse, Breach, Contravene, Defile, Desecrate, Fract, Infraction, > **INFRINGE**, March-treason, Outrage, Peccant, Rape, Ravish, Stuprate, Transgress, Trespass

Violence, Violent(ly) Amain, Attentat, Berserk, Brutal, Drastic, Extreme, Fierce, Flagrant, Force, Frenzied, Furious, Heady, Het, High, Hot, Mighty, Onset, Rage, Rampage, Rampant, Rough, Rough stuff, Rude, Severe, Slap, Stormy, Ta(r)tar, Tearaway, Terrorism, Thuggery, Tinderbox, Vehement, Vie, Wrath

▶ **Violet** *see* **VIOLA**

Violin(ist), Violin-maker, Violin-shaped Alto, Amati, Cremona, Fiddle, Griddle, Gu(e), Guarneri(us), Guarnieri, Kennedy, Kit, Kubelik, Leader, Luthier, Menuhin, Nero, Oistrakh, Paganini, Pandurate, Rebeck, Rote, Stradivarius

VIP Bashaw, Bigshot, Bigwig, Brass, Cheese, Cob, Effendi, Envoy, Grandee, Imago, Magnate, Magnifico, Mugwump, Nabob, Nib, Nob, Pot, Snob, Someone, Swell, Tuft, Tycoon, Worthy

Viper Asp, Gaboon, Horned, Pit, Rattlesnake, Russell's, Sand, Saw-scaled, > **SNAKE**, Traitor, Villain

Virago Amazon, Battle-axe, Beldam(e), Harpy, Shrew

Virgil Maro

Virgin(al), Virginity Airline, Blessed, Celibate, Chaste, Cherry, Extra, Intact, Maiden, Maidenhead, Maidenhood, May, New, Parthenos, Pietà, Pucel(l)age, Pucelle, Pure, Queen, Snood, Tarpeia, Untainted, Vestal

Virginia(n) Creeper, Old Dominion, Tuckahoe, Va, Wade

Virile, Virility Energetic, Machismo, Macho, Manly, Red-blooded

Virtu Curio

Virtue(s), Virtuous Angelic, Assay-piece, Attribute, Cardinal, Caritas, Charity, Chastity, Continent, Dharma, Efficacy, Ethical, Excellent, Faith, Fortitude, Good, Goody-goody, Grace, Hope, Justice, Moral(ity), Natural, Patience, Plaster-saint, Principal, Prudence, Qua, Say-piece, Temperance, Theological, Upright, Worth

Virtuosity, Virtuoso Artist, Bravura, Excellence, Executant, Maestro, Paganini, Savant

Virulent Acrimonious, Deadly, Hostile, Malign, Noxious, Toxic, Vitriolic, Waspish

Virus Antigen, Arbovirus, Bacteriophaze, Capsid, Contagium, Coxsackie, EB, Ebola, Echo, Epstein-Barr, Filterable, Fowlpest, Germ, Granulosis, Hantavirus, Herpes, HIV negative, HIV positive, Lassa, Latent, Leaf-mosaic, Lentivirus, Michelangelo, Oncogen, Parainfluenza, Parvo(virus), Pathogen, Peach-yellow, Picornavirus, Polyoma, Prophage, Reovirus, Retrovirus, Rhabdovirus, Rhinovirus, Ross River, Rotavirus, SARS, Shingles, Slow, Street, SV40, Varicella, Virion, Zoster

Visa Transit

Viscera Bowels, Entrails, Giblets, Guts, Harigal(d)s, Haslet, Innards, Omentum, Splanchnic, Umbles, Vitals

Viscount Vis

Viscous (liquid), Viscosity Glaireous, Gluey, Gummy, Slab, Sticky, Stoke, Tacky, Tar, Thick, Thixotropic

Visible Clear, Conspicuous, Evident, Explicit, Obvious

Visigoth Asaric

Vision(ary) Aery, Aisling, Apparition, Beatific, Bourignian, Double, Dream(er), Emmetropia, Fancy, Idealist, Image, Kef, Moonshine, Mouse-sight, Mystic, Ocular, Phantasm(a), Phantom, Pholism, Photopia, Rainbow-chaser,

Romantic, Seeing, Seer, Sight, Stereo, Sweven, Tunnel, Twenty-twenty

Visit(or) Affliction, Alien, Caller, ET, Event, First-foot, Frequent, Gam, Guest, Habitue, Haunt, Health, Kursaal, Manuhic, Prison, See, Sightseer, Stranger, Take

Visor, Vizor Eyeshade, Mesail, Mezail, Umbrel, Umbr(i)ere, Umbril, Vent(ayle)

Vista Enfilade, Outlook, Scene, View

Visual(ise) Envisage, Ocular, Optical, Visible

Vital(ity) Alive, Central, Critical, Crucial, Energy, Esprit, Essential, Existent, Foison, Gusto, Indispensable, Key, Kick, Life-blood, Linchpin, Lung, Mites, Momentous, Necessary, Oomph, Organ, Pizzazz, Salvation, Sap, Viable, Vigour, Zing, Zoetic

Vitals Numbles, Umbles, Viscera

Vitamin(s) A, Aneurin, Axerophthol, B, Bioflavonoid, Biotin, C, Calciferol, Calcitriol, Citrin, Cobalamin, D, E, Ergocalciferol, Folacin, H, Inositol, K, Linoleic, Menadione, Menaquinone, Niacin, P, Pan(to)thenol, Phylloquinone, Phytonadione, Pyridoxine, Retinene, Retinol, Riboflavin, Ribose, Thiamin(e), Tocopherol, Torulin, Tretinoin

Vitiate(d) Flaw(ed)

Vitreous Glassy, Hyaline

Vitriol(ic) Acid, Acrimonious, Biting, Blue, Caustic, Green, Mordant, White

Vituperate Abuse, Berate, Castigate, Censure, Defame, Inveigh, Lash, Rail, Scold

Viva Oral

Vivacity, Vivacious Animation, Brio, Esprit, Exuberant, Spirit, Verve

Vivid Bright, Brilliant, Dramatic, Eidectic, Fresh, Graphic, Keen, Live, Pictorial, Picturesque, Sharp, Violent

Vixen Catamaran, Harridan, Shrew, Virago

Viz Sc, Videlicet

Vizier Pheazar, Wazir

▶ **Vizor** *see* VISOR

Vocabulary Active, Glottochronology, Idiolect, Idioticon, Jargon, (Kata)kana, Lexicon, Lexis, Meta-language, Nomenclator, Passive, Wordbook

Vocal(isation), Vocalist Articulate, Eloquent, Minstrel, Oral, Singer, Sprechgesang

Vocation Call, Métier, Mission, Priesthood, Profession, Shop

Vociferous(ly) Clamant, Loud, Ore rotundo, Strident

Vogue Chic, Day, > FASHION, It, Mode, Rage, Style, Ton

Vogul Ugrian, Ugric

Voice(d) Active, Air, Alto, Ancestral, Bass, Chest, Contralto, Countertenor, Edh, Emit, Eth, Express, Falsetto, Glottis, Harp, Head, Lyric, Mezzo-soprano, Mouth, Opinion, Passive, Phonic, Pipe, Presa, Quill, Say, Sonant, Soprano, Speak, Spinto, Sprechstimme, Steven, Syrinx, Tais(c)h, Tenor, Throat, Tone, > TONGUE, Treble, Utter, White

Voiceless Aphonia, Aphony, Dumb, Edh, Eth, Mute, Silent, Tacit

Void Abyss, Annul, Belch, Blank, Chasm, Defeasance, Defecate, Diriment, Empty, Evacuate, Gap, Hollow, Inane, Invalid, Irritate, Lapse, Nullify, Quash, Space, Vacuum

Volatile Excitable, Explosive, Latin, Live(ly), Mercurial, Temperamental, Terpene

Volcanic, Volcano Aa, Agglomerate, Amygdale, Andesite, Aniakchak, Antisana, Aragats, Ararat, Askja, Aso(san), Cameroon, Chimborazo, Citlaltépetl, Comoros, Cone, Conic, Corcovado, Cotopaxi, Demavend, Egmont, El Misti,

Erclyas Dagi, Erebus, Etna, Fernando de Noronha, Fuji, Fumarole, Haleakala, Hekla, Hornito, Huasca(ra)n, Ice, Idocrase, Igneous, Ignimbrite, Iliamna, Ischia, Iwo Jima, Katmai, Kauai, Kazbek, Kilimanjaro, Krakatoa, Lassen Peak, Lipari, Maui, Mauna Kea, Mauna Loa, Mayon, Misti, Mofette, Montserrat, Mount Erebos, Mount Katmai, Mount St Helens, Mt Suribachi, Mud, National Park, Nevada de Colima, Nevada de Toluca, Nyamuragira, Nyiragongo, Obsidian, Okmok, Olympus Mons, Paricutin, Pele, Pelée, Pico de Teide, Pico de Teyde, Plinian, Popocatepetl, Pozz(u)olana, Pumice, Puy, Puzzolana, Ruapehu, St Helena, St Helens, St Kilda, Salse, Sandblow, Semeroe, Semeru, Shield, Soffioni, Solfatara, Soufrière Hills, Stromboli, Taal, Tambora, Tangariro, Taraniki, Thira, Tolima, Trass, Tuff, Vesuvius, Warrumbungle Range

Vole Arvicola, Muskrat, Musquash, Ondatra

Volition Velleity, Will

Volley Barrage, Boom, Broadside, Platoon, Salvo, Tirade, Tire

Volt(age) BeV, Bias, HT

Voltaire Arouet

Volte face U-turn

Voluble Fluent, Glib

Volume Band, Barrel, Book, Bushel, Capacity, CC, Code(x), Content, Critical, Cubage, Gallon, Hin, Loudness, Mass, Ml, Molecular, Omnibus, Peck, Pint, Quart, Quart(o), Roll, Roul(e), Size, Space, Specific, Stere, Swept, Tidal, Tome, Vol

Voluntary, Volunteer Enlist, Fencible, Free, Free-will, Honorary, Offer, Postlude, Reformado, Spontaneous, Tender, Tennessee, Terrier, TN, Ultroneous, Yeoman

Voluptuary, Voluptuous Carnal, Hedonist, Houri, Luscious, Sensuist, Sensuous, Sybarite

Volute Helix, Roll

Vomit(ing) Anacatharsis, Barf, Boak, Boke, Cascade, Cat, Chunder, Disgorge, Egist, Egurgitate, Emesis, Fetch-up, Haematemesis, Honk, Keck, Parbreak, Posset, Puke, Ralph, Regurgitate, Retch, Rolf, Spew, Throw up, Upchuck

Voodoo Charm, Jettatura, Kurdaitcha, Macumba, Mambo, Obeah, Sorcery, Zombi(e)

Voracious, Voracity Bulimia, Edacity, Gluttony, Greed, Ravenous, Serrasalmo

Vortex Charybdis, Eddy, Gyre, Trailing, Whirlpool

Votary Adherent, Cenobite, Devotee, Disciple, Fan, Nun, Swinger, Zealot

Vote(r), Votes, Voting Alternative, Aye, Ballot, Block, Card, Casting, Choose, Colonist, Coopt, Cross, Cumulative, Division, Donkey, Fag(g)ot, Floating, Franchise, Free, Grey, Informal, Mandate, Nay, No, Opt, People, Placet, Plebiscite, Plump, Plural, Poll, Postal, Pot-wabbler, Pot-waller, Pot-walloner, Pot-walloper, Pot-wobbler, PR, Preferential, Referendum, Return, Scrutiny, Side, Straw(-poll), Suffrage, Swinging, Tactical, Ten-pounder, Theta, Ticket, Token, Transferable, Voice, X, Yea, Yes

Vote-catcher Pork

Vouch(er), Vouchsafe Accredit, Assure, Attest, Book token, Chit, Coupon, Endorse, Gift, Guarantee, Luncheon, Meal-ticket, Receipt, Ticket, Token, Warrant

Voussoir Quoin, Wedge

Vow Baptismal, Behight, Behot(e), Earnest, Ex voto, Hecht, Hest, I do, Nuncupate, > OATH, Pledge, Plight, Promise, Simple, Solemn, Swear, Troth, Vum

Vowel(s) Ablaut, Anaptyxis, Aphesis, Breve, Cardinal, Diphthong, Gradation,

Indeterminate, Monophthong, Mutation, Point, Rhyme, S(c)hwa, Seg(h)ol,
Svarabhakti, Triphthong

Voyage(r) Anson, Course, Cruise, Launch, Maiden, Passage, Peregrinate,
Sinbad, Travel

Voyeur Scopophiliac

VTOL Convertiplane

Vulcan(ite) Blacksmith, Ebonite, Fire, Mulciber, Spock, Wayland

Vulgar(ian) Banausic, Barbaric, Base, Blatant, Blue, Brassy, Buffoon, Canaille,
Cheap, Cit, Coarse, Common, Crude, Demotic, Flash, Forward, Gaudy, General,
Gent, Gross, Heel, Hussy, Ignorant, Indecent, Laddish, Lewd, Low(-life), Naff,
Obscene, Ostentatious, Pandemian, Plebby, Plebeian, Popular, Proletarian,
Raffish, Riff-raff, Scaff, Tacky, Tawdry, Threepenny, Tiger, Tink, Upstart, Vulg

Vulnerable Exposed, Open, Susceptible, Unguarded, Wide-open

Vulture Aasvogel, Bird, Buzzard, California (condor), Condor, Culture, Falcon,
Gallinazo, Gier, Griffon, Gripe, Grype, Lammergeier, Lammergeyer, Ossifrage,
Predator, Turkey, Urubu, Zopilote

Ww

W Watt, West, Whisky, Women
Wad(ding) Batting, Lump, Pad, Pledget, Roll, Swab, Wodge
Waddle Toddle, Waggle
Waddy Club, Cowboy, Stick
Wade(r), Wading Antigropelo(e)s, Curlew, Dikkop, Egret, Flamingo, Gallae,
   Godwit, Grallatorial, Greenshank, Heron, Ibis, Jacksnipe, Limpkin,
   Oyster-catcher, Paddle, Phalarope, Plodge, Sarus, Seriema, Shoebill, Splodge,
   Stilt(bird), Terek, Virginia
Waesucks Ewhow, O(c)hone
Wafer Biscuit, Cracker, Crisp, Gaufer, Gaufre, Gofer, Gopher, Host, Papad, Seal
Waff Flap, Flutter, Wave
Waffle Adlib, Blather, Equivocate, Gas, Gaufer, Gaufre, Gofer, Gopher, Hedge,
   Poppycock, Prate, Rabbit
Waft(ing) Airborne, Aura, Blow, Drift, Float
Wag(gish), Waggle Arch, Card, Comedian, Facetious, Joker, Lick,
   Niddle-noddle, Nod, Rogue, Shake, Sway, Wit(snapper), Wobble
Wage(s) Ante, Fee, Hire, Living, Meed, Minimum, Pay, Portage, Practise,
   Prosecute, Rate, Salary, Screw, Subsistence
Wage-earner Breadwinner, Employee, Proletariat(e)
Wager Ante, Back, > BET, Gamble, Lay, Pascal's, Stake, Wed
Wagon(er) Ar(a)ba, Aroba, Bootes, Boxcar, Brake, Buck, Buckboard, Buggy,
   Caisson, Carriage, Cart, Cattle truck, Chuck, Cocopan, Conestoga, Corf,
   Covered, Democrat, Dray, Flatcar, Fourgon, Gambo, Go-cart, Hopper, Hutch,
   Low-loader, Mammy, Paddy, Palabra, Patrol, Plaustral, Police, Prairie schooner,
   Rave, Reefer, Rubberneck, Shandry, Station, Tank, Tartana, Telega, Tender,
   Trap, Trekker, Truck, Van, Victoria, Wain, Water
Waif Arab, Foundling, Jetsam, Stray, Victoria, Wastrel, Water, Weft
Wail(er) Banshee, Bawl, Blubber, Howl, Keen, Lament, Moan, Skirl, Threnody,
   Threnos, Ululate, Vagitus, Wah-wah, Yammer
Wain Cart, Dray, Wagon
Waist(band) Belt, Cummerbund, Girdlestead, Girth, Hour-glass, Middle,
   Midship, Obi, Sash, Shash, Wasp, Zoster
Waistcoat Gilet, Jerkin, Lorica, MB, Pressure, Sayon, Shawl, Vest, Weskit
Wait(er) Abid(e), Ambush, Barista, Bide, Busboy, Butler, Buttle, Carhop,
   Commis, Cupbearer, Dally, Delay, Estragon, Expect, Flunkey, Frist, Garçon,
   Hang on, Hesitate, Hover, Interval, Khidmutgar, Lime, Linger, Lurch, Maitre
   d', Maitre d'hôtel, Minority, Omnibus, Pannier, Pause, Remain, Serve(r),
   Sommelier, Stay, Steward, Suspense, Taihoa, Tarry, Tend(ance), Tray, Vladimir,
   Wine, Won
Waitress Hebe, Miss, Mousme(e), Nippy, Server
Waive Abandon, Defer, Overlook, Postpone, Relinquish, Renounce
Wake(n) Abrade, Abraid, Abray, Aftermath, Alert, American, Animate, Arouse,
   Astern, Deathwatch, Excite, Hereward, Keen, Knock-up, Like, Lyke, Prod, Rear,

> ROUSE, Train, Wash
Waldo Emerson
Wale(r) Prop, Ridge, Weal
Wales Cambria, Cymru, Dyfed, Principality
Walk(er), Walking, Walkabout, Walkway Alameda, Alley, Alure, Amble,
Ambulate, Arcade, Berceau, Birdcage, Charity, Cloister, Clump, Constitutional,
Dander, Dauner, Emu, Esplanade, EVA, Expatiate, Flanerie, Frescade, Gait,
Gallery, Ghost, Go, Gradient, Gressorial, Heel and toe, Hike, Hookey, Hump,
Lambeth, Leg, Lumber, Mainstreeting, Mall, March, Mince, Mosey, Pace,
Pad, Pasear, Paseo, Passage, Path, Ped, Perambulate, Pergola, Pipe-opener,
Prance, Prom(enade), Rack, Ramble, Rampart, Random, Routemarch, Sashay,
Shamble, Sidle, Slommock, Space, Spanish, Sponsored, Stalk, Step, Striddle,
Stroll, Strut, Stump, Terrace, Toddle, Tramp, Trash, Travolator, Tread, Trog,
Truck, Trudge, Turn, Wend, Widow's, Xyst
Walk-over Doddle, Pie, Scratch
Wall Antonine, Bail, Bailey, Barrier, Berlin, Berm, Cavity, Cell, Chinese,
Climbing, Countermure, Curtain, Dado, Dam, Dike, Dry-stone, Enceinte,
Epispore, Exine, Fail-dike, Fourth, Fronton, Frustule, Gable, Great, Hadrian's,
Hanging, Hangman, Head, Immure, Intine, Mahjongg, Mani, Merlon,
Myocardium, Non-bearing, Parapet, Parietal, Parie(te)s, Parpane, Parpen(d),
Parpent, Parpoint, Partition, Party, Peribolos, Pericarp, Perpend, Perpent,
Pleuron, Puteal, Qibla, Retaining, Revet(ment), Ring, Roman, Roughcast, Sea,
Septum, Severus, Side, Somatopleure, Spandrel, Spandril, Street, Tambour,
Tariff, Trumeau, Vallation, Vallum, Video, Wa', Wailing, Western, Zooecia
Wallaby Brusher, Dama, Kangaroo, Pad(d)ymelon, Pademelon, Quokka,
Tammar, Whiptail
Wallah Competition
Wallaroo Euro
Wall-covering, Wallpaper Anaglypta®, Arras, Burlap, Flock, Lincrusta, Paper,
Tapestry, Tapet
Waller Fats, Mason
Wallet Billfold, Case, Notecase, Pochette, Pocket-book, Purse, Scrip
Wallflower Crucifer, Dowd(y), Pariah
Wall-game Eton, Mahjongg
Wallop Bash, Baste, Batter, Beat, Biff, Clout, Cob, > HIT, Lam, Lounder, Polt,
Pound, Slog, Strap, Swinge, Tan, Tat, Trounce
Wallow(ing) Bask, Flounder, Luxuriate, Revel, Roll, Splash, Swelter, Tolter,
Volutation, Welter
Wall-painting Fresco, Graffiti, Grisaille
▶ **Wallpaper** *see* WALL-COVERING
Wall-plate Tassel, Torsel
Wall-support Beam, Foundation, Pier, Rear-arch, Rere-arch
Wally Dipstick
Walnut Black, Butternut, Hickory, Juglans, Satin, White
Walrus Morse, Moustache, Pinniped, Rosmarine, Sea-horse, Tash
Walter Bruno, Mitty, Pater, Scott
Waltz Anniversary, Blue Danube, Boston, Dance, Hesitation, Rotate, Valse
Wampum Peag, Shell-money
Wan Pale, Pallid, Pasty, Sanguine, Sorry
Wanchancy Unlucky
Wand Baton, Caduceus, Rod, Runic, Stick, Thyrse, Thyrsus, Vara, Vare
Wander(er), Wandering Aberrance, Amble, Bedouin, Berber, Bum, Caird,

Delirious, Desultory, Deviate, Digress, Divagate, Drift, Errant, Estray, Evagation, Excursive, Expatiate, Extravagate, Gad(about), Grope, Hobo, Jew, Landloper, Maunder, Meander, Meandrian, Mill, Moon, Nomad(e), Odysseus, Pedder, Peregrine, Peripatetic, Polar, Rache, Ramble, Range, Ratch, Roamer, Romany, Room, Rove, Solivagant, Stooge, Straggle, Stravaig, Stray, Strayve, Streel, Stroam, Stroll, Swan, Ta(i)ver, Tramp, Troll, Tuareg, Vagabond, Vagrant, Vague, Waif, Wend, Wheel, Wilder, Wolves

▷ **Wandering** *may indicate* an anagram

Wane Decline, Decrease, Diminish, Ebb

Wangle Arrange, Finagle, Trick

Want(ing), Wants Absence, Conative, Covet, Crave, Dearth, Defect, Deficient, Derth, Desiderata, > DESIRE, Destitution, Envy, Hardship, Indigent, Itch, Lack, Long, Mental, Need, Penury, Require, Scarceness, Scarcity, Shortfall, Shy, Void, Wish, Yen

Wanton(ness) Bona-roba, Cadgy, Chamber, Cocotte, Colt's tooth, Deliberate, Demirep, Filly, Flirt-gill, Gammerstang, Giglet, Giglot, Gillflirt, Hussy, Jay, Jezebel, Jillflirt, Lewd, Licentious, Loose, Nice, Protervity, Rig, Roué, Slut, Smicker, Sportive, Sybarite, Toyish, Twigger, Unchaste, Wayward

Wap Blow, Knock, Strike

War(fare), Wars American Civil, American Independence, Ares, Armageddon, Arms, Attrition, Barons', Bate, Battle, Biological, Bishop, Chemical, Civil, Clash, Class, Cod, Cold, Combat, Conflict, Crescentade, Crimean, Crusade, Electronic, Emergency, Feud, > FIGHT, Flame, Food, Franco-Prussian, Fray, Germ, Gigantomachy, Great, Guer(r)illa, Gulf, Holy, Hostilities, Hot, Hundred Years', Information, Internecine, Jehad, Jenkins' ear, Jihad, Jugurthine, Korean, Krieg, Mars, Mexican, Napoleonic, Nuclear, Opium, Peasants', Peloponnesian, Peninsular, Phony, Price, Private, Psychological, Punic, Push-button, Queen Anne's, Rebellion, Revolutionary, Roses, Russo-Japanese, Secession, Seven Years', Six Day, Social, Spam, Spanish-American, Spanish Civil, Star, Stoush, Sword, Terrapin, Theomachy, Thirty Years', Total, Trench, Trojan, Turf, Vietnam, Winter, World, Yom Kippur

Warble(r) Carol, Chiff-chaff, Chirl, Fauvette, Peggy, Record, Rel(l)ish, Trill, Vibrate, Yodel, Yodle

War-chant, War-cry Alalagmos, Haka, Slogan

Ward (off) Artemus, Averruncate, Care, Casual, Charge, Defend, District, Fend, Guard, Hand-off, Maternity, Nightingale, Oppose, Parry, Protégé, Pupil, Soc, Soken, Vintry, Wear, Weir

Warden Caretaker, Concierge, Constable, Crossing, Curator, Custodian, Game, Guardian, Keeper, Maori, Meter maid, Ranger, Septimus, Spooner, Steward, Traffic, Way

Warder Beefeater, Gaoler, Guardian, Keeper, Provost, Screw, Turnkey, Twirl

Wardrobe Almirah, Capsule, Closet, Clothes, Garderobe, Outfit, Vestuary

Ware(s) Arretine, Beware, Biscuit, Cameo, Canton, Chelsea, China, Etruria, Faience, Goods, Lustre, Merchandise, Palissy, Samian, Sanitary, Satsuma, Shippo, Truck, Wemyss

Warehouse Bonded, Data, Depository, Entrepôt, Freight-shed, Go-down, Hong, Store

▶ **Warfare** *see* WAR

War-game Kriegs(s)piel

War-god Ares, Mars, Tiu, Tiw, Tyr

Warhead Atomic, Supremo

Warhorse Charger, Destrier, Fighter

Wariness, Wary Ca'canny, Cagey, Careful, Cautel, Caution, Chary, Discreet, Distrust, Guarded, Leery, Mealy-mouthed, Prudent, Sceptical, Tentie, Tenty, Vigilant

Warlike Battailous, Bellicose, Gung-ho, Lachlan, Martial, Militant

Warlord Haw-haw, Kitchener, Shogun

Warm(er), Warming, Warmth Abask, Admonish, Air, Ardour, Balmy, British, Calefacient, Calid(ity), Chambré, Cordial, Empressement, Enchafe, Fervour, Foment, Gemutlich, Genial, Global, Glow, > **HEAT**, Hot, Incalescent, Kang, Lew, Logic, Loving, Muff, Muggy, Mull, Tepid, Thermal, Toast, Toasty

Warm-blooded Homothermal, Homothermic, Homothermous, Idiothermous

Warmonger Hawk

Warn(ing) Admonish, Alarum, Alert, Amber, Aposematic, Apprise, Beacon, Bleep, Buoy, Caution, Caveat, Caveat emptor, Commination, Cone, Counsel, Document, Early, En garde, Example, Foghorn, Fore, Foretoken, Gardyloo, Garnishment, Harbinger, Hazchem, Heads up, Hoot, Horn, Klaxon, Larum, Lesson, Light, Maroon, Monition, Nix, Nota bene, Notice, Omen, Pi-jaw, Portent, Premonitory, Presage, Prodromal, Profit, Rumble strip, Scaldings, Scarborough, Sematic, Shore, Signal, Storm, Tattler, Threat, Tip-off, Token, Vigia, Vor, Yellow card

Warner Alarm, Fore, Plum, Siren

Warp(ed) Bias, Buckle, Cast, Contort, Distort, Kam, Kedge, Pandation, Time, Twist, Weft

Warpath Rampage

▷ **Warped** *may indicate* an anagram

Warrant(y) Able, Authorise, Bench, Caption, Certificate, Death, Detainer, Distress, General, Guarantee, Justify, Mittimus, Permit, Precept, Royal, Search, Sepad, Special, Swear, Transire, Vouch, Warn

Warren Burrow, Colony, Hastings

Warrior Achilles, Agamemnon, Ajax, Amazon, Anzac, Berserk(er), Brave, Cossack, Crusader, Eorl, Fianna, Fighter, Geronimo, Ghazi, Heimdall, Housecarl, Impi, Myrmidon, Nestor, Rainbow, Rajpoot, Rajput, Samurai, Soldier, Tatar, Unknown, Warhorse, Zulu

Warship Battleship, Castle, Cog, Corvette, Cruiser, Destroyer, Drake, Dromon(d), Frigate, Invincible, Man-o-war, Mine-layer, Monitor, Privateer, Ram, Wooden Walls

Wart(y) Anbury, Angleberry, Blemish, Keratose, Muricate, Plantar, Tuberous, Verruca, Wen

Warwick Kingmaker

▶ **Wary** *see* **WARINESS**

Was Erat, Existed, Lived, Past

Wash(ed), Washer, Washing (up), Wash out Ablution, Affusion, Alluvion, Bath, Bay(e), Bidet, Bubble-dancing, Bur(r), Calcimine, Circlip, Clean(se), Cradle, D, Dashwheel, Dele(te), Dip, Edulcorate, Elute, Elutriate, Enema, Fen, Flush, Freshen, Gargle, Grommet, Grummet, Irrigate, Kalsomine, Lap, > **LAUNDER**, Lave, Leather, Lip, Lotion, Marsh, Maundy, Mop, Nipter, Pan, Pigswill, Poss, Purify, Rinse, Scrub, Shampoo, Shim, Sind, Sloosh, Sluice, Soogee, Soojee, Soojey, Squeegie, Stream, Sujee, Swab, Synd, Tie, Toilette, Top and tail, Twin tub, Tye, Wake, Wudu, Yellow

Washbasin, Washtub, Washhouse Copper, Lavabo, Steamie

Washerman, Washerwoman Dhobi, Laundress

Washington Wa

Wasn't Nas, Wasna

Wasp(ish) Appledrain, Bembex, Bink, Bite, Chalcid, Cuckoo-fly, Cynipidae, Cynips, Digger, European, Fig, Fretful, Gall(-fly), Gold, Hornet, Horntail, Hoverfly, Irritable, Marabunta, Mason, Miffy, Muddauber, Paper, Peevish, Pompilid, Potter, Ruby-tail, Sand, Seed, Solitary, Spider, Velvet ant, Vespa, Wood, Yellow jacket

Wasp's nest Bike, Bink, Byke

Wassail Carouse, Pledge, Toast

Wast Wert

Wastage, Waste(d), Wasting, Wasteland Atrophy, Blue, Cesspit, Cirrhosis, Consume, Contabescent, Cotton, Crud, Culm, Decay, Dejecta, Desert, Detritus, Devastate, Dilapidate, Dissipate, Dross, Dung, Dwindle, Dwine, Dystrophy, Effluent, Egesta, Emaciate, Erode, Estrepe, Excrement, Exhaust, Expend, Exudate, Faeces, Flue, Forpine, Fribble, Fritter, Garbage, Gash, Gob, Gunge, Haggard, Havoc, Hazardous, Knub, Lavish, Loose, Lose, Loss, Low-level, Marasmus, Merino, Misspent, Moor, Moulder, Muir, Mullock, Mungo, Natural, Novalia, Nub, Nuclear, Offal, Oller, Ordure, Pellagra, Phthisis, Pigswill, Pine, Prodigalise, Radioactive, Rammel, Ravage, Recrement, Red mud, Red tape, > **REFUSE**, Reif, Rubble, Ruderal, Schappe, Scissel, Scoria, Scrap, Sewage, Slag, Slurry, Spend, Spill, Spoil(age), Squander, Sullage, Syntexis, Tabes, Tailing, Thin, Ureal, Urine, Uropoiesis, Vast, Wanze, Wear, Wilderness, Yearn

▷ **Wasted** *may indicate* an anagram

Wastrel Idler, Profligate, Scattergood, Spend-all, Spendthrift, Stalko, Vagabond

Watch(er) Accutron®, Analog(ue), Analogon, Argus, Await, Bark, Behold, Bird-dog, Black, Clock, Coastguard, Cock-crow, Digital, Dog, Espy, Fob, Glom, Gregory, Guard, Half-hunter, Huer, Hunter, Kettle, Latewake, Lever, Lo, Look, Look-out, Middle, Monitor, Morning, Nark, Neighbourhood, Night, Nit, Note, Nuremberg egg, Observe, Overeye, Patrol, Pernoctation, Posse, Quartz, Regard, Repeater, Rolex®, Scout, Sentinel, Sentry, Shadow, Spectate, Spotter, Stemwinder, Surveillance, Tend, Ticker, Timekeeper, Timepiece, Timer, Tompion, Tout, Turnip, Vedette, > **VIGIL**, Voyeur, Wait, Wake, Wrist(let)

Watch-chain Albert, Slang

Watch-control Escapement

Watchful(ness) Alert, Aware, Care, Dragon, Ira, Jealous, Vigilant, Wary

Watchman Bellman, Charley, Charlie, Chok(e)y, Cho(w)kidar, Guard, Sentinel, Sentry, Speculator, Tompion, Viewer

Watch-tower Atalaya, Barbican, Beacon, Mirador, Sentry-go

Watchword Cry, Password, Shibboleth, Slogan

Water(ed), Waters, Watery Adam's ale, Adam's wine, Amrit, Apollinaris, Aq(ua), Aquatic, Aqueous, Barley, Bayou, Bedabble, Bilge, Bound, Brine, Broads, Brook, Burn, Canal, Cancer, Chresard, Chuck, Cold, Compensation, Conductivity, Dead, Deaw, Deg, Demersal, Dew, Dill, Dilute, Dribble, Drinking, Eau, Ebb, Echard, Element, Ennerdale, Epilimnion, Euphotic, Evian®, First, Flood, Ford, Fossil, Gallise, Gallize, Ganga jal, Grey, Gripe, Ground, Hard, Heavy, Hectum, Hellespont, High, Holy, Hot, Hungary, Hydatoid, Irrigate, Javel(le), Kuroshio, Kyle, Lagoon, Lagune, Lake, Lant, Lavender, Leachate, Lentic, Light, Limnology, Lithia, Lode, Lotic, Lough, Low, Lubricated, Lymph, Meteoric, Mineral, Miner's inch, Moiré, Nappe, North, Oasis®, Oedema, Overfall, Pawnee, Pee, Perrier®, Phreatic, Pisces, Polly, Polynia, Polynya, Poppy, Potash, Potass, Pump, Purest, Quinine, Rain, Rapids, Rate, Reach, Rip, Riverine, Rose, Runny, Rydal, Saltchuck, Scorpio, Sea, Seltzer, Sera, Serous, Serum, Shower, Simpson, Skinkling, Slack, Slick, Sluice, Soda, Sodden, Soft, Solent, Sound, Souse, Stream, Surface, Table, Tam, Tap, Tar, Territorial, Thin, Tide, Toilet,

Tonic, Urine, Vadose, Vichy, Viscous, Vlei, Vly, Wash(y), Weak, Wee, Whey, White, White coal, Wild, Wishy-washy

Waterbaby Moses, Tom

Water-boa Anaconda

Water-boatman Notonecta

Water-brash Pyrosis

Water-buckets Noria

Water-carrier Aqueduct, Bheestie, Bheesty, Bhistee, Bhisti, Bucket, Carafe, Chatty, Furphy, Hose, Hydra, Kirbeh, Pail, Pitcher

Water-chestnut Saligot

Water-colour Aquarelle, Painting, Pastel, RI

Water-course Arroyo, Billabong, Canal, Ditch, Dyke, Falaj, Furrow, Gutter, Khor, Lead, Nala, Nulla, Rean, Rhine, Riverway, Shott, Spruit, Wadi, Whelm

Water-device Shadoof, Shaduf

Water-diviner Dowser, Hydrostat

Waterfall Angel (Falls), Cataract, Churchill, Chute, Cuquenan, Force, Foss, Iguaçú, Kabiwa, Kaieteur, Kile, Lasher, Lin(n), Mardel, Mtarazi, Niagara, Overfall, Rapid, Sault, Sutherland, Takakkaw, Tugela, Victoria, Yellowstone, Yosemite

Water-fern Marsilea, Salvinia

Water-gate Penstock, Sluice, Sluse

Water-god Aleion, Aleyin, Alpheus

Water-hen Gallinule

Water-hole Bore, Gilgai, Oasis

Water-lily Lotus, Nenuphar, Nuphar, Spatterdock

Waterloo Rout

Waterman Aquarius, Bargee, Ferryman, Oarsman

Water-monster Nicker

Water-nymph Kelpie, Kelpy, Naiad, Ondine, Rusalka

Water-parsnip Sium, Skirret

Water-plant Alisma, Aquatic, Cress, Crowfoot, Elodea, Gulfweed, Lace-leaf, Lattice-leaf, Nelumbo, Nenuphar, Nuphar, Ouvirandra, Pontederia, Quillwort, Reate, Sea-mat, Sedge, Seg, Stratiotes, Urtricularia, Vallisneria

Waterproof, Water-tight Caisson, Caulk, Cofferdam, Dampcourse, Dubbin(g), Groundsheet, Loden, Mac, Mino, Oilers, Oilskin, Pay, Seaworthy, Stank, Sta(u)nch, Tarp, Waders

Water-rat Arvicola, Musk-rat, Ratty, Vole

Watershed Divide, Hilltop

Water-spout Gargoyle, Geyser, Hurricano

Water-sprite Kelpie, Kelpy, Nix(ie), Nixy, Tangie, Undine, Water-nymph

Water supply Dewpond, H, Hydrant, Spring, Tank, Tap

Waterway Aqueduct, Billabong, Canal, Channel, Culvert, Ditch, Igarapé, Illinois, Intracoastal, Lode, River, Sound, Straight, Suez

Water-wheel Noria, Pelton, Sakia, Saki(y)eh

Wattle(s) Acacia, Boobialla, Boree, Dewlap, Gills, Mimosa, Mulga, Sallow, Savanna, Snot

Wave(s), Waved, Wavelength, Wavy Alfven, Alpha, Beachcomber, Beam, Beck, Beta, Billow, Bore, Bow, Brain, Brandish, Breaker, Carrier, Circular polarisation, Clapotis, Comber, Complex, Continuous, Crenulate, Crest, Crime, Crimp, Cymotrichous, De Broglie, Decuman, Delta, Dominant, Dumper, Electromagnetic, Finger, Flap, Flaunt, Float, Flote, Flourish, Gesticulate, Gravitational, Gravity, Graybeard, Ground, Groundswell, Gyrose, Harmonic,

Haystack, Heat, Hertzian, Internal, Ionospheric, Lee, Long, Longitudinal, Marcel, Matter, Medium, Mexican, Nebule, New, Oundy, Peristalsis, Perm(anent), Plunger, Primary, Pulse, Radar, Radiation, Radio, Rayleigh, Repand, Rip, Ripple, Roller, Rooster, Sastrugi, Scrub, Sea, Secondary, Seiche, Seismic, Shock, Short, Sine, Sky, Snaky, Soliton, Sound, Spiller, Square, Squiggle, Standing, Stationary, Stream, Supplementary, Surf, Surge, Sway, Tabby, Theta, Third, Thought, Tidal, Tidal bore, Tide, Train, Transverse, Travelling, Tsunami, Ultrasonic, Undate, Unde, Undulate, Vermicular, Waffle, Waft, Wag, Waive, Wash, Waw, Whitecap, White-horse, Wigwag

▷ **Wave(s)** *may indicate* an anagram

Wave-band Channel

Wave-detector Coherer

Wavelength Band, De Broglie

Waver(ing), Waverer Dither, Falter, Flag, Gutter, Halt, Hesitate, Oscillate, Stagger, Sway, Swither, Teeter, Trimmer, Vacillate, Waffle, Wet, Wow

Wax(ed), Waxing, Waxy Adipocere, Ambergris, Appal, Bate, Bees, Bone, Brazilian, Candelilla, Carna(h)uba, Cere, Ceresin, Cerumen, Chinese, Cobbler's, Cutin, Earth, Effuse, Enseam, Gr(e)aves, Grow, Heelball, Honeycomb, Increase, Increscent, Inseam, Ire, Japan, Kiss, Lecithin, Lipide, Livid, Lost, Lyrical, Mineral, Montan, Mummy, Ozocerite, Ozokerite, Paraffin, Parmacitie, Pela, Petroleum, Propolis, Pruina, Rage, Seal, Sealing, Spermaceti, Suberin, Tallow, Tantrum, Temper, Toxaphene, Vegetable, White, Yielding

Waxwing Cedar-bird, Icarus

Way(s), Wayside Access, Agate, Appian, Autobahn, Avenue, Borstal(l), Bypass, Companion, Course, Crescent, Direction, Door, Draw, E, Each, Entrance, Family, Fashion, Flaminian, Foss(e), Gate, Habit, Hatch, Hedge, High, Hither, How, Lane, Manner, Means, Method, Milky, Mo, Mode, Modus, N, Pass, Path, Pennine, Permanent, Pilgrim's, Procedure, Railroad, Regimen, Ridge, > **ROAD**, Route, S, Sallypost, St(reet), Style, System, Taoism, Third, Thoroughfare, Thus, Trace, Trail, Troade, Turnpike, Underpass, Untrodden, Via, W, Wise

Wayfarer Commuter, Piepowder, Pilgrim, Traveller, Voyager

Waylay Accost, Ambuscade, Ambush, Beset, Bushwhack, Buttonhole, Molest, Obstruct, Stick up

Way-out Advanced, Bizarre, Egress, Esoteric, Exit, Exotic, Extreme, Offbeat, Trendy

Wayward Capricious, Disobedient, Errant, Erratic, Loup-the-dyke, Obstreperous, Perverse, Stray, Unruly, Wilful

We I and I, Oo, Royal, Us

Weak(er), Weaken(ing), Weakest, Weakness Achilles' heel, Acrasia, Antimnemonic, Aphesis, Appal, Arsis, Asthenia, Attenuate, Blot, Brickle, Brittle, Cachexia, Cataplexy, Chink, Cripple(d), Debile, Debilitate, Decrease, Delay, Delicate, Dilute, Disable, Effete, Emasculate, Enervate, Enfeeble, Entender, Fade, Faible, Failing, Faint, Fatigue, Feeble, Fissile, Flag, Flaw, Flimsy, Foible, Fragile, Frail(tee), Frailty, Give, Gone, Ham, Hamartia, Helpless, Honeycomb, Impair, Impotence, Infirm, Knock-kneed, Labefaction, Lassitude, Leptosomatic, Low, Low ebb, Meagre, Mild, Milk and water, Myasthenia, Namby-pamby, Pale, Pall, Paraparesis, Paresis, Puny, Push-over, Pusillanimous, Reckling, Reduce, Simp, Slack, Tenuous, Thesis, Thin, Thready, Tottery, Unable, Underdog, Undermine, Unnerve, Unstable, Vapid, Velleity, Vessel, Vulnerability, W, Washy, Water(y), Wish(y)-wash(y), Wuss(y)

Weakling Dilling, Drip, Milksop, Nerd, Nisgul, Reed, Softie, Wuss

Weal Ridge, Stripe, Wealth, Welfare, Welt, Whelk

Wealth(y) Abundance, Affluence, Bullion, Croesus, Fat-cat, Fortune, Golconda, Jet-set, Klondike, Klondyke, Load(s'a), Loaded, Lolly, Mammon, Means, Mine, Mint, Moneyed, Nabob, Opulence, Ore, Pelf, Plutocrat, Reich, Rich, Ritzy, Solid, Substance, Treasure, Untold, Well-heeled, Well-off, Well-to-do

Wean Ablactation, Bairn, Spain, Spane, Spean

Weapon Airgun, Alderman, Arbalest, Arblast, Arm, Armalite®, Arquebus(e), Arrow, Arsenal, Assegai, Ataghan, Backsword, Ballista, Baton, Battleaxe, Bayonet, Bazooka, Bill, Binary, Blowgun, Blowpipe, Bludgeon, Bolo, Bomb, Bondook, Broadsword, Caliver, Calthrop, Caltrap, Caltrop, Carbine, Catapult, Catchpole, Cestus, Chainshot, Club, Co(e)horn, Cosh, Creese, Cudgel, Culverin, Cutlass, Dag(ger), Dart, Derringer, Deterrent, Doodlebug, Dragon, Dragoon, Duster, Elf-arrow, Enfield, Estoc, Excalibur, Flail, Flamethrower, Flintlock, Forty-five, Fougade, Fougasse, Gad(e), Gaid, Gingal(l), Gisarme, Glaive, Grenade, Halberd, Halbert, Harpoon, Harquebus, Hoplology, Howitzer, Javelin, Jingal, Katana, Knife, Knuckleduster, Kris, Lance, Life-preserver, Longbow, Long-range, Machete, Mangonel, Manrikigusari, Matchet, Mauser®, Maxim, Mere, Missile, Morgenstern, Mortar, Munition, Musket, Nuclear, Nuke, Nunchaku (sticks), Onager, Orgue, Partisan, Pea-shooter, Petrary, Petronel, Pike, Pilum, Pistol, Poleaxe, Quarterstaff, Revolver, Rifle, Sabre, Saker, Sandbag, Sarbacane, Shotgun, Sidearm, Skean-dhu, Skene-dhu, Slingshot, Smallsword, Snickersnee, Sparke, Sparth, Spat, Spontoon, Sten, Stiletto, Sting, Stinkpot, Sword, Taiaha, Taser®, Theatre, Throw-stick, Tomboc, Torpedo, Traditional, Trebuchet, Trident, Truncheon, V1, Vou(l)ge, Whirl-bat, Whorl-bat

Wear(ing), Wear Out Abate, Ablative, Abrade, Air, Attrition, Chafe, Corrade, Corrode, Deteriorate, Detrition, Efface, Erode, Erosion, Fashion, For(e)spend, Fray, Frazzle, Fret, Garb, Impair, In, Pack, Scuff, Sport, Stand, Tedy, Utility

▷ **Wear** *may indicate* the NE (eg Sunderland)

Weariness, Wearisome, Weary Beat, Bejade, Bore, Cloy, Dog-tired, Ennui, Ennuyé, Exhaust, Fag, Fatigate, Fatigue, Harass, Hech, Irk, Jade, Lacklustre, Lassitude, Pall, Puny, Ramfeezle, Sleepy, Spent, Tire, Trash, Try, Tucker, Wabbit, Worn

Weasel Beech-marten, Cane, Delundung, Ermine, Ferret, Glutton, Grison, Kolinsky, Marten, Mink, Mustela, Pekan, Polecat, Stoat, Taira, Tayra, Vermin, Whitterick, Whit(t)ret, Whittrick, Wolverine, Woodshock

Weather, Weather forecast Atmosphere, Climate, Cyclone, Discolour, Ecoclimate, Elements, El Nino, Endure, Met, Sky, Stand, Survive, Tiros, Undergo, Withstand

Weathercock Barometer, Fane, Vane

Weave(r), Weaves, Weaving Arachne, Basket, Cane, Complect, Entwine, Finch, Fishnet, Folk, Heald, Heddle, Interlace, Lace, Lease, Leno, Lion, Loom, Marner, Pick, Plain, Raddle, Ripstop, Rya, Shuttle, Sparrow, Spider, Splice, Taha, Texture, Throstle, Tissue, Tweel, Twill, Twine, Wabster, Waggle, Webster, Zigzag

Weaver-bird Amadavat, Avadavat, Quelea, Rice-bird, Taha

Web(bed), Webbing, Web-footed, Web-site Aranea, Fissipalmate, Food, Fourchette, Infomediary, Internet, Mat, Maze, Mesh(work), Offset, Palama, Palmate, Palmiped, Patagium, Pinnatiped, Retiary, Skein, Snare, Spider, Tear, Tela, Tissue, Toil, Totipalmate, World Wide

Webster Spider, Weaver

Wed(ding), Wedlock Alliance, Bet, Diamond, Espousal, Golden, Hymen, Join, Knobstick, Link, Marriage, Marry, Mate, Matrimony, Me(i)nt, Meng(e), Meynt, Ming, Monkey's, Nuptials, Pair, Penny, Ruby, Shotgun, Silver, Spousal,

> **UNION**, Unite, White, Y

Wedge(d) Accretionary, Canting-coin, Chock, Chunk, Cleat, Cotter, Cuneal, Doorstop, Feather, Forelock, Gagger, Gib, Impacted, Jack, Jam, Key, Niblick, Pitching, Prop, Quoin, Sand, Scotch, Shim, Sphenic, Stick, Trig, Vomerine, Voussoir, Whipstock

Wedgwood Benn, China®

Wednesday Ash, Midweek, Pulver, Spy

Wee Leak, Little, Pee, Sma(ll), Tiny, Urinate, Widdle

Weed(y) Adderwort, Agrestal, Alga, Allseed, Anacharis, Arenaria, Bedstraw, Bell-bind, Blinks, Burdock, Carpetweed, Catch, Charlock, Chickweed, Chlorella, Cigar(ette), Cissy, Clover, Cobbler's pegs, Cockle, Colonist, Coltsfoot, Corncockle, Couch, Daisy, Dallop, Darnel, Dock, Dollop, Dulse, Elodea, Ers, Fag, Fat hen, Femitar, Fenitar, Fucoid, Fumitory, Groundsel, Helodea, Hoe, Indian, Joe-pye, Knapweed, Knawel, Knot-grass, Lemna, Mare's-tail, Marijuana, Matfelon, Mayweed, Nard, Nettle, Nipplewort, Nostoc, Onion, Oxygen, Paterson's curse, Pearlwort, Pilewort, Piri-piri, Plantain, Potamogeton, Purslane, Ragi, Ragwort, Reate, Rest-harrow, Ribwort, Ruderal, Runch, Sagittaria, Sargasso, Scal(l)awag, Scallywag, Senecio, Softy, Sorrel, Spurge, Spurrey, Sudd, Sun-spurge, Swine's-cress, Tansy, Tare, Thistle, Tine, Tobacco, Tormentil, Twitch, Ulotrichale, Ulva, Vetch, Viper's bugloss, Wartcress, Widow's, Winnow, Yarr

Weedkiller Arsenic, Atrazine, Dalapon, Diquat, Diuron, Herbicide, Paraquat®, Selective, Simazine

Week(ly) Ember, Expectation, Great, Hebdomadary, Holy, Orientation, Ouk, Oulk, Passion, Periodical, Rag, Rogation, Sennight, Working

Weekday Feria

Weekend K, Sat, Sun

Weep(er), Weepy, Wept Bawl, Blubber, Cry, Grat, Greet, Lachrymose, Lament, Loser, Maudlin, Niobe, Ooze, Pipe, Screet, Seep, Sob, Wail

Weevil Anthonomous, Bean, Boll, Bug, Cornworm, Curculio, Diamond-beetle, Grain, Insect, Pea, Rice, Seed

Weft Roon, Shot, Texture, Warp, Woof

Weigh(ing), Weigh down, Weight(y) All-up, Apothecaries', Arroba, Artal, As, Atomic, Avoirdupois, Balance, Bantam, Baric, Bob, Bulk, Burden, Candie, Candy, Cantar, Carat, Catty, Cental, Centner, Clove, Consider, Count, Counterpoise, Cruiser, Ct, Dead, Decagram(me), Deliberate, Derham, Dirham, Dirhem, Drail, Dumbbell, Emphasis, Equivalent, Feather, Fother, G, Gerah, Grain, Gram, Grammage, Gross, Heft, Importance, Impost, Incumbent, Journey, Kandy, Kantar, Kat(i), Katti, Kerb, Khat, Kin, Kip, Last, Libra, Lisp(o)und, Load, Mark, Massive, Maund, Metage, Mina, Mna, Molecular, Moment, Mouse, Nail, Nett, Obol, Oke, Onerous, Oppress, Ounce, Overpoise, Oz, Pease, Peaze, Peck, Peise, Peize, Perpend, Peyse, Pikul, Plummet, Poise, Ponderal, Pood, Pound, Pregnant, Preponderance, Prey, Pud, Pudge, Quintal, Recul, Rod, Rotolo, Sash, Scruple, Seer, Semuncia, Ser, Sinker, Sit, Slang, Slung-shot, Stone, Stress, Talent, Tare, Throw, Tical, Tod, Tola, Ton(nage), Tonne, Tophamper, Troy, Trutinate, Unce, Unmoor, Welter, Wey, Wt

Weighing machine Bismar, Scales, Steelyard, Tron(e)

Weightless Agravic

Weight-lifter Crane, Lewis, Windlass

Weir Cauld, Dam, Garth, Kiddle, Kidel, Lasher, Pen, Watergate

Weird Bizarre, Curious, Dree, Eerie, Eery, Eldritch, Kookie, Offbeat, Spectral, Strange, Supernatural, Taisch, Uncanny, Zany

Welch, Welsh Abscond, Cheat, Default, Embezzle, Levant, Rat, Reneg(u)e, Renig, Skedaddle, Weasel

Welcome, Welcoming Aloha, Ave, Bel-accoyle, Ciao, Embrace, Entertain, Glad-hand, Greet, Haeremai, Hallo, Halse, Hello, Hi, Hospitable, How, Hullo, Karanga, Powhiri, Receive, Reception, Salute, Yellow-ribbon

Weld(ing) Arc, Explosion, Fillet, Friction, Gas, Join, Merge, MIG, Resistance, Seam, Sinter, Stud, Tack, TIG, Ultrasonic, Unite

Welfare Advantage, Alms, Benison, Ha(y)le, Heal, Health, Sarvodaya, Social, Weal

Welkin Firmament, Sky

Well (done) Artesian, Atweel, Aweel, Bien, Bore(hole), Bravo, Cenote, Development, Dropping, Dry hole, Euge, Famously, Fine, Fit, Gas, Gasser, Good, Gosh, Gusher, Hale, > **HEALTHY**, Hot, Inkpot, Kapa haka, Law, My, Namma hole, Odso, Oh, Oil, Phreatic, Potential, Pump, So, Source, Spa, Spring, Sump, Surge, Um, Upflow, Zemzem

Wellbeing Atweel, Bien-être, Comfort, Euphoria, Euphory, Good, Health, Oomph, Welfare

Well-bred Genteel

Well-built Sturdy, Tight

Well-covered Chubby, Padded

Well-curb Puteal

Welles Orson

Wellington, Welly Accelerate, Boot, Green, Gumboot, Iron Duke, Nosey

Well-known Famous, Illustrious, Notorious, Notour, Prominent

Well-off Affluent, Far, Rich, Wealthy

Well part Bucket, Shadoof, Shaduf

Wells Bombardier, Fargo, Sadler's

Well-wisher Friend

▶ **Welsh** *see* WELCH

Welsh(man) Briton, Brittonic, Brython, Cake, Cambrian, Celtic, Cog, Cym(ric), Cymry, Dai, Ebbw, Emlyn, Evan, Fluellen, Gareth, Harp, Idris, Ifor, Keltic, P-Celtic, P-Keltic, Rabbit, Rarebit, Rees, Rhys, Sion, Taffy, Tudor, W

Wen Cyst, Talpa, Tumour, Wart

Wench Blowze, Court, Girl, Gouge, Hussy, Maid, Ramp, Rig, Smock, Strumpet

Wend Meander, Sorb, Steer

Wendy Darling, House

Went Left

Werewolf Loup-garou, Lycanthrope, Nazi, Turnskin, Vampire

Wesleyan Epworth, Methodist

West(ern), Westerly Ang mo, Far, Favonian, Hesperian, Mae, Middle, Movie, Oater, Occidental, Ponent, Spaghetti, Sunset, W, Wild

West African Fantee, Fanti, Kroo, Wolof

▷ **West end** *may indicate* 't' *or* 'W1'

West Indian Carib, Creole, Jamaican, Taino

Westminster SW1

Wet(ting) Bedabble, Bedraggled, Clammy, Daggle, Damp, Dank, Dew, Dip, Douse, Dowse, Drench, Drip(ping), Drook, Drouk, Embrue, Enuresis, Feeble, Humect, Humid, Hyetal, Imbue, Irrigate, Irriguous, Madefy, Madid, Marshy, Moil, Moist(en), Molly, Namby-pamby, Pee, Piddle, Pouring, Rainy, Ret(t), Roral, Roric, Runny, Saturate, Shower, Simp(leton), Sipe, Sluice, > **SOAK**, Sodden, Sopping, Sour, Steep, Tiddle, Tipsy, Urinate, Wat, Wee, Widdle, Wimpy, Wringing

Whack(ed) Belt, Bemaul, Biff, Deadbeat, Joll, Joule, Jowl, Lambast, Lounder, Swish, Thump

Whale(meat), Whaling Baleen, Beaked, Beluga, Black, Blower, Blubber, Blue, Bottlehead, Bottlenose, Bowhead, Bull, Cachalot, Calf, Cetacea(n), Cete, Cow, Cowfish, Dolphin, Dorado, Fall, Fin(back), Finner, Gam, Glutton, Grampus, Greenland, Grey, Greyback, Humpback, Killer, Kreng, Leviathan, Manatee, Minke, Monodon, Mysticeti, Narwhal, Odontoceti, Paste, Physeter, Pilot, Pod, Porpoise, Right, Rorqual, School, Scrag, Sea-canary, Sea-unicorn, Sei, Social, Sperm, Spouter, Sulphur-bottom, Thrasher, Toothed, Toothless, White, Zeuglodon(t)

▷ **Whale** *may indicate* an anagram

Whalebone Busk

Whaler Ahab, Harpooner, Ship, Specksioneer, Specktioneer, Waister

Whales' meat Clio

Wham Bang, Collide

Whang Blow, Flog, Thrash, Whack

Wharf(inger) Dock(er), Jetty, Key, Landing, Pier, Quay, Roustabout, Rouster, Staith(e)

What Anan, Eh, How, Pardon, Que, Siccan, That, Which

Whatnot, What's-its-name Dinges, Dingus, Doings, Etagère, Gismo, Jiggamaree, Jiggumbob, Thingamy, Thingumajig, Thingumbob, Thingummy, Timenoguy

Wheat Amelcorn, Blé, Bulg(h)ur, Cone, Couscous, Cracked, Durum, Einkorn, Emmer, Federation, Fromenty, Frumenty, Furme(n)ty, Furmity, Grain, Hard, Mummy, Rivet, Sarrasin, Sarrazin, Seiten, Semolina, Sharps, Soft, Spelt, Spring, Triticum, Winter

Wheatsheaf Bale, Gerbe, Stook

Wheedle Banter, Barney, Blandish, Butter up, Cajole, Coax, Cog, Cuiter, Cuittle, Flatter, Inveigle, Tweedle, Whilly(whaw)

Wheel(er) Balance, Bedel, Bevel, Bogy, Buff(ing), Caracol(e), Caster, Castor, Catherine, Chain, Chark(h)a, Circle, Cistern, Crown, Cycle, Daisy, Disc, Driving, Emery, Epicycloidal, Escape, Fan, Felloe, Felly, Ferris, Fifth, Fortune, Gear, Grinding, Helm, Hurl, Idle(r), Jagger, Kick, Lantern, Magnate, Medicine, Mortimer, Nabob, Nose, Paddle, Pattern, Pedal, Pelton, Perambulator, Persian, Pin, Pinion, Pitch, Pivot, Planet, Potter's, Prayer, Pulley, Rag, Ratchet, Rhomb, Roll, Rotate, Roulette, Rowel, Sheave, Snail, Spider, Spinning, Sprocket, Spur, Star, Steering, Stepney, Stitch, Tail, Throwing-table, Tread, Trindle, Trochus, Trolley, Truckle, Trundle, > TURN, Tympan(um), Water, Web, Wharve, Wire, Worm, Zoetrope

Wheelbarrow Monotroch

Wheelhouse Caravan, Paddle-box

Wheel-hub Axle, Nave

Wheelman Cyclist, Ixion

Wheelwright Spokesman

Wheeze Asthma, Jape, Joke, Pant, Ploy, Rale, Reak, Reik, Rhonchus, Ruse, Stridor, Trick, Whaisle, Whaizle

Whelk Buckie, Limpet, Shellfish, Stromb, Triton

Whelm Nalla(h), Nulla(h)

Whelp Bear, Bra(t)chet, Pup

When(ever) Although, As, If, Once, Though, Time

Where(abouts) Location, Neighbourhood, Place, Site, Vicinity, Whaur, Whither

Wherefore Cause, Reason, Why

Whereupon So, When
Wherewithal Finance, Means, Money, Needful, Resources
Wherry Barge, Rowboat
Whet(stone) Coticular, Excite, Hone, Sharpen, Stimulate
Whether Conditional, If
Whey Serum, Whig
Which(ever), Which is Anyway, As, QE, Whatna, Whilk, Who
Whiff Breath, Cigarette, Gust, Hum, Puff, Redolence, Smatch, Sniff, Trace, Waft
Whig Adullamite, Jig, Rascal, Tory, Whey
While Although, As, Interim, Since, Space, Span, Though, Throw, Time, When, Whenas, Yet
Whim(s), Whimsical, Whimsy Bizarre, Caprice, Conceit, Crotchet, Fad, Fancy, Fantastic, Fey, Flisk, Impulse, Kicksy-wicksy, Kink, Notion, Quaint, Quirk, Tick, Toy, Vagary
Whimper Cry, Grizzle, Mewl, Pule, Snivel, Whine
Whin Furze, Gorse, Ulex
Whine, Whinge Cant, Carp, Complain, Cry, Grumble, Kvetch, Mewl, Moan, Peenge, Pule, Snivel, Whimper, Yammer
Whinny Neigh, Nicker, Whicker
Whip(ped), Whip out, Whipping Beat, Braid, Brede, Bullwhack, Bullwhip, Cat, Cat o' nine tails, Chabouk, Chantilly, Chastise, Chief, Cilium, Colt, Crop, Drive, Feague, Firk, Five-line, Flagellate, Flagellum, Flay, Gad, Hide, Jambok, Knout, K(o)urbash, Larrup, > LASH, Leather, Limber, Lunge, Quirt, Rawhide, Riem, Scourge, Sjambok, Slash, Steal, Stock, Strap-oil, Swinge, Swish, Switch, Taw, Thong, Three-line, Trounce, Welt, West country, Whap, Whop
Whippersnapper Dandiprat, Dandyprat, Pup, Squirt
Whirl(er), Whirling Bullroarer, Circumgyrate, Dervish, Eddy, Gyrate, > IN A WHIRL, Pivot, Reel, Spin, Swing, Swirl, Vortex, Vortical, Vorticose, Vortiginous, Whirry
Whirlpool Eddy, Gulf, Gurge, Maelstrom, Moulin, Sea purse, Swelchie, Vorago, Vortex, Weel, Wiel
Whirlwind Cyclone, Dust devil, Eddy, Sand-devil, Tornado, Tourbillion, Typho(o)n, Vortex, Willy-willy
Whisk Chowri, Chowry, Swish, Switch, Whid, Whip
Whisker(s) Beard, Beater, Burnsides, Cat's, Dundreary, Hackle, Hair, Moustache, Mutton-chop, Samuel, Satyric tuft, Side(-boards), Side-burns, Vibrissa
Whisk(e)y Alcohol, Barley-bree, Barley-broo, Barley-broth, Bond, Bourbon, Canadian, Cape Smoke, Chain lighting, Corn, Cratur, Crayther, Creature, Fife, Fire-water, Hard tack, Highball, Hokonui, Hoo(t)ch, Irish, Malt, Monongahela, Moonshine, Morning, Mountain dew, Nip, Peat-reek, Pot(h)een, Ragwater, Red eye, Rye, Scotch, Sourmash, Spunkie, Tanglefoot, Tarantula juice, Usquebaugh, Wheech, Whiss
▷ **Whisky** *may indicate* an anagram
Whisper Breath(e), Bur(r), Hark, Hint, Innuendo, Murmur, Round, Rumour, Rustle, Sigh, Stage, Susurrus, Tittle, Undertone
Whist Dummy, Hush, Long, Quiet, Sh, Short, Solo
Whistle(r) Blow, Boatswain's, Calliope, Feedback, Flageolet, Hiss, Marmot, Penny, Ping, Pipe, Ref, Siffle(ur), Sowf(f), Sowth, Steam, Stop, Stridor, Swab(ber), Tin, Toot, Tweedle, Tweet, Warbler, Wheeple, Wheugh, Whew, Whiffle, Wolf
Whit Atom, Doit, Figo, Haet, Iota, Jot, Particle, Pentecost, Point, Red cent, Straw

White(n), Whitener, Whiteness Agene, Agenise, Alabaster, Albedo, Albescent, Albino, Albugineous, Albumen, Argent, Ashen, Au lit, Bakra, Blameless, Blanch, Blanco, Bleach, Buckra, Cabbage, Calm, Cam, Camstone, Candid, Candour, Canescent, Canities, Caucasian, Caum, China, Chinese, Christmas, Cliffs, Collar, Company, Dealbate, Egg, Elephant, Ermine, European, Fang, Fard, Feather, Flag, Flake, French, Glair, Gwen(da), Gwendolen, Honorary, Hore, House, Innocent, Ivory, Large, Leucoma, Lie, Lily, Livid, Man, Marbled, Mealy, Niveous, Opal, Oyster, Pakeha, Pale(face), Pallor, Paper, Paris, Pearl, Poor, Pure, Redleg, Russian, Sclerotic, Selborne, Sheep, Silver, Small, Snow(y), Spanish, Taw, Vitiligo, Wan, Wedding, Zinc

Whitefish Menominee

Whitefriars Alsatia

Whitehall Ministry

Whitehead Milium

White horses Skipper's daughters

White man Anglo, Ba(c)kra, Buckra, Caucasian, Gub(bah), Haole, Honkie, Honky, Kabloona, Larney, Mzungu, Occidental, Ofay, Pakeha, Paleface, Redleg, Redneck, Umlungu, WASP

Whitewash Calcimine, Excuse, Kalsomine, Lime, Skunk, Trounce

Whitlow Ancome, Felon, Panaritium, Paronychia

Whitsun Pinkster, Pinxter

Whittle Carve, Pare, Sharpen

Whizz Wheech

Who As, Doctor

Whodunit Mystery

Whole, Wholehearted, Wholeness, Wholly All, Eager, Entire(ty), Entity, Fully, Hale, Indiscrete, Intact, Integer, Integrity, Largely, Lot, Sum, Systemic, Thoroughly, Total, Unbroken, Uncut

Wholesale(r) Cutprice, En bloc, Engrosser, Jobber, Root and branch, Supplier, Sweeping

Wholesome Clean, Good, Healthy, Physical, Sound

Whoop(er), Whooping cough Alew, Celebrate, Chincough, Crane, Cry, Excite, Kink(cough), Kink-hoast, Pertussis, Swan, War

Whoopee Carouse, Evoe, Hey-go-mad, Roister

Whoosh Birr, Swish

Whopper, Whopping Barn, Crammer, Huge, Immense, Jumbo, Lie, Lig, Oner, Out and outer, Scrouger, Slapper, Slockdolager, Soc(k)dalager, Soc(k)dolager, Soc(k)doliger, Soc(k)dologer, Sogdolager, Sogdoliger, Sogdologer, Stonker, Tale, Taradiddle

Whore Drab, Harlot, Loose woman, Pinnace, Pro, Quail, Road, Strumpet, Tart

Whorl Corolla, Eucyclic, Spiral, Swirl, Verticil, Volute

Why Reason, Yogh

Wick Farm, Rush, Snaste, Vill(age)

Wicked(ness) Adharma, Atrocity, > **BAD**, Candle, Criminal, Cru(i)sie, Crusy, Depravity, Devilish, Evil, Facinorous, Flagitious, Goaty, Godless, Heinous, High-viced, Immoral, Impious, Improbity, Iniquity, Lantern, Nefarious, Night-light, Ponerology, Pravity, Rush, Satanic, Scelerate, Sin(ful), Taper, Turpitude, Unholy, Vile

▷ **Wicked** *may indicate* containing a wick

Wicker(work) Basketry, Sale, Seal

Wicket Gate, Hatch, Infield, Pitch, Square, Sticky, Stool, Stump, Yate

Wicket-keeper Stumper

Wide, Widen(ing), Width Abroad, Ample, Bay, Broad, Dilate, Drib, Eclectic, Expand, Extend, Far, Flanch, Flange, Flare, Flaunch, Ga(u)ge, General, Latitude, Miss, Prevalent, Roomy, Spacious, Spread, Sundry, Sweeping, Vast

Wide-awake Alert, Fly, Hat, Wary, Watchful

Widespread Catholic, Diffuse, Epidemic, Extensive, General, Pandemic, Panoramic, Prevalent, Prolate, Rife, Routh(ie), Sweeping

Widow(ed) Bereft, Black, Dame, Dowager, Golf, Grass, Hempen, Jointress, Relict, Sati, Sneerwell, Suttee, Vidual, Viduous, Whydah-bird, Widdy

Wield Brandish, Control, Exercise, Handle, > MANIPULATE, Ply, Sound

Wife, Wives Bride, Concubine, Consort, Devi, Dutch, Enid, Evadne, Feme, Feme covert, Fiere, Frau, Haram, Harem, Harim, Helpmate, Helpmeet, Hen, Her indoors, Kali, Kickie-wickie, Kicksy-wicksy, Kloo(t)chman, Lakshmi, Little woman, Mate, Memsahib, Missis, Missus, Mrs, Mummer's, Partner, Penelope, Pirrauru, Potiphar's, Rib, Seraglio, Spouse, Squaw, Trophy, Trouble and strife, Umfazi, Ux(or), W

Wig Adonis, Bagwig, Bob(wig), Brigadier, Brutus, Buzz-wig, Cadogan, Campaign, Carpet, Cauliflower, Caxon, Chevelure, Chide, Cockernony, Dalmahoy, Fright, Full-bottomed, Gizz, Gooseberry, Gorgone, Gregorian, Hair(piece), Heare, Jas(e)y, Jazey, Jiz, Macaroni, Major, Periwig, Peruke, Postiche, Ramil(l)ie(s), Rate, Reprimand, Rug, Scold, Scratch, Sheitel, Spencer, Targe, Tie, Toupee, Toupet, Tour

Wiggle, Wiggly Jiggle, Scoleciform, Wobble, Wriggle

Wight Man, Vectis

Wigwam Te(e)pee

Wild Aberrant, Agrestal, Barbarous, Berserk, Bundu, Bush, Chimeric, Crazy, Dionysian, Earl, Errant, Erratic, Farouche, Feral, Frantic, Frenetic, Haggard, Hectic, Lawless, Mad(cap), Manic, Meshugge, Myall, Natural, Rampant, Raver, Riotous, > SAVAGE, Unmanageable, Unruly, Violent, Warrigal, West, Woolly

▷ **Wild(ly)** *may indicate* an anagram

Wild beast Eyra, Sapi-utan, Scrubber

Wildcat Lion, Manul, Ocelot, Strike, Tiger

Wilderness Bush, Desert, Ruderal, Sinai, Solitude, Waste

Wild goose Chase, Greylag

Wild oats Haver

Wile, Wily Art, Artful, Artifice, Astute, Braide, > CUNNING, Deceit, Foxy, Peery, Ruse, Shifty, Shrewd, Slee, > SLY, Spider, Stratagem, Streetwise, Subtle, Trick, Versute, Wide

Wilful Deliberate, Headstrong, Heady, Obstinate, Recalcitrant, Wayward

Will, Willing(ly) Alsoon, Amenable, Bard, Bequeath, Bewildered, Bill(y), Complaisant, Compliant, Conation, Content, Desire, Devise, Fain, Force, Free, Game, General, Hay, Holographic, Leave, Legator, Leve, Lief, Lieve, Living, Noncupative, Obedient, On, Please, Prone, Purpose, Raring, Rather, Ready, Receptive, Scarlet, Soon, Spirit, Swan, Testament, Testate, Volition, Voluntary, Volunteer, Way, Wimble, Woot

▷ **Will** *may indicate* an anagram

William(s) Bill(y), Conqueror, Occam, Orange, Pear, Rufus, Silent, Sweet, Tell, Tennessee

Will o' the wisp Fen-fire, Friar's lantern, Ignis-fatuus, Jack o'lantern, Min min, Nightfire, Rush

Willow(ing), Willowy Crack, Diamond, Lissom(e), Lithe, Osier, Poplar, Port Jackson, Pussy, Salix, Sallow, Sauch, Saugh, Supple, Twilly, Weeping, Withy

Willpower Ab(o)uha, Determination, Strength

Willy-nilly Nolens volens, Perforce
Wilt Decline, Droop, Fade, Flag, Sap, Shalt, Wither
Wiltshireman Moonraker
▶ **Wily** *see* WILE
Wimple Gorget, Meander, Ripple, Turn
▷ **Wimple** *may indicate* an anagram
Win(ner), Winning Achieve, > BEAT, Capot, Champion, Conciliate, Conquer,
  Cup, Cute, Decider, Disarming, Dormie, Dormy, Earn, Endearing, First, Gain,
  Gammon, Hit, Jackpot, Land, Laureate, Lead, Medallist, Motser, Motza, Nice,
  Pile, Pot, Prevail, Profit, Purler, Repique, Result, Rubicon, Shoo-in, Slam, Snip,
  Success, Sweet, Take, > TRIUMPH, Up, Vellet, Velvet, Victor(y), Vole, Walk over,
  Wrest
Wince Blench, Cringe, Flinch, Recoil
Winch Crab, Crane, Jack, Windlass
Winchester® Rifle
Wind(er), Winding(s), Windy Aeolian, Air, Airstream, Ambages, Anabatic,
  Anfractuous, Anti-trade, Aquilo(n), Argestes, Auster, Backing, Baguio, Bend,
  Berg, Bise, Blore, Blow, Bluster, Bora, Boreas, Bottom, Bourasque, Brass,
  Breeze, Brickfielder, Buran, Burp, Buster, Cape doctor, Capstan, Carminative,
  Caurus, Chili, Chill, Chinook, Coil, Colic, Cordonazo, Corus, Crank, Creeky,
  Curl, Cyclone, Downwash, Draught, Draw, Dust devil, Easterly, Etesian,
  Euraquilo, Euroclydon, Eurus, Evagation, Favonian, Favonius, Fearful, Firn,
  Flatulence, Flatus, Flaw, Fo(e)hn, Gale, Gas, G(h)ibli, Gregale, Gust, Haboob,
  Harmattan, Heaves, Hurricane, Hurricano, Jet stream, Kamseen, Katabatic,
  K(h)amsin, Knee-swell, Levant(er), Libecc(h)io, Libs, Link, Meander, Meltemi,
  Mistral, Monsoon, Muzzler, Nervous, Noreast, Norther, Nor(th)wester(ly),
  Noser, Notus, Pampero, Periodic, Ponent, Poop, Prevailing, Puna, Purl, Quill,
  Reeds, Reel, Rip-snorter, Roll, Samiel, Sciroc, Scirocco, Screw, Sea, Second,
  Series, Serpentine, Shamal, Shimaal, Simoom, Simoon, Sinuous, Sirocco,
  Slant, Snake, Snifter, Snorter, Solano, Solar, Sough, Souther, Southerly buster,
  Spiral, Spool, Squall, Stellar, Sumatra, Surface, Swirl, Tail, Tehuantepecer,
  Thread, Throw, Tornado, Tortuous, Tourbillon, Trade, Tramontana, Trend,
  Turn, Twaddle, Twine, Twister, Twisty, Typhon, Typhoon, Vayu, Veer,
  Veering, Ventose, Volturnus, Waffle, Weave, Wester, Westerly, Whirlblast,
  White squall, Williwaw, Willy-willy, Winch, Woold, Wrap, Wreathe, Wrest,
  Wuthering, Zephyr(us), Zonda
Windbag Balloon, Bore, Drogue, Prattler, Whoopee cushion, Zeppelin
Windfall Bonanza, Buckshee, Caduac, Fortune, Godsend, Manna
Windflower Anemone
Windlass Differential, Spanish, Whim, Winch
Windmill Post, Smock, Whirligig
Window(s) Atmosphere, Bay, Bow, Casement, Catherine-wheel, Companion,
  Compass, Day, Deadlight, Dormer, Dream-hole, Eye, Eyelids, Fanlight,
  Fenestella, Fenestra, French, Gable, Garret, Glaze, Guichet, Jalousie, Jesse,
  Judas, Lancet, Lattice, Launch, Loop-light, Louver, Louvre, Lozen, Lucarne,
  Lunette, Luthern, Lychnoscope, Marigold, Mezzanine, Mirador, Monial,
  Mullion, Oculus, Oeil-de-boeuf, Ogive, Orb, Oriel, Ox-eye, Pane, Pede,
  Picture, Porthole, Quarterlight, Radio, Re-entry, Rosace, Rose, Sash, Sexfoil,
  Spyhole, Storm, Transom, Trellis, Ventana, Weather, Wheel, Wicket, Windock,
  Winnock
Window-bar, Window-fastening Astragal, Espagnolette
Windpipe Bronchus, Gular, Throat, Trachea, Weasand

Windscale Beaufort
Windsock Drogue, Sleeve
Windswept Scud
Wind-up End, Fright, Liquidate, Span
Windward Ahold, Aloof, Laveer, Luff, Up
Wine Bin, Cup, Essence, Fortified, Low, Must, Piece, Premier cru, Prisage, Rotgut, Rouge, The grape, Vat, Vintage

● **WINES**

● **2 letters:**
● It

● **3 letters:**
● Dao
● Red
● Sec
● Tun
● Vin

● **4 letters:**
● Asti
● Brut
● Cava
● Hock
● Mull
● Palm
● Pipe
● Port
● Race
● Rosé
● Rosy
● Sack
● Sekt
● Stum
● Tent
● Tutu
● Vino

● **5 letters:**
● Anjou
● Anker
● Biddy
● Blanc
● Bombo
● Comet
● Cuvée
● Gallo
● Macon
● Medoc
● Mirin
● Mosel

Negus
Pinot
Plonk
Rhine
Rioja
Soave
Straw
Syrah
Table
Tavel
Toddy
Tokay
White
Xeres

6 letters:
Barley
Barolo
Barsac
Beaune
Bishop
Bubbly
Canary
Claret
Ginger
Graves
Lisbon
Malaga
Merlot
Muscat
Piment
Plotty
Red Ned
Shiraz

7 letters:
Alicant
Amoroso
Auslese
Bastard
Catawba
Chablis

Chateau
Chianti
Cowslip
Demi-sec
Dessert
Eiswein
Fendant
Icewine
Madeira
Malmsey
Margaux
Marsala
Moselle
Oenomel
Orvieto
Pomerol
Pommard
Retsina
Rhenish
Sangria
Terroir
Vouvray

8 letters:
Bordeaux
Bucellas
Buckfast®
Burgundy
Cabernet
Champers
Charneco
Dubonnet®
Espumoso
Essencia
Frascati
Gluhwein
Jerepigo
Kabinett
Log-juice
Malvasia
Malvesie
Montilla

Mountain
Muscadel
Muscadet
Muscatel
Oenology
Pinotage
Pradikat
Red biddy
Resinata
Rheingau
Riesling
Sancerre
Sangaree
Sauterne
Semillon
Spätlese
Spumante
St Julien
Sylvaner
Verdelho
Vermouth

9 letters:
Bacharach
Bardolino
Champagne
En primeur
Falernian
Gladstone
Hermitage
Hippocras
Hoccamore
Inglenook
Lambrusco
Languedoc
Loll-shrob
Malvoisie
Meersault
Muscadine
Ordinaire
Pinot noir
Sauvignon

- Sauvignon
- Sparkling
- St Emilion
- Tafelwein
- Tarragona
- Zinfandel

10 letters:
- Beaujolais
- Bull's blood
- Chambertin
- Chardonnay
- Constantia
- Elderberry
- Genevrette
- Hochheimer
- Loll-shraub

Manzanilla
Montrachet
Muscadelle
Napa Valley
Peter-see-me
Piesporter
Vinho verde

11 letters:
Amontillado
Dom Perignon
Niersteiner
Pouilly-Fume
Rudesheimer
Scuppernong
Steinberger

12 letters:
Johannisberg
Marcobrunner
Supernaculum
Valpolicella
Vin ordinaire

13 letters:
Beerenauslese
Entre-Deux-Mers
Liebfraumilch
Pouilly-Fousse

14 letters:
Gewürztraminer
Johannisberger

15 letters:
Lachryma Christi

17 letters:
Cabernet
Sauvignon
Chateaux
cardboard
Nuits Saint
Georges

20 letters:
Trockenbeeren-
auslese

Wine-cellar, Wine-shop Bistro, Bodega, Vault, Vaut(e)
Wine-glass Flute
Wine-making Gallising, Remuage
Wing(ed), Winger, Wings, Wing-like Aerofoil, Ala(r), Alula, Annexe, Appendage,
  Arm, Bastard, > BIRD, Branch, Canard, Cellar, Corium, Coulisse, Delta,
  Dipteral, El(l), Elevon, Elytral, Elytriform, Elytron, Elytrum, Fender, Flap, Flew,
  Flex, Flipper, Flying, Forward, Gull, Halteres, Hurt, Left, Limb, Parascenia,
  Parascenium, Patagium, Pennate, Pennon, Pinero, Pinion, Pip, Pterygoid,
  Putto, Right, Rogallo, Sail, Samariform, Scent-scale, Segreant, Seraphim, Split,
  Standard, Sweepback, Sweptback, Sweptwing, Swift, Swingwing, Tailplane,
  Tectrix, Tegmen, Transept, Van, Vol(et), Wound(ed)
Winged sandals Talaria
▷ **Winger** *may indicate* a bird
Wing-footed Aliped, Fleet, Swift
Wingless Apteral
Wink (at) Atone, Bat, Condone, Connive, Eyelid, Flicker, Ignore, Instant, Nap,
  Nictitate, Pink, Twinkle
Winnie Pooh
Winnow Fan, Riddle, Separate, Sift, Van, Wecht
Winsome Bonny, Engaging, Gay, Pleasant
Winter, Wintry Blackthorn, Bleak, Brumal, Cold, Dec, Fimbul, Frigid, Frore,
  Hibernate, Hiemal, Hiems, Hodiernal, Jack Frost, Jasmine, Nuclear, Snowy, W
Winter cherry Chinese lantern
Wintergreen Sarcodes
Winter pear Nelis
Winter-sport Ski
Wipe (out), Wiping Abolish, Abrogate, Absterge, Amortise, Cancel, Cleanse,
  Demolish, Destroy, Deterge, Dicht, Dight, Eradicate, Expunge, Hanky, Mop,
  Nose-rag, Null, Purge, Raze, Reroussage, Slorm, Sponge, Tersion, Tissue
Wire(s), Wiry Aerial, Barb(ed), Cable, Cat's whiskers, Chicken, Coil, Earth,
  Fencing, Filament, Filar, File, Heald, Heddle, High, Kirschner, Lean, Lecher,
  Live, Marconigram, Mil, Nichrome®, Nipper, Piano, Pickpocket, Razor, Sevice,
  Shroud, Sinewy, Snake, Solenoid, Spit, Staple, Stilet, Strand, String, Stylet,
  Telegram, Telegraph, Thoth, Thread, Trace

Wireless (operator), Wireless part Baffle, Set, Sparks, Valve

Wise(acre), Wisdom Advisedly, Ancient, Astute, Athena, Athene, Canny, Depth, Ernie, Ganesa, Gothamite, Hep, Hindsight, Judgement, Judicious, Learned, Long-headed, Lore, Manner, Mimir, Minerva, Norman, Oracle, Owl, Penny, Philosopher, Philosophy, Politic, Polymath, Prajna, Profound, Prudence, Sagacity, Sage, Salomonic, Sapience, Savvy, Shrewd, Smartie, Solomon, Solon, Sophia, Wice

Wisecrack Dig, One-liner

Wise man Balthazar, Caspar, Heptad, Melchior, Nestor, Sage, Sapient, Seer, Solomon, Swami, Thales, Tohunga, Worldly

Wish(es) Crave, Death, Desiderate, > DESIRE, Hope, List, Long, Pant, Pleasure, Precatory, Regards, Velleity, Want, Yearn

Wishbone Furcula, Marriage-bone, Merrythought, Skipjack

Wishy-washy Bland, Feeble, Insipid, Irresolute, Milksop, Weak, Wheyey

Wisp(y) Cirrate, Frail, Scrap, Shred, Virga, Wase

Wit(s), Witticism, Witty Acumen, Attic, Badinage, Banter, Brevity, Commonsense, Concetto, Cunning, Dry, Epigram, Esprit, Estimation, Eutrapelia, Eutrapely, Facetious, Fantasy, Hartford, Humour, Imagination, Intelligence, Irony, Jest, Jeu d'esprit, Joke, Marbles, Marinism, Memory, Mind, Mot, Mother, Native, Nous, Pawky, Pun, Repartee, Rogue, Sally, Salt, Saut, Sconce, > SENSE, Shaft, Smart, Videlicet, Viz, Wag, Weet, Wisecrack, Word-play

Witch(craft) Broomstick, Cantrip, Carline, Circe, Coven, Craigfluke, Crone, Cutty Sark, Enchantress, Ensorcell, Galdragon, Glamour, Goety, Gramary(e), Gyre-carlin, Hag, Hecat(e), Hex, Invultuation, Lamia, Magic, Medea, Myal(ism), Necromancy, Night-hag, Obeahism, Obiism, Pythoness, Salem, Selim, Sibyl, Sieve, Sorceress, Speller, Sycorax, Trout, Valkyrie, Vaudoo, Vilia, Voodoo, Weird, Wicca

Witch-doctor Boyla, Medicine man, Mganga, Obi, Pawaw, Powwow, Sangoma, Shaman

Witch-hazel Fothergilla, Platan(e), Winter-bloom

Witch-hunter McCarthy

With And, By, Con, Cum, Hereby, In, Mit, Of, Plus, W

Withdraw(al), Withdrawn Abdicate, Alienate, Aloof, Cold turkey, Cry off, Detach, Disengage, Distrait, Enshell, Evacuate, Hive off, Inshell, Introvert, Offish, Palinode, Preserve, Recant, Recoil, Repair, Resile, Reticent, Retire, Retract(ion), Retreat, Revoke, Revulsion, Scratch, Secede, Sequester, Shrink, Shy, Stand down, Subduct, Unreeve, Unsay

Wither(ed), Withering, Withers Arefy, Atrophy, Blight, Burn, Corky, Die, Droop, Dry, Evanish, Fade, Forpine, Googie, Languish, Marcescent, Miff, Nose, Scram, Sere, Shrink, Shrivel, Welk, Welt

Withershins Eastlin(g)s

▷ **With gaucherie** *may indicate* an anagram

Withhold(ing) Abstain, Conceal, Curt, Deny, Detain, Detinue, Hide, Keep, > RESERVE, Trover

Within Enclosed, Endo-, Immanent, Indoors, Inside, Interior, Intra

With it Hep, Hip, Syn, Trendy, W

Without Bar, Beyond, Ex, Lack(ing), Less, Minus, Orb, Outdoors, Outside, Sans, Save, Sen, Senza, Sine, X

▷ **Without** *may indicate* one word surrounding another

▷ **Without restraint** *may indicate* an anagram

Without stimulus Nastic

Withstand Blight, Brave, Contest, Defy, Endure, Oppose, Resist, Weather

Witness Attest, Bystander, Compurgator, Crown, Deponent, Depose, Evidence, Expert, Hostile, Jehovah's, Martyr, Material, Muggletonian, Observe, Obtest, Onlooker, Proof, > SEE, Testament, Teste, Testify, Testimony

Witness-box Peter, Stand

▶ **Witticism** *see* WIT

Wizard (priest) Archimage, Carpathian, Conjuror, Expert, Gandalf, Hex, Magician, Merlin, Oz, Prospero, Shaman, Sorcerer, Super, Warlock, > WITCH-DOCTOR

Wizen(ed) Dehydrate, Dry, Sere, Shrivel, Sphacelate, Wither

Woad Anil, Dye, Indigo, Isatis, Pastel, Pastil

Wobble, Wobbling, Wobbly Chandler's, Coggle, Precess, Quaver, Reel, Rock, Shoggle, Shoogle, Totter, Tremble, Trillo, Unstable, Wag, Waggle, Walty, Waver, Wibble

Wodehouse Plum

Woe(ful) Alack, Alas, Bale, Bane, Distress, Doole, Dule, Ewhow, Gram, Grief, Jeremiad, Lack-a-day, Misery, Pain, Plague, > SORROW, Torment, Tribulation, Unhappy

Wolf(ish), Wolf-like Akela, Assyrian, Bolt, Cancer, Casanova, Coyote, Cram, Dangler, Earth, Engorge, Fenrir, Fenris, Gorge, Grey, Ise(n)grim, Lobo, Lone, Lothario, Lupine, Luster, Lycanthrope, MI, Michigan, Pack, Prairie, Rake, Ravenous, Red, Rip, Roué, Rout, Rye, Scoff, Sea, Strand, Tasmanian, Thylacine, Tiger, Timber, Wanderer, Were, Whistler

Wolfram Tungsten

Wolf's bane Aconite, Friar's-cap

Wolseley Sir Garnet

Woman(hood), Women Anile, Bellibone, Besom, Biddy, Bimbo, Bint, Boiler, Broad, Cailleach, Callet, Chai, Chapess, Chook, Citess, Crone, Cummer, Dame, Daughter, Distaff, Doe, Dona(h), Dorcas, Doris, Drab, Eve, F, Fair, Fair sex, > FEMALE, Feme, Flapper, Floozy, Frail, Frow, Gammer, Gimmer, Gin, Girl, Gyno-, -gyny, Harpy, Harridan, Hen, Her, Inner, Jade, Jane, Lady, Liberated, Lilith, Lorette, Madam(e), Mademoiselle, Maenad, Mary, Miladi, Milady, Mob, Mort, Ms, Muliebrity, Pandora, Peat, Pict, Piece, Piece of goods, Placket, Popsy, Quean, Queen, Ramp, Rib, Ribibe, Ronyon, Rudas, Runnion, Sabine, Sakti, Scarlet, Shakti, She, Skirt, Sort, Squaw, Tail, Tedesca, Tib, Tiring, Tit, Tottie, Totty, Trot, Umfazi, Vahine, Wahine, Weaker sex, Wifie

Womaniser Casanova, Lady-killer, Poodle-faker, Wolf

Womb Belly, Matrix, Metritis, Side, Uterus, Ventricle

Women's club, Women's lib S(h)akti, Soroptimist

Won Chon, W

Wonder(s) Admire, Agape, Amazement, AR, Arkansas, Arrah, Awe, Colossus, Ferly, Grape-seed, Marle, > MARVEL, Meteor, Mirabilia, Miracle, Muse, Nine-day, Phenomenon, Prodigy, Seven, Speculate, Stupor, Suppose, Surprise, Wheugh, Whew, Wow

Wonderful(ly) Amazing, Bees' knees, Bitchin(g), Chinless, Épatant, Fantastic, Far-out, Ferly, Geason, Gee-whiz, Glorious, Gramercy, Great, Keen, Lal(l)apalooza, Magic, Mirable, Old, Purely, Ripping, Smashing, Sublime, Superb

Wonder-worker Fakir, Thaumaturgist, Thaumaturgus

Wonky Cockeyed

Wont(ed) Accustomed, Apt, Custom, Habit, Shan't, Used, Winna

Woo(er) Address, Beau, Carve, Court, Seduce, Suitor, Swain

Wood(en), Woodland, Woody Arboretum, Batten, Beam, Board, Boord(e),

Brake, Cask, Channel, Chipboard, Clapboard, Conductor, Dead, Deadpan, Expressionless, Fathom, Fire, Fish, Funk, Furious, Gantry, Gauntree, Hanger, Hard, Hyle, Kindling, Knee, Lath, Lumber, Nemoral, Nemorous, Offcut, Pallet, Plastic, Pulpwood, Punk, Silvan, Slat, Spinney, Splat, Spline, Splint, Stolid, Sylvan, Three-ply, Timber, Tinder, Touch, Treen, Trees, Twiggy, Vert, Xylem, Xyloid

WOOD

3 letters:
Ash
Box
Cam
Elm
Log
Mad
Red

4 letters:
Beef
Bent
Bowl
Carr
Cord
Cork
Deal
Eugh
Gapó
Holt
Iron
King
Lana
Lima
Lime
Rata
Rock
Shaw
Soft
Spar
Wild
Yang

5 letters:
Agila
Algum
Almug
Balsa
Bavin
Beech
Cedar
Copse
Drive

Ebony
Elfin
Firth
Frith
Green
Grove
Heben
Hurst
Igapó
Iroko
Jarul
Joist
Kokra
Lance
Maple
Mazer
Myall
Opepe
Peach
Plane
Ramin
Rowan
Sapan
Spoon
Stink
Taiga
Thorn
Tiger
Tulip
Zante
Zebra

6 letters:
Alerce
Bamboo
Beaver
Birnam
Bocage
Brazil
Canary
Carapa
Cheese
Citron

Citrus
Dingle
Forest
Fustet
Fustic
Fustoc
Gaboon
Gopher
Jarool
Jarrah
Letter
Lignum
Loggat
Manuka
Miombo
Obeche
Orache
Orange
Paddle
Poplar
Raddle
Sabele
Sabicu
Sandal
Sapele
Sappan
Sissoo
Sponge
Tallow
Waboom
Walnut
Wandoo
Yellow

7 letters:
Amboina
Baywood
Boscage
Brassie
Cambium
Coppice
Dudgeon
Dunnage

Duramen
Gambrel
Gumwood
Hadrome
Hickory
Leopard
Meranti
Palmyra
Paranym
Pimento
Sanders
Sapwood
Shawnee
Shittim
Wallaba

8 letters:
Agalloch
Alburnum
Basswood
Bushveld
Caatinga
Coulisse
Harewood
Hornbeam
Kingwood
Laburnum
Ligneous
Mahogany
Pyengadu
Pyinkado
Rosewood
Sapucaia
Shagbark
Southern
Tamarack

9 letters:
Briarwood
Butternut
Caliature
Campeachy
Cocuswood

- Eaglewood
- Fruitwood
- Heartwood
- Ivorywood
- Krummholz
- Matchwood
- Partridge
- Porcupine

Quebracho
Satinwood

10 letters:
Afrormosia
Blockboard
Bulletwood
Calamander

Candlewood
Chittagong
Coromandel
Fiddlewood
Greenheart
Hackmatack
Nettle-tree
Palisander

Springwood
Summerwood

11 letters:
Lignum-vitae
Sanderswood
Slippery elm

▷ **Wood** *may indicate* an anagram (in sense of mad)
Wood-carver Bodger, Gibbons, Whittler
Woodchuck Bobac, Marmot
Woodcock Becasse, Beccaccia, Snipe
Woodlouse Isopod, Oniscus, Slater
Woodman Ali (Baba), Feller, Forester, Hewer, Logger, Lumberjack, Sawyer
Woodpecker Bird, Flicker, Hickwall, Picarian, Rainbird, Sapsucker, Saurognathae, Witwall, Woodwale, Yaffle
Wood-pigeon Bird, Cushat, Que(e)st, Qu(o)ist
Wood-sorrel Oca
Wood-tar Furan, Furfuran
Woodwind Bassoon, Clarinet, Cornet, Flute, Oboe, Piccolo, Pipe, Recorder, Reed
Woodwork(er) Sloid, Sloyd, Tarsia, Termite
Woodworm Gribble, Termes
Wookey Stalactite
Wool(len), Woolly Alpaca, Angora, Aran, Ardil, Bainin, Barège, Beige, Berlin, Botany, Bouclé, Calamanco, Cardi(gan), Cashmere, Cas(s)imere, Clip, Cotton, Crutchings, Daglock, Delaine, Doeskin, Dog, Doily, Down, Doyley, Drugget, Duffel, Fadge, Fingering, Fleece, Flock, Frib, Frieze, Fuzz, Glass, Greasy, Guernsey, Hank, Hause-lock, Hogget, Indumentum, Jaeger, Jersey, Kashmir, Ket, Lanate, Laniferous, Lanigerous, Lanose, Lock, Loden, Merino, Mineral, Mortling, Moul, Mullein, New, Noil(s), Nun's-veiling, Offsorts, Oo, Pashm, Pelage, Persian, Qiviut, Rock, Rolag, Sagathy, Saxon, Say, Shahtoosh, Shalloon, Shamina, Shetland, Shoddy, Skein, Slipe, Slip-on, Slub, Spencer, Staple, Steel, Strouding, Swansdown, Tamise, Tammy, Thibet, Three-ply, Tod, Tricot, Tweed, Twin set, Vicuna, Virgin, Wire, Wood, Worcester, Yarn, Zephyr, Zibel(l)ine
Wool-gather(er), Woolgathering Argo, Dreamer, Reverie
Wool-holder, Woolsack Bale, Distaff
Woolly-bear Tiger-moth, Woubit
Wool-oil Yolk
Wooster Bertie
Woozy Drunk, Vague, Woolly
Worcester Wigorn
Word(s), Wording, Wordy Appellative, Bahuvrihi, Buzz, Cheville, Claptrap, Clipped, Code, Comment, Content, Dick, Dit(t), Echoic, Embolalia, Enclitic, Epos, Etymon, Faith, Four-letter, Function, Ghost, Grace, Hard, Heteronym, Hint, Homograph, Homonym, Household, Hyponym, > **IN A WORD,** > **IN TWO WORDS,** Janus, Jonah, Key, Last, Lexeme, Lexicon, Lexis, Loan, Logia, Logos, Long-winded, Lyrics, Mantra, Message, Morpheme, Mot, Neologism, News, Nonce, Nonsense, Noun, Oracle, Order, Palabra, Paragram, Parole, Paroxytone, Particle, Perissology, Phrase, Piano, Pledge, Pleonasm, Polysemen, Portmanteau, Preposition, Prolix, Promise, Pronoun, Reserved, Rhematic, Rumour, Saying, Selah, Semantics, Signal, Subtitle, Surtitle, Term, Tetragram,

Text, Trigger, Trope, Typewriter, Verb, Verbiage, Verbose, Vogue, Warcry, Weasel, Wort, Written

Word-blindness Alexia, Dyslexia

Word-play Charade, Paronomasia, Pun

Workable Feasible, Practical

Workaholic, Work(er), Working(-class), Workmen, Works, Workman(ship) Act(ivate), Ant, Appliqué, Apronman, Artefact, Artel, Artifact, Artificer, Artisan, Beaver, Bee, Blue-collar, Bohunk, Boondoggle, Bull, Business, Careerist, Casual, Char, Chargehand, Chore, Claim, Clock, Coolie, Corvée, Crew, Darg, Do, Dog, Dogsbody, Droil, Drudge, Drug, Dung, Earn, Effect, Effort, Em, Erg(ataner), Ergatoid, Erg-nine, Ergon, Ergonomics, Erg-ten, Eta, Evince, Exercise, Exploit, Factotum, Facture, Fat, Fettler, Field, Floruit, Fret, Fuller, > **FUNCTION**, Gastarbeiter, Gel, Go, Graft, Grass, Grind, Grisette, Hand, Harness, Hat, Hobo, Horse, Hunky, Industry, Innards, Job, Journeyman, Key, Knead, Kolhoznik, Labour, Laid, Luddite, Lump, Machinist, Man, Manipulate, Manpower, Mechanic, Meng, Menial, Midinette, Mine, Ming, MO, Moider, Moil, Moonlight, Movement, Navvy, Neuter, Number, Oeuvre, On, Op, Opera(tion), Operative, Operator, Opus, Opusc(u)le, Outside, Ouvrier, Ox, Parergon, Part, Peasant, Peg, Pensum, Peon, Ply, Portfolio, Potboiler, Practise, Production, Prole(tariat), Prud'homme, Public, Pursuit, Red-neck, Rep, Ride, Robot, Roughneck, Rouseabout, Roustabout, Run, Samiti, Satisfactory, Scabble, Scapple, Serve, Service, Servile, Shift, Shop, Situation, Slogger, Smithy, Social, Staff, Stakhanovite, Stevedore, Stint, Strap, Straw, Strive, Support, Surface, Swaggie, Swagman, Sweat, Swink, Take, Tamper, Task, Temp, Tenail(le), Tenaillon, Termite, Tew, Tick, Till, Toccata, Toil, Toreutic, Travail, Treatise, Trojan, TU, Tut, Typto, Uphill, Wage plug, Walla(h), Wark, White-collar, Wobblies, Yacker, Yakka, Yakker

Work-basket, Workbox Caba(s), Nécessaire

Workbench Siege

Workhouse Casual ward, Spike, Union

▷ **Working** *may indicate* an anagram

Working-party Bee, Quilting-bee, Sewing-bee, Squad

Workmate Yokefellow

Work out Deduce

Works, Workshop Atelier, Engine, Factory, Forge, Foundry, Garage, Hacienda, Hangar, Innards, Lab, Mill, Passage, Plant, Public, Shed, Shop, Skylab, Smithy, Studio, Sweatshop, Telecottage, Time, Tin, Upper

Workshy Sweer(ed), Sweert, Sweir(t)

World(ly), Worldwide Carnal, Chthonic, Cosmopolitan, Cosmos, Dream, Earth, Fleshly, Fourth, Free, Ge, Globe, Kingdom, Lay, Lower, Mappemond, Microcosm, Mondaine, Mondial, Mould, Mundane, Nether, New, Old, Orb, Other, Oyster, Planet, Possible, Secular, Sensual, Society, Sphere, Spirit, Temporal, Terra, Terrene, Terrestrial, Third, Universe, Vale, Web, Welt

Worm(-like), Worms, Wormy Acorn, Anguillula, Annelid, Annulata, Apod(e), Apodous, Army, Arrow, Articulata, Ascarid, Bilharzia, Bladder, Blind, Blood, Bob, Bootlace, Brandling, Bristle, Caddis, Capeworm, Caseworm, Catworm, Cestode, Cestoid, Chaetopod, Clamworm, Copper, Dew, Diet, Diplozoon, Edge, Enteropneust, Fan, Filander, Filaria, Flag, Flat, Fluke, Galley, Gape, Gilt-tail, Gordius, Gourd, Guinea, Hair-eel, Hairworm, Heartworm, Helminth, Hemichordata, Hookworm, Horsehair, Idle, Inchworm, Leech, Liver-fluke, Lob, Lumbricus, Lytta, Maw, Measuring, Merosome, Miner's, Mopani, Nematoda, Nematode, Nemertea, Nereid, Night-crawler, Oligochaete,

Paddle, Palmer, Palolo, Paste-eel, Peripatus, Piper, Planarian, Platyhelminth, Polychaete, Ragworm, Ribbon, Roundworm, Sabella, Sand-mason, Schistosome, Scleciform, Scolex, Seamouse, Serpula, Servile, Ship, Sipunculacea, Sipunculoidea, Stomach, Strawworm, Strongyl(e), Taenia, Tag-tail, Taint, Tapeworm, Tenioid, Teredo, Termite, Threadworm, Tiger tail, Tongue, Toxocara, Trematode, Trichina, Trichin(ell)a, Trichinosed, Triclad, Tube, Tubifex, Turbellaria, Vermiform, Vinegar, Vinegar eel, Wheat-eel, Wheatworm, Whipworm

Wormkiller Anthelmintic, Santonin

Wormwood Absinth, Appleringie, Artemisia, Mugwort, Santonica, Southernwood

Worn (out) Attrite, Bare, Decrepit, Detrition, Effete, Epuisé, Exhausted, Forfairn, Forfoughten, Forjaskit, Forjeskit, Frazzled, Knackered, Old, On, Passé, Raddled, Rag, Seedy, Shabby, Shot, Spent, Stale, Tired, Traikit, Trite, Used, Weathered, Whacked

Worried, Worrier, Worry Agonise, Angst, Annoy, Anxiety, Badger, Bait, Beset, Bother, Care(worn), Cark, Chafe, Concern, Deave, Deeve, Distress, Disturb, Dog, Eat, Exercise, Feeze, Frab, Fret, Fuss, Harass, Harry, Headache, Hyp, Inquietude, Knag, Nag, Perturb, Pester, Pheese, Pheeze, Phese, Pingle, Pium, Preoccupy, Rile, Sool, Stew, Tew, Touse, Towse, Trouble, Unease, Unnerve, Vex, Wherrit, Worn

▷ **Worried** *may indicate* an anagram

Worse(n) Adversely, Degenerate, Deteriorate, Exacerbate, Impair, Inflame, Pejorate, Regress, War(re), Waur

Worship(per) Adore, Adulation, Ancestor, Angelolatry, Autolatry, Bless, Churchgoer, Cult, Deify, Devotion, Douleia, Dulia, Epeolatry, Exercise, Fetish, Glorify, Gurdwara, Happy-clappy, Henotheism, Hero, Idolatry, Idolise, Latria, Lauds, Lionise, Liturgics, Lordolatry, Mariolatry, Oncer, Orant, Praise, Puja, Revere, Sabaism, Sakta, Service, Shacharis, Shakta, Sun, Synaxis, Thiasus, Vaishnava, Venerate, Votary, Wodenism

Worst Beat, Best, Defeat, Get, Nadir, Outdo, Overpower, Pessimum, Rock-bottom, Scum, Severest, The pits, Throw, Trounce

Worsted Caddis, Caddyss, Challis, Coburg, Genappe, Lea, Ley, Serge, Shalli, Tamin(e), Whipcord

▷ **Worsted** *may indicate* an anagram

Wort Laser, Parkleaves, Plant, Tutsan

Worth(while), Worthy, Worthies Admirable, Asset, Be, Cop, Cost, Deserving, Eligible, Estimable, Feck, > MERIT, Nine, Notable, Substance, Tanti, Use, Value, Venerable, Virtuous, Wealth

Worthless (person) Base, Beggarly, Bilge, Blown, Bodger, Bootless, Bum, Catchpenny, Cheapjack, Crumb, Cypher, Damn, Despicable, Docken, Dodkin, Doit, Doitkin, Draffish, Draffy, Dreck, Dross, Fallal, Footra, Fouter, Foutre, Frippery, Gimcrack, Gingerbread, Glop, Gubbins, Hilding, Javel, Jimcrack, Left, Light, Lorel, Lorrell, Losel, Lozell, Manky, Mare's nest, Mud, Nugatory, Nyaff, Obol, Orra, Otiose, Paltry, Pin, Poxy, Punk, Raca, Rag, Rap, Riffraff, Rubbishy, Scabby, Scum, Shinkin, Shotten, Siwash, Sorry, Straw, Tinhorn, Tinpot, Tinsel, Tittle, Toerag, Trangam, Trashy, Trumpery, Tuppenny, Twat, Two-bit, Twopenny, Useless, Vain, Vile, Waff, Wanworthy, Wauff

Wotchermean Anan

Would be Assumed, Pseudo, Soi-disant

Wouldn't Nould(e)

Wound(ed) Battery, Bite, Bless, Blighty, Bruise, Chagrin, Coiled, Crepance,

Cut, Dere, Engore, Flesh, Ganch, Gash, Gaunch, Gore, Harm, Hurt, Injury,
Lacerate, Lesion, Maim, Molest, Mortify, Offend, Pip, Sabre-cut, Scab, Scar,
Scath, Scotch, Scratch, Shoot, Snaked, Snub, Sore, Stab, Sting, Trauma, Twined,
Umbrage, Vuln, Vulnerary, Walking, Wing, Wint

Woven Faconne, Knitted, Pirnit, Textile, Wattle

Wow Amaze, Howl, My, Success

Wrack Destroy, Downfall, Kelp, Ore, Torment, Varec(h), Vengeance

Wraith Apparition, Fetch, Ghost, Phantom, Shadow, Spectre

Wrangle(r), Wrangling Altercate, Argie-bargie, > ARGUE, Bandy, Bicker, Brangle,
Broil, Dispute, Haggle, Mathematical, Rag, Second, Senior, Vitilitigation

Wrap(per), Wrapping, Wrap up Amice, Amis, Bind, Body, Bubble, Bundle,
Cellophane®, Cere, Clingfilm, Cloak, Clothe, Cocoon, Conclude, Emboss,
Enfold, Enrol(l), Ensheath(e), Envelop(e), Foil, Folio, Furl, Hap, Hem, Kimono,
Kraft, Lag, Lap, Mail, Mob, Muffle, Negligee, Nori, Parcel, Roll, Rug, Shawl,
Sheath(e), Stole, Swaddle, Swathe, Throw, Tinfoil, Tsutsumu, Velamen, Wap,
Wimple

Wrasse Conner, Cunner, Parrot-fish, Scar

Wrath Anger, Cape, Fury, Ire, Passion, Vengeance

Wreak Avenge, Indulge, Inflict

Wreath(e) Adorn, Anadem, Bridal, Chaplet, Coronal, Crown, Entwine, Festoon,
Garland, Laurel, Lei, Torse, Tortile, Twist

Wreathe(d) Hederated

Wreck(age), Wrecked, Wrecker Blotto, Crab, Debris, Demolish, Devastate,
Flotsam, Founder, Goner, Hesperus, Hulk, Lagan, Ligan, Loss, Luddite,
Mutilate, Nervous, Ruin(ate), Sabotage, Shambles, Shatter, Sink, Smash,
Subvert, Torpedo, Trash, Wrack

▷ **Wrecked** *may indicate* an anagram

Wren Architect, Bird, Golden-crested, Hannah, Jenny, Kinglet, Rifleman-bird,
Sailor, Willow

Wrench Allen, Bobbejaan, Box, Fit, Jerk, Lug, Mole, Monkey, Pin, Pipe, Pull,
Socket, Spanner, Spider, Sprain, Stillson®, Strain, Strap, T-bar, Tear, Torque,
Twist, Windlass, Wrest

Wrestle(r), Wrestling All-in, Antaeus, Arm, Basho, Catch-as-catch-can,
Catchweight, Clinch, Featherweight, Flying mare, Folding-press, Freestyle,
Full-nelson, Grapple, Grovet, Half-nelson, Hammerlock, Haystacks, Headlock,
Hip-lock, Indian, Judo, Knee-drop, Makunouchi, Milo, Monkey climb, Mud,
Nelson, Niramiai, Ozeki, Palaestral, Pancratium, Pinfall, Posting, Rikishi,
Sambo, Stable, Struggle, Sumo, Sumotori, Tag, Tag (team), Tussle, Whip,
Wraxle, Wristlock, Writhe, Yokozuna

Wretch(ed) Bally, Blackguard, Blue, Caitiff, Chap-fallen, Cullion, Donder,
Forlorn, Git, Hapless, Lorn, Low, Measly, Miser, Miserable, Peelgarlic,
Pilgarlick, Pipsqueak, Pitiable, Poltroon, Poor, Punk, Rat, Scoundrel, Scroyle,
Seely, Snake, Unblest, Wo(e), Woeful

▷ **Wretched** *may indicate* an anagram

Wriggle Hirsle, Shimmy, Squirm, Twine, Wiggle, Writhe

Wring(er) Drain, Extort, Mangle, Screw, Squeeze, Twist

Wrinkle(d), Wrinkly Clue, Cockle, Corrugate, Crease, Crepy, Crimple, Crimpy,
Crinkle, Crow's-foot, Crumple, Fold, Frounce, Frown, Frumple, Furrow, Gen,
Groove, Headline, Hint, Idea, Line, Lirk, Plissé, Plough, Pucker, Purse, Ridge,
Rimple, Rivel, Rop(e)y, Ruck(le), Rugose, Rumple, Runkle, Seamy, Shrivel,
Sulcus, Time-worn, Tip, Whelk

Wrist Carpus, Radialia, Shackle-bone

Writ(s) Audita querela, Capias, Certiorari, Cursitor, Dedimus, Distringas, Elegit, Fieri facias, Filacer, Habeas corpus, Holy, Injunction, Jury process, Latitat, Law-burrows, Mandamus, Mise, Mittimus, Noverint, Praemunire, Process, Quo warranto, Replevin, Scirefacias, Significat, Subpoena, Summons, Supersedeas, Supplicavit, Tolt, Venire, Venire facias, Warrant

Write(r), Writing Allograph, Amphigory, Annotator, Apocrypha, > **AUTHOR**, Automatic, Ballpoint, Biographer, Biro®, Bloomsbury Group, Book-hand, Boustrophedon, Calligraphy, Causerie, Cento, Charactery, Clerk, Clinquant, Collectanea, Columnist, Copperplate, Creative, Cuneiform, Cursive, Diarist, Dite, Draft, > **DRAMATIST**, Elohist, Endorse, Endoss, Engross, Epigrammatise, Epistle, > **ESSAYIST**, Expatiate, Festschrift, Fist, Form, Formulary, Freelance, Ghost, Gongorism, Graffiti, Grammatology, Graphite, Hack, Hairline, Hand, Haplography, Hieratic, Hieroglyphics, Hiragana, Indite, Ink, Inkhorn-mate, Ink-jerker, Inkslinger, Inscribe, Join-hand, Jot(tings), Journalese, Journalist, Journo, Kalakana, Kaleyard School, Kana, Kanji, Katakana, Keelivine, Keelyvine, Leader, Lexigraphy, Lexis, Linear A, Lipogram, Litterateur, Longhand, Lucubrate, Marivaudage, Minoan, Mirror, Ms(s), Nesk(h), Nib, Notary, Notate, Novelese, > **NOVELIST**, Paragraphia, Pasigraphy, Pen, Pencil, Penmanship, Penne, Penny-a-liner, Pentel®, Picture, Pinyin, Planchette, > **POET**, Polemic, Pot-hook, Proser, Pseudepigrapha, Purana, Purple patch, Quill, Roundhand, Samizdat, Sanskrit, Sci-fi, Scissorer, Scratch, Screed, Screeve, Scribe, Scrip(t), Scripture, Scrivener, Scrow, Scytale, Secretary, Shaster, Shastra, Sign, Sling-ink, Space, Spirit, Stichometry, Style, Subscript, Superscribe, Sutra, Syllabary, Syllabic, Syllabism, Syngraph, Tantra, Transcribe, Treatise, Tushery, Uncial, Wordsmith, Zend-Avesta

WRITERS

3 letters:	Lang	Blake	Innes
APH	Loos	Caine	James
Eco	Loti	Camus	Joyce
Lee	Lyly	Corvo	Kafka
Paz	Mann	Crane	Lewis
Poe	More	Defoe	Lodge
RLS	Nash	Doyle	Lorca
	Opie	Dumas	Mason
4 letters:	Ovid	Eliot	Milne
Amis	Pope	Ellis	Munro
Asch	Saki	Genet	Musil
Aymé	Sand	Gogol	Nashe
Bede	Shaw	Gorky	Orczy
Behn	Snow	Gosse	Ouida
Bolt	Ward	Greer	Pater
Cary	West	Grimm	Paton
Dahl	Zola	Hardy	Pliny
Elia		Harte	Pound
Gide	5 letters:	Henty	Powys
Hope	Acton	Hesse	Reade
Hugo	Albee	Heyer	Renan
Hunt	Auden	Homer	Rilke
King	Ayres	Hoyle	Sagan
Lamb	Bates	Ibsen	Scott

Seuss
Shute
Spark
Stark
Stein
Swift
Synge
Twain
Verne
Vidal
Waugh
Wells
White
Wilde
Woolf
Yates
Yonge

6 letters:
Ambler
Arnold
Artaud
Asimov
Austen
Balzac
Baring
Barrie
Belloc
Bellow
Borges
Borrow
Braine
Bronte
Buchan
Bunyan
Butler
Capote
Cicero
Clarke
Conrad
Cowper
Cronin
Daudet
Dryden
Engels
Fowles
France
Gibbon
Goethe
Graves
Greene
Heller

Hobbes
Hughes
Huxley
Jerome
Jonson
Le Fanu
London
Lucian
Lytton
Mailer
Malory
Mannin
Miller
Milton
Morgan
Nerval
Onions
Orwell
Proust
Racine
Runyon
Ruskin
Sapper
Sappho
Sayers
Sendac
Sewell
Smiles
Steele
Sterne
Stoker
Storey
Thomas
Updike
Virgil
Walton
Wilder

7 letters:
Addison
Aldrich
Aretino
Bagehot
Ballard
Beckett
Bennett
Bentley
Boileau
Boswell
Burgess
Carlyle
Chaucer

Chekhov
Cobbett
Colette
Collins
Cookson
Coppard
Corelli
Cranmer
Deeping
Dickens
Drabble
Dreiser
Durrell
Emerson
Fenelon
Forster
Gissing
Golding
Haggard
Herbert
Hichens
Johnson
Kipling
Lardner
Marryat
Maugham
Mauriac
Mérimée
Mitford
Moravia
Murdoch
Nabokov
Naipaul
Peacock
Pushkin
Pynchon
Ransome
Rostand
Rushdie
Saroyan
Sassoon
Shelley
Simenon
Sitwell
Surtees
Terence
Thoreau
Tolkien
Tolstoy
Travers
Wallace
Walpole

Wharton
Whitman
Wyndham

8 letters:
Andersen
Beaumont
Bradbury
Browning
Caldwell
Cartland
Chandler
Childers
Christie
Constant
De la Mare
Disraeli
Faulkner
Fielding
Flaubert
Forester
Goncourt
Ishiguro
Kingsley
Langland
Lawrence
Mannheim
Meredith
Perrault
Plutarch
Proudhon
Rabelais
Rattigan
Remarque
Rousseau
Salinger
Schiller
Sillitoe
Smollett
Stendhal
Taffrail
Traherne
Trollope
Turgenev
Voltaire
Williams

9 letters:
Aeschylus
Ainsworth
Blackmore
Boccaccio

- Burroughs
- Cervantes
- Dos Passos
- Du Maurier
- Edgeworth
- Goldsmith
- Hawthorne
- Hemingway
- Isherwood
- Lermontov
- Linklater
- Mackenzie
- Madariaga

Mansfield
Martineau
Oppenheim
Pasternak
Priestley
Santayana
Sholokhov
Steinbeck
Stevenson
Thackeray
Wodehouse

10 letters:
Ballantyne
Chesterton
Dostoevsky
Fitzgerald
Galsworthy
Mandeville
Maupassant
Richardson

11 letters:
Machiavelli
Maeterlinck

Shakespeare

12 letters:
Aristophanes
Solzhenitsyn

13 letters:
Chateaubriand
Sackville-West

15 letters:
Somerset
Maugham

Write-off Amortise, Annul, Cancel, Scrap
Writhe, Writhing Athetosis, Contort, Curl, Scriggle, Squirm, Thraw, Twist, Wriggle
▷ **Writhing** *may indicate* an anagram
Writing-case Kalamdan
Writing-room Scriptorium
Wrong Aggrieve, Agley, Amiss, Astray, Awry, Bad, Bum, Chout, Delict, Disservice, Err, Fallacious, False, Falsism, Harm, Ill, Immoral, Improper, Incorrect, Injury, Mischief, Misintelligence, Misled, Mistake(n), Misuse, Nocent, Offbase, Offend, Peccadillo, Perverse, Private, Public, Sin(ful), Tort, Transgress, Unethical, Unright, Unsuitable, Withershins, Wryly, X
▷ **Wrong** *may indicate* an anagram
Wrong opinion Cacodoxy
Wrought (up) Agitated, Beaten, Carved, Created, Excited, Filigree, Freestone, Shaped
Wrung Twisted, Withers
Wry Askew, Contrary, Devious, Distort, Droll, Grimace, Ironic
Wryneck Iynx, Jynx, Torticollis, Yunx
Wycliffian Lollard
Wyoming Wy

Xx

X(-shaped) Buss, By, Chi, Christ, Cross, Decussate, Drawn, Kiss, Ten, Times, Unknown, X-ray

Xant(h)ippe Battle-axe, Dragon

Xenon Xe

Xerophyte, Xerophytic Cactus, Cereus, Mesquite, Tamaricaceae, Tamarisk

Xhosan Caffre, Kaf(f)ir

Ximenes Cardinal

▶ **Xmas** *see* CHRISTMAS

X-ray Angiogram, Anticathode, C(A)T-scanner, Cholangiography, Emi-Scanner, Encephalogram, Encephalograph, Fermi, Grenz, Mammogram, Plate, Pyelogram, Radioscopy, Rem, Roentgen, Sciagram, Screening, Skiagram, Tomography, Venogram, Xeroradiography

Xylophone Marimba, Sticcado, Sticcato

Yy

Y Samian, Unknown, Yankee, Yard, Year, Yen, Yttrium

Yacht Britannia, Dragon, Ice, Keelboat, Ketch, Knockabout, Land, Maxi, Sailboat, Sand

Yachtsman, Yachtsmen Chichester, RYS

Yak Gup, Talk

Yale® Key, Lock

Yam Adjigo, Batata, Breadroot, Camote, Dioscorea, Diosgenin, Kumara

Yank(ee) Bet, Carpetbagger, Hitch, Jerk, Jonathan, Lug, Northerner, Pluck, Pull, Rug, Schlep(p), So(o)le, Sowl(e), > **TUG**, Tweak, Twitch, Wrench, Wrest

▷ **Yank** *may indicate* an anagram

Yap Bark, Yelp

Yard Area, CID, Close, Court, Farm-toun, Garden, Haw, Hof, Kail, Knacker's, Main, Marshalling, Mast, Measure, Navy, Patio, Poultry, Prison, Ree(d), Scotland, Spar, Sprit, Steel, Stick, Stride, Switch, Tilt, Timber, Victualling, Y, Yd

Yarn(s) Abb, Berlin, Bouclé, Caddice, Caddis, Chenille, Clew, Clue, Cop, Cord, Crewel, Fib, Fibroline, Fingering, Genappe, Gimp, Gingham, Guimp(e), Gymp, Homespun, Jaw, Knittle, Knot, Lay, Lea, Ley, Line, Lisle, Lurex®, Marl, Merino, Mohair, Nylon, Organzine, Orlon®, Ply, Rigmarole, Ripping, Rogue's, Rope, Saxony, Schappe, Sennit, Sinnet, Skein, Spun, Story, Strand, Tale, Taradiddle, Thread, Thrid, Thrum(my), Tram, Warp, Weft, Woof, Wool, Worsted, Zephyr

Yarrow Milfoil

Yashmak Veil

Yaw(s) Boba, Buba, Deviate, Framboesia, Lean, Morula, Tack, Veer

Yawn(ing) Boredom, Chasmy, Fissure, Gant, Gape, Gaunt, Greys, Hiant, Oscitation, Pandiculation, Rictus

Yea Certainly, Truly, Verily, Yes

Year(ly), Years A, Age, Anno, Annual, Anomalistic, Astronomical, Calendar, Canicular, Civil, Common, Cosmic, Decennium, Donkey's, Dot, Ecclesiastical, Egyptian, Embolismic, Equinoctial, Financial, Fiscal, Gap, Great, Hebrew, Holy, Indiction, Julian, Leap, Legal, Light, Lunar, Lunisolar, Natural, PA, Perfect, Platonic, Riper, Sabbatical, School, Sidereal, Solar, Sothic, Summer, Sun, Tax, Theban, Time, Towmon(d), Towmont, Tropical, Twelvemonth, Vintage, Wander

Yearbook Annual

Yearling Colt, Hogget, Stirk, Teg

Yearn(ing) Ache, Ake, Aspire, Brame, Burn, Covet, Crave, Curdle, Desire, Erne, Greed, Hanker, Hone, > **LONG**, Nostalgia, Pant, Pine, Sigh

▷ **Yearning** *may indicate* an anagram

Year's end Dec

Yeast Barm, Bees, Brewer's, Ferment, Flor, Leaven, Saccharomycete, Torula, Vegemite®

Yell Cry, Hue, Shout, Skelloch, Thunder, Tiger, Waul, Yoick

Yellow(ish) Abram, Amber, Anthoclore, Auburn, Back, Beige, Bisque, Bistre,

Buff, Butternut, Cadmium, Canary, Chicken, Chrome, Citrine, Cowardly, Craven, Curcumin(e), Daffodil, Etiolin, Fallow, Fever, Filemot, Flavescent, Flavin(e), Flavon, Flaxen, Fulvous, Gamboge, Gold, Icteric, Isabel(le), Isabella, Jack, Jaundiced, Lammer, Lemon(y), Lupulin, Lutein, Lutescent, Mustard, Nankeen, Naples, Oaker, Ochery, Ochre(y), Or(eide), Oroide, Pages, Peril, Pink, Primrose, Queen's, River, Saffron, Sallow, Sand, Sear, Spineless, Straw, Sulphur, Tawny, Topaz, Tow, Vitelline, Weld, Xanthous, Yolk

Yellowhammer Bunting, Yeldring, Yeldrock, Yite, Yoldring

Yellow-wood Gopher

Yelp Cry, Squeal, Whee, Ya(w)p

Yemeni Adeni, Saba, Sabean, Sheba

Yen Desire, Itch, Longing, Urge, Y, Yearn

Yeoman Beefeater, Exon, Goodman, Goodwife, Salvation

Yep OK, Yes

Yes Ay(e), Da, Indeed, Ja, Jokol, Nod, OK, Oke, Quite, Sure, Truly, Uh-huh, Wilco, Yea, Yokul, Yup

Yesterday Démodé, Eve, Hesternal, Pridian

Yet But, Even, How-be, Moreover, Nay, Nevertheless, Now, Still, Though

Yeti Abominable snowman, Sasquatch

Yew Taxus

Yibbles A(i)blins

Yield(ing) Abandon, Afford, Bend, Bow, Breed, Capitulate, Catch, Cede, Come, Comply, Concede, Crack, Crop, Defer, Dividend, Docile, Ductile, Easy, Elastic, Exert, Facile, Flaccid, Flexible, Give, Harvest, Interest, Knuckle, Knuckle under, Meek, Meltith, Mess, Output, Pan, Pay, Pliant, Produce, Redemption, Relent, Render, Return, Sag, Soft, > **SUBMIT**, Succumb, Surrender, Susceptible, Truckle, Weak-kneed

Yodel Song, Warble

Yoga, Yogi As(h)tanga, Bear, Bhakti, Fakir, Hatha, Maha, Power, Raja, Sid(d)ha, Sivananda

Yog(h)urt Madzoon, Matzoon, Tzatziki

Yoke Bow, Cang(ue), Collar, Couple, Harness, Inspan, Jugal, Oxbow, Pair, Span, Square, Tucker

Yokel Boor, Bumpkin, Chaw(-bacon), Clumperton, Hayseed, Hick, Jake, Jock, Peasant, Rustic

Yolk Parablast, Vitellicle, Vitellus, Yellow

Yon(der) Distant, Further, O'erby, Thae, There, Thether, Thither

Yore Agone, Olden, Past

Yorick Sterne

York(shire), Yorkshireman Batter, Bowl, Ebor, Pudding, Ridings, Tyke

Yorker Tice

You One, Sie, Thee, Thou, Usted, Ye

Young (person), Youngster, Youth(ful) Adolescent, Ageless, Amorino, Bev(an), Bodgie, Boy, Boyhood, Brigham, Bub, Buckie, Calf-time, Ch, Charver, Chick, Chicken, Child, Chile, Cockerel, Cockle, Colt, Comsomol, Cornstalk, Cub, DJ, Early, Ephebe, Ephebus, Esquire, Flapper, Fledgling, Foetus, Fry, Gigolo, Gilded, Gillet, Girl, Gunsel, Halfling, Hebe, Hobbledehoy, Immature, Imp, Infant, Issue, Junior, Juvenal, Juvenesce, Juvenile, Keral, Kid, Kiddo, Kiddy, Kipper, Knave-bairn, Komsomol, Lad, Lamb, Latter-day, Leaping-time, Less, Litter, Little, Loretta, Middle, Minor, Misspent, Mod, Mormon, Nance, Neanic, Neophyte, Nestling, New, New Romantic, Nipper, Nymph, Plant, (Pre-)pubescent, Progeny, Protégé(e), Punk, Pup, Sapling, Scent,

Scion, Shaveling, Shaver, Skinhead, Slip, Son, Spawn, Sprig, Springal(d), Stripling, Swain, Syen, Ted, Teenager, Teens, Teenybopper, Toyboy, Vernal, Well-preserved, Whelp, Whippersnapper, Wigga, Wigger, Yippy, Yoof, Yopper, Younker, Yumpie, Yuppie

Younger, Youngest Baby, Benjamin, Cadet, Last born, Less, Minimus, Seneca, Wallydrag, Wallydraigle, Yr

Your(s) Thee, Thine, Thy

▶ **Youth** *see* YOUNG PERSON

Yo-yo Bandalore

Ytterbium Yb

Yttrium Y

Yucatan Maya

Yucca Adam's needle

Yucky Gooey, Grooly, Sickly, Sticky

Yugoslav Croat(ian), Serb, Slovene, Ustashi

Yukon YT

Yuletide Advent, Dec, Noel, Xmas

Zz

Z Izzard, Izzet, Zambia, Zebra
Zamenhof Esperanto
Zander Fogash, Sander
Zany Bor(r)el, Comic, Cuckoo, Idiotic, Mad
Zeal(ous) Ardour, Bigotry, Devotion, Eager, Enthusiasm, Evangelic, Fervour, Fire, Perfervid, Study
Zealot Bigot, Devotee, Fan(atic), St Simon, Votary
Zebra Convict, Quagga
Zenith Acme, Apogee, Height, Pole, Summit
Zeno Colonnade, Elea, Stoic
Zeolite Analcime, Analcite, Gmelinite
Zephyr Breeze, Wind
Zeppelin Airship, Balloon, Dirigible
Zero Absolute, Blob, Cipher, Donut, Ground, Nil, Nothing, Nought, O, Status, Z
Zest Condiment, Crave, Élan, Gusto, Pep, Piquancy, Relish, Spark, Spice, Tang, Zap, Zing
Ziegfeld Flo
Zigzag Crémaillère, Crinkle-crankle, Dancette, Feather-stitch, Indent, Major Mitchell, Ric-rac, Slalom, Stagger, Switchback, Tack, Traverse, Yaw
Zinc Blende, Gahnite, Mossy, Sherardise, Spelter, Sphalerite, Tutenag, Tutty, Willemite, Wurtzite, Zn
Zip(per) Dash, Energy, Fastener, Fly, Go, Oomph, Presto, Stingo, Vim, Vivacity, Whirry, Zero
Zircon Hyacinth, Jacinth, Jargo(o)n
Zirconium Baddeleyite, Zr
Zither Cithara, Kantela, Kantele, Koto
Zodiac(al) Aquarius, Archer, Aries, Bull, Cancer, Capricorn, Counter-glow, Crab, Fish, Gegenschein, Gemini, Goat, Horoscope, Leo, Libra, Lion, Ophiuchus, Pisces, Ram, Sagittarius, Scales, Scorpio(n), Taurus, Twins, Virgin, Virgo, Watercarrier
Zola Budd, Emile, Nana, Realism
Zombie Catatonic, Dolt, Robot
Zone(s) Abyssal, Acid, Anacoustic, Area, Band, Bathyal, Belt, Benioff, Buffer, Canal, Climate, Collision, Comfort, Convergence, Crumple, Drop, Economic, Ecotone, End, Enterprise, Erogenous, Euro, Exclusion, F layer, Fracture, Free, Fresnel, Frigid, Hadal, Hot, Impact, Krumhole, Low velocity, Neutral, No-fly, Nuclear-free, Precinct, > **REGION**, Rift, Ring, Sahel, Sector, Shear, Skip, Smokeless, Stratopause, Strike, Subduction, Temperate, Time, Tolerance, Torrid, Tundra, Twilight
Zoo Bedlam, Circus, Menagerie, Vivarium, Whipsnade
Zoologist, Zoology Biologist, Botanist, Cetology, Naturalist
Zoom Close-up, Speed
Zoroastrian Gabar, Gheber, Ghebre, Gueber, Guebre, Magus, Mazdaist,

Mazdean, Ormazd, Ormuzd, Parsee, Parsi
Zulu Chaka, Impi, Inkatha, Matabele, Niger, Shaka, Warrior
Zut Crimini